KEY TO WORLD MAP PAGES

COUNTRY INDEX

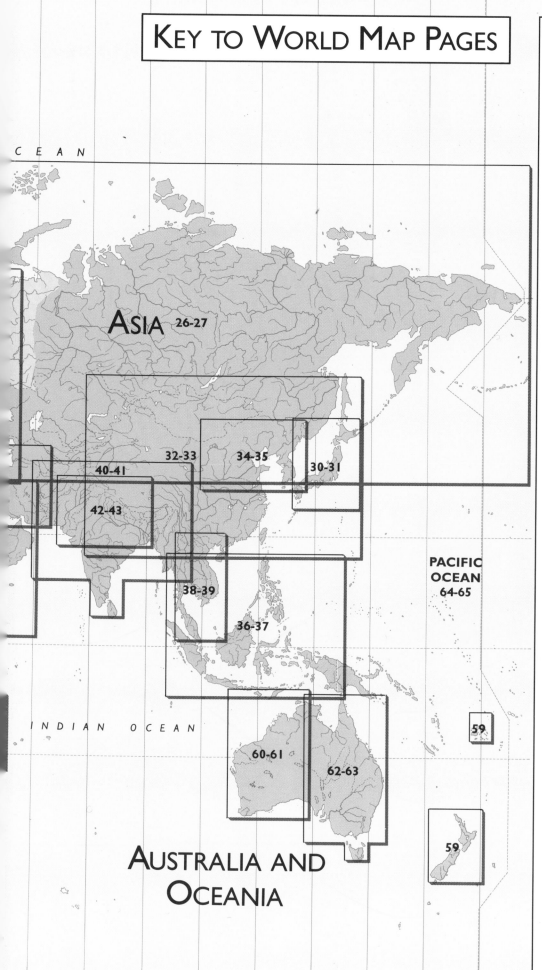

OCEAN

ASIA 26-27

32-33 34-35 30-31

40-41

42-43

38-39

36-37

INDIAN OCEAN

PACIFIC
OCEAN
64-65

60-61

62-63

AUSTRALIA AND
OCEANIA

59

59

WORLD ATLAS

REVISED EDITION

The World in Focus
Cartography by Philip's

Picture Acknowledgements
Page 14
Science Photo Library/NOAA

Illustrations
Stefan Chabluk

CONSULTANTS
Philip's are grateful to the following people for acting as specialist
geography consultants on 'The World in Focus' front section:

Professor D. Brunsden, Kings College, University of London, UK
Dr C. Clarke, Oxford University, UK
Dr I. S. Evans, Durham University, UK
Professor P. Haggett, University of Bristol, UK
Professor K. McLachlan, University of London, UK
Professor M. Monmonier, Syracuse University, New York, USA
Professor M-L. Hsu, University of Minnesota, Minnesota, USA
Professor M. J. Tooley, University of St Andrews, UK
Dr T. Unwin, Royal Holloway, University of London, UK

This edition first published in the UK
in 1999 by Philip's for
WHSmith, Greenbridge Road,
Swindon SN3 3RX

Copyright © 1999, 2001 Philip's
Reprinted with revisions 2002

Cover design © 1999 WHSmith Limited

Cartography by Philip's

ISBN 0-540-07821-2

A CIP catalogue record for this book is available from the British Library.

Printed in Hong Kong

Details of other Philip's titles and services can be found on our website at: www.philips-maps.co.uk

WORLD ATLAS

REVISED EDITION

Contents

v

World Statistics: Countries

This alphabetical list includes all the countries and territories of the world. If a territory is not completely independent, then the country it is associated with is named. The area figures give the total area of land, inland water and ice. The population figures are 2000 estimates. The annual income is the Gross National Product per capita in US dollars. The figures are the latest available, usually 1998.

Country/Territory	Area km² Thousands	Area miles² Thousands	Population Thousands	Capital	Annual Income US $
Afghanistan	652	252	26,511	Kabul	800
Albania	28.8	11.1	3,795	Tirana	810
Algeria	2,382	920	32,904	Algiers	1,550
American Samoa (US)	0.20	0.08	39	Pago Pago	2,600
Andorra	0.45	0.17	49	Andorra La Vella	18,000
Angola	1,247	481	13,295	Luanda	340
Anguilla (UK)	0.1	0.04	8	The Valley	6,800
Antigua & Barbuda	0.44	0.17	79	St John's	8,300
Argentina	2,767	1,068	36,238	Buenos Aires	8,970
Armenia	29.8	11.5	3,968	Yerevan	480
Aruba (Netherlands)	0.19	0.07	58	Oranjestad	22,000
Australia	7,687	2,968	18,855	Canberra	20,300
Austria	83.9	32.4	7,613	Vienna	26,850
Azerbaijan	86.6	33.4	8,324	Baku	490
Azores (Portugal)	2.2	0.87	238	Ponta Delgada	–
Bahamas	13.9	5.4	295	Nassau	20,100
Bahrain	0.68	0.26	683	Manama	7,660
Bangladesh	144	56	150,589	Dhaka	350
Barbados	0.43	0.17	265	Bridgetown	7,890
Belarus	207.6	80.1	10,697	Minsk	2,200
Belgium	30.5	11.8	9,832	Brussels	25,380
Belize	23	8.9	230	Belmopan	2,610
Benin	113	43	6,369	Porto-Novo	380
Bermuda (UK)	0.05	0.02	62	Hamilton	34,000
Bhutan	47	18.1	1,906	Thimphu	1,000
Bolivia	1,099	424	9,724	La Paz/Sucre	1,000
Bosnia-Herzegovina	51	20	4,601	Sarajevo	1,720
Botswana	582	225	1,822	Gaborone	3,600
Brazil	8,512	3,286	179,487	Brasília	4,570
Brunei	5.8	2.2	333	Bandar Seri Begawan	24,000
Bulgaria	111	43	9,071	Sofia	1,230
Burkina Faso	274	106	12,092	Ouagadougou	240
Burma (= Myanmar)	677	261	51,129	Rangoon	1,200
Burundi	27.8	10.7	7,358	Bujumbura	140
Cambodia	181	70	10,046	Phnom Penh	280
Cameroon	475	184	16,701	Yaoundé	610
Canada	9,976	3,852	28,488	Ottawa	20,020
Canary Is. (Spain)	7.3	2.8	1,494	Las Palmas/Santa Cruz	–
Cape Verde Is.	4	1.6	515	Praia	1,060
Cayman Is. (UK)	0.26	0.10	35	George Town	20,000
Central African Republic	623	241	4,074	Bangui	300
Chad	1,284	496	7,337	Ndjaména	230
Chile	757	292	15,272	Santiago	4,810
China	9,597	3,705	1,299,180	Beijing	750
Colombia	1,139	440	39,397	Bogotá	2,600
Comoros	2.2	0.86	670	Moroni	370
Congo	342	132	3,167	Brazzaville	690
Congo (Dem. Rep. of the)	2,345	905	49,190	Kinshasa	110
Cook Is. (NZ)	0.24	0.09	17	Avarua	900
Costa Rica	51.1	19.7	3,711	San José	2,780
Croatia	56.5	21.8	4,960	Zagreb	4,520
Cuba	111	43	11,504	Havana	1,560
Cyprus	9.3	3.6	762	Nicosia	13,000
Czech Republic	78.9	30.4	10,500	Prague	5,040
Denmark	43.1	16.6	5,153	Copenhagen	33,260
Djibouti	23.2	9	552	Djibouti	1,200
Dominica	0.75	0.29	87	Roseau	3,010
Dominican Republic	48.7	18.8	8,621	Santo Domingo	1,770
Ecuador	284	109	13,319	Quito	1,530
Egypt	1,001	387	64,210	Cairo	1,290
El Salvador	21	8.1	6,739	San Salvador	1,850
Equatorial Guinea	28.1	10.8	455	Malabo	1,500
Eritrea	94	36	4,523	Asmara	200
Estonia	44.7	17.3	1,647	Tallinn	3,390
Ethiopia	1,128	436	61,841	Addis Ababa	100
Faroe Is. (Denmark)	1.4	0.54	49	Tórshavn	16,000
Fiji	18.3	7.1	883	Suva	2,110
Finland	338	131	5,077	Helsinki	24,110
France	552	213	58,145	Paris	24,940
French Guiana (France)	90	34.7	130	Cayenne	6,000
French Polynesia (France)	4	1.5	268	Papeete	10,800
Gabon	268	103	1,612	Libreville	3,950
Gambia, The	11.3	4.4	1,119	Banjul	340
Georgia	69.7	26.9	5,777	Tbilisi	930
Germany	357	138	76,962	Berlin	25,850
Ghana	239	92	20,564	Accra	390
Gibraltar (UK)	0.007	0.003	32	Gibraltar Town	5,000
Greece	132	51	10,193	Athens	11,650
Greenland (Denmark)	2,176	840	60	Nuuk (Godthåb)	16,100
Grenada	0.34	0.13	83	St George's	3,170
Guadeloupe (France)	1.7	0.66	365	Basse-Terre	9,200
Guam (US)	0.55	0.21	128	Agana	19,000
Guatemala	109	42	12,222	Guatemala City	1,640
Guinea	246	95	7,830	Conakry	540
Guinea-Bissau	36.1	13.9	1,197	Bissau	160
Guyana	215	83	891	Georgetown	770
Haiti	27.8	10.7	8,003	Port-au-Prince	410
Honduras	112	43	6,846	Tegucigalpa	730
Hong Kong (China)	1.1	0.40	6,336	–	23,670
Hungary	93	35.9	10,531	Budapest	4,510
Iceland	103	40	274	Reykjavik	28,010
India	3,288	1,269	1,041,543	New Delhi	430
Indonesia	1,905	735	218,661	Jakarta	680
Iran	1,648	636	68,759	Tehran	1,770
Iraq	438	169	26,339	Baghdad	2,400
Ireland	70.3	27.1	4,086	Dublin	18,340
Israel	27	10.3	5,321	Jerusalem	15,940
Italy	301	116	57,195	Rome	20,250
Ivory Coast (Côte d'Ivoire)	322	125	17,600	Yamoussoukro	700
Jamaica	11	4.2	2,735	Kingston	1,680
Japan	378	146	128,470	Tokyo	32,380
Jordan	89.2	34.4	5,558	Amman	1,520
Kazakstan	2,717	1,049	19,006	Astana	1,310
Kenya	580	224	35,060	Nairobi	330
Kiribati	0.72	0.28	72	Tarawa	1,180
Korea, North	121	47	26,117	Pyŏngyang	1,000
Korea, South	99	38.2	46,403	Seoul	7,970
Kuwait	17.8	6.9	2,639	Kuwait City	22,700
Kyrgyzstan	198.5	76.6	5,403	Bishkek	350
Laos	237	91	5,463	Vientiane	330
Latvia	65	25	2,768	Riga	2,430
Lebanon	10.4	4	3,327	Beirut	3,560
Lesotho	30.4	11.7	2,370	Maseru	570
Liberia	111	43	3,575	Monrovia	1,000
Libya	1,760	679	6,500	Tripoli	6,700
Liechtenstein	0.16	0.06	28	Vaduz	50,000
Lithuania	65.2	25.2	3,935	Vilnius	2,440
Luxembourg	2.6	1	377	Luxembourg	43,570
Macau (China)	0.02	0.006	656	Macau	16,000
Macedonia (F.Y.R.O.M.)	25.7	9.9	2,157	Skopje	1,290
Madagascar	587	227	16,627	Antananarivo	260
Madeira (Portugal)	0.81	0.31	253	Funchal	–
Malawi	118	46	12,458	Lilongwe	200
Malaysia	330	127	21,983	Kuala Lumpur	3,600
Maldives	0.30	0.12	283	Malé	1,230
Mali	1,240	479	12,685	Bamako	250
Malta	0.32	0.12	366	Valletta	9,440
Marshall Is.	0.18	0.07	70	Dalap-Uliga-Darrit	1,540
Martinique (France)	1.1	0.42	362	Fort-de-France	10,700
Mauritania	1,030	412	2,702	Nouakchott	410
Mauritius	2.0	0.72	1,201	Port Louis	3,700
Mayotte (France)	0.37	0.14	141	Mamoundzou	1,430
Mexico	1,958	756	107,233	Mexico City	3,970
Micronesia, Fed. States of	0.70	0.27	110	Palikir	1,800
Moldova	33.7	13	4,707	Chişinău	410
Monaco	0.002	0.0001	30	Monaco	25,000
Mongolia	1,567	605	2,847	Ulan Bator	400
Montserrat (UK)	0.10	0.04	13	Plymouth	4,500
Morocco	447	172	31,559	Rabat	1,250
Mozambique	802	309	20,493	Maputo	210
Namibia	825	318	2,437	Windhoek	1,940
Nauru	0.02	0.008	10	Yaren District	10,000
Nepal	141	54	24,084	Katmandu	210
Netherlands	41.5	16	15,829	Amsterdam/The Hague	24,760
Netherlands Antilles (Neths)	0.99	0.38	203	Willemstad	11,500
New Caledonia (France)	18.6	7.2	195	Nouméa	11,400
New Zealand	269	104	3,662	Wellington	14,700
Nicaragua	130	50	5,261	Managua	390
Niger	1,267	489	10,752	Niamey	190
Nigeria	924	357	105,000	Abuja	300
Northern Mariana Is. (US)	0.48	0.18	50	Saipan	9,300
Norway	324	125	4,331	Oslo	34,330
Oman	212	82	2,176	Muscat	7,900
Pakistan	796	307	162,409	Islamabad	480
Palau	0.46	0.18	18	Koror	8,800
Panama	77.1	29.8	2,893	Panama City	3,080
Papua New Guinea	463	179	4,845	Port Moresby	890
Paraguay	407	157	5,538	Asunción	1,760
Peru	1,285	496	26,276	Lima	2,460
Philippines	300	116	77,473	Manila	1,050
Poland	313	121	40,366	Warsaw	3,900
Portugal	92.4	35.7	10,587	Lisbon	10,690
Puerto Rico (US)	9	3.5	3,836	San Juan	9,000
Qatar	11	4.2	499	Doha	17,100
Réunion (France)	2.5	0.97	692	Saint-Denis	4,800
Romania	238	92	24,000	Bucharest	1,390
Russia	17,075	6,592	155,096	Moscow	2,300
Rwanda	26.3	10.2	10,200	Kigali	230
St Kitts & Nevis	0.36	0.14	44	Basseterre	6,130
St Lucia	0.62	0.24	177	Castries	3,410
St Vincent & Grenadines	0.39	0.15	128	Kingstown	2,420
Samoa	2.8	1.1	171	Apia	1,020
San Marino	0.06	0.02	25	San Marino	20,000
São Tomé & Príncipe	0.96	0.37	151	São Tomé	280
Saudi Arabia	2,150	830	20,697	Riyadh	9,000
Senegal	197	76	8,716	Dakar	530
Seychelles	0.46	0.18	75	Victoria	6,450
Sierra Leone	71.7	27.7	5,437	Freetown	140
Singapore	0.62	0.24	3,000	Singapore	30,060
Slovak Republic	49	18.9	5,500	Bratislava	3,700
Slovenia	20.3	7.8	2,055	Ljubljana	9,760
Solomon Is.	28.9	11.2	429	Honiara	750
Somalia	638	246	9,736	Mogadishu	600
South Africa	1,220	471	43,666	C. Town/Pretoria/Bloem.	2,880
Spain	505	195	40,667	Madrid	14,080
Sri Lanka	65.6	25.3	19,416	Colombo	810
Sudan	2,506	967	33,625	Khartoum	290
Surinam	163	63	497	Paramaribo	1,660
Swaziland	17.4	6.7	1,121	Mbabane	1,400
Sweden	450	174	8,560	Stockholm	25,620
Switzerland	41.3	15.9	6,762	Bern	40,080
Syria	185	71	17,826	Damascus	1,020
Taiwan	36	13.9	22,000	Taipei	12,400
Tajikistan	143.1	55.2	7,041	Dushanbe	350
Tanzania	945	365	39,639	Dodoma	210
Thailand	513	198	63,670	Bangkok	2,200
Togo	56.8	21.9	4,861	Lomé	330
Tonga	0.75	0.29	92	Nuku'alofa	1,690
Trinidad & Tobago	5.1	2	1,484	Port of Spain	4,430
Tunisia	164	63	9,924	Tunis	2,050
Turkey	779	301	66,789	Ankara	3,160
Turkmenistan	488.1	188.5	4,585	Ashkhabad	1,630
Turks & Caicos Is. (UK)	0.43	0.17	12	Cockburn Town	5,000
Tuvalu	0.03	0.01	11	Fongafale	600
Uganda	236	91	26,958	Kampala	320
Ukraine	603.7	233.1	52,558	Kiev	850
United Arab Emirates	83.6	32.3	1,951	Abu Dhabi	18,220
United Kingdom	243.3	94	58,393	London	21,400
United States of America	9,373	3,619	266,096	Washington, DC	29,340
Uruguay	177	68	3,274	Montevideo	6,180
Uzbekistan	447.4	172.7	26,044	Tashkent	870
Vanuatu	12.2	4.7	206	Port-Vila	1,270
Venezuela	912	352	24,715	Caracas	350
Vietnam	332	127	82,427	Hanoi	330
Virgin Is. (UK)	0.15	0.06	15	Road Town	–
Virgin Is. (US)	0.34	0.13	135	Charlotte Amalie	12,500
Wallis & Futuna Is. (France)	0.20	0.08	26	Mata-Utu	–
Western Sahara	266	103	228	El Aaiún	300
Yemen	528	204	13,219	Sana	300
Yugoslavia	102.3	39.5	10,761	Belgrade	2,300
Zambia	753	291	12,267	Lusaka	330
Zimbabwe	391	151	13,123	Harare	610

World Statistics: Physical Dimensions

Each topic list is divided into continents and within a continent the items are listed in order of size. The bottom part of many of the lists is selective in order to give examples from as many different countries as possible. The order of the continents is the same as in the atlas, beginning with Europe and ending with South America. The figures are rounded as appropriate.

World, Continents, Oceans

	km²	miles²	%
The World	509,450,000	196,672,000	–
Land	149,450,000	57,688,000	29.3
Water	360,000,000	138,984,000	70.7
Asia	44,500,000	17,177,000	29.8
Africa	30,302,000	11,697,000	20.3
North America	24,241,000	9,357,000	16.2
South America	17,793,000	6,868,000	11.9
Antarctica	14,100,000	5,443,000	9.4
Europe	9,957,000	3,843,000	6.7
Australia & Oceania	8,557,000	3,303,000	5.7
Pacific Ocean	179,679,000	69,356,000	49.9
Atlantic Ocean	92,373,000	35,657,000	25.7
Indian Ocean	73,917,000	28,532,000	20.5
Arctic Ocean	14,090,000	5,439,000	3.9

Ocean Depths

	m	ft
Atlantic Ocean		
Puerto Rico (Milwaukee) Deep	9,220	30,249
Cayman Trench	7,680	25,197
Gulf of Mexico	5,203	17,070
Mediterranean Sea	5,121	16,801
Black Sea	2,211	7,254
North Sea	660	2,165
Indian Ocean		
Java Trench	7,450	24,442
Red Sea	2,635	8,454
Pacific Ocean		
Mariana Trench	11,022	36,161
Tonga Trench	10,882	35,702
Japan Trench	10,554	34,626
Kuril Trench	10,542	34,587
Arctic Ocean		
Molloy Deep	5,608	18,399

Mountains

		m	ft
Europe			
Elbrus	*Russia*	5,642	18,510
Mont Blanc	*France/Italy*	4,807	15,771
Monte Rosa	*Italy/Switzerland*	4,634	15,203
Dom	*Switzerland*	4,545	14,911
Liskamm	*Switzerland*	4,527	14,852
Weisshorn	*Switzerland*	4,505	14,780
Taschorn	*Switzerland*	4,490	14,730
Matterhorn/Cervino	*Italy/Switzerland*	4,478	14,691
Mont Maudit	*France/Italy*	4,465	14,649
Dent Blanche	*Switzerland*	4,356	14,291
Nadelhorn	*Switzerland*	4,327	14,196
Grandes Jorasses	*France/Italy*	4,208	13,806
Jungfrau	*Switzerland*	4,158	13,642
Grossglockner	*Austria*	3,797	12,457
Mulhacén	*Spain*	3,478	11,411
Zugspitze	*Germany*	2,962	9,718
Olympus	*Greece*	2,917	9,570
Triglav	*Slovenia*	2,863	9,393
Gerlachovka	*Slovak Republic*	2,655	8,711
Galdhöpiggen	*Norway*	2,468	8,100
Kebnekaise	*Sweden*	2,117	6,946
Ben Nevis	*UK*	1,343	4,406
Asia		m	ft
Everest	*China/Nepal*	8,850	29,035
K2 (Godwin Austen)	*China/Kashmir*	8,611	28,251
Kanchenjunga	*India/Nepal*	8,598	28,208
Lhotse	*China/Nepal*	8,516	27,939
Makalu	*China/Nepal*	8,481	27,824
Cho Oyu	*China/Nepal*	8,201	26,906
Dhaulagiri	*Nepal*	8,172	26,811
Manaslu	*Nepal*	8,156	26,758
Nanga Parbat	*Kashmir*	8,126	26,660
Annapurna	*Nepal*	8,078	26,502
Gasherbrum	*China/Kashmir*	8,068	26,469
Broad Peak	*China/Kashmir*	8,051	26,414
Xixabangma	*China*	8,012	26,286
Kangbachen	*India/Nepal*	7,902	25,925
Trivor	*Pakistan*	7,720	25,328
Pik Kommunizma	*Tajikistan*	7,495	24,590
Demavend	*Iran*	5,604	18,386
Ararat	*Turkey*	5,165	16,945
Gunong Kinabalu	*Malaysia (Borneo)*	4,101	13,455
Fuji-San	*Japan*	3,776	12,388
Africa		m	ft
Kilimanjaro	*Tanzania*	5,895	19,340
Mt Kenya	*Kenya*	5,199	17,057
Ruwenzori (Margherita)	*Ug./Congo (D.R.)*	5,109	16,762
Ras Dashan	*Ethiopia*	4,620	15,157
Meru	*Tanzania*	4,565	14,977
Karisimbi	*Rwanda/Congo (D.R.)*	4,507	14,787
Mt Elgon	*Kenya/Uganda*	4,321	14,176
Batu	*Ethiopia*	4,307	14,130
Toubkal	*Morocco*	4,165	13,665
Mt Cameroon	*Cameroon*	4,070	13,353
Oceania		m	ft
Puncak Jaya	*Indonesia*	5,029	16,499
Puncak Trikora	*Indonesia*	4,750	15,584
Puncak Mandala	*Indonesia*	4,702	15,427
Mt Wilhelm	*Papua New Guinea*	4,508	14,790
Mauna Kea	*USA (Hawaii)*	4,205	13,796
Mauna Loa	*USA (Hawaii)*	4,169	13,681
Mt Cook (Aoraki)	*New Zealand*	3,753	12,313
Mt Kosciuszko	*Australia*	2,237	7,339
North America		m	ft
Mt McKinley (Denali)	*USA (Alaska)*	6,194	20,321
Mt Logan	*Canada*	5,959	19,551
Citlaltepetl	*Mexico*	5,700	18,701
Mt St Elias	*USA/Canada*	5,489	18,008
Popocatepetl	*Mexico*	5,452	17,887
Mt Foraker	*USA (Alaska)*	5,304	17,401
Ixtaccihuatl	*Mexico*	5,286	17,342
Lucania	*Canada*	5,227	17,149
Mt Steele	*Canada*	5,073	16,644
Mt Bona	*USA (Alaska)*	5,005	16,420
Mt Whitney	*USA*	4,418	14,495
Tajumulco	*Guatemala*	4,220	13,845
Chirripó Grande	*Costa Rica*	3,837	12,589
Pico Duarte	*Dominican Rep.*	3,175	10,417
South America		m	ft
Aconcagua	*Argentina*	6,960	22,834
Bonete	*Argentina*	6,872	22,546
Ojos del Salado	*Argentina/Chile*	6,863	22,516
Pissis	*Argentina*	6,779	22,241
Mercedario	*Argentina/Chile*	6,770	22,211
Huascaran	*Peru*	6,768	22,204
Llullaillaco	*Argentina/Chile*	6,723	22,057
Nudo de Cachi	*Argentina*	6,720	22,047
Yerupaja	*Peru*	6,632	21,758
Sajama	*Bolivia*	6,542	21,463
Chimborazo	*Ecuador*	6,267	20,561
Pico Colon	*Colombia*	5,800	19,029
Pico Bolivar	*Venezuela*	5,007	16,427
Antarctica		m	ft
Vinson Massif		4,897	16,066
Mt Kirkpatrick		4,528	14,855

Rivers

		km	miles
Europe			
Volga	*Caspian Sea*	3,700	2,300
Danube	*Black Sea*	2,850	1,770
Ural	*Caspian Sea*	2,535	1,575
Dnepr (Dnipro)	*Black Sea*	2,285	1,420
Kama	*Volga*	2,030	1,260
Don	*Black Sea*	1,990	1,240
Petchora	*Arctic Ocean*	1,790	1,110
Oka	*Volga*	1,480	920
Dnister (Dniester)	*Black Sea*	1,400	870
Vyatka	*Kama*	1,370	850
Rhine	*North Sea*	1,320	820
N. Dvina	*Arctic Ocean*	1,290	800
Elbe	*North Sea*	1,145	710
Asia		km	miles
Yangtze	*Pacific Ocean*	6,380	3,960
Yenisey–Angara	*Arctic Ocean*	5,550	3,445
Huang He	*Pacific Ocean*	5,464	3,395
Ob–Irtysh	*Arctic Ocean*	5,410	3,360
Mekong	*Pacific Ocean*	4,500	2,795
Amur	*Pacific Ocean*	4,400	2,730
Lena	*Arctic Ocean*	4,400	2,730
Irtysh	*Ob*	4,250	2,640
Yenisey	*Arctic Ocean*	4,090	2,540
Ob	*Arctic Ocean*	3,680	2,285
Indus	*Indian Ocean*	3,100	1,925
Brahmaputra	*Indian Ocean*	2,900	1,800
Syrdarya	*Aral Sea*	2,860	1,775
Salween	*Indian Ocean*	2,800	1,740
Euphrates	*Indian Ocean*	2,700	1,675
Amudarya	*Aral Sea*	2,540	1,575
Africa		km	miles
Nile	*Mediterranean*	6,670	4,140
Congo	*Atlantic Ocean*	4,670	2,900
Niger	*Atlantic Ocean*	4,180	2,595
Zambezi	*Indian Ocean*	3,540	2,200
Oubangi/Uele	*Congo (D.R.)*	2,250	1,400
Kasai	*Congo (D.R.)*	1,950	1,210
Shaballe	*Indian Ocean*	1,930	1,200
Orange	*Atlantic Ocean*	1,860	1,155
Cubango	*Okavango Swamps*	1,800	1,120
Limpopo	*Indian Ocean*	1,600	995
Senegal	*Atlantic Ocean*	1,600	995
Australia		km	miles
Murray–Darling	*Indian Ocean*	3,750	2,330
Darling	*Murray*	3,070	1,905
Murray	*Indian Ocean*	2,575	1,600
Murrumbidgee	*Murray*	1,690	1,050
North America		km	miles
Mississippi–Missouri	*Gulf of Mexico*	6,020	3,740
Mackenzie	*Arctic Ocean*	4,240	2,630
Mississippi	*Gulf of Mexico*	3,780	2,350
Missouri	*Mississippi*	3,780	2,350
Yukon	*Pacific Ocean*	3,185	1,980
Rio Grande	*Gulf of Mexico*	3,030	1,880
Arkansas	*Mississippi*	2,340	1,450
Colorado	*Pacific Ocean*	2,330	1,445
		m	ft
Red	*Mississippi*	2,040	1,270
Columbia	*Pacific Ocean*	1,950	1,210
Saskatchewan	*Lake Winnipeg*	1,940	1,205
South America		km	miles
Amazon	*Atlantic Ocean*	6,450	4,010
Paraná–Plate	*Atlantic Ocean*	4,500	2,800
Purus	*Amazon*	3,350	2,080
Madeira	*Amazon*	3,200	1,990
São Francisco	*Atlantic Ocean*	2,900	1,800
Paraná	*Plate*	2,800	1,740
Tocantins	*Atlantic Ocean*	2,750	1,710
Paraguay	*Paraná*	2,550	1,580
Orinoco	*Atlantic Ocean*	2,500	1,550
Pilcomayo	*Paraná*	2,500	1,550
Araguaia	*Tocantins*	2,250	1,400

Lakes

		km²	miles²
Europe			
Lake Ladoga	*Russia*	17,700	6,800
Lake Onega	*Russia*	9,700	3,700
Saimaa system	*Finland*	8,000	3,100
Vänern	*Sweden*	5,500	2,100
Asia		km²	miles²
Caspian Sea	*Asia*	371,800	143,550
Lake Baykal	*Russia*	30,500	11,780
Aral Sea	*Kazakstan/Uzbekistan*	28,687	11,086
Tonlé Sap	*Cambodia*	20,000	7,700
Lake Balqash	*Kazakstan*	18,500	7,100
Africa		km²	miles²
Lake Victoria	*East Africa*	68,000	26,000
Lake Tanganyika	*Central Africa*	33,000	13,000
Lake Malawi/Nyasa	*East Africa*	29,600	11,430
Lake Chad	*Central Africa*	25,000	9,700
Lake Turkana	*Ethiopia/Kenya*	8,500	3,300
Lake Volta	*Ghana*	8,500	3,300
Australia		km²	miles²
Lake Eyre	*Australia*	8,900	3,400
Lake Torrens	*Australia*	5,800	2,200
Lake Gairdner	*Australia*	4,800	1,900
North America		km²	miles²
Lake Superior	*Canada/USA*	82,350	31,800
Lake Huron	*Canada/USA*	59,600	23,010
Lake Michigan	*USA*	58,000	22,400
Great Bear Lake	*Canada*	31,800	12,280
Great Slave Lake	*Canada*	28,500	11,000
Lake Erie	*Canada/USA*	25,700	9,900
Lake Winnipeg	*Canada*	24,400	9,400
Lake Ontario	*Canada/USA*	19,500	7,500
Lake Nicaragua	*Nicaragua*	8,200	3,200
South America		km²	miles²
Lake Titicaca	*Bolivia/Peru*	8,300	3,200
Lake Poopo	*Peru*	2,800	1,100

Islands

		km²	miles²
Europe			
Great Britain	*UK*	229,880	88,700
Iceland	*Atlantic Ocean*	103,000	39,800
Ireland	*Ireland/UK*	84,400	32,600
Novaya Zemlya (N.)	*Russia*	48,200	18,600
Sicily	*Italy*	25,500	9,800
Corsica	*France*	8,700	3,400
Asia		km²	miles²
Borneo	*Southeast Asia*	744,360	287,400
Sumatra	*Indonesia*	473,600	182,860
Honshu	*Japan*	230,500	88,980
Sulawesi (Celebes)	*Indonesia*	189,000	73,000
Java	*Indonesia*	126,700	48,900
Luzon	*Philippines*	104,700	40,400
Hokkaido	*Japan*	78,400	30,300
Africa		km²	miles²
Madagascar	*Indian Ocean*	587,040	226,660
Socotra	*Indian Ocean*	3,600	1,400
Réunion	*Indian Ocean*	2,500	965
Oceania		km²	miles²
New Guinea	*Indonesia/Papua NG*	821,030	317,000
New Zealand (S.)	*Pacific Ocean*	150,500	58,100
New Zealand (N.)	*Pacific Ocean*	114,700	44,300
Tasmania	*Australia*	67,800	26,200
Hawaii	*Pacific Ocean*	10,450	4,000
North America		km²	miles²
Greenland	*Atlantic Ocean*	2,175,600	839,800
Baffin Is.	*Canada*	508,000	196,100
Victoria Is.	*Canada*	212,200	81,900
Ellesmere Is.	*Canada*	212,000	81,800
Cuba	*Caribbean Sea*	110,860	42,800
Hispaniola	*Dominican Rep./Haiti*	76,200	29,400
Jamaica	*Caribbean Sea*	11,400	4,400
Puerto Rico	*Atlantic Ocean*	8,900	3,400
South America		km²	miles²
Tierra del Fuego	*Argentina/Chile*	47,000	18,100
Falkland Is. (E.)	*Atlantic Ocean*	6,800	2,600

Philip's World Maps

The reference maps which form the main body of this atlas have been prepared in accordance with the highest standards of international cartography to provide an accurate and detailed representation of the Earth. The scales and projections used have been carefully chosen to give balanced coverage of the world, while emphasizing the most densely populated and economically significant regions. A hallmark of Philip's mapping is the use of hill shading and relief colouring to create a graphic impression of landforms: this makes the maps exceptionally easy to read. However, knowledge of the key features employed in the construction and presentation of the maps will enable the reader to derive the fullest benefit from the atlas.

Map sequence

The atlas covers the Earth continent by continent: first Europe; then its land neighbour Asia (mapped north before south, in a clockwise sequence), then Africa, Australia and Oceania, North America and South America. This is the classic arrangement adopted by most cartographers since the 16th century. For each continent, there are maps at a variety of scales. First, physical relief and political maps of the whole continent; then a series of larger-scale maps of the regions within the continent, each followed, where required, by still larger-scale maps of the most important or densely populated areas. The governing principle is that by turning the pages of the atlas, the reader moves steadily from north to south through each continent, with each map overlapping its neighbours. A key map showing this sequence, and the area covered by each map, can be found on the endpapers of the atlas.

Map presentation

With very few exceptions (e.g. for the Arctic and Antarctica), the maps are drawn with north at the top, regardless of whether they are presented upright or sideways on the page. In the borders will be found the map title; a locator diagram showing the area covered and the page numbers for maps of adjacent areas; the scale; the projection used; the degrees of latitude and longitude; and the letters and figures used in the index for locating place names and geographical features. Physical relief maps also have a height reference panel identifying the colours used for each layer of contouring.

Map symbols

Each map contains a vast amount of detail which can only be conveyed clearly and accurately by the use of symbols. Points and circles of varying sizes locate and identify the relative importance of towns and cities; different styles of type are employed for administrative, geographical and regional place names. A variety of pictorial symbols denote features such as glaciers and marshes, as well

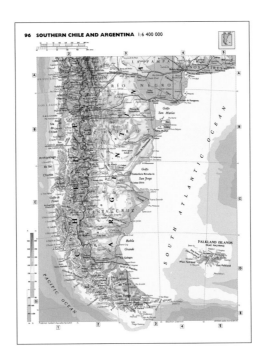

as man-made structures including roads, railways, airports and canals. International borders are shown by red lines. Where neighbouring countries are in dispute, for example in the Middle East, the maps show the *de facto* boundary between nations, regardless of the legal or historical situation. The symbols are explained on the first page of the World Maps section of the atlas.

Map scales

The scale of each map is given in the numerical form known as the 'representative fraction'. The first figure is always one, signifying one unit of distance on the map; the second figure, usually in millions, is the number by which the map unit must be multiplied to give the equivalent distance on the Earth's surface. Calculations can easily be made in centimetres and kilometres, by dividing the Earth units figure by 100 000 (i.e. deleting the last five 0s). Thus 1:1 000 000 means 1 cm = 10 km. The calculation for inches and miles is more laborious, but 1 000 000 divided by 63 360 (the number of inches in a mile) shows that the ratio 1:1 000 000 means approximately 1 inch = 16 miles. The table below provides distance equivalents for scales down to 1:50 000 000.

LARGE SCALE		
1:1 000 000	1 cm = 10 km	1 inch = 16 miles
1:2 500 000	1 cm = 25 km	1 inch = 39.5 miles
1:5 000 000	1 cm = 50 km	1 inch = 79 miles
1:6 000 000	1 cm = 60 km	1 inch = 95 miles
1:8 000 000	1 cm = 80 km	1 inch = 126 miles
1:10 000 000	1 cm = 100 km	1 inch = 158 miles
1:15 000 000	1 cm = 150 km	1 inch = 237 miles
1:20 000 000	1 cm = 200 km	1 inch = 316 miles
1:50 000 000	1 cm = 500 km	1 inch = 790 miles
SMALL SCALE		

Measuring distances

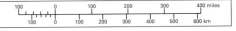

Although each map is accompanied by a scale bar, distances cannot always be measured with confidence because of the distortions involved in portraying the curved surface of the Earth on a flat page. As a general rule, the larger the map scale (i.e. the lower the number of Earth units in the representative fraction), the more accurate and reliable will be the distance measured. On small-scale maps such as those of the world and of entire continents, measurement may only be accurate along the 'standard parallels', or central axes, and should not be attempted without considering the map projection.

Latitude and longitude

Accurate positioning of individual points on the Earth's surface is made possible by reference to the geometrical system of latitude and longitude. Latitude *parallels* are drawn west–east around the Earth and numbered by degrees north and south of the Equator, which is designated 0° of latitude. Longitude *meridians* are drawn north–south and numbered by degrees east and west of the *prime meridian*, 0° of longitude, which passes through Greenwich in England. By referring to these co-ordinates and their subdivisions of minutes ($1/60$th of a degree) and seconds ($1/60$th of a minute), any place on Earth can be located to within a few hundred metres. Latitude and longitude are indicated by blue lines on the maps; they are straight or curved according to the projection employed. Reference to these lines is the easiest way of determining the relative positions of places on different maps, and for plotting compass directions.

Name forms

For ease of reference, both English and local name forms appear in the atlas. Oceans, seas and countries are shown in English throughout the atlas; country names may be abbreviated to their commonly accepted form (e.g. Germany, not The Federal Republic of Germany). Conventional English forms are also used for place names on the smaller-scale maps of the continents. However, local name forms are used on all large-scale and regional maps, with the English form given in brackets only for important cities – the large-scale map of Russia and Central Asia thus shows Moskva (Moscow). For countries which do not use a Roman script, place names have been transcribed according to the systems adopted by the British and US Geographic Names Authorities. For China, the Pin Yin system has been used, with some more widely known forms appearing in brackets, as with Beijing (Peking). Both English and local names appear in the index, the English form being cross-referenced to the local form.

THE
WORLD
IN FOCUS

Planet Earth

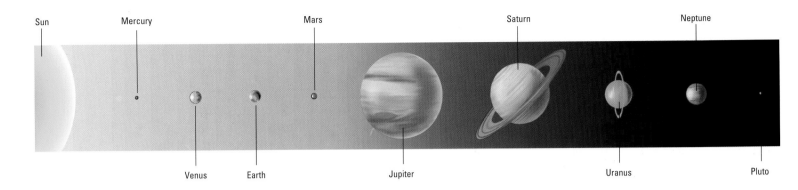

Sun · Mercury · Venus · Earth · Mars · Jupiter · Saturn · Uranus · Neptune · Pluto

The Solar System

A minute part of one of the billions of galaxies (collections of stars) that comprises the Universe, the Solar System lies some 27,000 light-years from the centre of our own galaxy, the 'Milky Way'. Thought to be about 4,600 million years old, it consists of a central sun with nine planets and their moons revolving around it, attracted by its gravitational pull. The planets orbit the Sun in the same direction – anti-clockwise when viewed from the Northern Heavens – and almost in the same plane. Their orbital paths, however, vary enormously.

The Sun's diameter is 109 times that of Earth, and the temperature at its core – caused by continuous thermonuclear fusions of hydrogen into helium – is estimated to be 15 million degrees Celsius. It is the Solar System's only source of light and heat.

Profile of the Planets

	Mean distance from Sun (million km)	Mass (Earth = 1)	Period of orbit (Earth years)	Period of rotation (Earth days)	Equatorial diameter (km)	Number of known satellites
Mercury	57.9	0.055	0.24 years	58.67	4,878	0
Venus	108.2	0.815	0.62 years	243.00	12,104	0
Earth	149.6	1.0	1.00 years	1.00	12,756	1
Mars	227.9	0.107	1.88 years	1.03	6,787	2
Jupiter	778.3	317.8	11.86 years	0.41	142,800	28
Saturn	1,427	95.2	29.46 years	0.43	120,000	30
Uranus	2,871	14.5	84.01 years	0.75	51,118	21
Neptune	4,497	17.1	164.80 years	0.80	49,528	8
Pluto	5,914	0.002	248.50 years	6.39	2,320	1

All planetary orbits are elliptical in form, but only Pluto and Mercury follow paths that deviate noticeably from a circular one. Near perihelion – its closest approach to the Sun – Pluto actually passes inside the orbit of Neptune, an event that last occurred in 1983. Pluto did not regain its station as outermost planet until February 1999.

The Seasons

Seasons occur because the Earth's axis is tilted at a constant angle of 23½°. When the northern hemisphere is tilted to a maximum extent towards the Sun, on 21 June, the Sun is overhead at the Tropic of Cancer (latitude 23½° North). This is midsummer, or the summer solstice, in the northern hemisphere.

On 22 or 23 September, the Sun is overhead at the Equator, and day and night are of equal length throughout the world. This is the autumn equinox in the northern hemisphere. On 21 or 22 December, the Sun is overhead at the Tropic of Capricorn (23½° South), the winter solstice in the northern hemisphere. The overhead Sun then tracks north until, on 21 March, it is overhead at the Equator. This is the spring (vernal) equinox in the northern hemisphere.

In the southern hemisphere, the seasons are the reverse of those in the north.

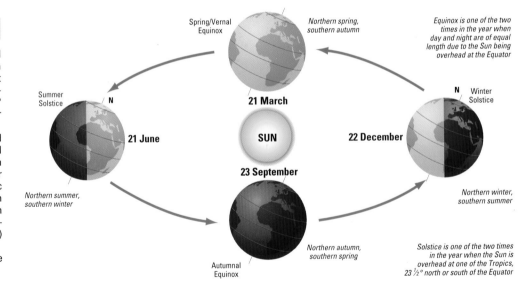

Spring/Vernal Equinox — Northern spring, southern autumn — 21 March

Equinox is one of the two times in the year when day and night are of equal length due to the Sun being overhead at the Equator

Summer Solstice — N — 21 June — SUN — 22 December — N — Winter Solstice

Northern summer, southern winter

23 September

Autumnal Equinox — Northern autumn, southern spring

Northern winter, southern summer

Solstice is one of the two times in the year when the Sun is overhead at one of the Tropics, 23½° north or south of the Equator

Day and Night

The Sun appears to rise in the east, reach its highest point at noon, and then set in the west, to be followed by night. In reality, it is not the Sun that is moving but the Earth rotating from west to east. The moment when the Sun's upper limb first appears above the horizon is termed sunrise; the moment when the Sun's upper limb disappears below the horizon is sunset.

At the summer solstice in the northern hemisphere (21 June), the Arctic has total daylight and the Antarctic total darkness. The opposite occurs at the winter solstice (21 or 22 December). At the Equator, the length of day and night are almost equal all year.

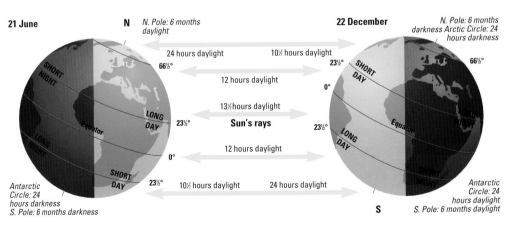

21 June — N — N. Pole: 6 months daylight — SHORT NIGHT — 66½° — LONG DAY — 23½° — Equator — LONG NIGHT — 0° — SHORT DAY — 23½° — Antarctic Circle: 24 hours darkness — S. Pole: 6 months darkness

24 hours daylight — 66½° — 12 hours daylight — 13½ hours daylight — Sun's rays — 12 hours daylight — 0° — 10½ hours daylight

22 December — N. Pole: 6 months darkness Arctic Circle: 24 hours darkness — SHORT DAY — 66½° — 23½° — 0° — Equator — LONG DAY — 23½° — Antarctic Circle: 24 hours daylight — S. Pole: 6 months daylight — S

10½ hours daylight — 23½° — 24 hours daylight

Time

Year: The time taken by the Earth to revolve around the Sun, or 365.24 days.

Leap Year: A calendar year of 366 days, 29 February being the additional day. It offsets the difference between the calendar and the solar year.

Month: The approximate time taken by the Moon to revolve around the Earth. The 12 months of the year in fact vary from 28 (29 in a Leap Year) to 31 days.

Week: An artificial period of 7 days, not based on astronomical time.

Day: The time taken by the Earth to complete one rotation on its axis.

Hour: 24 hours make one day. Usually the day is divided into hours AM (ante meridiem or before noon) and PM (post meridiem or after noon), although most timetables now use the 24-hour system, from midnight to midnight.

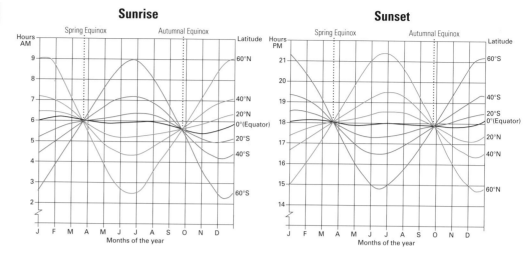

The Moon

The Moon rotates more slowly than the Earth, making one complete turn on its axis in just over 27 days. Since this corresponds to its period of revolution around the Earth, the Moon always presents the same

Phases of the Moon

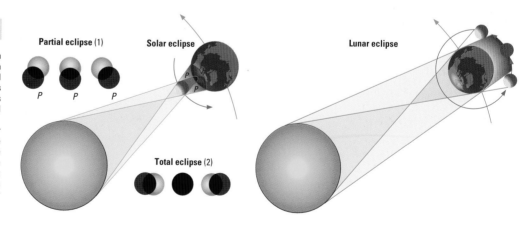

Distance from Earth: 356,410 km – 406,685 km; Mean diameter: 3,475.1 km; Mass: approx. 1/81 that of Earth; Surface gravity: one-sixth of Earth's; Daily range of temperature at lunar equator: 200°C; Average orbital speed: 3,683 km/h

hemisphere or face to us, and we never see 'the dark side'. The interval between one full Moon and the next (and between new Moons) is about 29½ days – a lunar month. The apparent changes in the shape of the Moon are caused by its changing position in relation to the Earth; like the planets, it produces no light of its own and shines only by reflecting the rays of the Sun.

Eclipses

When the Moon passes between the Sun and the Earth it causes a partial eclipse of the Sun (1) if the Earth passes through the Moon's outer shadow (P), or a total eclipse (2) if the inner cone shadow crosses the Earth's surface. In a lunar eclipse, the Earth's shadow crosses the Moon and, again, provides either a partial or total eclipse.

Eclipses of the Sun and the Moon do not occur every month because of the 5° difference between the plane of the Moon's orbit and the plane in which the Earth moves. In the 1990s only 14 lunar eclipses were possible, for example, seven partial and seven total; each was visible only from certain, and variable, parts of the world. The same period witnessed 13 solar eclipses – six partial (or annular) and seven total.

Tides

The daily rise and fall of the ocean's tides are the result of the gravitational pull of the Moon and that of the Sun, though the effect of the latter is only 46.6% as strong as that of the Moon. This effect is greatest on the hemisphere facing the Moon and causes a tidal 'bulge'. When the Sun, Earth and Moon are in line, tide-raising forces are at a maximum and Spring tides occur: high tide reaches the highest values, and low tide falls to low levels. When lunar and solar forces are least coincidental with the Sun and Moon at an angle (near the Moon's first and third quarters), Neap tides occur, which have a small tidal range.

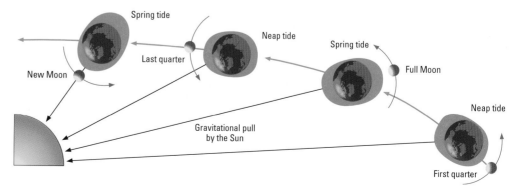

Restless Earth

The Earth's Structure

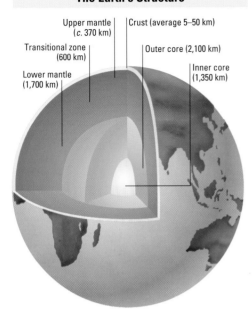

Upper mantle (c. 370 km)
Crust (average 5–50 km)
Transitional zone (600 km)
Outer core (2,100 km)
Lower mantle (1,700 km)
Inner core (1,350 km)

Continental Drift

About 200 million years ago the original Pangaea landmass began to split into two continental groups, which further separated over time to produce the present-day configuration.

135 million years ago

180 million years ago

Laurasia
Tethys Sea
Gondwanaland

Present day

Trench
Rift
New ocean floor
Zones of slippage

Notable Earthquakes Since 1900

Year	Location	Richter Scale	Deaths
1906	San Francisco, USA	8.3	503
1906	Valparaiso, Chile	8.6	22,000
1908	Messina, Italy	7.5	83,000
1915	Avezzano, Italy	7.5	30,000
1920	Gansu (Kansu), China	8.6	180,000
1923	Yokohama, Japan	8.3	143,000
1927	Nan Shan, China	8.3	200,000
1932	Gansu (Kansu), China	7.6	70,000
1933	Sanriku, Japan	8.9	2,990
1934	Bihar, India/Nepal	8.4	10,700
1935	Quetta, India (now Pakistan)	7.5	60,000
1939	Chillan, Chile	8.3	28,000
1939	Erzincan, Turkey	7.9	30,000
1960	Agadir, Morocco	5.8	12,000
1962	Khorasan, Iran	7.1	12,230
1968	N.E. Iran	7.4	12,000
1970	N. Peru	7.7	66,794
1972	Managua, Nicaragua	6.2	5,000
1974	N. Pakistan	6.3	5,200
1976	Guatemala	7.5	22,778
1976	Tangshan, China	8.2	255,000
1978	Tabas, Iran	7.7	25,000
1980	El Asnam, Algeria	7.3	20,000
1980	S. Italy	7.2	4,800
1985	Mexico City, Mexico	8.1	4,200
1988	N.W. Armenia	6.8	55,000
1990	N. Iran	7.7	36,000
1993	Maharashtra, India	6.4	30,000
1994	Los Angeles, USA	6.6	51
1995	Kobe, Japan	7.2	5,000
1995	Sakhalin Is., Russia	7.5	2,000
1997	N.E. Iran	7.1	2,500
1998	Takhar, Afghanistan	6.1	4,200
1998	Rostaq, Afghanistan	7.0	5,000
1999	Izmit, Turkey	7.4	15,000
1999	Taipei, Taiwan	7.6	1,700
2001	Gujarat, India	7.7	18,600

Earthquakes

Earthquake magnitude is usually rated according to either the Richter or the Modified Mercalli scale, both devised by seismologists in the 1930s. The Richter scale measures absolute earthquake power with mathematical precision: each step upwards represents a tenfold increase in shockwave amplitude. Theoretically, there is no upper limit, but the largest earthquakes measured have been rated at between 8.8 and 8.9. The 12–point Mercalli scale, based on observed effects, is often more meaningful, ranging from I (earthquakes noticed only by seismographs) to XII (total destruction); intermediate points include V (people awakened at night; unstable objects overturned), VII (collapse of ordinary buildings; chimneys and monuments fall) and IX (conspicuous cracks in ground; serious damage to reservoirs).

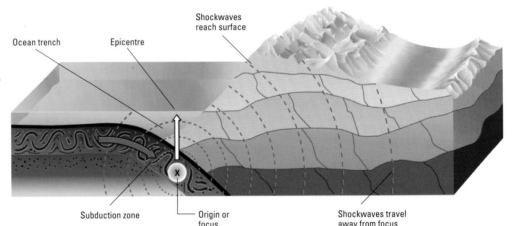

Ocean trench
Epicentre
Shockwaves reach surface
Subduction zone
Origin or focus
Shockwaves travel away from focus

Structure and Earthquakes

Mobile land areas
Submarine zones of mobile land areas
Stable land platforms
Submarine extensions of stable land platforms
Mid-oceanic volcanic ridges
Oceanic platforms

1976 ○ Principal earthquakes and dates

Earthquakes are a series of rapid vibrations originating from the slipping or faulting of parts of the Earth's crust when stresses within build up to breaking point. They usually happen at depths varying from 8 km to 30 km. Severe earthquakes cause extensive damage when they take place in populated areas, destroying structures and severing communications. Most initial loss of life occurs due to secondary causes such as falling masonry, fires and flooding.

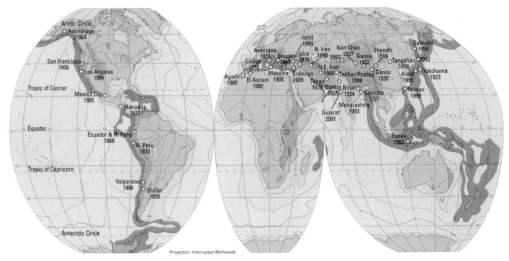

Projection: Interrupted Mollweide

Plate Tectonics

—— Plate boundaries   PACIFIC Major plates

➤ Direction of plate movements and rate of movement (cm/year)

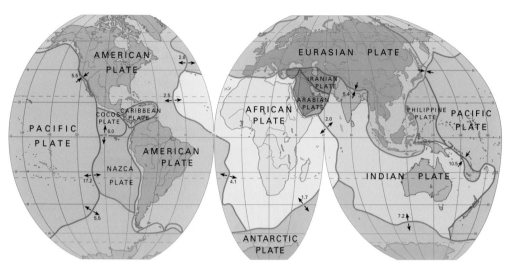

The drifting of the continents is a feature that is unique to Planet Earth. The complementary, almost jigsaw-puzzle fit of the coastlines on each side of the Atlantic Ocean inspired Alfred Wegener's theory of continental drift in 1915. The theory suggested that the ancient super-continent, which Wegener named Pangaea, incorporated all of the Earth's landmasses and gradually split up to form today's continents.

The original debate about continental drift was a prelude to a more radical idea: plate tectonics. The basic theory is that the Earth's crust is made up of a series of rigid plates which float on a soft layer of the mantle and are moved about by continental convection currents within the Earth's interior. These plates diverge and converge along margins marked by seismic activity. Plates diverge from mid-ocean ridges where molten lava pushes upwards and forces the plates apart at rates of up to 40 mm [1.6 in] a year.

The three diagrams, left, give some examples of plate boundaries from around the world. Diagram (a) shows sea-floor spreading at the Mid-Atlantic Ridge as the American and African plates slowly diverge. The same thing is happening in (b) where sea-floor spreading at the Mid-Indian Ocean Ridge is forcing the Indian plate to collide into the Eurasian plate. In (c) oceanic crust (sima) is being subducted beneath lighter continental crust (sial).

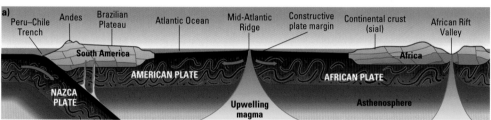

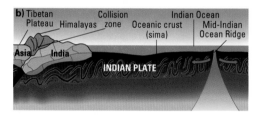

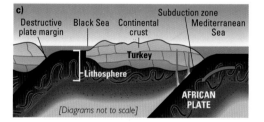

Volcanoes

Volcanoes occur when hot liquefied rock beneath the Earth's crust is pushed up by pressure to the surface as molten lava. Some volcanoes erupt in an explosive way, throwing out rocks and ash, whilst others are effusive and lava flows out of the vent. There are volcanoes which are both, such as Mount Fuji. An accumulation of lava and cinders creates cones of variable size and shape. As a result of many eruptions over centuries, Mount Etna in Sicily has a circumference of more than 120 km [75 miles].

Climatologists believe that volcanic ash, if ejected high into the atmosphere, can influence temperature and weather for several years afterwards. The 1991 eruption of Mount Pinatubo in the Philippines ejected more than 20 million tonnes of dust and ash 32 km [20 miles] into the atmosphere and is believed to have accelerated ozone depletion over a large part of the globe.

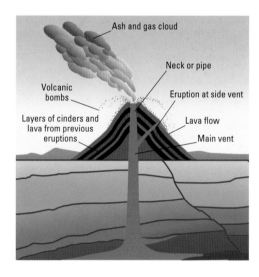

Distribution of Volcanoes

Volcanoes today may be the subject of considerable scientific study but they remain both dramatic and unpredictable: in 1991 Mount Pinatubo, 100 km [62 miles] north of the Philippines capital Manila, suddenly burst into life after lying dormant for more than six centuries. Most of the world's active volcanoes occur in a belt around the Pacific Ocean, on the edge of the Pacific plate, called the 'ring of fire'. Indonesia has the greatest concentration with 90 volcanoes, 12 of which are active. The most famous, Krakatoa, erupted in 1883 with such force that the resulting tidal wave killed 36,000 people and tremors were felt as far away as Australia.

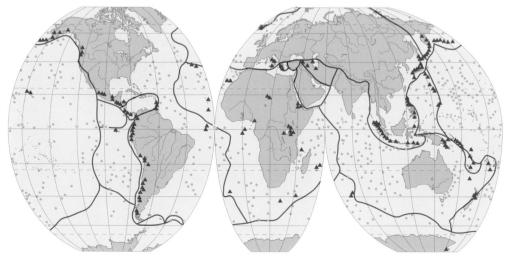

⬤ Submarine volcanoes

▲ Land volcanoes active since 1700

—— Boundaries of tectonic plates

Landforms

The Rock Cycle

James Hutton first proposed the rock cycle in the late 1700s after he observed the slow but steady effects of erosion.

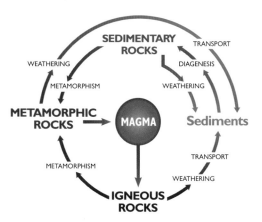

Above and below the surface of the oceans, the features of the Earth's crust are constantly changing. The phenomenal forces generated by convection currents in the molten core of our planet carry the vast segments or 'plates' of the crust across the globe in an endless cycle of creation and destruction. A continent may travel little more than 25 mm [1 in] per year, yet in the vast span of geological time this process throws up giant mountain ranges and creates new land.

Destruction of the landscape, however, begins as soon as it is formed. Wind, water, ice and sea, the main agents of erosion, mount a constant assault that even the most resistant rocks cannot withstand. Mountain peaks may dwindle by as little as a few millimetres each year, but if they are not uplifted by further movements of the crust they will eventually be reduced to rubble and transported away.

Water is the most powerful agent of erosion – it has been estimated that 100 billion tonnes of sediment are washed into the oceans every year. Three

Asian rivers account for 20% of this total, the Huang He, in China, and the Brahmaputra and Ganges in Bangladesh.

Rivers and glaciers, like the sea itself, generate much of their effect through abrasion – pounding the land with the debris they carry with them. But as well as destroying they also create new landforms, many of them spectacular: vast deltas like those of the Mississippi and the Nile, or the deep fjords cut by glaciers in British Columbia, Norway and New Zealand.

Geologists once considered that landscapes evolved from 'young', newly uplifted mountainous areas, through a 'mature' hilly stage, to an 'old age' stage when the land was reduced to an almost flat plain, or peneplain. This theory, called the 'cycle of erosion', fell into disuse when it became evident that so many factors, including the effects of plate tectonics and climatic change, constantly interrupt the cycle, which takes no account of the highly complex interactions that shape the surface of our planet.

Mountain Building

Mountains are formed when pressures on the Earth's crust caused by continental drift become so intense that the surface buckles or cracks. This happens where oceanic crust is subducted by continental crust or, more dramatically, where two tectonic plates collide: the Rockies, Andes, Alps, Urals and Himalayas resulted from such impacts. These are all known as fold mountains because they were formed by the compression of the rocks, forcing the surface to bend and fold like a crumpled rug. The Himalayas are formed from the folded former sediments of the Tethys Sea which was trapped in the collision zone between the Indian and Eurasian plates.

The other main mountain-building process occurs when the crust fractures to create faults, allowing rock to be forced upwards in large blocks; or when the pressure of magma within the crust forces the surface to bulge into a dome, or erupts to form a volcano. Large mountain ranges may reveal a combination of those features; the Alps, for example, have been compressed so violently that the folds are fragmented by numerous faults and intrusions of molten igneous rock.

Over millions of years, even the greatest mountain ranges can be reduced by the agents of erosion (most notably rivers) to a low rugged landscape known as a peneplain.

Types of faults: Faults occur where the crust is being stretched or compressed so violently that the rock strata break in a horizontal or vertical movement. They are classified by the direction in which the blocks of rock have moved. A normal fault results when a vertical movement causes the surface to break apart; compression causes a reverse fault. Horizontal movement causes shearing, known as a strike-slip fault. When the rock breaks in two places, the central block may be pushed up in a horst fault, or sink (creating a rift valley) in a graben fault.

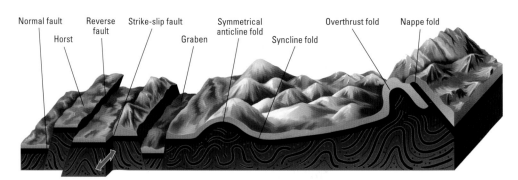

Types of fold: Folds occur when rock strata are squeezed and compressed. They are common therefore at destructive plate margins and where plates have collided, forcing the rocks to buckle into mountain ranges. Geographers give different names to the degrees of fold that result from continuing pressure on the rock. A simple fold may be symmetric, with even slopes on either side, but as the pressure builds up, one slope becomes steeper and the fold becomes asymmetric. Later, the ridge or 'anticline' at the top of the fold may slide over the lower ground or 'syncline' to form a recumbent fold. Eventually, the rock strata may break under the pressure to form an overthrust and finally a nappe fold.

Continental Glaciation

Ice sheets were at their greatest extent about 200,000 years ago. The maximum advance of the last Ice Age was about 18,000 years ago, when ice covered virtually all of Canada and reached as far south as the Bristol Channel in Britain.

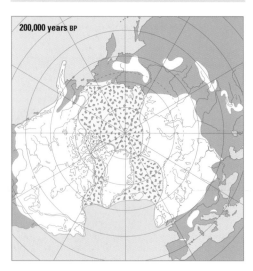

200,000 years BP

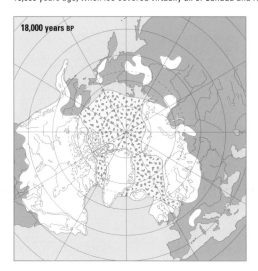

18,000 years BP

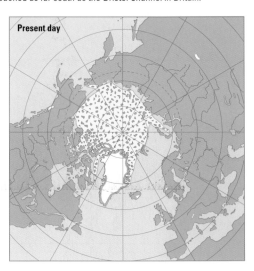

Present day

Natural Landforms

A stylized diagram to show a selection of landforms found in the mid-latitudes.

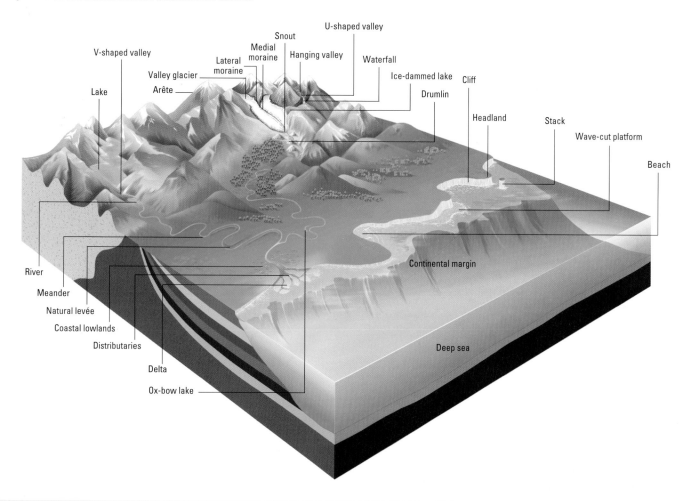

Labels (clockwise from top): U-shaped valley, Snout, Medial moraine, Hanging valley, Waterfall, Ice-dammed lake, Lateral moraine, Valley glacier, Arête, V-shaped valley, Lake, Drumlin, Cliff, Headland, Stack, Wave-cut platform, Beach, River, Meander, Natural levée, Coastal lowlands, Distributaries, Delta, Ox-bow lake, Continental margin, Deep sea

Desert Landscapes

The popular image that deserts are all huge expanses of sand is wrong. Despite harsh conditions, deserts contain some of the most varied and interesting landscapes in the world. They are also one of the most extensive environments – the hot and cold deserts together cover almost 40% of the Earth's surface.

The three types of hot desert are known by their Arabic names: sand desert, called *erg*, covers only about one-fifth of the world's desert; the rest is divided between *hammada* (areas of bare rock) and *reg* (broad plains covered by loose gravel or pebbles).

In areas of *erg*, such as the Namib Desert, the shape of the dunes reflects the character of local winds. Where winds are constant in direction, crescent-shaped *barchan* dunes form. In areas of bare rock, wind-blown sand is a major agent of erosion. The erosion is mainly confined to within 2 m [6.5 ft] of the surface, producing characteristic, mushroom-shaped rocks.

Erg

Hammada

Reg

Surface Processes

Catastrophic changes to natural landforms are periodically caused by such phenomena as avalanches, landslides and volcanic eruptions, but most of the processes that shape the Earth's surface operate extremely slowly in human terms. One estimate, based on a study in the United States, suggested that 1 m [3 ft] of land was removed from the entire surface of the country, on average, every 29,500 years. However, the time-scale varies from 1,300 years to 154,200 years depending on the terrain and climate.

In hot, dry climates, mechanical weathering, a result of rapid temperature changes, causes the outer layers of rock to peel away, while in cold mountainous regions, boulders are prised apart when water freezes in cracks in rocks. Chemical weathering, at its greatest in warm, humid regions, is responsible for hollowing out limestone caves and decomposing granites.

The erosion of soil and rock is greatest on sloping land and the steeper the slope, the greater the tendency for mass wasting – the movement of soil and rock downhill under the influence of gravity. The mechanisms of mass wasting (ranging from very slow to very rapid) vary with the type of material, but the presence of water as a lubricant is usually an important factor.

Running water is the world's leading agent of erosion and transportation. The energy of a river depends on several factors, including its velocity and volume, and its erosive power is at its peak when it is in full flood. Sea waves also exert tremendous erosive power during storms when they hurl pebbles against the shore, undercutting cliffs and hollowing out caves.

Glacier ice forms in mountain hollows and spills out to form valley glaciers, which transport rocks shattered by frost action. As glaciers move, rocks embedded into the ice erode steep-sided, U-shaped valleys. Evidence of glaciation in mountain regions includes cirques, knife-edged ridges, or arêtes, and pyramidal peaks.

Oceans

The Great Oceans

Relative sizes of the world's oceans

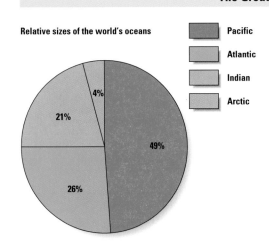

- Pacific
- Atlantic
- Indian
- Arctic

4%
21%
49%
26%

In a strict geographical sense there are only three true oceans – the Atlantic, Indian and Pacific. The legendary 'Seven Seas' would require these to be divided at the Equator and the addition of the Arctic Ocean – which accounts for less than 4% of the total sea area. The International Hydrographic Bureau does not recognize the Antarctic Ocean (even less the 'Southern Ocean') as a separate entity.

The Earth is a watery planet: more than 70% of its surface – over 360,000,000 sq km [140,000,000 sq miles] – is covered by the oceans and seas. The mighty Pacific alone accounts for nearly 36% of the total, and 49% of the sea area. Gravity holds in around 1,400 million cu. km [320 million cu. miles] of water, of which over 97% is saline.

The vast underwater world starts in the shallows of the seaside and plunges to depths of more than 11,000 m [36,000 ft]. The continental shelf, part of the landmass, drops gently to around 200 m [650 ft]; here the seabed falls away suddenly at an angle of 3° to 6° – the continental slope. The third stage, called the continental rise, is more gradual with gradients varying from 1 in 100 to 1 in 700. At an average depth of 5,000 m [16,500 ft] there begins the aptly-named abyssal plain – massive submarine depths where sunlight fails to penetrate and few creatures can survive.

From these plains rise volcanoes which, taken from base to top, rival and even surpass the tallest continental mountains in height. Mount Kea, on Hawaii, reaches a total of 10,203 m [33,400 ft], some 1,355 m [4,500 ft] more than Mount Everest, though scarcely 40% is visible above sea level.

In addition, there are underwater mountain chains up to 1,000 km [600 miles] across, whose peaks sometimes appear above sea level as islands such as Iceland and Tristan da Cunha.

The Ocean Depths

Average and maximum depths of the world's great oceans, in metres

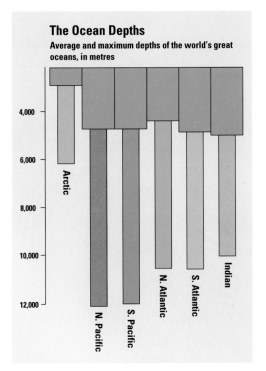

4,000
6,000
8,000
10,000
12,000

Arctic
N. Pacific
S. Pacific
N. Atlantic
S. Atlantic
Indian

Ocean Currents

January temperatures and ocean currents

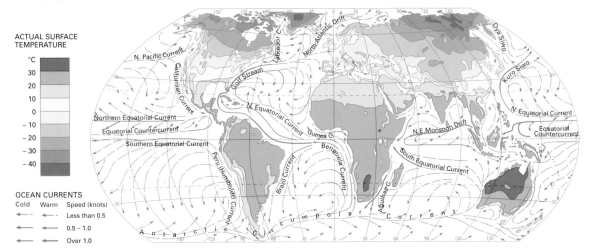

ACTUAL SURFACE TEMPERATURE

°C
30
20
10
0
- 10
- 20
- 30
- 40

OCEAN CURRENTS
Cold Warm Speed (knots)
Less than 0.5
0.5 – 1.0
Over 1.0

July temperatures and ocean currents

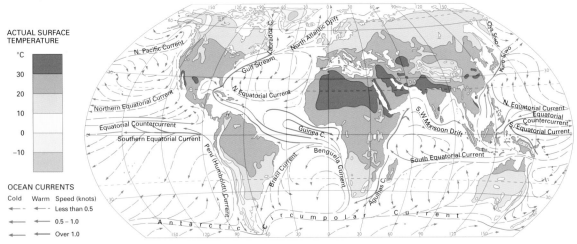

ACTUAL SURFACE TEMPERATURE

°C
30
20
10
0
-10

OCEAN CURRENTS
Cold Warm Speed (knots)
Less than 0.5
0.5 – 1.0
Over 1.0

Moving immense quantities of energy as well as billions of tonnes of water every hour, the ocean currents are a vital part of the great heat engine that drives the Earth's climate. They themselves are produced by a twofold mechanism. At the surface, winds push huge masses of water before them; in the deep ocean, below an abrupt temperature gradient that separates the churning surface waters from the still depths, density variations cause slow vertical movements.

The pattern of circulation of the great surface currents is determined by the displacement known as the Coriolis effect. As the Earth turns beneath a moving object – whether it is a tennis ball or a vast mass of water – it appears to be deflected to one side. The deflection is most obvious near the Equator, where the Earth's surface is spinning eastwards at 1,700 km/h [1,050 mph]; currents moving polewards are curved clockwise in the northern hemisphere and anti-clockwise in the southern.

The result is a system of spinning circles known as gyres. The Coriolis effect piles up water on the left of each gyre, creating a narrow, fast-moving stream that is matched by a slower, broader returning current on the right. North and south of the Equator, the fastest currents are located in the west and in the east respectively. In each case, warm water moves from the Equator and cold water returns to it. Cold currents often bring an upwelling of nutrients with them, supporting the world's most economically important fisheries.

Depending on the prevailing winds, some currents on or near the Equator may reverse their direction in the course of the year – a seasonal variation on which Asian monsoon rains depend, and whose occasional failure can bring disaster to millions.

World Fishing Areas

Main commercial fishing areas (numbered FAO regions)

Catch by top marine fishing areas, thousand tonnes (1997)

1.	Pacific, NW	[61]	26,785	28.7%
2.	Pacific, SE	[87]	15,717	16.8%
3.	Atlantic, NE	[27]	12,721	13.6%
4.	Pacific, WC	[71]	9,753	10.5%
5.	Indian, W	[51]	4,461	4.8%
6.	Indian, E	[57]	4,228	4.5%
7.	Atlantic, EC	[34]	3,873	4.2%
8.	Pacific, NE	[67]	3,042	3.3%

Principal fishing areas

Leading fishing nations

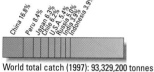

China 16.8% Peru 8.4% Japan 6.3% Chile 6.2% U.S.A. 5.4% Russia 5.0% India 3.9% Indonesia 3.9%

World total catch (1997): 93,329,200 tonnes
(Marine catch 91.7% Inland catch 8.3%)

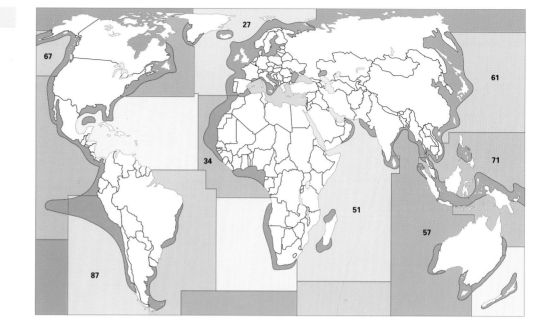

Marine Pollution

Sources of marine oil pollution (latest available year)

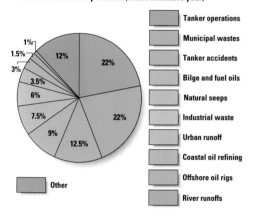

1% 1.5% 3% 3.5% 6% 7.5% 9% 12.5% 12% 22% 22%

- Tanker operations
- Municipal wastes
- Tanker accidents
- Bilge and fuel oils
- Natural seeps
- Industrial waste
- Urban runoff
- Coastal oil refining
- Offshore oil rigs
- River runoffs

Other

Oil Spills

Major oil spills from tankers and combined carriers

Year	Vessel	Location	Spill (barrels)**	Cause
1979	Atlantic Empress	West Indies	1,890,000	collision
1983	Castillo De Bellver	South Africa	1,760,000	fire
1978	Amoco Cadiz	France	1,628,000	grounding
1991	Haven	Italy	1,029,000	explosion
1988	Odyssey	Canada	1,000,000	fire
1967	Torrey Canyon	UK	909,000	grounding
1972	Sea Star	Gulf of Oman	902,250	collision
1977	Hawaiian Patriot	Hawaiian Is.	742,500	fire
1979	Independenta	Turkey	696,350	collision
1993	Braer	UK	625,000	grounding
1996	Sea Empress	UK	515,000	grounding

Other sources of major oil spills

1983	Nowruz oilfield	The Gulf	4,250,000†	war
1979	Ixtoc 1 oilwell	Gulf of Mexico	4,200,000	blow-out
1991	Kuwait	The Gulf	2,500,000†	war

** 1 barrel = 0.136 tonnes/159 lit./35 Imperial gal./42 US gal. † estimated

River Pollution

Sources of river pollution, USA (latest available year)

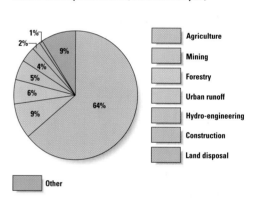

1% 2% 4% 5% 6% 9% 9% 64%

- Agriculture
- Mining
- Forestry
- Urban runoff
- Hydro-engineering
- Construction
- Land disposal

Other

Water Pollution

- Severely polluted sea areas and lakes
- Polluted sea areas and lakes
- Areas of frequent oil pollution by shipping

- ▲ Major oil tanker spills
- ▲ Major oil rig blow-outs
- ▼ Offshore dumpsites for industrial and municipal waste
- — Severely polluted rivers and estuaries

The most notorious tanker spillage of the 1980s occurred when the *Exxon Valdez* ran aground in Prince William Sound, Alaska, in 1989, spilling 267,000 barrels of crude oil close to shore in a sensitive ecological area. This rates as the world's 28th worst spill in terms of volume.

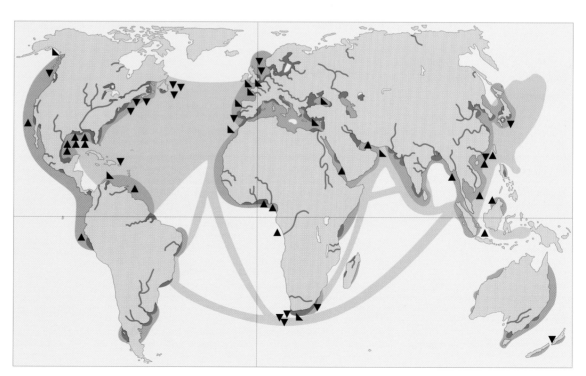

Climate

Climatic Regions

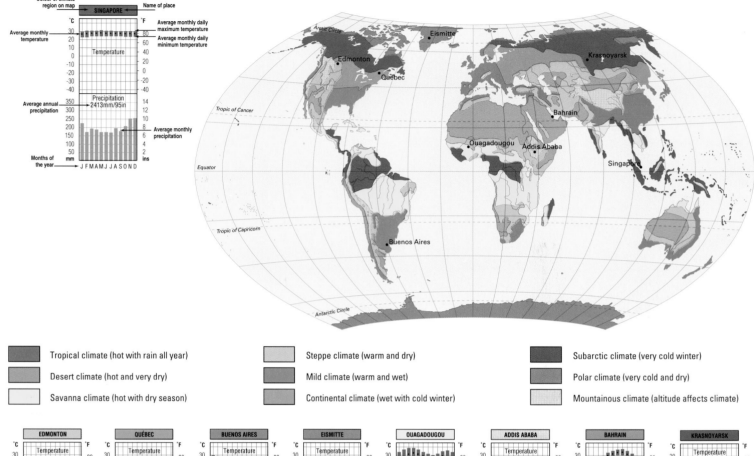

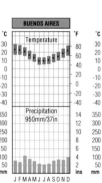
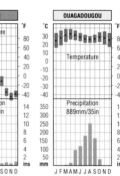
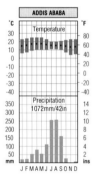
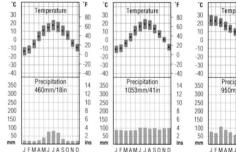
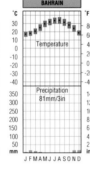
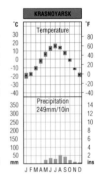

Tropical climate (hot with rain all year)

Desert climate (hot and very dry)

Savanna climate (hot with dry season)

Steppe climate (warm and dry)

Mild climate (warm and wet)

Continental climate (wet with cold winter)

Subarctic climate (very cold winter)

Polar climate (very cold and dry)

Mountainous climate (altitude affects climate)

Climate Records

Temperature
Highest recorded shade temperature: Al Aziziyah, Libya, 58°C [136.4°F], 13 September 1922.

Highest mean annual temperature: Dallol, Ethiopia, 34.4°C [94°F], 1960–66.

Longest heatwave: Marble Bar, W. Australia, 162 days over 38°C [100°F], 23 October 1923 to 7 April 1924.

Lowest recorded temperature (outside poles): Verkhoyansk, Siberia, –68°C [–90°F], 6 February 1933.

Lowest mean annual temperature: Plateau Station, Antarctica, –56.6°C [–72.0°F]

Pressure
Longest drought: Calama, N. Chile, no recorded rainfall in 400 years to 1971.

Wettest place (12 months): Cherrapunji, Meghalaya, N. E. India, 26,470 mm [1,040 in], August 1860 to August 1861. Cherrapunji also holds the record for the most rainfall in one month: 2,930 mm [115 in], July 1861.

Wettest place (average): Mawsynram, India, mean annual rainfall 11,873 mm [467.4 in].

Wettest place (24 hours): Cilaos, Réunion, Indian Ocean, 1,870 mm [73.6 in], 15–16 March 1952.

Heaviest hailstones: Gopalganj, Bangladesh, up to 1.02 kg [2.25 lb], 14 April 1986 (killed 92 people).

Heaviest snowfall (continuous): Bessans, Savoie, France, 1,730 mm [68 in] in 19 hours, 5–6 April 1969.

Heaviest snowfall (season/year): Paradise Ranger Station, Mt Rainier, Washington, USA, 31,102 mm [1,224.5 in], 19 February 1971 to 18 February 1972.

Pressure and winds
Highest barometric pressure: Agata, Siberia (at 262 m [862 ft] altitude), 1,083.8 mb, 31 December 1968.

Lowest barometric pressure: Typhoon Tip, Guam, Pacific Ocean, 870 mb, 12 October 1979.

Highest recorded wind speed: Mt Washington, New Hampshire, USA, 371 km/h [231 mph], 12 April 1934. This is three times as strong as hurricane force on the Beaufort Scale.

Windiest place: Commonwealth Bay, Antarctica, where gales frequently reach over 320 km/h [200 mph].

Climate

Climate is weather in the long term: the seasonal pattern of hot and cold, wet and dry, averaged over time (usually 30 years). At the simplest level, it is caused by the uneven heating of the Earth. Surplus heat at the Equator passes towards the poles, levelling out the energy differential. Its passage is marked by a ceaseless churning of the atmosphere and the oceans, further agitated by the Earth's diurnal spin and the motion it imparts to moving air and water. The heat's means of transport – by winds and ocean currents, by the continual evaporation and recondensation of water molecules – is the weather itself. There are four basic types of climate, each of which can be further subdivided: tropical, desert (dry), temperate and polar.

Composition of Dry Air

Nitrogen	78.09%	Sulphur dioxide	trace
Oxygen	20.95%	Nitrogen oxide	trace
Argon	0.93%	Methane	trace
Water vapour	0.2–4.0%	Dust	trace
Carbon dioxide	0.03%	Helium	trace
Ozone	0.00006%	Neon	trace

El Niño

In a normal year, south-easterly trade winds drive surface waters westwards off the coast of South America, drawing cold, nutrient-rich water up from below. In an El Niño year (which occurs every 2–7 years), warm water from the west Pacific suppresses upwelling in the east, depriving the region of nutrients. The water is warmed by as much as 7°C [12°F], disturbing the tropical atmospheric circulation. During an intense El Niño, the south-east trade winds change direction and become equatorial westerlies, resulting in climatic extremes in many regions of the world, such as drought in parts of Australia and India, and heavy rainfall in south-eastern USA. An intense El Niño occurred in 1997–8, with resultant freak weather conditions across the entire Pacific region.

Normal year

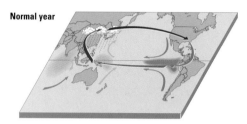

El Niño event

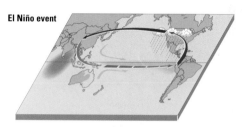

Beaufort Wind Scale

Named after the 19th-century British naval officer who devised it, the Beaufort Scale assesses wind speed according to its effects. It was originally designed as an aid for sailors, but has since been adapted for use on the land.

Scale	Wind speed km/h	mph	Effect
0	0–1	0–1	**Calm** Smoke rises vertically
1	1–5	1–3	**Light air** Wind direction shown only by smoke drift
2	6–11	4–7	**Light breeze** Wind felt on face; leaves rustle; vanes moved by wind
3	12–19	8–12	**Gentle breeze** Leaves and small twigs in constant motion; wind extends small flag
4	20–28	13–18	**Moderate** Raises dust and loose paper; small branches move
5	29–38	19–24	**Fresh** Small trees in leaf sway; wavelets on inland waters
6	39–49	25–31	**Strong** Large branches move; difficult to use umbrellas
7	50–61	32–38	**Near gale** Whole trees in motion; difficult to walk against wind
8	62–74	39–46	**Gale** Twigs break from trees; walking very difficult
9	75–88	47–54	**Strong gale** Slight structural damage
10	89–102	55–63	**Storm** Trees uprooted; serious structural damage
11	103–117	64–72	**Violent storm** Widespread damage
12	118+	73+	**Hurricane**

Conversions
°C = (°F − 32) × 5/9; °F = (°C × 9/5) + 32; 0°C = 32°F
1 in = 25.4 mm; 1 mm = 0.0394 in; 100 mm = 3.94 in

Temperature

Average temperature in January

Temperature
- 30°C
- 20°C
- 10°C
- 0°C
- −10°C
- −20°C
- −30°C
- −40°C

Average temperature in July

Temperature
- 30°C
- 20°C
- 10°C
- 0°C
- −10°C

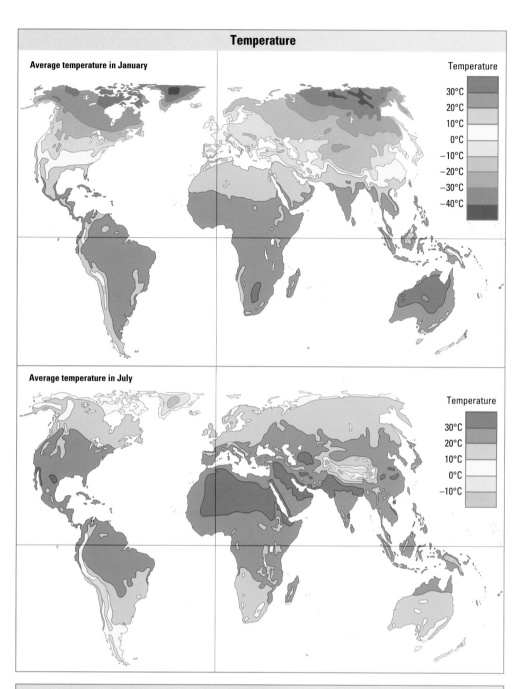

Precipitation

Average annual precipitation
- 3,000 mm
- 2,000 mm
- 1,000 mm
- 500 mm
- 250 mm

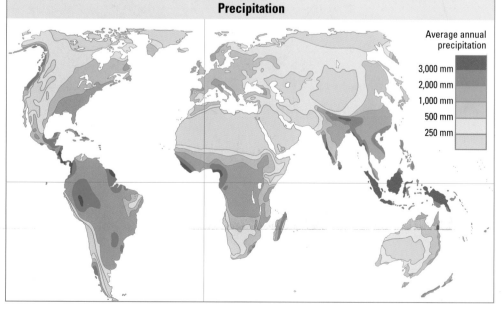

Water and Vegetation

The Hydrological Cycle

The world's water balance is regulated by the constant recycling of water between the oceans, atmosphere and land. The movement of water between these three reservoirs is known as the hydrological cycle. The oceans play a vital role in the hydrological cycle: 74% of the total precipitation falls over the oceans and 84% of the total evaporation comes from the oceans.

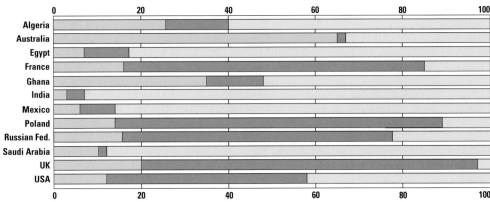

Water Distribution

The distribution of planetary water, by percentage. Oceans and ice-caps together account for more than 99% of the total; the breakdown of the remainder is estimated.

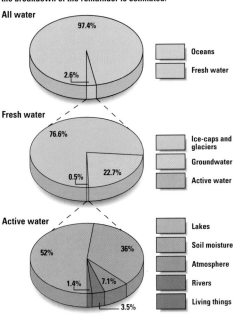

All water
- 97.4% Oceans
- 2.6% Fresh water

Fresh water
- 76.6% Ice-caps and glaciers
- 22.7% Groundwater
- 0.5% Active water

Active water
- 52% Lakes
- 36% Soil moisture
- 7.1% Atmosphere
- 3.5% Rivers
- 1.4% Living things

Water Utilization

Domestic   Industrial   Agriculture

The percentage breakdown of water usage by sector, selected countries (1996)

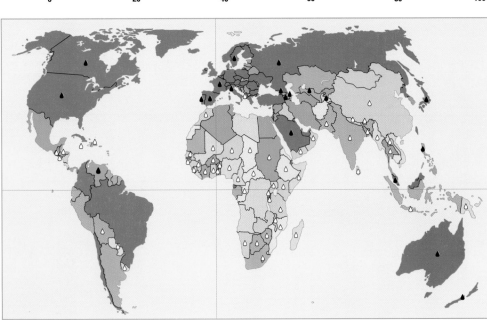

Algeria
Australia
Egypt
France
Ghana
India
Mexico
Poland
Russian Fed.
Saudi Arabia
UK
USA

Water Usage

Almost all the world's water is 3,000 million years old, and all of it cycles endlessly through the hydrosphere, though at different rates. Water vapour circulates over days, even hours, deep ocean water circulates over millennia, and ice-cap water remains solid for millions of years.

Fresh water is essential to all terrestrial life. Humans cannot survive more than a few days without it, and even the hardiest desert plants and animals could not exist without some water. Agriculture requires huge quantities of fresh water: without large-scale irrigation most of the world's people would starve. In the USA, agriculture uses 42% and industry 45% of all water withdrawals.

The United States is one of the heaviest users of water in the world. According to the latest figures the average American uses 380 litres a day and the average household uses 415,000 litres a year. This is two to four times more than in Western Europe.

Water Supply

Percentage of total population with access to safe drinking water (1995)

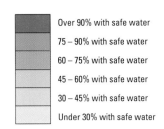

- Over 90% with safe water
- 75 – 90% with safe water
- 60 – 75% with safe water
- 45 – 60% with safe water
- 30 – 45% with safe water
- Under 30% with safe water

◊ Under 80 litres per person per day domestic water consumption

♦ Over 320 litres per person per day domestic water consumption

NB: 80 litres of water a day is considered necessary for a reasonable quality of life.

Least well-provided countries

Paraguay	8%	Central Afr. Rep	18%
Afghanistan	10%	Bhutan	21%
Cambodia	13%	Congo (D. Rep.)	25%

Natural Vegetation

Regional variation in vegetation

- Tundra and mountain vegetation
- Needleleaf evergreen forest
- Mixed needleleaf evergreen & broadleaf deciduous trees
- Broadleaf deciduous woodland
- Mid-latitude grassland
- Evergreen broadleaf and deciduous trees & shrubs
- Semi-desert scrub
- Desert
- Tropical grassland (savanna)
- Tropical broadleaf rainforest and monsoon forest
- Subtropical broadleaf and needleleaf forest

The map shows the natural 'climax vegetation' of regions, as dictated by climate and topography. In most cases, however, agricultural activity has drastically altered the vegetation pattern. Western Europe, for example, lost most of its broadleaf forest many centuries ago, while irrigation has turned some natural semi-desert into productive land.

Land Use by Continent

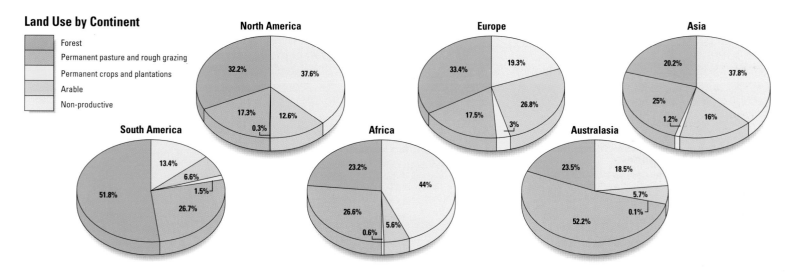

- Forest
- Permanent pasture and rough grazing
- Permanent crops and plantations
- Arable
- Non-productive

North America
37.6%, 12.6%, 0.3%, 17.3%, 32.2%

Europe
19.3%, 26.8%, 3%, 17.5%, 33.4%

Asia
37.8%, 16%, 1.2%, 25%, 20.2%

South America
13.4%, 6.6%, 1.5%, 26.7%, 51.8%

Africa
23.2%, 44%, 5.6%, 0.6%, 26.6%

Australasia
23.5%, 18.5%, 5.7%, 0.1%, 52.2%

Forestry: Production

Forest and woodland (million hectares)		Annual production (1996, million cubic metres)	
		Fuelwood and charcoal	Industrial roundwood*
World	**3,987.9**	**1,864.8**	**1,489.5**
S. America	829.3	193.0	129.9
N. & C. America	709.8	155.4	600.4
Africa	684.6	519.9	67.9
Asia	131.8	905.2	280.2
Europe	157.3	82.4	369.7
Australasia	157.2	8.7	41.5

Paper and Board

Top producers (1996)**		Top exporters (1996)**	
USA	85,173	Canada	13,393
China	30,253	USA	9,113
Japan	30,014	Finland	8,529
Canada	18,414	Sweden	7,483
Germany	14,733	Germany	6,319

* roundwood is timber as it is felled
** in thousand tonnes

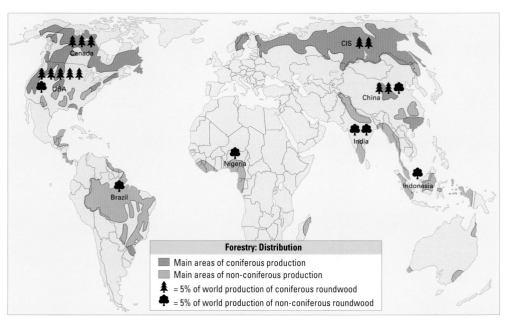

Forestry: Distribution

- Main areas of coniferous production
- Main areas of non-coniferous production
- 🌲 = 5% of world production of coniferous roundwood
- ♣ = 5% of world production of non-coniferous roundwood

Environment

Humans have always had a dramatic effect on their environment, at least since the development of agriculture almost 10,000 years ago. Generally, the Earth has accepted human interference without obvious ill effects: the complex systems that regulate the global environment have been able to absorb substantial damage while maintaining a stable and comfortable home for the planet's trillions of lifeforms. But advancing human technology and the rapidly-expanding populations it supports are now threatening to overwhelm the Earth's ability to compensate.

Industrial wastes, acid rainfall, desertification and large-scale deforestation all combine to create environmental change at a rate far faster than the great slow cycles of planetary evolution can accommodate. As a result of overcultivation, overgrazing and overcutting of groundcover for firewood, desertification is affecting as much as 60% of the world's croplands. In addition, with fire and chain-saws, humans are destroying more forest in a day than their ancestors could have done in a century, upsetting the balance between plant and animal, carbon dioxide and oxygen, on which all life ultimately depends.

The fossil fuels that power industrial civilization have pumped enough carbon dioxide and other so-called greenhouse gases into the atmosphere to make climatic change a near-certainty. As a result of the combination of these factors, the Earth's average temperature has risen by approximately 0.5°C [1°F] since the beginning of the 20th century, and it is still rising.

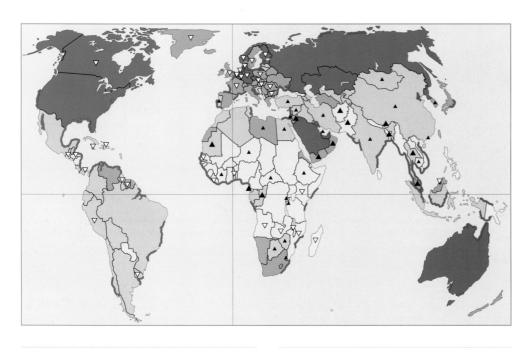

Global Warming

Carbon dioxide emissions in tonnes per person per year (1996)

- Over 10 tonnes of CO_2
- 5 – 10 tonnes of CO_2
- 1 – 5 tonnes of CO_2
- Under 1 tonne of CO_2
- No data available

Changes in CO_2 emissions 1980–90

- ▲ Over 100% increase in emissions
- ▲ 50–100% increase in emissions
- ▽ Reduction in emissions
- — Coastal areas in danger of flooding from rising sea levels caused by global warming

High atmospheric concentrations of heat-absorbing gases, appear to be causing a rise in average temperatures worldwide – up to 1.5°C [3°F] by the year 2020, according to some estimates. Global warming is likely to bring about a rise in sea levels that may flood some of the world's densely populated coastal areas.

Greenhouse Power

Relative contributions to the Greenhouse Effect by the major heat-absorbing gases in the atmosphere.

The chart combines greenhouse potency and volume. Carbon dioxide has a greenhouse potential of only 1, but its concentration of 350 parts per million makes it predominate. CFC 12, with 25,000 times the absorption capacity of CO_2, is present only as 0.00044 ppm.

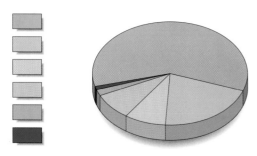

Ozone Layer

The ozone 'hole' over the northern hemisphere on 12 March 1995.

The colours represent Dobson Units (DU). The ozone 'hole' is seen as the dark blue and purple patch in the centre, where ozone values are around 120 DU or lower. Normal levels are around 280 DU. The ozone 'hole' over Antarctica is much larger.

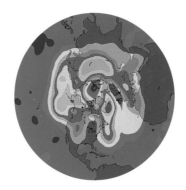

Carbon Dioxide

Cumulative carbon emissions, million tonnes of carbon (1950–96)

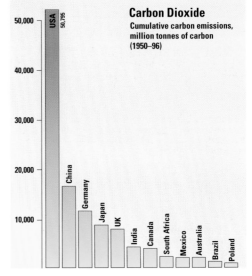

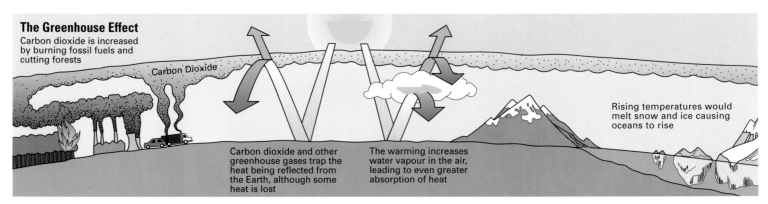

The Greenhouse Effect

Carbon dioxide is increased by burning fossil fuels and cutting forests

Carbon Dioxide

Carbon dioxide and other greenhouse gases trap the heat being reflected from the Earth, although some heat is lost

The warming increases water vapour in the air, leading to even greater absorption of heat

Rising temperatures would melt snow and ice causing oceans to rise

Desertification

- Existing deserts
- Areas with a high risk of desertification
- Areas with a moderate risk of desertification
- Former areas of rainforest
- Existing rainforest

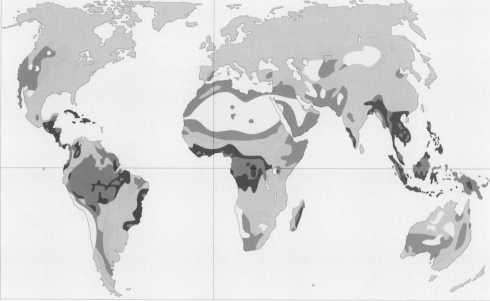

Forest Clearance

Thousands of hectares of forest cleared annually, tropical countries surveyed 1981–85 and 1987–90. Loss as a percentage of remaining stocks is shown in figures on each column.

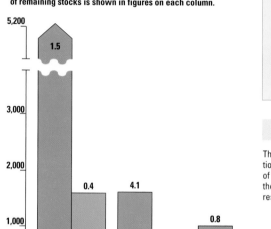

Deforestation

The Earth's remaining forests are under attack from three directions: expanding agriculture, logging, and growing consumption of fuelwood, often in combination. Sometimes deforestation is the direct result of government policy, as in the efforts made to resettle the urban poor in some parts of Brazil; just as often, it comes about despite state attempts at conservation. Loggers, licensed or unlicensed, blaze a trail into virgin forest, often destroying twice as many trees as they harvest. Landless farmers follow, burning away most of what remains to plant their crops, completing the destruction.

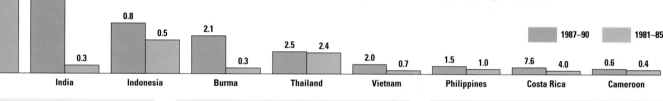

Ozone Depletion

The ozone layer, 25–30 km [15–18 miles] above sea level, acts as a barrier to most of the Sun's harmful ultra-violet radiation, protecting us from the ionizing radiation that can cause skin cancer and cataracts. In recent years, however, two holes in the ozone layer have been observed during winter: one over the Arctic and the other, the size of the USA, over Antarctica. By 1996, ozone had been reduced to around a half of its 1970 amount. The ozone (O_3) is broken down by chlorine released into the atmosphere as CFCs (chlorofluorocarbons) – chemicals used in refrigerators, packaging and aerosols.

Air Pollution

Sulphur dioxide is the main pollutant associated with industrial cities. According to the World Health Organization, at least 600 million people live in urban areas where sulphur dioxide concentrations regularly reach damaging levels. One of the world's most dangerously polluted urban areas is Mexico City, due to a combination of its enclosed valley location, 3 million cars and 60,000 factories. In May 1998, this lethal cocktail was added to by nearby forest fires and the resultant air pollution led to over 20% of the population (3 million people) complaining of respiratory problems.

Acid Rain

Killing trees, poisoning lakes and rivers and eating away buildings, acid rain is mostly produced by sulphur dioxide emissions from industry and volcanic eruptions. By the mid 1990s, acid rain had sterilized 4,000 or more of Sweden's lakes and left 45% of Switzerland's alpine conifers dead or dying, while the monuments of Greece were dissolving in Athens' smog. Prevailing wind patterns mean that the acids often fall many hundred kilometres from where the original pollutants were discharged. In parts of Europe acid deposition has slightly decreased, following reductions in emissions, but not by enough.

World Pollution

Acid rain and sources of acidic emissions (latest available year)

Acid rain is caused by high levels of sulphur and nitrogen in the atmosphere. They combine with water vapour and oxygen to form acids (H_2SO_4 and HNO_3) which fall as precipitation.

- Regions where sulphur and nitrogen oxides are released in high concentrations, mainly from fossil fuel combustion
- Major cities with high levels of air pollution (including nitrogen and sulphur emissions)

Areas of heavy acid deposition

pH numbers indicate acidity, decreasing from a neutral 7. Normal rain, slightly acid from dissolved carbon dioxide, never exceeds a pH of 5.6.

- pH less than 4.0 (most acidic)
- pH 4.0 to 4.5
- pH 4.5 to 5.0
- Areas where acid rain is a potential problem

Population

Demographic Profiles

Developed nations such as the UK have populations evenly spread across the age groups and, usually, a growing proportion of elderly people. The great majority of the people in developing nations, however, are in the younger age groups, about to enter their most fertile years. In time, these population profiles should resemble the world profile (even Kenya has made recent progress with reducing its birth rate), but the transition will come about only after a few more generations of rapid population growth.

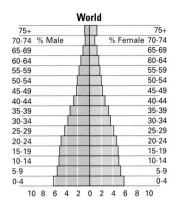

World

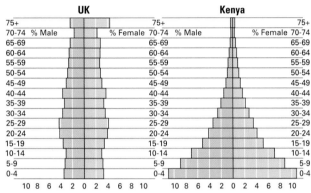

UK / **Kenya**

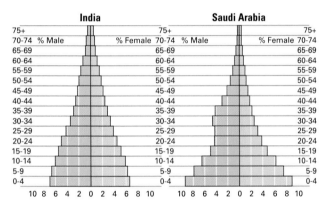

India / **Saudi Arabia**

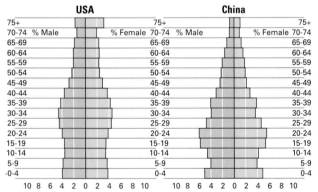

USA / **China**

Most Populous Nations [in millions (2000 estimates)]

1.	China	1,299	9.	Japan	128	17. Egypt	64
2.	India	1,041	10.	Mexico	107	18. Thailand	63
3.	USA	266	11.	Nigeria	105	19. Ethiopia	61
4.	Indonesia	218	12.	Vietnam	82	20. France	58
5.	Brazil	179	13.	Philippines	77	21. UK	58
6.	Pakistan	162	14.	Germany	76	22. Italy	57
7.	Russia	155	15.	Iran	68	23. Ukraine	52
8.	Bangladesh	150	16.	Turkey	66	24. Burma (Myanmar)	51

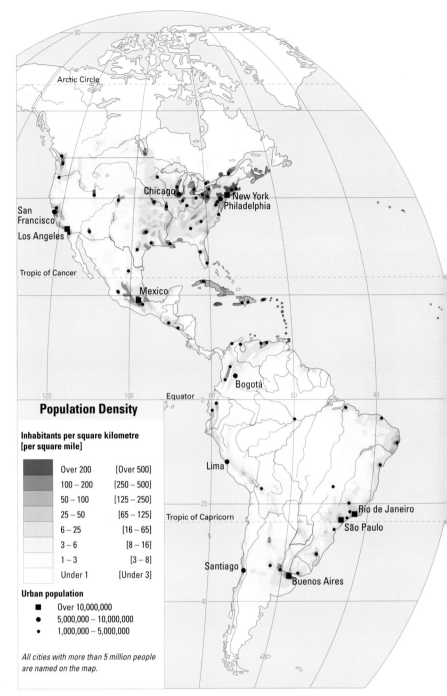

Population Density

Inhabitants per square kilometre [per square mile]

Over 200	[Over 500]
100 – 200	[250 – 500]
50 – 100	[125 – 250]
25 – 50	[65 – 125]
6 – 25	[16 – 65]
3 – 6	[8 – 16]
1 – 3	[3 – 8]
Under 1	[Under 3]

Urban population
- ■ Over 10,000,000
- ● 5,000,000 – 10,000,000
- • 1,000,000 – 5,000,000

All cities with more than 5 million people are named on the map.

Continental Comparisons

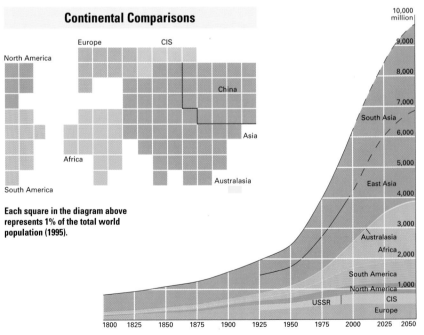

Each square in the diagram above represents 1% of the total world population (1995).

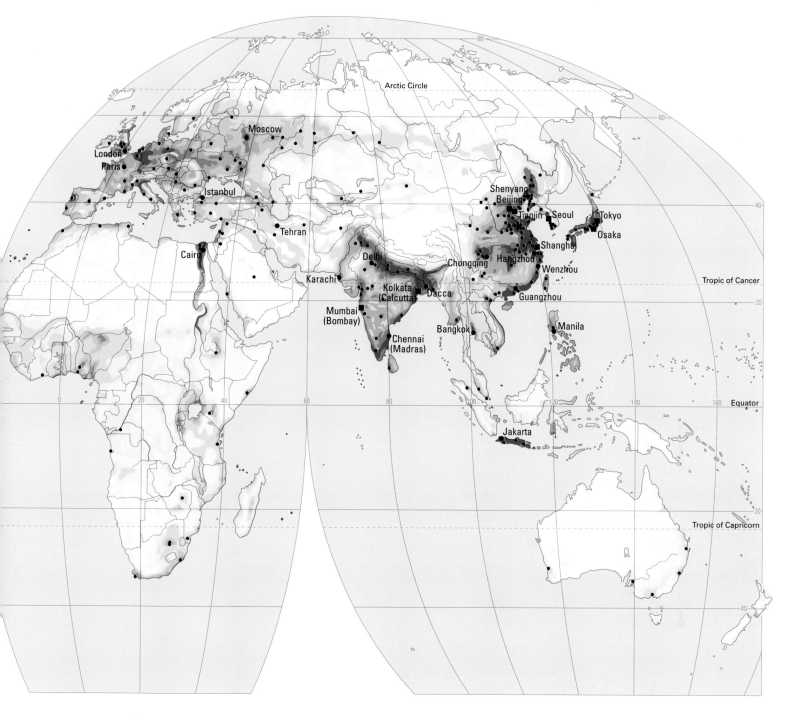

Arctic Circle

Moscow

London
Paris

Istanbul

Tehran

Cairo

Shenyang
Beijing
Tianjin
Seoul
Tokyo
Osaka
Shanghai
Hangzhou
Wenzhou

Delhi

Karachi

Chongqing

Kolkata
(Calcutta)
Dacca

Mumbai
(Bombay)

Chennai
(Madras)

Bangkok

Guangzhou

Manila

Tropic of Cancer

Equator

Jakarta

Tropic of Capricorn

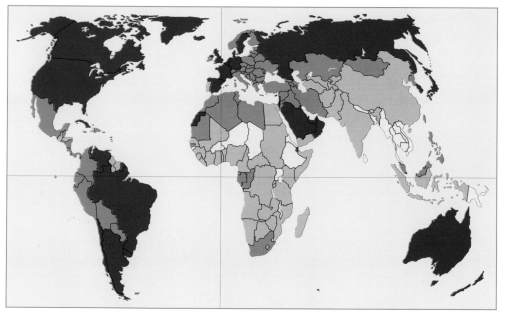

Urban Population

Percentage of total population living in towns and cities (1997)

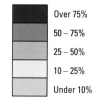

Over 75%

50 – 75%

25 – 50%

10 – 25%

Under 10%

Most urbanized		**Least urbanized**	
Singapore	100%	Rwanda	6%
Belgium	97%	Bhutan	8%
Israel	91%	Burundi	8%
Uruguay	91%	Nepal	11%
Netherlands	89%	Swaziland	12%

[UK 89%]

The Human Family

Predominant Languages

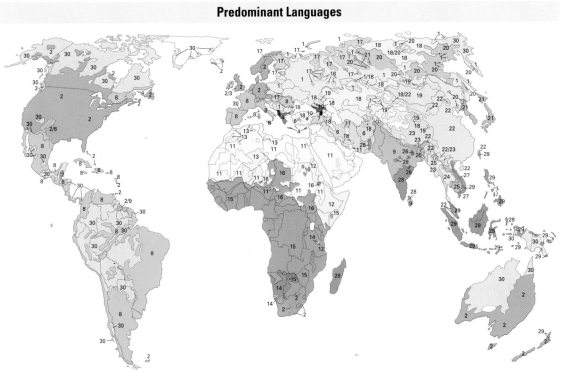

Languages of the World

Language can be classified by ancestry and structure. For example, the Romance and Germanic groups are both derived from an Indo-European language believed to have been spoken 5,000 years ago.

First-language speakers, 1999 (in millions)
Mandarin Chinese 885, Spanish 332, English 322, Bengali 189, Hindi 182, Portuguese 170, Russian 170, Japanese 125, German 98, Wu Chinese 77, Javanese 76, Korean 75, French 72, Vietnamese 68, Yue Chinese 66, Marathi 65, Tamil 63, Turkish 59, Urdu 58.

Official languages (% of total population)
English 27%, Chinese 19%, Hindi 13.5%, Spanish 5.4%, Russian 5.2%, French 4.2%, Arabic 3.3%, Portuguese 3%, Malay 3%, Bengali 2.9%, Japanese 2.3%.

INDO-EUROPEAN FAMILY

1 Balto-Slavic group (incl. Russian, Ukrainian)
2 Germanic group (incl. English, German)
3 Celtic group
4 Greek
5 Albanian
6 Iranian group
7 Armenian
8 Romance group (incl. Spanish, Portuguese, French, Italian)
9 Indo-Aryan group (incl. Hindi, Bengali, Urdu, Punjabi, Marathi)
10 CAUCASIAN FAMILY

AFRO-ASIATIC FAMILY

11 Semitic group (incl. Arabic)
12 Kushitic group
13 Berber group

14 KHOISAN FAMILY

15 NIGER-CONGO FAMILY

16 NILO-SAHARAN FAMILY

17 URALIC FAMILY

ALTAIC FAMILY

18 Turkic group
19 Mongolian group
20 Tungus-Manchu group
21 Japanese and Korean

SINO-TIBETAN FAMILY

22 Sinitic (Chinese) languages
23 Tibetic-Burmic languages

24 TAI FAMILY

AUSTRO-ASIATIC FAMILY

25 Mon-Khmer group
26 Munda group
27 Vietnamese

28 DRAVIDIAN FAMILY (incl. Telugu, Tamil)

29 AUSTRONESIAN FAMILY (incl. Malay-Indonesian)

30 OTHER LANGUAGES

Predominant Religions

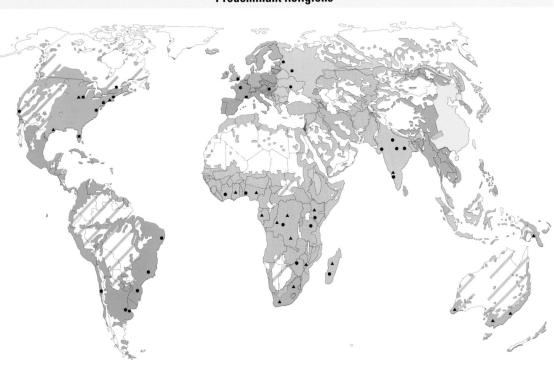

Religious Adherents

Religious adherents in millions (1998)

Christianity	1,980	Buddhist	360
Roman Catholic	*1,300*	Chinese Trad.	225
Orthodox	*240*	Indigenous	190
African sects	*110*	Sikh	23
Pentecostal	*105*	Yoruba	20
Others	*225*	Juche	19
Islam	1,300	Spiritism	14
Sunni	*940*	Judaism	14
Shiite	*120*	Baha'i	6
Others	*240*	Jainism	4
Hindu	900	Shinto	4
Secular	850		

 Roman Catholicism

 Orthodox and other Eastern Churches

Protestantism

Sunni Islam

Shiite Islam

Buddhism

Hinduism

Confucianism

Judaism

Shintoism

Tribal Religions

United Nations

Created in 1945 to promote peace and co-operation and based in New York, the United Nations is the world's largest international organization, with 185 members and an annual budget of US $2.6 billion (1996–97). Each member of the General Assembly has one vote, while the permanent members of the 15-nation Security Council – USA, Russia, China, UK and France – hold a veto. The Secretariat is the UN's principal administrative arm. The 54 members of the Economic and Social Council are responsible for economic, social, cultural, educational, health and related matters. The UN has 16 specialized agencies – based in Canada, France, Switzerland and Italy, as well as the USA – which help members in fields such as education (UNESCO), agriculture (FAO), medicine (WHO) and finance (IFC). By the end of 1994, all the original 11 trust territories of the Trusteeship Council had become independent.

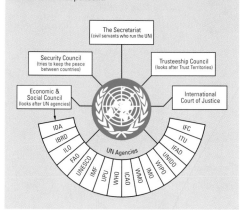

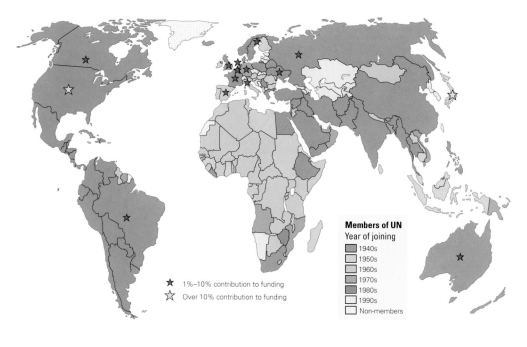

Members of UN
Year of joining
- 1940s
- 1950s
- 1960s
- 1970s
- 1980s
- 1990s
- Non-members

★ 1%–10% contribution to funding

☆ Over 10% contribution to funding

MEMBERSHIP OF THE UN In 1945 there were 51 members; by 2000 membership had increased to 188 following the admission of Kiribati, Nauru and Tonga. There are 4 independent states which are not members of the UN – Switzerland, Taiwan, Tuvalu and the Vatican City. All the successor states of the former USSR had joined by the end of 1992. The official languages of the UN are Chinese, English, French, Russian, Spanish and Arabic.

FUNDING The UN budget for 1996–97 was US $2.6 billion. Contributions are assessed by the members' ability to pay, with the maximum 25% of the total, the minimum 0.01%. Contributions for 1996 were: USA 25.0%, Japan 15.4%, Germany 9.0%, France 6.4%, UK 5.3%, Italy 5.2%, Russia 4.5%, Canada 3.1%, Spain 2.4%, Brazil 1.6%, Netherlands 1.6%, Australia 1.5%, Sweden 1.2%, Ukraine 1.1%, Belgium 1.0%.

International Organizations

EU European Union (evolved from the European Community in 1993). The 15 members – Austria, Belgium, Denmark, Finland, France, Germany, Greece, Ireland, Italy, Luxembourg, Netherlands, Portugal, Spain, Sweden and the UK – aim to integrate economies, co-ordinate social developments and bring about political union. These members of what is now the world's biggest market share agricultural and industrial policies and tariffs on trade. The original body, the European Coal and Steel Community (ECSC), was created in 1951 following the signing of the Treaty of Paris.

EFTA European Free Trade Association (formed in 1960). Portugal left the original 'Seven' in 1989 to join what was then the EC, followed by Austria, Finland and Sweden in 1995. Only 4 members remain: Norway, Iceland, Switzerland and Liechtenstein.

ACP African-Caribbean-Pacific (formed in 1963). Members have economic ties with the EU.

NATO North Atlantic Treaty Organization (formed in 1949). It continues after 1991 despite the winding up of the Warsaw Pact. The Czech Republic, Hungary and Poland were the latest members to join in 1999.

OAS Organization of American States (formed in 1948). It aims to promote social and economic co-operation between developed countries of North America and developing nations of Latin America.

ASEAN Association of South-east Asian Nations (formed in 1967). Cambodia joined in 1999.

OAU Organization of African Unity (formed in 1963). Its 53 members represent over 94% of Africa's population. Arabic, French, Portuguese and English are recognized as working languages.

LAIA Latin American Integration Association (1980). Its aim is to promote freer regional trade.

OECD Organization for Economic Co-operation and Development (formed in 1961). It comprises the 29 major Western free-market economies. Poland, Hungary and South Korea joined in 1996. 'G8' is its 'inner group' comprising Canada, France, Germany, Italy, Japan, Russia, the UK and the USA.

COMMONWEALTH The Commonwealth of Nations evolved from the British Empire; it comprises 16 Queen's realms, 32 republics and 5 indigenous monarchies, giving a total of 53.

OPEC Organization of Petroleum Exporting Countries (formed in 1960). It controls about three-quarters of the world's oil supply. Gabon left the organization in 1996.

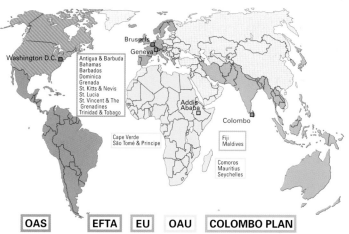

OAS EFTA EU OAU COLOMBO PLAN

ARAB LEAGUE (formed in 1945). The League's aim is to promote economic, social, political and military co-operation. There are 21 member nations.

COLOMBO PLAN (formed in 1951). Its 26 members aim to promote economic and social development in Asia and the Pacific.

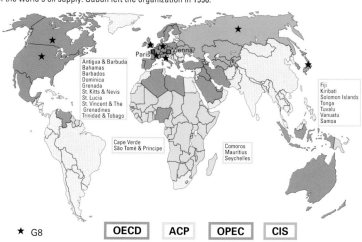

★ G8

OECD ACP OPEC CIS

NATO LAIA ARAB LEAGUE COMMONWEALTH ASEAN

Wealth

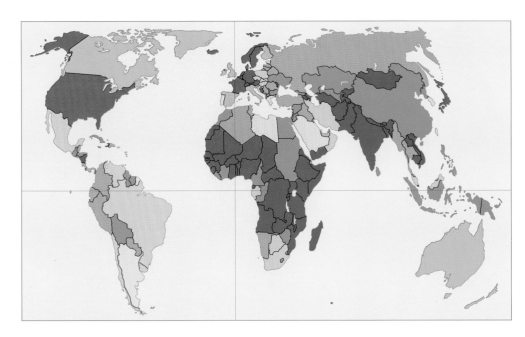

Gross National Product per capita: the value of total production divided by the population (1997)

Over 400% of world average

200 – 400% of world average

100 – 200% of world average

[World average wealth per person US $6,316]

50 – 100% of world average

25 – 50% of world average

10 – 25% of world average

Under 10% of world average

GNP per capita growth rate (%), selected countries, 1985–94

Thailand	8.2	Brazil	−0.4
Chile	6.9	Zimbabwe	−0.6
Japan	3.2	USA	−1.3
Germany	1.9	UK	−1.4
Australia	1.2	Armenia	−12.9

Wealth Creation

The Gross National Product (GNP) of the world's largest economies, US $ million (1998)

#	Country	GNP	#	Country	GNP
1.	USA	7,922,651	23.	Saudi Arabia	186,000
2.	Japan	4,089,910	24.	Denmark	176,374
3.	Germany	2,122,673	25.	Hong Kong	158,286
4.	Italy	1,666,178	26.	Norway	152,082
5.	France	1,466,014	27.	Poland	150,798
6.	UK	1,263,777	28.	Indonesia	138,501
7.	China	928,950	29.	Thailand	134,433
8.	Botswana	758,043	30.	Finland	124,293
9.	Canada	612,332	31.	Greece	122,880
10.	Spain	553,690	32.	South Africa	119,001
11.	India	421,259	33.	Iran	109,645
12.	Netherlands	388,682	34.	Portugal	106,376
13.	Mexico	380,917	35.	Colombia	106,090
14.	Australia	380,625	36.	Israel	95,179
15.	South Korea	369,890	37.	Singapore	95,095
16.	Russia	337,914	38.	Venezuela	81,347
17.	Argentina	324,084	39.	Malaysia	79,848
18.	Switzerland	284,808	40.	Egypt	79,208
19.	Belgium	259,045	41.	Philippines	78,896
20.	Sweden	226,861	42.	Chile	71,294
21.	Austria	217,163	43.	Ireland	67,491
22.	Turkey	200,505	44.	Pakistan	63,159

The Wealth Gap

The world's richest and poorest countries, by Gross National Product per capita in US $ (1999 estimates)

#	Country	GNP	#	Country	GNP
1.	Liechtenstein	50,000	1.	Ethiopia	100
2.	Luxembourg	44,640	2.	Congo (D. Rep.)	110
3.	Switzerland	38,350	3.	Burundi	120
4.	Bermuda	35,590	4.	Sierra Leone	130
5.	Norway	32,880	5.	Guinea-Bissau	160
6.	Japan	32,230	6.	Niger	190
7.	Denmark	32,030	7.	Malawi	190
8.	USA	30,600	8.	Eritrea	200
9.	Singapore	29,610	9.	Chad	200
10.	Iceland	29,280	10.	Nepal	220
11.	Austria	25,970	11.	Angola	220
12.	Germany	25,350	12.	Mozambique	230
13.	Sweden	25,040	13.	Tanzania	240
14.	Monaco	25,000	14.	Burkina Faso	240
15.	Belgium	24,510	15.	Mali	240
16.	Brunei	24,630	16.	Rwanda	250
17.	Netherlands	24,320	17.	Madagascar	250
18.	Finland	23,780	18.	Cambodia	260
19.	Hong Kong	23,520	19.	São Tomé & Principe	270
20.	France	23,480	20.	Laos	280

GNP per capita is calculated by dividing a country's Gross National Product by its total population.

Continental Shares

Shares of population and of wealth (GNP) by continent

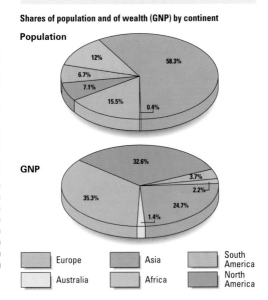

Population

GNP

Europe	Asia	South America
Australia	Africa	North America

Inflation

Average annual rate of inflation (1998–99)

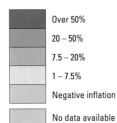

Over 50%

20 – 50%

7.5 – 20%

1 – 7.5%

Negative inflation

No data available

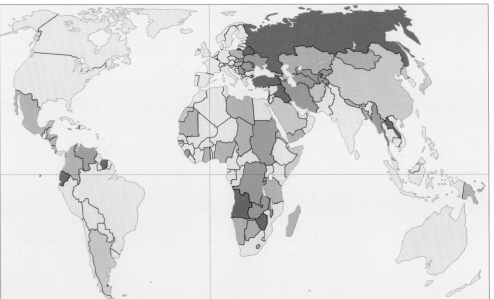

Highest average inflation

Belarus	295%
Angola	270%
Surinam	170%
Laos	140%
Iraq	135%

Lowest average inflation

Azerbaijan	−6.8%
Nauru	−3.6%
Argentina	−2.0%
China	−1.3%
Saudi Arabia	−1.2%

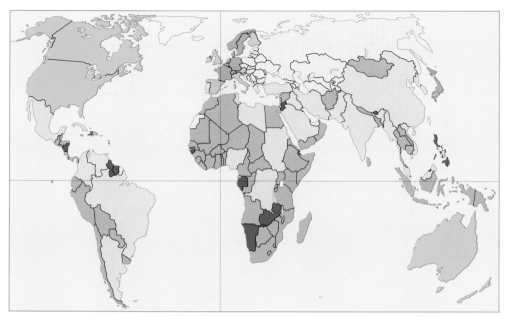

International Aid

Aid provided or received, divided by the total population, in US $ (1995)

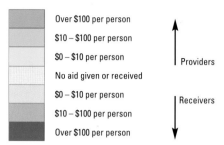

- Over $100 per person
- $10 – $100 per person
- $0 – $10 per person
- No aid given or received — Providers
- $0 – $10 per person
- $10 – $100 per person — Receivers
- Over $100 per person

Top 5 providers per capita (1994)		Top 5 receivers per capita (1994)	
France	$279	São Tomé & P.	$378
Denmark	$260	Cape Verde	$314
Norway	$247	Djibouti	$235
Sweden	$201	Surinam	$198
Germany	$166	Mauritania	$153

Debt and Aid

International debtors and the aid they receive (1996)

Although aid grants make a vital contribution to many of the world's poorer countries, they are usually dwarfed by the burden of debt that the developing economies are expected to repay. In 1992, they had to pay US $160,000 million in debt service charges alone – more than two and a half times the amount of Official Development Assistance (ODA) the developing countries were receiving, and US $60,000 million more than total private flows of aid in the same year. In 1990, the debts of Mozambique, one of the world's poorest countries, were estimated to be 75 times its entire earnings from exports.

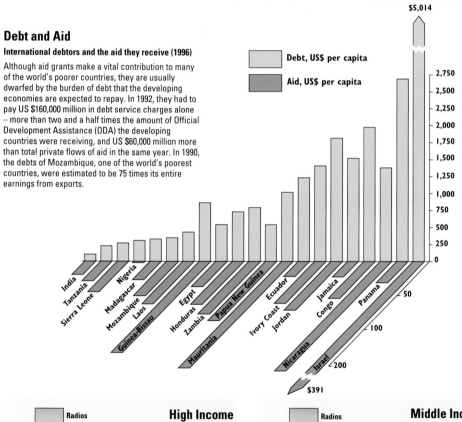

- Debt, US$ per capita
- Aid, US$ per capita

Distribution of Spending

Percentage share of household spending, selected countries

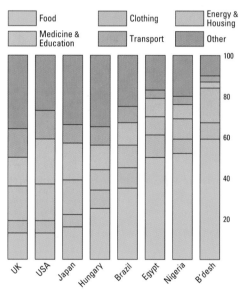

- Food
- Medicine & Education
- Clothing
- Transport
- Energy & Housing
- Other

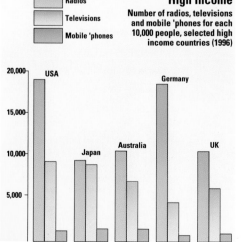

High Income

Number of radios, televisions and mobile 'phones for each 10,000 people, selected high income countries (1996)

- Radios
- Televisions
- Mobile 'phones

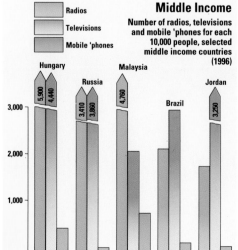

Middle Income

Number of radios, televisions and mobile 'phones for each 10,000 people, selected middle income countries (1996)

- Radios
- Televisions
- Mobile 'phones

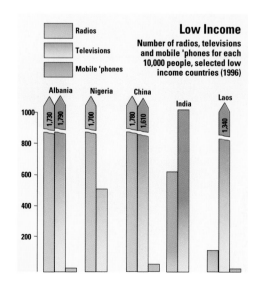

Low Income

Number of radios, televisions and mobile 'phones for each 10,000 people, selected low income countries (1996)

- Radios
- Televisions
- Mobile 'phones

Quality of Life

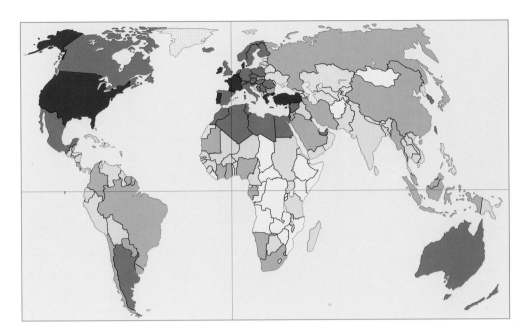

Daily Food Consumption

Average daily food intake in calories per person (1995)

■	Over 3,500 calories per person
■	3,000 – 3,500 calories per person
■	2,500 – 3,000 calories per person
■	2,000 – 2,500 calories per person
□	Under 2,000 calories per person
▦	No available data

Top 5 countries
Cyprus .... 3,708 cal.
Denmark.................... 3,704 cal.
Portugal.................... 3,639 cal.
Ireland....................... 3,638 cal.
USA .... 3,603 cal.

Bottom 5 countries
Congo (D.Rep.).......... 1,879 cal.
Djibouti...................... 1,831 cal.
Togo .... 1,754 cal.
Burundi .... 1,749 cal.
Mozambique .... 1,678 cal.

[UK 3,149 calories]

Hospital Capacity

Hospital beds available for each 1,000 people (1996)

Highest capacity		Lowest capacity	
Switzerland	20.8	Benin	0.2
Japan	16.2	Nepal	0.2
Tajikistan	16.0	Afghanistan	0.3
Norway	13.5	Bangladesh	0.3
Belarus	12.4	Ethiopia	0.3
Kazakstan	12.2	Mali	0.4
Moldova	12.2	Burkina Faso	0.5
Ukraine	12.2	Niger	0.5
Latvia	11.9	Guinea	0.6
Russia	11.8	India	0.6

[UK 4.9] [USA 4.2]

Although the ratio of people to hospital beds gives a good approximation of a country's health provision, it is not an absolute indicator. Raw numbers may mask inefficiency and other weaknesses: the high availability of beds in Kazakstan, for example, has not prevented infant mortality rates over three times as high as in the United Kingdom and the United States.

Life Expectancy

Years of life expectancy at birth, selected countries (1997)

The chart shows combined data for both sexes. On average, women live longer than men worldwide, even in developing countries with high maternal mortality rates. Overall, life expectancy is steadily rising, though the difference between rich and poor nations remains dramatic.

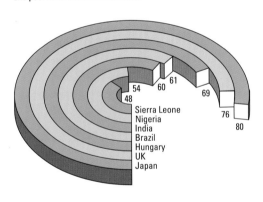

54 Sierra Leone
48
60 Nigeria
61 India
Brazil
Hungary
69 UK
76 Japan
80

Causes of Death

Causes of death for selected countries by % (1992–94)

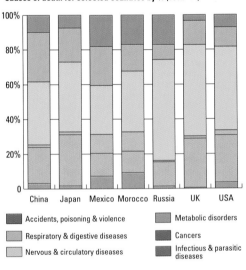

China Japan Mexico Morocco Russia UK USA

■	Accidents, poisoning & violence
□	Respiratory & digestive diseases
□	Nervous & circulatory diseases
■	Metabolic disorders
■	Cancers
■	Infectious & parasitic diseases

Child Mortality

Number of babies who will die under the age of one, per 1,000 births (average 1990–95)

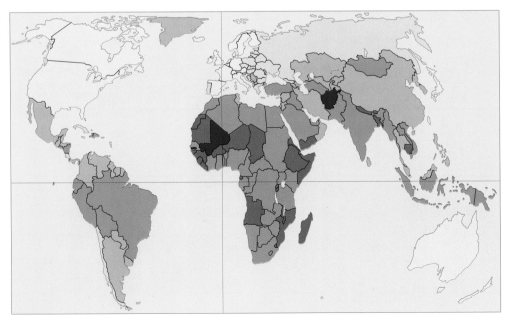

■	Over 150 deaths per 1,000 births
■	100 – 150 deaths per 1,000 births
■	50 – 100 deaths per 1,000 births
■	20 – 50 deaths per 1,000 births
□	10 – 20 deaths per 1,000 births
□	Under 10 deaths per 1,000 births

Highest child mortality		Lowest child mortality	
Afghanistan	162	Hong Kong	6
Mali	159	Denmark	6
Sierra Leone	143	Japan	5
Guinea-Bissau	140	Iceland	5
Malawi	138	Finland	5

[UK 8 deaths]

Illiteracy

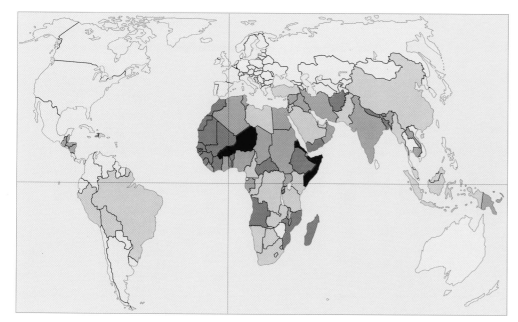

Percentage of the total population unable to read or write (1996)

Over 75% of population illiterate

50 – 75% of population illiterate

25 – 50% of population illiterate

10 – 25% of population illiterate

Under 10% of population illiterate

Educational expenditure per person (latest available year)

Top 5 countries		Bottom 5 countries	
Sweden	$997	Chad	$2
Qatar	$989	Bangladesh	$3
Canada	$983	Ethiopia	$3
Norway	$971	Nepal	$4
Switzerland	$796	Somalia	$4

[UK $447]

Fertility and Education

Fertility rates compared with female education, selected countries (1992–95)

Percentage of females aged 12–17 in secondary education

Fertility rate: average number of children borne per woman

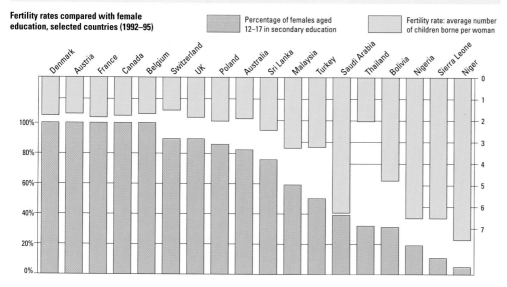

Living Standards

At first sight, most international contrasts in living standards are swamped by differences in wealth. The rich not only have more money, they have more of everything, including years of life. Those with only a little money are obliged to spend most of it on food and clothing, the basic maintenance costs of their existence; air travel and tourism are unlikely to feature on their expenditure lists. However, poverty and wealth are both relative: slum dwellers living on social security payments in an affluent industrial country have far more resources at their disposal than an average African peasant, but feel their own poverty nonetheless. A middle-class Indian lawyer cannot command a fraction of the earnings of a counterpart living in New York, London or Rome; nevertheless, he rightly sees himself as prosperous.

The rich not only live longer, on average, than the poor, they also die from different causes. Infectious and parasitic diseases, all but eliminated in the developed world, remain a scourge in the developing nations. On the other hand, more than two-thirds of the populations of OECD nations eventually succumb to cancer or circulatory disease.

Women in the Workforce

Women in paid employment as a percentage of the total workforce (1997)

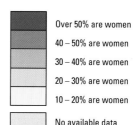

Over 50% are women

40 – 50% are women

30 – 40% are women

20 – 30% are women

10 – 20% are women

No available data

Most women in the workforce		Fewest women in the workforce	
Rwanda	56%	Oman	14%
Cambodia	53%	Saudi Arabia	13%
Ghana	51%	UAE	13%
Ukraine	50%	Qatar	13%
Vietnam	49%	Pakistan	13%

[USA 45%] [UK 44%]

Energy

Production

[Each square represents 1% of world energy production]

North America
Europe
CIS
Middle East
Japan
Africa
Asia
South America
Australasia

Consumption

[Each square represents 1% of world energy consumption]

North America
Europe
CIS
Middle East
Japan
Africa
Asia
South America
Australasia

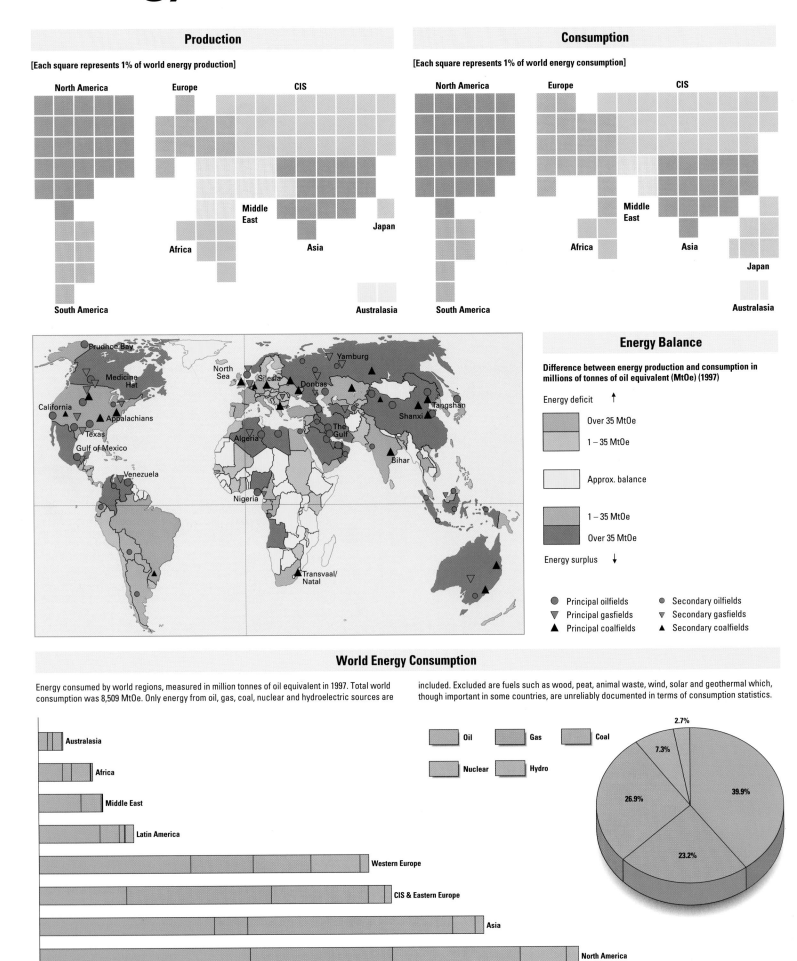

Prudhoe Bay
Medicine Hat
California
Appalachians
Texas
Gulf of Mexico
Venezuela
North Sea
Silesia
Donbas
Yamburg
Tangshan
Shanxi
The Gulf
Algeria
Bihar
Nigeria
Transvaal/Natal

Energy Balance

Difference between energy production and consumption in millions of tonnes of oil equivalent (MtOe) (1997)

Energy deficit ↑

- Over 35 MtOe
- 1 – 35 MtOe
- Approx. balance
- 1 – 35 MtOe
- Over 35 MtOe

Energy surplus ↓

- ● Principal oilfields   ● Secondary oilfields
- ▽ Principal gasfields   ▽ Secondary gasfields
- ▲ Principal coalfields   ▲ Secondary coalfields

World Energy Consumption

Energy consumed by world regions, measured in million tonnes of oil equivalent in 1997. Total world consumption was 8,509 MtOe. Only energy from oil, gas, coal, nuclear and hydroelectric sources are included. Excluded are fuels such as wood, peat, animal waste, wind, solar and geothermal which, though important in some countries, are unreliably documented in terms of consumption statistics.

- Oil
- Gas
- Coal
- Nuclear
- Hydro

Australasia
Africa
Middle East
Latin America
Western Europe
CIS & Eastern Europe
Asia
North America

5   10   15   20   25

2.7%
7.3%
39.9%
26.9%
23.2%

Energy

Energy is used to keep us warm or cool, fuel our industries and our transport systems, and even feed us; high-intensity agriculture, with its use of fertilizers, pesticides and machinery, is heavily energy-dependent. Although we live in a high-energy society, there are vast discrepancies between rich and poor; for example, a North American consumes 13 times as much energy as a Chinese person. But even developing nations have more power at their disposal than was imaginable a century ago.

The distribution of energy supplies, most importantly fossil fuels (coal, oil and natural gas), is very uneven. In addition, the diagrams and map opposite show that the largest producers of energy are not necessarily the largest consumers. The movement of energy supplies around the world is therefore an important component of international trade. In 1995, total world movements in oil amounted to 1,815 million tonnes.

As the finite reserves of fossil fuels are depleted, renewable energy sources, such as solar, hydro-thermal, wind, tidal and biomass, will become increasingly important around the world.

Nuclear Power

Percentage of nuclear in total domestic electricity generation, leading nations (1998)

1.	France	77%
2.	Sweden	47%
3.	Ukraine	44%
4.	Korea, South	38%
5.	Japan	32%
6.	Germany	29%
7.	UK	28%
8.	USA	19%
9.	Canada	13%
10.	Russia	13%

Although the 1980s were a bad time for the nuclear power industry (major projects ran over budget, and fears of long-term environmental damage were heavily reinforced by the 1986 disaster at Chernobyl), the industry picked up in the early 1990s. However, whilst the number of reactors is still increasing, orders for new plants have shrunk. This is partly due to the increasingly difficult task of disposing of nuclear waste.

Hydroelectricity

Percentage of hydroelectricity in total domestic electricity generation, leading nations (1998)

1.	Norway	99.4%
2.	Brazil	90.6%
3.	Canada	59.1%
4.	Sweden	47.0%
5.	Russia	19.3%
6.	China	17.4%
7.	India	16.8%
8.	France	12.9%
9.	Japan	9.8%
10.	USA	8.4%

Countries heavily reliant on hydroelectricity are usually small and non-industrial: a high proportion of hydroelectric power more often reflects a modest energy budget than vast hydroelectric resources. The USA, for instance, produces only 8.4% of power requirements from hydroelectricity; yet that 8.4% amounts to more than three times the hydropower generated by all of Africa.

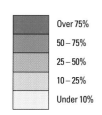

Fuel Exports

Fuels as a percentage of total value of exports (1996)

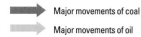

- Over 75%
- 50 – 75%
- 25 – 50%
- 10 – 25%
- Under 10%

Direction of Trade

- Major movements of coal
- Major movements of oil

Conversion Rates

1 barrel = 0.136 tonnes or 159 litres or 35 Imperial gallons or 42 US gallons

1 tonne = 7.33 barrels or 1,185 litres or 256 Imperial gallons or 261 US gallons

1 tonne oil = 1.5 tonnes hard coal or 3.0 tonnes lignite or 12,000 kWh

1 Imperial gallon = 1.201 US gallons or 4.546 litres or 277.4 cubic inches

Measurements

For historical reasons, oil is traded in 'barrels'. The weight and volume equivalents (shown right) are all based on average-density 'Arabian light' crude oil.

The energy equivalents given for a tonne of oil are also somewhat imprecise: oil and coal of different qualities will have varying energy contents, a fact usually reflected in their price on world markets.

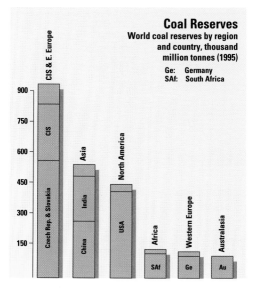

Coal Reserves
World coal reserves by region and country, thousand million tonnes (1995)

Ge: Germany
SAf: South Africa

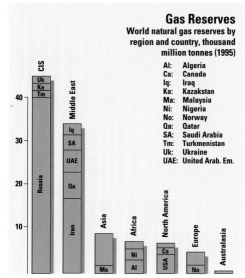

Gas Reserves
World natural gas reserves by region and country, thousand million tonnes (1995)

Al:	Algeria
Ca:	Canada
Iq:	Iraq
Ka:	Kazakstan
Ma:	Malaysia
Ni:	Nigeria
No:	Norway
Qa:	Qatar
SA:	Saudi Arabia
Tm:	Turkmenistan
Uk:	Ukraine
UAE:	United Arab. Em.

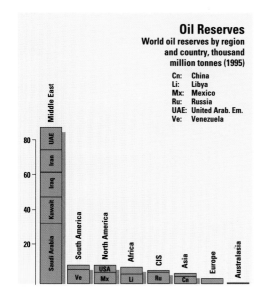

Oil Reserves
World oil reserves by region and country, thousand million tonnes (1995)

Cn:	China
Li:	Libya
Mx:	Mexico
Ru:	Russia
UAE:	United Arab. Em.
Ve:	Venezuela

Production

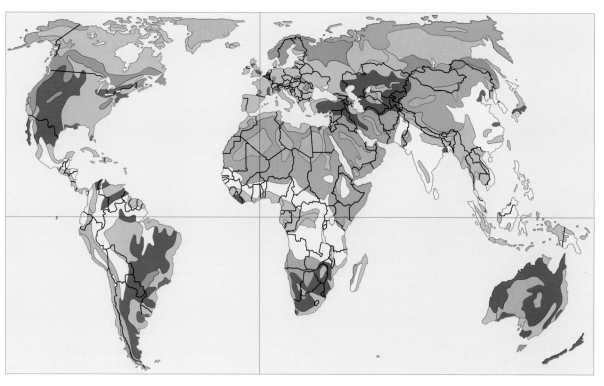

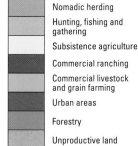
The development of agriculture has transformed human existence more than any other. The whole business of farming is constantly developing: due mainly to the new varieties of rice and wheat, world grain production has increased by over 70% since 1965. New machinery and modern agricultural techniques enable relatively few farmers to produce enough food for the world's 6 billion or so people.

Staple Crops

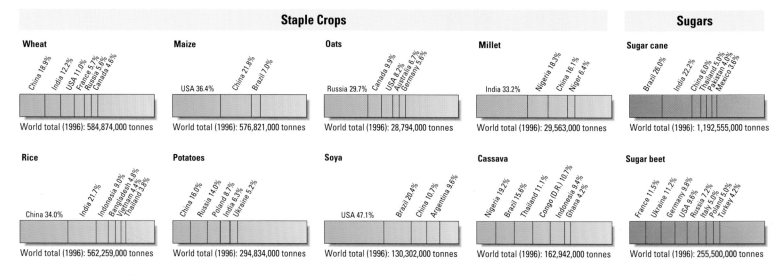

Wheat

China 18.9% | India 12.2% | USA 11.0% | France 5.7% | Russia 5.6% | Canada 4.6%

World total (1996): 584,874,000 tonnes

Maize

USA 36.4% | China 21.8% | Brazil 7.0%

World total (1996): 576,821,000 tonnes

Oats

Russia 29.7% | Canada 9.9% | USA 8.2% | Australia 6.7% | Germany 5.6%

World total (1996): 28,794,000 tonnes

Millet

India 33.2% | Nigeria 18.3% | China 16.1% | Niger 6.4%

World total (1996): 29,563,000 tonnes

Rice

China 34.0% | India 21.7% | Indonesia 9.0% | Bangladesh 4.8% | Vietnam 4.4% | Thailand 3.6%

World total (1996): 562,259,000 tonnes

Potatoes

China 16.0% | Russia 14.0% | Poland 8.7% | India 6.3% | Ukraine 5.2%

World total (1996): 294,834,000 tonnes

Soya

USA 47.1% | Brazil 20.4% | China 10.7% | Argentina 9.6%

World total (1996): 130,302,000 tonnes

Cassava

Nigeria 19.2% | Brazil 15.6% | Thailand 11.1% | Congo (D.R.) 10.7% | Indonesia 9.4% | Ghana 4.2%

World total (1996): 162,942,000 tonnes

Sugars

Sugar cane

Brazil 26.0% | India 22.2% | China 6.0% | Thailand 5.0% | Pakistan 4.0% | Mexico 3.5%

World total (1996): 1,192,555,000 tonnes

Sugar beet

France 11.5% | Ukraine 11.2% | Germany 9.6% | USA 9.4% | Russia 7.2% | Italy 5.0% | Poland 5.0% | Turkey 4.2%

World total (1996): 255,500,000 tonnes

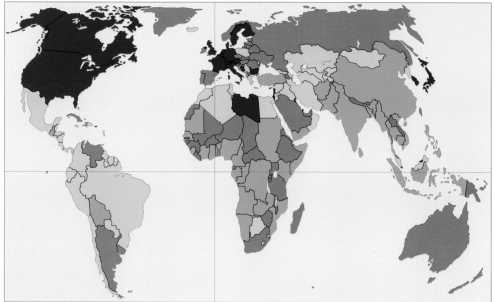

Employment

The number of workers employed in manufacturing for every 100 workers engaged in agriculture (1997)

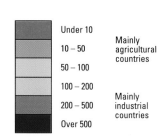

- Under 10 — Mainly agricultural countries
- 10 – 50
- 50 – 100
- 100 – 200 — Mainly industrial countries
- 200 – 500
- Over 500

Selected countries (latest available year)

Singapore	8,860	Germany	800
Hong Kong	3,532	Kuwait	767
UK	1,270	Bahrain	660
Belgium	820	USA	657
Yugoslavia	809	Israel	633

Mineral Production

***Figures for aluminium are for refined metal; all other figures refer to ore production.**

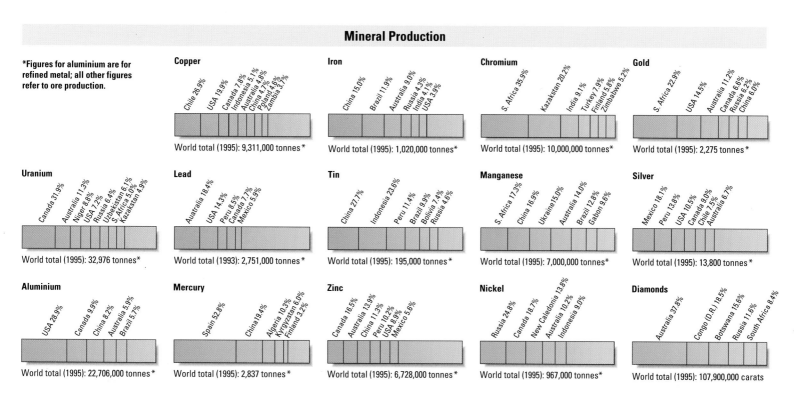

Copper

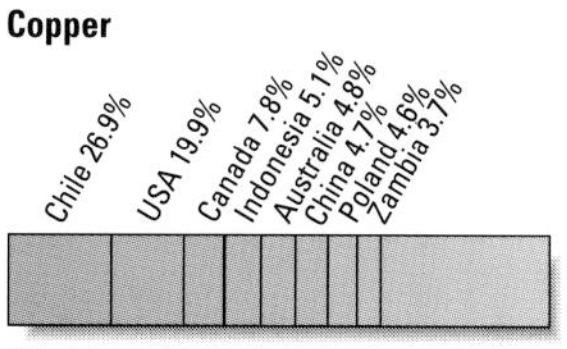
Chile 26.9%
USA 19.9%
Canada 7.8%
Indonesia 5.1%
Australia 4.8%
China 4.7%
Poland 4.6%
Zambia 3.7%

World total (1995): 9,311,000 tonnes*

Iron

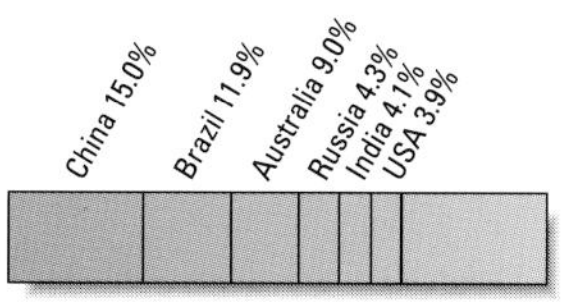
China 15.0%
Brazil 11.9%
Australia 9.0%
Russia 4.3%
India 4.1%
USA 3.9%

World total (1995): 1,020,000 tonnes*

Chromium

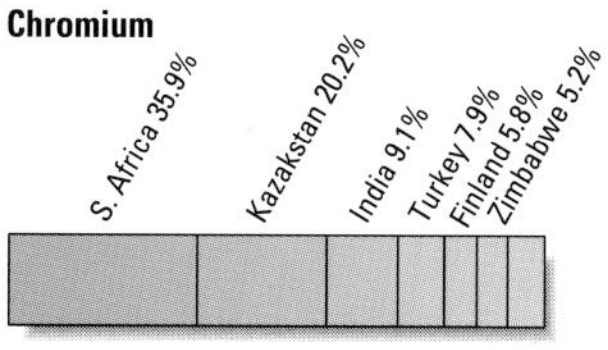
S. Africa 35.9%
Kazakstan 20.2%
India 9.1%
Turkey 7.9%
Finland 5.8%
Zimbabwe 5.2%

World total (1995): 10,000,000 tonnes*

Gold

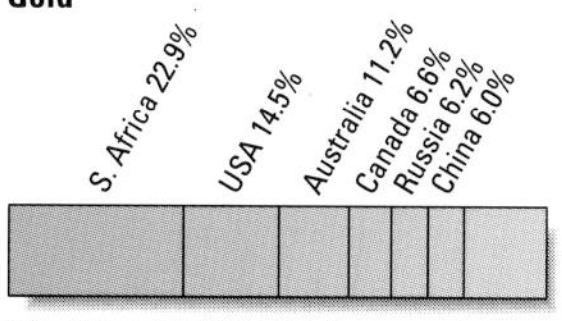
S. Africa 22.9%
USA 14.5%
Australia 11.2%
Canada 6.6%
Russia 6.2%
China 6.0%

World total (1995): 2,275 tonnes*

Uranium

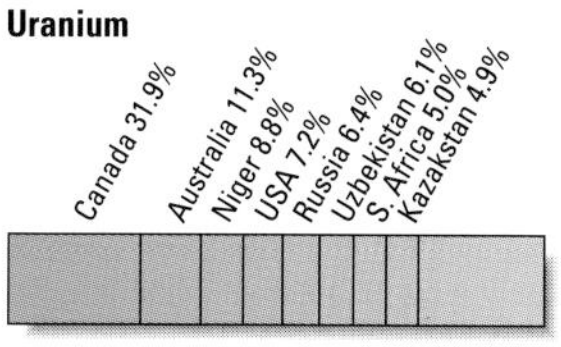
Canada 31.9%
Australia 11.3%
Niger 8.8%
USA 7.2%
Russia 6.4%
Uzbekistan 6.1%
S. Africa 5.0%
Kazakstan 4.9%

World total (1995): 32,976 tonnes*

Lead

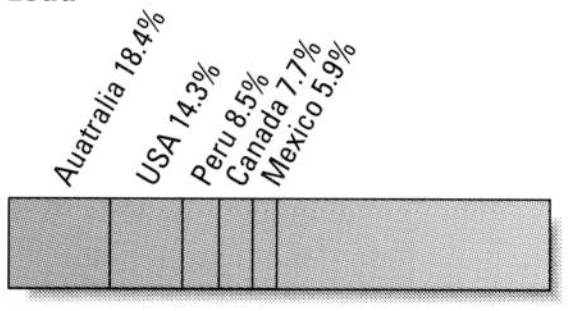
Auatralia 18.4%
USA 14.3%
Peru 8.5%
Canada 7.7%
Mexico 5.9%

World total (1993): 2,751,000 tonnes*

Tin

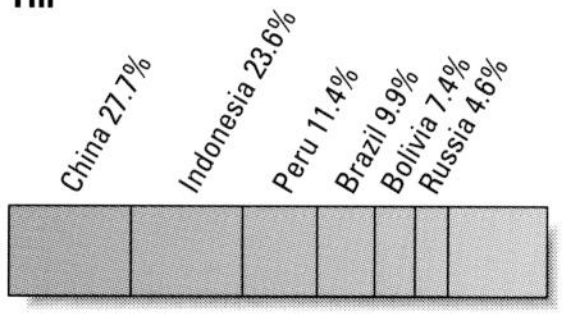
China 27.7%
Indonesia 23.6%
Peru 11.4%
Brazil 9.9%
Bolivia 7.4%
Russia 4.6%

World total (1995): 195,000 tonnes*

Manganese

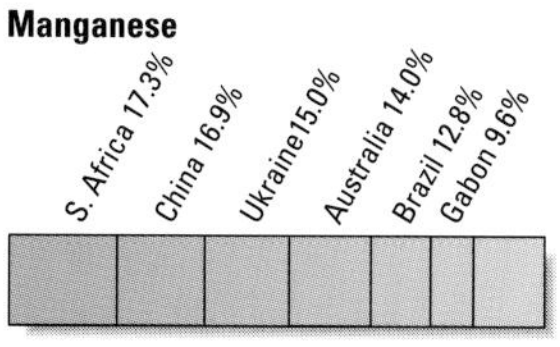
S. Africa 17.3%
China 16.9%
Ukraine15.0%
Australia 14.0%
Brazil 12.8%
Gabon 9.6%

World total (1995): 7,000,000 tonnes*

Silver

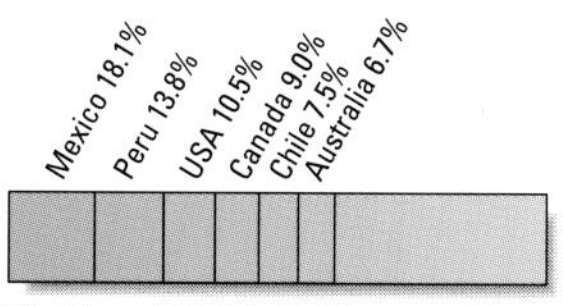
Mexico 18.1%
Peru 13.8%
USA 10.5%
Canada 9.0%
Chile 7.5%
Australia 6.7%

World total (1995): 13,800 tonnes*

Aluminium

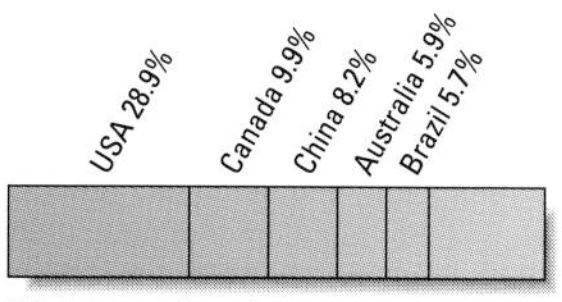
USA 28.9%
Canada 9.9%
China 8.2%
Australia 5.9%
Brazil 5.7%

World total (1995): 22,706,000 tonnes*

Mercury

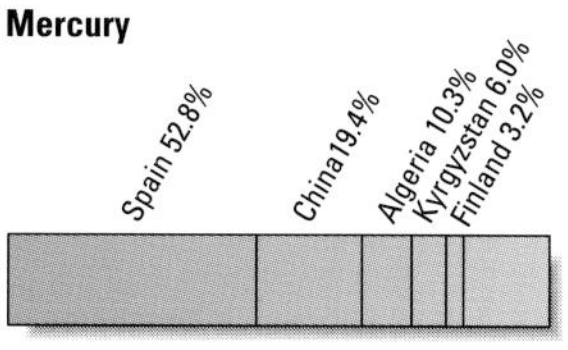
Spain 52.8%
China19.4%
Algeria 10.3%
Kyrgyzstan 6.0%
Finland 3.2%

World total (1995): 2,837 tonnes*

Zinc

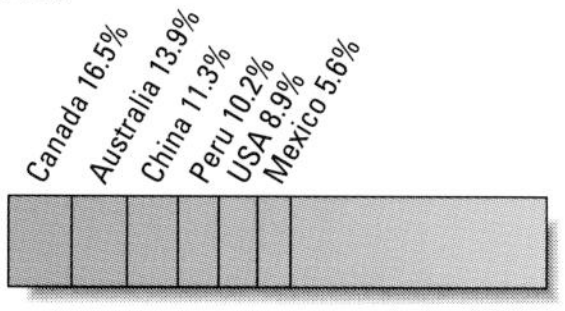
Canada 16.5%
Australia 13.9%
China 11.3%
Peru 10.2%
USA 8.9%
Mexico 5.6%

World total (1995): 6,728,000 tonnes*

Nickel

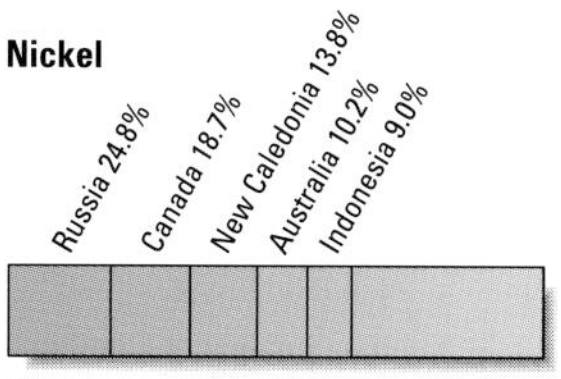
Russia 24.8%
Canada 18.7%
New Caledonia 13.8%
Australia 10.2%
Indonesia 9.0%

World total (1995): 967,000 tonnes*

Diamonds

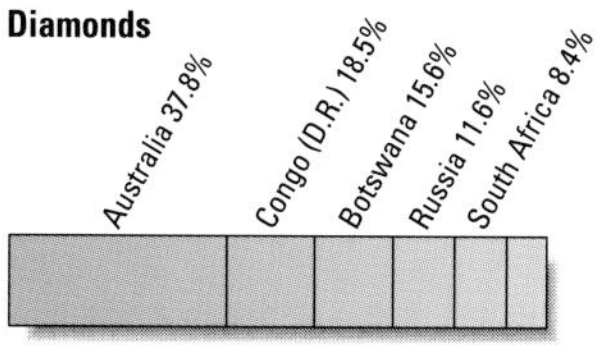
Australia 37.8%
Congo (D.R.) 18.5%
Botswana 15.6%
Russia 11.6%
South Africa 8.4%

World total (1995): 107,900,000 carats

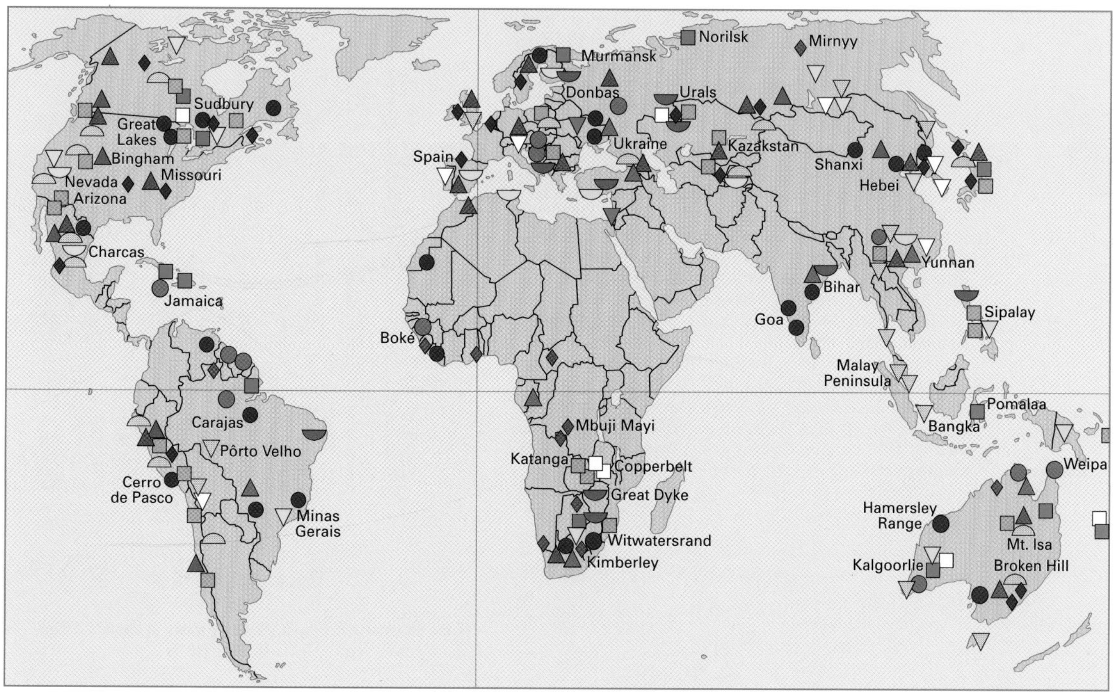
Norilsk
Mirnyy
Murmansk
Donbas
Urals
Sudbury
Great Lakes
Bingham
Missouri
Nevada
Arizona
Spain
Ukraine
Kazakstan
Shanxi
Hebei
Charcas
Jamaica
Yunnan
Bihar
Goa
Sipalay
Boke
Malay Peninsula
Pomalaa
Bangka
Carajas
Pôrto Velho
Mbuji Mayi
Katanga
Copperbelt
Great Dyke
Weipa
Cerro de Pasco
Minas Gerais
Hamersley Range
Witwatersrand
Kimberley
Kalgoorlie
Mt. Isa
Broken Hill

Mineral Distribution

The map shows the richest sources of the most important minerals. Major mineral locations are named.

- Gold
- Silver
- Diamonds
- Tungsten
- Iron Ore
- Nickel
- Chrome
- Manganese
- Cobalt
- Molybdenum
- Copper
- Lead
- Bauxite
- Tin
- Zinc
- Mercury

The map does not show undersea deposits, most of which are considered inaccessible.

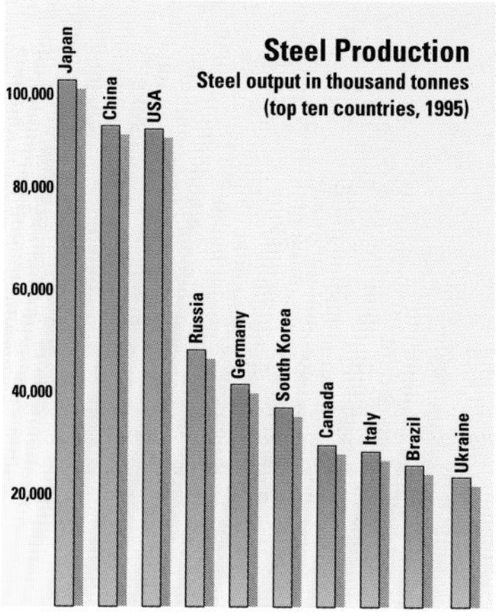
Japan
China
USA
Russia
Germany
South Korea
Canada
Italy
Brazil
Ukraine
100,000
80,000
60,000
40,000
20,000

Steel Production
Steel output in thousand tonnes (top ten countries, 1995)

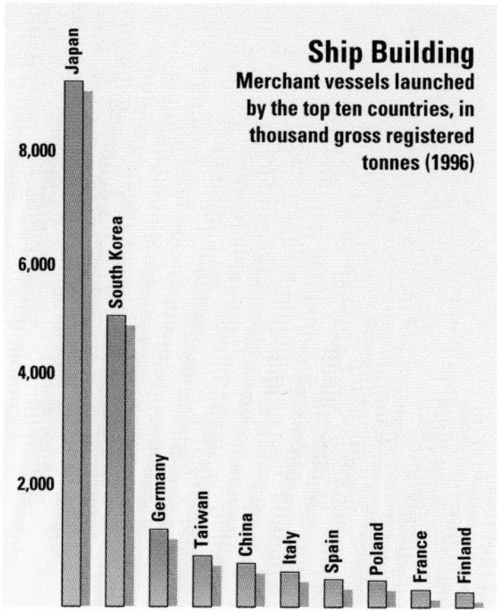
Japan
South Korea
Germany
Taiwan
China
Italy
Spain
Poland
France
Finland
8,000
6,000
4,000
2,000

Ship Building
Merchant vessels launched by the top ten countries, in thousand gross registered tonnes (1996)

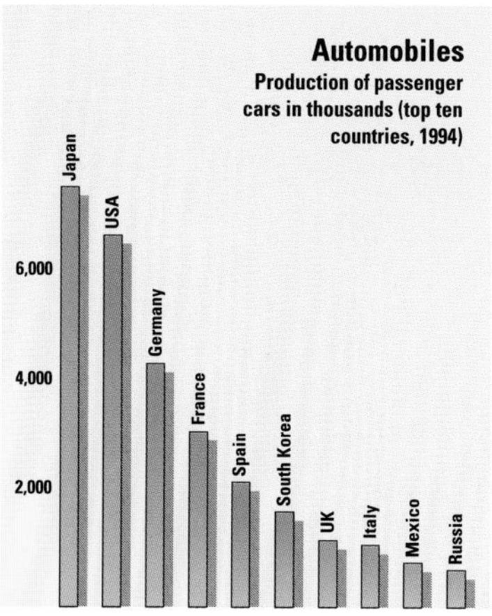
Japan
USA
Germany
France
Spain
South Korea
UK
Italy
Mexico
Russia
6,000
4,000
2,000

Automobiles
Production of passenger cars in thousands (top ten countries, 1994)

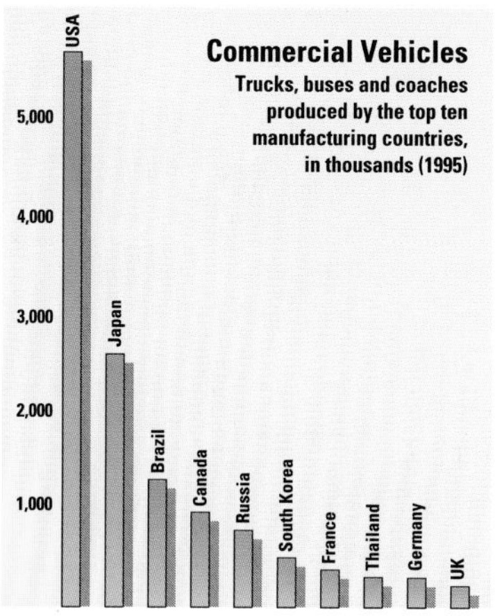
USA
Japan
Brazil
Canada
Russia
South Korea
France
Thailand
Germany
UK
5,000
4,000
3,000
2,000
1,000

Commercial Vehicles
Trucks, buses and coaches produced by the top ten manufacturing countries, in thousands (1995)

Trade

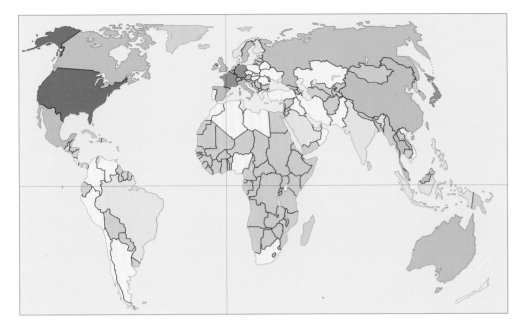

- Over 10% of world trade
- 5 – 10% of world trade
- 1 – 5% of world trade
- 0.5 – 1% of world trade
- 0.1 – 0.5% of world trade
- Under 0.1% of world trade

International trade is dominated by a handful of powerful maritime nations. The members of 'G8', the inner circle of OECD (see page 19), and the top seven countries listed in the diagram below, account for more than half the total. The majority of nations – including all but four in Africa – contribute less than one quarter of 1% to the worldwide total of exports; the EU countries account for 40%, the Pacific Rim nations over 35%.

The Main Trading Nations

The imports and exports of the top ten trading nations as a percentage of world trade (1994). Each country's trade in manufactured goods is shown in dark blue.

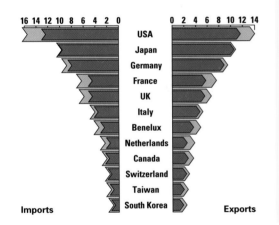

16 14 12 10 8 6 4 2 0   0 2 4 6 8 10 12 14

- USA
- Japan
- Germany
- France
- UK
- Italy
- Benelux
- Netherlands
- Canada
- Switzerland
- Taiwan
- South Korea

Imports   Exports

Patterns of Trade

Thriving international trade is the outward sign of a healthy world economy, the obvious indicator that some countries have goods to sell and others the means to buy them. Global exports expanded to an estimated US $3.92 trillion in 1994, an increase due partly to economic recovery in industrial nations but also to export-led growth strategies in many developing nations and lowered regional trade barriers. International trade remains dominated, however, by the rich, industrialized countries of the Organization for Economic Development: between them, OECD members account for almost 75% of world imports and exports in most years. However, continued rapid economic growth in some developing countries is altering global trade patterns. The 'tiger economies' of South-east Asia are particularly vibrant, averaging more than 8% growth between 1992 and 1994. The size of the largest trading economies means that imports and exports usually represent only a small percentage of their total wealth. In export-concious Japan, for example, trade in goods and services amounts to less than 18% of GDP. In poorer countries, trade – often in a single commodity – may amount to 50% of GDP.

Traded Products
Top ten manufactures traded, by value in billions of US $ (latest available year)

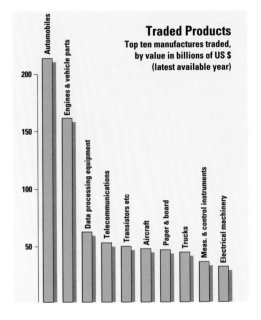

- Automobiles
- Engines & vehicle parts
- Data processing equipment
- Telecommunications
- Transistors etc
- Aircraft
- Paper & board
- Trucks
- Meas. & control instruments
- Electrical machinery

Balance of Trade

Value of exports in proportion to the value of imports (1995)

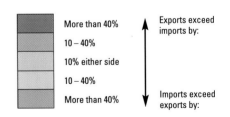

- More than 40%
- 10 – 40%
- 10% either side
- 10 – 40%
- More than 40%

Exports exceed imports by:

Imports exceed exports by:

The total world trade balance should amount to zero, since exports must equal imports on a global scale. In practice, at least $100 billion in exports go unrecorded, leaving the world with an apparent deficit and many countries in a better position than public accounting reveals. However, a favourable trade balance is not necessarily a sign of prosperity: many poorer countries must maintain a high surplus in order to service debts, and do so by restricting imports below the levels needed to sustain successful economies.

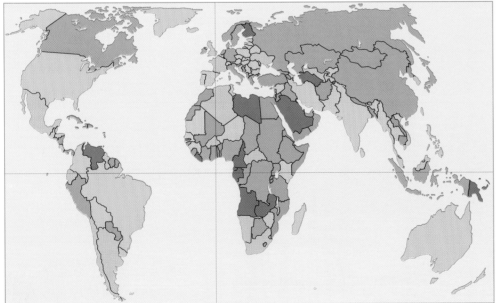

Seaborne Freight

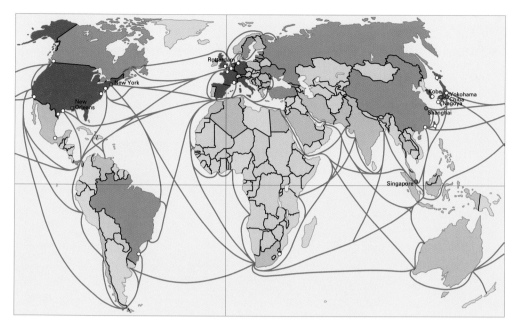

Freight unloaded in millions of tonnes (latest available year)

- Over 100
- 50 – 100
- 10 – 50
- 5 – 10
- Under 5
- Landlocked countries

Major seaports

- ● Over 100 million tonnes per year
- ○ 50–100 million tonnes per year
- ── Major shipping routes

Cargoes

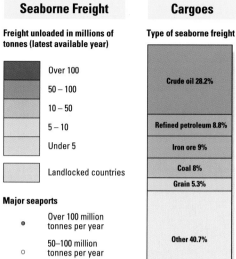

Type of seaborne freight

- Crude oil 28.2%
- Refined petroleum 8.8%
- Iron ore 9%
- Coal 8%
- Grain 5.3%
- Other 40.7%

Merchant Fleets

Merchant fleets in thousand gross tonnage (1996). A large number of vessels are registered in Liberia and Panama but they are not part of the national fleet.

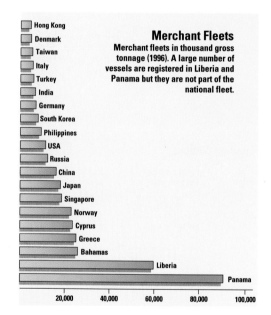

Hong Kong, Denmark, Taiwan, Italy, Turkey, India, Germany, South Korea, Philippines, USA, Russia, China, Japan, Singapore, Norway, Cyprus, Greece, Bahamas, Liberia, Panama

20,000 40,000 60,000 80,000 100,000

The Great Ports

Total Cargo Traffic (1995) '000 tonnes

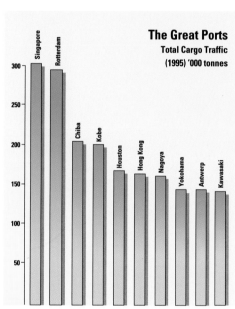

Singapore, Rotterdam, Chiba, Kobe, Houston, Hong Kong, Nagoya, Yokohama, Antwerp, Kawasaki

World Shipping

World merchant fleet by type of vessel and deadweight tonnage (latest available year)

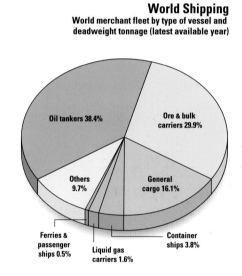

- Oil tankers 38.4%
- Ore & bulk carriers 29.9%
- General cargo 16.1%
- Others 9.7%
- Container ships 3.8%
- Liquid gas carriers 1.6%
- Ferries & passenger ships 0.5%

Dependence on Trade

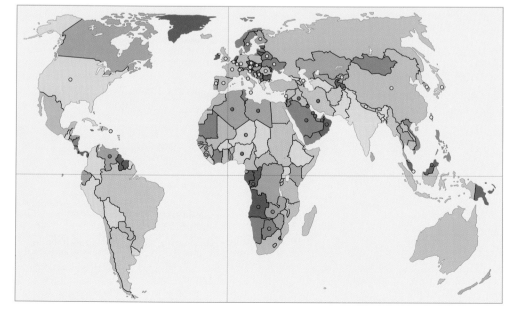

Value of exports as a percentage of Gross Domestic Product (1997)

- Over 50% GDP from exports
- 40 – 50% GDP from exports
- 30 – 40% GDP from exports
- 20 – 30% GDP from exports
- 10 – 20% GDP from exports
- Under 10% GDP from exports

- ○ Most dependent on industrial exports (over 75% of total exports)
- ● Most dependent on fuel exports (over 75% of total exports)
- ● Most dependent on mineral and metal exports (over 75% of total exports)

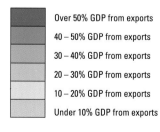

Travel and Tourism

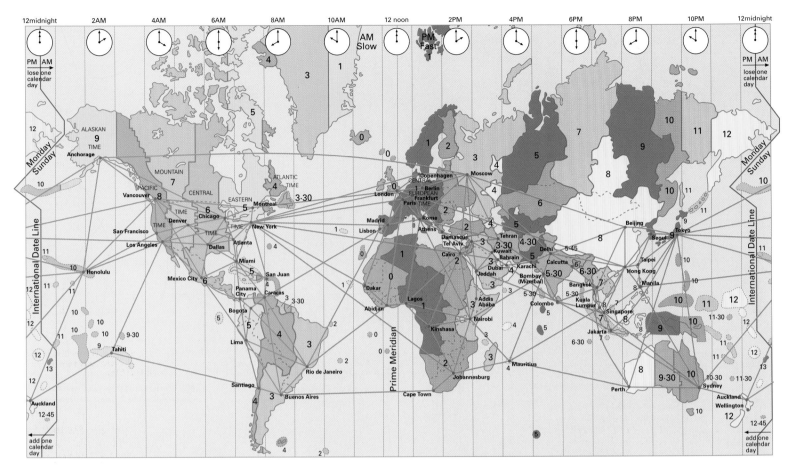

Time Zones

▨ Zones using GMT	▨ Zones fast of GMT
▨ Zones slow of GMT	▨ Half-hour zones
- - - - International boundaries	—— Time zone boundaries
10 Hours slow or fast of GMT	—— International Date Line
	—— Selected air routes

Certain time zones are affected by the incidence of 'summer time' in countries where it is adopted.

Actual Solar Time, when it is noon at Greenwich, is shown along the top of the map.

The world is divided into 24 time zones, each centred on meridians at 15° intervals, which is the longitudinal distance the sun travels every hour. The meridian running through Greenwich, London, passes through the middle of the first zone.

Rail and Road: The Leading Nations

Total rail network ('000 km) (1995)	Passenger km per head per year	Total road network ('000 km)	Vehicle km per head per year	Number of vehicles per km of roads
1. USA 235.7	Japan 2,017	USA 6,277.9	USA..................12,505	Hong Kong 284
2. Russia 87.4	Belarus.............1,880	India 2,962.5	Luxembourg 7,989	Taiwan 211
3. India 62.7	Russia 1,826	Brazil 1,824.4	Kuwait 7,251	Singapore 152
4. China 54.6	Switzerland 1,769	Japan 1,130.9	France 7,142	Kuwait 140
5. Germany 41.7	Ukraine 1,456	China 1,041.1	Sweden 6,991	Brunei 96
6. Australia 35.8	Austria 1,168	Russia 884.0	Germany 6,806	Italy 91
7. Argentina 34.2	France 1,011	Canada 849.4	Denmark 6,764	Israel 87
8. France.............31.9	Netherlands 994	France 811.6	Austria...............6,518	Thailand 73
9. Mexico............26.5	Latvia 918	Australia 810.3	Netherlands 5,984	Ukraine................73
10. South Africa.......26.3	Denmark 884	Germany 636.3	UK 5,738	UK 67
11. Poland.............24.9	Slovak Rep. 862	Romania.............461.9	Canada 5,493	Netherlands 66
12. Ukraine 22.6	Romania 851	Turkey 388.1	Italy.....................4,852	Germany 62

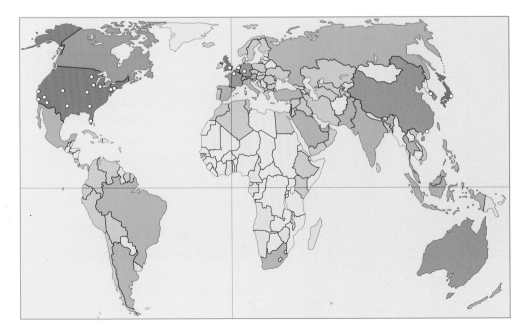

Air Travel

Passenger kilometres flown (the number of passengers – international and domestic – multiplied by the distance flown by each passenger from the airport of origin) (1997)

▨	Over 100,000 million
▨	50,000 – 100,000 million
▨	10,000 – 50,000 million
▨	1,000 – 10,000 million
▨	500 – 1,000 million
▨	Under 500 million
○	Major airports (handling over 25 million passengers in 2000)

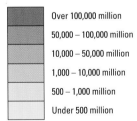

World's busiest airports (total passengers)	World's busiest airports (international passengers)
1. Atlanta (Hartsfield)	1. London (Heathrow)
2. Chicago (O'Hare)	2. Tokyo (Haneda)
3. Los Angeles (Intern'l)	3. Frankfurt (International)
4. London (Heathrow)	4. Paris (De Gaulle)
5. Dallas (Dallas/Ft Worth)	5. Amsterdam (Schipol)

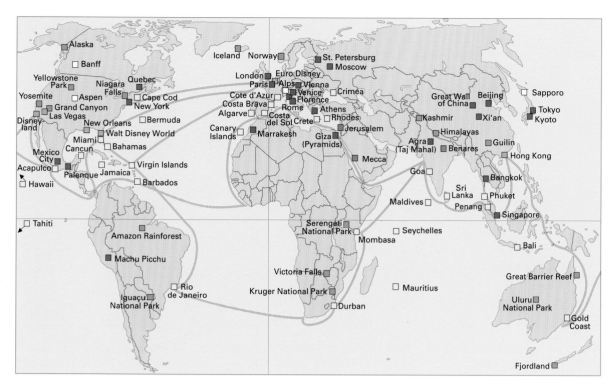

Destinations

■	Cultural and historical centres
☐	Coastal resorts
□	Ski resorts
■	Centres of entertainment
■	Places of pilgrimage
■	Places of great natural beauty
⁓	Popular holiday cruise routes

Visitors to the USA

Overseas travellers to the USA, thousands (1997 estimates)

1.	Canada	13,900
2.	Mexico	12,370
3.	Japan	4,640
4.	UK	3,350
5.	Germany	1,990
6.	France	1,030
7.	Taiwan	885
8.	Venezuela	860
9.	South Korea	800
10.	Brazil	785

In 1996, the USA earned the most from tourism, with receipts of more than US $75 billion.

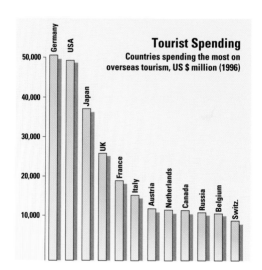

Tourist Spending
Countries spending the most on overseas tourism, US $ million (1996)

Importance of Tourism

		Arrivals from abroad (1996)	% of world total (1996)
1.	France	66,800,000	10.2%
2.	USA	49,038,000	7.5%
3.	Spain	43,403,000	6.6%
4.	Italy	34,087,000	5.2%
5.	UK	25,960,000	3.9%
6.	China	23,770,000	3.6%
7.	Poland	19,514,000	3.0%
8.	Mexico	18,667,000	2.9%
9.	Canada	17,610,000	2.7%
10.	Czech Republic	17,400,000	2.7%
11.	Hungary	17,248,000	2.6%
12.	Austria	16,642,000	2.5%

In 1996, there was a 4.6% rise, to 593 million, in the total number of people travelling abroad. Small economies in attractive areas are often completely dominated by tourism: in some West Indian islands, for example, tourist spending provides over 90% of total income.

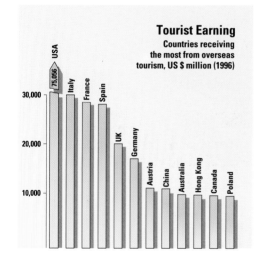

Tourist Earning
Countries receiving the most from overseas tourism, US $ million (1996)

Tourism

Tourism receipts as a percentage of Gross National Product (1996)

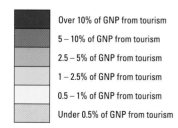

■	Over 10% of GNP from tourism
■	5 – 10% of GNP from tourism
■	2.5 – 5% of GNP from tourism
■	1 – 2.5% of GNP from tourism
□	0.5 – 1% of GNP from tourism
■	Under 0.5% of GNP from tourism

Countries spending the most on promoting tourism, millions of US $ (1996)

Germany	51
USA	49
Japan	37
UK	25
France	18

Countries with largest tourism receipts, millions of US $ (1996)

USA	75
Italy	30
France	28
Spain	27
UK	21

The World In Focus: **Index**

WORLD
MAPS

SETTLEMENTS

■ PARIS   ■ Berne   ◉ Livorno   ◉ Brugge   ◉ Algeciras   ◦ Frejus   ○ Oberammergau   ○ Thira

Settlement symbols and type styles vary according to the scale of each map and indicate the importance
of towns on the map rather than specific population figures

∴ Ruins or Archæological Sites   ⌣ Wells in Desert

ADMINISTRATION

——— International Boundaries

– – – International Boundaries
(Undefined or Disputed)

········· Internal Boundaries

National Parks

Country Names
NICARAGUA

Administrative
Area Names
KENT
CALABRIA

International boundaries show the *de facto* situation where there are rival claims to territory

COMMUNICATIONS

——— Principal Roads

——— Other Roads

+--+ Road Tunnels

⌣ Passes

⊕ Airfields

——— Principal Railways

–~–– Railways
Under Construction

——— Other Railways

+--+ Railway Tunnels

·········· Principal Canals

PHYSICAL FEATURES

——— Perrenial Streams

– – – Intermittent Streams

⬭ Perennial Lakes

⬭ Intermittent Lakes

Swamps and Marshes

Permanent Ice
and Glaciers

▲ 8848 Elevations in metres

▼ 8500 Sea Depths in metres

1134 Height of Lake Surface
Above Sea Level in metres

ELEVATION AND DEPTH TINTS

Height of Land above Sea Level   Land Below Sea Level   Depth of Sea

in feet	6000	4000	3000	2000	1500	1000	400	200	0						

in feet: 6000 4000 3000 2000 1500 1000 400 200 0   6000 12 000 15 000 18 000 24 000 in feet

in metres: 18 000 12 000 9000 6000 4500 3000 1200 600   0 200 2000 4000 5000 6000 8000 in metres

Some of the maps have different contours to highlight and clarify the principal relief features

Projection: *Hammer Equal Area*

A R C T I C   O C E A N

Svalbard
(Nor.)

Barents   Novaya
Sea   Zemlya   Kara   Severnaya
Sea   Zemlya   Laptev Sea   New Siberian Is.   East Siberian
Sea   Wrangel I.   Arctic Circle   A

Murmansk   Norilsk   Verkhoyansk   Lena

NORWAY   Arkhangelsk   Salekhard   Ob   Yenisei   Yakutsk   Okhotsk   Magadan   Bering
Oslo   SWEDEN   FINLAND   Sea of   Sea
Helsinki   R U S S I A   Okhotsk   Petropavlovsk-   B
Stockholm   EST.   ST.PETERSBURG   Perm   Yekaterinburg   Tomsk   Krasnoyarsk   Irkutsk   Ulan Ude   Komsomolsk   Kamchatsky   International
DENMARK   LATVIA   Volga   Kazan   L. Baikal   Khabarovsk   Date Line
Copenhagen   LITH.   MOSCOW   Samara   Chelyabinsk   Omsk   Novosibirsk   Barnaul   Irtysh   Amur   Sakhalin
amburg   NETH.   BELARUS   Saratov   Astana   Harbin   Vladivostok   Sapporo
nsterdam   Berlin   POLAND   Minsk   Kiev   Qaraghandy   Ulan Bator   Changchun   Kuril
ons   Brussels   GERMANY   Warsaw   UKRAINE   Volgograd   KAZAKSTAN   MONGOLIA   SHENYANG   NORTH   P'yongyang   JAPAN
PARIS   LUX.   Vienna CZECH REP.   Astrakhan   Aral   L. Balkhash   Ürümqi   BEIJING   TIANJIN   KOREA   SEOUL   TŌKYŌ   PACIFIC
SW.   AUSTRIA   Budapest   Sea   Almaty   Dalian   SOUTH   Ōsaka
Milan   SLOV. HUNG.   ROMANIA   Caspian   Bishkek   KYRGYZSTAN   Lanzhou   Taiyuan   KOREA   Kitakyūshū   OCEAN
Marseille   ITALY   CROATIA   Belgrade   Bucharest   UZBEKISTAN   Tashkent   C H I N A   Xi'an   Nanjing   C
arcelona   Rome   YUG.   BULGARIA   Black   GEORGIA   Baku   Samarkand   Dushanbe   TAJIKISTAN   Hoang Ho   SHANGHAI
Naples   ALB.   Sofia   Sea   Tbilisi   Yerevan   ARM.   AZER.   TURKMENISTAN   Chengdu   Wuhan   East China
Algiers   Sardinia   ISTANBUL   Ankara   Ashkhabad   Lhasa   CHONGQING   Sea
Tunis   Sicily   GREECE   TURKEY   Izmir   Tabriz   T I B E T   Ryukyu Is.
ERIA   Malta   Athens   Crete   CYPRUS   SYRIA   TEHRĀN   Mashhad   Kābul   Islamabad   Kunming   Fuzhou   Taipei   Bonin Is.
Mediterranean   Damascus   Baghdād   Esfahān   AFGHANISTAN   Lahore   GUANGZHOU   TAIWAN   (Japan)   Tropic of Cancer
Benghazi   LEB.   Beirut   Ammān   IRAQ   IRAN   JAMMU & KASHMIR   DELHI   NEPAL Katmandu   HONG KONG   Volcano Is.   Marcus I.
Alexandria   ISR.   Jerusalem   JORDAN   Shīrāz   New Delhi   BHU.   Hanoi   (Japan)   (Japan)
CAIRO   KUWAIT   The Gulf   PAKISTAN   Ganges   BANGLA-   DACCA   Hainan   NORTHERN   Wake I.
L I B Y A   Riyadh   BAHRAIN   Abu Dhabi   I N D I A   DESH   KOLKATA   BURMA   South   MARIANAS   (U.S.A.)
EGYPT   QATAR   Muscat   KARACHI   (Calcutta)   MYANMAR   Hanoi   China   (U.S.A.)
Aswân   Mecca   U.A.E.   Ahmadabad   Nagpur   Bay of   Rangoon   Vientiane   VIET-   Sea   MANILA
Red   SAUDI   OMAN   Arabian   MUMBAI   Bengal   Andaman Is.   BANGKOK   NAM   PHILIPPINES   GUAM
N I G E R   Omdurmân   Sea   ARABIA   Sea   (Bombay)   Hyderabad   (India)   THAILAND   CAMBODIA   (U.S.A.)
Niamey   Khartoum   Asmara   Sana'   YEMEN   Bangalore   CHENNAI   Phnom   Ho Chi Minh   MARSHALL IS.   D
C H A D   Ndjamena   ERITREA   Aden   (Madras)   Andaman Is.   Penh   City   FEDERATED STATES
Kano   L. Chad   DJIBOUTI   G. of Aden   SRI LANKA   (India)   Yap   Truk   Pohnpei
NIGERIA   S U D A N   Addis Ababa   Socotra   Lakshadweep Is.   Nicobar Is.   OF MICRONESIA
Ibadan   ETHIOPIA   SOMALI   (Yemen)   (India)   Colombo   (India)   M A L A Y S I A   PALAU   Caroline Is.
Abuja   CENTRAL   REP.   MALDIVES   Medan   SABAH
Lagos   CAMEROON   AFRICAN   Kuala Lumpur   BRUNEI   Gilbert Is.
EQUATORIAL   Douala   REP.   L. Turkana   Mogadishu   PEN. MALAYSIA   NAURU   KIRIBATI
GUINEA   Yaoundé   Bangui   UGANDA   Kisangani   Sumatra   SINGAPORE   Borneo   Equator
nea   Libreville   GABON   CONGO   Kampala   KENYA   I N D I A N   Palembang   I N D O N E S I A   IRIAN   New
SÃO TOMÉ   (Zaïre)   Kigali   RWANDA   Nairobi   Banjarmasin   JAYA   Ireland
& PRINCIPE   CONGO   DEM. REP. OF THE   BURUNDI   Mombasa   O C E A N   JAKARTA   Ujung Pandang   PAPUA   New   E
Brazzaville   Kananga   Bujumbura   Dodoma   SEYCHELLES   Bandung   Java   Surabaya   NEW   Britain
Kinshasa   CABINDA   L. Tanganyika   Zanzibar   Amirante   Chagos Arch.   GUINEA   SOLOMON
Luanda   (Angola)   TANZANIA   Dar es Salaam   Is.   Diego Garcia   (U.K.)   Timor   Port   IS.   Santa Cruz I.
Lubumbashi   Aldabra Is.   Agalega Is.   Arafura Sea   Moresby   SANTA CRUZ
A N G O L A   COMOROS   C. York   VANUATU
Benguela   Mayotte   Cocos Is.   Christmas I.   Darwin   New
ZAMBIA   Malawi   (Fr.)   Cargados Carajos   (Austral.)   (Austral.)   CALEDONIA   FIJI
Lusaka   Lilongwe   MADAGASCAR   Cairns   (Fr.)   Suva
ZIMBABWE   MALAWI   Antananarivo   Rodriguez   Townsville   Port Hedland   Alice Springs   Rockhampton
NAMIBIA   Harare   MOZAMBIQUE   RÉUNION   MAURITIUS   Tropic of Capricorn   A U S T R A L I A
Windhoek   Bulawayo   (Fr.)   Geraldton   Brisbane
BOTSWANA   Mozambique Channel   Kalgoorlie-   Lord Howe I.
Gaborone   Pretoria   Boulder   Newcastle   (Austral.)   F
Johannesburg   Maputo   Amsterdam I.   Perth   Great   Norfolk I.
SOUTH   SWAZILAND   (Fr.)   Fremantle   Australian   Adelaide   Darling   Sydney   (Austral.)
LESOTHO   St.Paul (Fr.)   Bight   Canberra   Auckland
AFRICA   Durban   Melbourne   Tasman   North I.
Cape Town   Port Elizabeth   Prince Edward Is.   Crozet Is.   Sea   NEW
C. of Good Hope   (S.Africa)   (Fr.)   Tasmania   Wellington   ZEALAND
Kerguelen   Hobart   Christchurch
S O U T H E R N   O C E A N   (Fr.)   South I.
McDonald Is.   Heard I.   Stewart I.   Dunedin
Bouvet I.   (Austral.)   (Austral.)   Bounty Is.   (N.Z.)
(Nor.)   Macquarie I.   Campbell I.   Antipodes Is.   G
(Austral.)   (N.Z.)   (N.Z.)
Antarctic Circle   Ross Sea   H

Hanoi ◉ Capital Cities

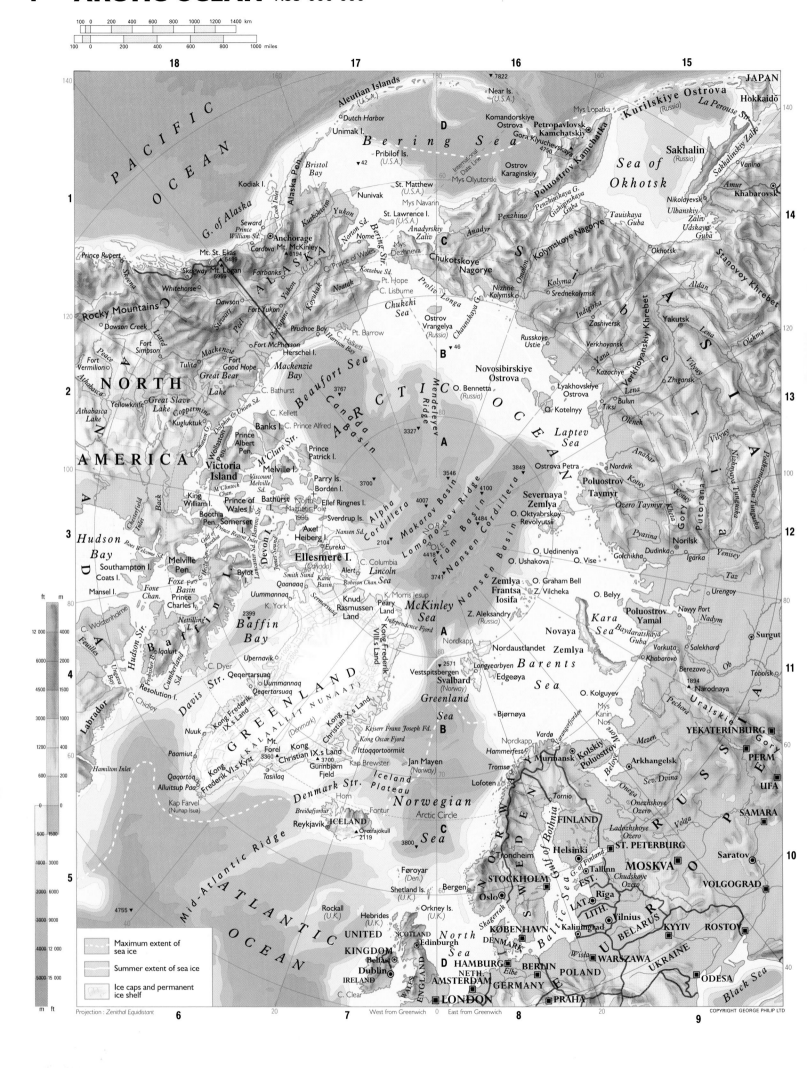

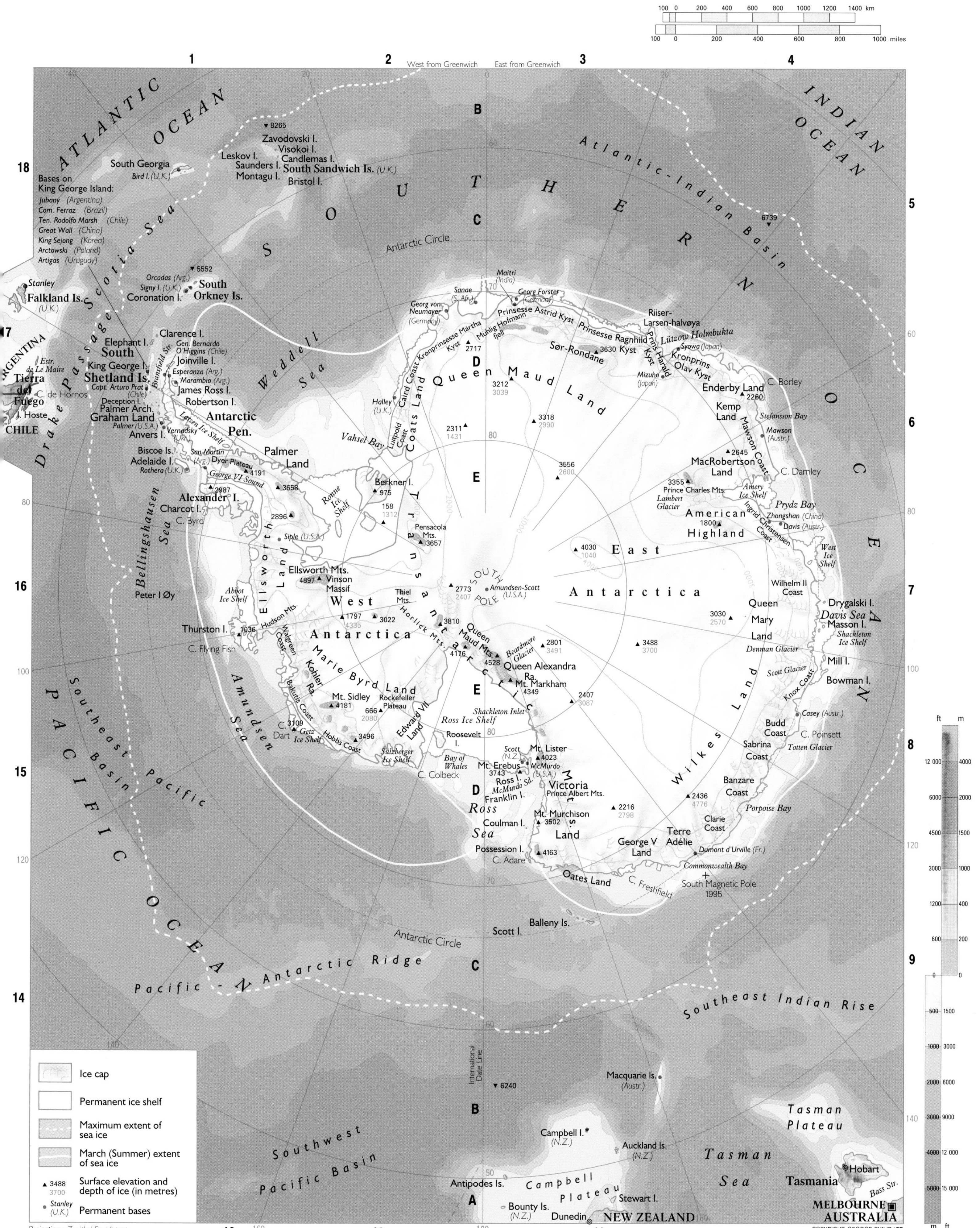

100 0 200 400 600 800 1000 1200 1400 km
100 0 200 400 600 800 1000 miles

ATLANTIC OCEAN

INDIAN OCEAN

West from Greenwich | East from Greenwich

S O U T H E R N   O C E A N

Atlantic-Indian Basin

Antarctic Circle

South Georgia
Bird I. (U.K.)

Bases on King George Island:
Jubany (Argentina)
Com. Ferraz (Brazil)
Ten. Rodolfo Marsh (Chile)
Great Wall (China)
King Sejong (Korea)
Arctowski (Poland)
Artigas (Uruguay)

Leskov I.
Visokoi I.
Zavodovski I.
Candlemas I.
Saunders I.
Montagu I.
South Sandwich Is. (U.K.)
Bristol I.

▼ 8265

Scotia Sea

Orcadas (Arg.)
Signy I. (U.K.)
Coronation I.
South Orkney Is.
▲ 5552

Stanley
Falkland Is. (U.K.)

Sanae (S. Afr.)
Maitri (India)
Georg von Neumayer (Germany)
Georg Forster (Germany)
Prinsesse Astrid Kyst
Prinsesse Ragnhild Kyst
Riiser-Larsen-halvøya
Lützow Holmbukta
Syowa (Japan)
Kronprins Olav Kyst
Prins Harald Kyst

Weddell Sea

ARGENTINA
Tierra del Fuego
C. de Hornos
J. Hoste
CHILE

Elephant I.
Clarence I.
Gen. Bernardo O'Higgins (Chile)
Joinville I.
Esperanza (Arg.)
Marambio (Arg.)
James Ross I.
Robertson I.
South Shetland Is.
King George I.
Capt. Arturo Prat (Chile)
Deception I.
Palmer Arch.
Graham Land
Palmer (U.S.A.)
Anvers I.
Vernadsky (U.K.)

Bransfield Str.

Antarctic Pen.

Larsen Ice Shelf

Queen Maud Land

Mühlig Hofmann fjell
Kronprinsesse Martha Kyst
Sør-Rondane
▲ 2717
▲ 3630
Kemp Land
Enderby Land
C. Borley
▲ 2260
Mizuho (Japan)
Stefansson Bay
Mawson (Austr.)
C. Darnley

Coats Land
Caird Coast
Luitpold Coast

Halley (U.K.)
Vahsel Bay
Berkner I.
Ronne Ice Shelf

▲ 3212 / 3039
▲ 2311 / 1431
▲ 3318 / 2990
▲ 3656 / 2600

MacRobertson Land
▲ 2645
Prince Charles Mts.
▲ 3355
Lambert Glacier
Amery Ice Shelf
Zhongshan (China)
Davis (Austr.)
Prydz Bay

Biscoe Is.
Adelaide I.
Rothera (U.K.)
San Martin (Arg.)
Dyer Plateau
Palmer Land
George VI Sound
▲ 4191

Alexander I.
▲ 2987
▲ 2896
C. Byrd
Charcot I.
Siple (U.S.A.)
▲ 3658
158 / 1312
975

Pensacola Mts.
▲ 3657

▲ 4030 / 1040

East Antarctica

American Highland
▲ 1800 / 2570

Bellingshausen Sea

Peter I Øy

Ellsworth Land
Ellsworth Mts.
Vinson Massif ▲ 4897
West Antarctica

Thiel Mts.
▲ 1797 / 4335
▲ 3022
▲ 3810
Queen Maud Mts.
▲ 4176
▲ 4528

Amundsen-Scott (U.S.A.)
SOUTH POLE
2773 / 2407

Horlick Mts.

Wilhelm II Coast
Drygalski I.
Davis Sea
Masson I.
Mill I.
Bowman I.

Queen Mary Land
▲ 3030 / 2570
▲ 3488 / 3700

Thurston I.
▲ 1036
C. Flying Fish

Amundsen Sea

Walgreen Coast
Bakutis Coast
Kohler Ra.
Marie Byrd Land
Mt. Sidley ▲ 4181
Rockefeller Plateau
666 / 2080
▲ 3108
Dart
Getz Ice Shelf
▲ 3496
Hobbs Coast
Sulzberger Ice Shelf
Abbot Ice Shelf
Hudson Mts.

Beardmore Glacier
▲ 2801 / 3491
Queen Alexandra Ra.
Mt. Markham ▲ 4349
▲ 2407 / 3087

Budd Coast
Sabrina Coast
Banzare Coast
Totten Glacier
Scott Glacier
Knox Coast
Denman Glacier
Casey (Austr.)
C. Poinsett
Wilkes Land

Shackleton Inlet
Shackleton Ice Shelf
West Ice Shelf

Edward VII Land
Roosevelt I.
Ross Ice Shelf

Bay of Whales
C. Colbeck
Scott (N.Z.)
McMurdo (U.S.A.)
Mt. Erebus ▲ 3743
Ross I.
McMurdo Sd.
Mt. Lister ▲ 4023
Franklin I.

Victoria Land
Prince Albert Mts.
Mt. Murchison ▲ 3502
Clarie Coast
▲ 2436 / 4776
▲ 2216 / 2798

Coulman I.
Ross Sea
Possession I.
▲ 4163
C. Adare

Terre Adélie
George V Land
Dumont d'Urville (Fr.)
Commonwealth Bay
+ South Magnetic Pole 1995
Porpoise Bay

Oates Land
C. Freshfield

Balleny Is.
Scott I.

Antarctic Circle

Pacific-Antarctic Ridge

PACIFIC OCEAN
Southeast Pacific Basin

Southeast Indian Rise

Macquarie Is. (Austr.)
▼ 6240

Campbell I. (N.Z.)
Auckland Is. (N.Z.)

Tasman Plateau
Tasman Sea

Southwest Pacific Basin

Antipodes Is.
Bounty Is. (N.Z.)
Campbell Plateau
Stewart I.
Dunedin
NEW ZEALAND

Hobart
Tasmania
Bass Str.
MELBOURNE
AUSTRALIA
COPYRIGHT GEORGE PHILIP LTD

Legend:

Ice cap
Permanent ice shelf
Maximum extent of sea ice
March (Summer) extent of sea ice
▲ 3488 / 3700 Surface elevation and depth of ice (in metres)
• Stanley (U.K.) Permanent bases

Projection: Zenithal Equidistant

The Antarctic Treaty was signed in Washington in 1959 so that scientific and technical research could continue unhampered by international politics.

All territorial claims covering land areas south of latitude 60°S have been suspended. Those claims were:

Norwegian claim	45°E – 20°W
Australian claims	45°E – 136°E
	142°E – 160°E
French claim	136°E – 142°E
New Zealand claim	160°E – 150°W
Chilean claim	90°W – 53°W
British claim	80°W – 20°W
Argentine claim	74°W – 53°W

ft   m
12 000 / 4000
6000 / 2000
4500 / 1500
3000 / 1000
1200 / 400
600 / 200
0
500 / 1500
1000 / 3000
2000 / 6000
3000 / 9000
4000 / 12 000
5000 / 15 000
m   ft

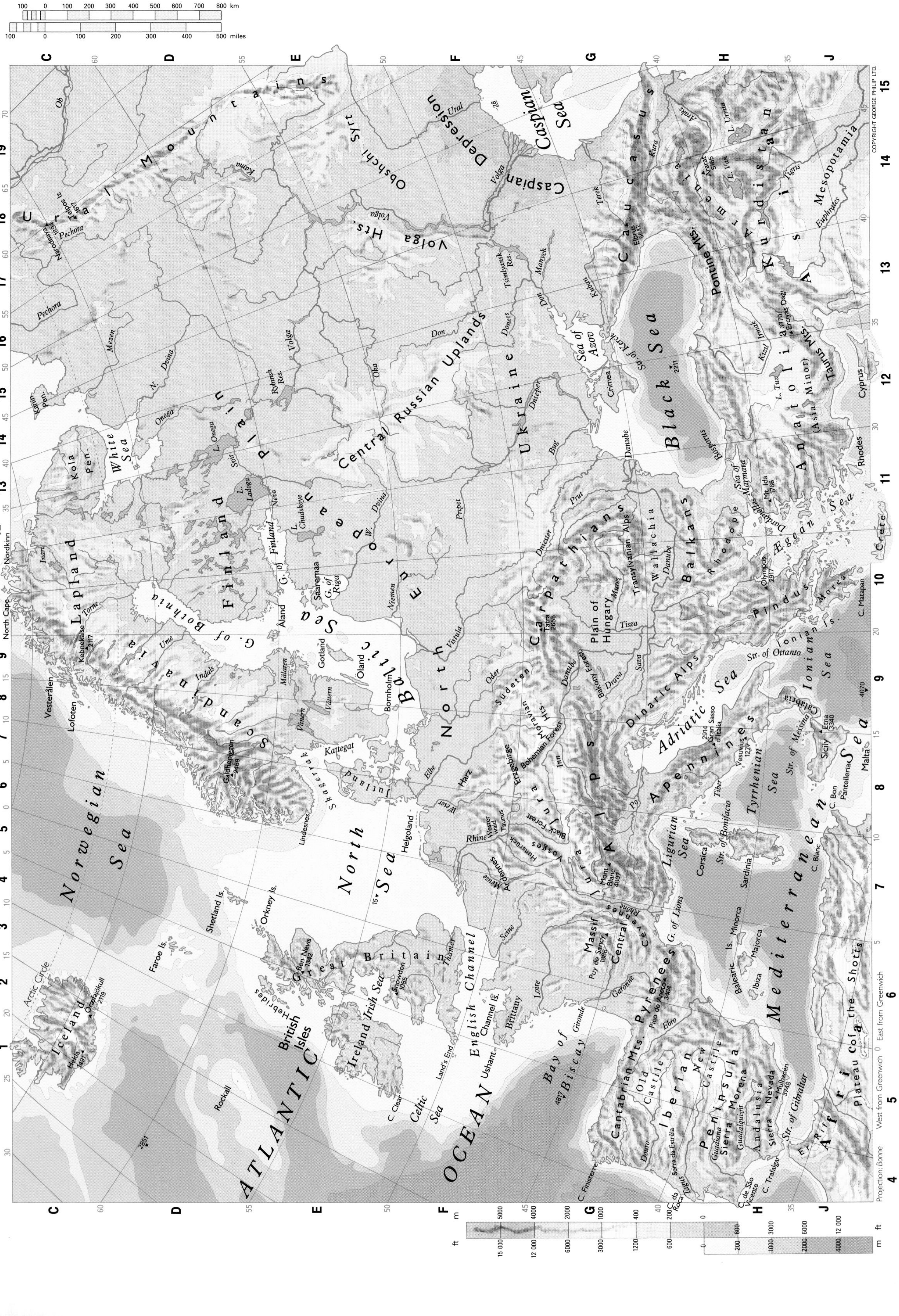

100 0 100 200 300 400 500 600 700 800 km
100 0 100 200 300 400 500 miles

Ural Mountains
Ob
Ural
Caspian Sea
Caspian Depression
Obshchi Syrt
Volga
Kama
Kanin Pen.
Pechora
Narodnaya 1894
Telpos Iz 1617
Pechora
Mezen
N. Dvina
Volga Hts.
Volga
Terek
Kuma
Timlyansk Res.
Don
Donets
Caucasus
Kura
Araks
Elbruz 5642
L. Urmia
Armenia
Kurdistan
L. Van
Ararat 5165
Erciyas Dağ 3916
Tigris
Euphrates
Mesopotamia

White Sea
Kola Pen.
L. Onega
Seir
Rybinsk Res.
Onega
Oka
Central Russian Uplands
Sea of Azov
Str. of Kerch
Crimea
Dnieper
Ukraine
Danube
Black Sea
Pontine Mts.
Taurus Mts. (Asia Minor)
Kizil Irmak
Kesti
L. Tuz
Anatolia (Asia Minor)
Rhodes
Cyprus

Laplan
Finland
L. Ladoga
Neva
L. Chudskoye
Russian Plain
W. Dvina
Pripet
European
Dniester
Prut
Wallachia
Transylvanian Alps
Carpathians
Balkans
Rhodope
Olympus 2917
Mt. Ida 1766
Sea of Marmara
Bosporus
Dardanelles
Ægean Sea
Morea
C. Matapan
Crete

Lapland
Nordkinn
North Cape
Inari
Kepheklsee
Kebnekaise 2117
Torne
Scandinavia
Saaremaa
G. of Riga
Niemen
Vistula
Oder
Sudeten
Moravia
Moravian Hts.
Bohemian Forest
Tatra 2655
Plain of Hungary
Tisza
Drave
Sava
Danube
Dinaric Alps
Adriatic Sea
Pindus
Str. of Otranto
Ionian Is.
Ionian Sea

Vesterålen
Lofoten
G. of Bothnia
Ume
Indals
Uddem
Galdhopiggen 2469
Gotland
Öland
Bornholm
Baltic Sea
North Sea
Elbe
Harz
Erzgebirge
Inn
Alps
Po
Apennines
Gran Sasso d'Italia 2914
Vesuvius 1277
Tiber
Tyrrhenian Sea
Str. of Messina
Sicily
Etna 3340
Calabria
C. Bon
Pantelleria
Malta

Norwegian Sea
Jutland
Skagerrak
Kattegat
Vänern
Vättern
Lindesnes
Helgoland
Weser
Rhine
Black Forest
Vosges
Jura
Mont Blanc 4807
Alps
Rhône
Ligurian Sea
Corsica
Str. of Bonifacio
Sardinia
Mediterranean Sea

Iceland
Öraefajökull 2119
Hekla 1491
Arctic Circle
Shetland Is.
Orkney Is.
Faroe Is.
Great Britain
Ben Nevis 1343
Pennine
Snowdon 1085
Thames
English Channel
Channel Is.
Brittany
Seine
Loire
Ardennes
Meuse
Rhine
Westerwald
Hunsrück
Central Massif
Cévennes
Garonne
Pyrenees
Puy de Sancy 1886
G. of Lions
Pico de Aneto 3404
Balearic Is.
Minorca
Majorca
Ibiza

ATLANTIC OCEAN
British Isles
Hebrides
Ireland
Irish Sea
Land's End
C. Clear
Celtic Sea
Ushant
Bay of Biscay
Gironde
Cantabrian Mts.
Iberian Peninsula
Old Castile
New Castile
Duero
Sierra de Estrela
Tagus
Sierra Morena
Guadalquivir
Guadiana
Andalusia
Sierra Nevada
Mulhacén 3478
C. de São Vicente
C. Trafalgar
Str. of Gibraltar
Plateau of the Shotts
Africa
C. Finisterre
C. da Roca

Rockall

West from Greenwich 0 East from Greenwich

Projection: Bonne

m: 5000 4000 3000 2000 1000 400 200 0
ft: 15 000 12 000 9000 6000 3000 1200 600 0
m: 200 600 1000 3000 6000 12 000
ft: 600 2000 6000 12 000

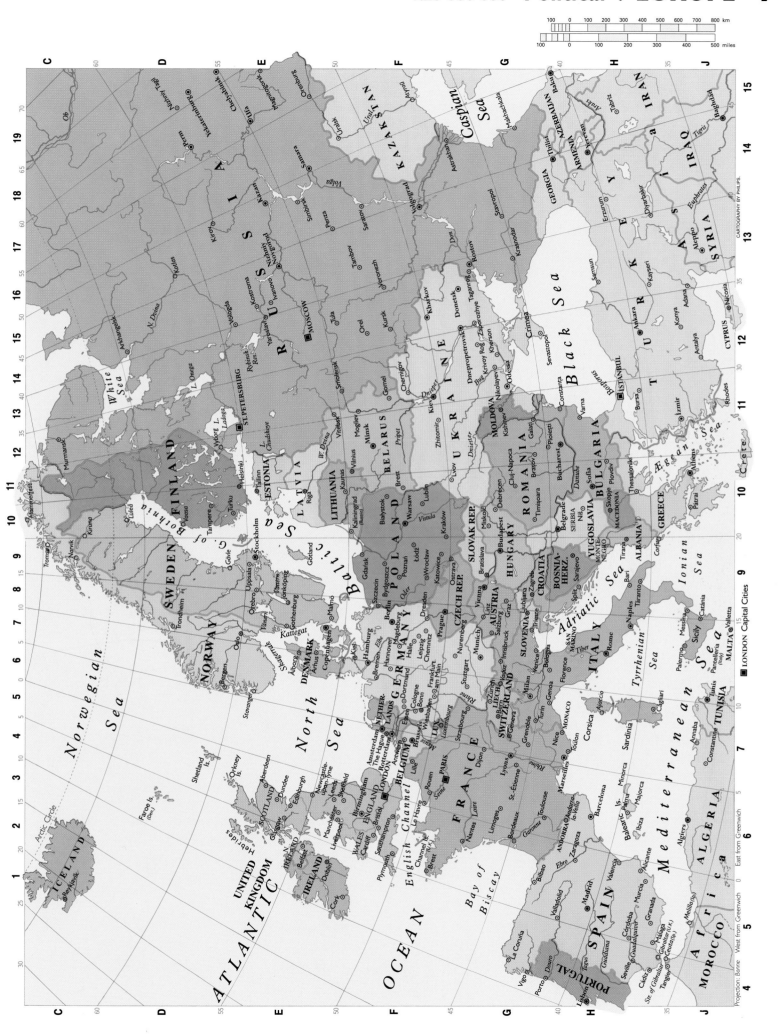

CARTOGRAPHY BY PHILIP'S.

Projection: Bonne   West from Greenwich   East from Greenwich

■ LONDON Capital Cities

SCANDINAVIA 1:5 000 000

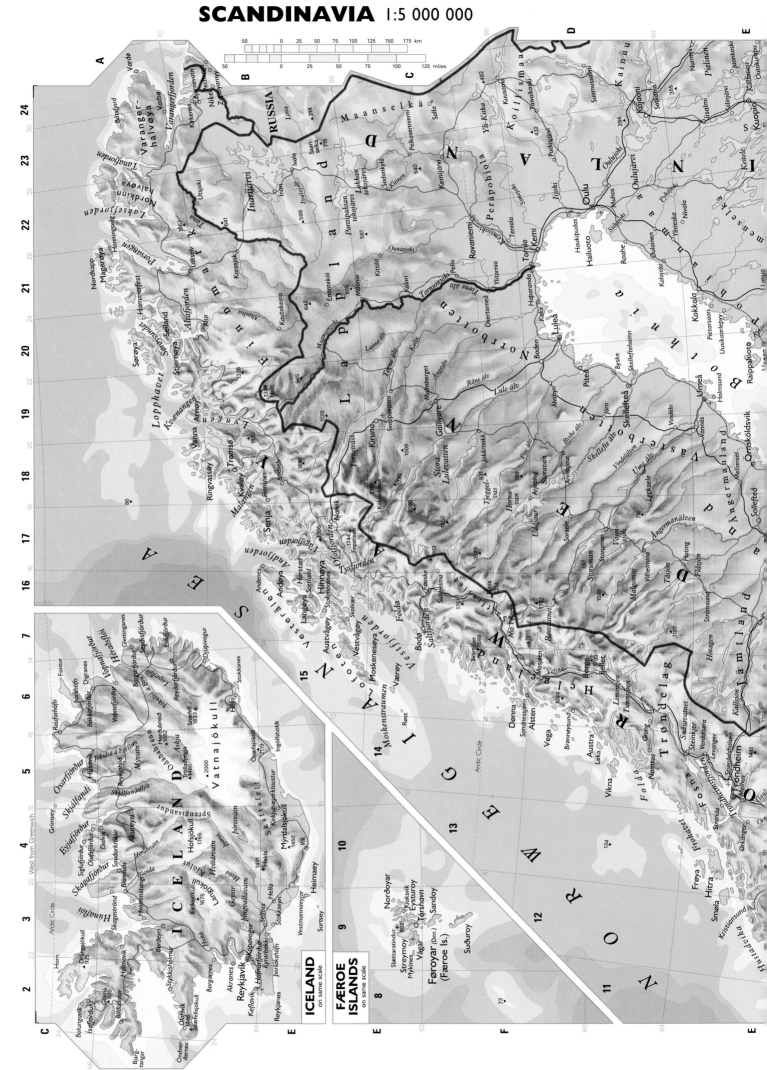

50   0 25 50 75 100 125 150 175 km
50   0   25   50   75   100   125 miles

ICELAND
on same scale

FÆROE
ISLANDS
on same scale

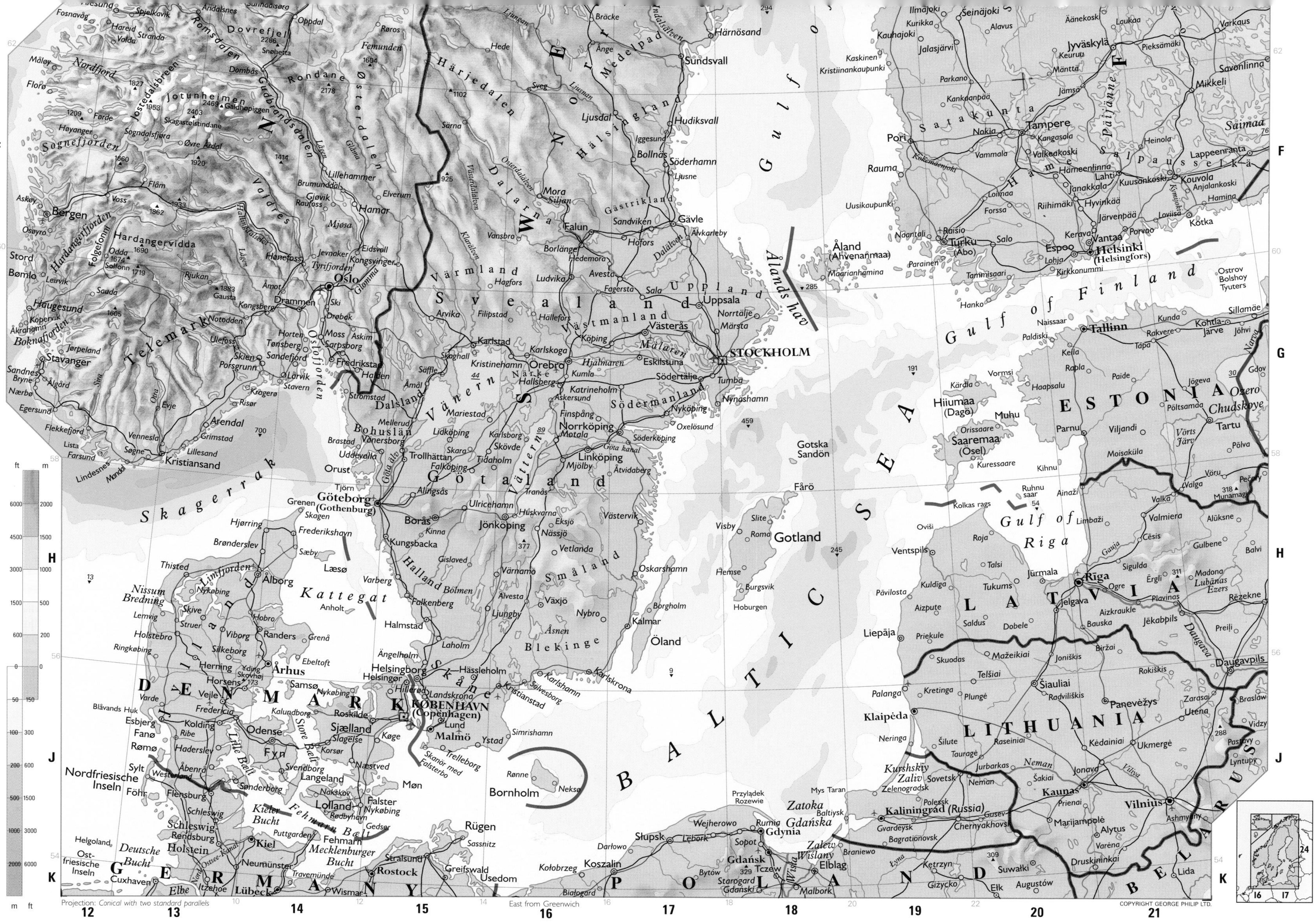

ESTONIA

LATVIA

LITHUANIA

FINLAND

SWEDEN

DENMARK

GERMANY

POLAND

RUSSIA

BELA

Gulf of Finland

Gulf of Riga

BALTIC SEA

STOCKHOLM

Helsinki (Helsingfors)

Tallinn

Riga

Vilnius

Kaunas

Kaliningrad (Russia)

Gdańsk

KØBENHAVN (Copenhagen)

Göteborg (Gothenburg)

Oslo

Bergen

Gotland

Öland

Bornholm

Rügen

Åland (Ahvenanmaa)

Skagerrak

Kattegat

Projection: Conical with two standard parallels

East from Greenwich

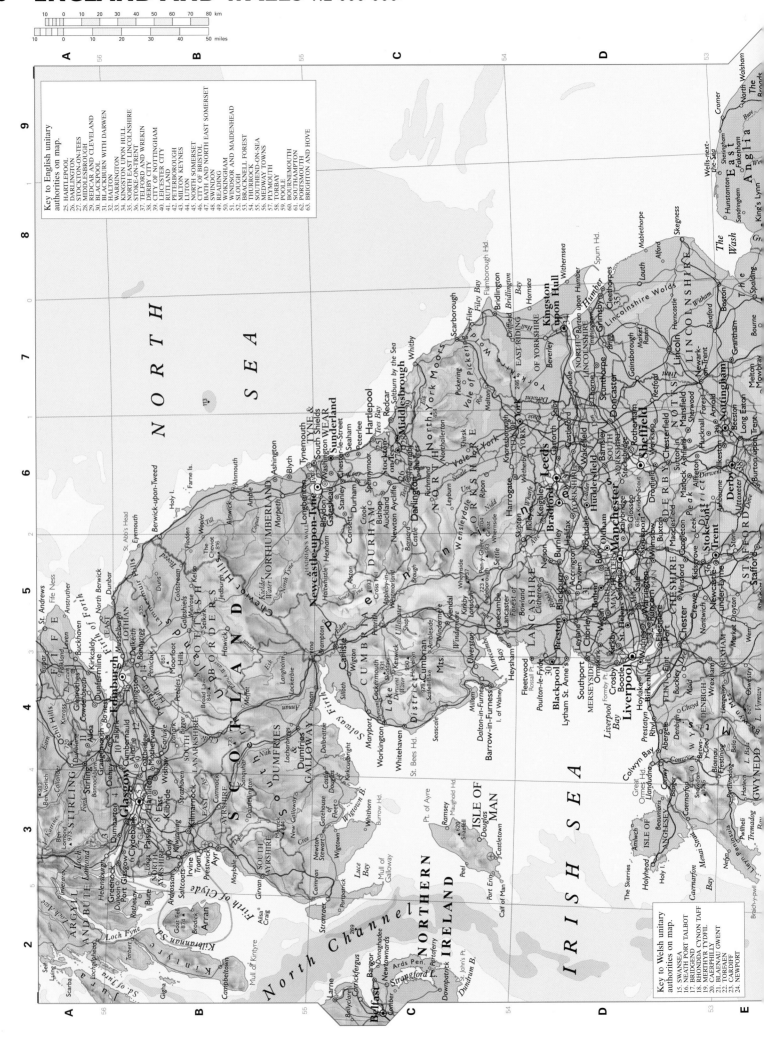

Key to English unitary authorities on map.

25. HARTLEPOOL
26. DARLINGTON
27. STOCKTON-ON-TEES
28. MIDDLESBROUGH
29. REDCAR AND CLEVELAND
30. BLACKPOOL
31. BLACKBURN WITH DARWEN
32. HALTON
33. WARRINGTON
34. KINGSTON UPON HULL
35. NORTH EAST LINCOLNSHIRE
36. STOKE-ON-TRENT
37. TELFORD AND WREKIN
38. DERBY CITY
39. CITY OF NOTTINGHAM
40. LEICESTER CITY
41. RUTLAND
42. PETERBOROUGH
43. MILTON KEYNES
44. LUTON
45. NORTH SOMERSET
46. CITY OF BRISTOL
47. BATH AND NORTH EAST SOMERSET
48. SWINDON
49. READING
50. WOKINGHAM
51. WINDSOR AND MAIDENHEAD
52. SLOUGH
53. BRACKNELL FOREST
54. THURROCK
55. SOUTHEND-ON-SEA
56. MEDWAY TOWNS
57. PLYMOUTH
58. TORBAY
59. POOLE
60. BOURNEMOUTH
61. SOUTHAMPTON
62. PORTSMOUTH
63. BRIGHTON AND HOVE

Key to Welsh unitary authorities on map.

15. SWANSEA
16. NEATH PORT TALBOT
17. BRIDGEND
18. RHONDDA CYNON TAFF
19. MERTHYR TYDFIL
20. CAERPHILLY
21. BLAENAU GWENT
22. TORFAEN
23. CARDIFF
24. NEWPORT

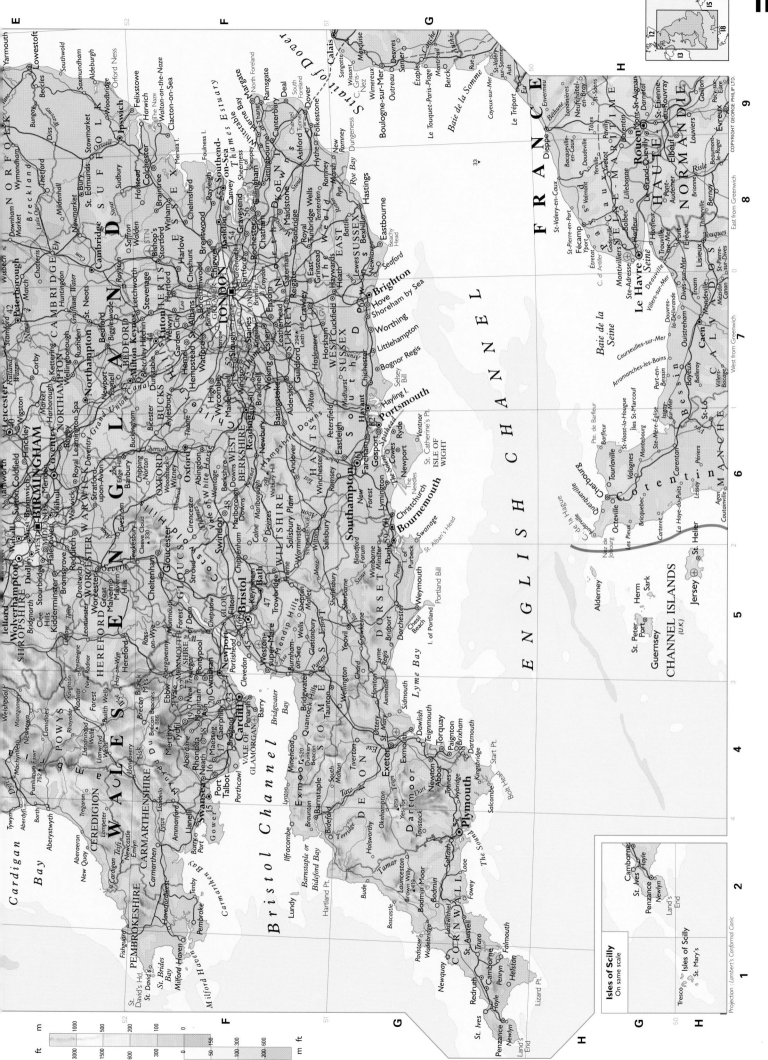

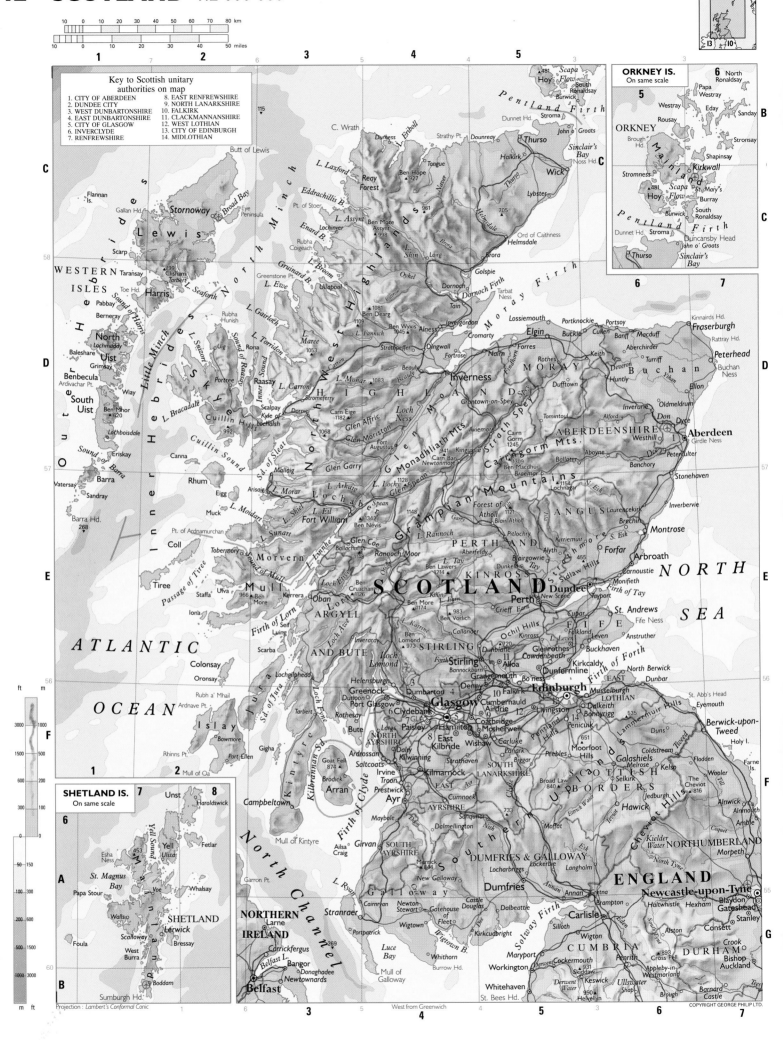

10 0 10 20 30 40 50 60 70 80 km
10 0 10 20 30 40 50 miles

Key to Scottish unitary authorities on map
1. CITY OF ABERDEEN
2. DUNDEE CITY
3. WEST DUNBARTONSHIRE
4. EAST DUNBARTONSHIRE
5. CITY OF GLASGOW
6. INVERCLYDE
7. RENFREWSHIRE
8. EAST RENFREWSHIRE
9. NORTH LANARKSHIRE
10. FALKIRK
11. CLACKMANNANSHIRE
12. WEST LOTHIAN
13. CITY OF EDINBURGH
14. MIDLOTHIAN

ORKNEY IS.
On same scale

SHETLAND IS.
On same scale

Projection: Lambert's Conformal Conic

West from Greenwich

COPYRIGHT GEORGE PHILIP LTD.

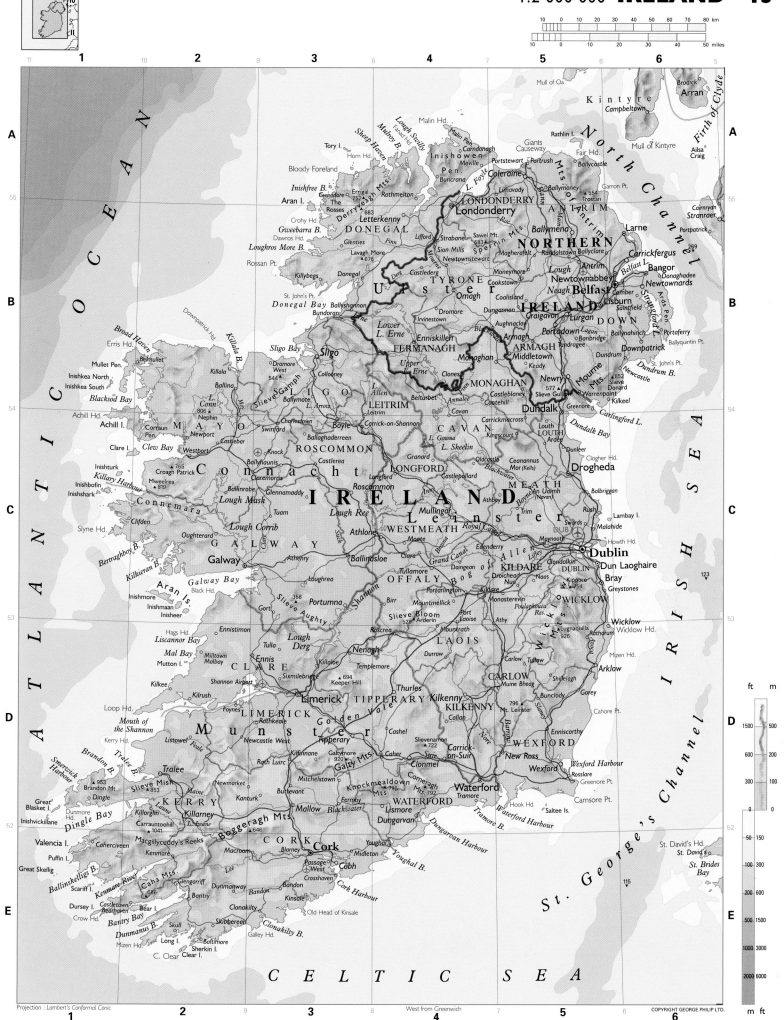

A

B

C

D

E

55

54

53

52

O C E A N

A T L A N T I C

North Channel

Firth of Clyde

IRISH SEA

St. George's Channel

C E L T I C   S E A

Mull of Oa
Kintyre
Campbeltown
Brodick
Arran
Mull of Kintyre
Ailsa Craig
Cairnryan
Stranraer
Portpatrick

Malin Hd.
Lough Swilly
Fanad Hd.
Malin Pen.
Carndonagh
Moville
Giants Causeway
Rathlin I.
Fair Hd.
Ballycastle
Garron Pt.
Trostan ▲554
269 ▲

Tory I.
Horn Hd.
Sheep Haven
Mulroy B.
Inishowen Pen.
Buncrana
L. Foyle
Coleraine
Portstewart
Portrush
Ballymoney
Limavady

Bloody Foreland
Inishfree B.
Aran I.
Gweedore
The Rosses
Errigal 752▲
Derryveagh Mts.
Rathmelton
Letterkenny
LONDONDERRY
Londonderry
Strabane
Sion Mills
Newtownstewart
Sawel Mt. 683▲
Speerin Mts.
Magherafelt
Randalstown
Ballymena
Antrim
Lough Neagh
Ballyclare
Larne
Carrickfergus
Belfast L.
Bangor
Donaghadee
Newtownards

Crohy Hd.
Gweebarra B.
Dawros Hd.
Glenties
683▲
Lavagh More 676▲
Finn
Lifford
DONEGAL
Moneymore
Cookstown
Coalisland
Dungannon
NORTHERN
Belfast
Lisburn
Comber
Strangford L.
Ards Pen.
Saintfield
Portaferry

Loughros More B.
Rossan Pt.
Killybegs
Donegal
St. John's Pt.
Castlederg
Derg
TYRONE
Omagh
IRELAND
Craigavon
Lurgan
Portadown
Lagan
Banbridge
Ballynahinch
DOWN
Portaferry
Ballyquintin Pt.

Broad Haven
Erris Hd.
Belmullet
Donegal Bay
Ballyshannon
Bundoran
Erne
Lower L. Erne
Enniskillen
FERMANAGH
Upper L. Erne
Irvinestown
Dromore
Armagh
ARMAGH
Middletown
Keady
Newry
Mourne Mts.
577▲
Slieve Gullion
852▲
Slieve Donard
Newcastle
Dundrum B.
Kilkeel

Mullet Pen.
Inishkea North
Inishkea South
Blacksod Bay
Achill Hd.
Killala B.
Dromore West
Sligo Bay
Sligo
Ballymote
L. Arrow
544▲
SLIGO
Collooney
L. Gill
Monaghan
MONAGHAN
Clones
Belturbet
Annalee
Castleblaney
Cootehill
Warrenpoint
Greenore
Carlingford L.
Clogher Hd.

Achill I.
Clare I.
Corraun Pen.
Newport
Castlebar
MAYO
Ballina
Nephin ▲806
L. Conn
Moy
Slieve Gamph
Swinford
Charlestown
Boyle
L. Allen
LEITRIM
Leitrim
Carrick-on-Shannon
Carrickmacross
Kingscourt
Cavan
L. Gowna
CAVAN
L. Sheelin
Oldcastle
Dundalk
LOUTH
Louth
Ardee
Dunleer
Dundalk Bay

Inishturk
Inishbofin
Inishshark
Clew Bay
Westport
765▲
Croagh Patrick
Mweelrea ▲819
Knock
Ballyhaunis
Claremorris
Ballaghaderreen
ROSCOMMON
Castlerea
Ballinrobe
Glennamaddy
Roscommon
LONGFORD
Longford
Granard
Castlepollard
Ceanannus Mor (Kells)
Blackwater
An Uaimh (Navan)
Clogher Hd.
Drogheda
Balbriggan

Slyne Hd.
Killary Harbour
Connemara
Clifden
Bertraghboy B.
Kilkieran B.
C o n n a c h t
Lough Mask
Lough Corrib
Tuam
Oughterard
Lough Ree
IRELAND
Athlone
Mullingar
WESTMEATH
Trim
MEATH
Boyne
Athboy
Royal Canal
Swords
Rush
Lambay I.
Malahide

Galway Bay
Aran Is.
Inishmore
Inishmaan
Inisheer
Black Hd.
GALWAY
Galway
Clare
Athenry
Ballinasloe
Loughrea
368▲
Slieve Aughty
Portumna
Shannon
Birr
OFFALY
Tullamore
Clara
Grand Canal
Daingean
Bog of Allen
Edenderry
Portarlington
Kildare
KILDARE
Maynooth
DUB
Clondalkin
DUBLIN
Dun Laoghaire
Howth Hd.
Dublin
Bray
Greystones

Hags Hd.
Liscannor Bay
Ennistimon
Mal Bay
Mutton I.
Milltown Malbay
Gort
Lough Derg
Nenagh
Roscrea
Slieve Bloom
528▲
Arderin
Mountrath
Port Laoise
LAOIS
Mountmellick
Monasterevin
Naas
Poulaphouca Res.
WICKLOW
Lugnaquilla ▲926
Wicklow Mts.
Rathdrum
Avoca
Wicklow
Wicklow Hd.
123

Loop Hd.
Mouth of the Shannon
Kilrush
Kilkee
Kerry Hd.
CLARE
Ennis
Sixmilebridge
Shannon Airport
694▲
Keeper Hill
Killaloe
Templemore
Thurles
Durrow
TIPPERARY
Tipperary
Golden Vale
Cashel
Slievenamon ▲722
Carrick-on-Suir
Clonmel
Comeragh Mts. 792▲
Mizen Hd.
Arklow

Brandon B.
Tralee B.
Smerwick Harbour
Brandon Mt. ▲953
Dingle
Slieve Mish 853▲
Tralee
Listowel
Feale
Foynes
Newcastle West
Rathkeale
Limerick
LIMERICK
Maine
Newmarket
Abbeyfeale
Kilfinnane
Galty Mts.
Galtymore ▲920
Caher
Kilkenny
KILKENNY
Callan
Mt. Leinster 796▲
Bunclody
Gorey
Cahore Pt.

Dunmore Hd.
Great Blasket I.
Dingle Bay
KERRY
Killorglin
Killarney
L. Leane
Carrauntoohill ▲1041
Macgillycuddy's Reeks
Kenmare
Boggeragh Mts. ▲646
CORK
Mallow
Blackwater
Fermoy
Mitchelstown
Buttevant
Kanturk
Knockmealdown Mts. 795▲
Lismore
WATERFORD
Dungarvan
Clonmel
New Ross
WEXFORD
Enniscorthy
Wexford
Wexford Harbour
Rosslare
Greenore Pt.
Carnsore Pt.

Inishvickillane
Valencia I.
Puffin I.
Great Skellig
Cahersiveen
Caha Mts. ▲686
Glengarriff
Dunmanway
Bandon
Lee
Macroom
Blarney
Cork
Passage West
Cobh
Midleton
Youghal
Youghal B.
Waterford
Tramore
Tramore B.
Waterford Harbour
Hook Hd.
Saltee Is.
Dungarvan Harbour

Ballinskelligs B.
Scariff I.
Dursey I.
Castletown Bearhaven
Bear I.
Bantry Bay
Kenmare River
Bantry
Kinsale
Clonakilty
Old Head of Kinsale
Cork Harbour
Crosshaven
St. David's Hd.
St. David's
St. Brides Bay
115

Crow Hd.
Dunmanus B.
Long I.
Skull
Baltimore
Sherkin I.
Clear I.
C. Clear
Skibbereen
Clonakilty B.
Galley Hd.
Mizen Hd.

U l s t e r

L e i n s t e r

M u n s t e r

ft   m
1500   500
600   200
300   100
0   0
50   150
100   300
200   600
500   1500
1000   3000
2000   6000
m   ft

ATLANTIC OCEAN

NORWAY
Bergen
Askøy
Osøyro
Stord
Bømlo
Leirvig
Haugesund
Kopervik
Åkrahamn
Boknafjd
Stavanger
Sandnes
Bryne
Nærbø

Shetland Is.
Yell
Unst
Fetlar
Foula
Mainland
Lerwick
Fair Isle

Orkney Is.
Westray
Sanday
Stronsay
Mainland
Kirkwall
Hoy
South Ronaldsay

C. Wrath
Pentland Firth
Thurso
Wick
Helmsdale

Lewis
Stornoway
North Minch
Harris
St. Kilda
789
Ullapool
Lairg
Golspie

North Uist
Benbecula
Portree
Skye
L. Ness
Inverness
Invergordon
Dingwall
Moray Firth
Nairn
Elgin
Buckie
Banff
Fraserburgh
Peterhead

South Uist
Barra
Rhum
Eigg
Mallaig
Fort William
1182
Aviemore
Spey
Don
Huntly
Inverurie
Aberdeen

Coll
Tiree
Tobermory
Oban
Mull
Ben Nevis
1342
1311
Dee
Ballater
Stonehaven

SCOTLAND
Grampian Mts.
1214
Forfar
Montrose
Arbroath

Colonsay
Jura
Islay
L. Lomond
973
Perth
Dundee
St. Andrews

Greenock
Stirling
Glenrothes
Kirkcaldy
Dunfermline
Dunbar

Paisley
Glasgow
Edinburgh
Berwick-upon-Tweed
East Kilbride
Hamilton
Campbeltown
Arran
Irvine
Kilmarnock
Galashiels
Southern Uplands
840
Jedburgh
816
Alnwick
Ayr
Hawick
Cheviot Hills

NORTH SEA

Malin Hd.
Buncrana
Coleraine
North Channel

Aran I.
Letterkenny
Londonderry
Ballymena
Larne
Donegal
Lifford
Omagh
NORTHERN IRELAND
Ulster
Antrim
Bangor
Belfast
Girvan
Dumfries
Kirkcudbright
Annan
Hexham
893
Newcastle-upon-Tyne
South Shields
Sunderland
Gateshead
Durham
Hartlepool
Redcar
Darlington
Middlesbrough
Stockton-on-Tees
Scarborough

Bundoran
Lower L. Erne
Enniskillen
Lough Neagh
Portadown
Lurgan
Armagh
Newry
Stranraer
Workington
Whitehaven
Carlisle
Pennines
Cumbrian Mts.
978
Barrow-in-Furness
Bridlington

Ballina
Sligo
Leitrim
Clones
Cavan
Castleblaney
Douglas
I. of Man
Lancaster
Harrogate
York
Kingston upon Hull
Beverley

Achill I.
L. Conn
Castlebar
Roscommon
Longford
Ceanannus Mor
Boyne
Drogheda
Blackpool
Keighley
Leeds
Preston
Bradford
Halifax
Huddersfield
Scunthorpe
Grimsby

Westport
Lough Mask
Lough Corrib
Athlone
Lough Ree
Mullingar
Boyne
Blackburn
Bolton
636
Oldham
Rotherham
Doncaster
Barnsley

Connemara
Galway B.
Galway
Ballinasloe
Tullamore
Liffey
Dublin
Dun Laoghaire
Holyhead
Anglesey
Bangor
Liverpool
Manchester
Stockport
Sheffield
Lincoln
Louth

Aran Is.
Ennis
Lough Derg
Birr
Port Laoise
Athy
Bray
Colwyn Bay
Chester
Crewe
Chesterfield
Mansfield
Skegness

IRELAND
IRISH SEA
Nenagh
Thurles
Carlow
Kilkenny
Arklow
Snowdon
1085
Wrexham
Stoke-on-Trent
Derby
Nottingham
Grantham
The Wash
Cromer

Limerick
Tipperary
926
Wicklow Mts.
Wexford
Rosslare
Cambrian Mts.
Shrewsbury
Stafford
Trent
Boston
King's Lynn

953
Listowel
Clonmel
Carrick-on-Suir
Welshpool
Telford
Nuneaton
Leicester
Peterborough
Norwich
Great Yarmouth
Lowestoft

Dingle
Tralee
Mallow
Clonmel
Waterford
Cardigan Bay
Aberystwyth
Wolverhampton
BIRMINGHAM
Coventry
Corby
Northampton
Ely
Thetford
Bury St. Edmunds
Ipswich

Killarney
1041
Carrauntoohill
Blackwater
Dungarvan
Youghal
Redditch
Worcester
Royal Leamington Spa
Rugby
Bedford
Cambridge
Harwich
Felixstowe

Macgillycuddy's Reeks
Cork
Cobh
WALES
Carmarthen
Brecon
Hereford
Cheltenham
Gloucester
Oxford
High Wycombe
Stevenage
Milton Keynes
Luton
Harlow
Colchester
Chelmsford

Valencia I.
Bantry
Kinsale
Fishguard
Haverfordwest
Milford Haven
Pembroke
Merthyr Tydfil
Neath
Llanelli
Rhondda
Newport
Cwmbran
Hemel Hempstead
Watford
Slough
Reading
Basildon
Southend-on-Sea

C. Clear
99
Swansea
Port Talbot
Barry
Cardiff
Bristol
Bath
Swindon
Newbury
LONDON
Thames
Chatham
Margate
Reigate
Maidstone
Canterbury
Dover

618
Bristol Channel
Weston-super-Mare
Salisbury
Basingstoke
Guildford
Crawley
Ashford
Folkestone
Str. of Dover

Barnstaple
Exmoor
Taunton
Yeovil
Winchester
Fareham
Hastings
Eastbourne
Boulogne

Bude
Dartmoor
Exeter
Bournemouth
Poole
Portsmouth
Worthing
Brighton
Newquay
Truro
St. Austell
Plymouth
Torbay
Exmouth
Weymouth
Isle of Wight
Newport

Land's End
Penzance
Falmouth
English Channel

CELTIC SEA

Isles of Scilly

Alderney
C. de la Hague
Pte. de Barfleur
Fécamp
Le Tréport
Dieppe
Abbeville
Amiens

Guernsey
St. Peter Port
Sark
Cherbourg
Valognes
Trouville-sur-Mer
Le Havre
Bolbec
Rouen
FRANCE
Picardie
St-Quentin

Channel Is. (U.K.)
St. Helier
Jersey
Bayeux
Caen
Lisieux
Elbeuf
Seine

NORTH SEA
Texel
Den Helder
NETHERLANDS
Haarlem
's-Gravenhage (Den Haag)
ROTTERDAM
Dordrecht
Alkmaar
Hoek van Holland

Vlissingen
Zeebrugge
Oostende
Antwerpen
Brugge
Gent
Mechelen
BELGIUM
BRUSSEL (Bruxelles)
Dunkerque
Calais
Gris Nez
Lille
Tournai

ft m
3000 1000
1500 500
600 200
0 0
50 150
100 300
200 600
500 1500
1000 3000
2000 6000
m ft

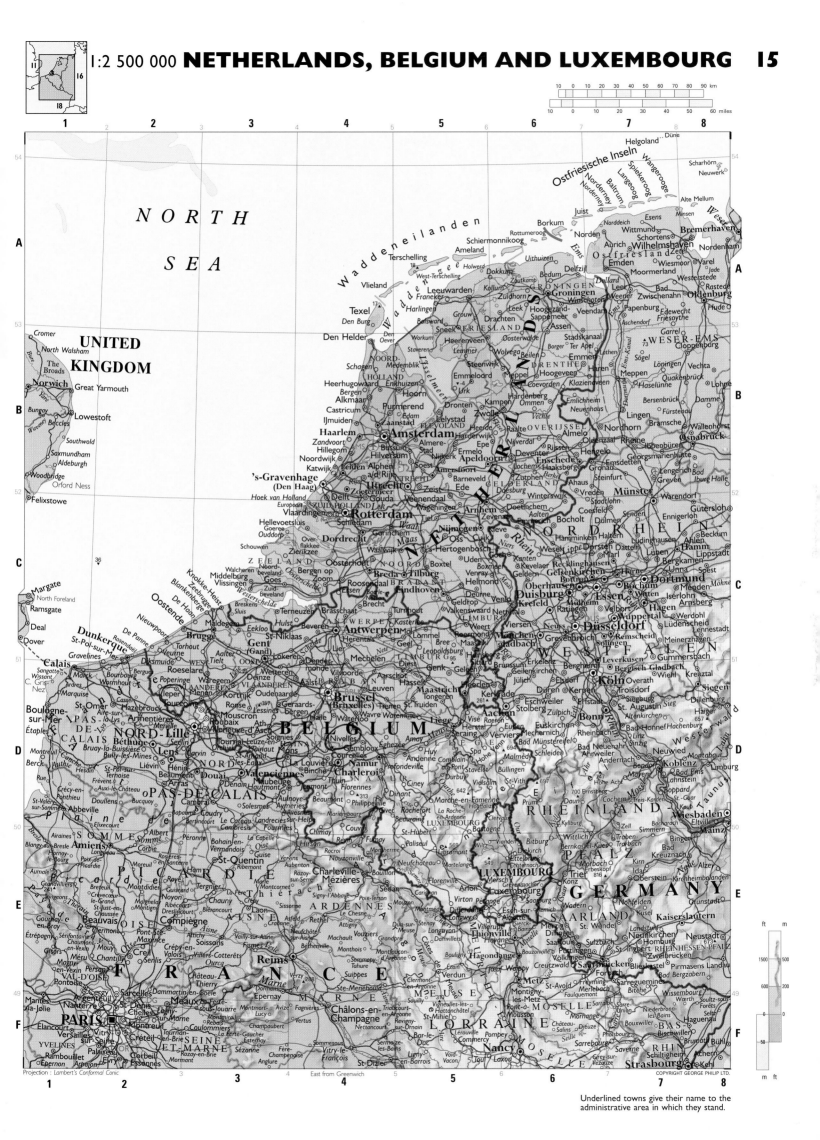

NORTH SEA

UNITED KINGDOM

NETHERLANDS

BELGIUM

GERMANY

LUXEMBOURG

FRANCE

PARIS

Projection : Lambert's Conformal Conic

East from Greenwich

COPYRIGHT GEORGE PHILIP LTD.

Underlined towns give their name to the
administrative area in which they stand.

Zatoka
Baltiysk
Gdańska
Kaliningrad (Russia)
LITHUANIA
Vilnius
BELARUS
MINSK
Mahilyow

POLAND

WARSZAWA (Warsaw)

Brest

UKRAINE

KYYIV (Kiev)

Lviv (Lvov)

SLOVAK REP.

Bratislava

BUDAPEST

HUNGARY

CZECH REP.

MOLDOVA

Chișinău

Tiraspol

ROMANIA

BUCUREȘTI (Bucharest)

BULGARIA

YUGOSLAVIA

BEOGRAD (Belgrade)

BOSNIA-

HERZEGOVINA

Sarajevo

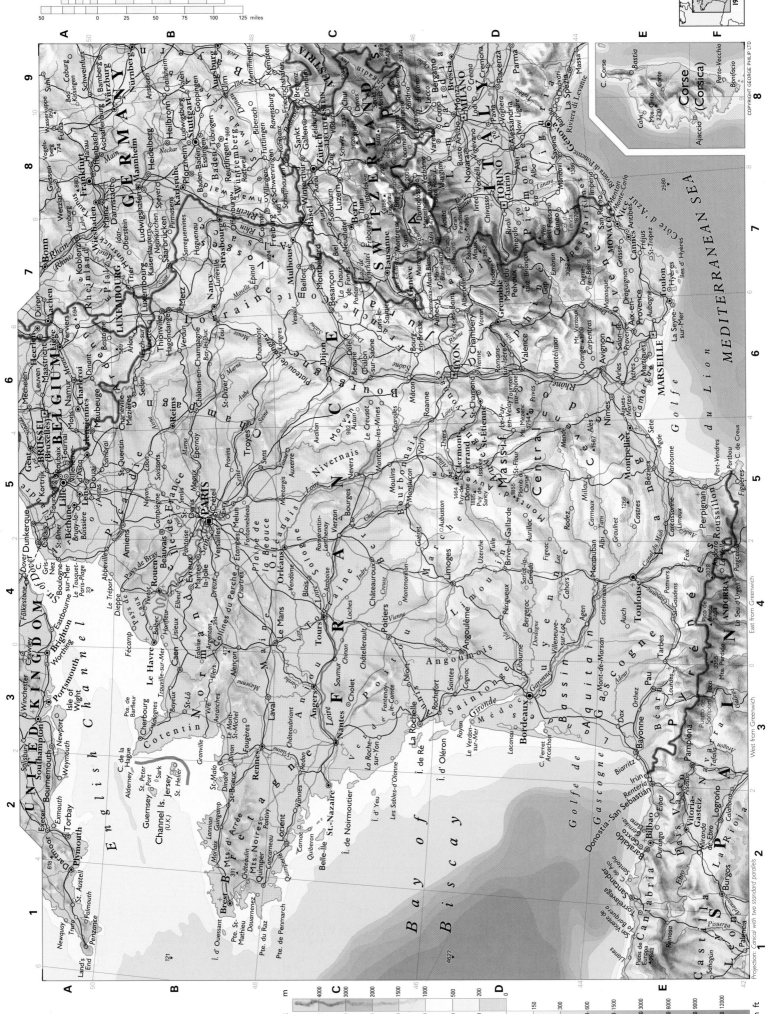

Corse (Corsica)

Projection: Conical with two standard parallels

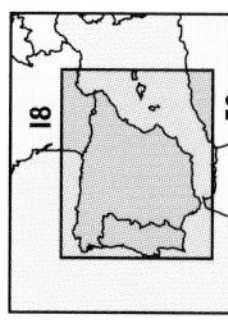

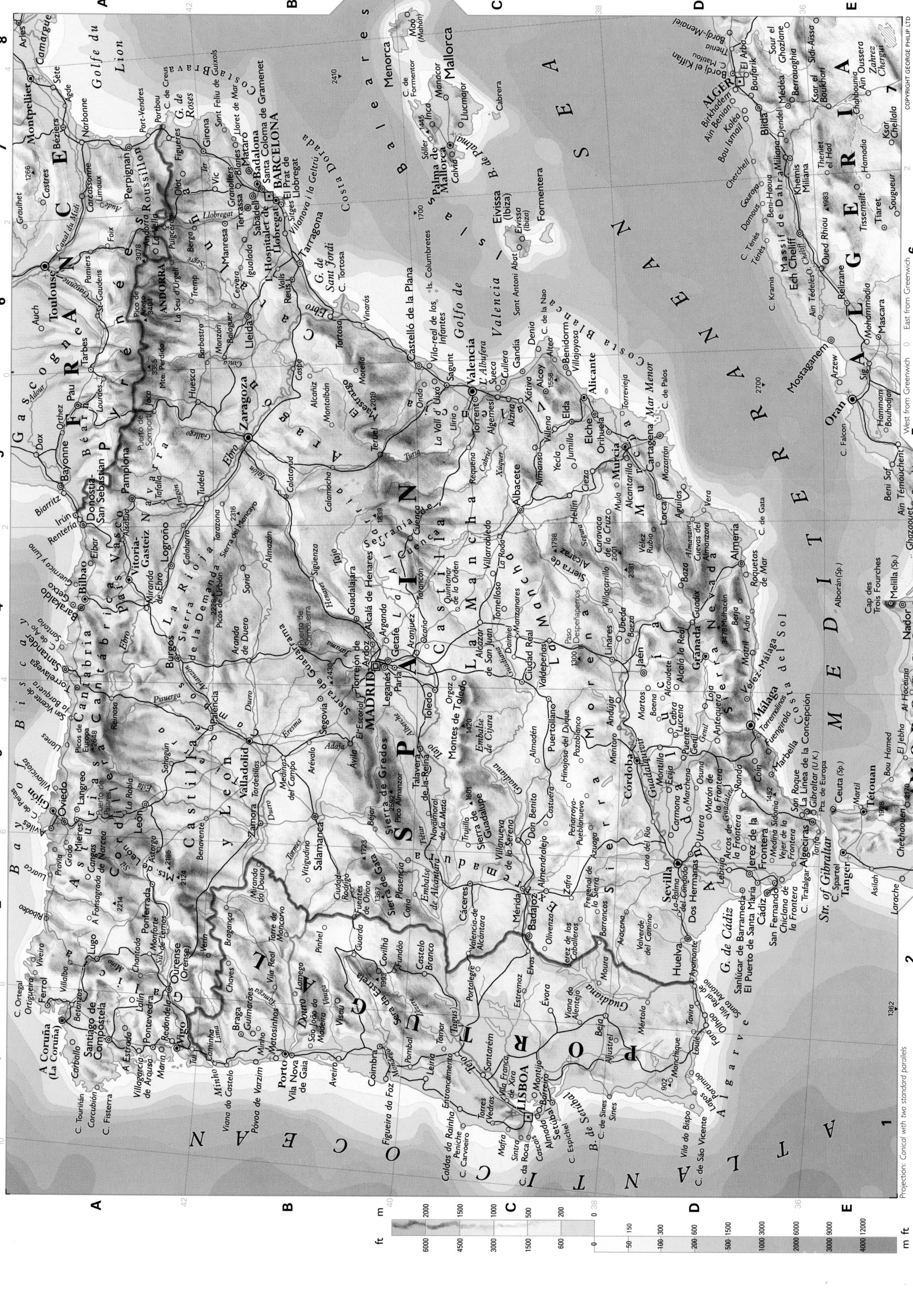

50 0 25 50 75 100 125 150 175 km
50 0 25 50 75 100 125 miles

FRANCE

SPAIN

PORTUGAL

MOROCCO

ALGERIA

MEDITERRANEAN SEA

Balearic Is

Mallorca

Menorca

Eivissa (Ibiza)

MADRID

BARCELONA

Zaragoza

Valencia

Sevilla

LISBOA

Porto

Bilbao

Málaga

Murcia

Toulouse

Montpellier

ANDORRA

ALGER

Oran

Golfe du Lion

Golfe de Valencia

Bay of Biscay

ATLANTIC OCEAN

Str. of Gibraltar

Projection: Conical with two standard parallels

West from Greenwich   0   East from Greenwich

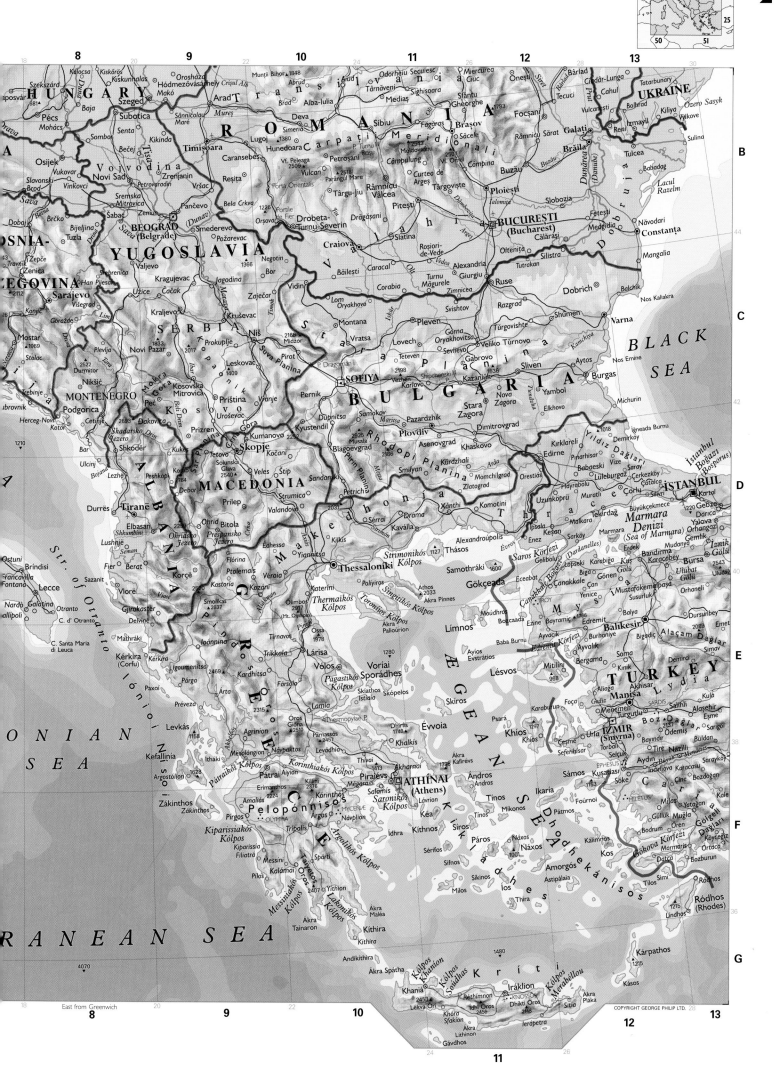

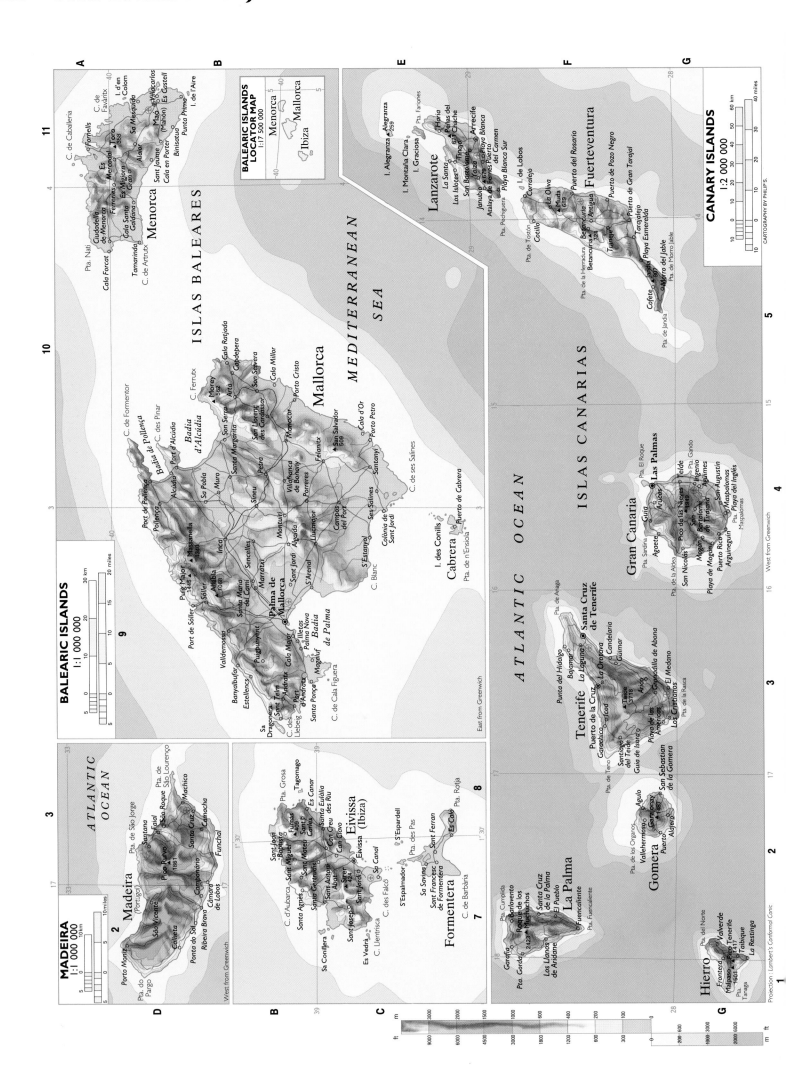

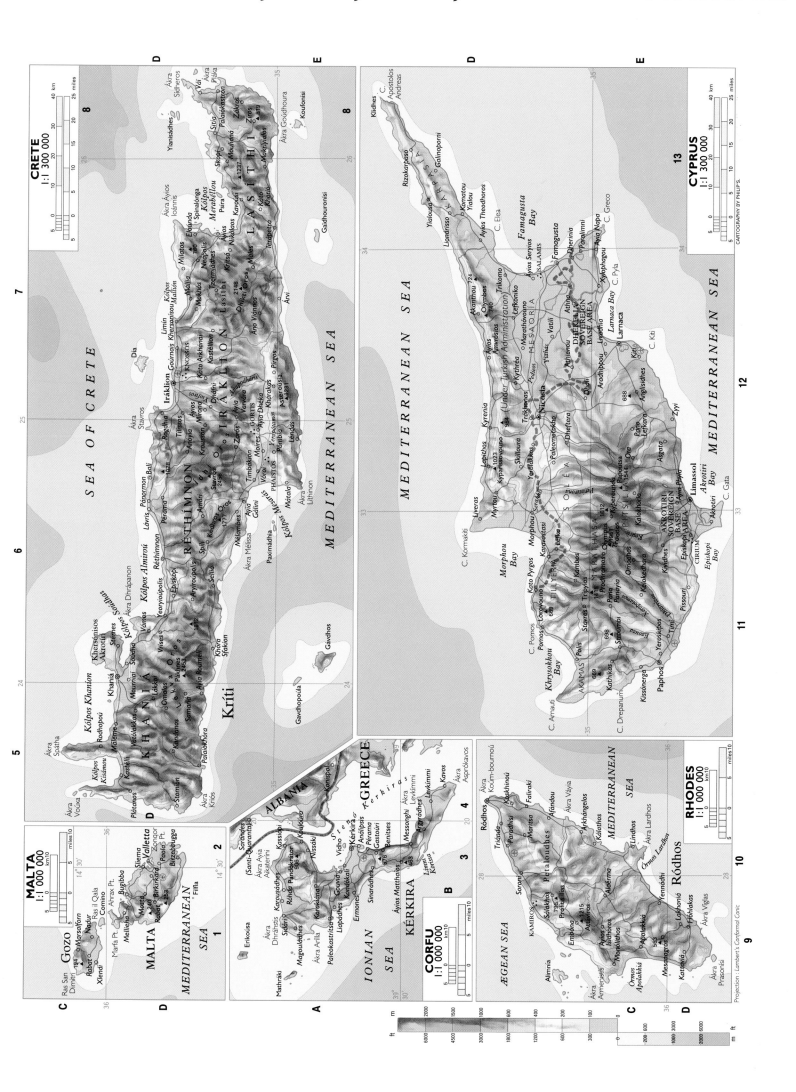

CRETE
1:1 300 000

MALTA
1:1 000 000

CORFU
1:1 000 000

RHODES
1:1 000 000

CYPRUS
1:1 300 000

CARTOGRAPHY BY PHILIP'S.

Projection : Lambert's Conformal Conic

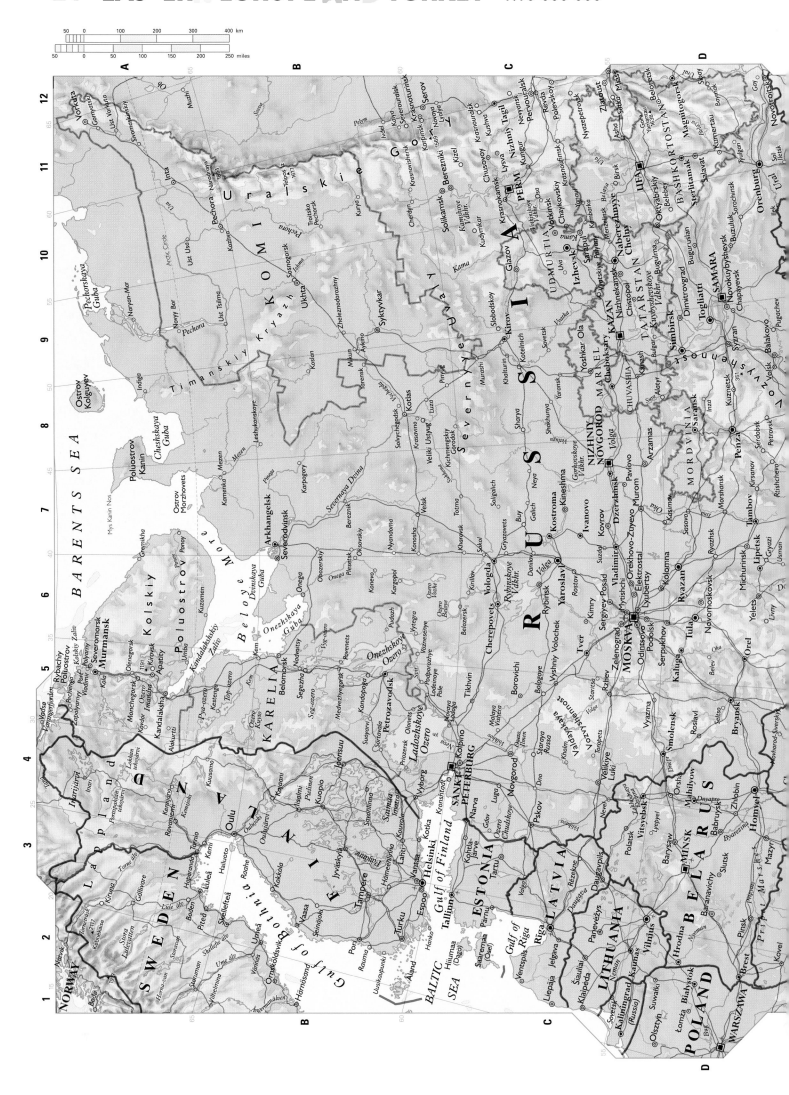

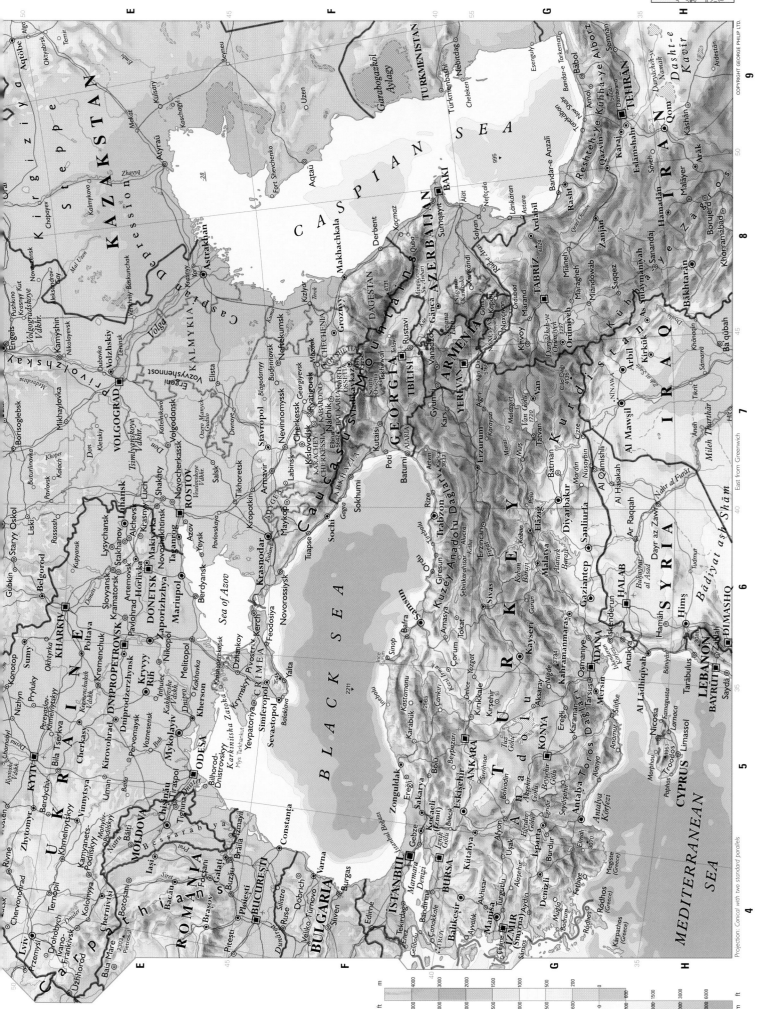

RUSSIA
1 Adygea
2 Karachey-Cherkessia
3 Kabardino-Balkaria
4 North Ossetia
5 Ingushetia
6 Chechenia
7 Dagestan
8 Mordvinia
9 Chuvashia
10 Mari El
11 Tatarstan
12 Udmurtia
13 Khakassia
AZERBAIJAN
14 Naxçivan
GEORGIA
15 Ajaria
16 Abkhazia
UKRAINE
17 Crimea

Projection: Conical Orthomorphic with two standard parallels

East from Greenwich

A
B
C
D
E
F

8 9 10 11 12 13 14 15 16 17 18 19

Mys Dezhneva
(East C.)

Uelen

Chukchi Sea

Vankarem

Providenya

Ostrov Vrangelya
Ostrov Gennyyetsy
Ostrova Delonga
Ostrov Zhokhova

St. Lawrence I.
(U.S.A.)

Beringovskiy

Anadyrskiy Zaliv

60

3800

Mys Arkticheskiy

Chukotskoye Nagorye

Ostrov Shmidta

Ostrov Komsomolets

Ostrova
Bennetta
Ostrov Faddeyevskiy

East Siberian Sea

Perek

Ust Chaun

Egvekinot

Ostrov Oktyabrskoy Revolyutsii

Ostrov
Pioner

Ostrov Bolshevik

965

Ostrov Novaya Sibir

Ostrova
Medvezhi

Ambarchik

Bilibino

Markovo

Koryakskoye Nagorye

2652

Khadyrka

Severnaya Zemlya

Novosibirskiye Ostrova

Ostrov Malyy Lyakhovskiy

Nizhne Kolymsk

Chersky

Bolshoy Anuy

Penzhino

Kamenskoye

OCEAN

Laptev Sea

Ostrov Belkovskiy

Ostrov Bolshoy Lyakhovskiy

Srednekolymsk

Oloy

Anadyr

Sredinnyy

Ossora

Karaginskiy

Bering Sea

Proliv Vilkitskogo

Mys Chelyuskin

Poluostrov Byrranga
Gory Taymyr

1146

Ostrov Bolshoy Begichev

574

Ostrov Kotelnyy

Chokurdakh

Indigirka

Khonuu

Kolyma

Taskan

Evensk

Gizhiginskaya Guba

Uka

Komandorskiye Ostrova

Oz. Taymyr

Nordvik

Ust Olenek

Lyakhovskiye Ostrova

Kazachye

Ust Kuyga

Druzhina

Zyryanka

Pobeda

Omsukchan

Orotukan

Poluostrov

Kamchatka

D

Volochanka

Kheta

Khatanga

Saskylakh

Olenek

Tit-Ary

Bulun

Kyusyur

Yana

Deputatskiy

Gora Chen 2682

Ust-Nera 3147

Susuman

Yagodnoye

Magadan

Petropavlovsk-Kamchatskiy

3621

4750 Gora Khodutka

Klyuchevskaya

3456

Khatyrka

Norilsk

Gory Putorana 1701

Novorybnoye

Zhilinda

Anabar

Olenek

Verkhoyansk

Batagai

2389

Khandyga

Seymchan

Nyukzha

Atka

Palatka

Ust-Omchug

Ust Khayryuzovo

Sea of Okhotsk

Tigil

Kirovskiy

Ust-Bolsheretsk

50

Yessey

Zhigansk

2295

Kystatym

Oymyakon 2959

Omsukchan

Severo-Kurilsk

Ostrov Paramushir

Nyurba

Sangar

Batamay

Okhotsky Perevoz

Ulya

Ayan

Okha

Ostrov Onekotan

arukhansk

Kostroma

962

Arctic Circle

Vilyuysk

Verkhnevilyuysk

Namtsy

Yakutsk

Ytyk-Kyuyel

Ust Maya

Aimo

Nelkan

Ostrov Bolshoy Shantar

Nikolayevsk-na-Amure

Sakhalinskiy Zaliv

Sakhalin

Aleksandrovsk-Sakhalinskiy

Kurilskiye Ostrova

Noginsk

Tura

Yerbogachen

Mirnyy

Suntar

Pokrovsk

Amga

Maya

Chagda

Uchur

Khrebet Dzhugdzur

1780

Ostrov Iturup

Ostrov Kunashir

Nishnyaya Tunguska

Chernysheyskiy

Olekminsk

Sinsk

Ust-Mil

Aldan

Neryungri

Nogornyy

Khrebet

Chumikan

Uda

Tuguro

Poronaysk

Yuzhno-Sakhalinsk

Kholmsk

Korsakov

Ostrov Simushir

R U S S I A

Lensk

Vitim

Yenyuka

Olekma

Aldan

2246

Stanovoy Khrebet

Tynda

Zeya

Gora Lopatina

Vanino

Ostrov Urup

Yartsevo

Severo-Yeniseyskiy

1104

Kuyumba

Mutoray

Vanavara

Kezhma

Korshunovo

Mama

Bodaybo

Chara

2999

Ust-Nyukzha

Skovorodino

Zeya

Norsk

Shimanovsk

Selemdzha

2640

2078

Nikolayevsk

Sikhote Alin

Amgu

Terney

Yeniseysk

Angara

Boguchany

Ust-Ilimsk

Makarovo

Ust-Kut

Kirensk

Magistralnyy

Nizhneangarsk

Bodgarin

2840

Mogocha

Shilka

Dzhalinda

Ushumun

Svobodnyy

Belogorsk

Chegdomyn

Komsomolsk

Amursk

Lesozavodsk

Dalnerechensk

Strelka

Kansk

Achinsk

Krasnoyarsk

Ilanskiy

Tayshet

Bratsk

Zheleznogorsk-Ilimskiy

Lena

Kalakan

Chita

Nerchinsk

Sretensk

1054

Shilka

Argun

Poyarkovo

Raychikhinsk

Obluchye

Birobidzhan

Smidovich

Khabarovsk

Bikin

Dalniy

Ussuriysk

Artem

Olga

Vostochnyy Sayan

Nizhneudinsk

Tulun

Zima

Cheremkhovo

Angarsk

1620

Bukachacha

Mogocha

Blagoveshchensk

Wolochayevka

Lazo

Kroskino

Vladivostok

Nakhodka

Artemovsk

Vostochnyy

Minusinsk

Abakan

padnyy Sayan

Irkutsk

455

Usolye Sibirskoye

Munku-Sardyk 3491

Slyudyanka

Ulan Ude

Petrovsk-Zabaykalskiy

Aginskoye

Khilok

Olovyannaya

Borzya

Zabaykalsk

Hailar

Dа Hinggan Ling

Nenjiang

Hegang

Jiamusi

Dalnerechensk

Dolniy

Terney

E

Chernogorsk

Kyzyl

Chadan

Toora-Khem

Hovsgol Nuur

Hatgal

Gusinoozersk

Zakamensk

Darhan

Kyakhta

Khapcheranga

Manzhouli

Hulun Nur

Choybalsan

Ang'angxi

Nen Jiang

QIQIHAR

Jianusi

Lesozavodsk

Dalnerechensk

Spassk

Dolniy

Ussuriysk

Hokkaido

Otaru

SAPPORO

Samagaltay

Erzin

Hentiyn Nuruu

Ondörhaan

Tamsagbulag

Songhua

HARBIN

Mudanjiang

Yanji

Vladivostok

Nakhodka

Kroskino

Abashiri

Obihiro

2290

Hakodate

Uvs Nuur

Uliastay

Hangayn Nuruu

2800

Lun

Ulaanbaatar

Tsetserleg

Choybalsan

Ondörhaan

Dongbei

JILIN

Songhua

Chongjin

Sea of

Hachinohe

Aomori

40

Hyargas Nuur

Döröö Nuur

MONGOLIA

Tao'an

Siping

CHANGCHUN

4714

Wonsan

Kansong

Honshū

Akita

Niigata

Altay

Xilinhot

Linxi

Chifeng

Tongliao

FUSHUN

SHENYANG

ANSHAN

NORTH KOREA

Dandong

Nampo

PYONGYANG

SEOUL

Japan

Kanazawa

Fuji-San 3776

JAPAN

OSAKA

4266

Hami

3957

Dalandzadgad

Saynshand

Erenhot

Chengde

Yingkou

Zhangjiakou

Hohhot

C H I N A

Gobi

Baotou

BEIJING

DALIAN

INCH'ON

SOUTH KOREA

TAEJON

TAEGU

PUSAN

Gaxun Nur

62

10 100 11 110 12 120 13 130 14

COPYRIGHT GEORGE PHILIP LTD.

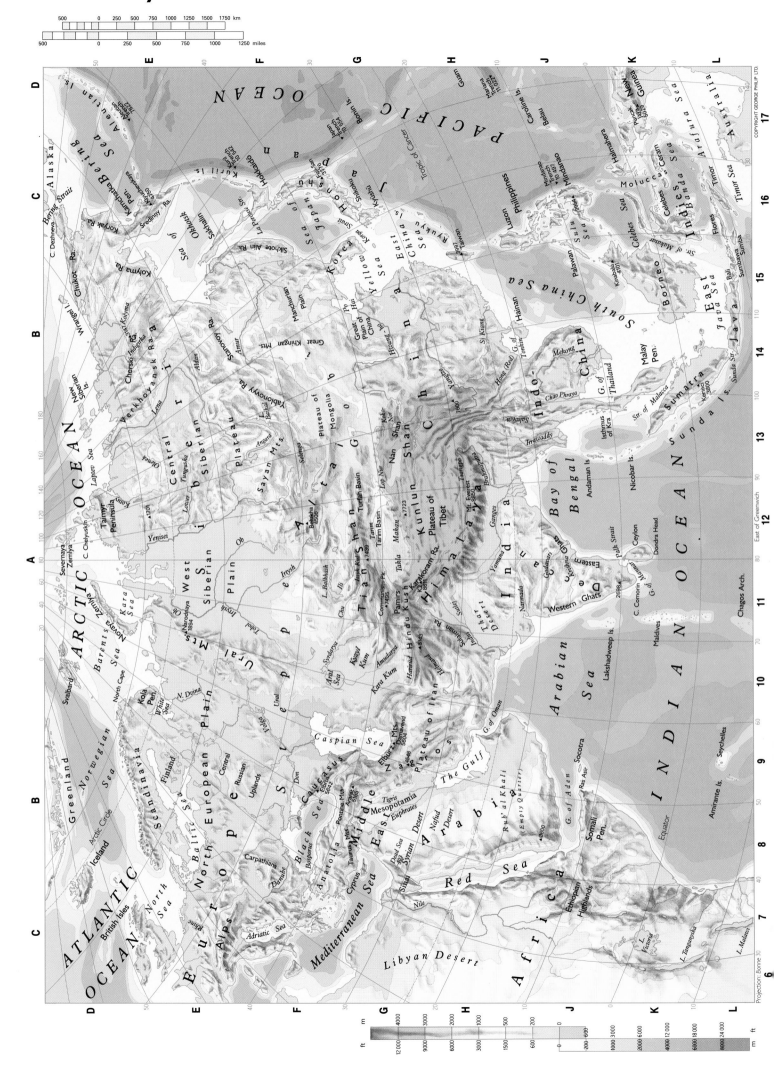

Projection: Bonne 30

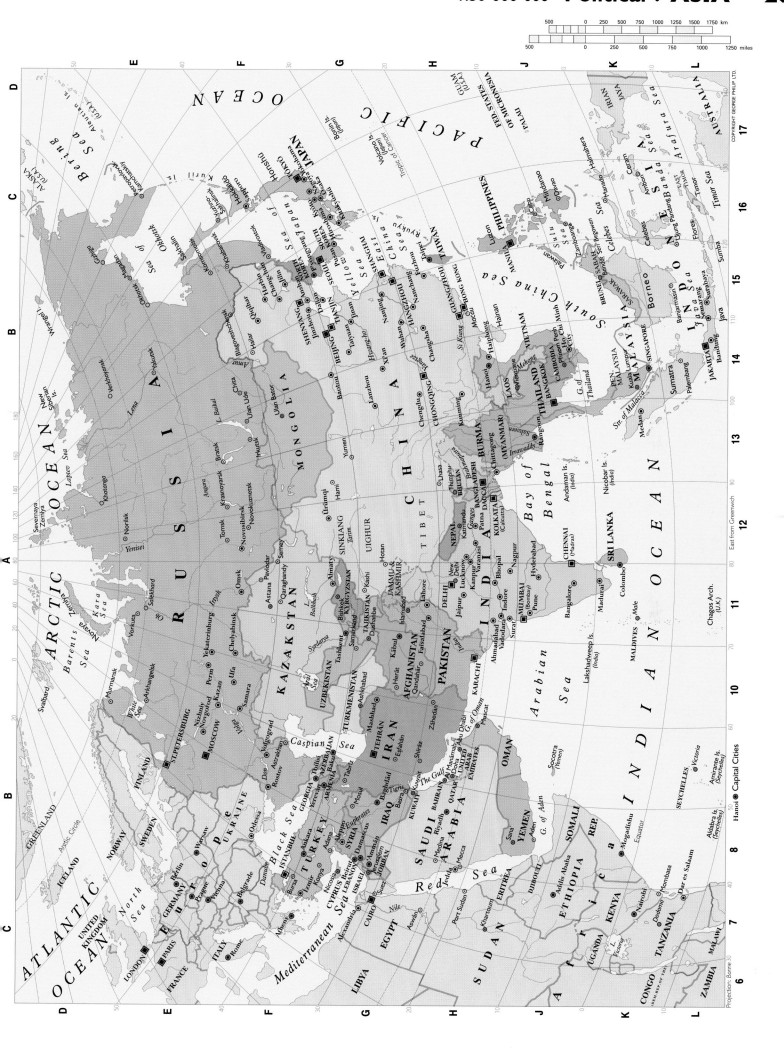

500   0   250   500   750   1000   1250   1500   1750 km
500   0   250   500   750   1000   1250 miles

COPYRIGHT GEORGE PHILIP LTD.

D

E   50   F   40   G   30   H   20   J   10   K   0   L

PACIFIC   OCEAN

GUAM (USA)

FED. STATES OF MICRONESIA

PALAU

D   17

ALASKA (U.S.A.)

Bering Sea

Aleutian Is. (USA)

Wrangel I.

New Siberian Is.

Severnaya Zemlya

Novaya Zemlya

Svalbard

ARCTIC   OCEAN

ATLANTIC   OCEAN

GREENLAND

ICELAND

NORWAY

UNITED KINGDOM

North Sea

LONDON

PARIS

FRANCE

ITALY

Rome

Prague

Berlin

GERMANY

Warsaw

Belgrade

Athens

Mediterranean Sea

C   16

Kamchatka

Petropavlovsk

Sea of Okhotsk

Sakhalin

Kuril Is.

Magadan

JAPAN

Hokkaido

Honshu

TOKYO

Yokohama

Kyoto

Osaka

Vladivostok

NORTH KOREA

SOUTH KOREA

SEOUL

Pusan

Sapporo

RUSSIA

Yakutsk

Lena

Laptev Sea

Kara Sea

Barents Sea

White Sea

Murmansk

Arkhangelsk

Vorkuta

St PETERSBURG

MOSCOW

FINLAND

SWEDEN

B   15

Sea of Japan

Niigata

Sea of Japan

Harbin

Changchun

Jilin

Qiqihar

Hailar

SHENYANG

Anshan

Dalian

Jinzhou

BEIJING

TIANJIN

TAIYUAN

Jinan

Yellow Sea

East China Sea

SHANGHAI

HANGZHOU

Nanjing

Wuhan

Nanchang

Fuzhou

Ryukyu Is.

TAIWAN

Taipei

Blagoveshchensk

Komsomolsk

Amur

Ulan Bator

MONGOLIA

L. Baikal

Ulan Ude

Irkutsk

Chita

Baotou

Lanzhou

CHINA

Huang-ho

Xian

Chengdu

CHONGQING

Kunming

Si Kiang

GUANGZHOU

HONG KONG

Macau

Hainan

Changsha

Yangtze

B   14

INDONESIA

JAVA

IRIAN JAYA

AUSTRALIA

Arafura Sea

Timor Sea

Banda Sea

EAST TIMOR

Ceram

Ambon

Halmahera

Celebes Sea

Celebes

Manado

Ujung Pandang

Flores

Sumba

Java

Bandung

JAKARTA

Surabaya

Semarang

Banjarmasin

Borneo

SARAWAK

SABAH

BRUNEI

Bandar Seri Begawan

Kuching

Palembang

Sumatra

Medan

SINGAPORE

PEN. MALAYSIA

MALAYSIA

Kuala Lumpur

Str. of Malacca

South China Sea

VIETNAM

Ho Chi Minh City

Phnom Penh

CAMBODIA

Da Nang

Hanoi

Haiphong

LAOS

Vientiane

BANGKOK

THAILAND

G. of Thailand

Mekong

PHILIPPINES

MANILA

Luzon

Cebu

Mindanao

Davao

Zamboanga

Sulu Sea

Palawan

Volcano Is. (Japan)

Tropic of Cancer

Bonin Is. (Japan)

C   B   A   B   C

180   160   140   10   20   30   40   Projection: Bonne

D   E   50   F   40   G   30   H   20   J   10   K   0   L

East from Greenwich

Hanoi ● Capital Cities

Novosibirsk

Novokuznetsk

Tomsk

Krasnoyarsk

Bratsk

Angara

Yenisei

Norilsk

Khatanga

Oleněk

Olekminsk

Viljujsk

Omsk

KAZAKSTAN

Astana

Pavlodar

Semey

Qaraghandy

L. Balkhash

Almaty

KYRGYZSTAN

Bishkek

Aral Sea

Syrdarye

Tashkent

UZBEKISTAN

TAJIKISTAN

Dushanbe

Samarkand

TURKMENISTAN

Ashkhabad

Kashi

Hotan

Urumqi

SINKIANG UIGHUR

Tarim

TIBET

Lhasa

Kashi

JAMMU & KASHMIR

Islamabad

Lahore

New Delhi

DELHI

Jaipur

Kanpur

Lucknow

Varanasi

NEPAL

Kathmandu

BHUTAN

Thimphu

Patna

DACCA

BANGLADESH

Chittagong

Ganges

Brahmaputra

KOLKATA (Calcutta)

Bay of Bengal

Andaman Is. (India)

Nicobar Is. (India)

BURMA (MYANMAR)

Rangoon

Irrawaddy

Salween

A   13

A   12

INDIA

Bhopal

Nagpur

Hyderabad

CHENNAI (Madras)

Bangalore

Madurai

SRI LANKA

Colombo

Chagos Arch. (U.K.)

Male

MALDIVES

Lakshadweep Is. (India)

Mandalay

B   11

Ekaterinburg

Chelyabinsk

Nizhniy Novgorod

Kazan

Ufa

Perm

Samara

Volga

Salekhard

Irtysh

Astrakhan

Rostov

Volgograd

Don

Caspian Sea

AZERBAIJAN

Baku

GEORGIA

Tbilisi

ARMENIA

Yerevan

Tabriz

TEHRAN

Mashhad

IRAN

Esfahan

Shiraz

Zahedan

AFGHANISTAN

Kabul

Herat

Qandahar

PAKISTAN

Faisalabad

KARACHI

Ahmadabad

MUMBAI (Bombay)

Pune

Surat

Vadodara

Indore

Arabian Sea

Indus

B   10

Odessa

Kiev

UKRAINE

Black Sea

ISTANBUL

Ankara

Bursa

Izmir

Konya

TURKEY

CYPRUS

Nicosia

LEBANON

Beirut

SYRIA

Aleppo

Damascus

Jerusalem

ISRAEL

Amman

JORDAN

Euphrates

Tigris

Mosul

Baghdad

IRAQ

Basra

KUWAIT

The Gulf

BAHRAIN

QATAR

Doha

Abu Dhabi

U.A.E.

ARAB EMIRATES

Manamah

Riyadh

SAUDI ARABIA

Medina

Mecca

Jedda

OMAN

Muscat

G. of Oman

Victoria

Amirante Is. (Seychelles)

SEYCHELLES

Aldabra Is. (Seychelles)

Socotra (Yemen)

YEMEN

Sana

Aden

G. of Aden

SOMALI REP.

Mogadishu

B   8

EUROPE

Danube

Nile

Aswan

Alexandria

CAIRO

Suez

EGYPT

LIBYA

Red Sea

SUDAN

Khartoum

ERITREA

DJIBOUTI

Aden

Port Sudan

ETHIOPIA

Addis Ababa

Africa

KENYA

Nairobi

UGANDA

L. Victoria

TANZANIA

Dodoma

Dar es Salaam

Mombasa

CONGO (DEM. REP. OF THE)

ZAMBIA

MALAWI

Equator

C   7

C   6

D   E   50   F   40   G   30   H   20   J   10   K   0   L

JAPAN 1:5 000 000

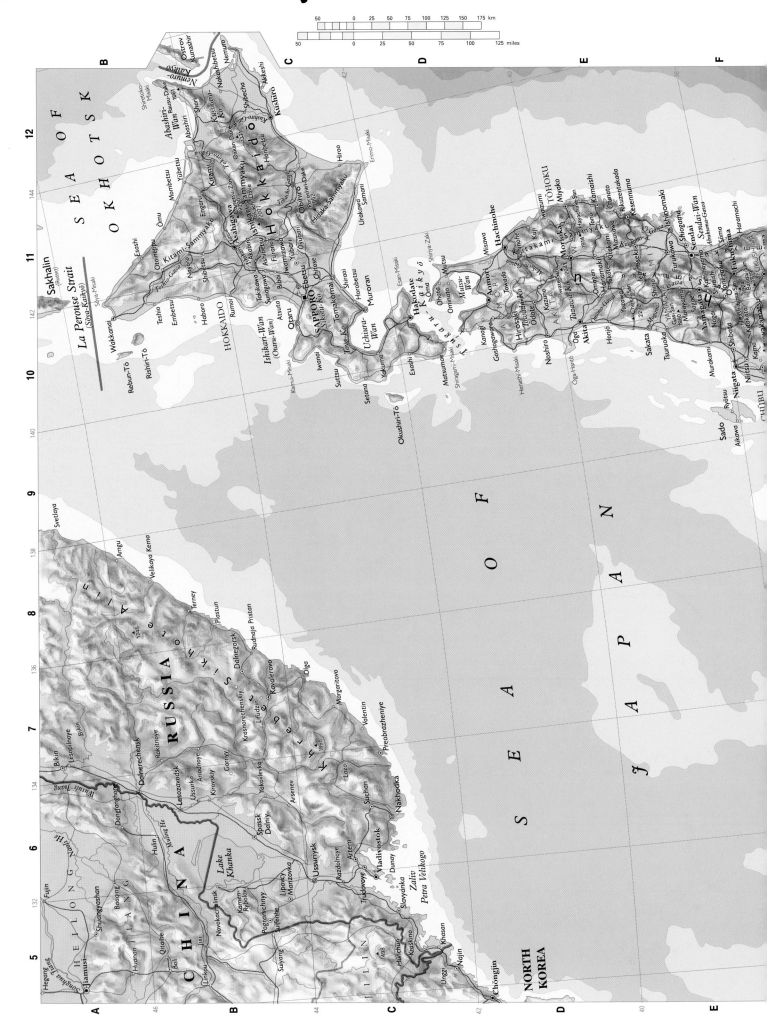

SEA OF OKHOTSK

Ostrov Kunashir

Nemuro-Kaikyō

Shiretoko-Misaki
Rausu-Dake 1661
Abashiri-Wan
Abashiri
Shari
Kushiro-Ko
Kitami
Honbetsu
Obihiro 2052

Sakhalin (Russia)

La Perouse Strait (Sōya-Kaikyō)

Sōya-Misaki

Wakkanai

Rebun-Tō
Rishiri-Tō

Teshio
Embetsu
Haboro
Rumoi

HOKKAIDO

Ōmu
Mombetsu
Yūbetsu
Esashi
Otoineppu
Nayoro
Shibetsu
Kitami-Sammyaku
Asahigawa
Akabira
Ashibetsu
Furano
Bibai
Takikawa
Sunagawa
Iwamizawa
Yūbari

Tenpoku-Ginga

Hiroo
Erimo-Misaki

Samani
Urakawa
Shiraoi
Hidaka-Sammyaku

SAPPORO
Shikotsu-Ko
Chitose
Ebetsu

Otaru
Ishikari-Wan (Otaru-Wan)

Kamu-Misaki

Iwanai
Suttsu
Setana
Okushiri-Tō

Tomakomai
Muroran
Horobetsu
Uchiura-Wan
Yakumo
Esashi
Matsumae-Misaki
Shiragami-Misaki

Tōyo-Ko
Toyako-Onsen
Esan-Misaki
Hakodate
Tsugaru-Kaikyō
Ōma

Ōhata
Ominato
Mutsu
Mutsu-Wan
Shiriya-Zaki

Henashi-Misaki
Oga-Hantō
Oga

TŌHOKU
Miyako
Iwaizumi
Hachinohe
Towada
Misawa
Kitakami-Gawa
Morioka
Hayachine-San 1914
Kamaishi
Ōfunato
Rikuzentakada
Kesennuma
Ishinomaki
Sendai-Wan

Aomori
Towada-Ko
Hirosaki
Ōdate
Kazuno
Gojōme
Akita
Honjō

HONSHU

Kanagi
Goshogawara
Omagari
Yokote
Shinjō
Yamagata
Mogami-Gawa
Sakata

Tsuruoka
Murakami
Shibata
Niitsu

Noshiro
Sada
Aikawa
Ryōtsu
Niigata

CHŪBU

FUKUSHIMA
Sōma
Haramachi

SEA OF JAPAN

RUSSIA

Svetlaya
Amgu
Velikaya Kema
Terney
Plastun
Rudnaja Pristan
Dalnegorsk

Sikhote

1745

Olga
Kavalerovo

Margaritovo
Valentin
Preobrazheniye

Krasnorechensky
Lifudzin
Gornyy
Yakovlevka
Arsenev
Lazo
Suchan

Dalnerechensk
Rakitnoye
Lesozavodsk

Ussuri
Ussurka
Aradnoye
Kirovka

Olga

Bikin
Lesopilnoye
Bikin

CHINA

HEILONGJIANG

Hegang
 Jiamusi
Songhua Jiang
Huanan
Shuangyashan
Boli
Linkou
Qitaihe

Fujin

Sungach' He
Mulang He
Wusuli Jiang

Hulin
Dongfanghong

Baoqing

JILIN

Muling
Suiyang

Spassk Dalniy
Kamen-Rybolov
Pogranichny
Luifenhe

Lake Khanka

Novokachalinsk

Zaliv Petra Velikogo
Vladivostok
Artem
Razdolnoye
Ussuriysk

Trudovoye
Dunay
Nakhodka
Slavyanka
Livovcy
Manzovka

Hunchun
1498

Kraskino
Khasan

Ungji
Najin

NORTH KOREA

Chŏngjin

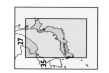

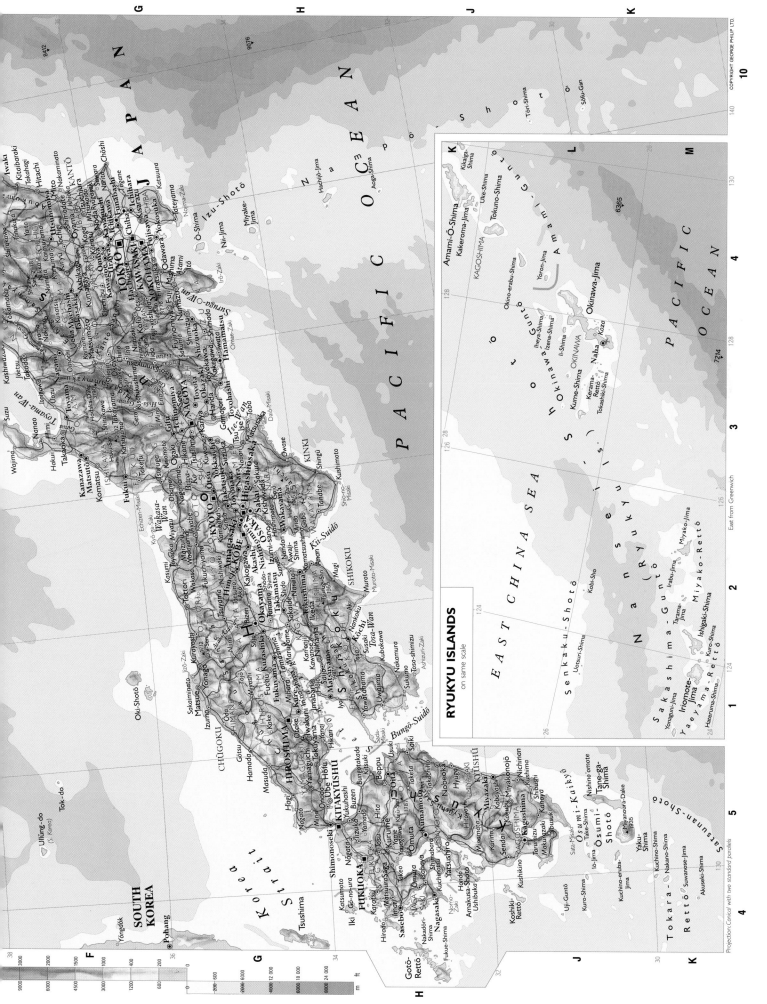

SOUTH KOREA

Yŏngdŏk

Pohang

Ulleung-do (S. Korea)

Tok-do

JAPAN

RYUKYU ISLANDS
on same scale

EAST CHINA SEA

Amami-O-Shima

Kakeroma-Shima

KAGOSHIMA

Kikaiga-Shima

Uke-Shima

Tokuno-Shima

Okino-erabu-Shima

Yoron-Jima

Iheya-Shima
Izena-Shima

Ii-Shima

OKINAWA

Kume-Shima

Kerama-Rettō

Okinawa-Jima
Naha
Koza

Tokashiki-Shima

N a n s e i - s h o t ō   (R y u k y u)

Senkaku-Shotō

Uotsuri-Shima

Kobi-Sho

Miyako-Rettō

Tarama-Jima

Irabu-Jima

Miyako-Jima

Sakashima-Guntō

Ishigaki-Shima

Kuro-Shima

Yaeyama-Rettō

Iriomote

Yonaguni-Jima

Hateruma-Shima

PACIFIC OCEAN

Tori-Shima

Sōfu-Gan

PACIFIC OCEAN

COPYRIGHT GEORGE PHILIP LTD.

East from Greenwich

Projection: Conical with two standard parallels

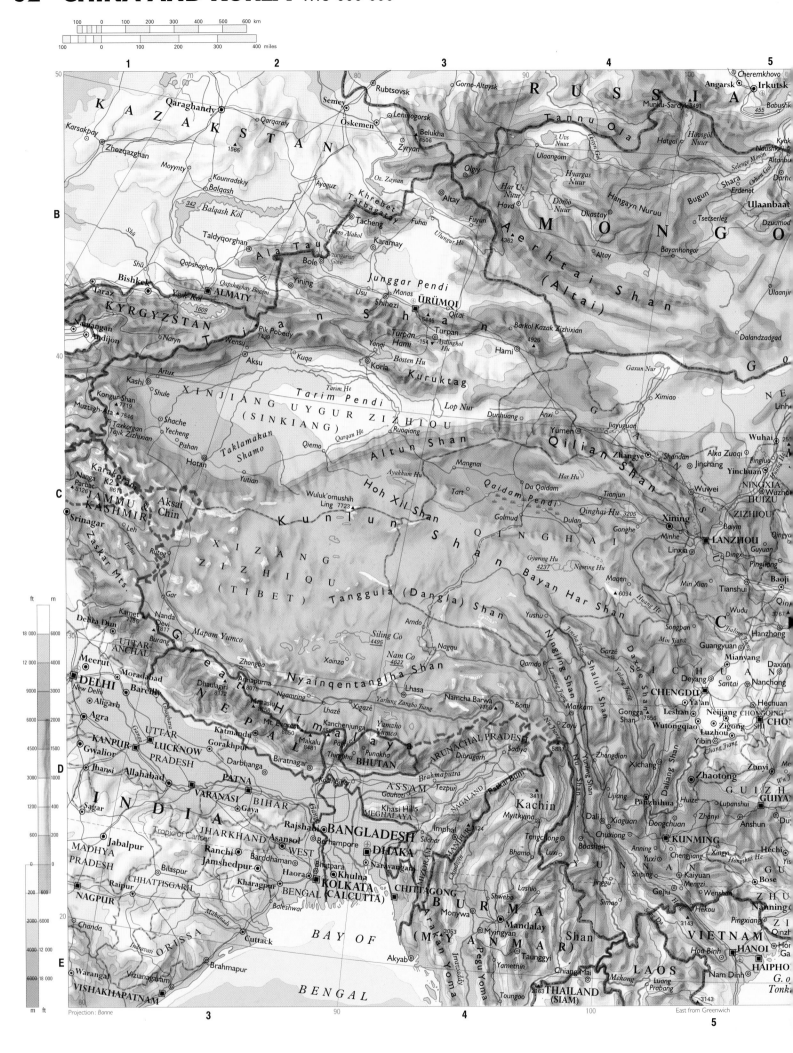

100 0 100 200 300 400 500 600 km
100 0 100 200 300 400 miles

ft   m

18 000 6000
12 000 4000
9000   3000
6000   2000
4500   1500
3000   1000
1200   400
600   200
0   0
200   600
2000   6000
4000   12 000
6000   18 000

m   ft

Projection: Bonne

East from Greenwich

27
40
38 37

6   7   8   9

Oz. Baykal
Ulan Ude
Chita
Sretensk
Bukachacha
Nerchinsk
Olovyannaya
Borzya
Petrovsk-zabaykalskiy
Hentiyn Nuruu
Manzhouli
Hailar
Kerulen
Choybalsan
Buir Nur
Tamsagbulag
Arxan
Horqin Youyi Qianqi
Solon
Butha Qi
Nenjiang
Bei'an
Anda
Daqing
Suihua
Gulian
Shimanovsk
Svobodnyy
Chegdomyn
Aihui
Blagoveshchensk
Bureya
Ozero Bolon
Komsomolsk
Amur
Aleksandrovsk-Sakhalinskiy
Vanino
Poronaysk
Mys Terpeniya
Sakhalin
Khabarovsk
Birobidzhan
Yichun
Hegang
Jiamusi
Shuangyashan
Bikin
Hulin
Kholmsk
Yuzhno-Sakhalinsk
La Perouse Str.
Wakkanai

B

LIA
MONGGOL ZIZHIQU (INNER MONGOLIA)
Saynshand
Borhoyn Tal
Erenhot
Sonid Youqi
Xilinhot
Duolun
Linxi
Chifeng
Huolin Gol
Tao'an
Baicheng
QIQIHAR
Shuangcheng
HARBIN
Mudanjiang
Jixi
L. Khanka
Mishan
Ussuriysk
Artem
Nakhodka
Hunchun
Vladivostok
Partizansk
Dunhua
JILIN
CHANGCHUN
Shuangliao
Siping
Liaoyuan
Tongliao
Yanji
Changbai Shan
Chŏngjin
SEA OF
JAPAN
Hokkaidō
SAPPORO
Otaru
Hakodate
Aomori
Hachinohe
Kitami
Asahigawa
Muroran
Erimo-misaki
Tsugaru-Kaikyō
Akita
Morioka

Bayan Obo
Baotou
Hohhot
Datong
Jining
Zhangjiakou
Xuanhua
Chengde
Chaoyang
Fuxin
Tieling
FUSHUN
SHENYANG
Benxi
Anshan
LIAONING
Jinzhou
Yingkou
Dandong
Hamhŭng
Hŭngnam
Wŏnsan
Kimchaek
Sado
Yamagata
Sendai
Fukushima
Niigata
Kōriyama
Utsunomiya
Mito

BEIJING (PEKING)
BEIJING SHI
Anci
Baoding
HEBEI
TAIYUAN
SHANXI
Yangquan
Yuci
TIANJIN
TIANJINN SHI
Cangzhou
Bo Hai
Qinhuangdao
Liaodong Wan
Liaodong Bandao
DALIAN
Namp'o
P'YŎNGYANG
Haeju
Kaesŏng
Ch'unch'ŏn
Kangnŭng
SŎUL (SEOUL)
INCH'ŎN
SOUTH KOREA
Takaoka
TOKYO
KAWASAKI
YOKOHAMA
NAGOYA
Kanazawa
Komatsu
Toyama
Wajima
Jōetsu

C

SHIJIAZHUANG
Fenyang
Yangquan
Dezhou
JINAN
SHANDONG
ZIBO
Weifang
Yantai
Weihai
Shandong Bandao
QINGDAO
YELLOW SEA
TAEJŎN
Kunsan
Chŏnju
TAEGU
PUSAN
Masan
KWANGJU
Mokp'o
Cheju-do
Fuji-San
Shizuoka
Hamamatsu
KYŌTO
ŌSAKA
KŌBE
Sakai
Okayama
Matsue
Kure
Shikoku
Kōchi
Wakayama
HIROSHIMA
Tsushima
Shimonoseki
KITAKYUSHU
FUKUOKA
Matsuyama
Sasebo
Kumamoto
Nagasaki
Kyūshū
Miyazaki
Kagoshima
Tane-ga-Shima
Yaku-Shima
JAPAN

Yuanping
3058
Linfen
Tongchuan
Luoyang
Kaifeng
Xinxiang
Jincheng
ZHENGZHOU
HENAN
Pingdingshan
Nanyang
Han Shui
Zhumadian
XI'AN
Changzhi
Jining
Zaozhuang
Xuzhou
Qingjiang
Lianyungang
JIANGSU
Yancheng
Shangqiu
Huaibei
Shangshui
Fuyang
Bengbu
Huainan
ANHUI
Taizhou
Yangzhou
NANJING
Changzhou
Nantong
Wuxi
SHANGHAI
Suzhou
SHANGHAI SHI
HEFEI
Ma'anshan
Wuhu
Wuxing
Jiaxing

30

XI'AN
Xiangfan
Shivan
Ankang
Dable Shan
Xinyang
Zhongxiang
Tongling
HUBEI
WUHAN
Anqing
Huangshi
Shashi
Yichang
Enshi
Changde
Yueyang
Dongting Hu
Jiujiang
Jingdezhen
Tunxi
Shaoxing
NINGBO
ZHEJIANG
LINHAI
Jinhua
Quzhou
Shangrao
NANCHANG
CHANGSHA
HANGZHOU
Hangzhou Wan
EAST CHINA SEA
Amami-Ō-Shima
Tokuno-Shima

D

HUNAN
Xiangtan
Yiyang
Shaoyang
Hengyang
Hongjiang
JIANGXI
Pingxiang
Linchuan
Wuyi Shan
2120
Nanping
Ji'an
Min Jiang
Sanming
FUJIAN
FUZHOU
Pútian
Quanzhou
Chilung
T'AIPEI
Hsinchu
T'aichung
Changhua
Chiai
Yu Shan
3997
TAIWAN (FORMOSA)
T'ainan
T'aitung
P'ingtung
KAOHSIUNG
Taiwan Strait
Wenzhou
Ryūkyū-rettō
Sakishima-Guntō
Miyako-Jima
Ishigaki-Shima
Iriomote-Jima
Naha
Okinawa-Jima
7507
Tropic of Cancer
PACIFIC OCEAN

Guilin
Hongjiang
GUANGXI
Wuzhou
Zhaoqing
Yangjiang
GUANGDONG
GUANGZHOU (CANTON)
Foshan
Jiangmen
Huizhou
Mei Xian
Chaozhou
Zhangzhou
Xiamen
Longyan
Ruijin
Shaoguan
Ganzhou
Xing'an
Nan Ling
Shantou
HONG KONG
Macau
Zhujiang Kou
Chilung
Batan Is.

E

Maoming
Zhanjiang
Haikou
Hainan Dao
1879
Yacheng
HAINAN
SOUTH CHINA SEA
PHILIPPINES
Babuyan Is.
Batan Is.

110   6   120   7   130   8

COPYRIGHT GEORGE PHILIP LTD.

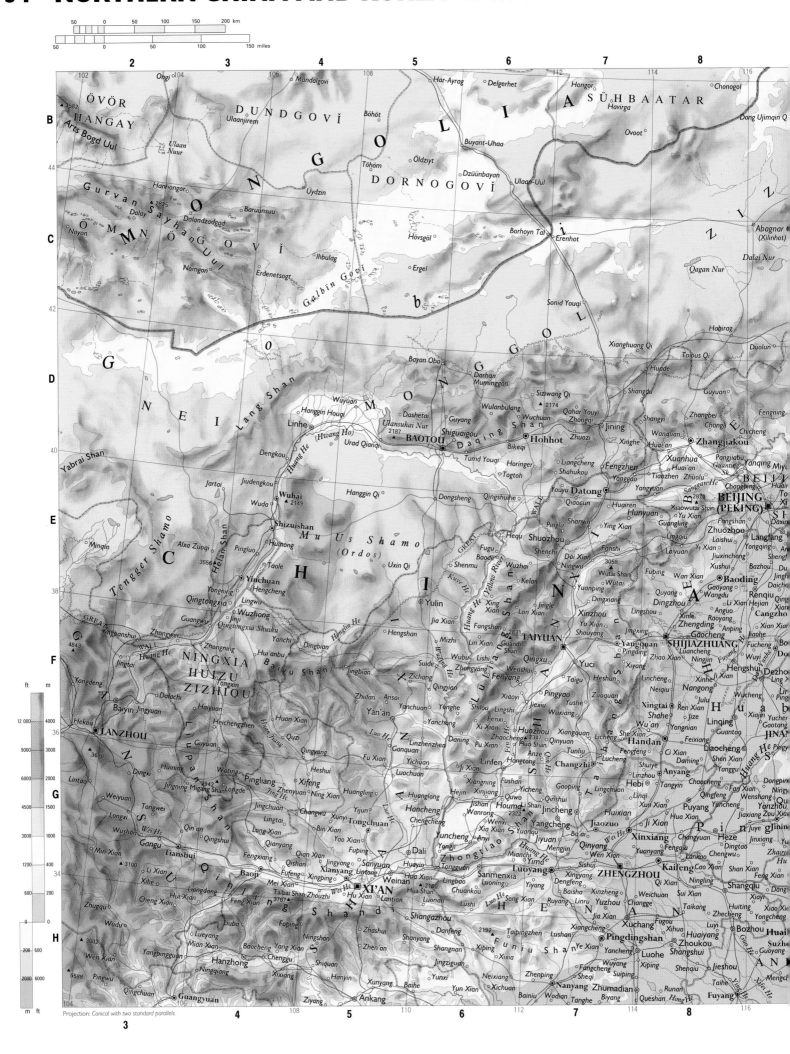

B

HEILONGJIANG

HARBIN   Bin Xian   Turiy Rog   Ozero
Horqin Youyi Qianqi   Zhenlai   Nen   Yanshou   Linkou   Jixi   Khanka
(Ulanhot)   Maoxing   Zhaodong   Shuangcheng   Acheng   Shangzhi   RUSSIA
Baicheng   Da'an   Changchunling   Lalin   Yimianpo   Hengdaohezi   Muling   Maqiaohe
Taonan   Tuquan   Anguang   Sanchahe   Wuchang   Hailin   Mudanjiang   Xiachengzi   Suifenhe   Pogranichnyy
Qagan   Fuyu   Beitaolaizhao   Yushu   Shanhetun   Shulan   1690   Ning'an   Dongning   Golenki
Qian an   Nur Qian   Gorlos   Kaoshan   Dehui   Huangsongdian   Dongjingcheng   Suyang   Ussuriysk
Jarud Qi   Tongyu   Shenjingzi   Nong'an   Wulajie   Jingbo   Luozigou   Razdolnoye
Zhanyu   Beizhengzhen   Fulongquan   Jiutai   Gangyao   Emu   Hu   Tavrichanka
Changling   Horqin Zuoyi   Maolin   Huaidezhen   Jiaohe   Xinzhan   Huadian   Dunhua   Daxinggou   Mingyuegue   Tumen   Hunchun   Vladivostok
Xinkai He   Zhongqi   CHANGCHUN   JILIN   Xianzhan   Wangqing   Yanji   Namyang   Hoeamdong   Slavyanka
Fanjiatun   Songhua   Chunyang   Longjing   Kraskino   Posyet
Kailu   Tongliao   Lishu   Gongzhuling   Yitong   Hu   Panshi   Antu   Helong   Hoeryong   Unggi   Najin

100   0   100   200   300   400   500 km
100   0   50   100   150   200   250   300   350 miles

1 **2** **3** **4** **5**

A

Letpadan
Tharrawaddy
Thoen
Uttaradit
Vientiane (Viangchan)
Nong Khai
Loei
Udon Thani
Muang Khammouan
Ba Don
Dong Hoi
Insein
BURMA
Sawankhalok
Phitsanulok
Nakhon Phanom
Savannakhet
Quang Tri
RANGOON (YANGON)
Thaton
Moulmein
Tak
Mae Sot
Phong
THAILAND
Sakon Nakhon
Hue
Ma-ubin
Pyapon
Kyaikkami
Phetchabun
Khon Kaen
Khemmarat
Saravan
Quang Ngai
Da Nang
Hoi An
(MYANMAR)
Ye
Nakhon Sawan
Chaiyaphum
Roi Et
Ubon Ratchasima
Sisaket
Pakxe
Chau O
2598
Kon Tum

15

Natkyizin
Nan Tok
Phra Nakhon Si Ayutthaya
Saraburi
Nakhon Ratchasima
Khu Khan
Phnom Dangrek
Muang Khong
Bong Son
Binh Dinh
Qui Nhon
Song Cau
Tavoy
Kanchanaburi
2075
BANGKOK
Samut Songkhram
Samut Prakan
Aranyaprathet
Cheom Ksan
761
Plei Ku
A Yun Pa

B

Moscos Islands
Phet Buri
Chon Buri
Pattaya
Kulen
Siemreab
Stoeng Treng
2405
Buon Me Thuot
Mui Nay
4424
Mali Kyun
Rayong
Batdambang
Pouthisat
Kampong Thom
Kracheh
Nha Trang
Kadan Kyun
Hua Hin
Ko Chang
Tonle Sap
Kampong Chhnang
Kampong Cham
Cam Ranh
Mergui
Chanthaburi
Trat
1813
Phnom Penh (Phnum Penh)
Prey Veng
Da Lat
Phan Rang
Tanintharyi
Ko Kut
Krong Koh Kong
Kaoh Kong
Takeo
Svay Rieng
Mui Dinh
Letsôk-aw Kyun
Prachuap Khiri Khan
Bang Saphan
Chaak Kampong Saom
Sre Ambel
Kampot
Long Xuyen
THANH PHO HO CHI MINH
Myeik
Bokpyin
Kampong Saom
Hon Chong
My Tho
Lambi Kyun
Chumphon
Gulf
Phumi Koh Kong
Phan Thiet
Bien Hoa
Kyunzu
Maliwun
Kho Khot Kra
Dao Phu Quoc
Sa Dec
Can Tho
Vung Tau

10

Zadetkyi Kyun
Ranong
Ko Phangan
of
Rach Gia
Soc Trang
Ko Samui
Thailand
Bac Lieu
Con Son
Surat Thani
Ca Mau
Mui Ca Mau
1835
Nakhon Si Thammarat
Phangnga
Pak Phanang

C

Thung Song
Phatthalung
Thale Luang
Phuket
Trang
Songkhla
Kantang
Hat Yai
Pattani
Narathiwat
Tumpat
Tarutao
Satun
Yala
Kota Baharu
We
Langkawi
Alor Setar
Pasir Mas
Perhentian
Sabang
Banda Aceh
Meureudu
Bireuen
Sungai Petani
Redang
Sigli
ACEH
Lhokseumawe
Idi
Butterworth
Pinang
Kuala Terengganu
Meulaboh
Peureulak
George Town
Kuala

5

Lhokkruet
Calang
Takengon
G. Leuser
Langsa
3381
Pangkalanbrandan
Belawan
Taiping
Ipoh
PENINSULAR MALAYSIA
Gunong Tahan
2190
Dungun
Tenggol
Kuala
MALAYSIA
Kepulauan Natuna Besar
Telukbutun
Natuna Besar
Bandar Seri Begawan
BRUNEI
Kota Kinabalu
Ranau
4101
SABAH
Melalap
Binjai
MEDAN
Tebingtinggi
Teluk Intan
Kampar
Kuala Lipis
Temerloh
Kuantan
Pulau Labuan
Kuala Belait
Miri
Seria
Kota Belud
Beaufort
Papar
Kudat
Langkon
Jembon
Kabanjahe
Pematangsiantar
Kuala Kubu Baharu
Kuala
Seri
Niah
Tenom
Lawas
Limbang
Sibu
Kanowit
Kapit
2438
Tanjungselor

D

Prapat
Danau Toba
Siaksriindrapura
Segamat
Mersing
Laut
Midai
Subi
Kepulauan Natuna Selatan
Serasan
SARAWAK
Bintulu
Oya
Mukah
Bintangor
Sarikei
Saratok
Betung
Nangapinoh
Gunung Hose
1701
Longnawan
2988
Tanjungredeb
Tanjungbaru
Tapaktuan
Tarutung
Port Dickson
Bagansiapiapi
Muar
Keluang
Kota Tinggi
Tanjung Datu
Kuching
Lundu
Niut
Tebakong
Serian
Bandar Sri Aman
Liangpran
2240
**KALIMAN
TAN TIMUR**
Simeulue
Sinabang
Rantauprapat
Dumai
Bengkalis
Batu Pahat
Johor Baharu
Ngabang
Sambas
Singkawang
SINGAPORE
Bintan
Tanjungpinang
Kepulauan Tambelan
Kepulauan Badas
Mempawah
Sambas
Sanggau
Sintang
Semitau
Putussibau
Pegunungan Kapuas Hulu
Sangkulirang
Bonta
Nias
Lahewa
Gunungsitoli
Telukdalem
Pekanbaru
Bangkinang
Lubuksikaping
Kepulauan Riau
Lingga
Kepulauan Lingga
Pontianak
BARAT
G. Saran
1758
Nangapinoh
Pegunungan Schwaner
2278
Kapuas
Longiram
Muarakaman
Muaratewe
Tenggarong
Balikpapa
Kepulauan Batu
Padangsidempuan
RIAU
Rupat
Kampar
Muarabungo
3805
Kerinci
Samarin
Pini
Lubuklinggau
Singkep
Pasirkuning
Kepulauan Karimata
Sukadana
Ketapang
Purukcahu
Muaratewe
Kualakuran

0

Tanahmasa
Tanahbala
Bukittinggi
Payakumbuh
Rengat
Belinyu
Sungailiat
Pangkalpinang
Muarajuloi
Buntok
Tanahgrogot
Siberut
Sabulubbek
Padang
Painan
Sawahlunto
Solok
Jambi
Muaratembesi
Bangka
Muntok
Pangkalanbuun
Sampit
Kumai
Kuala Kapuas
Kandangan
Besar
1892
Kepulauan Balabalan

E

Kepulauan Mentawai
BARAT
Padangpanjang
Bangko
Mukomuko
Sarolangun
Kualajelai
Semuda
SELATAN
Banjarmasin
Kotabaru
Sipura
Sungaipenuh
Sekayu
Sungaigerong
Tanjungpandan
Manggar
Belitung
Martapura
Sebuku
Pulau Pagai Utara
Lubuklinggau
Curup
PALEMBANG
Toboali
Dendang
Kualapembuang
Pelaihari
Karambu
Pulau Pagai Selatan
Tebintinggi
SELATAN
Perabumulih
Muaraenim
Tg. Lumut
Teluk Sampit
Jorong
Pagatan
Satui
Pulau Laut
Bengkulu
Lahat
3159
Dempo
Baturaja
Tanjung Pasir
Tanjung Puting
Tg. Seletan
Menggala

5

BENGKULU
Manna
Baturaja
Martapura
Kotabumi
Greater Sunda Islan
Tanjung Sambar
Kepulauan Laut Kecil
Kepulauan Masalima
6073
J
a
v
a
SEA
Enggano
LAMPUNG
Tanjungkarang Telukbetung
Kalianda
Kepulauan Seribu
Bawean
Kepulauan Karimunjawa
Kepulauan Masalembo
Merak
Serang
Kepulauan Kangean

F

INDIAN
Selat Sunda
Pulau Rakata (Krakatau)
Panaitan
Teluk Pelabuhan Ratu
JAKARTA
Bogor
Sukabumi
Purwakarta
Cirebon
Tegal
Pemalong
Pekalongan
Kendal
Tanjung Bugel
Bangkalan
Madura
Sampang
Tuban
Bojonegoro
Gresik
SURABAYA
Sangkapura
OCEAN
BANDUNG
Garut
Slamet
3428
TENGAH
Magelang
Madiun
Kediri
Pasuruan
Probolinggo
Lesser
Tasikmalaya
Cilacap
Kebumen
3265
Yogyakarta
Surakarta
3670
Semeru
Jember
Singaraja
3142
Lombok
6650
Kediri
Tulungagung
Blitar
Malang
Banyuwangi
BALI
Agung
3726
Mataram
Sumbawa Besar
J
a
v
a
TIMUR
Denpasar
Penida
2563
Amperan
Praya
Taliwang
NUSA TENGGARA BARAT

ANDAMAN SEA

SOUTH CHINA SEA
Paracel Is.
Nanshan I.
Loaita I.
Itu Aba I.
Sin Cowe I.
Spratly Is.
Spratly I.
Amboyna Cay
208
Mt. Mantalingajan
C. Buliluyan
Bugsuk
Balabac I.
Balabac Str.
Baragi

VIETNAM
LAOS

CAMBODIA

MALAYSIA
Pulau Tioman
Matak
Siantan
Kepulauan Anambas

Borneo
KALIMANTAN
TENGAH
Palangkaraya

INDONESIA

Strait of Malacca
Sumatra

Selat Karimata
Selat Bangka
Selat Berhala

Java Trench

Projection: Mercator

ft   m
12 000   4000
9000   3000
6000   2000
4500   1500
3000   1000
1200   400
600   200
0   0
200   600
2000   6000
4000   12 000
6000   18 000
8000   24 000
m   ft

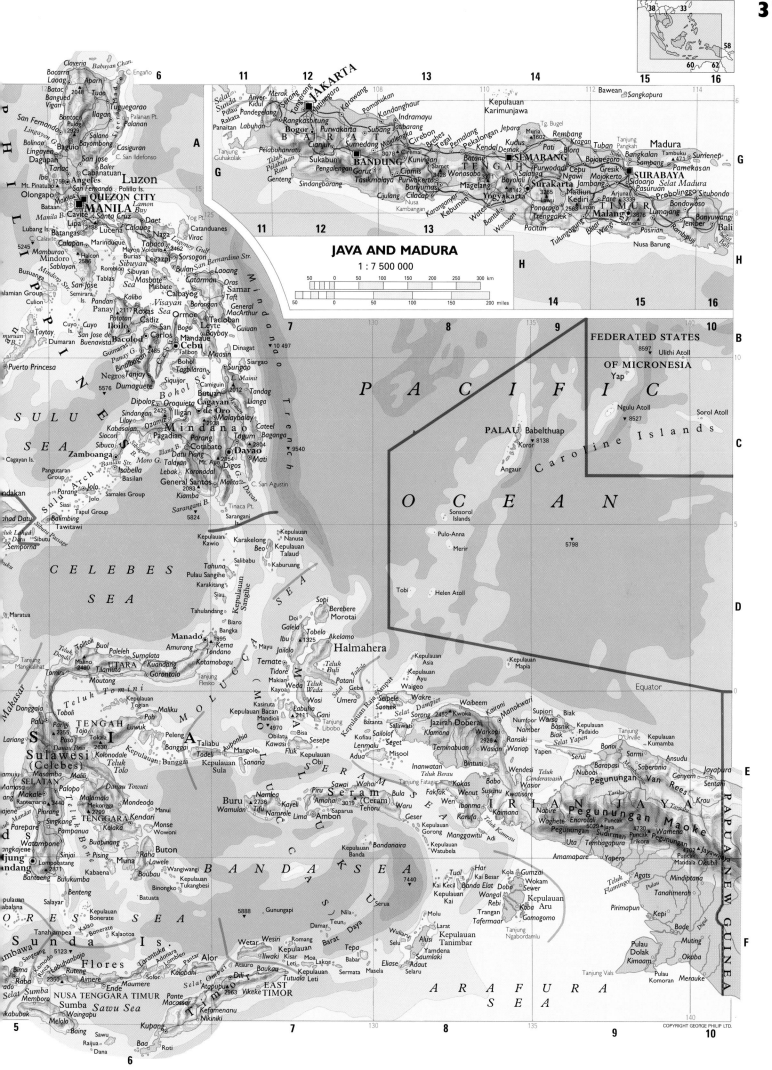

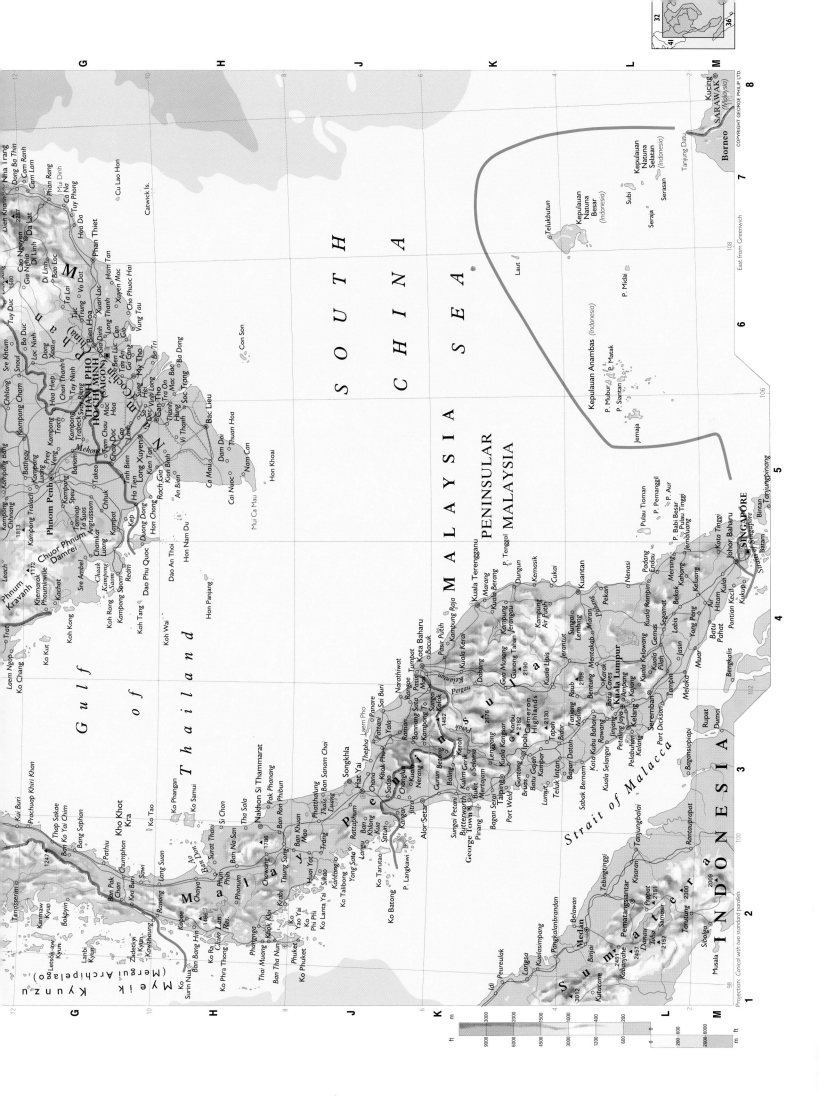

1 2 3 4 5 6 7 8 9 10 11

TURKMENISTAN

3020 · Torbat-e Jām · 61 · Meymaneh · Tokzar · TAKHĀR · NĀRIN

Gushgy · Bālā Morghāb · FĀRYĀB · Sar-e Pol · SAMANGĀN · BAGHLĀN · PĀRVĀN HINDU · BADAKHSHĀN · Mastuj · Ishkumān · Disteghil Sar · 4709 · Aghil Pass

Gonābad · Khvāf · Kūhestān · BADGHĪSĀT · Meqdīsh · Morghāb · Naryn · Tinch Mir · Chitral · Gilgit · Northern · Karakoram Pass · K2 · 8611 · 4779 · Khadzhilyang

HERĀT · Safīd Kūh · Koti-i-Baba · Kābul · Charikar · KĀPISĀ · LAGHMĀN · KONARHA · NORTH WEST · Saidu · Chilas · Nanga · 8126 · Skardu · 5575 · Aksai Chin

Qāyen · Yazdān · GHOWR · BĀMIĀN · 5143 · Nayak · Bāmiān · Kābul · Jalālābad · FRONTIER · Mardan · Malakand · Besal · Parbat · Dasu · **KASHMIR** · Saser · 7672

Birjand · 2886 · Anār Darreh · 4148 · ORUZGĀN · VARDAK · KĀBUL · NANGARHĀR · Peshawar · Mansehra · Baramula · Kargil · Leh · Shyok · Lanak La · 5486

A F G H A N I S T A N · Shindand · Ghazni · Khyber Pass · Attock · Wah · Abbottabad · Punch · Anantnag · Rutog · Bangong Co

Dasht-e Khāsh · Khāsh · Ghazap · GHAZNĪ · PAKTIĀ · Landi Kotal · Kohat · Jand · Srinagar · Nunkun · Chushul · Hanle

I R A N · Nehbandān · Lash-e Joveyn · Vāshīr · 3787 · Ali Khēl · Gardēz · Thal · Nowshera · Jhelum · **JAMMU** · Nurkun 7135 · Chamba · Gangbar

Farāh · Mūsa Qal'eh · Argandāb · Khōwst · Bannu · Kalabagh · Chakwal · Jammu · Udhampur · HIMACHAL · Dankhar · Gompa

Datyāchen- ye Seistan · Zābol · Chakhānsūr · Khāsh · Gereshk · QANDAHĀR · Qamruddin Karez · Mianwah · Daud · Gujrat · Sialkot · Pathankot · Palampur · 7026 · Gar

Zaranj · Dasht-e Mārgow · HELMAND · Qalāt · ZĀBOL · Zhob · Wazirabad · Khushab · Sargodha · Chiniot · Shekhupura · **Gujranwala** · PRADESH · Kulu · Jogindar Nagar · 7817

NĪMRŪZ · Kirteh · Rīgestān · Chaman · Khojak Pass · Hindubagh · Toba Kakar · Musa Khel · Hafizabad · **LAHORE** · Amritsar · Hoshiarpur · Simla

Mirābād · Chahar · Burjak · Helmand · Landay · Khost · Shahrig · Duki · Loralai · Dera Ghazi Khan · FAISALABAD · Gojra · Okara · Jullundur · Phagwara · Ludhiana · Chakrata · 7756

Ribat · Gowd-e Zirreh · Chāh Gay · **Quetta** · 3593 · Bolan Pass · Mekhtar · Multan · Sāhīwal · Firozpur · Fazilka · Muktsar · **PUNJAB** · Chandigarh · Mussoorie · Badarinath

Zāhedān · Qila Sefed · 2462 · Hāmūn-i-Lora · Nushki · Mastung · Sibi · Mach · Muzaffargarh · Kasur · Ambala · Dehra Dun · Rishikesh · 7817 · Nanda Devi

Mirjāveh · 4042 · Mashki Chāh · Kalat · Gandava · Kharian · Dhuri · Patiala · Jagadhri · Saharanpur · Haridwar · UTTARANCHAL

Lādiz · Nok Kundi · Dālbandin · Kalat · Nasirabad · Jacobabad · Ubauro · Panjnad Barrage · Bahawalnagar · Fort Abbas · Bahawalpur · Hanumangarh · Sirsa · Karnal · Muzaffarnagar · Najibabad · Roorkee · Bijnor

Khāsh · Hāmūn-i-Māshkel · Rōd · Kharan Kalat · Shikarpur · Rahimyar Khan · **Bikaner** · Churu · Loharu · Rewari · Muzaffarnagar · Amroha · Moradabad

Bāmpūr · Zāboli · Mashkid · 146 · Kūhak · Siahan Range · Panjgur · Khuzdar · 2480 · Shahdadkot · Sukkur Barrage · Guddu Barrage · Loharu · Jhunjhunu · Sikar · 1052 · Sardarshahr · Alwar · Bharatpur · Mathura · Fatehgarh · Mainpuri

2093 · Central Makran Range · Tump · Jhal Jhao · Bela · Dadu · Naushahro · Ramgarh · Koloyat · Nagaur · Sambhar · Ringas · **Jaipur** · Agra · Firozabad · Etawah · Kannauj

Bāhū Kalāt · Turbat · Pasni · Kandrach · Hingol · Sonmiani · Kotri · Hala · Tando Adam · Tharad · Sirohi · Nathdwara · Beawar · Ajmer · Tonk · Dausa · Bhind · **Gwalior** · Orai · Mau · Ranipur · Kanpur

Gavāter · Gwādar · Ormara · C. Monze · Hab Nadi Chauki · Ghulam Mohammad Barrage · Mirpur Khas · Umarkot · Nagar Parkar · 1722 · Udaipur · Bhilwara · Bundi · Kota · Shivpuri · Jhansi · Chhatarpur · Panna

A R A B I A N S E A · **KARACHI** · Tatta · Badin · Nara · Rann of Kachchh · Disa · Palanpur · Kherala · Khed Brahma · Nimach · Chittaurgarh · Guna · Lalitpur · Tikamgarh

Mouths of the Indus · Khavda · Lakhpat · Kori Creek · Patan · Mahesana · Himatnagar · Banswara · Jaora · Mandsaur · Ratlam · Sironj · Bina-Etawah · Banda

I N D I A · Indus · **GUJARAT** · Bhuj · Bhachau · Little Rann · Virangam · Shajapur · Vidisha · Sagar · Damoh

Tropic of Cancer · 2 · 62 · 3 · 64 · 4 · 66 · Bhuj · Kandla · Dhrol · Halvad · Chotila · Dewas · **MADHYA** · Bhanrer Ranges

M

GOA · Gop · Londa · Tungabhadra · Hospet · Gadag · Kurnool · Adoni · Erramala Hills · Cumbum · Chirala · Gulf of Kachchh · Okha · Dwarka · Jamnagar · Rajkot · Gondal · Godhra · Nadiad · **Ahmadabad** · Dahod · Ujjain · Sehore · Bhopal · Hoshangabad · Narsimhapur · **Jabalpur**

Dandeli · Dharwad · Ranibennur · Davangere · Anantapur · Kotturu · Rayadurg · Proddatur · Nellore · Gulf of Khambhat · Porbandar · Amreli · **KATHIAWAR** · Bhavnagar · Petlad · Khambhat · **Vadodara (Baroda)** · Dhar · Mhow · **Indore** · Kannod · Gadarwara · Nainpur

Karwar · 1100 · Shimoga · Bhadravati · Hindupur · Cuddapah · Gudur · Saradiya · Junagadh · Palitana · Bharuch · Nandurbar · Khargon · Khandwa · Harda · 1353 · Betul · Chhindwara · Balaghat

Sagar · Coondapoor · **KARNATAKA** · Chik Ballapur · 1255 · Tirupati · Pulicat L. · Veraval · Diu · Narmada · Amalner · Dhule · Malegaon · Burhanpur · Achalpur · Ramtek · Titodi · **Nagpur**

Udupi · Chikmagalur · Birur · Tumkur · Kolar · Vellore · Chittoor · **Chennai (Madras)** · Gulf of Khambhat · Daman · Tapi · Jalgaon · Bhusawal · Amravati · Wardha · Bramhapuri

Mangalore · Hassan · **Bangalore** · Gold Fields · Kanchipuram · Victor · Navsari · Valsad · Satmala Hills · Akola · Yavatmal · Wardha · Hinganghat · Chandrapur

Kasaragod · Madikeri · Mandya · Channapatna · Arcot · Kumbakonam · DADRA AND NAGAR HAVELI · Nasik · Yeola · Aurangabad · Jalna · Washim · Hingoli · Pusad · Adilabad · Asifabad

1745 · **Mysore** · Melagiri Hills · Dharmapuri · Tiruvannamalai · Madurantakam · Villupuram · Chalisgaon · 741 · Ajanta Range · Manmad · Deolali · Sangamner · Parbhani · Nanded · Nizamabad · Jagtial

Cannanore · Tellicherry · Udagamandalam · Salem · Attur · Pondicherry · Bhiwandi · Kalyan · Thane · **MAHARASHTRA** · Bir · Palam · Udgir · Nizamabad · Manthani · Karimnagar

Badagara · 2637 · Coimbatore · Erode · Cauvery · Cuddalore · Chidambaram · **MUMBAI (BOMBAY)** · Ulhasnagar · Balaghat Range · Latur · Bodhan · **ANDHRA**

Calicut (Kozhikode) · Palghat · Tiruppur · **TAMIL NADU** · Karaikal · Nagapattinam · Pune (Poona) · Kirkee · Kharda · Daund · Barsi · Osmanabad · Bidar · Sangareddi · **HYDERABAD**

Ponnani · Trichur · Pollachi · Dindigul · Pudukkottai · 796 · Mahabaleshwar · Kurduvadi · Madha · **PRADESH**

Cochin (Kochi) · Palani Hills · 2698 · **Tiruchchirappalli** · Thanjavur · Karaikkudi · 1438 · Satara · Pandharpur · **Solapur** · Gulbarga

Mattancheri · Madurai · Devakottai · Palk Strait · Point Pedro · Ratnagiri · Karad · Bhima · Nalgonda · Suriapet

Alleppey (Alappuzha) · Virudunagar · Ramanathapuram · Jaffna · Mullaittivu · Sangli · Miraj · Bijapur · Yadgir · Mahbubnagar · Krishna

Changanacheri · **KERALA** · Rajapalaiyam · Pamban I. · Mannar · Mankulam · Kolhapur · Jamkhandi · Raichur · Gadwal

Quilon (Kollam) · Cardamom Hills · Tenkasi · Palayankottai · Adam's Bridge · Anuradhapura · Trincomalee · Malvan · Bijapur · Bagalkot · Kurnool · Adoni

Tirunelveli · 1654 · Gulf of Mannar · Mannar · Batticaloa · Foul Pt. · Panaji · **GOA** · Gadag · Hospet · Bellary · Erramala Hills

Trivandrum (Thiruvananthapuram) · Tuticorin · Kulasekarappattinam · Galoya · Vengurla · 1053 · Dharwad · 1100 · Guntakal · Cumbum

Nagercoil · C. Comorin · Puttalam · Maho · 766 · **SRI LANKA** · Kurunegala · Matale · Kandy · Kalmunai · Marmagao · Panaji · Londa · Nandyal · Nallamalai Hills

Chilaw · Negombo · Pidurutalagala · 2524 · Bodulla · Pottuvil · Karwar · Ranibennur · Kotturu

Colombo · Ragama · Adam's Peak · 2243 · Opanake

Moratuwa · Kalutara · Matara · Hambantota · Dondra Head

ft · m · 18 000 · 6000 · 12 000 · 4000 · 9000 · 3000 · 6000 · 2000 · 4500 · 1500 · 3000 · 1000 · 1200 · 400 · 600 · 200 · 0 · 0 · 200 · 600 · m · ft

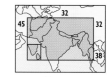

B

34

C

32

D

30

E

28

F

26

G

24

H

22

J

20

K

18

L

16

M

14

NJIANG UYGUR
ZIZHIQU Shan
Kunlun

XIZANG

ZIZHIQU
(TIBET)

Gangdisê Shan

Huh Xil Shan

Dogai Coring

QINGHAI
Bayan Har Shan

Ngoring Hu
Gyaring Hu

Ngoring Hu

Dainkog

Yushu

Nangqen

Gamtog

Garzê

Baiyü

Xinlong

SICHUAN
Yidun   Litang   Yajiang

CHINA

Tanggula (Dangla) Shan
Tanggula
Shankou   5180

Siling Co

Nagqu

Dêngqên

Qamdo

Ombu
Gyaring Co   Xainza
Tangra
Yumco
Coqên

Nam Co

Lhari

Nu Jiang

Lhorong

Yushu

Zhaxizê

Gongbo'gyamda
Goqên

Ningjing

Muli Zangzu
Zizhixian

Maquan He (Tsangpo)

Lhasa

Nyainqentanglha Shan
7088   Lhinzub

Jido

Riga   7756

Mainkung

Weixi   5600
Zhongdian

Lijiang

Jianchuan

Mapam
Yumco
Tanggula Kangri

Simikot   7059
Mugu   Zhongba   Saga
4944

Xigazê   Nang Xian

Yarlung Zangbo Jiang

Brahmaputra

Subansiri

Minutang

Hkakabo Razi
(Thala La)

Zizhixian

Namse
Shankou
8122

Mustang
Maquan He
Gyala Shankou

Lhazê
Dinggyê   Gamba

Comai   Cona

Thunkar   7089   Kangto

Murkangselek
Dum Duma

Ipunggen Pass
Saikhoa
Ghat   3072   Putao   Konglu

Chaukan Pass
2432   Bumpha Bum

Jianchuan

Dhaulagiri   Nuwakot   Gurkha   Nawakot
Xixabangma
Feng   8013
5602

Mt Everest
8850
Kanchenjunga
8598

Nyalam

7314   7554

Towang

North
Lakhimpur   Dibrugarh   Tinsukia

Sibsagar

Tipongpani

Patkai Bum

Kawngdim

Hukawng
Valley   3411

KACHIN

Lawng Pit

YUNNAN

Unlong

NEPAL
Katmandu   Bhaktapur   Gangtok   BHUTAN
Chisapani   Ramechhap

SIKKIM
Thimphu
Punakha   Tongsa

Rupa   ARUNACHAL PRADESH

Jorhat   Moingkwan
Maingkwan   Singkaling
Hkamti   2424

Mogaung   Myitkyina   Sadon   Baoshon

Tengchong   Longling

Changning

Siwalik
Range
Nepalganj   Balrampur   Gonda   Basti   Gorakhpur   Deoria
Faizabad

Darjiling   Jayanti   Taga Dzong
Tashigang

Bakla
Duar   Bomdila   Baipara

Rangia   Tezpur   Silghat   M

Dergaon   Nowgong

Mokakchung

NAGALAND
Kohima   3824   Kamon Bum   Homalin

Hkamti

Katha   Bhamo

Shwegu

ESH
Lucknow   Sultanpur   Azamgarh   Siwan
Rae Bareli   Fatehpur   Jaunpur   Bela

Siliguri   Jalpaiguri
Koch Bihar
Barpeta   Mairabari   Gauhati

Dhubri   Dhubun   Goalpara   Shillong   1981

Haflong
Barakhola

Baril Range

Ukhrul   Tamenglong   Thaungdut   Tigyaing   Man Na

Kunlang
Hsenwi

Pang-Long

Allahabad   Varanasi   Ghazipur   Patna   Bankipore   Mekama   Barsoi   Katihar

MEGHALAYA   Cherrapunji   SYLHET

MANIPUR
Churachandpur

Tamu   Wuntho

Kunlong

Bawdwin   Namtu   Lashio   Kawnto

Mirzapur   Jahanabad   Bihar   Jamalpur   Bhagalpur   Dinajpur   Rangpur   Tura   Sylhet

Lala Ghat   Kolasib   SAGAING   Mingin   Shwebo
2299   Madaya   Gokteik   Pang-Yang   Mong Yai   Muang   2693

Mong Mawk

A   BIHAR
Aurangabad   Gaya
Deoghar

Ganga   Saidpur   Pabna   Mymensingh

Bogra   Sirajganj

Dhubri   Comilla   Agartala   Aizawl   Sairang

Kennedy   2704   Tiddim   Kyunhla   Kalewa

Karnaphuli
Res.   Kyaukse

Ye-u   Budalin   Alon   Monywa
Sagaing   Mandalay

Mong Kung   Mong Hsu

Keng Tung

Deoghar   Rampur
Siuri   Baharampur   Hat   Ranghat   Chandpur
Kushtia   Jessore   Madaripur

MIZORAM
Dimagiri   Lunglei   Belonia

Kaladan   CHIN   Gangaw
Minbu   Yinmabin   Yamèthin

Mong Yak   Mong Ton

Hazaribag   Barhi   Giridih   Gomoh   Ranganj   Durgapur
Dhanbad   Asansol   Barddhaman   Krishnanagar   Narayanganj

DHAKA   Balla   Brahmanbaria

Chandpur   Khulna   Bhola

WEST   BENGAL
JHARKHAND   Lohardaga   Ramgarh   1366   Puruliya
Ranchi   Bankura

Chittagong
Dohazari

CHIN   Mt.
Victoria   3053   Pauk   Pakokku   Myingyan

Meiktila   Thazi   Taunggyi   2519   Heho   Mong Nai   Mong Ton

Mong Pan   Mawk Mai   2296
Lol-kaw   2183   Muang
Chiang Rai

Birmitrapur
Raurkela   Chakradharpur   Gua   Chaibasa   Medinipur   Haora   KOLKATA
Jamshedpur   Shrirampur
Barakpur   Port Canning   Barisal   Patuakhali   Hatia

Paletwa   Kanpetlet   Minbu   Magwe   Pyinmana

Kyaukpadaung   Thayetmyo

Yenangyaung

Bawlake   Loikaw   2620

Chiang Mai
Muang Lamphun   Lampang

1127
CHHATTISGARH   Khairagarh   Sarangarh   Hirakud
Dam   Sambalpur
Durg   Raipur   Sonepur   1187   Keonjhargarh

Baleshwar   Contai
Diamond
Harbour   Haldia
Lakshmikantapur

Sundarbans   Mouths of the Ganges

Cox's Bazar

Sittwe
(Akyab)   ARAKAN   Kyaukpyu   Ramree I.   Letpan

Thazi   Taungdwingyi   Pyu   Taungoo

KAYAH   2576   Muang
2620

THAILAND

Balangir   Talcher   Brahmani   Dhenkanal
Kanker   Dhamtari   Kendrapara
Mahanadi   Paradip

ORISSA   Cuttack   Bhubaneswar   Chilka L.
1001   Titlagarh   Russellkonda   Puri
Bhawanipatna

Brahmapur   Chatrapur

Arakan
Coast   Sandoway   Cheduba I.   Myanaung   Letpadan   Tharrawaddy

Prome   Okpo   Madauk
Henzada   Kyongpyaw

Pegu   Thaton

Bassein   Insein   RANGOON
(YANGON)   Pa-an   Moulmein

Tak

Papun

Ghats   Bastar   Rayagada   1501
Indravati   Jeypore   Ichchapuram
Jagdalpur   1240   Salur   Bobbili   Srikakulam
Konta   1680   Parvatipuram   Tekkali   Vizianagaram

BAY OF BENGAL

Gwa   Kyongpyaw   Yondoon   Ma-ubin   Pegu   Thaton
Myaungmya   Bassein

IRRAWADDY   Rangon   Pyapon   G. of Martaban   Pegu Yoma
Yandoon

hmundri   Pithapuram
Kakinada   Godavari Point
Narasapur

Anakopalle
Vishakhapatnam

INDIAN OCEAN

Maudin Sun

Preparis North Channel

Pariparit Kyun
(Burma)

Preparis South Channel

Koko Kyunzu
(Burma)

Mouths of the Irrawaddy

Moscos Is.
Maungmagan
Kyunzu

Launglon Boki

MON

Kalegauk
Kyun   Lamaing
Ye   Sangkhla
Buri

Natkyizin   Sangkhla

Nam Tok

Yèbyu   2080
Tavay

Mai Klong

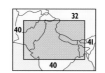

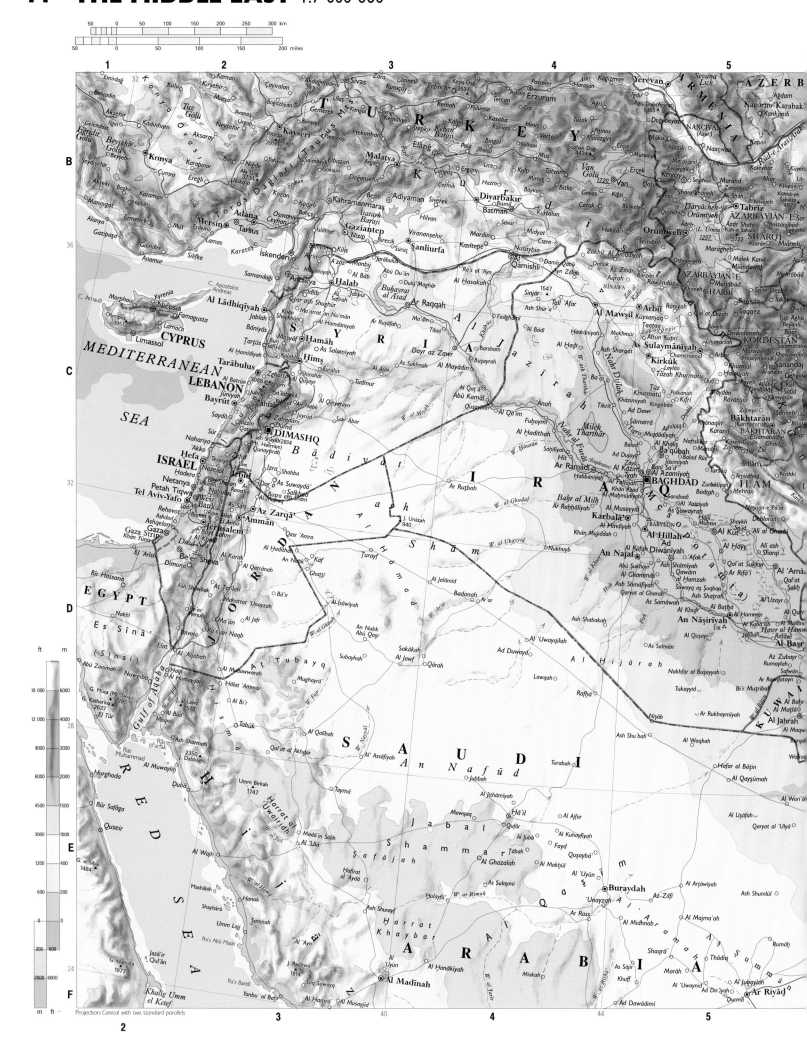

ft   m
18 000   6000
12 000   4000
9000   3000
6000   2000
4500   1500
3000   1000
1200   400
600   200
0   0
200   600
2000   6000
m   ft

Projection: Conical with two standard parallels

TURKEY

Emirdağ   Belkadın   Kaman   Kırşehir   Mucur   Akdağmadeni   Sivas   Zara   İmirenli   Erzincan   Keşiş Dağı 3537   Pasinler   Kağızman   Yerevan   ARMENIA   Sevana Lich   AZERB

Konya Ovası   Tuz Gölü   Çayıralan   Boğazlıyan   Gemerek   Ulaş   Kangal   Kuruçay   Erzurum   Ağrı Dağı (Ararat) 5165   NAXCIVAN (Azer)   Nagorno-Karabakh   Xankändi

MEDITERRANEAN   SEA

CYPRUS   Nicosia   Limassol   Larnaca   Famagusta

LEBANON   Tarābulus   Bayrūt   Saydā   Sūr

ISRAEL   Ḥefa   Nahariya   ‘Akko   Netanya   Tel Aviv-Yafo   Jerusalem   Gaza Strip   Gaza

EGYPT   (Sinai)   Es Sînâ'   Gulf of Aqaba   RED SEA

SYRIA   DIMASHQ   Ḥamāh   Ḥimş   Ḥalab   Idlib   Ar Raqqah   Dayr az Zawr

JORDAN   ‘Ammān   Az Zarqā'   Al Karak   Ma'ān   Al ‘Aqabah

IRAQ   BAGHDAD   Al Mawşil   Arbil   Kirkūk   As Sulaymānīyah   Al Baṣrah   An Nāşirīyah   Karbalā'   An Najaf

KUWAIT   Al Jahrah

SAUDI   ARABIA   An Nafūd   Jabal Shammar   Ḥā'il   Buraydah   Ar Riyāḍ   Al Madīnah   Taymā'

AZARBĀYJĀN-E SARQĪ   Tabriz   Orūmīyeh   KORDESTĀN   Sanandaj   BAKHTARĀN

ĪLĀM

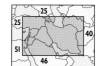

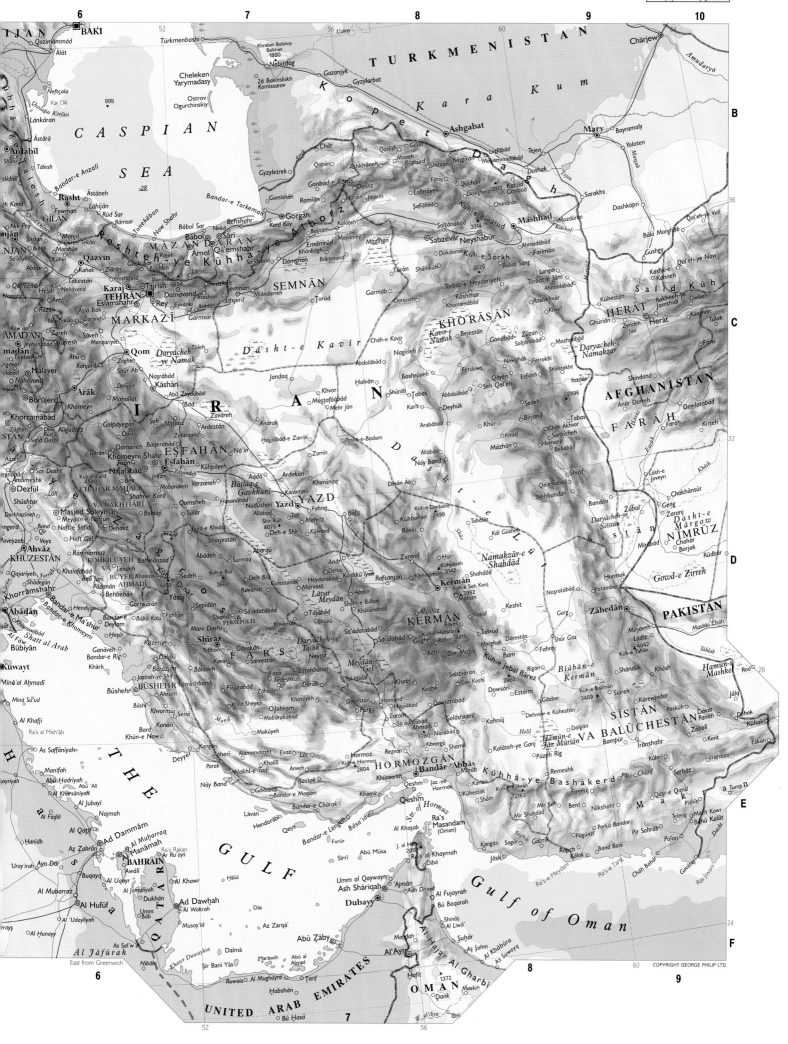

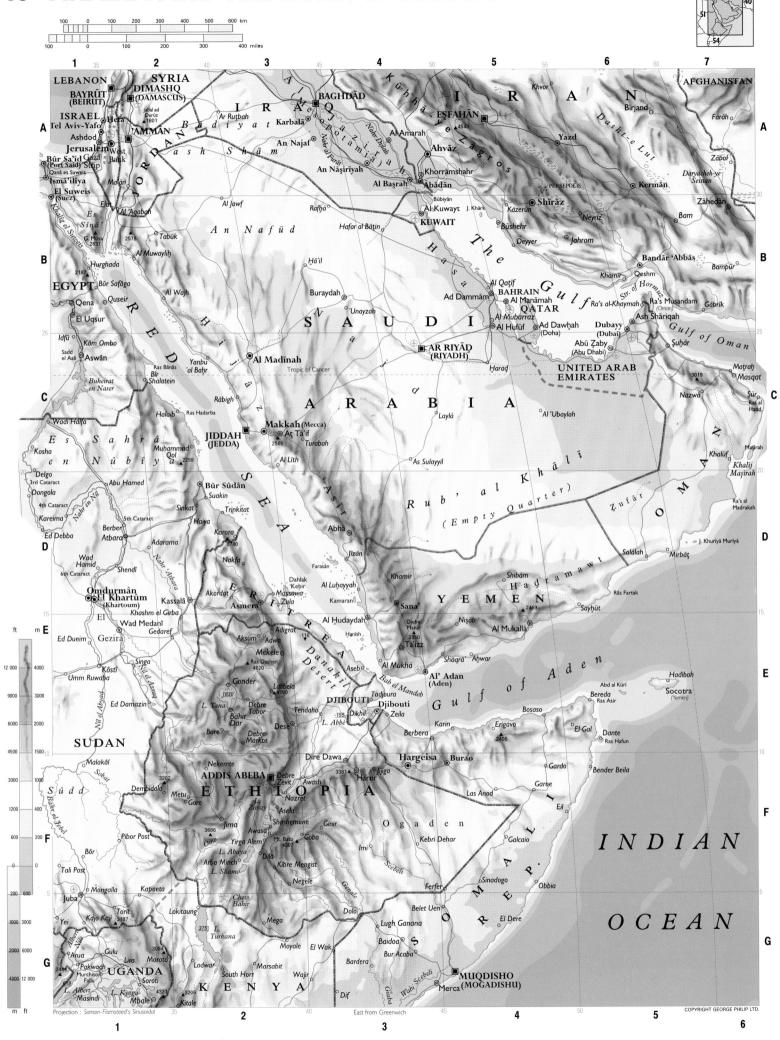

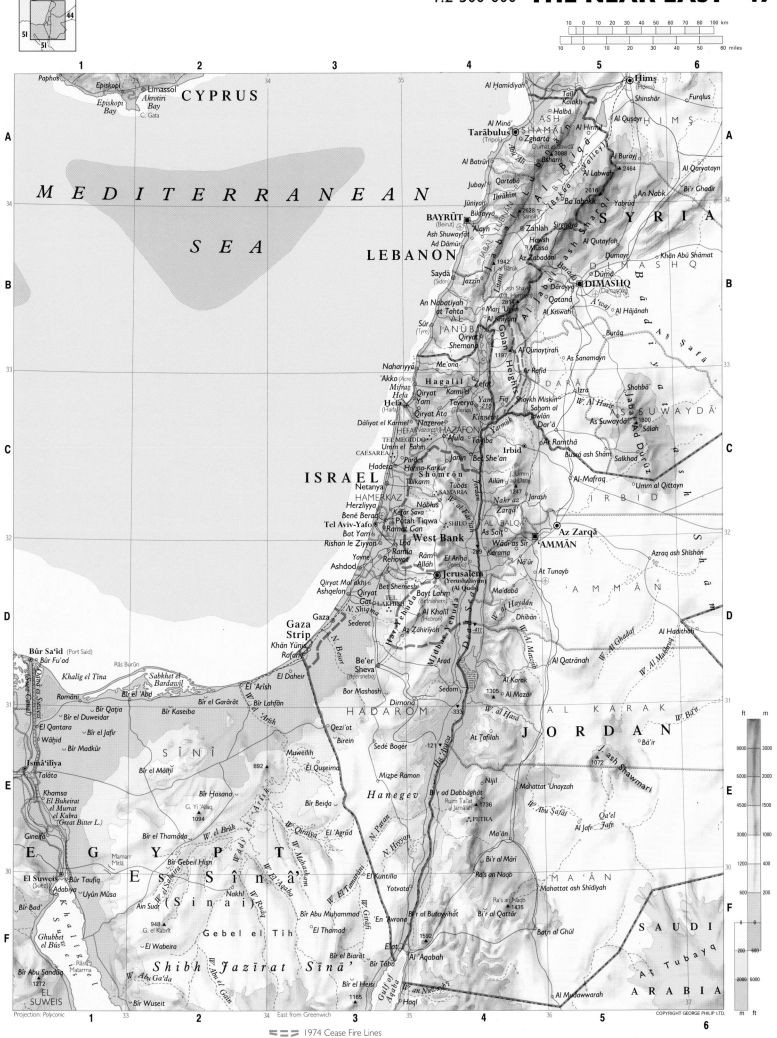

44
44
51
51

10 0 10 20 30 40 50 60 70 80 100 km
10 0 10 20 30 40 50 60 miles

Paphos
Episkopi   ○Limassol
Episkopi   *Akrotiri*   **CYPRUS**
Bay   *Bay*
                   C. Gata

M E D I T E R R A N E A N

S E A

Al Hamidiyah   ◉Himş
                               (Homs)
Tall
Kalakh   Shinshâr   Furqlus

Al Minâ'   ASH   Halbâ
Tarābulus SHAMĀL Al Hirmil   Al Quşayr
(Tripoli)○ Zgharta   ḤIMŞ
Qurnat as Sawdâ
Al Batrûn   3088   Al Labwah   An Nabk   Bi'r Ghadir
Bsharri
Jubayl   Qartabâ   2616   Al Qaryatayn
                              Yabrūd
Jūniyah Ibrāhīm   Ba'labakk   Al Burayj
                        2464
BAYRŪT Bikfayyā   2628
(Beirut)   Zahlah   Sannīn   **SYRIA**
Ash Shuwayfāt   Sirghāyā   Khān Abū Shāmat
Ad Dāmūr   'Alayh Hawsh   DIMASHQ
            Mussā Az Zabadānī   ◉Dūmā
LEBANON Saydā   Jazzīn   Barada **DIMASHQ**
(Sidon) ash Shayh   Qatanā   (Damascus)
An Nabatīyah   Mt. Hermon   Dārayyā   A'waj
at Tahta   2814   Marj 'Uyūn Al Kiswah   Al Hājānah
AL   Sūr   Qanā   Burāq
     (Tyre) JANŪB Qiryat
           Shemona   Al Qunayṭirah   As Sanamayn
Nahariyya   Me'ona   Golan 1197   Ar Rafid   W. Al Harīr Shahbā
'Akko (Acre) Zefat Heights   Fīq   Shaykh Miskīn   Izra AS SUWAYDĀ
Mifraz   Hagalil Karmi'el   Yam   Sahām al
Hefa   Qiryat   Teverya -210 Jawlān Dar'ā As Suwaydā 1800
Hefa Yam   (Tiberias) Kinneret   Yarmūk   Buşrá ash Shām Sālah
(Haifa) Qiryat Ata 'Nazerat   T-aîba   At Ramthā Salkhad
Dāliyat el Karmel   HAZAFON   J. Umm   J. AD DURŪZ
TEL MEGIDDO 'Afula   ad Daraj Al-Mafraq Umm al Qittayn
Umm el Fahm   Janin   1247
CAESAREA   Bet She'an   Ailūn   IRBID
Hadera   Pardes   Tūbās Jordan Nahr az   Jarash
ISRAEL Hanna-Karkur SAMARIA Zarqā
Netanya   Tulkarm W. al Far'ūn   Irbid
HAMERKAZ   Nāblus   AL BALQA
Herzliyya   Kfar Sava SHILO As Salt   **Az Zarqā**
Benē Beraq   Petah Tiqwa   Wādī as Sīr   **AMMĀN**
Tel Aviv-Yafo Ramat Gan   269   Karama   Azraq ash Shīshān
Bat Yam   **West Bank** Na'ūr   'AMMĀN
Rishon le Ziyyon Rām   El Arīha At Tunayb
Yavne   Rehovot   Allāh (Jericho) Ma'dabā
Ashdod   Qiryat Mol'akhi   Bet Shemesh Bayt Lahm Al Haydān   Dhibān
Ashqelon   Qiryat **Jerusalem**
Gat LAKHISH (Yerushalayim) W. al Mawjib   Al Hadithah
TEL (Al Quds)
N. Shiqma   Az Zāhiriyāh Al Khalīl   W. al Ghadaf
Gaza   Sederot   (Hebron) 411   Al Qatrānah
Strip Khān Yūnis   Arad   Al Karak W. Ba'ir
Rafah   Be'er   JORDAN
   Sheva   Sedom   1305   Al Mazár   AL KARAK
El Daheir   (Beersheba)   Al Karak   W. al Hasā
Bor Mashash   -333
Dimona   Mahattat 'Unayzah
HADAROM   W. al Hasā
At Tafilah   Bā'ir
Qezi'ot   Birein   Sedé Boqér
   -121   Nijil
Mizpe Ramon   Bi'r ad Dabbāghāt   MA'ĀN
G. Yi 'Allaq   Rujm Tal'at 1736
1094   al Jamā'īn W. Abu Şafāt
Ha negev   PETRA   Qa'el
   Ma'ān   Al Jafr   Jafr
El Kuntilla   Ra's an Naqb   MA'ĀN
Yotvata   Mahattat ash Shīdīyah
'En 'Avrona   Bi'r al Māri
Bi'r al Butayyiḥāt   1435   Bi'r al Qattār
1592   Boṭn al Ghūl
Elat   **SAUDI**
Al 'Aqabah
Hagl   Al Mudawwarah   **ARABIA**
At Tubayq

EGYPT
S I N Î
Bûr Sa'îd (Port Said)
○Bûr Fu'ad
Khalîg el Tîna   Râs Burûn
Sabkhet el   Bir el 'Abd
Bardawîl
Români   Bîr el Duweidar   Bîr el Garârât   Bîr Lahfân
El Qantara   Bîr Qatia   'Arish   Bîr Kaseiba
Wāhid   Bîr el Jafir
Bîr Madkûr
Ismâ'iliya   892   El Quseima
Talâta   Bîr el Mâlhi
Khamsa   Bîr Hasana   Bîr Beiḍa
El Buheirat   el Agrûd
el Murrat   Muweilih
el Kubra   948   El 'Arîsh
(Great Bitter L.)   Mamarr   Bîr Gebeil Hisn
Mitlâ
Gineifa   Nakhl   El Thamâda   W. el Bruk   Oraiya   El 'Arîsh
E G Y P T   Ain Sudr   W el Mahasham   N. Paran
   W. Qiraiya
E s   S î n â'   W. El 'â'   Bîr Abu Muhammad
(S i n a i)   Bîr el Biarât
El Suweis   Bûr Taufîq   W. El Tamarâni
(Suez)   Bîr Tôba
Adabiya   Uyûn Mûsa   El Wabeira
Bîr Bad'   948   G. el Kabrît   El Thamad   N. Hiyyon
Ghubbet   Gebel el Tîh   Bîr el Heisi
el Bûs   Râs
Matarma   1165
Bîr Abu Sandûq   *Shibh Jazîrat Sînâ'*   W. an Nitiyat
1272   W. Abu Ga'da   W. Abu el Gafr
EL
SUWEIS   Bîr Wuseit

ft   m
9000   3000
6000   2000
4500   1500
3000   1000
1200   400
600   200
0   0
200   600
2000   6000
m   ft

Projection: Polyconic   East from Greenwich   COPYRIGHT GEORGE PHILIP LTD.

⊏⊐⊏ 1974 Cease Fire Lines

See page 177 World: Regions in the News
for a map showing the areas under Palestinian control.

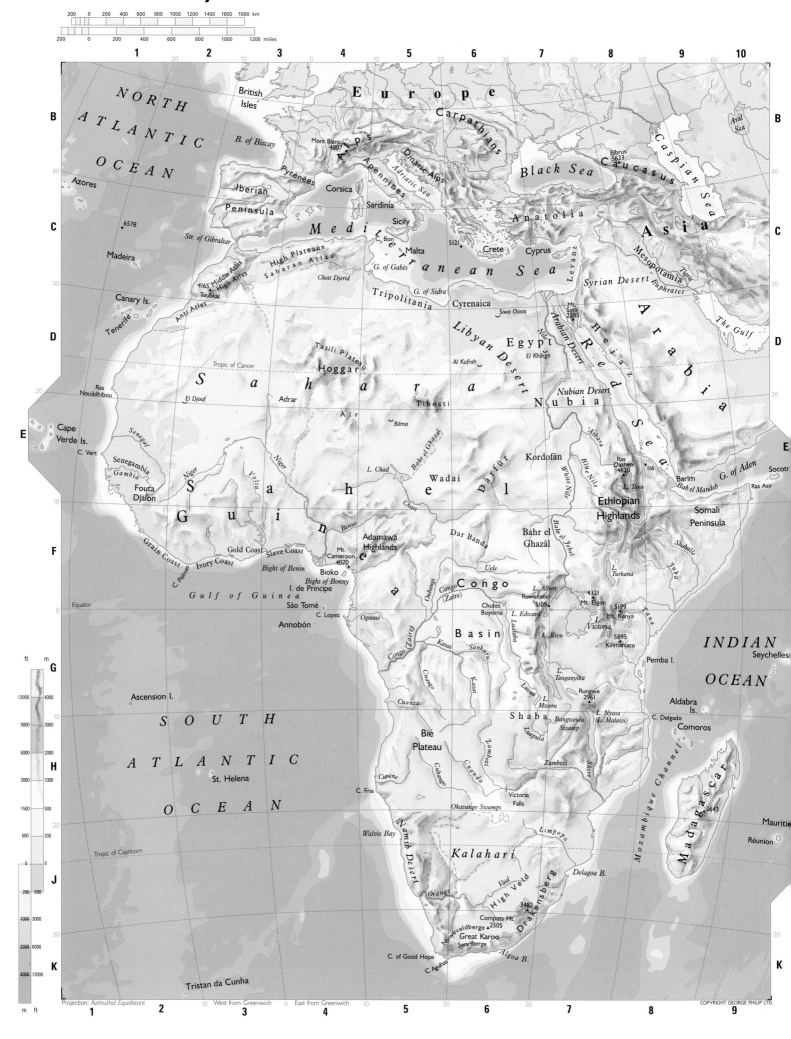

200 0 200 400 600 800 1000 1200 1400 1600 1800 km
200 0 200 400 600 800 1000 1200 miles

1   **2**   **3**   **4**   **5**   **6**   **7**   **8**   **9**   **10**

NORTH ATLANTIC OCEAN

Azores *(Port.)*

Madeira *(Port.)*

Canary Is. *(Sp.)*

B

B. of Biscay

UNITED KINGDOM
LONDON
NETH.
BELG.
PARIS
FRANCE
SWITZ.
GERMANY
POLAND
Warsaw
Prague
CZECH REP.
Vienna
SLOVAK REP.
AUSTRIA HUNGARY
CROATIA
BOS.-HERZ.
YUG.
ROMANIA
BULGARIA
ALB.
MAC.
GREECE
Athens
Kiev
UKRAINE
Odessa
Black Sea
GEORGIA
ARM. AZER.
RUSSIA
Volgograd
KAZAKSTAN
Aral Sea
Baku
Caspian Sea
TURKMEN.

Corsica
Rome
ITALY
Sardinia
Sicily
MALTA
Crete
CYPRUS
Ankara
TURKEY
SYRIA
Aleppo
LEB.
Damascus
ISRAEL
Tel Aviv-Jaffa
Jerusalem
JORDAN
Mosul
Tigris
Euphrates
Baghdad
IRAQ
KUWAIT
Esfahān
TEHRĀN
IRAN

C

Lisbon
Madrid
SPAIN
PORTUGAL
Rabat
Casablanca
Fés
Tétouan
Algiers
Annaba
Constantine
Tunis
Sfax
TUNISIA
Tripoli
Misrätah
Mediterranean Sea
Benghazi
Alexandria
Port Said
Suez
CAIRO
El Faiyûm
Asyût
Syrian Desert
SAUDI
ARABIA
BAHRAIN
QATAR
Riyadh
The Gulf

D

MOROCCO
Marrakesh
Dakhla
Fdérik
El Aaiûn
WESTERN SAHARA
Tropic of Cancer
S a h a r a
ALGERIA
In Salah
LIBYA
Marzûq
Al Jawf
EGYPT
Aswân
Red Sea
Wadi Halfa
Medina
Jedda
Mecca
Port Sudan

E

Ras Nouâdhibou
MAURITANIA
Nouakchott
Tombouctou
MALI
Niger
NIGER
Agadés
CHAD
L. Chad
Abéché
Omdurmân
Khartoum
Atbara
'Atbara
SUDAN
El Fâsher
El Obeid
Wâd Medani
White Nile
Blue Nile
Asmera
Mesewa
ERITREA
L. Tana
YEMEN
Socotra *(Yemen)*
G. of Aden
DJIBOUTI
Djibouti
Ras Asir

PE VERDE IS.
St-Louis
C. Vert
Dakar
SENEGAL
GAMBIA
Banjul
GUINEA-BISSAU
Bissau
Conakry
Freetown
SIERRA LEONE
GUINEA
Bamako
Niamey
BURKINA FASO
Ouagadougou
Bobo-Dioulasso
Kano
Maiduguri
Ndjamena
NIGERIA
Abuja
Chari
Ndamena
CENTRAL AFRICAN REP.
Wau
Malakâl
Bahr el Jebel
Addis Ababa
Harer
Berbera
ETHIOPIA
SOMALI REP.
Praia

F

LIBERIA
Monrovia
IVORY COAST
Yamoussoukro
Bouaké
Abidjan
Sekondi-Takoradi
GHANA
Kumasi
Accra
TOGO
Lomé
Lagos
Porto Novo
BENIN
Ibadan
Enugu
Benue
Port Harcourt
CAMEROON
Douala
Malabo
Yaoundé
Bangui
Oubangi
Congo (Zaïre)
Mbandaka
Kisangani
L. Albert
UGANDA
Kampala
L. Edward
L. Kivu
RWANDA
Kigali
BURUNDI
Bujumbura
Kisumu
L. Victoria
Nairobi
KENYA
L. Turkana
Juba
Shabelle
Mogadishu
Kismayu

Bight of Benin
Gulf of Guinea
EQUATORIAL GUINEA
SÃO TOMÉ & PRINCIPE
C. Lopez
Annobón
GABON
Libreville
Pointe-Noire
CABINDA *(Angola)*
CONGO
Brazzaville
Kinshasa
Matadi
CONGO (DEM. REP. OF THE)
Kasai
Kananga
TANZANIA
Dodoma
Zanzibar
Dar es Salaam
Mombasa
INDIAN OCEAN
SEYCHELLES

Equator **0**

G

Ascension I. *(U.K.)*
Luanda
Lobito
Namibe
C. Fria
ANGOLA
Huambo
Cunene
Cubango
L. Mweru
Likasi
Lubumbashi
Ndola
L. Tanganyika
L. Malawi
C. Delgado
COMOROS
Moroni
Mamoudzou
Mayotte *(Fr.)*
Antsiranana

H

SOUTH ATLANTIC OCEAN
St. Helena *(U.K.)*
ZAMBIA
Lusaka
Lilongwe
MALAWI
Blantyre
Zambezi
Moçambique
MOZAMBIQUE
Mozambique Channel
Mahajanga
Toamasina
Livingstone
Harare
ZIMBABWE
Beira
Bulawayo
Limpopo
MADAGASCAR
Antananarivo
MAURITIUS
St-Denis
Port Louis
Réunion *(Fr.)*
Fianarantsoa

Tropic of Capricorn

J

NAMIBIA
Windhoek
BOTSWANA
Gaborone
Pretoria
Johannesburg
Maputo
Mbabane
SWAZ.
Vaal
Orange
Kimberley
Maseru
LESOTHO
Durban

K

SOUTH AFRICA
Cape Town
C. of Good Hope
C. Agulhas
East London
Port Elizabeth

Tristan da Cunha *(U.K.)*

Projection: Azimuthal Equidistant

West from Greenwich East from Greenwich

● Dakar Capital Cities

COPYRIGHT GEORGE PHILIP LTD.

1   **2**   **3**   **4**   **5**   **6**   **7**   **8**   **9**

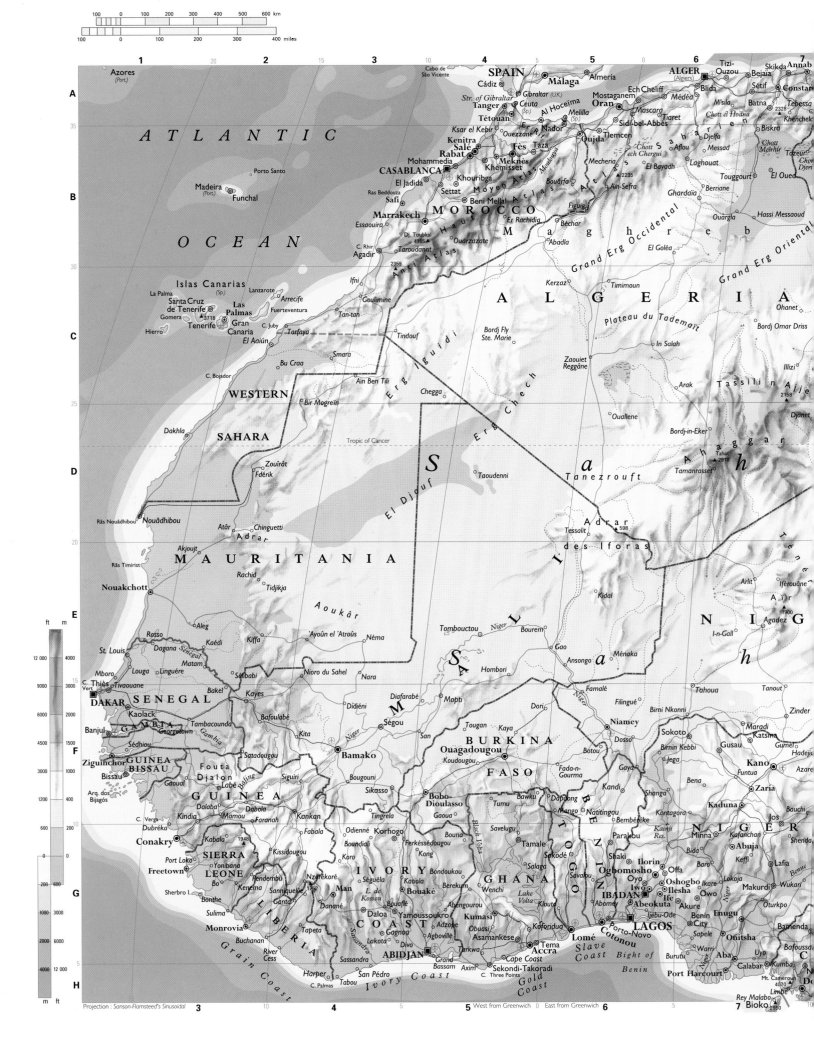

ATLANTIC

OCEAN

SPAIN

Azores
(Port.)

Madeira
(Port.)
Porto Santo
Funchal

Islas Canarias
(Sp.)
La Palma
Lanzarote
Santa Cruz
de Tenerife
Arrecife
Gomera
3718
Las
Palmas
Fuerteventura
Hierro
Tenerife
Gran
Canaria
C. Juby
El Aaiún
Tarfaya

Cabo de
São Vicente
Cádiz
Gibraltar (U.K.)
Málaga
Almería
Str. of Gibraltar
Ceuta (Sp.)
Tanger
Al Hoceïma
Melilla (Sp.)
Tétouan
Oran
Ksar el Kebir
Oujda
Kenitra
Salé
Fès
Taza
Rabat
Tlemcen
Mohammedia
Meknès
CASABLANCA
Khemisset
El Jadida
Khouriba
Settat
Ras Beddouza
Beni Mellal
Safi
MOROCCO
Marrakech
Essaouira
Er Rachidia
C. Rhir
Dj. Toubkal
4165
Ouarzazate
Agadir
2359
Taroudannt
Ifni
Goulimine
Tan-tan

ALGER
(Algiers)
Blida
Tizi-
Ouzou
Bejaïa
Skikda
Annaba
Ech Cheliff
Médéa
Sétif
Constan
Mostaganem
Mascara
Tiaret
M'sila
Batna
Sidi-bel-Abbès
2328
Tébessa
Djelfa
Aflou
Messad
Biskra
Mecheria
Chott
ech Chergui
El Bayadh
Laghouat
Tazen
Aïn-Sefra
Berriane
Ghardaïa
El Oued
Figuig
Ouargla
Hassi Messaoud
Béchar
Abadla
El Goléa
Ohanet
Grand Erg Occidental
Bordj Omar Driss
Kerzaz
Timimoun
Plateau du Tademaït
In Salah
Zaouiet
Reggâne
Bordj-in-Eker
Arak
Tamanrasser
Tahat
2918
Illizi
2158
Djanet
Tassili n Ajjer
Ahaggar

WESTERN

SAHARA
Smara
Bu Craa
C. Bojador
Bir Mogreïn
Aïn Ben Tili
Tindouf
Chegga
Erg Iguidi
Chech
Erg
Tropic of Cancer
Dakhla
Zouîrât
Fdérik
El Djouf
Taoudenni
Tanezrouft

Râs Nouâdhibou
Nouâdhibou
Atâr
Chinguetti
Adrar
Tessalit
598
Adrar
des Iforas

Râs Timirist
MAURITANIA
Rachid
Tidjikja
Akjoujt
Kidal
Arlit
Iférouâne
Aïr
1900
Nouakchott
Aoukâr
Agadez
NIGER
In-Gall
Sahel
St. Louis
Rosso
Aleg
'Ayoûn el 'Atroûs
Néma
Tombouctou
Niger
Bourem
Rosso
Kaédi
Kiffa
Gao
Tahoua
Tanout
Dagana
Senegal
Matam
Ansongo
Ménaka
Louga
Linguère
Sélibabi
Nioro du Sahel
Nara
Hombori
Famalé
Filingué
Zinder
Mboro
Thiès
Tivaouane
Bakel
Kayes
Diafarabé
Dori
Birni Nkonni
Maradi
Katsina
DAKAR
C. Vert
SENEGAL
Kaolack
Tambacounda
Bafoulabé
Didiéni
Mopti
Ségou
Tougan
Kaya
Niamey
Dosso
Sokoto
Gusau
Banjul
GAMBIA
Georgetown
Gambia
Kita
Niger
San
Ouagadougou
Botou
Gaya
Birnin Kebbi
Jega
Katsina
Kaduna
Ziguinchor
Sédhiou
GUINEA
BISSAU
Fouta
Djalon
Satadougou
Bamako
Bougouni
BURKINA
FASO
Fada-n-Gourma
Kandi
Shanga
Funtua
Zaria
Kano
Azare
Bissau
Arq. dos
Bijagós
Labé
Bafing
Siguiri
Sikasso
Bobo-
Dioulasso
Gaoua
Tumu
Bawku
Dapaong
Mango
Natitingou
Bembéréke
Kontagora
Minna
Abuja
Bauchi
Jos
GUINEA
Dalaba
Mamou
Dabola
Kankan
Tingrela
Odienné
Korhogo
Bouna
Savelugu
Bida
Baro
Keffi
Lafia
Makurdi
Wukari
C. Verga
Kindia
Dubréka
Faranah
Fabala
Boundiali
Kong
Tamale
Sokodé
Shaki
Ilorin
Oyo
Kainji
Res.
Ikare
Benin
City
Enugu
Conakry
Kabala
1948
Kissidougou
Koro
Ferkéssédougou
Salaga
Ogbomosho
Offa
Owo
Onitsha
Port Loko
SIERRA
Yonibana
Koidu
Nzérékoré
Séguéla
Katiola
Bouaké
Bondoukou
Berekum
Wenchi
GHANA
Kumasi
TOGO
Saloga
Lokoja
Iwo
Oshogbo
Ilesha
Ife
Akure
Aba
Freetown
LEONE
Bo
Kenema
Man
L. de
Kossou
Abengourou
Lake
Volta
Klouto
IBADAN
Abeokuta
Ijebu-Ode
Sapele
Warri
Uyo
Sherbro I.
Bonthe
Sulima
Danané
Bouaflé
Yamoussoukro
Obuasi
Asamankese
Koforidua
Benin
City
Calabar
LIBERIA
Ganta
Tapeta
Daloa
Divo
Gagnoa
Adzope
Agboville
Abomey
Porto-Novo
Cotonou
LAGOS
Lomé
Burutu
Monrovia
Buchanan
River Cess
Sassandra
IVORY
COAST
Lakota
ABIDJAN
Grand
Bassam
Accra
Tema
Bight of
Port Harcourt
Grain Coast
Harper
C. Palmas
Tabou
San Pédro
Ivory Coast
Axim
Sekondi-Takoradi
C. Three Points
Cape Coast
Gold Coast
Slave
Coast
Benin
Rey Malabo
Bioko
2850
Mt. Cameroon
4070
Limbe

Sa
S
a
h
a
r
a
SAHEL
Maghreb
Moyen Atlas
Haut Atlas
Anti Atlas
Saharien
Atlas

ft m
12 000 4000
9000 3000
6000 1500
4500 1200
3000 1000
600 400
0 200
0 0
200 600
1000 3000
2000 6000
4000 12 000
m ft

MEDITERRANEAN SEA

GREECE

TURKEY

CYPRUS

SYRIA

LEBANON

ISRAEL

IRAQ

JORDAN

EGYPT

LIBYA

SAUDI ARABIA

RED SEA

Sahrâ' Lîbîya

Sahrâ' Rebiana

CHAD

NIGER

SUDAN

ERITREA

Es Sahrâ en Nûbîya

ETHIOPIA

CENTRAL AFRICAN REPUBLIC

CAMEROON

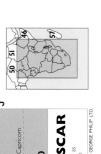

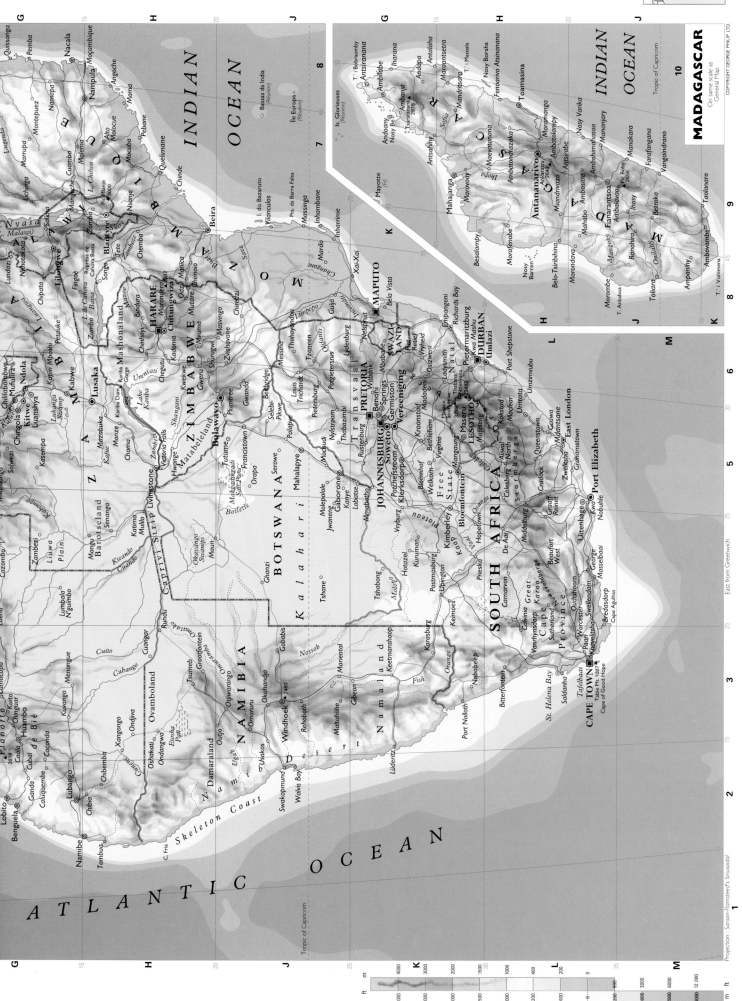

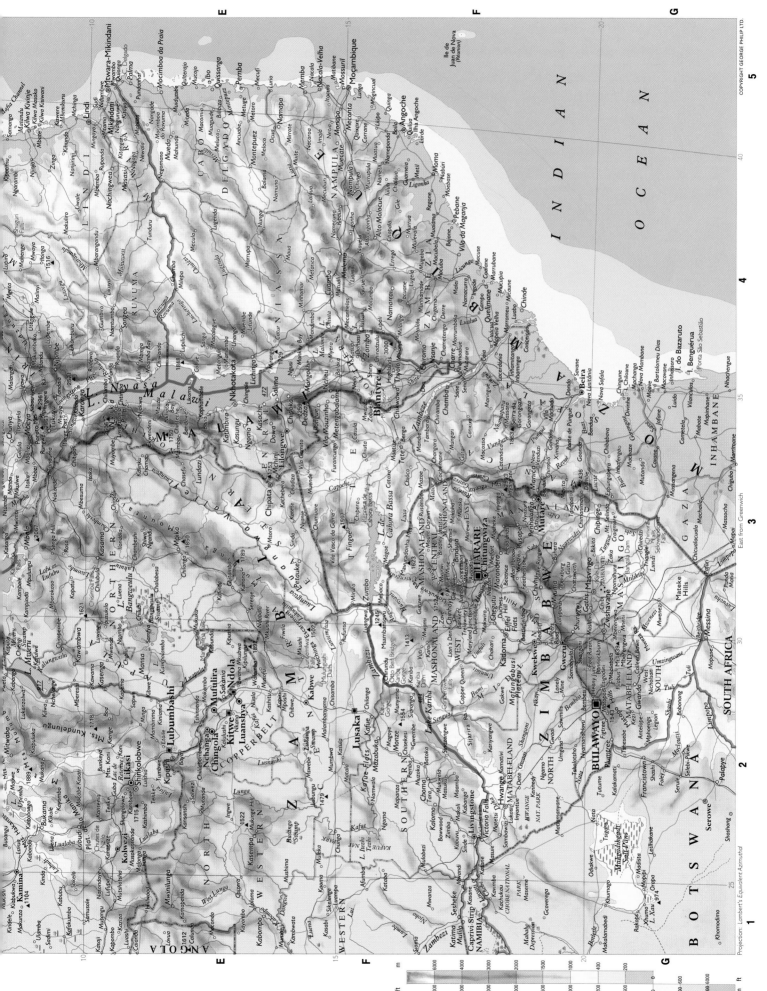

Projection: Lambert's Equivalent Azimuthal

East from Greenwich

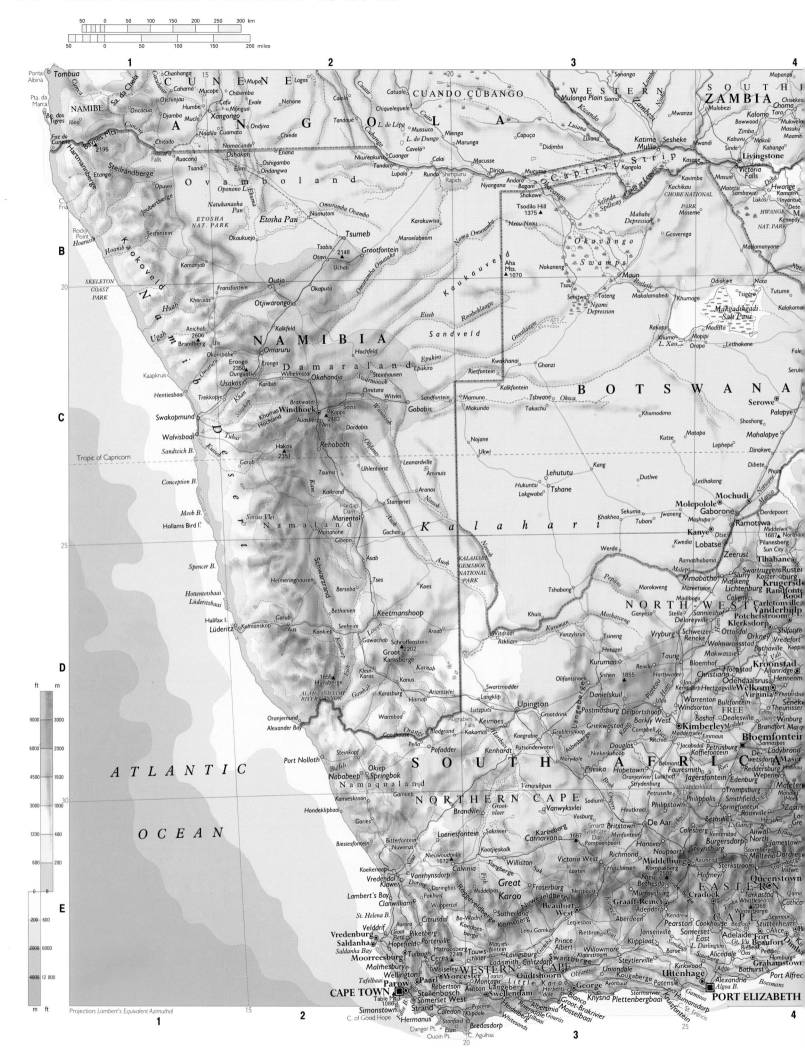

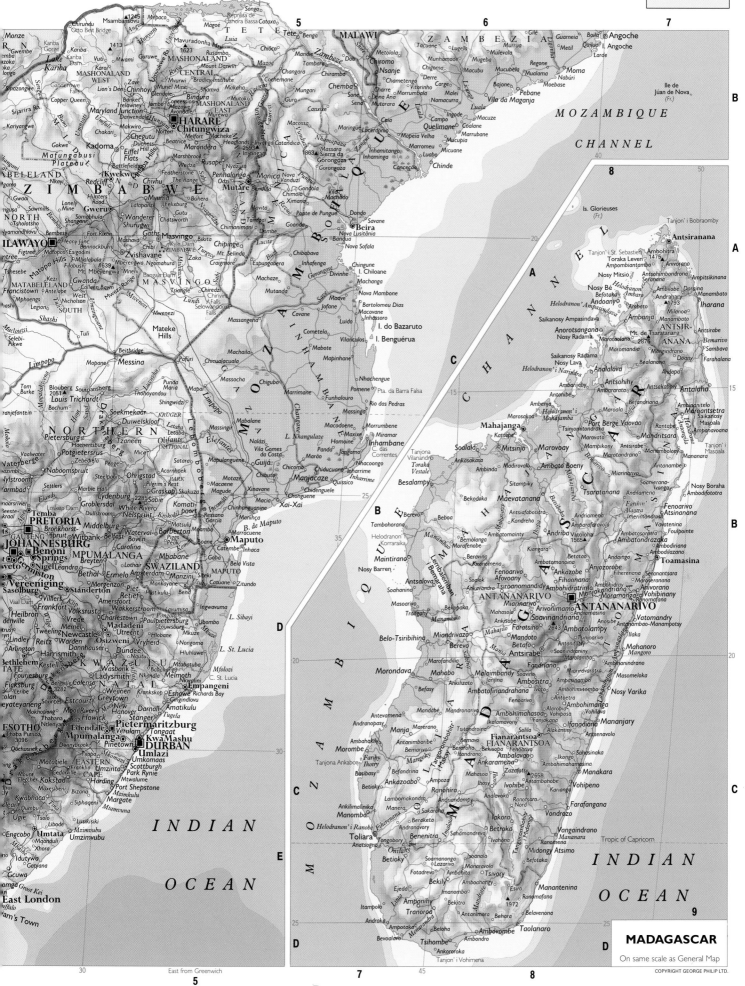

MADAGASCAR

On same scale as General Map

COPYRIGHT GEORGE PHILIP LTD.

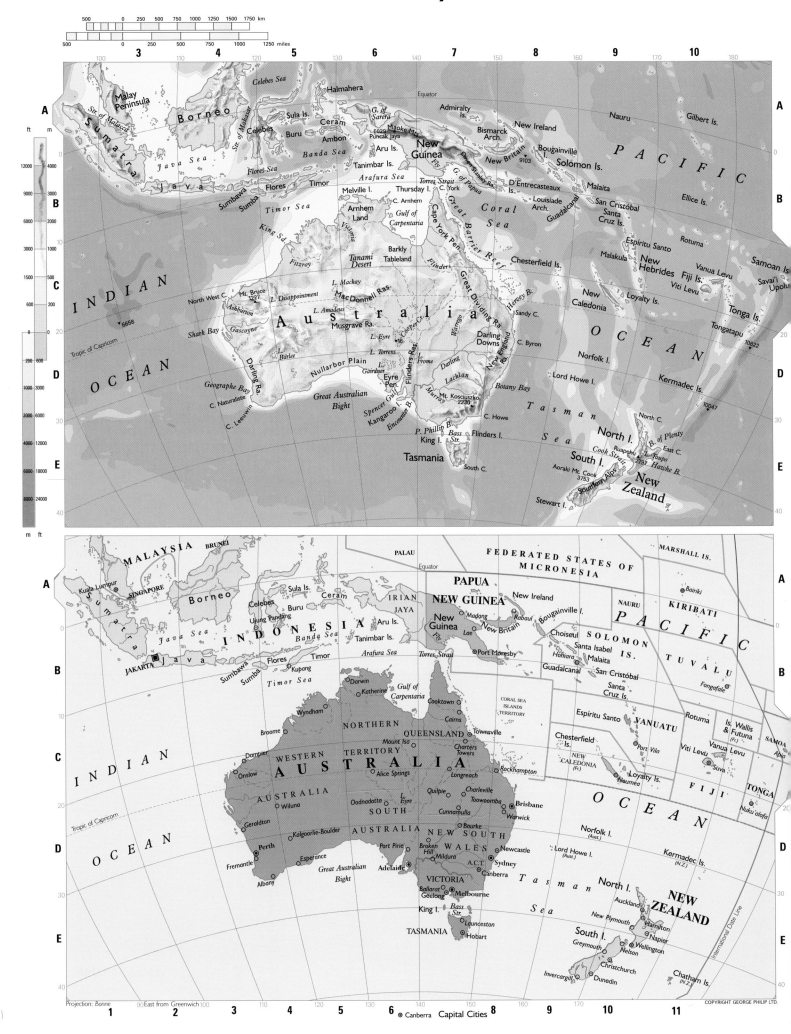

Physical map (top):

500 0 250 500 750 1000 1250 1500 1750 km
500 0 250 750 1000 1250 miles

ft m
12000 4000
9000 3000
6000 2000
3000 1000
1500 500
600 200
0 0
200 600
1000 3000
2000 6000
4000 12000
6000 18000
8000 24000
m ft

Malay Peninsula
Str. of Malacca
Sumatra
Borneo
Celebes Sea
Halmahera
Equator
Admiralty Is.
Nauru
Gilbert Is.
P A C I F I C
New Ireland
Bismarck Arch.
Bougainville
Sula Is.
Ceram
G. of Sarera
Maoke Mts.
5029 Puncak Jaya
New Britain 9103
Solomon Is.
Celebes
Buru
Ambon
New Guinea
Malaita
San Cristóbal
Ellice Is.
Java Sea
Aru Is.
Fly
G. of Papua
D'Entrecasteaux Is.
Santa Cruz Is.
Banda Sea
Tanimbar Is.
Owen Stanley Ra.
Guadalcanal
Java
Flores Sea
Timor
Arafura Sea
Torres Strait
Thursday I.
C. York
Great Barrier Reef
Coral Sea
Espíritu Santo
Rotuma
Samoan Is.
Sumbawa
Sumba
Flores
Melville I.
C. Arnhem
Malakula
New Hebrides
Vanua Levu
Savai'i
Timor Sea
Arnhem Land
Gulf of Carpentaria
Cape York Pen.
Chesterfield Is.
Viti Levu
Fiji Is.
Upolu
King Sd.
Victoria
Barkly Tableland
Flinders
Hervey B.
New Caledonia
Loyalty Is.
Tonga Is.
Fitzroy
Tanami Desert
MacDonnell Ras.
Great Dividing Ra.
Tongatapu
North West C.
Mt. Bruce 1227
L. Disappointment
L. Mackay
Sandy C.
Ashburton
L. Amadeus
Musgrave Ra.
Warrego
Darling Downs
C. Byron
Norfolk I.
6658
Shark Bay
Gascoyne
L. Eyre
Cooper Cr.
16
New England Ra.
Darling
Tropic of Capricorn
Australia
O C E A N
L. Barlee
Nullarbor Plain
L. Torrens
Flinders Ras.
L. Frome
Lachlan
Botany Bay
Lord Howe I.
Kermadec Is.
INDIAN
Darling Ra.
L. Gairdner
Murray
Mt. Kosciuszko 2230
OCEAN
Géographe Bay
Eyre Pen.
10047
C. Naturaliste
Great Australian Bight
Spencer Gulf
Kangaroo I.
Encounter B.
C. Howe
Tasman Sea
North C.
C. Leeuwin
King I.
Bass Str.
Flinders I.
North I.
B. of Plenty
East C.
Tasmania
South C.
South I.
Ruapehu 2797
L. Taupo
Hawke B.
Cook Strait
Aoraki Mt. Cook 3753
Southern Alps
New Zealand
Stewart I.

Political map (bottom):

Projection: Bonne
90 East from Greenwich 100
MALAYSIA
BRUNEI
PALAU
FEDERATED STATES OF MICRONESIA
MARSHALL IS.
Kuala Lumpur
SINGAPORE
Borneo
Sula Is.
Ceram
IRIAN JAYA
PAPUA NEW GUINEA
New Ireland
NAURU
Bairiki
KIRIBATI
Equator
Sumatra
Celebes
Buru
Madang
Rabaul
Bougainville I.
P A C I F I C
Ujung Pandang
INDONESIA
Aru Is.
New Guinea
Lae
New Britain
Choiseul
SOLOMON IS.
TUVALU
Java Sea
Banda Sea
Santa Isabel
Honiara
Malaita
JAKARTA
Java
Tanimbar Is.
Arafura Sea
Torres Strait
Port Moresby
Guadalcanal
San Cristóbal
Fongafale
Sumbawa
Flores
Kupang
Timor Sea
Darwin
Santa Cruz Is.
Sumba
Katherine
Gulf of Carpentaria
Cooktown
CORAL SEA ISLANDS TERRITORY
Espíritu Santo
Rotuma
Is. Wallis & Futuna (Fr.)
SAMOA
Wyndham
NORTHERN
Cairns
VANUATU
Apia
Broome
QUEENSLAND
Townsville
Chesterfield Is.
Port Vila
Viti Levu
Vanua Levu
Dampier
WESTERN
TERRITORY
Mount Isa
Charters Towers
NEW CALEDONIA (Fr.)
Suva
Onslow
AUSTRALIA
Alice Springs
Longreach
Rockhampton
Noumea
Loyalty Is.
FIJI
INDIAN
Wiluna
AUSTRALIA
Oodnadatta
Quilpie
Charleville
Toowoomba
Brisbane
TONGA
Geraldton
SOUTH
Cunnamulla
Warwick
O C E A N
Kalgoorlie-Boulder
AUSTRALIA
L. Eyre
Bourke
NEW SOUTH
Norfolk I. (Aust.)
Nuku'alofa
OCEAN
Perth
Esperance
Port Pirie
Broken Hill
WALES
Newcastle
Lord Howe I. (Aust.)
Kermadec Is. (N.Z.)
Fremantle
Great Australian Bight
Adelaide
Mildura
A.C.T.
Sydney
Canberra
Tasman
Tropic of Capricorn
Albany
VICTORIA
Ballarat
Geelong
Melbourne
Sea
North I.
Auckland
NEW ZEALAND
King I.
Bass Str.
New Plymouth
Hamilton
Launceston
Napier
TASMANIA
Hobart
South I.
Wellington
Greymouth
Nelson
Christchurch
Invercargill
Dunedin
Chatham Is. (N.Z.)
International Date Line

COPYRIGHT GEORGE PHILIP LTD.

Canberra ● Capital Cities

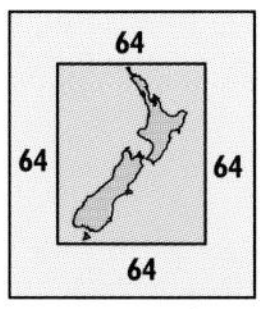

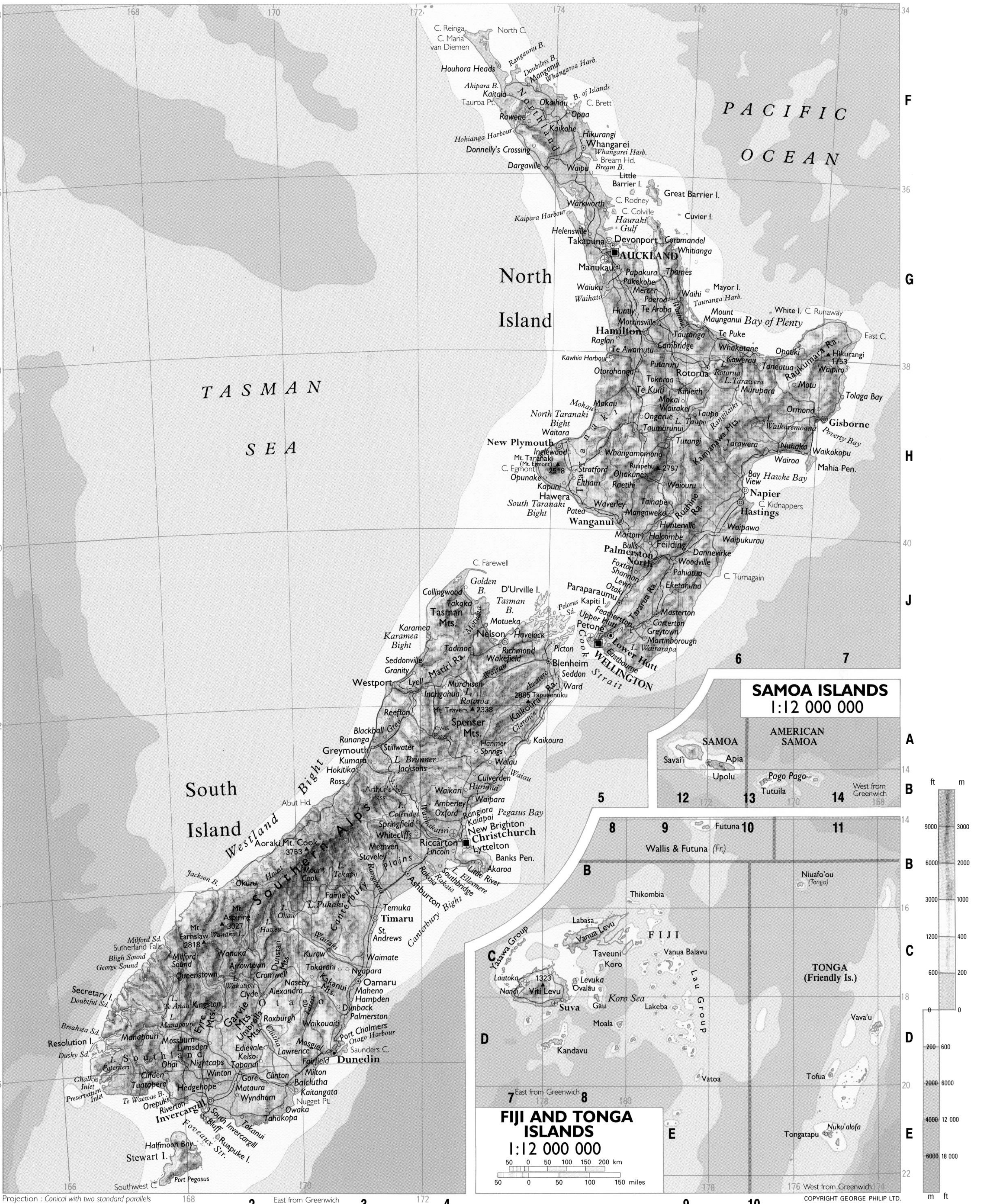

50   0   50   100   150   200 km
50   0   50   100   150 miles

PACIFIC

OCEAN

TASMAN

SEA

North

Island

C. Reinga
C. Maria
van Diemen
North C.
Houhora Heads
Rangaunu B.
Doubtless B.
Mangonui
Whangaroa Harb.
Ahipara B.
Kaitaia
Tauroa Pt.
Okaihau
C. Brett
Rawene
Opua
B. of Islands
Hokianga Harbour
Kaikohe
Hikurangi
Donnelly's Crossing
Whangarei
Whangarei Harb.
Dargaville
Waipu
Bream Hd.
Bream B.
Little
Barrier I.
Great Barrier I.
Warkworth
C. Rodney
Cuvier I.
Kaipara Harbour
C. Colville
Helensville
Hauraki
Coromandel
Takapuna
Gulf
Whitianga
Manukau
Devonport
■ AUCKLAND
Papakura
Thames
Waiuku
Pukekohe
Mayor I.
Waikato
Mercer
Waihi
Mount
Huntly
Paeroa
Tauranga Harb.
Maunganui
Morrinsville
White I. C. Runaway
Te Aroha
Bay of Plenty
Raglan
Hamilton
Tauranga
Te Puke
Whakatane
Cambridge
Kawerau
Opotiki
Raukumara Ra.
Te Awamutu
Rotorua
Taneatua
Hikurangi
Kawhia Harbour
Otorohanga
Kinleith
L. Rotorua
Murupara
1753
Waipiro
Mokau
Putaruru
L. Tarawera
Motu
North Taranaki
Mokau
Tokoroa
Wairakei
Tolaga Bay
Bight
Te Kuiti
Taupo
Rangitaiki
Waitara
Ongarue
L. Taupo
Waikaremoana
New Plymouth
Whangamomona
Taumarunui
Turangi
Tarawera
Nuhaka
Gisborne
Inglewood
Mt. Taranaki
Ruapehu 2797
Waiotapu
Poverty Bay
C. Egmont
(Mt. Egmont)
Stratford
Ohakune
Waikokopu
Mahia Pen.
2518
Opunake
Eltham
Raetihi
Waiouru
Bay
Hawke Bay
Kapuni
View
Hawera
Waverley
Taihape
Napier
South Taranaki
Patea
Mangaweka
Ruahine Ra.
C. Kidnappers
Bight
Wanganui
Hunterville
Hastings
Marton
Halcombe
Waipawa
Bulls
Feilding
Waipukurau
Palmerston
Danneyirke
North
Woodville
Foxton
Shannon
Pahiatua
Levin
Eketahuna
Paraparaumu
C. Turnagain
Otaki
Kapiti I.
Featherston
Upper Hutt
Masterton
C. Farewell
Pelorus Sd.
Cartarton
Golden
D'Urville I.
Greytown
Collingwood
B.
Tasman
Eastbourne
Martinborough
Takaka
B.
Motueka
Kapiti
WELLINGTON
L. Wairarapa
Tasman
Mts.
Nelson
Picton
Lower Hutt
Petone
Karamea
Richmond
Havelock
Cook
Karamea
Wakefield
Blenheim
Strait
Bight
Murchison
Waitara
Seddon
Seddonville
Lyell
L. Rotoroa
Anatoki
Ward
Granity
Inangahua
2885 Tapuaenuku
Westport
Reefton
Mt. Travers ▲ 2338
Kaikoura
Spenser
Clarence
Blackball
Mts.
Runanga
Hanmer
Greymouth
Stillwater
Springs
Kaikoura
Kumara
Waiau
Hokitika
L. Brunner
Culverden
Ross
Jacksons
Hurunui
Waipara
Arthur's
Waikari
Pass
Rangiora
Pegasus Bay
Coleridge
Amberley
Springfield
Kaiapoi
New Brighton
Whitecliffs
Oxford
Christchurch
Aoraki Mt. Cook
Methven
Riccarton
Lyttelton
3753 ▲
Staveley
Lincoln
Banks Pen.
Jackson B.
Mount
Plains
L. Ellesmere
Little River
Cook
L. Tekapo
Akaroa
Okuru
Ashburton
Haast
Rakaia
Rangitata
Fairlie
L. Pukaki
Mt.
Temuka
Aspiring ▲ 3027
Ohau
Timaru
Milford Sd.
Wanaka
St.
Sutherland Falls
Earnslaw
Wanaka L.
Andrews
2818 ▲
Milford
Hawea
Waimate
Bligh Sound
Sound
George Sound
Wonaka
Kurow
Waitaki
Queenstown
Arrowtown
Cromwell
Tokarahi
Ngapara
Secretary I.
Wakatipu
Clyde
Oamaru
Doubtful Sd.
Te Anau
Kingston
Alexandra
Naseby
Maheno
Dunback
L. Te Anau
L. Manapouri
Garvie
Waikouaiti
Breaksea Sd.
Manapouri
Mts.
Roxburgh
Port Chalmers
Dusky Sd.
Mossburn
Dumback
Palmerston
Resolution I.
Ohai
Edievale
Lawrence
Saunders C.
Otago Harbour
Chalky
Lumsden
Kelso
Dunedin
Inlet
Nightcaps
Tapanui
Milton
Preservation
Clifden
Winton
Clinton
Te Waewae B.
Tuatapere
Gore
Balclutha
Orepuki
Mataura
Kaitangata
Riverton
Hedgehope
Owaka
Invercargill
Wyndham
Tahakopa
Bluff
Ruapuke I.
South Invercargill
Foveaux Str.
Nugget Pt.
Halfmoon Bay
Stewart I.
Southwest C.
Port Pegasus

South

Island

Westland Bight

Southern Alps

Kanui Mts.
Otago
Dunstan Mts.
Canterbury Bight
Canterbury

Projection : Conical with two standard parallels
166   168   170   172   174
East from Greenwich
1   2   3   4

SAMOA ISLANDS
1:12 000 000

SAMOA
AMERICAN
SAMOA
Savai'i
Apia
Upolu
Pago Pago
Tutuila
West from
Greenwich
12   13   14
A   B
172   170   168

FIJI AND TONGA
ISLANDS
1:12 000 000

8   9   Futuna   10   11
Wallis & Futuna (Fr.)
Niuafo'ou
(Tonga)
Thikombia
Labasa
Vanua Levu
Yasawa Group
Vanua Balavu
Lautoka
1323
FIJI
Taveuni
Koro
Nandi
Viti Levu
Levuka
Lau Group
Ovalau
Vava'u
Gau
Suva
Koro Sea
Lakeba
Moala
TONGA
(Friendly Is.)
Kandavu
Tofua
Vatoa
Tongatapu
Nuku'alofa
East from Greenwich
180
West from Greenwich
7   8   9   10   11

50   0   50   100   150   200 km
50   0   50   100   150 miles

ft   m
9000   3000
6000   2000
3000   1000
1200   400
600   200
0   0
200   600
2000   6000
4000   12 000
6000   18 000
m   ft

50 0 50 100 150 200 250 300 km
50 0 50 100 150 200 miles

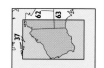

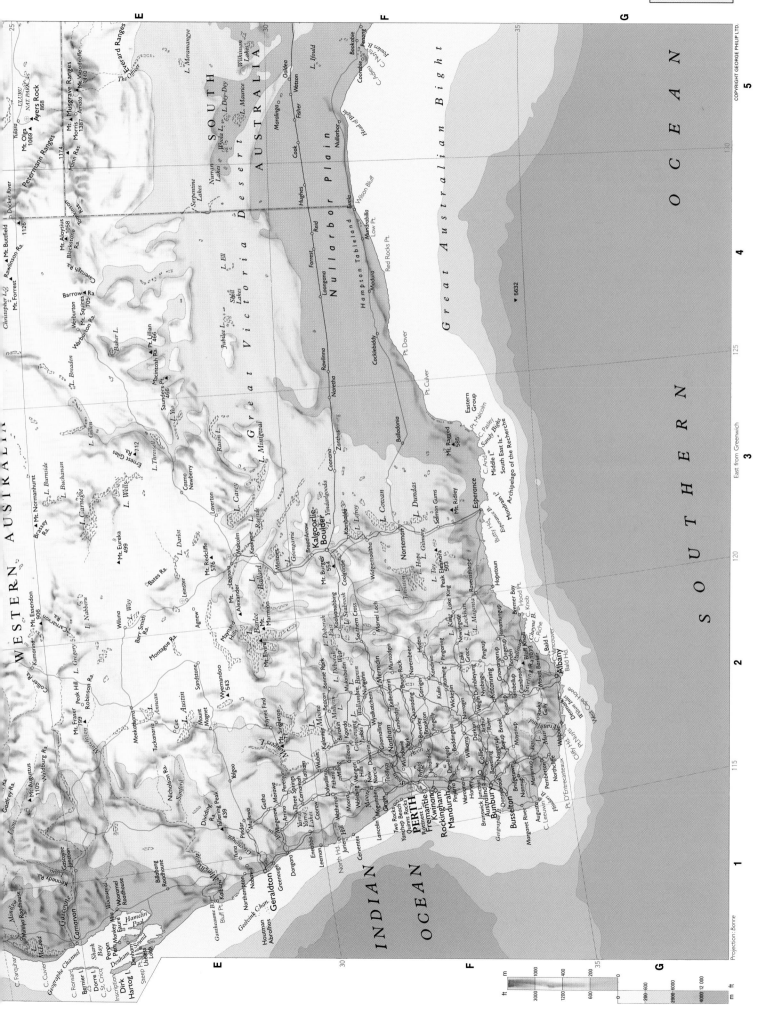

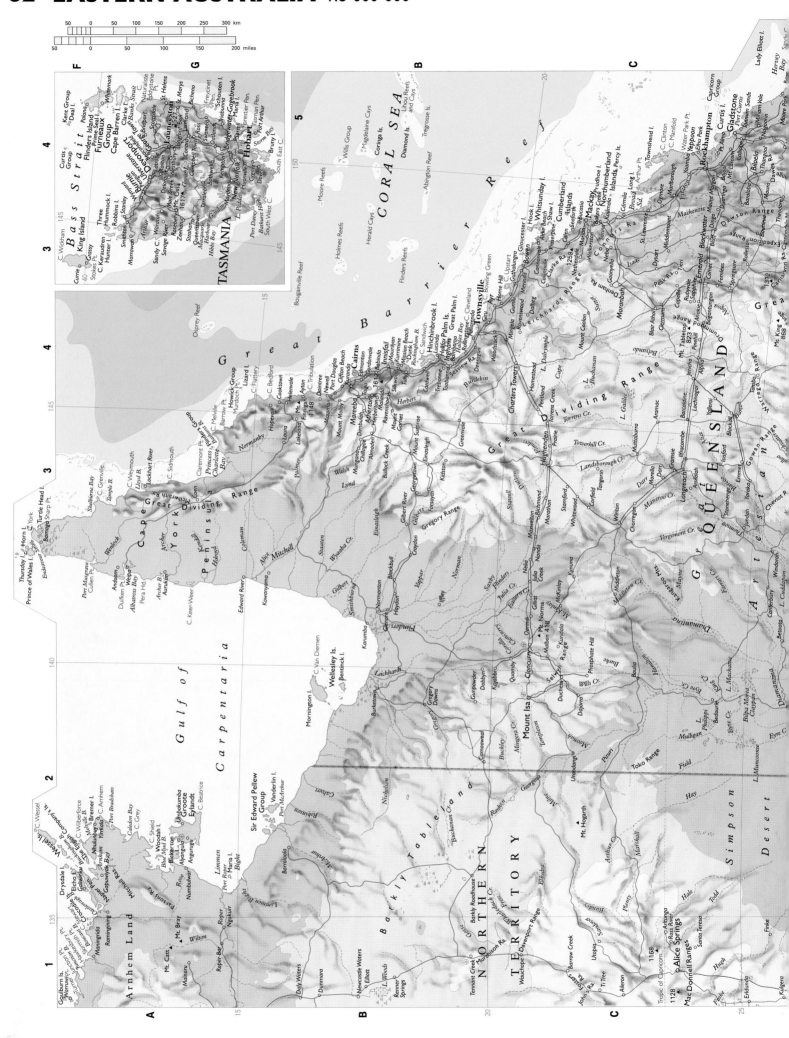

37 64
60 61

COPYRIGHT, GEORGE PHILIP LTD.

SOUTH AUSTRALIA

NEW SOUTH WALES

BRISBANE
Gold Coast
Tweed Heads

Lismore
Ballina
Coffs Harbour
Nambucca Heads
Port Macquarie
Taree
Tuncurry-Forster

Newcastle
Gosford
SYDNEY
Campbelltown
Wollongong
Shellharbour
Kiama
Nowra-Bomaderry
Batemans Bay

CANBERRA
Queanbeyan

Albury
Wodonga

MELBOURNE
Geelong
Ballarat
Bendigo

Darling Range

Darling Downs

Basin

Grey Range

Barrier Range

Flinders Ranges

Lake Eyre (North)
Lake Eyre (South)
Lake Torrens
Lake Gairdner
Lake Frome
Lake Blanche

ADELAIDE
Port Pirie
Port Augusta
Whyalla
Port Lincoln
Mount Gambier
Warrnambool

Eyre Peninsula
Yorke Peninsula
Kangaroo I.
Spencer Gulf
Gulf St. Vincent

Darling R.

Murray R.
Mildura
Broken Hill
Dubbo
Tamworth
Armidale
Grafton

Bourke

Cobar
Parkes
Orange
Bathurst

Goulburn
Katoomba

Griffith
Wagga Wagga
Shepparton

Flinders Island
Furneaux Group
Cape Barren I.
King Island
Bass Strait

T A S M A N   S E A

SOUTHERN   OCEAN

East from Greenwich

Projection: Bonne

m / ft scale bar
1500 1000 400 200 0 200 600 2000 4000 12000
4500 3000 1200 600 0 200 2000 6000 12000

135   140   145   150

30   35   40

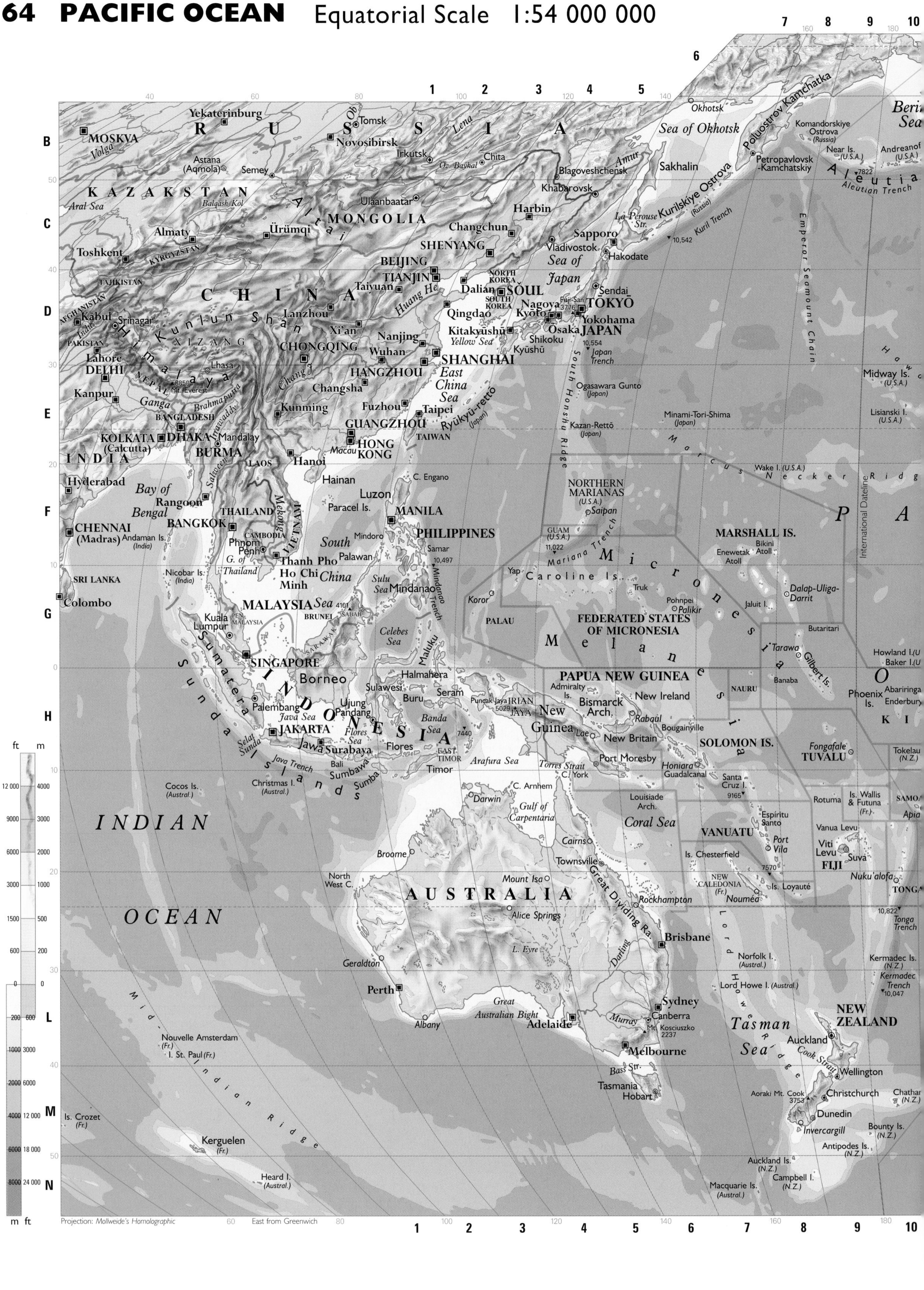

6

7 8 9 10

1 2 3 4 5

B

R U S S I A

MOSKVA
Volga
Yekaterinburg
Tomsk
Novosibirsk
Ob
Irkutsk
Lena
Chita
Oz. Baykal
Astana
(Aqmola)
Semey
Blagoveshchensk
Amur
Khabarovsk
Sakhalin
Okhotsk
Sea of Okhotsk
Poluostrov Kamchatka
Komandorskiye Ostrova
(Russia)
Near Is.
(U.S.A.)
Beri
Sea
Andreanof
(U.S.A.)

KAZAKSTAN
Aral Sea
Balqash Köl
Altay
MONGOLIA
Ulaanbaatar
La Pérouse Str.
Kuril'skiye Ostrova
(Russia)
Petropavlovsk-Kamchatskiy
7822
Kuril Trench
A l e u t i a
Aleutian Trench

C

Almaty
Ürümqi
KYRGYZSTAN
Toshkent
TAJIKISTAN
Changchun
SHENYANG
Sapporo
Vladivostok
Hakodate
10,542
Emperor Seamount Chain

BEIJING
TIANJIN
Taiyuan
NORTH KOREA
SŌUL
SOUTH KOREA
Sea of Japan
Sendai
Nagoya
Fuji-San 3776
TŌKYŌ

D

Kabul
Srinagar
AFGHANISTAN
Indus
PAKISTAN
Lahore
DELHI
Kunlun Shan
XIZANG
Lanzhou
Xi'an
CHINA
Huang He
Dalian
Qingdao
Kyōto
Osaka
Kitakyūshū
Shikoku
Kyūshū
Yellow Sea
Yokohama
JAPAN
10,554
Japan Trench
Midway Is.
(U.S.A.)

Himalaya
Lhasa
8850 Mt. Everest
NEPAL
CHONGQING
Wuhan
Nanjing
SHANGHAI
HANGZHOU
East China Sea
Ogasawara Gunto
(Japan)
Lisianski I.
(U.S.A.)

Kanpur
Ganga
Brahmaputra
Chang
Changsha
Fuzhou
Taipei
Ryūkyū-rettō
(Japan)
Minami-Tori-Shima
(Japan)

E

KOLKATA
(Calcutta)
DHAKA
BANGLADESH
Kunming
GUANGZHOU
HONG KONG
Macau
TAIWAN
Kazan-Rettō
(Japan)

INDIA
BURMA
Mandalay
Irrawaddy
Salween
Hanoi
LAOS
Hainan
C. Engano
Marcus
Necker Ridge
P A

Hyderabad
Bay of
Bengal
Rangoon
Mekong
THAILAND
BANGKOK
Luzon
Paracel Is.
MANILA
Wake I. (U.S.A.)

F

CHENNAI
(Madras)
Andaman Is.
(India)
CAMBODIA
Phnom Penh
PHILIPPINES
Mindoro
Samar
10,497
NORTHERN MARIANAS
(U.S.A.)
Saipan
GUAM
(U.S.A.)
11,022
MARSHALL IS.
Bikini
Enewetak Atoll

SRI LANKA
Nicobar Is.
(India)
G. of Thailand
South China Sea
Thanh Pho Ho Chi Minh
Palawan
Yap
Koror
Caroline Is.
Micronesia

G

Colombo
Kuala Lumpur
MALAYSIA
SINGAPORE
Sea
Sulu Sea
Mindanao
4101
Mindanao Trench
PALAU
Palikir
Pohnpei
Truk
Jaluit I.
Dalap-Uliga-Darrit
Butaritari

Sumatera
INDONESIA
SARAWAK
BRUNEI
SABAH
Borneo
Celebes Sea
FEDERATED STATES OF MICRONESIA
M e l a
NAURU
Tarawa
Gilbert Is.
Howland I.(U
Baker I.(U
Phoenix Is.
Abariringa
Enderbury
KI

H

Sunda Islands
Palembang
Java Sea
JAKARTA
Jawa
Surabaya
Ujung Pandang
Sulawesi
Buru
Halmahera
Seram
Banda Sea
Maluku
7440
Puncak Jaya 5029
IRIAN JAYA
New Guinea
Admiralty Is.
Bismarck Arch.
New Ireland
Rabaul
PAPUA NEW GUINEA
Bougainville
New Britain
Lae
SOLOMON IS.
Fongafale
TUVALU
Tokelau
(N.Z.)
O
n e s i a

Selat Sunda
Java Trench
Flores Sea
Bali
Sumbawa
Flores
Sumba
EAST TIMOR
Timor
Arafura Sea
Torres Strait
C. York
Port Moresby
Honiara
Guadalcanal
Santa Cruz I.
9165
Rotuma
Is. Wallis & Futuna
(Fr.)
SAMO
Apia

L

ft m
INDIAN
12 000 4000
9000 3000
6000 2000
3000 1000
1500 500
600 200
200 600
Cocos Is.
(Austral.)
Christmas I.
(Austral.)
C. Arnhem
Darwin
Gulf of Carpentaria
Cairns
Broome
North West C.
Louisiade Arch.
Coral Sea
Espiritu Santo
VANUATU
Port Vila
Is. Chesterfield
7570
Vanua Levu
Viti Levu
Suva
FIJI
Nuku'alofa
TONGA

OCEAN
Mount Isa
AUSTRALIA
Alice Springs
L. Eyre
NEW CALEDONIA
(Fr.)
Nouméa
Is. Loyauté
10,822
Tonga Trench

Townsville
Rockhampton
Brisbane
Norfolk I.
(Austral.)
Kermadec Is.
(N.Z.)

1000 3000
Geraldton
Darling
Sydney
Canberra
Mt. Kosciuszko 2237
Lord Howe I. (Austral.)
NEW ZEALAND
Kermadec Trench
10,047

Perth
Great Australian Bight
Albany
Adelaide
Murray
Melbourne
Bass Str.
Tasman Sea
Auckland
Cook Strait
Wellington

2000 6000
Nouvelle Amsterdam
(Fr.)
I. St. Paul (Fr.)
Mid-Indian Ridge

M

4000 12 000
Is. Crozet
(Fr.)
Tasmania
Hobart
Aoraki Mt. Cook 3753
Christchurch
Chatha
(N.Z.)
Dunedin

6000 18 000
Kerguelen
(Fr.)
Invercargill
Bounty Is.
(N.Z.)
Antipodes Is.
(N.Z.)

N

8000 24 000
Heard I.
(Austral.)
Auckland Is.
(N.Z.)
Macquarie I.
(Austral.)
Campbell I.
(N.Z.)

m ft

Arctic Circle

ALASKA
(U.S.A.)
Anchorage
Bristol Bay
Gulf of Alaska
Juneau

Is. (U.S.A.)

Prince of Wales I.
(U.S.A.) Prince Rupert
Queen Charlotte Is.
(Canada)

15

16 17 18 19 20

C A N A D A

R O C K Y

L. Winnipeg

Edmonton

Calgary Regina Winnipeg

Vancouver
Vancouver I. Victoria
Seattle
Portland

Snake

Boise

L. Superior

Newfoundland

St. Lawrence

Québec
St. John's

Montréal
Ottawa

N O R T H

B

C

Minneapolis
Missouri
L. Huron
L. Michigan Toronto Buffalo Boston
Detroit
CHICAGO L. Erie
Pittsburgh NEW YORK CITY
Kansas City Cincinnati PHILADELPHIA
St. Louis Baltimore
Washington D.C.

Salt Lake
City Denver

Colorado

C. Mendocino

Sacramento

SAN FRANCISCO

6741

4418

UNITED STATES
Oklahoma City Memphis
Phoenix
Dallas

Atlanta

Appalachian Mts.

C. Hatteras

A T L A N T I C

D

LOS ANGELES
San Diego

Guadalupe
(Mex.)

C. San Lucas

Baja California

Ciudad
Juárez

M

Golfo de California

Houston
San Antonio

Monterrey

New
Orleans

Mississippi

Gulf of Mexico

Jacksonville

Miami

Bermuda
(U.K.)

Sargasso Sea

BAHAMAS

O C E A N

Tropic of Cancer

Honolulu
Oahu 4205
Hawaii
HAWAIIAN IS.
(U.S.A.)

Johnston I.
(U.S.A.)

E

La Habana
CUBA

West Indies

Guadalajara
E Puebla
MEXICO
Acapulco

Is. Revilla Gigedo
(Mex.)

Mérida

5700

O

BELIZE
GUATEMALA HONDURAS
Guatemala
San Salvador NICARAGUA
EL SALVADOR
Managua

7680

Canal de Yucatán

Florida Str.

JAMAICA
Kingston

HAITI

9200

DOMINICAN REP.

PUERTO
RICO
(U.S.A.)

Leeward
Is.

Caribbean Sea

BARBADOS
Windward Is.

F

P A C I F I C

North West Christmas Ridge

Palmyra Is.
(U.S.A.)

O

Teraina
Tabuaeran
Kiritimati

I. Clipperton
(Fr.)

COSTA
RICA
PANAMA

San José
Barranquilla
Colón Panamá

Maracaibo

Caracas

Orinoco

VENEZUELA

G

I L B E R T

Jarvis I.
(U.S.A.)

E A N

Malden I.

Starbuck I.

Equator

Galápagos
(Ecuador)

I. del Coco
(Costa Rica) Medellín

I. de Malpelo
(Colombia)

Bogotá

Cali

COLOMBIA

Quito
ECUADOR

Kiritimati

ER.
MOA
S.A.)

K I R I B A T I

Tongareva

Pukapuka Manihiki
Caroline I.
Vostok I.
Flint I.

Is. Marquises

Guayaquil

C. Pariñas

Iquitos

Amazonas

BRAZIL

H

Suwarrow Is.
Is. de la
Société

Is. Tuamotu

Trujillo

6369

PERU

10

Cook Is.
(N.Z.)

Tahiti
Papeete

FRENCH POLYNESIA

LIMA

Cuzco

L. Titicaca

Nevada Ancohuma
6550

J

ue
Z.)

Rarotonga

Is. Tubuai

Tuamotu

Murūroa

Arequipa
6866

Peru-

Iquique

La Paz

BOLIVIA

Austral Seamount Chain

Ridge

Ducie I.

Pitcairn I.
(U.K.)

Rapa

Tropic of Capricorn

Sala-y-Gómez
(Chile)
I. de Pascua
(Chile)

East Pacific Ridge

San Felix
(Chile)

San Ambrosio
(Chile)

8050
Trench

Arica

Chile

Antofagasta

PARAGUAY

Asunción

San Miguel
de Tucumán

K

Arch. de
Juan Fernández
(Chile)

Valparaíso

SANTIAGO

Concepción

Chile Rise

Aconcagua
6960
ANDES

Córdoba

Rosario

BUENOS
AIRES

ARGENTINA

URUGUAY
Montevideo

Río de la Plata

Pôrto
Alegre

L

SOUTH

M

Patagonia

Pacific-Antarctic Ridge

6212

ATLANTIC

OCEAN

Punta Arenas
Est. de Magallanes
Tierra del Fuego
C. de Hornos

Falkland Is.
(U.K.)

South Georgia
(U.K.)

N

West from Greenwich

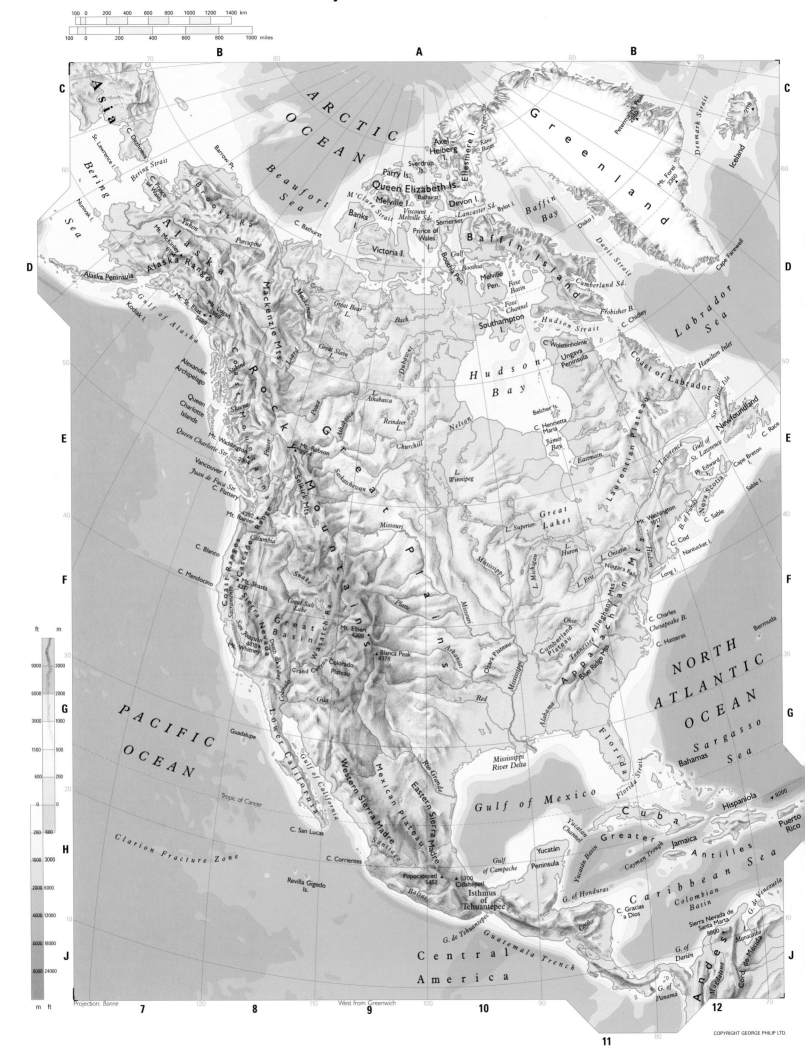

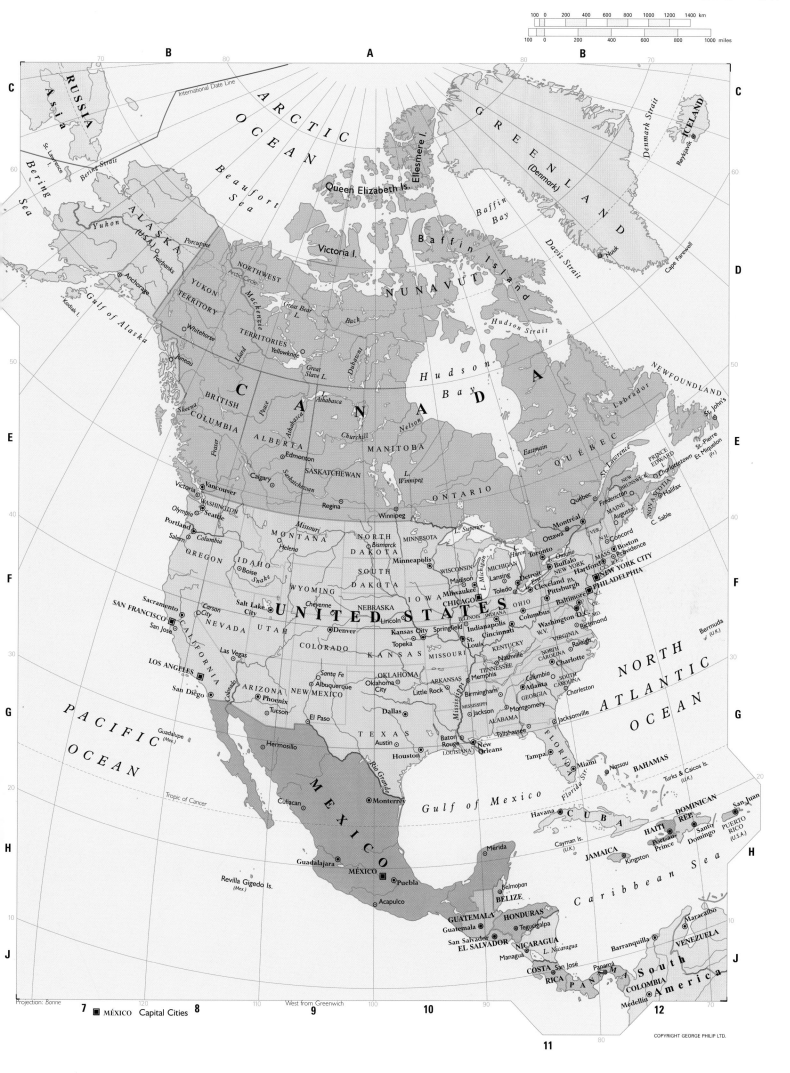

100 0 200 400 600 800 1000 1200 1400 km
100 0 200 400 600 800 1000 miles

C **RUSSIA** Asia
Asia
St. Lawrence I.
Bering Strait
Bering
Sea
International Date Line
ARCTIC
OCEAN
Beaufort
Sea
Queen Elizabeth Is.
Ellesmere I.
GREENLAND
(Denmark)
Denmark Strait
ICELAND
Reykjavik
C

ALASKA
(USA)
Yukon
Porcupine
Fairbanks
Anchorage
Kodiak I.
Gulf of Alaska
Whitehorse
Juneau
YUKON
TERRITORY
Arctic Circle
NORTHWEST
Mackenzie
Great Bear
L.
Victoria I.
Baffin
Bay
NUNAVUT
Baffin Island
Nuuk
Davis Strait
Cape Farewell
D

Skeena
BRITISH
COLUMBIA
Liard
TERRITORIES
Yellowknife
Great
Slave L.
Back
Dubawnt
Hudson Strait
NEWFOUNDLAND
E

Fraser
ALBERTA
Peace
Athabasca
Athabasca L.
C A N A D A
Churchill
MANITOBA
Nelson
Hudson
Bay
Eastmain
Labrador
St-Pierre
Et Miquelon
(Fr.)
E

Victoria
Vancouver
Calgary
Edmonton
SASKATCHEWAN
Saskatchewan
Regina
L.
Winnipeg
Winnipeg
ONTARIO
QUÉBEC
St. Lawrence
Québec
PRINCE
EDWARD
Charlottetown
NEW
BRUNSWICK
Fredericton
NOVA SCOTIA
Halifax
C. Sable
St John's

WASHINGTON
Seattle
Olympia
Portland
Salem
Columbia
OREGON
Missouri
MONTANA
Helena
NORTH
DAKOTA
Bismarck
MINNESOTA
Minneapolis
WISCONSIN
Madison
L. Superior
L. Huron
L. Michigan
Toronto
Ottawa
Montréal
MAINE
Augusta
VER.
N.H.
Concord
MASS.
Boston
Providence
F

IDAHO
Boise
Snake
WYOMING
SOUTH
DAKOTA
Lansing
MICHIGAN
Milwaukee
Detroit
Cleveland
Erie
Buffalo
NEW YORK
Hartford
NEW YORK CITY
PHILADELPHIA
N.J.
Sacramento
SAN FRANCISCO
San Jose
Carson
City
Salt Lake
City
NEVADA
UTAH
U N I T E D S T A T E S
NEBRASKA
Lincoln
IOWA
Chicago
ILLINOIS
INDIANA
Indianapolis
OHIO
Columbus
Toledo
Pittsburgh
PA.
Baltimore
Washington D.C.
W.V.
MD.
DE.
F

Las Vegas
CALIFORNIA
Denver
COLORADO
KANSAS
Kansas City
Topeka
Springfield
St.
Louis
MISSOURI
Cincinnati
KENTUCKY
Nashville
VIRGINIA
Richmond
NORTH
CAROLINA
Raleigh
Bermuda
(U.K.)
NORTH
LOS ANGELES
San Diego
ARIZONA
Phoenix
Tucson
Santa Fe
Albuquerque
NEW MEXICO
OKLAHOMA
Oklahoma
City
ARKANSAS
Little Rock
Memphis
TENNESSEE
Birmingham
Atlanta
GEORGIA
SOUTH
CAROLINA
Charlotte
Charleston
ATLANTIC
G

Colorado
El Paso
Dallas
T E X A S
Austin
Mississippi
MISSISSIPPI
Jackson
ALABAMA
Montgomery
Jacksonville
OCEAN
PACIFIC
Guadalupe
(Mex.)
Hermosillo
Houston
Baton
Rouge
LOUISIANA
New
Orleans
FLORIDA
Tampa
Tallahassee
G

OCEAN
Tropic of Cancer
Culiacan
M É X I C O
Monterrey
Rio Grande
Gulf of Mexico
Miami
Nassau
BAHAMAS
Turks & Caicos Is.
(U.K.)
Florida Str.
H

Guadalajara
MÉXICO
Puebla
Revilla Gigedo Is.
(Mex.)
Acapulco
Mérida
Cayman Is.
(U.K.)
Havana
CUBA
JAMAICA
Kingston
HAITI
Port-au-
Prince
DOMINICAN
REP.
Santo
Domingo
PUERTO
RICO
(U.S.A.)
San Juan
Caribbean Sea
H

Belmopan
BELIZE
GUATEMALA
Guatemala
HONDURAS
Tegucigalpa
San Salvador
EL SALVADOR
NICARAGUA
L. Nicaragua
Managua
COSTA
RICA
San José
PANAMA
Panama
Maracaibo
Barranquilla
VENEZUELA
COLOMBIA
Medellín
South
America
J

Projection: Bonne
7 ■ MÉXICO Capital Cities 8
120
110
West from Greenwich
9
10
90
80
11
12
70

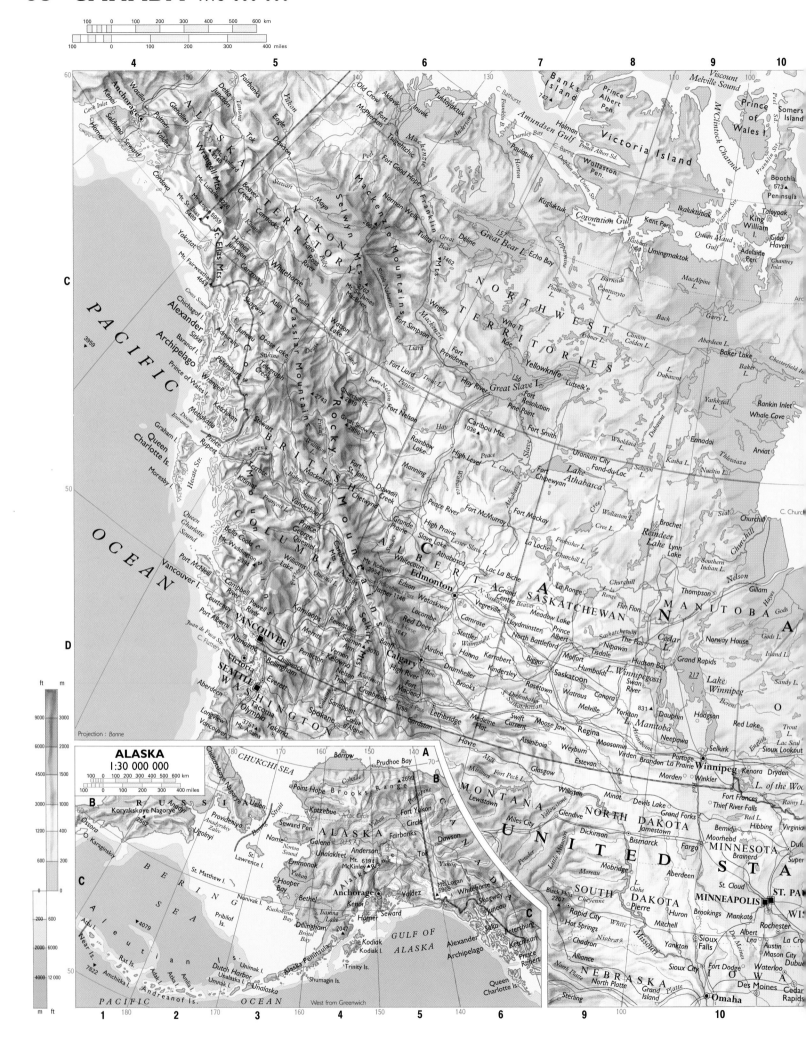

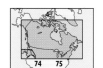

Projection: Lambert's Equivalent Azimuthal

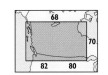

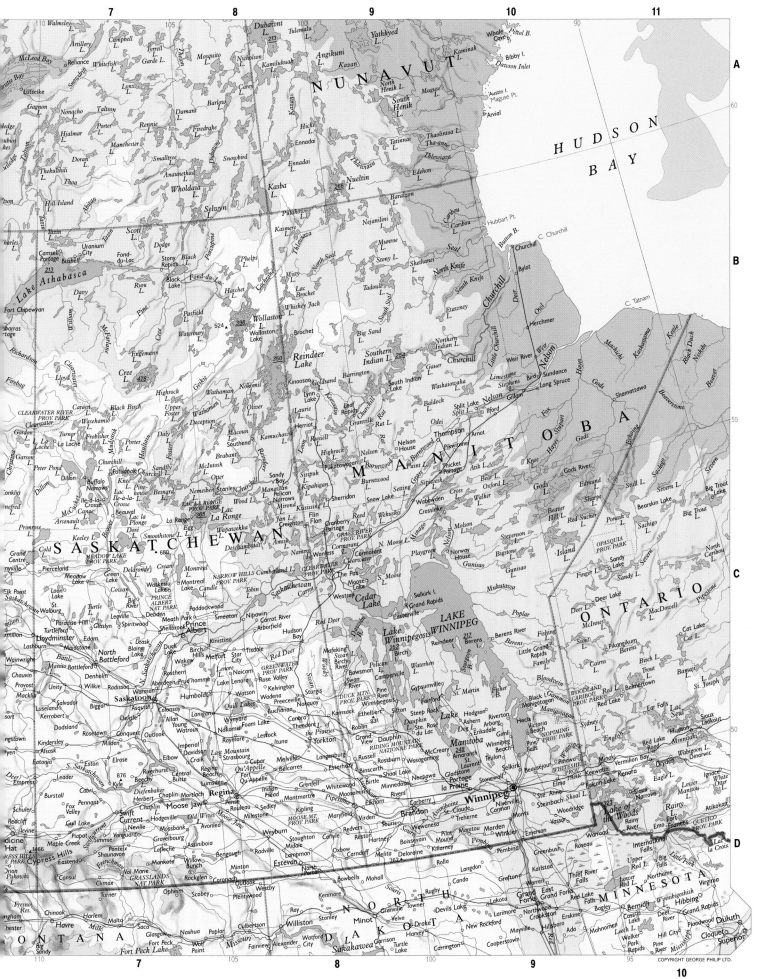

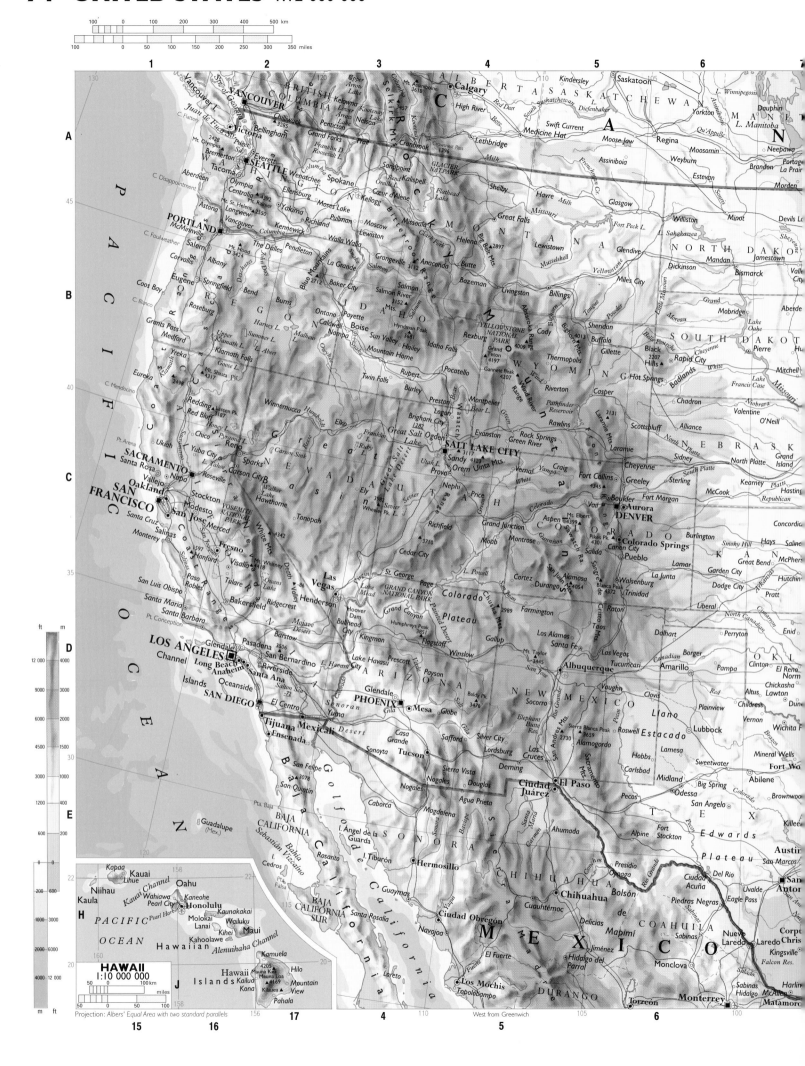

Projection: Albers' Equal Area with two standard parallels

HAWAII
1:10 000 000

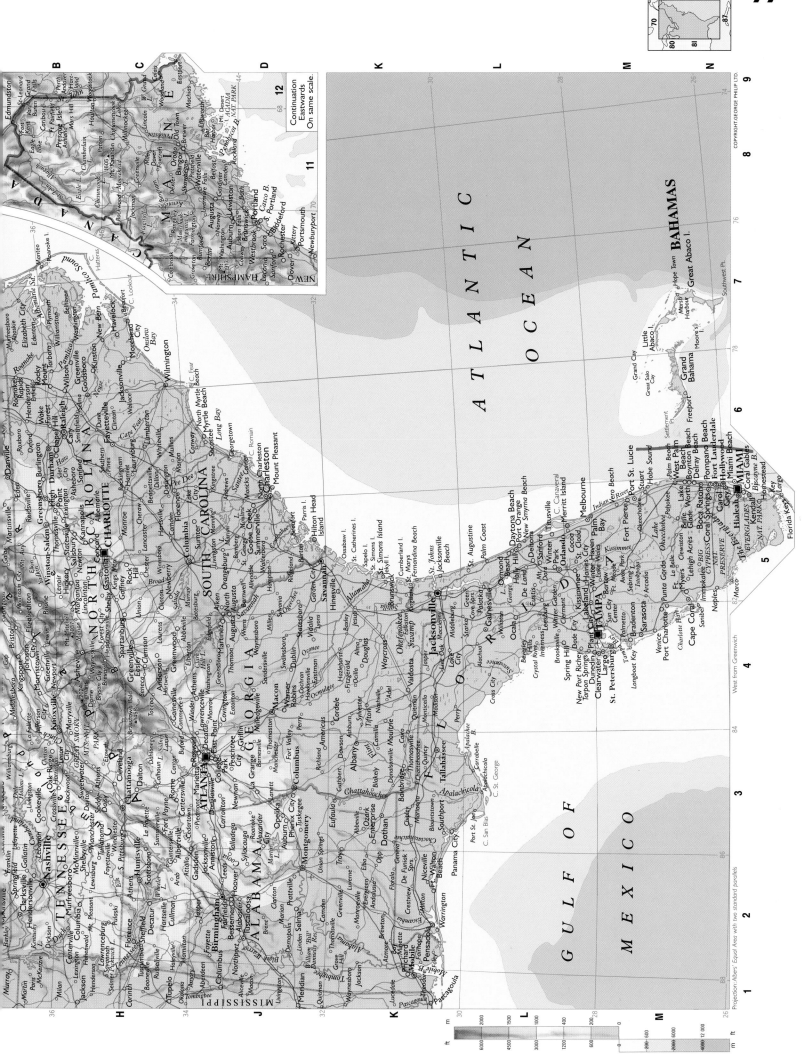

ATLANTIC OCEAN

GULF OF MEXICO

BAHAMAS

Great Abaco I.

Little Abaco I.

Grand Bahama

TENNESSEE

NORTH CAROLINA

SOUTH CAROLINA

GEORGIA

ALABAMA

MISSISSIPPI

FLORIDA

CHARLOTTE

ATLANTA

TAMPA

MIAMI

Nashville

Birmingham

Montgomery

Jacksonville

Tallahassee

Columbia

CANADA

MAINE

NEW HAMPSHIRE

Continuation
Eastwards
On same scale.

Projection: Albers' Equal Area with two standard parallels

COPYRIGHT GEORGE PHILIP LTD.

West from Greenwich

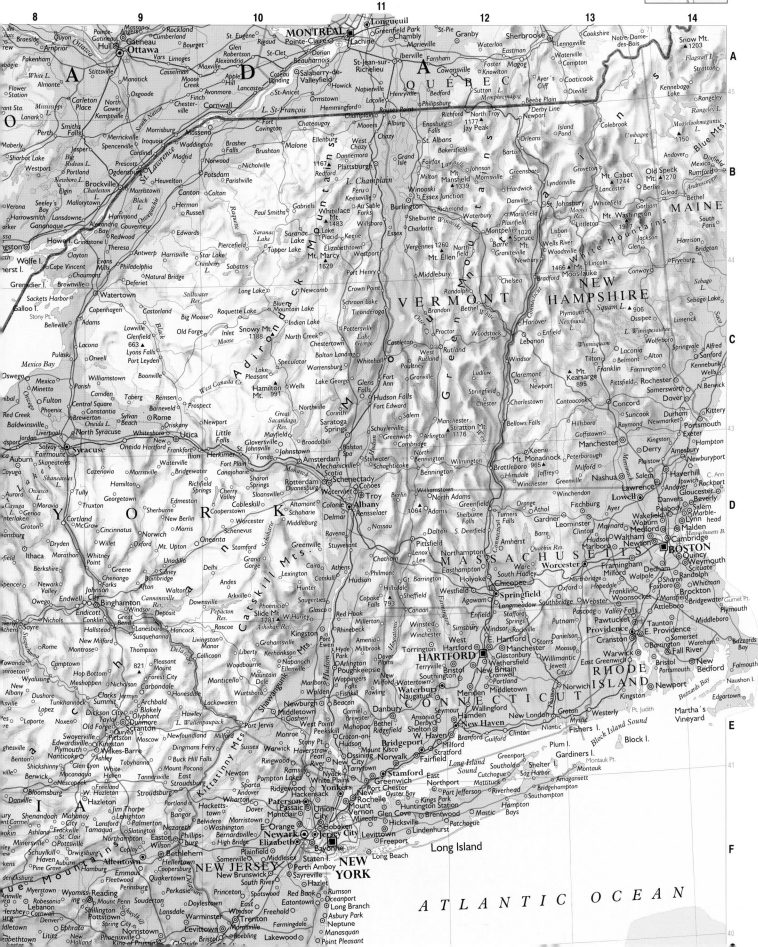

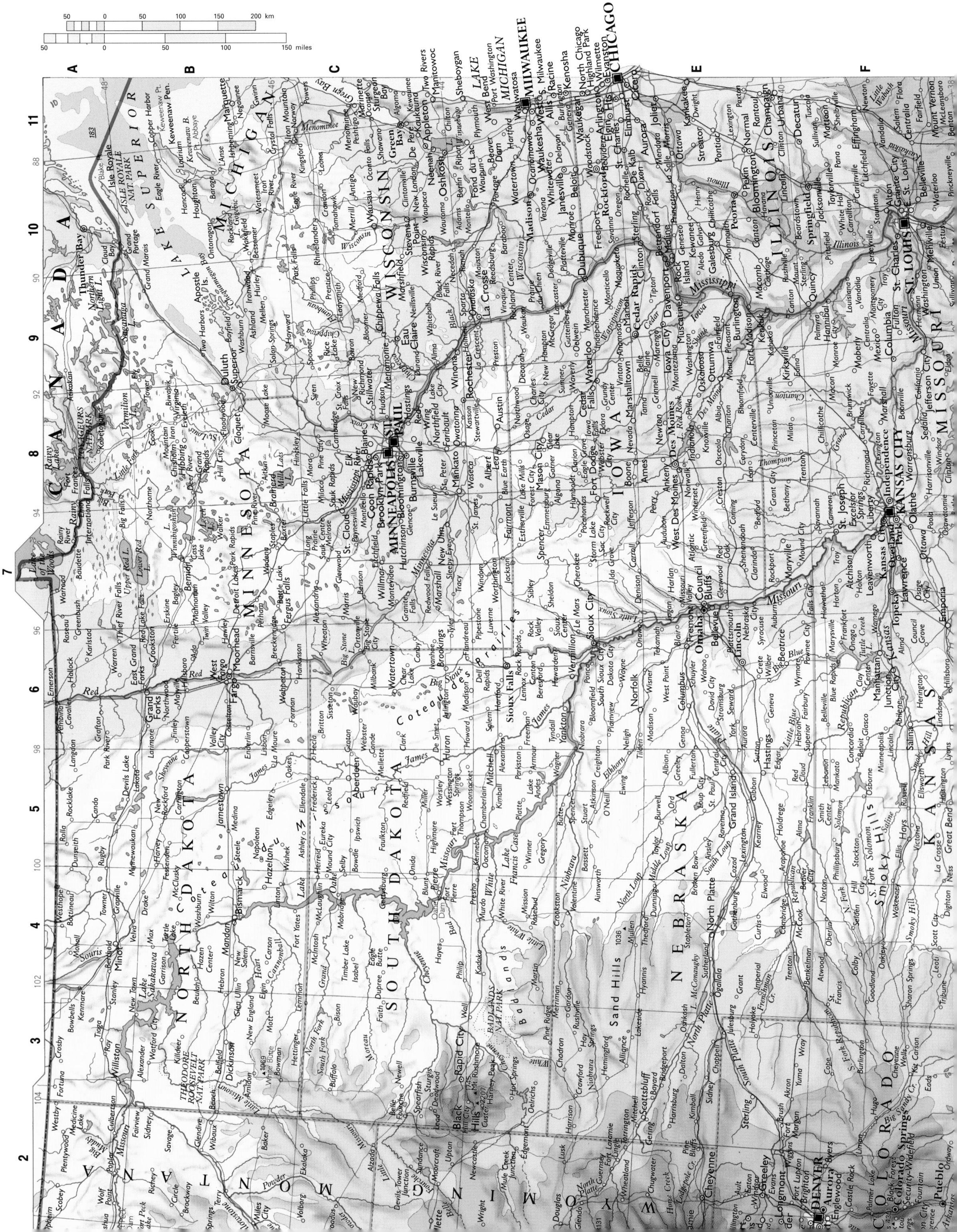

CANADA

LAKE SUPERIOR

MICHIGAN · WISCONSIN · MINNESOTA · IOWA · ILLINOIS

NORTH DAKOTA · SOUTH DAKOTA · NEBRASKA · KANSAS · MISSOURI

MONTANA · WYOMING · COLORADO

LAKE MICHIGAN

CHICAGO · MILWAUKEE · MINNEAPOLIS · ST. PAUL · KANSAS CITY · ST. LOUIS · DENVER · DULUTH · OMAHA · Lincoln · Des Moines · Sioux Falls · Bismarck · Rapid City · Topeka

THEODORE ROOSEVELT NAT. PARK · BADLANDS NAT. PARK · Black Hills · Mt. Rushmore

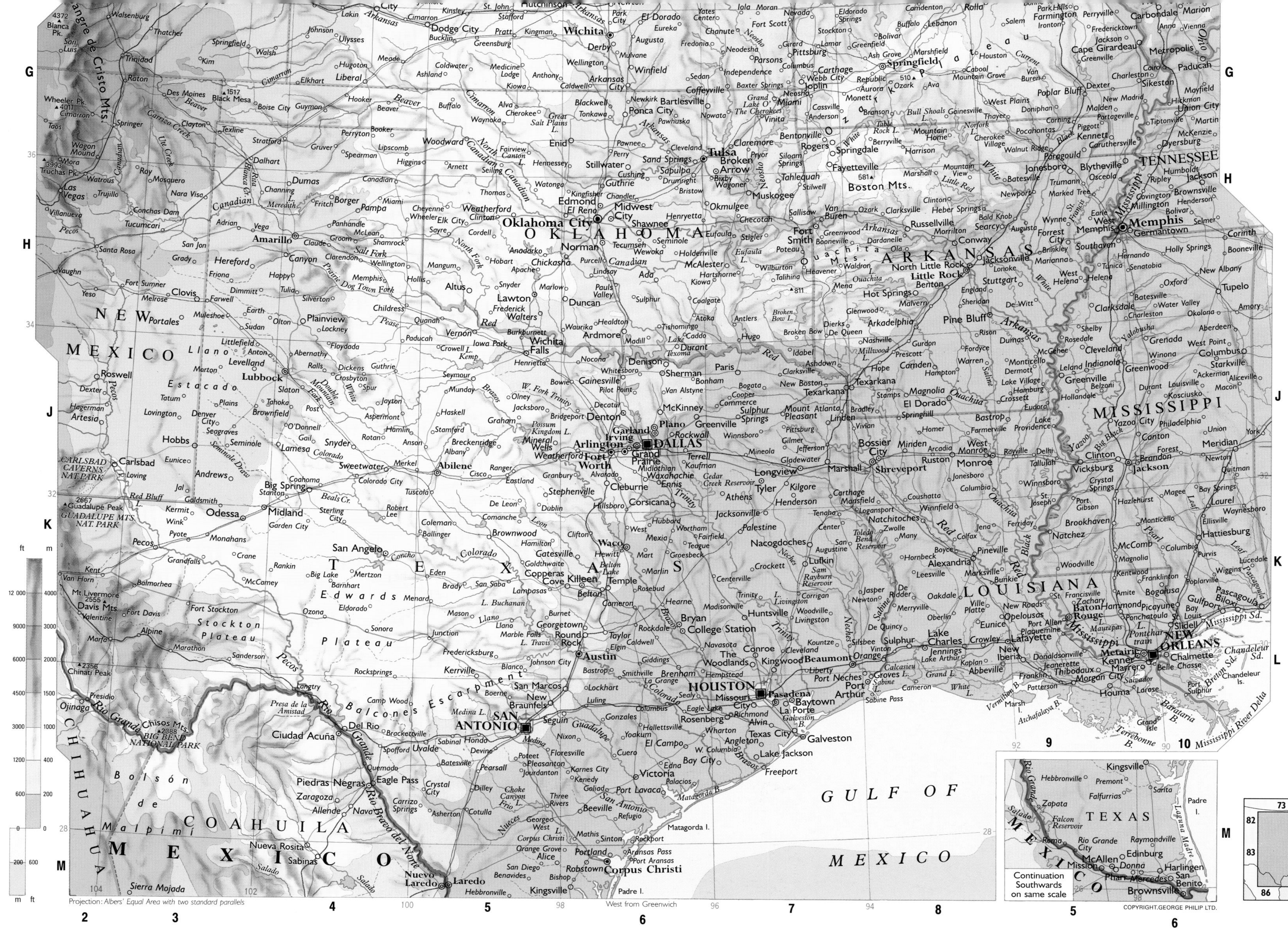

TENNESSEE

MISSISSIPPI

ARKANSAS

LOUISIANA

OKLAHOMA

T E X A S

NEW MEXICO

COAHUILA

CHIHUAHUA

M E X I C O

GULF OF MEXICO

Memphis

Springfield

Little Rock

Tulsa

Oklahoma City

Wichita

Dallas

Fort Worth

Houston

SAN ANTONIO

Austin

Corpus Christi

Laredo

Nuevo Laredo

Brownsville

NEW ORLEANS

Shreveport

Baton Rouge

Beaumont

Galveston

Amarillo

Lubbock

Odessa

Midland

San Angelo

Abilene

Del Rio

Ciudad Acuña

Piedras Negras

Eagle Pass

Rio Grande

Rio Bravo del Norte

Pecos

Red R.

Arkansas

Mississippi

Edwards Plateau

Llano Estacado

Balcones Escarpment

Stockton Plateau

BIG BEND NATIONAL PARK

CARLSBAD CAVERNS NAT. PARK

GUADALUPE MTS. NAT. PARK

Guadalupe Peak 2667

Sangre de Cristo Mts.

Sierra Madre

Laguna Madre

Padre I.

Mississippi River Delta

Chandeleur Sd.

COPYRIGHT GEORGE PHILIP LTD.

West from Greenwich

Projection: Albers' Equal Area with two standard parallels

Continuation Southwards on same scale

m ft
12 000
9000
6000
4500
3000
1500
600
200
0

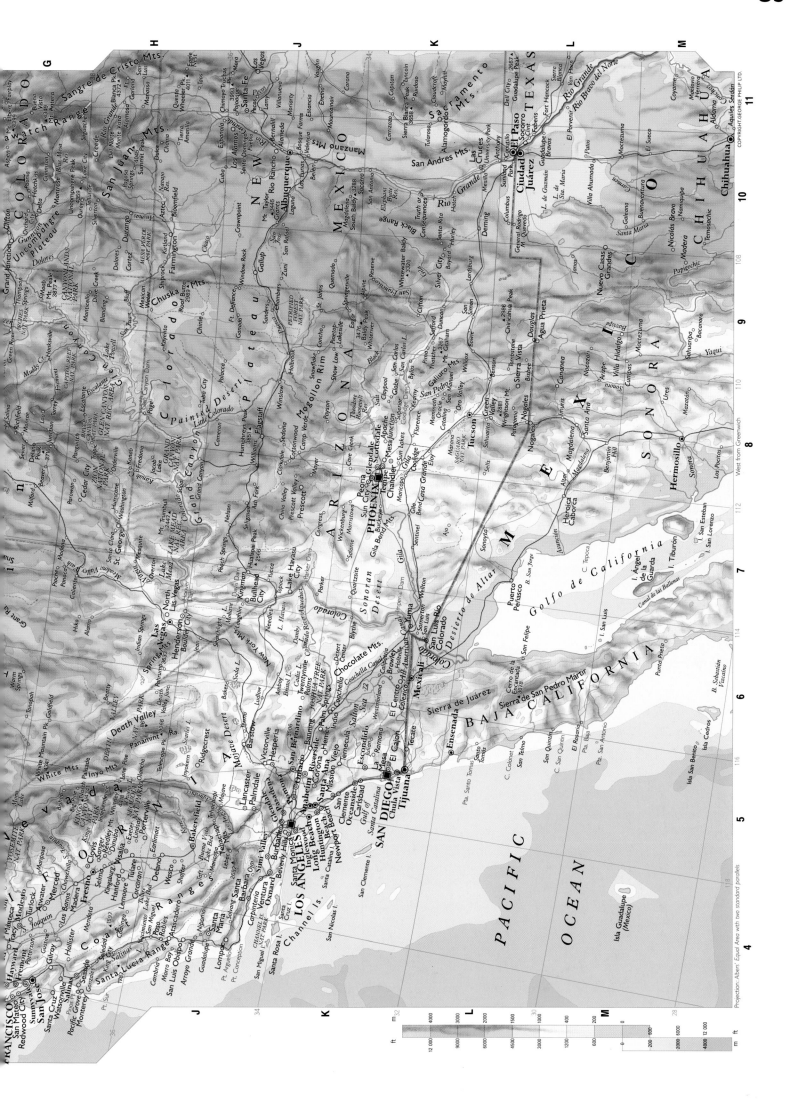

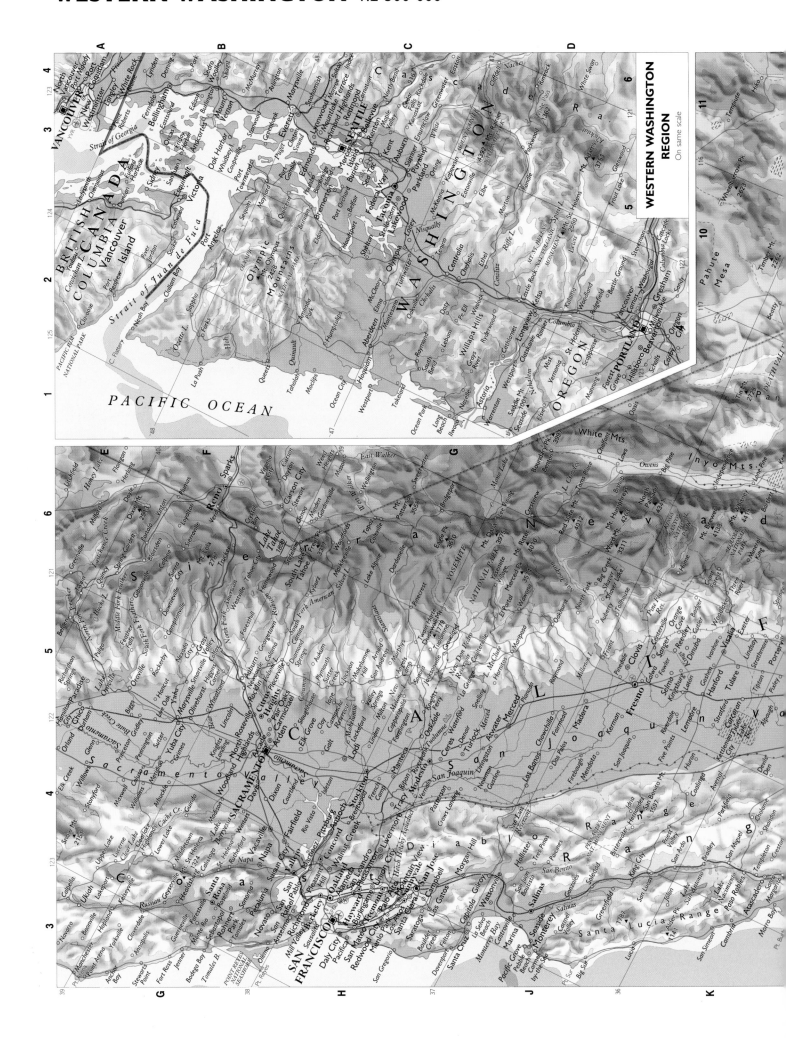

WESTERN WASHINGTON
REGION
On same scale

10 0 10 20 30 40 50 60 70 80 90 km

10 0 10 20 30 40 50 60 miles

H J K L M

13

14

15

12

11

16

10

17

9

18

8

N E V A D A

A R I Z O N A

M E X I C O

BAJA CALIFORNIA

C A L I F O R N I A

M o j a v e   D e s e r t

S o n o r a n   D e s e r t

Death Valley

Amargosa Range

Lake Mead

Colorado

Las Vegas
Henderson
North Las Vegas
Boulder City

Bakersfield

LOS ANGELES

Santa Barbara
Ventura
Oxnard

Long Beach
Santa Monica
Anaheim
Santa Ana
Irvine
Costa Mesa
Newport Beach
Huntington Beach

San Bernardino
Riverside
Moreno Valley
Redlands
Ontario
Pomona
Fontana
Corona

Lancaster
Palmdale
Victorville
Hesperia
Apple Valley
Barstow

Palm Springs
Palm Desert
Indio
Coachella

Salton Sea

Imperial Valley
El Centro
Brawley
Calexico
Mexicali

San Diego
Chula Vista
National City
Coronado
El Cajon
Escondido
Oceanside
Carlsbad
Vista
San Marcos
Poway

Tijuana

Chocolate Mts.

Providence Mts.

San Gabriel Mts.

Tehachapi Mts.

Lake Havasu City

Bullhead City
Needles
Kingman

Blythe
Parker

Yuma

Joshua Tree

Twentynine Palms

Channel Islands

Santa Catalina I.

San Clemente I.

San Nicolas I.

Santa Cruz I.
Santa Rosa I.
San Miguel I.

P A C I F I C   O C E A N

Santa Barbara Channel

San Pedro Channel

Gulf of Santa Catalina

50 0 50 100 150 200 250 300 km
50 0 50 100 150 200 miles

ft m
12 000 4000
9000 3000
6000 2000
4500 1500
3000 1000
1200 400
600 200
0 0
200 600
2000 6000
4000 12 000
m ft

PACIFIC

OCEAN

REFERENCE TO NUMBERS

1 Distrito Federal   5 México
2 Aguascalientes   6 Morelos
3 Guanajuato   7 Querétaro
4 Hidalgo   8 Tlaxcala

Projection: Bi-polar oblique Conical Orthomorphic

West from Greenwich

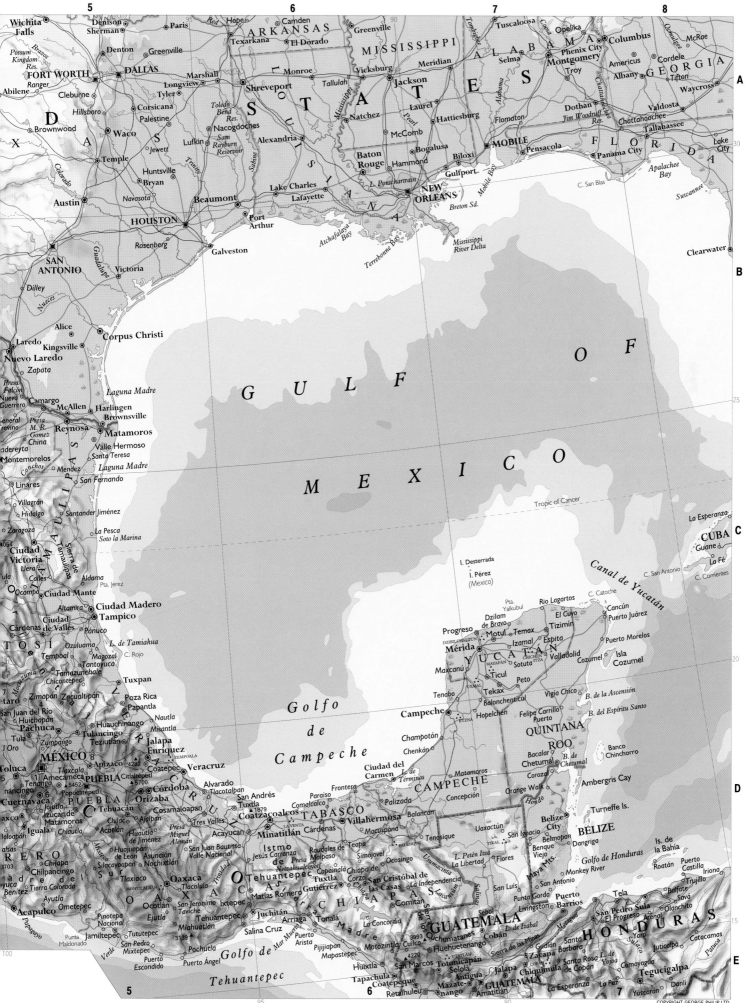

Projection: Conical with two standard parallels

87
92 93

50 0 50 100 150 200 250 300 km
50 0 50 100 150 200 miles

5 **6** **7** **8**

75 70 65 60 25 A

AMAS

arthur's Town

The Bight
Cat I.
San Salvador I.
Conception I.
Rum Cay
Long I.
andy Clarence
Town Samana Cay
Cay
Crooked I. Passage
Crooked I.
Plana Cays
Albert Snug Mayaguana I.
Town Corner
Acklins I.
Cay Verde Mira por vos Cay
Caicos Passage

A T L A N T I C

O C E A N

Tropic of Cancer

B

12 000 4000

9000 3000

6000 2000

C

4500 1500

Turks & Caicos
(U.K.)
Caicos Is.
Turks Is.

3000 1000

Cay Santa
Domingo
Hogsty Reef
Little Inagua I.
anes Lake Rosa
Great
Antilla Inagua I.
Moa Matthew
Town
Mayarí

Baracoa
Pta. de
Maisí Î. de la
Maisí Tortue
Guantánamo Paso de los Vientos Monte
(Windward Passage) Cristi LA ISABELA
Cap- Santiago de los Cabelleros
Haïtien San Francisco de Macorís
Jean Rabel Port-de- Puerto Milwaukee Puerto Rico Trench
Paix Plata Deep
Cap-à- Fort Liberté La Vega 9200
Foux Gonaïves Central Nagua Samaná
G. de la Cord. La Vega Sabana de la Mar
Gonâve Hinche 3175 Sánchez
St-Marc Bayamón SAN JUAN
HAITI DOMINICAN Arecibo Carolina Virgin Gorda Anegada Sombrero (U.K.)
Jérémie Î. de la Gonâve REP. San Pedro Hato Mayor St. Thomas Tortola Virgin Is. Anegada
PORT- de Macorís Higüey Fajardo Road Town (U.K.) Passage Anguilla (U.K.)
avassa I. AU-PRINCE San Juan Higüey 1338 Carolina Virgin Is. St.-Martin (Fr.)
(U.S.A.) Dame Massif de la Hotte L. Enriquillo C. Engaño Aguadilla Ponce Caguas Charlotte (U.S.A.) St. Maarten St.-Barthélemy (Fr.)
Marie Petit SANTO Azua de B. de Mayagüez Guayama Amalie St. Eustatius (Neth.) Saba (Neth.) Barbuda
Les Cayes Aquin Goâve Jacmel DOMINGO Compostela Yuma Isla Frederiksted St. Croix (Neth.) ST. KITTS ANTIGUA
Î. à Vache Pedernales San Cristóbal Barahona I. Saona Mona PUERTO Christiansted Basseterre & NEVIS & BARBUDA
Pointe-à-Gravois Barahona (U.S.A.) RICO Nevis Redonda ST. John's
H i s p a n i o l a (U.S.A.) Soufrière Antigua
I. Beata Montserrat Hills Guadeloupe Passage
C. Beata A n t i l l e s (U.K.) Ste.-Rose Le Moule
Le Moule La Désirade
GUADELOUPE Pointe-à-Pitre Marie-Galante (Fr.)
(Fr.) Grand-Bourg
Basse-Terre
I. de Aves I. des Saintes Dominica Passage
(Venezuela) (Fr.) Portsmouth DOMINICA
Roseau
B E A N S E A Martinique Passage
Mt. Pelée Ste.-Marie
1397 Le François
Fort-de- Rivière-Pilote
France MARTINIQUE
St. Lucia Channel (Fr.)
Castries
ST. LUCIA
Soufrière
St. Vincent Passage
La Soufrière 1234 ST. VINCENT
Speightstown
Kingstown Bridgetown
& THE BARBADOS
Hillsborough GRENADINES
Grenadines

15 m ft
200 600
2000 6000
4000 12 000
8000 24 000
m ft

Lesser
L e s s e r A n t i l l e s
Aruba
Oranjestad (Neth.)
Curaçao
C. San Román NETH. Bonaire I. Blanquilla (Ven.)
Pta. Gallinas Pen. de Willemstad ANTILLES I. Los Hermanos
Pta. Pen. de I. Las Aves (Ven.)
Pta. de la Espada Paraguaná Punta (Ven.) I. Orchila St. George's GRENADA
Guajira Fijo Puerto Cardón (Ven.) Is. Los Testigos
Ríohacha Uribia Cumarebo La Vela de Coro Is. Los Roques (Ven.) D
SANTA GUAJIRA Coro (Ven.) Tobago
MARTA Cumarebo I. de Margarita Scarborough
ARRAN- Ciénaga San FALCÓN Tucacas La Asunción NUEVA Port of
QUILLA Soledad Rafael Altagracia Tucacas La Guaira Porlamar ESPARTA Spain Galera
LÁNTICO Sabanalarga Sierra Nevada de MARACAIBO Mene de Mauroa Puerto Maracay CARACAS La Tortuga Río Pen. de Paria Point Trinidad
Santa Marta Cabello DISTRITO FEDERAL (Ven.) Carúpano Caribe Arima
Fundación 5800 La Concepción Santa Rita Baragua Giatire C. Codera SUCRE Caripe Río Claro
Calamar Cabimas Carora San Felipe YARACUY Higuerote Cumaná Carúpano G. de Paria San Fernando TRINIDAD
Valledupar Villa del Ciudad CARABOBO VALENCIA Los Teques Río Chico Puerto Caripe & TOBAGO
MAGDALENA Agustín Rosario Ojeda Mene Grande LARA Yaritagua de ARAGUA San Juan Ocumare del Tuy La Cruz Barcelona Caicara Maturín Serpent's Mouth
Plato CÉSAR Codazzi BARQUISIMETO los Morros Villa de Barcelona Maturín
Zambrano Machiques Lago de TRUJILLO Acarigua San Carlos de Cura Aragua de MONAGAS DELTA
ce- Corozal ZULIA Maracaibo El Tocuyo COJEDES Altagracia de Orituco Anaco Caicara Tucupita
jo Sincé Magangué Betijoque Valera El Baúl San Sombrero Aragua de Cantaura AMACURO
San Sahagún El Banco Trujillo PORTUGUESA El Baúl Santa María Barcelona Unare El Tigre
Marcos Mompós Encontrados San Carlos Guanare Portuguesa Calabozo de Ipire El Pao
Planeta NORTE del Zulia GUÁRICO Valle de Los Barrancos
Ayapel Majagual DE MÉRIDA Barinas la Pascua Ciudad Guayana
QBA BOLÍVAR Simití Ocaña Cord. de Mérida Ciudad Pariaguán Soledad Sierra Imataca
Caucasia SANTANDER Santa Bolivia Libertad ANZOÁTEGUI Ciudad Upata
Cúcuta TÁCHIRA Bárbara BARINAS San Fernando Orinoco Bolívar
Bruzual Puerto de Nutrias de Apure Mapire Embalse de Guri Guasipati El Callao
V E N E Z U E L A Achaguas Apure Caicara Caroní Tumeremo

5 West from Greenwich 6 65 7 COPYRIGHT GEORGE PHILIP LTD

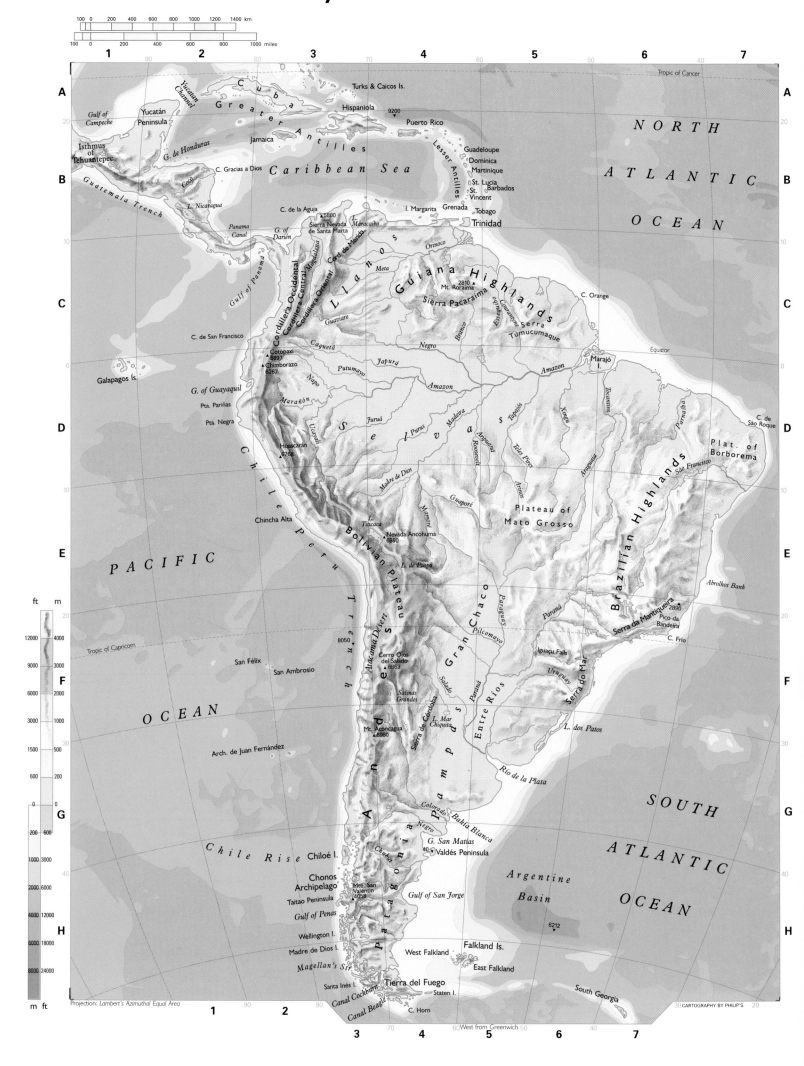

100 0 200 400 600 800 1000 1200 1400 km
100 0 200 400 600 800 1000 miles

1 **2** **3** **4** **5** **6** **7**

A
Tropic of Cancer

NORTH

ATLANTIC

OCEAN

Gulf of
Campeche
Yucatán
Peninsula
Yucatán
Channel
Cuba
Greater
Antilles
Turks & Caicos Is.
Hispaniola
9200
Puerto Rico
Guadeloupe
Dominica
Martinique
St. Lucia
Barbados
St.
Vincent
Grenada
Tobago
Trinidad

B
Isthmus
of
Tehuantepec
G. de Honduras
Jamaica
C. Gracias a Dios
Coco
L. Nicaragua
Guatemala Trench
Caribbean Sea
Lesser
Antilles
I. Margarita

Panama
Canal
C. de la Aguja
Sierra Nevada
de Santa Marta
5800
L.
Maracaibo
Orinoco

C
G. of
Darién
Gulf of Panama
Cordillera Occidental
Cordillera Central
Cordillera Oriental
Crd. de Mérida
Meta
Llanos
Guiana Highlands
Mt. Roraima
2810
C. Orange
Sierra Pacaraima
Serra
Tumucumaque
Caroní
Caura
Ventuari

C. de San Francisco
Guaviare
Caquetá
Negro
Branco
Equator

0
Cotopaxi
5897
Chimborazo
6267
Putumayo
Japurá
Amazon
Marajó
I.
Galapagos Is.
Napo
Amazon
Tocantins

D
G. of Guayaquil
Pta. Pariñas
Pta. Negra
Marañón
Ucayali
Juruá
Purus
Madeira
Roosevelt
Aripuanã
S. Tapajós
Teles Pires
Xingu
Araguaia
Parnaíba
C. de
São Roque
Selvas
Plat. of
Borborema

Huascarán
6768
Madre de Dios
Guaporé
Mamoré
Arinos
São Francisco
Brazilian Highlands

E
Chincha Alta
L.
Titicaca
Nevada Ancohuma
6550
Bolivian Plateau
L. de Poopó
Plateau of
Mato Grosso
Abrolhos Bank

PACIFIC
Chile Peru Trench
Gran Chaco
Paraguay
Paraná
Serra da Mantiqueira
2890
Pico da
Bandeira

F
Tropic of Capricorn
San Félix
San Ambrosio
8050
Atacama Desert
Cerro Ojos
del Salado
6863
Salinas
Grandes
Salado
Pilcomayo
Entre Ríos
Iguaçu Falls
Uruguay
Serra do Mar
C. Frio

OCEAN
Andes

G
Arch. de Juan Fernández
Mt. Aconcagua
6960
Sierra de Córdoba
L. Mar
Chiquita
Pampas
Paraná
Río de la Plata
L. dos Patos

SOUTH

Colorado
Bahía Blanca
Negro
ATLANTIC

H
Chile Rise
Chiloé I.
Chonos
Archipelago
Taitao Peninsula
Gulf of Penas
Wellington I.
Madre de Dios I.
Mte. San
Valentín
4058
Patagonia
Chubut
G. San Matías
40
Valdés Peninsula
Gulf of San Jorge
Argentine
Basin
6212
OCEAN

Magellan's Str.
Santa Inés I.
Canal Cockburn
Tierra del Fuego
Staten I.
Falkland Is.
West Falkland
East Falkland
South Georgia
Canal Beagle
C. Horn

ft m
12000 4000
9000 3000
6000 2000
3000 1000
1500 500
600 200
0 0
200 600
1000 3000
2000 6000
4000 12000
6000 18000
8000 24000
m ft

Projection: Lambert's Azimuthal Equal Area

CARTOGRAPHY BY PHILIP'S.

1 **2** **3** **4** **5** **6** **7**
West from Greenwich

100 0 200 400 600 800 1000 1200 1400 km
100 0 200 400 600 800 1000 miles

1   2   3   4   5   6   7

Tropic of Cancer

A   A

Havana BAHAMAS   Turks & Caicos Is.   *NORTH*
CUBA   (U.K.)
Virgin Is.
HAITI   San Juan   (U.K.)   *ATLANTIC*
JAMAICA Port-au-   PUERTO   ANTIGUA &
Kingston Prince   RICO   BARBUDA
DOMINICAN   (U.S.A.)   ST. KITTS   *OCEAN*
REP.   & NEVIS GUADELOUPE
B   Basse-Terre (Fr.)   B
Caribbean Sea   DOMINICA MARTINIQUE
MEXICO   Fort-de-France (Fr.)
Castries ST. LUCIA
GUATEMALA HONDURAS   ST. VINCENT   BARBADOS
Guatemala Tegucigalpa   Aruba   Kingstown   Bridgetown
San Salvador NICARAGUA   Curaçao GRENADA St. George's
EL SALVADOR   C. de   Port of
Managua   la Aguja Maracaibo   Caracas Spain TRINIDAD &
COSTA San José Barranquilla   Valencia   TOBAGO
Panamá RICA   Cartagena Barquisimeto
Gulf of   PANAMA   Cúcuta San Cristóbal   Ciudad Guayana   Georgetown
Darién   *Orinoco*   Paramaribo
Medellín   Bucaramanga   VENEZUELA   GUYANA   Cayenne
C   SURINAM   C. Orange C
Bogotá   FRENCH
Cali   COLOMBIA   RORAIMA   GUIANA
Magdalena   *Branco* *Essequibo*
AMAPÁ
Galapagos Is.   *Marajó*   Equator
(Ecuador) Quito   *Japurá*   *Amazon* *I.* Belém
ECUADOR   *Napo* *Putumayo*   Santarém
0   Manaus   0
Guayaquil   *Marañón* Iquitos   AMAZONAS   PARÁ *Tocantins* São Luís
G. of Guayaquil   *Tapajós*   Fortaleza
Juruá   *Amazon* *Madeira* *Xingu*   MARANHÃO Teresina   C. de
Chiclayo   CEARÁ São Roque
D   *Purus*   *Parnaíba*   RIO G. Natal D
Trujillo *Ucayali*   Pôrto Velho   PIAUÍ DO NORTE
Chimbote PERU *ACRE*   RONDÔNIA   *Araguaia*   PARAÍBA
Madre de Dios   BRAZIL   TOCANTINS   Campina Grande Recife
Callao LIMA   ALAGOAS PERNAMBUCO Maceió
Mamoré   MATO GROSSO   SERGIPE
Cuzco   BAHÍA   Aracaju
10   L.   GOIÁS   *São Francisco*   Salvador 10
Titicaca   Cuiabá DIS. FED. Brasília
BOLIVIA   Goiânia
Arequipa La Paz Cochabamba   MATO GROSSO   MINAS GERAIS
Sucre   Santa Cruz   DO SUL   Belo
Iquique   Ribeirão Horizonte   ESPÍRITO
E   Prêto   *Paraná* SANTO E
Paraguay   Juiz   Vitória
PARAGUAY   SÃO PAULO de Fora Campos
Antofagasta   *Pilcomayo*   *Paraná* Campinas R. DE J.
Asunción PARANÁ SÃO Niterói
San Miguel   Curitiba PAULO RIO DE
de Tucumán Salta   JANEIRO
F   San Félix Resistencia   SANTA CATARINA   F
(Chile) San Ambrosio   Corrientes *Uruguay*
(Chile)   *Salado*   RIO GRANDE
Córdoba Santa Fe   DO SUL
O C E A N   San Juan Paraná   Pelotas Pôrto Alegre
Arch. de Juan Fernández Mendoza Rosario   URUGUAY
(Chile) Viña del Mar   A Montevideo
Valparaíso   BUENOS AIRES Montevideo *SOUTH*
SANTIAGO   R   La Plata Rio de la Plata
Talca G   *ATLANTIC*
Concepción E   Bahía Mar del Plata
N *Colorado* Blanca   *OCEAN*
G   Valdivia T   G
I *Negro* Viedma
Puerto Montt N
A
Chubut
Comodoro Rivadavia
Gulf of San Jorge
Gulf of Penas
H   H
West Falkland FALKLAND IS.
(U.K.)
Magellan's Str.   Stanley
East Falkland
Punta Arenas Tierra del Fuego   South Georgia
(U.K.)
C. Horn

Tropic of Capricorn

PACIFIC

Projection: Lambert's Azimuthal Equal Area

1   2

■ LIMA Capital Cities

90 80   70   60 West from Greenwich 50   40   30 20

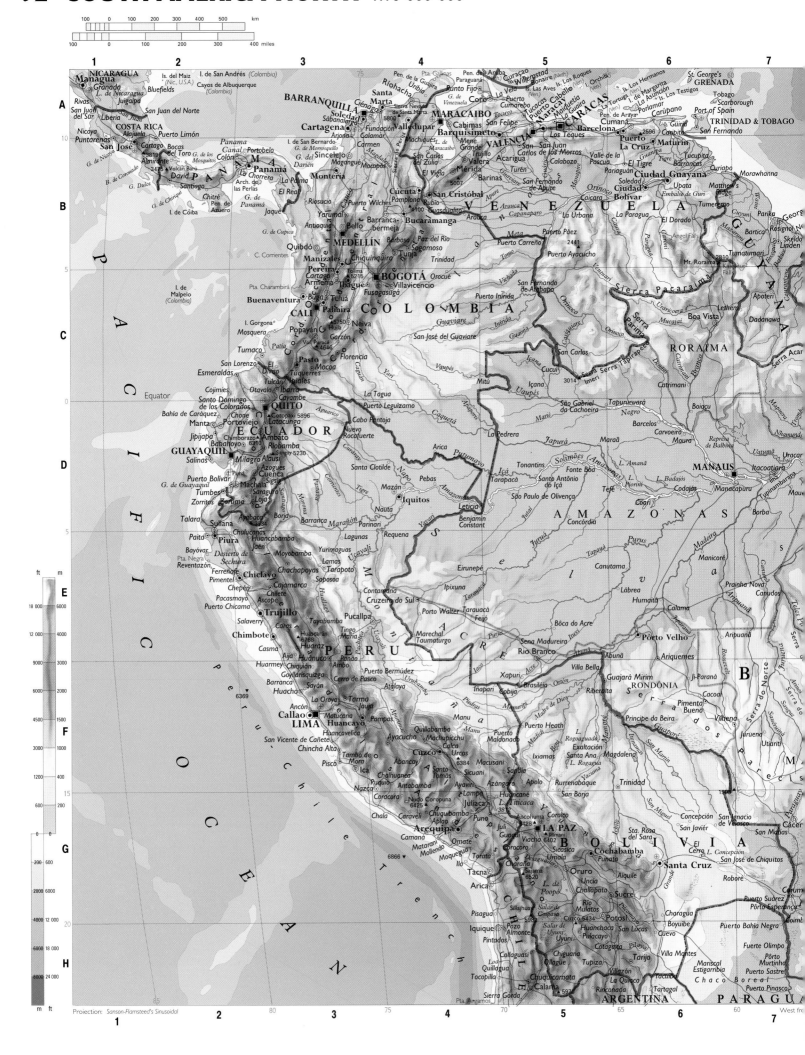

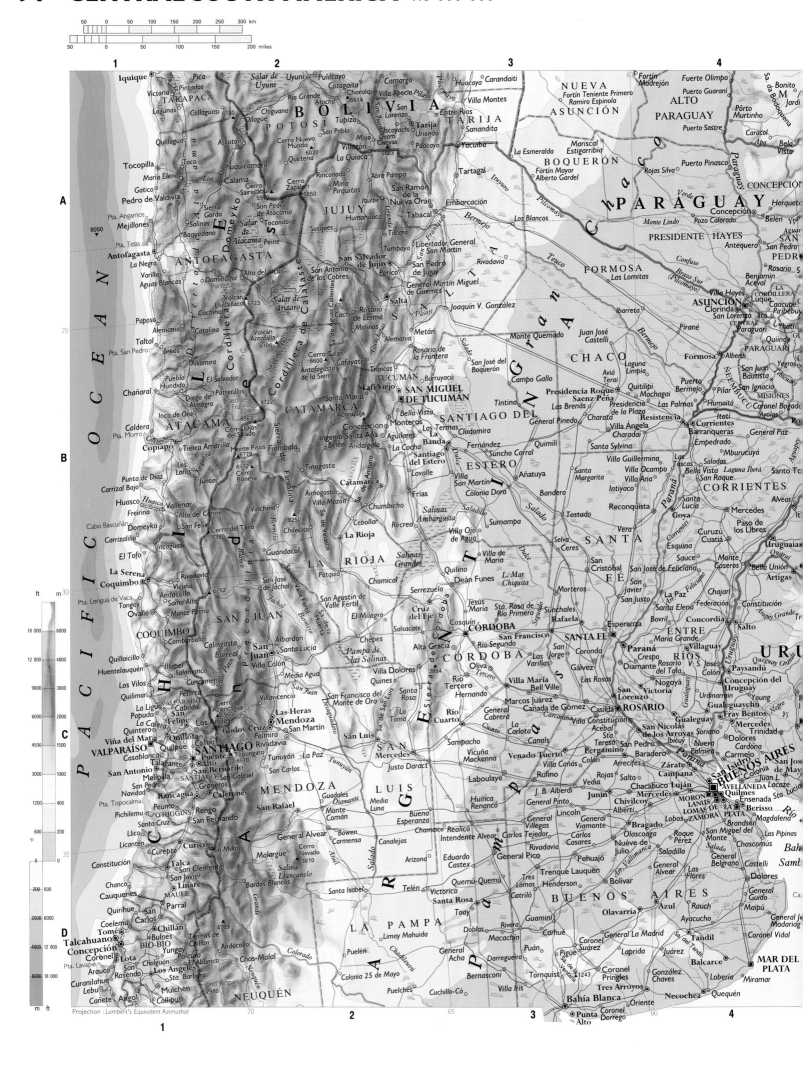

92 93
96

BELO HORIZONTE
Nova Lima
Itabirito

5   6   7

Vitória
Itaquari
Vila Velha
Guarapari

Sidrolândia
Nioaque
Três Lagoas
Andradina
Mirasso
São José do Rio Prêto
Olímpia
Batatais
Passos
Congonhas
Oliveira
Conselheiro
Ouro Prêto
Ponte Nova
Pico da Bandeira 2880
Castelo
Cachoeiro de Itapemirim

TO GROSSO
Xavantina
Mirandópolis
Araçatuba
Catanduva
Bebedouro
São Sebastião do Paraíso
Campo Belo
São João del Rei
Carangola
Alegre

DO SUL
Tiête
Novo
Taquaritinga
Ribeirão
Prêto
Guaxupé
Três
Pontas
Lavras
Barbacena
Cataguases
Muriaé
Itaperuna

Guia Lopes da Laguna
Panorama
Presidente
Epitácio
Birigui
Penápolis
Lins
Jaboticabal
Novo Horizonte
Mococa
Alfenas
Pouso Alegre
Dumont
Leopoldina
Cambuci
Guarus

Maracaju
Nova Alvorada do Sul
Adamantina
Tupã
Bauru
Garça
Barin
Poços de Caldas
Varginha
Três Corações
Juiz de Fora
Três Rios
Paraíba do Sul
CAMPOS

Dourados
Ivinhema
Presidente Prudente
Marília
Jaú
Rio Claro
Araras
Ouro Fino
Itajubá
Volta Redonda
Barra do Pirai
Nova Friburgo
Cabo de São Tomé

Ponta Porã
Pedro Juan Caballero
Euclides da Cunha Paulista
Rancharia
Assis
Piracicaba
CAMPINAS
Americana
Serra
Cruzeiro
Mansa
Barra
Macaé

Navirai
Esperança
Rolândia
Cambará
Ourinhos
Avaré
Botucatu
Itu
Bragança Paulista
Guaratinguetá
RIO DE JANEIRO

Mundo Novo
Paranavaí
Londrina
Sertanópolis
Jacarèzinho
Tatui
Sorocaba
Moji das Cruzes
NOVA IGUAÇU
DUQUE DE CAXIAS
SÃO GONÇALO

Umuarama
Cianorte
Apucarana
Joaquim Távora
Itaporanga
SÃO PAULO
São José dos
Jacarei
NITERÓI

Maringá
Arapongas
Mandaguari
Ibaiti
Itapeva
SANTO ANDRÉ
São Bernardo do Campo
Angra dos Reis
Cabo Frio

Cruzeiro do Oeste
Goio-Erê
Campo Mourão
Itararé
Paranapiacaba
SANTOS
Ilha Grande
Tropic of Capricorn

BRAZIL
PARANÁ
Cândido de Abreu
Tibagi
Juquiá
São Vicente
Guarujá
Itanhaém
Ilha de São Sebastião

Foz do Iguaçu
Prudentópolis
Ponta Grossa
Castro
Registro
Iguape

Ciudad del Este
Guarapuava
Palmeira
Ilha Comprida

PARANA
Irati
CURITIBA
Antonina
Ilha do Cardoso   25

Francisco Beltrão
Pato Branco
União da Vitória
Lapa
Paranaguá
Matinhos
Guaratuba

Palmas
São Mateus do Sul
Rio Negro
Joinville

MISIONES
Xanxerê
Chapecó
Pôrto União
Mafra
São Francisco do Sul

Caçador
Blumenau
Itajaí

SANTA CATARINA
Santa Cecília
Brusque

Erechim
Curitibanos
Rio do Sul

Lajes
São José
Ilha de Santa Catarina
Florianópolis

RIO GRANDE
Vacaria
Laguna
Cabo Santa Marta Grande

Caxías do Sul
Tubarão
Criciúma

Santa Maria
Bento Gonçalves
Araranguá
Torres

DO SUL
Nôvo Hamburgo
São Leopoldo
Osorio

PÔRTO ALEGRE
Viamão

ATLANTIC
Lagoa dos Patos

UAY
Pelotas
Rio Grande
São José do Norte

OCEAN

West from Greenwich   6   45   7   40   COPYRIGHT GEORGE PHILIP LTD

5

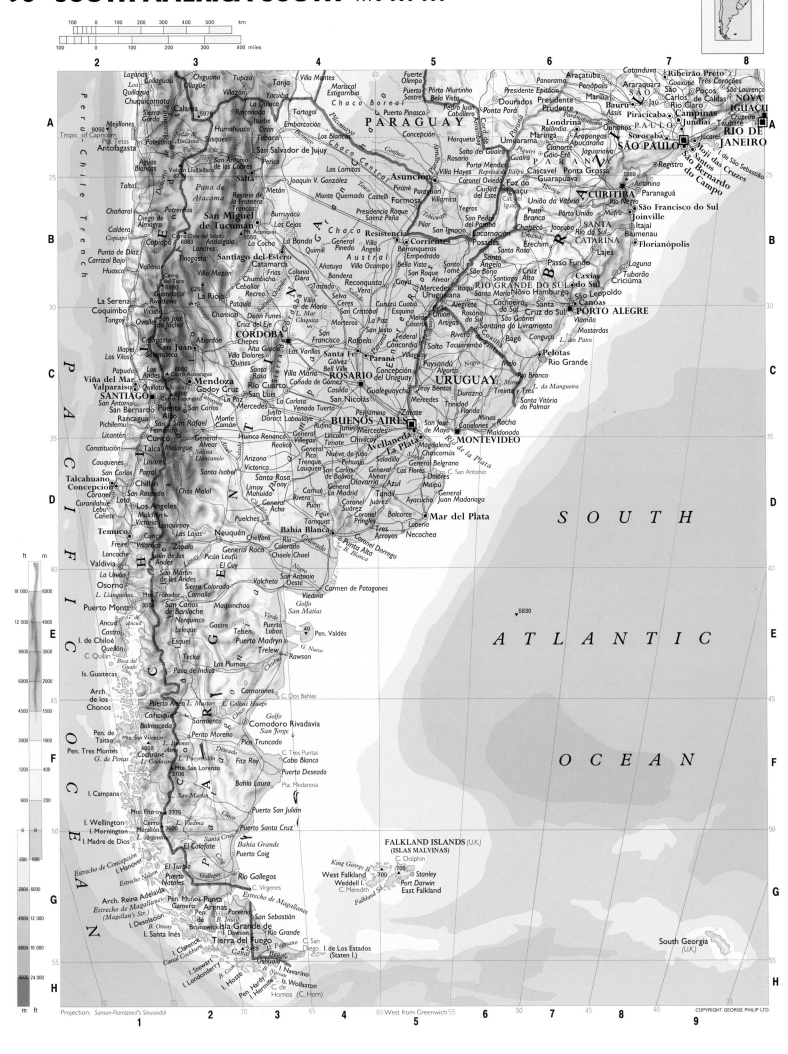

PARAGUAY

BRAZIL

SÃO PAULO

RIO DE JANEIRO

CURITIBA

SANTA CATARINA

RIO GRANDE DO SUL

PORTO ALEGRE

URUGUAY

MONTEVIDEO

CÓRDOBA

ROSARIO

BUENOS AIRES

Mar del Plata

Bahía Blanca

SANTIAGO

Valparaíso

Mendoza

Talcahuano
Concepción

S O U T H

A T L A N T I C

O C E A N

FALKLAND ISLANDS (U.K.)
(ISLAS MALVINAS)
West Falkland
East Falkland
Stanley
Port Darwin

South Georgia
(U.K.)

P A C I F I C   O C E A N

Tierra del Fuego

Projection: Sanson-Flamsteed's Sinusoidal

West from Greenwich

COPYRIGHT GEORGE PHILIP LTD.

INDEX

The index contains the names of all the principal places and features shown on the World Maps. Each name is followed by an additional entry in italics giving the country or region within which it is located. The alphabetical order of names composed of two or more words is governed primarily by the first word and then by the second. This is an example of the rule:

Mīr Kūh, *Iran*	**45 E8**	26 22N	58 55 E
Mīr Shahdād, *Iran*	**45 E8**	26 15N	58 29 E
Mira, *Italy*	**20 B5**	45 26N	12 8 E
Mira por vos Cay, *Bahamas* .	**89 B5**	22 9N	74 30W
Miraj, *India*	**40 L9**	16 50N	74 45 E

Physical features composed of a proper name (Erie) and a description (Lake) are positioned alphabetically by the proper name. The description is positioned after the proper name and is usually abbreviated:

Erie, L., *N. Amer.*	**78 D4**	42 15N	81 0W

Where a description forms part of a settlement or administrative name however, it is always written in full and put in its true alphabetic position:

Mount Morris, *U.S.A.*	**78 D7**	42 44N	77 52W

Names beginning with M' and Mc are indexed as if they were spelled Mac. Names beginning St. are alphabetised under Saint, but Sankt, Sint, Sant', Santa and San are all spelt in full and are alphabetised accordingly. If the same place name occurs twice or more times in the index and all are in the same country, each is followed by the name of the administrative subdivision in which it is located. The names are placed in the alphabetical order of the subdivisions. For example:

Jackson, *Ky., U.S.A.*	**76 G4**	37 33N	83 23W
Jackson, *Mich., U.S.A.*	**76 D3**	42 15N	84 24W
Jackson, *Minn., U.S.A.*	**80 D7**	43 37N	95 1W

The number in bold type which follows each name in the index refers to the number of the map page where that feature or place will be found. This is usually the largest scale at which the place or feature appears.

The letter and figure which are in bold type immediately after the page number give the grid square on the map page, within which the feature is situated. The letter represents the latitude and the figure the longitude.

In some cases the feature itself may fall within the specified square, while the name is outside. This is usually the case only with features which are larger than a grid square.

For a more precise location the geographical coordinates which follow the letter/figure references give the latitude and the longitude of each place. The first set of figures represent the latitude which is the distance north or south of the Equator measured as an angle at the centre of the earth. The Equator is latitude 0°, the North Pole is 90°N, and the South Pole 90°S.

The second set of figures represent the longitude, which is the distance East or West of the prime meridian, which runs through Greenwich, England. Longitude is also measured as an angle at the centre of the earth and is given East or West of the prime meridian, from 0° to 180° in either direction.

The unit of measurement for latitude and longitude is the degree, which is subdivided into 60 minutes. Each index entry states the position of a place in degrees and minutes, a space being left between the degrees and the minutes.

The latitude is followed by N(orth) or S(outh) and the longitude by E(ast) or W(est).

Rivers are indexed to their mouths or confluences, and carry the symbol ⇀ after their names. A solid square ■ follows the name of a country, while an open square □ refers to a first order administrative area.

Abbreviations used in the index

A.C.T. – Australian Capital Territory
Afghan. – Afghanistan
Ala. – Alabama
Alta. – Alberta
Amer. – America(n)
Arch. – Archipelago
Ariz. – Arizona
Ark. – Arkansas
Atl. Oc. – Atlantic Ocean
B. – Baie, Bahía, Bay, Bucht, Bugt
B.C. – British Columbia
Bangla. – Bangladesh
Barr. – Barrage
Bos.-H. – Bosnia-Herzegovina
C. – Cabo, Cap, Cape, Coast
C.A.R. – Central African Republic
C. Prov. – Cape Province
Calif. – California
Cent. – Central
Chan. – Channel
Colo. – Colorado
Conn. – Connecticut
Cord. – Cordillera
Cr. – Creek
Czech. – Czech Republic
D.C. – District of Columbia
Del. – Delaware
Dep. – Dependency
Des. – Desert
Dist. – District
Dj. – Djebel
Domin. – Dominica
Dom. Rep. – Dominican Republic
E. – East

E. Salv. – El Salvador
Eq. Guin. – Equatorial Guinea
Fla. – Florida
Falk. Is. – Falkland Is.
G. – Golfe, Golfo, Gulf, Guba, Gebel
Ga. – Georgia
Gt. – Great, Greater
Guinea-Biss. – Guinea-Bissau
H.K. – Hong Kong
H.P. – Himachal Pradesh
Hants. – Hampshire
Harb. – Harbor, Harbour
Hd. – Head
Hts. – Heights
I.(s). – Île, Ilha, Insel, Isla, Island, Isle
Ill. – Illinois
Ind. – Indiana
Ind. Oc. – Indian Ocean
Ivory C. – Ivory Coast
J. – Jabal, Jebel, Jazira
Junc. – Junction
K. – Kap, Kapp
Kans. – Kansas
Kep. – Kepulauan
Ky. – Kentucky
L. – Lac, Lacul, Lago, Lagoa, Lake, Limni, Loch, Lough
La. – Louisiana
Liech. – Liechtenstein
Lux. – Luxembourg
Mad. P. – Madhya Pradesh
Madag. – Madagascar
Man. – Manitoba
Mass. – Massachusetts

Md. – Maryland
Me. – Maine
Medit. S. – Mediterranean Sea
Mich. – Michigan
Minn. – Minnesota
Miss. – Mississippi
Mo. – Missouri
Mont. – Montana
Mozam. – Mozambique
Mt.(e) – Mont, Monte, Monti, Montaña, Mountain
N. – Nord, Norte, North, Northern, Nouveau
N.B. – New Brunswick
N.C. – North Carolina
N. Cal. – New Caledonia
N. Dak. – North Dakota
N.H. – New Hampshire
N.I. – North Island
N.J. – New Jersey
N. Mex. – New Mexico
N.S. – Nova Scotia
N.S.W. – New South Wales
N.W.T. – North West Territory
N.Y. – New York
N.Z. – New Zealand
Nebr. – Nebraska
Neths. – Netherlands
Nev. – Nevada
Nfld. – Newfoundland
Nic. – Nicaragua
O. – Oued, Ouadi
Occ. – Occidentale
Okla. – Oklahoma
Ont. – Ontario
Or. – Orientale

Oreg. – Oregon
Os. – Ostrov
Oz. – Ozero
P. – Pass, Passo, Pasul, Pulau
P.E.I. – Prince Edward Island
Pa. – Pennsylvania
Pac. Oc. – Pacific Ocean
Papua N.G. – Papua New Guinea
Pass. – Passage
Pen. – Peninsula, Péninsule
Phil. – Philippines
Pk. – Park, Peak
Plat. – Plateau
Prov. – Province, Provincial
Pt. – Point
Pta. – Ponta, Punta
Pte. – Pointe
Qué. – Québec
Queens. – Queensland
R. – Rio, River
R.I. – Rhode Island
Ra.(s). – Range(s)
Raj. – Rajasthan
Reg. – Region
Rep. – Republic
Res. – Reserve, Reservoir
S. – San, South, Sea
Si. Arabia – Saudi Arabia
S.C. – South Carolina
S. Dak. – South Dakota
S.I. – South Island
S. Leone – Sierra Leone
Sa. – Serra, Sierra
Sask. – Saskatchewan
Scot. – Scotland
Sd. – Sound

Sev. – Severnaya
Sib. – Siberia
Sprs. – Springs
St. – Saint
Sta. – Santa, Station
Ste. – Sainte
Sto. – Santo
Str. – Strait, Stretto
Switz. – Switzerland
Tas. – Tasmania
Tenn. – Tennessee
Tex. – Texas
Tg. – Tanjung
Trin. & Tob. – Trinidad & Tobago
U.A.E. – United Arab Emirates
U.K. – United Kingdom
U.S.A. – United States of America
Ut. P. – Uttar Pradesh
Va. – Virginia
Vdkhr. – Vodokhranilishche
Vf. – Vîrful
Vic. – Victoria
Vol. – Volcano
Vt. – Vermont
W. – Wadi, West
W. Va. – West Virginia
Wash. – Washington
Wis. – Wisconsin
Wlkp. – Wielkopolski
Wyo. – Wyoming
Yorks. – Yorkshire
Yug. – Yugoslavia

A Coruña

A

A Coruña, Spain 19 A1 43 20N 8 25W
A Estrada, Spain 19 A1 42 43N 8 27W
A Fonsagrada, Spain 19 A2 43 8N 7 4W
Aachen, Germany 16 C4 50 45N 6 6 E
Aalborg = Ålborg, Denmark 9 H13 57 2N 9 54 E
Aalen, Germany 16 D6 48 51N 10 6 E
Aalst, Belgium 15 D4 50 56N 4 2 E
Aalten, Neths. 15 C6 51 56N 6 35 E
Aalter, Belgium 15 C3 51 5N 3 28 E
Äänekoski, Finland 9 E21 62 36N 25 44 E
Aarau, Switz. 18 C8 47 23N 8 4 E
Aare →, Switz. 18 C8 47 33N 8 14 E
Aarhus = Århus, Denmark 9 H14 56 8N 10 11 E
Aarschot, Belgium 15 D4 50 59N 4 49 E
Aba, Dem. Rep. of the Congo 54 B3 3 58N 30 17 E
Aba, Nigeria 50 G7 5 10N 7 19 E
Ābādān, Iran 45 D6 30 22N 48 20 E
Ābādeh, Iran 45 D7 31 8N 52 40 E
Abadla, Algeria 50 B5 31 2N 2 45W
Abaetetuba, Brazil 93 D9 1 40S 48 50W
Abagnar Qi, China 34 C9 43 52N 116 2 E
Abai, Paraguay 95 B4 25 58S 55 54W
Abakan, Russia 27 D10 53 40N 91 10 E
Abancay, Peru 92 F4 13 35S 72 55W
Abariringa, Kiribati 64 H10 2 50S 171 40W
Abarqū, Iran 45 D7 31 10N 53 20 E
Abashiri, Japan 30 B12 44 0N 144 15 E
Abashiri-Wan, Japan 30 C12 44 0N 144 30 E
Ābay = Nîl el Azraq →, Sudan 51 E12 15 38N 32 31 E
Abay, Kazakstan 26 E8 49 38N 72 53 E
Abaya, L., Ethiopia 46 F2 6 30N 37 50 E
Abaza, Russia 26 D9 52 39N 90 6 E
'Abbāsābād, Iran 45 C8 33 34N 58 23 E
Abbay = Nîl el Azraq →, Sudan 51 E12 15 38N 32 31 E
Abbaye, Pt., U.S.A. 76 B1 46 58N 88 8W
Abbé, L., Ethiopia 46 E3 11 8N 41 47 E
Abbeville, France 18 A4 50 6N 1 49 E
Abbeville, Ala., U.S.A. 77 K3 31 34N 85 15W
Abbeville, La., U.S.A. 81 L8 29 58N 92 8W
Abbeville, S.C., U.S.A. 77 H4 34 11N 82 23W
Abbot Ice Shelf, Antarctica 5 D16 73 0S 92 0W
Abbottabad, Pakistan 42 B5 34 10N 73 15 E
Abd al Kūrī, Yemen 46 E5 12 5N 52 20 E
Ābdar, Iran 45 D7 30 16N 55 19 E
'Abdolābād, Iran 45 C8 34 12N 56 30 E
Abdulpur, Bangla. 43 G13 24 15N 88 59 E
Abéché, Chad 51 F10 13 50N 20 35 E
Abengourou, Ivory C. 50 G5 6 42N 3 27W
Åbenrå, Denmark 9 J13 55 3N 9 25 E
Abeokuta, Nigeria 50 G6 7 3N 3 19 E
Aber, Uganda 54 B3 2 12N 32 25 E
Aberaeron, U.K. 11 E3 52 15N 4 15W
Aberayron = Aberaeron, U.K. 11 E3 52 15N 4 15W
Aberchirder, U.K. 12 D6 57 34N 2 37W
Abercorn = Mbala, Zambia 55 D3 8 46S 31 24 E
Abercorn, Australia 63 D5 25 12S 151 5 E
Aberdare, U.K. 11 F4 51 43N 3 27W
Aberdare Ra., Kenya 54 C4 0 15S 36 50 E
Aberdeen, Australia 63 E5 32 9S 150 56 E
Aberdeen, Canada 73 C7 52 20N 106 8W
Aberdeen, S. Africa 56 E3 32 28S 24 2 E
Aberdeen, U.K. 12 D6 57 9N 2 5W
Aberdeen, Ala., U.S.A. 77 J1 33 49N 88 33W
Aberdeen, Idaho, U.S.A. 82 E7 42 57N 112 50W
Aberdeen, Md., U.S.A. 76 F7 39 31N 76 10W
Aberdeen, S. Dak., U.S.A. 80 C5 45 28N 98 29W
Aberdeen, Wash., U.S.A. 84 D3 46 59N 123 50W
Aberdeen, City of □, U.K. 12 D6 57 10N 2 10W
Aberdeenshire □, U.K. 12 D6 57 17N 2 36W
Aberdovey = Aberdyfi, U.K. 11 E3 52 33N 4 3W
Aberdyfi, U.K. 11 E3 52 33N 4 3W
Aberfeldy, U.K. 12 E5 56 37N 3 51W
Abergavenny, U.K. 11 F4 51 49N 3 1W
Abergele, U.K. 10 D4 53 17N 3 35W
Abernathy, U.S.A. 81 J4 33 50N 101 51W
Abert, L., U.S.A. 82 E3 42 38N 120 14W
Aberystwyth, U.K. 11 E3 52 25N 4 5W
Abhā, Si. Arabia 46 D3 18 0N 42 34 E
Abhar, Iran 45 B6 36 9N 49 13 E
Abhayapuri, India 43 F14 26 24N 90 38 E
Abidjan, Ivory C. 50 G5 5 26N 3 58W
Abilene, Kans., U.S.A. 80 F6 38 55N 97 13W
Abilene, Tex., U.S.A. 81 J5 32 28N 99 43W
Abingdon, U.K. 11 F6 51 40N 1 17W
Abingdon, U.S.A. 77 G5 36 43N 81 59W
Abington Reef, Australia 62 B4 18 0S 149 35 E
Abitau →, Canada 73 B7 59 53N 109 3W
Abitibi →, Canada 70 B3 51 3N 80 55W
Abitibi, L., Canada 70 C4 48 40N 79 40W
Abkhaz Republic = Abkhazia □, Georgia 25 F7 43 12N 41 5 E
Abkhazia □, Georgia 25 F7 43 12N 41 5 E
Abminga, Australia 63 D1 26 8S 134 51 E
Åbo = Turku, Finland 9 F20 60 30N 22 19 E
Abohar, India 42 D6 30 10N 74 10 E
Abomey, Benin 50 G6 7 10N 2 5 E
Abong-Mbang, Cameroon 52 D2 4 0N 13 8 E
Abou-Deïa, Chad 51 F9 11 20N 19 20 E
Aboyne, U.K. 12 D6 57 4N 2 47W
Abra Pampa, Argentina 94 A2 22 43S 65 42W
Abraham L., Canada 72 C5 52 15N 116 35W
Abreojos, Pta., Mexico 86 B2 26 50N 113 40W
Abrud, Romania 17 E12 46 19N 23 5 E
Absaroka Range, U.S.A. 82 D9 44 45N 109 50W
Abu, India 42 G5 24 41N 72 50 E
Abū al Abyad, U.A.E. 45 E7 24 11N 53 50 E
Abū al Khaşīb, Iraq 45 D6 30 25N 48 0 E
Abū 'Alī, Si. Arabia 45 E6 27 20N 49 27 E
Abū 'Alī →, Lebanon 47 A4 34 25N 35 50 E
Abu Dhabi = Abū Ẓāby, U.A.E. 46 C5 24 28N 54 22 E
Abū Du'ān, Syria 44 B3 36 25N 38 15 E
Abu el Gairi, W. →, Egypt 47 F2 29 35N 33 30 E
Abu Ga'da, W. →, Egypt 47 F1 29 15N 32 53 E
Abū Ḩadrīyah, Si. Arabia 45 E6 27 20N 48 58 E
Abu Hamed, Sudan 51 E12 19 32N 33 13 E
Abū Kamāl, Syria 44 C4 34 30N 41 0 E
Abū Madd, Ra's, Si. Arabia 44 E3 24 50N 37 7 E
Abū Mūsā, U.A.E. 45 E7 25 52N 55 3 E
Abū Qaşr, Si. Arabia 44 D3 30 21N 38 34 E
Abu Şafāt, W. →, Jordan 47 E5 30 24N 36 7 E
Abu Simbel, Egypt 51 D12 22 18N 31 40 E
Abū Şukhayr, Iraq 44 D5 31 54N 44 30 E
Abu Zabad, Sudan 51 F11 12 25N 29 10 E
Abū Ẓāby, U.A.E. 46 C5 24 28N 54 22 E
Abū Zeydābād, Iran 45 C6 33 54N 51 45 E
Abuja, Nigeria 50 G7 9 5N 7 32 E
Abukuma-Gawa →, Japan 30 E10 38 6N 140 52 E
Abukuma-Sammyaku, Japan 30 F10 37 30N 140 45 E
Abunã, Brazil 92 E5 9 40S 65 20W
Abunã →, Brazil 92 E5 9 41S 65 20W
Aburo, Dem. Rep. of the Congo 54 B3 2 4N 30 53 E
Abut Hd., N.Z. 59 K3 43 7S 170 15 E
Acadia Nat. Park, U.S.A. 77 C11 44 20N 68 13W
Açailândia, Brazil 93 D9 4 57S 47 0W
Acajutla, El Salv. 88 D2 13 36N 89 50W
Acámbaro, Mexico 86 D4 20 0N 100 40W
Acaponeta, Mexico 86 C3 22 30N 105 20W
Acapulco, Mexico 87 D5 16 51N 99 56W
Acarai, Serra, Brazil 92 C7 1 50N 57 50W
Acarigua, Venezuela 92 B5 9 33N 69 12W
Acatlán, Mexico 87 D5 18 10N 98 3W
Acayucan, Mexico 87 D6 17 59N 94 58W
Accomac, U.S.A. 76 G8 37 43N 75 40W
Accra, Ghana 50 G5 5 35N 0 6W
Accrington, U.K. 10 D5 53 45N 2 22W
Acebal, Argentina 94 C3 33 20S 60 50W
Aceh □, Indonesia 36 D1 4 15N 97 30 E
Achalpur, India 40 J10 21 22N 77 32 E
Acheng, China 35 B14 45 30N 126 58 E
Acher, India 42 H5 23 10N 72 32 E
Achill Hd., Ireland 13 C1 53 58N 10 15W
Achill I., Ireland 13 C1 53 58N 10 1W
Achinsk, Russia 27 D10 56 20N 90 20 E
Acireale, Italy 20 F6 37 37N 15 10 E
Ackerman, U.S.A. 81 J10 33 19N 89 11W
Acklins I., Bahamas 89 B5 22 30N 74 0W
Acme, Canada 72 C6 51 33N 113 30W
Acme, U.S.A. 78 F5 40 8N 79 26W
Aconcagua, Cerro, Argentina 94 C2 32 39S 70 0W
Aconquija, Mt., Argentina 94 B2 27 0S 66 0W
Açores, Is. dos, Atl. Oc. 50 A1 38 0N 27 0W
Acornhoek, S. Africa 57 C5 24 37S 31 2 E
Acraman, L., Australia 63 E2 32 2S 135 23 E
Acre = 'Akko, Israel 47 C4 32 55N 35 4 E
Acre □, Brazil 92 E4 9 1S 71 0W
Acre →, Brazil 92 E5 8 45S 67 22W
Acton, Canada 78 C4 43 38N 80 3W
Acuña, Mexico 86 B4 29 18N 100 55W
Ad Dammām, Si. Arabia 45 E6 26 20N 50 5 E
Ad Dāmūr, Lebanon 47 B4 33 44N 35 27 E
Ad Dawādimī, Si. Arabia 44 E5 24 35N 44 15 E
Ad Dawḩah, Qatar 46 B5 25 15N 51 35 E
Ad Dawr, Iraq 44 C4 34 27N 43 47 E
Ad Dir'īyah, Si. Arabia 44 E5 24 44N 46 35 E
Ad Dīwānīyah, Iraq 44 D5 32 0N 45 0 E
Ad Dujayl, Iraq 44 C5 33 51N 44 14 E
Ad Duwayd, Si. Arabia 44 D4 30 15N 42 17 E
Ada, Minn., U.S.A. 80 B6 47 18N 96 31W
Ada, Okla., U.S.A. 81 H6 34 46N 96 41W
Adabiya, Egypt 47 F1 29 53N 32 28 E
Adair, C., Canada 69 A12 71 31N 71 24W
Adaja →, Spain 19 B3 41 32N 4 52W
Adak I., U.S.A. 68 C2 51 45N 176 45W
Adamaoua, Massif de l', Cameroon 51 G7 7 20N 12 20 E
Adamawa Highlands = Adamaoua, Massif de l', Cameroon 51 G7 7 20N 12 20 E
Adamello, Mte., Italy 18 C9 46 9N 10 30 E
Adaminaby, Australia 63 F4 36 0S 148 45 E
Adams, Mass., U.S.A. 79 D11 42 38N 73 7W
Adams, N.Y., U.S.A. 79 C8 43 49N 76 1W
Adams, Wis., U.S.A. 80 D10 43 57N 89 49W
Adam's Bridge, Sri Lanka 40 Q11 9 15N 79 40 E
Adams L., Canada 72 C5 51 10N 119 40W
Adams Mt., U.S.A. 84 D5 46 12N 121 30W
Adam's Peak, Sri Lanka 40 R12 6 48N 80 30 E
Adana, Turkey 25 G6 37 0N 35 16 E
Adapazarı = Sakarya, Turkey 25 F5 40 48N 30 25 E
Adarama, Sudan 51 E12 17 10N 34 52 E
Adare, C., Antarctica 5 D11 71 0S 171 0 E
Adaut, Indonesia 37 F8 8 8S 131 7 E
Adavale, Australia 63 D3 25 52S 144 32 E
Adda →, Italy 18 D8 45 8N 9 53 E
Addis Ababa = Addis Abeba, Ethiopia 46 F2 9 2N 38 42 E
Addis Abeba, Ethiopia 46 F2 9 2N 38 42 E
Addison, U.S.A. 78 D7 42 1N 77 14W
Addo, S. Africa 56 E4 33 32S 25 45 E
Ādeh, Iran 44 B5 37 42N 45 11 E
Adel, U.S.A. 77 K4 31 8N 83 25W
Adelaide, Australia 63 E2 34 52S 138 30 E
Adelaide, Bahamas 88 A4 25 4N 77 31W
Adelaide, S. Africa 56 E4 32 42S 26 20 E
Adelaide I., Antarctica 5 C17 67 15S 68 30W
Adelaide Pen., Canada 68 B10 68 15N 97 30W
Adelaide River, Australia 60 B5 13 15S 131 7 E
Adelanto, U.S.A. 85 L9 34 35N 117 22W
Adele I., Australia 60 C3 15 32S 123 9 E
Adélie, Terre, Antarctica 5 C10 68 0S 140 0 E
Adélie Land = Adélie, Terre, Antarctica 5 C10 68 0S 140 0 E
Aden = Al 'Adan, Yemen 46 E4 12 45N 45 0 E
Aden, G. of, Asia 46 E4 12 30N 47 30 E
Adendorp, S. Africa 56 E3 32 15S 24 30 E
Adh Dhayd, U.A.E. 45 E7 25 17N 55 53 E
Adhoi, India 42 H4 23 26N 70 32 E
Adi, Indonesia 37 E8 4 15S 133 30 E
Adieu, C., Australia 61 F5 32 0S 132 10 E
Adieu Pt., Australia 60 C3 15 14S 124 35 E
Adige →, Italy 20 B5 45 9N 12 20 E
Adigrat, Ethiopia 46 E2 14 20N 39 26 E
Adilabad, India 40 K11 19 33N 78 20 E
Adirondack Mts., U.S.A. 79 C10 44 0N 74 0W
Adjumani, Uganda 54 B3 3 20N 31 50 E
Adlavik Is., Canada 71 B8 55 0N 58 40W
Admiralty G., Australia 60 B4 14 20S 125 55 E
Admiralty I., U.S.A. 72 B2 57 30N 134 30W
Admiralty Is., Papua N. G. 64 H6 2 0S 147 0 E
Adonara, Indonesia 37 F6 8 15S 123 5 E
Adoni, India 40 M10 15 33N 77 18 E
Adour →, France 18 E3 43 32N 1 32W
Adra, India 43 H12 23 30N 86 42 E
Adra, Spain 19 D4 36 43N 3 3W
Adrano, Italy 20 F6 37 40N 14 50 E
Adrar, Mauritania 50 D3 20 30N 7 30 E
Adrar des Iforas, Algeria 50 C5 27 51N 0 11 E
Adrian, Mich., U.S.A. 76 E3 41 54N 84 2W
Adrian, Tex., U.S.A. 81 H3 35 16N 102 40W
Adriatic Sea, Medit. S. 20 C6 43 0N 16 0 E
Adua, Indonesia 37 E7 1 45S 129 50 E
Adwa, Ethiopia 46 E2 14 15N 38 52 E
Adygea □, Russia 25 F7 45 0N 40 0 E
Adzhar Republic = Ajaria □, Georgia 25 F7 41 30N 42 0 E
Adzopé, Ivory C. 50 G5 6 7N 3 49W
Ægean Sea, Medit. S. 21 E11 38 30N 25 0 E
Aerhtai Shan, Mongolia 32 B4 46 40N 92 45 E
'Afak, Iraq 44 C5 32 4N 45 15 E
Afándou, Greece 23 C10 36 18N 28 12 E
Afghanistan ■, Asia 40 C4 33 0N 65 0 E
Aflou, Algeria 50 B6 34 7N 2 3 E
Africa 48 E6 10 0N 20 0 E
'Afrīn, Syria 44 B3 36 32N 36 50 E
Afton, N.Y., U.S.A. 79 D9 42 14N 75 32W
Afton, Wyo., U.S.A. 82 E8 42 44N 110 56W
Afuá, Brazil 93 D8 0 15S 50 20W
'Afula, Israel 47 C4 32 37N 35 17 E
Afyon, Turkey 25 G5 38 45N 30 33 E
Afyonkarahisar = Afyon, Turkey 25 G5 38 45N 30 33 E
Agadès = Agadez, Niger 50 E7 16 58N 7 59 E
Agadez, Niger 50 E7 16 58N 7 59 E
Agadir, Morocco 50 B4 30 28N 9 55W
Agaete, Canary Is. 22 F4 28 6N 15 43W
Agar, India 42 H7 23 40N 76 2 E
Agartala, India 41 H17 23 50N 91 23 E
Agassiz, Canada 72 D4 49 14N 121 46W
Agats, Indonesia 37 F9 5 33S 138 0 E
Agawam, U.S.A. 79 D12 42 5N 72 37W
Agboville, Ivory C. 50 G5 5 55N 4 15W
Ağdam, Azerbaijan 44 B5 40 0N 46 58 E
Agde, France 18 E5 43 19N 3 28 E
Agen, France 18 D4 44 12N 0 38 E
Āgh Kand, Iran 45 B6 37 15N 48 4 E
Aginskoye, Russia 27 D12 51 6N 114 32 E
Agnew, Australia 61 E3 28 1S 120 31 E
Agori, India 43 G10 24 33N 82 57 E
Agra, India 42 F7 27 17N 77 58 E
Ağri, Turkey 25 G7 39 44N 43 3 E
Agri →, Italy 20 D7 40 13N 16 44 E
Ağrı Dağı, Turkey 25 G7 39 50N 44 15 E
Ağri Karakose = Ağri, Turkey 25 G7 39 44N 43 3 E
Agrigento, Italy 20 F5 37 19N 13 34 E
Agrinion, Greece 21 E9 38 37N 21 27 E
Agua Caliente, Baja Calif., Mexico 85 N10 32 29N 116 59W
Agua Caliente, Sinaloa, Mexico 86 B3 26 30N 108 20W
Agua Caliente Springs, U.S.A. 85 N10 32 56N 116 19W
Água Clara, Brazil 93 H8 20 25S 52 45W
Agua Hechicero, Mexico 85 N10 32 26N 116 14W
Agua Prieta, Mexico 86 A3 31 20N 109 32W
Aguadilla, Puerto Rico 89 C6 18 26N 67 10W
Aguadulce, Panama 88 E3 8 15N 80 32W
Aguanga, U.S.A. 85 M10 33 27N 116 51W
Aguanish, Canada 71 B7 50 14N 62 2W
Aguanus →, Canada 71 B7 50 13N 62 5W
Aguapey →, Argentina 94 B4 29 7S 56 36W
Aguaray Guazú →, Paraguay 94 A4 24 47S 57 19W
Aguarico →, Ecuador 92 D3 0 59S 75 11W
Aguas Blancas, Chile 94 A2 24 15S 69 55W
Aguas Calientes, Sierra de, Argentina 94 B2 25 26S 66 40W
Aguascalientes, Mexico 86 C4 21 53N 102 12W
Aguascalientes □, Mexico 86 C4 22 0N 102 20W
Aguilares, Argentina 94 B2 27 26S 65 35W
Aguilas, Spain 19 D5 37 23N 1 35W
Agüimes, Canary Is. 22 G4 27 58N 15 27W
Aguja, C. de la, Colombia 90 B3 11 18N 74 12W
Agulhas, C., S. Africa 56 E3 34 52S 20 0 E
Agulo, Canary Is. 22 F2 28 11N 17 12W
Agung, Gunung, Indonesia 36 F5 8 20S 115 28 E
Agur, Uganda 54 B3 2 28N 32 55 E
Agusan →, Phil. 37 C7 9 0N 125 30 E
Aha Mts., Botswana 56 B3 19 45S 21 0 E
Ahaggar, Algeria 50 D7 23 0N 6 30 E
Ahar, Iran 44 B5 38 35N 47 0 E
Ahipara B., N.Z. 59 F4 35 5S 173 5 E
Ahiri, India 40 K12 19 30N 80 0 E
Ahmad Wal, Pakistan 42 E1 29 18N 65 58 E
Ahmadabad, India 42 H5 23 0N 72 40 E
Aḩmadābād, Khorāsān, Iran 45 C9 35 3N 60 50 E
Aḩmadābād, Khorāsān, Iran 45 C8 35 49N 59 42 E
Aḩmadī, Iran 45 E8 27 56N 56 42 E
Ahmadnagar, India 40 K9 19 7N 74 46 E
Ahmadpur, Pakistan 42 E4 29 12N 71 10 E
Ahmadpur Lamma, Pakistan 42 E4 28 19N 70 3 E
Ahmedabad = Ahmadabad, India 42 H5 23 0N 72 40 E
Ahmednagar = Ahmadnagar, India 40 K9 19 7N 74 46 E
Ahome, Mexico 86 B3 25 55N 109 11W
Ahoskie, U.S.A. 77 G7 36 17N 76 59W
Ahram, Iran 45 D6 28 52N 51 16 E
Ahrax Pt., Malta 23 D1 36 0N 14 22 E
Āhū, Iran 45 C6 34 33N 50 2 E
Ahuachapán, El Salv. 88 D2 13 54N 89 52W
Ahvāz, Iran 45 D6 31 20N 48 40 E
Ahvenanmaa = Åland, Finland 9 F19 60 15N 20 0 E
Aḩwar, Yemen 46 E4 13 30N 46 40 E
Ai →, India 43 F14 26 26N 90 44 E
Ai-Ais, Namibia 56 D2 27 54S 17 59 E
Aichi □, Japan 31 G8 35 0N 137 15 E
Aigua, Uruguay 95 C5 34 13S 54 46W
Aigues-Mortes, France 18 E6 43 35N 4 12 E
Aihui, China 33 A7 50 10N 127 30 E
Aija, Peru 92 E3 9 50S 77 45W
Aikawa, Japan 30 E9 38 2N 138 15 E
Aiken, U.S.A. 77 J5 33 34N 81 43W
Aileron, Australia 62 C1 22 39S 133 20 E
Aillik, Canada 71 A8 55 11N 59 18W
Ailsa Craig, U.K. 12 F3 55 15N 5 6W
'Ailūn, Jordan 47 C4 32 18N 35 47 E
Aim, Russia 27 D14 59 0N 133 55 E
Aimere, Indonesia 37 F6 8 45S 121 3 E
Aimogasta, Argentina 94 B2 28 33S 66 50W
Aïn Ben Tili, Mauritania 50 C4 25 59N 9 27W
Aïn Sefra, Algeria 50 B5 32 47N 0 37W
Ain Sudr, Egypt 47 F2 29 50N 33 6 E
Ainaži, Latvia 9 H21 57 50N 24 24 E
Ainsworth, U.S.A. 80 D5 42 33N 99 52W
Aiquile, Bolivia 92 G5 18 10S 65 10W
Aïr, Niger 50 E7 18 30N 8 0 E
Air Force I., Canada 69 B12 67 58N 74 5W
Air Hitam, Malaysia 39 M4 1 55N 103 11 E
Airdrie, Canada 72 C6 51 18N 114 2W
Airdrie, U.K. 12 F5 55 52N 3 57W
Aire →, U.K. 10 D7 53 43N 0 55W
Aire, I. de l', Spain 22 B11 39 48N 4 16 E
Airlie Beach, Australia 62 C4 20 16S 148 43 E
Aisne →, France 18 B5 49 26N 2 50 E
Ait, India 43 G8 25 54N 79 14 E
Aitkin, U.S.A. 80 B8 46 32N 93 42W
Aiud, Romania 17 E12 46 19N 23 44 E
Aix-en-Provence, France 18 E6 43 32N 5 27 E
Aix-la-Chapelle = Aachen, Germany 16 C4 50 45N 6 6 E
Aix-les-Bains, France 18 D6 45 41N 5 53 E
Aíyion, Greece 21 E10 38 15N 22 5 E
Aizawl, India 41 H18 23 40N 92 44 E
Aizkraukle, Latvia 9 H21 56 36N 25 11 E
Aizpute, Latvia 9 H19 56 43N 21 40 E
Aizuwakamatsu, Japan 30 F9 37 30N 139 56 E
Ajaccio, France 18 F8 41 55N 8 40 E
Ajaigarh, India 43 G9 24 52N 80 16 E
Ajalpan, Mexico 87 D5 18 22N 97 15W
Ajanta Ra., India 40 J9 20 28N 75 50 E
Ajari Rep. = Ajaria □, Georgia 25 F7 41 30N 42 0 E
Ajaria □, Georgia 25 F7 41 30N 42 0 E
Ajax, Canada 78 C5 43 50N 79 1W
Ajdābiyā, Libya 51 B10 30 54N 20 4 E
Ajka, Hungary 17 E9 47 4N 17 31 E
'Ajmān, U.A.E. 45 E7 25 25N 55 30 E
Ajmer, India 42 F6 26 28N 74 37 E
Ajnala, India 42 D6 31 50N 74 48 E
Ajo, U.S.A. 83 K7 32 22N 112 52W
Ajo, C. de, Spain 19 A4 43 31N 3 35W
Akabira, Japan 30 C11 43 33N 142 5 E
Akamas, Cyprus 23 D11 35 3N 32 18 E
Akanthou, Cyprus 23 D12 35 22N 33 45 E
Akaroa, N.Z. 59 K4 43 49S 172 59 E
Akashi, Japan 31 G7 34 45N 134 58 E
Akbarpur, Bihar, India 43 G10 24 39N 83 58 E
Akbarpur, Ut. P., India 43 F10 26 25N 82 32 E
Akelamo, Indonesia 37 D7 1 35N 129 40 E
Aketi, Dem. Rep. of the Congo 52 D4 2 38N 23 47 E
Akharnaí, Greece 21 E10 38 5N 23 44 E
Akhelóös →, Greece 21 E9 38 19N 21 7 E
Akhisar, Turkey 21 E12 38 56N 27 48 E
Akhnur, India 43 C6 32 52N 74 45 E
Akhtyrka = Okhtyrka, Ukraine 25 D5 50 25N 35 0 E
Aki, Japan 31 H6 33 30N 133 54 E
Akimiski I., Canada 70 B3 52 50N 81 30W
Akita, Japan 30 E10 39 45N 140 7 E
Akita □, Japan 30 E10 39 40N 140 30 E
Akjoujt, Mauritania 50 E3 19 45N 14 15W
Akkeshi, Japan 30 C12 43 2N 144 51 E
'Akko, Israel 47 C4 32 55N 35 4 E
Aklavik, Canada 68 B6 68 12N 135 0W
Aklera, India 42 G7 24 26N 76 32 E
Akmolinsk = Astana, Kazakstan 26 D8 51 10N 71 30 E
Akō, Japan 31 G7 34 45N 134 24 E
Akola, India 40 J10 20 42N 77 2 E
Akordat, Eritrea 46 D2 15 30N 37 40 E
Akpatok I., Canada 69 B13 60 25N 68 8W
Åkrahamn, Norway 9 G11 59 15N 5 10 E
Akranes, Iceland 8 D2 64 19N 22 5W
Akron, Colo., U.S.A. 80 E3 40 10N 103 13W
Akron, Ohio, U.S.A. 78 E3 41 5N 81 31W
Akrotiri, Cyprus 23 E11 34 36N 32 57 E
Akrotiri Bay, Cyprus 23 E12 34 35N 33 10 E
Aksai Chin, China 43 B8 35 15N 79 55 E
Aksaray, Turkey 25 G5 38 25N 34 2 E
Aksay, Kazakstan 25 D9 51 11N 53 0 E
Akşehir, Turkey 44 B1 38 18N 31 30 E
Akşehir Gölü, Turkey 25 G5 38 30N 31 25 E
Aksu, China 32 B3 41 5N 80 10 E
Aksum, Ethiopia 46 E2 14 5N 38 40 E
Aktogay, Kazakstan 26 E8 46 57N 79 40 E
Aktsyabrski, Belarus 17 B15 52 38N 28 53 E
Aktyubinsk = Aqtöbe, Kazakstan 25 D10 50 17N 57 10 E
Akure, Nigeria 50 G7 7 15N 5 5 E
Akureyri, Iceland 8 D4 65 40N 18 6W
Akuseki-Shima, Japan 31 K4 29 27N 129 37 E
Akyab = Sittwe, Burma 41 J18 20 18N 92 45 E
Al 'Adan, Yemen 46 E4 12 45N 45 0 E
Al Aḩsā = Hasa □, Si. Arabia 45 E6 25 50N 49 0 E
Al Ajfar, Si. Arabia 44 E4 27 26N 43 0 E
Al Amādīyah, Iraq 44 B4 37 5N 43 30 E
Al 'Amārah, Iraq 44 D5 31 55N 47 15 E
Al 'Aqabah, Jordan 47 F4 29 31N 35 0 E
Al Arak, Syria 44 C3 34 38N 38 35 E
Al 'Aramah, Si. Arabia 44 E5 25 30N 46 0 E
Al Arṭāwīyah, Si. Arabia 44 E5 26 31N 45 20 E
Al 'Āşimah = 'Ammān □, Jordan 47 D5 31 40N 36 30 E
Al 'Assāfīyah, Si. Arabia 44 D3 28 17N 38 59 E
Al 'Ayn, Oman 45 E7 24 15N 55 45 E
Al 'Ayn, Si. Arabia 44 E3 25 4N 38 6 E
Al 'Azamīyah, Iraq 44 C5 33 22N 44 22 E
Al 'Azīzīyah, Iraq 44 C5 32 54N 45 4 E
Al Bāb, Syria 44 B3 36 23N 37 29 E
Al Bad', Si. Arabia 44 D2 28 28N 35 1 E
Al Bādī, Iraq 44 C4 35 56N 41 32 E
Al Baḩrah, Kuwait 44 D5 29 40N 47 52 E
Al Baḩral Mayyit = Dead Sea, Asia 47 D4 31 30N 35 30 E
Al Balqā' □, Jordan 47 C4 32 5N 35 45 E
Al Bārūk, J., Lebanon 47 B4 33 39N 35 40 E
Al Başrah, Iraq 44 D5 30 30N 47 50 E
Al Baṭḩā, Iraq 44 D5 31 6N 45 53 E
Al Batrūn, Lebanon 47 A4 34 15N 35 40 E
Al Bayḑā, Libya 51 B10 32 50N 21 44 E
Al Biqā, Lebanon 47 A5 34 10N 36 10 E
Al Bi'r, Si. Arabia 44 D3 28 51N 36 16 E
Al Burayj, Syria 47 A5 34 15N 36 46 E
Al Faḑilī, Si. Arabia 45 E6 26 58N 49 10 E
Al Fallūjah, Iraq 44 C4 33 20N 43 55 E
Al Fāw, Iraq 45 D6 30 0N 48 30 E
Al Fujayrah, U.A.E. 45 E8 25 7N 56 18 E
Al Ghadaf, W. →, Jordan 47 D5 31 26N 36 43 E
Al Ghammās, Iraq 44 D5 31 45N 44 37 E

Amakusa-Shotō

Al Ghazālah, Si. Arabia 44 E4 26 48N 41 19 E
Al Ḩadīthah, Iraq 44 C4 34 0N 41 13 E
Al Ḩadīthah, Si. Arabia 47 D6 31 28N 37 8 E
Al Ḩaḑr, Iraq 44 C4 35 35N 42 44 E
Al Hājānah, Syria 47 B5 33 20N 36 33 E
Al Ḩajar al Gharbī, Oman 45 E8 24 10N 56 15 E
Al Hāmad, Si. Arabia 44 D3 31 30N 39 30 E
Al Hamdāniyah, Syria 44 C3 35 25N 36 50 E
Al Ḩamīdīyah, Syria 47 A4 34 42N 35 57 E
Al Ḩammār, Iraq 44 D5 30 57N 46 51 E
Al Ḩamrā', Si. Arabia 44 E3 24 2N 38 55 E
Al Ḩanākīyah, Si. Arabia 44 E4 24 51N 40 31 E
Al Ḩarīr, W. →, Syria 47 C4 32 44N 35 59 E
Al Ḩasā, W. →, Jordan 47 D4 31 4N 35 29 E
Al Ḩasakah, Syria 44 B4 36 35N 40 45 E
Al Haydān, W. →, Jordan 47 D4 31 29N 35 34 E
Al Ḩayy, Iraq 44 C5 32 5N 46 5 E
Al Ḩijarah, Asia 44 D4 30 0N 44 0 E
Al Ḩillah, Iraq 44 C5 32 30N 44 25 E
Al Ḩillah, Si. Arabia 46 B4 23 35N 46 50 E
Al Hindīyah, Iraq 44 C5 32 30N 44 10 E
Al Hirmil, Lebanon 47 A5 34 26N 36 24 E
Al Hoceïma, Morocco 50 A5 35 8N 3 58W
Al Ḩudaydah, Yemen 46 E3 14 50N 43 0 E
Al Hufūf, Si. Arabia 46 B4 25 25N 49 45 E
Al Ḩumayḑah, Si. Arabia 44 D2 29 14N 34 56 E
Al Ḩunayy, Si. Arabia 45 E6 25 58N 48 45 E
Al Īsāwīyah, Si. Arabia 44 D3 30 43N 37 59 E
Al Jafr, Jordan 47 E5 30 18N 36 14 E
Al Jāfūrah, Si. Arabia 45 E7 25 0N 50 15 E
Al Jaghbūb, Libya 51 C10 29 42N 24 38 E
Al Jahrah, Kuwait 44 D5 29 25N 47 40 E
Al Jalāmīd, Si. Arabia 44 D3 31 20N 40 6 E
Al Jamalīyah, Qatar 45 E6 25 37N 51 5 E
Al Janūb □, Lebanon 47 B4 33 20N 35 20 E
Al Jawf, Libya 51 D10 24 10N 23 24 E
Al Jawf, Si. Arabia 44 D3 29 55N 39 40 E
Al Jazirah, Iraq 44 C5 33 30N 44 0 E
Al Jithāmīyah, Si. Arabia 44 E4 27 41N 41 43 E
Al Jubayl, Si. Arabia 45 E6 27 0N 49 50 E
Al Jubaylah, Si. Arabia 44 E5 24 55N 46 25 E
Al Jubb, Si. Arabia 44 E4 27 11N 42 17 E
Al Junaynah, Sudan 51 F10 13 27N 22 45 E
Al Kabā'ish, Iraq 44 D5 30 58N 47 0 E
Al Karak, Jordan 47 D4 31 11N 35 42 E
Al Karak □, Jordan 47 E5 31 0N 36 0 E
Al Kāzim Tyah, Iraq 44 C5 33 22N 44 12 E
Al Khābūra, Oman 45 F8 23 57N 57 5 E
Al Khafji, Si. Arabia 45 E6 28 24N 48 29 E
Al Khalīl, West Bank 47 D4 31 32N 35 6 E
Al Khāliş, Iraq 44 C5 33 49N 44 32 E
Al Kharsānīyah, Si. Arabia 45 E6 27 13N 49 18 E
Al Khaşab, Oman 45 E8 26 14N 56 15 E
Al Khawr, Qatar 45 E6 25 41N 51 30 E
Al Khiḑr, Iraq 44 D5 31 12N 45 33 E
Al Khiyām, Lebanon 47 B4 33 20N 35 36 E
Al Kiswah, Syria 47 B5 33 23N 36 14 E
Al Kūfah, Iraq 44 C5 32 2N 44 24 E
Al Kufrah, Libya 51 D10 24 17N 23 15 E
Al Kuhayfīyah, Si. Arabia 44 E4 27 12N 43 3 E
Al Kūt, Iraq 44 C5 32 30N 46 0 E
Al Kuwayt, Kuwait 46 B4 29 30N 48 0 E
Al Labwah, Lebanon 47 A5 34 11N 36 20 E
Al Lādhiqīyah, Syria 44 C2 35 30N 35 45 E
Al Līth, Si. Arabia 46 C3 20 9N 40 15 E
Al Liwā', Oman 45 E8 24 31N 56 36 E
Al Luḩayyah, Yemen 46 D3 15 45N 42 40 E
Al Madīnah, Iraq 44 D5 30 57N 47 16 E
Al Madīnah, Si. Arabia 46 C2 24 35N 39 52 E
Al Mafraq, Jordan 47 C5 32 17N 36 14 E
Al Maḩmūdīyah, Iraq 44 C5 33 3N 44 21 E
Al Majma'ah, Si. Arabia 44 E5 25 57N 45 22 E
Al Makhruq, W. →, Jordan 47 D6 31 28N 37 0 E
Al Makḩūl, Si. Arabia 44 E4 26 37N 42 39 E
Al Manāmah, Bahrain 46 B5 26 10N 50 30 E
Al Maqwa', Kuwait 44 D5 29 10N 47 59 E
Al Marj, Libya 51 B10 32 25N 20 30 E
Al Maţlā, Kuwait 44 D5 29 24N 47 40 E
Al Mawjib, W. →, Jordan 47 D4 31 28N 35 36 E
Al Mawşil, Iraq 44 B4 36 15N 43 5 E
Al Mayādin, Syria 44 C4 35 1N 40 27 E
Al Mazār, Jordan 47 D4 31 4N 35 41 E
Al Midhnab, Si. Arabia 44 E5 25 50N 44 18 E
Al Minā', Lebanon 47 A4 34 24N 35 49 E
Al Miqdādīyah, Iraq 44 C5 34 0N 45 0 E
Al Mubarraz, Si. Arabia 45 E6 25 30N 49 40 E
Al Mudawwarah, Jordan 47 F5 29 19N 36 0 E
Al Mughayrā', U.A.E. 45 E7 24 5N 53 32 E
Al Muḩarraq, Bahrain 45 E6 26 15N 50 40 E
Al Mukallā, Yemen 46 E4 14 33N 49 2 E
Al Mukhā, Yemen 46 E3 13 18N 43 15 E
Al Musayjīd, Si. Arabia 44 E3 24 5N 39 5 E
Al Musayyib, Iraq 44 C5 32 49N 44 20 E
Al Muwaylih, Si. Arabia 44 E2 27 40N 35 30 E
Al Qā'im, Iraq 44 C4 34 21N 41 7 E
Al Qalībah, Si. Arabia 44 D3 28 24N 37 42 E
Al Qāmishlī, Syria 44 B4 37 2N 41 14 E
Al Qaryatayn, Syria 47 A6 34 12N 37 13 E
Al Qaşīm, Si. Arabia 44 E4 26 0N 43 0 E
Al Qaţ'ā, Syria 44 C4 34 40N 40 48 E
Al Qaţīf, Si. Arabia 45 E6 26 35N 50 0 E
Al Qatrānah, Jordan 47 D5 31 12N 36 6 E
Al Qaţrūn, Libya 51 D9 24 56N 15 3 E
Al Qayşūmah, Si. Arabia 44 D5 28 20N 46 7 E
Al Quds = Jerusalem, Israel 47 D4 31 47N 35 10 E
Al Qunayţirah, Syria 47 C4 32 55N 35 45 E
Al Qurnah, Iraq 44 D5 31 1N 47 25 E
Al Quşayr, Iraq 44 D5 30 39N 45 50 E
Al Quşayr, Syria 47 A5 34 31N 36 34 E
Al Quţayfah, Syria 47 B5 33 44N 36 36 E
Al 'Ubaylah, Si. Arabia 46 C5 21 59N 50 57 E
Al 'Uḑaylīyah, Si. Arabia 45 E6 25 8N 49 18 E
Al 'Ulā, Si. Arabia 44 E3 26 35N 38 0 E
Al 'Uqayr, Si. Arabia 45 E6 25 40N 50 15 E
Al 'Uwaynid, Si. Arabia 44 E5 24 50N 46 0 E
Al 'Uwayqīlah, Si. Arabia 44 D4 30 30N 42 10 E
Al 'Uyūn, Ḩijāz, Si. Arabia 44 E3 24 33N 39 35 E
Al 'Uyūn, Najd, Si. Arabia 44 E4 26 30N 43 50 E
Al 'Uzayr, Iraq 44 D5 31 19N 47 25 E
Al Wajh, Si. Arabia 44 E3 26 10N 36 30 E
Al Wakrah, Qatar 45 E6 25 10N 51 40 E
Al Waqbah, Si. Arabia 44 D5 28 48N 45 33 E
Al Wari'āh, Si. Arabia 44 E5 27 51N 47 25 E
Ala Dağ, Turkey 44 B2 37 44N 35 9 E
Ala Tau Shankou = Dzungarian Gates, Asia 32 B3 45 0N 82 0 E
Alabama □, U.S.A. 77 J2 33 0N 87 0W
Alabama →, U.S.A. 77 K2 31 8N 87 57W
Alabaster, U.S.A. 77 J2 33 15N 86 49W
Alaçam Dağları, Turkey 21 E13 39 18N 28 49 E
Alachua, U.S.A. 77 L4 29 47N 82 30W
Alaérma, Greece 23 C9 36 9N 27 57 E
Alagoa Grande, Brazil 93 E11 7 3S 35 35W
Alagoas □, Brazil 93 E11 9 0S 36 0W
Alagoinhas, Brazil 93 F11 12 7S 38 20W
Alaior, Spain 22 B11 39 57N 4 8 E
Alajero, Canary Is. 22 F2 28 3N 17 13W
Alajuela, Costa Rica 88 D3 10 2N 84 8W
Alakamisy, Madag. 57 C8 21 19S 47 14 E
Alaknanda →, India 43 D8 30 8N 78 36 E
Alakurtti, Russia 24 A5 67 0N 30 30 E
Alamarvdasht, Iran 45 E7 27 37N 52 59 E
Alameda, Calif., U.S.A. 84 H4 37 46N 122 15W
Alameda, N. Mex., U.S.A. 83 J10 35 11N 106 37W
Alamo, U.S.A. 85 J11 37 22N 115 10W
Alamo Crossing, U.S.A. 85 L13 34 16N 113 33W
Alamogordo, U.S.A. 83 K11 32 54N 105 57W
Alamos, Mexico 86 B3 27 0N 109 0W
Alamosa, U.S.A. 83 H11 37 28N 105 52W
Åland, Finland 9 F19 60 15N 20 0 E
Ålands hav, Sweden 9 F18 60 0N 19 30 E
Alania = North Ossetia □, Russia 25 F7 43 30N 44 30 E
Alanya, Turkey 25 G5 36 38N 32 0 E
Alaotra, Farihin', Madag. 57 B8 17 30S 48 30 E
Alapayevsk, Russia 26 D7 57 52N 61 42 E
Alappuzha = Alleppey, India 40 Q10 9 30N 76 28 E
Alarobia-Vohiposa, Madag. 57 C8 20 59S 47 9 E
Alaşehir, Turkey 21 E13 38 23N 28 30 E
Alaska □, U.S.A. 68 B5 64 0N 154 0W
Alaska, G. of, Pac. Oc. 68 C5 58 0N 145 0W
Alaska Peninsula, U.S.A. 68 C4 56 0N 159 0W
Alaska Range, U.S.A. 68 B4 62 50N 151 0W
Älät, Azerbaijan 25 G8 39 58N 49 25 E
Alatyr, Russia 24 D8 54 55N 46 35 E
Alausi, Ecuador 92 D3 2 0S 78 50W
Alava, C., U.S.A. 82 B1 48 10N 124 44W
Alavus, Finland 9 E20 62 35N 23 36 E
Alawoona, Australia 63 E3 34 45S 140 30 E
'Alayh, Lebanon 47 B4 33 46N 35 33 E
Alba, Italy 18 D8 44 42N 8 2 E
Alba-Iulia, Romania 17 E12 46 8N 23 39 E
Albacete, Spain 19 C5 39 0N 1 50W
Albacutya, L., Australia 63 F3 35 45S 141 58 E
Albanel, L., Canada 70 B5 50 55N 73 12W
Albania ■, Europe 21 D9 41 0N 20 0 E
Albany, Australia 61 G2 35 1S 117 58 E
Albany, Ga., U.S.A. 77 K3 31 35N 84 10W
Albany, N.Y., U.S.A. 79 D11 42 39N 73 45W
Albany, Oreg., U.S.A. 82 D2 44 38N 123 6W
Albany, Tex., U.S.A. 81 J5 32 44N 99 18W
Albany →, Canada 70 B3 52 17N 81 31W
Albardón, Argentina 94 C2 31 20S 68 30W
Albatross B., Australia 62 A3 12 45S 141 30 E
Albemarle, U.S.A. 77 H5 35 21N 80 11W
Albemarle Sd., U.S.A. 77 H7 36 5N 76 0W
Alberche →, Spain 19 C3 39 58N 4 46W
Alberdi, Paraguay 94 B4 26 14S 58 20W
Albert, L., Africa 54 B3 1 30N 31 0 E
Albert, L., Australia 63 F2 35 30S 139 10 E
Albert Edward Ra., Australia 60 C4 18 17S 127 57 E
Albert Lea, U.S.A. 80 D8 43 39N 93 22W
Albert Nile →, Uganda 54 B3 3 36N 32 2 E
Albert Town, Bahamas 89 B5 22 37N 74 33W
Alberta □, Canada 72 C6 54 40N 115 0W
Alberti, Argentina 94 D3 35 1S 60 16W
Albertinia, S. Africa 56 E3 34 11S 21 34 E
Alberton, Canada 71 C7 46 50N 64 0W
Albertville = Kalemie, Dem. Rep. of the Congo 54 D2 5 55S 29 9 E
Albertville, France 18 D7 45 40N 6 22 E
Albertville, U.S.A. 77 H2 34 16N 86 13W
Albi, France 18 E5 43 56N 2 9 E
Albia, U.S.A. 80 E8 41 2N 92 48W
Albina, Surinam 93 B8 5 37N 54 15W
Albina, Ponta, Angola 56 B1 15 52S 11 44 E
Albion, Mich., U.S.A. 76 D3 42 15N 84 45W
Albion, Nebr., U.S.A. 80 E6 41 42N 98 0W
Albion, Pa., U.S.A. 78 E4 41 53N 80 22W
Alborán, Medit. S. 19 E4 35 57N 3 0W
Ålborg, Denmark 9 H13 57 2N 9 54 E
Alborz, Reshteh-ye Kūhhā-ye, Iran 45 C7 36 0N 52 0 E
Albuquerque, U.S.A. 83 J10 35 5N 106 39W
Albuquerque, Cayos de, Caribbean 88 D3 12 10N 81 50W
Alburg, U.S.A. 79 B11 44 59N 73 18W
Albury = Albury-Wodonga, Australia 63 F4 36 3S 146 56 E
Albury-Wodonga, Australia 63 F4 36 3S 146 56 E
Alcalá de Henares, Spain 19 B4 40 28N 3 22W
Alcalá la Real, Spain 19 D4 37 27N 3 57W
Álcamo, Italy 20 F5 37 59N 12 55 E
Alcañiz, Spain 19 B5 41 2N 0 8W
Alcântara, Brazil 93 D10 2 20S 44 30W
Alcántara, Embalse de, Spain 19 C2 39 44N 6 50W
Alcantarilla, Spain 19 D5 37 59N 1 12W
Alcaraz, Sierra de, Spain 19 C4 38 40N 2 20W
Alcaudete, Spain 19 D3 37 35N 4 5W
Alcázar de San Juan, Spain 19 C4 39 24N 3 12W
Alchevsk, Ukraine 25 E6 48 30N 38 45 E
Alcira = Alzira, Spain 19 C5 39 9N 0 30W
Alcova, U.S.A. 82 E10 42 34N 106 43W
Alcoy, Spain 19 C5 38 43N 0 30W
Alcúdia, Spain 22 B10 39 51N 3 7 E
Alcúdia, B. d', Spain 22 B10 39 47N 3 15 E
Aldabra Is., Seychelles 49 G8 9 22S 46 28 E
Aldama, Mexico 87 C5 23 0N 98 4W
Aldan, Russia 27 D13 58 40N 125 30 E
Aldan →, Russia 27 C13 63 28N 129 35 E
Aldea, Pta. de la, Canary Is. 22 G4 28 0N 15 50W
Aldeburgh, U.K. 11 E9 52 10N 1 37 E
Alder Pk., U.S.A. 84 K5 35 53N 121 22W
Alderney, U.K. 11 H5 49 42N 2 11W
Aldershot, U.K. 11 F7 51 15N 0 44W
Aledo, U.S.A. 80 E9 41 12N 90 45W
Aleg, Mauritania 50 E3 17 3N 13 55W
Alegranza, Canary Is. 22 E6 29 23N 13 32W
Alegranza, I., Canary Is. 22 E6 29 23N 13 32W
Alegre, Brazil 95 A7 20 50S 41 30W
Alegrete, Brazil 95 B4 29 40S 56 0W
Aleisk, Russia 26 D9 52 40N 83 0 E
Aleksandriya = Oleksandriya, Ukraine 17 C14 50 37N 26 19 E
Aleksandrov Gay, Russia 25 D8 50 9N 48 34 E
Aleksandrovsk-Sakhalinskiy, Russia 27 D15 50 50N 142 20 E
Além Paraíba, Brazil 95 A7 21 52S 42 41W
Alemania, Argentina 94 B2 25 40S 65 30W
Alemania, Chile 94 B2 25 10S 69 55W
Alençon, France 18 B4 48 27N 0 4 E
Alenquer, Brazil 93 D8 1 56S 54 46W
Alenuihaha Channel, U.S.A. 74 H17 20 30N 156 0W
Aleppo = Ḩalab, Syria 44 B3 36 10N 37 15 E
Alès, France 18 D6 44 9N 4 5 E
Alessándria, Italy 18 D8 44 54N 8 37 E
Ålesund, Norway 9 E12 62 28N 6 12 E
Aleutian Is., Pac. Oc. 68 C2 52 0N 175 0W
Aleutian Trench, Pac. Oc. 64 C10 48 0N 180 0 E
Alexander, U.S.A. 80 B3 47 51N 103 39W
Alexander, Mt., Australia 61 E3 28 58S 120 16 E
Alexander Arch., U.S.A. 68 C6 56 0N 136 0W
Alexander Bay, S. Africa 56 D2 28 40S 16 30 E
Alexander City, U.S.A. 77 J3 32 56N 85 58W
Alexander I., Antarctica 5 C17 69 0S 70 0W
Alexandra, Australia 63 F4 37 8S 145 40 E
Alexandra, N.Z. 59 L2 45 14S 169 25 E
Alexandra Falls, Canada 72 A5 60 29N 116 18W
Alexandria = El Iskandarîya, Egypt 51 B11 31 13N 29 58 E
Alexandria, B.C., Canada 72 C4 52 35N 122 27W
Alexandria, Ont., Canada 79 A10 45 19N 74 38W
Alexandria, Romania 17 G13 43 57N 25 24 E
Alexandria, S. Africa 56 E4 33 38S 26 28 E
Alexandria, U.K. 12 F4 55 59N 4 35W
Alexandria, La., U.S.A. 81 K8 31 18N 92 27W
Alexandria, Minn., U.S.A. 80 C7 45 53N 95 22W
Alexandria, S. Dak., U.S.A. 80 D6 43 39N 97 47W
Alexandria, Va., U.S.A. 76 F7 38 48N 77 3W
Alexandria Bay, U.S.A. 79 B9 44 20N 75 55W
Alexandrina, L., Australia 63 F2 35 25S 139 10 E
Alexandroúpolis, Greece 21 D11 40 50N 25 54 E
Alexis →, Canada 71 B8 52 33N 56 8W
Alexis Creek, Canada 72 C4 52 10N 123 20W
Alfabia, Spain 22 B9 39 44N 2 44 E
Alfenas, Brazil 95 A6 21 20S 46 10W
Alford, Aberds., U.K. 12 D6 57 14N 2 41W
Alford, Lincs., U.K. 10 D8 53 15N 0 10 E
Alfred, Maine, U.S.A. 79 C14 43 29N 70 43W
Alfred, N.Y., U.S.A. 78 D7 42 16N 77 48W
Alfreton, U.K. 10 D6 53 6N 1 24W
Alga, Kazakstan 25 E10 49 53N 57 20 E
Algaida, Spain 22 B9 39 33N 2 53 E
Ålgård, Norway 9 G11 58 46N 5 53 E
Algarve, Portugal 19 D1 36 58N 8 20W
Algeciras, Spain 19 D3 36 9N 5 28W
Algemesí, Spain 19 C5 39 11N 0 27W
Alger, Algeria 50 A6 36 42N 3 8 E
Algeria ■, Africa 50 C6 28 30N 2 0 E
Alghero, Italy 20 D3 40 33N 8 19 E
Algiers = Alger, Algeria 50 A6 36 42N 3 8 E
Algoa B., S. Africa 56 E4 33 50S 25 45 E
Algoma, U.S.A. 76 C2 44 36N 87 26W
Algona, U.S.A. 80 D7 43 4N 94 14W
Algonac, U.S.A. 78 D2 42 37N 82 32W
Algonquin Prov. Park, Canada 70 C4 45 50N 78 30W
Algorta, Uruguay 96 C5 32 25S 57 23W
Alhambra, U.S.A. 85 L8 34 8N 118 6W
Alhucemas = Al Hoceïma, Morocco 50 A5 35 8N 3 58W
'Alī al Gharbī, Iraq 44 C5 32 30N 46 45 E
'Alī ash Sharqī, Iraq 44 C5 32 7N 46 44 E
'Alī Khēl, Afghan. 42 C3 33 57N 69 43 E
Alī Shāh, Iran 44 B5 38 9N 45 50 E
'Alīābād, Khorāsān, Iran 45 C8 32 30N 57 30 E
'Alīābād, Kordestān, Iran 44 C5 35 4N 46 58 E
'Alīābād, Yazd, Iran 45 D7 31 41N 53 49 E
Aliağa, Turkey 21 E12 38 47N 26 59 E
Aliákmon →, Greece 21 D10 40 30N 22 36 E
Alicante, Spain 19 C5 38 23N 0 30W
Alice, S. Africa 56 E4 32 48S 26 55 E
Alice, U.S.A. 81 M5 27 45N 98 5W
Alice →, Queens., Australia 62 C3 24 2S 144 50 E
Alice →, Queens., Australia 62 B3 15 35S 142 20 E
Alice Arm, Canada 72 B3 55 29N 129 31W
Alice Springs, Australia 62 C1 23 40S 133 50 E
Alicedale, S. Africa 56 E4 33 15S 26 4 E
Aliceville, U.S.A. 77 J1 33 8N 88 9W
Aliganj, India 43 F8 27 30N 79 10 E
Aligarh, Raj., India 42 G7 25 55N 76 15 E
Aligarh, Ut. P., India 42 F8 27 55N 78 10 E
Alīgūdarz, Iran 45 C6 33 25N 49 45 E
Alimnía, Greece 23 C9 36 16N 27 43 E
Alingsås, Sweden 9 H15 57 56N 12 31 E
Alipur, Pakistan 42 E4 29 25N 70 55 E
Alipur Duar, India 41 F16 26 30N 89 35 E
Aliquippa, U.S.A. 78 F4 40 37N 80 15W
Alitus = Alytus, Lithuania 9 J21 54 24N 24 3 E
Aliwal North, S. Africa 56 E4 30 45S 26 45 E
Alix, Canada 72 C6 52 24N 113 11W
Aljustrel, Portugal 19 D1 37 55N 8 10W
Alkmaar, Neths. 15 B4 52 37N 4 45 E
All American Canal, U.S.A. 83 K6 32 45N 115 15W
Allagash →, U.S.A. 77 B11 47 5N 69 3W
Allah Dad, Pakistan 42 G2 25 38N 67 34 E
Allahabad, India 43 G9 25 25N 81 58 E
Allan, Canada 73 C7 51 53N 106 4W
Allanridge, S. Africa 56 D4 27 45S 26 40 E
Allegany, U.S.A. 78 D6 42 6N 78 30W
Allegheny →, U.S.A. 78 F5 40 27N 80 1W
Allegheny Mts., U.S.A. 76 G6 38 15N 80 10W
Allegheny Reservoir, U.S.A. 78 E6 41 50N 79 0W
Allen, Bog of, Ireland 13 C5 53 15N 7 0W
Allen, L., Ireland 13 B3 54 8N 8 4W
Allendale, U.S.A. 77 J5 33 1N 81 18W
Allende, Mexico 86 B4 28 20N 100 50W
Allentown, U.S.A. 79 F9 40 37N 75 29W
Alleppey, India 40 Q10 9 30N 76 28 E
Aller →, Germany 16 B5 52 56N 9 12 E
Alliance, Nebr., U.S.A. 80 D3 42 6N 102 52W
Alliance, Ohio, U.S.A. 78 F3 40 55N 81 6W
Allier →, France 18 C5 46 57N 3 4 E
Alliford Bay, Canada 72 C2 53 12N 131 58W
Alliston, Canada 78 B5 44 9N 79 52W
Alloa, U.K. 12 E5 56 7N 3 47W
Allora, Australia 63 D5 28 2S 152 0 E
Alluitsup Paa, Greenland 4 C5 60 30N 45 35W
Alma, Canada 71 C5 48 35N 71 40W
Alma, Ga., U.S.A. 77 K4 31 33N 82 28W
Alma, Kans., U.S.A. 80 F6 39 1N 96 17W
Alma, Mich., U.S.A. 76 D3 43 23N 84 39W
Alma, Nebr., U.S.A. 80 E5 40 6N 99 22W
Alma Ata = Almaty, Kazakstan 26 E8 43 15N 76 57 E
Almada, Portugal 19 C1 38 40N 9 9W
Almaden, Australia 62 B3 17 22S 144 40 E
Almadén, Spain 19 C3 38 49N 4 52W
Almanor, L., U.S.A. 82 F3 40 14N 121 9W
Almansa, Spain 19 C5 38 51N 1 5W
Almanzor, Pico, Spain 19 B3 40 15N 5 18W
Almanzora →, Spain 19 D5 37 14N 1 46W
Almaty, Kazakstan 26 E8 43 15N 76 57 E
Almazán, Spain 19 B4 41 30N 2 30W
Almeirim, Brazil 93 D8 1 30S 52 34W
Almelo, Neths. 15 B6 52 22N 6 42 E
Almendralejo, Spain 19 C2 38 41N 6 26W
Almere-Stad, Neths. 15 B5 52 20N 5 15 E
Almería, Spain 19 D4 36 52N 2 27W
Almirante, Panama 88 E3 9 10N 82 30W
Almiroú, Kólpos, Greece 23 D6 35 23N 24 20 E
Almond, U.S.A. 78 D7 42 19N 77 44W
Almont, U.S.A. 78 D1 42 55N 83 3W
Almonte, Canada 79 A8 45 14N 76 12W
Almora, India 43 E8 29 38N 79 40 E
Alness, U.K. 12 D4 57 41N 4 16W
Alnmouth, U.K. 10 B6 55 24N 1 37W
Alnwick, U.K. 10 B6 55 24N 1 42W
Aloi, Uganda 54 B3 2 16N 33 10 E
Alon, Burma 41 H19 22 12N 95 5 E
Alor, Indonesia 37 F6 8 15S 124 30 E
Alor Setar, Malaysia 39 J3 6 7N 100 22 E
Alot, India 42 H6 23 56N 75 40 E
Aloysius, Mt., Australia 61 E4 26 0S 128 38 E
Alpaugh, U.S.A. 84 K7 35 53N 119 29W
Alpena, U.S.A. 76 C4 45 4N 83 27W
Alpha, Australia 62 C4 23 39S 146 37 E
Alphen aan den Rijn, Neths. 15 B4 52 7N 4 40 E
Alpine, Ariz., U.S.A. 83 K9 33 51N 109 9W
Alpine, Calif., U.S.A. 85 N10 32 50N 116 46W
Alpine, Tex., U.S.A. 81 K3 30 22N 103 40W
Alps, Europe 18 C8 46 30N 9 30 E
Alsace, France 18 B7 48 15N 7 25 E
Alsask, Canada 73 C7 51 21N 109 59W
Alsasua, Spain 19 A4 42 54N 2 10W
Alsek →, U.S.A. 72 B1 59 10N 138 12W
Alsten, Norway 8 D15 65 58N 12 40 E
Alston, U.K. 10 C5 54 49N 2 25W
Alta, Norway 8 B20 69 57N 23 10 E
Alta Gracia, Argentina 94 C3 31 40S 64 30W
Alta Sierra, U.S.A. 85 K8 35 42N 118 33W
Altaelva →, Norway 8 B20 69 54N 23 17 E
Altafjorden, Norway 8 A20 70 5N 23 5 E
Altai = Aerhtai Shan, Mongolia 32 B4 46 40N 92 45 E
Altamaha →, U.S.A. 77 K5 31 20N 81 20W
Altamira, Brazil 93 D8 3 12S 52 10W
Altamira, Chile 94 B2 25 47S 69 51W
Altamira, Mexico 87 C5 22 24N 97 55W
Altamont, U.S.A. 79 D10 42 43N 74 3W
Altamura, Italy 20 D7 40 49N 16 33 E
Altanbulag, Mongolia 32 A5 50 16N 106 30 E
Altar, Mexico 86 A2 30 40N 111 50W
Altar, Desierto de, Mexico 86 B2 30 10N 112 0W
Altata, Mexico 86 C3 24 30N 108 0W
Altavista, U.S.A. 76 G6 37 6N 79 17W
Altay, China 32 B3 47 48N 88 10 E
Altea, Spain 19 C5 38 38N 0 2W
Altiplano = Bolivian Plateau, S. Amer. 90 E4 20 0S 67 30W
Alto Araguaia, Brazil 93 G8 17 15S 53 20W
Alto Cuchumatanes = Cuchumatanes, Sierra de los, Guatemala 88 C1 15 35N 91 25W
Alto del Carmen, Chile 94 B1 28 46S 70 30W
Alto del Inca, Chile 94 A2 24 10S 68 10W
Alto Ligonha, Mozam. 55 F4 15 30S 38 11 E
Alto Molocue, Mozam. 55 F4 15 50S 37 35 E
Alto Paraguay □, Paraguay 94 A4 21 0S 58 30W
Alto Paraná □, Paraguay 95 B5 25 30S 54 50W
Alton, Canada 78 C4 43 54N 80 5W
Alton, U.K. 11 F7 51 9N 0 59W
Alton, Ill., U.S.A. 80 F9 38 53N 90 11W
Alton, N.H., U.S.A. 79 C13 43 27N 71 13W
Altoona, U.S.A. 78 F6 40 31N 78 24W
Altūn Kūprī, Iraq 44 C5 35 45N 44 9 E
Altun Shan, China 32 C3 38 30N 88 0 E
Alturas, U.S.A. 82 F3 41 29N 120 32W
Altus, U.S.A. 81 H5 34 38N 99 20W
Alucra, Turkey 25 F6 40 22N 38 47 E
Alūksne, Latvia 9 H22 57 24N 27 3 E
Alunite, U.S.A. 85 K12 35 59N 114 55W
Alusi, Indonesia 37 F8 7 35S 131 40 E
Alva, U.S.A. 81 G5 36 48N 98 40W
Alvarado, Mexico 87 D5 18 40N 95 50W
Alvarado, U.S.A. 81 J6 32 24N 97 13W
Alvaro Obregón, Presa, Mexico 86 B3 27 55N 109 52W
Alvear, Argentina 94 B4 29 5S 56 30W
Alvesta, Sweden 9 H16 56 54N 14 35 E
Alvin, U.S.A. 81 L7 29 26N 95 15W
Alvinston, Canada 78 D3 42 49N 81 52W
Älvkarleby, Sweden 9 F17 60 34N 17 26 E
Alvord Desert, U.S.A. 82 E4 42 30N 118 25W
Älvsbyn, Sweden 8 D19 65 40N 21 0 E
Alwar, India 42 F7 27 38N 76 34 E
Alxa Zuoqi, China 34 E3 38 50N 105 40 E
Alyangula, Australia 62 A2 13 55S 136 30 E
Alyata = Älät, Azerbaijan 25 G8 39 58N 49 25 E
Alyth, U.K. 12 E5 56 38N 3 13W
Alytus, Lithuania 9 J21 54 24N 24 3 E
Alzada, U.S.A. 80 C2 45 2N 104 25W
Alzira, Spain 19 C5 39 9N 0 30W
Am Timan, Chad 51 F10 11 0N 20 10 E
Amadeus, L., Australia 61 D5 24 54S 131 0 E
Amadi, Dem. Rep. of the Congo 54 B2 3 40N 26 40 E
Amâdi, Sudan 51 G12 5 29N 30 25 E
Amadjuak L., Canada 69 B12 65 0N 71 8W
Amagansett, U.S.A. 79 F12 40 59N 72 9W
Amagasaki, Japan 31 G7 34 42N 135 20 E
Amahai, Indonesia 37 E7 3 20S 128 55 E
Amakusa-Shotō, Japan 31 H5 32 15N 130 10 E

Åmål, Sweden 9 G15 59 3N 12 42 E
Amaliás, Greece 21 F9 37 47N 21 22 E
Amalner, India 40 J9 21 5N 75 5 E
Amamapare, Indonesia 37 E9 4 53S 136 38 E
Amambaí, Brazil 95 A4 23 5S 55 13W
Amambaí →, Brazil 95 A5 23 22S 53 56W
Amambay □, Paraguay 95 A4 23 0S 56 0W
Amambay, Cordillera de, S. Amer. 95 A4 23 0S 55 45W
Amami-Guntō, Japan 31 L4 27 16N 129 21 E
Amami-Ō-Shima, Japan 31 L4 28 0N 129 0 E
Amaná, L., Brazil 92 D6 2 35S 64 40W
Amanat →, India 43 G11 24 7N 84 4 E
Amanda Park, U.S.A. 84 C3 47 28N 123 55W
Amangeldy, Kazakstan 26 D7 50 10N 65 10 E
Amapá, Brazil 93 C8 2 5N 50 50W
Amapá □, Brazil 93 C8 1 40N 52 0W
Amarante, Brazil 93 E10 6 14S 42 50W
Amaranth, Canada 73 C9 50 36N 98 43W
Amargosa →, U.S.A. 85 J10 36 14N 116 51W
Amargosa Range, U.S.A. 85 J10 36 20N 116 45W
Amári, Greece 23 D6 35 13N 24 40 E
Amarillo, U.S.A. 81 H4 35 13N 101 50W
Amarkantak, India 43 H9 22 40N 81 45 E
Amaro, Mte., Italy 20 C6 42 5N 14 5 E
Amarpur, India 43 G12 25 5N 87 0 E
Amarwara, India 43 H8 22 18N 79 10 E
Amasya □, Turkey 25 F6 40 40N 35 50 E
Amata, Australia 61 E5 26 9S 131 9 E
Amatikulu, S. Africa 57 D5 29 3S 31 33 E
Amatitlán, Guatemala 88 D1 14 29N 90 38W
Amay, Belgium 15 D5 50 33N 5 19 E
Amazon = Amazonas →, S. Amer. 93 D9 0 5S 50 0W
Amazonas □, Brazil 92 E6 5 0S 65 0W
Amazonas →, S. Amer. 93 D9 0 5S 50 0W
Ambah, India 42 F8 26 43N 78 13 E
Ambahakily, Madag. 57 C7 21 36S 43 41 E
Ambahita, Madag. 57 C8 24 1S 45 16 E
Ambala, India 42 D7 30 23N 76 56 E
Ambalavao, Madag. 57 C8 21 50S 46 56 E
Ambanja, Madag. 57 A8 13 40S 48 27 E
Ambararata, Madag. 57 B8 15 3S 48 33 E
Ambarchik, Russia 27 C17 69 40N 162 20 E
Ambarijeby, Madag. 57 A8 14 56S 47 41 E
Ambaro, Helodranon', Madag. 57 A8 13 23S 48 38 E
Ambato, Ecuador 92 D3 1 5S 78 42W
Ambato, Madag. 57 A8 13 24S 48 29 E
Ambato, Sierra de, Argentina 94 B2 28 25S 66 10W
Ambato Boeny, Madag. 57 B8 16 28S 46 43 E
Ambatofinandrahana, Madag. 57 C8 20 33S 46 48 E
Ambatolampy, Madag. 57 B8 19 20S 47 35 E
Ambatomainty, Madag. 57 B8 17 41S 45 40 E
Ambatomanoina, Madag. 57 B8 18 18S 47 37 E
Ambatondrazaka, Madag. 57 B8 17 55S 48 28 E
Ambatosoratra, Madag. 57 B8 17 37S 48 31 E
Ambenja, Madag. 57 B8 15 17S 46 58 E
Amberg, Germany 16 D6 49 26N 11 52 E
Ambergris Cay, Belize 87 D7 18 0N 88 0W
Amberley, N.Z. 59 K4 43 9S 172 44 E
Ambikapur, India 43 H10 23 15N 83 15 E
Ambilobé, Madag. 57 A8 13 10S 49 3 E
Ambinanindrano, Madag. 57 C8 20 5S 48 23 E
Ambinanitelo, Madag. 57 B8 15 21S 49 35 E
Ambinda, Madag. 57 B8 16 25S 45 52 E
Amble, U.K. 10 B6 55 20N 1 36W
Ambleside, U.K. 10 C5 54 26N 2 58W
Ambo, Peru 92 F3 10 5S 76 10W
Amboahangy, Madag. 57 C8 24 15S 46 22 E
Ambodifototra, Madag. 57 B8 16 59S 49 52 E
Ambodilazana, Madag. 57 B8 18 6S 49 10 E
Ambodiriana, Madag. 57 B8 17 55S 49 18 E
Ambohidratrimo, Madag. 57 B8 18 50S 47 26 E
Ambohidray, Madag. 57 B8 18 36S 48 18 E
Ambohimahamasina, Madag. 57 C8 21 56S 47 11 E
Ambohimahasoa, Madag. 57 C8 21 7S 47 13 E
Ambohimanga, Madag. 57 C8 20 52S 47 36 E
Ambohimitombo, Madag. 57 C8 20 43S 47 26 E
Ambohitra, Madag. 57 A8 12 30S 49 10 E
Amboise, France 18 C4 47 24N 1 2 E
Ambon, Indonesia 37 E7 3 43S 128 12 E
Ambondro, Madag. 57 D8 25 13S 45 44 E
Amboseli, L., Kenya 54 C4 2 40S 37 10 E
Ambositra, Madag. 57 C8 20 31S 47 25 E
Ambovombe, Madag. 57 D8 25 11S 46 5 E
Amboy, U.S.A. 85 L11 34 33N 115 45W
Amboyna Cay, S. China Sea 36 C4 7 50N 112 50 E
Ambridge, U.S.A. 78 F4 40 36N 80 14W
Ambriz, Angola 52 F2 7 48S 13 8 E
Amchitka I., U.S.A. 68 C1 51 32N 179 0 E
Amderma, Russia 26 C7 69 45N 61 30 E
Amdhi, India 43 H9 23 51N 81 27 E
Ameca, Mexico 86 C4 20 30N 104 0W
Ameca →, Mexico 86 C3 20 40N 105 15W
Amecameca, Mexico 87 D5 19 7N 98 46W
Ameland, Neths. 15 A5 53 27N 5 45 E
Amenia, U.S.A. 79 E11 41 51N 73 33W
American Falls, U.S.A. 82 E7 42 47N 112 51W
American Falls Reservoir, U.S.A. 82 E7 42 47N 112 52W
American Fork, U.S.A. 82 F8 40 23N 111 48W
American Highland, Antarctica 5 D6 73 0S 75 0 E
American Samoa ■, Pac. Oc. 59 B13 14 20S 170 40W
Americana, Brazil 95 A6 22 45S 47 20W
Americus, U.S.A. 77 K3 32 4N 84 14W
Amersfoort, Neths. 15 B5 52 9N 5 23 E
Amersfoort, S. Africa 57 D4 26 59S 29 53 E
Amery Ice Shelf, Antarctica 5 C6 69 30S 72 0 E
Ames, U.S.A. 80 E8 42 2N 93 37W
Amesbury, U.S.A. 79 D14 42 51N 70 56W
Amet, India 42 G5 25 18N 73 56 E
Amga, Russia 27 C14 60 50N 132 0 E
Amga →, Russia 27 C14 62 38N 134 32 E
Amgu, Russia 27 E14 45 45N 137 15 E
Amgun →, Russia 27 D14 52 56N 139 38 E
Amherst, Canada 71 C7 45 48N 64 8W
Amherst, Mass., U.S.A. 79 D12 42 23N 72 31W
Amherst, N.Y., U.S.A. 78 D6 42 59N 78 48W
Amherst, Ohio, U.S.A. 78 E2 41 24N 82 14W
Amherst I., Canada 79 B8 44 8N 76 43W
Amherstburg, Canada 70 D3 42 6N 83 6W
Amiata, Mte., Italy 20 C4 42 53N 11 37 E
Amidon, U.S.A. 80 B3 46 29N 103 19W
Amiens, France 18 B5 49 54N 2 16 E
Aminuis, Namibia 56 C2 23 43S 19 21 E
Amīrābād, Iran 44 C5 33 20N 46 16 E
Amirante Is., Seychelles 28 K9 6 0S 53 0 E
Amisk L., Canada 73 C8 54 35N 102 15W
Amistad, Presa de la, Mexico 86 B4 29 24N 101 0W
Amite, U.S.A. 81 K9 30 44N 90 30W
Amla, India 42 J8 21 56N 78 7 E
Amlia I., U.S.A. 68 C2 52 4N 173 30W
Amlwch, U.K. 10 D3 53 24N 4 20W
'Ammān, Jordan 47 D4 31 57N 35 52 E
'Ammān □, Jordan 47 D5 31 40N 36 30 E
Ammanford, U.K. 11 F4 51 48N 3 59W
Ammassalik = Tasiilaq, Greenland 4 C6 65 40N 37 20W
Ammochostos = Famagusta, Cyprus 23 D12 35 8N 33 55 E
Ammon, U.S.A. 82 E8 43 28N 111 58W
Amnat Charoen, Thailand 38 E5 15 51N 104 38 E
Amnura, Bangla. 43 G13 24 37N 88 25 E
Āmol, Iran 45 B7 36 23N 52 20 E
Amorgós, Greece 21 F11 36 50N 25 57 E
Amory, U.S.A. 77 J1 33 59N 88 29W
Amos, Canada 70 C4 48 35N 78 5W
Åmot, Norway 9 G13 59 57N 9 54 E
Amoy = Xiamen, China 33 D6 24 25N 118 4 E
Ampanavoana, Madag. 57 B9 15 41S 50 22 E
Ampang, Malaysia 39 L3 3 8N 101 45 E
Ampangalana, Lakandranon', Madag. 57 C8 22 48S 47 50 E
Ampanihy, Madag. 57 C7 24 40S 44 45 E
Amparafaravola, Madag. 57 B8 17 35S 48 13 E
Ampasinambo, Madag. 57 C8 20 31S 48 0 E
Ampasindava, Helodranon', Madag. 57 A8 13 40S 48 15 E
Ampasindava, Saikanosy, Madag. 57 A8 13 42S 47 55 E
Ampenan, Indonesia 36 F5 8 34S 116 4 E
Amper →, Germany 16 D6 48 29N 11 55 E
Ampitsikinana, Réunion 57 A8 12 57S 49 49 E
Ampombiantambo, Madag. 57 A8 12 42S 48 57 E
Ampotaka, Madag. 57 D7 25 3S 44 41 E
Ampoza, Madag. 57 C7 22 20S 44 44 E
Amqui, Canada 71 C6 48 28N 67 27W
Amravati, India 40 J10 20 55N 77 45 E
Amreli, India 42 J4 21 35N 71 17 E
Amritsar, India 42 D6 31 35N 74 57 E
Amroha, India 43 E8 28 53N 78 30 E
Amsterdam, Neths. 15 B4 52 23N 4 54 E
Amsterdam, U.S.A. 79 D10 42 56N 74 11W
Amsterdam, I. = Nouvelle-Amsterdam, I., Ind. Oc. 3 F13 38 30S 77 30 E
Amstetten, Austria 16 D8 48 7N 14 51 E
Amudarya →, Uzbekistan 26 E6 43 58N 59 34 E
Amundsen Gulf, Canada 68 A7 71 0N 124 0W
Amundsen Sea, Antarctica 5 D15 72 0S 115 0W
Amuntai, Indonesia 36 E5 2 28S 115 25 E
Amur →, Russia 27 D15 52 56N 141 10 E
Amurang, Indonesia 37 D6 1 5N 124 40 E
Amursk, Russia 27 D14 50 14N 136 54 E
Amyderya = Amudarya →, Uzbekistan 26 E6 43 58N 59 34 E
An Bien, Vietnam 39 H5 9 45N 105 0 E
An Hoa, Vietnam 38 E7 15 40N 108 5 E
An Nabatīyah at Tahta, Lebanon 47 B4 33 23N 35 27 E
An Nabk, Si. Arabia 44 D3 31 20N 37 20 E
An Nabk, Syria 47 A5 34 2N 36 44 E
An Nafūd, Si. Arabia 44 D4 28 15N 41 0 E
An Najaf, Iraq 44 C5 32 3N 44 15 E
An Nāṣirīyah, Iraq 44 D5 31 0N 46 15 E
An Nhon, Vietnam 38 F7 13 55N 109 7 E
An Nu'ayrīyah, Si. Arabia 45 E6 27 30N 48 30 E
An Nuwayb'ī, W. →, Si. Arabia 47 F3 29 18N 34 57 E
An Thoi, Dao, Vietnam 39 H4 9 58N 104 0 E
An Uaimh, Ireland 13 C5 53 39N 6 41W
Anabar →, Russia 27 B12 73 8N 113 36 E
'Anabtā, West Bank 47 C4 32 19N 35 7 E
Anaconda, U.S.A. 82 C7 46 8N 112 57W
Anacortes, U.S.A. 84 B4 48 30N 122 37W
Anadarko, U.S.A. 81 H5 35 4N 98 15W
Anadolu, Turkey 25 G5 39 0N 30 0 E
Anadyr, Russia 27 C18 64 35N 177 20 E
Anadyr →, Russia 27 C18 64 55N 176 5 E
Anadyrskiy Zaliv, Russia 27 C19 64 0N 180 0 E
Anaga, Pta. de, Canary Is. 22 F3 28 34N 16 9W
'Ānah, Iraq 44 C4 34 25N 42 0 E
Anaheim, U.S.A. 85 M9 33 50N 117 55W
Anahim Lake, Canada 72 C3 52 28N 125 18W
Anáhuac, Mexico 86 B4 27 14N 100 9W
Anakapalle, India 41 L13 17 42N 83 6 E
Anakie, Australia 62 C4 23 32S 147 45 E
Analalava, Madag. 57 A8 14 35S 48 0 E
Analavoka, Madag. 57 C8 22 23S 46 30 E
Análipsis, Greece 23 A3 39 36N 19 55 E
Anambar →, Pakistan 42 D3 30 15N 68 50 E
Anambas, Kepulauan, Indonesia 39 L6 3 20N 106 30 E
Anambas Is. = Anambas, Kepulauan, Indonesia 39 L6 3 20N 106 30 E
Anamosa, U.S.A. 80 D9 42 7N 91 17W
Anamur, Turkey 25 G5 36 8N 32 58 E
Anan, Japan 31 H7 33 54N 134 40 E
Anand, India 42 H5 22 32N 72 59 E
Anantnag, India 43 C6 33 45N 75 10 E
Ananyiv, Ukraine 17 E15 47 44N 29 58 E
Anapodháris →, Greece 23 E7 34 59N 25 20 E
Anápolis, Brazil 93 G9 16 15S 48 50W
Anapu →, Brazil 93 D8 1 53S 50 53W
Anār, Iran 45 D7 30 55N 55 13 E
Anārak, Iran 45 C7 33 25N 53 40 E
Anas →, India 42 H5 23 26N 74 0 E
Anatolia = Anadolu, Turkey 25 G5 39 0N 30 0 E
Anatsogno, Madag. 57 C7 23 33S 43 46 E
Añatuya, Argentina 94 B3 28 20S 62 50W
Anaunethad L., Canada 73 A8 60 55N 104 25W
Anbyŏn, N. Korea 35 E14 39 1N 127 35 E
Ancaster, Canada 78 C5 43 13N 79 59W
Anchor Bay, U.S.A. 84 G3 38 48N 123 34W
Anchorage, U.S.A. 68 B5 61 13N 149 54W
Anci, China 34 E9 39 20N 116 40 E
Ancohuma, Nevada, Bolivia 92 G5 16 0S 68 50W
Ancón, Peru 92 F3 11 50S 77 10W
Ancona, Italy 20 C5 43 38N 13 30 E
Ancud, Chile 96 E2 42 0S 73 50W
Ancud, G. de, Chile 96 E2 42 0S 73 0W
Anda, China 33 B7 46 24N 125 19 E
Andacollo, Argentina 94 D1 37 10S 70 42W
Andacollo, Chile 94 C1 30 14S 71 6W
Andaingo, Madag. 57 B8 18 12S 48 17 E
Andalgalá, Argentina 94 B2 27 40S 66 30W
Åndalsnes, Norway 9 E12 62 35N 7 43 E
Andalucía □, Spain 19 D3 37 35N 5 0W
Andalusia = Andalucía □, Spain 19 D3 37 35N 5 0W
Andalusia, U.S.A. 77 K2 31 18N 86 29W
Andaman Is., Ind. Oc. 29 H13 12 30N 92 45 E
Andaman Sea, Ind. Oc. 36 B1 13 0N 96 0 E
Andamooka Opal Fields, Australia 63 E2 30 27S 137 9 E
Andapa, Madag. 57 A8 14 39S 49 39 E
Andara, Namibia 56 B3 18 2S 21 9 E
Andenes, Norway 8 B17 69 19N 16 18 E
Andenne, Belgium 15 D5 50 28N 5 5 E
Anderson, Alaska, U.S.A. 68 B5 64 25N 149 15W
Anderson, Calif., U.S.A. 82 F2 40 27N 122 18W
Anderson, Ind., U.S.A. 76 E3 40 10N 85 41W
Anderson, Mo., U.S.A. 81 G7 36 39N 94 27W
Anderson, S.C., U.S.A. 77 H4 34 31N 82 39W
Anderson →, Canada 68 B7 69 42N 129 0W
Andes, U.S.A. 79 D10 42 12N 74 47W
Andes, Cord. de los, S. Amer. 92 H5 20 0S 68 0W
Andfjorden, Norway 8 B17 69 10N 16 20 E
Andhra Pradesh □, India 40 L11 18 0N 79 0 E
Andijon, Uzbekistan 26 E8 41 10N 72 15 E
Andikíthira, Greece 21 G10 35 52N 23 15 E
Andilamena, Madag. 57 B8 17 1S 48 35 E
Andīmeshk, Iran 45 C6 32 27N 48 21 E
Andizhan = Andijon, Uzbekistan 26 E8 41 10N 72 15 E
Andoany, Madag. 57 A8 13 25S 48 16 E
Andong, S. Korea 35 F15 36 40N 128 43 E
Andongwei, China 35 G10 35 6N 119 20 E
Andoom, Australia 62 A3 12 25S 141 53 E
Andorra ■, Europe 18 E4 42 30N 1 30 E
Andorra La Vella, Andorra 18 E4 42 31N 1 32 E
Andover, U.K. 11 F6 51 12N 1 29W
Andover, Maine, U.S.A. 79 B14 44 38N 70 45W
Andover, Mass., U.S.A. 79 D13 42 40N 71 8W
Andover, N.J., U.S.A. 79 F10 40 59N 74 45W
Andover, N.Y., U.S.A. 78 D7 42 10N 77 48W
Andover, Ohio, U.S.A. 78 E4 41 36N 80 34W
Andøya, Norway 8 B16 69 10N 15 50 E
Andradina, Brazil 93 H8 20 54S 51 23W
Andrahary, Mt., Madag. 57 A8 13 37S 49 17 E
Andramasina, Madag. 57 B8 19 11S 47 35 E
Andranopasy, Madag. 57 C7 21 17S 43 44 E
Andranovory, Madag. 57 C7 23 8S 44 10 E
Andratx, Spain 22 B9 39 39N 2 25 E
Andreanof Is., U.S.A. 68 C2 51 30N 176 0W
Andrews, S.C., U.S.A. 77 J6 33 27N 79 34W
Andrews, Tex., U.S.A. 81 J3 32 19N 102 33W
Ándria, Italy 20 D7 41 13N 16 17 E
Andriamena, Madag. 57 B8 17 26S 47 30 E
Andriandampy, Madag. 57 C8 22 45S 45 41 E
Andriba, Madag. 57 B8 17 30S 46 58 E
Androka, Madag. 57 C7 24 58S 44 2 E
Andropov = Rybinsk, Russia 24 C6 58 5N 38 50 E
Ándros, Greece 21 F11 37 50N 24 57 E
Andros I., Bahamas 88 B4 24 30N 78 0W
Andros Town, Bahamas 88 B4 24 43N 77 47W
Androscoggin →, U.S.A. 79 C14 43 58N 70 0W
Andselv, Norway 8 B18 69 4N 18 34 E
Andújar, Spain 19 C3 38 3N 4 5W
Andulo, Angola 52 G3 11 25S 16 45 E
Anegada I., Br. Virgin Is. 89 C7 18 45N 64 20W
Anegada Passage, W. Indies 89 C7 18 15N 63 45W
Aneto, Pico de, Spain 19 A6 42 37N 0 40 E
Ang Thong, Thailand 38 E3 14 35N 100 31 E
Angamos, Punta, Chile 94 A1 23 1S 70 32W
Angara →, Russia 27 D10 58 5N 94 20 E
Angarsk, Russia 27 D11 52 30N 104 0 E
Angas Hills, Australia 60 D4 23 0S 127 50 E
Angaston, Australia 63 E2 34 30S 139 8 E
Ånge, Sweden 9 E16 62 31N 15 35 E
Ángel, Salto = Angel Falls, Venezuela 92 B6 5 57N 62 30W
Ángel de la Guarda, I., Mexico 86 B2 29 30N 113 30W
Angel Falls, Venezuela 92 B6 5 57N 62 30W
Angeles, Phil. 37 A6 15 9N 120 33 E
Ängelholm, Sweden 9 H15 56 15N 12 58 E
Angels Camp, U.S.A. 84 G6 38 4N 120 32W
Ångermanälven →, Sweden 8 E17 62 40N 18 0 E
Ångermanland, Sweden 8 E18 63 36N 17 45 E
Angers, Canada 79 A9 45 31N 75 29W
Angers, France 18 C3 47 30N 0 35W
Ängesån →, Sweden 8 C20 66 16N 22 47 E
Angikuni L., Canada 73 A9 62 0N 100 0W
Angkor, Cambodia 38 F4 13 22N 103 50 E
Anglesey, Isle of □, U.K. 10 D3 53 16N 4 18W
Angleton, U.S.A. 81 L7 29 10N 95 26W
Anglisidhes, Cyprus 23 E12 34 51N 33 27 E
Angmagssalik = Tasiilaq, Greenland 4 C6 65 40N 37 20W
Ango, Dem. Rep. of the Congo 54 B2 4 10N 26 5 E
Angoche, Mozam. 55 F4 16 8S 39 55 E
Angoche, I., Mozam. 55 F4 16 20S 39 50 E
Angol, Chile 94 D1 37 56S 72 45W
Angola, Ind., U.S.A. 76 E3 41 38N 85 0W
Angola, N.Y., U.S.A. 78 D5 42 38N 79 2W
Angola ■, Africa 53 G3 12 0S 18 0 E
Angoulême, France 18 D4 45 39N 0 10 E
Angoumois, France 18 D3 45 50N 0 25 E
Angra dos Reis, Brazil 95 A7 23 0S 44 10W
Angren, Uzbekistan 26 E8 41 1N 70 12 E
Angtassom, Cambodia 39 G5 11 1N 104 41 E
Angu, Dem. Rep. of the Congo 54 B1 3 23N 24 30 E
Anguang, China 35 B12 45 15N 123 45 E
Anguilla ■, W. Indies 89 C7 18 14N 63 5W
Anguo, China 34 E8 38 28N 115 15 E
Angurugu, Australia 62 A2 14 0S 136 25 E
Angus □, U.K. 12 E6 56 46N 2 56W
Angwa →, Zimbabwe 57 B5 16 0S 30 23 E
Anhanduí →, Brazil 95 A5 21 46S 52 9W
Anholt, Denmark 9 H14 56 42N 11 33 E
Anhui □, China 33 C6 32 0N 117 0 E
Anhwei = Anhui □, China 33 C6 32 0N 117 0 E
Anichab, Namibia 56 C1 21 0S 14 46 E
Animas →, U.S.A. 83 H9 36 43N 108 13W
Anivorano, Madag. 57 B8 18 44S 48 58 E
Anjalankoski, Finland 9 F22 60 45N 26 51 E
Anjar, India 42 H4 23 6N 70 10 E
Anjou, France 18 C3 47 20N 0 15W
Anjozorobe, Madag. 57 B8 18 22S 47 52 E
Anju, N. Korea 35 E13 39 36N 125 40 E
Ankaboa, Tanjona, Madag. 57 C7 21 58S 43 20 E
Ankang, China 34 H5 32 40N 109 1 E
Ankara, Turkey 25 G5 39 57N 32 54 E
Ankaramena, Madag. 57 C8 21 57S 46 39 E
Ankaratra, Madag. 53 H9 19 25S 47 12 E
Ankasakasa, Madag. 57 B7 16 21S 44 52 E
Ankavandra, Madag. 57 B8 18 46S 45 18 E
Ankazoabo, Madag. 57 C7 22 18S 44 31 E
Ankazobe, Madag. 57 B8 18 20S 47 10 E
Ankeny, U.S.A. 80 E8 41 44N 93 36W
Ankilimalinika, Madag. 57 C7 22 58S 43 45 E
Ankilizato, Madag. 57 C8 20 25S 45 1 E
Ankisabe, Madag. 57 B8 19 17S 46 29 E
Ankoro, Dem. Rep. of the Congo 54 D2 6 45S 26 55 E
Ankororoka, Madag. 57 D8 25 30S 45 11 E
Anmyŏn-do, S. Korea 35 F14 36 25N 126 25 E
Ann, C., U.S.A. 79 D14 42 38N 70 35W
Ann Arbor, U.S.A. 76 D4 42 17N 83 45W
Anna, U.S.A. 81 G10 37 28N 89 15W
Annaba, Algeria 50 A7 36 50N 7 46 E
Annalee →, Ireland 13 B4 54 2N 7 24W
Annam, Vietnam 38 E7 16 0N 108 0 E
Annamitique, Chaîne, Asia 38 D6 17 0N 106 0 E
Annan, U.K. 12 G5 54 59N 3 16W
Annan →, U.K. 12 G5 54 58N 3 16W
Annapolis, U.S.A. 76 F7 38 59N 76 30W
Annapolis Royal, Canada 71 D6 44 44N 65 32W
Annapurna, Nepal 43 E10 28 34N 83 50 E
Annean, L., Australia 61 E2 26 54S 118 14 E
Annecy, France 18 D7 45 55N 6 8 E
Anning, China 32 D5 24 55N 102 26 E
Anniston, U.S.A. 77 J3 33 39N 85 50W
Annobón, Atl. Oc. 49 G4 1 25S 5 36 E
Annotto Bay, Jamaica 88 C4 18 17N 76 45W
Annville, U.S.A. 79 F8 40 20N 76 31W
Áno Viánnos, Greece 23 D7 35 2N 25 21 E
Anorotsangana, Madag. 57 A8 13 56S 47 55 E
Anosibe, Madag. 57 B8 19 26S 48 13 E
Anóyia, Greece 23 D6 35 16N 24 52 E
Anping, Hebei, China 34 E8 38 15N 115 30 E
Anping, Liaoning, China 35 D12 41 5N 123 30 E
Anqing, China 33 C6 30 30N 117 3 E
Anqiu, China 35 F10 36 25N 119 10 E
Ansai, China 34 F5 36 50N 109 20 E
Ansbach, Germany 16 D6 49 28N 10 34 E
Anshan, China 35 D12 41 5N 122 58 E
Anshun, China 32 D5 26 18N 105 57 E
Ansley, U.S.A. 80 E5 41 18N 99 23W
Anson, U.S.A. 81 J5 32 45N 99 54W
Anson B., Australia 60 B5 13 20S 130 6 E
Ansongo, Mali 50 E6 15 25N 0 35 E
Ansonia, U.S.A. 79 E11 41 21N 73 5W
Anstruther, U.K. 12 E6 56 14N 2 41W
Ansudu, Indonesia 37 E9 2 11S 139 22 E
Antabamba, Peru 92 F4 14 40S 73 0W
Antakya, Turkey 25 G6 36 14N 36 10 E
Antalaha, Madag. 57 A9 14 57S 50 20 E
Antalya, Turkey 25 G5 36 52N 30 45 E
Antalya Körfezi, Turkey 25 G5 36 15N 31 30 E
Antambohobe, Madag. 57 C8 22 20S 46 47 E
Antanambao-Manampotsy, Madag. 57 B8 19 29S 48 34 E
Antanambe, Madag. 57 B8 16 26S 49 52 E
Antananarivo, Madag. 57 B8 18 55S 47 31 E
Antananarivo □, Madag. 57 B8 19 0S 47 0 E
Antanifotsy, Madag. 57 B8 19 39S 47 19 E
Antanimbaribe, Madag. 57 C7 21 30S 44 48 E
Antanimora, Madag. 57 C8 24 49S 45 40 E
Antarctic Pen., Antarctica 5 C18 67 0S 60 0W
Antarctica 5 E3 90 0S 0 0W
Antelope, Zimbabwe 55 G2 21 2S 28 31 E
Antequera, Paraguay 94 A4 24 8S 57 7W
Antequera, Spain 19 D3 37 5N 4 33W
Antero, Mt., U.S.A. 83 G10 38 41N 106 15W
Antevamena, Madag. 57 C7 21 2S 44 8 E
Anthony, Kans., U.S.A. 81 G5 37 9N 98 2W
Anthony, N. Mex., U.S.A. 83 K10 32 0N 106 36W
Anti Atlas, Morocco 50 C4 30 0N 8 30W
Anti-Lebanon = Ash Sharqi, Al Jabal, Lebanon 47 B5 33 40N 36 10 E
Antibes, France 18 E7 43 34N 7 6 E
Anticosti, Î. d', Canada 71 C7 49 30N 63 0W
Antigo, U.S.A. 80 C10 45 9N 89 9W
Antigonish, Canada 71 C7 45 38N 61 58W
Antigua, Canary Is. 22 F5 28 24N 14 1W
Antigua, Guatemala 88 D1 14 34N 90 41W
Antigua, W. Indies 89 C7 17 0N 61 50W
Antigua & Barbuda ■, W. Indies 89 C7 17 20N 61 48W
Antilla, Cuba 88 B4 20 40N 75 50W
Antilles = West Indies, Cent. Amer. 89 D7 15 0N 65 0W
Antioch, U.S.A. 84 G5 38 1N 121 48W
Antioquia, Colombia 92 B3 6 40N 75 55W
Antipodes Is., Pac. Oc. 64 M9 49 45S 178 40 E
Antlers, U.S.A. 81 H7 34 14N 95 37W
Antoetra, Madag. 57 C8 20 46S 47 20 E
Antofagasta, Chile 94 A1 23 50S 70 30W
Antofagasta □, Chile 94 A2 24 0S 69 0W
Antofagasta de la Sierra, Argentina 94 B2 26 5S 67 20W
Antofalla, Argentina 94 B2 25 30S 68 5W
Antofalla, Salar de, Argentina 94 B2 25 40S 67 45W
Anton, U.S.A. 81 J3 33 49N 102 10W
Antongila, Helodrano, Madag. 57 B8 15 30S 49 50 E
Antonibé, Madag. 57 B8 15 7S 47 24 E
Antonibé, Presqu'île d', Madag. 57 A8 14 55S 47 20 E
Antonina, Brazil 95 B6 25 26S 48 42W
Antrim, U.K. 13 B5 54 43N 6 14W
Antrim, U.S.A. 78 F3 40 7N 81 21W
Antrim □, U.K. 13 B5 54 56N 6 25W
Antrim, Mts. of, U.K. 13 A5 55 3N 6 14W
Antrim Plateau, Australia 60 C4 18 8S 128 20 E
Antsakabary, Madag. 57 B8 15 3S 48 56 E
Antsalova, Madag. 57 B7 18 40S 44 37 E

Āshkhāneh

Āshkhāneh, *Iran*	**45 B8**	37 26N	56 55 E
Ashland, *Kans., U.S.A.*	**81 G5**	37 11N	99 46W
Ashland, *Ky., U.S.A.*	**76 F4**	38 28N	82 38W
Ashland, *Mont., U.S.A.*	**82 D10**	45 36N	106 16W
Ashland, *Ohio, U.S.A.*	**78 F2**	40 52N	82 19W
Ashland, *Oreg., U.S.A.*	**82 E2**	42 12N	122 43W
Ashland, *Pa., U.S.A.*	**79 F8**	40 45N	76 22W
Ashland, *Va., U.S.A.*	**76 G7**	37 46N	77 29W
Ashland, *Wis., U.S.A.*	**80 B9**	46 35N	90 53W
Ashley, *N. Dak., U.S.A.*	**80 B5**	46 2N	99 22W
Ashley, *Pa., U.S.A.*	**79 E9**	41 12N	75 55W
Ashmore Reef, *Australia*	**60 B3**	12 14S	123 5 E
Ashmyany, *Belarus*	**9 J21**	54 26N	25 52 E
Ashokan Reservoir, *U.S.A.*	**79 E10**	41 56N	74 13W
Ashqelon, *Israel*	**47 D3**	31 42N	34 35 E
Ashta, *India*	**42 H7**	23 1N	76 43 E
Ashtabula, *U.S.A.*	**78 E4**	41 52N	80 47W
Ashton, *S. Africa*	**56 E3**	33 50S	20 5 E
Ashton, *U.S.A.*	**82 D8**	44 4N	111 27W
Ashuanipi, L., *Canada*	**71 B6**	52 45N	66 15W
Ashville, *U.S.A.*	**78 F6**	40 34N	78 33W
Asia	**28 E11**	45 0N	75 0 E
Asia, Kepulauan, *Indonesia*	**37 D8**	1 0N	131 13 E
Āsīā Bak, *Iran*	**45 C6**	35 19N	50 30 E
Asifabad, *India*	**40 K11**	19 20N	79 24 E
Asinara, *Italy*	**20 D3**	41 4N	8 16 E
Asinara, G. dell', *Italy*	**20 D3**	41 0N	8 30 E
Asino, *Russia*	**26 D9**	57 0N	86 0 E
Asipovichy, *Belarus*	**17 B15**	53 19N	28 33 E
'Asīr □, *Si. Arabia*	**46 D3**	18 40N	42 30 E
Asir, Ras, *Somali Rep.*	**46 E5**	11 55N	51 10 E
Askersund, *Sweden*	**9 G16**	58 53N	14 55 E
Askham, *S. Africa*	**56 D3**	26 59S	20 47 E
Askim, *Norway*	**9 G14**	59 35N	11 10 E
Askja, *Iceland*	**8 D5**	65 3N	16 48W
Askøy, *Norway*	**9 F11**	60 29N	5 10 E
Asmara = Asmera, *Eritrea*	**46 D2**	15 19N	38 55 E
Asmera, *Eritrea*	**46 D2**	15 19N	38 55 E
Åsnen, *Sweden*	**9 H16**	56 37N	14 45 E
Aspen, *U.S.A.*	**83 G10**	39 11N	106 49W
Aspermont, *U.S.A.*	**81 J4**	33 8N	100 14W
Aspiring, Mt., *N.Z.*	**59 L2**	44 23S	168 46 E
Asprókavos, Ákra, *Greece*	**23 B4**	39 21N	20 6 E
Aspur, *India*	**42 H6**	23 58N	74 7 E
Asquith, *Canada*	**73 C7**	52 8N	107 13W
Assab = Aseb, *Eritrea*	**46 E3**	13 0N	42 40 E
Assam □, *India*	**41 G18**	26 0N	93 0 E
Asse, *Belgium*	**15 D4**	50 24N	4 10 E
Assen, *Neths.*	**15 A6**	53 0N	6 35 E
Assiniboia, *Canada*	**73 D7**	49 40N	105 59W
Assiniboine →, *Canada*	**73 D9**	49 53N	97 8W
Assiniboine, Mt., *Canada*	**72 C5**	50 52N	115 39W
Assis, *Brazil*	**95 A5**	22 40S	50 20W
Assisi, *Italy*	**20 C5**	43 4N	12 37 E
Assynt, L., *U.K.*	**12 C3**	58 10N	5 3W
Astana, *Kazakstan*	**26 D8**	51 10N	71 30 E
Āstāneh, *Iran*	**45 B6**	37 17N	49 59 E
Astara, *Azerbaijan*	**25 G8**	38 30N	48 50 E
Asteroúsia, *Greece*	**23 E7**	34 59N	25 3 E
Asti, *Italy*	**18 D8**	44 54N	8 12 E
Astipálaia, *Greece*	**21 F12**	36 32N	26 22 E
Astorga, *Spain*	**19 A2**	42 29N	6 8W
Astoria, *U.S.A.*	**84 D3**	46 11N	123 50W
Astrakhan, *Russia*	**25 E8**	46 25N	48 5 E
Asturias □, *Spain*	**19 A3**	43 15N	6 0W
Asunción, *Paraguay*	**94 B4**	25 10S	57 30W
Asunción Nochixtlán, *Mexico*	**87 D5**	17 28N	97 14W
Aswa →, *Uganda*	**54 B3**	3 43N	31 55 E
Aswân, *Egypt*	**51 D12**	24 4N	32 57 E
Aswân High Dam = Sadd el Aali, *Egypt*	**51 D12**	23 54N	32 54 E
Asyût, *Egypt*	**51 C12**	27 11N	31 4 E
At Ţafīlah, *Jordan*	**47 E4**	30 45N	35 30 E
Aţ Tā'if, *Si. Arabia*	**46 C3**	21 5N	40 27 E
Aţ Ţirāq, *Si. Arabia*	**44 E5**	27 19N	44 33 E
Aţ Tubayq, *Si. Arabia*	**44 D3**	29 30N	37 0 E
Atacama □, *Chile*	**94 B2**	27 30S	70 0W
Atacama, Desierto de, *Chile*	**94 A2**	24 0S	69 20W
Atacama, Salar de, *Chile*	**94 A2**	23 30S	68 20W
Atalaya, *Peru*	**92 F4**	10 45S	73 50W
Atalaya de Femes, *Canary Is.*	**22 F6**	28 56N	13 47W
Atami, *Japan*	**31 G9**	35 5N	139 4 E
Atapupu, *E. Timor*	**37 F6**	9 0S	124 51 E
Atâr, *Mauritania*	**50 D3**	20 30N	13 5W
Atari, *Pakistan*	**42 D6**	30 56N	74 2 E
Atascadero, *U.S.A.*	**84 K6**	35 29N	120 40W
Atasu, *Kazakstan*	**26 E8**	48 30N	71 0 E
Atatürk Barajı, *Turkey*	**25 G6**	37 28N	38 30 E
Atauro, *E. Timor*	**37 F7**	8 10S	125 30 E
'Atbara, *Sudan*	**51 E12**	17 42N	33 59 E
'Atbara, Nahr →, *Sudan*	**51 E12**	17 40N	33 56 E
Atbasar, *Kazakstan*	**26 D7**	51 48N	68 20 E
Atchafalaya B., *U.S.A.*	**81 L9**	29 25N	91 25W
Atchison, *U.S.A.*	**80 F7**	39 34N	95 7W
Āteshān, *Iran*	**45 C7**	35 35N	52 37 E
Ath, *Belgium*	**15 D3**	50 38N	3 47 E
Athabasca, *Canada*	**72 C6**	54 45N	113 20W
Athabasca →, *Canada*	**73 B6**	58 40N	110 50W
Athabasca, L., *Canada*	**73 B7**	59 15N	109 15W
Athboy, *Ireland*	**13 C5**	53 37N	6 56W
Athenry, *Ireland*	**13 C3**	53 18N	8 44W
Athens = Athínai, *Greece*	**21 F10**	37 58N	23 46 E
Athens, *Ala., U.S.A.*	**77 H2**	34 48N	86 58W
Athens, *Ga., U.S.A.*	**77 J4**	33 57N	83 23W
Athens, *N.Y., U.S.A.*	**79 D11**	42 16N	73 49W
Athens, *Ohio, U.S.A.*	**76 F4**	39 20N	82 6W
Athens, *Pa., U.S.A.*	**79 E8**	41 57N	76 31W
Athens, *Tenn., U.S.A.*	**77 H3**	35 27N	84 36W
Athens, *Tex., U.S.A.*	**81 J7**	32 12N	95 51W
Atherley, *Canada*	**78 B5**	44 37N	79 20W
Atherton, *Australia*	**62 B4**	17 17S	145 30 E
Athienou, *Cyprus*	**23 D12**	35 3N	33 32 E
Athínai, *Greece*	**21 F10**	37 58N	23 46 E
Athlone, *Ireland*	**13 C4**	53 25N	7 56W
Athna, *Cyprus*	**23 D12**	35 3N	33 47 E
Athol, *U.S.A.*	**79 D12**	42 36N	72 14W
Atholl, Forest of, *U.K.*	**12 E5**	56 51N	3 50W
Atholville, *Canada*	**71 C6**	47 59N	66 43W
Áthos, *Greece*	**21 D11**	40 9N	24 22 E
Athy, *Ireland*	**13 C5**	53 0N	7 0W
Ati, *Chad*	**51 F9**	13 13N	18 20 E
Atiak, *Uganda*	**54 B3**	3 12N	32 2 E
Atik L., *Canada*	**73 B9**	55 15N	96 0W
Atikameg →, *Canada*	**70 B3**	52 30N	82 46W
Atikokan, *Canada*	**70 C1**	48 45N	91 37W
Atikonak L., *Canada*	**71 B7**	52 40N	64 32W
Atka, *Russia*	**27 C16**	60 50N	151 48 E
Atka I., *U.S.A.*	**68 C2**	52 7N	174 30W
Atkinson, *U.S.A.*	**80 D5**	42 32N	98 59W
Atlanta, *Ga., U.S.A.*	**77 J3**	33 45N	84 23W
Atlanta, *Tex., U.S.A.*	**81 J7**	33 7N	94 10W
Atlantic, *U.S.A.*	**80 E7**	41 24N	95 1W
Atlantic City, *U.S.A.*	**76 F8**	39 21N	74 27W
Atlantic Ocean	**2 E9**	0 0	20 0W
Atlas Mts. = Haut Atlas, *Morocco*	**50 B4**	32 30N	5 0W
Atlin, *Canada*	**72 B2**	59 31N	133 41W
Atlin, L., *Canada*	**72 B2**	59 26N	133 45W
Atlin Prov. Park, *Canada*	**72 B2**	59 10N	134 30W
Atmore, *U.S.A.*	**77 K2**	31 2N	87 29W
Atoka, *U.S.A.*	**81 H6**	34 23N	96 8W
Atolia, *U.S.A.*	**85 K9**	35 19N	117 37W
Atrai →, *Bangla.*	**43 G13**	24 7N	89 22 E
Atrak = Atrek →, *Turkmenistan*	**45 B8**	37 35N	53 58 E
Atrauli, *India*	**42 E8**	28 2N	78 20 E
Atrek →, *Turkmenistan*	**45 B8**	37 35N	53 58 E
Atsuta, *Japan*	**30 C10**	43 24N	141 26 E
Attalla, *U.S.A.*	**77 H2**	34 1N	86 6W
Attapu, *Laos*	**38 E6**	14 48N	106 50 E
Attáviros, *Greece*	**23 C9**	36 12N	27 50 E
Attawapiskat, *Canada*	**70 B3**	52 56N	82 24W
Attawapiskat →, *Canada*	**70 B3**	52 57N	82 18W
Attawapiskat L., *Canada*	**70 B2**	52 18N	87 54W
Attica, *Ind., U.S.A.*	**76 E2**	40 18N	87 15W
Attica, *Ohio, U.S.A.*	**78 E2**	41 4N	82 53W
Attikamagen L., *Canada*	**71 B6**	55 0N	66 30W
Attleboro, *U.S.A.*	**79 E13**	41 57N	71 17W
Attock, *Pakistan*	**42 C5**	33 52N	72 20 E
Attopeu = Attapu, *Laos*	**38 E6**	14 48N	106 50 E
Attu I., *U.S.A.*	**68 C1**	52 55N	172 55 E
Attur, *India*	**40 P11**	11 35N	78 30 E
Atuel →, *Argentina*	**94 D2**	36 17S	66 50W
Åtvidaberg, *Sweden*	**9 G17**	58 12N	16 0 E
Atwater, *U.S.A.*	**84 H6**	37 21N	120 37W
Atwood, *Canada*	**78 C3**	43 40N	81 1W
Atwood, *U.S.A.*	**80 F4**	39 48N	101 3W
Atyraū, *Kazakstan*	**25 E9**	47 5N	52 0 E
Au Sable, *U.S.A.*	**78 B1**	44 25N	83 20W
Au Sable →, *U.S.A.*	**76 C4**	44 25N	83 20W
Au Sable Forks, *U.S.A.*	**79 B11**	44 27N	73 41W
Au Sable Pt., *U.S.A.*	**78 B1**	44 20N	83 20W
Aubagne, *France*	**18 E6**	43 17N	5 37 E
Aubarca, C. d', *Spain*	**22 B7**	39 4N	1 22 E
Aube →, *France*	**18 B5**	48 34N	3 43 E
Auberry, *U.S.A.*	**84 H7**	37 7N	119 29W
Auburn, *Ala., U.S.A.*	**77 J3**	32 36N	85 29W
Auburn, *Calif., U.S.A.*	**84 G5**	38 54N	121 4W
Auburn, *Ind., U.S.A.*	**76 E3**	41 22N	85 4W
Auburn, *Maine, U.S.A.*	**77 C10**	44 6N	70 14W
Auburn, *N.Y., U.S.A.*	**79 D8**	42 56N	76 34W
Auburn, *Nebr., U.S.A.*	**80 E7**	40 23N	95 51W
Auburn, *Pa., U.S.A.*	**79 F8**	40 36N	76 6W
Auburn, *Wash., U.S.A.*	**84 C4**	47 18N	122 14W
Auburn Ra., *Australia*	**63 D5**	25 15S	150 30 E
Auburndale, *U.S.A.*	**77 L5**	28 4N	81 48W
Aubusson, *France*	**18 D5**	45 57N	2 11 E
Auch, *France*	**18 E4**	43 39N	0 36 E
Auckland, *N.Z.*	**59 G5**	36 52S	174 46 E
Auckland Is., *Pac. Oc.*	**64 N8**	50 40S	166 5 E
Aude →, *France*	**18 E5**	43 13N	3 14 E
Auden, *Canada*	**70 B2**	50 14N	87 53W
Audubon, *U.S.A.*	**80 E7**	41 43N	94 56W
Augathella, *Australia*	**63 D4**	25 48S	146 35 E
Aughnacloy, *U.K.*	**13 B5**	54 25N	6 59W
Augrabies Falls, *S. Africa*	**56 D3**	28 35S	20 20 E
Augsburg, *Germany*	**16 D6**	48 25N	10 52 E
Augusta, *Australia*	**61 F2**	34 19S	115 9 E
Augusta, *Italy*	**20 F6**	37 13N	15 13 E
Augusta, *Ark., U.S.A.*	**81 H9**	35 17N	91 22W
Augusta, *Ga., U.S.A.*	**77 J5**	33 28N	81 58W
Augusta, *Kans., U.S.A.*	**81 G6**	37 41N	96 59W
Augusta, *Maine, U.S.A.*	**69 D13**	44 19N	69 47W
Augusta, *Mont., U.S.A.*	**82 C7**	47 30N	112 24W
Augustów, *Poland*	**17 B12**	53 51N	23 0 E
Augustus, Mt., *Australia*	**61 D2**	24 20S	116 50 E
Augustus I., *Australia*	**60 C3**	15 20S	124 30 E
Aukum, *U.S.A.*	**84 G6**	38 34N	120 43W
Auld, L., *Australia*	**60 D3**	22 25S	123 50 E
Ault, *U.S.A.*	**80 E2**	40 35N	104 44W
Aunis, *France*	**18 C3**	46 5N	0 50W
Auponhia, *Indonesia*	**37 E7**	1 58S	125 27 E
Aur, Pulau, *Malaysia*	**39 L5**	2 35N	104 10 E
Auraiya, *India*	**43 F8**	26 28N	79 33 E
Aurangabad, *Bihar, India*	**43 G11**	24 45N	84 18 E
Aurangabad, *Maharashtra, India*	**40 K9**	19 50N	75 23 E
Aurich, *Germany*	**16 B4**	53 28N	7 28 E
Aurillac, *France*	**18 D5**	44 55N	2 26 E
Aurora, *Canada*	**78 C5**	44 0N	79 28W
Aurora, *S. Africa*	**56 E2**	32 40S	18 29 E
Aurora, *Colo., U.S.A.*	**80 F2**	39 44N	104 52W
Aurora, *Ill., U.S.A.*	**76 E1**	41 45N	88 19W
Aurora, *Mo., U.S.A.*	**81 G8**	36 58N	93 43W
Aurora, *N.Y., U.S.A.*	**79 D8**	42 45N	76 42W
Aurora, *Nebr., U.S.A.*	**80 E6**	40 52N	98 0W
Aurora, *Ohio, U.S.A.*	**78 E3**	41 21N	81 20W
Aurukun, *Australia*	**62 A3**	13 20S	141 45 E
Aus, *Namibia*	**56 D2**	26 35S	16 12 E
Ausable →, *Canada*	**78 C3**	43 19N	81 46W
Auschwitz = Oświęcim, *Poland*	**17 C10**	50 2N	19 11 E
Austin, *Minn., U.S.A.*	**80 D8**	43 40N	92 58W
Austin, *Nev., U.S.A.*	**82 G5**	39 30N	117 4W
Austin, *Pa., U.S.A.*	**78 E6**	41 38N	78 6W
Austin, *Tex., U.S.A.*	**81 K6**	30 17N	97 45W
Austin, L., *Australia*	**61 E2**	27 40S	118 0 E
Austin I., *Canada*	**73 A10**	61 10N	94 0W
Austra, *Norway*	**8 D14**	65 8N	11 55 E
Austral Is. = Tubuai Is., *Pac. Oc.*	**65 K13**	25 0S	150 0W
Austral Seamount Chain, *Pac. Oc.*	**65 K13**	24 0S	150 0W
Australia ■, *Oceania*	**64 K5**	23 0S	135 0 E
Australian Capital Territory □, *Australia*	**63 F4**	35 30S	149 0 E
Australind, *Australia*	**61 F2**	33 17S	115 42 E
Austria ■, *Europe*	**16 E8**	47 0N	14 0 E
Austvågøy, *Norway*	**8 B16**	68 20N	14 40 E
Autlán, *Mexico*	**86 D4**	19 40N	104 30W
Autun, *France*	**18 C6**	46 58N	4 17 E
Auvergne, *France*	**18 D5**	45 20N	3 15 E
Auvergne, Mts. d', *France*	**18 D5**	45 20N	2 55 E
Auxerre, *France*	**18 C5**	47 48N	3 32 E
Ava, *U.S.A.*	**81 G8**	36 57N	92 40W
Avallon, *France*	**18 C5**	47 30N	3 53 E
Avalon, *U.S.A.*	**85 M8**	33 21N	118 20W
Avalon Pen., *Canada*	**71 C9**	47 30N	53 20W
Avanos, *Turkey*	**44 B2**	38 43N	34 51 E
Avaré, *Brazil*	**95 A6**	23 4S	48 58W
Avawatz Mts., *U.S.A.*	**85 K10**	35 40N	116 30W
Aveiro, *Brazil*	**93 D7**	3 10S	55 5W
Aveiro, *Portugal*	**19 B1**	40 37N	8 38W
Āvej, *Iran*	**45 C6**	35 40N	49 15 E
Avellaneda, *Argentina*	**94 C4**	34 50S	58 10W
Avellino, *Italy*	**20 D6**	40 54N	14 47 E
Avenal, *U.S.A.*	**84 K6**	36 0N	120 8W
Aversa, *Italy*	**20 D6**	40 58N	14 12 E
Avery, *U.S.A.*	**82 C6**	47 15N	115 49W
Aves, Is. las, *Venezuela*	**89 D6**	12 0N	67 30W
Avesta, *Sweden*	**9 F17**	60 9N	16 10 E
Avezzano, *Italy*	**20 C5**	42 2N	13 25 E
Aviá Terai, *Argentina*	**94 B3**	26 45S	60 50W
Aviemore, *U.K.*	**12 D5**	57 12N	3 50W
Avignon, *France*	**18 E6**	43 57N	4 50 E
Ávila, *Spain*	**19 B3**	40 39N	4 43W
Avila Beach, *U.S.A.*	**85 K6**	35 11N	120 44W
Avilés, *Spain*	**19 A3**	43 35N	5 57W
Avis, *U.S.A.*	**78 E7**	41 11N	77 19W
Avoca, *U.S.A.*	**78 D7**	42 25N	77 25W
Avoca →, *Australia*	**63 F3**	35 40S	143 43 E
Avoca →, *Ireland*	**13 D5**	52 48N	6 10W
Avola, *Canada*	**72 C5**	51 45N	119 19W
Avola, *Italy*	**20 F6**	36 56N	15 7 E
Avon, *U.S.A.*	**78 D7**	42 55N	77 45W
Avon →, *Australia*	**61 F2**	31 40S	116 7 E
Avon →, *Bristol, U.K.*	**11 F5**	51 29N	2 41W
Avon →, *Dorset, U.K.*	**11 G6**	50 44N	1 46W
Avon →, *Warks., U.K.*	**11 E5**	52 0N	2 8W
Avon Park, *U.S.A.*	**77 M5**	27 36N	81 31W
Avondale, *Zimbabwe*	**55 F3**	17 43S	30 58 E
Avonlea, *Canada*	**73 D8**	50 0N	105 0W
Avonmore, *Canada*	**79 A10**	45 10N	74 58W
Avranches, *France*	**18 B3**	48 40N	1 20W
A'waj →, *Syria*	**47 B5**	33 23N	36 20 E
Awaji-Shima, *Japan*	**31 G7**	34 30N	134 50 E
'Awālī, *Bahrain*	**45 E6**	26 0N	50 30 E
Awantipur, *India*	**43 C6**	33 55N	75 3 E
Awasa, *Ethiopia*	**46 F2**	7 2N	38 28 E
Awash, *Ethiopia*	**46 F3**	9 1N	40 10 E
Awatere →, *N.Z.*	**59 J5**	41 37S	174 10 E
Awbārī, *Libya*	**51 C8**	26 46N	12 57 E
Awe, L., *U.K.*	**12 E3**	56 17N	5 16W
Awjilah, *Libya*	**51 C10**	29 8N	21 7 E
Axe →, *U.K.*	**11 F5**	50 42N	3 4W
Axel Heiberg I., *Canada*	**4 B3**	80 0N	90 0W
Axim, *Ghana*	**50 H5**	4 51N	2 15W
Axiós →, *Greece*	**21 D10**	40 57N	22 35 E
Axminster, *U.K.*	**11 G4**	50 46N	3 0W
Ayabaca, *Peru*	**92 D3**	4 40S	79 53W
Ayabe, *Japan*	**31 G7**	35 20N	135 20 E
Ayacucho, *Argentina*	**94 D4**	37 5S	58 20W
Ayacucho, *Peru*	**92 F4**	13 0S	74 0W
Ayaguz, *Kazakstan*	**26 E9**	48 10N	80 10 E
Ayamonte, *Spain*	**19 D2**	37 12N	7 24W
Ayan, *Russia*	**27 D14**	56 30N	138 16 E
Ayaviri, *Peru*	**92 F4**	14 50S	70 35W
Aydın, *Turkey*	**21 F12**	37 51N	27 51 E
Aydin □, *Turkey*	**25 G4**	37 50N	28 0 E
Ayer, *U.S.A.*	**79 D13**	42 34N	71 35W
Ayer's Cliff, *Canada*	**79 A12**	45 10N	72 3W
Ayers Rock, *Australia*	**61 E5**	25 23S	131 5 E
Ayia Aikateríni, Ákra, *Greece*	**23 A3**	39 50N	19 50 E
Ayia Dhéka, *Greece*	**23 D6**	35 3N	24 58 E
Ayia Gálini, *Greece*	**23 D6**	35 6N	24 41 E
Áyia Napa, *Cyprus*	**23 E13**	34 59N	34 0 E
Áyia Phyla, *Cyprus*	**23 E12**	34 43N	33 1 E
Ayia Varvára, *Greece*	**23 D7**	35 8N	25 1 E
Áyios Amvrósios, *Cyprus*	**23 D12**	35 20N	33 35 E
Áyios Evstrátios, *Greece*	**21 E11**	39 34N	24 58 E
Áyios Ioánnis, Ákra, *Greece*	**23 D7**	35 20N	25 40 E
Áyios Isidhoros, *Greece*	**23 C9**	36 9N	27 51 E
Áyios Matthaíos, *Greece*	**23 B3**	39 30N	19 47 E
Áyios Nikólaos, *Greece*	**23 D7**	35 11N	25 41 E
Áyios Seryios, *Cyprus*	**23 D12**	35 12N	33 53 E
Áyios Theodhoros, *Cyprus*	**23 D13**	35 22N	34 1 E
Aykino, *Russia*	**24 B8**	62 15N	49 56 E
Aylesbury, *U.K.*	**11 F7**	51 49N	0 49W
Aylmer, *Canada*	**78 D4**	42 46N	80 59W
Aylmer, L., *Canada*	**68 B8**	64 0N	110 8W
'Ayn, Wādī al, *Oman*	**45 F7**	22 15N	55 28 E
Ayn Dār, *Si. Arabia*	**45 E7**	25 55N	49 10 E
Ayn Zālah, *Iraq*	**44 B4**	36 45N	42 35 E
Ayolas, *Paraguay*	**94 B4**	27 10S	56 59W
Ayon, Ostrov, *Russia*	**27 C17**	69 50N	169 0 E
'Ayoûn el 'Atroûs, *Mauritania*	**50 E4**	16 38N	9 37W
Ayr, *Australia*	**62 B4**	19 35S	147 25 E
Ayr, *Canada*	**78 C4**	43 17N	80 27W
Ayr, *U.K.*	**12 F4**	55 28N	4 38W
Ayr →, *U.K.*	**12 F4**	55 28N	4 38W
Ayre, Pt. of, *U.K.*	**10 C3**	54 25N	4 21W
Ayton, *Australia*	**62 B4**	15 56S	145 22 E
Aytos, *Bulgaria*	**21 C12**	42 42N	27 16 E
Ayu, Kepulauan, *Indonesia*	**37 D8**	0 35N	131 5 E
Ayutla, *Guatemala*	**88 D1**	14 40N	92 10W
Ayutla, *Mexico*	**87 D5**	16 58N	99 17W
Ayvacık, *Turkey*	**21 E12**	39 36N	26 24 E
Ayvalık, *Turkey*	**21 E12**	39 20N	26 46 E
Az Zabadānī, *Syria*	**47 B5**	33 43N	36 5 E
Aẓ Ẓāhirīyah, *West Bank*	**47 D3**	31 25N	34 58 E
Aẓ Ẓahrān, *Si. Arabia*	**45 E6**	26 10N	50 7 E
Az Zarqā, *Jordan*	**47 C5**	32 5N	36 4 E
Az Zarqā', *U.A.E.*	**45 E7**	24 53N	53 4 E
Az Zībār, *Iraq*	**44 B5**	36 52N	44 4 E
Az Zilfī, *Si. Arabia*	**44 E5**	26 12N	44 52 E
Az Zubayr, *Iraq*	**44 D5**	30 26N	47 40 E
Azamgarh, *India*	**43 F10**	26 5N	83 13 E
Azangaro, *Peru*	**92 F4**	14 55S	70 13W
Āzār Shahr, *Iran*	**44 B5**	37 45N	45 59 E
Azarān, *Iran*	**44 B5**	37 25N	47 16 E
Azärbayjan = Azerbaijan ■, *Asia*	**25 F8**	40 20N	48 0 E
Āzarbāyjān-e Gharbī □, *Iran*	**44 B5**	37 0N	44 30 E
Āzarbāyjān-e Sharqī □, *Iran*	**44 B5**	37 20N	47 0 E
Azare, *Nigeria*	**50 F8**	11 55N	10 10 E
A'zāz, *Syria*	**44 B3**	36 36N	37 4 E
Azbine = Aïr, *Niger*	**50 E7**	18 30N	8 0 E
Azerbaijan ■, *Asia*	**25 F8**	40 20N	48 0 E
Azerbaijchan = Azerbaijan ■, *Asia*	**25 F8**	40 20N	48 0 E
Azimganj, *India*	**43 G13**	24 14N	88 16 E
Azogues, *Ecuador*	**92 D3**	2 35S	78 0W
Azores = Açores, Is. dos, *Atl. Oc.*	**50 A1**	38 0N	27 0W
Azov, *Russia*	**25 E6**	47 3N	39 25 E
Azov, Sea of, *Europe*	**25 E6**	46 0N	36 30 E
Azovskoye More = Azov, Sea of, *Europe*	**25 E6**	46 0N	36 30 E
Azraq ash Shīshān, *Jordan*	**47 D5**	31 50N	36 49 E
Aztec, *U.S.A.*	**83 H10**	36 49N	107 59W
Azúa de Compostela, *Dom. Rep.*	**89 C5**	18 25N	70 44W
Azuaga, *Spain*	**19 C3**	38 16N	5 39W
Azuero, Pen. de, *Panama*	**88 E3**	7 30N	80 30W
Azul, *Argentina*	**94 D4**	36 42S	59 43W
Azusa, *U.S.A.*	**85 L9**	34 8N	117 52W

B

Ba Don, *Vietnam*	**38 D6**	17 45N	106 26 E
Ba Dong, *Vietnam*	**39 H6**	9 40N	106 33 E
Ba Ngoi = Cam Lam, *Vietnam*	**39 G7**	11 54N	109 10 E
Ba Tri, *Vietnam*	**39 G6**	10 2N	106 36 E
Ba Xian = Bazhou, *China*	**34 E9**	39 8N	116 22 E
Baa, *Indonesia*	**37 F6**	10 50S	123 0 E
Baardeere = Bardera, *Somali Rep.*	**46 G3**	2 20N	42 27 E
Baarle-Nassau, *Belgium*	**15 C4**	51 27N	4 56 E
Bab el Mandeb, *Red Sea*	**46 E3**	12 35N	43 25 E
Bābā, Koh-i-, *Afghan.*	**40 B5**	34 30N	67 0 E
Baba Burnu, *Turkey*	**21 E12**	39 29N	26 2 E
Bābā Kalū, *Iran*	**45 D6**	30 7N	50 49 E
Babadag, *Romania*	**17 F15**	44 53N	28 44 E
Babadayhan, *Turkmenistan*	**26 F7**	37 42N	60 23 E
Babaeski, *Turkey*	**21 D12**	41 26N	27 6 E
Babahoyo, *Ecuador*	**92 D3**	1 40S	79 30W
Babai = Sarju →, *India*	**43 F9**	27 21N	81 23 E
Babar, *Indonesia*	**37 F7**	8 0S	129 30 E
Babar, *Pakistan*	**42 D3**	31 7N	69 32 E
Babarkach, *Pakistan*	**42 E3**	29 45N	68 0 E
Babb, *U.S.A.*	**82 B7**	48 51N	113 27W
Baberu, *India*	**43 G9**	25 33N	80 43 E
Babi Besar, Pulau, *Malaysia*	**39 L4**	2 25N	103 59 E
Babinda, *Australia*	**62 B4**	17 20S	145 56 E
Babine, *Canada*	**72 B3**	55 22N	126 37W
Babine →, *Canada*	**72 B3**	55 45N	127 44W
Babine L., *Canada*	**72 C3**	54 48N	126 0W
Babo, *Indonesia*	**37 E8**	2 30S	133 30 E
Bābol, *Iran*	**45 B7**	36 40N	52 50 E
Bābol Sar, *Iran*	**45 B7**	36 45N	52 45 E
Babruysk, *Belarus*	**17 B15**	53 10N	29 15 E
Babuhri, *India*	**42 F3**	26 49N	69 43 E
Babusar Pass, *Pakistan*	**43 B5**	35 12N	73 59 E
Babuyan Chan., *Phil.*	**37 A6**	18 40N	121 30 E
Babylon, *Iraq*	**44 C5**	32 34N	44 22 E
Bac Can, *Vietnam*	**38 A5**	22 8N	105 49 E
Bac Giang, *Vietnam*	**38 B6**	21 16N	106 11 E
Bac Lieu, *Vietnam*	**39 H5**	9 17N	105 43 E
Bac Ninh, *Vietnam*	**38 B6**	21 13N	106 4 E
Bac Phan, *Vietnam*	**38 B5**	22 0N	105 0 E
Bac Quang, *Vietnam*	**38 A5**	22 30N	104 48 E
Bacabal, *Brazil*	**93 D10**	4 15S	44 45W
Bacalar, *Mexico*	**87 D7**	18 50N	87 27W
Bacan, Kepulauan, *Indonesia*	**37 E7**	0 35S	127 30 E
Bacarra, *Phil.*	**37 A6**	18 15N	120 37 E
Bacău, *Romania*	**17 E14**	46 35N	26 55 E
Bacerac, *Mexico*	**86 A3**	30 18N	108 50W
Bach Long Vi, Dao, *Vietnam*	**38 B6**	20 10N	107 40 E
Bachelina, *Russia*	**26 D7**	57 45N	67 20 E
Bachhwara, *India*	**43 G11**	25 35N	85 54 E
Back →, *Canada*	**68 B9**	65 10N	104 0W
Bacolod, *Phil.*	**37 B6**	10 40N	122 57 E
Bacuk, *Malaysia*	**39 J4**	6 4N	102 25 E
Bād, *Iran*	**45 C7**	33 41N	52 1 E
Bad →, *U.S.A.*	**80 C4**	44 21N	100 22W
Bad Axe, *U.S.A.*	**78 C2**	43 48N	83 0W
Bad Ischl, *Austria*	**16 E7**	47 44N	13 38 E
Bad Kissingen, *Germany*	**16 C6**	50 11N	10 4 E
Bad Lands, *U.S.A.*	**80 D3**	43 40N	102 10W
Bada Barabil, *India*	**43 H11**	22 7N	85 24 E
Badagara, *India*	**40 P9**	11 35N	75 40 E
Badajós, L., *Brazil*	**92 D6**	3 15S	62 50W
Badajoz, *Spain*	**19 C2**	38 50N	6 59W
Badalona, *Spain*	**19 B7**	41 26N	2 15 E
Badalzai, *Afghan.*	**42 E1**	29 50N	65 35 E
Badampahar, *India*	**41 H15**	22 10N	86 10 E
Badanah, *Si. Arabia*	**44 D4**	30 58N	41 30 E
Badarinath, *India*	**43 D8**	30 45N	79 30 E
Badas, Kepulauan, *Indonesia*	**36 D3**	0 45N	107 5 E
Baddo →, *Pakistan*	**40 F4**	28 0N	64 20 E
Bade, *Indonesia*	**37 F9**	7 10S	139 35 E
Baden, *Austria*	**16 D9**	48 1N	16 13 E
Baden, *U.S.A.*	**78 F4**	40 38N	80 14W
Baden-Baden, *Germany*	**16 D5**	48 44N	8 13 E
Baden-Württemberg □, *Germany*	**16 D5**	48 20N	8 40 E
Badgastein, *Austria*	**16 E7**	47 7N	13 9 E
Badger, *Canada*	**71 C8**	49 0N	56 4W
Badger, *U.S.A.*	**84 J7**	36 38N	119 1W
Bādghīs □, *Afghan.*	**40 B3**	35 0N	63 0 E
Badgom, *India*	**43 B6**	34 1N	74 45 E
Badin, *Pakistan*	**42 G3**	24 38N	68 54 E
Badlands Nat. Park, *U.S.A.*	**80 D3**	43 38N	102 56W
Badrah, *Iraq*	**44 C5**	33 6N	45 58 E
Badrinath, *India*	**43 D8**	30 44N	79 29 E
Badulla, *Sri Lanka*	**40 R12**	7 1N	81 7 E
Baena, *Spain*	**19 D3**	37 37N	4 20W
Baeza, *Spain*	**19 D4**	37 57N	3 25W
Baffin B., *Canada*	**69 A13**	72 0N	64 0W
Baffin I., *Canada*	**69 B12**	68 0N	75 0W
Bafing →, *Mali*	**50 F3**	13 49N	10 50W
Bafliyūn, *Syria*	**44 B3**	36 37N	36 59 E
Bafoulabé, *Mali*	**50 F3**	13 50N	10 55W
Bāfq, *Iran*	**45 D7**	31 40N	55 25 E
Bafra, *Turkey*	**25 F6**	41 34N	35 54 E
Bāft, *Iran*	**45 D8**	29 15N	56 38 E
Bafwasende, *Dem. Rep. of the Congo*	**54 B2**	1 3N	27 5 E

Biaora

Behala, *India*	**43 H13**	22 30N	88 20 E
Behara, *Madag.*	**57 C8**	24 55S	46 20 E
Behbehān, *Iran*	**45 D6**	30 30N	50 15 E
Behm Canal, *U.S.A.*	**72 B2**	55 10N	131 0W
Behshahr, *Iran*	**45 B7**	36 45N	53 35 E
Bei Jiang →, *China*	**33 D6**	23 2N	112 58 E
Bei'an, *China*	**33 B7**	48 10N	126 20 E
Beihai, *China*	**33 D5**	21 28N	109 6 E
Beijing, *China*	**34 E9**	39 55N	116 20 E
Beijing □, *China*	**34 E9**	39 55N	116 20 E
Beilen, *Neths.*	**15 B6**	52 52N	6 27 E
Beilpajah, *Australia*	**63 E3**	32 54S	143 52 E
Beinn na Faoghla = Benbecula, *U.K.*	**12 D1**	57 26N	7 21W
Beipiao, *China*	**35 D11**	41 52N	120 32 E
Beira, *Mozam.*	**55 F3**	19 50S	34 52 E
Beirut = Bayrūt, *Lebanon*	**47 B4**	33 53N	35 31 E
Beiseker, *Canada*	**72 C6**	51 23N	113 32W
Beitaolaizhao, *China*	**35 B13**	44 58N	125 58 E
Beitbridge, *Zimbabwe*	**55 G3**	22 12S	30 0 E
Beizhen = Binzhou, *China*	**35 F10**	37 20N	118 2 E
Beizhen, *China*	**35 D11**	41 38N	121 54 E
Beizhengzhen, *China*	**35 B12**	44 31N	123 30 E
Beja, *Portugal*	**19 C2**	38 2N	7 53W
Béja, *Tunisia*	**51 A7**	36 43N	9 12 E
Bejaïa, *Algeria*	**50 A7**	36 42N	5 2 E
Béjar, *Spain*	**19 B3**	40 23N	5 46W
Bejestān, *Iran*	**45 C8**	34 30N	58 5 E
Békéscsaba, *Hungary*	**17 E11**	46 40N	21 5 E
Bekily, *Madag.*	**57 C8**	24 13S	45 19 E
Bekisopa, *Madag.*	**57 C8**	21 40S	45 54 E
Bekitro, *Madag.*	**57 C8**	24 33S	45 18 E
Bekodoka, *Madag.*	**57 B8**	16 58S	45 7 E
Bekok, *Malaysia*	**39 L4**	2 20N	103 7 E
Bekopaka, *Madag.*	**57 B7**	19 9S	44 48 E
Bela, *India*	**43 G10**	25 50N	82 0 E
Bela, *Pakistan*	**42 F2**	26 12N	66 20 E
Bela Crkva, *Serbia, Yug.*	**21 B9**	44 55N	21 27 E
Bela Vista, *Brazil*	**94 A4**	22 12S	56 20W
Bela Vista, *Mozam.*	**57 D5**	26 10S	32 44 E
Belan →, *India*	**43 G9**	24 2N	81 45 E
Belarus ■, *Europe*	**17 B14**	53 30N	27 0 E
Belau = Palau ■, *Pac. Oc.*	**28 J17**	7 30N	134 30 E
Belavenona, *Madag.*	**57 C8**	24 50S	47 4 E
Belawan, *Indonesia*	**36 D1**	3 33N	98 32 E
Belaya →, *Russia*	**24 C9**	54 40N	56 0 E
Belaya Tserkov = Bila Tserkva, *Ukraine*	**17 D16**	49 45N	30 10 E
Belcher Is., *Canada*	**70 A3**	56 15N	78 45W
Belden, *U.S.A.*	**84 E5**	40 2N	121 17W
Belebey, *Russia*	**24 D9**	54 7N	54 7 E
Beled Weyne = Belet Uen, *Somali Rep.*	**46 G4**	4 30N	45 5 E
Belém, *Brazil*	**93 D9**	1 20S	48 30W
Belén, *Argentina*	**94 B2**	27 40S	67 5W
Belén, *Paraguay*	**94 A4**	23 30S	57 6W
Belen, *U.S.A.*	**83 J10**	34 40N	106 46W
Belet Uen, *Somali Rep.*	**46 G4**	4 30N	45 5 E
Belev, *Russia*	**24 D6**	53 50N	36 5 E
Belfair, *U.S.A.*	**84 C4**	47 27N	122 50W
Belfast, *S. Africa*	**57 D5**	25 42S	30 2 E
Belfast, *U.K.*	**13 B6**	54 37N	5 56W
Belfast, *Maine, U.S.A.*	**77 C11**	44 26N	69 1W
Belfast, *N.Y., U.S.A.*	**78 D6**	42 21N	78 7W
Belfast L., *U.K.*	**13 B6**	54 40N	5 50W
Belfield, *U.S.A.*	**80 B3**	46 53N	103 12W
Belfort, *France*	**18 C7**	47 38N	6 50 E
Belfry, *U.S.A.*	**82 D9**	45 9N	109 1W
Belgaum, *India*	**40 M9**	15 55N	74 35 E
Belgium ■, *Europe*	**15 D4**	50 30N	5 0 E
Belgorod, *Russia*	**25 D6**	50 35N	36 35 E
Belgorod-Dnestrovskiy = Bilhorod-Dnistrovskyy, *Ukraine*	**25 E5**	46 11N	30 23 E
Belgrade = Beograd, *Serbia, Yug.*	**21 B9**	44 50N	20 37 E
Belgrade, *U.S.A.*	**82 D8**	45 47N	111 11W
Belhaven, *U.S.A.*	**77 H7**	35 33N	76 37W
Beli Drim →, *Europe*	**21 C9**	42 6N	20 25 E
Belinyu, *Indonesia*	**36 E3**	1 35S	105 50 E
Beliton Is. = Belitung, *Indonesia*	**36 E3**	3 10S	107 50 E
Belitung, *Indonesia*	**36 E3**	3 10S	107 50 E
Belize ■, *Cent. Amer.*	**87 D7**	17 0N	88 30W
Belize City, *Belize*	**87 D7**	17 25N	88 0W
Belkovskiy, Ostrov, *Russia*	**27 B14**	75 32N	135 44 E
Bell →, *Canada*	**70 C4**	49 48N	77 38W
Bell I., *Canada*	**71 B8**	50 46N	55 35W
Bell-Irving →, *Canada*	**72 B3**	56 12N	129 5W
Bell Peninsula, *Canada*	**69 B11**	63 50N	82 0W
Bell Ville, *Argentina*	**94 C3**	32 40S	62 40W
Bella Bella, *Canada*	**72 C3**	52 10N	128 10W
Bella Coola, *Canada*	**72 C3**	52 25N	126 40W
Bella Unión, *Uruguay*	**94 C4**	30 15S	57 40W
Bella Vista, *Corrientes, Argentina*	**94 B4**	28 33S	59 0W
Bella Vista, *Tucuman, Argentina*	**94 B2**	27 10S	65 25W
Bellaire, *U.S.A.*	**78 F4**	40 1N	80 45W
Bellary, *India*	**40 M10**	15 10N	76 56 E
Bellata, *Australia*	**63 D4**	29 53S	149 46 E
Belle-Chasse, *U.S.A.*	**81 L10**	29 51N	89 59W
Belle Fourche, *U.S.A.*	**80 C3**	44 40N	103 51W
Belle Fourche →, *U.S.A.*	**80 C3**	44 26N	102 18W
Belle Glade, *U.S.A.*	**77 M5**	26 41N	80 40W
Belle-Île, *France*	**18 C2**	47 20N	3 10W
Belle Isle, *Canada*	**71 B8**	51 57N	55 25W
Belle Isle, Str. of, *Canada*	**71 B8**	51 30N	56 30W
Belle Plaine, *U.S.A.*	**80 E8**	41 54N	92 17W
Bellefontaine, *U.S.A.*	**76 E4**	40 22N	83 46W
Bellefonte, *U.S.A.*	**78 F7**	40 55N	77 47W
Belleoram, *Canada*	**71 C8**	47 31N	55 25W
Belleville, *Canada*	**78 B7**	44 10N	77 23W
Belleville, *Ill., U.S.A.*	**80 F10**	38 31N	89 59W
Belleville, *Kans., U.S.A.*	**80 F6**	39 50N	97 38W
Belleville, *N.Y., U.S.A.*	**79 C8**	43 46N	76 10W
Bellevue, *Canada*	**72 D6**	49 35N	114 22W
Bellevue, *Idaho, U.S.A.*	**82 E6**	43 28N	114 16W
Bellevue, *Nebr., U.S.A.*	**80 E7**	41 8N	95 53W
Bellevue, *Ohio, U.S.A.*	**78 E2**	41 17N	82 51W
Bellevue, *Wash., U.S.A.*	**84 C4**	47 37N	122 12W
Bellin = Kangirsuk, *Canada*	**69 B13**	60 0N	70 0W
Bellingen, *Australia*	**63 E5**	30 25S	152 50 E
Bellingham, *U.S.A.*	**68 D7**	48 46N	122 29W
Bellingshausen Sea, *Antarctica*	**5 C17**	66 0S	80 0W
Bellinzona, *Switz.*	**18 C8**	46 11N	9 1 E
Bello, *Colombia*	**92 B3**	6 20N	75 33W
Bellows Falls, *U.S.A.*	**79 C12**	43 8N	72 27W
Bellpat, *Pakistan*	**42 E3**	29 0N	68 5 E
Belluno, *Italy*	**20 A5**	46 9N	12 13 E
Bellwood, *U.S.A.*	**78 F6**	40 36N	78 20W
Belmont, *Canada*	**78 D3**	42 53N	81 5W
Belmont, *S. Africa*	**56 D3**	29 28S	24 22 E
Belmont, *U.S.A.*	**78 D6**	42 14N	78 2W
Belmonte, *Brazil*	**93 G11**	16 0S	39 0W
Belmopan, *Belize*	**87 D7**	17 18N	88 30W
Belmullet, *Ireland*	**13 B2**	54 14N	9 58W
Belo Horizonte, *Brazil*	**93 G10**	19 55S	43 56W
Belo-sur-Mer, *Madag.*	**57 C7**	20 42S	44 0 E
Belo-Tsiribihina, *Madag.*	**57 B7**	19 40S	44 30 E
Belogorsk, *Russia*	**27 D13**	51 0N	128 20 E
Beloha, *Madag.*	**57 D8**	25 10S	45 3 E
Beloit, *Kans., U.S.A.*	**80 F5**	39 28N	98 6W
Beloit, *Wis., U.S.A.*	**80 D10**	42 31N	89 2W
Belokorovichi, *Ukraine*	**17 C15**	51 7N	28 2 E
Belomorsk, *Russia*	**24 B5**	64 35N	34 54 E
Belonia, *India*	**41 H17**	23 15N	91 30 E
Beloretsk, *Russia*	**24 D10**	53 58N	58 24 E
Belorussia = Belarus ■, *Europe*	**17 B14**	53 30N	27 0 E
Belovo, *Russia*	**26 D9**	54 30N	86 0 E
Beloye, Ozero, *Russia*	**24 B6**	60 10N	37 35 E
Beloye More, *Russia*	**24 A6**	66 30N	38 0 E
Belozersk, *Russia*	**24 B6**	60 1N	37 45 E
Belpre, *U.S.A.*	**76 F5**	39 17N	81 34W
Belrain, *India*	**43 E9**	28 23N	80 55 E
Belt, *U.S.A.*	**82 C8**	47 23N	110 55W
Beltana, *Australia*	**63 E2**	30 48S	138 25 E
Belterra, *Brazil*	**93 D8**	2 45S	55 0W
Belton, *U.S.A.*	**81 K6**	31 3N	97 28W
Belton L., *U.S.A.*	**81 K6**	31 8N	97 32W
Beltsy = Bălţi, *Moldova*	**17 E14**	47 48N	27 58 E
Belturbet, *Ireland*	**13 B4**	54 6N	7 26W
Belukha, *Russia*	**26 E9**	49 50N	86 50 E
Beluran, *Malaysia*	**36 C5**	5 48N	117 35 E
Belvidere, *Ill., U.S.A.*	**80 D10**	42 15N	88 50W
Belvidere, *N.J., U.S.A.*	**79 F9**	40 50N	75 5W
Belyando →, *Australia*	**62 C4**	21 38S	146 50 E
Belyy, Ostrov, *Russia*	**26 B8**	73 30N	71 0 E
Belyy Yar, *Russia*	**26 D9**	58 26N	84 39 E
Belzoni, *U.S.A.*	**81 J9**	33 11N	90 29W
Bemaraha, Lembalemban' i, *Madag.*	**57 B7**	18 40S	44 45 E
Bemarivo, *Madag.*	**57 C7**	21 45S	44 45 E
Bemarivo →, *Antsiranana, Madag.*	**57 A9**	14 9S	50 9 E
Bemarivo →, *Mahajanga, Madag.*	**57 B8**	15 27S	47 40 E
Bemavo, *Madag.*	**57 C8**	21 33S	45 25 E
Bembéréke, *Benin*	**50 F6**	10 11N	2 43 E
Bembesi, *Zimbabwe*	**55 G2**	20 0S	28 58 E
Bembesi →, *Zimbabwe*	**55 F2**	18 57S	27 47 E
Bemetara, *India*	**43 J9**	21 42N	81 32 E
Bemidji, *U.S.A.*	**80 B7**	47 28N	94 53W
Bemolanga, *Madag.*	**57 B8**	17 44S	45 6 E
Ben, *Iran*	**45 C6**	32 32N	50 45 E
Ben Cruachan, *U.K.*	**12 E3**	56 26N	5 8W
Ben Dearg, *U.K.*	**12 D4**	57 47N	4 56W
Ben Hope, *U.K.*	**12 C4**	58 25N	4 36W
Ben Lawers, *U.K.*	**12 E4**	56 32N	4 14W
Ben Lomond, *N.S.W., Australia*	**63 E5**	30 1S	151 43 E
Ben Lomond, *Tas., Australia*	**62 G4**	41 38S	147 42 E
Ben Lomond, *U.K.*	**12 E4**	56 11N	4 38W
Ben Luc, *Vietnam*	**39 G6**	10 39N	106 29 E
Ben Macdhui, *U.K.*	**12 D5**	57 4N	3 40W
Ben Mhor, *U.K.*	**12 D1**	57 15N	7 18W
Ben More, *Arg. & Bute, U.K.*	**12 E2**	56 26N	6 1W
Ben More, *Stirl., U.K.*	**12 E4**	56 23N	4 32W
Ben More Assynt, *U.K.*	**12 C4**	58 8N	4 52W
Ben Nevis, *U.K.*	**12 E3**	56 48N	5 1W
Ben Quang, *Vietnam*	**38 D6**	17 3N	106 55 E
Ben Vorlich, *U.K.*	**12 E4**	56 21N	4 14W
Ben Wyvis, *U.K.*	**12 D4**	57 40N	4 35W
Bena, *Nigeria*	**50 F7**	11 20N	5 50 E
Benalla, *Australia*	**63 F4**	36 30S	146 0 E
Benares = Varanasi, *India*	**43 G10**	25 22N	83 0 E
Benavente, *Spain*	**19 A3**	42 2N	5 43W
Benavides, *U.S.A.*	**81 M5**	27 36N	98 25W
Benbecula, *U.K.*	**12 D1**	57 26N	7 21W
Benbonyathe, *Australia*	**63 E2**	30 25S	139 11 E
Bend, *U.S.A.*	**82 D3**	44 4N	121 19W
Bender Beila, *Somali Rep.*	**46 F5**	9 30N	50 48 E
Bendery = Tighina, *Moldova*	**17 E15**	46 50N	29 30 E
Bendigo, *Australia*	**63 F3**	36 40S	144 15 E
Benē Beraq, *Israel*	**47 C3**	32 6N	34 51 E
Benenitra, *Madag.*	**57 C8**	23 27S	45 5 E
Benevento, *Italy*	**20 D6**	41 8N	14 45 E
Benga, *Mozam.*	**55 F3**	16 11S	33 40 E
Bengal, Bay of, *Ind. Oc.*	**41 M17**	15 0N	90 0 E
Bengbu, *China*	**35 H9**	32 58N	117 20 E
Benghazi = Banghāzī, *Libya*	**51 B10**	32 11N	20 3 E
Bengkalis, *Indonesia*	**36 D2**	1 30N	102 10 E
Bengkulu, *Indonesia*	**36 E2**	3 50S	102 12 E
Bengkulu □, *Indonesia*	**36 E2**	3 48S	102 16 E
Bengough, *Canada*	**73 D7**	49 25N	105 10W
Benguela, *Angola*	**53 G2**	12 37S	13 25 E
Benguérua, I., *Mozam.*	**57 C6**	21 58S	35 28 E
Beni, *Dem. Rep. of the Congo*	**54 B2**	0 30N	29 27 E
Beni →, *Bolivia*	**92 F5**	10 23S	65 24W
Beni Mellal, *Morocco*	**50 B4**	32 21N	6 21W
Beni Suef, *Egypt*	**51 C12**	29 5N	31 6 E
Beniah L., *Canada*	**72 A6**	63 23N	112 17W
Benicia, *U.S.A.*	**84 G4**	38 3N	122 9W
Benidorm, *Spain*	**19 C5**	38 33N	0 9W
Benin ■, *Africa*	**50 G6**	10 0N	2 0 E
Benin, Bight of, *W. Afr.*	**50 H6**	5 0N	3 0 E
Benin City, *Nigeria*	**50 G7**	6 20N	5 31 E
Benitses, *Greece*	**23 A3**	39 32N	19 55 E
Benjamin Aceval, *Paraguay*	**94 A4**	24 58S	57 34W
Benjamin Constant, *Brazil*	**92 D4**	4 40S	70 15W
Benjamin Hill, *Mexico*	**86 A2**	30 10N	111 10W
Benkelman, *U.S.A.*	**80 E4**	40 3N	101 32W
Bennett, *Canada*	**72 B2**	59 56N	134 53W
Bennett, L., *Australia*	**60 D5**	22 50S	131 2 E
Bennetta, Ostrov, *Russia*	**27 B15**	76 21N	148 56 E
Bennettsville, *U.S.A.*	**77 H6**	34 37N	79 41W
Bennington, *N.H., U.S.A.*	**79 D11**	43 0N	71 55W
Bennington, *Vt., U.S.A.*	**79 D11**	42 53N	73 12W
Benoni, *S. Africa*	**57 D4**	26 11S	28 18 E
Benque Viejo, *Belize*	**87 D7**	17 5N	89 8W
Benson, *Ariz., U.S.A.*	**83 L8**	31 58N	110 18W
Benson, *Minn., U.S.A.*	**80 C7**	45 19N	95 36W
Bent, *Iran*	**45 E8**	26 20N	59 31 E
Benteng, *Indonesia*	**37 F6**	6 10S	120 30 E
Bentinck I., *Australia*	**62 B2**	17 3S	139 35 E
Bento Gonçalves, *Brazil*	**95 B5**	29 10S	51 31W
Benton, *Ark., U.S.A.*	**81 H8**	34 34N	92 35W
Benton, *Calif., U.S.A.*	**84 H8**	37 48N	118 32W
Benton, *Ill., U.S.A.*	**80 G10**	38 0N	88 55W
Benton, *Pa., U.S.A.*	**79 E8**	41 12N	76 23W
Benton Harbor, *U.S.A.*	**76 D2**	42 6N	86 27W
Bentonville, *U.S.A.*	**81 G7**	36 22N	94 13W
Bentung, *Malaysia*	**39 L3**	3 31N	101 55 E
Benue →, *Nigeria*	**50 G7**	7 48N	6 46 E
Benxi, *China*	**35 D12**	41 20N	123 48 E
Beo, *Indonesia*	**37 D7**	4 25N	126 50 E
Beograd, *Serbia, Yug.*	**21 B9**	44 50N	20 37 E
Beppu, *Japan*	**31 H5**	33 15N	131 30 E
Beqaa Valley = Al Biqā, *Lebanon*	**47 A5**	34 10N	36 10 E
Ber Mota, *India*	**42 H3**	23 27N	68 34 E
Berach →, *India*	**42 G6**	25 15N	75 2 E
Beraketa, *Madag.*	**57 C7**	23 7S	44 25 E
Berat, *Albania*	**21 D8**	40 43N	19 59 E
Berau, Teluk, *Indonesia*	**37 E8**	2 30S	132 30 E
Beravina, *Madag.*	**57 B8**	18 10S	45 14 E
Berber, *Sudan*	**51 E12**	18 0N	34 0 E
Berbera, *Somali Rep.*	**46 E4**	10 30N	45 2 E
Berbérati, *C.A.R.*	**52 D3**	4 15N	15 40 E
Berbice →, *Guyana*	**92 B7**	6 20N	57 32W
Berdichev = Berdychiv, *Ukraine*	**17 D15**	49 57N	28 30 E
Berdsk, *Russia*	**26 D9**	54 47N	83 2 E
Berdyansk, *Ukraine*	**25 E6**	46 45N	36 50 E
Berdychiv, *Ukraine*	**17 D15**	49 57N	28 30 E
Berea, *U.S.A.*	**76 G3**	37 34N	84 17W
Berebere, *Indonesia*	**37 D7**	2 25N	128 45 E
Bereda, *Somali Rep.*	**46 E5**	11 45N	51 0 E
Berehove, *Ukraine*	**17 D12**	48 15N	22 35 E
Berekum, *Ghana*	**50 G5**	7 29N	2 34W
Berens →, *Canada*	**73 C9**	52 25N	97 2W
Berens I., *Canada*	**73 C9**	52 18N	97 18W
Berens River, *Canada*	**73 C9**	52 25N	97 0W
Beresford, *U.S.A.*	**80 D6**	43 5N	96 47W
Berestechko, *Ukraine*	**17 C13**	50 22N	25 5 E
Berevo, *Mahajanga, Madag.*	**57 B7**	17 14S	44 17 E
Berevo, *Toliara, Madag.*	**57 B7**	19 44S	44 58 E
Bereza = Byaroza, *Belarus*	**17 B13**	52 31N	24 51 E
Berezhany, *Ukraine*	**17 D13**	49 26N	24 58 E
Berezina = Byarezina →, *Belarus*	**17 B16**	52 33N	30 14 E
Bereznik, *Russia*	**24 B7**	62 51N	42 40 E
Berezniki, *Russia*	**24 C10**	59 24N	56 46 E
Berezovo, *Russia*	**26 C7**	64 0N	65 0 E
Berga, *Spain*	**19 A6**	42 6N	1 48 E
Bergama, *Turkey*	**21 E12**	39 8N	27 11 E
Bérgamo, *Italy*	**18 D8**	45 41N	9 43 E
Bergen, *Neths.*	**15 B4**	52 40N	4 43 E
Bergen, *Norway*	**9 F11**	60 20N	5 20 E
Bergen, *U.S.A.*	**78 C7**	43 5N	77 57W
Bergen op Zoom, *Neths.*	**15 C4**	51 28N	4 18 E
Bergerac, *France*	**18 D4**	44 51N	0 30 E
Bergholz, *U.S.A.*	**78 F4**	40 31N	80 53W
Bergisch Gladbach, *Germany*	**15 D7**	50 59N	7 8 E
Bergville, *S. Africa*	**57 D4**	28 52S	29 18 E
Berhala, Selat, *Indonesia*	**36 E2**	1 0S	104 15 E
Berhampore = Baharampur, *India*	**43 G13**	24 2N	88 27 E
Berhampur = Brahmapur, *India*	**41 K14**	19 15N	84 54 E
Bering Sea, *Pac. Oc.*	**68 C1**	58 0N	171 0 E
Bering Strait, *Pac. Oc.*	**68 B3**	65 30N	169 0W
Beringovskiy, *Russia*	**27 C18**	63 3N	179 19 E
Berisso, *Argentina*	**94 C4**	34 56S	57 50W
Berja, *Spain*	**19 D4**	36 50N	2 56W
Berkeley, *U.S.A.*	**84 H4**	37 52N	122 16W
Berkner I., *Antarctica*	**5 D18**	79 30S	50 0W
Berkshire, *U.S.A.*	**79 D8**	42 19N	76 11W
Berkshire Downs, *U.K.*	**11 F6**	51 33N	1 29W
Berlin, *Germany*	**16 B7**	52 30N	13 25 E
Berlin, *Md., U.S.A.*	**76 F8**	38 20N	75 13W
Berlin, *N.H., U.S.A.*	**79 B13**	44 28N	71 11W
Berlin, *N.Y., U.S.A.*	**79 D11**	42 42N	73 23W
Berlin, *Wis., U.S.A.*	**76 D1**	43 58N	88 57W
Berlin L., *U.S.A.*	**78 E4**	41 3N	81 0W
Bermejo →, *Formosa, Argentina*	**94 B4**	26 51S	58 23W
Bermejo →, *San Juan, Argentina*	**94 C2**	32 30S	67 30W
Bermen, L., *Canada*	**71 B6**	53 35N	68 55W
Bermuda ■, *Atl. Oc.*	**66 F13**	32 45N	65 0W
Bern, *Switz.*	**18 C7**	46 57N	7 28 E
Bernalillo, *U.S.A.*	**83 J10**	35 18N	106 33W
Bernardo de Irigoyen, *Argentina*	**95 B5**	26 15S	53 40W
Bernardo O'Higgins □, *Chile*	**94 C1**	34 15S	70 45W
Bernardsville, *U.S.A.*	**79 F10**	40 43N	74 34W
Bernasconi, *Argentina*	**94 D3**	37 55S	63 44W
Bernburg, *Germany*	**16 C6**	51 47N	11 44 E
Berne = Bern, *Switz.*	**18 C7**	46 57N	7 28 E
Berneray, *U.K.*	**12 D1**	57 43N	7 11W
Bernier I., *Australia*	**61 D1**	24 50S	113 12 E
Bernina, Piz, *Switz.*	**18 C8**	46 20N	9 54 E
Beroroha, *Madag.*	**57 C8**	21 40S	45 10 E
Beroun, *Czech Rep.*	**16 D8**	49 57N	14 5 E
Berri, *Australia*	**63 E3**	34 14S	140 35 E
Berriane, *Algeria*	**50 B6**	32 50N	3 46 E
Berry, *Australia*	**63 E5**	34 46S	150 43 E
Berry, *France*	**18 C5**	46 50N	2 0 E
Berry Is., *Bahamas*	**88 A4**	25 40N	77 50W
Berryessa L., *U.S.A.*	**84 G4**	38 31N	122 6W
Berryville, *U.S.A.*	**81 G8**	36 22N	93 34W
Berseba, *Namibia*	**56 D2**	26 0S	17 46 E
Bershad, *Ukraine*	**17 D15**	48 22N	29 31 E
Berthold, *U.S.A.*	**80 A4**	48 19N	101 44W
Berthoud, *U.S.A.*	**80 E2**	40 19N	105 5W
Bertoua, *Cameroon*	**52 D2**	4 30N	13 45 E
Bertraghboy B., *Ireland*	**13 C2**	53 22N	9 54W
Berwick, *U.S.A.*	**79 E8**	41 3N	76 14W
Berwick-upon-Tweed, *U.K.*	**10 B6**	55 46N	2 0W
Berwyn Mts., *U.K.*	**10 E4**	52 54N	3 26W
Besal, *Pakistan*	**43 B5**	35 4N	73 56 E
Besalampy, *Madag.*	**57 B7**	16 43S	44 29 E
Besançon, *France*	**18 C7**	47 15N	6 2 E
Besar, *Indonesia*	**36 E5**	2 40S	116 0 E
Besnard L., *Canada*	**73 B7**	55 25N	106 0W
Besni, *Turkey*	**44 B3**	37 41N	37 52 E
Besor, N. →, *Egypt*	**47 D3**	31 28N	34 22 E
Bessarabiya, *Moldova*	**17 E15**	47 0N	28 10 E
Bessarabka = Basarabeasca, *Moldova*	**17 E15**	46 21N	28 58 E
Bessemer, *Ala., U.S.A.*	**77 J2**	33 24N	86 58W
Bessemer, *Mich., U.S.A.*	**80 B9**	46 29N	90 3W
Bessemer, *Pa., U.S.A.*	**78 F4**	40 59N	80 30W
Beswick, *Australia*	**60 B5**	14 34S	132 53 E
Bet She'an, *Israel*	**47 C4**	32 30N	35 30 E
Bet Shemesh, *Israel*	**47 D4**	31 44N	35 0 E
Betafo, *Madag.*	**57 B8**	19 50S	46 51 E
Betancuria, *Canary Is.*	**22 F5**	28 25N	14 3W
Betanzos, *Spain*	**19 A1**	43 15N	8 12W
Bétaré Oya, *Cameroon*	**52 C2**	5 40N	14 5 E
Betatao, *Madag.*	**57 B8**	18 11S	47 52 E
Bethal, *S. Africa*	**57 D4**	26 27S	29 28 E
Bethanien, *Namibia*	**56 D2**	26 31S	17 8 E
Bethany, *Canada*	**78 B6**	44 11N	78 34W
Bethany, *U.S.A.*	**80 E7**	40 16N	94 2W
Bethel, *Alaska, U.S.A.*	**68 B3**	60 48N	161 45W
Bethel, *Conn., U.S.A.*	**79 E11**	41 22N	73 25W
Bethel, *Maine, U.S.A.*	**79 B14**	44 25N	70 47W
Bethel, *Vt., U.S.A.*	**79 C12**	43 50N	72 38W
Bethel Park, *U.S.A.*	**78 F4**	40 20N	80 1W
Bethlehem = Bayt Lahm, *West Bank*	**47 D4**	31 43N	35 12 E
Bethlehem, *S. Africa*	**57 D4**	28 14S	28 18 E
Bethlehem, *U.S.A.*	**79 F9**	40 37N	75 23W
Bethulie, *S. Africa*	**56 E4**	30 30S	25 59 E
Béthune, *France*	**18 A5**	50 30N	2 38 E
Betioky, *Madag.*	**57 C7**	23 48S	44 20 E
Betong, *Thailand*	**39 K3**	5 45N	101 5 E
Betoota, *Australia*	**62 D3**	25 45S	140 42 E
Betroka, *Madag.*	**57 C8**	23 16S	46 0 E
Betsiamites, *Canada*	**71 C6**	48 56N	68 40W
Betsiamites →, *Canada*	**71 C6**	48 56N	68 38W
Betsiboka →, *Madag.*	**57 B8**	16 3S	46 36 E
Bettendorf, *U.S.A.*	**80 E9**	41 32N	90 30W
Bettiah, *India*	**43 F11**	26 48N	84 33 E
Betul, *India*	**40 J10**	21 58N	77 59 E
Betung, *Malaysia*	**36 D4**	1 24N	111 31 E
Betws-y-Coed, *U.K.*	**10 D4**	53 5N	3 48W
Beulah, *Mich., U.S.A.*	**76 C2**	44 38N	86 6W
Beulah, *N. Dak., U.S.A.*	**80 B4**	47 16N	101 47W
Beveren, *Belgium*	**15 C4**	51 12N	4 16 E
Beverley, *Australia*	**61 F2**	32 9S	116 56 E
Beverley, *U.K.*	**10 D7**	53 51N	0 26W
Beverley Hills, *U.S.A.*	**77 L4**	28 56N	82 28W
Beverly, *U.S.A.*	**79 D14**	42 33N	70 53W
Beverly Hills, *U.S.A.*	**85 L8**	34 4N	118 25W
Bevoalavo, *Madag.*	**57 D7**	25 13S	45 26 E
Bewas →, *India*	**43 H8**	23 59N	79 21 E
Bexhill, *U.K.*	**11 G8**	50 51N	0 29 E
Beyānlū, *Iran*	**44 C5**	36 0N	47 51 E
Beyneu, *Kazakstan*	**25 E10**	45 18N	55 9 E
Beypazarı, *Turkey*	**25 F5**	40 10N	31 56 E
Beyşehir Gölü, *Turkey*	**25 G5**	37 41N	31 33 E
Béziers, *France*	**18 E5**	43 20N	3 12 E
Bezwada = Vijayawada, *India*	**41 L12**	16 31N	80 39 E
Bhabua, *India*	**43 G10**	25 3N	83 37 E
Bhachau, *India*	**40 H7**	23 20N	70 16 E
Bhadar →, *Gujarat, India*	**42 H5**	22 17N	72 20 E
Bhadar →, *Gujarat, India*	**42 J3**	21 27N	69 47 E
Bhadarwah, *India*	**43 C6**	32 58N	75 46 E
Bhadohi, *India*	**43 G10**	25 25N	82 34 E
Bhadra, *India*	**42 E6**	29 8N	75 14 E
Bhadrakh, *India*	**41 J15**	21 10N	86 30 E
Bhadran, *India*	**42 H5**	22 19N	72 6 E
Bhadravati, *India*	**40 N9**	13 49N	75 40 E
Bhag, *Pakistan*	**42 E2**	29 2N	67 49 E
Bhagalpur, *India*	**43 G12**	25 10N	87 0 E
Bhagirathi →, *Uttaranchal, India*	**43 D8**	30 8N	78 35 E
Bhagirathi →, *W. Bengal, India*	**43 H13**	23 25N	88 23 E
Bhakkar, *Pakistan*	**42 D4**	31 40N	71 5 E
Bhakra Dam, *India*	**42 D7**	31 30N	76 45 E
Bhaktapur, *Nepal*	**43 F11**	27 38N	85 24 E
Bhamo, *Burma*	**41 G20**	24 15N	97 15 E
Bhandara, *India*	**40 J11**	21 5N	79 42 E
Bhanpura, *India*	**42 G6**	24 31N	75 44 E
Bhanrer Ra., *India*	**43 H8**	23 40N	79 45 E
Bhaptiahi, *India*	**43 F12**	26 19N	86 44 E
Bharat = India ■, *Asia*	**40 K11**	20 0N	78 0 E
Bharatpur, *Chhattisgarh, India*	**43 H9**	23 44N	81 46 E
Bharatpur, *Raj., India*	**42 F7**	27 15N	77 30 E
Bharno, *India*	**43 H11**	23 14N	84 53 E
Bhatinda, *India*	**42 D6**	30 15N	74 57 E
Bhatpara, *India*	**43 H13**	22 50N	88 25 E
Bhattu, *India*	**42 E6**	29 36N	75 19 E
Bhaun, *Pakistan*	**42 C5**	32 55N	72 40 E
Bhaunagar = Bhavnagar, *India*	**40 J8**	21 45N	72 10 E
Bhavnagar, *India*	**40 J8**	21 45N	72 10 E
Bhawari, *India*	**42 G5**	25 42N	73 4 E
Bhayavadar, *India*	**42 J4**	21 51N	70 15 E
Bhera, *Pakistan*	**42 C5**	32 29N	72 57 E
Bhikangaon, *India*	**42 J6**	21 52N	75 57 E
Bhilsa = Vidisha, *India*	**42 H7**	23 28N	77 53 E
Bhilwara, *India*	**42 G6**	25 25N	74 38 E
Bhima →, *India*	**40 L10**	16 25N	77 17 E
Bhimbar, *Pakistan*	**43 C6**	32 59N	74 3 E
Bhind, *India*	**43 F8**	26 30N	78 46 E
Bhinga, *India*	**43 F9**	27 43N	81 56 E
Bhinmal, *India*	**42 G5**	25 0N	72 15 E
Bhiwandi, *India*	**40 K8**	19 20N	73 0 E
Bhiwani, *India*	**42 E7**	28 50N	76 9 E
Bhogava →, *India*	**42 H5**	22 26N	72 20 E
Bhola, *Bangla.*	**41 H17**	22 45N	90 35 E
Bholari, *Pakistan*	**42 G3**	25 19N	68 13 E
Bhopal, *India*	**42 H7**	23 20N	77 30 E
Bhubaneshwar, *India*	**41 J14**	20 15N	85 50 E
Bhuj, *India*	**42 H3**	23 15N	69 49 E
Bhusaval, *India*	**40 J9**	21 3N	75 46 E
Bhutan ■, *Asia*	**41 F17**	27 25N	90 30 E
Biafra, B. of = Bonny, Bight of, *Africa*	**52 D1**	3 30N	9 20 E
Biak, *Indonesia*	**37 E9**	1 10S	136 6 E
Biała Podlaska, *Poland*	**17 B12**	52 4N	23 6 E
Białogard, *Poland*	**16 A8**	54 2N	15 58 E
Białystok, *Poland*	**17 B12**	53 10N	23 10 E
Biaora, *India*	**42 H7**	23 56N	76 56 E

Bīārjmand

Bīārjmand, Iran 45 B7 36 6N 55 53 E
Biaro, Indonesia 37 D7 2 5N 125 26 E
Biarritz, France 18 E3 43 29N 1 33W
Bibai, Japan 30 C10 43 19N 141 52 E
Bibby I., Canada 73 A10 61 55N 93 0W
Biberach, Germany 16 D5 48 5N 9 47 E
Bibungwa, Dem. Rep. of the Congo 54 C2 2 40S 28 15 E
Bic, Canada 71 C6 48 20N 68 41W
Bicester, U.K. 11 F6 51 54N 1 9W
Bicheno, Australia 62 G4 41 52S 148 18 E
Bichia, India 43 H9 22 27N 80 42 E
Bickerton I., Australia 62 A2 13 45S 136 10 E
Bida, Nigeria 50 G7 9 3N 5 58 E
Bidar, India 40 L10 17 55N 77 35 E
Biddeford, U.S.A. 77 D10 43 30N 70 28W
Bideford, U.K. 11 F3 51 1N 4 13W
Bideford Bay, U.K. 11 F3 51 5N 4 20W
Bidhuna, India 43 F8 26 49N 79 31 E
Bidor, Malaysia 39 K3 4 6N 101 15 E
Bié, Planalto de, Angola 53 G3 12 0S 16 0 E
Bieber, U.S.A. 82 F3 41 7N 121 8W
Biel, Switz. 18 C7 47 8N 7 14 E
Bielefeld, Germany 16 B5 52 1N 8 33 E
Biella, Italy 18 D8 45 34N 8 3 E
Bielsk Podlaski, Poland 17 B12 52 47N 23 12 E
Bielsko-Biała, Poland 17 D10 49 50N 19 2 E
Bien Hoa, Vietnam 39 G6 10 57N 106 49 E
Bienne = Biel, Switz. 18 C7 47 8N 7 14 E
Bienville, L., Canada 70 A5 55 5N 72 40W
Biesiesfontein, S. Africa 56 E2 30 57S 17 58 E
Big →, Canada 71 B8 54 50N 58 55W
Big B., Canada 71 A7 55 43N 60 35W
Big Bear City, U.S.A. 85 L10 34 16N 116 51W
Big Bear Lake, U.S.A. 85 L10 34 15N 116 56W
Big Belt Mts., U.S.A. 82 C8 46 30N 111 25W
Big Bend, Swaziland 57 D5 26 50S 31 58 E
Big Bend Nat. Park, U.S.A. 81 L3 29 20N 103 5W
Big Black →, U.S.A. 81 K9 32 3N 91 4W
Big Blue →, U.S.A. 80 F6 39 35N 96 34W
Big Creek, U.S.A. 84 H7 37 11N 119 14W
Big Cypress Nat. Preserve, U.S.A. 77 M5 26 0N 81 10W
Big Cypress Swamp, U.S.A. 77 M5 26 15N 81 30W
Big Falls, U.S.A. 80 A8 48 12N 93 48W
Big Fork →, U.S.A. 80 A8 48 31N 93 43W
Big Horn Mts. = Bighorn Mts., U.S.A. 82 D10 44 30N 107 30W
Big I., Canada 72 A5 61 7N 116 45W
Big Lake, U.S.A. 81 K4 31 12N 101 28W
Big Moose, U.S.A. 79 C10 43 49N 74 58W
Big Muddy Cr. →, U.S.A. 80 A2 48 8N 104 36W
Big Pine, U.S.A. 84 H8 37 10N 118 17W
Big Piney, U.S.A. 82 E8 42 32N 110 7W
Big Rapids, U.S.A. 76 D3 43 42N 85 29W
Big Rideau L., Canada 79 B8 44 40N 76 15W
Big River, Canada 73 C7 53 50N 107 0W
Big Run, U.S.A. 78 F6 40 57N 78 55W
Big Sable Pt., U.S.A. 76 C2 44 3N 86 1W
Big Salmon →, Canada 72 A2 61 52N 134 55W
Big Sand L., Canada 73 B9 57 45N 99 45W
Big Sandy, U.S.A. 82 B8 48 11N 110 7W
Big Sandy →, U.S.A. 76 F4 38 25N 82 36W
Big Sandy Cr. →, U.S.A. 80 F3 38 7N 102 29W
Big Sioux →, U.S.A. 80 D6 42 29N 96 27W
Big Spring, U.S.A. 81 J4 32 15N 101 28W
Big Stone City, U.S.A. 80 C6 45 18N 96 28W
Big Stone Gap, U.S.A. 77 G4 36 52N 82 47W
Big Stone L., U.S.A. 80 C6 45 30N 96 35W
Big Sur, U.S.A. 84 J5 36 15N 121 48W
Big Timber, U.S.A. 82 D9 45 50N 109 57W
Big Trout L., Canada 70 B2 53 40N 90 0W
Big Trout Lake, Canada 70 B2 53 45N 90 0W
Biğa, Turkey 21 D12 40 13N 27 14 E
Bigadiç, Turkey 21 E13 39 22N 28 7 E
Biggar, Canada 73 C7 52 4N 108 0W
Biggar, U.K. 12 F5 55 38N 3 32W
Bigge I., Australia 60 B4 14 35S 125 10 E
Biggenden, Australia 63 D5 25 31S 152 4 E
Biggleswade, U.K. 11 E7 52 5N 0 14W
Biggs, U.S.A. 84 F5 39 25N 121 43W
Bighorn, U.S.A. 82 C10 46 10N 107 27W
Bighorn →, U.S.A. 82 C10 46 10N 107 28W
Bighorn L., U.S.A. 82 D9 44 55N 108 15W
Bighorn Mts., U.S.A. 82 D10 44 30N 107 30W
Bigstone L., Canada 73 C9 53 42N 95 44W
Bigwa, Tanzania 54 D4 7 10S 39 10 E
Bihać, Bos.-H. 16 F8 44 49N 15 57 E
Bihar, India 43 G11 25 5N 85 40 E
Bihar □, India 43 G12 25 0N 86 0 E
Biharamulo, Tanzania 54 C3 2 25S 31 25 E
Bihariganj, India 43 G12 25 44N 86 59 E
Bihor, Munţii, Romania 17 E12 46 29N 22 47 E
Bijagós, Arquipélago dos, Guinea-Biss. 50 F2 11 15N 16 10W
Bijaipur, India 42 F7 26 2N 77 20 E
Bijapur, Chhattisgarh, India 41 K12 18 50N 80 50 E
Bijapur, Karnataka, India 40 L9 16 50N 75 55 E
Bījār, Iran 44 C5 35 52N 47 35 E
Bijawar, India 43 G8 24 38N 79 30 E
Bijeljina, Bos.-H. 21 B8 44 46N 19 14 E
Bijnor, India 42 E8 29 27N 78 11 E
Bikaner, India 42 E5 28 2N 73 18 E
Bikapur, India 43 F10 26 30N 82 7 E
Bikeqi, China 34 D6 40 43N 111 20 E
Bikfayyā, Lebanon 47 B4 33 55N 35 41 E
Bikin, Russia 27 E14 46 50N 134 20 E
Bikin →, Russia 30 A7 46 51N 134 2 E
Bikini Atoll, Marshall Is. 64 F8 12 0N 167 30 E
Bikita, Zimbabwe 57 C5 20 6S 31 41 E
Bila Tserkva, Ukraine 17 D16 49 45N 30 10 E
Bilara, India 42 F5 26 14N 73 53 E
Bilaspur, Chhattisgarh, India 43 H10 22 2N 82 15 E
Bilaspur, Punjab, India 42 D7 31 19N 76 50 E
Bilauk Taungdan, Thailand 38 F2 13 0N 99 0 E
Bilbao, Spain 19 A4 43 16N 2 56W
Bilbo = Bilbao, Spain 19 A4 43 16N 2 56W
Bíldudalur, Iceland 8 D2 65 41N 23 36W
Bílé Karpaty, Europe 17 D9 49 5N 18 0 E
Bilecik, Turkey 25 F5 40 5N 30 5 E
Bilgram, India 43 F9 27 11N 80 2 E
Bilhaur, India 43 F9 26 51N 80 5 E
Bilhorod-Dnistrovskyy, Ukraine 25 E5 46 11N 30 23 E
Bilibino, Russia 27 C17 68 3N 166 20 E
Bilibiza, Mozam. 55 E5 12 30S 40 20 E
Billabalong Roadhouse, Australia 61 E2 27 25S 115 49 E
Billiluna, Australia 60 C4 19 37S 127 41 E
Billings, U.S.A. 82 D9 45 47N 108 30W
Billiton Is. = Belitung, Indonesia 36 E3 3 10S 107 50 E
Bilma, Niger 51 E8 18 50N 13 30 E
Biloela, Australia 62 C5 24 24S 150 31 E
Biloxi, U.S.A. 81 K10 30 24N 88 53W
Bilpa Morea Claypan, Australia 62 D3 25 0S 140 0 E
Biltine, Chad 51 F10 14 40N 20 50 E
Bima, Indonesia 37 F5 8 22S 118 49 E
Bimini Is., Bahamas 88 A4 25 42N 79 25W
Bin Xian, Heilongjiang, China 35 B14 45 42N 127 32 E
Bin Xian, Shaanxi, China 34 G5 35 2N 108 4 E
Bina-Etawah, India 42 G8 24 13N 78 14 E
Bināb, Iran 45 B6 36 35N 48 41 E
Binalbagan, Phil. 37 B6 10 12N 122 50 E
Binalong, Australia 63 E4 34 40S 148 39 E
Bīnālūd, Kūh-e, Iran 45 B8 36 30N 58 30 E
Binatang = Bintangor, Malaysia 36 D4 2 10N 111 40 E
Binche, Belgium 15 D4 50 26N 4 10 E
Bindki, India 43 F9 26 2N 80 36 E
Bindura, Zimbabwe 55 F3 17 18S 31 18 E
Bingara, Australia 63 D5 29 52S 150 36 E
Bingham, U.S.A. 77 C11 45 3N 69 53W
Binghamton, U.S.A. 79 D9 42 6N 75 55W
Bingöl, Turkey 44 B4 38 53N 40 29 E
Binh Dinh = An Nhon, Vietnam 38 F7 13 55N 109 7 E
Binh Khe, Vietnam 38 F7 13 57N 108 51 E
Binh Son, Vietnam 38 E7 15 20N 108 40 E
Binhai, China 35 G10 34 2N 119 49 E
Binisatua, Spain 22 B11 39 50N 4 11 E
Binjai, Indonesia 36 D3 3 20N 98 30 E
Binnaway, Australia 63 E4 31 28S 149 24 E
Binongko, Indonesia 37 F6 5 57S 124 2 E
Binscarth, Canada 73 C8 50 37N 101 17W
Bintan, Indonesia 36 D2 1 0N 104 0 E
Bintangor, Malaysia 36 D4 2 10N 111 40 E
Bintulu, Malaysia 36 D4 3 10N 113 0 E
Bintuni, Indonesia 37 E8 2 7S 133 32 E
Binzert = Bizerte, Tunisia 51 A7 37 15N 9 50 E
Binzhou, China 35 F10 37 20N 118 2 E
Bío Bío □, Chile 94 D1 37 35S 72 0W
Bioko, Eq. Guin. 52 D1 3 30N 8 40 E
Bir, India 40 K9 19 4N 75 46 E
Bîr Abu Muḥammad, Egypt 47 F3 29 44N 34 14 E
Bi'r ad Dabbāghāt, Jordan 47 E4 30 26N 35 32 E
Bi'r al Butayyihāt, Jordan 47 F4 29 47N 35 20 E
Bi'r al Mārī, Jordan 47 E4 30 4N 35 33 E
Bi'r al Qattār, Jordan 47 F4 29 47N 35 32 E
Bir Atrun, Sudan 51 E11 18 15N 26 40 E
Bîr Beiḍa, Egypt 47 E3 30 25N 34 29 E
Bîr el 'Abd, Egypt 47 D2 31 2N 33 0 E
Bîr el Biarât, Egypt 47 F3 29 30N 34 43 E
Bîr el Duweidar, Egypt 47 E1 30 56N 32 32 E
Bîr el Garârât, Egypt 47 D2 31 3N 33 34 E
Bîr el Heisi, Egypt 47 F3 29 22N 34 36 E
Bîr el Jafir, Egypt 47 E1 30 50N 32 41 E
Bîr el Mâlḥi, Egypt 47 E2 30 38N 33 19 E
Bîr el Thamâda, Egypt 47 E2 30 12N 33 27 E
Bîr Gebeil Ḥiṣn, Egypt 47 E2 30 2N 33 18 E
Bi'r Ghadīr, Syria 47 A6 34 6N 37 3 E
Bîr Ḥasana, Egypt 47 E2 30 29N 33 46 E
Bîr Kaseiba, Egypt 47 E2 31 0N 33 17 E
Bîr Lahfân, Egypt 47 E2 31 0N 33 51 E
Bîr Madkûr, Egypt 47 E1 30 44N 32 33 E
Bîr Mogreïn, Mauritania 50 C3 25 10N 11 25W
Bi'r Muṭribah, Kuwait 44 D5 29 54N 47 17 E
Bîr Qaṭia, Egypt 47 E1 30 58N 32 45 E
Bîr Shalatein, Egypt 51 D13 23 5N 35 25 E
Biratnagar, Nepal 43 F12 26 27N 87 17 E
Birawa, Dem. Rep. of the Congo 54 C2 2 20S 28 48 E
Birch →, Canada 72 B6 58 28N 112 17W
Birch Hills, Canada 73 C7 52 59N 105 25W
Birch I., Canada 73 C9 52 26N 99 54W
Birch L., N.W.T., Canada 72 A5 62 4N 116 33W
Birch L., Ont., Canada 70 B1 51 23N 92 18W
Birch Mts., Canada 72 B6 57 30N 113 10W
Birch River, Canada 73 C8 52 24N 101 6W
Birchip, Australia 63 F3 35 56S 142 55 E
Bird, Canada 73 B10 56 30N 94 13W
Bird I. = Las Aves, Is., W. Indies 89 C7 15 45N 63 55W
Birdsville, Australia 62 D2 25 51S 139 20 E
Birdum Cr. →, Australia 60 C5 15 14S 133 0 E
Birecik, Turkey 44 B3 37 2N 38 0 E
Birein, Israel 47 E3 30 50N 34 28 E
Bireuen, Indonesia 36 C1 5 14N 96 39 E
Birigui, Brazil 95 A5 21 18S 50 16W
Birjand, Iran 45 C8 32 53N 59 13 E
Birkenhead, U.K. 10 D4 53 23N 3 2W
Bîrlad = Bârlad, Romania 17 E14 46 15N 27 38 E
Birmingham, U.K. 11 E6 52 29N 1 52W
Birmingham, U.S.A. 77 J2 33 31N 86 48W
Birmitrapur, India 41 H14 22 24N 84 46 E
Birni Nkonni, Niger 50 F7 13 55N 5 15 E
Birnin Kebbi, Nigeria 50 F6 12 32N 4 12 E
Birobidzhan, Russia 27 E14 48 50N 132 50 E
Birr, Ireland 13 C4 53 6N 7 54W
Birrie →, Australia 63 D4 29 43S 146 37 E
Birsilpur, India 42 E5 28 11N 72 15 E
Birsk, Russia 24 C10 55 25N 55 30 E
Birtle, Canada 73 C8 50 30N 101 5W
Birur, India 40 N9 13 30N 75 55 E
Biržai, Lithuania 9 H21 56 11N 24 45 E
Birzebbugga, Malta 23 D2 35 50N 14 32 E
Bisa, Indonesia 37 E7 1 15S 127 28 E
Bisalpur, India 43 E8 28 14N 79 48 E
Bisbee, U.S.A. 83 L9 31 27N 109 55W
Biscay, B. of, Atl. Oc. 18 D1 45 0N 2 0W
Biscayne B., U.S.A. 77 N5 25 40N 80 12W
Biscoe Bay, Antarctica 5 D13 77 0S 152 0W
Biscoe Is., Antarctica 5 C17 66 0S 67 0W
Biscostasing, Canada 70 C3 47 18N 82 9W
Bishkek, Kyrgyzstan 26 E8 42 54N 74 46 E
Bishnupur, India 43 H12 23 8N 87 20 E
Bisho, S. Africa 57 E4 32 50S 27 23 E
Bishop, Calif., U.S.A. 84 H8 37 22N 118 24W
Bishop, Tex., U.S.A. 81 M6 27 35N 97 48W
Bishop Auckland, U.K. 10 C6 54 39N 1 40W
Bishop's Falls, Canada 71 C8 49 2N 55 30W
Bishop's Stortford, U.K. 11 F8 51 52N 0 10 E
Bisina, L., Uganda 54 B3 1 38N 33 56 E
Biskra, Algeria 50 B7 34 50N 5 44 E
Bismarck, U.S.A. 80 B4 46 48N 100 47W
Bismarck Arch., Papua N. G. 64 H7 2 30S 150 0 E
Biso, Uganda 54 B3 1 44N 31 26 E
Bison, U.S.A. 80 C3 45 31N 102 28W
Bīsotūn, Iran 44 C5 34 23N 47 26 E
Bissagos = Bijagós, Arquipélago dos, Guinea-Biss. 50 F2 11 15N 16 10W
Bissau, Guinea-Biss. 50 F2 11 45N 15 45W
Bistcho L., Canada 72 B5 59 45N 118 50W
Bistriţa, Romania 17 E13 47 9N 24 35 E
Bistriţa →, Romania 17 E14 46 30N 26 57 E
Biswan, India 43 F9 27 29N 81 2 E
Bitlis, Turkey 44 B4 38 20N 42 3 E
Bitola, Macedonia 21 D9 41 1N 21 20 E
Bitolj = Bitola, Macedonia 21 D9 41 1N 21 20 E
Bitter Creek, U.S.A. 82 F9 41 33N 108 33W
Bitterfontein, S. Africa 56 E2 31 1S 18 32 E
Bitterroot →, U.S.A. 82 C6 46 52N 114 7W
Bitterroot Range, U.S.A. 82 D6 46 0N 114 20W
Bitterwater, U.S.A. 84 J6 36 23N 121 0W
Biu, Nigeria 51 F8 10 40N 12 3 E
Biwa-Ko, Japan 31 G8 35 15N 136 10 E
Biwabik, U.S.A. 80 B8 47 32N 92 21W
Bixby, U.S.A. 81 H7 35 57N 95 53W
Biyang, China 34 H7 32 38N 113 21 E
Biysk, Russia 26 D9 52 40N 85 0 E
Bizana, S. Africa 57 E4 30 50S 29 52 E
Bizen, Japan 31 G7 34 43N 134 8 E
Bizerte, Tunisia 51 A7 37 15N 9 50 E
Bjargtangar, Iceland 8 D1 65 30N 24 30W
Bjelovar, Croatia 20 B7 45 56N 16 49 E
Bjørnevatn, Norway 8 B23 69 40N 30 0 E
Bjørnøya, Arctic 4 B8 74 30N 19 0 E
Black = Da →, Vietnam 38 B5 21 15N 105 20 E
Black →, Canada 78 B5 44 42N 79 19W
Black →, Ariz., U.S.A. 83 K8 33 44N 110 13W
Black →, Ark., U.S.A. 81 H9 35 38N 91 20W
Black →, Mich., U.S.A. 78 D2 42 59N 82 27W
Black →, N.Y., U.S.A. 79 C8 43 59N 76 4W
Black →, Wis., U.S.A. 80 D9 43 57N 91 22W
Black Bay Pen., Canada 70 C2 48 38N 88 21W
Black Birch L., Canada 73 B7 56 53N 107 45W
Black Diamond, Canada 72 C6 50 45N 114 14W
Black Duck →, Canada 70 A2 56 51N 89 2W
Black Forest = Schwarzwald, Germany 16 D5 48 30N 8 20 E
Black Forest, U.S.A. 80 F2 39 0N 104 43W
Black Hd., Ireland 13 C2 53 9N 9 16W
Black Hills, U.S.A. 80 D3 44 0N 103 45W
Black I., Canada 73 C9 51 12N 96 30W
Black L., Canada 73 B7 59 12N 105 15W
Black L., Mich., U.S.A. 76 C3 45 28N 84 16W
Black L., N.Y., U.S.A. 79 B9 44 31N 75 36W
Black Lake, Canada 73 B7 59 11N 105 20W
Black Mesa, U.S.A. 81 G3 36 58N 102 58W
Black Mt. = Mynydd Du, U.K. 11 F4 51 52N 3 50W
Black Mts., U.K. 11 F4 51 55N 3 7W
Black Range, U.S.A. 83 K10 33 15N 107 50W
Black River, Jamaica 88 C4 18 0N 77 50W
Black River Falls, U.S.A. 80 C9 44 18N 90 51W
Black Sea, Eurasia 25 F6 43 30N 35 0 E
Black Tickle, Canada 71 B8 53 28N 55 45W
Black Volta →, Africa 50 G5 8 41N 1 33W
Black Warrior →, U.S.A. 77 J2 32 32N 87 51W
Blackall, Australia 62 C4 24 25S 145 45 E
Blackball, N.Z. 59 K3 42 22S 171 26 E
Blackbull, Australia 62 B3 17 55S 141 45 E
Blackburn, U.K. 10 D5 53 45N 2 29W
Blackburn with Darwen □, U.K. 10 D5 53 45N 2 29W
Blackfoot, U.S.A. 82 E7 43 11N 112 21W
Blackfoot →, U.S.A. 82 C7 46 52N 113 53W
Blackfoot River Reservoir, U.S.A. 82 E8 43 0N 111 43W
Blackpool, U.K. 10 D4 53 49N 3 3W
Blackpool □, U.K. 10 D4 53 49N 3 3W
Blackriver, U.S.A. 78 B1 44 46N 83 17W
Blacks Harbour, Canada 71 C6 45 3N 66 49W
Blacksburg, U.S.A. 76 G5 37 14N 80 25W
Blacksod B., Ireland 13 B1 54 6N 10 0W
Blackstone, U.S.A. 76 G7 37 4N 78 0W
Blackstone Ra., Australia 61 E4 26 0S 128 30 E
Blackwater, Australia 62 C4 23 35S 148 53 E
Blackwater →, Meath, Ireland 13 C4 53 39N 6 41W
Blackwater →, Waterford, Ireland 13 D4 52 4N 7 52W
Blackwater →, U.K. 13 B5 54 31N 6 35W
Blackwell, U.S.A. 81 G6 36 48N 97 17W
Blackwells Corner, U.S.A. 85 K7 35 37N 119 47W
Blaenau Ffestiniog, U.K. 10 E4 53 0N 3 56W
Blaenau Gwent □, U.K. 11 F4 51 48N 3 12W
Blagodarnoye = Blagodarnyy, Russia 25 E7 45 7N 43 37 E
Blagodarnyy, Russia 25 E7 45 7N 43 37 E
Blagoevgrad, Bulgaria 21 C10 42 2N 23 5 E
Blagoveshchensk, Russia 27 D13 50 20N 127 30 E
Blain, U.S.A. 78 F7 40 20N 77 31W
Blaine, Minn., U.S.A. 80 C8 45 10N 93 13W
Blaine, Wash., U.S.A. 84 B4 48 59N 122 45W
Blaine Lake, Canada 73 C7 52 51N 106 52W
Blair, U.S.A. 80 E6 41 33N 96 8W
Blair Athol, Australia 62 C4 22 42S 147 31 E
Blair Atholl, U.K. 12 E5 56 46N 3 50W
Blairgowrie, U.K. 12 E5 56 35N 3 21W
Blairsden, U.S.A. 84 F6 39 47N 120 37W
Blairsville, U.S.A. 78 F5 40 26N 79 16W
Blake Pt., U.S.A. 80 A10 48 11N 88 25W
Blakely, Ga., U.S.A. 77 K3 31 23N 84 56W
Blakely, Pa., U.S.A. 79 E9 41 28N 75 37W
Blanc, C., Spain 22 B9 39 21N 2 51 E
Blanc, Mont, Alps 18 D7 45 48N 6 50 E
Blanc-Sablon, Canada 71 B8 51 24N 57 12W
Blanca, B., Argentina 96 D4 39 10S 61 30W
Blanca Peak, U.S.A. 83 H11 37 35N 105 29W
Blanche, C., Australia 63 E1 33 1S 134 9 E
Blanche, L., S. Austral., Australia 63 D2 29 15S 139 40 E
Blanche, L., W. Austral., Australia 60 D3 22 25S 123 17 E
Blanco, S. Africa 56 E3 33 55S 22 23 E
Blanco, U.S.A. 81 K5 30 6N 98 25W
Blanco →, Argentina 94 C2 30 20S 68 42W
Blanco, C., Costa Rica 88 E2 9 34N 85 8W
Blanco, C., U.S.A. 82 E1 42 51N 124 34W
Blanda →, Iceland 8 D3 65 37N 20 9W
Blandford Forum, U.K. 11 G5 50 51N 2 9W
Blanding, U.S.A. 83 H9 37 37N 109 29W
Blanes, Spain 19 B7 41 40N 2 48 E
Blankenberge, Belgium 15 C3 51 20N 3 9 E
Blanquilla, I., Venezuela 89 D7 11 51N 64 37W
Blanquillo, Uruguay 95 C4 32 53S 55 37W
Blantyre, Malawi 55 F4 15 45S 35 0 E
Blarney, Ireland 13 E3 51 56N 8 33W
Blasdell, U.S.A. 78 D6 42 48N 78 50W
Blåvands Huk, Denmark 9 J13 55 33N 8 4 E
Blaydon, U.K. 10 C6 54 58N 1 42W
Blayney, Australia 63 E4 33 32S 149 14 E
Blaze, Pt., Australia 60 B5 12 56S 130 11 E
Blekinge, Sweden 9 H16 56 25N 15 20 E
Blenheim, Canada 78 D3 42 20N 82 0W
Blenheim, N.Z. 59 J4 41 38S 173 57 E
Bletchley, U.K. 11 F7 51 59N 0 44W
Blida, Algeria 50 A6 36 30N 2 49 E
Bligh Sound, N.Z. 59 L1 44 47S 167 32 E
Blind River, Canada 70 C3 46 10N 82 58W
Bliss, Idaho, U.S.A. 82 E6 42 56N 114 57W
Bliss, N.Y., U.S.A. 78 D6 42 34N 78 15W
Blissfield, U.S.A. 78 F3 40 24N 81 58W
Blitar, Indonesia 37 H15 8 5S 112 11 E
Block I., U.S.A. 79 E13 41 11N 71 35W
Block Island Sd., U.S.A. 79 E13 41 15N 71 40W
Bloemfontein, S. Africa 56 D4 29 6S 26 7 E
Bloemhof, S. Africa 56 D4 27 38S 25 32 E
Blois, France 18 C4 47 35N 1 20 E
Blönduós, Iceland 8 D3 65 40N 20 12W
Bloodvein →, Canada 73 C9 51 47N 96 43W
Bloody Foreland, Ireland 13 A3 55 10N 8 17W
Bloomer, U.S.A. 80 C9 45 6N 91 29W
Bloomfield, Canada 78 C7 43 59N 77 14W
Bloomfield, Iowa, U.S.A. 80 E8 40 45N 92 25W
Bloomfield, N. Mex., U.S.A. 83 H10 36 43N 107 59W
Bloomfield, Nebr., U.S.A. 80 D6 42 36N 97 39W
Bloomington, Ill., U.S.A. 80 E10 40 28N 89 0W
Bloomington, Ind., U.S.A. 76 F2 39 10N 86 32W
Bloomington, Minn., U.S.A. 80 C8 44 50N 93 17W
Bloomsburg, U.S.A. 79 F8 41 0N 76 27W
Blora, Indonesia 37 G14 6 57S 111 25 E
Blossburg, U.S.A. 78 E7 41 41N 77 4W
Blouberg, S. Africa 57 C4 23 8S 28 59 E
Blountstown, U.S.A. 77 K3 30 27N 85 3W
Blue Earth, U.S.A. 80 D8 43 38N 94 6W
Blue Mesa Reservoir, U.S.A. 83 G10 38 28N 107 20W
Blue Mountain Lake, U.S.A. 79 C10 43 52N 74 30W
Blue Mts., Maine, U.S.A. 79 B14 44 50N 70 35W
Blue Mts., Oreg., U.S.A. 82 D4 45 15N 119 0W
Blue Mts., Pa., U.S.A. 79 F8 40 30N 76 30W
Blue Mud B., Australia 62 A2 13 30S 136 0 E
Blue Nile = Nîl el Azraq →, Sudan 51 E12 15 38N 32 31 E
Blue Rapids, U.S.A. 80 F6 39 41N 96 39W
Blue Ridge Mts., U.S.A. 77 G5 36 30N 80 15W
Blue River, Canada 72 C5 52 6N 119 18W
Bluefield, U.S.A. 76 G5 37 15N 81 17W
Bluefields, Nic. 88 D3 12 20N 83 50W
Bluff, Australia 62 C4 23 35S 149 4 E
Bluff, N.Z. 59 M2 46 37S 168 20 E
Bluff, U.S.A. 83 H9 37 17N 109 33W
Bluff Knoll, Australia 61 F2 34 24S 118 15 E
Bluff Pt., Australia 61 E1 27 50S 114 5 E
Bluffton, U.S.A. 76 E3 40 44N 85 11W
Blumenau, Brazil 95 B6 27 0S 49 0W
Blunt, U.S.A. 80 C5 44 31N 99 59W
Bly, U.S.A. 82 E3 42 24N 121 3W
Blyth, Canada 78 C3 43 44N 81 26W
Blyth, U.K. 10 B6 55 8N 1 31W
Blythe, U.S.A. 85 M12 33 37N 114 36W
Blytheville, U.S.A. 81 H10 35 56N 89 55W
Bo, S. Leone 50 G3 7 55N 11 50W
Bo Duc, Vietnam 39 G6 11 58N 106 50 E
Bo Hai, China 35 E10 39 0N 119 0 E
Bo Xian = Bozhou, China 34 H8 33 55N 115 41 E
Boa Vista, Brazil 92 C6 2 48N 60 30W
Boaco, Nic. 88 D2 12 29N 85 35W
Bo'ai, China 34 G7 35 10N 113 3 E
Boalsburg, U.S.A. 78 F7 40 46N 77 47W
Boane, Mozam. 57 D5 26 6S 32 19 E
Boardman, U.S.A. 78 E4 41 2N 80 40W
Bobadah, Australia 63 E4 32 19S 146 41 E
Bobbili, India 41 K13 18 35N 83 30 E
Bobcaygeon, Canada 78 B6 44 33N 78 33W
Bobo-Dioulasso, Burkina Faso 50 F5 11 8N 4 13W
Bóbr →, Poland 16 B8 52 4N 15 4 E
Bobraomby, Tanjon' i, Madag. 57 A8 12 40S 49 10 E
Bobruysk = Babruysk, Belarus 17 B15 53 10N 29 15 E
Boby, Pic, Madag. 53 J9 22 12S 46 55 E
Bôca do Acre, Brazil 92 E5 8 50S 67 27W
Boca Raton, U.S.A. 77 M5 26 21N 80 5W
Bocas del Toro, Panama 88 E3 9 15N 82 20W
Bochnia, Poland 17 D11 49 58N 20 27 E
Bochum, Germany 16 C4 51 28N 7 13 E
Bocoyna, Mexico 86 B3 27 52N 107 35W
Bodaybo, Russia 27 D12 57 50N 114 0 E
Boddam, U.K. 12 B7 59 56N 1 17W
Boddington, Australia 61 F2 32 50S 116 30 E
Bodega Bay, U.S.A. 84 G3 38 20N 123 3W
Boden, Sweden 8 D19 65 50N 21 42 E
Bodensee, Europe 18 C8 47 35N 9 25 E
Bodhan, India 40 K10 18 40N 77 44 E
Bodmin, U.K. 11 G3 50 28N 4 43W
Bodmin Moor, U.K. 11 G3 50 33N 4 36W
Bodø, Norway 8 C16 67 17N 14 24 E
Bodrog →, Hungary 17 D11 48 11N 21 22 E
Bodrum, Turkey 21 F12 37 3N 27 30 E
Boende, Dem. Rep. of the Congo 52 E4 0 24S 21 12 E
Boerne, U.S.A. 81 L5 29 47N 98 44W
Boesmans →, S. Africa 56 E4 33 42S 26 39 E
Bogalusa, U.S.A. 81 K10 30 47N 89 52W
Bogan →, Australia 63 D4 29 59S 146 17 E
Bogan Gate, Australia 63 E4 33 7S 147 49 E
Bogantungan, Australia 62 C4 23 41S 147 17 E
Bogata, U.S.A. 81 J7 33 28N 95 13W
Boggabilla, Australia 63 D5 28 36S 150 24 E

Brewster

Brewster, *Ohio, U.S.A.* **78 F3** 40 43N 81 36W
Brewster, *Wash., U.S.A.* **82 B4** 48 6N 119 47W
Brewster, Kap = Kangikajik, *Greenland* **4 B6** 70 7N 22 0W
Brewton, *U.S.A.* **77 K2** 31 7N 87 4W
Breyten, *S. Africa* **57 D5** 26 16S 30 0 E
Brezhnev = Naberezhnyye Chelny, *Russia* **24 C9** 55 42N 52 19 E
Briançon, *France* **18 D7** 44 54N 6 39 E
Bribie I., *Australia* **63 D5** 27 0S 153 10 E
Bribri, *Costa Rica* **88 E3** 9 38N 82 50W
Bridgehampton, *U.S.A.* **79 F12** 40 56N 72 19W
Bridgend, *U.K.* **11 F4** 51 30N 3 34W
Bridgend □, *U.K.* **11 F4** 51 36N 3 36W
Bridgeport, *Calif., U.S.A.* **84 G7** 38 15N 119 14W
Bridgeport, *Conn., U.S.A.* **79 E11** 41 11N 73 12W
Bridgeport, *Nebr., U.S.A.* **80 E3** 41 40N 103 6W
Bridgeport, *Tex., U.S.A.* **81 J6** 33 13N 97 45W
Bridger, *U.S.A.* **82 D9** 45 18N 108 55W
Bridgeton, *U.S.A.* **76 F8** 39 26N 75 14W
Bridgetown, *Australia* **61 F2** 33 58S 116 7 E
Bridgetown, *Barbados* **89 D8** 13 5N 59 30W
Bridgetown, *Canada* **71 D6** 44 55N 65 18W
Bridgewater, *Canada* **71 D7** 44 25N 64 31W
Bridgewater, *Mass., U.S.A.* **79 E14** 41 59N 70 58W
Bridgewater, *N.Y., U.S.A.* **79 D9** 42 53N 75 15W
Bridgewater, C., *Australia* **63 F3** 38 23S 141 23 E
Bridgewater-Gagebrook, *Australia* **62 G4** 42 44S 147 14 E
Bridgnorth, *U.K.* **11 E5** 52 32N 2 25W
Bridgton, *U.S.A.* **79 B14** 44 3N 70 42W
Bridgwater, *U.K.* **11 F5** 51 8N 2 59W
Bridgwater B., *U.K.* **11 F4** 51 15N 3 15W
Bridlington, *U.K.* **10 C7** 54 5N 0 12W
Bridlington B., *U.K.* **10 C7** 54 4N 0 10W
Bridport, *Australia* **62 G4** 40 59S 147 23 E
Bridport, *U.K.* **11 G5** 50 44N 2 45W
Brig, *Switz.* **18 C7** 46 18N 7 59 E
Brigg, *U.K.* **10 D7** 53 34N 0 28W
Brigham City, *U.S.A.* **82 F7** 41 31N 112 1W
Bright, *Australia* **63 F4** 36 42S 146 56 E
Brighton, *Australia* **63 F2** 35 5S 138 30 E
Brighton, *Canada* **78 B7** 44 2N 77 44W
Brighton, *U.K.* **11 G7** 50 49N 0 7W
Brighton, *Colo., U.S.A.* **80 F2** 39 59N 104 49W
Brighton, *N.Y., U.S.A.* **78 C7** 43 8N 77 34W
Brilliant, *U.S.A.* **78 F4** 40 15N 80 39W
Brindisi, *Italy* **21 D7** 40 39N 17 55 E
Brinkley, *U.S.A.* **81 H9** 34 53N 91 12W
Brinnon, *U.S.A.* **84 C4** 47 41N 122 54W
Brion, I., *Canada* **71 C7** 47 46N 61 26W
Brisbane, *Australia* **63 D5** 27 25S 153 2 E
Brisbane →, *Australia* **63 D5** 27 24S 153 9 E
Bristol, *U.K.* **11 F5** 51 26N 2 35W
Bristol, *Conn., U.S.A.* **79 E12** 41 40N 72 57W
Bristol, *Pa., U.S.A.* **79 F10** 40 6N 74 51W
Bristol, *R.I., U.S.A.* **79 E13** 41 40N 71 16W
Bristol, *Tenn., U.S.A.* **77 G4** 36 36N 82 11W
Bristol, City of □, *U.K.* **11 F5** 51 27N 2 36W
Bristol B., *U.S.A.* **68 C4** 58 0N 160 0W
Bristol Channel, *U.K.* **11 F3** 51 18N 4 30W
Bristol I., *Antarctica* **5 B1** 58 45S 28 0W
Bristol L., *U.S.A.* **83 J5** 34 23N 116 50W
Bristow, *U.S.A.* **81 H6** 35 50N 96 23W
Britain = Great Britain, *Europe* **6 E5** 54 0N 2 15W
British Columbia □, *Canada* **72 C3** 55 0N 125 15W
British Indian Ocean Terr. = Chagos Arch., *Ind. Oc.* **29 K11** 6 0S 72 0 E
British Isles, *Europe* **6 E5** 54 0N 4 0W
Brits, *S. Africa* **57 D4** 25 37S 27 48 E
Britstown, *S. Africa* **56 E3** 30 37S 23 30 E
Britt, *Canada* **70 C3** 45 46N 80 34W
Brittany = Bretagne, *France* **18 B2** 48 10N 3 0W
Britton, *U.S.A.* **80 C6** 45 48N 97 45W
Brive-la-Gaillarde, *France* **18 D4** 45 10N 1 32 E
Brixen = Bressanone, *Italy* **20 A4** 46 43N 11 39 E
Brixham, *U.K.* **11 G4** 50 23N 3 31W
Brno, *Czech Rep.* **17 D9** 49 10N 16 35 E
Broad →, *U.S.A.* **77 J5** 34 1N 81 4W
Broad Arrow, *Australia* **61 F3** 30 23S 121 15 E
Broad B., *U.K.* **12 C2** 58 14N 6 18W
Broad Haven, *Ireland* **13 B2** 54 20N 9 55W
Broad Law, *U.K.* **12 F5** 55 30N 3 21W
Broad Sd., *Australia* **62 C4** 22 0S 149 45 E
Broadalbin, *U.S.A.* **79 C10** 43 4N 74 12W
Broadback →, *Canada* **70 B4** 51 21N 78 52W
Broadhurst Ra., *Australia* **60 D3** 22 30S 122 30 E
Broads, The, *U.K.* **10 E9** 52 45N 1 30 E
Broadus, *U.S.A.* **80 C2** 45 27N 105 25W
Brochet, *Canada* **73 B8** 57 53N 101 40W
Brochet, L., *Canada* **73 B8** 58 36N 101 35W
Brocken, *Germany* **16 C6** 51 47N 10 37 E
Brockport, *U.S.A.* **78 C7** 43 13N 77 56W
Brockton, *U.S.A.* **79 D13** 42 5N 71 1W
Brockville, *Canada* **79 B9** 44 35N 75 41W
Brockway, *Mont., U.S.A.* **80 B2** 47 18N 105 45W
Brockway, *Pa., U.S.A.* **78 E6** 41 15N 78 47W
Brocton, *U.S.A.* **78 D5** 42 23N 79 26W
Brodeur Pen., *Canada* **69 A11** 72 30N 88 10W
Brodhead, Mt., *U.S.A.* **78 E7** 41 39N 77 47W
Brodick, *U.K.* **12 F3** 55 35N 5 9W
Brodnica, *Poland* **17 B10** 53 15N 19 25 E
Brody, *Ukraine* **17 C13** 50 5N 25 10 E
Brogan, *U.S.A.* **82 D5** 44 15N 117 31W
Broken Arrow, *U.S.A.* **81 G7** 36 3N 95 48W
Broken Bow, *Nebr., U.S.A.* **80 E5** 41 24N 99 38W
Broken Bow, *Okla., U.S.A.* **81 H7** 34 2N 94 44W
Broken Bow Lake, *U.S.A.* **81 H7** 34 9N 94 40W
Broken Hill = Kabwe, *Zambia* **55 E2** 14 30S 28 29 E
Broken Hill, *Australia* **63 E3** 31 58S 141 29 E
Bromley □, *U.K.* **11 F8** 51 24N 0 2 E
Bromsgrove, *U.K.* **11 E5** 52 21N 2 2W
Brønderslev, *Denmark* **9 H13** 57 16N 9 57 E
Bronkhorstspruit, *S. Africa* **57 D4** 25 46S 28 45 E
Brønnøysund, *Norway* **8 D15** 65 28N 12 14 E
Brook Park, *U.S.A.* **78 E4** 41 24N 81 51W
Brookhaven, *U.S.A.* **81 K9** 31 35N 90 26W
Brookings, *Oreg., U.S.A.* **82 E1** 42 3N 124 17W
Brookings, *S. Dak., U.S.A.* **80 C6** 44 19N 96 48W
Brooklin, *Canada* **78 C6** 43 55N 78 55W
Brooklyn Park, *U.S.A.* **80 C8** 45 6N 93 23W
Brooks, *Canada* **72 C6** 50 35N 111 55W
Brooks Range, *U.S.A.* **68 B5** 68 0N 152 0W
Brooksville, *U.S.A.* **77 L4** 28 33N 82 23W
Brookton, *Australia* **61 F2** 32 22S 117 0 E
Brookville, *U.S.A.* **78 E5** 41 10N 79 5W
Broom, L., *U.K.* **12 D3** 57 55N 5 15W
Broome, *Australia* **60 C3** 18 0S 122 15 E
Brora, *U.K.* **12 C5** 58 0N 3 52W
Brora →, *U.K.* **12 C5** 58 0N 3 51W
Brosna →, *Ireland* **13 C4** 53 14N 7 58W
Brothers, *U.S.A.* **82 E3** 43 49N 120 36W
Brough, *U.K.* **10 C5** 54 32N 2 18W
Brough Hd., *U.K.* **12 B5** 59 8N 3 20W
Broughton Island = Qikiqtarjuaq, *Canada* **69 B13** 67 33N 63 0W
Brown, L., *Australia* **61 F2** 31 5S 118 15 E
Brown, Pt., *Australia* **63 E1** 32 32S 133 50 E
Brown City, *U.S.A.* **78 C2** 43 13N 82 59W
Brown Willy, *U.K.* **11 G3** 50 35N 4 37W
Brownfield, *U.S.A.* **81 J3** 33 11N 102 17W
Browning, *U.S.A.* **82 B7** 48 34N 113 1W
Brownsville, *Oreg., U.S.A.* **82 D2** 44 24N 122 59W
Brownsville, *Pa., U.S.A.* **78 F5** 40 1N 79 53W
Brownsville, *Tenn., U.S.A.* **81 H10** 35 36N 89 16W
Brownsville, *Tex., U.S.A.* **81 N6** 25 54N 97 30W
Brownville, *U.S.A.* **79 C9** 44 0N 75 59W
Brownwood, *U.S.A.* **81 K5** 31 43N 98 59W
Browse I., *Australia* **60 B3** 14 7S 123 33 E
Bruas, *Malaysia* **39 K3** 4 30N 100 47 E
Bruay-la-Buissière, *France* **18 A5** 50 29N 2 33 E
Bruce, Mt., *Australia* **60 D2** 22 37S 118 8 E
Bruce Pen., *Canada* **78 B3** 45 0N 81 30W
Bruce Rock, *Australia* **61 F2** 31 52S 118 8 E
Bruck an der Leitha, *Austria* **17 D9** 48 1N 16 47 E
Bruck an der Mur, *Austria* **16 E8** 47 24N 15 16 E
Brue →, *U.K.* **11 F5** 51 13N 2 59W
Bruges = Brugge, *Belgium* **15 C3** 51 13N 3 13 E
Brugge, *Belgium* **15 C3** 51 13N 3 13 E
Bruin, *U.S.A.* **78 E5** 41 3N 79 43W
Brûlé, *Canada* **72 C5** 53 15N 117 58W
Brumado, *Brazil* **93 F10** 14 14S 41 40W
Brumunddal, *Norway* **9 F14** 60 53N 10 56 E
Bruneau, *U.S.A.* **82 E6** 42 53N 115 48W
Bruneau →, *U.S.A.* **82 E6** 42 56N 115 57W
Brunei = Bandar Seri Begawan, *Brunei* **36 C4** 4 52N 115 0 E
Brunei ■, *Asia* **36 D4** 4 50N 115 0 E
Brunner, L., *N.Z.* **59 K3** 42 37S 171 27 E
Brunssum, *Neths.* **15 D5** 50 57N 5 59 E
Brunswick = Braunschweig, *Germany* **16 B6** 52 15N 10 31 E
Brunswick, *Ga., U.S.A.* **77 K5** 31 10N 81 30W
Brunswick, *Maine, U.S.A.* **77 D11** 43 55N 69 58W
Brunswick, *Md., U.S.A.* **76 F7** 39 19N 77 38W
Brunswick, *Mo., U.S.A.* **80 F8** 39 26N 93 8W
Brunswick, *Ohio, U.S.A.* **78 E3** 41 14N 81 51W
Brunswick, Pen. de, *Chile* **96 G2** 53 30S 71 30W
Brunswick B., *Australia* **60 C3** 15 15S 124 50 E
Brunswick Junction, *Australia* **61 F2** 33 15S 115 50 E
Bruny I., *Australia* **62 G4** 43 20S 147 15 E
Brus Laguna, *Honduras* **88 C3** 15 47N 84 35W
Brush, *U.S.A.* **80 E3** 40 15N 103 37W
Brushton, *U.S.A.* **79 B10** 44 50N 74 31W
Brusque, *Brazil* **95 B6** 27 5S 49 0W
Brussel, *Belgium* **15 D4** 50 51N 4 21 E
Brussels = Brussel, *Belgium* **15 D4** 50 51N 4 21 E
Brussels, *Canada* **78 C3** 43 44N 81 15W
Bruthen, *Australia* **63 F4** 37 42S 147 50 E
Bruxelles = Brussel, *Belgium* **15 D4** 50 51N 4 21 E
Bryan, *Ohio, U.S.A.* **76 E3** 41 28N 84 33W
Bryan, *Tex., U.S.A.* **81 K6** 30 40N 96 22W
Bryan, Mt., *Australia* **63 E2** 33 30S 139 0 E
Bryansk, *Russia* **24 D4** 53 13N 34 25 E
Bryce Canyon Nat. Park, *U.S.A.* **83 H7** 37 30N 112 10W
Bryne, *Norway* **9 G11** 58 44N 5 38 E
Bryson City, *U.S.A.* **77 H4** 35 26N 83 27W
Bsharri, *Lebanon* **47 A5** 34 15N 36 0 E
Bū Baqarah, *U.A.E.* **45 E8** 25 35N 56 25 E
Bu Craa, *W. Sahara* **50 C3** 26 45N 12 50W
Bū Ḩasā, *U.A.E.* **45 F7** 23 30N 53 20 E
Bua Yai, *Thailand* **38 E4** 15 33N 102 26 E
Buapinang, *Indonesia* **37 E6** 4 40S 121 30 E
Bubanza, *Burundi* **54 C2** 3 6S 29 23 E
Būbiyān, *Kuwait* **46 B4** 29 45N 48 15 E
Bucaramanga, *Colombia* **92 B4** 7 0N 73 0W
Bucasia, *Australia* **62 C4** 21 2S 149 10 E
Buccaneer Arch., *Australia* **60 C3** 16 7S 123 20 E
Buchach, *Ukraine* **17 D13** 49 5N 25 25 E
Buchan, *U.K.* **12 D6** 57 32N 2 21W
Buchan Ness, *U.K.* **12 D7** 57 29N 1 46W
Buchanan, *Canada* **73 C8** 51 40N 102 45W
Buchanan, *Liberia* **50 G3** 5 57N 10 2W
Buchanan, L., *Queens., Australia* **62 C4** 21 35S 145 52 E
Buchanan, L., *W. Austral., Australia* **61 E3** 25 33S 123 2 E
Buchanan, L., *U.S.A.* **81 K5** 30 45N 98 25W
Buchanan Cr. →, *Australia* **62 B2** 19 13S 136 33 E
Buchans, *Canada* **71 C8** 48 50N 56 52W
Bucharest = Bucureşti, *Romania* **17 F14** 44 27N 26 10 E
Buchon, Pt., *U.S.A.* **84 K6** 35 15N 120 54W
Buck Hill Falls, *U.S.A.* **79 E9** 41 11N 75 16W
Buckeye, *U.S.A.* **83 K7** 33 22N 112 35W
Buckeye Lake, *U.S.A.* **78 G2** 39 55N 82 29W
Buckhannon, *U.S.A.* **76 F5** 39 0N 80 8W
Buckhaven, *U.K.* **12 E5** 56 11N 3 3W
Buckhorn L., *Canada* **78 B6** 44 29N 78 23W
Buckie, *U.K.* **12 D6** 57 41N 2 58W
Buckingham, *Canada* **70 C4** 45 37N 75 24W
Buckingham, *U.K.* **11 F7** 51 59N 0 57W
Buckingham B., *Australia* **62 A2** 12 10S 135 40 E
Buckinghamshire □, *U.K.* **11 F7** 51 53N 0 55W
Buckle Hd., *Australia* **60 B4** 14 26S 127 52 E
Buckleboo, *Australia* **63 E2** 32 54S 136 12 E
Buckley, *U.K.* **10 D4** 53 10N 3 5W
Buckley →, *Australia* **62 C2** 20 10S 138 49 E
Bucklin, *U.S.A.* **81 G5** 37 33N 99 38W
Bucks L., *U.S.A.* **84 F5** 39 54N 121 12W
Buctouche, *Canada* **71 C7** 46 30N 64 45W
Bucureşti, *Romania* **17 F14** 44 27N 26 10 E
Bucyrus, *U.S.A.* **76 E4** 40 48N 82 59W
Budalin, *Burma* **41 H19** 22 20N 95 10 E
Budapest, *Hungary* **17 E10** 47 29N 19 5 E
Budaun, *India* **43 E8** 28 5N 79 10 E
Budd Coast, *Antarctica* **5 C8** 68 0S 112 0 E
Bude, *U.K.* **11 G3** 50 49N 4 34W
Budennovsk, *Russia* **25 F7** 44 50N 44 10 E
Budge Budge = Baj Baj, *India* **43 H13** 22 30N 88 5 E
Budgewoi, *Australia* **63 E5** 33 13S 151 34 E
Budjala, *Dem. Rep. of the Congo* **52 D3** 2 50N 19 40 E
Buellton, *U.S.A.* **85 L6** 34 37N 120 12W
Buena Esperanza, *Argentina* **94 C2** 34 45S 65 15W
Buena Park, *U.S.A.* **85 M9** 33 52N 117 59W
Buena Vista, *Colo., U.S.A.* **83 G10** 38 51N 106 8W
Buena Vista, *Va., U.S.A.* **76 G6** 37 44N 79 21W
Buena Vista Lake Bed, *U.S.A.* **85 K7** 35 12N 119 18W
Buenaventura, *Colombia* **92 C3** 3 53N 77 4W
Buenaventura, *Mexico* **86 B3** 29 50N 107 30W
Buenos Aires, *Argentina* **94 C4** 34 30S 58 20W
Buenos Aires, *Costa Rica* **88 E3** 9 10N 83 20W
Buenos Aires □, *Argentina* **94 D4** 36 30S 60 0W
Buenos Aires, L., *Chile* **96 F2** 46 35S 72 30W
Buffalo, *Mo., U.S.A.* **81 G8** 37 39N 93 6W
Buffalo, *N.Y., U.S.A.* **78 D6** 42 53N 78 53W
Buffalo, *Okla., U.S.A.* **81 G5** 36 50N 99 38W
Buffalo, *S. Dak., U.S.A.* **80 C3** 45 35N 103 33W
Buffalo, *Wyo., U.S.A.* **82 D10** 44 21N 106 42W
Buffalo →, *Canada* **72 A5** 60 5N 115 5W
Buffalo →, *S. Africa* **57 D5** 28 43S 30 37 E
Buffalo Head Hills, *Canada* **72 B5** 57 25N 115 55W
Buffalo L., *Alta., Canada* **72 C6** 52 27N 112 54W
Buffalo L., *N.W.T., Canada* **72 A5** 60 12N 115 25W
Buffalo Narrows, *Canada* **73 B7** 55 51N 108 29W
Buffels →, *S. Africa* **56 D2** 29 36S 17 3 E
Buford, *U.S.A.* **77 H4** 34 10N 84 0W
Bug = Buh →, *Ukraine* **25 E5** 46 59N 31 58 E
Bug →, *Poland* **17 B11** 52 31N 21 5 E
Buga, *Colombia* **92 C3** 4 0N 76 15W
Bugala I., *Uganda* **54 C3** 0 40S 32 20 E
Buganda, *Uganda* **54 C3** 0 0 31 30 E
Buganga, *Uganda* **54 C3** 0 3S 32 0 E
Bugel, Tanjung, *Indonesia* **37 G14** 6 26S 111 3 E
Bugibba, *Malta* **23 D1** 35 57N 14 25 E
Bugsuk, *Phil.* **36 C5** 8 15N 117 15 E
Bugulma, *Russia* **24 D9** 54 33N 52 48 E
Bugun Shara, *Mongolia* **32 B5** 49 0N 104 0 E
Buguruslan, *Russia* **24 D9** 53 39N 52 26 E
Buh →, *Ukraine* **25 E5** 46 59N 31 58 E
Buhera, *Zimbabwe* **57 B5** 19 18S 31 29 E
Buhl, *U.S.A.* **82 E6** 42 36N 114 46W
Builth Wells, *U.K.* **11 E4** 52 9N 3 25W
Buir Nur, *Mongolia* **33 B6** 47 50N 117 42 E
Bujumbura, *Burundi* **54 C2** 3 16S 29 18 E
Bukachacha, *Russia* **27 D12** 52 55N 116 50 E
Bukama, *Dem. Rep. of the Congo* **55 D2** 9 10S 25 50 E
Bukavu, *Dem. Rep. of the Congo* **54 C2** 2 20S 28 52 E
Bukene, *Tanzania* **54 C3** 4 15S 32 48 E
Bukhara = Bukhoro, *Uzbekistan* **26 F7** 39 48N 64 25 E
Bukhoro, *Uzbekistan* **26 F7** 39 48N 64 25 E
Bukima, *Tanzania* **54 C3** 1 50S 33 25 E
Bukit Mertajam, *Malaysia* **39 K3** 5 22N 100 28 E
Bukittinggi, *Indonesia* **36 E2** 0 20S 100 20 E
Bukoba, *Tanzania* **54 C3** 1 20S 31 49 E
Bukuya, *Uganda* **54 B3** 0 40N 31 52 E
Būl, Kuh-e, *Iran* **45 D7** 30 48N 52 45 E
Bula, *Indonesia* **37 E8** 3 6S 130 30 E
Bulahdelah, *Australia* **63 E5** 32 23S 152 13 E
Bulan, *Phil.* **37 B6** 12 40N 123 52 E
Bulandshahr, *India* **42 E7** 28 28N 77 51 E
Bulawayo, *Zimbabwe* **55 G2** 20 7S 28 32 E
Buldan, *Turkey* **21 E13** 38 2N 28 50 E
Bulgar, *Russia* **24 D8** 54 57N 49 4 E
Bulgaria ■, *Europe* **21 C11** 42 35N 25 30 E
Buli, Teluk, *Indonesia* **37 D7** 0 48N 128 25 E
Buliluyan, C., *Phil.* **36 C5** 8 20N 117 15 E
Bulkley →, *Canada* **72 B3** 55 15N 127 40W
Bull Shoals L., *U.S.A.* **81 G8** 36 22N 92 35W
Bullhead City, *U.S.A.* **85 K12** 35 8N 114 32W
Büllingen, *Belgium* **15 D6** 50 25N 6 16 E
Bullock Creek, *Australia* **62 B3** 17 43S 144 31 E
Bulloo →, *Australia* **63 D3** 28 43S 142 30 E
Bulloo L., *Australia* **63 D3** 28 43S 142 25 E
Bulls, *N.Z.* **59 J5** 40 10S 175 24 E
Bulnes, *Chile* **94 D1** 36 42S 72 19W
Bulsar = Valsad, *India* **40 J8** 20 40N 72 58 E
Bultfontein, *S. Africa* **56 D4** 28 18S 26 10 E
Bulukumba, *Indonesia* **37 F6** 5 33S 120 11 E
Bulun, *Russia* **27 B13** 70 37N 127 30 E
Bumba, *Dem. Rep. of the Congo* **52 D4** 2 13N 22 30 E
Bumbiri I., *Tanzania* **54 C3** 1 40S 31 55 E
Bumhpa Bum, *Burma* **41 F20** 26 51N 97 14 E
Bumi →, *Zimbabwe* **55 F2** 17 0S 28 20 E
Buna, *Kenya* **54 B4** 2 58N 39 30 E
Bunazi, *Tanzania* **54 C3** 1 3S 31 23 E
Bunbury, *Australia* **61 F2** 33 20S 115 35 E
Bunclody, *Ireland* **13 D5** 52 39N 6 40W
Buncrana, *Ireland* **13 A4** 55 8N 7 27W
Bundaberg, *Australia* **63 C5** 24 54S 152 22 E
Bundey →, *Australia* **62 C2** 21 46S 135 37 E
Bundi, *India* **42 G6** 25 30N 75 35 E
Bundoran, *Ireland* **13 B3** 54 28N 8 16W
Bung Kan, *Thailand* **38 C4** 18 23N 103 37 E
Bungay, *U.K.* **11 E9** 52 27N 1 28 E
Bungil Cr. →, *Australia* **63 D4** 27 5S 149 5 E
Bungo-Suidō, *Japan* **31 H6** 33 0N 132 15 E
Bungoma, *Kenya* **54 B3** 0 34N 34 34 E
Bungotakada, *Japan* **31 H5** 33 35N 131 25 E
Bungu, *Tanzania* **54 D4** 7 35S 39 0 E
Bunia, *Dem. Rep. of the Congo* **54 B3** 1 35N 30 20 E
Bunji, *Pakistan* **43 B6** 35 45N 74 40 E
Bunkie, *U.S.A.* **81 K8** 30 57N 92 11W
Bunnell, *U.S.A.* **77 L5** 29 28N 81 16W
Buntok, *Indonesia* **36 E4** 1 40S 114 58 E
Bunyu, *Indonesia* **36 D5** 3 35N 117 50 E
Buol, *Indonesia* **37 D6** 1 15N 121 32 E
Buon Brieng, *Vietnam* **38 F7** 13 9N 108 12 E
Buon Ma Thuot, *Vietnam* **38 F7** 12 40N 108 3 E
Buong Long, *Cambodia* **38 F6** 13 44N 106 59 E
Buorkhaya, Mys, *Russia* **27 B14** 71 50N 132 40 E
Buqayq, *Si. Arabia* **45 E6** 26 0N 49 45 E
Bur Acaba, *Somali Rep.* **46 G3** 3 12N 44 20 E
Būr Safāga, *Egypt* **44 E2** 26 43N 33 57 E
Būr Sa'īd, *Egypt* **51 B12** 31 16N 32 18 E
Būr Sūdān, *Sudan* **51 E13** 19 32N 37 9 E
Bura, *Kenya* **54 C4** 1 4S 39 58 E
Burakin, *Australia* **61 F2** 30 31S 117 10 E
Burao, *Somali Rep.* **46 F4** 9 32N 45 32 E
Burāq, *Syria* **47 B5** 33 11N 36 29 E
Buraydah, *Si. Arabia* **44 E4** 26 20N 43 59 E
Burbank, *U.S.A.* **85 L8** 34 11N 118 19W
Burda, *India* **42 G6** 25 50N 77 35 E
Burdekin →, *Australia* **62 B4** 19 38S 147 25 E
Burdur, *Turkey* **25 G5** 37 45N 30 17 E
Burdwan = Barddhaman, *India* **43 H12** 23 14N 87 39 E
Bure, *Ethiopia* **46 E2** 10 40N 37 4 E
Bure →, *U.K.* **10 E9** 52 38N 1 43 E
Bureya →, *Russia* **27 E13** 49 27N 129 30 E
Burford, *Canada* **78 C4** 43 7N 80 27W
Burgas, *Bulgaria* **21 C12** 42 33N 27 29 E
Burgeo, *Canada* **71 C8** 47 37N 57 38W
Burgersdorp, *S. Africa* **56 E4** 31 0S 26 20 E
Burges, Mt., *Australia* **61 F3** 30 50S 121 5 E
Burgos, *Spain* **19 A4** 42 21N 3 41W
Burgsvik, *Sweden* **9 H18** 57 3N 18 19 E
Burgundy = Bourgogne, *France* **18 C6** 47 0N 4 50 E
Burhaniye, *Turkey* **21 E12** 39 30N 26 58 E
Burhanpur, *India* **40 J10** 21 18N 76 14 E
Burhi Gandak →, *India* **43 G12** 25 20N 86 37 E
Burhner →, *India* **43 H9** 22 43N 80 31 E
Burias I., *Phil.* **37 B6** 12 55N 123 5 E
Burica, Pta., *Costa Rica* **88 E3** 8 3N 82 51W
Burien, *U.S.A.* **84 C4** 47 28N 122 21W
Burigi, L., *Tanzania* **54 C3** 2 2S 31 22 E
Burin, *Canada* **71 C8** 47 1N 55 14W
Buriram, *Thailand* **38 E4** 15 0N 103 0 E
Burj Sāfitā, *Syria* **44 C3** 34 48N 36 7 E
Burkburnett, *U.S.A.* **81 H5** 34 6N 98 34W
Burke →, *Australia* **62 C2** 23 12S 139 33 E
Burke Chan., *Canada* **72 C3** 52 10N 127 30W
Burketown, *Australia* **62 B2** 17 45S 139 33 E
Burkina Faso ■, *Africa* **50 F5** 12 0N 1 0W
Burk's Falls, *Canada* **70 C4** 45 37N 79 24W
Burleigh Falls, *Canada* **78 B6** 44 33N 78 12W
Burley, *U.S.A.* **82 E7** 42 32N 113 48W
Burlingame, *U.S.A.* **84 H4** 37 35N 122 21W
Burlington, *Canada* **78 C5** 43 18N 79 45W
Burlington, *Colo., U.S.A.* **80 F3** 39 18N 102 16W
Burlington, *Iowa, U.S.A.* **80 E9** 40 49N 91 14W
Burlington, *Kans., U.S.A.* **80 F7** 38 12N 95 45W
Burlington, *N.C., U.S.A.* **77 G6** 36 6N 79 26W
Burlington, *N.J., U.S.A.* **79 F10** 40 4N 74 51W
Burlington, *Vt., U.S.A.* **79 B11** 44 29N 73 12W
Burlington, *Wash., U.S.A.* **84 B4** 48 28N 122 20W
Burlington, *Wis., U.S.A.* **76 D1** 42 41N 88 17W
Burlyu-Tyube, *Kazakstan* **26 E8** 46 30N 79 10 E
Burma ■, *Asia* **41 J20** 21 0N 96 30 E
Burnaby I., *Canada* **72 C2** 52 25N 131 19W
Burnet, *U.S.A.* **81 K5** 30 45N 98 14W
Burney, *U.S.A.* **82 F3** 40 53N 121 40W
Burnham, *U.S.A.* **78 F7** 40 38N 77 34W
Burnham-on-Sea, *U.K.* **11 F5** 51 14N 3 0W
Burnie, *Australia* **62 G4** 41 4S 145 56 E
Burnley, *U.K.* **10 D5** 53 47N 2 14W
Burns, *U.S.A.* **82 E4** 43 35N 119 3W
Burns Lake, *Canada* **72 C3** 54 20N 125 45W
Burnside →, *Canada* **68 B9** 66 51N 108 4W
Burnside, L., *Australia* **61 E3** 25 22S 123 0 E
Burnsville, *U.S.A.* **80 C8** 44 47N 93 17W
Burnt L., *Canada* **71 B7** 53 35N 64 4W
Burnt River, *Canada* **78 B6** 44 41N 78 42W
Burntwood →, *Canada* **73 B9** 56 8N 96 34W
Burntwood L., *Canada* **73 B8** 55 22N 100 26W
Burqān, *Kuwait* **44 D5** 29 0N 47 57 E
Burra, *Australia* **63 E2** 33 40S 138 55 E
Burray, *U.K.* **12 C6** 58 51N 2 54W
Burren Junction, *Australia* **63 E4** 30 7S 148 59 E
Burrinjuck Res., *Australia* **63 F4** 35 0S 148 36 E
Burro, Serranías del, *Mexico* **86 B4** 29 0N 102 0W
Burrow Hd., *U.K.* **12 G4** 54 41N 4 24W
Burruyacú, *Argentina* **94 B3** 26 30S 64 40W
Burry Port, *U.K.* **11 F3** 51 41N 4 15W
Bursa, *Turkey* **21 D13** 40 15N 29 5 E
Burstall, *Canada* **73 C7** 50 39N 109 54W
Burton, *Ohio, U.S.A.* **78 E3** 41 28N 81 8W
Burton, *S.C., U.S.A.* **77 J5** 32 25N 80 45W
Burton, L., *Canada* **70 B4** 54 45N 78 20W
Burton upon Trent, *U.K.* **10 E6** 52 48N 1 38W
Buru, *Indonesia* **37 E7** 3 30S 126 30 E
Burûn, Râs, *Egypt* **47 D2** 31 14N 33 7 E
Burundi ■, *Africa* **54 C3** 3 15S 30 0 E
Bururi, *Burundi* **54 C2** 3 57S 29 37 E
Burutu, *Nigeria* **50 G7** 5 20N 5 29 E
Burwell, *U.S.A.* **80 E5** 41 47N 99 8W
Burwick, *U.K.* **12 C5** 58 45N 2 58W
Bury, *U.K.* **10 D5** 53 35N 2 17W
Bury St. Edmunds, *U.K.* **11 E8** 52 15N 0 43 E
Buryatia □, *Russia* **27 D11** 53 0N 110 0 E
Busan = Pusan, *S. Korea* **35 G15** 35 5N 129 0 E
Busango Swamp, *Zambia* **55 E2** 14 15S 25 45 E
Buşayrah, *Syria* **44 C4** 35 9N 40 26 E
Būshehr, *Iran* **45 D6** 28 55N 50 55 E
Būshehr □, *Iran* **45 D6** 28 20N 51 45 E
Bushell, *Canada* **73 B7** 59 31N 108 45W
Bushenyi, *Uganda* **54 C3** 0 35S 30 10 E
Bushire = Būshehr, *Iran* **45 D6** 28 55N 50 55 E
Businga, *Dem. Rep. of the Congo* **52 D4** 3 16N 20 59 E
Buşra ash Shām, *Syria* **47 C5** 32 30N 36 25 E
Busselton, *Australia* **61 F2** 33 42S 115 15 E
Bussum, *Neths.* **15 B5** 52 16N 5 10 E
Busto Arsízio, *Italy* **18 D8** 45 37N 8 51 E
Busu Djanoa, *Dem. Rep. of the Congo* **52 D4** 1 43N 21 23 E
Busuanga I., *Phil.* **37 B5** 12 10N 120 0 E
Buta, *Dem. Rep. of the Congo* **54 B1** 2 50N 24 53 E
Butare, *Rwanda* **54 C2** 2 31S 29 52 E
Butaritari, *Kiribati* **64 G9** 3 30N 174 0 E
Bute, *U.K.* **12 F3** 55 48N 5 2W
Bute Inlet, *Canada* **72 C4** 50 40N 124 53W
Butemba, *Uganda* **54 B3** 1 9N 31 37 E
Butembo, *Dem. Rep. of the Congo* **54 B2** 0 9N 29 18 E
Butha Qi, *China* **33 B7** 48 0N 122 32 E
Butiaba, *Uganda* **54 B3** 1 50N 31 20 E
Butler, *Mo., U.S.A.* **80 F7** 38 16N 94 20W
Butler, *Pa., U.S.A.* **78 F5** 40 52N 79 54W
Buton, *Indonesia* **37 E6** 5 0S 122 45 E
Butte, *Mont., U.S.A.* **82 C7** 46 0N 112 32W
Butte, *Nebr., U.S.A.* **80 D5** 42 58N 98 51W

Canyonville

Butte Creek →, U.S.A. 84 F5 39 12N 121 56W
Butterworth = Gcuwa, S. Africa 57 E4 32 20S 28 11 E
Butterworth, Malaysia 39 K3 5 24N 100 23 E
Buttevant, Ireland 13 D3 52 14N 8 40W
Buttfield, Mt., Australia 61 D4 24 45S 128 9 E
Button B., Canada 73 B10 58 45N 94 23W
Buttonwillow, U.S.A. 85 K7 35 24N 119 28W
Butty Hd., Australia 61 F3 33 54S 121 39 E
Butuan, Phil. 37 C7 8 57N 125 33 E
Butung = Buton, Indonesia 37 E6 5 0S 122 45 E
Buturlinovka, Russia 25 D7 50 50N 40 35 E
Buur Hakaba = Bur Acaba, Somali Rep. 46 G3 3 12N 44 20 E
Buxa Duar, India 43 F13 27 45N 89 35 E
Buxar, India 43 G10 25 34N 83 58 E
Buxtehude, Germany 16 B5 53 28N 9 39 E
Buxton, U.K. 10 D6 53 16N 1 54W
Buy, Russia 24 C7 58 28N 41 28 E
Büyük Menderes →, Turkey 21 F12 37 28N 27 11 E
Büyükçekmece, Turkey 21 D13 41 2N 28 35 E
Buzău, Romania 17 F14 45 10N 26 50 E
Buzău →, Romania 17 F14 45 26N 27 44 E
Buzen, Japan 31 H5 33 35N 131 5 E
Buzi →, Mozam. 55 F3 19 50S 34 43 E
Buzuluk, Russia 24 D9 52 48N 52 12 E
Buzzards B., U.S.A. 79 E14 41 45N 70 37W
Buzzards Bay, U.S.A. 79 E14 41 44N 70 37W
Bwana Mkubwe, Dem. Rep. of the Congo 55 E2 13 8S 28 38 E
Byarezina →, Belarus 17 B16 52 33N 30 14 E
Byaroza, Belarus 17 B13 52 31N 24 51 E
Bydgoszcz, Poland 17 B9 53 10N 18 0 E
Byelarus = Belarus ■, Europe 17 B14 53 30N 27 0 E
Byelorussia = Belarus ■, Europe 17 B14 53 30N 27 0 E
Byers, U.S.A. 80 F2 39 43N 104 14W
Byesville, U.S.A. 78 G3 39 58N 81 32W
Byford, Australia 61 F2 32 15S 116 0 E
Bykhaw, Belarus 17 B16 53 31N 30 14 E
Bykhov = Bykhaw, Belarus 17 B16 53 31N 30 14 E
Bylas, U.S.A. 83 K8 33 8N 110 7W
Bylot, Canada 73 B10 58 25N 94 8W
Bylot I., Canada 69 A12 73 13N 78 34W
Byrd, C., Antarctica 5 C17 69 38S 76 7W
Byrock, Australia 63 E4 30 40S 146 27 E
Byron Bay, Australia 63 D5 28 43S 153 37 E
Byrranga, Gory, Russia 27 B11 75 0N 100 0 E
Byrranga Mts. = Byrranga, Gory, Russia 27 B11 75 0N 100 0 E
Byske, Sweden 8 D19 64 57N 21 11 E
Byske älv →, Sweden 8 D19 64 57N 21 13 E
Bytom, Poland 17 C10 50 25N 18 54 E
Bytów, Poland 17 A9 54 10N 17 30 E
Byumba, Rwanda 54 C3 1 35S 30 4 E

C

Ca →, Vietnam 38 C5 18 45N 105 45 E
Ca Mau, Vietnam 39 H5 9 7N 105 8 E
Ca Mau, Mui, Vietnam 39 H5 8 38N 104 44 E
Ca Na, Vietnam 39 G7 11 20N 108 54 E
Caacupé, Paraguay 94 B4 25 23S 57 5W
Caála, Angola 53 G3 12 46S 15 30 E
Caamano Sd., Canada 72 C3 52 55N 129 25W
Caazapá, Paraguay 94 B4 26 8S 56 19W
Caazapá □, Paraguay 95 B4 26 10S 56 0W
Caballeria, C. de, Spain 22 A11 40 5N 4 5 E
Cabanatuan, Phil. 37 A6 15 30N 120 58 E
Cabano, Canada 71 C6 47 40N 68 56W
Cabazon, U.S.A. 85 M10 33 55N 116 47W
Cabedelo, Brazil 93 E12 7 0S 34 50W
Cabildo, Chile 94 C1 32 30S 71 5W
Cabimas, Venezuela 92 A4 10 23N 71 25W
Cabinda, Angola 52 F2 5 33S 12 11 E
Cabinda □, Angola 52 F2 5 0S 12 30 E
Cabinet Mts., U.S.A. 82 C6 48 0N 115 30W
Cabo Blanco, Argentina 96 F3 47 15S 65 47W
Cabo Frio, Brazil 95 A7 22 51S 42 3W
Cabo Pantoja, Peru 92 D3 1 0S 75 10W
Cabonga, Réservoir, Canada 70 C4 47 20N 76 40W
Cabool, U.S.A. 81 G8 37 7N 92 6W
Caboolture, Australia 63 D5 27 5S 152 58 E
Cabora Bassa Dam = Cahora Bassa, Reprêsa de, Mozam. 55 F3 15 20S 32 50 E
Caborca, Mexico 86 A2 30 40N 112 10W
Cabot, Mt., U.S.A. 79 B13 44 30N 71 25W
Cabot Hd., Canada 78 A3 45 14N 81 17W
Cabot Str., Canada 71 C8 47 15N 59 40W
Cabra, Spain 19 D3 37 30N 4 28W
Cabrera, Spain 22 B9 39 8N 2 57 E
Cabri, Canada 73 C7 50 35N 108 25W
Cabriel →, Spain 19 C5 39 14N 1 3W
Caçador, Brazil 95 B5 26 47S 51 0W
Čačak, Serbia, Yug. 21 C9 43 54N 20 20 E
Caçapava do Sul, Brazil 95 C5 30 30S 53 30W
Cáceres, Brazil 92 G7 16 5S 57 40W
Cáceres, Spain 19 C2 39 26N 6 23W
Cache Bay, Canada 70 C4 46 22N 80 0W
Cache Cr. →, U.S.A. 84 G5 38 42N 121 42W
Cache Creek, Canada 72 C4 50 48N 121 19W
Cachi, Argentina 94 B2 25 5S 66 10W
Cachimbo, Serra do, Brazil 93 E7 9 30S 55 30W
Cachinal de la Sierra, Chile 94 A2 24 58S 69 32W
Cachoeira, Brazil 93 F11 12 30S 39 0W
Cachoeira do Sul, Brazil 95 C5 30 3S 52 53W
Cachoeiro de Itapemirim, Brazil 95 A7 20 51S 41 7W
Cacoal, Brazil 92 F6 11 32S 61 18W
Cacólo, Angola 52 G3 10 9S 19 21 E
Caconda, Angola 53 G3 13 48S 15 8 E
Caddo, U.S.A. 81 H6 34 7N 96 16W
Cader Idris, U.K. 11 E4 52 42N 3 53W
Cadereyta, Mexico 86 B5 25 36N 100 0W
Cadibarrawirracanna, L., Australia 63 D2 28 52S 135 27 E
Cadillac, U.S.A. 76 C3 44 15N 85 24W
Cadiz, Phil. 37 B6 10 57N 123 15 E
Cádiz, Spain 19 D2 36 30N 6 20W
Cadiz, Calif., U.S.A. 85 L11 34 30N 115 28W
Cadiz, Ohio, U.S.A. 78 F4 40 22N 81 0W
Cádiz, G. de, Spain 19 D2 36 40N 7 0W
Cadiz L., U.S.A. 83 J6 34 18N 115 24W
Cadney Park, Australia 63 D1 27 55S 134 3 E
Cadomin, Canada 72 C5 53 2N 117 20W
Cadotte Lake, Canada 72 B5 56 26N 116 23W
Cadoux, Australia 61 F2 30 46S 117 7 E
Caen, France 18 B3 49 10N 0 22W
Caernarfon, U.K. 10 D3 53 8N 4 16W
Caernarfon B., U.K. 10 D3 53 4N 4 40W
Caernarvon = Caernarfon, U.K. 10 D3 53 8N 4 16W
Caerphilly, U.K. 11 F4 51 35N 3 13W
Caerphilly □, U.K. 11 F4 51 37N 3 12W
Caesarea, Israel 47 C3 32 30N 34 53 E
Caetité, Brazil 93 F10 13 50S 42 32W
Cafayate, Argentina 94 B2 26 2S 66 0W
Cafu, Angola 56 B2 16 30S 15 8 E
Cagayan de Oro, Phil. 37 C6 8 30N 124 40 E
Cagayan Is., Phil. 37 C5 9 40N 121 16 E
Cágliari, Italy 20 E3 39 13N 9 7 E
Cágliari, G. di, Italy 20 E3 39 8N 9 11 E
Caguán →, Colombia 92 D4 0 8S 74 18W
Caguas, Puerto Rico 89 C6 18 14N 66 2W
Caha Mts., Ireland 13 E2 51 45N 9 40W
Cahama, Angola 56 B1 16 17S 14 19 E
Caher, Ireland 13 D4 52 22N 7 56W
Caherciveen, Ireland 13 E1 51 56N 10 14W
Cahora Bassa, L. de, Mozam. 55 F3 15 35S 32 0 E
Cahora Bassa, Reprêsa de, Mozam. 55 F3 15 20S 32 50 E
Cahore Pt., Ireland 13 D5 52 33N 6 12W
Cahors, France 18 D4 44 27N 1 27 E
Cahul, Moldova 17 F15 45 50N 28 15 E
Cai Bau, Dao, Vietnam 38 B6 21 10N 107 27 E
Cai Nuoc, Vietnam 39 H5 8 56N 105 1 E
Caia, Mozam. 55 F4 17 51S 35 24 E
Caianda, Angola 55 E1 11 2S 23 31 E
Caibarién, Cuba 88 B4 22 30N 79 30W
Caicara, Venezuela 92 B5 7 38N 66 10W
Caicó, Brazil 93 E11 6 20S 37 0W
Caicos Is., Turks & Caicos 89 B5 21 40N 71 40W
Caicos Passage, W. Indies 89 B5 22 45N 72 45W
Caird Coast, Antarctica 5 D1 75 0S 25 0W
Cairn Gorm, U.K. 12 D5 57 7N 3 39W
Cairngorm Mts., U.K. 12 D5 57 6N 3 42W
Cairnryan, U.K. 12 G3 54 59N 5 1W
Cairns, Australia 62 B4 16 57S 145 45 E
Cairns L., Canada 73 C10 51 42N 94 30W
Cairo = El Qâhira, Egypt 51 B12 30 1N 31 14 E
Cairo, Ga., U.S.A. 77 K3 30 52N 84 13W
Cairo, Ill., U.S.A. 81 G10 37 0N 89 11W
Cairo, N.Y., U.S.A. 79 D11 42 18N 74 0W
Caithness, Ord of, U.K. 12 C5 58 8N 3 36W
Cajamarca, Peru 92 E3 7 5S 78 28W
Cajàzeiras, Brazil 93 E11 6 52S 38 30W
Cala d'Or, Spain 22 B10 39 23N 3 14 E
Cala en Porter, Spain 22 B11 39 52N 4 8 E
Cala Figuera, C. de, Spain 22 B9 39 27N 2 31 E
Cala Forcat, Spain 22 B10 40 0N 3 47 E
Cala Major, Spain 22 B9 39 33N 2 37 E
Cala Mezquida = Sa Mesquida, Spain 22 B11 39 55N 4 16 E
Cala Millor, Spain 22 B10 39 35N 3 22 E
Cala Ratjada, Spain 22 B10 39 43N 3 27 E
Cala Santa Galdana, Spain 22 B10 39 56N 3 58 E
Calabar, Nigeria 50 H7 4 57N 8 20 E
Calabogie, Canada 79 A8 45 18N 76 43W
Calabozo, Venezuela 92 B5 9 0N 67 28W
Calábria □, Italy 20 E7 39 0N 16 30 E
Calafate, Argentina 96 G2 50 19S 72 15W
Calahorra, Spain 19 A5 42 18N 1 59W
Calais, France 18 A4 50 57N 1 56 E
Calais, U.S.A. 77 C12 45 11N 67 17W
Calalaste, Cord. de, Argentina 94 B2 25 0S 67 0W
Calama, Brazil 92 E6 8 0S 62 50W
Calama, Chile 94 A2 22 30S 68 55W
Calamar, Colombia 92 A4 10 15N 74 55W
Calamian Group, Phil. 37 B5 11 50N 119 55 E
Calamocha, Spain 19 B5 40 50N 1 17W
Calang, Indonesia 36 D1 4 37N 95 37 E
Calapan, Phil. 37 B6 13 25N 121 7 E
Călăraşi, Romania 17 F14 44 12N 27 20 E
Calatayud, Spain 19 B5 41 20N 1 40W
Calauag, Phil. 37 B6 13 55N 122 15 E
Calavite, C., Phil. 37 B6 13 26N 120 20 E
Calbayog, Phil. 37 B6 12 4N 124 38 E
Calca, Peru 92 F4 13 22S 72 0W
Calcasieu L., U.S.A. 81 L8 29 55N 93 18W
Calcutta = Kolkata, India 43 H13 22 36N 88 24 E
Calcutta, U.S.A. 78 F4 40 40N 80 34W
Caldas da Rainha, Portugal 19 C1 39 24N 9 8W
Calder →, U.K. 10 D6 53 44N 1 22W
Caldera, Chile 94 B1 27 5S 70 55W
Caldwell, Idaho, U.S.A. 82 E5 43 40N 116 41W
Caldwell, Kans., U.S.A. 81 G6 37 2N 97 37W
Caldwell, Tex., U.S.A. 81 K6 30 32N 96 42W
Caledon, S. Africa 56 E2 34 14S 19 26 E
Caledon →, S. Africa 56 E4 30 31S 26 5 E
Caledon B., Australia 62 A2 12 45S 137 0 E
Caledonia, Canada 78 C5 43 7N 79 58W
Caledonia, U.S.A. 78 D7 42 58N 77 51W
Calemba, Angola 56 B2 16 0S 15 44 E
Calen, Australia 62 C4 20 56S 148 48 E
Caletones, Chile 94 C1 34 6S 70 27W
Calexico, U.S.A. 85 N11 32 40N 115 30W
Calf of Man, U.K. 10 C3 54 3N 4 48W
Calgary, Canada 72 C6 51 0N 114 10W
Calheta, Madeira 22 D2 32 44N 17 11W
Calhoun, U.S.A. 77 H3 34 30N 84 57W
Cali, Colombia 92 C3 3 25N 76 35W
Calicut, India 40 P9 11 15N 75 43 E
Caliente, U.S.A. 83 H6 37 37N 114 31W
California, Mo., U.S.A. 80 F8 38 38N 92 34W
California, Pa., U.S.A. 78 F5 40 4N 79 54W
California □, U.S.A. 84 H7 37 30N 119 30W
California, Baja, Mexico 86 A1 32 10N 115 12W
California, Baja, T.N. = Baja California □, Mexico 86 B2 30 0N 115 0W
California, Baja, T.S. = Baja California Sur □, Mexico 86 B2 25 50N 111 50W
California, G. de, Mexico 86 B2 27 0N 111 0W
California City, U.S.A. 85 K9 35 10N 117 55W
California Hot Springs, U.S.A. 85 K8 35 51N 118 41W
Calingasta, Argentina 94 C2 31 15S 69 30W
Calipatria, U.S.A. 85 M11 33 8N 115 31W
Calistoga, U.S.A. 84 G4 38 35N 122 35W
Calitzdorp, S. Africa 56 E3 33 33S 21 42 E
Callabonna, L., Australia 63 D3 29 40S 140 5 E
Callan, Ireland 13 D4 52 32N 7 24W
Callander, U.K. 12 E4 56 15N 4 13W
Callao, Peru 92 F3 12 0S 77 0W
Calles, Mexico 87 C5 23 2N 98 42W
Callicoon, U.S.A. 79 E9 41 46N 75 3W
Calling Lake, Canada 72 B6 55 15N 113 12W
Calliope, Australia 62 C5 24 0S 151 16 E
Calne, U.K. 11 F6 51 26N 2 0W
Calola, Angola 56 B2 16 25S 17 48 E
Caloundra, Australia 63 D5 26 45S 153 10 E
Calpella, U.S.A. 84 F3 39 14N 123 12W
Calpine, U.S.A. 84 F6 39 40N 120 27W
Calstock, Canada 70 C3 49 47N 84 9W
Caltagirone, Italy 20 F6 37 14N 14 31 E
Caltanissetta, Italy 20 F6 37 29N 14 4 E
Calulo, Angola 52 G2 10 1S 14 56 E
Calvert →, Australia 62 B2 16 17S 137 44 E
Calvert I., Canada 72 C3 51 30N 128 0W
Calvert Ra., Australia 60 D3 24 0S 122 30 E
Calvi, France 18 E8 42 34N 8 45 E
Calviá, Spain 19 C7 39 34N 2 31 E
Calvillo, Mexico 86 C4 21 51N 102 43W
Calvinia, S. Africa 56 E2 31 28S 19 45 E
Calwa, U.S.A. 84 J7 36 42N 119 46W
Cam →, U.K. 11 E8 52 21N 0 16 E
Cam Lam, Vietnam 39 G7 11 54N 109 10 E
Cam Pha, Vietnam 38 B6 21 7N 107 18 E
Cam Ranh, Vietnam 39 G7 11 54N 109 12 E
Cam Xuyen, Vietnam 38 C6 18 15N 106 0 E
Camabatela, Angola 52 F3 8 20S 15 26 E
Camacha, Madeira 22 D3 32 41N 16 49W
Camacho, Mexico 86 C4 24 25N 102 18W
Camacupa, Angola 53 G3 11 58S 17 22 E
Camagüey, Cuba 88 B4 21 20N 78 0W
Camaná, Peru 92 G4 16 30S 72 50W
Camanche Reservoir, U.S.A. 84 G6 38 14N 121 1W
Camaquã, Brazil 95 C5 30 51S 51 49W
Camaquã →, Brazil 95 C5 31 17S 51 47W
Câmara de Lobos, Madeira 22 D3 32 39N 16 59W
Camargo, Mexico 87 B5 26 19N 98 50W
Camargue, France 18 E6 43 34N 4 34 E
Camarillo, U.S.A. 85 L7 34 13N 119 2W
Camarón, C., Honduras 88 C2 16 0N 85 5W
Camarones, Argentina 96 E3 44 50S 65 40W
Camas, U.S.A. 84 E4 45 35N 122 24W
Camas Valley, U.S.A. 82 E2 43 2N 123 40W
Camballin, Australia 60 C3 17 59S 124 12 E
Cambará, Brazil 95 A5 23 2S 50 5W
Cambay = Khambhat, India 42 H5 22 23N 72 33 E
Cambay, G. of = Khambhat, G. of, India 40 J8 20 45N 72 30 E
Cambodia ■, Asia 38 F5 12 15N 105 0 E
Camborne, U.K. 11 G2 50 12N 5 19W
Cambrai, France 18 A5 50 11N 3 14 E
Cambria, U.S.A. 84 K5 35 34N 121 5W
Cambrian Mts., U.K. 11 E4 52 3N 3 57W
Cambridge, Canada 78 C4 43 23N 80 15W
Cambridge, Jamaica 88 C4 18 18N 77 54W
Cambridge, N.Z. 59 G5 37 54S 175 29 E
Cambridge, U.K. 11 E8 52 12N 0 8 E
Cambridge, Mass., U.S.A. 79 D13 42 22N 71 6W
Cambridge, Minn., U.S.A. 80 C8 45 34N 93 13W
Cambridge, N.Y., U.S.A. 79 C11 43 2N 73 22W
Cambridge, Nebr., U.S.A. 80 E4 40 17N 100 10W
Cambridge, Ohio, U.S.A. 78 F3 40 2N 81 35W
Cambridge Bay = Ikaluktutiak, Canada 68 B9 69 10N 105 0W
Cambridge G., Australia 60 B4 14 55S 128 15 E
Cambridge Springs, U.S.A. 78 E4 41 48N 80 4W
Cambridgeshire □, U.K. 11 E7 52 25N 0 7W
Cambuci, Brazil 95 A7 21 35S 41 55W
Cambundi-Catembo, Angola 52 G3 10 10S 17 35 E
Camden, Ala., U.S.A. 77 K2 31 59N 87 17W
Camden, Ark., U.S.A. 81 J8 33 35N 92 50W
Camden, Maine, U.S.A. 77 C11 44 13N 69 4W
Camden, N.J., U.S.A. 79 G9 39 56N 75 7W
Camden, N.Y., U.S.A. 79 C9 43 20N 75 45W
Camden, S.C., U.S.A. 77 H5 34 16N 80 36W
Camden Sd., Australia 60 C3 15 27S 124 25 E
Camdenton, U.S.A. 81 F8 38 1N 92 45W
Cameron, Ariz., U.S.A. 83 J8 35 53N 111 25W
Cameron, La., U.S.A. 81 L8 29 48N 93 20W
Cameron, Mo., U.S.A. 80 F7 39 44N 94 14W
Cameron, Tex., U.S.A. 81 K6 30 51N 96 59W
Cameron Highlands, Malaysia 39 K3 4 27N 101 22 E
Cameron Hills, Canada 72 B5 59 48N 118 0W
Cameroon ■, Africa 52 C2 6 0N 12 30 E
Cameroun, Mt., Cameroon 52 D1 4 13N 9 10 E
Cametá, Brazil 93 D9 2 12S 49 30W
Camiguin I., Phil. 37 C6 18 56N 121 55 E
Camilla, U.S.A. 77 K3 31 14N 84 12W
Caminha, Portugal 19 B1 41 50N 8 50W
Camino, U.S.A. 84 G6 38 44N 120 41W
Camira Creek, Australia 63 D5 29 15S 152 58 E
Cammal, U.S.A. 78 E7 41 24N 77 28W
Camocim, Brazil 93 D10 2 55S 40 50W
Camooweal, Australia 62 B2 19 56S 138 7 E
Camopi, Fr. Guiana 93 C8 3 12N 52 17W
Camp Borden, Canada 78 B5 44 18N 79 56W
Camp Hill, U.S.A. 78 F8 40 14N 76 55W
Camp Nelson, U.S.A. 85 J8 36 8N 118 39W
Camp Pendleton, U.S.A. 85 M9 33 16N 117 23W
Camp Verde, U.S.A. 83 J8 34 34N 111 51W
Camp Wood, U.S.A. 81 L5 29 40N 100 1W
Campana, Argentina 94 C4 34 10S 58 55W
Campana, I., Chile 96 F1 48 20S 75 20W
Campanário, Madeira 22 D2 32 39N 17 2W
Campánia □, Italy 20 D6 41 0N 14 30 E
Campbell, S. Africa 56 D3 28 48S 23 44 E
Campbell, Calif., U.S.A. 84 H5 37 17N 121 57W
Campbell, Ohio, U.S.A. 78 E4 41 5N 80 37W
Campbell I., Pac. Oc. 64 N8 52 30S 169 0 E
Campbell L., Canada 73 A7 63 14N 106 55W
Campbell River, Canada 72 C3 50 5N 125 20W
Campbell Town, Australia 62 G4 41 52S 147 30 E
Campbellford, Canada 78 B7 44 18N 77 48W
Campbellpur, Pakistan 42 C5 33 46N 72 26 E
Campbellsville, U.S.A. 76 G3 37 21N 85 20W
Campbellton, Canada 71 C6 47 57N 66 43W
Campbelltown, Australia 63 E5 34 4S 150 49 E
Campbeltown, U.K. 12 F3 55 26N 5 36W
Campeche, Mexico 87 D6 19 50N 90 32W
Campeche □, Mexico 87 D6 19 50N 90 32W
Campeche, Golfo de, Mexico 87 D6 19 30N 93 0W
Camperdown, Australia 63 F3 38 14S 143 9 E
Camperville, Canada 73 C8 51 59N 100 9W
Câmpina, Romania 17 F13 45 10N 25 45 E
Campina Grande, Brazil 93 E11 7 20S 35 47W
Campinas, Brazil 95 A6 22 50S 47 0W
Campo Grande, Brazil 93 H8 20 25S 54 40W
Campo Maíor, Brazil 93 D10 4 50S 42 12W
Campo Mourão, Brazil 95 A5 24 3S 52 22W
Campobasso, Italy 20 D6 41 34N 14 39 E
Campos, Brazil 95 A7 21 50S 41 20W
Campos Belos, Brazil 93 F9 13 10S 47 3W
Campos del Port, Spain 22 B10 39 26N 3 1 E
Campos Novos, Brazil 95 B5 27 21S 51 50W
Camptonville, U.S.A. 84 F5 39 27N 121 3W
Camptown, U.S.A. 79 E8 41 44N 76 14W
Câmpulung, Romania 17 F13 45 17N 25 3 E
Camrose, Canada 72 C6 53 0N 112 50W
Camsell Portage, Canada 73 B7 59 37N 109 15W
Çan, Turkey 21 D12 40 2N 27 3 E
Can Clavo, Spain 22 C7 38 57N 1 27 E
Can Creu, Spain 22 C7 38 58N 1 28 E
Can Gio, Vietnam 39 G6 10 25N 106 58 E
Can Tho, Vietnam 39 G5 10 2N 105 46 E
Canaan, U.S.A. 79 D11 42 2N 73 20W
Canada ■, N. Amer. 68 C10 60 0N 100 0W
Cañada de Gómez, Argentina 94 C3 32 40S 61 30W
Canadian, U.S.A. 81 H4 35 55N 100 23W
Canadian →, U.S.A. 81 H7 35 28N 95 3W
Canajoharie, U.S.A. 79 D10 42 54N 74 35W
Çanakkale, Turkey 21 D12 40 8N 26 24 E
Çanakkale Boğazı, Turkey 21 D12 40 17N 26 32 E
Canal Flats, Canada 72 C5 50 10N 115 48W
Canalejas, Argentina 94 D2 35 15S 66 34W
Canals, Argentina 94 C3 33 35S 62 53W
Canandaigua, U.S.A. 78 D7 42 54N 77 17W
Canandaigua L., U.S.A. 78 D7 42 47N 77 19W
Cananea, Mexico 86 A2 31 0N 110 20W
Canarias, Is., Atl. Oc. 22 F4 28 30N 16 0W
Canarreos, Arch. de los, Cuba 88 B3 21 35N 81 40W
Canary Is. = Canarias, Is., Atl. Oc. 22 F4 28 30N 16 0W
Canaseraga, U.S.A. 78 D7 42 27N 77 45W
Canatlán, Mexico 86 C4 24 31N 104 47W
Canaveral, C., U.S.A. 77 L5 28 27N 80 32W
Canavieiras, Brazil 93 G11 15 39S 39 0W
Canberra, Australia 63 F4 35 15S 149 8 E
Canby, Calif., U.S.A. 82 F3 41 27N 120 52W
Canby, Minn., U.S.A. 80 C6 44 43N 96 16W
Canby, Oreg., U.S.A. 84 E4 45 16N 122 42W
Cancún, Mexico 87 C7 21 8N 86 44W
Candelaria, Argentina 95 B4 27 29S 55 44W
Candelaria, Canary Is. 22 F3 28 22N 16 22W
Candelo, Australia 63 F4 36 47S 149 43 E
Candia = Iráklion, Greece 23 D7 35 20N 25 12 E
Candle L., Canada 73 C7 53 50N 105 18W
Candlemas I., Antarctica 5 B1 57 3S 26 40W
Cando, U.S.A. 80 A5 48 32N 99 12W
Canea = Khaniá, Greece 23 D6 35 30N 24 4 E
Canelones, Uruguay 95 C4 34 32S 56 17W
Cañete, Chile 94 D1 37 50S 73 30W
Cañete, Peru 92 F3 13 8S 76 30W
Cangas de Narcea, Spain 19 A2 43 10N 6 32W
Canguaretama, Brazil 93 E11 6 20S 35 5W
Canguçu, Brazil 95 C5 31 22S 52 43W
Canguçu, Serra do, Brazil 95 C5 31 20S 52 40W
Cangzhou, China 34 E9 38 19N 116 52 E
Caniapiscau →, Canada 71 A6 56 40N 69 30W
Caniapiscau, Rés. de, Canada 71 B6 54 10N 69 55W
Canicattì, Italy 20 F5 37 21N 13 51 E
Canim Lake, Canada 72 C4 51 47N 120 54W
Canindeyu □, Paraguay 95 A5 24 10S 55 0W
Canisteo, U.S.A. 78 D7 42 16N 77 36W
Canisteo →, U.S.A. 78 D7 42 7N 77 8W
Cañitas, Mexico 86 C4 23 36N 102 43W
Çankırı, Turkey 25 F5 40 40N 33 37 E
Cankuzo, Burundi 54 C3 3 10S 30 31 E
Canmore, Canada 72 C5 51 7N 115 18W
Cann River, Australia 63 F4 37 35S 149 7 E
Canna, U.K. 12 D2 57 3N 6 33W
Cannanore, India 40 P9 11 53N 75 27 E
Cannes, France 18 E7 43 32N 7 1 E
Canning Town = Port Canning, India 43 H13 22 23N 88 40 E
Cannington, Canada 78 B5 44 20N 79 2W
Cannock, U.K. 11 E5 52 41N 2 1W
Cannon Ball →, U.S.A. 80 B4 46 20N 100 38W
Cannondale Mt., Australia 62 D4 25 13S 148 57 E
Cannonsville Reservoir, U.S.A. 79 D9 42 4N 75 22W
Cannonvale, Australia 62 C4 20 17S 148 43 E
Canoas, Brazil 95 B5 29 56S 51 11W
Canoe L., Canada 73 B7 55 10N 108 15W
Canon City, U.S.A. 80 F2 38 27N 105 14W
Canora, Canada 73 C8 51 40N 102 30W
Canowindra, Australia 63 E4 33 35S 148 38 E
Canso, Canada 71 C7 45 20N 61 0W
Cantabria □, Spain 19 A4 43 10N 4 0W
Cantabrian Mts. = Cantábrica, Cordillera, Spain 19 A3 43 0N 5 10W
Cantábrica, Cordillera, Spain 19 A3 43 0N 5 10W
Cantal, Plomb du, France 18 D5 45 3N 2 45 E
Canterbury, Australia 62 D3 25 23S 141 53 E
Canterbury, U.K. 11 F9 51 16N 1 6 E
Canterbury Bight, N.Z. 59 L3 44 16S 171 55 E
Canterbury Plains, N.Z. 59 K3 43 55S 171 22 E
Cantil, U.S.A. 85 K9 35 18N 117 58W
Canton = Guangzhou, China 33 D6 23 5N 113 10 E
Canton, Ga., U.S.A. 77 H3 34 14N 84 29W
Canton, Ill., U.S.A. 80 E9 40 33N 90 2W
Canton, Miss., U.S.A. 81 J9 32 37N 90 2W
Canton, Mo., U.S.A. 80 E9 40 8N 91 32W
Canton, N.Y., U.S.A. 79 B9 44 36N 75 10W
Canton, Ohio, U.S.A. 78 F3 40 48N 81 23W
Canton, Pa., U.S.A. 78 E8 41 39N 76 51W
Canton, S. Dak., U.S.A. 80 D6 43 18N 96 35W
Canton L., U.S.A. 81 G5 36 6N 98 35W
Canudos, Brazil 92 E7 7 13S 58 5W
Canumã →, Brazil 92 D7 3 55S 59 10W
Canutama, Brazil 92 E6 6 30S 64 20W
Canutillo, U.S.A. 83 L10 31 55N 106 36W
Canvey, U.K. 11 F8 51 31N 0 37 E
Canyon, U.S.A. 81 H4 34 59N 101 55W
Canyonlands Nat. Park, U.S.A. 83 G9 38 15N 110 0W
Canyonville, U.S.A. 82 E2 42 56N 123 17W

Cao Bang

Cao Bang, *Vietnam* **38 A6** 22 40N 106 15 E
Cao He →, *China* **35 D13** 40 10N 124 32 E
Cao Lanh, *Vietnam* **39 G5** 10 27N 105 38 E
Cao Xian, *China* **34 G8** 34 50N 115 35 E
Cap-aux-Meules, *Canada* **71 C7** 47 23N 61 52W
Cap-Chat, *Canada* **71 C6** 49 6N 66 40W
Cap-de-la-Madeleine, *Canada* **70 C5** 46 22N 72 31W
Cap-Haïtien, *Haiti* **89 C5** 19 40N 72 20W
Capac, *U.S.A.* **78 C2** 43 1N 82 56W
Capanaparo →, *Venezuela* **92 B5** 7 1N 67 7W
Cape →, *Australia* **62 C4** 20 59S 146 51 E
Cape Barren I., *Australia* **62 G4** 40 25S 148 15 E
Cape Breton Highlands Nat. Park, *Canada* **71 C7** 46 50N 60 40W
Cape Breton I., *Canada* **71 C7** 46 0N 60 30W
Cape Charles, *U.S.A.* **76 G8** 37 16N 76 1W
Cape Coast, *Ghana* **50 G5** 5 5N 1 15W
Cape Coral, *U.S.A.* **77 M5** 26 33N 81 57W
Cape Dorset, *Canada* **69 B12** 64 14N 76 32W
Cape Fear →, *U.S.A.* **77 H6** 33 53N 78 1W
Cape Girardeau, *U.S.A.* **81 G10** 37 19N 89 32W
Cape May, *U.S.A.* **76 F8** 38 56N 74 56W
Cape May Point, *U.S.A.* **76 F8** 38 56N 74 58W
Cape Province, *S. Africa* **53 L3** 32 0S 23 0 E
Cape Tormentine, *Canada* **71 C7** 46 8N 63 47W
Cape Town, *S. Africa* **56 E2** 33 55S 18 22 E
Cape Verde Is. ■, *Atl. Oc.* **49 E1** 16 0N 24 0W
Cape Vincent, *U.S.A.* **79 B8** 44 8N 76 20W
Cape York Peninsula, *Australia* **62 A3** 12 0S 142 30 E
Capela, *Brazil* **93 F11** 10 30S 37 0W
Capella, *Australia* **62 C4** 23 2S 148 1 E
Capim →, *Brazil* **93 D9** 1 40S 47 47W
Capitan, *U.S.A.* **83 K11** 33 35N 105 35W
Capitol Reef Nat. Park, *U.S.A.* **83 G8** 38 15N 111 10W
Capitola, *U.S.A.* **84 J5** 36 59N 121 57W
Capoche →, *Mozam.* **55 F3** 15 35S 33 0 E
Capraia, *Italy* **18 E8** 43 2N 9 50 E
Capreol, *Canada* **70 C3** 46 43N 80 56W
Capri, *Italy* **20 D6** 40 33N 14 14 E
Capricorn Group, *Australia* **62 C5** 23 30S 151 55 E
Capricorn Ra., *Australia* **60 D2** 23 20S 116 50 E
Caprivi Strip, *Namibia* **56 B3** 18 0S 23 0 E
Captain's Flat, *Australia* **63 F4** 35 35S 149 27 E
Caquetá →, *Colombia* **92 D5** 1 15S 69 15W
Caracal, *Romania* **17 F13** 44 8N 24 22 E
Caracas, *Venezuela* **92 A5** 10 30N 66 55W
Caracol, *Mato Grosso do Sul, Brazil* **94 A4** 22 18S 57 1W
Caracol, *Piauí, Brazil* **93 E10** 9 15S 43 22W
Carajas, *Brazil* **93 E8** 6 5S 50 23W
Carajás, Serra dos, *Brazil* **93 E8** 6 0S 51 30W
Carangola, *Brazil* **95 A7** 20 44S 42 5W
Caransebeş, *Romania* **17 F12** 45 28N 22 18 E
Caraquet, *Canada* **71 C6** 47 48N 64 57W
Caras, *Peru* **92 E3** 9 3S 77 47W
Caratasca, L., *Honduras* **88 C3** 15 20N 83 40W
Caratinga, *Brazil* **93 G10** 19 50S 42 10W
Caraúbas, *Brazil* **93 E11** 5 43S 37 33W
Caravaca = Caravaca de la Cruz, *Spain* **19 C5** 38 8N 1 52W
Caravaca de la Cruz, *Spain* **19 C5** 38 8N 1 52W
Caravelas, *Brazil* **93 G11** 17 45S 39 15W
Caraveli, *Peru* **92 G4** 15 45S 73 25W
Caràzinho, *Brazil* **95 B5** 28 16S 52 46W
Carballo, *Spain* **19 A1** 43 13N 8 41W
Carberry, *Canada* **73 D9** 49 50N 99 25W
Carbó, *Mexico* **86 B2** 29 42N 110 58W
Carbonara, C., *Italy* **20 E3** 39 6N 9 31 E
Carbondale, *Colo., U.S.A.* **82 G10** 39 24N 107 13W
Carbondale, *Ill., U.S.A.* **81 G10** 37 44N 89 13W
Carbondale, *Pa., U.S.A.* **79 E9** 41 35N 75 30W
Carbonear, *Canada* **71 C9** 47 42N 53 13W
Carbónia, *Italy* **20 E3** 39 10N 8 30 E
Carcajou, *Canada* **72 B5** 57 47N 117 6W
Carcarana →, *Argentina* **94 C3** 32 27S 60 48W
Carcasse, C., *Haiti* **89 C5** 18 30N 74 28W
Carcassonne, *France* **18 E5** 43 13N 2 20 E
Carcross, *Canada* **72 A2** 60 13N 134 45W
Cardamon Hills, *India* **40 Q10** 9 30N 77 15 E
Cárdenas, *Cuba* **88 B3** 23 0N 81 30W
Cárdenas, *San Luis Potosí, Mexico* **87 C5** 22 0N 99 41W
Cárdenas, *Tabasco, Mexico* **87 D6** 17 59N 93 21W
Cardiff, *U.K.* **11 F4** 51 29N 3 10W
Cardiff □, *U.K.* **11 F4** 51 31N 3 12W
Cardiff-by-the-Sea, *U.S.A.* **85 M9** 33 1N 117 17W
Cardigan, *U.K.* **11 E3** 52 5N 4 40W
Cardigan B., *U.K.* **11 E3** 52 30N 4 30W
Cardinal, *Canada* **79 B9** 44 47N 75 23W
Cardona, *Uruguay* **94 C4** 33 53S 57 18W
Cardoso, Ilha do, *Brazil* **95 B5** 25 8S 47 58W
Cardston, *Canada* **72 D6** 49 15N 113 20W
Cardwell, *Australia* **62 B4** 18 14S 146 2 E
Careen L., *Canada* **73 B7** 57 0N 108 11W
Carei, *Romania* **17 E12** 47 40N 22 29 E
Careme = Ciremai, *Indonesia* **37 G13** 6 55S 108 27 E
Carey, *U.S.A.* **82 E7** 43 19N 113 57W
Carey, L., *Australia* **61 E3** 29 0S 122 15 E
Carey L., *Canada* **73 A8** 62 12N 102 55W
Carhué, *Argentina* **94 D3** 37 10S 62 50W
Caria, *Turkey* **21 F13** 37 20N 28 10 E
Cariacica, *Brazil* **93 H10** 20 16S 40 25W
Caribbean Sea, *W. Indies* **89 D5** 15 0N 75 0W
Cariboo Mts., *Canada* **72 C4** 53 0N 121 0W
Caribou, *U.S.A.* **77 B12** 46 52N 68 1W
Caribou →, *Man., Canada* **73 B10** 59 20N 94 44W
Caribou →, *N.W.T., Canada* **72 A3** 61 27N 125 45W
Caribou I., *Canada* **70 C2** 47 22N 85 49W
Caribou Is., *Canada* **72 A6** 61 55N 113 15W
Caribou L., *Man., Canada* **73 B9** 59 21N 96 10W
Caribou L., *Ont., Canada* **70 B2** 50 25N 89 5W
Caribou Mts., *Canada* **72 B5** 59 12N 115 40W
Carichic, *Mexico* **86 B3** 27 56N 107 3W
Carillo, *Mexico* **86 B4** 26 50N 103 55W
Carinda, *Australia* **63 E4** 30 28S 147 41 E
Carinhanha, *Brazil* **93 F10** 14 15S 44 46W
Carinhanha →, *Brazil* **93 F10** 14 20S 43 47W
Carinthia = Kärnten □, *Austria* **16 E8** 46 52N 13 30 E
Caripito, *Venezuela* **92 A6** 10 8N 63 6W
Carleton, Mt., *Canada* **71 C6** 47 23N 66 53W
Carleton Place, *Canada* **79 A8** 45 8N 76 9W
Carletonville, *S. Africa* **56 D4** 26 23S 27 22 E
Carlin, *U.S.A.* **82 F5** 40 43N 116 7W
Carlingford L., *U.K.* **13 B5** 54 3N 6 9W
Carlinville, *U.S.A.* **80 F10** 39 17N 89 53W
Carlisle, *U.K.* **10 C5** 54 54N 2 56W
Carlisle, *U.S.A.* **78 F7** 40 12N 77 12W
Carlos Casares, *Argentina* **94 D3** 35 32S 61 20W
Carlos Tejedor, *Argentina* **94 D3** 35 25S 62 25W
Carlow, *Ireland* **13 D5** 52 50N 6 56W
Carlow □, *Ireland* **13 D5** 52 43N 6 50W
Carlsbad, *Calif., U.S.A.* **85 M9** 33 10N 117 21W
Carlsbad, *N. Mex., U.S.A.* **81 J2** 32 25N 104 14W
Carlsbad Caverns Nat. Park, *U.S.A.* **81 J2** 32 10N 104 35W
Carluke, *U.K.* **12 F5** 55 45N 3 50W
Carlyle, *Canada* **73 D8** 49 40N 102 20W
Carmacks, *Canada* **68 B6** 62 5N 136 16W
Carman, *Canada* **73 D9** 49 30N 98 0W
Carmarthen, *U.K.* **11 F3** 51 52N 4 19W
Carmarthen B., *U.K.* **11 F3** 51 40N 4 30W
Carmarthenshire □, *U.K.* **11 F3** 51 55N 4 13W
Carmaux, *France* **18 D5** 44 3N 2 10 E
Carmel, *U.S.A.* **79 E11** 41 26N 73 41W
Carmel-by-the-Sea, *U.S.A.* **84 J5** 36 33N 121 55W
Carmel Valley, *U.S.A.* **84 J5** 36 29N 121 43W
Carmelo, *Uruguay* **94 C4** 34 0S 58 20W
Carmen, *Colombia* **92 B3** 9 43N 75 8W
Carmen, *Paraguay* **95 B4** 27 13S 56 12W
Carmen →, *Mexico* **86 A3** 30 42N 106 29W
Carmen, I., *Mexico* **86 B2** 26 0N 111 20W
Carmen de Patagones, *Argentina* **96 E4** 40 50S 63 0W
Carmensa, *Argentina* **94 D2** 35 15S 67 40W
Carmi, *Canada* **72 D5** 49 36N 119 8W
Carmi, *U.S.A.* **76 F1** 38 5N 88 10W
Carmichael, *U.S.A.* **84 G5** 38 38N 121 19W
Carmila, *Australia* **62 C4** 21 55S 149 24 E
Carmona, *Costa Rica* **88 E2** 10 0N 85 15W
Carmona, *Spain* **19 D3** 37 28N 5 42W
Carn Ban, *U.K.* **12 D4** 57 7N 4 15W
Carn Eige, *U.K.* **12 D3** 57 17N 5 8W
Carnac, *France* **18 C2** 47 35N 3 6W
Carnamah, *Australia* **61 E2** 29 41S 115 53 E
Carnarvon, *Australia* **61 D1** 24 51S 113 42 E
Carnarvon, *S. Africa* **56 E3** 30 56S 22 8 E
Carnarvon Ra., *Queens., Australia* **62 D4** 25 15S 148 30 E
Carnarvon Ra., *W. Austral., Australia* **61 E3** 25 20S 120 45 E
Carnation, *U.S.A.* **84 C5** 47 39N 121 55W
Carndonagh, *Ireland* **13 A4** 55 16N 7 15W
Carnduff, *Canada* **73 D8** 49 10N 101 50W
Carnegie, *U.S.A.* **78 F4** 40 24N 80 5W
Carnegie, L., *Australia* **61 E3** 26 5S 122 30 E
Carnic Alps = Karnische Alpen, *Europe* **16 E7** 46 36N 13 0 E
Carniche Alpi = Karnische Alpen, *Europe* **16 E7** 46 36N 13 0 E
Carnot, *C.A.R.* **52 D3** 4 59N 15 56 E
Carnot, C., *Australia* **63 E2** 34 57S 135 38 E
Carnot B., *Australia* **60 C3** 17 20S 122 15 E
Carnoustie, *U.K.* **12 E6** 56 30N 2 42W
Carnsore Pt., *Ireland* **13 D5** 52 10N 6 22W
Caro, *U.S.A.* **76 D4** 43 29N 83 24W
Carol City, *U.S.A.* **77 N5** 25 56N 80 16W
Carolina, *Brazil* **93 E9** 7 10S 47 30W
Carolina, *Puerto Rico* **89 C6** 18 23N 65 58W
Carolina, *S. Africa* **57 D5** 26 5S 30 6 E
Caroline I., *Kiribati* **65 H12** 9 58S 150 13W
Caroline Is., *Micronesia* **28 J17** 8 0N 150 0 E
Caroni →, *Venezuela* **92 B6** 8 21N 62 43W
Caronie = Nébrodi, Monti, *Italy* **20 F6** 37 54N 14 35 E
Caroona, *Australia* **63 E5** 31 24S 150 26 E
Carpathians, *Europe* **17 D11** 49 30N 21 0 E
Carpaţii Meridionali, *Romania* **17 F13** 45 30N 25 0 E
Carpentaria, G. of, *Australia* **62 A2** 14 0S 139 0 E
Carpentras, *France* **18 D6** 44 3N 5 2 E
Carpi, *Italy* **20 B4** 44 47N 10 53 E
Carpinteria, *U.S.A.* **85 L7** 34 24N 119 31W
Carr Boyd Ra., *Australia* **60 C4** 16 15S 128 35 E
Carrabelle, *U.S.A.* **77 L3** 29 51N 84 40W
Carranza, Presa V., *Mexico* **86 B4** 27 20N 100 50W
Carrara, *Italy* **18 D9** 44 5N 10 6 E
Carrauntoohill, *Ireland* **13 D2** 52 0N 9 45W
Carrick-on-Shannon, *Ireland* **13 C3** 53 57N 8 5W
Carrick-on-Suir, *Ireland* **13 D4** 52 21N 7 24W
Carrickfergus, *U.K.* **13 B6** 54 43N 5 49W
Carrickmacross, *Ireland* **13 C5** 53 59N 6 43W
Carrieton, *Australia* **63 E2** 32 25S 138 31 E
Carrington, *U.S.A.* **80 B5** 47 27N 99 8W
Carrizal Bajo, *Chile* **94 B1** 28 5S 71 20W
Carrizalillo, *Chile* **94 B1** 29 5S 71 30W
Carrizo Cr. →, *U.S.A.* **81 G3** 36 55N 103 55W
Carrizo Springs, *U.S.A.* **81 L5** 28 31N 99 52W
Carrizozo, *U.S.A.* **83 K11** 33 38N 105 53W
Carroll, *U.S.A.* **80 D7** 42 4N 94 52W
Carrollton, *Ga., U.S.A.* **77 J3** 33 35N 85 5W
Carrollton, *Ill., U.S.A.* **80 F9** 39 18N 90 24W
Carrollton, *Ky., U.S.A.* **76 F3** 38 41N 85 11W
Carrollton, *Mo., U.S.A.* **80 F8** 39 22N 93 30W
Carrollton, *Ohio, U.S.A.* **78 F3** 40 34N 81 5W
Carron →, *U.K.* **12 D4** 57 53N 4 22W
Carron, L., *U.K.* **12 D3** 57 22N 5 35W
Carrot →, *Canada* **73 C8** 53 50N 101 17W
Carrot River, *Canada* **73 C8** 53 17N 103 35W
Carruthers, *Canada* **73 C7** 52 52N 109 16W
Carson, *Calif., U.S.A.* **85 M8** 33 48N 118 17W
Carson, *N. Dak., U.S.A.* **80 B4** 46 25N 101 34W
Carson →, *U.S.A.* **84 F8** 39 45N 118 40W
Carson City, *U.S.A.* **84 F7** 39 10N 119 46W
Carson Sink, *U.S.A.* **82 G4** 39 50N 118 25W
Cartagena, *Colombia* **92 A3** 10 25N 75 33W
Cartagena, *Spain* **19 D5** 37 38N 0 59W
Cartago, *Colombia* **92 C3** 4 45N 75 55W
Cartago, *Costa Rica* **88 E3** 9 50N 83 55W
Cartersville, *U.S.A.* **77 H3** 34 10N 84 48W
Carterton, *N.Z.* **59 J5** 41 2S 175 31 E
Carthage, *Tunisia* **51 A8** 36 50N 10 21 E
Carthage, *Ill., U.S.A.* **80 E9** 40 25N 91 8W
Carthage, *Mo., U.S.A.* **81 G7** 37 11N 94 19W
Carthage, *N.Y., U.S.A.* **76 D8** 43 59N 75 37W
Carthage, *Tex., U.S.A.* **81 J7** 32 9N 94 20W
Cartier I., *Australia* **60 B3** 12 31S 123 29 E
Cartwright, *Canada* **71 B8** 53 41N 56 58W
Caruaru, *Brazil* **93 E11** 8 15S 35 55W
Carúpano, *Venezuela* **92 A6** 10 39N 63 15W
Caruthersville, *U.S.A.* **81 G10** 36 11N 89 39W
Carvoeiro, *Brazil* **92 D6** 1 30S 61 59W
Carvoeiro, C., *Portugal* **19 C1** 39 21N 9 24W
Cary, *U.S.A.* **77 H6** 35 47N 78 46W
Casa Grande, *U.S.A.* **83 K8** 32 53N 111 45W
Casablanca, *Chile* **94 C1** 33 20S 71 25W
Casablanca, *Morocco* **50 B4** 33 36N 7 36W
Cascade, *Idaho, U.S.A.* **82 D5** 44 31N 116 2W
Cascade, *Mont., U.S.A.* **82 C8** 47 16N 111 42W
Cascade Locks, *U.S.A.* **84 E5** 45 40N 121 54W
Cascade Ra., *U.S.A.* **84 D5** 47 0N 121 30W
Cascade Reservoir, *U.S.A.* **82 D5** 44 32N 116 3W
Cascais, *Portugal* **19 C1** 38 41N 9 25W
Cascavel, *Brazil* **95 A5** 24 57S 53 28W
Cáscina, *Italy* **20 C4** 43 41N 10 33 E
Casco B., *U.S.A.* **77 D10** 43 45N 70 0W
Caserta, *Italy* **20 D6** 41 4N 14 20 E
Caseyr, Raas = Asir, Ras, *Somali Rep.* **46 E5** 11 55N 51 10 E
Cashel, *Ireland* **13 D4** 52 30N 7 53W
Casiguran, *Phil.* **37 A6** 16 22N 122 7 E
Casilda, *Argentina* **94 C3** 33 10S 61 10W
Casino, *Australia* **63 D5** 28 52S 153 3 E
Casiquiare →, *Venezuela* **92 C5** 2 1N 67 7W
Casma, *Peru* **92 E3** 9 30S 78 20W
Casmalia, *U.S.A.* **85 L6** 34 50N 120 32W
Caspe, *Spain* **19 B5** 41 14N 0 1W
Casper, *U.S.A.* **82 E10** 42 51N 106 19W
Caspian Depression, *Eurasia* **25 E8** 47 0N 48 0 E
Caspian Sea, *Eurasia* **25 F9** 43 0N 50 0 E
Cass Lake, *U.S.A.* **80 B7** 47 23N 94 37W
Cassadaga, *U.S.A.* **78 D5** 42 20N 79 19W
Casselman, *Canada* **79 A9** 45 19N 75 5W
Casselton, *U.S.A.* **80 B6** 46 54N 97 13W
Cassiar, *Canada* **72 B3** 59 16N 129 40W
Cassiar Mts., *Canada* **72 B2** 59 30N 130 30W
Cassino, *Italy* **20 D5** 41 30N 13 49 E
Cassville, *U.S.A.* **81 G8** 36 41N 93 52W
Castaic, *U.S.A.* **85 L8** 34 30N 118 38W
Castalia, *U.S.A.* **78 E2** 41 24N 82 49W
Castanhal, *Brazil* **93 D9** 1 18S 47 55W
Castellammare di Stábia, *Italy* **20 D6** 40 42N 14 29 E
Castelli, *Argentina* **94 D4** 36 7S 57 47W
Castelló de la Plana, *Spain* **19 C5** 39 58N 0 3W
Castelo, *Brazil* **95 A7** 20 33S 41 14W
Castelo Branco, *Portugal* **19 C2** 39 50N 7 31W
Castelsarrasin, *France* **18 E4** 44 2N 1 7 E
Castelvetrano, *Italy* **20 F5** 37 41N 12 47 E
Casterton, *Australia* **63 F3** 37 30S 141 30 E
Castile, *U.S.A.* **78 D6** 42 38N 78 3W
Castilla-La Mancha □, *Spain* **19 C4** 39 30N 3 30W
Castilla y Leon □, *Spain* **19 B3** 42 0N 5 0W
Castillos, *Uruguay* **95 C5** 34 12S 53 52W
Castle Dale, *U.S.A.* **82 G8** 39 13N 111 1W
Castle Douglas, *U.K.* **12 G5** 54 56N 3 56W
Castle Rock, *Colo., U.S.A.* **80 F2** 39 22N 104 51W
Castle Rock, *Wash., U.S.A.* **84 D4** 46 17N 122 54W
Castlebar, *Ireland* **13 C2** 53 52N 9 18W
Castleblaney, *Ireland* **13 B5** 54 7N 6 44W
Castlederg, *U.K.* **13 B4** 54 42N 7 35W
Castleford, *U.K.* **10 D6** 53 43N 1 21W
Castlegar, *Canada* **72 D5** 49 20N 117 40W
Castlemaine, *Australia* **63 F3** 37 2S 144 12 E
Castlepollard, *Ireland* **13 C4** 53 41N 7 19W
Castlerea, *Ireland* **13 C3** 53 46N 8 29W
Castlereagh →, *Australia* **63 E4** 30 12S 147 32 E
Castlereagh B., *Australia* **62 A2** 12 10S 135 10 E
Castleton, *U.S.A.* **79 C11** 43 37N 73 11W
Castletown, *U.K.* **10 C3** 54 5N 4 38W
Castletown Bearhaven, *Ireland* **13 E2** 51 39N 9 55W
Castor, *Canada* **72 C6** 52 15N 111 50W
Castor →, *Canada* **70 B4** 53 24N 78 58W
Castorland, *U.S.A.* **79 C9** 43 53N 75 31W
Castres, *France* **18 E5** 43 37N 2 13 E
Castricum, *Neths.* **15 B4** 52 33N 4 40 E
Castries, *St. Lucia* **89 D7** 14 2N 60 58W
Castro, *Brazil* **95 A6** 24 45S 50 0W
Castro, *Chile* **96 E2** 42 30S 73 50W
Castro Alves, *Brazil* **93 F11** 12 46S 39 33W
Castroville, *U.S.A.* **84 J5** 36 46N 121 45W
Castuera, *Spain* **19 C3** 38 43N 5 37W
Cat Ba, Dao, *Vietnam* **38 B6** 20 50N 107 0 E
Cat I., *Bahamas* **89 B4** 24 30N 75 30W
Cat L., *Canada* **70 B1** 51 40N 91 50W
Cat Lake, *Canada* **70 B1** 51 40N 91 50W
Catacamas, *Honduras* **88 D2** 14 54N 85 56W
Cataguases, *Brazil* **95 A7** 21 23S 42 39W
Catalão, *Brazil* **93 G9** 18 10S 47 57W
Çatalca, *Turkey* **21 D13** 41 8N 28 27 E
Catalina, *Canada* **71 C9** 48 31N 53 4W
Catalina, *Chile* **94 B2** 25 13S 69 43W
Catalina, *U.S.A.* **83 K8** 32 30N 110 50W
Catalonia = Cataluña □, *Spain* **19 B6** 41 40N 1 15 E
Cataluña □, *Spain* **19 B6** 41 40N 1 15 E
Catamarca, *Argentina* **94 B2** 28 30S 65 50W
Catamarca □, *Argentina* **94 B2** 27 0S 65 50W
Catanduanes □, *Phil.* **37 B6** 13 50N 124 20 E
Catanduva, *Brazil* **95 A6** 21 5S 48 58W
Catánia, *Italy* **20 F6** 37 30N 15 6 E
Catanzaro, *Italy* **20 E7** 38 54N 16 35 E
Catarman, *Phil.* **37 B6** 12 28N 124 35 E
Cateel, *Phil.* **37 C7** 7 47N 126 24 E
Catembe, *Mozam.* **57 D5** 26 0S 32 33 E
Caterham, *U.K.* **11 F7** 51 15N 0 4W
Cathcart, *S. Africa* **56 E4** 32 18S 27 10 E
Cathlamet, *U.S.A.* **84 D3** 46 12N 123 23W
Catlettsburg, *U.S.A.* **76 F4** 38 25N 82 36W
Catoche, C., *Mexico* **87 C7** 21 40N 87 8W
Catriló, *Argentina* **94 D3** 36 26S 63 24W
Catrimani, *Brazil* **92 C6** 0 27N 61 41W
Catrimani →, *Brazil* **92 C6** 0 28N 61 44W
Catskill, *U.S.A.* **79 D11** 42 14N 73 52W
Catskill Mts., *U.S.A.* **79 D10** 42 10N 74 25W
Catt, Mt., *Australia* **62 A1** 13 49S 134 23 E
Cattaraugus, *U.S.A.* **78 D6** 42 22N 78 52W
Catuala, *Angola* **56 B2** 16 25S 19 2 E
Catuane, *Mozam.* **57 D5** 26 48S 32 18 E
Catur, *Mozam.* **55 E4** 13 45S 35 30 E
Catwick Is., *Vietnam* **39 G7** 10 0N 109 0 E
Cauca →, *Colombia* **92 B4** 8 54N 74 28W
Caucaia, *Brazil* **93 D11** 3 40S 38 35W
Caucasus Mountains, *Eurasia* **25 F7** 42 50N 44 0 E
Caungula, *Angola* **52 F3** 8 26S 18 38 E
Cauquenes, *Chile* **94 D1** 36 0S 72 22W
Caura →, *Venezuela* **92 B6** 7 38N 64 53W
Cauresi →, *Mozam.* **55 F3** 17 8S 33 0 E
Causapscal, *Canada* **71 C6** 48 19N 67 12W
Cauvery →, *India* **40 P11** 11 9N 78 52 E
Caux, Pays de, *France* **18 B4** 49 38N 0 35 E
Cavalier, *U.S.A.* **80 A6** 48 48N 97 37W
Cavan, *Ireland* **13 B4** 54 0N 7 22W
Cavan □, *Ireland* **13 C4** 54 1N 7 16W
Cave Creek, *U.S.A.* **83 K7** 33 50N 111 57W
Cavenagh Ra., *Australia* **61 E4** 26 12S 127 55 E
Cavendish, *Australia* **63 F3** 37 31S 142 2 E
Caviana, I., *Brazil* **93 C8** 0 10N 50 10W
Cavite, *Phil.* **37 B6** 14 29N 120 55 E
Cawndilla L., *Australia* **63 E3** 32 30S 142 15 E
Cawnpore = Kanpur, *India* **43 F9** 26 28N 80 20 E
Caxias, *Brazil* **93 D10** 4 55S 43 20W
Caxias do Sul, *Brazil* **95 B5** 29 10S 51 10W
Cay Sal Bank, *Bahamas* **88 B4** 23 45N 80 0W
Cayambe, *Ecuador* **92 C3** 0 3N 78 8W
Cayenne, *Fr. Guiana* **93 B8** 5 5N 52 18W
Cayman Brac, *Cayman Is.* **88 C4** 19 43N 79 49W
Cayman Is. ■, *W. Indies* **88 C3** 19 40N 80 30W
Cayo Romano, *Cuba* **88 B4** 22 0N 78 0W
Cayuga, *Canada* **78 D5** 42 59N 79 50W
Cayuga, *U.S.A.* **79 D8** 42 54N 76 44W
Cayuga L., *U.S.A.* **79 D8** 42 41N 76 41W
Cazenovia, *U.S.A.* **79 D9** 42 56N 75 51W
Cazombo, *Angola* **53 G4** 11 54S 22 56 E
Ceanannus Mor, *Ireland* **13 C5** 53 44N 6 53W
Ceará = Fortaleza, *Brazil* **93 D11** 3 45S 38 35W
Ceará □, *Brazil* **93 E11** 5 0S 40 0W
Ceará Mirim, *Brazil* **93 E11** 5 38S 35 25W
Cebaco, I. de, *Panama* **88 E3** 7 33N 81 9W
Cebollar, *Argentina* **94 B2** 29 10S 66 35W
Cebu, *Phil.* **37 B6** 10 18N 123 54 E
Cecil Plains, *Australia* **63 D5** 27 30S 151 11 E
Cedar →, *U.S.A.* **80 E9** 41 17N 91 21W
Cedar City, *U.S.A.* **83 H7** 37 41N 113 4W
Cedar Creek Reservoir, *U.S.A.* **81 J6** 32 11N 96 4W
Cedar Falls, *Iowa, U.S.A.* **80 D8** 42 32N 92 27W
Cedar Falls, *Wash., U.S.A.* **84 C5** 47 25N 121 45W
Cedar Key, *U.S.A.* **77 L4** 29 8N 83 2W
Cedar L., *Canada* **73 C9** 53 10N 100 0W
Cedar Rapids, *U.S.A.* **80 E9** 41 59N 91 40W
Cedartown, *U.S.A.* **77 H3** 34 1N 85 15W
Cedarvale, *Canada* **72 B3** 55 1N 128 22W
Cedarville, *S. Africa* **57 E4** 30 23S 29 3 E
Cedral, *Mexico* **86 C4** 23 50N 100 42W
Cedro, *Brazil* **93 E11** 6 34S 39 3W
Cedros, I. de, *Mexico* **86 B1** 28 10N 115 20W
Ceduna, *Australia* **63 E1** 32 7S 133 46 E
Ceerigaabo = Erigavo, *Somali Rep.* **46 E4** 10 35N 47 20 E
Cefalù, *Italy* **20 E6** 38 2N 14 1 E
Cegléd, *Hungary* **17 E10** 47 11N 19 47 E
Celaya, *Mexico* **86 C4** 20 31N 100 37W
Celebes Sea, *Indonesia* **37 D6** 3 0N 123 0 E
Celina, *U.S.A.* **76 E3** 40 33N 84 35W
Celje, *Slovenia* **16 E8** 46 16N 15 18 E
Celle, *Germany* **16 B6** 52 37N 10 4 E
Cenderwasih, Teluk, *Indonesia* **37 E9** 3 0S 135 20 E
Center, *N. Dak., U.S.A.* **80 B4** 47 7N 101 18W
Center, *Tex., U.S.A.* **81 K7** 31 48N 94 11W
Centerburg, *U.S.A.* **78 F2** 40 18N 82 42W
Centerville, *Calif., U.S.A.* **84 J7** 36 44N 119 30W
Centerville, *Iowa, U.S.A.* **80 E8** 40 44N 92 52W
Centerville, *Pa., U.S.A.* **78 F5** 40 3N 79 59W
Centerville, *Tenn., U.S.A.* **77 H2** 35 47N 87 28W
Centerville, *Tex., U.S.A.* **81 K7** 31 16N 95 59W
Central □, *Kenya* **54 C4** 0 30S 37 30 E
Central □, *Malawi* **55 E3** 13 30S 33 30 E
Central □, *Zambia* **55 E2** 14 25S 28 50 E
Central, Cordillera, *Colombia* **92 C4** 5 0N 75 0W
Central, Cordillera, *Costa Rica* **88 D3** 10 10N 84 5W
Central, Cordillera, *Dom. Rep.* **89 C5** 19 15N 71 0W
Central African Rep. ■, *Africa* **52 C4** 7 0N 20 0 E
Central America, *America* **66 H11** 12 0N 85 0W
Central Butte, *Canada* **73 C7** 50 48N 106 31W
Central City, *Colo., U.S.A.* **82 G11** 39 48N 105 31W
Central City, *Ky., U.S.A.* **76 G2** 37 18N 87 7W
Central City, *Nebr., U.S.A.* **80 E6** 41 7N 98 0W
Central I., *Kenya* **54 B4** 3 30N 36 0 E
Central Makran Range, *Pakistan* **40 F4** 26 30N 64 15 E
Central Patricia, *Canada* **70 B1** 51 30N 90 9W
Central Point, *U.S.A.* **82 E2** 42 23N 122 55W
Central Russian Uplands, *Europe* **6 E13** 54 0N 36 0 E
Central Siberian Plateau, *Russia* **28 C14** 65 0N 105 0 E
Central Square, *U.S.A.* **79 C8** 43 17N 76 9W
Centralia, *Ill., U.S.A.* **80 F10** 38 32N 89 8W
Centralia, *Mo., U.S.A.* **80 F8** 39 13N 92 8W
Centralia, *Wash., U.S.A.* **84 D4** 46 43N 122 58W
Cephalonia = Kefallinía, *Greece* **21 E9** 38 15N 20 30 E
Cepu, *Indonesia* **37 G14** 7 9S 111 35 E
Ceram = Seram, *Indonesia* **37 E7** 3 10S 129 0 E
Ceram Sea = Seram Sea, *Indonesia* **37 E7** 2 30S 128 30 E
Ceredigion □, *U.K.* **11 E3** 52 16N 4 15W
Ceres, *Argentina* **94 B3** 29 55S 61 55W
Ceres, *S. Africa* **56 E2** 33 21S 19 18 E
Ceres, *U.S.A.* **84 H6** 37 35N 120 57W
Cerignola, *Italy* **20 D6** 41 17N 15 53 E
Cerigo = Kíthira, *Greece* **21 F10** 36 8N 23 0 E
Çerkezköy, *Turkey* **21 D12** 41 17N 28 0 E
Cerralvo, I., *Mexico* **86 C3** 24 20N 109 45W
Cerritos, *Mexico* **86 C4** 22 27N 100 20W
Cerro Chato, *Uruguay* **95 C4** 33 6S 55 8W
Cerventes, *Australia* **61 F2** 30 31S 115 3 E
Cervera, *Spain* **19 B6** 41 40N 1 16 E
Cesena, *Italy* **20 B5** 44 8N 12 15 E
Cēsis, *Latvia* **9 H21** 57 18N 25 15 E
České Budějovice, *Czech Rep.* **16 D8** 48 55N 14 25 E
Českomoravská Vrchovina, *Czech Rep.* **16 D8** 49 30N 15 40 E
Çeşme, *Turkey* **21 E12** 38 20N 26 23 E
Cessnock, *Australia* **63 E5** 32 50S 151 21 E
Cetinje, *Montenegro, Yug.* **21 C8** 42 23N 18 59 E
Cetraro, *Italy* **20 E6** 39 31N 15 55 E
Ceuta, *N. Afr.* **19 E3** 35 52N 5 18W
Cévennes, *France* **18 D5** 44 10N 3 50 E
Ceyhan, *Turkey* **44 B2** 37 4N 35 47 E
Ceylon = Sri Lanka ■, *Asia* **40 R12** 7 30N 80 50 E

Chicopee

Cha-am, *Thailand* **38 F2** 12 48N 99 58 E
Cha Pa, *Vietnam* **38 A4** 22 20N 103 47 E
Chacabuco, *Argentina* **94 C3** 34 40S 60 27W
Chachapoyas, *Peru* **92 E3** 6 15S 77 50W
Chachoengsao, *Thailand* **38 F3** 13 42N 101 5 E
Chachran, *Pakistan* **40 E7** 28 55N 70 30 E
Chachro, *Pakistan* **42 G4** 25 5N 70 15 E
Chaco □, *Argentina* **94 B3** 26 30S 61 0W
Chaco □, *Paraguay* **94 B4** 26 0S 60 0W
Chaco →, *U.S.A.* **83 H9** 36 46N 108 39W
Chaco Austral, *S. Amer.* **96 B4** 27 0S 61 30W
Chaco Boreal, *S. Amer.* **92 H6** 22 0S 60 0W
Chaco Central, *S. Amer.* **96 A4** 24 0S 61 0W
Chacon, C., *U.S.A.* **72 C2** 54 42N 132 0W
Chad ■, *Africa* **51 F8** 15 0N 17 15 E
Chad, L. = Tchad, L., *Chad* **51 F8** 13 30N 14 30 E
Chadan, *Russia* **27 D10** 51 17N 91 35 E
Chadileuvú →, *Argentina* **94 D2** 37 46S 66 0W
Chadiza, *Zambia* **55 E3** 14 45S 32 27 E
Chadron, *U.S.A.* **80 D3** 42 50N 103 0W
Chadyr-Lunga = Ciadâr-Lunga, *Moldova* **17 E15** 46 3N 28 51 E
Chae Hom, *Thailand* **38 C2** 18 43N 99 35 E
Chaem →, *Thailand* **38 C2** 18 11N 98 38 E
Chaeryŏng, *N. Korea* **35 E13** 38 24N 125 36 E
Chagai Hills = Chāh Gay Hills, *Afghan.* **40 E3** 29 30N 64 0 E
Chagda, *Russia* **27 D14** 58 45N 130 38 E
Chagos Arch., *Ind. Oc.* **29 K11** 6 0S 72 0 E
Chagrin Falls, *U.S.A.* **78 E3** 41 26N 81 24W
Chāh Ākhvor, *Iran* **45 C8** 32 41N 59 40 E
Chāh Bahar, *Iran* **45 E9** 25 20N 60 40 E
Chāh-e Kavīr, *Iran* **45 C8** 34 29N 56 52 E
Chāh Gay Hills, *Afghan.* **40 E3** 29 30N 64 0 E
Chahar Burjak, *Afghan.* **40 D3** 30 15N 62 0 E
Chahār Mahāll va Bakhtīarī □, *Iran* **45 C6** 32 0N 49 0 E
Chaibasa, *India* **41 H14** 22 42N 85 49 E
Chainat, *Thailand* **38 E3** 15 11N 100 8 E
Chaiya, *Thailand* **39 H2** 9 23N 99 14 E
Chaj Doab, *Pakistan* **42 C5** 32 15N 73 0 E
Chajari, *Argentina* **94 C4** 30 42S 58 0W
Chak Amru, *Pakistan* **42 C6** 32 22N 75 11 E
Chakar →, *Pakistan* **42 E3** 29 29N 68 2 E
Chakari, *Zimbabwe* **57 B4** 18 5S 29 51 E
Chake Chake, *Tanzania* **54 D4** 5 15S 39 45 E
Chakhānsūr, *Afghan.* **40 D3** 31 10N 62 0 E
Chakonipau, L., *Canada* **71 A6** 56 18N 68 30W
Chakradharpur, *India* **43 H11** 22 45N 85 40 E
Chakrata, *India* **42 D7** 30 42N 77 51 E
Chakwal, *Pakistan* **42 C5** 32 56N 72 53 E
Chala, *Peru* **92 G4** 15 48S 74 20W
Chalchihuites, *Mexico* **86 C4** 23 29N 103 53W
Chalcis = Khalkís, *Greece* **21 E10** 38 27N 23 42 E
Chaleur B., *Canada* **71 C6** 47 55N 65 30W
Chalfant, *U.S.A.* **84 H8** 37 32N 118 21W
Chalhuanca, *Peru* **92 F4** 14 15S 73 15W
Chalisgaon, *India* **40 J9** 20 30N 75 10 E
Chalk River, *Canada* **70 C4** 46 1N 77 27W
Chalky Inlet, *N.Z.* **59 M1** 46 3S 166 31 E
Challapata, *Bolivia* **92 G5** 18 53S 66 50W
Challis, *U.S.A.* **82 D6** 44 30N 114 14W
Chalmette, *U.S.A.* **81 L10** 29 56N 89 58W
Chalon-sur-Saône, *France* **18 C6** 46 48N 4 50 E
Châlons-en-Champagne, *France* **18 B6** 48 58N 4 20 E
Chalyaphum, *Thailand* **38 E4** 15 48N 102 2 E
Cham, Cu Lao, *Vietnam* **38 E7** 15 57N 108 30 E
Chama, *U.S.A.* **83 H10** 36 54N 106 35W
Chamaicó, *Argentina* **94 D3** 35 3S 64 58W
Chaman, *Pakistan* **40 D5** 30 58N 66 25 E
Chamba, *India* **42 C7** 32 35N 76 10 E
Chamba, *Tanzania* **55 E4** 11 37S 37 0 E
Chambal →, *India* **43 F8** 26 29N 79 15 E
Chamberlain, *U.S.A.* **80 D5** 43 49N 99 20W
Chamberlain →, *Australia* **60 C4** 15 30S 127 54 E
Chamberlain L., *U.S.A.* **77 B11** 46 14N 69 19W
Chambers, *U.S.A.* **83 J9** 35 11N 109 26W
Chambersburg, *U.S.A.* **76 F7** 39 56N 77 40W
Chambéry, *France* **18 D6** 45 34N 5 55 E
Chambeshi →, *Zambia* **52 G6** 11 53S 29 48 E
Chambly, *Canada* **79 A11** 45 27N 73 17W
Chambord, *Canada* **71 C5** 48 25N 72 6W
Chamchamal, *Iraq* **44 C5** 35 32N 44 50 E
Chamela, *Mexico* **86 D3** 19 32N 105 5W
Chamical, *Argentina* **94 C2** 30 22S 66 27W
Chamkar Luong, *Cambodia* **39 G4** 11 0N 103 45 E
Chamoli, *India* **43 D8** 30 24N 79 21 E
Chamonix-Mont Blanc, *France* **18 D7** 45 55N 6 51 E
Chamouchouane →, *Canada* **70 C5** 48 37N 72 20W
Champa, *India* **43 H10** 22 2N 82 43 E
Champagne, *Canada* **72 A1** 60 49N 136 30W
Champagne, *France* **18 B6** 48 40N 4 20 E
Champaign, *U.S.A.* **76 E1** 40 7N 88 15W
Champassak, *Laos* **38 E5** 14 53N 105 52 E
Champawat, *India* **43 E9** 29 20N 80 6 E
Champdoré, L., *Canada* **71 A6** 55 55N 65 49W
Champion, *U.S.A.* **78 E4** 41 19N 80 51W
Champlain, *U.S.A.* **79 B11** 44 59N 73 27W
Champlain, L., *U.S.A.* **79 B11** 44 40N 73 20W
Champotón, *Mexico* **87 D6** 19 20N 90 50W
Champua, *India* **43 H11** 22 5N 85 40 E
Chana, *Thailand* **39 J3** 6 55N 100 44 E
Chañaral, *Chile* **94 B1** 26 23S 70 40W
Chanārān, *Iran* **45 B8** 36 39N 59 6 E
Chanasma, *India* **42 H5** 23 44N 72 5 E
Chanco, *Chile* **94 D1** 35 44S 72 32W
Chand, *India* **43 J8** 21 57N 79 7 E
Chandan, *India* **43 G12** 24 38N 86 40 E
Chandan Chauki, *India* **43 E9** 28 33N 80 47 E
Chandannagar, *India* **43 H13** 22 52N 88 24 E
Chandausi, *India* **43 E8** 28 27N 78 49 E
Chandeleur Is., *U.S.A.* **81 L10** 29 55N 88 57W
Chandeleur Sd., *U.S.A.* **81 L10** 29 55N 89 0W
Chandigarh, *India* **42 D7** 30 43N 76 47 E
Chandil, *India* **43 H12** 22 58N 86 3 E
Chandler, *Australia* **63 D1** 27 0S 133 19 E
Chandler, *Canada* **71 C7** 48 18N 64 46W
Chandler, *Ariz., U.S.A.* **83 K8** 33 18N 111 50W
Chandler, *Okla., U.S.A.* **81 H6** 35 42N 96 53W
Chandod, *India* **42 J5** 21 59N 73 28 E
Chandpur, *Bangla.* **41 H17** 23 8N 90 45 E
Chandrapur, *India* **40 K11** 19 57N 79 25 E
Chānf, *Iran* **45 E9** 26 38N 60 29 E
Chang, *Pakistan* **42 F3** 26 59N 68 30 E
Chang, Ko, *Thailand* **39 F4** 12 0N 102 23 E
Ch'ang Chiang = Chang Jiang →, *China* **33 C7** 31 48N 121 10 E
Chang Jiang →, *China* **33 C7** 31 48N 121 10 E
Changa, *India* **43 C7** 33 53N 77 35 E
Changanacheri, *India* **40 Q10** 9 25N 76 31 E
Changane →, *Mozam.* **57 C5** 24 30S 33 30 E
Changbai, *China* **35 D15** 41 25N 128 5 E
Changbai Shan, *China* **35 C15** 42 20N 129 0 E
Changchiak'ou = Zhangjiakou, *China* **34 D8** 40 48N 114 55 E
Ch'angchou = Changzhou, *China* **33 C6** 31 47N 119 58 E
Changchun, *China* **35 C13** 43 57N 125 17 E
Changchunling, *China* **35 B13** 45 18N 125 27 E
Changde, *China* **33 D6** 29 4N 111 35 E
Changdo-ri, *N. Korea* **35 E14** 38 30N 127 40 E
Changhai = Shanghai, *China* **33 C7** 31 15N 121 26 E
Changhua, *Taiwan* **33 D7** 24 2N 120 30 E
Changhŭng, *S. Korea* **35 G14** 34 41N 126 52 E
Changhŭngni, *N. Korea* **35 D15** 40 24N 128 19 E
Changjiang, *China* **38 C7** 19 20N 108 55 E
Changjin, *N. Korea* **35 D14** 40 23N 127 15 E
Changjin-chŏsuji, *N. Korea* **35 D14** 40 30N 127 15 E
Changli, *China* **35 E10** 39 40N 119 13 E
Changling, *China* **35 B12** 44 20N 123 58 E
Changlun, *Malaysia* **39 J3** 6 25N 100 26 E
Changping, *China* **34 D9** 40 14N 116 12 E
Changsha, *China* **33 D6** 28 12N 113 0 E
Changwu, *China* **34 G4** 35 10N 107 45 E
Changyi, *China* **35 F10** 36 40N 119 30 E
Changyŏn, *N. Korea* **35 E13** 38 15N 125 6 E
Changyuan, *China* **34 G8** 35 15N 114 42 E
Changzhi, *China* **34 F7** 36 10N 113 6 E
Changzhou, *China* **33 C6** 31 47N 119 58 E
Chanhanga, *Angola* **56 B1** 16 0S 14 8 E
Channapatna, *India* **40 N10** 12 40N 77 15 E
Channel Is., *U.K.* **11 H5** 49 19N 2 24W
Channel Is., *U.S.A.* **85 M7** 33 40N 119 15W
Channel Islands Nat. Park, *U.S.A.* **85 M8** 33 30N 119 0W
Channel-Port aux Basques, *Canada* **71 C8** 47 30N 59 9W
Channel Tunnel, *Europe* **11 F9** 51 0N 1 30 E
Channing, *U.S.A.* **81 H3** 35 41N 102 20W
Chantada, *Spain* **19 A2** 42 36N 7 46W
Chanthaburi, *Thailand* **38 F4** 12 38N 102 12 E
Chantrey Inlet, *Canada* **68 B10** 67 48N 96 20W
Chanute, *U.S.A.* **81 G7** 37 41N 95 27W
Chao Phraya →, *Thailand* **38 F3** 13 32N 100 36 E
Chao Phraya Lowlands, *Thailand* **38 E3** 15 30N 100 0 E
Chaocheng, *China* **34 F8** 36 4N 115 37 E
Chaoyang, *China* **35 D11** 41 35N 120 22 E
Chaozhou, *China* **33 D6** 23 42N 116 32 E
Chapais, *Canada* **70 C5** 49 47N 74 51W
Chapala, *Mozam.* **55 F4** 15 50S 37 35 E
Chapala, L. de, *Mexico* **86 C4** 20 10N 103 20W
Chapayev, *Kazakstan* **25 D9** 50 25N 51 10 E
Chapayevsk, *Russia* **24 D8** 53 0N 49 40 E
Chapecó, *Brazil* **95 B5** 27 14S 52 41W
Chapel Hill, *U.S.A.* **77 H6** 35 55N 79 4W
Chapleau, *Canada* **70 C3** 47 50N 83 24W
Chaplin, *Canada* **73 C7** 50 28N 106 40W
Chaplin L., *Canada* **73 C7** 50 22N 106 36W
Chappell, *U.S.A.* **80 E3** 41 6N 102 28W
Chapra = Chhapra, *India* **43 G11** 25 48N 84 44 E
Chara, *Russia* **27 D12** 56 54N 118 20 E
Charadai, *Argentina* **94 B4** 27 35S 59 55W
Charagua, *Bolivia* **92 G6** 19 45S 63 10W
Charambirá, Punta, *Colombia* **92 C3** 4 16N 77 32W
Charaña, *Bolivia* **92 G5** 17 30S 69 25W
Charanwala, *India* **42 F5** 27 51N 72 10 E
Charata, *Argentina* **94 B3** 27 13S 61 14W
Charcas, *Mexico* **86 C4** 23 10N 101 20W
Chard, *U.K.* **11 G5** 50 52N 2 58W
Chardon, *U.S.A.* **78 E3** 41 35N 81 12W
Chardzhou = Chārjew, *Turkmenistan* **26 F7** 39 6N 63 34 E
Charente →, *France* **18 D3** 45 57N 1 5W
Chari →, *Chad* **51 F8** 12 58N 14 31 E
Chārīkār, *Afghan.* **40 B6** 35 0N 69 10 E
Chariton →, *U.S.A.* **80 F8** 39 19N 92 58W
Chārjew, *Turkmenistan* **26 F7** 39 6N 63 34 E
Charkhari, *India* **43 G8** 25 24N 79 45 E
Charkhi Dadri, *India* **42 E7** 28 37N 76 17 E
Charleroi, *Belgium* **15 D4** 50 24N 4 27 E
Charleroi, *U.S.A.* **78 F5** 40 9N 79 57W
Charles, C., *U.S.A.* **76 G8** 37 7N 75 58W
Charles City, *U.S.A.* **80 D8** 43 4N 92 41W
Charles L., *Canada* **73 B6** 59 50N 110 33W
Charles Town, *U.S.A.* **76 F7** 39 17N 77 52W
Charleston, *Ill., U.S.A.* **76 F1** 39 30N 88 10W
Charleston, *Miss., U.S.A.* **81 H9** 34 1N 90 4W
Charleston, *Mo., U.S.A.* **81 G10** 36 55N 89 21W
Charleston, *S.C., U.S.A.* **77 J6** 32 46N 79 56W
Charleston, *W. Va., U.S.A.* **76 F5** 38 21N 81 38W
Charleston L., *Canada* **79 B9** 44 32N 76 0W
Charleston Peak, *U.S.A.* **85 J11** 36 16N 115 42W
Charlestown, *Ireland* **13 C3** 53 58N 8 48W
Charlestown, *S. Africa* **57 D4** 27 26S 29 53 E
Charlestown, *Ind., U.S.A.* **76 F3** 38 27N 85 40W
Charlestown, *N.H., U.S.A.* **79 C12** 43 14N 72 25W
Charleville = Rath Luirc, *Ireland* **13 D3** 52 21N 8 40W
Charleville, *Australia* **63 D4** 26 24S 146 15 E
Charleville-Mézières, *France* **18 B6** 49 44N 4 40 E
Charlevoix, *U.S.A.* **76 C3** 45 19N 85 16W
Charlotte, *Mich., U.S.A.* **76 D3** 42 34N 84 50W
Charlotte, *N.C., U.S.A.* **77 H5** 35 13N 80 51W
Charlotte, *Vt., U.S.A.* **79 B11** 44 19N 73 14W
Charlotte Amalie, *U.S. Virgin Is.* **89 C7** 18 21N 64 56W
Charlotte Harbor, *U.S.A.* **77 M4** 26 50N 82 10W
Charlotte L., *Canada* **72 C3** 52 12N 125 19W
Charlottesville, *U.S.A.* **76 F6** 38 2N 78 30W
Charlottetown, *Nfld., Canada* **71 B8** 52 46N 56 7W
Charlottetown, *P.E.I., Canada* **71 C7** 46 14N 63 8W
Charlton, *Australia* **63 F3** 36 16S 143 24 E
Charlton, *U.S.A.* **80 E8** 40 59N 93 20W
Charlton I., *Canada* **70 B4** 52 0N 79 20W
Charny, *Canada* **71 C5** 46 43N 71 15W
Charolles, *France* **18 C6** 46 27N 4 16 E
Charre, *Mozam.* **55 F4** 17 13S 35 10 E
Charsadda, *Pakistan* **42 B4** 34 7N 71 45 E
Charters Towers, *Australia* **62 C4** 20 5S 146 13 E
Chartres, *France* **18 B4** 48 29N 1 30 E
Chascomús, *Argentina* **94 D4** 35 30S 58 0W
Chasefu, *Zambia* **55 E3** 11 55S 33 8 E
Chashma Barrage, *Pakistan* **42 C4** 32 27N 71 20 E
Chāt, *Iran* **45 B7** 37 59N 55 16 E
Châteaubriant, *France* **18 C3** 47 43N 1 23W
Chateaugay, *U.S.A.* **79 B10** 44 56N 74 5W
Châteauguay, L., *Canada* **71 A5** 56 26N 70 3W
Châteaulin, *France* **18 B1** 48 11N 4 8W
Châteauroux, *France* **18 C4** 46 50N 1 40 E
Châtellerault, *France* **18 C4** 46 50N 0 30 E
Chatham = Miramichi, *Canada* **71 C6** 47 2N 65 28W
Chatham, *Canada* **78 D2** 42 24N 82 11W
Chatham, *U.K.* **11 F8** 51 22N 0 32 E
Chatham, *U.S.A.* **79 D11** 42 21N 73 36W
Chatham Is., *Pac. Oc.* **64 M10** 44 0S 176 40W
Chatmohar, *Bangla.* **43 G13** 24 15N 89 15 E
Chatra, *India* **43 G11** 24 12N 84 56 E
Chatrapur, *India* **41 K14** 19 22N 85 2 E
Chats, L. des, *Canada* **79 A8** 45 30N 76 20W
Chatsu, *India* **42 F6** 26 36N 75 57 E
Chatsworth, *Canada* **78 B4** 44 27N 80 54W
Chatsworth, *Zimbabwe* **55 F3** 19 38S 31 13 E
Chattahoochee, *U.S.A.* **77 K3** 30 42N 84 51W
Chattahoochee →, *U.S.A.* **77 K3** 30 54N 84 57W
Chattanooga, *U.S.A.* **77 H3** 35 3N 85 19W
Chatteris, *U.K.* **11 E8** 52 28N 0 2 E
Chaturat, *Thailand* **38 E3** 15 40N 101 51 E
Chau Doc, *Vietnam* **39 G5** 10 42N 105 7 E
Chaukan Pass, *Burma* **41 F20** 27 0N 97 15 E
Chaumont, *France* **18 B6** 48 7N 5 8 E
Chaumont, *U.S.A.* **79 B8** 44 4N 76 8W
Chautauqua L., *U.S.A.* **78 D5** 42 10N 79 24W
Chauvin, *Canada* **73 C6** 52 45N 110 10W
Chaves, *Brazil* **93 D9** 0 15S 49 55W
Chaves, *Portugal* **19 B2** 41 45N 7 32W
Chawang, *Thailand* **39 H2** 8 25N 99 30 E
Chaykovskiy, *Russia* **24 C9** 56 47N 54 9 E
Chazy, *U.S.A.* **79 B11** 44 53N 73 26W
Cheb, *Czech Rep.* **16 C7** 50 9N 12 28 E
Cheboksary, *Russia* **24 C8** 56 8N 47 12 E
Cheboygan, *U.S.A.* **76 C3** 45 39N 84 29W
Chech, Erg, *Africa* **50 D5** 25 0N 2 15W
Chechenia □, *Russia* **25 F8** 43 30N 45 29 E
Checheno-Ingush Republic = Chechenia □, *Russia* **25 F8** 43 30N 45 29 E
Chechnya = Chechenia □, *Russia* **25 F8** 43 30N 45 29 E
Chech'ŏn, *S. Korea* **35 F15** 37 8N 128 12 E
Checotah, *U.S.A.* **81 H7** 35 28N 95 31W
Chedabucto B., *Canada* **71 C7** 45 25N 61 8W
Cheduba I., *Burma* **41 K18** 18 45N 93 40 E
Cheepie, *Australia* **63 D4** 26 33S 145 1 E
Chegdomyn, *Russia* **27 D14** 51 7N 133 1 E
Chegga, *Mauritania* **50 C4** 25 27N 5 40W
Chegutu, *Zimbabwe* **55 F3** 18 10S 30 14 E
Chehalis, *U.S.A.* **84 D4** 46 40N 122 58W
Chehalis →, *U.S.A.* **84 D3** 46 57N 123 50W
Cheju do, *S. Korea* **35 H14** 33 29N 126 34 E
Chekiang = Zhejiang □, *China* **33 D7** 29 0N 120 0 E
Chela, Sa. da, *Angola* **56 B1** 16 20S 13 20 E
Chelan, *U.S.A.* **82 C4** 47 51N 120 1W
Chelan, L., *U.S.A.* **82 B3** 48 11N 120 30W
Cheleken, *Turkmenistan* **25 G9** 39 34N 53 16 E
Cheleken Yarymadasy, *Turkmenistan* **45 B7** 39 30N 53 15 E
Chelforó, *Argentina* **96 D3** 39 0S 66 33W
Chelkar = Shalqar, *Kazakstan* **26 E6** 47 48N 59 39 E
Chelkar Tengiz, Solonchak, *Kazakstan* **26 E7** 48 5N 63 7 E
Chełm, *Poland* **17 C12** 51 8N 23 30 E
Chełmno, *Poland* **17 B10** 53 20N 18 30 E
Chelmsford, *U.K.* **11 F8** 51 44N 0 29 E
Chelsea, *U.S.A.* **79 C12** 43 59N 72 27W
Cheltenham, *U.K.* **11 F5** 51 54N 2 4W
Chelyabinsk, *Russia* **26 D7** 55 10N 61 24 E
Chelyuskin, C., *Russia* **28 B14** 77 30N 103 0 E
Chemainus, *Canada* **84 B3** 48 55N 123 42W
Chemba, *Mozam.* **53 H6** 17 9S 34 53 E
Chemnitz, *Germany* **16 C7** 50 51N 12 54 E
Chemult, *U.S.A.* **82 E3** 43 14N 121 47W
Chen, Gora, *Russia* **27 C15** 65 16N 141 50 E
Chenab →, *Pakistan* **42 D4** 30 23N 71 2 E
Chenango Forks, *U.S.A.* **79 D9** 42 15N 75 51W
Cheney, *U.S.A.* **82 C5** 47 30N 117 35W
Cheng Xian, *China* **34 H3** 33 43N 105 42 E
Chengcheng, *China* **34 G5** 35 8N 109 56 E
Chengchou = Zhengzhou, *China* **34 G7** 34 45N 113 34 E
Chengde, *China* **35 D9** 40 59N 117 58 E
Chengdu, *China* **32 C5** 30 38N 104 2 E
Chenggu, *China* **34 H4** 33 10N 107 21 E
Chengjiang, *China* **32 D5** 24 39N 103 0 E
Ch'engmai, *China* **38 C7** 19 50N 109 58 E
Ch'engtu = Chengdu, *China* **32 C5** 30 38N 104 2 E
Chengwu, *China* **34 G8** 34 58N 115 50 E
Chengyang, *China* **35 F11** 36 18N 120 21 E
Chenjiagang, *China* **35 G10** 34 23N 119 47 E
Chenkán, *Mexico* **87 D6** 19 8N 90 58W
Chennai, *India* **40 N12** 13 8N 80 19 E
Cheo Reo, *Vietnam* **36 B3** 13 25N 108 28 E
Cheom Ksan, *Cambodia* **38 E5** 14 13N 104 56 E
Chepén, *Peru* **92 E3** 7 15S 79 23W
Chepes, *Argentina* **94 C2** 31 20S 66 35W
Chepo, *Panama* **88 E4** 9 10N 79 6W
Chepstow, *U.K.* **11 F5** 51 38N 2 41W
Cheptulil, Mt., *Kenya* **54 B4** 1 25N 35 35 E
Chequamegon B., *U.S.A.* **80 B9** 46 40N 90 30W
Cher →, *France* **18 C4** 47 21N 0 29 E
Cheraw, *U.S.A.* **77 H6** 34 42N 79 53W
Cherbourg, *France* **18 B3** 49 39N 1 40W
Cherdyn, *Russia* **24 B10** 60 24N 56 29 E
Cheremkhovo, *Russia* **27 D11** 53 8N 103 1 E
Cherepanovo, *Russia* **26 D9** 54 15N 83 30 E
Cherepovets, *Russia* **24 C6** 59 5N 37 55 E
Chergui, Chott ech, *Algeria* **50 B6** 34 21N 0 25 E
Cherikov = Cherykaw, *Belarus* **17 B16** 53 32N 31 20 E
Cherkasy, *Ukraine* **25 E5** 49 27N 32 4 E
Cherkessk, *Russia* **25 F7** 44 15N 42 5 E
Cherlak, *Russia* **26 D8** 54 15N 74 55 E
Chernaya, *Russia* **27 B9** 70 30N 89 10 E
Chernigov = Chernihiv, *Ukraine* **24 D5** 51 28N 31 20 E
Chernihiv, *Ukraine* **24 D5** 51 28N 31 20 E
Chernivtsi, *Ukraine* **17 D13** 48 15N 25 52 E
Chernobyl = Chornobyl, *Ukraine* **17 C16** 51 20N 30 15 E
Chernogorsk, *Russia* **27 D10** 53 49N 91 18 E
Chernovtsy = Chernivtsi, *Ukraine* **17 D13** 48 15N 25 52 E
Chernyakhovsk, *Russia* **9 J19** 54 36N 21 48 E
Chernysheyskiy, *Russia* **27 C12** 63 0N 112 30 E
Cherokee, *Iowa, U.S.A.* **80 D7** 42 45N 95 33W
Cherokee, *Okla., U.S.A.* **81 G5** 36 45N 98 21W
Cherokee Village, *U.S.A.* **81 G9** 36 17N 91 30W
Cherokees, Grand Lake O' The, *U.S.A.* **81 G7** 36 28N 95 2W
Cherrapunji, *India* **41 G17** 25 17N 91 47 E
Cherry Valley, *Calif., U.S.A.* **85 M10** 33 59N 116 57W
Cherry Valley, *N.Y., U.S.A.* **79 D10** 42 48N 74 45W
Cherskiy, *Russia* **27 C17** 68 45N 161 18 E
Cherskogo Khrebet, *Russia* **27 C15** 65 0N 143 0 E
Cherven, *Belarus* **17 B15** 53 45N 28 28 E
Chervonohrad, *Ukraine* **17 C13** 50 25N 24 10 E
Cherwell →, *U.K.* **11 F6** 51 44N 1 14W
Cherykaw, *Belarus* **17 B16** 53 32N 31 20 E
Chesapeake, *U.S.A.* **76 G7** 36 50N 76 17W
Chesapeake B., *U.S.A.* **76 G7** 38 0N 76 10W
Cheshire □, *U.K.* **10 D5** 53 14N 2 30W
Cheshskaya Guba, *Russia* **24 A8** 67 20N 47 0 E
Cheshunt, *U.K.* **11 F7** 51 43N 0 1W
Chesil Beach, *U.K.* **11 G5** 50 37N 2 33W
Chesley, *Canada* **78 B3** 44 17N 81 5W
Chester, *U.K.* **10 D5** 53 12N 2 53W
Chester, *Calif., U.S.A.* **82 F3** 40 19N 121 14W
Chester, *Ill., U.S.A.* **81 G10** 37 55N 89 49W
Chester, *Mont., U.S.A.* **82 B8** 48 31N 110 58W
Chester, *Pa., U.S.A.* **76 F8** 39 51N 75 22W
Chester, *S.C., U.S.A.* **77 H5** 34 43N 81 12W
Chester, *Vt., U.S.A.* **79 C12** 43 16N 72 36W
Chester, *W. Va., U.S.A.* **78 F4** 40 37N 80 34W
Chester-le-Street, *U.K.* **10 C6** 54 51N 1 34W
Chesterfield, *U.K.* **10 D6** 53 15N 1 25W
Chesterfield, Is., *N. Cal.* **64 J7** 19 52S 158 15 E
Chesterfield Inlet, *Canada* **68 B10** 63 30N 90 45W
Chesterton Ra., *Australia* **63 D4** 25 30S 147 27 E
Chestertown, *U.S.A.* **79 C11** 43 40N 73 48W
Chesterville, *Canada* **79 A9** 45 6N 75 14W
Chestnut Ridge, *U.S.A.* **78 F5** 40 20N 79 10W
Chesuncook L., *U.S.A.* **77 C11** 46 0N 69 21W
Chéticamp, *Canada* **71 C7** 46 37N 60 59W
Chetumal, *Mexico* **87 D7** 18 30N 88 20W
Chetumal, B. de, *Mexico* **87 D7** 18 40N 88 10W
Chetwynd, *Canada* **72 B4** 55 45N 121 36W
Cheviot, The, *U.K.* **10 B5** 55 29N 2 9W
Cheviot Hills, *U.K.* **10 B5** 55 20N 2 30W
Cheviot Ra., *Australia* **62 D3** 25 20S 143 45 E
Chew Bahir, *Ethiopia* **46 G2** 4 40N 36 50 E
Chewelah, *U.S.A.* **82 B5** 48 17N 117 43W
Cheyenne, *Okla., U.S.A.* **81 H5** 35 37N 99 40W
Cheyenne, *Wyo., U.S.A.* **80 E2** 41 8N 104 49W
Cheyenne →, *U.S.A.* **80 C4** 44 41N 101 18W
Cheyenne Wells, *U.S.A.* **80 F3** 38 49N 102 21W
Cheyne B., *Australia* **61 F2** 34 35S 118 50 E
Chhabra, *India* **42 G7** 24 40N 76 54 E
Chhaktala, *India* **42 H6** 22 6N 74 11 E
Chhapra, *India* **43 G11** 25 48N 84 44 E
Chhata, *India* **42 F7** 27 42N 77 30 E
Chhatarpur, *Jharkhand, India* **43 G11** 24 23N 84 11 E
Chhatarpur, *Mad. P., India* **43 G8** 24 55N 79 35 E
Chhattisgarh □, *India* **43 J10** 22 0N 82 0 E
Chhep, *Cambodia* **38 F5** 13 45N 105 24 E
Chhindwara, *Mad. P., India* **43 H8** 23 3N 79 29 E
Chhindwara, *Mad. P., India* **43 H8** 22 2N 78 59 E
Chhlong, *Cambodia* **39 F5** 12 15N 105 58 E
Chhota Tawa →, *India* **42 H7** 22 14N 76 36 E
Chhoti Kali Sindh →, *India* **42 G6** 24 2N 75 31 E
Chhuikhadan, *India* **43 J9** 21 32N 80 59 E
Chhuk, *Cambodia* **39 G5** 10 46N 104 28 E
Chi →, *Thailand* **38 E5** 15 11N 104 43 E
Chiai, *Taiwan* **33 D7** 23 29N 120 25 E
Chiamboni, *Somali Rep.* **52 E8** 1 39S 41 35 E
Chiamussu = Jiamusi, *China* **33 B8** 46 40N 130 26 E
Chiang Dao, *Thailand* **38 C2** 19 22N 98 58 E
Chiang Kham, *Thailand* **38 C3** 19 32N 100 18 E
Chiang Khan, *Thailand* **38 D3** 17 52N 101 36 E
Chiang Khong, *Thailand* **38 B3** 20 17N 100 24 E
Chiang Mai, *Thailand* **38 C2** 18 47N 98 59 E
Chiang Rai, *Thailand* **38 C2** 19 52N 99 50 E
Chiang Saen, *Thailand* **38 B3** 20 16N 100 5 E
Chiapa →, *Mexico* **87 D6** 16 42N 93 0W
Chiapa de Corzo, *Mexico* **87 D6** 16 42N 93 0W
Chiapas □, *Mexico* **87 D6** 17 0N 92 45W
Chiautla, *Mexico* **87 D5** 18 18N 98 34W
Chiávari, *Italy* **18 D8** 44 19N 9 19 E
Chiavenna, *Italy* **18 C8** 46 19N 9 24 E
Chiba, *Japan* **31 G10** 35 30N 140 7 E
Chiba □, *Japan* **31 G10** 35 30N 140 20 E
Chibabava, *Mozam.* **57 C5** 20 17S 33 35 E
Chibemba, *Cunene, Angola* **53 H2** 15 48S 14 8 E
Chibemba, *Huila, Angola* **56 B2** 16 20S 15 20 E
Chibi, *Zimbabwe* **57 C5** 20 18S 30 25 E
Chibia, *Angola* **53 H2** 15 10S 13 42 E
Chibougamau, *Canada* **70 C5** 49 56N 74 24W
Chibougamau, L., *Canada* **70 C5** 49 50N 74 20W
Chibuto, *Mozam.* **57 C5** 24 40S 33 33 E
Chic-Chocs, Mts., *Canada* **71 C6** 48 55N 66 0W
Chicacole = Srikakulam, *India* **41 K13** 18 14N 83 58 E
Chicago, *U.S.A.* **76 E2** 41 53N 87 38W
Chicago Heights, *U.S.A.* **76 E2** 41 30N 87 38W
Chichagof I., *U.S.A.* **68 C6** 57 30N 135 30W
Chichén-Itzá, *Mexico* **87 C7** 20 40N 88 36W
Chicheng, *China* **34 D8** 40 55N 115 55 E
Chichester, *U.K.* **11 G7** 50 50N 0 47W
Chichester Ra., *Australia* **60 D2** 22 12S 119 15 E
Chichibu, *Japan* **31 F9** 35 59N 139 10 E
Ch'ich'ihaerh = Qiqihar, *China* **27 E13** 47 26N 124 0 E
Chicholi, *India* **42 H8** 22 1N 77 40 E
Chickasha, *U.S.A.* **81 H6** 35 3N 97 58W
Chiclana de la Frontera, *Spain* **19 D2** 36 26N 6 9W
Chiclayo, *Peru* **92 E3** 6 42S 79 50W
Chico, *U.S.A.* **84 F5** 39 44N 121 50W
Chico →, *Chubut, Argentina* **96 E3** 44 0S 67 0W
Chico →, *Santa Cruz, Argentina* **96 G3** 50 0S 68 30W
Chicomo, *Mozam.* **57 C5** 24 31S 34 6 E
Chicontepec, *Mexico* **87 C5** 20 58N 98 10W
Chicopee, *U.S.A.* **79 D12** 42 9N 72 37W

Chicoutimi

Chicoutimi, *Canada* **71 C5** 48 28N 71 5W
Chicualacuala, *Mozam.* **57 C5** 22 6S 31 42 E
Chidambaram, *India* **40 P11** 11 20N 79 45 E
Chidenguele, *Mozam.* **57 C5** 24 55S 34 11 E
Chidley, C., *Canada* **69 B13** 60 23N 64 26W
Chiducuane, *Mozam.* **57 C5** 24 35S 34 25 E
Chiede, *Angola* **56 B2** 17 15S 16 22 E
Chiefs Pt., *Canada* **78 B3** 44 41N 81 18W
Chiem Hoa, *Vietnam* **38 A5** 22 12N 105 17 E
Chiemsee, *Germany* **16 E7** 47 53N 12 28 E
Chiengi, *Zambia* **55 D2** 8 45S 29 10 E
Chiengmai = Chiang Mai, *Thailand* **38 C2** 18 47N 98 59 E
Chiese →, *Italy* **18 D9** 45 8N 10 25 E
Chieti, *Italy* **20 C6** 42 21N 14 10 E
Chifeng, *China* **35 C10** 42 18N 118 58 E
Chignecto B., *Canada* **71 C7** 45 30N 64 40W
Chiguana, *Bolivia* **94 A2** 21 0S 67 58W
Chigwell, *U.K.* **11 F8** 51 37N 0 5 E
Chiha-ri, *N. Korea* **35 E14** 38 40N 126 30 E
Chihli, G. of = Bo Hai, *China* **35 E10** 39 0N 119 0 E
Chihuahua, *Mexico* **86 B3** 28 40N 106 3W
Chihuahua □, *Mexico* **86 B3** 28 40N 106 3W
Chiili = Shīeli, *Kazakstan* **26 E7** 44 20N 66 15 E
Chik Bollapur, *India* **40 N10** 13 25N 77 45 E
Chikmagalur, *India* **40 N9** 13 15N 75 45 E
Chikwawa, *Malawi* **55 F3** 16 2S 34 50 E
Chilac, *Mexico* **87 D5** 18 20N 97 24W
Chilam Chavki, *Pakistan* **43 B6** 35 5N 75 5 E
Chilanga, *Zambia* **55 F2** 15 33S 28 16 E
Chilapa, *Mexico* **87 D5** 17 40N 99 11W
Chilas, *Pakistan* **43 B6** 35 25N 74 5 E
Chilaw, *Sri Lanka* **40 R11** 7 30N 79 50 E
Chilcotin →, *Canada* **72 C4** 51 44N 122 23W
Childers, *Australia* **63 D5** 25 15S 152 17 E
Childress, *U.S.A.* **81 H4** 34 25N 100 13W
Chile ■, *S. Amer.* **96 D2** 35 0S 72 0W
Chile Rise, *Pac. Oc.* **65 L18** 38 0S 92 0W
Chilecito, *Argentina* **94 B2** 29 10S 67 30W
Chilete, *Peru* **92 E3** 7 10S 78 50W
Chililabombwe, *Zambia* **55 E2** 12 18S 27 43 E
Chilin = Jilin, *China* **35 C14** 43 44N 126 30 E
Chilka L., *India* **41 K14** 19 40N 85 25 E
Chilko →, *Canada* **72 C4** 52 0N 123 40W
Chilko L., *Canada* **72 C4** 51 20N 124 10W
Chillagoe, *Australia* **62 B3** 17 7S 144 33 E
Chillán, *Chile* **94 D1** 36 40S 72 10W
Chillicothe, *Ill., U.S.A.* **80 E10** 40 55N 89 29W
Chillicothe, *Mo., U.S.A.* **80 F8** 39 48N 93 33W
Chillicothe, *Ohio, U.S.A.* **76 F4** 39 20N 82 59W
Chilliwack, *Canada* **72 D4** 49 10N 121 54W
Chilo, *India* **42 F5** 27 25N 73 32 E
Chiloane, I., *Mozam.* **57 C5** 20 40S 34 55 E
Chiloé, I. de, *Chile* **96 E2** 42 30S 73 50W
Chilpancingo, *Mexico* **87 D5** 17 30N 99 30W
Chiltern Hills, *U.K.* **11 F7** 51 40N 0 53W
Chilton, *U.S.A.* **76 C1** 44 2N 88 10W
Chilubi, *Zambia* **55 E2** 11 5S 29 58 E
Chilubula, *Zambia* **55 E3** 10 14S 30 51 E
Chilumba, *Malawi* **55 E3** 10 28S 34 12 E
Chilung, *Taiwan* **33 D7** 25 3N 121 45 E
Chilwa, L., *Malawi* **55 F4** 15 15S 35 40 E
Chimaltitán, *Mexico* **86 C4** 21 46N 103 50W
Chimán, *Panama* **88 E4** 8 45N 78 40W
Chimanimani, *Zimbabwe* **57 B5** 19 48S 32 52 E
Chimay, *Belgium* **15 D4** 50 3N 4 20 E
Chimayo, *U.S.A.* **83 H11** 36 0N 105 56W
Chimbay, *Uzbekistan* **26 E6** 42 57N 59 47 E
Chimborazo, *Ecuador* **92 D3** 1 29S 78 55W
Chimbote, *Peru* **92 E3** 9 0S 78 35W
Chimkent = Shymkent, *Kazakstan* **26 E7** 42 18N 69 36 E
Chimoio, *Mozam.* **55 F3** 19 4S 33 30 E
Chimpembe, *Zambia* **55 D2** 9 31S 29 33 E
Chin □, *Burma* **41 J18** 22 0N 93 0 E
Chin Ling Shan = Qinling Shandi, *China* **34 H5** 33 50N 108 10 E
China, *Mexico* **87 B5** 25 40N 99 20W
China ■, *Asia* **33 C6** 30 0N 110 0 E
China Lake, *U.S.A.* **85 K9** 35 44N 117 37W
Chinan = Jinan, *China* **34 F9** 36 38N 117 1 E
Chinandega, *Nic.* **88 D2** 12 35N 87 12W
Chinati Peak, *U.S.A.* **81 L2** 29 57N 104 29W
Chincha Alta, *Peru* **92 F3** 13 25S 76 7W
Chinchaga →, *Canada* **72 B5** 58 53N 118 20W
Chinchilla, *Australia* **63 D5** 26 45S 150 38 E
Chinchorro, Banco, *Mexico* **87 D7** 18 35N 87 20W
Chinchou = Jinzhou, *China* **35 D11** 41 5N 121 3 E
Chincoteague, *U.S.A.* **76 G8** 37 56N 75 23W
Chinde, *Mozam.* **55 F4** 18 35S 36 30 E
Chindo, *S. Korea* **35 G14** 34 28N 126 15 E
Chindwin →, *Burma* **41 J19** 21 26N 95 15 E
Chineni, *India* **43 C6** 33 2N 75 15 E
Chinga, *Mozam.* **55 F4** 15 13S 38 35 E
Chingola, *Zambia* **55 E2** 12 31S 27 53 E
Chingole, *Malawi* **55 E3** 13 4S 34 17 E
Ch'ingtao = Qingdao, *China* **35 F11** 36 5N 120 20 E
Chinguetti, *Mauritania* **50 D3** 20 25N 12 24W
Chingune, *Mozam.* **57 C5** 20 33S 34 58 E
Chinhae, *S. Korea* **35 G15** 35 9N 128 47 E
Chinhanguanine, *Mozam.* **57 D5** 25 21S 32 30 E
Chinhoyi, *Zimbabwe* **55 F3** 17 20S 30 8 E
Chini, *India* **42 D8** 31 32N 78 15 E
Chiniot, *Pakistan* **42 D5** 31 45N 73 0 E
Chinipas, *Mexico* **86 B3** 27 22N 108 32W
Chinji, *Pakistan* **42 C5** 32 42N 72 22 E
Chinju, *S. Korea* **35 G15** 35 12N 128 2 E
Chinle, *U.S.A.* **83 H9** 36 9N 109 33W
Chinnampo = Namp'o, *N. Korea* **35 E13** 38 52N 125 10 E
Chino, *Japan* **31 G9** 35 59N 138 9 E
Chino, *U.S.A.* **85 L9** 34 1N 117 41W
Chino Valley, *U.S.A.* **83 J7** 34 45N 112 27W
Chinon, *France* **18 C4** 47 10N 0 15 E
Chinook, *U.S.A.* **82 B9** 48 35N 109 14W
Chinsali, *Zambia* **55 E3** 10 30S 32 2 E
Chióggia, *Italy* **20 B5** 45 13N 12 17 E
Chíos = Khíos, *Greece* **21 E12** 38 27N 26 9 E
Chipata, *Zambia* **55 E3** 13 38S 32 28 E
Chipinge, *Zimbabwe* **55 G3** 20 13S 32 28 E
Chipley, *U.S.A.* **77 K3** 30 47N 85 32W
Chipman, *Canada* **71 C6** 46 6N 65 53W
Chipoka, *Malawi* **55 E3** 13 57S 34 28 E
Chippenham, *U.K.* **11 F5** 51 27N 2 6W
Chippewa →, *U.S.A.* **80 C8** 44 25N 92 5W
Chippewa Falls, *U.S.A.* **80 C9** 44 56N 91 24W
Chipping Norton, *U.K.* **11 F6** 51 56N 1 32W
Chiputneticook Lakes, *U.S.A.* **77 C11** 45 35N 67 35W
Chiquián, *Peru* **92 F3** 10 10S 77 0W
Chiquimula, *Guatemala* **88 D2** 14 51N 89 37W
Chiquinquira, *Colombia* **92 B4** 5 37N 73 50W
Chirala, *India* **40 M12** 15 50N 80 26 E
Chiramba, *Mozam.* **55 F3** 16 55S 34 39 E
Chirawa, *India* **42 E6** 28 14N 75 42 E
Chirchiq, *Uzbekistan* **26 E7** 41 29N 69 35 E
Chiredzi, *Zimbabwe* **57 C5** 21 0S 31 38 E
Chiricahua Peak, *U.S.A.* **83 L9** 31 51N 109 18W
Chiriquí, G. de, *Panama* **88 E3** 8 0N 82 10W
Chiriquí, L. de, *Panama* **88 E3** 9 10N 82 0W
Chirivira Falls, *Zimbabwe* **55 G3** 21 10S 32 12 E
Chirmiri, *India* **41 H13** 23 15N 82 20 E
Chirripó Grande, Cerro, *Costa Rica* **88 E3** 9 29N 83 29W
Chirundu, *Zimbabwe* **57 B4** 16 3S 28 50 E
Chisamba, *Zambia* **55 E2** 14 55S 28 20 E
Chisapani Garhi, *Nepal* **41 F14** 27 30N 84 2 E
Chisasibi, *Canada* **70 B4** 53 50N 79 0W
Chisholm, *Canada* **72 C6** 54 55N 114 10W
Chisholm, *U.S.A.* **80 B8** 47 29N 92 53W
Chishtian Mandi, *Pakistan* **42 E5** 29 50N 72 55 E
Chisimaio, *Somali Rep.* **49 G8** 0 22S 42 32 E
Chisimba Falls, *Zambia* **55 E3** 10 12S 30 56 E
Chişinău, *Moldova* **17 E15** 47 2N 28 50 E
Chisos Mts., *U.S.A.* **81 L3** 29 5N 103 15W
Chistopol, *Russia* **24 C9** 55 25N 50 38 E
Chita, *Russia* **27 D12** 52 0N 113 35 E
Chitipa, *Malawi* **55 D3** 9 41S 33 19 E
Chitose, *Japan* **30 C10** 42 49N 141 39 E
Chitral, *Pakistan* **40 B7** 35 50N 71 56 E
Chitré, *Panama* **88 E3** 7 59N 80 27W
Chittagong, *Bangla.* **41 H17** 22 19N 91 48 E
Chittagong □, *Bangla.* **41 G17** 24 5N 91 0 E
Chittaurgarh, *India* **42 G6** 24 52N 74 38 E
Chittoor, *India* **40 N11** 13 15N 79 5 E
Chitungwiza, *Zimbabwe* **55 F3** 18 0S 31 6 E
Chiusi, *Italy* **20 C4** 43 1N 11 57 E
Chivasso, *Italy* **18 D7** 45 11N 7 53 E
Chivhu, *Zimbabwe* **55 F3** 19 2S 30 52 E
Chivilcoy, *Argentina* **94 C4** 34 55S 60 0W
Chiwanda, *Tanzania* **55 E3** 11 23S 34 55 E
Chizarira, *Zimbabwe* **55 F2** 17 36S 27 45 E
Chizera, *Zambia* **55 E2** 13 10S 25 0 E
Chkalov = Orenburg, *Russia* **24 D10** 51 45N 55 6 E
Chloride, *U.S.A.* **85 K12** 35 25N 114 12W
Cho Bo, *Vietnam* **38 B5** 20 46N 105 10 E
Cho-do, *N. Korea* **35 E13** 38 30N 124 40 E
Cho Phuoc Hai, *Vietnam* **39 G6** 10 26N 107 18 E
Choba, *Kenya* **54 B4** 2 30N 38 5 E
Choch'iwŏn, *S. Korea* **35 F14** 36 37N 127 18 E
Chocolate Mts., *U.S.A.* **85 M11** 33 15N 115 15W
Choctawhatchee →, *U.S.A.* **77 K3** 30 25N 86 8W
Choele Choel, *Argentina* **96 D3** 39 11S 65 40W
Choix, *Mexico* **86 B3** 26 40N 108 23W
Chojnice, *Poland* **17 B9** 53 42N 17 32 E
Chōkai-San, *Japan* **30 E10** 39 6N 140 3 E
Choke Canyon L., *U.S.A.* **81 L5** 28 30N 98 20W
Chokurdakh, *Russia* **27 B15** 70 38N 147 55 E
Cholame, *U.S.A.* **84 K6** 35 44N 120 18W
Cholet, *France* **18 C3** 47 4N 0 52W
Cholguan, *Chile* **94 D1** 37 10S 72 3W
Choluteca, *Honduras* **88 D2** 13 20N 87 14W
Choluteca →, *Honduras* **88 D2** 13 0N 87 20W
Chom Bung, *Thailand* **38 F2** 13 37N 99 36 E
Chom Thong, *Thailand* **38 C2** 18 25N 98 41 E
Choma, *Zambia* **55 F2** 16 48S 26 59 E
Chomun, *India* **42 F6** 27 15N 75 40 E
Chomutov, *Czech Rep.* **16 C7** 50 28N 13 23 E
Chon Buri, *Thailand* **38 F3** 13 21N 101 1 E
Chon Thanh, *Vietnam* **39 G6** 11 24N 106 36 E
Ch'onan, *S. Korea* **35 F14** 36 48N 127 9 E
Chone, *Ecuador* **92 D3** 0 40S 80 0W
Chong Kai, *Cambodia* **38 F4** 13 57N 103 35 E
Chong Mek, *Thailand* **38 E5** 15 10N 105 27 E
Chŏngdo, *S. Korea* **35 G15** 35 38N 128 42 E
Chŏngha, *S. Korea* **35 F15** 36 12N 129 21 E
Chŏngjin, *N. Korea* **35 D15** 41 47N 129 50 E
Chŏngju, *S. Korea* **35 F14** 36 39N 127 27 E
Chŏngju, *N. Korea* **35 E13** 39 40N 125 5 E
Chongli, *China* **34 D8** 40 58N 115 15 E
Chongqing, *China* **32 D5** 29 35N 106 25 E
Chongqing Shi □, *China* **32 C5** 30 0N 108 0 E
Chonguene, *Mozam.* **57 C5** 25 3S 33 49 E
Chŏngŭp, *S. Korea* **35 G14** 35 35N 126 50 E
Chŏnju, *S. Korea* **35 G14** 35 50N 127 4 E
Chonos, Arch. de los, *Chile* **96 F2** 45 0S 75 0W
Chop, *Ukraine* **17 D12** 48 26N 22 12 E
Chopim →, *Brazil* **95 B5** 25 35S 53 5W
Chor, *Pakistan* **42 G3** 25 31N 69 46 E
Chorbat La, *India* **43 B7** 34 42N 76 37 E
Chorley, *U.K.* **10 D5** 53 39N 2 38W
Chornobyl, *Ukraine* **17 C16** 51 20N 30 15 E
Chorolque, Cerro, *Bolivia* **94 A2** 20 59S 66 5W
Chorregon, *Australia* **62 C3** 22 40S 143 32 E
Chortkiv, *Ukraine* **17 D13** 49 2N 25 46 E
Ch'ŏrwon, *S. Korea* **35 E14** 38 15N 127 10 E
Chorzów, *Poland* **17 C10** 50 18N 18 57 E
Chos-Malal, *Argentina* **94 D1** 37 20S 70 15W
Ch'osan, *N. Korea* **35 D13** 40 50N 125 47 E
Choszczno, *Poland* **16 B8** 53 7N 15 25 E
Choteau, *U.S.A.* **82 C7** 47 49N 112 11W
Chotila, *India* **42 H4** 22 23N 71 15 E
Chotta Udepur, *India* **42 H6** 22 19N 74 1 E
Chowchilla, *U.S.A.* **84 H6** 37 7N 120 16W
Choybalsan, *Mongolia* **33 B6** 48 4N 114 30 E
Christchurch, *N.Z.* **59 K4** 43 33S 172 47 E
Christchurch, *U.K.* **11 G6** 50 44N 1 47W
Christian I., *Canada* **78 B4** 44 50N 80 12W
Christiana, *S. Africa* **56 D4** 27 52S 25 8 E
Christiansted, *U.S. Virgin Is.* **89 C7** 17 45N 64 42W
Christie B., *Canada* **73 A6** 62 32N 111 10W
Christina →, *Canada* **73 B6** 56 40N 111 3W
Christmas Cr. →, *Australia* **60 C4** 18 29S 125 23 E
Christmas I. = Kiritimati, *Kiribati* **65 G12** 1 58N 157 27W
Christmas I., *Ind. Oc.* **64 J2** 10 30S 105 40 E
Christopher L., *Australia* **61 D4** 24 49S 127 42 E
Chtimba, *Malawi* **55 E3** 10 35S 34 13 E
Chu = Shū, *Kazakstan* **26 E8** 43 36N 73 42 E
Chu →, *Vietnam* **38 C5** 19 53N 105 45 E
Chu Lai, *Vietnam* **38 E7** 15 28N 108 45 E
Ch'uanchou = Quanzhou, *China* **33 D6** 24 55N 118 34 E
Chuankou, *China* **34 G6** 34 20N 110 59 E
Chubbuck, *U.S.A.* **82 E7** 42 55N 112 28W
Chūbu □, *Japan* **31 F8** 36 45N 137 30 E
Chubut →, *Argentina* **96 E3** 43 20S 65 5W
Chuchi L., *Canada* **72 B4** 55 12N 124 30W
Chuda, *India* **42 H4** 22 29N 71 41 E
Chudskoye, Ozero, *Russia* **9 G22** 58 13N 27 30 E
Chūgoku □, *Japan* **31 G6** 35 0N 133 0 E
Chūgoku-Sanchi, *Japan* **31 G6** 35 0N 133 0 E
Chugwater, *U.S.A.* **80 E2** 41 46N 104 50W
Chukchi Sea, *Russia* **27 C19** 68 0N 175 0W
Chukotskoye Nagorye, *Russia* **27 C18** 68 0N 175 0 E
Chula Vista, *U.S.A.* **85 N9** 32 39N 117 5W
Chulucanas, *Peru* **92 E2** 5 8S 80 10W
Chulym →, *Russia* **26 D9** 57 43N 83 51 E
Chum Phae, *Thailand* **38 D4** 16 40N 102 6 E
Chum Saeng, *Thailand* **38 E3** 15 55N 100 15 E
Chumar, *India* **43 C8** 32 40N 78 35 E
Chumbicha, *Argentina* **94 B2** 29 0S 66 10W
Chumikan, *Russia* **27 D14** 54 40N 135 10 E
Chumphon, *Thailand* **39 G2** 10 35N 99 14 E
Chumuare, *Mozam.* **55 E3** 14 31S 31 50 E
Chumunjin, *S. Korea* **35 F15** 37 55N 128 54 E
Chuna →, *Russia* **27 D10** 57 47N 94 37 E
Ch'unch'ŏn, *S. Korea* **35 F14** 37 58N 127 44 E
Chunchura, *India* **43 H13** 22 53N 88 27 E
Chunga, *Zambia* **55 F2** 15 0S 26 2 E
Chunggang-ŭp, *N. Korea* **35 D14** 41 48N 126 48 E
Chunghwa, *N. Korea* **35 E13** 38 52N 125 47 E
Ch'ungju, *S. Korea* **35 F14** 36 58N 127 58 E
Chungking = Chongqing, *China* **32 D5** 29 35N 106 25 E
Ch'ungmu, *S. Korea* **35 G15** 34 50N 128 20 E
Chungt'iaoshan = Zhongtiao Shan, *China* **34 G6** 35 0N 111 10 E
Chunian, *Pakistan* **42 D6** 30 57N 74 0 E
Chunya, *Tanzania* **55 D3** 8 30S 33 27 E
Chunyang, *China* **35 C15** 43 38N 129 23 E
Chuquibamba, *Peru* **92 G4** 15 47S 72 44W
Chuquicamata, *Chile* **94 A2** 22 15S 69 0W
Chur, *Switz.* **18 C8** 46 52N 9 32 E
Churachandpur, *India* **41 G18** 24 20N 93 40 E
Churchill, *Canada* **73 B10** 58 47N 94 11W
Churchill →, *Man., Canada* **73 B10** 58 47N 94 12W
Churchill →, *Nfld., Canada* **71 B7** 53 19N 60 10W
Churchill, C., *Canada* **73 B10** 58 46N 93 12W
Churchill Falls, *Canada* **71 B7** 53 36N 64 19W
Churchill L., *Canada* **73 B7** 55 55N 108 20W
Churchill Pk., *Canada* **72 B3** 58 10N 125 10W
Churki, *India* **43 H10** 23 50N 83 12 E
Churu, *India* **42 E6** 28 20N 74 50 E
Churún Merú = Angel Falls, *Venezuela* **92 B6** 5 57N 62 30W
Chushal, *India* **43 C8** 33 40N 78 40 E
Chuska Mts., *U.S.A.* **83 H9** 36 15N 108 50W
Chusovoy, *Russia* **24 C10** 58 22N 57 50 E
Chute-aux-Outardes, *Canada* **71 C6** 49 7N 68 24W
Chuuronjang, *N. Korea* **35 D15** 41 35N 129 40 E
Chuvash Republic = Chuvashia □, *Russia* **24 C8** 55 30N 47 0 E
Chuvashia □, *Russia* **24 C8** 55 30N 47 0 E
Chuwārtah, *Iraq* **44 C5** 35 43N 45 34 E
Chūy = Shū →, *Kazakstan* **28 E10** 45 0N 67 44 E
Chuy, *Uruguay* **95 C5** 33 41S 53 27W
Ci Xian, *China* **34 F8** 36 20N 114 25 E
Ciadâr-Lunga, *Moldova* **17 E15** 46 3N 28 51 E
Ciamis, *Indonesia* **37 G13** 7 20S 108 21 E
Cianjur, *Indonesia* **37 G12** 6 49S 107 8 E
Cianorte, *Brazil* **95 A5** 23 37S 52 37W
Cibola, *U.S.A.* **85 M12** 33 17N 114 42W
Cicero, *U.S.A.* **76 E2** 41 51N 87 45W
Ciechanów, *Poland* **17 B11** 52 52N 20 38 E
Ciego de Avila, *Cuba* **88 B4** 21 50N 78 50W
Ciénaga, *Colombia* **92 A4** 11 1N 74 15W
Cienfuegos, *Cuba* **88 B3** 22 10N 80 30W
Cieszyn, *Poland* **17 D10** 49 45N 18 35 E
Cieza, *Spain* **19 C5** 38 17N 1 23W
Cihuatlán, *Mexico* **86 D4** 19 14N 104 35W
Cijara, Embalse de, *Spain* **19 C3** 39 18N 4 52W
Cijulang, *Indonesia* **37 G13** 7 42S 108 27 E
Cilacap, *Indonesia* **37 G13** 7 43S 109 0 E
Cill Chainnigh = Kilkenny, *Ireland* **13 D4** 52 39N 7 15W
Cilo Dağı, *Turkey* **25 G7** 37 28N 43 55 E
Cima, *U.S.A.* **85 K11** 35 14N 115 30W
Cimarron, *Kans., U.S.A.* **81 G4** 37 48N 100 21W
Cimarron, *N. Mex., U.S.A.* **81 G2** 36 31N 104 55W
Cimarron →, *U.S.A.* **81 G6** 36 10N 96 17W
Cimişlia, *Moldova* **17 E15** 46 34N 28 44 E
Cimone, Mte., *Italy* **20 B4** 44 12N 10 42 E
Cinca →, *Spain* **19 B6** 41 26N 0 21 E
Cincar, *Bos.-H.* **20 C7** 43 55N 17 5 E
Cincinnati, *U.S.A.* **76 F3** 39 6N 84 31W
Cincinnatus, *U.S.A.* **79 D9** 42 33N 75 54W
Çine, *Turkey* **21 F13** 37 37N 28 2 E
Ciney, *Belgium* **15 D5** 50 18N 5 5 E
Cinto, Mte., *France* **18 E8** 42 24N 8 54 E
Circle, *Alaska, U.S.A.* **68 B5** 65 50N 144 4W
Circle, *Mont., U.S.A.* **80 B2** 47 25N 105 35W
Circleville, *U.S.A.* **76 F4** 39 36N 82 57W
Cirebon, *Indonesia* **36 F3** 6 45S 108 32 E
Ciremai, *Indonesia* **37 G13** 6 55S 108 27 E
Cirencester, *U.K.* **11 F6** 51 43N 1 57W
Cirium, *Cyprus* **23 E11** 34 40N 32 53 E
Cisco, *U.S.A.* **81 J5** 32 23N 98 59W
Citlaltépetl, *Mexico* **87 D5** 19 0N 97 20W
Citrus Heights, *U.S.A.* **84 G5** 38 42N 121 17W
Citrusdal, *S. Africa* **56 E2** 32 35S 19 0 E
Città di Castello, *Italy* **20 C5** 43 27N 12 14 E
Ciudad Altamirano, *Mexico* **86 D4** 18 20N 100 40W
Ciudad Bolívar, *Venezuela* **92 B6** 8 5N 63 36W
Ciudad Camargo, *Mexico* **86 B3** 27 41N 105 10W
Ciudad de Valles, *Mexico* **87 C5** 22 0N 99 0W
Ciudad del Carmen, *Mexico* **87 D6** 18 38N 91 50W
Ciudad del Este, *Paraguay* **95 B5** 25 30S 54 50W
Ciudad Delicias = Delicias, *Mexico* **86 B3** 28 10N 105 30W
Ciudad Guayana, *Venezuela* **92 B6** 8 0N 62 30W
Ciudad Guerrero, *Mexico* **86 B3** 28 33N 107 28W
Ciudad Guzmán, *Mexico* **86 D4** 19 40N 103 30W
Ciudad Juárez, *Mexico* **86 A3** 31 40N 106 28W
Ciudad Madero, *Mexico* **87 C5** 22 19N 97 50W
Ciudad Mante, *Mexico* **87 C5** 22 50N 99 0W
Ciudad Obregón, *Mexico* **86 B3** 27 28N 109 59W
Ciudad Real, *Spain* **19 C4** 38 59N 3 55W
Ciudad Rodrigo, *Spain* **19 B2** 40 35N 6 32W
Ciudad Trujillo = Santo Domingo, *Dom. Rep.* **89 C6** 18 30N 69 59W
Ciudad Victoria, *Mexico* **87 C5** 23 41N 99 9W
Ciudadela, *Spain* **22 B10** 40 0N 3 50 E
Civitanova Marche, *Italy* **20 C5** 43 18N 13 44 E
Civitavécchia, *Italy* **20 C4** 42 6N 11 48 E
Cizre, *Turkey* **25 G7** 37 19N 42 10 E
Clackmannanshire □, *U.K.* **12 E5** 56 10N 3 43W
Clacton-on-Sea, *U.K.* **11 F9** 51 47N 1 11 E
Claire, L., *Canada* **72 B6** 58 35N 112 5W
Clairton, *U.S.A.* **78 F5** 40 18N 79 53W
Clallam Bay, *U.S.A.* **84 B2** 48 15N 124 16W
Clanton, *U.S.A.* **77 J2** 32 51N 86 38W
Clanwilliam, *S. Africa* **56 E2** 32 11S 18 52 E
Clara, *Ireland* **13 C4** 53 21N 7 37W
Claraville, *U.S.A.* **85 K8** 35 24N 118 20W
Clare, *Australia* **63 E2** 33 50S 138 37 E
Clare, *U.S.A.* **76 D3** 43 49N 84 46W
Clare □, *Ireland* **13 D3** 52 45N 9 0W
Clare →, *Ireland* **13 C2** 53 20N 9 2W
Clare I., *Ireland* **13 C1** 53 49N 10 0W
Claremont, *Calif., U.S.A.* **85 L9** 34 6N 117 43W
Claremont, *N.H., U.S.A.* **79 C12** 43 23N 72 20W
Claremont Pt., *Australia* **62 A3** 14 1S 143 41 E
Claremore, *U.S.A.* **81 G7** 36 19N 95 36W
Claremorris, *Ireland* **13 C3** 53 45N 9 0W
Clarence →, *Australia* **63 D5** 29 25S 153 22 E
Clarence →, *N.Z.* **59 K4** 42 10S 173 56 E
Clarence, I., *Chile* **96 G2** 54 0S 72 0W
Clarence I., *Antarctica* **5 C18** 61 10S 54 0W
Clarence Str., *Australia* **60 B5** 12 0S 131 0 E
Clarence Town, *Bahamas* **89 B5** 23 6N 74 59W
Clarendon, *Pa., U.S.A.* **78 E5** 41 47N 79 6W
Clarendon, *Tex., U.S.A.* **81 H4** 34 56N 100 53W
Clarenville, *Canada* **71 C9** 48 10N 54 1W
Claresholm, *Canada* **72 D6** 50 0N 113 33W
Clarie Coast, *Antarctica* **5 C9** 68 0S 135 0 E
Clarinda, *U.S.A.* **80 E7** 40 44N 95 2W
Clarion, *Iowa, U.S.A.* **80 D8** 42 44N 93 44W
Clarion, *Pa., U.S.A.* **78 E5** 41 13N 79 23W
Clarion →, *U.S.A.* **78 E5** 41 7N 79 41W
Clark, *U.S.A.* **80 C6** 44 53N 97 44W
Clark, Pt., *Canada* **78 B3** 44 4N 81 45W
Clark Fork, *U.S.A.* **82 B5** 48 9N 116 11W
Clark Fork →, *U.S.A.* **82 B5** 48 9N 116 15W
Clarkdale, *U.S.A.* **83 J7** 34 46N 112 3W
Clarke City, *Canada* **71 B6** 50 12N 66 38W
Clarke I., *Australia* **62 G4** 40 32S 148 10 E
Clarke Ra., *Australia* **62 C4** 20 40S 148 30 E
Clark's Fork →, *U.S.A.* **82 D9** 45 39N 108 43W
Clark's Harbour, *Canada* **71 D6** 43 25N 65 38W
Clarks Hill L., *U.S.A.* **77 J4** 33 40N 82 12W
Clarks Summit, *U.S.A.* **79 E9** 41 30N 75 42W
Clarksburg, *U.S.A.* **76 F5** 39 17N 80 30W
Clarksdale, *U.S.A.* **81 H9** 34 12N 90 35W
Clarksville, *Ark., U.S.A.* **81 H8** 35 28N 93 28W
Clarksville, *Tenn., U.S.A.* **77 G2** 36 32N 87 21W
Clarksville, *Tex., U.S.A.* **81 J7** 33 37N 95 3W
Clatskanie, *U.S.A.* **84 D3** 46 6N 123 12W
Claude, *U.S.A.* **81 H4** 35 7N 101 22W
Claveria, *Phil.* **37 A6** 18 37N 121 4 E
Clay, *U.S.A.* **84 G5** 38 17N 121 10W
Clay Center, *U.S.A.* **80 F6** 39 23N 97 8W
Claypool, *U.S.A.* **83 K8** 33 25N 110 51W
Claysburg, *U.S.A.* **78 F6** 40 17N 78 27W
Claysville, *U.S.A.* **78 F4** 40 7N 80 25W
Clayton, *N. Mex., U.S.A.* **81 G3** 36 27N 103 11W
Clayton, *N.Y., U.S.A.* **79 B8** 44 14N 76 5W
Clear, C., *Ireland* **13 E2** 51 25N 9 32W
Clear, L., *Canada* **78 A7** 45 26N 77 12W
Clear Hills, *Canada* **72 B5** 56 40N 119 30W
Clear I., *Ireland* **13 E2** 51 26N 9 30W
Clear L., *U.S.A.* **84 F4** 39 2N 122 47W
Clear Lake, *Iowa, U.S.A.* **80 D8** 43 8N 93 23W
Clear Lake, *S. Dak., U.S.A.* **80 C6** 44 45N 96 41W
Clear Lake Reservoir, *U.S.A.* **82 F3** 41 56N 121 5W
Clearfield, *Pa., U.S.A.* **78 E6** 41 2N 78 27W
Clearfield, *Utah, U.S.A.* **82 F8** 41 7N 112 2W
Clearlake, *U.S.A.* **82 G2** 38 57N 122 38W
Clearlake Highlands, *U.S.A.* **84 G4** 38 57N 122 38W
Clearwater, *Canada* **72 C4** 51 38N 120 2W
Clearwater, *U.S.A.* **77 M4** 27 58N 82 48W
Clearwater →, *Alta., Canada* **72 C6** 52 22N 114 57W
Clearwater →, *Alta., Canada* **73 B6** 56 44N 111 23W
Clearwater L., *Canada* **73 C9** 53 34N 99 49W
Clearwater Mts., *U.S.A.* **82 C6** 46 5N 115 20W
Clearwater Prov. Park, *Canada* **73 C8** 54 0N 101 0W
Clearwater River Prov. Park, *Canada* **73 B7** 56 55N 109 10W
Cleburne, *U.S.A.* **81 J6** 32 21N 97 23W
Clee Hills, *U.K.* **11 E5** 52 26N 2 35W
Cleethorpes, *U.K.* **10 D7** 53 33N 0 3W
Cleeve Cloud, *U.K.* **11 F6** 51 56N 2 0W
Clemson, *U.S.A.* **77 H4** 34 41N 82 50W
Clerke Reef, *Australia* **60 C2** 17 22S 119 20 E
Clermont, *Australia* **62 C4** 22 49S 147 39 E
Clermont, *U.S.A.* **77 L5** 28 33N 81 46W
Clermont-Ferrand, *France* **18 D5** 45 46N 3 4 E
Clervaux, *Lux.* **15 D6** 50 4N 6 2 E
Clevedon, *U.K.* **11 F5** 51 26N 2 52W
Cleveland, *Miss., U.S.A.* **81 J9** 33 45N 90 43W
Cleveland, *Ohio, U.S.A.* **78 E3** 41 30N 81 42W
Cleveland, *Okla., U.S.A.* **81 G6** 36 19N 96 28W
Cleveland, *Tenn., U.S.A.* **77 H3** 35 10N 84 53W
Cleveland, *Tex., U.S.A.* **81 K7** 30 21N 95 5W
Cleveland, C., *Australia* **62 B4** 19 11S 147 1 E
Cleveland, Mt., *U.S.A.* **82 B7** 48 56N 113 51W
Cleveland Heights, *U.S.A.* **78 E3** 41 30N 81 34W
Clevelândia, *Brazil* **95 B5** 26 24S 52 23W
Clew B., *Ireland* **13 C2** 53 50N 9 49W
Clewiston, *U.S.A.* **77 M5** 26 45N 80 56W
Clifden, *Ireland* **13 C1** 53 29N 10 1W
Clifden, *N.Z.* **59 M1** 46 1S 167 42 E
Cliffdell, *U.S.A.* **84 D5** 46 56N 121 5W
Cliffy Hd., *Australia* **61 G2** 35 1S 116 29 E
Clifton, *Australia* **63 D5** 27 59S 151 53 E
Clifton, *Ariz., U.S.A.* **83 K9** 33 3N 109 18W
Clifton, *Colo., U.S.A.* **83 G9** 39 7N 108 25W
Clifton, *Tex., U.S.A.* **81 K6** 31 47N 97 35W
Clifton Beach, *Australia* **62 B4** 16 46S 145 39 E
Climax, *Canada* **73 D7** 49 10N 108 20W

Coral Sea

Clinch →, U.S.A. 77 H3 35 53N 84 29W
Clingmans Dome, U.S.A. 77 H4 35 34N 83 30W
Clint, U.S.A. 83 L10 31 35N 106 14W
Clinton, B.C., Canada 72 C4 51 6N 121 35W
Clinton, Ont., Canada 78 C3 43 37N 81 32W
Clinton, N.Z. 59 M2 46 12S 169 23 E
Clinton, Ark., U.S.A. 81 H8 35 36N 92 28W
Clinton, Conn., U.S.A. 79 E12 41 17N 72 32W
Clinton, Ill., U.S.A. 80 E10 40 9N 88 57W
Clinton, Ind., U.S.A. 76 F2 39 40N 87 24W
Clinton, Iowa, U.S.A. 80 E9 41 51N 90 12W
Clinton, Mass., U.S.A. 79 D13 42 25N 71 41W
Clinton, Miss., U.S.A. 81 J9 32 20N 90 20W
Clinton, Mo., U.S.A. 80 F8 38 22N 93 46W
Clinton, N.C., U.S.A. 77 H6 35 0N 78 22W
Clinton, Okla., U.S.A. 81 H5 35 31N 98 58W
Clinton, S.C., U.S.A. 77 H5 34 29N 81 53W
Clinton, Tenn., U.S.A. 77 G3 36 6N 84 8W
Clinton, Wash., U.S.A. 84 C4 47 59N 122 21W
Clinton C., Australia 62 C5 22 30S 150 45 E
Clinton Colden L., Canada 68 B9 63 58N 107 27W
Clintonville, U.S.A. 80 C10 44 37N 88 46W
Clipperton, I., Pac. Oc. 65 F17 10 18N 109 13W
Clisham, U.K. 12 D2 57 57N 6 49W
Clitheroe, U.K. 10 D5 53 53N 2 22W
Clo-oose, Canada 84 B2 48 39N 124 49W
Cloates, Pt., Australia 60 D1 22 43S 113 40 E
Clocolan, S. Africa 57 D4 28 55S 27 34 E
Clodomira, Argentina 94 B3 27 35S 64 14W
Clogher Hd., Ireland 13 C5 53 48N 6 14W
Clonakilty, Ireland 13 E3 51 37N 8 53W
Clonakilty B., Ireland 13 E3 51 35N 8 51W
Cloncurry, Australia 62 C3 20 40S 140 28 E
Cloncurry →, Australia 62 B3 18 37S 140 40 E
Clondalkin, Ireland 13 C5 53 19N 6 25W
Clones, Ireland 13 B4 54 11N 7 15W
Clonmel, Ireland 13 D4 52 21N 7 42W
Cloquet, U.S.A. 80 B8 46 43N 92 28W
Clorinda, Argentina 94 B4 25 16S 57 45W
Cloud Bay, Canada 70 C2 48 5N 89 26W
Cloud Peak, U.S.A. 82 D10 44 23N 107 11W
Cloudcroft, U.S.A. 83 K11 32 58N 105 45W
Cloverdale, U.S.A. 84 G4 38 48N 123 1W
Clovis, Calif., U.S.A. 84 J7 36 49N 119 42W
Clovis, N. Mex., U.S.A. 81 H3 34 24N 103 12W
Cloyne, Canada 78 B7 44 49N 77 11W
Cluj-Napoca, Romania 17 E12 46 47N 23 38 E
Clunes, Australia 63 F3 37 20S 143 45 E
Clutha →, N.Z. 59 M2 46 20S 169 49 E
Clwyd →, U.K. 10 D4 53 19N 3 31W
Clyde, Canada 72 C6 54 9N 113 39W
Clyde, N.Z. 59 L2 45 12S 169 20 E
Clyde, U.S.A. 78 C8 43 5N 76 52W
Clyde →, U.K. 12 F4 55 55N 4 30W
Clyde, Firth of, U.K. 12 F3 55 22N 5 1W
Clyde River, Canada 69 A13 70 30N 68 30W
Clydebank, U.K. 12 F4 55 54N 4 23W
Clymer, N.Y., U.S.A. 78 D5 42 1N 79 37W
Clymer, Pa., U.S.A. 78 D5 40 40N 79 1W
Coachella, U.S.A. 85 M10 33 41N 116 10W
Coachella Canal, U.S.A. 85 N12 32 43N 114 57W
Coahoma, U.S.A. 81 J4 32 18N 101 18W
Coahuayana →, Mexico 86 D4 18 41N 103 45W
Coahuila □, Mexico 86 B4 27 0N 103 0W
Coal →, Canada 72 B3 59 39N 126 57W
Coalane, Mozam. 55 F4 17 48S 37 2 E
Coalcomán, Mexico 86 D4 18 40N 103 10W
Coaldale, Canada 72 D6 49 45N 112 35W
Coalgate, U.S.A. 81 H6 34 32N 96 13W
Coalinga, U.S.A. 84 J6 36 9N 120 21W
Coalisland, U.K. 13 B5 54 33N 6 42W
Coalville, U.K. 10 E6 52 44N 1 23W
Coalville, U.S.A. 82 F8 40 55N 111 24W
Coari, Brazil 92 D6 4 8S 63 7W
Coast □, Kenya 54 C4 2 40S 39 45 E
Coast Mts., Canada 72 C3 55 0N 129 20W
Coast Ranges, U.S.A. 84 G4 39 0N 123 0W
Coatbridge, U.K. 12 F4 55 52N 4 6W
Coatepec, Mexico 87 D5 19 27N 96 58W
Coatepeque, Guatemala 88 D1 14 46N 91 55W
Coatesville, U.S.A. 76 F8 39 59N 75 50W
Coaticook, Canada 79 A13 45 10N 71 46W
Coats I., Canada 69 B11 62 30N 83 0W
Coats Land, Antarctica 5 D1 77 0S 25 0W
Coatzacoalcos, Mexico 87 D6 18 7N 94 25W
Cobalt, Canada 70 C4 47 25N 79 42W
Cobán, Guatemala 88 C1 15 30N 90 21W
Cobar, Australia 63 E4 31 27S 145 48 E
Cóbh, Ireland 13 E3 51 51N 8 17W
Cobija, Bolivia 92 F5 11 0S 68 50W
Cobleskill, U.S.A. 79 D10 42 41N 74 29W
Coboconk, Canada 78 B6 44 39N 78 48W
Cobourg, Canada 78 C6 43 58N 78 10W
Cobourg Pen., Australia 60 B5 11 20S 132 15 E
Cobram, Australia 63 F4 35 54S 145 40 E
Cóbué, Mozam. 55 E3 12 0S 34 58 E
Coburg, Germany 16 C6 50 15N 10 58 E
Cocanada = Kakinada, India 41 L13 16 57N 82 11 E
Cochabamba, Bolivia 92 G5 17 26S 66 10W
Cochemane, Mozam. 55 F3 17 0S 32 54 E
Cochin, India 40 Q10 9 58N 76 20 E
Cochin China = Nam-Phan, Vietnam 39 G6 10 30N 106 0 E
Cochran, U.S.A. 77 J4 32 23N 83 21W
Cochrane, Alta., Canada 72 C6 51 11N 114 30W
Cochrane, Ont., Canada 70 C3 49 0N 81 0W
Cochrane, Chile 96 F2 47 15S 72 33W
Cochrane →, Canada 73 B8 59 0N 103 40W
Cochrane, L., Chile 96 F2 47 10S 72 0W
Cochranton, U.S.A. 78 E4 41 31N 80 3W
Cockburn, Australia 63 E3 32 5S 141 0 E
Cockburn, Canal, Chile 96 G2 54 30S 72 0W
Cockburn I., Canada 70 C3 45 55N 83 22W
Cockburn Ra., Australia 60 C4 15 46S 128 0 E
Cockermouth, U.K. 10 C4 54 40N 3 22W
Cocklebiddy, Australia 61 F4 32 0S 126 3 E
Coco →, Cent. Amer. 88 D3 15 0N 83 8W
Coco, I. del, Pac. Oc. 65 G19 5 25N 87 55W
Cocoa, U.S.A. 77 L5 28 21N 80 44W
Cocobeach, Gabon 52 D1 0 59N 9 34 E
Cocos Is., Ind. Oc. 64 J1 12 10S 96 55 E
Cod, C., U.S.A. 76 D10 42 5N 70 10W
Codajás, Brazil 92 D6 3 55S 62 0W
Codó, Brazil 93 D10 4 30S 43 55W
Cody, U.S.A. 82 D9 44 32N 109 3W
Coe Hill, Canada 78 B7 44 52N 77 50W
Coelemu, Chile 94 D1 36 30S 72 48W
Coen, Australia 62 A3 13 52S 143 12 E
Cœur d'Alene, U.S.A. 82 C5 47 45N 116 51W
Cœur d'Alene L., U.S.A. 82 C5 47 32N 116 48W
Coevorden, Neths. 15 B6 52 40N 6 44 E
Cofete, Canary Is. 22 F5 28 6N 14 23W
Coffeyville, U.S.A. 81 G7 37 2N 95 37W
Coffin B., Australia 63 E2 34 38S 135 28 E
Coffin Bay, Australia 63 E2 34 37S 135 29 E
Coffin Bay Peninsula, Australia 63 E2 34 32S 135 15 E
Coffs Harbour, Australia 63 E5 30 16S 153 5 E
Cognac, France 18 D3 45 41N 0 20W
Cohocton, U.S.A. 78 D7 42 30N 77 30W
Cohocton →, U.S.A. 78 D7 42 9N 77 6W
Cohoes, U.S.A. 79 D11 42 46N 73 42W
Cohuna, Australia 63 F3 35 45S 144 15 E
Coiba, I., Panama 88 E3 7 30N 81 40W
Coig →, Argentina 96 G3 51 0S 69 10W
Coigeach, Rubha, U.K. 12 C3 58 6N 5 26W
Coihaique, Chile 96 F2 45 30S 71 45W
Coimbatore, India 40 P10 11 2N 76 59 E
Coimbra, Brazil 92 G7 19 55S 57 48W
Coimbra, Portugal 19 B1 40 15N 8 27W
Coín, Spain 19 D3 36 40N 4 48W
Coipasa, Salar de, Bolivia 92 G5 19 26S 68 9W
Cojimies, Ecuador 92 C3 0 20N 80 0W
Cojutepequé, El Salv. 88 D2 13 41N 88 54W
Cokeville, U.S.A. 82 E8 42 5N 110 57W
Colac, Australia 63 F3 38 21S 143 35 E
Colatina, Brazil 93 G10 19 32S 40 37W
Colbeck, C., Antarctica 5 D13 77 6S 157 48W
Colborne, Canada 78 C7 44 0N 77 53W
Colby, U.S.A. 80 F4 39 24N 101 3W
Colchester, U.K. 11 F8 51 54N 0 55 E
Cold L., Canada 73 C7 54 33N 110 5W
Coldstream, Canada 72 C5 50 13N 119 11W
Coldstream, U.K. 12 F6 55 39N 2 15W
Coldwater, Canada 78 B5 44 42N 79 40W
Coldwater, Kans., U.S.A. 81 G5 37 16N 99 20W
Coldwater, Mich., U.S.A. 76 E3 41 57N 85 0W
Colebrook, U.S.A. 79 B13 44 54N 71 30W
Coleman, U.S.A. 81 K5 31 50N 99 26W
Coleman →, Australia 62 B3 15 6S 141 38 E
Colenso, S. Africa 57 D4 28 44S 29 50 E
Coleraine, Australia 63 F3 37 36S 141 40 E
Coleraine, U.K. 13 A5 55 8N 6 41W
Coleridge, L., N.Z. 59 K3 43 17S 171 30 E
Colesberg, S. Africa 56 E4 30 45S 25 5 E
Coleville, U.S.A. 84 G7 38 34N 119 30W
Colfax, Calif., U.S.A. 84 F6 39 6N 120 57W
Colfax, La., U.S.A. 81 K8 31 31N 92 42W
Colfax, Wash., U.S.A. 82 C5 46 53N 117 22W
Colhué Huapi, L., Argentina 96 F3 45 30S 69 0W
Coligny, S. Africa 57 D4 26 17S 26 15 E
Colima, Mexico 86 D4 19 14N 103 43W
Colima □, Mexico 86 D4 19 10N 103 40W
Colima, Nevado de, Mexico 86 D4 19 35N 103 45W
Colina, Chile 94 C1 33 13S 70 45W
Colinas, Brazil 93 E10 6 0S 44 10W
Coll, U.K. 12 E2 56 39N 6 34W
Collaguasi, Chile 94 A2 21 5S 68 45W
Collarenebri, Australia 63 D4 29 33S 148 34 E
Colleen Bawn, Zimbabwe 55 G2 21 0S 29 12 E
College Park, U.S.A. 77 J3 33 40N 84 27W
College Station, U.S.A. 81 K6 30 37N 96 21W
Collie, Australia 61 F2 33 22S 116 8 E
Collier B., Australia 60 C3 16 10S 124 15 E
Collier Ra., Australia 61 D2 24 45S 119 10 E
Collina, Passo di, Italy 20 B4 44 2N 10 56 E
Collingwood, Canada 78 B4 44 29N 80 13W
Collingwood, N.Z. 59 J4 40 41S 172 40 E
Collins, Canada 70 B2 50 17N 89 27W
Collinsville, Australia 62 C4 20 30S 147 56 E
Collipulli, Chile 94 D1 37 55S 72 30W
Collooney, Ireland 13 B3 54 11N 8 29W
Colmar, France 18 B7 48 5N 7 20 E
Colo →, Australia 63 E5 33 25S 150 52 E
Cologne = Köln, Germany 16 C4 50 56N 6 57 E
Colom, I. d'en, Spain 22 B11 39 58N 4 16 E
Coloma, U.S.A. 84 G6 38 48N 120 53W
Colomb-Béchar = Béchar, Algeria 50 B5 31 38N 2 18W
Colombia ■, S. Amer. 92 C4 3 45N 73 0W
Colombian Basin, S. Amer. 66 H12 14 0N 76 0W
Colombo, Sri Lanka 40 R11 6 56N 79 58 E
Colón, Buenos Aires, Argentina 94 C3 33 53S 61 7W
Colón, Entre Ríos, Argentina 94 C4 32 12S 58 10W
Colón, Cuba 88 B3 22 42N 80 54W
Colón, Panama 88 E4 9 20N 79 54W
Colònia de Sant Jordi, Spain 22 B9 39 19N 2 59 E
Colonia del Sacramento, Uruguay 94 C4 34 25S 57 50W
Colonia Dora, Argentina 94 B3 28 34S 62 59W
Colonial Beach, U.S.A. 76 F7 38 15N 76 58W
Colonie, U.S.A. 79 D11 42 43N 73 50W
Colonsay, Canada 73 C7 51 59N 105 52W
Colonsay, U.K. 12 E2 56 5N 6 12W
Colorado □, U.S.A. 83 G10 39 30N 105 30W
Colorado →, Argentina 96 D4 39 50S 62 8W
Colorado →, N. Amer. 83 L6 31 45N 114 40W
Colorado →, U.S.A. 81 L7 28 36N 95 59W
Colorado City, U.S.A. 81 J4 32 24N 100 52W
Colorado Plateau, U.S.A. 83 H8 37 0N 111 0W
Colorado River Aqueduct, U.S.A. 85 L12 34 17N 114 10W
Colorado Springs, U.S.A. 80 F2 38 50N 104 49W
Colotlán, Mexico 86 C4 22 6N 103 16W
Colstrip, U.S.A. 82 D10 45 53N 106 38W
Colton, U.S.A. 79 B10 44 33N 74 56W
Columbia, Ky., U.S.A. 76 G3 37 6N 85 18W
Columbia, La., U.S.A. 81 J8 32 6N 92 5W
Columbia, Miss., U.S.A. 81 K10 31 15N 89 50W
Columbia, Mo., U.S.A. 80 F8 38 57N 92 20W
Columbia, Pa., U.S.A. 79 F8 40 2N 76 30W
Columbia, S.C., U.S.A. 77 J5 34 0N 81 2W
Columbia, Tenn., U.S.A. 77 H2 35 37N 87 2W
Columbia →, N. Amer. 84 D2 46 15N 124 5W
Columbia, C., Canada 4 A4 83 0N 70 0W
Columbia, District of □, U.S.A. 76 F7 38 55N 77 0W
Columbia, Mt., Canada 72 C5 52 8N 117 20W
Columbia Basin, U.S.A. 82 C4 46 45N 119 5W
Columbia Falls, U.S.A. 82 B6 48 23N 114 11W
Columbia Mts., Canada 72 C5 52 0N 119 0W
Columbia Plateau, U.S.A. 82 D5 44 0N 117 30W
Columbiana, U.S.A. 78 F4 40 53N 80 42W
Columbretes, Is., Spain 19 C6 39 50N 0 50 E
Columbus, Ga., U.S.A. 77 J3 32 28N 84 59W
Columbus, Ind., U.S.A. 76 F3 39 13N 85 55W
Columbus, Kans., U.S.A. 81 G7 37 10N 94 50W
Columbus, Miss., U.S.A. 77 J1 33 30N 88 25W
Columbus, Mont., U.S.A. 82 D9 45 38N 109 15W
Columbus, N. Mex., U.S.A. 83 L10 31 50N 107 38W
Columbus, Nebr., U.S.A. 80 E6 41 26N 97 22W
Columbus, Ohio, U.S.A. 76 F4 39 58N 83 0W
Columbus, Tex., U.S.A. 81 L6 29 42N 96 33W
Colusa, U.S.A. 84 F4 39 13N 122 1W
Colville, U.S.A. 82 B5 48 33N 117 54W
Colville →, U.S.A. 68 A4 70 25N 150 30W
Colville, C., N.Z. 59 G5 36 29S 175 21 E
Colwood, Canada 84 B3 48 26N 123 29W
Colwyn Bay, U.K. 10 D4 53 18N 3 44W
Comácchio, Italy 20 B5 44 42N 12 11 E
Comalcalco, Mexico 87 D6 18 16N 93 13W
Comallo, Argentina 96 E2 41 0S 70 5W
Comanche, U.S.A. 81 K5 31 54N 98 36W
Comayagua, Honduras 88 D2 14 25N 87 37W
Combahee →, U.S.A. 77 J5 32 30N 80 31W
Combarbalá, Chile 94 C1 31 11S 71 2W
Comber, Canada 78 D2 42 14N 82 33W
Comber, U.K. 13 B6 54 33N 5 45W
Combermere, Canada 78 A7 45 22N 77 37W
Comblain-au-Pont, Belgium 15 D5 50 29N 5 35 E
Comeragh Mts., Ireland 13 D4 52 18N 7 34W
Comet, Australia 62 C4 23 36S 148 38 E
Comilla, Bangla. 41 H17 23 28N 91 10 E
Comino, Malta 23 C1 36 1N 14 20 E
Comino, C., Italy 20 D3 40 32N 9 49 E
Comitán, Mexico 87 D6 16 18N 92 9W
Commerce, Ga., U.S.A. 77 H4 34 12N 83 28W
Commerce, Tex., U.S.A. 81 J7 33 15N 95 54W
Committee B., Canada 69 B11 68 30N 86 30W
Commonwealth B., Antarctica 5 C10 67 0S 144 0 E
Commoron Cr. →, Australia 63 D5 28 22S 150 8 E
Communism Pk. = Kommunizma, Pik, Tajikistan 26 F8 39 0N 72 2 E
Como, Italy 18 D8 45 47N 9 5 E
Como, Lago di, Italy 18 D8 46 0N 9 11 E
Comodoro Rivadavia, Argentina 96 F3 45 50S 67 40W
Comorin, C., India 40 Q10 8 3N 77 40 E
Comoro Is. = Comoros ■, Ind. Oc. 49 H8 12 10S 44 15 E
Comoros ■, Ind. Oc. 49 H8 12 10S 44 15 E
Comox, Canada 72 D4 49 42N 124 55W
Compiègne, France 18 B5 49 24N 2 50 E
Compostela, Mexico 86 C4 21 15N 104 53W
Comprida, I., Brazil 95 A6 24 50S 47 42W
Compton, Canada 79 A13 45 14N 71 49W
Compton, U.S.A. 85 M8 33 54N 118 13W
Comrat, Moldova 17 E15 46 18N 28 40 E
Con Cuong, Vietnam 38 C5 19 2N 104 54 E
Con Son, Vietnam 39 H6 8 41N 106 37 E
Conakry, Guinea 50 G3 9 29N 13 49W
Conara, Australia 62 G4 41 50S 147 26 E
Concarneau, France 18 C2 47 52N 3 56W
Conceição, Mozam. 55 F4 18 47S 36 7 E
Conceição da Barra, Brazil 93 G11 18 35S 39 45W
Conceição do Araguaia, Brazil 93 E9 8 0S 49 2W
Concepción, Argentina 94 B2 27 20S 65 35W
Concepción, Bolivia 92 G6 16 15S 62 8W
Concepción, Chile 94 D1 36 50S 73 0W
Concepción, Mexico 87 D6 18 15N 90 5W
Concepción, Paraguay 94 A4 23 22S 57 26W
Concepción □, Chile 94 D1 37 0S 72 30W
Concepción →, Mexico 86 A2 30 32N 113 2W
Concepción, Est. de, Chile 96 G2 50 30S 74 55W
Concepción, L., Bolivia 92 G6 17 20S 61 20W
Concepción, Punta, Mexico 86 B2 26 55N 111 59W
Concepción del Oro, Mexico 86 C4 24 40N 101 30W
Concepción del Uruguay, Argentina 94 C4 32 35S 58 20W
Conception, Pt., U.S.A. 85 L6 34 27N 120 28W
Conception B., Canada 71 C9 47 45N 53 0W
Conception B., Namibia 56 C1 23 55S 14 22 E
Conception I., Bahamas 89 B4 23 52N 75 9W
Concession, Zimbabwe 55 F3 17 27S 30 56 E
Conchas Dam, U.S.A. 81 H2 35 22N 104 11W
Concho, U.S.A. 83 J9 34 28N 109 36W
Concho →, U.S.A. 81 K5 31 34N 99 43W
Conchos →, Chihuahua, Mexico 86 B4 29 32N 105 0W
Conchos →, Tamaulipas, Mexico 87 B5 25 9N 98 35W
Concord, Calif., U.S.A. 84 H4 37 59N 122 2W
Concord, N.C., U.S.A. 77 H5 35 25N 80 35W
Concord, N.H., U.S.A. 79 C13 43 12N 71 32W
Concordia, Argentina 94 C4 31 20S 58 2W
Concórdia, Brazil 92 D5 4 36S 66 36W
Concordia, Mexico 86 C3 23 18N 106 2W
Concordia, U.S.A. 80 F6 39 34N 97 40W
Concrete, U.S.A. 82 B3 48 32N 121 45W
Condamine, Australia 63 D5 26 56S 150 9 E
Conde, U.S.A. 80 C5 45 9N 98 6W
Condeúba, Brazil 93 F10 14 52S 42 0W
Condobolin, Australia 63 E4 33 4S 147 6 E
Condon, U.S.A. 82 D3 45 14N 120 11W
Conegliano, Italy 20 B5 45 53N 12 18 E
Conejera, I. = Conills, I. des, Spain 22 B9 39 11N 2 58 E
Conejos, Mexico 86 B4 26 14N 103 53W
Confuso →, Paraguay 94 B4 25 9S 57 34W
Congleton, U.K. 10 D5 53 10N 2 13W
Congo (Kinshasa) = Congo, Dem. Rep. of the ■, Africa 52 E4 3 0S 23 0 E
Congo ■, Africa 52 E3 1 0S 16 0 E
Congo →, Africa 52 F2 6 4S 12 24 E
Congo, Dem. Rep. of the ■, Africa 52 E4 3 0S 23 0 E
Congo Basin, Africa 52 E4 0 10S 24 30 E
Congonhas, Brazil 95 A7 20 30S 43 52W
Congress, U.S.A. 83 J7 34 9N 112 51W
Conills, I. des, Spain 22 B9 39 11N 2 58 E
Coniston, Canada 70 C3 46 29N 80 51W
Conjeeveram = Kanchipuram, India 40 N11 12 52N 79 45 E
Conklin, Canada 73 B6 55 38N 111 5W
Conklin, U.S.A. 79 D9 42 2N 75 49W
Conn, L., Ireland 13 B2 54 3N 9 15W
Connacht □, Ireland 13 C2 53 43N 9 12W
Conneaut, U.S.A. 78 E4 41 57N 80 34W
Connecticut □, U.S.A. 79 E12 41 30N 72 45W
Connecticut →, U.S.A. 79 E12 41 16N 72 20W
Connell, U.S.A. 82 C4 46 40N 118 52W
Connellsville, U.S.A. 78 F5 40 1N 79 35W
Connemara, Ireland 13 C2 53 29N 9 45W
Connemaugh →, U.S.A. 78 F5 40 28N 79 19W
Connersville, U.S.A. 76 F3 39 39N 85 8W
Connors Ra., Australia 62 C4 21 40S 149 10 E
Conquest, Canada 73 C7 51 32N 107 14W
Conrad, U.S.A. 82 B8 48 10N 111 57W
Conran, C., Australia 63 F4 37 49S 148 44 E
Conroe, U.S.A. 81 K7 30 19N 95 27W
Consecon, Canada 78 C7 44 0N 77 31W
Conselheiro Lafaiete, Brazil 95 A7 20 40S 43 48W
Consett, U.K. 10 C6 54 51N 1 50W
Consort, Canada 73 C6 52 1N 110 46W
Constance = Konstanz, Germany 16 E5 47 40N 9 10 E
Constance, L. = Bodensee, Europe 18 C8 47 35N 9 25 E
Constanța, Romania 17 F15 44 14N 28 38 E
Constantia, U.S.A. 79 C8 43 15N 76 1W
Constantine, Algeria 50 A7 36 25N 6 42 E
Constitución, Chile 94 D1 35 20S 72 30W
Constitución, Uruguay 94 C4 31 0S 57 50W
Consul, Canada 73 D7 49 20N 109 30W
Contact, U.S.A. 82 F6 41 46N 114 45W
Contai, India 43 J12 21 54N 87 46 E
Contamana, Peru 92 E4 7 19S 74 55W
Contas →, Brazil 93 F11 14 17S 39 1W
Contoocook, U.S.A. 79 C13 43 13N 71 45W
Contra Costa, Mozam. 57 D5 25 9S 33 30 E
Contwoyto L., Canada 68 B8 65 42N 110 50W
Conway = Conwy, U.K. 10 D4 53 17N 3 50W
Conway = Conwy →, U.K. 10 D4 53 17N 3 50W
Conway, Ark., U.S.A. 81 H8 35 5N 92 26W
Conway, N.H., U.S.A. 79 C13 43 59N 71 7W
Conway, S.C., U.S.A. 77 J6 33 51N 79 3W
Conway, L., Australia 63 D2 28 17S 135 35 E
Conwy, U.K. 10 D4 53 17N 3 50W
Conwy □, U.K. 10 D4 53 10N 3 44W
Conwy →, U.K. 10 D4 53 17N 3 50W
Coober Pedy, Australia 63 D1 29 1S 134 43 E
Cooch Behar = Koch Bihar, India 41 F16 26 22N 89 29 E
Cooinda, Australia 60 B5 13 15S 130 5 E
Cook, Australia 61 F5 30 37S 130 25 E
Cook, U.S.A. 80 B8 47 49N 92 39W
Cook, B., Chile 96 H3 55 10S 70 0W
Cook, C., Canada 72 C3 50 8N 127 55W
Cook, Mt. = Aoraki Mount Cook, N.Z. 59 K3 43 36S 170 9 E
Cook Inlet, U.S.A. 68 C4 60 0N 152 0W
Cook Is., Pac. Oc. 65 J12 17 0S 160 0W
Cook Strait, N.Z. 59 J5 41 15S 174 29 E
Cookeville, U.S.A. 77 G3 36 10N 85 30W
Cookhouse, S. Africa 56 E4 32 44S 25 47 E
Cookshire, Canada 79 A13 45 25N 71 38W
Cookstown, U.K. 13 B5 54 39N 6 45W
Cooksville, Canada 78 C5 43 36N 79 35W
Cooktown, Australia 62 B4 15 30S 145 16 E
Coolabah, Australia 63 E4 31 1S 146 43 E
Cooladdi, Australia 63 D4 26 37S 145 23 E
Coolah, Australia 63 E4 31 48S 149 41 E
Coolamon, Australia 63 E4 34 46S 147 8 E
Coolgardie, Australia 61 F3 30 55S 121 8 E
Coolidge, U.S.A. 83 K8 32 59N 111 31W
Coolidge Dam, U.S.A. 83 K8 33 0N 110 20W
Cooma, Australia 63 F4 36 12S 149 8 E
Coon Rapids, U.S.A. 80 C8 45 9N 93 19W
Coonabarabran, Australia 63 E4 31 14S 149 18 E
Coonamble, Australia 63 E4 30 56S 148 27 E
Coonana, Australia 61 F3 31 0S 123 0 E
Coondapoor, India 40 N9 13 42N 74 40 E
Cooninie, L., Australia 63 D2 26 4S 139 59 E
Cooper, U.S.A. 81 J7 33 23N 95 42W
Cooper Cr. →, Australia 63 D2 28 29S 137 46 E
Cooperstown, N. Dak., U.S.A. 80 B5 47 27N 98 8W
Cooperstown, N.Y., U.S.A. 79 D10 42 42N 74 56W
Coorabie, Australia 61 F5 31 54S 132 18 E
Coorong, The, Australia 63 F2 35 50S 139 20 E
Coorow, Australia 61 E2 29 53S 116 2 E
Cooroy, Australia 63 D5 26 22S 152 54 E
Coos Bay, U.S.A. 82 E1 43 22N 124 13W
Coosa →, U.S.A. 77 J2 32 30N 86 16W
Cootamundra, Australia 63 E4 34 36S 148 1 E
Cootehill, Ireland 13 B4 54 4N 7 5W
Copahue Paso, Argentina 94 D1 37 49S 71 8W
Copainalá, Mexico 87 D6 17 8N 93 11W
Copake Falls, U.S.A. 79 D11 42 7N 73 31W
Copán, Honduras 88 D2 14 50N 89 9W
Cope, U.S.A. 80 F3 39 40N 102 51W
Copenhagen = København, Denmark 9 J15 55 41N 12 34 E
Copenhagen, U.S.A. 79 C9 43 54N 75 41W
Copiapó, Chile 94 B1 27 30S 70 20W
Copiapó →, Chile 94 B1 27 19S 70 56W
Coplay, U.S.A. 79 F9 40 44N 75 29W
Copp L., Canada 72 A6 60 14N 114 40W
Coppename →, Surinam 93 B7 5 48N 55 55W
Copper Harbor, U.S.A. 76 B2 47 28N 87 53W
Copper Queen, Zimbabwe 55 F2 17 29S 29 18 E
Copperas Cove, U.S.A. 81 K6 31 8N 97 54W
Copperbelt □, Zambia 55 E2 13 15S 27 30 E
Coppermine = Kugluktuk, Canada 68 B8 67 50N 115 5W
Coppermine →, Canada 68 B8 67 49N 116 4W
Copperopolis, U.S.A. 84 H6 37 58N 120 38W
Coquet →, U.K. 10 B6 55 20N 1 32W
Coquille, U.S.A. 82 E1 43 11N 124 11W
Coquimbo, Chile 94 C1 30 0S 71 20W
Coquimbo □, Chile 94 C1 31 0S 71 0W
Corabia, Romania 17 G13 43 48N 24 30 E
Coracora, Peru 92 G4 15 5S 73 45W
Coraki, Australia 63 D5 28 59S 153 17 E
Coral, U.S.A. 78 F5 40 29N 79 10W
Coral Gables, U.S.A. 77 N5 25 45N 80 16W
Coral Harbour = Salliq, Canada 69 B11 64 8N 83 10W
Coral Sea, Pac. Oc. 64 J7 15 0S 150 0 E

115

East Providence

Donnybrook, Australia 61 F2 33 34S 115 48 E
Donnybrook, S. Africa 57 D4 29 59S 29 48 E
Donora, U.S.A. 78 F5 40 11N 79 52W
Donostia = Donostia-San Sebastián, Spain 19 A5 43 17N 1 58W
Donostia-San Sebastián, Spain 19 A5 43 17N 1 58W
Doon →, U.K. 12 F4 55 27N 4 39W
Dora, L., Australia 60 D3 22 0S 123 0 E
Dora Báltea →, Italy 18 D8 45 11N 8 3 E
Doran L., Canada 73 A7 61 13N 108 6W
Dorchester, U.K. 11 G5 50 42N 2 27W
Dorchester, C., Canada 69 B12 65 27N 77 27W
Dordabis, Namibia 56 C2 22 52S 17 38 E
Dordogne →, France 18 D3 45 2N 0 36W
Dordrecht, Neths. 15 C4 51 48N 4 39 E
Dordrecht, S. Africa 56 E4 31 20S 27 3 E
Doré L., Canada 73 C7 54 46N 107 17W
Doré Lake, Canada 73 C7 54 38N 107 36W
Dori, Burkina Faso 50 F5 14 3N 0 2W
Doring →, S. Africa 56 E2 31 54S 18 39 E
Doringbos, S. Africa 56 E2 31 59S 19 16 E
Dorion, Canada 79 A10 45 23N 74 3W
Dornbirn, Austria 16 E5 47 25N 9 45 E
Dornie, U.K. 12 D3 57 17N 5 31W
Dornoch, U.K. 12 D4 57 53N 4 2W
Dornoch Firth, U.K. 12 D4 57 51N 4 4W
Dornogovĭ □, Mongolia 34 C6 44 0N 110 0 E
Dorohoi, Romania 17 E14 47 56N 26 23 E
Döröö Nuur, Mongolia 32 B4 48 0N 93 0 E
Dorr, Iran 45 C6 33 17N 50 38 E
Dorre I., Australia 61 E1 25 13S 113 12 E
Dorrigo, Australia 63 E5 30 20S 152 44 E
Dorris, U.S.A. 82 F3 41 58N 121 55W
Dorset, Canada 78 A6 45 14N 78 54W
Dorset, U.S.A. 78 E4 41 40N 80 40W
Dorset □, U.K. 11 G5 50 45N 2 26W
Dortmund, Germany 16 C4 51 30N 7 28 E
Doruma, Dem. Rep. of the Congo 54 B2 4 42N 27 33 E
Dorūneh, Iran 45 C8 35 10N 57 18 E
Dos Bahías, C., Argentina 96 E3 44 58S 65 32W
Dos Hermanas, Spain 19 D3 37 16N 5 55W
Dos Palos, U.S.A. 84 J6 36 59N 120 37W
Dosso, Niger 50 F6 13 0N 3 13 E
Dothan, U.S.A. 77 K3 31 13N 85 24W
Doty, U.S.A. 84 D3 46 38N 123 17W
Douai, France 18 A5 50 21N 3 4 E
Douala, Cameroon 52 D1 4 0N 9 45 E
Douarnenez, France 18 B1 48 6N 4 21W
Double Island Pt., Australia 63 D5 25 56S 153 11 E
Double Mountain Fork →, U.S.A. 81 J4 33 16N 100 0W
Doubs →, France 18 C6 46 53N 5 1 E
Doubtful Sd., N.Z. 59 L1 45 20S 166 49 E
Doubtless B., N.Z. 59 F4 34 55S 173 26 E
Douglas, S. Africa 56 D3 29 4S 23 46 E
Douglas, U.K. 10 C3 54 10N 4 28W
Douglas, Ariz., U.S.A. 83 L9 31 21N 109 33W
Douglas, Ga., U.S.A. 77 K4 31 31N 82 51W
Douglas, Wyo., U.S.A. 80 D2 42 45N 105 24W
Douglas Chan., Canada 72 C3 53 40N 129 20W
Douglas Pt., Canada 78 B3 44 19N 81 37W
Douglasville, U.S.A. 77 J3 33 45N 84 45W
Dounreay, U.K. 12 C5 58 35N 3 44W
Dourada, Serra, Brazil 93 F9 13 10S 48 45W
Dourados, Brazil 95 A5 22 9S 54 50W
Dourados →, Brazil 95 A5 21 58S 54 18W
Dourados, Serra dos, Brazil 95 A5 23 30S 53 30W
Douro →, Europe 19 B1 41 8N 8 40W
Dove →, U.K. 10 E6 52 51N 1 36W
Dove Creek, U.S.A. 83 H9 37 46N 108 54W
Dover, Australia 62 G4 43 18S 147 2 E
Dover, U.K. 11 F9 51 7N 1 19 E
Dover, Del., U.S.A. 76 F8 39 10N 75 32W
Dover, N.H., U.S.A. 79 C14 43 12N 70 56W
Dover, N.J., U.S.A. 79 F10 40 53N 74 34W
Dover, Ohio, U.S.A. 78 F3 40 32N 81 29W
Dover, Pt., Australia 61 F4 32 32S 125 32 E
Dover, Str. of, Europe 11 G9 51 0N 1 30 E
Dover-Foxcroft, U.S.A. 77 C11 45 11N 69 13W
Dover Plains, U.S.A. 79 E11 41 43N 73 35W
Dovey = Dyfi →, U.K. 11 E3 52 32N 4 3W
Dovrefjell, Norway 9 E13 62 15N 9 33 E
Dow Rūd, Iran 45 C6 33 28N 49 4 E
Dowa, Malawi 55 E3 13 38S 33 58 E
Dowagiac, U.S.A. 76 E2 41 59N 86 6W
Dowerin, Australia 61 F2 31 12S 117 2 E
Dowgha'i, Iran 45 B8 36 54N 58 32 E
Dowlatābād, Iran 45 D8 28 20N 56 40 E
Down □, U.K. 13 B5 54 23N 6 2W
Downey, Calif., U.S.A. 85 M8 33 56N 118 7W
Downey, Idaho, U.S.A. 82 E7 42 26N 112 7W
Downham Market, U.K. 11 E8 52 37N 0 23 E
Downieville, U.S.A. 84 F6 39 34N 120 50W
Downpatrick, U.K. 13 B6 54 20N 5 43W
Downpatrick Hd., Ireland 13 B2 54 20N 9 21W
Downsville, U.S.A. 79 D10 42 5N 74 50W
Downton, Mt., Canada 72 C4 52 42N 124 52W
Dowsārī, Iran 45 D8 28 25N 57 59 E
Doyle, U.S.A. 84 E6 40 2N 120 6W
Doylestown, U.S.A. 79 F9 40 21N 75 10W
Dozois, Rés., Canada 70 C4 47 30N 77 5W
Dra Khel, Pakistan 42 F2 27 58N 66 45 E
Drachten, Neths. 15 A6 53 7N 6 5 E
Drăgăşani, Romania 17 F13 44 39N 24 17 E
Dragichyn, Belarus 17 B13 52 15N 25 8 E
Dragoman, Prokhod, Bulgaria 21 C10 42 58N 22 53 E
Draguignan, France 18 E7 43 32N 6 27 E
Drain, U.S.A. 82 E2 43 40N 123 19W
Drake, U.S.A. 80 B4 47 55N 100 23W
Drake Passage, S. Ocean 5 B17 58 0S 68 0W
Drakensberg, S. Africa 57 D4 31 0S 28 0 E
Dráma, Greece 21 D11 41 9N 24 10 E
Drammen, Norway 9 G14 59 42N 10 12 E
Drangajökull, Iceland 8 C2 66 9N 22 15W
Dras, India 43 B6 34 25N 75 48 E
Drau = Drava →, Croatia 21 B8 45 33N 18 55 E
Drava →, Croatia 21 B8 45 33N 18 55 E
Drayton Valley, Canada 72 C6 53 12N 114 58W
Drenthe □, Neths. 15 B6 52 52N 6 40 E
Drepanum, C., Cyprus 23 E11 34 54N 32 19 E
Dresden, Canada 78 D2 42 35N 82 11W
Dresden, Germany 16 C7 51 3N 13 44 E
Dreux, France 18 B4 48 44N 1 23 E
Driffield, U.K. 10 C7 54 0N 0 26W
Driftwood, U.S.A. 78 E6 41 20N 78 8W
Driggs, U.S.A. 82 E8 43 44N 111 6W
Drin →, Albania 21 C8 42 1N 19 38 E
Drina →, Bos.-H. 21 B8 44 53N 19 21 E
Drøbak, Norway 9 G14 59 39N 10 39 E
Drobeta-Turnu Severin, Romania 17 F12 44 39N 22 41 E
Drochia, Moldova 17 D14 48 2N 27 48 E
Drogheda, Ireland 13 C5 53 43N 6 22W
Drogichin = Dragichyn, Belarus 17 B13 52 15N 25 8 E
Drogobych = Drohobych, Ukraine 17 D12 49 20N 23 30 E
Drohobych, Ukraine 17 D12 49 20N 23 30 E
Droichead Atha = Drogheda, Ireland 13 C5 53 43N 6 22W
Droichead Nua, Ireland 13 C5 53 11N 6 48W
Droitwich, U.K. 11 E5 52 16N 2 8W
Dromedary, C., Australia 63 F5 36 17S 150 10 E
Dromore, U.K. 13 B4 54 31N 7 28W
Dromore West, Ireland 13 B3 54 15N 8 52W
Dronfield, U.K. 10 D6 53 19N 1 27W
Dronten, Neths. 15 B5 52 32N 5 43 E
Drumbo, Canada 78 C4 43 16N 80 35W
Drumheller, Canada 72 C6 51 25N 112 40W
Drummond, U.S.A. 82 C7 46 40N 113 9W
Drummond I., U.S.A. 76 C4 46 1N 83 39W
Drummond Pt., Australia 63 E2 34 9S 135 16 E
Drummond Ra., Australia 62 C4 23 45S 147 10 E
Drummondville, Canada 70 C5 45 55N 72 25W
Drumright, U.S.A. 81 H6 35 59N 96 36W
Druskininkai, Lithuania 9 J20 54 3N 23 58 E
Drut →, Belarus 17 B16 53 8N 30 5 E
Druzhina, Russia 27 C15 68 14N 145 18 E
Dry Tortugas, U.S.A. 88 B3 24 38N 82 55W
Dryden, Canada 73 D10 49 47N 92 50W
Dryden, U.S.A. 79 D8 42 30N 76 18W
Drygalski I., Antarctica 5 C7 66 0S 92 0 E
Drysdale →, Australia 60 B4 13 59S 126 51 E
Drysdale I., Australia 62 A2 11 41S 136 0 E
Du Bois, U.S.A. 78 E6 41 8N 78 46W
Du Gué →, Canada 70 A5 57 21N 70 45W
Du Quoin, U.S.A. 80 G10 38 1N 89 14W
Duanesburg, U.S.A. 79 D10 42 45N 74 11W
Duaringa, Australia 62 C4 23 42S 149 42 E
Ḑubā, Si. Arabia 44 E2 27 10N 35 40 E
Dubai = Dubayy, U.A.E. 46 B6 25 18N 55 20 E
Dubăsari, Moldova 17 E15 47 15N 29 10 E
Dubăsari Vdkhr., Moldova 17 E15 47 30N 29 0 E
Dubawnt →, Canada 73 A8 64 33N 100 6W
Dubawnt, L., Canada 73 A8 63 4N 101 42W
Dubayy, U.A.E. 46 B6 25 18N 55 20 E
Dubbo, Australia 63 E4 32 11S 148 35 E
Dubele, Dem. Rep. of the Congo 54 B2 2 56N 29 35 E
Dublin, Ireland 13 C5 53 21N 6 15W
Dublin, Ga., U.S.A. 77 J4 32 32N 82 54W
Dublin, Tex., U.S.A. 81 J5 32 5N 98 21W
Dublin □, Ireland 13 C5 53 24N 6 20W
Dubno, Ukraine 17 C13 50 25N 25 45 E
Dubois, U.S.A. 82 D7 44 10N 112 14W
Dubossary = Dubăsari, Moldova 17 E15 47 15N 29 10 E
Dubossary Vdkhr. = Dubăsari Vdkhr., Moldova 17 E15 47 30N 29 0 E
Dubovka, Russia 25 E7 49 5N 44 50 E
Dubrajpur, India 43 H12 23 48N 87 25 E
Dubréka, Guinea 50 G3 9 46N 13 31W
Dubrovitsa = Dubrovytsya, Ukraine 17 C14 51 31N 26 35 E
Dubrovnik, Croatia 21 C8 42 39N 18 6 E
Dubrovytsya, Ukraine 17 C14 51 31N 26 35 E
Dubuque, U.S.A. 80 D9 42 30N 90 41W
Duchesne, U.S.A. 82 F8 40 10N 110 24W
Duchess, Australia 62 C2 21 20S 139 50 E
Ducie I., Pac. Oc. 65 K15 24 40S 124 48W
Duck →, U.S.A. 77 G2 36 2N 87 52W
Duck Cr. →, Australia 60 D2 22 37S 116 53 E
Duck Lake, Canada 73 C7 52 50N 106 16W
Duck Mountain Prov. Park, Canada 73 C8 51 45N 101 0W
Duckwall, Mt., U.S.A. 84 H6 37 58N 120 7W
Dudhi, India 41 G13 24 15N 83 10 E
Dudinka, Russia 27 C9 69 30N 86 13 E
Dudley, U.K. 11 E5 52 31N 2 5W
Dudwa, India 43 E9 28 30N 80 41 E
Duero = Douro →, Europe 19 B1 41 8N 8 40W
Dufftown, U.K. 12 D5 57 27N 3 8W
Dūghī Kalā, Afghan. 40 C3 32 20N 62 50 E
Dugi Otok, Croatia 16 G8 44 0N 15 3 E
Duifken Pt., Australia 62 A3 12 33S 141 38 E
Duisburg, Germany 16 C4 51 26N 6 45 E
Duiwelskloof, S. Africa 57 C5 23 42S 30 10 E
Dūkdamīn, Iran 45 C8 35 59N 57 43 E
Dukelský Průsmyk, Slovak Rep. 17 D11 49 25N 21 42 E
Dukhān, Qatar 45 E6 25 25N 50 50 E
Duki, Pakistan 40 D6 30 14N 68 25 E
Duku, Nigeria 51 F8 10 43N 10 43 E
Dulce, U.S.A. 83 H10 36 56N 107 0W
Dulce →, Argentina 94 C3 30 32S 62 33W
Dulce, G., Costa Rica 88 E3 8 40N 83 20W
Dulf, Iraq 44 C5 35 7N 45 51 E
Dulit, Banjaran, Malaysia 36 D4 3 15N 114 30 E
Duliu, China 34 E9 39 2N 116 55 E
Dullewala, Pakistan 42 D4 31 50N 71 25 E
Dullstroom, S. Africa 57 D5 25 27S 30 7 E
Dulq Maghār, Syria 44 B3 36 22N 38 39 E
Duluth, U.S.A. 80 B8 46 47N 92 6W
Dum Dum, India 43 H13 22 39N 88 33 E
Dum Duma, India 41 F19 27 40N 95 40 E
Dūmā, Syria 47 B5 33 34N 36 24 E
Dumaguete, Phil. 37 C6 9 17N 123 15 E
Dumai, Indonesia 36 D2 1 35N 101 28 E
Dumaran, Phil. 37 B5 10 33N 119 50 E
Dumas, Ark., U.S.A. 81 J9 33 53N 91 29W
Dumas, Tex., U.S.A. 81 H4 35 52N 101 58W
Ḑumayr, Syria 47 B5 33 39N 36 42 E
Dumbarton, U.K. 12 F4 55 57N 4 33W
Dumbleyung, Australia 61 F2 33 17S 117 42 E
Dumfries, U.K. 12 F5 55 4N 3 37W
Dumfries & Galloway □, U.K. 12 F5 55 9N 3 58W
Dumka, India 43 G12 24 12N 87 15 E
Dumoine →, Canada 70 C4 46 13N 77 51W
Dumoine, L., Canada 70 C4 46 55N 77 55W
Dumraon, India 43 G11 25 33N 84 8 E
Dumyât, Egypt 51 B12 31 24N 31 48 E
Dún Dealgan = Dundalk, Ireland 13 B5 54 1N 6 24W
Dun Laoghaire, Ireland 13 C5 53 17N 6 8W
Duna = Dunărea →, Europe 17 F15 45 20N 29 40 E
Dunagiri, India 43 D8 30 31N 79 52 E
Dunaj = Dunărea →, Europe 17 F15 45 20N 29 40 E
Dunakeszi, Hungary 17 E10 47 37N 19 8 E
Dunărea →, Europe 17 F15 45 20N 29 40 E
Dunaújváros, Hungary 17 E10 46 58N 18 57 E
Dunav = Dunărea →, Europe 17 F15 45 20N 29 40 E
Dunay, Russia 30 C6 42 52N 132 22 E
Dunback, N.Z. 59 L3 45 23S 170 36 E
Dunbar, U.K. 12 E6 56 0N 2 31W
Dunblane, U.K. 12 E5 56 11N 3 58W
Duncan, Canada 72 D4 48 45N 123 40W
Duncan, Ariz., U.S.A. 83 K9 32 43N 109 6W
Duncan, Okla., U.S.A. 81 H6 34 30N 97 57W
Duncan, L., Canada 70 B4 53 29N 77 58W
Duncan L., Canada 72 A6 62 51N 113 58W
Duncan Town, Bahamas 88 B4 22 15N 75 45W
Duncannon, U.S.A. 78 F7 40 23N 77 2W
Duncansby Head, U.K. 12 C5 58 38N 3 1W
Duncansville, U.S.A. 78 F6 40 25N 78 26W
Dundalk, Canada 78 B4 44 10N 80 24W
Dundalk, Ireland 13 B5 54 1N 6 24W
Dundalk, U.S.A. 76 F7 39 16N 76 32W
Dundalk Bay, Ireland 13 C5 53 55N 6 15W
Dundas, Canada 78 C5 43 17N 79 59W
Dundas, L., Australia 61 F3 32 35S 121 50 E
Dundas I., Canada 72 C2 54 30N 130 50W
Dundas Str., Australia 60 B5 11 15S 131 35 E
Dundee, S. Africa 57 D5 28 11S 30 15 E
Dundee, U.K. 12 E6 56 28N 2 59W
Dundee, U.S.A. 78 D8 42 32N 76 59W
Dundee City □, U.K. 12 E6 56 30N 2 58W
Dundgovĭ □, Mongolia 34 B4 45 10N 106 0 E
Dundrum, U.K. 13 B6 54 16N 5 52W
Dundrum B., U.K. 13 B6 54 13N 5 47W
Dunedin, N.Z. 59 L3 45 50S 170 33 E
Dunedin, U.S.A. 77 L4 28 1N 82 47W
Dunfermline, U.K. 12 E5 56 5N 3 27W
Dungannon, Canada 78 C3 43 51N 81 36W
Dungannon, U.K. 13 B5 54 31N 6 46W
Dungarpur, India 42 H5 23 52N 73 45 E
Dungarvan, Ireland 13 D4 52 5N 7 37W
Dungarvan Harbour, Ireland 13 D4 52 4N 7 35W
Dungeness, U.K. 11 G8 50 54N 0 59 E
Dungo, L. do, Angola 56 B2 17 15S 19 0 E
Dungog, Australia 63 E5 32 22S 151 46 E
Dungu, Dem. Rep. of the Congo 54 B2 3 40N 28 32 E
Dungun, Malaysia 39 K4 4 45N 103 25 E
Dunhua, China 35 C15 43 20N 128 14 E
Dunhuang, China 32 B4 40 8N 94 36 E
Dunk I., Australia 62 B4 17 59S 146 29 E
Dunkeld, Australia 63 E4 33 25S 149 29 E
Dunkeld, U.K. 12 E5 56 34N 3 35W
Dunkerque, France 18 A5 51 2N 2 20 E
Dunkery Beacon, U.K. 11 F4 51 9N 3 36W
Dunkirk = Dunkerque, France 18 A5 51 2N 2 20 E
Dunkirk, U.S.A. 78 D5 42 29N 79 20W
Dúnleary = Dun Laoghaire, Ireland 13 C5 53 17N 6 8W
Dunleer, Ireland 13 C5 53 50N 6 24W
Dunmanus B., Ireland 13 E2 51 31N 9 50W
Dunmanway, Ireland 13 E2 51 43N 9 6W
Dunmara, Australia 62 B1 16 42S 133 25 E
Dunmore, U.S.A. 79 E9 41 25N 75 38W
Dunmore Hd., Ireland 13 D1 52 10N 10 35W
Dunmore Town, Bahamas 88 A4 25 30N 76 39W
Dunn, U.S.A. 77 H6 35 19N 78 37W
Dunnellon, U.S.A. 77 L4 29 3N 82 28W
Dunnet Hd., U.K. 12 C5 58 40N 3 21W
Dunning, U.S.A. 80 E4 41 50N 100 6W
Dunnville, Canada 78 D5 42 54N 79 36W
Dunolly, Australia 63 F3 36 51S 143 44 E
Dunoon, U.K. 12 F4 55 57N 4 56W
Dunphy, U.S.A. 82 F5 40 42N 116 31W
Duns, U.K. 12 F6 55 47N 2 20W
Dunseith, U.S.A. 80 A4 48 50N 100 3W
Dunsmuir, U.S.A. 82 F2 41 13N 122 16W
Dunstable, U.K. 11 F7 51 53N 0 32W
Dunstan Mts., N.Z. 59 L2 44 53S 169 35 E
Dunster, Canada 72 C5 53 8N 119 50W
Dunvegan L., Canada 73 A7 60 8N 107 10W
Duolun, China 34 C9 42 12N 116 28 E
Duong Dong, Vietnam 39 G4 10 13N 103 58 E
Dupree, U.S.A. 80 C4 45 4N 101 35W
Dupuyer, U.S.A. 82 B7 48 13N 112 30W
Duque de Caxias, Brazil 95 A7 22 45S 43 19W
Durack →, Australia 60 C4 15 33S 127 52 E
Durack Ra., Australia 60 C4 16 50S 127 40 E
Durance →, France 18 E6 43 55N 4 45 E
Durand, U.S.A. 80 C9 44 38N 91 58W
Durango, Mexico 86 C4 24 3N 104 39W
Durango, U.S.A. 83 H10 37 16N 107 53W
Durango □, Mexico 86 C4 25 0N 105 0W
Durant, Miss., U.S.A. 81 J10 33 4N 89 51W
Durant, Okla., U.S.A. 81 J6 33 59N 96 25W
Durazno, Uruguay 94 C4 33 25S 56 31W
Durazzo = Durrës, Albania 21 D8 41 19N 19 28 E
Durban, S. Africa 57 D5 29 49S 31 1 E
Durbuy, Belgium 15 D5 50 21N 5 28 E
Düren, Germany 16 C4 50 48N 6 29 E
Durg, India 41 J12 21 15N 81 22 E
Durgapur, India 43 H12 23 30N 87 20 E
Durham, Canada 78 B4 44 10N 80 49W
Durham, U.K. 10 C6 54 47N 1 34W
Durham, Calif., U.S.A. 84 F5 39 39N 121 48W
Durham, N.C., U.S.A. 77 H6 35 59N 78 54W
Durham, N.H., U.S.A. 79 C14 43 8N 70 56W
Durham □, U.K. 10 C6 54 42N 1 45W
Ḑurmā, Si. Arabia 44 E5 24 37N 46 8 E
Durmitor, Montenegro, Yug. 21 C8 43 10N 19 0 E
Durness, U.K. 12 C4 58 34N 4 45W
Durrës, Albania 21 D8 41 19N 19 28 E
Durrow, Ireland 13 D4 52 51N 7 24W
Dursey I., Ireland 13 E1 51 36N 10 12W
Dursunbey, Turkey 21 E13 39 35N 28 37 E
Duru, Dem. Rep. of the Congo 54 B2 4 14N 28 50 E
Durūz, Jabal ad, Jordan 47 C5 32 35N 36 40 E
D'Urville, Tanjung, Indonesia 37 E9 1 28S 137 54 E
D'Urville I., N.Z. 59 J4 40 50S 173 55 E
Duryea, U.S.A. 79 E9 41 20N 75 45W
Dushak, Turkmenistan 26 F7 37 13N 60 1 E
Dushanbe, Tajikistan 26 F7 38 33N 68 48 E
Dushore, U.S.A. 79 E8 41 31N 76 24W
Dusky Sd., N.Z. 59 L1 45 47S 166 30 E
Dussejour, C., Australia 60 B4 14 45S 128 13 E
Düsseldorf, Germany 16 C4 51 14N 6 47 E
Dutch Harbor, U.S.A. 68 C3 53 53N 166 32W
Dutlwe, Botswana 56 C3 23 58S 23 46 E
Dutton, Canada 78 D3 42 39N 81 30W
Dutton →, Australia 62 C3 20 44S 143 10 E
Duwayhin, Khawr, U.A.E. 45 E6 24 20N 51 25 E
Duyun, China 32 D5 26 18N 107 29 E
Duzdab = Zāhedān, Iran 45 D9 29 30N 60 50 E
Dvina, Severnaya →, Russia 24 B7 64 32N 40 30 E
Dvinsk = Daugavpils, Latvia 9 J22 55 53N 26 32 E
Dvinskaya Guba, Russia 24 B6 65 0N 39 0 E
Dwarka, India 42 H3 22 18N 69 8 E
Dwellingup, Australia 61 F2 32 43S 116 4 E
Dwight, Canada 78 A5 45 20N 79 1W
Dwight, U.S.A. 76 E1 41 5N 88 26W
Dyatlovo = Dzyatlava, Belarus 17 B13 53 28N 25 28 E
Dyce, U.K. 12 D6 57 13N 2 12W
Dyer, C., Canada 69 B13 66 40N 61 0W
Dyer Bay, Canada 78 A3 45 10N 81 20W
Dyer Plateau, Antarctica 5 D17 70 45S 65 30W
Dyersburg, U.S.A. 81 G10 36 3N 89 23W
Dyfi →, U.K. 11 E3 52 32N 4 3W
Dymer, Ukraine 17 C16 50 47N 30 18 E
Dysart, Australia 62 C4 22 32S 148 23 E
Dzamin Üüd = Borhoyn Tal, Mongolia 34 C6 43 50N 111 58 E
Dzerzhinsk, Russia 24 C7 56 14N 43 30 E
Dzhalinda, Russia 27 D13 53 26N 124 0 E
Dzhambul = Taraz, Kazakstan 26 E8 42 54N 71 22 E
Dzhankoy, Ukraine 25 E5 45 40N 34 20 E
Dzhezkazgan = Zhezqazghan, Kazakstan 26 E7 47 44N 67 40 E
Dzhizak = Jizzakh, Uzbekistan 26 E7 40 6N 67 50 E
Dzhugdzur, Khrebet, Russia 27 D14 57 30N 138 0 E
Dzhungarskiye Vorota = Dzungarian Gates, Asia 32 B3 45 0N 82 0 E
Działdowo, Poland 17 B11 53 15N 20 15 E
Dzibilchaltun, Mexico 87 C7 21 5N 89 36W
Dzierżoniów, Poland 17 C9 50 45N 16 39 E
Dzilam de Bravo, Mexico 87 C7 21 24N 88 53W
Dzungaria = Junggar Pendi, China 32 B3 44 30N 86 0 E
Dzungarian Gates, Asia 32 B3 45 0N 82 0 E
Dzuumod, Mongolia 32 B5 47 45N 106 58 E
Dzyarzhynsk, Belarus 17 B14 53 40N 27 1 E
Dzyatlava, Belarus 17 B13 53 28N 25 28 E

E

Eabamet L., Canada 70 B2 51 30N 87 46W
Eads, U.S.A. 80 F3 38 29N 102 47W
Eagar, U.S.A. 83 J9 34 6N 109 17W
Eagle, Alaska, U.S.A. 68 B5 64 47N 141 12W
Eagle, Colo., U.S.A. 82 G10 39 39N 106 50W
Eagle →, Canada 71 B8 53 36N 57 26W
Eagle Butte, U.S.A. 80 C4 45 0N 101 10W
Eagle Grove, U.S.A. 80 D8 42 40N 93 54W
Eagle L., Canada 73 D10 49 42N 93 13W
Eagle L., Calif., U.S.A. 82 F3 40 39N 120 45W
Eagle L., Maine, U.S.A. 77 B11 46 20N 69 22W
Eagle Lake, Canada 78 A6 45 8N 78 29W
Eagle Lake, Maine, U.S.A. 77 B11 47 3N 68 36W
Eagle Lake, Tex., U.S.A. 81 L6 29 35N 96 20W
Eagle Mountain, U.S.A. 85 M11 33 49N 115 27W
Eagle Nest, U.S.A. 83 H11 36 33N 105 16W
Eagle Pass, U.S.A. 81 L4 28 43N 100 30W
Eagle Pk., U.S.A. 84 G7 38 10N 119 25W
Eagle Pt., Australia 60 C3 16 11S 124 23 E
Eagle River, Mich., U.S.A. 76 B1 47 24N 88 18W
Eagle River, Wis., U.S.A. 80 C10 45 55N 89 15W
Eaglehawk, Australia 63 F3 36 44S 144 15 E
Eagles Mere, U.S.A. 79 E8 41 25N 76 33W
Ealing □, U.K. 11 F7 51 31N 0 20W
Ear Falls, Canada 73 C10 50 38N 93 13W
Earle, U.S.A. 81 H9 35 16N 90 28W
Earlimart, U.S.A. 85 K7 35 53N 119 16W
Earn →, U.K. 12 E5 56 21N 3 18W
Earn, L., U.K. 12 E4 56 23N 4 13W
Earnslaw, Mt., N.Z. 59 L2 44 32S 168 27 E
Earth, U.S.A. 81 H3 34 14N 102 24W
Easley, U.S.A. 77 H4 34 50N 82 36W
East Anglia, U.K. 10 E9 52 30N 1 0 E
East Angus, Canada 71 C5 45 30N 71 40W
East Aurora, U.S.A. 78 D6 42 46N 78 37W
East Ayrshire □, U.K. 12 F4 55 26N 4 11W
East Bengal, Bangla. 41 H17 24 0N 90 0 E
East Beskids = Vychodné Beskydy, Europe 17 D11 49 20N 22 0 E
East Brady, U.S.A. 78 F5 40 59N 79 36W
East C., N.Z. 59 G7 37 42S 178 35 E
East Chicago, U.S.A. 76 E2 41 38N 87 27W
East China Sea, Asia 33 D7 30 0N 126 0 E
East Coulee, Canada 72 C6 51 23N 112 27W
East Dereham, U.K. 11 E8 52 41N 0 57 E
East Dunbartonshire □, U.K. 12 F4 55 57N 4 13W
East Falkland, Falk. Is. 96 G5 51 30S 58 30W
East Grand Forks, U.S.A. 80 B6 47 56N 97 1W
East Greenwich, U.S.A. 79 E13 41 40N 71 27W
East Grinstead, U.K. 11 F8 51 7N 0 0W
East Hartford, U.S.A. 79 E12 41 46N 72 39W
East Helena, U.S.A. 82 C8 46 35N 111 56W
East Indies, Asia 28 K15 0 0 120 0 E
East Kilbride, U.K. 12 F4 55 47N 4 11W
East Lansing, U.S.A. 76 D3 42 44N 84 29W
East Liverpool, U.S.A. 78 F4 40 37N 80 35W
East London, S. Africa 57 E4 33 0S 27 55 E
East Lothian □, U.K. 12 F6 55 58N 2 44W
East Main = Eastmain, Canada 70 B4 52 10N 78 30W
East Northport, U.S.A. 79 F11 40 53N 73 20W
East Orange, U.S.A. 79 F10 40 46N 74 13W
East Pacific Ridge, Pac. Oc. 65 J17 15 0S 110 0W
East Palestine, U.S.A. 78 F4 40 50N 80 33W
East Pine, Canada 72 B4 55 48N 120 12W
East Point, U.S.A. 77 J3 33 41N 84 27W
East Providence, U.S.A. 79 E13 41 49N 71 23W

East Pt.

118

F

Farmington

Farmington, Mo., U.S.A. 81 G9 37 47N 90 25W
Farmington, N.H., U.S.A. ... 79 C13 43 24N 71 4W
Farmington, N. Mex., U.S.A. 83 H9 36 44N 108 12W
Farmington, Utah, U.S.A. ... 82 F8 41 0N 111 12W
Farmington →, U.S.A. 79 E12 41 51N 72 38W
Farmville, U.S.A. 76 G6 37 18N 78 24W
Farne Is., U.K. 10 B6 55 38N 1 37W
Farnham, Canada 79 A12 45 17N 72 59W
Farnham, Mt., Canada 72 C5 50 29N 116 30W
Faro, Brazil 93 D7 2 10S 56 39W
Faro, Canada 68 B6 62 11N 133 22W
Faro, Portugal 19 D2 37 2N 7 55W
Fårö, Sweden .... 9 H18 57 55N 19 5 E
Farquhar, C., Australia ..... 61 D1 23 50S 113 36 E
Farrars Cr. →, Australia .... 62 D3 25 35S 140 43 E
Farrāshband, Iran .... 45 D7 28 57N 52 5 E
Farrell, U.S.A. 78 E4 41 13N 80 30W
Farrokhī, Iran .... 45 C8 33 50N 59 31 E
Farruch, C. = Ferrutx, C., Spain .... 22 B10 39 47N 3 21 E
Fārs □, Iran .... 45 D7 29 30N 55 0 E
Fársala, Greece .... 21 E10 39 17N 22 23 E
Farson, U.S.A. 82 E9 42 6N 109 27W
Farsund, Norway .... 9 G12 58 5N 6 55 E
Fartak, Râs, Si. Arabia ...... 44 D2 28 5N 34 34 E
Fartak, Ra's, Yemen .... 46 D5 15 38N 52 15 E
Fartura, Serra da, Brazil 95 B5 26 21S 52 52W
Fārūj, Iran .... 45 B8 37 14N 58 14 E
Farvel, Kap = Nunap Isua, Greenland 69 C15 59 48N 43 55W
Farwell, U.S.A. 81 H3 34 23N 103 2W
Fasā, Iran .... 45 D7 29 0N 53 39 E
Fasano, Italy .... 20 D7 40 50N 17 22 E
Fastiv, Ukraine .... 17 C15 50 7N 29 57 E
Fastov = Fastiv, Ukraine .... 17 C15 50 7N 29 57 E
Fatagar, Tanjung, Indonesia 37 E8 2 46S 131 57 E
Fatehabad, Haryana, India .. 42 E6 29 31N 75 27 E
Fatehabad, Ut. P., India .... 42 F8 27 1N 78 19 E
Fatehgarh, India .... 43 F8 27 25N 79 35 E
Fatehpur, Bihar, India ...... 43 G11 24 38N 85 14 E
Fatehpur, Raj., India .... 42 F6 28 0N 74 40 E
Fatehpur, Ut. P., India ...... 43 G9 25 56N 81 13 E
Fatehpur, Ut. P., India ...... 43 F9 27 10N 81 13 E
Fatehpur Sikri, India .... 42 F6 27 6N 77 40 E
Fatima, Canada 71 C7 47 24N 61 53W
Faulkton, U.S.A. 80 C5 45 2N 99 8W
Faure I., Australia .... 61 E1 25 52S 113 50 E
Fauresmith, S. Africa .... 56 D4 29 44S 25 17 E
Fauske, Norway .... 8 C16 67 17N 15 25 E
Favara, Italy .... 20 F5 37 19N 13 39 E
Favàritx, C. de, Spain .... 22 B11 40 0N 4 15 E
Favignana, Italy .... 20 F5 37 56N 12 20 E
Fawcett, Pt., Australia ...... 60 B5 11 46S 130 2 E
Fawn →, Canada 70 A2 55 20N 87 35W
Fawnskin, U.S.A. 85 L10 34 16N 116 56W
Faxaflói, Iceland 8 D2 64 29N 23 0W
Faya-Largeau, Chad .... 51 E9 17 58N 19 6 E
Fayd, Si. Arabia .... 44 E4 27 1N 42 52 E
Fayette, Ala., U.S.A. 77 J2 33 41N 87 50W
Fayette, Mo., U.S.A. 80 F8 39 9N 92 41W
Fayetteville, Ark., U.S.A. 81 G7 36 4N 94 10W
Fayetteville, N.C., U.S.A. 77 H6 35 3N 78 53W
Fayetteville, Tenn., U.S.A. .. 77 H2 35 9N 86 34W
Fazilka, India .... 42 D6 30 27N 74 2 E
Fazilpur, Pakistan .... 42 E4 29 18N 70 29 E
Fdérik, Mauritania 50 D3 22 40N 12 45W
Feale →, Ireland 13 D2 52 27N 9 37W
Fear, C., U.S.A. 77 J7 33 50N 77 58W
Feather →, U.S.A. 82 G3 38 47N 121 36W
Feather Falls, U.S.A. 84 F5 39 36N 121 16W
Featherston, N.Z. .... 59 J5 41 6S 175 20 E
Featherstone, Zimbabwe .... 55 F3 18 42S 30 55 E
Fécamp, France .... 18 B4 49 45N 0 22 E
Fedala = Mohammedia, Morocco 50 B4 33 44N 7 21W
Federación, Argentina 94 C4 31 0S 57 55W
Féderal, Argentina 96 C5 30 57S 58 48W
Federal Way, U.S.A. 84 C4 47 18N 122 19W
Fedeshküh, Iran .... 45 D7 28 49N 53 50 E
Fehmarn, Germany .... 16 A6 54 27N 11 7 E
Fehmarn Bælt, Europe ..... 9 J14 54 35N 11 20 E
Fehmarn Belt = Fehmarn Bælt, Europe .... 9 J14 54 35N 11 20 E
Fei Xian, China .... 35 G9 35 18N 117 59 E
Feijó, Brazil 92 E4 8 9S 70 21W
Feilding, N.Z. .... 59 J5 40 13S 175 35 E
Feira de Santana, Brazil 93 F11 12 15S 38 57W
Feixiang, China .... 34 F8 36 30N 114 45 E
Felanitx, Spain .... 22 B10 39 28N 3 9 E
Feldkirch, Austria .... 16 E5 47 15N 9 37 E
Felipe Carrillo Puerto, Mexico 87 D7 19 38N 88 3W
Felixburg, Zimbabwe ...... 57 B5 19 29S 30 51 E
Felixstowe, U.K. .... 11 F9 51 58N 1 23 E
Felton, U.S.A. 84 H4 37 3N 122 4W
Femer Bælt = Fehmarn Bælt, Europe .... 9 J14 54 35N 11 20 E
Femunden, Norway .... 9 E14 62 10N 11 53 E
Fen He →, China .... 34 G6 35 36N 110 42 E
Fenelon Falls, Canada 78 B6 44 32N 78 45W
Feng Xian, Jiangsu, China .. 34 G9 34 43N 116 35 E
Feng Xian, Shaanxi, China .. 34 H4 33 54N 106 40 E
Fengcheng, China .... 35 D13 40 28N 124 5 E
Fengfeng, China .... 34 F8 36 28N 114 8 E
Fengning, China .... 34 D9 41 10N 116 33 E
Fengqiu, China .... 34 G8 35 2N 114 25 E
Fengrun, China .... 35 E10 39 48N 118 8 E
Fengtai, China .... 34 E9 39 50N 116 18 E
Fengxiang, China .... 34 G4 34 29N 107 25 E
Fengyang, China .... 35 H9 32 51N 117 29 E
Fengzhen, China .... 34 D7 40 25N 113 2 E
Fenoarivo, Fianarantsoa, Madag. .... 57 C8 21 43S 46 24 E
Fenoarivo, Fianarantsoa, Madag. .... 57 C8 20 52S 46 53 E
Fenoarivo Afovoany, Madag. 57 B8 18 26S 46 34 E
Fenoarivo Atsinanana, Madag. .... 57 B8 17 22S 49 25 E
Fens, The, U.K. 10 E7 52 38N 0 2W
Fenton, U.S.A. 76 D4 42 48N 83 42W
Fenxi, China .... 34 F6 36 40N 111 31 E
Fenyang, China .... 34 F6 37 18N 111 48 E
Feodosiya, Ukraine .... 25 E6 45 2N 35 16 E
Ferdows, Iran .... 45 C8 33 58N 58 2 E
Ferfer, Somali Rep. .... 46 F4 5 4N 45 9 E
Fergana = Farghona, Uzbekistan .... 26 E8 40 23N 71 19 E
Fergus, Canada 78 C4 43 43N 80 24W
Fergus Falls, U.S.A. 80 B6 46 17N 96 4W
Ferkéssédougou, Ivory C. ... 50 G4 9 35N 5 6W
Ferland, Canada 70 B2 50 19N 88 27W
Fermanagh □, U.K. 13 B4 54 21N 7 40W
Fermo, Italy .... 20 C5 43 9N 13 43 E
Fermont, Canada 71 B6 52 47N 67 5W
Fermoy, Ireland 13 D3 52 9N 8 16W
Fernández, Argentina 94 B3 27 55S 63 50W
Fernandina Beach, U.S.A. .. 77 K5 30 40N 81 27W
Fernando de Noronha, Brazil 93 D12 4 0S 33 10W
Fernando Póo = Bioko, Eq. Guin. .... 52 D1 3 30N 8 40 E
Ferndale, U.S.A. 84 B4 48 51N 122 36W
Fernie, Canada 72 D5 49 30N 115 5W
Fernlees, Australia .... 62 C4 23 51S 148 7 E
Fernley, U.S.A. 82 G4 39 36N 119 15W
Ferozepore = Firozpur, India 42 D6 30 55N 74 40 E
Ferrara, Italy .... 20 B4 44 50N 11 35 E
Ferreñafe, Peru 92 E3 6 42S 79 50W
Ferrerías, Spain .... 22 B11 39 59N 4 1 E
Ferret, C., France 18 D3 44 38N 1 15W
Ferriday, U.S.A. 81 K9 31 38N 91 33W
Ferrol, Spain 19 A1 43 29N 8 15W
Ferron, U.S.A. 83 G8 39 5N 111 8W
Ferrutx, C., Spain .... 22 B10 39 47N 3 21 E
Ferryland, Canada 71 C9 47 2N 52 53W
Fertile, U.S.A. 80 B6 47 32N 96 17W
Fès, Morocco 50 B5 34 0N 5 0W
Fessenden, U.S.A. 80 B5 47 39N 99 38W
Festus, U.S.A. 80 F9 38 13N 90 24W
Feteşti, Romania .... 17 F14 44 22N 27 51 E
Fethiye, Turkey .... 25 G4 36 36N 29 6 E
Fetlar, U.K. 12 A8 60 36N 0 52W
Feuilles →, Canada 69 C12 58 47N 70 4W
Fez = Fès, Morocco 50 B5 34 0N 5 0W
Fezzan, Libya .... 51 C8 27 0N 13 0 E
Fiambalá, Argentina 94 B2 27 45S 67 37W
Fianarantsoa, Madag. ...... 57 C8 21 26S 47 5 E
Fianarantsoa □, Madag. ..... 57 B8 19 30S 47 0 E
Ficksburg, S. Africa .... 57 D4 28 51S 27 53 E
Field →, Australia .... 62 C2 23 48S 138 0 E
Field I., Australia .... 60 B5 12 5S 132 23 E
Fier, Albania .... 21 D8 40 43N 19 33 E
Fife □, U.K. 12 E5 56 16N 3 1W
Fife Ness, U.K. 12 E6 56 17N 2 35W
Fifth Cataract, Sudan ...... 51 E12 18 22N 33 50 E
Figeac, France .... 18 D5 44 37N 2 2 E
Figtree, Zimbabwe .... 55 G2 20 22S 28 20 E
Figueira da Foz, Portugal ... 19 B1 40 7N 8 54W
Figueres, Spain .... 19 A7 42 18N 2 58 E
Figuig, Morocco 50 B5 32 5N 1 11W
Fihaonana, Madag. .... 57 B8 18 36S 47 12 E
Fiherenana, Madag. .... 57 B8 18 29S 48 24 E
Fiherenana →, Madag. ..... 57 C7 23 19S 43 37 E
Fiji ■, Pac. Oc. .... 59 C8 17 20S 179 0 E
Filabusi, Zimbabwe .... 57 C4 20 34S 29 20 E
Filey, U.K. 10 C7 54 12N 0 18W
Filey B., U.K. 10 C7 54 12N 0 15W
Filfla, Malta .... 23 D1 35 47N 14 24 E
Filiatrá, Greece .... 21 F9 37 9N 21 35 E
Filingué, Niger .... 50 F6 14 21N 3 22 E
Filipstad, Sweden .... 9 G16 59 43N 14 9 E
Fillmore, Calif., U.S.A. 85 L8 34 24N 118 55W
Fillmore, Utah, U.S.A. 83 G7 38 58N 112 20W
Finch, Canada 79 A9 45 11N 75 7W
Findhorn →, U.K. 12 D5 57 38N 3 38W
Findlay, U.S.A. 76 E4 41 2N 83 39W
Finger L., Canada 70 B1 53 33N 93 30W
Finger Lakes, U.S.A. 79 D8 42 40N 76 30W
Fingoè, Mozam. .... 55 E3 14 55S 31 50 E
Finisterre, C. = Fisterra, C., Spain 19 A1 42 50N 9 19W
Finke, Australia .... 62 D1 25 34S 134 35 E
Finland ■, Europe .... 8 E22 63 0N 27 0 E
Finland, G. of, Europe ...... 9 G21 60 0N 26 0 E
Finlay →, Canada 72 B3 57 0N 125 10W
Finley, Australia .... 63 F4 35 38S 145 35 E
Finley, U.S.A. 80 B6 47 31N 97 50W
Finn →, Ireland 13 B4 54 51N 7 28W
Finnigan, Mt., Australia .... 62 B4 15 49S 145 17 E
Finniss, C., Australia ...... 63 E1 33 8S 134 51 E
Finnmark, Norway .... 8 B20 69 37N 23 57 E
Finnsnes, Norway .... 8 B18 69 14N 18 0 E
Finspång, Sweden .... 9 G16 58 43N 15 47 E
Fiora →, Italy .... 20 C4 42 20N 11 34 E
Fiq, Syria .... 47 C4 32 46N 35 41 E
Firat = Furāt, Nahr al →, Asia 44 D5 31 0N 47 25 E
Firebag →, Canada 73 B6 57 45N 111 21W
Firebaugh, U.S.A. 84 J6 36 52N 120 27W
Firedrake L., Canada 73 A8 61 25N 104 30W
Firenze, Italy .... 20 C4 43 46N 11 15 E
Firk →, Iraq .... 44 D5 30 59N 44 34 E
Firozabad, India .... 43 F8 27 10N 78 25 E
Firozpur, India .... 42 D6 30 55N 74 40 E
Firozpur-Jhirka, India ...... 42 F7 27 48N 76 57 E
Fīrūzābād, Iran .... 45 D7 28 52N 52 35 E
Fīrūzkūh, Iran .... 45 C7 35 50N 52 50 E
Firvale, Canada 72 C3 52 27N 126 13W
Fish →, Namibia .... 56 D2 28 7S 17 10 E
Fish →, S. Africa .... 56 E3 31 30S 20 16 E
Fish River Canyon, Namibia . 56 D2 27 40S 17 35 E
Fisher, Australia .... 61 F5 30 30S 131 0 E
Fisher B., Canada 73 C9 51 35N 97 13W
Fishers I., U.S.A. 79 E13 41 15N 72 0W
Fishguard, U.K. 11 E3 52 0N 4 58W
Fishing L., Canada 73 C9 52 10N 95 24W
Fishkill, U.S.A. 79 E11 41 32N 73 53W
Fisterra, C., Spain 19 A1 42 50N 9 19W
Fitchburg, U.S.A. 79 D13 42 35N 71 48W
Fitz Roy, Argentina 96 F3 47 0S 67 0W
Fitzgerald, Canada 72 B6 59 51N 111 36W
Fitzgerald, U.S.A. 77 K4 31 43N 83 15W
Fitzmaurice →, Australia ... 60 B5 14 45S 130 5 E
Fitzroy →, Queens., Australia 62 C5 23 32S 150 52 E
Fitzroy →, W. Austral., Australia .... 60 C3 17 31S 123 35 E
Fitzroy, Mte., Argentina 96 F2 49 17S 73 5W
Fitzroy Crossing, Australia .. 60 C4 18 9S 125 38 E
Fitzwilliam I., Canada 78 A3 45 30N 81 45W
Fiume = Rijeka, Croatia .... 16 F8 45 20N 14 21 E
Five Points, U.S.A. 84 J6 36 26N 120 6W
Fizi, Dem. Rep. of the Congo 54 C2 4 17S 28 55 E
Flagstaff, U.S.A. 83 J8 35 12N 111 39W
Flagstaff L., U.S.A. 77 C10 45 12N 70 18W
Flaherty I., Canada 70 A4 56 15N 79 15W
Flåm, Norway .... 9 F12 60 50N 7 7 E
Flambeau →, U.S.A. 80 C9 45 18N 91 14W
Flamborough Hd., U.K. 10 C7 54 7N 0 5W
Flaming Gorge Reservoir, U.S.A. 82 F9 41 10N 109 25W
Flamingo, Teluk, Indonesia . 37 F9 5 30S 138 0 E
Flanders = Flandre, Europe . 18 A5 50 50N 2 30 E
Flandre, Europe .... 18 A5 50 50N 2 30 E
Flandre Occidentale = West-Vlaanderen □, Belgium ... 15 D2 51 0N 3 0 E
Flandre Orientale = Oost-Vlaanderen □, Belgium ... 15 C3 51 5N 3 50 E
Flandreau, U.S.A. 80 C6 44 3N 96 36W
Flanigan, U.S.A. 84 E7 40 10N 119 53W
Flannan Is., U.K. 12 C1 58 9N 7 52W
Flåsjön, Sweden .... 8 D16 64 5N 15 40 E
Flat →, Canada 72 A3 61 33N 125 18W
Flathead L., U.S.A. 82 C7 47 51N 114 8W
Flattery, C., Australia ...... 62 A4 14 58S 145 21 E
Flattery, C., U.S.A. 84 B2 48 23N 124 29W
Flatwoods, U.S.A. 76 F4 38 31N 82 43W
Fleetwood, U.K. 10 D4 53 55N 3 1W
Fleetwood, U.S.A. 79 F9 40 27N 75 49W
Flekkefjord, Norway .... 9 G12 58 18N 6 39 E
Flemington, U.S.A. 78 E7 41 7N 77 28W
Flensburg, Germany .... 16 A5 54 47N 9 27 E
Flers, France 18 B3 48 47N 0 33W
Flesherton, Canada 78 B4 44 16N 80 33W
Flesko, Tanjung, Indonesia . 37 D6 0 29N 124 30 E
Fleurieu Pen., Australia .... 63 F2 35 40S 138 5 E
Flevoland □, Neths. .... 15 B5 52 30N 5 30 E
Flin Flon, Canada 73 C8 54 46N 101 53W
Flinders →, Australia ...... 62 B3 17 36S 140 36 E
Flinders B., Australia ...... 61 F2 34 19S 115 19 E
Flinders Group, Australia ... 62 A3 14 11S 144 15 E
Flinders I., S. Austral., Australia .... 63 E1 33 44S 134 41 E
Flinders I., Tas., Australia .. 62 G4 40 0S 148 0 E
Flinders Ranges, Australia .. 63 E2 31 30S 138 30 E
Flinders Reefs, Australia .... 62 B4 17 37S 148 31 E
Flint, U.K. 10 D4 53 15N 3 8W
Flint, U.S.A. 76 D4 43 1N 83 41W
Flint →, U.S.A. 77 K3 30 57N 84 34W
Flint I., Kiribati 65 J12 11 26S 151 48W
Flintshire □, U.K. 10 D4 53 17N 3 17W
Flodden, U.K. 10 B5 55 37N 2 8W
Floodwood, U.S.A. 80 B8 46 55N 92 55W
Flora, U.S.A. 76 F1 38 40N 88 29W
Florala, U.S.A. 77 K2 31 0N 86 20W
Florence = Firenze, Italy .... 20 C4 43 46N 11 15 E
Florence, Ala., U.S.A. 77 H2 34 48N 87 41W
Florence, Ariz., U.S.A. 83 K8 33 2N 111 23W
Florence, Colo., U.S.A. 80 F2 38 23N 105 8W
Florence, Oreg., U.S.A. 82 E1 43 58N 124 7W
Florence, S.C., U.S.A. 77 H6 34 12N 79 46W
Florence, L., Australia ...... 63 D2 28 53S 138 9 E
Florencia, Colombia 92 C3 1 36N 75 36W
Florennes, Belgium .... 15 D4 50 15N 4 35 E
Florenville, Belgium .... 15 E5 49 40N 5 19 E
Flores, Guatemala 88 C2 16 59N 89 50W
Flores, Indonesia .... 37 F6 8 35S 121 0 E
Flores I., Canada 72 D3 49 20N 126 10W
Flores Sea, Indonesia ...... 37 F6 6 30S 120 0 E
Floreşti, Moldova .... 17 E15 47 53N 28 17 E
Floresville, U.S.A. 81 L5 29 8N 98 10W
Floriano, Brazil 93 E10 6 50S 43 0W
Florianópolis, Brazil 95 B6 27 30S 48 30W
Florida, Cuba 88 B4 21 32N 78 14W
Florida, Uruguay 95 C4 34 7S 56 10W
Florida □, U.S.A. 77 L5 28 0N 82 0W
Florida, Straits of, U.S.A. ... 88 B4 25 0N 80 0W
Florida B., U.S.A. 88 B3 25 0N 80 45W
Florida Keys, U.S.A. 77 N5 24 40N 81 0W
Flórina, Greece .... 21 D9 40 48N 21 26 E
Florø, Norway .... 9 F11 61 35N 5 1 E
Flower Station, Canada 79 A8 45 10N 76 41W
Flowerpot I., Canada 78 A3 45 18N 81 38W
Floydada, U.S.A. 81 J4 33 59N 101 20W
Fluk, Indonesia .... 37 E7 1 42S 127 44 E
Flushing = Vlissingen, Neths. 15 C3 51 26N 3 34 E
Flying Fish, C., Antarctica ... 5 D15 72 6S 102 29W
Foam Lake, Canada 73 C8 51 40N 103 32W
Foça, Turkey .... 21 E12 38 39N 26 46 E
Focşani, Romania .... 17 F14 45 41N 27 15 E
Fóggia, Italy .... 20 D6 41 27N 15 34 E
Fogo, Canada 71 C9 49 43N 54 17W
Fogo I., Canada 71 C9 49 40N 54 5W
Föhr, Germany .... 16 A5 54 43N 8 30 E
Foix, France .... 18 E4 42 58N 1 38 E
Folda, Nord-Trøndelag, Norway .... 8 D14 64 32N 10 30 E
Folda, Nordland, Norway .... 8 C16 67 38N 14 50 E
Foley, Botswana .... 56 C4 21 34S 27 21 E
Foley, U.S.A. 77 K2 30 24N 87 41W
Foleyet, Canada 70 C3 48 15N 82 25W
Folgefonni, Norway .... 9 F12 60 3N 6 23 E
Foligno, Italy .... 20 C5 42 57N 12 42 E
Folkestone, U.K. .... 11 F9 51 5N 1 12 E
Folkston, U.S.A. 77 K5 30 50N 82 0W
Follansbee, U.S.A. 78 F4 40 19N 80 35W
Folsom L., U.S.A. 84 G5 38 42N 121 9W
Fond-du-Lac, Canada 73 B7 59 19N 107 12W
Fond du Lac, U.S.A. 80 D10 43 47N 88 27W
Fond-du-Lac →, Canada 73 B7 59 17N 106 0W
Fonda, U.S.A. 79 D10 42 57N 74 22W
Fondi, Italy .... 20 D5 41 21N 13 25 E
Fongafale, Tuvalu .... 64 H9 8 31S 179 13 E
Fonsagrada = A Fonsagrada, Spain 19 A2 43 8N 7 4W
Fonseca, G. de, Cent. Amer. . 88 D2 13 10N 87 40W
Fontainebleau, France ..... 18 B5 48 24N 2 40 E
Fontana, U.S.A. 85 L9 34 6N 117 26W
Fontas →, Canada 72 B4 58 14N 121 48W
Fonte Boa, Brazil 92 D5 2 33S 66 0W
Fontenay-le-Comte, France . 18 C3 46 28N 0 48W
Fontenelle Reservoir, U.S.A. 82 E8 42 1N 110 3W
Fontur, Iceland 8 C6 66 23N 14 32W
Foochow = Fuzhou, China .. 33 D6 26 5N 119 16 E
Foping, China .... 34 H5 33 41N 108 0 E
Forbes, Australia .... 63 E4 33 22S 148 5 E
Forbesganj, India .... 43 F12 26 17N 87 18 E
Ford City, Calif., U.S.A. 85 K7 35 9N 119 27W
Ford City, Pa., U.S.A. 78 F5 40 46N 79 32W
Førde, Norway .... 9 F11 61 27N 5 53 E
Ford's Bridge, Australia .... 63 D4 29 41S 145 29 E
Fordyce, U.S.A. 81 J8 33 49N 92 25W
Forel, Mt., Greenland 4 C6 66 52N 36 55W
Foremost, Canada 72 D6 49 26N 111 34W
Forest, Canada 78 C3 43 6N 82 0W
Forest, U.S.A. 81 J10 32 22N 89 29W
Forest City, Iowa, U.S.A. 80 D8 43 16N 93 39W
Forest City, N.C., U.S.A. 77 H5 35 20N 81 52W
Forest City, Pa., U.S.A. 79 E9 41 39N 75 28W
Forest Grove, U.S.A. 84 E3 45 31N 123 7W
Forestburg, Canada 72 C6 52 35N 112 1W
Foresthill, U.S.A. 84 F6 39 1N 120 49W
Forestier Pen., Australia .... 62 G4 43 0S 148 0 E
Forestville, Canada 71 C6 48 48N 69 2W
Forestville, Calif., U.S.A. 84 G4 38 28N 122 54W
Forestville, N.Y., U.S.A. 78 D5 42 28N 79 10W
Forfar, U.K. 12 E6 56 39N 2 53W
Forks, U.S.A. 84 C2 47 57N 124 23W
Forksville, U.S.A. 79 E8 41 29N 76 35W
Forlì, Italy .... 20 B5 44 13N 12 3 E
Forman, U.S.A. 80 B6 46 7N 97 38W
Formby Pt., U.K. 10 D4 53 33N 3 6W
Formentera, Spain .... 22 C7 38 43N 1 27 E
Formentor, C. de, Spain .... 22 B10 39 58N 3 13 E
Former Yugoslav Republic of Macedonia = Macedonia ■, Europe .... 21 D9 41 53N 21 40 E
Fórmia, Italy .... 20 D5 41 15N 13 37 E
Formosa = Taiwan ■, Asia ... 33 D7 23 30N 121 0 E
Formosa, Argentina 94 B4 26 15S 58 10W
Formosa, Brazil 93 G9 15 32S 47 20W
Formosa □, Argentina 94 B4 25 0S 60 0W
Formosa, Serra, Brazil 93 F8 12 0S 55 0W
Formosa Bay, Kenya .... 54 C5 2 40S 40 20 E
Fornells, Spain .... 22 A11 40 3N 4 7 E
Føroyar, Atl. Oc. 8 F9 62 0N 7 0W
Forres, U.K. 12 D5 57 37N 3 37W
Forrest, Australia .... 61 F4 30 51S 128 6 E
Forrest, Mt., Australia ...... 61 D4 24 48S 127 45 E
Forrest City, U.S.A. 81 H9 35 1N 90 47W
Forsayth, Australia .... 62 B3 18 33S 143 34 E
Forssa, Finland .... 9 F20 60 49N 23 38 E
Forst, Germany .... 16 C8 51 45N 14 37 E
Forsyth, U.S.A. 82 C10 46 16N 106 41W
Fort Abbas, Pakistan ...... 42 E5 29 12N 72 52 E
Fort Albany, Canada 70 B3 52 15N 81 35W
Fort Ann, U.S.A. 79 C11 43 25N 73 30W
Fort Assiniboine, Canada ... 72 C6 54 20N 114 45W
Fort Augustus, U.K. 12 D4 57 9N 4 42W
Fort Beaufort, S. Africa .... 56 E4 32 46S 26 40 E
Fort Benton, U.S.A. 82 C8 47 49N 110 40W
Fort Bragg, U.S.A. 82 G2 39 26N 123 48W
Fort Bridger, U.S.A. 82 F8 41 19N 110 23W
Fort Chipewyan, Canada ... 73 B6 58 42N 111 8W
Fort Collins, U.S.A. 80 E2 40 35N 105 5W
Fort-Coulonge, Canada 70 C4 45 50N 76 45W
Fort Covington, U.S.A. 79 B10 44 59N 74 29W
Fort Davis, U.S.A. 81 K3 30 35N 103 54W
Fort-de-France, Martinique . 89 D7 14 36N 61 2W
Fort Defiance, U.S.A. 83 J9 35 45N 109 5W
Fort Dodge, U.S.A. 80 D7 42 30N 94 11W
Fort Edward, U.S.A. 79 C11 43 16N 73 35W
Fort Erie, Canada 78 D6 42 54N 78 56W
Fort Fairfield, U.S.A. 77 B12 46 46N 67 50W
Fort Frances, Canada 73 D10 48 36N 93 24W
Fort Garland, U.S.A. 83 H11 37 26N 105 26W
Fort George = Chisasibi, Canada 70 B4 53 50N 79 0W
Fort Good-Hope, Canada 68 B7 66 14N 128 40W
Fort Hancock, U.S.A. 83 L11 31 18N 105 51W
Fort Hertz = Putao, Burma .. 41 F20 27 28N 97 30 E
Fort Hope, Canada 70 B2 51 30N 88 0W
Fort Irwin, U.S.A. 85 K10 35 16N 116 34W
Fort Kent, U.S.A. 77 B11 47 15N 68 36W
Fort Klamath, U.S.A. 82 E3 42 42N 122 0W
Fort Laramie, U.S.A. 80 D2 42 13N 104 31W
Fort Lauderdale, U.S.A. 77 M5 26 7N 80 8W
Fort Liard, Canada 72 A4 60 14N 123 30W
Fort Liberté, Haiti 89 C5 19 42N 71 51W
Fort Lupton, U.S.A. 80 E2 40 5N 104 49W
Fort Mackay, Canada 72 B6 57 12N 111 41W
Fort Macleod, Canada 72 D6 49 45N 113 30W
Fort McMurray, Canada 72 B6 56 44N 111 7W
Fort McPherson, Canada 68 B6 67 30N 134 55W
Fort Madison, U.S.A. 80 E9 40 38N 91 27W
Fort Meade, U.S.A. 77 M5 27 45N 81 48W
Fort Morgan, U.S.A. 80 E3 40 15N 103 48W
Fort Myers, U.S.A. 77 M5 26 39N 81 52W
Fort Nelson, Canada 72 B4 58 50N 122 44W
Fort Nelson →, Canada 72 B4 59 32N 124 0W
Fort Norman = Tulita, Canada 68 B7 64 57N 125 30W
Fort Payne, U.S.A. 77 H3 34 26N 85 43W
Fort Peck, U.S.A. 82 B10 48 1N 106 27W
Fort Peck Dam, U.S.A. 82 C10 48 0N 106 26W
Fort Peck L., U.S.A. 82 C10 48 0N 106 26W
Fort Pierce, U.S.A. 77 M5 27 27N 80 20W
Fort Pierre, U.S.A. 80 C4 44 21N 100 22W
Fort Plain, U.S.A. 79 D10 42 56N 74 37W
Fort Portal, Uganda .... 54 B3 0 40N 30 20 E
Fort Providence, Canada 72 A5 61 3N 117 40W
Fort Qu'Appelle, Canada 73 C8 50 45N 103 50W
Fort Resolution, Canada 72 A6 61 10N 113 40W
Fort Rixon, Zimbabwe ..... 55 G2 20 2S 29 17 E
Fort Ross, U.S.A. 84 G3 38 32N 123 13W
Fort Rupert = Waskaganish, Canada 70 B4 51 30N 78 40W
Fort St. James, Canada 72 C4 54 30N 124 10W
Fort St. John, Canada 72 B4 56 15N 120 50W
Fort Saskatchewan, Canada . 72 C6 53 40N 113 15W
Fort Scott, U.S.A. 81 G7 37 50N 94 42W
Fort Severn, Canada 70 A2 56 0N 87 40W
Fort Shevchenko, Kazakstan 25 F9 44 35N 50 23 E
Fort Simpson, Canada 72 A4 61 45N 121 15W
Fort Smith, Canada 72 B6 60 0N 111 51W
Fort Smith, U.S.A. 81 H7 35 23N 94 25W
Fort Stockton, U.S.A. 81 K3 30 53N 102 53W
Fort Sumner, U.S.A. 81 H2 34 28N 104 15W
Fort Thompson, U.S.A. 80 C5 44 3N 99 26W
Fort Valley, U.S.A. 77 J4 32 33N 83 53W
Fort Vermilion, Canada 72 B5 58 24N 116 0W
Fort Walton Beach, U.S.A. .. 77 K2 30 25N 86 36W
Fort Wayne, U.S.A. 76 E3 41 4N 85 9W
Fort William, U.K. 12 E3 56 49N 5 7W
Fort Worth, U.S.A. 81 J6 32 45N 97 18W
Fort Yates, U.S.A. 80 B4 46 5N 100 38W

G

Garden Grove

Garden Grove, *U.S.A.* **85 M9** 33 47N 117 55W
Gardēz, *Afghan.* .... **42 C3** 33 37N 69 9 E
Gardiner, *Maine, U.S.A.* **77 C11** 44 14N 69 47W
Gardiner, *Mont., U.S.A.* **82 D8** 45 2N 110 22W
Gardiners I., *U.S.A.* **79 E12** 41 6N 72 6W
Gardner, *U.S.A.* **79 D13** 42 34N 71 59W
Gardner Canal, *Canada* **72 C3** 53 27N 128 8W
Gardnerville, *U.S.A.* **84 G7** 38 56N 119 45W
Gardo, *Somali Rep.* .... **46 F4** 9 30N 49 6 E
Garey, *U.S.A.* **85 L6** 34 53N 120 19W
Garfield, *U.S.A.* **82 C5** 47 1N 117 9W
Garforth, *U.K.* **10 D6** 53 47N 1 24W
Gargano, Mte., *Italy* .... **20 D6** 41 43N 15 43 E
Garibaldi Prov. Park, *Canada* **72 D4** 49 50N 122 40W
Gariep, L., *S. Africa* .... **56 E4** 30 40S 25 40 E
Garies, *S. Africa* .... **56 E2** 30 32S 17 59 E
Garigliano →, *Italy* .... **20 D5** 41 13N 13 45 E
Garissa, *Kenya* .... **54 C4** 0 25S 39 40 E
Garland, *Tex., U.S.A.* **81 J6** 32 55N 96 38W
Garland, *Utah, U.S.A.* **82 F7** 41 47N 112 10W
Garm, *Tajikistan* .... **26 F8** 39 0N 70 20 E
Garmāb, *Iran* .... **45 C8** 35 25N 56 45 E
Garmisch-Partenkirchen,
Germany .... **16 E6** 47 30N 11 6 E
Garmo, Qullai =
Kommunizma, Pik,
Tajikistan .... **26 F8** 39 0N 72 2 E
Garmsār, *Iran* .... **45 C7** 35 20N 52 25 E
Garner, *U.S.A.* **80 D8** 43 6N 93 36W
Garnett, *U.S.A.* **80 F7** 38 17N 95 14W
Garo Hills, *India* .... **43 G14** 25 30N 90 30 E
Garoe, *Somali Rep.* .... **46 F4** 8 25N 48 33 E
Garonne →, *France* **18 D3** 45 2N 0 36W
Garoowe = Garoe,
Somali Rep. .... **46 F4** 8 25N 48 33 E
Garot, *India* .... **42 G6** 24 19N 75 41 E
Garoua, *Cameroon* .... **51 G8** 9 19N 13 21 E
Garrauli, *India* .... **43 G8** 25 5N 79 22 E
Garrison, *Mont., U.S.A.* **82 C7** 46 31N 112 49W
Garrison, *N. Dak., U.S.A.* ... **80 B4** 47 40N 101 25W
Garrison Res. = Sakakawea,
L., *U.S.A.* **80 B4** 47 30N 101 25W
Garron Pt., *U.K.* **13 A6** 55 3N 5 59W
Garry →, *U.K.* **12 E5** 56 44N 3 47W
Garry, L., *Canada* **68 B9** 65 58N 100 18W
Garsen, *Kenya* .... **54 C5** 2 20S 40 5 E
Garson L., *Canada* **73 B6** 56 19N 110 2W
Garu, *India* .... **43 H11** 23 40N 84 14 E
Garub, *Namibia* .... **56 D2** 26 37S 16 0 E
Garut, *Indonesia* .... **37 G12** 7 14S 107 53 E
Garvie Mts., *N.Z.* .... **59 L2** 45 30S 168 50 E
Garwa = Garoua, *Cameroon* **51 G8** 9 19N 13 21 E
Garwa, *India* .... **43 G10** 24 11N 83 47 E
Gary, *U.S.A.* **76 E2** 41 36N 87 20W
Garzê, *China* .... **32 C5** 31 38N 100 1 E
Garzón, *Colombia* **92 C3** 2 10N 75 40W
Gas-San, *Japan* .... **30 E10** 38 32N 140 1 E
Gasan Kuli = Esenguly,
Turkmenistan .... **26 F6** 37 37N 53 59 E
Gascogne, *France* .... **18 E4** 43 45N 0 20 E
Gascogne, G. de, *Europe* ... **18 D2** 44 0N 2 0W
Gascony = Gascogne, *France* **18 E4** 43 45N 0 20 E
Gascoyne →, *Australia* .... **61 D1** 24 52S 113 37 E
Gascoyne Junction, *Australia* **61 E2** 25 2S 115 17 E
Gashaka, *Nigeria* .... **51 G8** 7 20N 11 29 E
Gasherbrum, *Pakistan* ..... **43 B7** 35 40N 76 40 E
Gashua, *Nigeria* .... **51 F8** 12 54N 11 0 E
Gaspé, *Canada* **71 C7** 48 52N 64 30W
Gaspé, C. de, *Canada* **71 C7** 48 48N 64 7W
Gaspé, Pén. de, *Canada* **71 C6** 48 45N 65 40W
Gaspésie, Parc de
Conservation de la, *Canada* **71 C6** 48 55N 65 50W
Gasteiz = Vitoria-Gasteiz,
Spain **19 A4** 42 50N 2 41W
Gastonia, *U.S.A.* **77 H5** 35 16N 81 11W
Gastre, *Argentina* **96 E3** 42 20S 69 15W
Gata, C., *Cyprus* .... **23 E12** 34 34N 33 2 E
Gata, C. de, *Spain* **19 D4** 36 41N 2 13W
Gata, Sierra de, *Spain* **19 B2** 40 20N 6 45W
Gataga →, *Canada* **72 B3** 58 35N 126 59W
Gatehouse of Fleet, *U.K.* **12 G4** 54 53N 4 12W
Gates, *U.S.A.* **78 C7** 43 9N 77 42W
Gateshead, *U.K.* **10 C6** 54 57N 1 35W
Gatesville, *U.S.A.* **81 K6** 31 26N 97 45W
Gaths, *Zimbabwe* .... **55 G3** 20 2S 30 32 E
Gatico, *Chile* **94 A1** 22 29S 70 20W
Gatineau, *Canada* **79 A9** 45 29N 75 38W
Gatineau →, *Canada* **70 C4** 45 27N 75 42W
Gatineau, Parc Nat. de la,
Canada **70 C4** 45 40N 76 0W
Gatton, *Australia* .... **63 D5** 27 32S 152 17 E
Gatun, L., *Panama* **88 E4** 9 7N 79 56W
Gatyana, *S. Africa* .... **57 E4** 32 16S 28 31 E
Gau, *Fiji* .... **59 D8** 18 2S 179 18 E
Gauer L., *Canada* **73 B9** 57 0N 97 50W
Gauhati = Guwahati, *India* .. **41 F17** 26 10N 91 45 E
Gauja →, *Latvia* .... **9 H21** 57 10N 24 16 E
Gaula →, *Norway* .... **8 E14** 63 21N 10 14 E
Gauri Phanta, *India* .... **43 E9** 28 41N 80 36 E
Gausta, *Norway* .... **9 G13** 59 48N 8 40 E
Gauteng □, *S. Africa* ...... **57 D4** 26 0S 28 0 E
Gāv Koshī, *Iran* .... **45 D8** 28 38N 57 12 E
Gāvakān, *Iran* .... **45 D7** 29 37N 53 10 E
Gavāter, *Iran* .... **45 E9** 25 10N 61 31 E
Gāvbandī, *Iran* .... **45 E7** 27 12N 53 4 E
Gavdhopoúla, *Greece* ...... **23 E6** 34 56N 24 0 E
Gávdhos, *Greece* .... **23 E6** 34 50N 24 5 E
Gaviota, *U.S.A.* **85 L6** 34 29N 120 13W
Gāvkhūnī, Bāţlāq-e, *Iran* .... **45 C7** 32 6N 52 52 E
Gävle, *Sweden* .... **9 F17** 60 40N 17 9 E
Gawachab, *Namibia* .... **56 D2** 27 4S 17 55 E
Gawilgarh Hills, *India* ...... **40 J10** 21 15N 76 45 E
Gawler, *Australia* .... **63 E2** 34 30S 138 42 E
Gaxun Nur, *China* .... **32 B5** 42 22N 100 30 E
Gay, *Russia* .... **24 D10** 51 27N 58 27 E
Gaya, *India* .... **43 G11** 24 47N 85 4 E
Gaya, *Niger* .... **50 F6** 11 52N 3 28 E
Gaylord, *U.S.A.* **76 C3** 45 2N 84 41W
Gayndah, *Australia* .... **63 D5** 25 35S 151 32 E
Gaysin = Haysyn, *Ukraine* .. **17 D15** 48 57N 29 25 E
Gayvoron = Hayvoron,
Ukraine .... **17 D15** 48 22N 29 52 E
Gaza, *Gaza Strip* .... **47 D3** 31 30N 34 28 E
Gaza □, *Mozam.* .... **57 C5** 23 10S 32 45 E
Gaza Strip □, *Asia* .... **47 D3** 31 29N 34 25 E
Gazanjyk, *Turkmenistan* .... **45 B7** 39 16N 55 32 E
Gāzbor, *Iran* .... **45 D8** 28 5N 58 51 E
Gazi, *Dem. Rep. of the Congo* **54 B1** 1 3N 24 30 E
Gaziantep, *Turkey* .... **25 G6** 37 6N 37 23 E
Gcoverega, *Botswana* ...... **56 B3** 19 8S 24 18 E
Gcuwa, *S. Africa* .... **57 E4** 32 20S 28 11 E
Gdańsk, *Poland* .... **17 A10** 54 22N 18 40 E
Gdańska, Zatoka, *Poland* .... **17 A10** 54 30N 19 20 E
Gdov, *Russia* .... **9 G22** 58 48N 27 55 E
Gdynia, *Poland* .... **17 A10** 54 35N 18 33 E
Gebe, *Indonesia* .... **37 D7** 0 5N 129 25 E
Gebze, *Turkey* .... **21 D13** 40 47N 29 25 E
Gedaref, *Sudan* .... **51 F13** 14 2N 35 28 E
Gediz →, *Turkey* .... **21 E12** 38 35N 26 48 E
Gedser, *Denmark* .... **9 J14** 54 35N 11 55 E
Geegully Cr. →, *Australia* .. **60 C3** 18 32S 123 41 E
Geel, *Belgium* .... **15 C4** 51 10N 4 59 E
Geelong, *Australia* .... **63 F3** 38 10S 144 22 E
Geelvink B. = Cenderwasih,
Teluk, *Indonesia* .... **37 E9** 3 0S 135 20 E
Geelvink Chan., *Australia* ... **61 E1** 28 30S 114 0 E
Geesthacht, *Germany* ...... **16 B6** 53 26N 10 22 E
Geidam, *Nigeria* .... **51 F8** 12 57N 11 57 E
Geikie →, *Canada* **73 B8** 57 45N 103 52W
Geistown, *U.S.A.* **78 F6** 40 18N 78 52W
Geita, *Tanzania* .... **54 C3** 2 48S 32 12 E
Gejiu, *China* .... **32 D5** 23 20N 103 10 E
Gel, Meydān-e, *Iran* .... **45 D7** 29 4N 54 50 E
Gela, *Italy* .... **20 F6** 37 4N 14 15 E
Gelderland □, *Neths.* ...... **15 B6** 52 5N 6 10 E
Geldrop, *Neths.* .... **15 C5** 51 25N 5 32 E
Geleen, *Neths.* .... **15 D5** 50 57N 5 49 E
Gelibolu, *Turkey* .... **21 D12** 40 28N 26 43 E
Gelsenkirchen, *Germany* .... **16 C4** 51 32N 7 6 E
Gemas, *Malaysia* .... **39 L4** 2 37N 102 36 E
Gembloux, *Belgium* .... **15 D4** 50 34N 4 43 E
Gemena, *Dem. Rep. of*
the Congo .... **52 D3** 3 13N 19 48 E
Gemerek, *Turkey* .... **44 B3** 39 15N 36 10 E
Gemlik, *Turkey* .... **21 D13** 40 26N 29 9 E
Genale →, *Ethiopia* .... **46 F2** 6 2N 39 1 E
General Acha, *Argentina* ... **94 D3** 37 20S 64 38W
General Alvear, *Buenos Aires,*
Argentina **94 D4** 36 0S 60 0W
General Alvear, *Mendoza,*
Argentina **94 D2** 35 0S 67 40W
General Artigas, *Paraguay* .. **94 B4** 26 52S 56 16W
General Belgrano, *Argentina* **94 D4** 36 35S 58 47W
General Cabrera, *Argentina* . **94 C3** 32 53S 63 52W
General Cepeda, *Mexico* **86 B4** 25 23N 101 27W
General Guido, *Argentina* .. **94 D4** 36 40S 57 50W
General Juan Madariaga,
Argentina **94 D4** 37 0S 57 0W
General La Madrid, *Argentina* **94 D3** 37 17S 61 20W
General MacArthur, *Phil.* .... **37 B7** 11 18N 125 28 E
General Martin Miguel de
Güemes, *Argentina* **94 A3** 24 50S 65 0W
General Paz, *Argentina* **94 B4** 27 45S 57 36W
General Pico, *Argentina* **94 D3** 35 45S 63 50W
General Pinedo, *Argentina* .. **94 B3** 27 15S 61 20W
General Pinto, *Argentina* ... **94 C3** 34 45S 61 50W
General Roca, *Argentina* **96 D3** 39 2S 67 35W
General Santos, *Phil.* ...... **37 C7** 6 5N 125 14 E
General Trevino, *Mexico* **87 B5** 26 14N 99 29W
General Trías, *Mexico* **86 B3** 28 21N 106 22W
General Viamonte, *Argentina* **94 D3** 35 1S 61 3W
General Villegas, *Argentina* . **94 D3** 35 5S 63 0W
Genesee, *Idaho, U.S.A.* **82 C5** 46 33N 116 56W
Genesee, *Pa., U.S.A.* **78 E7** 41 59N 77 54W
Genesee →, *U.S.A.* **78 C7** 43 16N 77 36W
Geneseo, *Ill., U.S.A.* **80 E9** 41 27N 90 9W
Geneseo, *N.Y., U.S.A.* **78 D7** 42 48N 77 49W
Geneva = Genève, *Switz.* ... **18 C7** 46 12N 6 9 E
Geneva, *Ala., U.S.A.* **77 K3** 31 2N 85 52W
Geneva, *N.Y., U.S.A.* **78 D8** 42 52N 76 59W
Geneva, *Nebr., U.S.A.* **80 E6** 40 32N 97 36W
Geneva, *Ohio, U.S.A.* **78 E4** 41 48N 80 57W
Geneva, L. = Léman, L.,
Europe .... **18 C7** 46 26N 6 30 E
Geneva, L., *U.S.A.* **76 D1** 42 38N 88 30W
Genève, *Switz.* .... **18 C7** 46 12N 6 9 E
Genil →, *Spain* **19 D3** 37 42N 5 19W
Genk, *Belgium* .... **15 D5** 50 58N 5 32 E
Gennargentu, Mti. del, *Italy* . **20 D3** 40 1N 9 19 E
Genoa = Gênova, *Italy* ..... **18 D8** 44 25N 8 57 E
Genoa, *Australia* .... **63 F4** 37 29S 149 35 E
Genoa, *N.Y., U.S.A.* **79 D8** 42 40N 76 32W
Genoa, *Nebr., U.S.A.* **80 E6** 41 27N 97 44W
Genoa, *Nev., U.S.A.* **84 F7** 39 2N 119 50W
Génova, *Italy* .... **18 D8** 44 25N 8 57 E
Génova, G. di, *Italy* .... **20 C3** 44 0N 9 0 E
Genriyetty, Ostrov, *Russia* .. **27 B16** 77 6N 156 30 E
Gent, *Belgium* .... **15 C3** 51 2N 3 42 E
Genteng, *Indonesia* .... **37 G12** 7 22S 106 24 E
Genyem, *Indonesia* .... **37 E10** 2 46S 140 12 E
Geographe B., *Australia* .... **61 F2** 33 30S 115 15 E
Geographe Chan., *Australia* . **61 D1** 24 30S 113 0 E
Georga, Zemlya, *Russia* ..... **26 A5** 80 30N 49 0 E
George, *S. Africa* .... **56 E3** 33 58S 22 29 E
George →, *Canada* **71 A6** 58 49N 66 10W
George, L., *N.S.W., Australia* **63 F4** 35 10S 149 25 E
George, L., *S. Austral.,*
Australia .... **63 F3** 37 25S 140 0 E
George, L., *W. Austral.,*
Australia .... **60 D3** 22 45S 123 40 E
George, L., *Uganda* .... **54 B3** 0 5N 30 10 E
George, L., *Fla., U.S.A.* **77 L5** 29 17N 81 36W
George, L., *N.Y., U.S.A.* **79 C11** 43 37N 73 33W
George Gill Ra., *Australia* ... **60 D5** 24 22S 131 45 E
George River =
Kangiqsualujjuaq, *Canada* **69 C13** 58 30N 65 59W
George Sound, *N.Z.* .... **59 L1** 44 52S 167 25 E
George Town, *Australia* ..... **62 G4** 41 6S 146 49 E
George Town, *Bahamas* **88 B4** 23 33N 75 47W
George Town, *Cayman Is.* ... **88 C3** 19 20N 81 24W
George Town, *Malaysia* ..... **39 K3** 5 25N 100 20 E
George V Land, *Antarctica* .. **5 C10** 69 0S 148 0 E
George VI Sound, *Antarctica* **5 D17** 71 0S 68 0W
George West, *U.S.A.* **81 L5** 28 20N 98 7W
Georgetown, *Australia* ...... **62 B3** 18 17S 143 33 E
Georgetown, *Ont., Canada* .. **78 C5** 43 40N 79 56W
Georgetown, *P.E.I., Canada* . **71 C7** 46 13N 62 24W
Georgetown, *Gambia* **50 F3** 13 30N 14 47W
Georgetown, *Guyana* **92 B7** 6 50N 58 12W
Georgetown, *Calif., U.S.A.* .. **84 G6** 38 54N 120 50W
Georgetown, *Colo., U.S.A.* .. **82 G11** 39 42N 105 42W
Georgetown, *Ky., U.S.A.* **76 F3** 38 13N 84 33W
Georgetown, *N.Y., U.S.A.* ... **79 D9** 42 46N 75 44W
Georgetown, *Ohio, U.S.A.* ... **76 F4** 38 52N 83 54W
Georgetown, *S.C., U.S.A.* ... **77 J6** 33 23N 79 17W
Georgetown, *Tex., U.S.A.* ... **81 K6** 30 38N 97 41W
Georgia □, *U.S.A.* **77 K5** 32 50N 83 15W
Georgia ■, *Asia* .... **25 F7** 42 0N 43 0 E
Georgia, Str. of, *Canada* **72 D4** 49 25N 124 0W
Georgian B., *Canada* **78 A4** 45 15N 81 0W
Georgina →, *Australia* ..... **62 C2** 23 30S 139 47 E
Georgina I., *Canada* **78 B5** 44 22N 79 17W
Georgiu-Dezh = Liski, *Russia* **25 D6** 51 3N 39 30 E
Georgiyevsk, *Russia* .... **25 F7** 44 12N 43 28 E
Gera, *Germany* .... **16 C7** 50 53N 12 4 E
Geraardsbergen, *Belgium* ... **15 D3** 50 45N 3 53 E
Geral, Serra, *Brazil* **95 B6** 26 25S 50 0W
Geral de Goiás, Serra, *Brazil* **93 F9** 12 0S 46 0W
Geraldine, *U.S.A.* **82 C8** 47 36N 110 16W
Geraldton, *Australia* .... **61 E1** 28 48S 114 32 E
Geraldton, *Canada* **70 C2** 49 44N 86 59W
Gereshk, *Afghan.* .... **40 D4** 31 47N 64 35 E
Gerik, *Malaysia* .... **39 K3** 5 50N 101 15 E
Gering, *U.S.A.* **80 E3** 41 50N 103 40W
Gerlach, *U.S.A.* **82 F4** 40 39N 119 21W
Germansen Landing, *Canada* **72 B4** 55 43N 124 40W
Germantown, *U.S.A.* **81 M10** 35 5N 89 49W
Germany ■, *Europe* .... **16 C6** 51 0N 10 0 E
Germī, *Iran* .... **45 B6** 39 1N 48 3 E
Germiston, *S. Africa* .... **57 D4** 26 15S 28 10 E
Gernika-Lumo, *Spain* **19 A4** 43 19N 2 40W
Gero, *Japan* .... **31 G8** 35 48N 137 14 E
Gerona = Girona, *Spain* .... **19 B7** 41 58N 2 46 E
Gerrard, *Canada* **72 C5** 50 30N 117 17W
Geser, *Indonesia* .... **37 E8** 3 50S 130 54 E
Getafe, *Spain* **19 B4** 40 18N 3 44W
Gettysburg, *Pa., U.S.A.* **76 F7** 39 50N 77 14W
Gettysburg, *S. Dak., U.S.A.* . **80 C5** 45 1N 99 57W
Getxo, *Spain* **19 A4** 43 21N 2 59W
Getz Ice Shelf, *Antarctica* ... **5 D14** 75 0S 130 0W
Geyser, *U.S.A.* **82 C8** 47 16N 110 30W
Geyserville, *U.S.A.* **84 G4** 38 42N 122 54W
Ghaggar →, *India* .... **42 E6** 29 30N 74 53 E
Ghaghara →, *India* .... **43 G11** 25 45N 84 40 E
Ghaghat →, *Bangla.* .... **43 G13** 25 19N 89 38 E
Ghagra, *India* .... **43 H11** 23 17N 84 33 E
Ghagra →, *India* .... **43 F9** 27 29N 81 9 E
Ghana ■, *W. Afr.* **50 G5** 8 0N 1 0W
Ghansor, *India* .... **43 H9** 22 39N 80 1 E
Ghanzi, *Botswana* .... **56 C3** 21 50S 21 34 E
Ghardaïa, *Algeria* .... **50 B6** 32 20N 3 37 E
Gharyān, *Libya* .... **51 B8** 32 10N 13 0 E
Ghat, *Libya* .... **51 D8** 24 59N 10 11 E
Ghatal, *India* .... **43 H12** 22 40N 87 46 E
Ghatampur, *India* .... **43 F9** 26 8N 80 13 E
Ghatsila, *India* .... **43 H12** 22 36N 86 29 E
Ghaţţī, *Si. Arabia* .... **44 D3** 31 16N 37 31 E
Ghawdex = Gozo, *Malta* .... **23 C1** 36 3N 14 15 E
Ghazal, Bahr el →, *Chad* .... **51 F9** 13 0N 15 47 E
Ghazâl, Bahr el →, *Sudan* .. **51 G12** 9 31N 30 25 E
Ghaziabad, *India* .... **42 E7** 28 42N 77 26 E
Ghazipur, *India* .... **43 G10** 25 38N 83 35 E
Ghaznī, *Afghan.* .... **42 C3** 33 30N 68 28 E
Ghaznī □, *Afghan.* .... **40 C6** 32 10N 68 20 E
Ghent = Gent, *Belgium* ..... **15 C3** 51 2N 3 42 E
Gheorghe Gheorghiu-Dej =
Oneşti, *Romania* .... **17 E14** 46 17N 26 47 E
Ghīnah, Wādī al →, *Si. Arabia* **44 D3** 30 27N 38 14 E
Ghizao, *Afghan.* .... **42 C1** 33 20N 65 44 E
Ghizar →, *Pakistan* .... **43 A5** 36 15N 73 43 E
Ghotaru, *India* .... **42 F4** 27 20N 70 1 E
Ghotki, *Pakistan* .... **42 E3** 28 5N 69 21 E
Ghowr □, *Afghan.* .... **40 C4** 34 0N 64 20 E
Ghudaf, W. al →, *Iraq* ...... **44 C4** 32 56N 43 30 E
Ghudāmis, *Libya* .... **49 C4** 30 11N 9 29 E
Ghughri, *India* .... **43 H9** 22 39N 80 41 E
Ghugus, *India* .... **40 K11** 19 58N 79 12 E
Ghulam Mohammad Barrage,
Pakistan .... **42 G3** 25 30N 68 20 E
Ghūriān, *Afghan.* .... **40 B2** 34 17N 61 25 E
Gia Dinh, *Vietnam* .... **39 G6** 10 49N 106 42 E
Gia Lai = Plei Ku, *Vietnam* .. **38 F7** 13 57N 108 0 E
Gia Nghia, *Vietnam* .... **39 G6** 11 58N 107 42 E
Gia Ngoc, *Vietnam* .... **38 E7** 14 50N 108 58 E
Gia Vuc, *Vietnam* .... **38 E7** 14 42N 108 34 E
Giant Forest, *U.S.A.* **84 J8** 36 36N 118 43W
Giants Causeway, *U.K.* **13 A5** 55 16N 6 29W
Giarabub = Al Jaghbūb, *Libya* **51 C10** 29 42N 24 38 E
Giarre, *Italy* .... **20 F6** 37 43N 15 11 E
Gibara, *Cuba* **88 B4** 21 9N 76 11W
Gibb River, *Australia* ...... **60 C4** 16 26S 126 26 E
Gibbon, *U.S.A.* **80 E5** 40 45N 98 51W
Gibeon, *Namibia* .... **56 D2** 25 9S 17 43 E
Gibraltar ■, *Europe* **19 D3** 36 7N 5 22W
Gibraltar, Str. of, *Medit. S.* .. **19 E3** 35 55N 5 40W
Gibson Desert, *Australia* .... **60 D4** 24 0S 126 0 E
Gibsons, *Canada* **72 D4** 49 24N 123 32W
Gibsonville, *U.S.A.* **84 F6** 39 46N 120 54W
Giddings, *U.S.A.* **81 K6** 30 11N 96 56W
Giebnegáisi = Kebnekaise,
Sweden .... **8 C18** 67 53N 18 33 E
Giessen, *Germany* .... **16 C5** 50 34N 8 41 E
Gīfān, *Iran* .... **45 B8** 37 54N 57 28 E
Gift Lake, *Canada* **72 B5** 55 53N 115 49W
Gifu, *Japan* .... **31 G8** 35 30N 136 45 E
Gifu □, *Japan* .... **31 G8** 35 40N 137 0 E
Giganta, Sa. de la, *Mexico* .. **86 B2** 25 30N 111 30W
Gigha, *U.K.* **12 F3** 55 42N 5 44W
Giglio, *Italy* .... **20 C4** 42 20N 10 52 E
Gijón, *Spain* **19 A3** 43 32N 5 42W
Gil I., *Canada* **72 C3** 53 12N 129 15W
Gila →, *U.S.A.* **83 K6** 32 43N 114 33W
Gila Bend, *U.S.A.* **83 K7** 32 57N 112 43W
Gila Bend Mts., *U.S.A.* **83 K7** 33 10N 113 0W
Gīlān □, *Iran* .... **45 B6** 37 0N 50 0 E
Gilbert →, *Australia* .... **62 B3** 16 35S 141 15 E
Gilbert Is., *Kiribati* .... **64 G9** 1 0N 172 0 E
Gilbert River, *Australia* ..... **62 B3** 18 9S 142 52 E
Gilead, *U.S.A.* **79 B14** 44 24N 70 59W
Gilford I., *Canada* **72 C3** 50 40N 126 30W
Gilgandra, *Australia* .... **63 E4** 31 43S 148 39 E
Gilgil, *Kenya* .... **54 C4** 0 30S 36 20 E
Gilgit, *India* .... **43 B6** 35 50N 74 15 E
Gilgit →, *Pakistan* .... **43 B6** 35 44N 74 37 E
Gillam, *Canada* **73 B10** 56 20N 94 40W
Gillen, L., *Australia* .... **61 E3** 26 11S 124 38 E
Gilles, L., *Australia* .... **63 E2** 32 50S 136 45 E
Gillette, *U.S.A.* **80 C2** 44 18N 105 30W
Gilliat, *Australia* .... **62 C3** 20 40S 141 28 E
Gillingham, *U.K.* .... **11 F8** 51 23N 0 33 E
Gilmer, *U.S.A.* **81 J7** 32 44N 94 57W
Gilmore, L., *Australia* ...... **61 F3** 32 29S 121 37 E
Gilroy, *U.S.A.* **84 H5** 37 1N 121 34W
Gimli, *Canada* **73 C9** 50 40N 97 0W
Gin Gin, *Australia* .... **63 D5** 25 0S 151 58 E
Gingin, *Australia* .... **61 F2** 31 22S 115 54 E
Gingindlovu, *S. Africa* ..... **57 D5** 29 2S 31 30 E
Ginir, *Ethiopia* .... **46 F3** 7 6N 40 40 E
Gióna, Óros, *Greece* .... **21 E10** 38 38N 22 14 E
Gir Hills, *India* .... **42 J4** 21 0N 71 0 E
Girab, *India* .... **42 F4** 26 2N 70 38 E
Girâfi, W. →, *Egypt* .... **47 F3** 29 58N 34 39 E
Girard, *Kans., U.S.A.* **81 G7** 37 31N 94 51W
Girard, *Ohio, U.S.A.* **78 E4** 41 9N 80 42W
Girard, *Pa., U.S.A.* **78 E4** 42 0N 80 19W
Girdle Ness, *U.K.* **12 D6** 57 9N 2 3W
Giresun, *Turkey* .... **25 F6** 40 55N 38 30 E
Girga, *Egypt* .... **51 C12** 26 17N 31 55 E
Giri →, *India* .... **42 D7** 30 28N 77 41 E
Giridih, *India* .... **43 G12** 24 10N 86 21 E
Girne = Kyrenia, *Cyprus* .... **23 D12** 35 20N 33 20 E
Girona, *Spain* .... **19 B7** 41 58N 2 46 E
Gironde →, *France* **18 D3** 45 32N 1 7W
Giru, *Australia* .... **62 B4** 19 30S 147 5 E
Girvan, *U.K.* **12 F4** 55 14N 4 51W
Gisborne, *N.Z.* .... **59 H7** 38 39S 178 5 E
Gisenyi, *Rwanda* .... **54 C2** 1 41S 29 15 E
Gislaved, *Sweden* .... **9 H15** 57 19N 13 32 E
Gitega, *Burundi* .... **54 C2** 3 26S 29 56 E
Giuba →, *Somali Rep.* ...... **46 G3** 1 30N 42 35 E
Giurgiu, *Romania* .... **17 G13** 43 52N 25 57 E
Giza = El Gîza, *Egypt* ...... **51 C12** 30 0N 31 10 E
Gizhiga, *Russia* .... **27 C17** 62 3N 160 30 E
Gizhiginskaya Guba, *Russia* . **27 C16** 61 0N 158 0 E
Giżycko, *Poland* .... **17 A11** 54 2N 21 48 E
Gjirokastër, *Albania* .... **21 D9** 40 7N 20 10 E
Gjoa Haven, *Canada* **68 B10** 68 20N 96 8W
Gjøvik, *Norway* .... **9 F14** 60 47N 10 43 E
Glace Bay, *Canada* **71 C8** 46 11N 59 58W
Glacier Bay Nat. Park and
Preserve, *U.S.A.* **72 B1** 58 45N 136 30W
Glacier Nat. Park, *Canada* ... **72 C5** 51 15N 117 30W
Glacier Nat. Park, *U.S.A.* **82 B7** 48 30N 113 18W
Glacier Peak, *U.S.A.* **82 B3** 48 7N 121 7W
Gladewater, *U.S.A.* **81 J7** 32 33N 94 56W
Gladstone, *Queens., Australia* **62 C5** 23 52S 151 16 E
Gladstone, *S. Austral.,*
Australia .... **63 E2** 33 15S 138 22 E
Gladstone, *Canada* **73 C9** 50 13N 98 57W
Gladstone, *U.S.A.* **76 C2** 45 51N 87 1W
Gladwin, *U.S.A.* **76 D3** 43 59N 84 29W
Glåma = Glomma →, *Norway* **9 G14** 59 12N 10 57 E
Gláma, *Iceland* **8 D2** 65 48N 23 0W
Glamis, *U.S.A.* **85 N11** 32 55N 115 5W
Glasco, *Kans., U.S.A.* **80 F6** 39 22N 97 50W
Glasco, *N.Y., U.S.A.* **79 D11** 42 3N 73 57W
Glasgow, *U.K.* **12 F4** 55 51N 4 15W
Glasgow, *Ky., U.S.A.* **76 G3** 37 0N 85 55W
Glasgow, *Mont., U.S.A.* **82 B10** 48 12N 106 38W
Glasgow, City of □, *U.K.* **12 F4** 55 51N 4 12W
Glaslyn, *Canada* **73 C7** 53 22N 108 21W
Glastonbury, *U.K.* **11 F5** 51 9N 2 43W
Glastonbury, *U.S.A.* **79 E12** 41 43N 72 37W
Glazov, *Russia* .... **24 C9** 58 9N 52 40 E
Gleichen, *Canada* **72 C6** 50 52N 113 3W
Gleiwitz = Gliwice, *Poland* .. **17 C10** 50 22N 18 41 E
Glen, *U.S.A.* **79 B13** 44 7N 71 11W
Glen Affric, *U.K.* **12 D3** 57 17N 5 1W
Glen Canyon, *U.S.A.* **83 H8** 37 30N 110 40W
Glen Canyon Dam, *U.S.A.* ... **83 H8** 36 57N 111 29W
Glen Canyon Nat. Recr. Area,
U.S.A. **83 H8** 37 15N 111 0W
Glen Coe, *U.K.* **12 E3** 56 40N 5 0W
Glen Cove, *U.S.A.* **79 F11** 40 52N 73 38W
Glen Garry, *U.K.* **12 D3** 57 3N 5 7W
Glen Innes, *Australia* ...... **63 D5** 29 44S 151 44 E
Glen Lyon, *U.S.A.* **79 E8** 41 10N 76 5W
Glen Mor, *U.K.* **12 D4** 57 9N 4 37W
Glen Moriston, *U.K.* **12 D4** 57 11N 4 52W
Glen Robertson, *Canada* **79 A10** 45 22N 74 30W
Glen Spean, *U.K.* **12 E4** 56 53N 4 40W
Glen Ullin, *U.S.A.* **80 B4** 46 49N 101 50W
Glencoe, *Canada* **78 D3** 42 45N 81 43W
Glencoe, *S. Africa* .... **57 D5** 28 11S 30 11 E
Glencoe, *U.S.A.* **80 C7** 44 46N 94 9W
Glendale, *Ariz., U.S.A.* **83 K7** 33 32N 112 11W
Glendale, *Calif., U.S.A.* **85 L8** 34 9N 118 15W
Glendale, *Zimbabwe* .... **55 F3** 17 22S 31 5 E
Glendive, *U.S.A.* **80 B2** 47 7N 104 43W
Glendo, *U.S.A.* **80 D2** 42 30N 105 2W
Glenelg →, *Australia* ...... **63 F3** 38 4S 140 59 E
Glenfield, *U.S.A.* **79 C9** 43 43N 75 24W
Glengarriff, *Ireland* **13 E2** 51 45N 9 34W
Glenmont, *U.S.A.* **78 F2** 40 31N 82 6W
Glenmorgan, *Australia* ..... **63 D4** 27 14S 149 42 E
Glenn, *U.S.A.* **84 F4** 39 31N 122 1W
Glennallen, *U.S.A.* **68 B5** 62 7N 145 33W
Glennamaddy, *Ireland* **13 C3** 53 37N 8 33W
Glenns Ferry, *U.S.A.* **82 E6** 42 57N 115 18W
Glenore, *Australia* .... **62 B3** 17 50S 141 12 E
Glenreagh, *Australia* .... **63 E5** 30 2S 153 1 E
Glenrock, *U.S.A.* **82 E11** 42 52N 105 52W
Glenrothes, *U.K.* **12 E5** 56 12N 3 10W
Glens Falls, *U.S.A.* **79 C11** 43 19N 73 39W
Glenside, *U.S.A.* **79 F9** 40 6N 75 9W
Glenties, *Ireland* **13 B3** 54 49N 8 16W
Glenville, *U.S.A.* **76 F5** 38 56N 80 50W
Glenwood, *Canada* **71 C9** 49 0N 54 58W
Glenwood, *Ark., U.S.A.* **81 H8** 34 20N 93 33W
Glenwood, *Iowa, U.S.A.* **80 E7** 41 3N 95 45W
Glenwood, *Minn., U.S.A.* **80 C7** 45 39N 95 23W
Glenwood, *Wash., U.S.A.* ... **84 D5** 46 1N 121 17W
Glenwood Springs, *U.S.A.* ... **82 G10** 39 33N 107 19W
Glettinganes, *Iceland* **8 D7** 65 30N 13 37W
Gliwice, *Poland* .... **17 C10** 50 22N 18 41 E
Globe, *U.S.A.* **83 K8** 33 24N 110 47W
Głogów, *Poland* .... **16 C9** 51 37N 16 5 E
Glomma →, *Norway* .... **9 G14** 59 12N 10 57 E
Glorieuses, Is., *Ind. Oc.* .... **57 A8** 11 30S 47 20 E
Glossop, *U.K.* **10 D6** 53 27N 1 56W

Green Valley

Green Valley, *U.S.A.* 83 L8 31 52N 110 56W
Greenbank, *U.S.A.* 84 B4 48 6N 122 34W
Greenbush, *Mich., U.S.A.* 78 B1 44 35N 83 19W
Greenbush, *Minn., U.S.A.* 80 A6 48 42N 96 11W
Greencastle, *U.S.A.* 76 F2 39 38N 86 52W
Greene, *U.S.A.* 79 D9 42 20N 75 46W
Greenfield, *Calif., U.S.A.* 84 J5 36 19N 121 15W
Greenfield, *Calif., U.S.A.* 85 K8 35 15N 119 0W
Greenfield, *Ind., U.S.A.* 76 F3 39 47N 85 46W
Greenfield, *Iowa, U.S.A.* 80 E7 41 18N 94 28W
Greenfield, *Mass., U.S.A.* 79 D12 42 35N 72 36W
Greenfield, *Mo., U.S.A.* 81 G8 37 25N 93 51W
Greenfield Park, *Canada* 79 A11 45 29N 73 29W
Greenland ■, *N. Amer.* 4 C5 66 0N 45 0W
Greenland Sea, *Arctic* 4 B7 73 0N 10 0W
Greenock, *U.K.* 12 F4 55 57N 4 46W
Greenore, *Ireland* 13 B5 54 2N 6 8W
Greenore Pt., *Ireland* 13 D5 52 14N 6 19W
Greenough, *Australia* 61 E1 28 58S 114 43 E
Greenough →, *Australia* 61 E1 28 51S 114 38 E
Greenough Pt., *Canada* 78 B3 44 58N 81 26W
Greenport, *U.S.A.* 79 E12 41 6N 72 22W
Greensboro, *Ga., U.S.A.* 77 J4 33 35N 83 11W
Greensboro, *N.C., U.S.A.* 77 G6 36 4N 79 48W
Greensboro, *Vt., U.S.A.* 79 B12 44 36N 72 18W
Greensburg, *Ind., U.S.A.* 76 F3 39 20N 85 29W
Greensburg, *Kans., U.S.A.* 81 G5 37 36N 99 18W
Greensburg, *Pa., U.S.A.* 78 F5 40 18N 79 33W
Greenstone Pt., *U.K.* 12 D3 57 55N 5 37W
Greenvale, *Australia* 62 B4 18 59S 145 7 E
Greenville, *Ala., U.S.A.* 77 K2 31 50N 86 38W
Greenville, *Calif., U.S.A.* 84 E6 40 8N 120 57W
Greenville, *Maine, U.S.A.* 77 C11 45 28N 69 35W
Greenville, *Mich., U.S.A.* 76 D3 43 11N 85 15W
Greenville, *Miss., U.S.A.* 81 J9 33 24N 91 4W
Greenville, *Mo., U.S.A.* 81 G9 37 8N 90 27W
Greenville, *N.C., U.S.A.* 77 H7 35 37N 77 23W
Greenville, *N.H., U.S.A.* 79 D13 42 46N 71 49W
Greenville, *N.Y., U.S.A.* 79 D10 42 25N 74 1W
Greenville, *Ohio, U.S.A.* 76 E3 40 6N 84 38W
Greenville, *Pa., U.S.A.* 78 E4 41 24N 80 23W
Greenville, *S.C., U.S.A.* 77 H4 34 51N 82 24W
Greenville, *Tenn., U.S.A.* 77 G4 36 13N 82 51W
Greenville, *Tex., U.S.A.* 81 J6 33 8N 96 7W
Greenwater Lake Prov. Park, *Canada* 73 C8 52 32N 103 30W
Greenwich, *Conn., U.S.A.* 79 E11 41 2N 73 38W
Greenwich, *N.Y., U.S.A.* 79 C11 43 5N 73 30W
Greenwich, *Ohio, U.S.A.* 78 E2 41 2N 82 31W
Greenwich □, *U.K.* 11 F8 51 29N 0 1 E
Greenwood, *Canada* 72 D5 49 10N 118 40W
Greenwood, *Ark., U.S.A.* 81 H7 35 13N 94 16W
Greenwood, *Ind., U.S.A.* 76 F2 39 37N 86 7W
Greenwood, *Miss., U.S.A.* 81 J9 33 31N 90 11W
Greenwood, *S.C., U.S.A.* 77 H4 34 12N 82 10W
Greenwood, Mt., *Australia* 60 B5 13 48S 130 4 E
Gregory, *U.S.A.* 80 D5 43 14N 99 20W
Gregory →, *Australia* 62 B2 17 53S 139 17 E
Gregory, L., *S. Austral., Australia* 63 D2 28 55S 139 0 E
Gregory, L., *W. Austral., Australia* 61 E2 25 38S 119 58 E
Gregory Downs, *Australia* 62 B2 18 35S 138 45 E
Gregory L., *Australia* 60 D4 20 0S 127 40 E
Gregory Ra., *Queens., Australia* 62 B3 19 30S 143 40 E
Gregory Ra., *W. Austral., Australia* 60 D3 21 20S 121 12 E
Greifswald, *Germany* 16 A7 54 5N 13 23 E
Greiz, *Germany* 16 C7 50 39N 12 10 E
Gremikha, *Russia* 24 A6 67 59N 39 47 E
Grenå, *Denmark* 9 H14 56 25N 10 53 E
Grenada, *U.S.A.* 81 J10 33 47N 89 49W
Grenada ■, *W. Indies* 89 D7 12 10N 61 40W
Grenadier I., *U.S.A.* 79 B8 44 3N 76 22W
Grenadines, *St. Vincent* 89 D7 12 40N 61 20W
Grenen, *Denmark* 9 H14 57 44N 10 40 E
Grenfell, *Australia* 63 E4 33 52S 148 8 E
Grenfell, *Canada* 73 C8 50 30N 102 56W
Grenoble, *France* 18 D6 45 12N 5 42 E
Grenville, C., *Australia* 62 A3 12 0S 143 13 E
Grenville Chan., *Canada* 72 C3 53 40N 129 46W
Gresham, *U.S.A.* 84 E4 45 30N 122 26W
Gresik, *Indonesia* 37 G15 7 13S 112 38 E
Gretna, *U.K.* 12 F5 55 0N 3 3W
Grevenmacher, *Lux.* 15 E6 49 41N 6 26 E
Grey →, *Canada* 71 C8 47 34N 57 6W
Grey →, *N.Z.* 59 K3 42 27S 171 12 E
Grey, C., *Australia* 62 A2 13 0S 136 35 E
Grey Ra., *Australia* 63 D3 27 0S 143 30 E
Greybull, *U.S.A.* 82 D9 44 30N 108 3W
Greymouth, *N.Z.* 59 K3 42 29S 171 13 E
Greystones, *Ireland* 13 C5 53 9N 6 5W
Greytown, *N.Z.* 59 J5 41 5S 175 29 E
Greytown, *S. Africa* 57 D5 29 1S 30 36 E
Gribbell I., *Canada* 72 C3 53 23N 129 0W
Gridley, *U.S.A.* 84 F5 39 22N 121 42W
Griekwastad, *S. Africa* 56 D3 28 49S 23 15 E
Griffin, *U.S.A.* 77 J3 33 15N 84 16W
Griffith, *Australia* 63 E4 34 18S 146 2 E
Griffith, *Canada* 78 A7 45 15N 77 10W
Griffith I., *Canada* 78 B4 44 50N 80 55W
Grimaylov = Hrymayliv, *Ukraine* 17 D14 49 20N 26 5 E
Grimes, *U.S.A.* 84 F5 39 4N 121 54W
Grimsay, *U.K.* 12 D1 57 29N 7 14W
Grimsby, *Canada* 78 C5 43 12N 79 34W
Grimsby, *U.K.* 10 D7 53 34N 0 5W
Grímsey, *Iceland* 8 C5 66 33N 17 58W
Grimshaw, *Canada* 72 B5 56 10N 117 40W
Grimstad, *Norway* 9 G13 58 20N 8 35 E
Grindstone I., *Canada* 79 B8 44 43N 76 14W
Grinnell, *U.S.A.* 80 E8 41 45N 92 43W
Gris-Nez, C., *France* 18 A4 50 52N 1 35 E
Groais I., *Canada* 71 B8 50 55N 55 35W
Groblersdal, *S. Africa* 57 D4 25 15S 29 25 E
Grodno = Hrodna, *Belarus* 17 B12 53 42N 23 52 E
Grodzyanka = Hrodzyanka, *Belarus* 17 B15 53 31N 28 42 E
Groesbeck, *U.S.A.* 81 K6 30 48N 96 31W
Grójec, *Poland* 17 C11 51 50N 20 58 E
Grong, *Norway* 8 D15 64 25N 12 8 E
Groningen, *Neths.* 15 A6 53 15N 6 35 E
Groningen □, *Neths.* 15 A6 53 16N 6 40 E
Groom, *U.S.A.* 81 H4 35 12N 101 6W
Groot →, *S. Africa* 56 E3 33 45S 24 36 E
Groot Berg →, *S. Africa* 56 E2 32 47S 18 8 E
Groot-Brakrivier, *S. Africa* 56 E3 34 2S 22 18 E
Groot Karasberge, *Namibia* 56 D2 27 20S 18 40 E
Groot-Kei →, *S. Africa* 57 E4 32 41S 28 22 E
Groot Vis →, *S. Africa* 56 E4 33 28S 27 5 E
Grootdrink, *S. Africa* 56 D3 28 33S 21 42 E
Groote Eylandt, *Australia* 62 A2 14 0S 136 40 E
Grootfontein, *Namibia* 56 B2 19 31S 18 6 E
Grootlaagte →, *Africa* 56 C3 20 55S 21 27 E
Grootvloer →, *S. Africa* 56 E3 30 0S 20 40 E
Gros C., *Canada* 72 A6 61 59N 113 32W
Gros Morne Nat. Park, *Canada* 71 C8 49 40N 57 50W
Grossa, Pta., *Spain* 22 B8 39 6N 1 36 E
Grosser Arber, *Germany* 16 D7 49 6N 13 8 E
Grosseto, *Italy* 20 C4 42 46N 11 8 E
Grossglockner, *Austria* 16 E7 47 5N 12 40 E
Groswater B., *Canada* 71 B8 54 20N 57 40W
Groton, *Conn., U.S.A.* 79 E12 41 21N 72 5W
Groton, *N.Y., U.S.A.* 79 D8 42 36N 76 22W
Groton, *S. Dak., U.S.A.* 80 C5 45 27N 98 6W
Grouard Mission, *Canada* 72 B5 55 33N 116 9W
Groundhog →, *Canada* 70 C3 48 45N 82 58W
Grouw, *Neths.* 15 A5 53 5N 5 51 E
Grove City, *U.S.A.* 78 E4 41 10N 80 5W
Grove Hill, *U.S.A.* 77 K2 31 42N 87 47W
Groveland, *U.S.A.* 84 H6 37 50N 120 14W
Grover City, *U.S.A.* 85 K6 35 7N 120 37W
Groves, *U.S.A.* 81 L8 29 57N 93 54W
Groveton, *U.S.A.* 79 B13 44 36N 71 31W
Groznyy, *Russia* 25 F8 43 20N 45 45 E
Grudziądz, *Poland* 17 B10 53 30N 18 47 E
Gruinard B., *U.K.* 12 D3 57 56N 5 35W
Grundy Center, *U.S.A.* 80 D8 42 22N 92 47W
Gruver, *U.S.A.* 81 G4 36 16N 101 24W
Gryazi, *Russia* 24 D6 52 30N 39 58 E
Gryazovets, *Russia* 24 C7 58 50N 40 10 E
Gua, *India* 41 H14 22 18N 85 20 E
Gua Musang, *Malaysia* 39 K3 4 53N 101 58 E
Guacanayabo, G. de, *Cuba* 88 B4 20 40N 77 20W
Guachípas →, *Argentina* 94 B2 25 40S 65 30W
Guadalajara, *Mexico* 86 C4 20 40N 103 20W
Guadalajara, *Spain* 19 B4 40 37N 3 12W
Guadalcanal, *Solomon Is.* 64 H8 9 32S 160 12 E
Guadales, *Argentina* 94 C2 34 30S 67 55W
Guadalete →, *Spain* 19 D2 36 35N 6 13W
Guadalquivir →, *Spain* 19 D2 36 47N 6 22W
Guadalupe = Guadeloupe ■, *W. Indies* 89 C7 16 20N 61 40W
Guadalupe, *Mexico* 85 N10 32 4N 116 32W
Guadalupe, *U.S.A.* 85 L6 34 59N 120 33W
Guadalupe →, *Mexico* 85 N10 32 6N 116 51W
Guadalupe →, *U.S.A.* 81 L6 28 27N 96 47W
Guadalupe, Sierra de, *Spain* 19 C3 39 28N 5 30W
Guadalupe Bravos, *Mexico* 86 A3 31 20N 106 10W
Guadalupe I., *Pac. Oc.* 66 G8 29 0N 118 50W
Guadalupe Mts. Nat. Park, *U.S.A.* 81 K2 32 0N 104 30W
Guadalupe Peak, *U.S.A.* 81 K2 31 50N 104 52W
Guadalupe y Calvo, *Mexico* 86 B3 26 6N 106 58W
Guadarrama, Sierra de, *Spain* 19 B4 41 0N 4 0W
Guadeloupe ■, *W. Indies* 89 C7 16 20N 61 40W
Guadeloupe Passage, *W. Indies* 89 C7 16 50N 62 15W
Guadiana →, *Portugal* 19 D2 37 14N 7 22W
Guadix, *Spain* 19 D4 37 18N 3 11W
Guafo, Boca del, *Chile* 96 E2 43 35S 74 0W
Guainía →, *Colombia* 92 C5 2 1N 67 7W
Guaíra, *Brazil* 95 A5 24 5S 54 10W
Guaíra □, *Paraguay* 94 B4 25 45S 56 30W
Guaitecas, Is., *Chile* 96 E2 44 0S 74 30W
Guajará-Mirim, *Brazil* 92 F5 10 50S 65 20W
Guajira, Pen. de la, *Colombia* 92 A4 12 0N 72 0W
Gualán, *Guatemala* 88 C2 15 8N 89 22W
Gualeguay, *Argentina* 94 C4 33 10S 59 14W
Gualeguaychú, *Argentina* 94 C4 33 3S 59 31W
Gualequay →, *Argentina* 94 C4 33 19S 59 39W
Guam ■, *Pac. Oc.* 64 F6 13 27N 144 45 E
Guaminí, *Argentina* 94 D3 37 1S 62 28W
Guamúchil, *Mexico* 86 B3 25 25N 108 3W
Guanabacoa, *Cuba* 88 B3 23 8N 82 18W
Guanacaste, Cordillera del, *Costa Rica* 88 D2 10 40N 85 4W
Guanaceví, *Mexico* 86 B3 25 40N 106 0W
Guanahani = San Salvador I., *Bahamas* 89 B5 24 0N 74 40W
Guanajay, *Cuba* 88 B3 22 56N 82 42W
Guanajuato, *Mexico* 86 C4 21 0N 101 20W
Guanajuato □, *Mexico* 86 C4 20 40N 101 20W
Guandacol, *Argentina* 94 B2 29 30S 68 40W
Guane, *Cuba* 88 B3 22 10N 84 7W
Guangdong □, *China* 33 D6 23 0N 113 0 E
Guangling, *China* 34 E8 39 47N 114 22 E
Guangrao, *China* 35 F10 37 5N 118 25 E
Guangwu, *China* 34 F3 37 48N 105 57 E
Guangxi Zhuangzu Zizhiqu □, *China* 33 D5 24 0N 109 0 E
Guangzhou, *China* 33 D6 23 5N 113 10 E
Guanipa →, *Venezuela* 92 B6 9 56N 62 26W
Guannan, *China* 35 G10 34 8N 119 21 E
Guantánamo, *Cuba* 89 B4 20 10N 75 14W
Guantao, *China* 34 F8 36 42N 115 25 E
Guanyun, *China* 35 G10 34 20N 119 18 E
Guápiles, *Costa Rica* 88 D3 10 10N 83 46W
Guaporé, *Brazil* 95 B5 28 51S 51 54W
Guaporé →, *Brazil* 92 F5 11 55S 65 4W
Guaqui, *Bolivia* 92 G5 16 41S 68 54W
Guarapari, *Brazil* 95 A7 20 40S 40 30W
Guarapuava, *Brazil* 95 B5 25 20S 51 30W
Guaratinguetá, *Brazil* 95 A6 22 49S 45 9W
Guaratuba, *Brazil* 95 B6 25 53S 48 38W
Guarda, *Portugal* 19 B2 40 32N 7 20W
Guardafui, C. = Asir, Ras, *Somali Rep.* 46 E5 11 55N 51 10 E
Guárico □, *Venezuela* 92 B5 8 40N 66 35W
Guarujá, *Brazil* 95 A6 24 2S 46 25W
Guarus, *Brazil* 95 A7 21 44S 41 20W
Guasave, *Mexico* 86 B3 25 34N 108 27W
Guasdualito, *Venezuela* 92 B4 7 15N 70 44W
Guatemala, *Guatemala* 88 D1 14 40N 90 22W
Guatemala ■, *Cent. Amer.* 88 C1 15 40N 90 30W
Guaviare →, *Colombia* 92 C5 4 3N 67 44W
Guaxupé, *Brazil* 95 A6 21 10S 47 5W
Guayama, *Puerto Rico* 89 C6 17 59N 66 7W
Guayaquil, *Ecuador* 92 D3 2 15S 79 52W
Guayaquil, G. de, *Ecuador* 92 D2 3 10S 81 0W
Guaymas, *Mexico* 86 B2 27 59N 110 54W
Guba, *Dem. Rep. of the Congo* 55 E2 10 38S 26 27 E
Gubkin, *Russia* 25 D6 51 17N 37 32 E
Gudbrandsdalen, *Norway* 9 F14 61 33N 10 10 E
Guddu Barrage, *Pakistan* 40 E6 28 30N 69 50 E
Gudur, *India* 40 M11 14 12N 79 55 E
Guecho = Getxo, *Spain* 19 A4 43 21N 2 59W
Guelmine = Goulimine, *Morocco* 50 C3 28 56N 10 0W
Guelph, *Canada* 78 C4 43 35N 80 20W
Guéret, *France* 18 C4 46 11N 1 51 E
Guerneville, *U.S.A.* 84 G4 38 30N 123 0W
Guernica = Gernika-Lumo, *Spain* 19 A4 43 19N 2 40W
Guernsey, *U.K.* 11 H5 49 26N 2 35W
Guernsey, *U.S.A.* 80 D2 42 19N 104 45W
Guerrero □, *Mexico* 87 D5 17 30N 100 0W
Gügher, *Iran* 45 D8 29 28N 56 27 E
Guhakolak, Tanjung, *Indonesia* 37 G11 6 50S 105 14 E
Guia, *Canary Is.* 22 F4 28 8N 15 38W
Guia de Isora, *Canary Is.* 22 F3 28 12N 16 46W
Guia Lopes da Laguna, *Brazil* 95 A4 21 26S 56 7W
Guiana, *S. Amer.* 90 C4 5 10N 60 40W
Guidónia-Montecélio, *Italy* 20 C5 42 1N 12 45 E
Guijá, *Mozam.* 57 C5 24 27S 33 0 E
Guildford, *U.K.* 11 F7 51 14N 0 34W
Guilford, *U.S.A.* 79 E12 41 17N 72 41W
Guilin, *China* 33 D6 25 18N 110 15 E
Guillaume-Delisle L., *Canada* 70 A4 56 15N 76 17W
Güímar, *Canary Is.* 22 F3 28 18N 16 24W
Guimarães, *Portugal* 19 B1 41 28N 8 24W
Guimaras □, *Phil.* 37 B6 10 35N 122 37 E
Guinda, *U.S.A.* 84 G4 38 50N 122 12W
Guinea, *Africa* 48 F4 8 0N 8 0 E
Guinea ■, *W. Afr.* 50 F3 10 20N 11 30W
Guinea, Gulf of, *Atl. Oc.* 49 F4 3 0N 2 30 E
Guinea-Bissau ■, *Africa* 50 F3 12 0N 15 0W
Güines, *Cuba* 88 B3 22 50N 82 0W
Guingamp, *France* 18 B2 48 34N 3 10W
Güiria, *Venezuela* 92 A6 10 32N 62 18W
Guiuan, *Phil.* 37 B7 11 5N 125 55 E
Guiyang, *China* 32 D5 26 32N 106 40 E
Guizhou □, *China* 32 D5 27 0N 107 0 E
Gujar Khan, *Pakistan* 42 C5 33 16N 73 19 E
Gujarat □, *India* 42 H4 23 20N 71 0 E
Gujranwala, *Pakistan* 42 C6 32 10N 74 12 E
Gujrat, *Pakistan* 42 C6 32 40N 74 2 E
Gulbarga, *India* 40 L10 17 20N 76 50 E
Gulbene, *Latvia* 9 H22 57 8N 26 52 E
Gulf, The, *Asia* 45 E6 27 0N 50 0 E
Gulfport, *U.S.A.* 81 K10 30 22N 89 6W
Gulgong, *Australia* 63 E4 32 20S 149 49 E
Gulistan, *Pakistan* 42 D2 30 30N 66 35 E
Gull Lake, *Canada* 73 C7 50 10N 108 29W
Güllük, *Turkey* 21 F12 37 14N 27 35 E
Gulmarg, *India* 43 B6 34 3N 74 25 E
Gulshad, *Kazakhstan* 26 E8 46 45N 74 25 E
Gulu, *Uganda* 54 B3 2 48N 32 17 E
Gulwe, *Tanzania* 54 D4 6 30S 36 25 E
Gumal →, *Pakistan* 42 D4 31 40N 71 50 E
Gumbaz, *Pakistan* 42 D3 30 2N 69 0 E
Gumel, *Nigeria* 50 F7 12 39N 9 22 E
Gumla, *India* 43 H11 23 3N 84 33 E
Gumlu, *Australia* 62 B4 19 53S 147 41 E
Gumma □, *Japan* 31 F9 36 30N 138 20 E
Gumzai, *Indonesia* 37 F8 5 28S 134 42 E
Guna, *India* 42 G7 24 40N 77 19 E
Gunisao →, *Canada* 73 C9 53 56N 97 53W
Gunisao L., *Canada* 73 C9 53 33N 96 15W
Gunjyal, *Pakistan* 42 C4 32 20N 71 55 E
Gunnbjørn Fjeld, *Greenland* 4 C6 68 55N 29 47W
Gunnedah, *Australia* 63 E5 30 59S 150 15 E
Gunnewin, *Australia* 63 D4 25 59S 148 33 E
Gunningbar Cr. →, *Australia* 63 E4 31 14S 147 6 E
Gunnison, *Colo., U.S.A.* 83 G10 38 33N 106 56W
Gunnison, *Utah, U.S.A.* 82 G8 39 9N 111 49W
Gunnison →, *U.S.A.* 83 G9 39 4N 108 35W
Gunpowder, *Australia* 62 B2 19 42S 139 22 E
Guntakal, *India* 40 M10 15 11N 77 27 E
Guntersville, *U.S.A.* 77 H2 34 21N 86 18W
Guntong, *Malaysia* 39 K3 4 36N 101 3 E
Guntur, *India* 41 L12 16 23N 80 30 E
Gunungapi, *Indonesia* 37 F7 6 45S 126 30 E
Gunungsitoli, *Indonesia* 36 D1 1 15N 97 30 E
Gunza, *Angola* 52 G2 10 50S 13 50 E
Guo He →, *China* 35 H9 32 59N 117 10 E
Guoyang, *China* 34 H9 33 32N 116 12 E
Gupis, *Pakistan* 43 A5 36 15N 73 20 E
Gurdaspur, *India* 42 C6 32 5N 75 31 E
Gurdon, *U.S.A.* 81 J8 33 55N 93 9W
Gurgaon, *India* 42 E7 28 27N 77 1 E
Gurgueia →, *Brazil* 93 E10 6 50S 43 24W
Gurha, *India* 42 G4 25 12N 71 39 E
Guri, Embalse de, *Venezuela* 92 B6 7 50N 62 52W
Gurkha, *Nepal* 43 E11 28 5N 84 40 E
Gurley, *Australia* 63 D4 29 45S 149 48 E
Gurnet Point, *U.S.A.* 79 D14 42 1N 70 34W
Guro, *Mozam.* 55 F3 17 26S 32 30 E
Gurué, *Mozam.* 55 F4 15 25S 36 58 E
Gurun, *Malaysia* 39 K3 5 49N 100 27 E
Gürün, *Turkey* 25 G6 38 43N 37 15 E
Gurupá, *Brazil* 93 D8 1 25S 51 35W
Gurupá, I. Grande de, *Brazil* 93 D8 1 25S 51 45W
Gurupi, *Brazil* 93 F9 11 43S 49 4W
Gurupi →, *Brazil* 93 D9 1 13S 46 6W
Guruwe, *Zimbabwe* 57 B5 16 40S 30 42 E
Guryev = Atyraū, *Kazakhstan* 25 E9 47 5N 52 0 E
Gusau, *Nigeria* 50 F7 12 12N 6 40 E
Gusev, *Russia* 9 J20 54 35N 22 10 E
Gushan, *China* 35 E12 39 50N 123 35 E
Gushgy, *Turkmenistan* 26 F7 35 20N 62 18 E
Gusinoozersk, *Russia* 27 D11 51 16N 106 27 E
Gustavus, *U.S.A.* 72 B1 58 25N 135 44W
Gustine, *U.S.A.* 84 H6 37 16N 121 0W
Güstrow, *Germany* 16 B7 53 47N 12 10 E
Gütersloh, *Germany* 16 C5 51 54N 8 24 E
Gutha, *Australia* 61 E2 28 58S 115 55 E
Guthalungra, *Australia* 62 B4 19 52S 147 50 E
Guthrie, *Okla., U.S.A.* 81 H6 35 53N 97 25W
Guthrie, *Tex., U.S.A.* 81 J4 33 37N 100 19W
Guttenberg, *U.S.A.* 80 D9 42 47N 91 6W
Gutu, *Zimbabwe* 57 B5 19 41S 31 9 E
Guwahati, *India* 41 F17 26 10N 91 45 E
Guyana ■, *S. Amer.* 92 C7 5 0N 59 0W
Guyane française = French Guiana ■, *S. Amer.* 93 C8 4 0N 53 0W
Guyang, *China* 34 D6 41 0N 110 5 E
Guyenne, *France* 18 D4 44 30N 0 40 E
Guymon, *U.S.A.* 81 G4 36 41N 101 29W
Guyra, *Australia* 63 E5 30 15S 151 40 E
Guyuan, *Hebei, China* 34 D8 41 37N 115 40 E
Guyuan, *Ningxia Huizu, China* 34 G4 36 0N 106 20 E
Guzhen, *China* 35 H9 33 22N 117 18 E
Guzmán, L. de, *Mexico* 86 A3 31 25N 107 25W
Gvardeysk, *Russia* 9 J19 54 39N 21 5 E
Gwa, *Burma* 41 L19 17 36N 94 34 E
Gwaai, *Zimbabwe* 55 F2 19 15S 27 45 E
Gwaai →, *Zimbabwe* 55 F2 17 59S 26 52 E
Gwabegar, *Australia* 63 E4 30 31S 149 0 E
Gwādar, *Pakistan* 40 G3 25 10N 62 18 E
Gwalior, *India* 42 F8 26 12N 78 10 E
Gwanda, *Zimbabwe* 55 G2 20 55S 29 0 E
Gwane, *Dem. Rep. of the Congo* 54 B2 4 45N 25 48 E
Gweebarra B., *Ireland* 13 B3 54 51N 8 23W
Gweedore, *Ireland* 13 A3 55 3N 8 13W
Gweru, *Zimbabwe* 55 F2 19 28S 29 45 E
Gwinn, *U.S.A.* 76 B2 46 19N 87 27W
Gwydir →, *Australia* 63 D4 29 27S 149 48 E
Gwynedd □, *U.K.* 10 E3 52 52N 4 10W
Gyandzha = Gäncä, *Azerbaijan* 25 F8 40 45N 46 20 E
Gyaring Hu, *China* 32 C4 34 50N 97 40 E
Gydanskiy Poluostrov, *Russia* 26 C8 70 0N 78 0 E
Gympie, *Australia* 63 D5 26 11S 152 38 E
Gyöngyös, *Hungary* 17 E10 47 48N 19 56 E
Győr, *Hungary* 17 E9 47 41N 17 40 E
Gypsum Pt., *Canada* 72 A6 61 53N 114 35W
Gypsumville, *Canada* 73 C9 51 45N 98 40W
Gyula, *Hungary* 17 E11 46 38N 21 17 E
Gyumri, *Armenia* 25 F7 40 47N 43 50 E
Gyzylarbat, *Turkmenistan* 26 F6 39 4N 56 23 E
Gyzyletrek, *Turkmenistan* 45 B7 37 36N 54 46 E

H

Ha 'Arava →, *Israel* 47 E4 30 50N 35 20 E
Ha Coi, *Vietnam* 38 B6 21 26N 107 46 E
Ha Dong, *Vietnam* 38 B5 20 58N 105 46 E
Ha Giang, *Vietnam* 38 A5 22 50N 104 59 E
Ha Tien, *Vietnam* 39 G5 10 23N 104 29 E
Ha Tinh, *Vietnam* 38 C5 18 20N 105 54 E
Ha Trung, *Vietnam* 38 C5 19 58N 105 50 E
Haaksbergen, *Neths.* 15 B6 52 9N 6 45 E
Haapsalu, *Estonia* 9 G20 58 56N 23 30 E
Haarlem, *Neths.* 15 B4 52 23N 4 39 E
Haast →, *N.Z.* 59 K2 43 50S 169 2 E
Haast Bluff, *Australia* 60 D5 23 22S 132 0 E
Hab →, *Pakistan* 42 G3 24 53N 66 41 E
Hab Nadi Chauki, *Pakistan* 42 G2 25 0N 66 50 E
Habaswein, *Kenya* 54 B4 1 2N 39 30 E
Habay, *Canada* 72 B5 58 50N 118 44W
Ḥabbānīyah, *Iraq* 44 C4 33 17N 43 29 E
Haboro, *Japan* 30 B10 44 22N 141 42 E
Ḥabshān, *U.A.E.* 45 F7 23 50N 53 37 E
Hachijō-Jima, *Japan* 31 H9 33 5N 139 45 E
Hachinohe, *Japan* 30 D10 40 30N 141 29 E
Hachiōji, *Japan* 31 G9 35 40N 139 20 E
Hachŏn, *N. Korea* 35 D15 41 29N 129 2 E
Hackensack, *U.S.A.* 79 F10 40 53N 74 3W
Hackettstown, *U.S.A.* 79 F10 40 51N 74 50W
Hadali, *Pakistan* 42 C5 32 16N 72 11 E
Hadarba, Ras, *Sudan* 51 D13 22 4N 36 51 E
Hadarom □, *Israel* 47 E4 31 0N 35 0 E
Ḥadd, Ra's al, *Oman* 46 C6 22 35N 59 50 E
Hadejia, *Nigeria* 50 F7 12 30N 10 5 E
Hadera, *Israel* 47 C3 32 27N 34 55 E
Hadera, N. →, *Israel* 47 C3 32 28N 34 52 E
Haderslev, *Denmark* 9 J13 55 15N 9 30 E
Hadhramaut = Ḥaḍramawt, *Yemen* 46 D4 15 30N 49 30 E
Hadiboh, *Yemen* 46 E5 12 39N 54 2 E
Hadong, *S. Korea* 35 G14 35 5N 127 44 E
Ḥaḍramawt, *Yemen* 46 D4 15 30N 49 30 E
Ḥadrānīyah, *Iraq* 44 C4 35 38N 43 14 E
Hadrian's Wall, *U.K.* 10 B5 55 0N 2 30W
Haeju, *N. Korea* 35 E13 38 3N 125 45 E
Haenam, *S. Korea* 35 G14 34 34N 126 35 E
Haenertsburg, *S. Africa* 57 C4 24 0S 29 50 E
Haerhpin = Harbin, *China* 35 B14 45 48N 126 40 E
Hafar al Bāṭin, *Si. Arabia* 44 D5 28 32N 45 52 E
Ḥafirat al 'Aydā, *Si. Arabia* 44 E3 26 26N 39 12 E
Ḥafit, *Oman* 45 F7 23 59N 55 49 E
Hafizabad, *Pakistan* 42 C5 32 5N 73 40 E
Haflong, *India* 41 G18 25 10N 93 5 E
Hafnarfjörður, *Iceland* 8 D3 64 4N 21 57W
Haft Gel, *Iran* 45 D6 31 30N 49 32 E
Hafun, Ras, *Somali Rep.* 46 E5 10 29N 51 30 E
Hagalil, *Israel* 47 C4 32 53N 35 18 E
Hagen, *Germany* 16 C4 51 21N 7 27 E
Hagerman, *U.S.A.* 81 J2 33 7N 104 20W
Hagerstown, *U.S.A.* 76 F7 39 39N 77 43W
Hagersville, *Canada* 78 D4 42 58N 80 3W
Hagfors, *Sweden* 9 F15 60 3N 13 45 E
Hagi, *Japan* 31 G5 34 30N 131 22 E
Hagolan, *Syria* 47 C4 33 0N 35 45 E
Hagondange, *France* 18 B7 49 16N 6 11 E
Hags Hd., *Ireland* 13 D2 52 57N 9 28W
Hague, C. de la, *France* 18 B3 49 44N 1 56W
Hague, The = 's-Gravenhage, *Neths.* 15 B4 52 7N 4 17 E
Haguenau, *France* 18 B7 48 49N 7 47 E
Hai Duong, *Vietnam* 38 B6 20 56N 106 19 E
Haicheng, *China* 35 D12 40 50N 122 45 E
Haidar Khel, *Afghan.* 42 C3 33 58N 68 38 E
Haidargarh, *India* 43 F9 26 37N 81 22 E
Haifa = Ḥefa, *Israel* 47 C4 32 46N 35 0 E
Haikou, *China* 33 D6 20 1N 110 16 E
Ḥā'il, *Si. Arabia* 44 E4 27 28N 41 45 E
Hailar, *China* 33 B6 49 10N 119 38 E
Hailey, *U.S.A.* 82 E6 43 31N 114 19W
Haileybury, *Canada* 70 C4 47 30N 79 38W
Hailin, *China* 35 B15 44 37N 129 30 E
Hailong, *China* 35 C13 42 32N 125 40 E

127

J

129

Jora, *India* **42 F6** 26 20N 77 49 E
Jordan, *Mont., U.S.A.* **82 C10** 47 19N 106 55W
Jordan, *N.Y., U.S.A.* **79 C8** 43 4N 76 29W
Jordan ■, *Asia* **47 E5** 31 0N 36 0 E
Jordan →, *Asia* **47 D4** 31 48N 35 32 E
Jordan Valley, *U.S.A.* **82 E5** 42 59N 117 3W
Jorhat, *India* **41 F19** 26 45N 94 12 E
Jörn, *Sweden* **8 D19** 65 4N 20 1 E
Jorong, *Indonesia* **36 E4** 3 58S 114 56 E
Jørpeland, *Norway* **9 G11** 59 3N 6 1 E
Jorquera →, *Chile* **94 B2** 28 3S 69 58W
Jos, *Nigeria* **50 G7** 9 53N 8 51 E
José Batlle y Ordóñez, *Uruguay* **95 C4** 33 20S 55 10W
Joseph, L., *Nfld., Canada* **71 B6** 52 45N 65 18W
Joseph, L., *Ont., Canada* **78 A5** 45 10N 79 44W
Joseph Bonaparte G., *Australia* **60 B4** 14 35S 128 50 E
Joshinath, *India* **43 D8** 30 34N 79 34 E
Joshua Tree, *U.S.A.* **85 L10** 34 8N 116 19W
Joshua Tree Nat. Park, *U.S.A.* **85 M10** 33 55N 116 0W
Jostedalsbreen, *Norway* **9 F12** 61 40N 6 59 E
Jotunheimen, *Norway* **9 F13** 61 35N 8 25 E
Joubertberge, *Namibia* **56 B1** 18 30S 14 0 E
Jourdanton, *U.S.A.* **81 L5** 28 55N 98 33W
Jovellanos, *Cuba* **88 B3** 22 40N 81 10W
Ju Xian, *China* **35 F10** 36 35N 118 20 E
Juan Aldama, *Mexico* **86 C4** 24 20N 103 23W
Juan Bautista Alberdi, *Argentina* **94 C3** 34 26S 61 48W
Juan de Fuca Str., *Canada* **84 B3** 48 15N 124 0W
Juan de Nova, *Ind. Oc.* **57 B7** 17 3S 43 45 E
Juan Fernández, Arch. de, *Pac. Oc.* **90 G2** 33 50S 80 0W
Juan José Castelli, *Argentina* **94 B3** 25 27S 60 57W
Juan L. Lacaze, *Uruguay* **94 C4** 34 26S 57 25W
Juankoski, *Finland* **8 E23** 63 3N 28 19 E
Juárez, *Argentina* **94 D4** 37 40S 59 43W
Juárez, *Mexico* **85 N11** 32 20N 115 57W
Juárez, Sierra de, *Mexico* **86 A1** 32 0N 116 0W
Juàzeiro, *Brazil* **93 E10** 9 30S 40 30W
Juàzeiro do Norte, *Brazil* **93 E11** 7 10S 39 18W
Juba = Giuba →, *Somali Rep.* **46 G3** 1 30N 42 35 E
Juba, *Sudan* **51 H12** 4 50N 31 35 E
Jubayl, *Lebanon* **47 A4** 34 5N 35 39 E
Jubbah, *Si. Arabia* **44 D4** 28 2N 40 56 E
Jubbal, *India* **42 D7** 31 5N 77 40 E
Jubbulpore = Jabalpur, *India* **43 H8** 23 9N 79 58 E
Jubilee L., *Australia* **61 E4** 29 0S 126 50 E
Juby, C., *Morocco* **50 C3** 28 0N 12 59W
Júcar = Xúquer →, *Spain* **19 C5** 39 5N 0 10W
Júcaro, *Cuba* **88 B4** 21 37N 78 51W
Juchitán, *Mexico* **87 D5** 16 27N 95 5W
Judaea = Har Yehuda, *Israel* **47 D3** 31 35N 34 57 E
Judith →, *U.S.A.* **82 C9** 47 44N 109 39W
Judith, Pt., *U.S.A.* **79 E13** 41 22N 71 29W
Judith Gap, *U.S.A.* **82 C9** 46 41N 109 45W
Jugoslavia = Yugoslavia ■, *Europe* **21 B9** 43 20N 20 0 E
Juigalpa, *Nic.* **88 D2** 12 6N 85 26W
Juiz de Fora, *Brazil* **95 A7** 21 43S 43 19W
Jujuy □, *Argentina* **94 A2** 23 20S 65 40W
Julesburg, *U.S.A.* **80 E3** 40 59N 102 16W
Juli, *Peru* **92 G5** 16 10S 69 25W
Julia Cr. →, *Australia* **62 C3** 20 0S 141 11 E
Julia Creek, *Australia* **62 C3** 20 39S 141 44 E
Juliaca, *Peru* **92 G4** 15 25S 70 10W
Julian, *U.S.A.* **85 M10** 33 4N 116 38W
Julian L., *Canada* **70 B4** 54 25N 77 57W
Julianatop, *Surinam* **93 C7** 3 40N 56 30W
Julianehåb = Qaqortoq, *Greenland* **69 B6** 60 43N 46 0W
Julimes, *Mexico* **86 B3** 28 25N 105 27W
Jullundur, *India* **42 D6** 31 20N 75 40 E
Julu, *China* **34 F8** 37 15N 115 2 E
Jumbo, *Zimbabwe* **55 F3** 17 30S 30 58 E
Jumbo Pk., *U.S.A.* **85 J12** 36 12N 114 11W
Jumentos Cays, *Bahamas* **88 B4** 23 0N 75 40W
Jumilla, *Spain* **19 C5** 38 28N 1 19W
Jumla, *Nepal* **43 E10** 29 15N 82 13 E
Jumna = Yamuna →, *India* **43 G9** 25 30N 81 53 E
Junagadh, *India* **42 J4** 21 30N 70 30 E
Junction, *Tex., U.S.A.* **81 K5** 30 29N 99 46W
Junction, *Utah, U.S.A.* **83 G7** 38 14N 112 13W
Junction B., *Australia* **62 A1** 11 52S 133 55 E
Junction City, *Kans., U.S.A.* **80 F6** 39 2N 96 50W
Junction City, *Oreg., U.S.A.* **82 D2** 44 13N 123 12W
Junction Pt., *Australia* **62 A1** 11 45S 133 50 E
Jundah, *Australia* **62 C3** 24 46S 143 2 E
Jundiaí, *Brazil* **95 A6** 24 30S 47 0W
Juneau, *U.S.A.* **72 B2** 58 18N 134 25W
Junee, *Australia* **63 E4** 34 53S 147 35 E
Jungfrau, *Switz.* **18 C7** 46 32N 7 58 E
Junggar Pendi, *China* **32 B3** 44 30N 86 0 E
Jungshahi, *Pakistan* **42 G2** 24 52N 67 44 E
Juniata →, *U.S.A.* **78 F7** 40 30N 77 40W
Junín, *Argentina* **94 C3** 34 33S 60 57W
Junín de los Andes, *Argentina* **96 D2** 39 45S 71 0W
Jūniyah, *Lebanon* **47 B4** 33 59N 35 38 E
Juntas, *Chile* **94 B2** 28 24S 69 58W
Juntura, *U.S.A.* **82 E4** 43 45N 118 5W
Jur, Nahr el →, *Sudan* **51 G11** 8 45N 29 15 E
Jura = Jura, Mts. du, *Europe* **18 C7** 46 40N 6 5 E
Jura = Schwäbische Alb, *Germany* **16 D5** 48 20N 9 30 E
Jura, *U.K.* **12 F3** 56 0N 5 50W
Jura, Mts. du, *Europe* **18 C7** 46 40N 6 5 E
Jura, Sd. of, *U.K.* **12 F3** 55 57N 5 45W
Jurbarkas, *Lithuania* **9 J20** 55 4N 22 46 E
Jurien, *Australia* **61 F2** 30 18S 115 2 E
Jūrmala, *Latvia* **9 H20** 56 58N 23 34 E
Juruá →, *Brazil* **92 D5** 2 37S 65 44W
Juruena, *Brazil* **92 F7** 13 0S 58 10W
Juruena →, *Brazil* **92 E7** 7 20S 58 3W
Juruti, *Brazil* **93 D7** 2 9S 56 4W
Justo Daract, *Argentina* **94 C2** 33 52S 65 12W
Jutaí →, *Brazil* **92 D5** 2 43S 66 57W
Juticalpa, *Honduras* **88 D2** 14 40N 86 12W
Jutland = Jylland, *Denmark* **9 H13** 56 25N 9 30 E
Juventud, I. de la, *Cuba* **88 B3** 21 40N 82 40W
Jūy Zar, *Iran* **44 C5** 33 50N 46 18 E
Juye, *China* **34 G9** 35 22N 116 5 E
Jwaneng, *Botswana* **53 J4** 24 45S 24 50 E
Jylland, *Denmark* **9 H13** 56 25N 9 30 E
Jyväskylä, *Finland* **9 E21** 62 14N 25 50 E

K

K2, *Pakistan* **43 B7** 35 58N 76 32 E
Kaap Plateau, *S. Africa* **56 D3** 28 30S 24 0 E
Kaapkruis, *Namibia* **56 C1** 21 55S 13 57 E
Kaapstad = Cape Town, *S. Africa* **56 E2** 33 55S 18 22 E
Kabaena, *Indonesia* **37 F6** 5 15S 122 0 E
Kabala, *S. Leone* **50 G3** 9 38N 11 37W
Kabale, *Uganda* **54 C3** 1 15S 30 0 E
Kabalo, *Dem. Rep. of the Congo* **54 D2** 6 0S 27 0 E
Kabambare, *Dem. Rep. of the Congo* **54 C2** 4 41S 27 39 E
Kabango, *Dem. Rep. of the Congo* **55 D2** 8 35S 28 30 E
Kabanjahe, *Indonesia* **36 D1** 3 6N 98 30 E
Kabardino-Balkar Republic = Kabardino-Balkaria □, *Russia* **25 F7** 43 30N 43 30 E
Kabardino-Balkaria □, *Russia* **25 F7** 43 30N 43 30 E
Kabarega Falls = Murchison Falls, *Uganda* **54 B3** 2 15N 31 30 E
Kabasalan, *Phil.* **37 C6** 7 47N 122 44 E
Kabetogama, *U.S.A.* **80 A8** 48 28N 92 59W
Kabin Buri, *Thailand* **38 F3** 13 57N 101 43 E
Kabinakagami L., *Canada* **70 C3** 48 54N 84 25W
Kabinda, *Dem. Rep. of the Congo* **52 F4** 6 19S 24 20 E
Kabompo, *Zambia* **55 E1** 13 36S 24 14 E
Kabompo →, *Zambia* **53 G4** 14 10S 23 11 E
Kabondo, *Dem. Rep. of the Congo* **55 D2** 8 58S 25 40 E
Kabongo, *Dem. Rep. of the Congo* **54 D2** 7 22S 25 33 E
Kabūd Gonbad, *Iran* **45 B8** 37 5N 59 45 E
Kābul, *Afghan.* **42 B3** 34 28N 69 11 E
Kābul □, *Afghan.* **40 B6** 34 30N 69 0 E
Kābul →, *Pakistan* **42 C5** 33 55N 72 14 E
Kabunga, *Dem. Rep. of the Congo* **54 C2** 1 38S 28 3 E
Kaburuang, *Indonesia* **37 D7** 3 50N 126 30 E
Kabwe, *Zambia* **55 E2** 14 30S 28 29 E
Kachchh, Gulf of, *India* **42 H3** 22 50N 69 15 E
Kachchh, Rann of, *India* **42 H4** 24 0N 70 0 E
Kachchhidhana, *India* **43 J8** 21 44N 78 46 E
Kachebera, *Zambia* **55 E3** 13 50S 32 50 E
Kachikau, *Botswana* **56 B3** 18 8S 24 26 E
Kachin □, *Burma* **41 G20** 26 0N 97 30 E
Kachira, L., *Uganda* **54 C3** 0 40S 31 7 E
Kachiry, *Kazakstan* **26 D8** 53 10N 75 50 E
Kachnara, *India* **42 H6** 23 50N 75 6 E
Kachot, *Cambodia* **39 G4** 11 30N 103 3 E
Kaçkar, *Turkey* **25 F7** 40 45N 41 10 E
Kadan Kyun, *Burma* **38 F2** 12 30N 98 20 E
Kadanai →, *Afghan.* **42 D1** 31 22N 65 45 E
Kadavu, *Fiji* **59 D8** 19 0S 178 15 E
Kadi, *India* **42 H5** 23 18N 72 23 E
Kadina, *Australia* **63 E2** 33 55S 137 43 E
Kadipur, *India* **43 F10** 26 10N 82 23 E
Kadirli, *Turkey* **44 B3** 37 23N 36 5 E
Kadiyevka = Stakhanov, *Ukraine* **25 E6** 48 35N 38 40 E
Kadoka, *U.S.A.* **80 D4** 43 50N 101 31W
Kadoma, *Zimbabwe* **55 F2** 18 20S 29 52 E
Kâdugli, *Sudan* **51 F11** 11 0N 29 45 E
Kaduna, *Nigeria* **50 F7** 10 30N 7 21 E
Kaédi, *Mauritania* **50 E3** 16 9N 13 28W
Kaeng Khoï, *Thailand* **38 E3** 14 35N 101 0 E
Kaesŏng, *N. Korea* **35 F14** 37 58N 126 35 E
Kāf, *Si. Arabia* **44 D3** 31 25N 37 29 E
Kafan = Kapan, *Armenia* **25 G8** 39 18N 46 27 E
Kafanchan, *Nigeria* **50 G7** 9 40N 8 20 E
Kafinda, *Zambia* **55 E3** 12 32S 30 20 E
Kafirévs, Ákra, *Greece* **21 E11** 38 9N 24 38 E
Kafue, *Zambia* **55 F2** 15 46S 28 9 E
Kafue →, *Zambia* **53 H5** 15 30S 29 0 E
Kafue Flats, *Zambia* **55 F2** 15 40S 27 25 E
Kafulwe, *Zambia* **55 D2** 9 0S 29 1 E
Kaga, *Afghan.* **42 B4** 34 14N 70 10 E
Kaga Bandoro, *C.A.R.* **52 C3** 7 0N 19 10 E
Kagan, *Uzbekistan* **26 F7** 39 43N 64 33 E
Kagawa □, *Japan* **31 G7** 34 15N 134 0 E
Kagera = Ziwa Maghariba □, *Tanzania* **54 C3** 2 0S 31 30 E
Kagera →, *Uganda* **54 C3** 0 57S 31 47 E
Kağızman, *Turkey* **44 B4** 40 5N 43 10 E
Kagoshima, *Japan* **31 J5** 31 35N 130 33 E
Kagoshima □, *Japan* **31 J5** 31 30N 130 30 E
Kagul = Cahul, *Moldova* **17 F15** 45 50N 28 15 E
Kahak, *Iran* **45 B6** 36 6N 49 46 E
Kahama, *Tanzania* **54 C3** 4 8S 32 30 E
Kahan, *Pakistan* **42 E3** 29 18N 68 54 E
Kahang, *Malaysia* **39 L4** 2 12N 103 32 E
Kahayan →, *Indonesia* **36 E4** 3 40S 114 0 E
Kahe, *Tanzania* **54 C4** 3 30S 37 25 E
Kahnūj, *Iran* **45 E8** 27 55N 57 40 E
Kahoka, *U.S.A.* **80 E9** 40 25N 91 44W
Kahoolawe, *U.S.A.* **74 H16** 20 33N 156 37W
Kahramanmaraş, *Turkey* **25 G6** 37 37N 36 53 E
Kahuta, *Pakistan* **42 C5** 33 35N 73 24 E
Kai, Kepulauan, *Indonesia* **37 F8** 5 55S 132 45 E
Kai Besar, *Indonesia* **37 F8** 5 35S 133 0 E
Kai Is. = Kai, Kepulauan, *Indonesia* **37 F8** 5 55S 132 45 E
Kai Kecil, *Indonesia* **37 F8** 5 45S 132 40 E
Kaiapoi, *N.Z.* **59 K4** 43 24S 172 40 E
Kaieteur Falls, *Guyana* **92 B7** 5 1N 59 10W
Kaifeng, *China* **34 G8** 34 48N 114 21 E
Kaikohe, *N.Z.* **59 F4** 35 25S 173 49 E
Kaikoura, *N.Z.* **59 K4** 42 25S 173 43 E
Kaikoura Ra., *N.Z.* **59 J4** 41 59S 173 41 E
Kailu, *China* **35 C11** 43 38N 121 18 E
Kailua Kona, *U.S.A.* **74 J17** 19 39N 155 59W
Kaimana, *Indonesia* **37 E8** 3 39S 133 45 E
Kaimanawa Mts., *N.Z.* **59 H5** 39 15S 175 56 E
Kaimganj, *India* **43 F8** 27 33N 79 24 E
Kaimur Hills, *India* **43 G10** 24 30N 82 0 E
Kainab →, *Namibia* **56 D2** 28 32S 19 34 E
Kainji Res., *Nigeria* **50 F6** 10 1N 4 40 E
Kainuu, *Finland* **8 D23** 64 30N 29 7 E
Kaipara Harbour, *N.Z.* **59 G5** 36 25S 174 14 E
Kaipokok B., *Canada* **71 B8** 54 54N 59 47W
Kaira, *India* **42 H5** 22 45N 72 50 E
Kairana, *India* **42 E7** 29 24N 77 15 E
Kaironi, *Indonesia* **37 E8** 0 47S 133 40 E
Kairouan, *Tunisia* **51 A8** 35 45N 10 5 E
Kaiserslautern, *Germany* **16 D4** 49 26N 7 45 E
Kaitaia, *N.Z.* **59 F4** 35 8S 173 17 E
Kaitangata, *N.Z.* **59 M2** 46 17S 169 51 E
Kaithal, *India* **42 E7** 29 48N 76 26 E
Kaitu →, *Pakistan* **42 C4** 33 10N 70 30 E
Kaiyuan, *China* **35 C13** 42 28N 124 1 E
Kajaani, *Finland* **8 D22** 64 17N 27 46 E
Kajabbi, *Australia* **62 C3** 20 0S 140 1 E
Kajana = Kajaani, *Finland* **8 D22** 64 17N 27 46 E
Kajang, *Malaysia* **39 L3** 2 59N 101 48 E
Kajiado, *Kenya* **54 C4** 1 53S 36 48 E
Kajo Kaji, *Sudan* **51 H12** 3 58N 31 40 E
Kakabeka Falls, *Canada* **70 C2** 48 24N 89 37W
Kakamas, *S. Africa* **56 D3** 28 45S 20 33 E
Kakamega, *Kenya* **54 B3** 0 20N 34 46 E
Kakanui Mts., *N.Z.* **59 L3** 45 10S 170 30 E
Kakdwip, *India* **43 J13** 21 53N 88 11 E
Kake, *Japan* **31 G6** 34 36N 132 19 E
Kake, *U.S.A.* **72 B2** 56 59N 133 57W
Kakegawa, *Japan* **31 G9** 34 45N 138 1 E
Kakeroma-Jima, *Japan* **31 K4** 28 8N 129 14 E
Kakhovka, *Ukraine* **25 E5** 46 45N 33 30 E
Kakhovske Vdskh., *Ukraine* **25 E5** 47 5N 34 0 E
Kakinada, *India* **41 L13** 16 57N 82 11 E
Kakisa →, *Canada* **72 A5** 61 3N 118 10W
Kakisa L., *Canada* **72 A5** 60 56N 117 43W
Kakogawa, *Japan* **31 G7** 34 46N 134 51 E
Kakwa →, *Canada* **72 C5** 54 37N 118 28W
Kāl Gūsheh, *Iran* **45 D8** 30 59N 58 12 E
Kal Safīd, *Iran* **44 C5** 34 52N 47 23 E
Kalaallit Nunaat = Greenland ■, *N. Amer.* **4 C5** 66 0N 45 0W
Kalabagh, *Pakistan* **42 C4** 33 0N 71 28 E
Kalabahi, *Indonesia* **37 F6** 8 13S 124 31 E
Kalach, *Russia* **25 D7** 50 22N 41 0 E
Kaladan →, *Burma* **41 J18** 20 20N 93 5 E
Kaladar, *Canada* **78 B7** 44 37N 77 5W
Kalahari, *Africa* **56 C3** 24 0S 21 30 E
Kalajoki, *Finland* **8 D20** 64 12N 24 10 E
Kālak, *Iran* **45 E8** 25 29N 59 22 E
Kalakamati, *Botswana* **57 C4** 20 40S 27 25 E
Kalakan, *Russia* **27 D12** 55 15N 116 45 E
K'alak'unlun Shank'ou = Karakoram Pass, *Asia* **43 B7** 35 33N 77 50 E
Kalam, *Pakistan* **43 B5** 35 34N 72 30 E
Kalama, *Dem. Rep. of the Congo* **54 C2** 2 52S 28 35 E
Kalama, *U.S.A.* **84 E4** 46 1N 122 51W
Kalámai, *Greece* **21 F10** 37 3N 22 10 E
Kalamata = Kalámai, *Greece* **21 F10** 37 3N 22 10 E
Kalamazoo, *U.S.A.* **76 D3** 42 17N 85 35W
Kalamazoo →, *U.S.A.* **76 D2** 42 40N 86 10W
Kalambo Falls, *Tanzania* **55 D3** 8 37S 31 35 E
Kalan, *Turkey* **44 B3** 39 7N 39 32 E
Kalannie, *Australia* **61 F2** 30 22S 117 5 E
Kalāntarī, *Iran* **45 C7** 32 10N 54 8 E
Kalao, *Indonesia* **37 F6** 7 21S 121 0 E
Kalaotoa, *Indonesia* **37 F6** 7 20S 121 50 E
Kalasin, *Thailand* **38 D4** 16 26N 103 30 E
Kalat, *Pakistan* **40 E5** 29 8N 66 31 E
Kalāteh, *Iran* **45 B7** 36 33N 55 41 E
Kalāteh-ye Ganj, *Iran* **45 E8** 27 31N 57 55 E
Kalbarri, *Australia* **61 E1** 27 40S 114 10 E
Kalce, *Slovenia* **16 F8** 45 54N 14 13 E
Kale, *Turkey* **21 F13** 37 27N 28 49 E
Kalegauk Kyun, *Burma* **41 M20** 15 33N 97 35 E
Kalehe, *Dem. Rep. of the Congo* **54 C2** 2 6S 28 50 E
Kalema, *Tanzania* **54 C3** 1 12S 31 55 E
Kalemie, *Dem. Rep. of the Congo* **54 D2** 5 55S 29 9 E
Kalewa, *Burma* **41 H19** 23 10N 94 15 E
Kaleybar, *Iran* **44 B5** 38 47N 47 2 E
Kalgan = Zhangjiakou, *China* **34 D8** 40 48N 114 55 E
Kalgoorlie-Boulder, *Australia* **61 F3** 30 40S 121 22 E
Kali →, *India* **43 F8** 27 6N 79 55 E
Kali Sindh →, *India* **42 G6** 25 32N 76 17 E
Kaliakra, Nos, *Bulgaria* **21 C13** 43 21N 28 30 E
Kalianda, *Indonesia* **36 F3** 5 50S 105 45 E
Kalibo, *Phil.* **37 B6** 11 43N 122 22 E
Kalima, *Dem. Rep. of the Congo* **54 C2** 2 33S 26 32 E
Kalimantan □, *Indonesia* **36 E4** 0 0 114 0 E
Kalimantan Barat □, *Indonesia* **36 E4** 0 0 110 30 E
Kalimantan Selatan □, *Indonesia* **36 E5** 2 30S 115 30 E
Kalimantan Tengah □, *Indonesia* **36 E4** 2 0S 113 30 E
Kalimantan Timur □, *Indonesia* **36 D5** 1 30N 116 30 E
Kálimnos, *Greece* **21 F12** 37 0N 27 0 E
Kalimpong, *India* **43 F13** 27 4N 88 35 E
Kalinin = Tver, *Russia* **24 C6** 56 55N 35 55 E
Kaliningrad, *Russia* **9 J19** 54 42N 20 32 E
Kalinkavichy, *Belarus* **17 B15** 52 12N 29 20 E
Kalinkovichi = Kalinkavichy, *Belarus* **17 B15** 52 12N 29 20 E
Kaliro, *Uganda* **54 B3** 0 56N 33 30 E
Kalispell, *U.S.A.* **82 B6** 48 12N 114 19W
Kalisz, *Poland* **17 C10** 51 45N 18 8 E
Kaliua, *Tanzania* **54 D3** 5 5S 31 48 E
Kalix, *Sweden* **8 D20** 65 53N 23 12 E
Kalix →, *Sweden* **8 D20** 65 50N 23 11 E
Kalka, *India* **42 D7** 30 46N 76 57 E
Kalkarindji, *Australia* **60 C5** 17 30S 130 47 E
Kalkaska, *U.S.A.* **76 C3** 44 44N 85 11W
Kalkfeld, *Namibia* **56 C2** 20 57S 16 14 E
Kalkfontein, *Botswana* **56 C3** 22 4S 20 57 E
Kalkrand, *Namibia* **56 C2** 24 1S 17 35 E
Kallavesi, *Finland* **8 E22** 62 58N 27 30 E
Kallsjön, *Sweden* **8 E15** 63 38N 13 0 E
Kalmar, *Sweden* **9 H17** 56 40N 16 20 E
Kalmyk Republic = Kalmykia □, *Russia* **25 E8** 46 5N 46 1 E
Kalmykia □, *Russia* **25 E8** 46 5N 46 1 E
Kalmykovo, *Kazakstan* **25 E9** 49 0N 51 47 E
Kalna, *India* **43 H13** 23 13N 88 25 E
Kalnai, *India* **43 H10** 22 46N 83 30 E
Kalocsa, *Hungary* **17 E10** 46 32N 19 0 E
Kalokhorio, *Cyprus* **23 E12** 34 51N 33 2 E
Kaloko, *Dem. Rep. of the Congo* **54 D2** 6 47S 25 48 E
Kalol, *Gujarat, India* **42 H5** 22 37N 73 31 E
Kalol, *Gujarat, India* **42 H5** 23 15N 72 33 E
Kalomo, *Zambia* **55 F2** 17 0S 26 30 E
Kalpi, *India* **43 F8** 26 8N 79 47 E
Kalu, *Pakistan* **42 G2** 25 5N 67 39 E
Kaluga, *Russia* **24 D6** 54 35N 36 10 E
Kalulushi, *Zambia* **55 E2** 12 50S 28 3 E
Kalundborg, *Denmark* **9 J14** 55 41N 11 5 E
Kalush, *Ukraine* **17 D13** 49 3N 24 23 E
Kalutara, *Sri Lanka* **40 R12** 6 35N 80 0 E
Kalya, *Russia* **24 B10** 60 15N 59 59 E
Kama, *Dem. Rep. of the Congo* **54 C2** 3 30S 27 5 E
Kama →, *Russia* **24 C9** 55 45N 52 0 E
Kamachumu, *Tanzania* **54 C3** 1 37S 31 37 E
Kamaishi, *Japan* **30 E10** 39 16N 141 53 E
Kamalia, *Pakistan* **42 D5** 30 44N 72 42 E
Kaman, *India* **42 F6** 27 39N 77 16 E
Kamanjab, *Namibia* **56 B2** 19 35S 14 51 E
Kamapanda, *Zambia* **55 E1** 12 5S 24 0 E
Kamarān, *Yemen* **46 D3** 15 21N 42 35 E
Kamativi, *Zimbabwe* **56 B4** 18 20S 27 6 E
Kambalda, *Australia* **61 F3** 31 10S 121 37 E
Kambar, *Pakistan* **42 F3** 27 37N 68 1 E
Kambarka, *Russia* **24 C9** 56 15N 54 11 E
Kambolé, *Zambia* **55 D3** 8 47S 30 48 E
Kambos, *Cyprus* **23 D11** 35 2N 32 44 E
Kambove, *Dem. Rep. of the Congo* **55 E2** 10 51S 26 33 E
Kamchatka, Poluostrov, *Russia* **27 D16** 57 0N 160 0 E
Kamchatka Pen. = Kamchatka, Poluostrov, *Russia* **27 D16** 57 0N 160 0 E
Kamchiya →, *Bulgaria* **21 C12** 43 4N 27 44 E
Kamen, *Russia* **26 D9** 53 50N 81 30 E
Kamen-Rybolov, *Russia* **30 B6** 44 46N 132 2 E
Kamenjak, Rt, *Croatia* **16 F7** 44 47N 13 55 E
Kamenka, *Russia* **24 A7** 65 58N 44 0 E
Kamenka Bugskaya = Kamyanka-Buzka, *Ukraine* **17 C13** 50 8N 24 16 E
Kamensk Uralskiy, *Russia* **26 D7** 56 25N 62 2 E
Kamenskoye, *Russia* **27 C17** 62 45N 165 30 E
Kameoka, *Japan* **31 G7** 35 0N 135 35 E
Kamiah, *U.S.A.* **82 C5** 46 14N 116 2W
Kamieskroon, *S. Africa* **56 E2** 30 9S 17 56 E
Kamilukuak, L., *Canada* **73 A8** 62 22N 101 40W
Kamin-Kashyrskyy, *Ukraine* **17 C13** 51 39N 24 56 E
Kamina, *Dem. Rep. of the Congo* **55 D2** 8 45S 25 0 E
Kaminak L., *Canada* **73 A10** 62 10N 95 0W
Kaministiquia, *Canada* **70 C1** 48 32N 89 35W
Kaminoyama, *Japan* **30 E10** 38 9N 140 17 E
Kamiros, *Greece* **23 C9** 36 20N 27 56 E
Kamituga, *Dem. Rep. of the Congo* **54 C2** 3 2S 28 10 E
Kamla →, *India* **43 G12** 25 35N 86 36 E
Kamloops, *Canada* **72 C4** 50 40N 120 20W
Kamo, *Japan* **30 F9** 37 39N 139 3 E
Kamoke, *Pakistan* **42 C6** 32 4N 74 4 E
Kampala, *Uganda* **54 B3** 0 20N 32 30 E
Kampang Chhnang, *Cambodia* **39 F5** 12 20N 104 35 E
Kampar, *Malaysia* **39 K3** 4 18N 101 9 E
Kampar →, *Indonesia* **36 D2** 0 30N 103 8 E
Kampen, *Neths.* **15 B5** 52 33N 5 53 E
Kampene, *Dem. Rep. of the Congo* **52 E5** 3 36S 26 40 E
Kamphaeng Phet, *Thailand* **38 D2** 16 28N 99 30 E
Kampolombo, L., *Zambia* **55 E2** 11 37S 29 42 E
Kampong Saom, *Cambodia* **39 G4** 10 38N 103 30 E
Kampong Saom, Chaak, *Cambodia* **39 G4** 10 50N 103 32 E
Kampong To, *Thailand* **39 J3** 6 3N 101 13 E
Kampot, *Cambodia* **39 G5** 10 36N 104 10 E
Kampuchea = Cambodia ■, *Asia* **38 F5** 12 15N 105 0 E
Kampung Air Putih, *Malaysia* **39 K4** 4 15N 103 10 E
Kampung Jerangau, *Malaysia* **39 K4** 4 50N 103 10 E
Kampung Raja, *Malaysia* **39 K4** 5 45N 102 35 E
Kampungbaru = Tolitoli, *Indonesia* **37 D6** 1 5N 120 50 E
Kamrau, Teluk, *Indonesia* **37 E8** 3 30S 133 36 E
Kamsack, *Canada* **73 C8** 51 34N 101 54W
Kamskoye Vdkhr., *Russia* **24 C10** 58 41N 56 7 E
Kamuchawie L., *Canada* **73 B8** 56 18N 101 59W
Kamui-Misaki, *Japan* **30 C10** 43 20N 140 21 E
Kamyanets-Podilskyy, *Ukraine* **17 D14** 48 45N 26 40 E
Kamyanka-Buzka, *Ukraine* **17 C13** 50 8N 24 16 E
Kāmyārān, *Iran* **44 C5** 34 47N 46 56 E
Kamyshin, *Russia* **25 D8** 50 10N 45 24 E
Kanaaupscow, *Canada* **70 B4** 54 2N 76 30W
Kanaaupscow →, *Canada* **69 C12** 53 39N 77 9W
Kanab, *U.S.A.* **83 H7** 37 3N 112 32W
Kanab →, *U.S.A.* **83 H7** 36 24N 112 38W
Kanagi, *Japan* **30 D10** 40 54N 140 27 E
Kanairiktok →, *Canada* **71 A7** 55 2N 60 18W
Kananga, *Dem. Rep. of the Congo* **52 F4** 5 55S 22 18 E
Kanash, *Russia* **24 C8** 55 30N 47 32 E
Kanaskat, *U.S.A.* **84 C5** 47 19N 121 54W
Kanastraíon, Ákra = Palioúrion, Ákra, *Greece* **21 E10** 39 57N 23 45 E
Kanawha →, *U.S.A.* **76 F4** 38 50N 82 9W
Kanazawa, *Japan* **31 F8** 36 30N 136 38 E
Kanchanaburi, *Thailand* **38 E2** 14 2N 99 31 E
Kanchenjunga, *Nepal* **43 F13** 27 50N 88 10 E
Kanchipuram, *India* **40 N11** 12 52N 79 45 E
Kandaghat, *India* **42 D7** 30 59N 77 7 E
Kandahar = Qandahār, *Afghan.* **40 D4** 31 32N 65 43 E
Kandalaksha, *Russia* **24 A5** 67 9N 32 30 E
Kandalakshkiy Zaliv, *Russia* **24 A6** 66 0N 35 0 E
Kandangan, *Indonesia* **36 E5** 2 50S 115 20 E
Kandanghaur, *Indonesia* **37 G13** 6 21S 108 6 E
Kandanos, *Greece* **23 D5** 35 19N 23 44 E
Kandavu = Kadavu, *Fiji* **59 D8** 19 0S 178 15 E
Kandhkot, *Pakistan* **42 E3** 28 16N 69 8 E
Kandhla, *India* **42 E7** 29 18N 77 19 E
Kandi, *Benin* **50 F6** 11 7N 2 55 E
Kandi, *India* **43 H13** 23 58N 88 5 E
Kandiaro, *Pakistan* **42 F3** 27 4N 68 13 E
Kandla, *India* **42 H4** 23 0N 70 10 E
Kandos, *Australia* **63 E4** 32 45S 149 58 E
Kandreho, *Madag.* **57 B8** 17 29S 46 6 E

Keene

Kandy, *Sri Lanka* **40 R12** 7 18N 80 43 E
Kane, *U.S.A.* **78 E6** 41 40N 78 49W
Kane Basin, *Greenland* **4 B4** 79 1N 70 0W
Kaneohe, *U.S.A.* **74 H16** 21 25N 157 48W
Kang, *Botswana* **56 C3** 23 41S 22 50 E
Kangān, *Fārs, Iran* **45 E7** 27 50N 52 3 E
Kangān, *Hormozgān, Iran* **45 E8** 25 48N 57 28 E
Kangar, *Malaysia* **39 J3** 6 27N 100 12 E
Kangaroo I., *Australia* **63 F2** 35 45S 137 0 E
Kangaroo Mts., *Australia* **62 C3** 23 29S 141 51 E
Kangasala, *Finland* **9 F21** 61 28N 24 4 E
Kangāvar, *Iran* **45 C6** 34 40N 48 0 E
Kangdong, *N. Korea* **35 E14** 39 9N 126 5 E
Kangean, Kepulauan, *Indonesia* **36 F5** 6 55S 115 23 E
Kangean Is. = Kangean, Kepulauan, *Indonesia* **36 F5** 6 55S 115 23 E
Kanggye, *N. Korea* **35 D14** 41 0N 126 35 E
Kanggyŏng, *S. Korea* **35 F14** 36 10N 127 0 E
Kanghwa, *S. Korea* **35 F14** 37 45N 126 30 E
Kangikajik, *Greenland* **4 B6** 70 7N 22 0W
Kangiqsliniq = Rankin Inlet, *Canada* **68 B10** 62 30N 93 0W
Kangiqsualujjuaq, *Canada* **69 C13** 58 30N 65 59W
Kangiqsujuaq, *Canada* **69 B12** 61 30N 72 0W
Kangiqtugaapik = Clyde River, *Canada* **69 A13** 70 30N 68 30W
Kangirsuk, *Canada* **69 B13** 60 0N 70 0W
Kangnŭng, *S. Korea* **35 F15** 37 45N 128 54 E
Kangping, *China* **35 C12** 42 43N 123 18 E
Kangra, *India* **42 C7** 32 6N 76 16 E
Kangto, *India* **41 F18** 27 50N 92 35 E
Kanhar →, *India* **43 G10** 24 28N 83 8 E
Kaniama, *Dem. Rep. of the Congo* **54 D1** 7 30S 24 12 E
Kaniapiskau = Caniapiscau →, *Canada* **71 A6** 56 40N 69 30W
Kaniapiskau, Res. = Caniapiscau, Rés. de, *Canada* **71 B6** 54 10N 69 55W
Kanin, Poluostrov, *Russia* **24 A8** 68 0N 45 0 E
Kanin Nos, Mys, *Russia* **24 A7** 68 39N 43 32 E
Kanin Pen. = Kanin, Poluostrov, *Russia* **24 A8** 68 0N 45 0 E
Kaniva, *Australia* **63 F3** 36 22S 141 18 E
Kanjut Sar, *Pakistan* **43 A6** 36 7N 75 25 E
Kankaanpää, *Finland* **9 F20** 61 44N 22 50 E
Kankakee, *U.S.A.* **76 E2** 41 7N 87 52W
Kankakee →, *U.S.A.* **76 E1** 41 23N 88 15W
Kankan, *Guinea* **50 F4** 10 23N 9 15W
Kankendy = Xankändi, *Azerbaijan* **25 G8** 39 52N 46 49 E
Kanker, *India* **41 J12** 20 10N 81 40 E
Kankroli, *India* **42 G5** 25 4N 73 53 E
Kannapolis, *U.S.A.* **77 H5** 35 30N 80 37W
Kannauj, *India* **43 F8** 27 3N 79 56 E
Kannod, *India* **40 H10** 22 45N 76 40 E
Kano, *Nigeria* **50 F7** 12 2N 8 30 E
Kan'onji, *Japan* **31 G6** 34 7N 133 39 E
Kanowit, *Malaysia* **36 D4** 2 14N 112 20 E
Kanoya, *Japan* **31 J5** 31 25N 130 50 E
Kanpetlet, *Burma* **41 J18** 21 10N 93 59 E
Kanpur, *India* **43 F9** 26 28N 80 20 E
Kansas □, *U.S.A.* **80 F6** 38 30N 99 0W
Kansas →, *U.S.A.* **80 F7** 39 7N 94 37W
Kansas City, *Kans., U.S.A.* **80 F7** 39 7N 94 38W
Kansas City, *Mo., U.S.A.* **80 F7** 39 6N 94 35W
Kansenia, *Dem. Rep. of the Congo* **55 E2** 10 20S 26 0 E
Kansk, *Russia* **27 D10** 56 20N 95 37 E
Kansŏng, *S. Korea* **35 E15** 38 24N 128 30 E
Kansu = Gansu □, *China* **34 G3** 36 0N 104 0 E
Kantaphor, *India* **42 H7** 22 35N 76 34 E
Kantharalak, *Thailand* **38 E5** 14 39N 104 39 E
Kantli →, *India* **42 E6** 28 20N 75 30 E
Kantō □, *Japan* **31 F9** 36 15N 139 30 E
Kantō-Sanchi, *Japan* **31 G9** 35 59N 138 50 E
Kanturk, *Ireland* **13 D3** 52 11N 8 54W
Kanuma, *Japan* **31 F9** 36 34N 139 42 E
Kanus, *Namibia* **56 D2** 27 50S 18 39 E
Kanye, *Botswana* **56 C4** 24 55S 25 28 E
Kanzenze, *Dem. Rep. of the Congo* **55 E2** 10 30S 25 12 E
Kanzi, Ras, *Tanzania* **54 D4** 7 1S 39 33 E
Kaohsiung, *Taiwan* **33 D7** 22 35N 120 16 E
Kaokoveld, *Namibia* **56 B1** 19 15S 14 30 E
Kaolack, *Senegal* **50 F2** 14 5N 16 8W
Kaoshan, *China* **35 B13** 44 38N 124 50 E
Kapaa, *U.S.A.* **74 G15** 22 5N 159 19W
Kapadvanj, *India* **42 H5** 23 5N 73 0 E
Kapan, *Armenia* **25 G8** 39 18N 46 27 E
Kapanga, *Dem. Rep. of the Congo* **52 F4** 8 30S 22 40 E
Kapchagai = Qapshaghay, *Kazakstan* **26 E8** 43 51N 77 14 E
Kapela = Velika Kapela, *Croatia* **16 F8** 45 10N 15 5 E
Kapema, *Dem. Rep. of the Congo* **55 E2** 10 45S 28 22 E
Kapfenberg, *Austria* **16 E8** 47 26N 15 18 E
Kapiri Mposhi, *Zambia* **55 E2** 13 59S 28 43 E
Kapiskau →, *Canada* **70 B3** 52 47N 81 55W
Kapit, *Malaysia* **36 D4** 2 0N 112 55 E
Kapiti I., *N.Z.* **59 J5** 40 50S 174 56 E
Kaplan, *U.S.A.* **81 K8** 30 0N 92 17W
Kapoe, *Thailand* **39 H2** 9 34N 98 32 E
Kapoeta, *Sudan* **51 H12** 4 50N 33 35 E
Kaposvár, *Hungary* **17 E9** 46 25N 17 47 E
Kapowsin, *U.S.A.* **84 D4** 46 59N 122 13W
Kapps, *Namibia* **56 C2** 22 32S 17 18 E
Kapsan, *N. Korea* **35 D15** 41 4N 128 19 E
Kapsukas = Marijampolė, *Lithuania* **9 J20** 54 33N 23 19 E
Kapuas →, *Indonesia* **36 E3** 0 25S 109 20 E
Kapuas Hulu, Pegunungan, *Malaysia* **36 D4** 1 30N 113 30 E
Kapuas Hulu Ra. = Kapuas Hulu, Pegunungan, *Malaysia* **36 D4** 1 30N 113 30 E
Kapulo, *Dem. Rep. of the Congo* **55 D2** 8 18S 29 15 E
Kapunda, *Australia* **63 E2** 34 20S 138 56 E
Kapuni, *N.Z.* **59 H5** 39 29S 174 8 E
Kapurthala, *India* **42 D6** 31 23N 75 25 E
Kapuskasing, *Canada* **70 C3** 49 25N 82 30W
Kapuskasing →, *Canada* **70 C3** 49 49N 82 0W
Kaputar, *Australia* **63 E5** 30 15S 150 10 E
Kaputir, *Kenya* **54 B4** 2 5N 35 28 E
Kara, *Russia* **26 C7** 69 10N 65 0 E
Kara Bogaz Gol, Zaliv = Garabogazköl Aylagy, *Turkmenistan* **25 F9** 41 0N 53 30 E
Kara Kalpak Republic = Qoraqalpoghistan □, *Uzbekistan* **26 E6** 43 0N 58 0 E
Kara Kum, *Turkmenistan* **26 F6** 39 30N 60 0 E
Kara Sea, *Russia* **26 B7** 75 0N 70 0 E
Karabiğa, *Turkey* **21 D12** 40 23N 27 17 E
Karabük, *Turkey* **25 F5** 41 12N 32 37 E
Karaburun, *Turkey* **21 E12** 38 41N 26 28 E
Karabutak = Qarabutaq, *Kazakstan* **26 E7** 49 59N 60 14 E
Karacabey, *Turkey* **21 D13** 40 12N 28 21 E
Karacasu, *Turkey* **21 F13** 37 43N 28 35 E
Karachey-Cherkessia □, *Russia* **25 F7** 43 40N 41 30 E
Karachi, *Pakistan* **42 G2** 24 53N 67 0 E
Karad, *India* **40 L9** 17 15N 74 10 E
Karaganda = Qaraghandy, *Kazakstan* **26 E8** 49 50N 73 10 E
Karagayly, *Kazakstan* **26 E8** 49 26N 76 0 E
Karaginskiy, Ostrov, *Russia* **27 D17** 58 45N 164 0 E
Karagiye, Vpadina, *Kazakstan* **25 F9** 43 27N 51 45 E
Karagiye Depression = Karagiye, Vpadina, *Kazakstan* **25 F9** 43 27N 51 45 E
Karagola Road, *India* **43 G12** 25 29N 87 23 E
Karaikal, *India* **40 P11** 10 59N 79 50 E
Karaikkudi, *India* **40 P11** 10 5N 78 45 E
Karaj, *Iran* **45 C6** 35 48N 51 0 E
Karak, *Malaysia* **39 L4** 3 25N 102 2 E
Karakalpakstan = Qoraqalpoghistan □, *Uzbekistan* **26 E6** 43 0N 58 0 E
Karakelong, *Indonesia* **37 D7** 4 35N 126 50 E
Karakitang, *Indonesia* **37 D7** 3 14N 125 28 E
Karaklis = Vanadzor, *Armenia* **25 F7** 40 48N 44 30 E
Karakol, *Kyrgyzstan* **26 E8** 42 30N 78 20 E
Karakoram Pass, *Asia* **43 B7** 35 33N 77 50 E
Karakoram Ra., *Pakistan* **43 B7** 35 30N 77 0 E
Karakuwisa, *Namibia* **56 B2** 18 56S 19 40 E
Karalon, *Russia* **27 D12** 57 5N 115 50 E
Karama, *Jordan* **47 D4** 31 57N 35 35 E
Karaman, *Turkey* **25 G5** 37 14N 33 13 E
Karamay, *China* **32 B3** 45 30N 84 58 E
Karambu, *Indonesia* **36 E5** 3 53S 116 6 E
Karamea Bight, *N.Z.* **59 J3** 41 22S 171 40 E
Karamnasa →, *India* **43 G10** 25 31N 83 52 E
Karand, *Iran* **44 C5** 34 16N 46 15 E
Karanganyar, *Indonesia* **37 G13** 7 38S 109 37 E
Karanjia, *India* **43 J11** 21 47N 85 58 E
Karasburg, *Namibia* **56 D2** 28 0S 18 44 E
Karasino, *Russia* **26 C9** 66 50N 86 50 E
Karasjok, *Norway* **8 B21** 69 27N 25 30 E
Karasuk, *Russia* **26 D8** 53 44N 78 2 E
Karasuyama, *Japan* **31 F10** 36 39N 140 9 E
Karatau, Khrebet = Qaratau, *Kazakstan* **26 E7** 43 30N 69 30 E
Karatsu, *Japan* **31 H4** 33 26N 129 58 E
Karaul, *Russia* **26 B9** 70 6N 82 15 E
Karauli, *India* **42 F7** 26 30N 77 4 E
Karavostasi, *Cyprus* **23 D11** 35 8N 32 50 E
Karawang, *Indonesia* **37 G12** 6 30S 107 15 E
Karawanken, *Europe* **16 E8** 46 30N 14 40 E
Karayazı, *Turkey* **25 G7** 39 41N 42 9 E
Karazhal, *Kazakstan* **26 E8** 48 2N 70 49 E
Karbalā', *Iraq* **44 C5** 32 36N 44 3 E
Karcag, *Hungary* **17 E11** 47 19N 20 57 E
Karcha →, *Pakistan* **43 B7** 34 45N 76 10 E
Karchana, *India* **43 G9** 25 17N 81 56 E
Kardhítsa, *Greece* **21 E9** 39 23N 21 54 E
Kärdla, *Estonia* **9 G20** 58 50N 22 40 E
Kareeberge, *S. Africa* **56 E3** 30 59S 21 50 E
Kareha →, *India* **43 G12** 25 44N 86 21 E
Kareima, *Sudan* **51 E12** 18 30N 31 49 E
Karelia □, *Russia* **24 A5** 65 30N 32 30 E
Karelian Republic = Karelia □, *Russia* **24 A5** 65 30N 32 30 E
Karera, *India* **42 G8** 25 32N 78 9 E
Kārevāndar, *Iran* **45 E9** 27 53N 60 44 E
Kargasok, *Russia* **26 D9** 59 3N 80 53 E
Kargat, *Russia* **26 D9** 55 10N 80 15 E
Kargil, *India* **43 B7** 34 32N 76 12 E
Kargopol, *Russia* **24 B6** 61 30N 38 58 E
Karhal, *India* **43 F8** 27 1N 78 57 E
Karīān, *Iran* **45 E8** 26 57N 57 14 E
Karianga, *Madag.* **57 C8** 22 25S 47 22 E
Kariba, *Zimbabwe* **55 F2** 16 28S 28 50 E
Kariba, L., *Zimbabwe* **55 F2** 16 40S 28 25 E
Kariba Dam, *Zimbabwe* **55 F2** 16 30S 28 35 E
Kariba Gorge, *Zambia* **55 F2** 16 30S 28 50 E
Karibib, *Namibia* **56 C2** 22 0S 15 56 E
Karimata, Kepulauan, *Indonesia* **36 E3** 1 25S 109 0 E
Karimata, Selat, *Indonesia* **36 E3** 2 0S 108 40 E
Karimata Is. = Karimata, Kepulauan, *Indonesia* **36 E3** 1 25S 109 0 E
Karimnagar, *India* **40 K11** 18 26N 79 10 E
Karimunjawa, Kepulauan, *Indonesia* **36 F4** 5 50S 110 30 E
Karin, *Somali Rep.* **46 E4** 10 50N 45 52 E
Karīt, *Iran* **45 C8** 33 29N 56 55 E
Kariya, *Japan* **31 G8** 34 58N 137 1 E
Kariyangwe, *Zimbabwe* **57 B4** 18 0S 27 38 E
Karkaralinsk = Qarqaraly, *Kazakstan* **26 E8** 49 26N 75 30 E
Karkheh →, *Iran* **44 D5** 31 2N 47 29 E
Karkinitska Zatoka, *Ukraine* **25 E5** 45 56N 33 0 E
Karkinitskiy Zaliv = Karkinitska Zatoka, *Ukraine* **25 E5** 45 56N 33 0 E
Karl-Marx-Stadt = Chemnitz, *Germany* **16 C7** 50 51N 12 54 E
Karlovac, *Croatia* **16 F8** 45 31N 15 36 E
Karlovo, *Bulgaria* **21 C11** 42 38N 24 47 E
Karlovy Vary, *Czech Rep.* **16 C7** 50 13N 12 51 E
Karlsbad = Karlovy Vary, *Czech Rep.* **16 C7** 50 13N 12 51 E
Karlsborg, *Sweden* **9 G16** 58 33N 14 33 E
Karlshamn, *Sweden* **9 H16** 56 10N 14 51 E
Karlskoga, *Sweden* **9 G16** 59 28N 14 33 E
Karlskrona, *Sweden* **9 H16** 56 10N 15 35 E
Karlsruhe, *Germany* **16 D5** 49 0N 8 23 E
Karlstad, *Sweden* **9 G15** 59 23N 13 30 E
Karlstad, *U.S.A.* **80 A6** 48 35N 96 31W
Karmi'el, *Israel* **47 C4** 32 55N 35 18 E
Karnak, *Egypt* **51 C12** 25 43N 32 39 E
Karnal, *India* **42 E7** 29 42N 77 2 E
Karnali →, *Nepal* **43 E9** 28 45N 81 16 E
Karnaphuli Res., *Bangla.* **41 H18** 22 40N 92 20 E
Karnaprayag, *India* **43 D8** 30 16N 79 15 E
Karnataka □, *India* **40 N10** 13 15N 77 0 E
Karnes City, *U.S.A.* **81 L6** 28 53N 97 54W
Karnische Alpen, *Europe* **16 E7** 46 36N 13 0 E
Kärnten □, *Austria* **16 E8** 46 52N 13 30 E
Karoi, *Zimbabwe* **55 F2** 16 48S 29 45 E
Karonga, *Malawi* **55 D3** 9 57S 33 55 E
Karoonda, *Australia* **63 F2** 35 1S 139 59 E
Karor, *Pakistan* **42 D4** 31 15N 70 59 E
Karora, *Sudan* **51 E13** 17 44N 38 15 E
Karpasia, *Cyprus* **23 D13** 35 32N 34 15 E
Kárpathos, *Greece* **21 G12** 35 37N 27 10 E
Karpinsk, *Russia* **24 C11** 59 45N 60 1 E
Karpogory, *Russia* **24 B7** 64 0N 44 27 E
Karpuz Burnu = Apostolos Andreas, C., *Cyprus* **23 D13** 35 42N 34 35 E
Karratha, *Australia* **60 D2** 20 53S 116 40 E
Kars, *Turkey* **25 F7** 40 40N 43 5 E
Karsakpay, *Kazakstan* **26 E7** 47 55N 66 40 E
Karshi = Qarshi, *Uzbekistan* **26 F7** 38 53N 65 48 E
Karsiyang, *India* **43 F13** 26 56N 88 18 E
Karsog, *India* **42 D7** 31 23N 77 12 E
Kartaly, *Russia* **26 D7** 53 3N 60 40 E
Kartapur, *India* **42 D6** 31 27N 75 32 E
Karthaus, *U.S.A.* **78 E6** 41 8N 78 9W
Karufa, *Indonesia* **37 E8** 3 50S 133 20 E
Karumba, *Australia* **62 B3** 17 31S 140 50 E
Karumo, *Tanzania* **54 C3** 2 25S 32 50 E
Karumwa, *Tanzania* **54 C3** 3 12S 32 38 E
Kārūn →, *Iran* **45 D6** 30 26N 48 10 E
Karungu, *Kenya* **54 C3** 0 50S 34 10 E
Karviná, *Czech Rep.* **17 D10** 49 53N 18 31 E
Karwan →, *India* **42 F8** 27 26N 78 4 E
Karwar, *India* **40 M9** 14 55N 74 13 E
Karwi, *India* **43 G9** 25 12N 80 57 E
Kasache, *Malawi* **55 E3** 13 25S 34 20 E
Kasai →, *Dem. Rep. of the Congo* **52 E3** 3 30S 16 10 E
Kasai-Oriental □, *Dem. Rep. of the Congo* **54 D1** 5 0S 24 30 E
Kasaji, *Dem. Rep. of the Congo* **55 E1** 10 25S 23 27 E
Kasama, *Zambia* **55 E3** 10 16S 31 9 E
Kasan-dong, *N. Korea* **35 D14** 41 18N 126 55 E
Kasane, *Namibia* **56 B3** 17 34S 24 50 E
Kasanga, *Tanzania* **55 D3** 8 30S 31 10 E
Kasaragod, *India* **40 N9** 12 30N 74 58 E
Kasba L., *Canada* **73 A8** 60 20N 102 10W
Kāseh Garān, *Iran* **44 C5** 34 5N 46 2 E
Kasempa, *Zambia* **55 E2** 13 30S 25 44 E
Kasenga, *Dem. Rep. of the Congo* **55 E2** 10 20S 28 45 E
Kasese, *Uganda* **54 B3** 0 13N 30 3 E
Kasewa, *Zambia* **55 E2** 14 28S 28 53 E
Kasganj, *India* **43 F8** 27 48N 78 42 E
Kashabowie, *Canada* **70 C1** 48 40N 90 26W
Kashaf, *Iran* **45 C9** 35 58N 61 7 E
Kāshān, *Iran* **45 C6** 34 5N 51 30 E
Kashechewan, *Canada* **70 B3** 52 18N 81 37W
Kashgar = Kashi, *China* **32 C2** 39 30N 76 2 E
Kashi, *China* **32 C2** 39 30N 76 2 E
Kashimbo, *Dem. Rep. of the Congo* **55 E2** 11 12S 26 19 E
Kashipur, *India* **43 E8** 29 15N 79 0 E
Kashiwazaki, *Japan* **31 F9** 37 22N 138 33 E
Kashk-e Kohneh, *Afghan.* **40 B3** 34 55N 62 30 E
Kashkū'īyeh, *Iran* **45 D7** 30 31N 55 40 E
Kāshmar, *Iran* **45 C8** 35 16N 58 26 E
Kashmir, *Asia* **43 C7** 34 0N 76 0 E
Kashmor, *Pakistan* **42 E3** 28 28N 69 32 E
Kashun Noerh = Gaxun Nur, *China* **32 B5** 42 22N 100 30 E
Kasiari, *India* **43 H12** 22 8N 87 14 E
Kasimov, *Russia* **24 D7** 54 55N 41 20 E
Kasinge, *Dem. Rep. of the Congo* **54 D2** 6 15S 26 58 E
Kasiruta, *Indonesia* **37 E7** 0 25S 127 12 E
Kaskaskia →, *U.S.A.* **80 G10** 37 58N 89 57W
Kaskattama →, *Canada* **73 B10** 57 3N 90 4W
Kaskinen, *Finland* **9 E19** 62 22N 21 15 E
Kaslo, *Canada* **72 D5** 49 55N 116 55W
Kasmere L., *Canada* **73 B8** 59 34N 101 10W
Kasongo, *Dem. Rep. of the Congo* **54 C2** 4 30S 26 33 E
Kasongo Lunda, *Dem. Rep. of the Congo* **52 F3** 6 35S 16 49 E
Kásos, *Greece* **21 G12** 35 20N 26 55 E
Kassalâ, *Sudan* **51 E13** 15 30N 36 0 E
Kassel, *Germany* **16 C5** 51 18N 9 26 E
Kassiópi, *Greece* **23 A3** 39 48N 19 53 E
Kasson, *U.S.A.* **80 C8** 44 2N 92 45W
Kastamonu, *Turkey* **25 F5** 41 25N 33 43 E
Kastélli, *Greece* **23 D5** 35 29N 23 38 E
Kastéllion, *Greece* **23 D7** 35 12N 25 20 E
Kasterlee, *Belgium* **15 C4** 51 15N 4 59 E
Kastoría, *Greece* **21 D9** 40 30N 21 19 E
Kasulu, *Tanzania* **54 C3** 4 37S 30 5 E
Kasumi, *Japan* **31 G7** 35 38N 134 38 E
Kasungu, *Malawi* **55 E3** 13 0S 33 29 E
Kasur, *Pakistan* **42 D6** 31 5N 74 25 E
Kataba, *Zambia* **55 F2** 16 5S 25 10 E
Katahdin, Mt., *U.S.A.* **77 C11** 45 54N 68 56W
Katako Kombe, *Dem. Rep. of the Congo* **54 C1** 3 25S 24 20 E
Katale, *Tanzania* **54 C3** 4 52S 31 7 E
Katanda, *Katanga, Dem. Rep. of the Congo* **54 D1** 7 52S 24 13 E
Katanda, *Nord-Kivu, Dem. Rep. of the Congo* **54 C2** 0 55S 29 21 E
Katanga □, *Dem. Rep. of the Congo* **54 D2** 8 0S 25 0 E
Katangi, *India* **40 J11** 21 56N 79 50 E
Katanning, *Australia* **61 F2** 33 40S 117 33 E
Katavi Swamp, *Tanzania* **54 D3** 6 50S 31 10 E
Kateríni, *Greece* **21 D10** 40 18N 22 37 E
Katghora, *India* **43 H10** 22 30N 82 33 E
Katha, *Burma* **41 G20** 24 10N 96 30 E
Katherîna, Gebel, *Egypt* **44 D2** 28 30N 33 57 E
Katherine, *Australia* **60 B5** 14 27S 132 20 E
Katherine Gorge, *Australia* **60 B5** 14 18S 132 28 E
Kathi, *India* **42 J6** 21 47N 74 3 E
Kathiawar, *India* **42 H4** 22 20N 71 0 E
Kathikas, *Cyprus* **23 E11** 34 55N 32 25 E
Kathmandu = Katmandu, *Nepal* **43 F11** 27 45N 85 20 E
Kathua, *India* **42 C6** 32 23N 75 34 E
Katihar, *India* **43 G12** 25 34N 87 36 E
Katima Mulilo, *Zambia* **56 B3** 17 28S 24 13 E
Katimbira, *Malawi* **55 E3** 12 40S 34 0 E
Katingan = Mendawai →, *Indonesia* **36 E4** 3 30S 113 0 E
Katiola, *Ivory C.* **50 G4** 8 10N 5 10W
Katmandu, *Nepal* **43 F11** 27 45N 85 20 E
Katni, *India* **43 H9** 23 51N 80 24 E
Káto Arkhánai, *Greece* **23 D7** 35 15N 25 10 E
Káto Khorió, *Greece* **23 D7** 35 3N 25 47 E
Káto Pyrgos, *Cyprus* **23 D11** 35 11N 32 41 E
Katompe, *Dem. Rep. of the Congo* **54 D2** 6 2S 26 23 E
Katonga →, *Uganda* **54 B3** 0 34N 31 50 E
Katoomba, *Australia* **63 E5** 33 41S 150 19 E
Katowice, *Poland* **17 C10** 50 17N 19 5 E
Katrine, L., *U.K.* **12 E4** 56 15N 4 30W
Katrineholm, *Sweden* **9 G17** 59 9N 16 12 E
Katsepe, *Madag.* **57 B8** 15 45S 46 15 E
Katsina, *Nigeria* **50 F7** 13 0N 7 32 E
Katsumoto, *Japan* **31 H4** 33 51N 129 42 E
Katsuura, *Japan* **31 G10** 35 10N 140 20 E
Katsuyama, *Japan* **31 F8** 36 3N 136 30 E
Kattaviá, *Greece* **23 D9** 35 57N 27 46 E
Kattegat, *Denmark* **9 H14** 56 40N 11 20 E
Katumba, *Dem. Rep. of the Congo* **54 D2** 7 40S 25 17 E
Katungu, *Kenya* **54 C5** 2 55S 40 3 E
Katwa, *India* **43 H13** 23 30N 88 5 E
Katwijk, *Neths.* **15 B4** 52 12N 4 24 E
Kauai, *U.S.A.* **74 H15** 22 3N 159 30W
Kauai Channel, *U.S.A.* **74 H15** 21 45N 158 50W
Kaufman, *U.S.A.* **81 J6** 32 35N 96 19W
Kauhajoki, *Finland* **9 E20** 62 25N 22 10 E
Kaukauna, *U.S.A.* **76 C1** 44 17N 88 17W
Kaukauveld, *Namibia* **56 C3** 20 0S 20 15 E
Kaunakakai, *U.S.A.* **74 H16** 21 6N 157 1W
Kaunas, *Lithuania* **9 J20** 54 54N 23 54 E
Kaunia, *Bangla.* **43 G13** 25 46N 89 26 E
Kautokeino, *Norway* **8 B20** 69 0N 23 4 E
Kauwapur, *India* **43 F10** 27 31N 82 18 E
Kavacha, *Russia* **27 C17** 60 16N 169 51 E
Kavalerovo, *Russia* **30 B7** 44 15N 135 4 E
Kavali, *India* **40 M12** 14 55N 80 1 E
Kaválla, *Greece* **21 D11** 40 57N 24 28 E
Kavār, *Iran* **45 D7** 29 11N 52 44 E
Kavi, *India* **42 H5** 22 12N 72 38 E
Kavimba, *Botswana* **56 B3** 18 2S 24 38 E
Kavīr, Dasht-e, *Iran* **45 C7** 34 30N 55 0 E
Kavos, *Greece* **23 B4** 39 23N 20 3 E
Kaw, *Fr. Guiana* **93 C8** 4 30N 52 15W
Kawagama L., *Canada* **78 A6** 45 18N 78 45W
Kawagoe, *Japan* **31 G9** 35 55N 139 29 E
Kawaguchi, *Japan* **31 G9** 35 52N 139 45 E
Kawambwa, *Zambia* **55 D2** 9 48S 29 3 E
Kawanoe, *Japan* **31 G6** 34 1N 133 34 E
Kawardha, *India* **43 J9** 22 0N 81 17 E
Kawasaki, *Japan* **31 G9** 35 35N 139 42 E
Kawasi, *Indonesia* **37 E7** 1 38S 127 28 E
Kawerau, *N.Z.* **59 H6** 38 7S 176 42 E
Kawhia Harbour, *N.Z.* **59 H5** 38 5S 174 51 E
Kawio, Kepulauan, *Indonesia* **37 D7** 4 30N 125 30 E
Kawnro, *Burma* **41 H21** 22 48N 99 8 E
Kawthaung, *Burma* **39 H2** 10 5N 98 36 E
Kawthoolei = Kayin □, *Burma* **41 L20** 18 0N 97 30 E
Kawthule = Kayin □, *Burma* **41 L20** 18 0N 97 30 E
Kaya, *Burkina Faso* **50 F5** 13 4N 1 10W
Kayah □, *Burma* **41 K20** 19 15N 97 15 E
Kayan →, *Indonesia* **36 D5** 2 55N 117 35 E
Kaycee, *U.S.A.* **82 E10** 43 43N 106 38W
Kayeli, *Indonesia* **37 E7** 3 20S 127 10 E
Kayenta, *U.S.A.* **83 H8** 36 44N 110 15W
Kayes, *Mali* **50 F3** 14 25N 11 30W
Kayin □, *Burma* **41 L20** 18 0N 97 30 E
Kayoa, *Indonesia* **37 D7** 0 1N 127 28 E
Kayomba, *Zambia* **55 E1** 13 11S 24 2 E
Kayseri, *Turkey* **25 G6** 38 45N 35 30 E
Kaysville, *U.S.A.* **82 F8** 41 2N 111 56W
Kazachye, *Russia* **27 B14** 70 52N 135 58 E
Kazakstan ■, *Asia* **26 E7** 50 0N 70 0 E
Kazan, *Russia* **24 C8** 55 50N 49 10 E
Kazan →, *Canada* **73 A9** 64 3N 95 35W
Kazan-Rettō, *Pac. Oc.* **64 E6** 25 0N 141 0 E
Kazanlŭk, *Bulgaria* **21 C11** 42 38N 25 20 E
Kazatin = Kozyatyn, *Ukraine* **17 D15** 49 45N 28 50 E
Kāzerūn, *Iran* **45 D6** 29 38N 51 40 E
Kazi Magomed = Qazimämmäd, *Azerbaijan* **45 A6** 40 3N 49 0 E
Kazuno, *Japan* **30 D10** 40 10N 140 45 E
Kazym →, *Russia* **26 C7** 63 54N 65 50 E
Kéa, *Greece* **21 F11** 37 35N 24 22 E
Keady, *U.K.* **13 B5** 54 15N 6 42W
Kearney, *U.S.A.* **80 E5** 40 42N 99 5W
Kearny, *U.S.A.* **83 K8** 33 3N 110 55W
Kearsarge, Mt., *U.S.A.* **79 C13** 43 22N 71 50W
Keban, *Turkey* **25 G6** 38 50N 38 50 E
Keban Barajı, *Turkey* **25 G6** 38 41N 38 33 E
Kebnekaise, *Sweden* **8 C18** 67 53N 18 33 E
Kebri Dehar, *Ethiopia* **46 F3** 6 45N 44 17 E
Kebumen, *Indonesia* **37 G13** 7 42S 109 40 E
Kechika →, *Canada* **72 B3** 59 41N 127 12W
Kecskemét, *Hungary* **17 E10** 46 57N 19 42 E
Kėdainiai, *Lithuania* **9 J21** 55 15N 24 2 E
Kedarnath, *India* **43 D8** 30 44N 79 4 E
Kedgwick, *Canada* **71 C6** 47 40N 67 20W
Kédhros Óros, *Greece* **23 D6** 35 11N 24 37 E
Kediri, *Indonesia* **36 F4** 7 51S 112 1 E
Keeler, *U.S.A.* **84 J9** 36 29N 117 52W
Keeley L., *Canada* **73 C7** 54 54N 108 8W
Keeling Is. = Cocos Is., *Ind. Oc.* **64 J1** 12 10S 96 55 E
Keelung = Chilung, *Taiwan* **33 D7** 25 3N 121 45 E
Keene, *Canada* **78 B6** 44 15N 78 10W
Keene, *Calif., U.S.A.* **85 K8** 35 13N 118 33W
Keene, *N.H., U.S.A.* **79 D12** 42 56N 72 17W

Keene

Keene, *N.Y., U.S.A.* **79 B11** 44 16N 73 46W
Keeper Hill, *Ireland* **13 D3** 52 45N 8 16W
Keer-Weer, C., *Australia* **62 A3** 14 0S 141 32 E
Keeseville, *U.S.A.* **79 B11** 44 29N 73 30W
Keetmanshoop, *Namibia* **56 D2** 26 35S 18 8 E
Keewatin, *Canada* **73 D10** 49 46N 94 34W
Keewatin →, *Canada* **73 B8** 56 29N 100 46W
Kefallinía, *Greece* **21 E9** 38 15N 20 30 E
Kefamenanu, *Indonesia* **37 F6** 9 28S 124 29 E
Kefar Sava, *Israel* **47 C3** 32 11N 34 54 E
Keffi, *Nigeria* **50 G7** 8 55N 7 43 E
Keflavík, *Iceland* **8 D2** 64 2N 22 35W
Keg River, *Canada* **72 B5** 57 54N 117 55W
Kegaska, *Canada* **71 B7** 50 9N 61 18W
Keighley, *U.K.* **10 D6** 53 52N 1 54W
Keila, *Estonia* **9 G21** 59 18N 24 25 E
Keimoes, *S. Africa* **56 D3** 28 41S 20 59 E
Keitele, *Finland* **8 E22** 63 10N 26 20 E
Keith, *Australia* **63 F3** 36 6S 140 20 E
Keith, *U.K.* **12 D6** 57 32N 2 57W
Keizer, *U.S.A.* **82 D2** 44 57N 123 1W
Kejimkujik Nat. Park, *Canada* **71 D6** 44 25N 65 25W
Kejserr Franz Joseph Fd., *Greenland* **4 B6** 73 30N 24 30W
Kekri, *India* **42 G6** 26 0N 75 10 E
Kelan, *China* **34 E6** 38 43N 111 31 E
Kelang, *Malaysia* **39 L3** 3 2N 101 26 E
Kelantan →, *Malaysia* **39 J4** 6 13N 102 14 E
Kelkit →, *Turkey* **25 F6** 40 45N 36 32 E
Kellerberrin, *Australia* **61 F2** 31 36S 117 38 E
Kellett, C., *Canada* **4 B1** 72 0N 126 0W
Kelleys I., *U.S.A.* **78 E2** 41 36N 82 42W
Kellogg, *U.S.A.* **82 C5** 47 32N 116 7W
Kells = Ceanannus Mor, *Ireland* **13 C5** 53 44N 6 53W
Kelokedhara, *Cyprus* **23 E11** 34 48N 32 39 E
Kelowna, *Canada* **72 D5** 49 50N 119 25W
Kelseyville, *U.S.A.* **84 G4** 38 59N 122 50W
Kelso, *N.Z.* **59 L2** 45 54S 169 15 E
Kelso, *U.K.* **12 F6** 55 36N 2 26W
Kelso, *U.S.A.* **84 D4** 46 9N 122 54W
Keluang, *Malaysia* **39 L4** 2 3N 103 18 E
Kelvington, *Canada* **73 C8** 52 10N 103 30W
Kem, *Russia* **24 B5** 65 0N 34 38 E
Kem →, *Russia* **24 B5** 64 57N 34 41 E
Kema, *Indonesia* **37 D7** 1 22N 125 8 E
Kemah, *Turkey* **44 B3** 39 32N 39 5 E
Kemaman, *Malaysia* **36 D2** 4 12N 103 18 E
Kemano, *Canada* **72 C3** 53 35N 128 0W
Kemasik, *Malaysia* **39 K4** 4 25N 103 27 E
Kemerovo, *Russia* **26 D9** 55 20N 86 5 E
Kemi, *Finland* **8 D21** 65 44N 24 34 E
Kemi älv = Kemijoki →, *Finland* **8 D21** 65 47N 24 32 E
Kemijärvi, *Finland* **8 C22** 66 43N 27 22 E
Kemijoki →, *Finland* **8 D21** 65 47N 24 32 E
Kemmerer, *U.S.A.* **82 F8** 41 48N 110 32W
Kemmuna = Comino, *Malta* **23 C1** 36 1N 14 20 E
Kemp, L., *U.S.A.* **81 J5** 33 46N 99 9W
Kemp Land, *Antarctica* **5 C5** 69 0S 55 0 E
Kempsey, *Australia* **63 E5** 31 1S 152 50 E
Kempt, L., *Canada* **70 C5** 47 25N 74 22W
Kempten, *Germany* **16 E6** 47 45N 10 17 E
Kempton, *Australia* **62 G4** 42 31S 147 12 E
Kemptville, *Canada* **79 B9** 45 0N 75 38W
Ken →, *India* **43 G9** 25 13N 80 27 E
Kenai, *U.S.A.* **68 B4** 60 33N 151 16W
Kendai, *India* **43 H10** 22 45N 82 37 E
Kendal, *Indonesia* **37 G14** 6 56S 110 14 E
Kendal, *U.K.* **10 C5** 54 20N 2 44W
Kendall, *Australia* **63 E5** 31 35S 152 44 E
Kendall, *U.S.A.* **77 N5** 25 41N 80 19W
Kendall →, *Australia* **62 A3** 14 4S 141 35 E
Kendallville, *U.S.A.* **76 E3** 41 27N 85 16W
Kendari, *Indonesia* **37 E6** 3 50S 122 30 E
Kendawangan, *Indonesia* **36 E4** 2 32S 110 17 E
Kendrapara, *India* **41 J15** 20 35N 86 30 E
Kendrew, *S. Africa* **56 E3** 32 32S 24 30 E
Kene Thao, *Laos* **38 D3** 17 44N 101 10 E
Kenedy, *U.S.A.* **81 L6** 28 49N 97 51W
Kenema, *S. Leone* **50 G3** 7 50N 11 14W
Keng Kok, *Laos* **38 D5** 16 26N 105 12 E
Keng Tawng, *Burma* **41 J21** 20 45N 98 18 E
Keng Tung, *Burma* **41 J21** 21 0N 99 30 E
Kengeja, *Tanzania* **54 D4** 5 26S 39 45 E
Kenhardt, *S. Africa* **56 D3** 29 19S 21 12 E
Kenitra, *Morocco* **50 B4** 34 15N 6 40W
Kenli, *China* **35 F10** 37 30N 118 20 E
Kenmare, *Ireland* **13 E2** 51 53N 9 36W
Kenmare, *U.S.A.* **80 A3** 48 41N 102 5W
Kenmare River, *Ireland* **13 E2** 51 48N 9 51W
Kennebago Lake, *U.S.A.* **79 A14** 45 4N 70 40W
Kennebec, *U.S.A.* **80 D5** 43 54N 99 52W
Kennebec →, *U.S.A.* **77 D11** 43 45N 69 46W
Kennebunk, *U.S.A.* **79 C14** 43 23N 70 33W
Kennedy, *Zimbabwe* **56 B4** 18 52S 27 10 E
Kennedy Ra., *Australia* **61 D2** 24 45S 115 10 E
Kennedy Taungdeik, *Burma* **41 H18** 23 15N 93 45 E
Kenner, *U.S.A.* **81 L9** 29 59N 90 15W
Kennet →, *U.K.* **11 F7** 51 27N 0 57W
Kenneth Ra., *Australia* **61 D2** 23 50S 117 8 E
Kennett, *U.S.A.* **81 G9** 36 14N 90 3W
Kennewick, *U.S.A.* **82 C4** 46 12N 119 7W
Kenogami →, *Canada* **70 B3** 51 6N 84 28W
Kenora, *Canada* **73 D10** 49 47N 94 29W
Kenosha, *U.S.A.* **76 D2** 42 35N 87 49W
Kensington, *Canada* **71 C7** 46 28N 63 34W
Kent, *Ohio, U.S.A.* **78 E3** 41 9N 81 22W
Kent, *Tex., U.S.A.* **81 K2** 31 4N 104 13W
Kent, *Wash., U.S.A.* **84 C4** 47 23N 122 14W
Kent □, *U.K.* **11 F8** 51 12N 0 40 E
Kent Group, *Australia* **62 F4** 39 30S 147 20 E
Kent Pen., *Canada* **68 B9** 68 30N 107 0W
Kentaū, *Kazakstan* **26 E7** 43 32N 68 36 E
Kentland, *U.S.A.* **76 E2** 40 46N 87 27W
Kenton, *U.S.A.* **76 E4** 40 39N 83 37W
Kentucky □, *U.S.A.* **76 G3** 37 0N 84 0W
Kentucky →, *U.S.A.* **76 F3** 38 41N 85 11W
Kentucky L., *U.S.A.* **77 G2** 37 1N 88 16W
Kentville, *Canada* **71 C7** 45 6N 64 29W
Kentwood, *U.S.A.* **81 K9** 30 56N 90 31W
Kenya ■, *Africa* **54 B4** 1 0N 38 0 E
Kenya, Mt., *Kenya* **54 C4** 0 10S 37 18 E
Keo Neua, Deo, *Vietnam* **38 C5** 18 23N 105 10 E
Keokuk, *U.S.A.* **80 E9** 40 24N 91 24W
Keonjhargarh, *India* **43 J11** 21 28N 85 35 E
Kep, *Cambodia* **39 G5** 10 29N 104 19 E
Kep, *Vietnam* **38 B6** 21 24N 106 16 E
Kepi, *Indonesia* **37 F9** 6 32S 139 19 E
Kerala □, *India* **40 P10** 11 0N 76 15 E
Kerama-Rettō, *Japan* **31 L3** 26 5N 127 15 E
Keran, *Pakistan* **43 B5** 34 35N 73 59 E
Kerang, *Australia* **63 F3** 35 40S 143 55 E
Keraudren, C., *Australia* **60 C2** 19 58S 119 45 E
Kerava, *Finland* **9 F21** 60 25N 25 5 E
Kerch, *Ukraine* **25 E6** 45 20N 36 20 E
Kerguelen, *Ind. Oc.* **3 G13** 49 15S 69 10 E
Kericho, *Kenya* **54 C4** 0 22S 35 15 E
Kerinci, *Indonesia* **36 E2** 1 40S 101 15 E
Kerki, *Turkmenistan* **26 F7** 37 50N 65 12 E
Kérkira, *Greece* **23 A3** 39 38N 19 50 E
Kerkrade, *Neths.* **15 D6** 50 53N 6 4 E
Kermadec Is., *Pac. Oc.* **64 L10** 30 0S 178 15W
Kermadec Trench, *Pac. Oc.* **64 L10** 30 30S 176 0W
Kermān, *Iran* **45 D8** 30 15N 57 1 E
Kerman, *U.S.A.* **84 J6** 36 43N 120 4W
Kermān □, *Iran* **45 D8** 30 0N 57 0 E
Kermān, Bīābān-e, *Iran* **45 D8** 28 45N 59 45 E
Kermānshāh = Bākhtarān, *Iran* **44 C5** 34 23N 47 0 E
Kermit, *U.S.A.* **81 K3** 31 52N 103 6W
Kern →, *U.S.A.* **85 K7** 35 16N 119 18W
Kernow = Cornwall □, *U.K.* **11 G3** 50 26N 4 40W
Kernville, *U.S.A.* **85 K8** 35 45N 118 26W
Keroh, *Malaysia* **39 K3** 5 43N 101 1 E
Kerrera, *U.K.* **12 E3** 56 24N 5 33W
Kerrobert, *Canada* **73 C7** 51 56N 109 8W
Kerrville, *U.S.A.* **81 K5** 30 3N 99 8W
Kerry □, *Ireland* **13 D2** 52 7N 9 35W
Kerry Hd., *Ireland* **13 D2** 52 25N 9 56W
Kerulen →, *Asia* **33 B6** 48 48N 117 0 E
Kerzaz, *Algeria* **50 C5** 29 29N 1 37W
Kesagami →, *Canada* **70 B4** 51 40N 79 45W
Kesagami L., *Canada* **70 B3** 50 23N 80 15W
Keşan, *Turkey* **21 D12** 40 49N 26 38 E
Kesennuma, *Japan* **30 E10** 38 54N 141 35 E
Keshit, *Iran* **45 D8** 29 43N 58 17 E
Kestell, *S. Africa* **57 D4** 28 17S 28 42 E
Kestenga, *Russia* **24 A5** 65 50N 31 45 E
Keswick, *U.K.* **10 C4** 54 36N 3 8W
Ket →, *Russia* **26 D9** 58 55N 81 32 E
Ketapang, *Indonesia* **36 E4** 1 55S 110 0 E
Ketchikan, *U.S.A.* **72 B2** 55 21N 131 39W
Ketchum, *U.S.A.* **82 E6** 43 41N 114 22W
Ketef, Khalîg Umm el, *Egypt* **44 F2** 23 40N 35 35 E
Keti Bandar, *Pakistan* **42 G2** 24 8N 67 27 E
Ketri, *India* **42 E6** 28 1N 75 50 E
Kętrzyn, *Poland* **17 A11** 54 7N 21 22 E
Kettering, *U.K.* **11 E7** 52 24N 0 43W
Kettering, *U.S.A.* **76 F3** 39 41N 84 10W
Kettle →, *Canada* **73 B11** 56 40N 89 34W
Kettle Falls, *U.S.A.* **82 B4** 48 37N 118 3W
Kettle Pt., *Canada* **78 C2** 43 13N 82 1W
Kettleman City, *U.S.A.* **84 J7** 36 1N 119 58W
Keuka L., *U.S.A.* **78 D7** 42 30N 77 9W
Keuruu, *Finland* **9 E21** 62 16N 24 41 E
Kewanee, *U.S.A.* **80 E10** 41 14N 89 56W
Kewaunee, *U.S.A.* **76 C2** 44 27N 87 31W
Keweenaw B., *U.S.A.* **76 B1** 47 0N 88 15W
Keweenaw Pen., *U.S.A.* **76 B2** 47 30N 88 0W
Keweenaw Pt., *U.S.A.* **76 B2** 47 25N 87 43W
Key Largo, *U.S.A.* **77 N5** 25 5N 80 27W
Key West, *U.S.A.* **75 F10** 24 33N 81 48W
Keynsham, *U.K.* **11 F5** 51 24N 2 29W
Keyser, *U.S.A.* **76 F6** 39 26N 78 59W
Kezhma, *Russia* **27 D11** 58 59N 101 9 E
Kezi, *Zimbabwe* **57 C4** 20 58S 28 32 E
Khabarovsk, *Russia* **27 E14** 48 30N 135 5 E
Khabr, *Iran* **45 D8** 28 51N 56 22 E
Khābūr →, *Syria* **44 C4** 35 17N 40 35 E
Khachmas = Xaçmaz, *Azerbaijan* **25 F8** 41 31N 48 42 E
Khachrod, *India* **42 H6** 23 25N 75 20 E
Khadro, *Pakistan* **42 F3** 26 11N 68 50 E
Khadzhilyangar, *China* **43 B8** 35 45N 79 20 E
Khaga, *India* **43 G9** 25 47N 81 7 E
Khagaria, *India* **43 G12** 25 30N 86 32 E
Khaipur, *Pakistan* **42 E5** 29 34N 72 17 E
Khair, *India* **42 F7** 27 57N 77 46 E
Khairabad, *India* **43 F9** 27 33N 80 47 E
Khairagarh, *India* **43 J9** 21 27N 81 2 E
Khairpur, *Pakistan* **42 F3** 27 32N 68 49 E
Khairpur Nathan Shah, *Pakistan* **42 F2** 27 6N 67 44 E
Khairwara, *India* **42 H5** 23 58N 73 38 E
Khaisor →, *Pakistan* **42 D3** 31 17N 68 59 E
Khajuri Kach, *Pakistan* **42 C3** 32 4N 69 51 E
Khakassia □, *Russia* **26 D9** 53 0N 90 0 E
Khakhea, *Botswana* **56 C3** 24 48S 23 22 E
Khalafābād, *Iran* **45 D6** 30 54N 49 24 E
Khalilabad, *India* **43 F10** 26 48N 83 5 E
Khalīlī, *Iran* **45 E7** 27 38N 53 17 E
Khalkhāl, *Iran* **45 B6** 37 37N 48 32 E
Khalkís, *Greece* **21 E10** 38 27N 23 42 E
Khalmer-Sede = Tazovskiy, *Russia* **26 C8** 67 30N 78 44 E
Khalmer Yu, *Russia* **26 C7** 67 58N 65 1 E
Khalturin, *Russia* **24 C8** 58 40N 48 50 E
Khalūf, *Oman* **46 C6** 20 30N 58 13 E
Kham Keut, *Laos* **38 C5** 18 15N 104 43 E
Khamaria, *India* **43 H9** 23 5N 80 48 E
Khambhaliya, *India* **42 H3** 22 14N 69 41 E
Khambhat, *India* **42 H5** 22 23N 72 33 E
Khambhat, G. of, *India* **40 J8** 20 45N 72 30 E
Khamīr, *Iran* **45 E7** 26 57N 55 36 E
Khamir, *Yemen* **46 D3** 16 2N 44 0 E
Khamsa, *Egypt* **47 E1** 30 27N 32 23 E
Khan →, *Namibia* **56 C2** 22 37S 14 56 E
Khān Abū Shāmat, *Syria* **47 B5** 33 39N 36 53 E
Khān Azād, *Iraq* **44 C5** 33 7N 44 22 E
Khān Mujiddah, *Iraq* **44 C4** 32 21N 43 48 E
Khān Shaykhūn, *Syria* **44 C3** 35 26N 36 38 E
Khān Yūnis, *Gaza Strip* **47 D3** 31 21N 34 18 E
Khanai, *Pakistan* **42 D2** 30 30N 67 8 E
Khānaqīn, *Iraq* **44 C5** 34 23N 45 25 E
Khānbāghī, *Iran* **45 B7** 36 10N 55 25 E
Khandwa, *India* **40 J10** 21 49N 76 22 E
Khandyga, *Russia* **27 C14** 62 42N 135 35 E
Khāneh, *Iran* **44 B5** 36 41N 45 8 E
Khanewal, *Pakistan* **42 D4** 30 20N 71 55 E
Khangah Dogran, *Pakistan* **42 D5** 31 50N 73 37 E
Khanh Duong, *Vietnam* **38 F7** 12 44N 108 44 E
Khaniá, *Greece* **23 D6** 35 30N 24 4 E
Khaniá □, *Greece* **23 D6** 35 30N 24 0 E
Khaniadhana, *India* **42 G8** 25 1N 78 8 E
Khanion, Kólpos, *Greece* **23 D5** 35 33N 23 55 E
Khanka, L., *Asia* **27 E14** 45 0N 132 24 E
Khankendy = Xankändi, *Azerbaijan* **25 G8** 39 52N 46 49 E
Khanna, *India* **42 D7** 30 42N 76 16 E
Khanozai, *Pakistan* **42 D2** 30 37N 67 19 E
Khanpur, *Pakistan* **42 E4** 28 42N 70 35 E
Khanty-Mansiysk, *Russia* **26 C7** 61 0N 69 0 E
Khapalu, *Pakistan* **43 B7** 35 10N 76 20 E
Khapcheranga, *Russia* **27 E12** 49 42N 112 24 E
Kharaghoda, *India* **42 H4** 23 11N 71 46 E
Kharagpur, *India* **43 H12** 22 20N 87 25 E
Khárakas, *Greece* **23 D7** 35 1N 25 7 E
Kharan Kalat, *Pakistan* **40 E4** 28 34N 65 21 E
Kharānaq, *Iran* **45 C7** 32 20N 54 45 E
Kharda, *India* **40 K9** 18 40N 75 34 E
Khardung La, *India* **43 B7** 34 20N 77 43 E
Khârga, El Wâhât-el, *Egypt* **51 C12** 25 10N 30 35 E
Khargon, *India* **40 J9** 21 45N 75 40 E
Khari →, *India* **42 G6** 25 54N 74 31 E
Kharian, *Pakistan* **42 C5** 32 49N 73 52 E
Khārk, Jazīreh-ye, *Iran* **45 D6** 29 15N 50 28 E
Kharkiv, *Ukraine* **25 E6** 49 58N 36 20 E
Kharkov = Kharkiv, *Ukraine* **25 E6** 49 58N 36 20 E
Kharovsk, *Russia* **24 C7** 59 56N 40 13 E
Kharsawangarh, *India* **43 H11** 22 48N 85 50 E
Kharta, *Turkey* **21 D13** 40 55N 29 7 E
Khartoum = El Khartûm, *Sudan* **51 E12** 15 31N 32 35 E
Khasan, *Russia* **30 C5** 42 25N 130 40 E
Khāsh, *Iran* **40 E2** 28 15N 61 15 E
Khashm el Girba, *Sudan* **51 F13** 14 59N 35 58 E
Khaskovo, *Bulgaria* **21 D11** 41 56N 25 30 E
Khatanga, *Russia* **27 B11** 72 0N 102 20 E
Khatanga →, *Russia* **27 B11** 72 55N 106 0 E
Khatauli, *India* **42 E7** 29 17N 77 43 E
Khatra, *India* **43 H12** 22 59N 86 51 E
Khātūnābād, *Iran* **45 D7** 30 1N 55 25 E
Khatyrka, *Russia* **27 C18** 62 3N 175 15 E
Khavda, *India* **42 H3** 23 51N 69 43 E
Khaybar, Ḥarrat, *Si. Arabia* **44 E4** 25 45N 40 0 E
Khayelitsha, *S. Africa* **53 L3** 34 5S 18 42 E
Khāzimiyah, *Iraq* **44 C4** 34 46N 43 37 E
Khe Bo, *Vietnam* **38 C5** 19 8N 104 41 E
Khe Long, *Vietnam* **38 B5** 21 29N 104 46 E
Khed Brahma, *India* **40 G8** 24 7N 73 5 E
Khekra, *India* **42 E7** 28 52N 77 20 E
Khemarak Phouminville, *Cambodia* **39 G4** 11 37N 102 59 E
Khemisset, *Morocco* **50 B4** 33 50N 6 1W
Khemmarat, *Thailand* **38 D5** 16 10N 105 15 E
Khenāmān, *Iran* **45 D8** 30 27N 56 29 E
Khenchela, *Algeria* **50 A7** 35 28N 7 11 E
Khersān →, *Iran* **45 D6** 31 33N 50 22 E
Kherson, *Ukraine* **25 E5** 46 35N 32 35 E
Khersónisos Akrotíri, *Greece* **23 D6** 35 30N 24 10 E
Kheta →, *Russia* **27 B11** 71 54N 102 6 E
Khewari, *Pakistan* **42 F3** 26 36N 68 52 E
Khilchipur, *India* **42 G7** 24 2N 76 34 E
Khilok, *Russia* **27 D12** 51 30N 110 45 E
Khíos, *Greece* **21 E12** 38 27N 26 9 E
Khirsadoh, *India* **43 H8** 22 11N 78 47 E
Khiuma = Hiiumaa, *Estonia* **9 G20** 58 50N 22 45 E
Khiva, *Uzbekistan* **26 E7** 41 30N 60 18 E
Khīyāv, *Iran* **44 B5** 38 30N 47 45 E
Khlong Khlung, *Thailand* **38 D2** 16 12N 99 43 E
Khmelnik, *Ukraine* **17 D14** 49 33N 27 58 E
Khmelnitskiy = Khmelnytskyy, *Ukraine* **17 D14** 49 23N 27 0 E
Khmelnytskyy, *Ukraine* **17 D14** 49 23N 27 0 E
Khmer Rep. = Cambodia ■, *Asia* **38 F5** 12 15N 105 0 E
Khoai, Hon, *Vietnam* **39 H5** 8 26N 104 50 E
Khodoriv, *Ukraine* **17 D13** 49 24N 24 19 E
Khodzent = Khŭjand, *Tajikistan* **26 E7** 40 17N 69 37 E
Khojak Pass, *Afghan.* **42 D2** 30 51N 66 34 E
Khok Kloi, *Thailand* **39 H2** 8 17N 98 19 E
Khok Pho, *Thailand* **39 J3** 6 43N 101 6 E
Kholm, *Russia* **24 C5** 57 10N 31 15 E
Kholmsk, *Russia* **27 E15** 47 40N 142 5 E
Khomas Hochland, *Namibia* **56 C2** 22 40S 16 0 E
Khomeyn, *Iran* **45 C6** 33 40N 50 7 E
Khomeynī Shahr, *Iran* **45 C6** 32 41N 51 31 E
Khomodino, *Botswana* **56 C3** 22 46S 23 52 E
Khon Kaen, *Thailand* **38 D4** 16 30N 102 47 E
Khong →, *Cambodia* **38 F5** 13 32N 105 58 E
Khong Sedone, *Laos* **38 E5** 15 34N 105 49 E
Khonuu, *Russia* **27 C15** 66 30N 143 12 E
Khoper →, *Russia* **25 D6** 49 30N 42 20 E
Khóra Sfakion, *Greece* **23 D6** 35 15N 24 9 E
Khorāsān □, *Iran* **45 C8** 34 0N 58 0 E
Khorat = Nakhon Ratchasima, *Thailand* **38 E4** 14 59N 102 12 E
Khorat, Cao Nguyen, *Thailand* **38 E4** 15 30N 102 50 E
Khorixas, *Namibia* **56 C1** 20 16S 14 59 E
Khorramābād, *Khorāsān, Iran* **45 C8** 35 6N 57 57 E
Khorramābād, *Lorestān, Iran* **45 C6** 33 30N 48 25 E
Khorrāmshahr, *Iran* **45 D6** 30 29N 48 15 E
Khorugh, *Tajikistan* **26 F8** 37 30N 71 36 E
Khosravī, *Iran* **45 D6** 30 48N 51 28 E
Khosrowābād, *Khuzestān, Iran* **45 D6** 30 10N 48 25 E
Khosrowābād, *Kordestān, Iran* **44 C5** 35 31N 47 38 E
Khost, *Pakistan* **42 D2** 30 13N 67 35 E
Khosūyeh, *Iran* **45 D7** 28 32N 54 26 E
Khotyn, *Ukraine* **17 D14** 48 31N 26 27 E
Khouribga, *Morocco* **50 B4** 32 58N 6 57W
Khowst, *Afghan.* **42 C3** 33 22N 69 58 E
Khoyniki, *Belarus* **17 C15** 51 54N 29 55 E
Khrysokhou B., *Cyprus* **23 D11** 35 6N 32 25 E
Khu Khan, *Thailand* **38 E5** 14 42N 104 12 E
Khudzhand = Khŭjand, *Tajikistan* **26 E7** 40 17N 69 37 E
Khuff, *Si. Arabia* **44 E5** 24 55N 44 53 E
Khūgīānī, *Afghan.* **42 D2** 31 37N 65 4 E
Khuis, *Botswana* **56 D3** 26 40S 21 49 E
Khuiyala, *India* **42 F4** 27 9N 70 25 E
Khŭjand, *Tajikistan* **26 E7** 40 17N 69 37 E
Khujner, *India* **42 H7** 23 47N 76 36 E
Khulna, *Bangla.* **41 H16** 22 45N 89 34 E
Khulna □, *Bangla.* **41 H16** 22 25N 89 35 E
Khumago, *Botswana* **56 C3** 20 26S 24 32 E
Khūnsorkh, *Iran* **45 E8** 27 9N 56 7 E
Khunti, *India* **43 H11** 23 5N 85 17 E
Khūr, *Iran* **45 C8** 32 55N 58 18 E
Khurai, *India* **42 G8** 24 3N 78 23 E
Khuraysۡ, *Si. Arabia* **45 E6** 25 6N 48 2 E
Khurīyā Murīyā, Jazā'ir, *Oman* **46 D6** 17 30N 55 58 E
Khurja, *India* **42 E7** 28 15N 77 58 E
Khūrmāl, *Iraq* **44 C5** 35 18N 46 2 E
Khurr, Wādī al, *Iraq* **44 C4** 32 3N 43 52 E
Khūsf, *Iran* **45 C8** 32 46N 58 53 E
Khush, *Afghan.* **40 C3** 32 55N 62 10 E
Khushab, *Pakistan* **42 C5** 32 20N 72 20 E
Khust, *Ukraine* **17 D12** 48 10N 23 18 E
Khuzdar, *Pakistan* **42 F2** 27 52N 66 30 E
Khūzestān □, *Iran* **45 D6** 31 0N 49 0 E
Khvāf, *Iran* **45 C9** 34 33N 60 8 E
Khvājeh, *Iran* **44 B5** 38 9N 46 35 E
Khvānsār, *Iran* **45 D7** 29 56N 54 8 E
Khvor, *Iran* **45 C7** 33 45N 55 0 E
Khvorgū, *Iran* **45 E8** 27 34N 56 27 E
Khvormūj, *Iran* **45 D6** 28 40N 51 30 E
Khvoy, *Iran* **44 B5** 38 35N 45 0 E
Khyber Pass, *Afghan.* **42 B4** 34 10N 71 8 E
Kiabukwa, *Dem. Rep. of the Congo* **55 D1** 8 40S 24 48 E
Kiama, *Australia* **63 E5** 34 40S 150 50 E
Kiamba, *Phil.* **37 C6** 6 2N 124 46 E
Kiambi, *Dem. Rep. of the Congo* **54 D2** 7 15S 28 0 E
Kiambu, *Kenya* **54 C4** 1 8S 36 50 E
Kiangara, *Madag.* **57 B8** 17 58S 47 2 E
Kiangsi = Jiangxi □, *China* **33 D6** 27 30N 116 0 E
Kiangsu = Jiangsu □, *China* **35 H11** 33 0N 120 0 E
Kibanga Port, *Uganda* **54 B3** 0 10N 32 58 E
Kibara, *Tanzania* **54 C3** 2 8S 33 30 E
Kibare, Mts., *Dem. Rep. of the Congo* **54 D2** 8 25S 27 10 E
Kibombo, *Dem. Rep. of the Congo* **54 C2** 3 57S 25 53 E
Kibondo, *Tanzania* **54 C3** 3 35S 30 45 E
Kibre Mengist, *Ethiopia* **46 F2** 5 54N 38 59 E
Kibumbu, *Burundi* **54 C2** 3 32S 29 45 E
Kibungo, *Rwanda* **54 C3** 2 10S 30 32 E
Kibuye, *Burundi* **54 C2** 3 39S 29 59 E
Kibuye, *Rwanda* **54 C2** 2 3S 29 21 E
Kibwesa, *Tanzania* **54 D2** 6 30S 29 58 E
Kibwezi, *Kenya* **54 C4** 2 27S 37 57 E
Kichha, *India* **43 E8** 28 53N 79 30 E
Kichha →, *India* **43 E8** 28 41N 79 18 E
Kichmengskiy Gorodok, *Russia* **24 B8** 59 59N 45 48 E
Kicking Horse Pass, *Canada* **72 C5** 51 28N 116 16W
Kidal, *Mali* **50 E6** 18 26N 1 22 E
Kidderminster, *U.K.* **11 E5** 52 24N 2 15W
Kidete, *Tanzania* **54 D4** 6 25S 37 17 E
Kidnappers, C., *N.Z.* **59 H6** 39 38S 177 5 E
Kidsgrove, *U.K.* **10 D5** 53 5N 2 14W
Kidston, *Australia* **62 B3** 18 52S 144 8 E
Kidugallo, *Tanzania* **54 D4** 6 49S 38 15 E
Kiel, *Germany* **16 A6** 54 19N 10 8 E
Kiel Canal = Nord-Ostsee-Kanal, *Germany* **16 A5** 54 12N 9 32 E
Kielce, *Poland* **17 C11** 50 52N 20 42 E
Kielder Water, *U.K.* **10 B5** 55 11N 2 31W
Kieler Bucht, *Germany* **16 A6** 54 35N 10 25 E
Kien Binh, *Vietnam* **39 H5** 9 55N 105 19 E
Kien Tan, *Vietnam* **39 G5** 10 7N 105 17 E
Kienge, *Dem. Rep. of the Congo* **55 E2** 10 30S 27 30 E
Kiev = Kyyiv, *Ukraine* **17 C16** 50 30N 30 28 E
Kiffa, *Mauritania* **50 E3** 16 37N 11 24W
Kifrī, *Iraq* **44 C5** 34 45N 45 0 E
Kigali, *Rwanda* **54 C3** 1 59S 30 4 E
Kigarama, *Tanzania* **54 C3** 1 1S 31 50 E
Kigoma □, *Tanzania* **54 D3** 5 0S 30 0 E
Kigoma-Ujiji, *Tanzania* **54 C2** 4 55S 29 36 E
Kigomasha, Ras, *Tanzania* **54 C4** 4 58S 38 58 E
Kığzı, *Turkey* **44 B4** 38 18N 43 25 E
Kihei, *U.S.A.* **74 H16** 20 47N 156 28W
Kihnu, *Estonia* **9 G21** 58 9N 24 1 E
Kii-Sanchi, *Japan* **31 G8** 34 20N 136 0 E
Kii-Suidō, *Japan* **31 H7** 33 40N 134 45 E
Kikaiga-Shima, *Japan* **31 K4** 28 19N 129 59 E
Kikinda, *Serbia, Yug.* **21 B9** 45 50N 20 30 E
Kikládhes, *Greece* **21 F11** 37 0N 24 30 E
Kikwit, *Dem. Rep. of the Congo* **52 E3** 5 0S 18 45 E
Kilar, *India* **42 C7** 33 6N 76 25 E
Kilauea Crater, *U.S.A.* **74 J17** 19 25N 155 17W
Kilbrannan Sd., *U.K.* **12 F3** 55 37N 5 26W
Kilchu, *N. Korea* **35 D15** 40 57N 129 25 E
Kilcoy, *Australia* **63 D5** 26 59S 152 30 E
Kildare, *Ireland* **13 C5** 53 9N 6 55W
Kildare □, *Ireland* **13 C5** 53 10N 6 50W
Kilfinnane, *Ireland* **13 D3** 52 21N 8 28W
Kilgore, *U.S.A.* **81 J7** 32 23N 94 53W
Kilifi, *Kenya* **54 C4** 3 40S 39 48 E
Kilimanjaro, *Tanzania* **54 C4** 3 7S 37 20 E
Kilimanjaro □, *Tanzania* **54 C4** 4 0S 38 0 E
Kilindini, *Kenya* **54 C4** 4 4S 39 40 E
Kilis, *Turkey* **44 B3** 36 42N 37 6 E
Kiliya, *Ukraine* **17 F15** 45 28N 29 16 E
Kilkee, *Ireland* **13 D2** 52 41N 9 39W
Kilkeel, *U.K.* **13 B5** 54 4N 6 0W
Kilkenny, *Ireland* **13 D4** 52 39N 7 15W
Kilkenny □, *Ireland* **13 D4** 52 35N 7 15W
Kilkieran B., *Ireland* **13 C2** 53 20N 9 41W
Kilkís, *Greece* **21 D10** 40 58N 22 57 E
Killala, *Ireland* **13 B2** 54 13N 9 12W
Killala B., *Ireland* **13 B2** 54 16N 9 8W
Killaloe, *Ireland* **13 D3** 52 48N 8 28W
Killaloe Station, *Canada* **78 A7** 45 33N 77 25W
Killarney, *Australia* **63 D5** 28 20S 152 18 E
Killarney, *Canada* **73 D9** 49 10N 99 40W
Killarney, *Ireland* **13 D2** 52 4N 9 30W
Killary Harbour, *Ireland* **13 C2** 53 38N 9 52W
Killdeer, *U.S.A.* **80 B3** 47 26N 102 48W
Killeen, *U.S.A.* **81 K6** 31 7N 97 44W
Killin, *U.K.* **12 E4** 56 28N 4 19W
Killíni, *Greece* **21 F10** 37 54N 22 25 E
Killorglin, *Ireland* **13 D2** 52 6N 9 47W
Killybegs, *Ireland* **13 B3** 54 38N 8 26W
Kilmarnock, *U.K.* **12 F4** 55 37N 4 29W
Kilmore, *Australia* **63 F3** 37 25S 144 53 E

Kondratyevo

Kilondo, Tanzania 55 D3 9 45S 34 20 E
Kilosa, Tanzania 54 D4 6 48S 37 0 E
Kilrush, Ireland 13 D2 52 38N 9 29W
Kilwa Kisiwani, Tanzania 55 D4 8 58S 39 32 E
Kilwa Kivinje, Tanzania 55 D4 8 45S 39 25 E
Kilwa Masoko, Tanzania 55 D4 8 55S 39 30 E
Kilwinning, U.K. 12 F4 55 39N 4 43W
Kim, U.S.A. 81 G3 37 15N 103 21W
Kimaam, Indonesia 37 F9 7 58S 138 53 E
Kimamba, Tanzania 54 D4 6 45S 37 10 E
Kimba, Australia 63 E2 33 8S 136 23 E
Kimball, Nebr., U.S.A. 80 E3 41 14N 103 40W
Kimball, S. Dak., U.S.A. 80 D5 43 45N 98 57W
Kimberley, Australia 60 C4 16 20S 127 0 E
Kimberley, Canada 72 D5 49 40N 115 59W
Kimberley, S. Africa 56 D3 28 43S 24 46 E
Kimberly, U.S.A. 82 E6 42 32N 114 22W
Kimch'aek, N. Korea 35 D15 40 40N 129 10 E
Kimch'ŏn, S. Korea 35 F15 36 11N 128 4 E
Kimje, S. Korea 35 G14 35 48N 126 45 E
Kimmirut, Canada 69 B13 62 50N 69 50W
Kimpese, Dem. Rep. of the Congo 52 F2 5 35S 14 26 E
Kimry, Russia 24 C6 56 55N 37 15 E
Kinabalu, Gunong, Malaysia 36 C5 6 3N 116 14 E
Kinaskan L., Canada 72 B2 57 38N 130 8W
Kinbasket L., Canada 72 C5 52 0N 118 10W
Kincardine, Canada 78 B3 44 10N 81 40W
Kincolith, Canada 72 B3 55 0N 129 57W
Kinda, Dem. Rep. of the Congo 55 D2 9 18S 25 4 E
Kinde, U.S.A. 78 C2 43 56N 83 0W
Kinder Scout, U.K. 10 D6 53 24N 1 52W
Kindersley, Canada 73 C7 51 30N 109 10W
Kindia, Guinea 50 F3 10 0N 12 52W
Kindu, Dem. Rep. of the Congo 54 C2 2 55S 25 50 E
Kineshma, Russia 24 C7 57 30N 42 5 E
Kinesi, Tanzania 54 C3 1 25S 33 50 E
King, L., Australia 61 F2 33 10S 119 35 E
King, Mt., Australia 62 D4 25 10S 147 30 E
King City, U.S.A. 84 J5 36 13N 121 8W
King Cr. →, Australia 62 C2 24 35S 139 30 E
King Edward →, Australia 60 B4 14 14S 126 35 E
King Frederick VI Land = Kong Frederik VI Kyst, Greenland 4 C5 63 0N 43 0W
King George B., Falk. Is. 96 G4 51 30S 60 30W
King George I., Antarctica 5 C18 60 0S 60 0W
King George Is., Canada 69 C11 57 20N 80 30W
King I. = Kadan Kyun, Burma 38 F2 12 30N 98 20 E
King I., Australia 62 F3 39 50S 144 0 E
King I., Canada 72 C3 52 10N 127 40W
King Leopold Ranges, Australia 60 C4 17 30S 125 45 E
King of Prussia, U.S.A. 79 F9 40 5N 75 23W
King Sd., Australia 60 C3 16 50S 123 20 E
King William I., Canada 68 B10 69 10N 97 25W
King William's Town, S. Africa 56 E4 32 51S 27 22 E
Kingaok = Bathurst Inlet, Canada 68 B9 66 50N 108 1W
Kingaroy, Australia 63 D5 26 32S 151 51 E
Kingfisher, U.S.A. 81 H6 35 52N 97 56W
Kingirbān, Iraq 44 C5 34 40N 44 54 E
Kingisepp = Kuressaare, Estonia 9 G20 58 15N 22 30 E
Kingman, Ariz., U.S.A. 85 K12 35 12N 114 4W
Kingman, Kans., U.S.A. 81 G5 37 39N 98 7W
Kingoonya, Australia 63 E2 30 55S 135 19 E
Kingri, Pakistan 42 D3 30 27N 69 49 E
Kings →, U.S.A. 84 J7 36 3N 119 50W
Kings Canyon Nat. Park, U.S.A. 84 J8 36 50N 118 40W
King's Lynn, U.K. 10 E8 52 45N 0 24 E
Kings Mountain, U.S.A. 77 H5 35 15N 81 20W
Kings Park, U.S.A. 79 F11 40 53N 73 16W
King's Peak, U.S.A. 82 F8 40 46N 110 27W
Kingsbridge, U.K. 11 G4 50 17N 3 47W
Kingsburg, U.S.A. 84 J7 36 31N 119 33W
Kingscote, Australia 63 F2 35 40S 137 38 E
Kingscourt, Ireland 13 C5 53 55N 6 48W
Kingsford, U.S.A. 76 C1 45 48N 88 4W
Kingsland, U.S.A. 77 K5 30 48N 81 41W
Kingsley, U.S.A. 80 D7 42 35N 95 58W
Kingsport, U.S.A. 77 G4 36 33N 82 33W
Kingston, Canada 79 B8 44 14N 76 30W
Kingston, Jamaica 88 C4 18 0N 76 50W
Kingston, N.Z. 59 L2 45 20S 168 43 E
Kingston, N.H., U.S.A. 79 D13 42 56N 71 3W
Kingston, N.Y., U.S.A. 79 E11 41 56N 73 59W
Kingston, Pa., U.S.A. 79 E9 41 16N 75 54W
Kingston, R.I., U.S.A. 79 E13 41 29N 71 30W
Kingston Pk., U.S.A. 85 K11 35 45N 115 54W
Kingston South East, Australia 63 F2 36 51S 139 55 E
Kingston upon Hull, U.K. 10 D7 53 45N 0 21W
Kingston upon Hull □, U.K. 10 D7 53 45N 0 21W
Kingston-upon-Thames □, U.K. 11 F7 51 24N 0 17W
Kingstown, St. Vincent 89 D7 13 10N 61 10W
Kingstree, U.S.A. 77 J6 33 40N 79 50W
Kingsville, Canada 78 D2 42 2N 82 45W
Kingsville, U.S.A. 81 M6 27 31N 97 52W
Kingussie, U.K. 12 D4 57 6N 4 2W
Kingwood, U.S.A. 81 K7 29 54N 95 18W
Kınık, Turkey 21 E12 39 6N 27 24 E
Kinistino, Canada 73 C7 52 57N 105 2W
Kinkala, Congo 52 E2 4 18S 14 49 E
Kinki □, Japan 31 H8 33 45N 136 0 E
Kinleith, N.Z. 59 H5 38 20S 175 56 E
Kinmount, Canada 78 B6 44 48N 78 45W
Kinna, Sweden 9 H15 57 32N 12 42 E
Kinnairds Hd., U.K. 12 D6 57 43N 2 1W
Kinnarodden, Norway 6 A11 71 8N 27 40 E
Kinngait = Cape Dorset, Canada 69 B12 64 14N 76 32W
Kino, Mexico 86 B2 28 45N 111 59W
Kinoje →, Canada 70 B3 52 8N 81 25W
Kinomoto, Japan 31 G8 35 30N 136 13 E
Kinoni, Uganda 54 C3 0 41S 30 28 E
Kinoosao, Canada 73 B8 57 5N 102 1W
Kinross, U.K. 12 E5 56 13N 3 25W
Kinsale, Ireland 13 E3 51 42N 8 31W
Kinsale, Old Hd. of, Ireland 13 E3 51 37N 8 33W
Kinsha = Chang Jiang →, China 33 C7 31 48N 121 10 E
Kinshasa, Dem. Rep. of the Congo 52 E3 4 20S 15 15 E
Kinsley, U.S.A. 81 G5 37 55N 99 25W
Kinsman, U.S.A. 78 E4 41 26N 80 35W
Kinston, U.S.A. 77 H7 35 16N 77 35W
Kintore Ra., Australia 60 D4 23 15S 128 47 E
Kintyre, U.K. 12 F3 55 30N 5 35W
Kintyre, Mull of, U.K. 12 F3 55 17N 5 47W
Kinushseo →, Canada 70 A3 55 15N 83 45W
Kinuso, Canada 72 B5 55 20N 115 25W
Kinyangiri, Tanzania 54 C3 4 25S 34 37 E
Kinzua, U.S.A. 78 E6 41 52N 78 58W
Kinzua Dam, U.S.A. 78 E6 41 53N 79 0W
Kiosk, Canada 70 C4 46 6N 78 53W
Kiowa, Kans., U.S.A. 81 G5 37 1N 98 29W
Kiowa, Okla., U.S.A. 81 H7 34 43N 95 54W
Kipahigan L., Canada 73 B8 55 20N 101 55W
Kipanga, Tanzania 54 D4 6 15S 35 20 E
Kiparissía, Greece 21 F9 37 15N 21 40 E
Kiparissiakós Kólpos, Greece 21 F9 37 25N 21 25 E
Kipawa, L., Canada 70 C4 46 50N 79 0W
Kipembawe, Tanzania 54 D3 7 38S 33 27 E
Kipengere Ra., Tanzania 55 D3 9 12S 34 15 E
Kipili, Tanzania 54 D3 7 28S 30 32 E
Kipini, Kenya 54 C5 2 30S 40 32 E
Kipling, Canada 73 C8 50 6N 102 38W
Kippure, Ireland 13 C5 53 11N 6 21W
Kipushi, Dem. Rep. of the Congo 55 E2 11 48S 27 12 E
Kiranomena, Madag. 57 B8 18 17S 46 2 E
Kirensk, Russia 27 D11 57 50N 107 55 E
Kirghizia = Kyrgyzstan ■, Asia 26 E8 42 0N 75 0 E
Kirghizstan = Kyrgyzstan ■, Asia 26 E8 42 0N 75 0 E
Kirgiziya Steppe, Eurasia 25 E10 50 0N 55 0 E
Kiribati ■, Pac. Oc. 64 H10 5 0S 180 0 E
Kırıkkale, Turkey 25 G5 39 51N 33 32 E
Kirillov, Russia 24 C6 59 49N 38 24 E
Kirin = Jilin, China 35 C14 43 44N 126 30 E
Kirinyaga = Kenya, Mt., Kenya 54 C4 0 10S 37 18 E
Kiritimati, Kiribati 65 G12 1 58N 157 27W
Kirkby, U.K. 10 D5 53 30N 2 54W
Kirkby Lonsdale, U.K. 10 C5 54 12N 2 36W
Kirkcaldy, U.K. 12 E5 56 7N 3 9W
Kirkcudbright, U.K. 12 G4 54 50N 4 2W
Kirkee, India 40 K8 18 34N 73 56 E
Kirkenes, Norway 8 B23 69 40N 30 5 E
Kirkfield, Canada 78 B6 44 34N 78 59W
Kirkjubæjarklaustur, Iceland 8 E4 63 47N 18 4W
Kirkkonummi, Finland 9 F21 60 8N 24 26 E
Kirkland Lake, Canada 70 C3 48 9N 80 2W
Kırklareli, Turkey 21 D12 41 44N 27 15 E
Kirksville, U.S.A. 80 E8 40 12N 92 35W
Kirkūk, Iraq 44 C5 35 30N 44 21 E
Kirkwall, U.K. 12 C6 58 59N 2 58W
Kirkwood, S. Africa 56 E4 33 22S 25 15 E
Kirov, Russia 24 C8 58 35N 49 40 E
Kirovabad = Gäncä, Azerbaijan 25 F8 40 45N 46 20 E
Kirovakan = Vanadzor, Armenia 25 F7 40 48N 44 30 E
Kirovograd = Kirovohrad, Ukraine 25 E5 48 35N 32 20 E
Kirovohrad, Ukraine 25 E5 48 35N 32 20 E
Kirovsk = Babadayhan, Turkmenistan 26 F7 37 42N 60 23 E
Kirovsk, Russia 24 A5 67 32N 33 41 E
Kirovskiy, Kamchatka, Russia 27 D16 54 27N 155 42 E
Kirovskiy, Primorsk, Russia 30 B6 45 7N 133 30 E
Kirriemuir, U.K. 12 E5 56 41N 3 1W
Kirsanov, Russia 24 D7 52 35N 42 40 E
Kırşehir, Turkey 25 G5 39 14N 34 5 E
Kirthar Range, Pakistan 42 F2 27 0N 67 0 E
Kirtland, U.S.A. 83 H9 36 44N 108 21W
Kiruna, Sweden 8 C19 67 52N 20 15 E
Kirundu, Dem. Rep. of the Congo 54 C2 0 50S 25 35 E
Kiryū, Japan 31 F9 36 24N 139 20 E
Kisaga, Tanzania 54 C3 4 30S 34 23 E
Kisalaya, Nic. 88 D3 14 40N 84 3W
Kisámou, Kólpos, Greece 23 D5 35 30N 23 38 E
Kisanga, Dem. Rep. of the Congo 54 B2 2 30N 26 35 E
Kisangani, Dem. Rep. of the Congo 54 B2 0 35N 25 15 E
Kisar, Indonesia 37 F7 8 5S 127 10 E
Kisarawe, Tanzania 54 D4 6 53S 39 0 E
Kisarazu, Japan 31 G9 35 23N 139 55 E
Kishanganga →, Pakistan 43 B5 34 18N 73 28 E
Kishanganj, India 43 F13 26 3N 88 14 E
Kishangarh, Raj., India 42 F6 26 34N 74 52 E
Kishangarh, Raj., India 42 F4 27 50N 70 30 E
Kishinev = Chişinău, Moldova 17 E15 47 2N 28 50 E
Kishiwada, Japan 31 G7 34 28N 135 22 E
Kishtwar, India 43 C6 33 20N 75 48 E
Kisii, Kenya 54 C3 0 40S 34 45 E
Kisiju, Tanzania 54 D4 7 23S 39 19 E
Kisizi, Uganda 54 C2 1 0S 29 58 E
Kiskőrös, Hungary 17 E10 46 37N 19 20 E
Kiskunfélegyháza, Hungary 17 E10 46 42N 19 53 E
Kiskunhalas, Hungary 17 E10 46 28N 19 37 E
Kislovodsk, Russia 25 F7 43 50N 42 45 E
Kismayu = Chisimaio, Somali Rep. 49 G8 0 22S 42 32 E
Kiso-Gawa →, Japan 31 G8 35 20N 136 45 E
Kiso-Sammyaku, Japan 31 G8 35 45N 137 45 E
Kisofukushima, Japan 31 G8 35 52N 137 43 E
Kisoro, Uganda 54 C2 1 17S 29 48 E
Kissidougou, Guinea 50 G3 9 5N 10 5W
Kissimmee, U.S.A. 77 L5 28 18N 81 24W
Kissimmee →, U.S.A. 77 M5 27 9N 80 52W
Kississing L., Canada 73 B8 55 10N 101 20W
Kissónerga, Cyprus 23 E11 34 49N 32 24 E
Kisumu, Kenya 54 C3 0 3S 34 45 E
Kiswani, Tanzania 54 C4 4 5S 37 57 E
Kiswere, Tanzania 55 D4 9 27S 39 30 E
Kit Carson, U.S.A. 80 F3 38 46N 102 48W
Kita, Mali 50 F4 13 5N 9 25W
Kitaibaraki, Japan 31 F10 36 50N 140 45 E
Kitakami, Japan 30 E10 39 20N 141 10 E
Kitakami-Gawa →, Japan 30 E10 38 25N 141 19 E
Kitakami-Sammyaku, Japan 30 E10 39 30N 141 30 E
Kitakata, Japan 30 F9 37 39N 139 52 E
Kitakyūshū, Japan 31 H5 33 50N 130 50 E
Kitale, Kenya 54 B4 1 0N 35 0 E
Kitami, Japan 30 C11 43 48N 143 54 E
Kitami-Sammyaku, Japan 30 B11 44 22N 142 43 E
Kitangiri, L., Tanzania 54 C3 4 5S 34 20 E
Kitaya, Tanzania 55 E5 10 38S 40 8 E
Kitchener, Canada 78 C4 43 27N 80 29W
Kitega = Gitega, Burundi 54 C2 3 26S 29 56 E
Kitengo, Dem. Rep. of the Congo 54 D1 7 26S 24 8 E
Kitgum, Uganda 54 B3 3 17N 32 52 E
Kíthira, Greece 21 F10 36 8N 23 0 E
Kíthnos, Greece 21 F11 37 26N 24 27 E
Kiti, Cyprus 23 E12 34 50N 33 34 E
Kiti, C., Cyprus 23 E12 34 48N 33 36 E
Kitimat, Canada 72 C3 54 3N 128 38W
Kitinen →, Finland 8 C22 67 14N 27 27 E
Kitsuki, Japan 31 H5 33 25N 131 37 E
Kittakittaooloo, L., Australia 63 D2 28 3S 138 14 E
Kittanning, U.S.A. 78 F5 40 49N 79 31W
Kittatinny Mts., U.S.A. 79 F10 41 0N 75 0W
Kittery, U.S.A. 77 D10 43 5N 70 45W
Kittilä, Finland 8 C21 67 40N 24 51 E
Kitui, Kenya 54 C4 1 17S 38 0 E
Kitwanga, Canada 72 B3 55 6N 128 4W
Kitwe, Zambia 55 E2 12 54S 28 13 E
Kivarli, India 42 G5 24 33N 72 46 E
Kivertsi, Ukraine 17 C13 50 50N 25 28 E
Kividhes, Cyprus 23 E11 34 46N 32 51 E
Kivu, L., Dem. Rep. of the Congo 54 C2 1 48S 29 0 E
Kiyev = Kyyiv, Ukraine 17 C16 50 30N 30 28 E
Kiyevskoye Vdkhr. = Kyyivske Vdskh., Ukraine 17 C16 51 0N 30 25 E
Kizel, Russia 24 C10 59 3N 57 40 E
Kiziguru, Rwanda 54 C3 1 46S 30 23 E
Kızıl Irmak →, Turkey 25 F6 41 44N 35 58 E
Kizil Jilga, China 43 B8 35 26N 78 50 E
Kızıltepe, Turkey 44 B4 37 12N 40 35 E
Kizimkazi, Tanzania 54 D4 6 28S 39 30 E
Kizlyar, Russia 25 F8 43 51N 46 40 E
Kizyl-Arvat = Gyzylarbat, Turkmenistan 26 F6 39 4N 56 23 E
Kjölur, Iceland 8 D4 64 50N 19 25W
Kladno, Czech Rep. 16 C8 50 10N 14 7 E
Klaeng, Thailand 38 F3 12 47N 101 39 E
Klagenfurt, Austria 16 E8 46 38N 14 20 E
Klaipėda, Lithuania 9 J19 55 43N 21 10 E
Klaksvík, Færoe Is. 8 E9 62 14N 6 35W
Klamath →, U.S.A. 82 F1 41 33N 124 5W
Klamath Falls, U.S.A. 82 E3 42 13N 121 46W
Klamath Mts., U.S.A. 82 F2 41 20N 123 0W
Klamono, Indonesia 37 E8 1 8S 131 30 E
Klappan →, Canada 72 B3 58 0N 129 43W
Klarälven →, Sweden 9 G15 59 23N 13 32 E
Klatovy, Czech Rep. 16 D7 49 23N 13 18 E
Klawer, S. Africa 56 E2 31 44S 18 36 E
Klazienaveen, Neths. 15 B6 52 44N 7 0 E
Kleena Kleene, Canada 72 C4 52 0N 124 59W
Klein-Karas, Namibia 56 D2 27 33S 18 7 E
Klerksdorp, S. Africa 56 D4 26 53S 26 38 E
Kletsk = Klyetsk, Belarus 17 B14 53 5N 26 45 E
Kletskiy, Russia 25 E7 49 16N 43 11 E
Klickitat, U.S.A. 82 D3 45 49N 121 9W
Klickitat →, U.S.A. 84 E5 45 42N 121 17W
Klidhes, Cyprus 23 D13 35 42N 34 36 E
Klinaklini →, Canada 72 C3 51 21N 125 40W
Klip →, S. Africa 57 D4 27 3S 29 3 E
Klipdale, S. Africa 56 E2 34 19S 19 57 E
Klipplaat, S. Africa 56 E3 33 1S 24 22 E
Kłodzko, Poland 17 C9 50 28N 16 38 E
Klouto, Togo 50 G6 6 57N 0 44 E
Kluane L., Canada 68 B6 61 15N 138 40W
Kluane Nat. Park, Canada 72 A1 60 45N 139 30W
Kluczbork, Poland 17 C10 50 58N 18 12 E
Klukwan, U.S.A. 72 B1 59 24N 135 54W
Klyetsk, Belarus 17 B14 53 5N 26 45 E
Klyuchevskaya, Gora, Russia 27 D17 55 50N 160 30 E
Knaresborough, U.K. 10 C6 54 1N 1 28W
Knee L., Man., Canada 70 A1 55 3N 94 45W
Knee L., Sask., Canada 73 B7 55 51N 107 0W
Knight Inlet, Canada 72 C3 50 45N 125 40W
Knighton, U.K. 11 E4 52 21N 3 3W
Knights Ferry, U.S.A. 84 H6 37 50N 120 40W
Knights Landing, U.S.A. 84 G5 38 48N 121 43W
Knob, C., Australia 61 F2 34 32S 119 16 E
Knock, Ireland 13 C3 53 48N 8 55W
Knockmealdown Mts., Ireland 13 D4 52 14N 7 56W
Knokke-Heist, Belgium 15 C3 51 21N 3 17 E
Knossós, Greece 23 D7 35 16N 25 10 E
Knowlton, Canada 79 A12 45 13N 72 31W
Knox, U.S.A. 76 E2 41 18N 86 37W
Knox Coast, Antarctica 5 C8 66 30S 108 0 E
Knoxville, Iowa, U.S.A. 80 E8 41 19N 93 6W
Knoxville, Pa., U.S.A. 78 E7 41 57N 77 27W
Knoxville, Tenn., U.S.A. 77 H4 35 58N 83 55W
Knysna, S. Africa 56 E3 34 2S 23 2 E
Ko Kha, Thailand 38 C2 18 11N 99 24 E
Koartac = Quaqtaq, Canada 69 B13 60 55N 69 40W
Koba, Indonesia 37 F8 6 37S 134 37 E
Kobarid, Slovenia 16 E7 46 15N 13 30 E
Kobayashi, Japan 31 J5 31 56N 130 59 E
Kobdo = Hovd, Mongolia 32 B4 48 2N 91 37 E
Kōbe, Japan 31 G7 34 45N 135 10 E
København, Denmark 9 J15 55 41N 12 34 E
Kōbi-Sho, Japan 31 M1 25 56N 123 41 E
Koblenz, Germany 16 C4 50 21N 7 36 E
Kobryn, Belarus 17 B13 52 15N 24 22 E
Kocaeli, Turkey 25 F4 40 45N 29 50 E
Kočani, Macedonia 21 D10 41 55N 22 25 E
Koch Bihar, India 41 F16 26 22N 89 29 E
Kochang, S. Korea 35 G14 35 41N 127 55 E
Kochas, India 43 G10 25 15N 83 56 E
Kochi = Cochin, India 40 Q10 9 58N 76 20 E
Kōchi, Japan 31 H6 33 30N 133 35 E
Kōchi □, Japan 31 H6 33 40N 133 30 E
Kochiu = Gejiu, China 32 D5 23 20N 103 10 E
Kodarma, India 43 G11 24 28N 85 36 E
Kodiak, U.S.A. 68 C4 57 47N 152 24W
Kodiak I., U.S.A. 68 C4 57 30N 152 45W
Kodinar, India 42 J4 20 46N 70 46 E
Koedoesberge, S. Africa 56 E3 32 40S 20 11 E
Koes, Namibia 56 D2 26 0S 19 15 E
Koffiefontein, S. Africa 56 D4 29 30S 25 0 E
Kofiau, Indonesia 37 E7 1 11S 129 50 E
Koforidua, Ghana 50 G5 6 3N 0 17W
Kōfu, Japan 31 G9 35 40N 138 30 E
Koga, Japan 31 F9 36 11N 139 43 E
Kogaluk →, Canada 71 A7 56 12N 61 44W
Køge, Denmark 9 J15 55 27N 12 11 E
Koh-i-Khurd, Afghan. 42 C1 33 30N 65 59 E
Koh-i-Maran, Pakistan 42 E2 29 18N 66 50 E
Kohat, Pakistan 42 C4 33 40N 71 29 E
Kohima, India 41 G19 25 35N 94 10 E
Kohkīlūyeh va Būyer Aḥmadi □, Iran 45 D6 31 30N 50 30 E
Kohler Ra., Antarctica 5 D15 77 0S 110 0W
Kohlu, Pakistan 42 E3 29 54N 69 15 E
Kohtla-Järve, Estonia 9 G22 59 20N 27 20 E
Koillismaa, Finland 8 D23 65 44N 28 36 E
Koin-dong, N. Korea 35 D14 40 28N 126 18 E
Kojō, N. Korea 35 E14 38 58N 127 58 E
Kojonup, Australia 61 F2 33 48S 117 10 E
Kojūr, Iran 45 B6 36 23N 51 43 E
Kokand = Qŭqon, Uzbekistan 26 E8 40 30N 70 57 E
Kokas, Indonesia 37 E8 2 42S 132 26 E
Kokchetav = Kökshetaū, Kazakstan 26 D7 53 20N 69 25 E
Kokemäenjoki →, Finland 9 F19 61 32N 21 44 E
Kokkola, Finland 8 E20 63 50N 23 8 E
Koko Kyunzu, Burma 41 M18 14 10N 93 25 E
Kokomo, U.S.A. 76 E2 40 29N 86 8W
Koksan, N. Korea 35 E14 38 46N 126 40 E
Kökshetaū, Kazakstan 26 D7 53 20N 69 25 E
Koksoak →, Canada 69 C13 58 30N 68 10W
Kokstad, S. Africa 57 E4 30 32S 29 29 E
Kokubu, Japan 31 J5 31 44N 130 46 E
Kola, Indonesia 37 F8 5 35S 134 30 E
Kola, Russia 24 A5 68 45N 33 8 E
Kola Pen. = Kolskiy Poluostrov, Russia 24 A6 67 30N 38 0 E
Kolachi →, Pakistan 42 F2 27 8N 67 2 E
Kolahoi, India 43 B6 34 12N 75 22 E
Kolaka, Indonesia 37 E6 4 3S 121 46 E
Kolar, India 40 N11 13 12N 78 15 E
Kolar Gold Fields, India 40 N11 12 58N 78 16 E
Kolaras, India 42 G6 25 14N 77 36 E
Kolari, Finland 8 C20 67 20N 23 48 E
Kolayat, India 40 F8 27 50N 72 50 E
Kolchugino = Leninsk-Kuznetskiy, Russia 26 D9 54 44N 86 10 E
Kolding, Denmark 9 J13 55 30N 9 29 E
Kolepom = Dolak, Pulau, Indonesia 37 F9 8 0S 138 30 E
Kolguyev, Ostrov, Russia 24 A8 69 20N 48 30 E
Kolhapur, India 40 L9 16 43N 74 15 E
Kolín, Czech Rep. 16 C8 50 2N 15 9 E
Kolkas rags, Latvia 9 H20 57 46N 22 37 E
Kolkata, India 43 H13 22 36N 88 24 E
Kollam = Quilon, India 40 Q10 8 50N 76 38 E
Kollum, Neths. 15 A6 53 17N 6 10 E
Kolmanskop, Namibia 56 D2 26 45S 15 14 E
Köln, Germany 16 C4 50 56N 6 57 E
Koło, Poland 17 B10 52 14N 18 40 E
Kołobrzeg, Poland 16 A8 54 10N 15 35 E
Kolomna, Russia 24 C6 55 8N 38 45 E
Kolomyya, Ukraine 17 D13 48 31N 25 2 E
Kolonodale, Indonesia 37 E6 2 0S 121 19 E
Kolosib, India 41 G18 24 15N 92 45 E
Kolpashevo, Russia 26 D9 58 20N 83 5 E
Kolpino, Russia 24 C5 59 44N 30 39 E
Kolskiy Poluostrov, Russia 24 A6 67 30N 38 0 E
Kolskiy Zaliv, Russia 24 A5 69 23N 34 0 E
Kolwezi, Dem. Rep. of the Congo 55 E2 10 40S 25 25 E
Kolyma →, Russia 27 C17 69 30N 161 0 E
Kolymskoye Nagorye, Russia 27 C16 63 0N 157 0 E
Kôm Ombo, Egypt 51 D12 24 25N 32 52 E
Komandorskiye Is. = Komandorskiye Ostrova, Russia 27 D17 55 0N 167 0 E
Komandorskiye Ostrova, Russia 27 D17 55 0N 167 0 E
Komárno, Slovak Rep. 17 E10 47 49N 18 5 E
Komatipoort, S. Africa 57 D5 25 25S 31 55 E
Komatou Yialou, Cyprus 23 D13 35 25N 34 8 E
Komatsu, Japan 31 F8 36 25N 136 30 E
Komatsushima, Japan 31 H7 34 0N 134 35 E
Komi □, Russia 24 B10 64 0N 55 0 E
Kommunarsk = Alchevsk, Ukraine 25 E6 48 30N 38 45 E
Kommunizma, Pik, Tajikistan 26 F8 39 0N 72 2 E
Komodo, Indonesia 37 F5 8 37S 119 20 E
Komoran, Pulau, Indonesia 37 F9 8 18S 138 45 E
Komoro, Japan 31 F9 36 19N 138 26 E
Komotini, Greece 21 D11 41 9N 25 26 E
Kompasberg, S. Africa 56 E3 31 45S 24 32 E
Kompong Bang, Cambodia 39 F5 12 24N 104 40 E
Kompong Cham, Cambodia 39 F5 12 0N 105 30 E
Kompong Chhnang = Kampang Chhnang, Cambodia 39 F5 12 20N 104 35 E
Kompong Chikreng, Cambodia 38 F5 13 5N 104 18 E
Kompong Kleang, Cambodia 38 F5 13 6N 104 8 E
Kompong Luong, Cambodia 39 G5 11 49N 104 48 E
Kompong Pranak, Cambodia 38 F5 13 35N 104 55 E
Kompong Som = Kampong Saom, Cambodia 39 G4 10 38N 103 30 E
Kompong Som, Chhung = Kampong Saom, Chaak, Cambodia 39 G4 10 50N 103 32 E
Kompong Speu, Cambodia 39 G5 11 26N 104 32 E
Kompong Sralao, Cambodia 38 E5 14 5N 105 46 E
Kompong Thom, Cambodia 38 F5 12 35N 104 51 E
Kompong Trabeck, Cambodia 38 F5 13 6N 105 14 E
Kompong Trabeck, Cambodia 39 G5 11 9N 105 28 E
Kompong Trach, Cambodia 39 G5 11 25N 105 48 E
Kompong Tralach, Cambodia 39 G5 11 54N 104 47 E
Komrat = Comrat, Moldova 17 E15 46 18N 28 40 E
Komsberg, S. Africa 56 E3 32 40S 20 45 E
Komsomolets, Ostrov, Russia 27 A10 80 30N 95 0 E
Komsomolsk, Russia 27 D14 50 30N 137 0 E
Kon Tum, Vietnam 38 E7 14 24N 108 0 E
Kon Tum, Plateau du, Vietnam 38 E7 14 30N 108 30 E
Konarhā □, Afghan. 40 B7 35 30N 71 3 E
Konārī, Iran 45 D6 28 13N 51 36 E
Konch, India 43 G8 26 0N 79 10 E
Konde, Tanzania 54 C4 4 57S 39 45 E
Kondinin, Australia 61 F2 32 34S 118 8 E
Kondoa, Tanzania 54 C4 4 55S 35 50 E
Kondókali, Greece 23 A3 39 38N 19 51 E
Kondopaga, Russia 24 B5 62 12N 34 17 E
Kondratyevo, Russia 27 D10 57 22N 98 15 E

Lanak La

Kut, Ko, Thailand 39 G4 11 40N 102 35 E
Kütahya, Turkey 25 G5 39 30N 30 2 E
Kutaisi, Georgia 25 F7 42 19N 42 40 E
Kutaraja = Banda Aceh, Indonesia 36 C1 5 35N 95 20 E
Kutch, Gulf of = Kachchh, Gulf of, India 42 H3 22 50N 69 15 E
Kutch, Rann of = Kachchh, Rann of, India 42 H4 24 0N 70 0 E
Kutiyana, India 42 J4 21 36N 70 2 E
Kutno, Poland 17 B10 52 15N 19 23 E
Kutse, Botswana 56 C3 21 7S 22 16 E
Kutu, Dem. Rep. of the Congo 52 E3 2 40S 18 11 E
Kutum, Sudan 51 F10 14 10N 24 40 E
Kuujjuaq, Canada 69 C13 58 6N 68 15W
Kuujjuarapik, Canada 70 A4 55 20N 77 35W
Kuŭp-tong, N. Korea 35 D14 40 45N 126 1 E
Kuusamo, Finland 8 D23 65 57N 29 8 E
Kuusankoski, Finland 9 F22 60 55N 26 38 E
Kuwait = Al Kuwayt, Kuwait 46 B4 29 30N 48 0 E
Kuwait ■, Asia 46 B4 29 30N 47 30 E
Kuwana, Japan 31 G8 35 5N 136 43 E
Kuwana →, India 43 F10 26 25N 83 15 E
Kuybyshev = Samara, Russia 24 D9 53 8N 50 6 E
Kuybyshev, Russia 26 D8 55 27N 78 19 E
Kuybyshevskoye Vdkhr., Russia 24 C8 55 2N 49 30 E
Kuye He →, China 34 E6 38 23N 110 46 E
Kūyeh, Iran 44 B5 38 45N 47 57 E
Kūysanjaq, Iraq 44 B5 36 5N 44 38 E
Kuyto, Ozero, Russia 24 B5 65 6N 31 20 E
Kuyumba, Russia 27 C10 60 58N 96 59 E
Kuzey Anadolu Dağları, Turkey 25 F6 41 30N 35 0 E
Kuznetsk, Russia 24 D8 53 12N 46 40 E
Kuzomen, Russia 24 A6 66 22N 36 50 E
Kvænangen, Norway 8 A19 70 5N 21 15 E
Kvaløy, Norway 8 B18 69 40N 18 30 E
Kvarner, Croatia 16 F8 44 50N 14 10 E
Kvarnerič, Croatia 16 F8 44 43N 14 37 E
Kwa-Nobuhle, S. Africa 53 L5 33 50S 25 22 E
Kwabhaca, S. Africa 57 E4 30 51S 29 0 E
Kwakhanai, Botswana 56 C3 21 39S 21 16 E
Kwakoegron, Surinam 93 B7 5 12N 55 25W
Kwale, Kenya 54 C4 4 15S 39 31 E
KwaMashu, S. Africa 57 D5 29 45S 30 58 E
Kwando →, Africa 56 B3 18 27S 23 32 E
Kwangdaeri, N. Korea 35 D14 40 31N 127 32 E
Kwangju, S. Korea 35 G14 35 9N 126 54 E
Kwango →, Dem. Rep. of the Congo 52 E3 3 14S 17 22 E
Kwangsi-Chuang = Guangxi Zhuangzu Zizhiqu □, China 33 D5 24 0N 109 0 E
Kwangtung = Guangdong □, China 33 D6 23 0N 113 0 E
Kwataboahegan →, Canada 70 B3 51 9N 80 50W
Kwatisore, Indonesia 37 E8 3 18S 134 50 E
KwaZulu Natal □, S. Africa 57 D5 29 0S 30 0 E
Kweichow = Guizhou □, China 32 D5 27 0N 107 0 E
Kwekwe, Zimbabwe 55 F2 18 58S 29 48 E
Kwidzyn, Poland 17 B10 53 44N 18 55 E
Kwinana New Town, Australia 61 F2 32 15S 115 47 E
Kwoka, Indonesia 37 E8 0 31S 132 27 E
Kyabra Cr. →, Australia 63 D3 25 36S 142 55 E
Kyabram, Australia 63 F4 36 19S 145 4 E
Kyaikto, Burma 38 D1 17 20N 97 3 E
Kyakhta, Russia 27 D11 50 30N 106 25 E
Kyancutta, Australia 63 E2 33 8S 135 33 E
Kyaukpadaung, Burma 41 J19 20 52N 95 8 E
Kyaukpyu, Burma 41 K18 19 28N 93 30 E
Kyaukse, Burma 41 J20 21 36N 96 10 E
Kyburz, U.S.A. 84 G6 38 47N 120 18W
Kyelang, India 42 C7 32 35N 77 2 E
Kyenjojo, Uganda 54 B3 0 40N 30 37 E
Kyle, Canada 73 C7 50 50N 108 2W
Kyle Dam, Zimbabwe 55 G3 20 15S 31 0 E
Kyle of Lochalsh, U.K. 12 D3 57 17N 5 44W
Kymijoki →, Finland 9 F22 60 30N 26 55 E
Kyneton, Australia 63 F3 37 10S 144 29 E
Kynuna, Australia 62 C3 21 37S 141 55 E
Kyō-ga-Saki, Japan 31 G7 35 45N 135 15 E
Kyoga, L., Uganda 54 B3 1 35N 33 0 E
Kyogle, Australia 63 D5 28 40S 153 0 E
Kyongju, S. Korea 35 G15 35 51N 129 14 E
Kyongpyaw, Burma 41 L19 17 12N 95 10 E
Kyŏngsŏng, N. Korea 35 D15 41 35N 129 36 E
Kyōto, Japan 31 G7 35 0N 135 45 E
Kyōto □, Japan 31 G7 35 15N 135 45 E
Kyparissovouno, Cyprus 23 D12 35 19N 33 10 E
Kyperounda, Cyprus 23 E11 34 56N 32 58 E
Kyrenia, Cyprus 23 D12 35 20N 33 20 E
Kyrgyzstan ■, Asia 26 E8 42 0N 75 0 E
Kyrönjoki →, Finland 8 E19 63 14N 21 45 E
Kystatyam, Russia 27 C13 67 20N 123 10 E
Kythréa, Cyprus 23 D12 35 15N 33 29 E
Kyunhla, Burma 41 H19 23 25N 95 15 E
Kyuquot Sound, Canada 72 D3 50 2N 127 22W
Kyūshū, Japan 31 H5 33 0N 131 0 E
Kyūshū □, Japan 31 H5 33 0N 131 0 E
Kyūshū-Sanchi, Japan 31 H5 32 35N 131 17 E
Kyustendil, Bulgaria 21 C10 42 16N 22 41 E
Kyusyur, Russia 27 B13 70 19N 127 30 E
Kyyiv, Ukraine 17 C16 50 30N 30 28 E
Kyyivske Vdskh., Ukraine 17 C16 51 0N 30 25 E
Kyzyl, Russia 27 D10 51 50N 94 30 E
Kyzyl Kum, Uzbekistan 26 E7 42 30N 65 0 E
Kyzyl-Kyya, Kyrgyzstan 26 E8 40 16N 72 8 E
Kzyl-Orda = Qyzylorda, Kazakstan 26 E7 44 48N 65 28 E

L

La Alcarria, Spain 19 B4 40 31N 2 45W
La Asunción, Venezuela 92 A6 11 2N 63 53W
La Baie, Canada 71 C5 48 19N 70 53W
La Banda, Argentina 94 B3 27 45S 64 10W
La Barca, Mexico 86 C4 20 20N 102 40W
La Barge, U.S.A. 82 E8 42 16N 110 12W
La Belle, U.S.A. 77 M5 26 46N 81 26W
La Biche →, Canada 72 B4 59 57N 123 50W
La Biche, L., Canada 72 C6 54 50N 112 5W
La Bomba, Mexico 86 A1 31 53N 115 2W
La Calera, Chile 94 C1 32 50S 71 10W
La Canal = Sa Canal, Spain 22 C7 38 51N 1 23 E
La Carlota, Argentina 94 C3 33 30S 63 20W
La Ceiba, Honduras 88 C2 15 40N 86 50W
La Chaux-de-Fonds, Switz. 18 C7 47 7N 6 50 E
La Chorrera, Panama 88 E4 8 53N 79 47W
La Cocha, Argentina 94 B2 27 50S 65 40W
La Concepción, Panama 88 E3 8 31N 82 37W
La Concordia, Mexico 87 D6 16 8N 92 38W
La Coruña = A Coruña, Spain 19 A1 43 20N 8 25W
La Crescent, U.S.A. 80 D9 43 50N 91 18W
La Crete, Canada 72 B5 58 11N 116 24W
La Crosse, Kans., U.S.A. 80 F5 38 32N 99 18W
La Crosse, Wis., U.S.A. 80 D9 43 48N 91 15W
La Cruz, Costa Rica 88 D2 11 4N 85 39W
La Cruz, Mexico 86 C3 23 55N 106 54W
La Désirade, Guadeloupe 89 C7 16 18N 61 3W
La Escondida, Mexico 86 C5 24 6N 99 55W
La Esmeralda, Paraguay 94 A3 22 16S 62 33W
La Esperanza, Cuba 88 B3 22 46N 83 44W
La Esperanza, Honduras 88 D2 14 15N 88 10W
La Estrada = A Estrada, Spain 19 A1 42 43N 8 27W
La Fayette, U.S.A. 77 H3 34 42N 85 17W
La Fé, Cuba 88 B3 22 2N 84 15W
La Follette, U.S.A. 77 G3 36 23N 84 7W
La Grande, U.S.A. 82 D4 45 20N 118 5W
La Grande →, Canada 70 B5 53 50N 79 0W
La Grande Deux, Rés., Canada 70 B4 53 40N 76 55W
La Grande Quatre, Rés., Canada 70 B5 54 0N 73 15W
La Grande Trois, Rés., Canada 70 B4 53 40N 75 10W
La Grange, Calif., U.S.A. 84 H6 37 42N 120 27W
La Grange, Ga., U.S.A. 77 J3 33 2N 85 2W
La Grange, Ky., U.S.A. 76 F3 38 25N 85 23W
La Grange, Tex., U.S.A. 81 L6 29 54N 96 52W
La Guaira, Venezuela 92 A5 10 36N 66 56W
La Habana, Cuba 88 B3 23 8N 82 22W
La Independencia, Mexico 87 D6 16 31N 91 47W
La Isabela, Dom. Rep. 89 C5 19 58N 71 2W
La Junta, U.S.A. 81 F3 37 59N 103 33W
La Laguna, Canary Is. 22 F3 28 28N 16 18W
La Libertad, Guatemala 88 C1 16 47N 90 7W
La Libertad, Mexico 86 B2 29 55N 112 41W
La Ligua, Chile 94 C1 32 30S 71 16W
La Línea de la Concepción, Spain 19 D3 36 15N 5 23W
La Loche, Canada 73 B7 56 29N 109 26W
La Louvière, Belgium 15 D4 50 27N 4 10 E
La Malbaie, Canada 71 C5 47 40N 70 10W
La Mancha, Spain 19 C4 39 10N 2 54W
La Martre, L., Canada 72 A5 63 15N 117 55W
La Mesa, U.S.A. 85 N9 32 46N 117 3W
La Misión, Mexico 86 A1 32 5N 116 50W
La Moure, U.S.A. 80 B5 46 21N 98 18W
La Negra, Chile 94 A1 23 46S 70 18W
La Oliva, Canary Is. 22 F6 28 36N 13 57W
La Orotava, Canary Is. 22 F3 28 22N 16 31W
La Oroya, Peru 92 F3 11 32S 75 54W
La Palma, Canary Is. 22 F2 28 40N 17 50W
La Palma, Panama 88 E4 8 15N 78 0W
La Palma del Condado, Spain 19 D2 37 21N 6 38W
La Paloma, Chile 94 C1 30 35S 71 0W
La Pampa □, Argentina 94 D2 36 50S 66 0W
La Paragua, Venezuela 92 B6 6 50N 63 20W
La Paz, Entre Ríos, Argentina 94 C4 30 50S 59 45W
La Paz, San Luis, Argentina 94 C2 33 30S 67 20W
La Paz, Bolivia 92 G5 16 20S 68 10W
La Paz, Honduras 88 D2 14 20N 87 47W
La Paz, Mexico 86 C2 24 10N 110 20W
La Paz Centro, Nic. 88 D2 12 20N 86 41W
La Pedrera, Colombia 92 D5 1 18S 69 43W
La Pérade, Canada 71 C5 46 35N 72 12W
La Perouse Str., Asia 30 B11 45 40N 142 0 E
La Pesca, Mexico 87 C5 23 46N 97 47W
La Piedad, Mexico 86 C4 20 20N 102 1W
La Pine, U.S.A. 82 E3 43 40N 121 30W
La Plata, Argentina 94 D4 35 0S 57 55W
La Pocatière, Canada 71 C5 47 22N 70 2W
La Porte, Ind., U.S.A. 76 E2 41 36N 86 43W
La Porte, Tex., U.S.A. 81 L7 29 39N 95 1W
La Purísima, Mexico 86 B2 26 10N 112 4W
La Push, U.S.A. 84 C2 47 55N 124 38W
La Quiaca, Argentina 94 A2 22 5S 65 35W
La Restinga, Canary Is. 22 G2 27 38N 17 59W
La Rioja, Argentina 94 B2 29 20S 67 0W
La Rioja □, Argentina 94 B2 29 30S 67 0W
La Rioja □, Spain 19 A4 42 20N 2 20W
La Robla, Spain 19 A3 42 50N 5 41W
La Roche-en-Ardenne, Belgium 15 D5 50 11N 5 35 E
La Roche-sur-Yon, France 18 C3 46 40N 1 25W
La Rochelle, France 18 C3 46 10N 1 9W
La Roda, Spain 19 C4 39 13N 2 15W
La Romana, Dom. Rep. 89 C6 18 27N 68 57W
La Ronge, Canada 73 B7 55 5N 105 20W
La Rumorosa, Mexico 85 N10 32 33N 116 4W
La Sabina = Sa Savina, Spain 22 C7 38 44N 1 25 E
La Salle, U.S.A. 80 E10 41 20N 89 6W
La Santa, Canary Is. 22 E6 29 5N 13 40W
La Sarre, Canada 70 C4 48 45N 79 15W
La Scie, Canada 71 C8 49 57N 55 36W
La Selva Beach, U.S.A. 84 J5 36 56N 121 51W
La Serena, Chile 94 B1 29 55S 71 10W
La Seu d'Urgell, Spain 19 A6 42 22N 1 23 E
La Seyne-sur-Mer, France 18 E6 43 7N 5 52 E
La Soufrière, St. Vincent 89 D7 13 20N 61 11W
La Spézia, Italy 18 D8 44 7N 9 50 E
La Tagua, Colombia 92 C4 0 3N 74 40W
La Tortuga, Venezuela 89 D6 11 0N 65 22W
La Tuque, Canada 70 C5 47 30N 72 50W
La Unión, Chile 96 E2 40 10S 73 0W
La Unión, El Salv. 88 D2 13 20N 87 50W
La Unión, Mexico 86 D4 17 58N 101 49W
La Urbana, Venezuela 92 B5 7 8N 66 56W
La Vall d'Uixó, Spain 19 C5 39 49N 0 15W
La Vega, Dom. Rep. 89 C5 19 20N 70 30W
La Vela de Coro, Venezuela 92 A5 11 27N 69 34W
La Venta, Mexico 87 D6 18 8N 94 3W
La Ventura, Mexico 86 C4 24 38N 100 54W
Laas Caanood = Las Anod, Somali Rep. 46 F4 8 26N 47 19 E
Labasa, Fiji 59 C8 16 30S 179 27 E
Labe = Elbe →, Europe 16 B5 53 50N 9 0 E
Labé, Guinea 50 F3 11 24N 12 16W
Laberge, L., Canada 72 A1 61 11N 135 12W
Labinsk, Russia 25 F7 44 40N 40 48 E
Labis, Malaysia 39 L4 2 22N 103 2 E
Laboulaye, Argentina 94 C3 34 10S 63 30W
Labrador, Canada 71 B7 53 20N 61 0W
Labrador City, Canada 71 B6 52 57N 66 55W
Labrador Sea, Atl. Oc. 69 C14 57 0N 54 0W
Lábrea, Brazil 92 E6 7 15S 64 51W
Labuan, Malaysia 36 C5 5 20N 115 14 E
Labuan, Pulau, Malaysia 36 C5 5 21N 115 13 E
Labuha, Indonesia 37 E7 0 30S 127 30 E
Labuhan, Indonesia 37 G11 6 22S 105 50 E
Labuhanbajo, Indonesia 37 F6 8 28S 119 54 E
Labuk, Telok, Malaysia 36 C5 6 10N 117 50 E
Labyrinth, L., Australia 63 E2 30 40S 135 11 E
Labytnangi, Russia 26 C7 66 39N 66 21 E
Lac Bouchette, Canada 71 C5 48 16N 72 11W
Lac Édouard, Canada 70 C5 47 40N 72 16W
Lac La Biche, Canada 72 C6 54 45N 111 58W
Lac la Martre = Wha Ti, Canada 68 B8 63 8N 117 16W
Lac La Ronge Prov. Park, Canada 73 B7 55 9N 104 41W
Lac-Mégantic, Canada 71 C5 45 35N 70 53W
Lac Thien, Vietnam 38 F7 12 25N 108 11 E
Lacanau, France 18 D3 44 58N 1 5W
Lacantúm →, Mexico 87 D6 16 36N 90 40W
Laccadive Is. = Lakshadweep Is., India 29 H11 10 0N 72 30 E
Lacepede B., Australia 63 F2 36 40S 139 40 E
Lacepede Is., Australia 60 C3 16 55S 122 0 E
Lacerdónia, Mozam. 55 F4 18 3S 35 35 E
Lacey, U.S.A. 84 C4 47 7N 122 49W
Lachhmangarh, India 42 F6 27 50N 75 4 E
Lachi, Pakistan 42 C4 33 25N 71 20 E
Lachine, Canada 79 A11 45 30N 73 40W
Lachlan →, Australia 63 E3 34 22S 143 55 E
Lachute, Canada 70 C5 45 39N 74 21W
Lackawanna, U.S.A. 78 D6 42 50N 78 50W
Lackawaxen, U.S.A. 79 E10 41 29N 74 59W
Lacolle, Canada 79 A11 45 5N 73 22W
Lacombe, Canada 72 C6 52 30N 113 44W
Lacona, U.S.A. 79 C8 43 39N 76 10W
Laconia, U.S.A. 79 C13 43 32N 71 28W
Ladakh Ra., India 43 C8 34 0N 78 0 E
Ladismith, S. Africa 56 E3 33 28S 21 15 E
Lādīz, Iran 45 D9 28 55N 61 15 E
Ladnun, India 42 F6 27 38N 74 25 E
Ladoga, L. = Ladozhskoye Ozero, Russia 24 B5 61 15N 30 30 E
Ladozhskoye Ozero, Russia 24 B5 61 15N 30 30 E
Lady Elliott I., Australia 62 C5 24 7S 152 42 E
Lady Grey, S. Africa 56 E4 30 43S 27 13 E
Ladybrand, S. Africa 56 D4 29 9S 27 29 E
Ladysmith, Canada 72 D4 49 0N 123 49W
Ladysmith, S. Africa 57 D4 28 32S 29 46 E
Ladysmith, U.S.A. 80 C9 45 28N 91 12W
Lae, Papua N. G. 64 H6 6 40S 147 2 E
Laem Ngop, Thailand 39 F4 12 10N 102 26 E
Laem Pho, Thailand 39 J3 6 55N 101 19 E
Læsø, Denmark 9 H14 57 15N 11 5 E
Lafayette, Colo., U.S.A. 80 F2 39 58N 105 12W
Lafayette, Ind., U.S.A. 76 E2 40 25N 86 54W
Lafayette, La., U.S.A. 81 K9 30 14N 92 1W
Lafayette, Tenn., U.S.A. 77 G2 36 31N 86 2W
Laferte →, Canada 72 A5 61 53N 117 44W
Lafia, Nigeria 50 G7 8 30N 8 34 E
Lafleche, Canada 73 D7 49 45N 106 40W
Lagan →, U.K. 13 B6 54 36N 5 55W
Lagarfljót →, Iceland 8 D6 65 40N 14 18W
Lågen →, Oppland, Norway 9 F14 61 8N 10 25 E
Lågen →, Vestfold, Norway 9 G14 59 3N 10 3 E
Laghouat, Algeria 50 B6 33 50N 2 59 E
Lagoa Vermelha, Brazil 95 B5 28 13S 51 32W
Lagonoy G., Phil. 37 B6 13 35N 123 50 E
Lagos, Nigeria 50 G6 6 25N 3 27 E
Lagos, Portugal 19 D1 37 5N 8 41W
Lagos de Moreno, Mexico 86 C4 21 21N 101 55W
Lagrange, Australia 60 C3 18 45S 121 43 E
Lagrange B., Australia 60 C3 18 38S 121 42 E
Laguna, Brazil 95 B6 28 30S 48 50W
Laguna, U.S.A. 83 J10 35 2N 107 25W
Laguna Beach, U.S.A. 85 M9 33 33N 117 47W
Laguna Limpia, Argentina 94 B4 26 32S 59 45W
Lagunas, Chile 94 A2 21 0S 69 45W
Lagunas, Peru 92 E3 5 10S 75 35W
Lahad Datu, Malaysia 37 C5 5 0N 118 20 E
Lahad Datu, Teluk, Malaysia 37 D5 4 50N 118 20 E
Lahan Sai, Thailand 38 E4 14 25N 102 52 E
Lahanam, Laos 38 D5 16 16N 105 16 E
Lahar, India 43 F8 26 12N 78 57 E
Laharpur, India 43 F9 27 43N 80 56 E
Lahat, Indonesia 36 E2 3 45S 103 30 E
Lahewa, Indonesia 36 D1 1 22N 97 12 E
Lāhījān, Iran 45 B6 37 10N 50 6 E
Lahn →, Germany 16 C4 50 19N 7 37 E
Laholm, Sweden 9 H15 56 30N 13 2 E
Lahore, Pakistan 42 D6 31 32N 74 22 E
Lahri, Pakistan 42 E3 29 11N 68 13 E
Lahti, Finland 9 F21 60 58N 25 40 E
Lahtis = Lahti, Finland 9 F21 60 58N 25 40 E
Laï, Chad 51 G9 9 25N 16 18 E
Lai Chau, Vietnam 38 A4 22 5N 103 3 E
Laila = Layla, Si. Arabia 46 C4 22 10N 46 40 E
Laingsburg, S. Africa 56 E3 33 9S 20 52 E
Lainio älv →, Sweden 8 C20 67 35N 22 40 E
Lairg, U.K. 12 C4 58 2N 4 24W
Laishui, China 34 E8 39 23N 115 45 E
Laiwu, China 35 F9 36 15N 117 40 E
Laixi, China 35 F11 36 50N 120 31 E
Laiyang, China 35 F11 36 59N 120 45 E
Laiyuan, China 34 E8 39 20N 114 40 E
Laizhou, China 35 F10 37 8N 119 57 E
Laizhou Wan, China 35 F10 37 30N 119 30 E
Laja →, Mexico 86 C4 20 55N 100 46W
Lajes, Brazil 95 B5 27 48S 50 20W
Lak Sao, Laos 38 C5 18 11N 104 59 E
Lakaband, Pakistan 42 D3 31 2N 69 15 E
Lake Alpine, U.S.A. 84 G7 38 29N 120 0W
Lake Andes, U.S.A. 80 D5 43 9N 98 32W
Lake Arthur, U.S.A. 81 K8 30 5N 92 41W
Lake Cargelligo, Australia 63 E4 33 15S 146 22 E
Lake Charles, U.S.A. 81 K8 30 14N 93 13W
Lake City, Colo., U.S.A. 83 G10 38 2N 107 19W
Lake City, Fla., U.S.A. 77 K4 30 11N 82 38W
Lake City, Mich., U.S.A. 76 C3 44 20N 85 13W
Lake City, Minn., U.S.A. 80 C8 44 27N 92 16W
Lake City, Pa., U.S.A. 78 D4 42 1N 80 21W
Lake City, S.C., U.S.A. 77 J6 33 52N 79 45W
Lake Cowichan, Canada 72 D4 48 49N 124 3W
Lake District, U.K. 10 C4 54 35N 3 20 E
Lake Elsinore, U.S.A. 85 M9 33 38N 117 20W
Lake George, U.S.A. 79 C11 43 26N 73 43W
Lake Grace, Australia 61 F2 33 7S 118 28 E
Lake Harbour = Kimmirut, Canada 69 B13 62 50N 69 50W
Lake Havasu City, U.S.A. 85 L12 34 27N 114 22W
Lake Hughes, U.S.A. 85 L8 34 41N 118 26W
Lake Isabella, U.S.A. 85 K8 35 38N 118 28W
Lake Jackson, U.S.A. 81 L7 29 3N 95 27W
Lake Junction, U.S.A. 82 D8 44 35N 110 28W
Lake King, Australia 61 F2 33 5S 119 45 E
Lake Lenore, Canada 73 C8 52 24N 104 59W
Lake Louise, Canada 72 C5 51 30N 116 10W
Lake Mead Nat. Recr. Area, U.S.A. 85 K12 36 15N 114 30W
Lake Mills, U.S.A. 80 D8 43 25N 93 32W
Lake Placid, U.S.A. 79 B11 44 17N 73 59W
Lake Pleasant, U.S.A. 79 C10 43 28N 74 25W
Lake Providence, U.S.A. 81 J9 32 48N 91 10W
Lake St. Peter, Canada 78 A6 45 18N 78 2W
Lake Superior Prov. Park, Canada 70 C3 47 45N 84 45W
Lake Village, U.S.A. 81 J9 33 20N 91 17W
Lake Wales, U.S.A. 77 M5 27 54N 81 35W
Lake Worth, U.S.A. 77 M5 26 37N 80 3W
Lakeba, Fiji 59 D9 18 13S 178 47W
Lakefield, Canada 78 B6 44 25N 78 16W
Lakehurst, U.S.A. 79 F10 40 1N 74 19W
Lakeland, Australia 62 B3 15 49S 144 57 E
Lakeland, U.S.A. 77 M5 28 3N 81 57W
Lakemba = Lakeba, Fiji 59 D9 18 13S 178 47W
Lakeport, Calif., U.S.A. 84 F4 39 3N 122 55W
Lakeport, Mich., U.S.A. 78 C2 43 7N 82 30W
Lakes Entrance, Australia 63 F4 37 50S 148 0 E
Lakeside, Ariz., U.S.A. 83 J9 34 9N 109 58W
Lakeside, Calif., U.S.A. 85 N10 32 52N 116 55W
Lakeside, Nebr., U.S.A. 80 D3 42 3N 102 26W
Lakeside, Ohio, U.S.A. 78 E2 41 32N 82 46W
Lakeview, U.S.A. 82 E3 42 11N 120 21W
Lakeville, U.S.A. 80 C8 44 39N 93 14W
Lakewood, Colo., U.S.A. 80 F2 39 44N 105 5W
Lakewood, N.J., U.S.A. 79 F10 40 6N 74 13W
Lakewood, N.Y., U.S.A. 78 D5 42 6N 79 19W
Lakewood, Ohio, U.S.A. 78 E3 41 29N 81 48W
Lakewood, Wash., U.S.A. 84 C4 47 11N 122 32W
Lakha, India 42 F4 26 9N 70 54 E
Lakhaniá, Greece 23 D9 35 58N 27 54 E
Lakhimpur, India 43 F9 27 57N 80 46 E
Lakhnadon, India 43 H8 22 36N 79 36 E
Lakhonpheng, Laos 38 E5 15 54N 105 34 E
Lakhpat, India 42 H3 23 48N 68 47 E
Lakin, U.S.A. 81 G4 37 57N 101 15W
Lakitusaki →, Canada 70 B3 54 21N 82 25W
Lakki, Pakistan 42 C4 32 36N 70 55 E
Lákkoi, Greece 23 D5 35 24N 23 57 E
Lakonikós Kólpos, Greece 21 F10 36 40N 22 40 E
Lakor, Indonesia 37 F7 8 15S 128 17 E
Lakota, Ivory C. 50 G4 5 50N 5 30W
Lakota, U.S.A. 80 A5 48 2N 98 21W
Laksar, India 42 E8 29 46N 78 3 E
Laksefjorden, Norway 8 A22 70 45N 26 50 E
Lakselv, Norway 8 A21 70 2N 25 0 E
Lakshadweep Is., India 29 H11 10 0N 72 30 E
Lakshmanpur, India 43 H10 22 58N 83 3 E
Lakshmikantapur, India 43 H13 22 5N 88 20 E
Lala Ghat, India 41 G18 24 30N 92 40 E
Lala Musa, Pakistan 42 C5 32 40N 73 57 E
Lalago, Tanzania 54 C3 3 28S 33 58 E
Lalapanzi, Zimbabwe 55 F3 19 20S 30 15 E
L'Albufera, Spain 19 C5 39 20N 0 27W
Lalganj, India 43 G11 25 52N 85 13 E
Lalgola, India 43 G13 24 25N 88 15 E
Lālī, Iran 45 C6 32 21N 49 6 E
Lalibela, Ethiopia 46 E2 12 3N 39 0 E
Lalin, China 35 B14 45 12N 127 0 E
Lalín, Spain 19 A1 42 40N 8 5W
Lalin He →, China 35 B13 45 32N 125 40 E
Lalitapur, Nepal 43 F11 27 40N 85 20 E
Lalitpur, India 43 G8 24 42N 78 28 E
Lalkua, India 43 E8 29 5N 79 31 E
Lalsot, India 42 F7 26 34N 76 20 E
Lam, Vietnam 38 B6 21 21N 106 31 E
Lam Pao Res., Thailand 38 D4 16 50N 103 15 E
Lamaing, Burma 41 M20 15 25N 97 53 E
Lamar, Colo., U.S.A. 80 F3 38 5N 102 37W
Lamar, Mo., U.S.A. 81 G7 37 30N 94 16W
Lamas, Peru 92 E3 6 28S 76 31W
Lambaréné, Gabon 52 E2 0 41S 10 12 E
Lambasa = Labasa, Fiji 59 C8 16 30S 179 27 E
Lambay I., Ireland 13 C5 53 29N 6 1W
Lambert Glacier, Antarctica 5 D6 71 0S 70 0 E
Lambert's Bay, S. Africa 56 E2 32 5S 18 17 E
Lambeth, Canada 78 D3 42 54N 81 18W
Lambomakondro, Madag. 57 C7 22 41S 44 44 E
Lame Deer, U.S.A. 82 D10 45 37N 106 40W
Lamego, Portugal 19 B2 41 5N 7 52W
Lamèque, Canada 71 C7 47 45N 64 38W
Lameroo, Australia 63 F3 35 19S 140 33 E
Lamesa, U.S.A. 81 J4 32 44N 101 58W
Lamía, Greece 21 E10 38 55N 22 26 E
Lammermuir Hills, U.K. 12 F6 55 50N 2 40W
Lamoille →, U.S.A. 79 B11 44 38N 73 13W
Lamon B., Phil. 37 B6 14 30N 122 20 E
Lamont, Canada 72 C6 53 46N 112 50W
Lamont, Calif., U.S.A. 85 K8 35 15N 118 55W
Lamont, Wyo., U.S.A. 82 E10 42 13N 107 29W
Lampa, Peru 92 G4 15 22S 70 22W
Lampang, Thailand 38 C2 18 16N 99 32 E
Lampasas, U.S.A. 81 K5 31 4N 98 11W
Lampazos de Naranjo, Mexico 86 B4 27 2N 100 32W
Lampedusa, Medit. S. 20 G5 35 36N 12 40 E
Lampeter, U.K. 11 E3 52 7N 4 4W
Lampione, Medit. S. 20 G5 35 33N 12 20 E
Lampman, Canada 73 D8 49 25N 102 50W
Lampung □, Indonesia 36 F2 5 30S 104 30 E
Lamta, India 43 H9 22 8N 80 7 E
Lamu, Kenya 54 C5 2 16S 40 55 E
Lamy, U.S.A. 83 J11 35 29N 105 53W
Lan Xian, China 34 E6 38 15N 111 35 E
Lanak La, China 43 B8 34 27N 79 32 E

Lanak'o Shank'ou

Lanak'o Shank'ou = Lanak La, China 43 B8 34 27N 79 32 E
Lanark, Canada 79 A8 45 1N 76 22W
Lanark, U.K. 12 F5 55 40N 3 47W
Lanbi Kyun, Burma 39 G2 10 50N 98 20 E
Lancang Jiang →, China 32 D5 21 40N 101 10 E
Lancashire □, U.K. 10 D5 53 50N 2 48W
Lancaster, Canada 79 A10 45 10N 74 30W
Lancaster, U.K. 10 C5 54 3N 2 48W
Lancaster, Calif., U.S.A. 85 L8 34 42N 118 8W
Lancaster, Ky., U.S.A. 76 G3 37 37N 84 35W
Lancaster, N.H., U.S.A. 79 B13 44 29N 71 34W
Lancaster, N.Y., U.S.A. 78 D6 42 54N 78 40W
Lancaster, Ohio, U.S.A. 76 F4 39 43N 82 36W
Lancaster, Pa., U.S.A. 79 F8 40 2N 76 19W
Lancaster, S.C., U.S.A. 77 H5 34 43N 80 46W
Lancaster, Wis., U.S.A. 80 D9 42 51N 90 43W
Lancaster Sd., Canada 69 A11 74 13N 84 0W
Lancelin, Australia 61 F2 31 0S 115 18 E
Lanchow = Lanzhou, China 34 F2 36 1N 103 52 E
Lanciano, Italy 20 C6 42 14N 14 23 E
Lancun, China 35 F11 36 25N 120 10 E
Landeck, Austria 16 E6 47 9N 10 34 E
Lander, U.S.A. 82 E9 42 50N 108 44W
Lander →, Australia 60 D5 22 0S 132 0 E
Landes, France 18 D3 44 0N 1 0W
Landi Kotal, Pakistan 42 B4 34 7N 71 6 E
Landisburg, U.S.A. 78 F7 40 21N 77 19W
Land's End, U.K. 11 G2 50 4N 5 44W
Landsborough Cr. →, Australia 62 C3 22 28S 144 35 E
Landshut, Germany 16 D7 48 34N 12 8 E
Landskrona, Sweden 9 J15 55 53N 12 50 E
Lanesboro, U.S.A. 79 E9 41 57N 75 34W
Lanett, U.S.A. 77 J3 32 52N 85 12W
Lang Qua, Vietnam 38 A5 22 16N 104 27 E
Lang Shan, China 34 D4 41 0N 106 30 E
Lang Son, Vietnam 38 B6 21 52N 106 42 E
Lang Suan, Thailand 39 H2 9 57N 99 4 E
La'nga Co, China 41 D12 30 45N 81 15 E
Langar, Iran 45 C9 35 23N 60 25 E
Langara I., Canada 72 C2 54 14N 133 1W
Langdon, U.S.A. 80 A5 48 45N 98 22W
Langeberg, S. Africa 56 E3 33 55S 21 0 E
Langeberge, S. Africa 56 D3 28 15S 22 33 E
Langeland, Denmark 9 J14 54 56N 10 48 E
Langenburg, Canada 73 C8 50 51N 101 43W
Langholm, U.K. 12 F5 55 9N 3 0W
Langjökull, Iceland 8 D3 64 39N 20 12W
Langkawi, Pulau, Malaysia 39 J2 6 25N 99 45 E
Langklip, S. Africa 56 D3 28 12S 20 20 E
Langkon, Malaysia 36 C5 6 30N 116 40 E
Langlade, St- P. & M. 71 C8 46 50N 56 20W
Langley, Canada 84 A4 49 7N 122 39W
Langøya, Norway 8 B16 68 45N 14 50 E
Langreo, Spain 19 A3 43 18N 5 40W
Langres, France 18 C6 47 52N 5 20 E
Langres, Plateau de, France 18 C6 47 45N 5 3 E
Langsa, Indonesia 36 D1 4 30N 97 57 E
Langtry, U.S.A. 81 L4 29 49N 101 34W
Langu, Thailand 39 J2 6 53N 99 47 E
Languedoc, France 18 E5 43 58N 3 55 E
Langxiangzhen, China 34 E9 39 43N 116 8 E
Lanigan, Canada 73 C7 51 51N 105 2W
Lankao, China 34 G8 34 48N 114 50 E
Länkäran, Azerbaijan 25 G8 38 48N 48 52 E
Lannion, France 18 B2 48 46N 3 29W
L'Annonciation, Canada 70 C5 46 25N 74 55W
Lansdale, U.S.A. 79 F9 40 14N 75 17W
Lansdowne, Australia 63 E5 31 48S 152 30 E
Lansdowne, Canada 79 B8 44 24N 76 1W
Lansdowne, India 43 E8 29 50N 78 41 E
Lansdowne House, Canada 70 B2 52 14N 87 53W
L'Anse, U.S.A. 76 B1 46 45N 88 27W
L'Anse au Loup, Canada 71 B8 51 32N 56 50W
L'Anse aux Meadows, Canada 71 B8 51 36N 55 32W
Lansford, U.S.A. 79 F9 40 50N 75 53W
Lansing, U.S.A. 76 D3 42 44N 84 33W
Lanta Yai, Ko, Thailand 39 J2 7 35N 99 3 E
Lantian, China 34 G5 34 11N 109 20 E
Lanus, Argentina 94 C4 34 44S 58 27W
Lanusei, Italy 20 E3 39 52N 9 34 E
Lanzarote, Canary Is. 22 F6 29 0N 13 40W
Lanzhou, China 34 F2 36 1N 103 52 E
Lao Bao, Laos 38 D6 16 35N 106 30 E
Lao Cai, Vietnam 38 A4 22 30N 103 57 E
Laoag, Phil. 37 A6 18 7N 120 34 E
Laoang, Phil. 37 B7 12 32N 125 8 E
Laoha He →, China 35 C11 43 25N 120 35 E
Laois □, Ireland 13 D4 52 57N 7 36W
Laon, France 18 B5 49 33N 3 35 E
Laona, U.S.A. 76 C1 45 34N 88 40W
Laos ■, Asia 38 D5 17 45N 105 0 E
Lapa, Brazil 95 B6 25 46S 49 44W
Lapeer, U.S.A. 76 D4 43 3N 83 19W
Lapithos, Cyprus 23 D12 35 21N 33 11 E
Lapland = Lappland, Europe 8 B21 68 7N 24 0 E
Laporte, U.S.A. 79 E8 41 25N 76 30W
Lappeenranta, Finland 9 F23 61 3N 28 12 E
Lappland, Europe 8 B21 68 7N 24 0 E
Laprida, Argentina 94 D3 37 34S 60 45W
Lapseki, Turkey 21 D12 40 20N 26 41 E
Laptev Sea, Russia 27 B13 76 0N 125 0 E
Lapua, Finland 8 E20 62 58N 23 0 E
L'Áquila, Italy 20 C5 42 22N 13 22 E
Lār, Āzarbājān-e Sharqī, Iran 44 B5 38 30N 47 52 E
Lār, Fārs, Iran 45 E7 27 40N 54 14 E
Laramie, U.S.A. 80 E2 41 19N 105 35W
Laramie →, U.S.A. 82 F11 42 13N 104 33W
Laramie Mts., U.S.A. 80 E2 42 0N 105 30W
Laranjeiras do Sul, Brazil 95 B5 25 23S 52 23W
Larantuka, Indonesia 37 F6 8 21S 122 55 E
Larat, Indonesia 37 F8 7 0S 132 0 E
Larde, Mozam. 55 F4 16 28S 39 43 E
Larder Lake, Canada 70 C4 48 5N 79 40W
Lardhos, Ákra = Líndhos, Ákra, Greece 23 C10 36 4N 28 10 E
Lardhos, Órmos, Greece 23 C10 36 4N 28 2 E
Laredo, U.S.A. 81 M5 27 30N 99 30W
Laredo Sd., Canada 72 C3 52 30N 128 53W
Largo, U.S.A. 77 M4 27 55N 82 47W
Largs, U.K. 12 F4 55 47N 4 52W
Lariang, Indonesia 37 E5 1 26S 119 17 E
Larimore, U.S.A. 80 B6 47 54N 97 38W
Lārīn, Iran 45 C7 35 55N 52 19 E
Lárisa, Greece 21 E10 39 36N 22 27 E
Larkana, Pakistan 42 F3 27 32N 68 18 E
Larnaca, Cyprus 23 E12 34 55N 33 38 E
Larnaca Bay, Cyprus 23 E12 34 53N 33 45 E
Larne, U.K. 13 B6 54 51N 5 51W
Larned, U.S.A. 80 F5 38 11N 99 6W
Larose, U.S.A. 81 L9 29 34N 90 23W
Larrimah, Australia 60 C5 15 35S 133 12 E
Larsen Ice Shelf, Antarctica 5 C17 67 0S 62 0W
Larvik, Norway 9 G14 59 4N 10 2 E
Las Animas, U.S.A. 80 F3 38 4N 103 13W
Las Anod, Somali Rep. 46 F4 8 26N 47 19 E
Las Aves, Is., W. Indies 89 C7 15 45N 63 55W
Las Brenãs, Argentina 94 B3 27 5S 61 7W
Las Cejas, Argentina 96 B4 26 53S 64 44W
Las Chimeneas, Mexico 85 N10 32 8N 116 5W
Las Cruces, U.S.A. 83 K10 32 19N 106 47W
Las Flores, Argentina 94 D4 36 10S 59 7W
Las Heras, Argentina 94 C2 32 51S 68 49W
Las Lajas, Argentina 96 D2 38 30S 70 25W
Las Lomitas, Argentina 94 A3 24 43S 60 35W
Las Palmas, Argentina 94 B4 27 8S 58 45W
Las Palmas, Canary Is. 22 F4 28 7N 15 26W
Las Palmas →, Mexico 85 N10 32 26N 116 54W
Las Piedras, Uruguay 95 C4 34 44S 56 14W
Las Pipinas, Argentina 94 D4 35 30S 57 19W
Las Plumas, Argentina 96 E3 43 40S 67 15W
Las Rosas, Argentina 94 C3 32 30S 61 35W
Las Tablas, Panama 88 E3 7 49N 80 14W
Las Termas, Argentina 94 B3 27 29S 64 52W
Las Toscas, Argentina 94 B4 28 21S 59 18W
Las Truchas, Mexico 86 D4 17 57N 102 13W
Las Varillas, Argentina 94 C3 31 50S 62 50W
Las Vegas, N. Mex., U.S.A. 83 J11 35 36N 105 13W
Las Vegas, Nev., U.S.A. 85 J11 36 10N 115 9W
Lascano, Uruguay 95 C5 33 35S 54 12W
Lash-e Joveyn, Afghan. 40 D2 31 45N 61 30 E
Lashburn, Canada 73 C7 53 10N 109 40W
Lashio, Burma 41 H20 22 56N 97 45 E
Lashkar, India 42 F8 26 10N 78 10 E
Lasíthi, Greece 23 D7 35 11N 25 31 E
Lasíthi □, Greece 23 D7 35 5N 25 50 E
Lāsjerd, Iran 45 C7 35 24N 53 4 E
Lassen Pk., U.S.A. 82 F3 40 29N 121 31W
Lassen Volcanic Nat. Park, U.S.A. 82 F3 40 30N 121 20W
Last Mountain L., Canada 73 C7 51 5N 105 14W
Lastchance Cr. →, U.S.A. 84 E5 40 2N 121 15W
Lastoursville, Gabon 52 E2 0 55S 12 38 E
Lastovo, Croatia 20 C7 42 46N 16 55 E
Lat Yao, Thailand 38 E2 15 45N 99 48 E
Latacunga, Ecuador 92 D3 0 50S 78 35W
Latakia = Al Lādhiqīyah, Syria 44 C2 35 30N 35 45 E
Latchford, Canada 70 C4 47 20N 79 50W
Latehar, India 43 H11 23 45N 84 30 E
Latham, Australia 61 E2 29 44S 116 20 E
Lathi, India 42 F4 27 43N 71 23 E
Lathrop Wells, U.S.A. 85 J10 36 39N 116 24W
Latina, Italy 20 D5 41 28N 12 52 E
Latium = Lazio □, Italy 20 C5 42 10N 12 30 E
Laton, U.S.A. 84 J7 36 26N 119 41W
Latouche Treville, C., Australia 60 C3 18 27S 121 49 E
Latrobe, Australia 62 G4 41 14S 146 30 E
Latrobe, U.S.A. 78 F5 40 19N 79 23W
Latvia ■, Europe 9 H20 56 50N 24 0 E
Lau Group, Fiji 59 C9 17 0S 178 30W
Lauchhammer, Germany 16 C7 51 29N 13 47 E
Laughlin, U.S.A. 83 J6 35 8N 114 35W
Laukaa, Finland 9 E21 62 24N 25 56 E
Launceston, Australia 62 G4 41 24S 147 8 E
Launceston, U.K. 11 G3 50 38N 4 22W
Laune →, Ireland 13 D2 52 7N 9 47W
Launglon Bok, Burma 38 F1 13 50N 97 54 E
Laura, Australia 62 B3 15 32S 144 32 E
Laurel, Miss., U.S.A. 81 K10 31 41N 89 8W
Laurel, Mont., U.S.A. 82 D9 45 40N 108 46W
Laurencekirk, U.K. 12 E6 56 50N 2 28W
Laurens, U.S.A. 77 H4 34 30N 82 1W
Laurentian Plateau, Canada 71 B6 52 0N 70 0W
Lauria, Italy 20 E6 40 2N 15 50 E
Laurie L., Canada 73 B8 56 35N 101 57W
Laurinburg, U.S.A. 77 H6 34 47N 79 28W
Laurium, U.S.A. 76 B1 47 14N 88 27W
Lausanne, Switz. 18 C7 46 32N 6 38 E
Laut, Indonesia 39 K6 4 45N 108 0 E
Laut, Pulau, Indonesia 36 E5 3 40S 116 10 E
Laut Kecil, Kepulauan, Indonesia 36 E5 4 45S 115 40 E
Lautoka, Fiji 59 C7 17 37S 177 27 E
Lavagh More, Ireland 13 B3 54 46N 8 6W
Laval, France 18 B3 48 4N 0 48W
Lavalle, Argentina 94 B2 28 15S 65 15W
Lavant Station, Canada 79 A8 45 3N 76 42W
Lāvar Meydān, Iran 45 D7 30 20N 54 30 E
Laverton, Australia 61 E3 28 44S 122 29 E
Lavras, Brazil 95 A7 21 20S 45 0W
Lávrion, Greece 21 F11 37 40N 24 4 E
Lávris, Greece 23 D6 35 25N 24 40 E
Lavumisa, Swaziland 57 D5 27 20S 31 55 E
Lawas, Malaysia 36 D5 4 55N 115 25 E
Lawele, Indonesia 37 F6 5 13S 122 57 E
Lawng Pit, Burma 41 G20 25 30N 97 25 E
Lawqah, Si. Arabia 44 D4 29 49N 42 45 E
Lawrence, N.Z. 59 L2 45 55S 169 41 E
Lawrence, Kans., U.S.A. 80 F7 38 58N 95 14W
Lawrence, Mass., U.S.A. 79 D13 42 43N 71 10W
Lawrenceburg, Ind., U.S.A. 76 F3 39 6N 84 52W
Lawrenceburg, Tenn., U.S.A. 77 H2 35 14N 87 20W
Lawrenceville, Ga., U.S.A. 77 J4 33 57N 83 59W
Lawrenceville, Pa., U.S.A. 78 E7 41 59N 77 8W
Laws, U.S.A. 84 H8 37 24N 118 20W
Lawton, U.S.A. 81 H5 34 37N 98 25W
Lawu, Indonesia 37 G14 7 40S 111 13 E
Laxford, L., U.K. 12 C3 58 24N 5 6W
Layla, Si. Arabia 46 C4 22 10N 46 40 E
Laylān, Iraq 44 C5 35 18N 44 31 E
Layton, U.S.A. 82 F7 41 4N 111 58W
Laytonville, U.S.A. 82 G2 39 41N 123 29W
Lazarivo, Madag. 57 C8 23 54S 44 59 E
Lazio □, Italy 20 C5 42 10N 12 30 E
Lazo, Russia 30 C6 43 25N 133 55 E
Le Creusot, France 18 C6 46 48N 4 24 E
Le François, Martinique 89 D7 14 38N 60 57W
Le Havre, France 18 B4 49 30N 0 5 E
Le Mans, France 18 C4 48 0N 0 10 E
Le Mars, U.S.A. 80 D6 42 47N 96 10W
Le Mont-St-Michel, France 18 B3 48 40N 1 30W
Le Moule, Guadeloupe 89 C7 16 20N 61 22W
Le Puy-en-Velay, France 18 D5 45 3N 3 52 E
Le Sueur, U.S.A. 80 C8 44 28N 93 55W
Le Thuy, Vietnam 38 D6 17 14N 106 49 E
Le Touquet-Paris-Plage, France 18 A4 50 30N 1 36 E
Le Tréport, France 18 A4 50 3N 1 20 E
Le Verdon-sur-Mer, France 18 D3 45 33N 1 4W
Lea →, U.K. 11 F8 51 31N 0 1 E
Leach, Cambodia 39 F4 12 21N 103 46 E
Lead, U.S.A. 80 C3 44 21N 103 46W
Leader, Canada 73 C7 50 50N 109 30W
Leadville, U.S.A. 83 G10 39 15N 106 18W
Leaf →, U.S.A. 81 K10 30 59N 88 44W
Leaf Rapids, Canada 73 B9 56 30N 99 59W
Leamington, Canada 78 D2 42 3N 82 36W
Leamington, U.S.A. 82 G7 39 32N 112 17W
Leamington Spa = Royal Leamington Spa, U.K. 11 E6 52 18N 1 31W
Leandro Norte Alem, Argentina 95 B4 27 34S 55 15W
Leane, L., Ireland 13 D2 52 2N 9 32W
Learmonth, Australia 60 D1 22 13S 114 10 E
Leask, Canada 73 C7 53 5N 106 45W
Leatherhead, U.K. 11 F7 51 18N 0 20W
Leavenworth, Kans., U.S.A. 80 F7 39 19N 94 55W
Leavenworth, Wash., U.S.A. 82 C3 47 36N 120 40W
Lebak, Phil. 37 C6 6 32N 124 5 E
Lebam, U.S.A. 84 D3 46 34N 123 33W
Lebanon, Ind., U.S.A. 76 E2 40 3N 86 28W
Lebanon, Kans., U.S.A. 80 F5 39 49N 98 33W
Lebanon, Ky., U.S.A. 76 G3 37 34N 85 15W
Lebanon, Mo., U.S.A. 81 G8 37 41N 92 40W
Lebanon, N.H., U.S.A. 79 C12 43 39N 72 15W
Lebanon, Oreg., U.S.A. 82 D2 44 32N 122 55W
Lebanon, Pa., U.S.A. 79 F8 40 20N 76 26W
Lebanon, Tenn., U.S.A. 77 G2 36 12N 86 18W
Lebanon ■, Asia 47 B5 34 0N 36 0 E
Lebec, U.S.A. 85 L8 34 50N 118 52W
Lebel-sur-Quévillon, Canada 70 C4 49 3N 76 59W
Lebomboberge, S. Africa 57 C5 24 30S 32 0 E
Lębork, Poland 17 A9 54 33N 17 46 E
Lebrija, Spain 19 D2 36 53N 6 5W
Lebu, Chile 94 D1 37 40S 73 47W
Lecce, Italy 21 D8 40 23N 18 11 E
Lecco, Italy 18 D8 45 51N 9 23 E
Lech →, Germany 16 D6 48 43N 10 56 E
Lecontes Mills, U.S.A. 78 E6 41 5N 78 17W
Łęczyca, Poland 17 B10 52 5N 19 15 E
Ledong, China 38 C7 18 41N 109 5 E
Leduc, Canada 72 C6 53 15N 113 30W
Lee, U.S.A. 79 D11 42 19N 73 15W
Lee →, Ireland 13 E3 51 53N 8 56W
Lee Vining, U.S.A. 84 H7 37 58N 119 7W
Leech L., U.S.A. 80 B7 47 10N 94 24W
Leechburg, U.S.A. 78 F5 40 37N 79 36W
Leeds, U.K. 10 D6 53 48N 1 33W
Leeds, U.S.A. 77 J2 33 33N 86 33W
Leek, Neths. 15 A6 53 10N 6 24 E
Leek, U.K. 10 D5 53 7N 2 1W
Leeman, Australia 61 E1 29 57S 114 58 E
Leeper, U.S.A. 78 E5 41 22N 79 18W
Leer, Germany 16 B4 53 13N 7 26 E
Leesburg, U.S.A. 77 L5 28 49N 81 53W
Leesville, U.S.A. 81 K8 31 9N 93 16W
Leeton, Australia 63 E4 34 33S 146 23 E
Leetonia, U.S.A. 78 F4 40 53N 80 45W
Leeu Gamka, S. Africa 56 E3 32 47S 21 59 E
Leeuwarden, Neths. 15 A5 53 15N 5 48 E
Leeuwin, C., Australia 61 F2 34 20S 115 9 E
Leeward Is., Atl. Oc. 89 C7 16 30N 63 30W
Lefka, Cyprus 23 D11 35 6N 32 51 E
Lefkoniko, Cyprus 23 D12 35 18N 33 44 E
Lefroy, Canada 78 B5 44 16N 79 34W
Lefroy, L., Australia 61 F3 31 21S 121 40 E
Leganés, Spain 19 B4 40 19N 3 45W
Legazpi, Phil. 37 B6 13 10N 123 45 E
Legendre I., Australia 60 D2 20 22S 116 55 E
Leghorn = Livorno, Italy 20 C4 43 33N 10 19 E
Legionowo, Poland 17 B11 52 25N 20 50 E
Legnago, Italy 20 B4 45 11N 11 18 E
Legnica, Poland 16 C9 51 12N 16 10 E
Leh, India 43 B7 34 9N 77 35 E
Lehigh Acres, U.S.A. 77 M5 26 36N 81 39W
Lehighton, U.S.A. 79 F9 40 50N 75 43W
Lehututu, Botswana 56 C3 23 54S 21 55 E
Leiah, Pakistan 42 D4 30 58N 70 58 E
Leicester, U.K. 11 E6 52 38N 1 8W
Leicester City □, U.K. 11 E6 52 38N 1 8W
Leicestershire □, U.K. 11 E6 52 41N 1 17W
Leichhardt →, Australia 62 B2 17 35S 139 48 E
Leichhardt Ra., Australia 62 C4 20 46S 147 40 E
Leiden, Neths. 15 B4 52 9N 4 30 E
Leie →, Belgium 15 C3 51 2N 3 45 E
Leine →, Germany 16 B5 52 43N 9 36 E
Leinster, Australia 61 E3 27 51S 120 36 E
Leinster □, Ireland 13 C4 53 3N 7 8W
Leinster, Mt., Ireland 13 D5 52 37N 6 46W
Leipzig, Germany 16 C7 51 18N 12 22 E
Leiria, Portugal 19 C1 39 46N 8 53W
Leirvik, Norway 9 G11 59 47N 5 28 E
Leisler, Mt., Australia 60 D4 23 23S 129 20 E
Leith, U.K. 12 F5 55 59N 3 11W
Leith Hill, U.K. 11 F7 51 11N 0 22W
Leitrim, Ireland 13 B3 54 0N 8 5W
Leitrim □, Ireland 13 B4 54 8N 8 0W
Leizhou Bandao, China 33 D6 21 0N 110 0 E
Lek →, Neths. 15 C4 51 54N 4 35 E
Leka, Norway 8 D14 65 5N 11 35 E
Lékva Óros, Greece 23 D6 35 18N 24 3 E
Leland, Mich., U.S.A. 76 C3 45 1N 85 45W
Leland, Miss., U.S.A. 81 J9 33 24N 90 54W
Leleque, Argentina 96 E2 42 28S 71 0W
Lelystad, Neths. 15 B5 52 30N 5 25 E
Léman, L., Europe 18 C7 46 26N 6 30 E
Lemera, Dem. Rep. of the Congo 54 C2 3 0S 28 55 E
Lemhi Ra., U.S.A. 82 D7 44 30N 113 30W
Lemmer, Neths. 15 B5 52 51N 5 43 E
Lemmon, U.S.A. 80 C3 45 57N 102 10W
Lemon Grove, U.S.A. 85 N9 32 45N 117 2W
Lemoore, U.S.A. 84 J7 36 18N 119 46W
Lemvig, Denmark 9 H13 56 33N 8 20 E
Lena →, Russia 27 B13 72 52N 126 40 E
Léndas, Greece 23 E6 34 56N 24 56 E
Lendeh, Iran 45 D6 30 58N 50 25 E
Lenggong, Malaysia 39 K3 5 6N 100 58 E
Lengua de Vaca, Pta., Chile 94 C1 30 14S 71 38W
Leninabad = Khŭjand, Tajikistan 26 E7 40 17N 69 37 E
Leninakan = Gyumri, Armenia 25 F7 40 47N 43 50 E
Leningrad = Sankt-Peterburg, Russia 24 C5 59 55N 30 20 E
Leninogorsk, Kazakstan 26 D9 50 20N 83 30 E
Leninsk, Russia 25 E8 48 40N 45 15 E
Leninsk-Kuznetskiy, Russia 26 D9 54 44N 86 10 E
Lenkoran = Länkäran, Azerbaijan 25 G8 38 48N 48 52 E
Lenmalu, Indonesia 37 E8 1 45S 130 15 E
Lennox, U.S.A. 80 D6 43 21N 96 53W
Lennoxville, Canada 79 A13 45 22N 71 51W
Lenoir, U.S.A. 77 H5 35 55N 81 32W
Lenoir City, U.S.A. 77 H3 35 48N 84 16W
Lenore L., Canada 73 C8 52 30N 104 59W
Lenox, U.S.A. 79 D11 42 22N 73 17W
Lens, France 18 A5 50 26N 2 50 E
Lensk, Russia 27 C12 60 48N 114 55 E
Lentini, Italy 20 F6 37 17N 15 0 E
Lenwood, U.S.A. 85 L9 34 53N 117 7W
Lenya, Burma 36 B1 11 33N 98 57 E
Leoben, Austria 16 E8 47 22N 15 5 E
Leodhas = Lewis, U.K. 12 C2 58 9N 6 40W
Leola, U.S.A. 80 C5 45 43N 98 56W
Leominster, U.K. 11 E5 52 14N 2 43W
Leominster, U.S.A. 79 D13 42 32N 71 46W
León, Mexico 86 C4 21 7N 101 40W
León, Nic. 88 D2 12 20N 86 51W
León, Spain 19 A3 42 38N 5 34W
Leon, U.S.A. 80 E8 40 44N 93 45W
Leon →, U.S.A. 81 K6 31 14N 97 28W
León, Montes de, Spain 19 A2 42 30N 6 18W
Leonardtown, U.S.A. 76 F7 38 17N 76 38W
Leonardville, Namibia 56 C2 23 29S 18 49 E
Leongatha, Australia 63 F4 38 30S 145 58 E
Leonora, Australia 61 E3 28 49S 121 19 E
Leopoldina, Brazil 95 A7 21 28S 42 40W
Leopoldsburg, Belgium 15 C5 51 7N 5 13 E
Leoti, U.S.A. 80 F4 38 29N 101 21W
Leova, Moldova 17 E15 46 28N 28 15 E
Leoville, Canada 73 C7 53 39N 107 33W
Lepel = Lyepyel, Belarus 24 D4 54 50N 28 40 E
Lépo, L. do, Angola 56 B2 17 0S 19 0 E
Leppävirta, Finland 9 E22 62 29N 27 46 E
Lerdo, Mexico 86 B4 25 32N 103 32W
Leribe, Lesotho 57 D4 28 51S 28 3 E
Lérida = Lleida, Spain 19 B6 41 37N 0 39 E
Lerwick, U.K. 12 A7 60 9N 1 9W
Les Cayes, Haiti 89 C5 18 15N 73 46W
Les Sables-d'Olonne, France 18 C3 46 30N 1 45W
Lesbos = Lésvos, Greece 21 E12 39 10N 26 20 E
Leshan, China 32 D5 29 33N 103 41 E
Leshukonskoye, Russia 24 B8 64 54N 45 46 E
Leskov I., Antarctica 5 B1 56 0S 28 0W
Leskovac, Serbia, Yug. 21 C9 43 0N 21 58 E
Lesopilnoye, Russia 30 A7 46 44N 134 20 E
Lesotho ■, Africa 57 D4 29 40S 28 0 E
Lesozavodsk, Russia 27 E14 45 30N 133 29 E
Lesse →, Belgium 15 D4 50 15N 4 54 E
Lesser Antilles, W. Indies 89 D7 15 0N 61 0W
Lesser Slave L., Canada 72 B5 55 30N 115 25W
Lesser Sunda Is., Indonesia 37 F6 8 0S 120 0 E
Lessines, Belgium 15 D3 50 42N 3 50 E
Lester, U.S.A. 84 C5 47 12N 121 29W
Lestock, Canada 73 C8 51 19N 103 59W
Lesuer I., Australia 60 B4 13 50S 127 17 E
Lésvos, Greece 21 E12 39 10N 26 20 E
Leszno, Poland 17 C9 51 50N 16 30 E
Letaba, S. Africa 57 C5 23 59S 31 50 E
Letchworth, U.K. 11 F7 51 59N 0 13W
Lethbridge, Canada 72 D6 49 45N 112 45W
Lethem, Guyana 92 C7 3 20N 59 50W
Leti, Kepulauan, Indonesia 37 F7 8 10S 128 0 E
Leti Is. = Leti, Kepulauan, Indonesia 37 F7 8 10S 128 0 E
Letiahau →, Botswana 56 C3 21 16S 24 0 E
Leticia, Colombia 92 D5 4 9S 70 0W
Leting, China 35 E10 39 23N 118 55 E
Letjiesbos, S. Africa 56 E3 32 34S 22 16 E
Letlhakane, Botswana 56 C4 21 27S 25 30 E
Letlhakeng, Botswana 56 C3 24 0S 24 59 E
Letong, Indonesia 36 D3 2 58N 105 42 E
Letpadan, Burma 41 L19 17 45N 95 45 E
Letpan, Burma 41 K19 19 28N 94 10 E
Letsôk-aw Kyun, Burma 39 G2 11 30N 98 25 E
Letterkenny, Ireland 13 B4 54 57N 7 45W
Leucadia, U.S.A. 85 M9 33 4N 117 18W
Leuser, G., Indonesia 36 D1 3 46N 97 12 E
Leuven, Belgium 15 D4 50 52N 4 42 E
Leuze-en-Hainaut, Belgium 15 D3 50 36N 3 37 E
Levádhia, Greece 21 E10 38 27N 22 54 E
Levanger, Norway 8 E14 63 45N 11 19 E
Levelland, U.S.A. 81 J3 33 35N 102 23W
Leven, U.K. 12 E6 56 12N 3 0W
Leven, L., U.K. 12 E5 56 12N 3 22W
Leven, Toraka, Madag. 57 A8 12 30S 47 45 E
Leveque C., Australia 60 C3 16 20S 123 0 E
Levice, Slovak Rep. 17 D10 48 13N 18 35 E
Levin, N.Z. 59 J5 40 37S 175 18 E
Lévis, Canada 71 C5 46 48N 71 9W
Levis, L., Canada 72 A5 62 37N 117 58W
Levittown, N.Y., U.S.A. 79 F11 40 44N 73 31W
Levittown, Pa., U.S.A. 79 F10 40 9N 74 51W
Levkás, Greece 21 E9 38 40N 20 43 E
Levkímmi, Greece 23 B4 39 25N 20 3 E
Levkímmi, Ákra, Greece 23 B4 39 29N 20 4 E
Levkôsia = Nicosia, Cyprus 23 D12 35 10N 33 25 E
Levskigrad = Karlovo, Bulgaria 21 C11 42 38N 24 47 E
Lewes, U.K. 11 G8 50 52N 0 1 E
Lewes, U.S.A. 76 F8 38 46N 75 9W
Lewis, U.K. 12 C2 58 9N 6 40W
Lewis →, U.S.A. 84 E4 45 51N 122 48W
Lewis, Butt of, U.K. 12 C2 58 31N 6 16W
Lewis Ra., Australia 60 D4 20 3S 128 50 E
Lewis Range, U.S.A. 82 C7 48 5N 113 5W
Lewis Run, U.S.A. 78 E6 41 52N 78 40W
Lewisburg, Pa., U.S.A. 78 F8 40 58N 76 54W
Lewisburg, Tenn., U.S.A. 77 H2 35 27N 86 48W
Lewisburg, W. Va., U.S.A. 76 G5 37 48N 80 27W
Lewisporte, Canada 71 C8 49 15N 55 3W
Lewiston, Idaho, U.S.A. 82 C5 46 25N 117 1W

Makwiro

Lynden, U.S.A. 84 B4 48 57N 122 27W
Lyndhurst, Australia 63 E2 30 15S 138 18 E
Lyndon →, Australia 61 D1 23 29S 114 6 E
Lyndonville, N.Y., U.S.A. 78 C6 43 20N 78 23W
Lyndonville, Vt., U.S.A. 79 B12 44 31N 72 1W
Lyngen, Norway 8 B19 69 45N 20 30 E
Lynher Reef, Australia 60 C3 15 27S 121 55 E
Lynn, U.S.A. 79 D14 42 28N 70 57W
Lynn Lake, Canada 73 B8 56 51N 101 3W
Lynnwood, U.S.A. 84 C4 47 49N 122 19W
Lynton, U.K. 11 F4 51 13N 3 50W
Lyntupy, Belarus 9 J22 55 4N 26 23 E
Lynx L., Canada 73 A7 62 25N 106 15W
Lyon, France 18 D6 45 46N 4 50 E
Lyonnais, France 18 D6 45 45N 4 15 E
Lyons = Lyon, France 18 D6 45 46N 4 50 E
Lyons, Ga., U.S.A. 77 J4 32 12N 82 19W
Lyons, Kans., U.S.A. 80 F5 38 21N 98 12W
Lyons, N.Y., U.S.A. 78 C8 43 5N 77 0W
Lyons →, Australia 61 E2 25 2S 115 9 E
Lyons Falls, U.S.A. 79 C9 43 37N 75 22W
Lys = Leie →, Belgium 15 C3 51 2N 3 45 E
Lysva, Russia 24 C10 58 7N 57 49 E
Lysychansk, Ukraine 25 E6 48 55N 38 30 E
Lytham St. Anne's, U.K. 10 D4 53 45N 3 0W
Lyttelton, N.Z. 59 K4 43 35S 172 44 E
Lytton, Canada 72 C4 50 13N 121 31W
Lyubertsy, Russia 24 C6 55 39N 37 50 E
Lyuboml, Ukraine 17 C13 51 11N 24 4 E

M

M.R. Gomez, Presa, Mexico 87 B5 26 10N 99 0W
Ma →, Vietnam 38 C5 19 47N 105 56 E
Ma'adaba, Jordan 47 E4 30 43N 35 47 E
Maamba, Zambia 56 B4 17 17S 26 28 E
Ma'ān, Jordan 47 E4 30 12N 35 44 E
Ma'ān □, Jordan 47 F5 30 0N 36 0 E
Maanselkä, Finland 8 C23 63 52N 28 32 E
Ma'anshan, China 33 C6 31 44N 118 29 E
Maarianhamina, Finland 9 F18 60 5N 19 55 E
Ma'arrat an Nu'mān, Syria 44 C3 35 43N 36 43 E
Maas →, Neths. 15 C4 51 45N 4 32 E
Maaseik, Belgium 15 C5 51 6N 5 45 E
Maasin, Phil. 37 B6 10 8N 124 50 E
Maastricht, Neths. 18 A6 50 50N 5 40 E
Maave, Mozam. 57 C5 21 4S 34 47 E
Mababe Depression, Botswana 56 B3 18 50S 24 15 E
Mabalane, Mozam. 57 C5 23 37S 32 31 E
Mabel L., Canada 72 C5 50 35N 118 43W
Mabenge, Dem. Rep. of the Congo 54 B1 4 15N 24 12 E
Maberly, Canada 79 B8 44 50N 76 32W
Mablethorpe, U.K. 10 D8 53 20N 0 15 E
Maboma, Dem. Rep. of the Congo 54 B2 2 30N 28 10 E
Mac Bac, Vietnam 39 H6 9 46N 106 7 E
Macachín, Argentina 94 D3 37 10S 63 43W
Macaé, Brazil 95 A7 22 20S 41 43W
McAlester, U.S.A. 81 H7 34 56N 95 46W
McAllen, U.S.A. 81 M5 26 12N 98 14W
MacAlpine L., Canada 68 B9 66 40N 102 50W
Macamic, Canada 70 C4 48 45N 79 0W
Macao = Macau, China 33 D6 22 12N 113 33 E
Macapá, Brazil 93 C8 0 5N 51 4W
McArthur →, Australia 62 B2 15 54S 136 40 E
McArthur, Port, Australia 62 B2 16 4S 136 23 E
Macau, Brazil 93 E11 5 15S 36 40W
Macau, China 33 D6 22 12N 113 33 E
McBride, Canada 72 C4 53 20N 120 19W
McCall, U.S.A. 82 D5 44 55N 116 6W
McCamey, U.S.A. 81 K3 31 8N 102 14W
McCammon, U.S.A. 82 E7 42 39N 112 12W
McCauley I., Canada 72 C2 53 40N 130 15W
McCleary, U.S.A. 84 C3 47 3N 123 16W
Macclenny, U.S.A. 77 K4 30 17N 82 7W
Macclesfield, U.K. 10 D5 53 15N 2 8W
M'Clintock Chan., Canada 68 A9 72 0N 102 0W
McClintock Ra., Australia 60 C4 18 44S 127 38 E
McCloud, U.S.A. 82 F2 41 15N 122 8W
McCluer I., Australia 60 B5 11 5S 133 0 E
McClure, U.S.A. 78 F7 40 42N 77 19W
McClure, L., U.S.A. 84 H6 37 35N 120 16W
M'Clure Str., Canada 4 B2 75 0N 119 0W
McClusky, U.S.A. 80 B4 47 29N 100 27W
McComb, U.S.A. 81 K9 31 15N 90 27W
McConaughy, L., U.S.A. 80 E4 41 14N 101 40W
McCook, U.S.A. 80 E4 40 12N 100 38W
McCreary, Canada 73 C9 50 47N 99 29W
McCullough Mt., U.S.A. 85 K11 35 35N 115 13W
McCusker →, Canada 73 B7 55 32N 108 39W
McDame, Canada 72 B3 59 44N 128 59W
McDermitt, U.S.A. 82 F5 41 59N 117 43W
McDonald, U.S.A. 78 F4 40 22N 80 14W
Macdonald, L., Australia 60 D4 23 30S 129 0 E
McDonald Is., Ind. Oc. 3 G13 53 0S 73 0 E
MacDonnell Ranges, Australia 60 D5 23 40S 133 0 E
MacDowell L., Canada 70 B1 52 15N 92 45W
Macduff, U.K. 12 D6 57 40N 2 31W
Macedonia = Makedhonía □, Greece 21 D10 40 39N 22 0 E
Macedonia, U.S.A. 78 E3 41 19N 81 31W
Macedonia ■, Europe 21 D9 41 53N 21 40 E
Maceió, Brazil 93 E11 9 40S 35 41W
Macerata, Italy 20 C5 43 18N 13 27 E
McFarland, U.S.A. 85 K7 35 41N 119 14W
McFarlane →, Canada 73 B7 59 12N 107 58W
Macfarlane, L., Australia 63 E2 32 0S 136 40 E
McGehee, U.S.A. 81 J9 33 38N 91 24W
McGill, U.S.A. 82 G6 39 23N 114 47W
Macgillycuddy's Reeks, Ireland 13 E2 51 58N 9 45W
McGraw, U.S.A. 79 D8 42 36N 76 8W
McGregor, U.S.A. 80 D9 43 1N 91 11W
McGregor Ra., Australia 63 D3 27 0S 142 45 E
Mach, Pakistan 40 E5 29 50N 67 20 E
Māch Kowr, Iran 45 E9 25 48N 61 28 E
Machado = Jiparaná →, Brazil 92 E6 8 3S 62 52W
Machagai, Argentina 94 B3 26 56S 60 2W
Machakos, Kenya 54 C4 1 30S 37 15 E
Machala, Ecuador 92 D3 3 20S 79 57W
Machanga, Mozam. 57 C6 20 59S 35 0 E
Machattie, L., Australia 62 C2 24 50S 139 48 E
Machava, Mozam. 57 D5 25 54S 32 28 E
Machece, Mozam. 55 F4 19 15S 35 32 E
Macheke, Zimbabwe 57 B5 18 5S 31 51 E
Machhu →, India 42 H4 23 6N 70 46 E
Machias, Maine, U.S.A. 77 C12 44 43N 67 28W
Machias, N.Y., U.S.A. 78 D6 42 25N 78 30W
Machichi →, Canada 73 B10 57 3N 92 6W
Machico, Madeira 22 D3 32 43N 16 44W
Machilipatnam, India 41 L12 16 12N 81 8 E
Machiques, Venezuela 92 A4 10 4N 72 34W
Machupicchu, Peru 92 F4 13 8S 72 30W
Machynlleth, U.K. 11 E4 52 35N 3 50W
Macia, Mozam. 57 D5 25 2S 33 8 E
McIlwraith Ra., Australia 62 A3 13 50S 143 20 E
McInnes L., Canada 73 C10 52 13N 93 45W
McIntosh, U.S.A. 80 C4 45 55N 101 21W
McIntosh L., Canada 73 B8 55 45N 105 0W
Macintosh Ra., Australia 61 E4 27 39S 125 32 E
Macintyre →, Australia 63 D5 28 37S 150 47 E
Mackay, Australia 62 C4 21 8S 149 11 E
Mackay, U.S.A. 82 E7 43 55N 113 37W
MacKay →, Canada 72 B6 57 10N 111 38W
Mackay, L., Australia 60 D4 22 30S 129 0 E
McKay Ra., Australia 60 D3 23 0S 122 30 E
McKeesport, U.S.A. 78 F5 40 21N 79 52W
McKellar, Canada 78 A5 45 30N 79 55W
McKenna, U.S.A. 84 D4 46 56N 122 33W
Mackenzie, Canada 72 B4 55 20N 123 5W
McKenzie, U.S.A. 77 G1 36 8N 88 31W
Mackenzie →, Australia 62 C4 23 38S 149 46 E
Mackenzie →, Canada 68 B6 69 10N 134 20W
McKenzie →, U.S.A. 82 D2 44 7N 123 6W
Mackenzie Bay, Canada 4 B1 69 0N 137 30W
Mackenzie City = Linden, Guyana 92 B7 6 0N 58 10W
Mackenzie Mts., Canada 68 B6 64 0N 130 0W
Mackinaw City, U.S.A. 76 C3 45 47N 84 44W
McKinlay, Australia 62 C3 21 16S 141 18 E
McKinlay →, Australia 62 C3 20 50S 141 28 E
McKinley, Mt., U.S.A. 68 B4 63 4N 151 0W
McKinley Sea, Arctic 4 A7 82 0N 0 0W
McKinney, U.S.A. 81 J6 33 12N 96 37W
Mackinnon Road, Kenya 54 C4 3 40S 39 1 E
McKittrick, U.S.A. 85 K7 35 18N 119 37W
Macklin, Canada 73 C7 52 20N 109 56W
Macksville, Australia 63 E5 30 40S 152 56 E
McLaughlin, U.S.A. 80 C4 45 49N 100 49W
Maclean, Australia 63 D5 29 26S 153 16 E
McLean, U.S.A. 81 H4 35 14N 100 36W
McLeansboro, U.S.A. 80 F10 38 6N 88 32W
Maclear, S. Africa 57 E4 31 2S 28 23 E
Macleay →, Australia 63 E5 30 56S 153 0 E
McLennan, Canada 72 B5 55 42N 116 50W
McLeod →, Canada 72 C5 54 9N 115 44W
MacLeod, B., Canada 73 A7 62 53N 110 0W
McLeod, L., Australia 61 D1 24 9S 113 47 E
MacLeod Lake, Canada 72 C4 54 58N 123 0W
McLoughlin, Mt., U.S.A. 82 E2 42 27N 122 19W
McMechen, U.S.A. 78 G4 39 57N 80 44W
McMinnville, Oreg., U.S.A. 82 D2 45 13N 123 12W
McMinnville, Tenn., U.S.A. 77 H3 35 41N 85 46W
McMurdo Sd., Antarctica 5 D11 77 0S 170 0 E
McMurray = Fort McMurray, Canada 72 B6 56 44N 111 7W
McMurray, U.S.A. 84 B4 48 19N 122 14W
Macodoene, Mozam. 57 C6 23 32S 35 5 E
Macomb, U.S.A. 80 E9 40 27N 90 40W
Mâcon, France 18 C6 46 19N 4 50 E
Macon, Ga., U.S.A. 77 J4 32 51N 83 38W
Macon, Miss., U.S.A. 77 J1 33 7N 88 34W
Macon, Mo., U.S.A. 80 F8 39 44N 92 28W
Macossa, Mozam. 55 F3 17 55S 33 56 E
Macoun L., Canada 73 B8 56 32N 103 40W
Macovane, Mozam. 57 C6 21 30S 35 2 E
McPherson, U.S.A. 80 F6 38 22N 97 40W
McPherson Pk., U.S.A. 85 L7 34 53N 119 53W
McPherson Ra., Australia 63 D5 28 15S 153 15 E
Macquarie →, Australia 63 E4 30 5S 147 30 E
Macquarie Harbour, Australia 62 G4 42 15S 145 23 E
Macquarie Is., Pac. Oc. 64 N7 54 36S 158 55 E
MacRobertson Land, Antarctica 5 D6 71 0S 64 0 E
Macroom, Ireland 13 E3 51 54N 8 57W
MacTier, Canada 78 A5 45 9N 79 46W
Macubela, Mozam. 55 F4 16 53S 37 49 E
Macuiza, Mozam. 55 F3 18 7S 34 29 E
Macusani, Peru 92 F4 14 4S 70 29W
Macuse, Mozam. 55 F4 17 45S 37 10 E
Macuspana, Mexico 87 D6 17 46N 92 36W
Macusse, Angola 56 B3 17 48S 20 23 E
Madadeni, S. Africa 57 D5 27 43S 30 3 E
Madagascar ■, Africa 57 C8 20 0S 47 0 E
Madā'in Sālih, Si. Arabia 44 E3 26 46N 37 57 E
Madama, Niger 51 D8 22 0N 13 40 E
Madame I., Canada 71 C7 45 30N 60 58W
Madaripur, Bangla. 41 H17 23 19N 90 15 E
Madauk, Burma 41 L20 17 56N 96 52 E
Madawaska, Canada 78 A7 45 30N 78 0W
Madawaska →, Canada 78 A8 45 27N 76 21W
Madaya, Burma 41 H20 22 12N 96 10 E
Maddalena, Italy 20 D3 41 16N 9 23 E
Madeira, Atl. Oc. 22 D3 32 50N 17 0W
Madeira →, Brazil 92 D7 3 22S 58 45W
Madeleine, Îs. de la, Canada 71 C7 47 30N 61 40W
Madera, Mexico 86 B3 29 12N 108 7W
Madera, Calif., U.S.A. 84 J6 36 57N 120 3W
Madera, Pa., U.S.A. 78 F6 40 49N 78 26W
Madha, India 40 L9 18 0N 75 30 E
Madhavpur, India 42 J3 21 15N 69 58 E
Madhepura, India 43 F12 26 11N 86 23 E
Madhubani, India 43 F12 26 21N 86 7 E
Madhupur, India 43 G12 24 16N 86 39 E
Madhya Pradesh □, India 42 J8 22 50N 78 0 E
Madidi →, Bolivia 92 F5 12 32S 66 52W
Madikeri, India 40 N9 12 30N 75 45 E
Madill, U.S.A. 81 H6 34 6N 96 46W
Madimba, Dem. Rep. of the Congo 52 E3 4 58S 15 5 E
Ma'din, Syria 44 C3 35 45N 39 36 E
Madingou, Congo 52 E2 4 10S 13 33 E
Madirovalo, Madag. 57 B8 16 26S 46 32 E
Madison, Calif., U.S.A. 84 G5 38 41N 121 59W
Madison, Fla., U.S.A. 77 K4 30 28N 83 25W
Madison, Ind., U.S.A. 76 F3 38 44N 85 23W
Madison, Nebr., U.S.A. 80 E6 41 50N 97 27W
Madison, Ohio, U.S.A. 78 E3 41 46N 81 3W
Madison, S. Dak., U.S.A. 80 D6 44 0N 97 7W
Madison, Wis., U.S.A. 80 D10 43 4N 89 24W
Madison →, U.S.A. 82 D8 45 56N 111 31W
Madison Heights, U.S.A. 76 G6 37 25N 79 8W
Madisonville, Ky., U.S.A. 76 G2 37 20N 87 30W
Madisonville, Tex., U.S.A. 81 K7 30 57N 95 55W
Madista, Botswana 56 C4 21 15S 25 6 E
Madiun, Indonesia 36 F4 7 38S 111 32 E
Madoc, Canada 78 B7 44 30N 77 28W
Madona, Latvia 9 H22 56 53N 26 5 E
Madrakah, Ra's al, Oman 46 D6 19 0N 57 50 E
Madras = Chennai, India 40 N12 13 8N 80 19 E
Madras = Tamil Nadu □, India 40 P10 11 0N 77 0 E
Madras, U.S.A. 82 D3 44 38N 121 8W
Madre, Laguna, U.S.A. 81 M6 27 0N 97 30W
Madre, Sierra, Phil. 37 A6 17 0N 122 0 E
Madre de Dios →, Bolivia 92 F5 10 59S 66 8W
Madre de Dios, I., Chile 96 G1 50 20S 75 10W
Madre del Sur, Sierra, Mexico 87 D5 17 30N 100 0W
Madre Occidental, Sierra, Mexico 86 B3 27 0N 107 0W
Madre Oriental, Sierra, Mexico 86 C5 25 0N 100 0W
Madri, India 42 G5 24 16N 73 32 E
Madrid, Spain 19 B4 40 25N 3 45W
Madrid, U.S.A. 79 B9 44 45N 75 8W
Madura, Australia 61 F4 31 55S 127 0 E
Madura, Indonesia 37 G15 7 30S 114 0 E
Madura, Selat, Indonesia 37 G15 7 30S 113 20 E
Madurai, India 40 Q11 9 55N 78 10 E
Madurantakam, India 40 N11 12 30N 79 50 E
Mae Chan, Thailand 38 B2 20 9N 99 52 E
Mae Hong Son, Thailand 38 C2 19 16N 97 56 E
Mae Khlong →, Thailand 38 F3 13 24N 100 0 E
Mae Phrik, Thailand 38 D2 17 27N 99 7 E
Mae Ramat, Thailand 38 D2 16 58N 98 31 E
Mae Rim, Thailand 38 C2 18 54N 98 57 E
Mae Sot, Thailand 38 D2 16 43N 98 34 E
Mae Suai, Thailand 38 C2 19 39N 99 33 E
Mae Tha, Thailand 38 C2 18 28N 99 8 E
Maebashi, Japan 31 F9 36 24N 139 4 E
Maesteg, U.K. 11 F4 51 36N 3 40W
Maestra, Sierra, Cuba 88 B4 20 15N 77 0W
Maevatanana, Madag. 57 B8 16 56S 46 49 E
Mafeking = Mafikeng, S. Africa 56 D4 25 50S 25 38 E
Mafeking, Canada 73 C8 52 40N 101 10W
Mafeteng, Lesotho 56 D4 29 51S 27 15 E
Maffra, Australia 63 F4 37 53S 146 58 E
Mafia I., Tanzania 54 D4 7 45S 39 50 E
Mafikeng, S. Africa 56 D4 25 50S 25 38 E
Mafra, Brazil 95 B6 26 10S 49 55W
Mafra, Portugal 19 C1 38 55N 9 20W
Mafungabusi Plateau, Zimbabwe 55 F2 18 30S 29 8 E
Magadan, Russia 27 D16 59 38N 150 50 E
Magadi, Kenya 54 C4 1 54S 36 19 E
Magadi, L., Kenya 54 C4 1 54S 36 19 E
Magaliesburg, S. Africa 57 D4 26 0S 27 32 E
Magallanes, Estrecho de, Chile 96 G2 52 30S 75 0W
Magangué, Colombia 92 B4 9 14N 74 45W
Magdalen Is. = Madeleine, Îs. de la, Canada 71 C7 47 30N 61 40W
Magdalena, Argentina 94 D4 35 5S 57 30W
Magdalena, Bolivia 92 F6 13 13S 63 57W
Magdalena, Mexico 86 A2 30 50N 112 0W
Magdalena, U.S.A. 83 J10 34 7N 107 15W
Magdalena →, Colombia 92 A4 11 6N 74 51W
Magdalena →, Mexico 86 A2 30 40N 112 25W
Magdalena, B., Mexico 86 C2 24 30N 112 10W
Magdalena, Llano de la, Mexico 86 C2 25 0N 111 30W
Magdeburg, Germany 16 B6 52 7N 11 38 E
Magdelaine Cays, Australia 62 B5 16 33S 150 18 E
Magee, U.S.A. 81 K10 31 52N 89 44W
Magelang, Indonesia 36 F4 7 29S 110 13 E
Magellan's Str. = Magallanes, Estrecho de, Chile 96 G2 52 30S 75 0W
Magenta, L., Australia 61 F2 33 30S 119 2 E
Magerøya, Norway 8 A21 71 3N 25 40 E
Maggiore, Lago, Italy 18 D8 45 57N 8 39 E
Maghâgha, Egypt 51 C12 28 38N 30 50 E
Magherafelt, U.K. 13 B5 54 45N 6 37W
Maghreb, N. Afr. 50 B5 32 0N 4 0W
Magistralnyy, Russia 27 D11 56 16N 107 36 E
Magnetic Pole (North) = North Magnetic Pole, Canada 4 B2 77 58N 102 8W
Magnetic Pole (South) = South Magnetic Pole, Antarctica 5 C9 64 8S 138 8 E
Magnitogorsk, Russia 24 D10 53 27N 59 4 E
Magnolia, Ark., U.S.A. 81 J8 33 16N 93 14W
Magnolia, Miss., U.S.A. 81 K9 31 9N 90 28W
Magog, Canada 79 A12 45 18N 72 9W
Magoro, Uganda 54 B3 1 45N 34 12 E
Magosa = Famagusta, Cyprus 23 D12 35 8N 33 55 E
Magouládhes, Greece 23 A3 39 45N 19 42 E
Magoye, Zambia 55 F2 16 1S 27 30 E
Magozal, Mexico 87 C5 21 34N 97 59W
Magpie, L., Canada 71 B7 51 0N 64 41W
Magrath, Canada 72 D6 49 25N 112 50W
Maguarinho, C., Brazil 93 D9 0 15S 48 30W
Magude, Mozam. 57 D5 25 2S 32 40 E
Mağusa = Famagusta, Cyprus 23 D12 35 8N 33 55 E
Maguse L., Canada 73 A9 61 40N 95 10W
Maguse Pt., Canada 73 A10 61 20N 93 50W
Magvana, India 42 H3 23 13N 69 22 E
Magwe, Burma 41 J19 20 10N 95 0 E
Maha Sarakham, Thailand 38 D4 16 12N 103 16 E
Mahābād, Iran 44 B5 36 50N 45 45 E
Mahabharat Lekh, Nepal 43 E10 28 30N 82 0 E
Mahabo, Madag. 57 C7 20 23S 44 40 E
Mahadeo Hills, India 43 H8 22 20N 78 30 E
Mahaffey, U.S.A. 78 F6 40 53N 78 44W
Mahagi, Dem. Rep. of the Congo 54 B3 2 20N 31 0 E
Mahajamba →, Madag. 57 B8 15 33S 47 8 E
Mahajamba, Helodranon' i, Madag. 57 B8 15 24S 47 5 E
Mahajan, India 42 E5 28 48N 73 56 E
Mahajanga, Madag. 57 B8 15 40S 46 25 E
Mahajanga □, Madag. 57 B8 17 0S 47 0 E
Mahajilo →, Madag. 57 B8 19 42S 45 22 E
Mahakam →, Indonesia 36 E5 0 35S 117 17 E
Mahalapye, Botswana 56 C4 23 1S 26 51 E
Maḩallāt, Iran 45 C6 33 55N 50 30 E
Māhān, Iran 45 D8 30 5N 57 18 E
Mahan →, India 43 H10 23 30N 82 50 E
Mahanadi →, India 41 J15 20 20N 86 25 E
Mahananda →, India 43 G12 25 12N 87 52 E
Mahanoro, Madag. 57 B8 19 54S 48 48 E
Mahanoy City, U.S.A. 79 F8 40 49N 76 9W
Maharashtra □, India 40 J9 20 30N 75 30 E
Mahari Mts., Tanzania 54 D3 6 20S 30 0 E
Mahasham, W. →, Egypt 47 E3 30 15N 34 10 E
Mahasoa, Madag. 57 C8 22 12S 46 6 E
Mahasolo, Madag. 57 B8 19 7S 46 22 E
Mahattat ash Shīdīyah, Jordan 47 F4 29 55N 35 55 E
Mahattat 'Unayzah, Jordan 47 E4 30 30N 35 47 E
Mahavavy →, Madag. 57 B8 15 57S 45 54 E
Mahaxay, Laos 38 D5 17 22N 105 12 E
Mahbubnagar, India 40 L10 16 45N 77 59 E
Maḩḑah, Oman 45 E7 24 24N 55 59 E
Mahdia, Tunisia 51 A8 35 28N 11 0 E
Mahe, India 43 C8 33 10N 78 32 E
Mahendragarh, India 42 E7 28 17N 76 14 E
Mahenge, Tanzania 55 D4 8 45S 36 41 E
Maheno, N.Z. 59 L3 45 10S 170 50 E
Mahesana, India 42 H5 23 39N 72 26 E
Maheshwar, India 42 H6 22 11N 75 35 E
Mahgawan, India 43 F8 26 29N 78 37 E
Mahi →, India 42 H5 22 15N 72 55 E
Mahia Pen., N.Z. 59 H6 39 9S 177 55 E
Mahilyow, Belarus 17 B16 53 55N 30 18 E
Mahmud Kot, Pakistan 42 D4 30 16N 71 0 E
Mahnomen, U.S.A. 80 B7 47 19N 95 58W
Mahoba, India 43 G8 25 15N 79 55 E
Mahón = Maó, Spain 22 B11 39 53N 4 16 E
Mahone Bay, Canada 71 D7 44 30N 64 20W
Mahopac, U.S.A. 79 E11 41 22N 73 45W
Mahuva, India 42 J4 21 5N 71 48 E
Mai-Ndombe, L., Dem. Rep. of the Congo 52 E3 2 0S 18 20 E
Mai-Sai, Thailand 38 B2 20 20N 99 55 E
Maicurú →, Brazil 93 D8 2 14S 54 17W
Maidan Khula, Afghan. 42 C3 33 36N 69 50 E
Maidenhead, U.K. 11 F7 51 31N 0 42W
Maidstone, Canada 73 C7 53 5N 109 20W
Maidstone, U.K. 11 F8 51 16N 0 32 E
Maiduguri, Nigeria 51 F8 12 0N 13 20 E
Maihar, India 43 G9 24 16N 80 45 E
Maijdi, Bangla. 41 H17 22 48N 91 10 E
Maikala Ra., India 41 J12 22 0N 81 0 E
Mailani, India 43 E9 28 17N 80 21 E
Mailsi, Pakistan 42 E5 29 48N 72 15 E
Main →, Germany 16 C5 50 0N 8 18 E
Main →, U.K. 13 B5 54 48N 6 18W
Maine, France 18 C3 48 20N 0 15W
Maine □, U.S.A. 77 C11 45 20N 69 0W
Maine →, Ireland 13 D2 52 9N 9 45W
Maingkwan, Burma 41 F20 26 15N 96 37 E
Mainit, L., Phil. 37 C7 9 31N 125 30 E
Mainland, Orkney, U.K. 12 C5 58 59N 3 8W
Mainland, Shet., U.K. 12 A7 60 15N 1 22W
Mainoru, Australia 62 A1 14 0S 134 6 E
Mainpuri, India 43 F8 27 18N 79 4 E
Maintirano, Madag. 57 B7 18 3S 44 1 E
Mainz, Germany 16 C5 50 1N 8 14 E
Maipú, Argentina 94 D4 36 52S 57 50W
Maiquetía, Venezuela 92 A5 10 36N 66 57W
Mairabari, India 41 F18 26 30N 92 22 E
Maisí, Cuba 89 B5 20 17N 74 9W
Maisí, Pta. de, Cuba 89 B5 20 10N 74 10W
Maitland, N.S.W., Australia 63 E5 32 33S 151 36 E
Maitland, S. Austral., Australia 63 E2 34 23S 137 40 E
Maitland →, Canada 78 C3 43 45N 81 43W
Maiz, Is. del, Nic. 88 D3 12 15N 83 4W
Maizuru, Japan 31 G7 35 25N 135 22 E
Majalengka, Indonesia 37 G13 6 50S 108 13 E
Majene, Indonesia 37 E5 3 38S 118 57 E
Majorca = Mallorca, Spain 22 B10 39 30N 3 0 E
Makaha, Zimbabwe 57 B5 17 20S 32 39 E
Makalamabedi, Botswana 56 C3 20 19S 23 51 E
Makale, Indonesia 37 E5 3 6S 119 51 E
Makamba, Burundi 54 C2 4 8S 29 49 E
Makarikari = Makgadikgadi Salt Pans, Botswana 56 C4 20 40S 25 45 E
Makarovo, Russia 27 D11 57 40N 107 45 E
Makasar = Ujung Pandang, Indonesia 37 F5 5 10S 119 20 E
Makasar, Selat, Indonesia 37 E5 1 0S 118 20 E
Makasar, Str. of = Makasar, Selat, Indonesia 37 E5 1 0S 118 20 E
Makat, Kazakstan 25 E9 47 39N 53 19 E
Makedhonía □, Greece 21 D10 40 39N 22 0 E
Makedonija = Macedonia ■, Europe 21 D9 41 53N 21 40 E
Makeyevka = Makiyivka, Ukraine 25 E6 48 0N 38 0 E
Makgadikgadi Salt Pans, Botswana 56 C4 20 40S 25 45 E
Makhachkala, Russia 25 F8 43 0N 47 30 E
Makhmūr, Iraq 44 C4 35 46N 43 35 E
Makian, Indonesia 37 D7 0 20N 127 20 E
Makindu, Kenya 54 C4 2 18S 37 50 E
Makinsk, Kazakstan 26 D8 52 37N 70 26 E
Makiyivka, Ukraine 25 E6 48 0N 38 0 E
Makkah, Si. Arabia 46 C2 21 30N 39 54 E
Makkovik, Canada 71 A8 55 10N 59 10W
Makó, Hungary 17 E11 46 14N 20 33 E
Makokou, Gabon 52 D2 0 40N 12 50 E
Makongo, Dem. Rep. of the Congo 54 B2 3 25N 26 17 E
Makoro, Dem. Rep. of the Congo 54 B2 3 10N 29 59 E
Makrai, India 40 H10 22 2N 77 0 E
Makran Coast Range, Pakistan 40 G4 25 40N 64 0 E
Makrana, India 42 F6 27 2N 74 46 E
Makriyialos, Greece 23 D7 35 2N 25 59 E
Mākū, Iran 44 B5 39 15N 44 31 E
Makunda, Botswana 56 C3 22 30S 20 7 E
Makurazaki, Japan 31 J5 31 15N 130 20 E
Makurdi, Nigeria 50 G7 7 43N 8 35 E
Makūyeh, Iran 45 D7 28 7N 53 9 E
Makwassie, S. Africa 56 D4 27 17S 26 0 E
Makwiro, Zimbabwe 57 B5 17 58S 30 25 E

Mal B., Ireland 13 D2 52 50N 9 30W
Mala, Pta., Panama 88 E3 7 28N 80 2W
Malabar Coast, India 40 P9 11 0N 75 0 E
Malabo = Rey Malabo, Eq. Guin. 52 D1 3 45N 8 50 E
Malacca, Str. of, Indonesia 39 L3 3 0N 101 0 E
Malad City, U.S.A. 82 E7 42 12N 112 15W
Maladzyechna, Belarus 17 A14 54 20N 26 50 E
Málaga, Spain 19 D3 36 43N 4 23W
Malagarasi, Tanzania 54 D3 5 5S 30 50 E
Malagarasi →, Tanzania 54 D2 5 12S 29 47 E
Malagasy Rep. = Madagascar ■, Africa 57 C8 20 0S 47 0 E
Malahide, Ireland 13 C5 53 26N 6 9W
Malaimbandy, Madag. 57 C8 20 20S 45 36 E
Malakâl, Sudan 51 G12 9 33N 31 40 E
Malakand, Pakistan 42 B4 34 40N 71 55 E
Malakwal, Pakistan 42 C5 32 34N 73 13 E
Malamala, Indonesia 37 E6 3 21S 120 55 E
Malanda, Australia 62 B4 17 22S 145 35 E
Malang, Indonesia 36 F4 7 59S 112 45 E
Malangen, Norway 8 B18 69 24N 18 37 E
Malanje, Angola 52 F3 9 36S 16 17 E
Mälaren, Sweden 9 G17 59 30N 17 10 E
Malargüe, Argentina 94 D2 35 32S 69 30W
Malartic, Canada 70 C4 48 9N 78 9W
Malaryta, Belarus 17 C13 51 50N 24 3 E
Malatya, Turkey 25 G6 38 25N 38 20 E
Malawi ■, Africa 55 E3 11 55S 34 0 E
Malawi, L. = Nyasa, L., Africa 55 E3 12 30S 34 30 E
Malay Pen., Asia 39 J3 7 25N 100 0 E
Malaya Vishera, Russia 24 C5 58 55N 32 25 E
Malaybalay, Phil. 37 C7 8 5N 125 7 E
Malāyer, Iran 45 C6 34 19N 48 51 E
Malaysia ■, Asia 39 K4 5 0N 110 0 E
Malazgirt, Turkey 25 G7 39 10N 42 33 E
Malbon, Australia 62 C3 21 5S 140 17 E
Malbooma, Australia 63 E1 30 41S 134 11 E
Malbork, Poland 17 B10 54 3N 19 1 E
Malcolm, Australia 61 E3 28 51S 121 25 E
Malcolm, Pt., Australia 61 F3 33 48S 123 45 E
Maldah, India 43 G13 25 2N 88 9 E
Maldegem, Belgium 15 C3 51 14N 3 26 E
Malden, Mass., U.S.A. 79 D13 42 26N 71 4W
Malden, Mo., U.S.A. 81 G10 36 34N 89 57W
Malden I., Kiribati 65 H12 4 3S 155 1W
Maldives ■, Ind. Oc. 29 J11 5 0N 73 0 E
Maldonado, Uruguay 95 C5 34 59S 55 0W
Maldonado, Punta, Mexico 87 D5 16 19N 98 35W
Malé, Maldives 29 J11 4 0N 73 28 E
Malé Karpaty, Slovak Rep. 17 D9 48 30N 17 20 E
Maléa, Ákra, Greece 21 F10 36 28N 23 7 E
Malegaon, India 40 J9 20 30N 74 38 E
Malei, Mozam. 55 F4 17 12S 36 58 E
Malek Kandī, Iran 44 B5 37 9N 46 6 E
Malela, Dem. Rep. of the Congo 54 C2 4 22S 26 8 E
Malema, Mozam. 55 E4 14 57S 37 20 E
Máleme, Greece 23 D5 35 31N 23 49 E
Maleny, Australia 63 D5 26 45S 152 52 E
Malerkotla, India 42 D6 30 32N 75 58 E
Máles, Greece 23 D7 35 6N 25 35 E
Malgomaj, Sweden 8 D17 64 40N 16 30 E
Malha, Sudan 51 E11 15 8N 25 10 E
Malhargarh, India 42 G6 24 17N 74 59 E
Malheur →, U.S.A. 82 D5 44 4N 116 59W
Malheur L., U.S.A. 82 E4 43 20N 118 48W
Mali ■, Africa 50 E5 17 0N 3 0W
Mali →, Burma 41 G20 25 40N 97 40 E
Mali Kyun, Burma 38 F2 13 0N 98 20 E
Malibu, U.S.A. 85 L8 34 2N 118 41W
Maliku, Indonesia 37 E6 0 39S 123 16 E
Malili, Indonesia 37 E6 2 42S 121 6 E
Malimba, Mts., Dem. Rep. of the Congo 54 D2 7 30S 29 30 E
Malin Hd., Ireland 13 A4 55 23N 7 23W
Malin Pen., Ireland 13 A4 55 20N 7 17W
Malindi, Kenya 54 C5 3 12S 40 5 E
Malines = Mechelen, Belgium 15 C4 51 2N 4 29 E
Malino, Indonesia 37 D6 1 0N 121 0 E
Malinyi, Tanzania 55 D4 8 56S 36 0 E
Malita, Phil. 37 C7 6 19N 125 39 E
Maliwun, Burma 36 B1 10 17N 98 40 E
Maliya, India 42 H4 23 5N 70 46 E
Malkara, Turkey 21 D12 40 53N 26 53 E
Mallacoota Inlet, Australia 63 F4 37 34S 149 40 E
Mallaig, U.K. 12 D3 57 0N 5 50W
Mallawan, India 43 F9 27 4N 80 12 E
Mallawi, Egypt 51 C12 27 44N 30 44 E
Mállia, Greece 23 D7 35 17N 25 32 E
Mallión, Kólpos, Greece 23 D7 35 19N 25 27 E
Mallorca, Spain 22 B10 39 30N 3 0 E
Mallorytown, Canada 79 B9 44 29N 75 53W
Mallow, Ireland 13 D3 52 8N 8 39W
Malmberget, Sweden 8 C19 67 11N 20 40 E
Malmédy, Belgium 15 D6 50 25N 6 2 E
Malmesbury, S. Africa 56 E2 33 28S 18 41 E
Malmö, Sweden 9 J15 55 36N 12 59 E
Malolos, Phil. 37 B6 14 50N 120 49 E
Malombe L., Malawi 55 E4 14 40S 35 15 E
Malone, U.S.A. 79 B10 44 51N 74 18W
Måløy, Norway 9 F11 61 57N 5 6 E
Malpaso, Canary Is. 22 G1 27 43N 18 3W
Malpelo, I. de, Colombia 92 C2 4 3N 81 35W
Malpur, India 42 H5 23 21N 73 27 E
Malpura, India 42 F6 26 17N 75 23 E
Malta, Idaho, U.S.A. 82 E7 42 18N 113 22W
Malta, Mont., U.S.A. 82 B10 48 21N 107 52W
Malta ■, Europe 23 D2 35 55N 14 26 E
Maltahöhe, Namibia 56 C2 24 55S 17 0 E
Malton, Canada 78 C5 43 42N 79 38W
Malton, U.K. 10 C7 54 8N 0 49W
Maluku, Indonesia 37 E7 1 0S 127 0 E
Maluku □, Indonesia 37 E7 3 0S 128 0 E
Maluku Sea = Molucca Sea, Indonesia 37 E6 0 0 125 0 E
Malvan, India 40 L8 16 2N 73 30 E
Malvern, U.S.A. 81 H8 34 22N 92 49W
Malvern Hills, U.K. 11 E5 52 0N 2 19W
Malvinas, Is. = Falkland Is. □, Atl. Oc. 96 G5 51 30S 59 0W
Malya, Tanzania 54 C3 3 5S 33 38 E
Malyn, Ukraine 17 C15 50 46N 29 3 E
Malyy Lyakhovskiy, Ostrov, Russia 27 B15 74 7N 140 36 E
Mama, Russia 27 D12 58 18N 112 54 E
Mamanguape, Brazil 93 E11 6 50S 35 4W
Mamarr Mitlā, Egypt 47 E1 30 2N 32 54 E
Mamasa, Indonesia 37 E5 2 55S 119 20 E
Mambasa, Dem. Rep. of the Congo 54 B2 1 22N 29 3 E
Mamberamo →, Indonesia 37 E9 2 0S 137 50 E
Mambilima Falls, Zambia 55 E2 10 31S 28 45 E
Mambirima, Dem. Rep. of the Congo 55 E2 11 25S 27 33 E
Mambo, Tanzania 54 C4 4 52S 38 22 E
Mambrui, Kenya 54 C5 3 5S 40 5 E
Mamburao, Phil. 37 B6 13 13N 120 39 E
Mameigwess L., Canada 70 B2 52 35N 87 50W
Mammoth, U.S.A. 83 K8 32 43N 110 39W
Mammoth Cave Nat. Park, U.S.A. 76 G3 37 8N 86 13W
Mamoré →, Bolivia 92 F5 10 23S 65 53W
Mamou, Guinea 50 F3 10 15N 12 0W
Mamoudzou, Mayotte 49 H8 12 48S 45 14 E
Mampikony, Madag. 57 B8 16 6S 47 38 E
Mamuju, Indonesia 37 E5 2 41S 118 50 E
Mamuno, Botswana 56 C3 22 16S 20 1 E
Man, Ivory C. 50 G4 7 30N 7 40W
Man, I. of, U.K. 10 C3 54 15N 4 30W
Man-Bazar, India 43 H12 23 4N 86 39 E
Man Na, Burma 41 H20 23 27N 97 19 E
Mana →, Fr. Guiana 93 B8 5 45N 53 55W
Manaar, G. of = Mannar, G. of, Asia 40 Q11 8 30N 79 0 E
Manacapuru, Brazil 92 D6 3 16S 60 37W
Manacor, Spain 22 B10 39 34N 3 13 E
Manado, Indonesia 37 D6 1 29N 124 51 E
Managua, Nic. 88 D2 12 6N 86 20W
Managua, L. de, Nic. 88 D2 12 20N 86 30W
Manakara, Madag. 57 C8 22 8S 48 1 E
Manali, India 42 C7 32 16N 77 10 E
Manama = Al Manāmah, Bahrain 46 B5 26 10N 50 30 E
Manambao →, Madag. 57 B7 17 35S 44 0 E
Manambato, Madag. 57 A8 13 43S 49 7 E
Manambolo →, Madag. 57 B7 19 18S 44 22 E
Manambolosy, Madag. 57 B8 16 2S 49 40 E
Mananara, Madag. 57 B8 16 10S 49 46 E
Mananara →, Madag. 57 C8 23 21S 47 42 E
Mananjary, Madag. 57 C8 21 13S 48 20 E
Manantenina, Madag. 57 C8 24 17S 47 19 E
Manaos = Manaus, Brazil 92 D7 3 0S 60 0W
Manapire →, Venezuela 92 B5 7 42N 66 7W
Manapouri, N.Z. 59 L1 45 34S 167 39 E
Manapouri, L., N.Z. 59 L1 45 32S 167 32 E
Manār, Jabal, Yemen 46 E3 14 2N 44 17 E
Manaravolo, Madag. 57 C8 23 59S 45 39 E
Manas, China 32 B3 44 17N 85 56 E
Manas →, India 41 F17 26 12N 90 40 E
Manaslu, Nepal 43 E11 28 33N 84 33 E
Manasquan, U.S.A. 79 F10 40 8N 74 3W
Manassa, U.S.A. 83 H11 37 11N 105 56W
Manaung, Burma 41 K18 18 45N 93 40 E
Manaus, Brazil 92 D7 3 0S 60 0W
Manawan L., Canada 73 B8 55 24N 103 14W
Manbij, Syria 44 B3 36 31N 37 57 E
Manchegorsk, Russia 26 C4 67 54N 32 58 E
Manchester, U.K. 10 D5 53 29N 2 12W
Manchester, Calif., U.S.A. 84 G3 38 58N 123 41W
Manchester, Conn., U.S.A. 79 E12 41 47N 72 31W
Manchester, Ga., U.S.A. 77 J3 32 51N 84 37W
Manchester, Iowa, U.S.A. 80 D9 42 29N 91 27W
Manchester, Ky., U.S.A. 76 G4 37 9N 83 46W
Manchester, N.H., U.S.A. 79 D13 42 59N 71 28W
Manchester, N.Y., U.S.A. 78 D7 42 56N 77 16W
Manchester, Pa., U.S.A. 79 F8 40 4N 76 43W
Manchester, Tenn., U.S.A. 77 H2 35 29N 86 5W
Manchester, Vt., U.S.A. 79 C11 43 10N 73 5W
Manchester L., Canada 73 A7 61 28N 107 29W
Manchhar L., Pakistan 42 F2 26 25N 67 39 E
Manchuria = Dongbei, China 35 D13 45 0N 125 0 E
Manchurian Plain, China 28 E16 47 0N 124 0 E
Mand →, India 43 J10 21 42N 83 15 E
Mand →, Iran 45 D7 28 20N 52 30 E
Manda, Ludewe, Tanzania 55 E3 10 30S 34 40 E
Manda, Mbeya, Tanzania 54 D3 7 58S 32 29 E
Manda, Mbeya, Tanzania 55 D3 8 30S 32 49 E
Mandabé, Madag. 57 C7 21 0S 44 55 E
Mandaguari, Brazil 95 A5 23 32S 51 42W
Mandah = Töhöm, Mongolia 34 B5 44 27N 108 2 E
Mandal, Norway 9 G12 58 2N 7 25 E
Mandala, Puncak, Indonesia 37 E10 4 44S 140 20 E
Mandalay, Burma 41 J20 22 0N 96 4 E
Mandale = Mandalay, Burma 41 J20 22 0N 96 4 E
Mandalgarh, India 42 G6 25 12N 75 6 E
Mandalgovi, Mongolia 34 B4 45 45N 106 10 E
Mandalī, Iraq 44 C5 33 43N 45 28 E
Mandan, U.S.A. 80 B4 46 50N 100 54W
Mandar, Teluk, Indonesia 37 E5 3 35S 119 15 E
Mandaue, Phil. 37 B6 10 20N 123 56 E
Mandera, Kenya 54 B5 3 55N 41 53 E
Mandi, India 42 D7 31 39N 76 58 E
Mandi Dabwali, India 42 E6 29 58N 74 42 E
Mandimba, Mozam. 55 E4 14 20S 35 40 E
Mandioli, Indonesia 37 E7 0 40S 127 20 E
Mandla, India 43 H9 22 39N 80 30 E
Mandorah, Australia 60 B5 12 32S 130 42 E
Mandoto, Madag. 57 B8 19 34S 46 17 E
Mandra, Pakistan 42 C5 33 23N 73 12 E
Mandrare →, Madag. 57 D8 25 10S 46 30 E
Mandritsara, Madag. 57 B8 15 50S 48 49 E
Mandronarivo, Madag. 57 C8 21 7S 45 38 E
Mandsaur, India 42 G6 24 3N 75 8 E
Mandurah, Australia 61 F2 32 36S 115 48 E
Mandvi, India 42 H3 22 51N 69 22 E
Mandya, India 40 N10 12 30N 77 0 E
Mandzai, Pakistan 42 D2 30 55N 67 6 E
Maneh, Iran 45 B8 37 39N 57 7 E
Manera, Madag. 57 C7 22 55S 44 20 E
Maneroo Cr. →, Australia 62 C3 23 21S 143 53 E
Manfalût, Egypt 51 C12 27 20N 30 52 E
Manfredónia, Italy 20 D6 41 38N 15 55 E
Mangabeiras, Chapada das, Brazil 93 F9 10 0S 46 30W
Mangalia, Romania 17 G15 43 50N 28 35 E
Mangalore, India 40 N9 12 55N 74 47 E
Mangan, India 43 F13 27 31N 88 32 E
Mangaung, S. Africa 53 K5 29 10S 26 25 E
Mangawan, India 43 G9 24 41N 81 33 E
Mangaweka, N.Z. 59 H5 39 48S 175 47 E
Manggar, Indonesia 36 E3 2 50S 108 10 E
Manggawitu, Indonesia 37 E8 4 8S 133 32 E
Mangindrano, Madag. 57 A8 14 17S 48 58 E
Mangkalihat, Tanjung, Indonesia 37 D5 1 2N 118 59 E
Mangla, Pakistan 42 C5 33 7N 73 39 E
Mangla Dam, Pakistan 43 C5 33 9N 73 44 E
Manglaur, India 42 E7 29 44N 77 49 E
Mangnai, China 32 C4 37 52N 91 43 E
Mango, Togo 50 F6 10 20N 0 30 E
Mangoche, Malawi 55 E4 14 25S 35 16 E
Mangoky →, Madag. 57 C7 21 29S 43 41 E
Mangole, Indonesia 37 E6 1 50S 125 55 E
Mangombe, Dem. Rep. of the Congo 54 C2 1 20S 26 48 E
Mangonui, N.Z. 59 F4 35 1S 173 32 E
Mangoro →, Madag. 57 B8 20 0S 48 45 E
Mangrol, Mad. P., India 42 J4 21 7N 70 7 E
Mangrol, Raj., India 42 G6 25 20N 76 31 E
Mangueira, L. da, Brazil 95 C5 33 0S 52 50W
Mangum, U.S.A. 81 H5 34 53N 99 30W
Mangyshlak Poluostrov, Kazakstan 26 E6 44 30N 52 30 E
Manhattan, U.S.A. 80 F6 39 11N 96 35W
Manhiça, Mozam. 57 D5 25 23S 32 49 E
Mania →, Madag. 57 B8 19 42S 45 22 E
Manica, Mozam. 57 B5 18 58S 32 59 E
Manica □, Mozam. 57 B5 19 10S 33 45 E
Manicaland □, Zimbabwe 55 F3 19 0S 32 30 E
Manicoré, Brazil 92 E6 5 48S 61 16W
Manicouagan →, Canada 71 C6 49 30N 68 30W
Manicouagan, Rés., Canada 71 B6 51 5N 68 40W
Maniema □, Dem. Rep. of the Congo 54 C2 3 0S 26 0 E
Manīfah, Si. Arabia 45 E6 27 44N 49 0 E
Manifold, C., Australia 62 C5 22 41S 150 50 E
Manigotagan, Canada 73 C9 51 6N 96 18W
Manigotagan →, Canada 73 C9 51 7N 96 20W
Manihari, India 43 G12 25 21N 87 38 E
Manihiki, Cook Is. 65 J11 10 24S 161 1W
Manika, Plateau de la, Dem. Rep. of the Congo 55 E2 10 0S 25 5 E
Manikpur, India 43 G9 25 4N 81 7 E
Manila, Phil. 37 B6 14 40N 121 3 E
Manila, U.S.A. 82 F9 40 59N 109 43W
Manila B., Phil. 37 B6 14 40N 120 35 E
Manilla, Australia 63 E5 30 45S 150 43 E
Maningrida, Australia 62 A1 12 3S 134 13 E
Manipur □, India 41 G19 25 0N 94 0 E
Manipur →, Burma 41 H19 23 45N 94 20 E
Manisa, Turkey 21 E12 38 38N 27 30 E
Manistee, U.S.A. 76 C2 44 15N 86 19W
Manistee →, U.S.A. 76 C2 44 15N 86 21W
Manistique, U.S.A. 76 C2 45 57N 86 15W
Manito L., Canada 73 C7 52 43N 109 43W
Manitoba □, Canada 73 B9 55 30N 97 0W
Manitoba, L., Canada 73 C9 51 0N 98 45W
Manitou, Canada 73 D9 49 15N 98 32W
Manitou, L., Canada 71 B6 50 55N 65 17W
Manitou Is., U.S.A. 76 C3 45 8N 86 0W
Manitou Springs, U.S.A. 80 F2 38 52N 104 55W
Manitoulin I., Canada 70 C3 45 40N 82 30W
Manitouwadge, Canada 70 C2 49 8N 85 48W
Manitowoc, U.S.A. 76 C2 44 5N 87 40W
Manizales, Colombia 92 B3 5 5N 75 32W
Manja, Madag. 57 C7 21 26S 44 20 E
Manjacaze, Mozam. 57 C5 24 45S 34 0 E
Manjakandriana, Madag. 57 B8 18 55S 47 47 E
Manjhand, Pakistan 42 G3 25 50N 68 10 E
Manjil, Iran 45 B6 36 46N 49 30 E
Manjimup, Australia 61 F2 34 15S 116 6 E
Manjra →, India 40 K10 18 49N 77 52 E
Mankato, Kans., U.S.A. 80 F5 39 47N 98 13W
Mankato, Minn., U.S.A. 80 C8 44 10N 94 0W
Mankayane, Swaziland 57 D5 26 40S 31 4 E
Mankera, Pakistan 42 D4 31 23N 71 26 E
Mankota, Canada 73 D7 49 25N 107 5W
Manlay = Üydzin, Mongolia 34 B4 44 9N 107 0 E
Manmad, India 40 J9 20 18N 74 28 E
Mann Ranges, Australia 61 E5 26 6S 130 5 E
Manna, Indonesia 36 E2 4 25S 102 55 E
Mannahill, Australia 63 E3 32 25S 140 0 E
Mannar, Sri Lanka 40 Q11 9 1N 79 54 E
Mannar, G. of, Asia 40 Q11 8 30N 79 0 E
Mannar I., Sri Lanka 40 Q11 9 5N 79 45 E
Mannheim, Germany 16 D5 49 29N 8 29 E
Manning, Canada 72 B5 56 53N 117 39W
Manning, Oreg., U.S.A. 84 E3 45 45N 123 13W
Manning, S.C., U.S.A. 77 J5 33 42N 80 13W
Manning Prov. Park, Canada 72 D4 49 5N 120 45W
Mannum, Australia 63 E2 34 50S 139 20 E
Manoharpur, India 43 H11 22 23N 85 12 E
Manokwari, Indonesia 37 E8 0 54S 134 0 E
Manombo, Madag. 57 C7 22 57S 43 28 E
Manono, Dem. Rep. of the Congo 54 D2 7 15S 27 25 E
Manosque, France 18 E6 43 49N 5 47 E
Manotick, Canada 79 A9 45 13N 75 41W
Manouane →, Canada 71 C5 49 30N 71 10W
Manouane, L., Canada 71 B5 50 45N 70 45W
Manp'o, N. Korea 35 D14 41 6N 126 24 E
Manpojin = Manp'o, N. Korea 35 D14 41 6N 126 24 E
Manpur, Chhattisgarh, India 43 H10 23 17N 83 35 E
Manpur, Mad. P., India 42 H6 22 26N 75 37 E
Manresa, Spain 19 B6 41 48N 1 50 E
Mansa, Gujarat, India 42 H5 23 27N 72 45 E
Mansa, Punjab, India 42 E6 30 0N 75 27 E
Mansa, Zambia 55 E2 11 13S 28 55 E
Mansehra, Pakistan 42 B5 34 20N 73 15 E
Mansel I., Canada 69 B11 62 0N 80 0W
Mansfield, Australia 63 F4 37 4S 146 6 E
Mansfield, U.K. 10 D6 53 9N 1 11W
Mansfield, La., U.S.A. 81 J8 32 2N 93 43W
Mansfield, Mass., U.S.A. 79 D13 42 2N 71 13W
Mansfield, Ohio, U.S.A. 78 F2 40 45N 82 31W
Mansfield, Pa., U.S.A. 78 E7 41 48N 77 5W
Mansfield, Mt., U.S.A. 79 B12 44 33N 72 49W
Manson Creek, Canada 72 B4 55 37N 124 32W
Manta, Ecuador 92 D2 1 0S 80 40W
Mantalingajan, Mt., Phil. 36 C5 8 55N 117 45 E
Mantare, Tanzania 54 C3 2 42S 33 13 E
Manteca, U.S.A. 84 H5 37 48N 121 13W
Manteo, U.S.A. 77 H8 35 55N 75 40W
Mantes-la-Jolie, France 18 B4 48 58N 1 41 E
Manthani, India 40 K11 18 40N 79 35 E
Manti, U.S.A. 82 G8 39 16N 111 38W
Mantiqueira, Serra da, Brazil 95 A7 22 0S 44 0W
Manton, U.S.A. 76 C3 44 25N 85 24W
Mántova, Italy 20 B4 45 9N 10 48 E
Mänttä, Finland 9 E21 62 0N 24 40 E
Mantua = Mántova, Italy 20 B4 45 9N 10 48 E
Manu, Peru 92 F4 12 10S 70 51W
Manu →, Peru 92 F4 12 16S 70 55W
Manu'a Is., Amer. Samoa 59 B14 14 13S 169 35W
Manuel Alves →, Brazil 93 F9 11 19S 48 28W
Manui, Indonesia 37 E6 3 35S 123 5 E
Manukau, N.Z. 59 G5 40 43S 175 13 E
Manuripi →, Bolivia 92 F5 11 6S 67 36W
Many, U.S.A. 81 K8 31 34N 93 29W
Manyara, L., Tanzania 54 C4 3 40S 35 50 E
Manych-Gudilo, Ozero, Russia 25 E7 46 24N 42 38 E
Manyonga →, Tanzania 54 C3 4 10S 34 15 E
Manyoni, Tanzania 54 D3 5 45S 34 55 E
Manzai, Pakistan 42 C4 32 12N 70 15 E
Manzanares, Spain 19 C4 39 2N 3 22W
Manzanillo, Cuba 88 B4 20 20N 77 31W
Manzanillo, Mexico 86 D4 19 0N 104 20W
Manzanillo, Pta., Panama 88 E4 9 30N 79 40W
Manzano Mts., U.S.A. 83 J10 34 40N 106 20W
Manzarīyeh, Iran 45 C6 34 53N 50 50 E
Manzhouli, China 33 B6 49 35N 117 25 E
Manzini, Swaziland 57 D5 26 30S 31 25 E
Mao, Chad 51 F9 14 4N 15 19 E
Maó, Spain 22 B11 39 53N 4 16 E
Maoke, Pegunungan, Indonesia 37 E9 3 40S 137 30 E
Maolin, China 35 C12 43 58N 123 30 E
Maoming, China 33 D6 21 50N 110 54 E
Maoxing, China 35 B13 45 28N 124 40 E
Mapam Yumco, China 32 C3 30 45N 81 28 E
Mapastepec, Mexico 87 D6 15 26N 92 54W
Mapia, Kepulauan, Indonesia 37 D8 0 50N 134 20 E
Mapimí, Mexico 86 B4 25 50N 103 50W
Mapimí, Bolsón de, Mexico 86 B4 27 30N 104 15W
Mapinga, Tanzania 54 D4 6 40S 39 12 E
Mapinhane, Mozam. 57 C6 22 20S 35 0 E
Maple Creek, Canada 73 D7 49 55N 109 29W
Maple Valley, U.S.A. 84 C4 47 25N 122 3W
Mapleton, U.S.A. 82 D2 44 2N 123 52W
Mapuera →, Brazil 92 D7 1 5S 57 2W
Mapulanguene, Mozam. 57 C5 24 29S 32 6 E
Maputo, Mozam. 57 D5 25 58S 32 32 E
Maputo □, Mozam. 57 D5 26 0S 32 25 E
Maputo, B. de, Mozam. 57 D5 25 50S 32 45 E
Maqiaohe, China 35 B16 44 40N 130 30 E
Maqnā, Si. Arabia 44 D2 28 25N 34 50 E
Maquela do Zombo, Angola 52 F3 6 0S 15 15 E
Maquinchao, Argentina 96 E3 41 15S 68 50W
Maquoketa, U.S.A. 80 D9 42 4N 90 40W
Mar, Serra do, Brazil 95 B6 25 30S 49 0W
Mar Chiquita, L., Argentina 94 C3 30 40S 62 50W
Mar del Plata, Argentina 94 D4 38 0S 57 30W
Mar Menor, Spain 19 D5 37 40N 0 45W
Mara, Tanzania 54 C3 1 30S 34 32 E
Mara □, Tanzania 54 C3 1 45S 34 20 E
Maraã, Brazil 92 D5 1 52S 65 25W
Marabá, Brazil 93 E9 5 20S 49 5W
Maracá, I. de, Brazil 93 C8 2 10N 50 30W
Maracaibo, Venezuela 92 A4 10 40N 71 37W
Maracaibo, L. de, Venezuela 92 B4 9 40N 71 30W
Maracaju, Brazil 95 A4 21 38S 55 9W
Maracay, Venezuela 92 A5 10 15N 67 28W
Maradi, Niger 50 F7 13 29N 7 20 E
Marāgheh, Iran 44 B5 37 30N 46 12 E
Marāh, Si. Arabia 44 E5 25 0N 45 35 E
Marajó, I. de, Brazil 93 D9 1 0S 49 30W
Marākand, Iran 44 B5 38 51N 45 16 E
Maralal, Kenya 54 B4 1 0N 36 38 E
Maralinga, Australia 61 F5 30 13S 131 32 E
Maran, Malaysia 39 L4 3 35N 102 45 E
Marana, U.S.A. 83 K8 32 27N 111 13W
Maranboy, Australia 60 B5 14 40S 132 39 E
Marand, Iran 44 B5 38 30N 45 45 E
Marang, Malaysia 39 K4 5 12N 103 13 E
Maranguape, Brazil 93 D11 3 55S 38 50W
Maranhão = São Luís, Brazil 93 D10 2 39S 44 15W
Maranhão □, Brazil 93 E9 5 0S 46 0W
Maranoa →, Australia 63 D4 27 50S 148 37 E
Marañón →, Peru 92 D4 4 30S 73 35W
Marão, Mozam. 57 C5 24 18S 34 2 E
Maraş = Kahramanmaraş, Turkey 25 G6 37 37N 36 53 E
Marathasa, Cyprus 23 E11 34 59N 32 51 E
Marathon, Australia 62 C3 20 51S 143 32 E
Marathon, Canada 70 C2 48 44N 86 23W
Marathon, N.Y., U.S.A. 79 D8 42 27N 76 2W
Marathon, Tex., U.S.A. 81 K3 30 12N 103 15W
Marathóvouno, Cyprus 23 D12 35 13N 33 37 E
Maratua, Indonesia 37 D5 2 10N 118 35 E
Maravatío, Mexico 86 D4 19 51N 100 25W
Marāwih, U.A.E. 45 E7 24 18N 53 18 E
Marbella, Spain 19 D3 36 30N 4 57W
Marble Bar, Australia 60 D2 21 9S 119 44 E
Marble Falls, U.S.A. 81 K5 30 35N 98 16W
Marblehead, U.S.A. 79 D14 42 30N 70 51W
Marburg, Germany 16 C5 50 47N 8 46 E
March, U.K. 11 E8 52 33N 0 5 E
Marche, France 18 C4 46 5N 1 20 E
Marche-en-Famenne, Belgium 15 D5 50 14N 5 19 E
Marchena, Spain 19 D3 37 18N 5 23W
Marco, U.S.A. 77 N5 25 58N 81 44W
Marcos Juárez, Argentina 94 C3 32 42S 62 5W
Marcus I. = Minami-Tori-Shima, Pac. Oc. 64 E7 24 20N 153 58 E
Marcus Necker Ridge, Pac. Oc. 64 F9 20 0N 175 0 E
Marcy, Mt., U.S.A. 79 B11 44 7N 73 56W
Mardan, Pakistan 42 B5 34 20N 72 0 E
Mardin, Turkey 25 G7 37 20N 40 43 E
Maree, L., U.K. 12 D3 57 40N 5 26W
Mareeba, Australia 62 B4 16 59S 145 28 E
Mareetsane, S. Africa 56 D4 26 9S 25 25 E
Marek = Stanke Dimitrov, Bulgaria 21 C10 42 17N 23 9 E
Marengo, U.S.A. 80 E8 41 48N 92 4W
Marenyi, Kenya 54 C4 4 22S 39 8 E
Marerano, Madag. 57 C7 21 23S 44 52 E
Marfa, U.S.A. 81 K2 30 19N 104 1W
Marfa Pt., Malta 23 D1 35 59N 14 19 E
Margaret →, Australia 60 C4 18 9S 125 41 E
Margaret Bay, Canada 72 C3 51 20N 127 35W

Mbala

Margaret L., *Canada* **72 B5** 58 56N 115 25W
Margaret River, *Australia* **61 F2** 33 57S 115 4 E
Margarita, I. de, *Venezuela* **92 A6** 11 0N 64 0W
Margaritovo, *Russia* **30 C7** 43 25N 134 45 E
Margate, *S. Africa* **57 E5** 30 50S 30 20 E
Margate, *U.K.* **11 F9** 51 23N 1 23 E
Mārgow, Dasht-e, *Afghan.* **40 D3** 30 40N 62 30 E
Marguerite, *Canada* **72 C4** 52 30N 122 25W
Mari El □, *Russia* **24 C8** 56 30N 48 0 E
Mari Indus, *Pakistan* **42 C4** 32 57N 71 34 E
Mari Republic = Mari El □, *Russia* **24 C8** 56 30N 48 0 E
María Elena, *Chile* **94 A2** 22 18S 69 40W
María Grande, *Argentina* **94 C4** 31 45S 59 55W
Maria I., *N. Terr., Australia* **62 A2** 14 52S 135 45 E
Maria I., *Tas., Australia* **62 G4** 42 35S 148 0 E
Maria van Diemen, C., *N.Z.* **59 F4** 34 29S 172 40 E
Mariakani, *Kenya* **54 C4** 3 50S 39 27 E
Marian, *Australia* **62 C4** 21 9S 148 57 E
Marian L., *Canada* **72 A5** 63 0N 116 15W
Mariana Trench, *Pac. Oc.* **28 H18** 13 0N 145 0 E
Marianao, *Cuba* **88 B3** 23 8N 82 24W
Marianna, *Ark., U.S.A.* **81 H9** 34 46N 90 46W
Marianna, *Fla., U.S.A.* **77 K3** 30 46N 85 14W
Marias →, *U.S.A.* **82 C8** 47 56N 110 30W
Mariato, Punta, *Panama* **88 E3** 7 12N 80 52W
Maribor, *Slovenia* **16 E8** 46 36N 15 40 E
Marico →, *Africa* **56 C4** 23 35S 26 57 E
Maricopa, *Ariz., U.S.A.* **83 K7** 33 4N 112 3W
Maricopa, *Calif., U.S.A.* **85 K7** 35 4N 119 24W
Marié →, *Brazil* **92 D5** 0 27S 66 26W
Marie Byrd Land, *Antarctica* **5 D14** 79 30S 125 0W
Marie-Galante, *Guadeloupe* **89 C7** 15 56N 61 16W
Mariecourt = Kangiqsujuaq, *Canada* **69 B12** 61 30N 72 0W
Mariembourg, *Belgium* **15 D4** 50 6N 4 31 E
Mariental, *Namibia* **56 C2** 24 36S 18 0 E
Marienville, *U.S.A.* **78 E5** 41 28N 79 8W
Mariestad, *Sweden* **9 G15** 58 43N 13 50 E
Marietta, *Ga., U.S.A.* **77 J3** 33 57N 84 33W
Marietta, *Ohio, U.S.A.* **76 F5** 39 25N 81 27W
Marieville, *Canada* **79 A11** 45 26N 73 10W
Mariinsk, *Russia* **26 D9** 56 10N 87 20 E
Marijampolė, *Lithuania* **9 J20** 54 33N 23 19 E
Marília, *Brazil* **95 A6** 22 13S 50 0W
Marín, *Spain* **19 A1** 42 23N 8 42W
Marina, *U.S.A.* **84 J5** 36 41N 121 48W
Marinduque, *Phil.* **37 B6** 13 25N 122 0 E
Marine City, *U.S.A.* **78 D2** 42 43N 82 30W
Marinette, *U.S.A.* **76 C2** 45 6N 87 38W
Maringá, *Brazil* **95 A5** 23 26S 52 2W
Marion, *Ala., U.S.A.* **77 J2** 32 38N 87 19W
Marion, *Ill., U.S.A.* **81 G10** 37 44N 88 56W
Marion, *Ind., U.S.A.* **76 E3** 40 32N 85 40W
Marion, *Iowa, U.S.A.* **80 D9** 42 2N 91 36W
Marion, *Kans., U.S.A.* **80 F6** 38 21N 97 1W
Marion, *N.C., U.S.A.* **77 H5** 35 41N 82 1W
Marion, *Ohio, U.S.A.* **76 E4** 40 35N 83 8W
Marion, *S.C., U.S.A.* **77 H6** 34 11N 79 24W
Marion, *Va., U.S.A.* **77 G5** 36 50N 81 31W
Marion, L., *U.S.A.* **77 J5** 33 28N 80 10W
Mariposa, *U.S.A.* **84 H7** 37 29N 119 58W
Mariscal Estigarribia, *Paraguay* **94 A3** 22 3S 60 40W
Maritime Alps = Maritimes, Alpes, *Europe* **18 D7** 44 10N 7 10 E
Maritimes, Alpes, *Europe* **18 D7** 44 10N 7 10 E
Maritsa = Évros →, *Greece* **21 D12** 41 40N 26 34 E
Maritsá, *Greece* **23 C10** 36 22N 28 8 E
Mariupol, *Ukraine* **25 E6** 47 5N 37 31 E
Marīvān, *Iran* **44 C5** 35 30N 46 25 E
Marj 'Uyūn, *Lebanon* **47 B4** 33 20N 35 35 E
Marka = Merca, *Somali Rep.* **46 G3** 1 48N 44 50 E
Markazī □, *Iran* **45 C6** 35 0N 49 30 E
Markdale, *Canada* **78 B4** 44 19N 80 39W
Marked Tree, *U.S.A.* **81 H9** 35 32N 90 25W
Market Drayton, *U.K.* **10 E5** 52 54N 2 29W
Market Harborough, *U.K.* **11 E7** 52 29N 0 55W
Market Rasen, *U.K.* **10 D7** 53 24N 0 20W
Markham, *Canada* **78 C5** 43 52N 79 16W
Markham, Mt., *Antarctica* **5 E11** 83 0S 164 0 E
Markleeville, *U.S.A.* **84 G7** 38 42N 119 47W
Markovo, *Russia* **27 C17** 64 40N 170 24 E
Marks, *Russia* **24 D8** 51 45N 46 50 E
Marksville, *U.S.A.* **81 K8** 31 8N 92 4W
Marla, *Australia* **63 D1** 27 19S 133 33 E
Marlbank, *Canada* **78 B7** 44 26N 77 6W
Marlboro, *Mass., U.S.A.* **79 D13** 42 19N 71 33W
Marlboro, *N.Y., U.S.A.* **79 E11** 41 36N 73 59W
Marlborough, *Australia* **62 C4** 22 46S 149 52 E
Marlborough, *U.K.* **11 F6** 51 25N 1 43W
Marlborough Downs, *U.K.* **11 F6** 51 27N 1 53W
Marlin, *U.S.A.* **81 K6** 31 18N 96 54W
Marlow, *U.S.A.* **81 H6** 34 39N 97 58W
Marmagao, *India* **40 M8** 15 25N 73 56 E
Marmara, *Turkey* **21 D12** 40 35N 27 34 E
Marmara, Sea of = Marmara Denizi, *Turkey* **21 D13** 40 45N 28 15 E
Marmara Denizi, *Turkey* **21 D13** 40 45N 28 15 E
Marmaris, *Turkey* **21 F13** 36 50N 28 14 E
Marmion, Mt., *Australia* **61 E2** 29 16S 119 50 E
Marmion L., *Canada* **70 C1** 48 55N 91 20W
Marmolada, Mte., *Italy* **20 A4** 46 26N 11 51 E
Marmora, *Canada* **78 B7** 44 28N 77 41W
Marne →, *France* **18 B5** 48 48N 2 24 E
Maroala, *Madag.* **57 B8** 15 23S 47 59 E
Maroantsetra, *Madag.* **57 B8** 15 26S 49 44 E
Maroelaboom, *Namibia* **56 B2** 19 15S 18 53 E
Marofandilia, *Madag.* **57 C7** 20 7S 44 34 E
Marolambo, *Madag.* **57 C8** 20 2S 48 7 E
Maromandia, *Madag.* **57 A8** 14 13S 48 5 E
Marondera, *Zimbabwe* **55 F3** 18 5S 31 42 E
Maroni →, *Fr. Guiana* **93 B8** 5 30N 54 0W
Maroochydore, *Australia* **63 D5** 26 29S 153 5 E
Maroona, *Australia* **63 F3** 37 27S 142 54 E
Marosakoa, *Madag.* **57 B8** 15 26S 46 38 E
Maroseranana, *Madag.* **57 B8** 18 32S 48 51 E
Marotandrano, *Madag.* **57 B8** 16 10S 48 50 E
Marotaolano, *Madag.* **57 A8** 12 47S 49 15 E
Maroua, *Cameroon* **51 F8** 10 40N 14 20 E
Marovato, *Madag.* **57 B8** 15 48S 48 5 E
Marovoay, *Madag.* **57 B8** 16 6S 46 39 E
Marquard, *S. Africa* **56 D4** 28 40S 27 28 E
Marquesas Is. = Marquises, Is., *Pac. Oc.* **65 H14** 9 30S 140 0W
Marquette, *U.S.A.* **76 B2** 46 33N 87 24W
Marquises, Is., *Pac. Oc.* **65 H14** 9 30S 140 0W
Marra, Djebel, *Sudan* **51 F10** 13 10N 24 22 E
Marracuene, *Mozam.* **57 D5** 25 45S 32 35 E
Marrakech, *Morocco* **50 B4** 31 9N 8 0W
Marrawah, *Australia* **62 G3** 40 55S 144 42 E
Marree, *Australia* **63 D2** 29 39S 138 1 E
Marrero, *U.S.A.* **81 L9** 29 54N 90 6W
Marrimane, *Mozam.* **57 C5** 22 58S 33 34 E
Marromeu, *Mozam.* **57 B6** 18 15S 36 25 E
Marrowie Cr. →, *Australia* **63 E4** 33 23S 145 40 E
Marrubane, *Mozam.* **55 F4** 18 0S 37 0 E
Marrupa, *Mozam.* **55 E4** 13 8S 37 30 E
Mars Hill, *U.S.A.* **77 B12** 46 31N 67 52W
Marsá Matrûh, *Egypt* **51 B11** 31 19N 27 9 E
Marsabit, *Kenya* **54 B4** 2 18N 38 0 E
Marsala, *Italy* **20 F5** 37 48N 12 26 E
Marsalforn, *Malta* **23 C1** 36 4N 14 16 E
Marsden, *Australia* **63 E4** 33 47S 147 32 E
Marseille, *France* **18 E6** 43 18N 5 23 E
Marseilles = Marseille, *France* **18 E6** 43 18N 5 23 E
Marsh I., *U.S.A.* **81 L9** 29 34N 91 53W
Marshall, *Ark., U.S.A.* **81 H8** 35 55N 92 38W
Marshall, *Mich., U.S.A.* **76 D3** 42 16N 84 58W
Marshall, *Minn., U.S.A.* **80 C7** 44 25N 95 45W
Marshall, *Mo., U.S.A.* **80 F8** 39 7N 93 12W
Marshall, *Tex., U.S.A.* **81 J7** 32 33N 94 23W
Marshall →, *Australia* **62 C2** 22 59S 136 59 E
Marshall Is. ■, *Pac. Oc.* **64 G9** 9 0N 171 0 E
Marshalltown, *U.S.A.* **80 D8** 42 3N 92 55W
Marshbrook, *Zimbabwe* **57 B5** 18 33S 31 9 E
Marshfield, *Mo., U.S.A.* **81 G8** 37 15N 92 54W
Marshfield, *Vt., U.S.A.* **79 B12** 44 20N 72 20W
Marshfield, *Wis., U.S.A.* **80 C9** 44 40N 90 10W
Marshūn, *Iran* **45 B6** 36 19N 49 23 E
Märsta, *Sweden* **9 G17** 59 37N 17 52 E
Mart, *U.S.A.* **81 K6** 31 33N 96 50W
Martaban, *Burma* **41 L20** 16 30N 97 35 E
Martaban, G. of, *Burma* **41 L20** 16 5N 96 30 E
Martapura, *Kalimantan, Indonesia* **36 E4** 3 22S 114 47 E
Martapura, *Sumatera, Indonesia* **36 E2** 4 19S 104 22 E
Martelange, *Belgium* **15 E5** 49 49N 5 43 E
Martha's Vineyard, *U.S.A.* **79 E14** 41 25N 70 38W
Martigny, *Switz.* **18 C7** 46 6N 7 3 E
Martigues, *France* **18 E6** 43 24N 5 4 E
Martin, *Slovak Rep.* **17 D10** 49 6N 18 58 E
Martin, *S. Dak., U.S.A.* **80 D4** 43 11N 101 44W
Martin, *Tenn., U.S.A.* **81 G10** 36 21N 88 51W
Martin L., *U.S.A.* **77 J3** 32 41N 85 55W
Martina Franca, *Italy* **20 D7** 40 42N 17 20 E
Martinborough, *N.Z.* **59 J5** 41 14S 175 29 E
Martinez, *Calif., U.S.A.* **84 G4** 38 1N 122 8W
Martinez, *Ga., U.S.A.* **77 J4** 33 31N 82 4W
Martinique ■, *W. Indies* **89 D7** 14 40N 61 0W
Martinique Passage, *W. Indies* **89 C7** 15 15N 61 0W
Martinópolis, *Brazil* **95 A5** 22 11S 51 12W
Martins Ferry, *U.S.A.* **78 F4** 40 6N 80 44W
Martinsburg, *Pa., U.S.A.* **78 F6** 40 19N 78 20W
Martinsburg, *W. Va., U.S.A.* **76 F7** 39 27N 77 58W
Martinsville, *Ind., U.S.A.* **76 F2** 39 26N 86 25W
Martinsville, *Va., U.S.A.* **77 G6** 36 41N 79 52W
Marton, *N.Z.* **59 J5** 40 4S 175 23 E
Martos, *Spain* **19 D4** 37 44N 3 58W
Marudi, *Malaysia* **36 D4** 4 11N 114 19 E
Maruf, *Afghan.* **40 D5** 31 30N 67 6 E
Marugame, *Japan* **31 G6** 34 15N 133 40 E
Marunga, *Angola* **56 B3** 17 28S 20 2 E
Marungu, Mts., *Dem. Rep. of the Congo* **54 D3** 7 30S 30 0 E
Marv Dasht, *Iran* **45 D7** 29 50N 52 40 E
Marvast, *Iran* **45 D7** 30 30N 54 15 E
Marvel Loch, *Australia* **61 F2** 31 28S 119 29 E
Marwar, *India* **42 G5** 25 43N 73 45 E
Mary, *Turkmenistan* **26 F7** 37 40N 61 50 E
Maryborough = Port Laoise, *Ireland* **13 C4** 53 2N 7 18W
Maryborough, *Queens., Australia* **63 D5** 25 31S 152 37 E
Maryborough, *Vic., Australia* **63 F3** 37 0S 143 44 E
Maryfield, *Canada* **73 D8** 49 50N 101 35W
Maryland □, *U.S.A.* **76 F7** 39 0N 76 30W
Maryland Junction, *Zimbabwe* **55 F3** 17 45S 30 31 E
Maryport, *U.K.* **10 C4** 54 44N 3 28W
Mary's Harbour, *Canada* **71 B8** 52 18N 55 51W
Marystown, *Canada* **71 C8** 47 10N 55 10W
Marysville, *Canada* **72 D5** 49 35N 116 0W
Marysville, *Calif., U.S.A.* **84 F5** 39 9N 121 35W
Marysville, *Kans., U.S.A.* **80 F6** 39 51N 96 39W
Marysville, *Mich., U.S.A.* **78 D2** 42 54N 82 29W
Marysville, *Ohio, U.S.A.* **76 E4** 40 14N 83 22W
Marysville, *Wash., U.S.A.* **84 B4** 48 3N 122 11W
Maryville, *Mo., U.S.A.* **80 E7** 40 21N 94 52W
Maryville, *Tenn., U.S.A.* **77 H4** 35 46N 83 58W
Marzūq, *Libya* **51 C8** 25 53N 13 57 E
Masahunga, *Tanzania* **54 C3** 2 6S 33 18 E
Masai Steppe, *Tanzania* **54 C4** 4 30S 36 30 E
Masaka, *Uganda* **54 C3** 0 21S 31 45 E
Masalembo, Kepulauan, *Indonesia* **36 F4** 5 35S 114 30 E
Masalima, Kepulauan, *Indonesia* **36 F5** 5 4S 117 5 E
Masamba, *Indonesia* **37 E6** 2 30S 120 15 E
Masan, *S. Korea* **35 G15** 35 11N 128 32 E
Masandam, Ra's, *Oman* **46 B6** 26 30N 56 30 E
Masasi, *Tanzania* **55 E4** 10 45S 38 52 E
Masaya, *Nic.* **88 D2** 12 0N 86 7W
Masbate, *Phil.* **37 B6** 12 21N 123 36 E
Mascara, *Algeria* **50 A6** 35 26N 0 6 E
Mascota, *Mexico* **86 C4** 20 30N 104 50W
Masela, *Indonesia* **37 F7** 8 9S 129 51 E
Maseru, *Lesotho* **56 D4** 29 18S 27 30 E
Mashaba, *Zimbabwe* **55 G3** 20 2S 30 29 E
Mashābih, *Si. Arabia* **44 E3** 25 35N 36 30 E
Masherbrum, *Pakistan* **43 B7** 35 38N 76 18 E
Mashhad, *Iran* **45 B8** 36 20N 59 35 E
Mashīz, *Iran* **45 D8** 29 56N 56 37 E
Mashkel, Hāmūn-i-, *Pakistan* **40 E3** 28 20N 62 56 E
Mashki Chāh, *Pakistan* **40 E3** 29 5N 62 30 E
Mashonaland, *Zimbabwe* **53 H6** 16 30S 31 0 E
Mashonaland Central □, *Zimbabwe* **57 B5** 17 30S 31 0 E
Mashonaland East □, *Zimbabwe* **57 B5** 18 0S 32 0 E
Mashonaland West □, *Zimbabwe* **57 B4** 17 30S 29 30 E
Mashrakh, *India* **43 F11** 26 7N 84 48 E
Masindi, *Uganda* **54 B3** 1 40N 31 43 E
Masindi Port, *Uganda* **54 B3** 1 43N 32 2 E
Maşīrah, *Oman* **46 C6** 21 0N 58 50 E
Maşīrah, Khalīj, *Oman* **46 C6** 20 10N 58 10 E
Masisi, *Dem. Rep. of the Congo* **54 C2** 1 23S 28 49 E
Masjed Soleyman, *Iran* **45 D6** 31 55N 49 18 E
Mask, L., *Ireland* **13 C2** 53 36N 9 22W
Maskin, *Oman* **45 F8** 23 30N 56 50 E
Masoala, Tanjon' i, *Madag.* **57 B9** 15 59S 50 13 E
Masoarivo, *Madag.* **57 B7** 19 3S 44 19 E
Masohi = Amahai, *Indonesia* **37 E7** 3 20S 128 55 E
Masomeloka, *Madag.* **57 C8** 20 17S 48 37 E
Mason, *Nev., U.S.A.* **84 G7** 38 56N 119 8W
Mason, *Tex., U.S.A.* **81 K5** 30 45N 99 14W
Mason City, *U.S.A.* **80 D8** 43 9N 93 12W
Maspalomas, *Canary Is.* **22 G4** 27 46N 15 35W
Maspalomas, Pta., *Canary Is.* **22 G4** 27 43N 15 36W
Masqat, *Oman* **46 C6** 23 37N 58 36 E
Massa, *Italy* **18 D9** 44 1N 10 9 E
Massachusetts □, *U.S.A.* **79 D13** 42 30N 72 0W
Massachusetts B., *U.S.A.* **79 D14** 42 20N 70 50W
Massakory, *Chad* **51 F9** 13 0N 15 49 E
Massanella, *Spain* **22 B9** 39 48N 2 51 E
Massangena, *Mozam.* **57 C5** 21 34S 33 0 E
Massango, *Angola* **52 F3** 8 2S 16 21 E
Massawa = Mitsiwa, *Eritrea* **46 D2** 15 35N 39 25 E
Massena, *U.S.A.* **79 B10** 44 56N 74 54W
Massénya, *Chad* **51 F9** 11 21N 16 9 E
Masset, *Canada* **72 C2** 54 2N 132 10W
Massif Central, *France* **18 D5** 44 55N 3 0 E
Massillon, *U.S.A.* **78 F3** 40 48N 81 32W
Massinga, *Mozam.* **57 C6** 23 15S 35 22 E
Massingir, *Mozam.* **57 C5** 23 51S 32 4 E
Masson, *Canada* **79 A9** 45 32N 75 25W
Masson I., *Antarctica* **5 C7** 66 10S 93 20 E
Mastanli = Momchilgrad, *Bulgaria* **21 D11** 41 33N 25 23 E
Masterton, *N.Z.* **59 J5** 40 56S 175 39 E
Mastic, *U.S.A.* **79 F12** 40 47N 72 54W
Mastuj, *Pakistan* **43 A5** 36 20N 72 36 E
Mastung, *Pakistan* **40 E5** 29 50N 66 56 E
Masty, *Belarus* **17 B13** 53 27N 24 38 E
Masuda, *Japan* **31 G5** 34 40N 131 51 E
Masvingo, *Zimbabwe* **55 G3** 20 8S 30 49 E
Masvingo □, *Zimbabwe* **55 G3** 21 0S 31 30 E
Maşyāf, *Syria* **44 C3** 35 4N 36 20 E
Matabeleland, *Zimbabwe* **53 H5** 18 0S 27 0 E
Matabeleland North □, *Zimbabwe* **55 F2** 19 0S 28 0 E
Matabeleland South □, *Zimbabwe* **55 G2** 21 0S 29 0 E
Matachewan, *Canada* **70 C3** 47 56N 80 39W
Matadi, *Dem. Rep. of the Congo* **52 F2** 5 52S 13 31 E
Matagalpa, *Nic.* **88 D2** 13 0N 85 58W
Matagami, *Canada* **70 C4** 49 45N 77 34W
Matagami, L., *Canada* **70 C4** 49 50N 77 40W
Matagorda B., *U.S.A.* **81 L6** 28 40N 96 0W
Matagorda I., *U.S.A.* **81 L6** 28 15N 96 30W
Matak, *Indonesia* **39 L6** 3 18N 106 16 E
Mátala, *Greece* **23 E6** 34 59N 24 45 E
Matam, *Senegal* **50 E3** 15 34N 13 17W
Matamoros, *Campeche, Mexico* **87 D6** 18 50N 90 50W
Matamoros, *Coahuila, Mexico* **86 B4** 25 33N 103 15W
Matamoros, *Tamaulipas, Mexico* **87 B5** 25 50N 97 30W
Ma'ṭan as Sarra, *Libya* **51 D10** 21 45N 22 0 E
Matandu →, *Tanzania* **55 D3** 8 45S 34 19 E
Matane, *Canada* **71 C6** 48 50N 67 33W
Matanomadh, *India* **42 H3** 23 33N 68 57 E
Matanzas, *Cuba* **88 B3** 23 0N 81 40W
Matapa, *Botswana* **56 C3** 23 11S 24 39 E
Matapan, C. = Taínaron, Ákra, *Greece* **21 F10** 36 22N 22 27 E
Matapédia, *Canada* **71 C6** 48 0N 66 59W
Matara, *Sri Lanka* **40 S12** 5 58N 80 30 E
Mataram, *Indonesia* **36 F5** 8 35S 116 7 E
Matarani, *Peru* **92 G4** 17 0S 72 10W
Mataranka, *Australia* **60 B5** 14 55S 133 4 E
Matarma, Râs, *Egypt* **47 E1** 30 27N 32 44 E
Mataró, *Spain* **19 B7** 41 32N 2 29 E
Matatiele, *S. Africa* **57 E4** 30 20S 28 49 E
Mataura, *N.Z.* **59 M2** 46 11S 168 51 E
Matehuala, *Mexico* **86 C4** 23 40N 100 40W
Mateke Hills, *Zimbabwe* **55 G3** 21 48S 31 0 E
Matera, *Italy* **20 D7** 40 40N 16 36 E
Matetsi, *Zimbabwe* **55 F2** 18 12S 26 0 E
Mathis, *U.S.A.* **81 L6** 28 6N 97 50W
Mathráki, *Greece* **23 A3** 39 48N 19 31 E
Mathura, *India* **42 F7** 27 30N 77 40 E
Mati, *Phil.* **37 C7** 6 55N 126 15 E
Matiali, *India* **43 F13** 26 56N 88 49 E
Matías Romero, *Mexico* **87 D5** 16 53N 95 2W
Matibane, *Mozam.* **55 E5** 14 49S 40 45 E
Matima, *Botswana* **56 C3** 20 15S 24 26 E
Matiri Ra., *N.Z.* **59 J4** 41 38S 172 20 E
Matjiesfontein, *S. Africa* **56 E3** 33 14S 20 35 E
Matla →, *India* **43 J13** 21 40N 88 40 E
Matlamanyane, *Botswana* **56 B4** 19 33S 25 57 E
Matli, *Pakistan* **42 G3** 25 2N 68 39 E
Matlock, *U.K.* **10 D6** 53 9N 1 33W
Mato Grosso □, *Brazil* **93 F8** 14 0S 55 0W
Mato Grosso, Planalto do, *Brazil* **93 G8** 15 0S 55 0W
Mato Grosso do Sul □, *Brazil* **93 G8** 18 0S 55 0W
Matochkin Shar, *Russia* **26 B6** 73 10N 56 40 E
Matopo Hills, *Zimbabwe* **55 G2** 20 36S 28 20 E
Matopos, *Zimbabwe* **55 G2** 20 20S 28 29 E
Matosinhos, *Portugal* **19 B1** 41 11N 8 42W
Matroosberg, *S. Africa* **56 E2** 33 23S 19 40 E
Maţruḩ, *Oman* **46 C6** 23 37N 58 30 E
Matsue, *Japan* **31 G6** 35 25N 133 10 E
Matsumae, *Japan* **30 D10** 41 26N 140 7 E
Matsumoto, *Japan* **31 F9** 36 15N 138 0 E
Matsusaka, *Japan* **31 G8** 34 34N 136 32 E
Matsuura, *Japan* **31 H4** 33 20N 129 49 E
Matsuyama, *Japan* **31 H6** 33 45N 132 45 E
Mattagami →, *Canada* **70 B3** 50 43N 81 29W
Mattancheri, *India* **40 Q10** 9 50N 76 15 E
Mattawa, *Canada* **70 C4** 46 20N 78 45W
Matterhorn, *Switz.* **18 D7** 45 58N 7 39 E
Matthew Town, *Bahamas* **89 B5** 20 57N 73 40W
Matthew's Ridge, *Guyana* **92 B6** 7 37N 60 10W
Mattice, *Canada* **70 C3** 49 40N 83 20W
Mattituck, *U.S.A.* **79 F12** 40 59N 72 32W
Mattō, *Japan* **31 F8** 36 31N 136 34 E
Mattoon, *U.S.A.* **76 F1** 39 29N 88 23W
Matuba, *Mozam.* **57 C5** 24 28S 32 49 E
Matucana, *Peru* **92 F3** 11 55S 76 25W
Matūn = Khowst, *Afghan.* **42 C3** 33 22N 69 58 E
Maturín, *Venezuela* **92 B6** 9 45N 63 11W
Mau, *Mad. P., India* **43 F8** 26 17N 78 41 E
Mau, *Ut. P., India* **43 G10** 25 56N 83 33 E
Mau, *Ut. P., India* **43 G9** 25 17N 81 23 E
Mau Escarpment, *Kenya* **54 C4** 0 40S 36 0 E
Mau Ranipur, *India* **43 G8** 25 16N 79 8 E
Maubeuge, *France* **18 A6** 50 17N 3 57 E
Maud, Pt., *Australia* **60 D1** 23 6S 113 45 E
Maude, *Australia* **63 E3** 34 29S 144 18 E
Maudin Sun, *Burma* **41 M19** 16 0N 94 30 E
Maués, *Brazil* **92 D7** 3 20S 57 45W
Mauganj, *India* **41 G12** 24 50N 81 55 E
Maughold Hd., *U.K.* **10 C3** 54 18N 4 18W
Maui, *U.S.A.* **74 H16** 20 48N 156 20W
Maulamyaing = Moulmein, *Burma* **41 L20** 16 30N 97 40 E
Maule □, *Chile* **94 D1** 36 5S 72 30W
Maumee, *U.S.A.* **76 E4** 41 34N 83 39W
Maumee →, *U.S.A.* **76 E4** 41 42N 83 28W
Maumere, *Indonesia* **37 F6** 8 38S 122 13 E
Maun, *Botswana* **56 C3** 20 0S 23 26 E
Mauna Kea, *U.S.A.* **74 J17** 19 50N 155 28W
Mauna Loa, *U.S.A.* **74 J17** 19 30N 155 35W
Maungmagan Kyunzu, *Burma* **38 E1** 14 0N 97 48 E
Maupin, *U.S.A.* **82 D3** 45 11N 121 5W
Maurepas, L., *U.S.A.* **81 K9** 30 15N 90 30W
Maurice, L., *Australia* **61 E5** 29 30S 131 0 E
Mauricie, Parc Nat. de la, *Canada* **70 C5** 46 45N 73 0W
Mauritania ■, *Africa* **50 E3** 20 50N 10 0W
Mauritius ■, *Ind. Oc.* **49 J9** 20 0S 57 0 E
Mauston, *U.S.A.* **80 D9** 43 48N 90 5W
Mavli, *India* **42 G5** 24 45N 73 55 E
Mavuradonha Mts., *Zimbabwe* **55 F3** 16 30S 31 30 E
Mawa, *Dem. Rep. of the Congo* **54 B2** 2 45N 26 40 E
Mawai, *India* **43 H9** 22 30N 81 4 E
Mawana, *India* **42 E7** 29 6N 77 58 E
Mawand, *Pakistan* **42 E3** 29 33N 68 38 E
Mawk Mai, *Burma* **41 J20** 20 14N 97 37 E
Mawlaik, *Burma* **41 H19** 23 40N 94 26 E
Mawlamyine = Moulmein, *Burma* **41 L20** 16 30N 97 40 E
Mawqaq, *Si. Arabia* **44 E4** 27 25N 41 8 E
Mawson Coast, *Antarctica* **5 C6** 68 30S 63 0 E
Max, *U.S.A.* **80 B4** 47 49N 101 18W
Maxcanú, *Mexico* **87 C6** 20 40N 92 0W
Maxesibeni, *S. Africa* **57 E4** 30 49S 29 23 E
Maxhamish L., *Canada* **72 B4** 59 50N 123 17W
Maxixe, *Mozam.* **57 C6** 23 54S 35 17 E
Maxville, *Canada* **79 A10** 45 17N 74 51W
Maxwell, *U.S.A.* **84 F4** 39 17N 122 11W
Maxwelton, *Australia* **62 C3** 20 43S 142 41 E
May, C., *U.S.A.* **76 F8** 38 56N 74 58W
May Pen, *Jamaica* **88 C4** 17 58N 77 15W
Maya →, *Russia* **27 D14** 60 28N 134 28 E
Maya Mts., *Belize* **87 D7** 16 30N 89 0W
Mayaguana, *Bahamas* **89 B5** 22 30N 72 44W
Mayagüez, *Puerto Rico* **89 C6** 18 12N 67 9W
Mayāmey, *Iran* **45 B7** 36 24N 55 42 E
Mayanup, *Australia* **61 F2** 33 57S 116 27 E
Mayapan, *Mexico* **87 C7** 20 30N 89 25W
Mayarí, *Cuba* **89 B4** 20 40N 75 41W
Maybell, *U.S.A.* **82 F9** 40 31N 108 5W
Maybole, *U.K.* **12 F4** 55 21N 4 42W
Maydān, *Iraq* **44 C5** 34 55N 45 37 E
Maydena, *Australia* **62 G4** 42 45S 146 30 E
Mayenne →, *France* **18 C3** 47 30N 0 32W
Mayer, *U.S.A.* **83 J7** 34 24N 112 14W
Mayerthorpe, *Canada* **72 C5** 53 57N 115 8W
Mayfield, *Ky., U.S.A.* **77 G1** 36 44N 88 38W
Mayfield, *N.Y., U.S.A.* **79 C10** 43 6N 74 16W
Mayhill, *U.S.A.* **83 K11** 32 53N 105 29W
Maykop, *Russia* **25 F7** 44 35N 40 10 E
Maymyo, *Burma* **38 A1** 22 2N 96 28 E
Maynard, *Mass., U.S.A.* **79 D13** 42 26N 71 27W
Maynard, *Wash., U.S.A.* **84 C4** 47 59N 122 55W
Maynard Hills, *Australia* **61 E2** 28 28S 119 49 E
Mayne →, *Australia* **62 C3** 23 40S 141 55 E
Maynooth, *Ireland* **13 C5** 53 23N 6 34W
Mayo, *Canada* **68 B6** 63 38N 135 57W
Mayo □, *Ireland* **13 C2** 53 53N 9 3W
Mayon Volcano, *Phil.* **37 B6** 13 15N 123 41 E
Mayor I., *N.Z.* **59 G6** 37 16S 176 17 E
Mayotte, *Ind. Oc.* **53 G9** 12 50S 45 10 E
Maysville, *U.S.A.* **76 F4** 38 39N 83 46W
Mayu, *Indonesia* **37 D7** 1 30N 126 30 E
Mayville, *N. Dak., U.S.A.* **80 B6** 47 30N 97 20W
Mayville, *N.Y., U.S.A.* **78 D5** 42 15N 79 30W
Mayya, *Russia* **27 C14** 61 44N 130 18 E
Mazabuka, *Zambia* **55 F2** 15 52S 27 44 E
Mazagán = El Jadida, *Morocco* **50 B4** 33 11N 8 17W
Mazagão, *Brazil* **93 D8** 0 7S 51 16W
Mazán, *Peru* **92 D4** 3 30S 73 0W
Māzandarān □, *Iran* **45 B7** 36 30N 52 0 E
Mazapil, *Mexico* **86 C4** 24 38N 101 34W
Mazara del Vallo, *Italy* **20 F5** 37 39N 12 35 E
Mazarrón, *Spain* **19 D5** 37 38N 1 19W
Mazaruni →, *Guyana* **92 B7** 6 25N 58 35W
Mazatán, *Mexico* **86 B2** 29 0N 110 8W
Mazatenango, *Guatemala* **88 D1** 14 35N 91 30W
Mazatlán, *Mexico* **86 C3** 23 13N 106 25W
Mažeikiai, *Lithuania* **9 H20** 56 20N 22 20 E
Māzhān, *Iran* **45 C8** 32 30N 59 0 E
Mazīnān, *Iran* **45 B8** 36 19N 56 56 E
Mazoe, *Mozam.* **55 F3** 16 42S 33 7 E
Mazoe →, *Mozam.* **55 F3** 16 20S 33 30 E
Mazowe, *Zimbabwe* **55 F3** 17 28S 30 58 E
Mazurian Lakes = Mazurski, Pojezierze, *Poland* **17 B11** 53 50N 21 0 E
Mazurski, Pojezierze, *Poland* **17 B11** 53 50N 21 0 E
Mazyr, *Belarus* **17 B15** 51 59N 29 15 E
Mbabane, *Swaziland* **57 D5** 26 18S 31 6 E
Mbaïki, *C.A.R.* **52 D3** 3 53N 18 1 E
Mbala, *Zambia* **55 D3** 8 46S 31 24 E

Mbalabala

Mbalabala, *Zimbabwe* .... **57 C4** 20 27S 29 3 E
Mbale, *Uganda* .... **54 B3** 1 8N 34 12 E
Mbalmayo, *Cameroon* .... **52 D2** 3 33N 11 33 E
Mbamba Bay, *Tanzania* .... **55 E3** 11 13S 34 49 E
Mbandaka, *Dem. Rep. of the Congo* .... **52 D3** 0 1N 18 18 E
Mbanza Congo, *Angola* .... **52 F2** 6 18S 14 16 E
Mbanza Ngungu, *Dem. Rep. of the Congo* .... **52 F2** 5 12S 14 53 E
Mbarangandu, *Tanzania* .... **55 D4** 10 11S 36 48 E
Mbarara, *Uganda* .... **54 C3** 0 35S 30 40 E
Mbashe →, *S. Africa* .... **57 E4** 32 15S 28 54 E
Mbenkuru →, *Tanzania* .... **55 D4** 9 25S 39 50 E
Mberengwa, *Zimbabwe* .... **55 G2** 20 29S 29 57 E
Mberengwa, Mt., *Zimbabwe* .... **55 G2** 20 37S 29 55 E
Mbesuma, *Zambia* .... **55 E3** 10 0S 32 2 E
Mbeya, *Tanzania* .... **55 D3** 8 54S 33 29 E
Mbeya □, *Tanzania* .... **54 D3** 8 15S 33 30 E
Mbinga, *Tanzania* .... **55 E4** 10 50S 35 0 E
Mbini = Río Muni □, *Eq. Guin.* **52 D2** 1 30N 10 0 E
Mbour, *Senegal* **50 F2** 14 22N 16 54W
Mbuji-Mayi, *Dem. Rep. of the Congo* .... **54 D1** 6 9S 23 40 E
Mbulu, *Tanzania* .... **54 C4** 3 45S 35 30 E
Mburucuyá, *Argentina* **94 B4** 28 1S 58 14W
Mchinja, *Tanzania* .... **55 D4** 9 44S 39 45 E
Mchinji, *Malawi* .... **55 E3** 13 47S 32 58 E
Mdantsane, *S. Africa* .... **53 L5** 32 56S 27 46 E
Mead, L., *U.S.A.* **85 J12** 36 1N 114 44W
Meade, *U.S.A.* **81 G4** 37 17N 100 20W
Meadow Lake, *Canada* **73 C7** 54 10N 108 26W
Meadow Lake Prov. Park, *Canada* **73 C7** 54 27N 109 0W
Meadow Valley Wash →, *U.S.A.* **85 J12** 36 40N 114 34W
Meadville, *U.S.A.* **78 E4** 41 39N 80 9W
Meaford, *Canada* **78 B4** 44 36N 80 35W
Mealy Mts., *Canada* **71 B8** 53 10N 58 0W
Meander River, *Canada* **72 B5** 59 2N 117 42W
Meares, C., *U.S.A.* **82 D2** 45 37N 124 0W
Mearim →, *Brazil* **93 D10** 3 4S 44 35W
Meath □, *Ireland* **13 C5** 53 40N 6 57W
Meath Park, *Canada* **73 C7** 53 27N 105 22W
Meaux, *France* .... **18 B5** 48 58N 2 50 E
Mebechi-Gawa →, *Japan* .... **30 D10** 40 31N 141 31 E
Mecanhelas, *Mozam.* .... **55 F4** 15 12S 35 54 E
Mecca = Makkah, *Si. Arabia* .... **46 C2** 21 30N 39 54 E
Mecca, *U.S.A.* **85 M10** 33 34N 116 5W
Mechanicsburg, *U.S.A.* **78 F8** 40 13N 77 1W
Mechanicville, *U.S.A.* **79 D11** 42 54N 73 41W
Mechelen, *Belgium* .... **15 C4** 51 2N 4 29 E
Mecheria, *Algeria* **50 B5** 33 35N 0 18W
Mecklenburg, *Germany* .... **16 B6** 53 33N 11 40 E
Mecklenburger Bucht, *Germany* .... **16 A6** 54 20N 11 40 E
Meconta, *Mozam.* .... **55 E4** 14 59S 39 50 E
Medan, *Indonesia* .... **36 D1** 3 40N 98 38 E
Medanosa, Pta., *Argentina* **96 F3** 48 8S 66 0W
Médéa, *Algeria* .... **50 A6** 36 12N 2 50 E
Medellín, *Colombia* **92 B3** 6 15N 75 35W
Medelpad, *Sweden* .... **9 E17** 62 33N 16 30 E
Medemblik, *Neths.* .... **15 B5** 52 46N 5 8 E
Medford, *Mass., U.S.A.* **79 D13** 42 25N 71 7W
Medford, *Oreg., U.S.A.* **82 E2** 42 19N 122 52W
Medford, *Wis., U.S.A.* **80 C9** 45 9N 90 20W
Medgidia, *Romania* .... **17 F15** 44 15N 28 19 E
Media Agua, *Argentina* **94 C2** 31 58S 68 25W
Media Luna, *Argentina* **94 C2** 34 45S 66 44W
Medianeira, *Brazil* **95 B5** 25 17S 54 5W
Mediaş, *Romania* .... **17 E13** 46 9N 24 22 E
Medicine Bow, *U.S.A.* **82 F10** 41 54N 106 12W
Medicine Bow Pk., *U.S.A.* **82 F10** 41 21N 106 19W
Medicine Bow Ra., *U.S.A.* **82 F10** 41 10N 106 25W
Medicine Hat, *Canada* **73 D6** 50 0N 110 45W
Medicine Lake, *U.S.A.* **80 A2** 48 30N 104 30W
Medicine Lodge, *U.S.A.* **81 G5** 37 17N 98 35W
Medina = Al Madīnah, *Si. Arabia* .... **46 C2** 24 35N 39 52 E
Medina, *N. Dak., U.S.A.* **80 B5** 46 54N 99 18W
Medina, *N.Y., U.S.A.* **78 C6** 43 13N 78 23W
Medina, *Ohio, U.S.A.* **78 E3** 41 8N 81 52W
Medina →, *U.S.A.* **81 L5** 29 16N 98 29W
Medina del Campo, *Spain* **19 B3** 41 18N 4 55W
Medina L., *U.S.A.* **81 L5** 29 32N 98 56W
Medina Sidonia, *Spain* **19 D3** 36 28N 5 57W
Medinipur, *India* .... **43 H12** 22 25N 87 21 E
Mediterranean Sea, *Europe* .... **49 C5** 35 0N 15 0 E
Médoc, *France* **18 D3** 45 10N 0 50W
Medveditsa →, *Russia* .... **25 E7** 49 35N 42 41 E
Medvezhi, Ostrava, *Russia* .... **27 B17** 71 0N 161 0 E
Medvezhyegorsk, *Russia* .... **24 B5** 63 0N 34 25 E
Medway □, *U.K.* .... **11 F8** 51 25N 0 32 E
Medway →, *U.K.* .... **11 F8** 51 27N 0 46 E
Meekatharra, *Australia* .... **61 E2** 26 32S 118 29 E
Meeker, *U.S.A.* **82 F10** 40 2N 107 55W
Meelpaeg Res., *Canada* **71 C8** 48 15N 56 33W
Meerut, *India* .... **42 E7** 29 1N 77 42 E
Meeteetse, *U.S.A.* **82 D9** 44 9N 108 52W
Mega, *Ethiopia* .... **46 G2** 3 57N 38 19 E
Mégara, *Greece* .... **21 F10** 37 58N 23 22 E
Megasini, *India* .... **43 J12** 21 38N 86 21 E
Meghalaya □, *India* .... **41 G17** 25 50N 91 0 E
Mégiscane, L., *Canada* **70 C4** 48 35N 75 55W
Meharry, Mt., *Australia* .... **60 D2** 22 59S 118 35 E
Mehlville, *U.S.A.* **80 F9** 38 30N 90 19W
Mehndawal, *India* .... **43 F10** 26 58N 83 5 E
Mehr Jān, *Iran* .... **45 C7** 33 50N 55 6 E
Mehrābād, *Iran* .... **44 B5** 36 53N 47 55 E
Mehrān, *Iran* .... **44 C5** 33 7N 46 10 E
Mehrīz, *Iran* .... **45 D7** 31 35N 54 28 E
Mei Xian, *China* .... **34 G4** 34 18N 107 55 E
Meiktila, *Burma* .... **41 J19** 20 53N 95 54 E
Meissen, *Germany* .... **16 C7** 51 9N 13 29 E
Meizhou, *China* .... **33 D6** 24 16N 116 6 E
Meja, *India* .... **43 G10** 25 9N 82 7 E
Mejillones, *Chile* **94 A1** 23 10S 70 30W
Mekele, *Ethiopia* .... **46 E2** 13 33N 39 30 E
Mekhtar, *Pakistan* .... **40 D6** 30 30N 69 15 E
Meknès, *Morocco* **50 B4** 33 57N 5 33W
Mekong →, *Asia* .... **39 H6** 9 30N 106 15 E
Mekongga, *Indonesia* .... **37 E6** 3 39S 121 15 E
Mekvari = Kür →, *Azerbaijan* **25 G8** 39 29N 49 15 E
Melagiri Hills, *India* .... **40 N10** 12 20N 77 30 E
Melaka, *Malaysia* .... **39 L4** 2 15N 102 15 E
Melalap, *Malaysia* .... **36 C5** 5 10N 116 5 E
Mélambes, *Greece* .... **23 D6** 35 8N 24 40 E
Melanesia, *Pac. Oc.* .... **64 H7** 4 0S 155 0 E
Melbourne, *Australia* .... **63 F4** 37 50S 145 0 E
Melbourne, *U.S.A.* **77 L5** 28 5N 80 37W
Melchor Múzquiz, *Mexico* **86 B4** 27 50N 101 30W
Melchor Ocampo, *Mexico* **86 C4** 24 52N 101 40W
Mélèzes →, *Canada* **70 A5** 57 40N 69 29W
Melfort, *Canada* **73 C8** 52 50N 104 37W
Melfort, *Zimbabwe* .... **55 F3** 18 0S 31 25 E
Melhus, *Norway* .... **8 E14** 63 17N 10 18 E
Melilla, *N. Afr.* **19 E4** 35 21N 2 57W
Melipilla, *Chile* **94 C1** 33 42S 71 15W
Mélissa, Ákra, *Greece* .... **23 D6** 35 6N 24 33 E
Melita, *Canada* **73 D8** 49 15N 101 0W
Melitopol, *Ukraine* .... **25 E6** 46 50N 35 22 E
Melk, *Austria* .... **16 D8** 48 13N 15 20 E
Mellansel, *Sweden* .... **8 E18** 63 25N 18 17 E
Mellen, *U.S.A.* **80 B9** 46 20N 90 40W
Mellerud, *Sweden* .... **9 G15** 58 41N 12 28 E
Mellette, *U.S.A.* **80 C5** 45 9N 98 30W
Mellieha, *Malta* .... **23 D1** 35 57N 14 22 E
Melo, *Uruguay* **95 C5** 32 20S 54 10W
Melolo, *Indonesia* .... **37 F6** 9 53S 120 40 E
Melouprey, *Cambodia* .... **38 F5** 13 48N 105 16 E
Melrose, *Australia* .... **63 E4** 32 42S 146 57 E
Melrose, *U.K.* **12 F6** 55 36N 2 43W
Melrose, *Minn., U.S.A.* **80 C7** 45 40N 94 49W
Melrose, *N. Mex., U.S.A.* **81 H3** 34 26N 103 38W
Melstone, *U.S.A.* **82 C10** 46 36N 107 52W
Melton Mowbray, *U.K.* **10 E7** 52 47N 0 54W
Melun, *France* .... **18 B5** 48 32N 2 39 E
Melville, *Canada* **73 C8** 50 55N 102 50W
Melville, C., *Australia* .... **62 A3** 14 11S 144 30 E
Melville, L., *Canada* **71 B8** 53 30N 60 0W
Melville B., *Australia* .... **62 A2** 12 0S 136 45 E
Melville I., *Australia* .... **60 B5** 11 30S 131 0 E
Melville I., *Canada* **4 B2** 75 30N 112 0W
Melville Pen., *Canada* **69 B11** 68 0N 84 0W
Memba, *Mozam.* .... **55 E5** 14 11S 40 30 E
Memboro, *Indonesia* .... **37 F5** 9 30S 119 30 E
Memel = Klaipėda, *Lithuania* .... **9 J19** 55 43N 21 10 E
Memel, *S. Africa* .... **57 D4** 27 38S 29 36 E
Memmingen, *Germany* .... **16 E6** 47 58N 10 10 E
Mempawah, *Indonesia* .... **36 D3** 0 30N 109 5 E
Memphis, *Mich., U.S.A.* **78 D2** 42 54N 82 46W
Memphis, *Tenn., U.S.A.* **81 H10** 35 8N 90 3W
Memphis, *Tex., U.S.A.* **81 H4** 34 44N 100 33W
Memphremagog, L., *U.S.A.* **79 B12** 45 0N 72 12W
Mena, *U.S.A.* **81 H7** 34 35N 94 15W
Menai Strait, *U.K.* **10 D3** 53 11N 4 13W
Ménaka, *Mali* .... **50 E6** 15 59N 2 18 E
Menan = Chao Phraya →, *Thailand* .... **38 F3** 13 32N 100 36 E
Menarandra →, *Madag.* .... **57 D7** 25 17S 44 30 E
Menard, *U.S.A.* **81 K5** 30 55N 99 47W
Mendawai →, *Indonesia* .... **36 E4** 3 30S 113 0 E
Mende, *France* .... **18 D5** 44 31N 3 30 E
Mendez, *Mexico* **87 B5** 25 7N 98 34W
Mendhar, *India* .... **43 C6** 33 35N 74 10 E
Mendip Hills, *U.K.* **11 F5** 51 17N 2 40W
Mendocino, *U.S.A.* **82 G2** 39 19N 123 48W
Mendocino, C., *U.S.A.* **82 F1** 40 26N 124 25W
Mendota, *Calif., U.S.A.* **84 J6** 36 45N 120 23W
Mendota, *Ill., U.S.A.* **80 E10** 41 33N 89 7W
Mendoza, *Argentina* **94 C2** 32 50S 68 52W
Mendoza □, *Argentina* **94 C2** 33 0S 69 0W
Mene Grande, *Venezuela* **92 B4** 9 49N 70 56W
Menemen, *Turkey* .... **21 E12** 38 34N 27 3 E
Menen, *Belgium* .... **15 D3** 50 47N 3 7 E
Menggala, *Indonesia* .... **36 E3** 4 30S 105 15 E
Mengjin, *China* .... **34 G7** 34 55N 112 45 E
Mengyin, *China* .... **35 G9** 35 40N 117 58 E
Mengzi, *China* .... **32 D5** 23 20N 103 22 E
Menihek, *Canada* **71 B6** 54 28N 56 36W
Menihek L., *Canada* **71 B6** 54 0N 67 0W
Menin = Menen, *Belgium* .... **15 D3** 50 47N 3 7 E
Menindee, *Australia* .... **63 E3** 32 20S 142 25 E
Menindee L., *Australia* .... **63 E3** 32 20S 142 25 E
Meningie, *Australia* .... **63 F2** 35 50S 139 18 E
Menlo Park, *U.S.A.* **84 H4** 37 27N 122 12W
Menominee, *U.S.A.* **76 C2** 45 6N 87 37W
Menominee →, *U.S.A.* **76 C2** 45 6N 87 36W
Menomonie, *U.S.A.* **80 C9** 44 53N 91 55W
Menongue, *Angola* .... **53 G3** 14 48S 17 52 E
Menorca, *Spain* .... **22 B11** 40 0N 4 0 E
Mentakab, *Malaysia* .... **39 L4** 3 29N 102 21 E
Mentawai, Kepulauan, *Indonesia* .... **36 E1** 2 0S 99 0 E
Menton, *France* .... **18 E7** 43 50N 7 29 E
Mentor, *U.S.A.* **78 E3** 41 40N 81 21W
Menzelinsk, *Russia* .... **24 C9** 55 47N 53 11 E
Menzies, *Australia* .... **61 E3** 29 40S 121 2 E
Meob B., *Namibia* .... **56 B2** 24 25S 14 34 E
Me'ona, *Israel* .... **47 B4** 33 1N 35 15 E
Meoqui, *Mexico* **86 B3** 28 17N 105 29W
Mepaco, *Mozam.* .... **55 F3** 15 57S 30 48 E
Meppel, *Neths.* .... **15 B6** 52 42N 6 12 E
Merabéllou, Kólpos, *Greece* .... **23 D7** 35 10N 25 50 E
Merak, *Indonesia* .... **37 F12** 6 10N 106 26 E
Meramangye, L., *Australia* .... **61 E5** 28 25S 132 13 E
Meran = Merano, *Italy* .... **20 A4** 46 40N 11 9 E
Merano, *Italy* .... **20 A4** 46 40N 11 9 E
Merauke, *Indonesia* .... **37 F10** 8 29S 140 24 E
Merbein, *Australia* .... **63 E3** 34 10S 142 2 E
Merca, *Somali Rep.* .... **46 G3** 1 48N 44 50 E
Merced, *U.S.A.* **84 H6** 37 18N 120 29W
Merced →, *U.S.A.* **84 H6** 37 21N 120 59W
Merced Pk., *U.S.A.* **84 H7** 37 36N 119 24W
Mercedes, *Buenos Aires, Argentina* **94 C4** 34 40S 59 30W
Mercedes, *Corrientes, Argentina* **94 B4** 29 10S 58 5W
Mercedes, *San Luis, Argentina* **94 C2** 33 40S 65 21W
Mercedes, *Uruguay* **94 C4** 33 12S 58 0W
Mercedes, *U.S.A.* **81 M6** 26 9N 97 55W
Merceditas, *Chile* **94 B1** 28 20S 70 35W
Mercer, *N.Z.* .... **59 G5** 37 16S 175 5 E
Mercer, *U.S.A.* **78 E4** 41 14N 80 15W
Mercer Island, *U.S.A.* **84 C4** 47 35N 122 15W
Mercury, *U.S.A.* **85 J11** 36 40N 115 58W
Mercy C., *Canada* **69 B13** 65 0N 63 30W
Mere, *U.K.* **11 F5** 51 6N 2 16W
Meredith, C., *Falk. Is.* **96 G4** 52 15S 60 40W
Meredith, L., *U.S.A.* **81 H4** 35 43N 101 33W
Mergui, *Burma* .... **38 F2** 12 26N 98 34 E
Mergui Arch. = Myeik Kyunzu, *Burma* .... **39 G1** 11 30N 97 30 E
Mérida, *Mexico* **87 C7** 20 58N 89 37W
Mérida, *Spain* **19 C2** 38 55N 6 25W
Mérida, *Venezuela* **92 B4** 8 24N 71 8W
Mérida, Cord. de, *Venezuela* **92 B4** 9 0N 71 0W
Meriden, *U.K.* **11 E6** 52 26N 1 38W
Meriden, *U.S.A.* **79 E12** 41 32N 72 48W
Meridian, *Calif., U.S.A.* **84 F5** 39 9N 121 55W
Meridian, *Idaho, U.S.A.* **82 E5** 43 37N 116 24W
Meridian, *Miss., U.S.A.* **77 J1** 32 22N 88 42W
Merinda, *Australia* .... **62 C4** 20 2S 148 11 E
Merir, *Pac. Oc.* .... **37 D8** 4 10N 132 30 E
Merirumã, *Brazil* **93 C8** 1 15N 54 50W
Merkel, *U.S.A.* **81 J5** 32 28N 100 1W
Mermaid Reef, *Australia* .... **60 C2** 17 6S 119 36 E
Merredin, *Australia* .... **61 F2** 31 28S 118 18 E
Merrick, *U.K.* **12 F4** 55 8N 4 28W
Merrickville, *Canada* **79 B9** 44 55N 75 50W
Merrill, *Oreg., U.S.A.* **82 E3** 42 1N 121 36W
Merrill, *Wis., U.S.A.* **80 C10** 45 11N 89 41W
Merrimack →, *U.S.A.* **79 D14** 42 49N 70 49W
Merriman, *U.S.A.* **80 D4** 42 55N 101 42W
Merritt, *Canada* **72 C4** 50 10N 120 45W
Merritt Island, *U.S.A.* **77 L5** 28 21N 80 42W
Merriwa, *Australia* .... **63 E5** 32 6S 150 22 E
Merry I., *Canada* **70 A4** 55 29N 77 31W
Merryville, *U.S.A.* **81 K8** 30 45N 93 33W
Mersch, *Lux.* .... **15 E6** 49 44N 6 7 E
Mersea I., *U.K.* .... **11 F8** 51 47N 0 58 E
Merseburg, *Germany* .... **16 C6** 51 22N 11 59 E
Mersey →, *U.K.* **10 D4** 53 25N 3 1W
Merseyside □, *U.K.* **10 D4** 53 31N 3 2W
Mersin, *Turkey* .... **25 G5** 36 51N 34 36 E
Mersing, *Malaysia* .... **39 L4** 2 25N 103 50 E
Merta, *India* .... **42 F6** 26 39N 74 4 E
Merta Road, *India* .... **42 F5** 26 43N 73 55 E
Merthyr Tydfil, *U.K.* **11 F4** 51 45N 3 22W
Merthyr Tydfil □, *U.K.* **11 F4** 51 46N 3 21W
Mértola, *Portugal* **19 D2** 37 40N 7 40W
Mertzon, *U.S.A.* **81 K4** 31 16N 100 49W
Meru, *Kenya* .... **54 B4** 0 3N 37 40 E
Meru, *Tanzania* .... **54 C4** 3 15S 36 46 E
Mesa, *U.S.A.* **83 K8** 33 25N 111 50W
Mesa Verde Nat. Park, *U.S.A.* **83 H9** 37 11N 108 29W
Mesanagrós, *Greece* .... **23 C9** 36 1N 27 49 E
Mesaoría, *Cyprus* .... **23 D12** 35 12N 33 14 E
Mesarás, Kólpos, *Greece* .... **23 D6** 35 6N 24 47 E
Mesgouez, L., *Canada* **70 B5** 51 20N 75 0W
Meshed = Mashhad, *Iran* .... **45 B8** 36 20N 59 35 E
Meshoppen, *U.S.A.* **79 E8** 41 36N 76 3W
Mesilinka →, *Canada* **72 B4** 56 6N 124 30W
Mesilla, *U.S.A.* **83 K10** 32 16N 106 48W
Mesolóngion, *Greece* .... **21 E9** 38 21N 21 28 E
Mesopotamia = Al Jazirah, *Iraq* .... **44 C5** 33 30N 44 0 E
Mesopotamia, *U.S.A.* **78 E4** 41 27N 80 57W
Mesquite, *U.S.A.* **83 H6** 36 47N 114 6W
Messaad, *Algeria* .... **50 B6** 34 8N 3 30 E
Messalo →, *Mozam.* .... **55 E4** 12 25S 39 15 E
Messina, *Italy* .... **20 E6** 38 11N 15 34 E
Messina, *S. Africa* .... **57 C5** 22 20S 30 5 E
Messina, Str. di, *Italy* .... **20 F6** 38 15N 15 35 E
Messíni, *Greece* .... **21 F10** 37 4N 22 1 E
Messiniakós Kólpos, *Greece* .... **21 F10** 36 45N 22 5 E
Messonghi, *Greece* .... **23 B3** 39 29N 19 56 E
Mesta →, *Bulgaria* .... **21 D11** 40 54N 24 49 E
Meta →, *S. Amer.* **92 B5** 6 12N 67 28W
Meta Incognita Peninsula, *Canada* **69 B13** 62 40N 68 0W
Metabetchouan, *Canada* **71 C5** 48 26N 71 52W
Metairie, *U.S.A.* **81 L9** 29 58N 90 10W
Metaline Falls, *U.S.A.* **82 B5** 48 52N 117 22W
Metán, *Argentina* **94 B3** 25 30S 65 0W
Metangula, *Mozam.* .... **55 E3** 12 40S 34 50 E
Metengobalame, *Mozam.* .... **55 E3** 14 49S 34 30 E
Methven, *N.Z.* .... **59 K3** 43 38S 171 40 E
Metil, *Mozam.* .... **55 F4** 16 24S 39 0 E
Metlakatla, *U.S.A.* **68 C6** 55 8N 131 35W
Metropolis, *U.S.A.* **81 G10** 37 9N 88 44W
Metu, *Ethiopia* .... **46 F2** 8 18N 35 35 E
Metz, *France* .... **18 B7** 49 8N 6 10 E
Meulaboh, *Indonesia* .... **36 D1** 4 11N 96 3 E
Meureudu, *Indonesia* .... **36 C1** 5 19N 96 10 E
Meuse →, *Europe* .... **18 A6** 50 45N 5 41 E
Mexia, *U.S.A.* **81 K6** 31 41N 96 29W
Mexiana, I., *Brazil* **93 D9** 0 0 49 30W
Mexicali, *Mexico* **85 N11** 32 40N 115 30W
Mexican Plateau, *Mexico* **66 G9** 25 0N 104 0W
Mexican Water, *U.S.A.* **83 H9** 36 57N 109 32W
México, *Mexico* **87 D5** 19 20N 99 10W
Mexico, *Maine, U.S.A.* **79 B14** 44 34N 70 33W
Mexico, *Mo., U.S.A.* **80 F9** 39 10N 91 53W
Mexico, *N.Y., U.S.A.* **79 C8** 43 28N 76 18W
México □, *Mexico* **87 D5** 19 20N 99 10W
Mexico ■, *Cent. Amer.* **86 C4** 25 0N 105 0W
Mexico, G. of, *Cent. Amer.* **87 C7** 25 0N 90 0W
Mexico B., *U.S.A.* **79 C8** 43 35N 76 20W
Meydān-e Naftūn, *Iran* .... **45 D6** 31 56N 49 18 E
Meydani, Ra's-e, *Iran* .... **45 E8** 25 24N 59 6 E
Meymaneh, *Afghan.* .... **40 B4** 35 53N 64 38 E
Mezen, *Russia* .... **24 A7** 65 50N 44 20 E
Mezen →, *Russia* .... **24 A7** 65 44N 44 22 E
Mézenc, Mt., *France* .... **18 D6** 44 54N 4 11 E
Mezhdurechenskiy, *Russia* .... **26 D7** 59 36N 65 56 E
Mezőkövesd, *Hungary* .... **17 E11** 47 49N 20 35 E
Mezőtúr, *Hungary* .... **17 E11** 47 1N 20 41 E
Mezquital, *Mexico* **86 C4** 23 29N 104 23W
Mfolozi →, *S. Africa* .... **57 D5** 28 25S 32 26 E
Mgeta, *Tanzania* .... **55 D4** 8 22S 36 6 E
Mhlaba Hills, *Zimbabwe* .... **55 F3** 18 30S 30 30 E
Mhow, *India* .... **42 H6** 22 33N 75 50 E
Miahuatlán, *Mexico* **87 D5** 16 21N 96 36W
Miami, *Fla., U.S.A.* **77 N5** 25 47N 80 11W
Miami, *Okla., U.S.A.* **81 G7** 36 53N 94 53W
Miami, *Tex., U.S.A.* **81 H4** 35 42N 100 38W
Miami Beach, *U.S.A.* **77 N5** 25 47N 80 8W
Mian Xian, *China* .... **34 H4** 33 10N 106 32 E
Mianchi, *China* .... **34 G6** 34 48N 111 48 E
Mīāndarreh, *Iran* .... **45 C7** 35 37N 53 39 E
Mīāndowāb, *Iran* .... **44 B5** 37 0N 46 5 E
Miandrivazo, *Madag.* .... **57 B8** 19 31S 45 29 E
Mīāneh, *Iran* .... **44 B5** 37 30N 47 40 E
Mianwali, *Pakistan* .... **42 C4** 32 38N 71 28 E
Miarinarivo, *Antananarivo, Madag.* .... **57 B8** 18 57S 46 55 E
Miarinarivo, *Toamasina, Madag.* .... **57 B8** 16 38S 48 15 E
Miariravaratra, *Madag.* .... **57 C8** 20 13S 47 31 E
Miass, *Russia* .... **24 D11** 54 59N 60 6 E
Mica, *S. Africa* .... **57 C5** 24 10S 30 48 E
Michalovce, *Slovak Rep.* .... **17 D11** 48 47N 21 58 E
Michigan □, *U.S.A.* **76 C3** 44 0N 85 0W
Michigan, L., *U.S.A.* **76 D2** 44 0N 87 0W
Michigan City, *U.S.A.* **76 E2** 41 43N 86 54W
Michipicoten I., *Canada* **70 C2** 47 40N 85 40W
Michoacan □, *Mexico* **86 D4** 19 0N 102 0W
Michurin, *Bulgaria* .... **21 C12** 42 9N 27 51 E
Michurinsk, *Russia* .... **24 D7** 52 58N 40 27 E
Mico, Pta., *Nic.* **88 D3** 12 0N 83 30W
Micronesia, *Pac. Oc.* .... **64 G7** 11 0N 160 0 E
Micronesia, Federated States of ■, *Pac. Oc.* .... **64 G7** 9 0N 150 0 E
Midai, *Indonesia* .... **39 L6** 3 0N 107 47 E
Midale, *Canada* **73 D8** 49 25N 103 20W
Middelburg, *Neths.* .... **15 C3** 51 30N 3 36 E
Middelburg, *Eastern Cape, S. Africa* .... **56 E4** 31 30S 25 0 E
Middelburg, *Mpumalanga, S. Africa* .... **57 D4** 25 49S 29 28 E
Middelpos, *S. Africa* .... **56 E3** 31 55S 20 13 E
Middelwit, *S. Africa* .... **56 C4** 24 51S 27 3 E
Middle Alkali L., *U.S.A.* **82 F3** 41 27N 120 5W
Middle Bass I., *U.S.A.* **78 E2** 41 41N 82 49W
Middle East, *Asia* .... **28 F7** 38 0N 40 0 E
Middle Fork Feather →, *U.S.A.* **84 F5** 38 33N 121 30W
Middle I., *Australia* .... **61 F3** 34 6S 123 11 E
Middle Loup →, *U.S.A.* **80 E5** 41 17N 98 24W
Middle Sackville, *Canada* **71 D7** 44 47N 63 42W
Middleboro, *U.S.A.* **79 E14** 41 54N 70 55W
Middleburg, *Fla., U.S.A.* **77 K5** 30 4N 81 52W
Middleburg, *N.Y., U.S.A.* **79 D10** 42 36N 74 20W
Middleburg, *Pa., U.S.A.* **78 F7** 40 47N 77 3W
Middlebury, *U.S.A.* **79 B11** 44 1N 73 10W
Middlemount, *Australia* .... **62 C4** 22 50S 148 40 E
Middleport, *N.Y., U.S.A.* **78 C6** 43 13N 78 29W
Middleport, *Ohio, U.S.A.* **76 F4** 39 0N 82 3W
Middlesboro, *U.S.A.* **77 G4** 36 36N 83 43W
Middlesbrough, *U.K.* **10 C6** 54 35N 1 13W
Middlesbrough □, *U.K.* **10 C6** 54 28N 1 13W
Middlesex, *Belize* **88 C2** 17 2N 88 31W
Middlesex, *N.J., U.S.A.* **79 F10** 40 36N 74 30W
Middlesex, *N.Y., U.S.A.* **78 D7** 42 42N 77 16W
Middleton, *Australia* .... **62 C3** 22 22S 141 32 E
Middleton, *Canada* **71 D6** 44 57N 65 4W
Middleton Cr. →, *Australia* .... **62 C3** 22 35S 141 51 E
Middletown, *U.K.* **13 B5** 54 17N 6 51W
Middletown, *Calif., U.S.A.* **84 G4** 38 45N 122 37W
Middletown, *Conn., U.S.A.* **79 E12** 41 34N 72 39W
Middletown, *N.Y., U.S.A.* **79 E10** 41 27N 74 25W
Middletown, *Ohio, U.S.A.* **76 F3** 39 31N 84 24W
Middletown, *Pa., U.S.A.* **79 F8** 40 12N 76 44W
Midhurst, *U.K.* **11 G7** 50 59N 0 44W
Midi, Canal du →, *France* .... **18 E4** 43 45N 1 21 E
Midland, *Canada* **78 B5** 44 45N 79 50W
Midland, *Calif., U.S.A.* **85 M12** 33 52N 114 48W
Midland, *Mich., U.S.A.* **76 D3** 43 37N 84 14W
Midland, *Pa., U.S.A.* **78 F4** 40 39N 80 27W
Midland, *Tex., U.S.A.* **81 K3** 32 0N 102 3W
Midlands □, *Zimbabwe* .... **55 F2** 19 40S 29 0 E
Midleton, *Ireland* **13 E3** 51 55N 8 10W
Midlothian, *U.S.A.* **81 J6** 32 30N 97 0W
Midlothian □, *U.K.* **12 F5** 55 51N 3 5W
Midongy, Tangorombohitr' i, *Madag.* .... **57 C8** 23 30S 47 0 E
Midongy Atsimo, *Madag.* .... **57 C8** 23 35S 47 1 E
Midway Is., *Pac. Oc.* **64 E10** 28 13N 177 22W
Midway Wells, *U.S.A.* **85 N11** 32 41N 115 7W
Midwest, *U.S.A.* **82 E10** 43 25N 106 16W
Midwest City, *U.S.A.* **81 H6** 35 27N 97 24W
Midyat, *Turkey* .... **44 B4** 37 25N 41 23 E
Midžor, *Bulgaria* .... **21 C10** 43 24N 22 40 E
Mie □, *Japan* .... **31 G8** 34 30N 136 10 E
Międzychód, *Poland* .... **16 B8** 52 35N 15 53 E
Międzyrzec Podlaski, *Poland* .... **17 C12** 51 58N 22 45 E
Mielec, *Poland* .... **17 C11** 50 15N 21 25 E
Mienga, *Angola* .... **56 B2** 17 12S 19 48 E
Miercurea-Ciuc, *Romania* .... **17 E13** 46 21N 25 48 E
Mieres, *Spain* **19 A3** 43 18N 5 48W
Mifflintown, *U.S.A.* **78 F7** 40 34N 77 24W
Mifraz Hefa, *Israel* .... **47 C4** 32 52N 35 0 E
Miguel Alemán, Presa, *Mexico* **87 D5** 18 15N 96 40W
Mihara, *Japan* .... **31 G6** 34 24N 133 5 E
Mikese, *Tanzania* .... **54 D4** 6 48S 37 55 E
Mikhaylovgrad = Montana, *Bulgaria* .... **21 C10** 43 27N 23 16 E
Mikhaylovka, *Russia* .... **25 D7** 50 3N 43 5 E
Mikkeli, *Finland* .... **9 F22** 61 43N 27 15 E
Mikkwa →, *Canada* **72 B6** 58 25N 114 46W
Mikonos, *Greece* .... **21 F11** 37 30N 25 25 E
Mikumi, *Tanzania* .... **54 D4** 7 26S 37 0 E
Mikun, *Russia* .... **24 B9** 62 20N 50 0 E
Milaca, *U.S.A.* **80 C8** 45 45N 93 39W
Milagro, *Ecuador* **92 D3** 2 11S 79 36W
Milan = Milano, *Italy* .... **18 D8** 45 28N 9 12 E
Milan, *Mo., U.S.A.* **80 E8** 40 12N 93 7W
Milan, *Tenn., U.S.A.* **77 H1** 35 55N 88 46W
Milange, *Mozam.* .... **55 F4** 16 3S 35 45 E
Milano, *Italy* .... **18 D8** 45 28N 9 12 E
Milanoa, *Madag.* .... **57 A8** 13 35S 49 47 E
Milâs, *Turkey* .... **21 F12** 37 20N 27 50 E
Milatos, *Greece* .... **23 D7** 35 18N 25 34 E
Milazzo, *Italy* .... **20 E6** 38 13N 15 15 E
Milbank, *U.S.A.* **80 C6** 45 13N 96 38W
Milbanke Sd., *Canada* **72 C3** 52 15N 128 35W
Milden, *Canada* **73 C7** 51 29N 107 32W
Mildenhall, *U.K.* .... **11 E8** 52 21N 0 32 E
Mildmay, *Canada* **78 B3** 44 3N 81 7W
Mildura, *Australia* .... **63 E3** 34 13S 142 9 E
Miles, *Australia* .... **63 D5** 26 40S 150 9 E
Miles City, *U.S.A.* **80 B2** 46 25N 105 51W
Milestone, *Canada* **73 D8** 49 59N 104 31W
Miletus, *Turkey* .... **21 F12** 37 30N 27 18 E
Milford, *Calif., U.S.A.* **84 E6** 40 10N 120 22W
Milford, *Conn., U.S.A.* **79 E11** 41 14N 73 3W
Milford, *Del., U.S.A.* **76 F8** 38 55N 75 26W
Milford, *Mass., U.S.A.* **79 D13** 42 8N 71 31W
Milford, *N.H., U.S.A.* **79 D13** 42 50N 71 39W
Milford, *Pa., U.S.A.* **79 E10** 41 19N 74 48W
Milford, *Utah, U.S.A.* **83 G7** 38 24N 113 1W

Mono L.

Milford Haven, U.K. 11 F2 51 42N 5 7W
Milford Sd., N.Z. 59 L1 44 41S 167 47 E
Milḥ, Baḥr al, Iraq 44 C4 32 40N 43 35 E
Milikapiti, Australia 60 B5 11 26S 130 40 E
Miling, Australia 61 F2 30 30S 116 17 E
Milk →, U.S.A. 82 B10 48 4N 106 19W
Milk River, Canada 72 D6 49 10N 112 5W
Mill I., Antarctica 5 C8 66 0S 101 30 E
Mill Valley, U.S.A. 84 H4 37 54N 122 32W
Millau, France 18 D5 44 8N 3 4 E
Millbridge, Canada 78 B7 44 41N 77 36W
Millbrook, Canada 78 B6 44 10N 78 29W
Millbrook, U.S.A. 79 E11 41 47N 73 42W
Mille Lacs, L. des, Canada 70 C1 48 45N 90 35W
Mille Lacs L., U.S.A. 80 B8 46 15N 93 39W
Milledgeville, U.S.A. 77 J4 33 5N 83 14W
Millen, U.S.A. 77 J5 32 48N 81 57W
Millennium I. = Caroline I., Kiribati 65 H12 9 58S 150 13W
Miller, U.S.A. 80 C5 44 31N 98 59W
Millersburg, Ohio, U.S.A. 78 F3 40 33N 81 55W
Millersburg, Pa., U.S.A. 78 F8 40 32N 76 58W
Millerton, U.S.A. 79 E11 41 57N 73 31W
Millerton L., U.S.A. 84 J7 37 1N 119 41W
Millheim, U.S.A. 78 F7 40 54N 77 29W
Millicent, Australia 63 F3 37 34S 140 21 E
Millington, U.S.A. 81 H10 35 20N 89 53W
Millinocket, U.S.A. 77 C11 45 39N 68 43W
Millmerran, Australia 63 D5 27 53S 151 16 E
Millom, U.K. 10 C4 54 13N 3 16W
Mills L., Canada 72 A5 61 30N 118 20W
Millsboro, U.S.A. 78 G5 40 0N 80 0W
Milltown Malbay, Ireland 13 D2 52 52N 9 24W
Millville, N.J., U.S.A. 76 F8 39 24N 75 2W
Millville, Pa., U.S.A. 79 E8 41 7N 76 32W
Millwood L., U.S.A. 81 J8 33 42N 93 58W
Milne →, Australia 62 C2 21 10S 137 33 E
Milo, U.S.A. 77 C11 45 15N 68 59W
Mílos, Greece 21 F11 36 44N 24 25 E
Milparinka, Australia 63 D3 29 46S 141 57 E
Milton, N.S., Canada 71 D7 44 4N 64 45W
Milton, Ont., Canada 78 C5 43 31N 79 53W
Milton, N.Z. 59 M2 46 7S 169 59 E
Milton, Calif., U.S.A. 84 G6 38 3N 120 51W
Milton, Fla., U.S.A. 77 K2 30 38N 87 3W
Milton, Pa., U.S.A. 78 F8 41 1N 76 51W
Milton, Vt., U.S.A. 79 B11 44 38N 73 7W
Milton-Freewater, U.S.A. 82 D4 45 56N 118 23W
Milton Keynes, U.K. 11 E7 52 1N 0 44W
Milton Keynes □, U.K. 11 E7 52 1N 0 44W
Milverton, Canada 78 C4 43 34N 80 55W
Milwaukee, U.S.A. 76 D2 43 2N 87 55W
Milwaukee Deep, Atl. Oc. 89 C6 19 50N 68 0W
Milwaukie, U.S.A. 84 E4 45 27N 122 38W
Min Jiang →, Fujian, China 33 D6 26 0N 119 35 E
Min Jiang →, Sichuan, China 32 D5 28 45N 104 40 E
Min Xian, China 34 G3 34 25N 104 5 E
Mina Pirquitas, Argentina 94 A2 22 40S 66 30W
Mīnā Su'ud, Si. Arabia 45 D6 28 45N 48 28 E
Mīnā'al Aḥmadī, Kuwait 45 D6 29 5N 48 10 E
Minago →, Canada 73 C9 54 33N 98 59W
Minaki, Canada 73 D10 49 59N 94 40W
Minamata, Japan 31 H5 32 10N 130 30 E
Minami-Tori-Shima, Pac. Oc. 64 E7 24 20N 153 58 E
Minas, Uruguay 95 C4 34 20S 55 10W
Minas, Sierra de las, Guatemala 88 C2 15 9N 89 31W
Minas Basin, Canada 71 C7 45 20N 64 12W
Minas Gerais □, Brazil 93 G9 18 50S 46 0W
Minatitlán, Mexico 87 D6 17 59N 94 31W
Minbu, Burma 41 J19 20 10N 94 52 E
Minchinabad, Pakistan 42 D5 30 10N 73 34 E
Mindanao, Phil. 37 C6 8 0N 125 0 E
Mindanao Sea = Bohol Sea, Phil. 37 C6 9 0N 124 0 E
Mindanao Trench, Pac. Oc. 37 B7 12 0N 126 6 E
Minden, Canada 78 B6 44 55N 78 43W
Minden, Germany 16 B5 52 17N 8 55 E
Minden, La., U.S.A. 81 J8 32 37N 93 17W
Minden, Nev., U.S.A. 84 G7 38 57N 119 46W
Mindiptana, Indonesia 37 F10 5 55S 140 22 E
Mindoro, Phil. 37 B6 13 0N 121 0 E
Mindoro Str., Phil. 37 B6 12 30N 120 30 E
Mine, Japan 31 G5 34 12N 131 7 E
Minehead, U.K. 11 F4 51 12N 3 29W
Mineola, N.Y., U.S.A. 79 F11 40 45N 73 39W
Mineola, Tex., U.S.A. 81 J7 32 40N 95 29W
Mineral King, U.S.A. 84 J8 36 27N 118 36W
Mineral Wells, U.S.A. 81 J5 32 48N 98 7W
Minersville, U.S.A. 79 F8 40 41N 76 16W
Minerva, U.S.A. 78 F3 40 44N 81 6W
Minetto, U.S.A. 79 C8 43 24N 76 28W
Mingäçevir Su Anbarı, Azerbaijan 25 F8 40 57N 46 50 E
Mingan, Canada 71 B7 50 20N 64 0W
Mingechaurskoye Vdkhr. = Mingäçevir Su Anbarı, Azerbaijan 25 F8 40 57N 46 50 E
Mingela, Australia 62 B4 19 52S 146 38 E
Mingenew, Australia 61 E2 29 12S 115 21 E
Mingera Cr. →, Australia 62 C2 20 38S 137 45 E
Mingin, Burma 41 H19 22 50N 94 30 E
Mingo Junction, U.S.A. 78 F4 40 19N 80 37W
Mingteke Daban = Mintaka Pass, Pakistan 43 A6 37 0N 74 58 E
Mingyuegue, China 35 C15 43 2N 128 50 E
Minho = Miño →, Spain 19 A2 41 52N 8 40W
Minho, Portugal 19 B1 41 25N 8 20W
Minidoka, U.S.A. 82 E7 42 45N 113 29W
Minigwal, L., Australia 61 E3 29 31S 123 14 E
Minilya →, Australia 61 D1 23 45S 114 0 E
Minilya Roadhouse, Australia 61 D1 23 55S 114 0 E
Minipi L., Canada 71 B7 52 25N 60 45W
Mink L., Canada 72 A5 61 54N 117 40W
Minna, Nigeria 50 G7 9 37N 6 30 E
Minneapolis, Kans., U.S.A. 80 F6 39 8N 97 42W
Minneapolis, Minn., U.S.A. 80 C8 44 59N 93 16W
Minnedosa, Canada 73 C9 50 14N 99 50W
Minnesota □, U.S.A. 80 B8 46 0N 94 15W
Minnesota →, U.S.A. 80 C8 44 54N 93 9W
Minnewaukan, U.S.A. 80 A5 48 4N 99 15W
Minnipa, Australia 63 E2 32 51S 135 9 E
Minnitaki L., Canada 70 C1 49 57N 92 10W
Mino, Japan 31 G8 35 32N 136 55 E
Miño →, Spain 19 A2 41 52N 8 40W
Minorca = Menorca, Spain 22 B11 40 0N 4 0 E
Minot, U.S.A. 80 A4 48 14N 101 18W
Minqin, China 34 E2 38 38N 103 20 E
Minsk, Belarus 17 B14 53 52N 27 30 E
Mińsk Mazowiecki, Poland 17 B11 52 10N 21 33 E
Mintabie, Australia 63 D1 27 15S 133 7 E
Mintaka Pass, Pakistan 43 A6 37 0N 74 58 E
Minto, Canada 71 C6 46 5N 66 5W
Minto, L., Canada 70 A5 57 13N 75 0W
Minton, Canada 73 D8 49 10N 104 35W
Minturn, U.S.A. 82 G10 39 35N 106 26W
Minusinsk, Russia 27 D10 53 43N 91 20 E
Minutang, India 41 E20 28 15N 96 30 E
Miquelon, Canada 70 C4 49 25N 76 27W
Miquelon, St- P. & M. 71 C8 47 8N 56 22W
Mīr Kūh, Iran 45 E8 26 22N 58 55 E
Mīr Shahdād, Iran 45 E8 26 15N 58 29 E
Mira, Italy 20 B5 45 26N 12 8 E
Mira por vos Cay, Bahamas 89 B5 22 9N 74 30W
Miraj, India 40 L9 16 50N 74 45 E
Miram Shah, Pakistan 42 C4 33 0N 70 2 E
Miramar, Argentina 94 D4 38 15S 57 50W
Miramar, Mozam. 57 C6 23 50S 35 35 E
Miramichi, Canada 71 C6 47 2N 65 28W
Miramichi B., Canada 71 C7 47 15N 65 0W
Miranda, Brazil 93 H7 20 10S 56 15W
Miranda →, Brazil 92 G7 19 25S 57 20W
Miranda de Ebro, Spain 19 A4 42 41N 2 57W
Miranda do Douro, Portugal 19 B2 41 30N 6 16W
Mirandópolis, Brazil 95 A5 21 9S 51 6W
Mirango, Malawi 55 E3 13 32S 34 58 E
Mirassol, Brazil 95 A6 20 46S 49 28W
Mirbāṭ, Oman 46 D5 17 0N 54 45 E
Miri, Malaysia 36 D4 4 23N 113 59 E
Miriam Vale, Australia 62 C5 24 20S 151 33 E
Mirim, L., S. Amer. 95 C5 32 45S 52 50W
Mirnyy, Russia 27 C12 62 33N 113 53 E
Mirokhan, Pakistan 42 F3 27 46N 68 6 E
Mirond L., Canada 73 B8 55 6N 102 47W
Mirpur, Pakistan 43 C5 33 32N 73 56 E
Mirpur Batoro, Pakistan 42 G3 24 44N 68 16 E
Mirpur Bibiwari, Pakistan 42 E2 28 33N 67 44 E
Mirpur Khas, Pakistan 42 G3 25 30N 69 0 E
Mirpur Sakro, Pakistan 42 G2 24 33N 67 41 E
Mirtağ, Turkey 44 B4 38 23N 41 56 E
Miryang, S. Korea 35 G15 35 31N 128 44 E
Mirzapur, India 43 G10 25 10N 82 34 E
Mirzapur-cum-Vindhyachal = Mirzapur, India 43 G10 25 10N 82 34 E
Misantla, Mexico 87 D5 19 56N 96 50W
Misawa, Japan 30 D10 40 41N 141 24 E
Miscou I., Canada 71 C7 47 57N 64 31W
Mish'āb, Ra's al, Si. Arabia 45 D6 28 15N 48 43 E
Mishan, China 33 B8 45 37N 131 48 E
Mishawaka, U.S.A. 76 E2 41 40N 86 11W
Mishima, Japan 31 G9 35 10N 138 52 E
Misión, Mexico 85 N10 32 6N 116 53W
Misiones □, Argentina 95 B5 27 0S 55 0W
Misiones □, Paraguay 94 B4 27 0S 56 0W
Miskah, Si. Arabia 44 E4 24 49N 42 56 E
Miskitos, Cayos, Nic. 88 D3 14 26N 82 50W
Miskolc, Hungary 17 D11 48 7N 20 50 E
Misoke, Dem. Rep. of the Congo 54 C2 0 42S 28 2 E
Misool, Indonesia 37 E8 1 52S 130 10 E
Mişrātah, Libya 51 B9 32 24N 15 3 E
Missanabie, Canada 70 C3 48 20N 84 6W
Missinaibi →, Canada 70 B3 50 43N 81 29W
Missinaibi L., Canada 70 C3 48 23N 83 40W
Mission, Canada 72 D4 49 10N 122 15W
Mission, S. Dak., U.S.A. 80 D4 43 18N 100 39W
Mission, Tex., U.S.A. 81 M5 26 13N 98 20W
Mission Beach, Australia 62 B4 17 53S 146 6 E
Mission Viejo, U.S.A. 85 M9 33 36N 117 40W
Missisa L., Canada 70 B2 52 20N 85 7W
Missisicabi →, Canada 70 B4 51 14N 79 31W
Mississagi →, Canada 70 C3 46 15N 83 9W
Mississauga, Canada 78 C5 43 32N 79 35W
Mississippi □, U.S.A. 81 J10 33 0N 90 0W
Mississippi →, U.S.A. 81 L10 29 9N 89 15W
Mississippi L., Canada 79 A8 45 5N 76 10W
Mississippi River Delta, U.S.A. 81 L9 29 10N 89 15W
Mississippi Sd., U.S.A. 81 K10 30 20N 89 0W
Missoula, U.S.A. 82 C7 46 52N 114 1W
Missouri □, U.S.A. 80 F8 38 25N 92 30W
Missouri →, U.S.A. 80 F9 38 49N 90 7W
Missouri City, U.S.A. 81 L7 29 37N 95 32W
Missouri Valley, U.S.A. 80 E7 41 34N 95 53W
Mist, U.S.A. 84 E3 45 59N 123 15W
Mistassibi →, Canada 71 B5 48 53N 72 13W
Mistassini, Canada 71 C5 48 53N 72 12W
Mistassini →, Canada 71 C5 48 42N 72 20W
Mistassini, L., Canada 70 B5 51 0N 73 30W
Mistastin L., Canada 71 A7 55 57N 63 20W
Mistinibi, L., Canada 71 A7 55 56N 64 17W
Misty L., Canada 73 B8 58 53N 101 40W
Misurata = Mişrātah, Libya 51 B9 32 24N 15 3 E
Mitchell, Australia 63 D4 26 29S 147 58 E
Mitchell, Canada 78 C3 43 28N 81 12W
Mitchell, Nebr., U.S.A. 80 E3 41 57N 103 49W
Mitchell, Oreg., U.S.A. 82 D3 44 34N 120 9W
Mitchell, S. Dak., U.S.A. 80 D6 43 43N 98 2W
Mitchell →, Australia 62 B3 15 12S 141 35 E
Mitchell, Mt., U.S.A. 77 H4 35 46N 82 16W
Mitchell Ranges, Australia 62 A2 12 49S 135 36 E
Mitchelstown, Ireland 13 D3 52 15N 8 16W
Mitha Tiwana, Pakistan 42 C5 32 13N 72 6 E
Mithi, Pakistan 42 G3 24 44N 69 48 E
Mithrao, Pakistan 42 F3 27 28N 69 40 E
Mitilíni, Greece 21 E12 39 6N 26 35 E
Mito, Japan 31 F10 36 20N 140 30 E
Mitrovica = Kosovska Mitrovica, Kosovo, Yug. 21 C9 42 54N 20 52 E
Mitsinjo, Madag. 57 B8 16 1S 45 52 E
Mitsiwa, Eritrea 46 D2 15 35N 39 25 E
Mitsukaidō, Japan 31 F9 36 1N 139 59 E
Mittagong, Australia 63 E5 34 28S 150 29 E
Mittimatalik = Pond Inlet, Canada 69 A12 72 40N 77 0W
Mitú, Colombia 92 C4 1 15N 70 13W
Mitumba, Tanzania 54 D3 7 8S 31 2 E
Mitumba, Mts., Dem. Rep. of the Congo 54 D2 7 0S 27 30 E
Mitwaba, Dem. Rep. of the Congo 55 D2 8 2S 27 17 E
Mityana, Uganda 54 B3 0 23N 32 2 E
Mixteco →, Mexico 87 D5 18 11N 98 30W
Miyagi □, Japan 30 E10 38 15N 140 45 E
Miyāh, W. el →, Syria 44 C3 34 44N 39 57 E
Miyake-Jima, Japan 31 G9 34 5N 139 30 E
Miyako, Japan 30 E10 39 40N 141 59 E
Miyako-Jima, Japan 31 M2 24 45N 125 20 E
Miyako-Rettō, Japan 31 M2 24 24N 125 0 E
Miyakonojō, Japan 31 J5 31 40N 131 5 E
Miyani, India 42 J3 21 50N 69 26 E
Miyanoura-Dake, Japan 31 J5 30 20N 130 31 E
Miyazaki, Japan 31 J5 31 56N 131 30 E
Miyazaki □, Japan 31 H5 32 30N 131 30 E
Miyazu, Japan 31 G7 35 35N 135 10 E
Miyet, Bahr el = Dead Sea, Asia 47 D4 31 30N 35 30 E
Miyoshi, Japan 31 G6 34 48N 132 51 E
Miyun, China 34 D9 40 28N 116 50 E
Miyun Shuiku, China 35 D9 40 30N 117 0 E
Mizdah, Libya 51 B8 31 30N 13 0 E
Mizen Hd., Cork, Ireland 13 E2 51 27N 9 50W
Mizen Hd., Wick., Ireland 13 D5 52 51N 6 4W
Mizhi, China 34 F6 37 47N 110 12 E
Mizoram □, India 41 H18 23 30N 92 40 E
Mizpe Ramon, Israel 47 E3 30 34N 34 49 E
Mizusawa, Japan 30 E10 39 8N 141 8 E
Mjölby, Sweden 9 G16 58 20N 15 10 E
Mjøsa, Norway 9 F14 60 40N 11 0 E
Mkata, Tanzania 54 D4 5 45S 38 20 E
Mkokotoni, Tanzania 54 D4 5 55S 39 15 E
Mkomazi, Tanzania 54 C4 4 40S 38 7 E
Mkomazi →, S. Africa 57 E5 30 12S 30 50 E
Mkulwe, Tanzania 55 D3 8 37S 32 20 E
Mkumbi, Ras, Tanzania 54 D4 7 38S 39 55 E
Mkushi, Zambia 55 E2 14 25S 29 15 E
Mkushi River, Zambia 55 E2 13 32S 29 45 E
Mkuze, S. Africa 57 D5 27 10S 32 0 E
Mladá Boleslav, Czech Rep. 16 C8 50 27N 14 53 E
Mlala Hills, Tanzania 54 D3 6 50S 31 40 E
Mlange = Mulanje, Malawi 55 F4 16 2S 35 33 E
Mlanje, Pic, Malawi 53 H7 15 57S 35 38 E
Mława, Poland 17 B11 53 9N 20 25 E
Mljet, Croatia 20 C7 42 43N 17 30 E
Mmabatho, S. Africa 56 D4 25 49S 25 30 E
Mo i Rana, Norway 8 C16 66 20N 14 7 E
Moa, Cuba 89 B4 20 40N 74 56W
Moa, Indonesia 37 F7 8 0S 128 0 E
Moab, U.S.A. 83 G9 38 35N 109 33W
Moala, Fiji 59 D8 18 36S 179 53 E
Moama, Australia 63 F3 36 7S 144 46 E
Moamba, Mozam. 57 D5 25 36S 32 15 E
Moapa, U.S.A. 85 J12 36 40N 114 37W
Moate, Ireland 13 C4 53 24N 7 44W
Moba, Dem. Rep. of the Congo 54 D2 7 0S 29 48 E
Mobārakābād, Iran 45 D7 28 24N 53 20 E
Mobaye, C.A.R. 52 D4 4 25N 21 5 E
Mobayi, Dem. Rep. of the Congo 52 D4 4 15N 21 8 E
Moberley Lake, Canada 72 B4 55 50N 121 44W
Moberly, U.S.A. 80 F8 39 25N 92 26W
Mobile, U.S.A. 77 K1 30 41N 88 3W
Mobile B., U.S.A. 77 K2 30 30N 88 0W
Mobridge, U.S.A. 80 C4 45 32N 100 26W
Mobutu Sese Seko, L. = Albert, L., Africa 54 B3 1 30N 31 0 E
Moc Chau, Vietnam 38 B5 20 50N 104 38 E
Moc Hoa, Vietnam 39 G5 10 46N 105 56 E
Mocabe Kasari, Dem. Rep. of the Congo 55 D2 9 58S 26 12 E
Moçambique, Mozam. 55 F5 15 3S 40 42 E
Moçâmedes = Namibe, Angola 53 H2 15 7S 12 11 E
Mocanaqua, U.S.A. 79 E8 41 9N 76 8W
Mochudi, Botswana 56 C4 24 27S 26 7 E
Mocimboa da Praia, Mozam. 55 E5 11 25S 40 20 E
Moclips, U.S.A. 84 C2 47 14N 124 13W
Mocoa, Colombia 92 C3 1 7N 76 35W
Mococa, Brazil 95 A6 21 28S 47 0W
Mocorito, Mexico 86 B3 25 30N 107 53W
Moctezuma, Mexico 86 B3 29 50N 109 0W
Moctezuma →, Mexico 87 C5 21 59N 98 34W
Mocuba, Mozam. 55 F4 16 54S 36 57 E
Mocúzari, Presa, Mexico 86 B3 27 10N 109 10W
Modane, France 18 D7 45 12N 6 40 E
Modasa, India 42 H5 23 30N 73 21 E
Modder →, S. Africa 56 D3 29 2S 24 37 E
Modderrivier, S. Africa 56 D3 29 2S 24 38 E
Módena, Italy 20 B4 44 40N 10 55 E
Modena, U.S.A. 83 H7 37 48N 113 56W
Modesto, U.S.A. 84 H6 37 39N 121 0W
Módica, Italy 20 F6 36 52N 14 46 E
Moe, Australia 63 F4 38 12S 146 19 E
Moebase, Mozam. 55 F4 17 3S 38 41 E
Moengo, Surinam 93 B8 5 45N 54 20W
Moffat, U.K. 12 F5 55 21N 3 27W
Moga, India 42 D6 30 48N 75 8 E
Mogadishu = Muqdisho, Somali Rep. 46 G4 2 2N 45 25 E
Mogador = Essaouira, Morocco 50 B4 31 32N 9 42W
Mogalakwena →, S. Africa 57 C4 22 38S 28 40 E
Mogami-Gawa →, Japan 30 E10 38 45N 140 0 E
Mogán, Canary Is. 22 G4 27 53N 15 43W
Mogaung, Burma 41 G20 25 20N 97 0 E
Mogi das Cruzes, Brazil 95 A6 23 31S 46 11W
Mogi-Guaçu →, Brazil 95 A6 20 53S 48 10W
Mogi-Mirim, Brazil 95 A6 22 29S 47 0W
Mogilev = Mahilyow, Belarus 17 B16 53 55N 30 18 E
Mogilev-Podolskiy = Mohyliv-Podilskyy, Ukraine 17 D14 48 26N 27 48 E
Mogincual, Mozam. 55 F5 15 35S 40 25 E
Mogocha, Russia 27 D12 53 40N 119 50 E
Mogok, Burma 41 H20 23 0N 96 40 E
Mogollon Rim, U.S.A. 83 J8 34 10N 110 50W
Mogumber, Australia 61 F2 31 2S 116 3 E
Mohács, Hungary 17 F10 45 58N 18 41 E
Mohales Hoek, Lesotho 56 E4 30 7S 27 26 E
Mohall, U.S.A. 80 A4 48 46N 101 31W
Moḥammadābād, Iran 45 B8 37 52N 59 5 E
Mohammedia, Morocco 50 B4 33 44N 7 21W
Mohana →, India 43 G11 24 43N 85 0 E
Mohanlalganj, India 43 F9 26 41N 80 58 E
Mohave, L., U.S.A. 85 K12 35 12N 114 34W
Mohawk →, U.S.A. 79 D11 42 47N 73 41W
Mohenjodaro, Pakistan 42 F3 27 19N 68 7 E
Mohicanville Reservoir, U.S.A. 78 F3 40 45N 82 0W
Mohoro, Tanzania 54 D4 8 6S 39 8 E
Mohyliv-Podilskyy, Ukraine 17 D14 48 26N 27 48 E
Moidart, L., U.K. 12 E3 56 47N 5 52W
Moira →, Canada 78 B7 44 21N 77 24W
Moires, Greece 23 D6 35 4N 24 56 E
Moisaküla, Estonia 9 G21 58 3N 25 12 E
Moisie, Canada 71 B6 50 12N 66 1W
Moisie →, Canada 71 B6 50 14N 66 5W
Mojave, U.S.A. 85 K8 35 3N 118 10W
Mojave Desert, U.S.A. 85 L10 35 0N 116 30W
Mojo, Bolivia 94 A2 21 48S 65 33W
Mojokerto, Indonesia 37 G15 7 28S 112 26 E
Mokai, N.Z. 59 H5 38 32S 175 56 E
Mokambo, Dem. Rep. of the Congo 55 E2 12 25S 28 20 E
Mokameh, India 43 G11 25 24N 85 55 E
Mokau, N.Z. 59 H5 38 42S 174 39 E
Mokelumne →, U.S.A. 84 G5 38 13N 121 28W
Mokelumne Hill, U.S.A. 84 G6 38 18N 120 43W
Mokhós, Greece 23 D7 35 16N 25 27 E
Mokhotlong, Lesotho 57 D4 29 22S 29 2 E
Mokokchung, India 41 F19 26 15N 94 30 E
Mokolo →, S. Africa 57 C4 23 14S 27 43 E
Mokp'o, S. Korea 35 G14 34 50N 126 25 E
Mokra Gora, Yugoslavia 21 C9 42 50N 20 30 E
Mol, Belgium 15 C5 51 11N 5 5 E
Molchanovo, Russia 26 D9 57 40N 83 50 E
Mold, U.K. 10 D4 53 9N 3 8W
Moldavia = Moldova ■, Europe 17 E15 47 0N 28 0 E
Molde, Norway 8 E12 62 45N 7 9 E
Moldova ■, Europe 17 E15 47 0N 28 0 E
Moldoveanu, Vf., Romania 17 F13 45 36N 24 45 E
Mole →, U.K. 11 F7 51 24N 0 21W
Mole Creek, Australia 62 G4 41 34S 146 24 E
Molepolole, Botswana 56 C4 24 28S 25 28 E
Molfetta, Italy 20 D7 41 12N 16 36 E
Moline, U.S.A. 80 E9 41 30N 90 31W
Molinos, Argentina 94 B2 25 28S 66 15W
Moliro, Dem. Rep. of the Congo 54 D3 8 12S 30 30 E
Mollendo, Peru 92 G4 17 0S 72 0W
Mollerin, L., Australia 61 F2 30 30S 117 35 E
Molodechno = Maladzyechna, Belarus 17 A14 54 20N 26 50 E
Molokai, U.S.A. 74 H16 21 8N 157 0W
Molong, Australia 63 E4 33 5S 148 54 E
Molopo →, Africa 56 D3 27 30S 20 13 E
Molotov = Perm, Russia 24 C10 58 0N 56 10 E
Molson L., Canada 73 C9 54 22N 96 40W
Molteno, S. Africa 56 E4 31 22S 26 22 E
Molu, Indonesia 37 F8 6 45S 131 40 E
Molucca Sea, Indonesia 37 E6 0 0 125 0 E
Moluccas = Maluku, Indonesia 37 E7 1 0S 127 0 E
Moma, Dem. Rep. of the Congo 54 C1 1 35S 23 52 E
Moma, Mozam. 55 F4 16 47S 39 4 E
Mombasa, Kenya 54 C4 4 2S 39 43 E
Mombetsu, Japan 30 B11 44 21N 143 22 E
Momchilgrad, Bulgaria 21 D11 41 33N 25 23 E
Momi, Dem. Rep. of the Congo 54 C2 1 42S 27 0 E
Mompós, Colombia 92 B4 9 14N 74 26W
Møn, Denmark 9 J15 54 57N 12 20 E
Mon □, Burma 41 L20 16 0N 97 30 E
Mona, Canal de la, W. Indies 89 C6 18 30N 67 45W
Mona, Isla, Puerto Rico 89 C6 18 5N 67 54W
Mona, Pta., Costa Rica 88 E3 9 37N 82 36W
Monaca, U.S.A. 78 F4 40 41N 80 17W
Monaco ■, Europe 18 E7 43 46N 7 23 E
Monadhliath Mts., U.K. 12 D4 57 10N 4 4W
Monadnock, Mt., U.S.A. 79 D12 42 52N 72 7W
Monaghan, Ireland 13 B5 54 15N 6 57W
Monaghan □, Ireland 13 B5 54 11N 6 56W
Monahans, U.S.A. 81 K3 31 36N 102 54W
Monapo, Mozam. 55 E5 14 56S 40 19 E
Monar, L., U.K. 12 D3 57 26N 5 8W
Monarch Mt., Canada 72 C3 51 55N 125 57W
Monashee Mts., Canada 72 C5 51 0N 118 43W
Monasterevin, Ireland 13 C4 53 8N 7 4W
Monastir = Bitola, Macedonia 21 D9 41 1N 21 20 E
Moncayo, Sierra del, Spain 19 B5 41 48N 1 50W
Monchegorsk, Russia 24 A5 67 54N 32 58 E
Mönchengladbach, Germany 16 C4 51 11N 6 27 E
Monchique, Portugal 19 D1 37 19N 8 38W
Moncks Corner, U.S.A. 77 J5 33 12N 80 1W
Monclova, Mexico 86 B4 26 50N 101 30W
Moncton, Canada 71 C7 46 7N 64 51W
Mondego →, Portugal 19 B1 40 9N 8 52W
Mondeodo, Indonesia 37 E6 3 34S 122 9 E
Mondovì, Italy 18 D7 44 23N 7 49 E
Mondrain I., Australia 61 F3 34 9S 122 14 E
Monessen, U.S.A. 78 F5 40 9N 79 54W
Monett, U.S.A. 81 G8 36 55N 93 55W
Moneymore, U.K. 13 B5 54 41N 6 40W
Monforte de Lemos, Spain 19 A2 42 31N 7 33W
Mong Hsu, Burma 41 J21 21 54N 98 30 E
Mong Kung, Burma 41 J20 21 35N 97 35 E
Mong Nai, Burma 41 J20 20 32N 97 46 E
Mong Pawk, Burma 41 H21 22 4N 99 16 E
Mong Ton, Burma 41 J21 20 17N 98 45 E
Mong Wa, Burma 41 J22 21 26N 100 27 E
Mong Yai, Burma 41 H21 22 21N 98 3 E
Mongalla, Sudan 51 G12 5 8N 31 42 E
Mongers, L., Australia 61 E2 29 25S 117 5 E
Monghyr = Munger, India 43 G12 25 23N 86 30 E
Mongibello = Etna, Italy 20 F6 37 50N 14 55 E
Mongo, Chad 51 F9 12 14N 18 43 E
Mongolia ■, Asia 27 E10 47 0N 103 0 E
Mongu, Zambia 53 H4 15 16S 23 12 E
Môngua, Angola 56 B2 16 43S 15 20 E
Monifieth, U.K. 12 E6 56 30N 2 48W
Monkey Bay, Malawi 55 E4 14 7S 35 1 E
Monkey Mia, Australia 61 E1 25 48S 113 43 E
Monkey River, Belize 87 D7 16 22N 88 29W
Monkoto, Dem. Rep. of the Congo 52 E4 1 38S 20 35 E
Monkton, Canada 78 C3 43 35N 81 5W
Monmouth, U.K. 11 F5 51 48N 2 42W
Monmouth, Ill., U.S.A. 80 E9 40 55N 90 39W
Monmouth, Oreg., U.S.A. 82 D2 44 51N 123 14W
Monmouthshire □, U.K. 11 F5 51 48N 2 54W
Mono L., U.S.A. 84 H7 38 1N 119 1W

Naju, *S. Korea* **35 G14** 35 3N 126 43 E
Nakadōri-Shima, *Japan* **31 H4** 32 57N 129 4 E
Nakalagba, *Dem. Rep. of the Congo* **54 B2** 2 50N 27 58 E
Nakaminato, *Japan* **31 F10** 36 21N 140 36 E
Nakamura, *Japan* **31 H6** 32 59N 132 56 E
Nakano, *Japan* **31 F9** 36 45N 138 22 E
Nakano-Shima, *Japan* **31 K4** 29 51N 129 52 E
Nakashibetsu, *Japan* **30 C12** 43 33N 144 59 E
Nakfa, *Eritrea* **46 D2** 16 40N 38 32 E
Nakhfar al Buşayyah, *Iraq* **44 D5** 30 0N 46 10 E
Nakhichevan = Naxçıvan, *Azerbaijan* **25 G8** 39 12N 45 15 E
Nakhichevan Republic = Naxçıvan □, *Azerbaijan* **25 G8** 39 25N 45 26 E
Nakhl, *Egypt* **47 F2** 29 55N 33 43 E
Nakhl-e Taqī, *Iran* **45 E7** 27 28N 52 36 E
Nakhodka, *Russia* **27 E14** 42 53N 132 54 E
Nakhon Nayok, *Thailand* **38 E3** 14 12N 101 13 E
Nakhon Pathom, *Thailand* **38 F3** 13 49N 100 3 E
Nakhon Phanom, *Thailand* **38 D5** 17 23N 104 43 E
Nakhon Ratchasima, *Thailand* **38 E4** 14 59N 102 12 E
Nakhon Sawan, *Thailand* **38 E3** 15 35N 100 10 E
Nakhon Si Thammarat, *Thailand* **39 H3** 8 29N 100 0 E
Nakhon Thai, *Thailand* **38 D3** 17 5N 100 44 E
Nakhtarana, *India* **42 H3** 23 20N 69 15 E
Nakina, *Canada* **70 B2** 50 10N 86 40W
Nakodar, *India* **42 D6** 31 8N 75 31 E
Nakskov, *Denmark* **9 J14** 54 50N 11 8 E
Naktong →, *S. Korea* **35 G15** 35 7N 128 57 E
Nakuru, *Kenya* **54 C4** 0 15S 36 4 E
Nakuru, L., *Kenya* **54 C4** 0 23S 36 5 E
Nakusp, *Canada* **72 C5** 50 20N 117 45W
Nal, *Pakistan* **42 F2** 27 40N 66 12 E
Nal →, *Pakistan* **42 G1** 25 20N 65 30 E
Nalázi, *Mozam.* **57 C5** 24 3S 33 20 E
Nalchik, *Russia* **25 F7** 43 30N 43 33 E
Nalgonda, *India* **40 L11** 17 6N 79 15 E
Nalhati, *India* **43 G12** 24 17N 87 52 E
Naliya, *India* **42 H3** 23 16N 68 50 E
Nallamalai Hills, *India* **40 M11** 15 30N 78 50 E
Nam Can, *Vietnam* **39 H5** 8 46N 104 59 E
Nam-ch'on, *N. Korea* **35 E14** 38 15N 126 26 E
Nam Co, *China* **32 C4** 30 30N 90 45 E
Nam Dinh, *Vietnam* **38 B6** 20 25N 106 5 E
Nam Du, Hon, *Vietnam* **39 H5** 9 41N 104 21 E
Nam Ngum Dam, *Laos* **38 C4** 18 35N 102 34 E
Nam-Phan, *Vietnam* **39 G6** 10 30N 106 0 E
Nam Phong, *Thailand* **38 D4** 16 42N 102 52 E
Nam Tha, *Laos* **38 B3** 20 58N 101 30 E
Nam Tok, *Thailand* **38 E2** 14 21N 99 4 E
Namacunde, *Angola* **56 B2** 17 18S 15 50 E
Namacurra, *Mozam.* **57 B6** 17 30S 36 50 E
Namak, Daryācheh-ye, *Iran* **45 C7** 34 30N 52 0 E
Namak, Kavir-e, *Iran* **45 C8** 34 30N 57 30 E
Namakzār, Daryācheh-ye, *Iran* **45 C9** 34 0N 60 30 E
Namaland, *Namibia* **56 C2** 26 0S 17 0 E
Namangan, *Uzbekistan* **26 E8** 41 0N 71 40 E
Namapa, *Mozam.* **55 E4** 13 43S 39 50 E
Namaqualand, *S. Africa* **56 E2** 30 0S 17 25 E
Namasagali, *Uganda* **54 B3** 1 2N 33 0 E
Namber, *Indonesia* **37 E8** 1 2S 134 49 E
Nambour, *Australia* **63 D5** 26 32S 152 58 E
Nambucca Heads, *Australia* **63 E5** 30 37S 153 0 E
Namcha Barwa, *China* **32 D4** 29 40N 95 10 E
Namche Bazar, *Nepal* **43 F12** 27 51N 86 47 E
Namchonjŏm = Nam-ch'on, *N. Korea* **35 E14** 38 15N 126 26 E
Namecunda, *Mozam.* **55 E4** 14 54S 37 37 E
Nameponda, *Mozam.* **55 F4** 15 50S 39 50 E
Nametil, *Mozam.* **55 F4** 15 40S 39 21 E
Namew L., *Canada* **73 C8** 54 14N 101 56W
Namgia, *India* **43 D8** 31 48N 78 40 E
Namib Desert, *Namibia* **56 C2** 22 30S 15 0 E
Namibe, *Angola* **53 H2** 15 7S 12 11 E
Namibe □, *Angola* **56 B1** 16 35S 12 30 E
Namibia ■, *Africa* **56 C2** 22 0S 18 9 E
Namibwoestyn = Namib Desert, *Namibia* **56 C2** 22 30S 15 0 E
Namlea, *Indonesia* **37 E7** 3 18S 127 5 E
Namoi →, *Australia* **63 E4** 30 12S 149 30 E
Nampa, *U.S.A.* **82 E5** 43 34N 116 34W
Namp'o, *N. Korea* **35 E13** 38 52N 125 10 E
Nampō-Shotō, *Japan* **31 J10** 32 0N 140 0 E
Nampula, *Mozam.* **55 F4** 15 6S 39 15 E
Namrole, *Indonesia* **37 E7** 3 46S 126 46 E
Namse Shankou, *China* **41 E13** 30 0N 82 25 E
Namsen →, *Norway* **8 D14** 64 28N 11 37 E
Namsos, *Norway* **8 D14** 64 29N 11 30 E
Namtsy, *Russia* **27 C13** 62 43N 129 37 E
Namtu, *Burma* **41 H20** 23 5N 97 28 E
Namtumbo, *Tanzania* **55 E4** 10 30S 36 4 E
Namu, *Canada* **72 C3** 51 52N 127 50W
Namur, *Belgium* **15 D4** 50 27N 4 52 E
Namur □, *Belgium* **15 D4** 50 17N 5 0 E
Namutoni, *Namibia* **56 B2** 18 49S 16 55 E
Namwala, *Zambia* **55 F2** 15 44S 26 30 E
Namwŏn, *S. Korea* **35 G14** 35 23N 127 23 E
Nan, *Thailand* **38 C3** 18 48N 100 46 E
Nan →, *Thailand* **38 E3** 15 42N 100 9 E
Nan-ch'ang = Nanchang, *China* **33 D6** 28 42N 115 55 E
Nanaimo, *Canada* **72 D4** 49 10N 124 0W
Nanam, *N. Korea* **35 D15** 41 44N 129 40 E
Nanango, *Australia* **63 D5** 26 40S 152 0 E
Nanao, *Japan* **31 F8** 37 0N 137 0 E
Nanchang, *China* **33 D6** 28 42N 115 55 E
Nanching = Nanjing, *China* **33 C6** 32 2N 118 47 E
Nanchong, *China* **32 C5** 30 43N 106 2 E
Nancy, *France* **18 B7** 48 42N 6 12 E
Nanda Devi, *India* **43 D8** 30 23N 79 59 E
Nanda Kot, *India* **43 D9** 30 17N 80 5 E
Nandan, *Japan* **31 G7** 34 10N 134 42 E
Nanded, *India* **40 K10** 19 10N 77 20 E
Nandewar Ra., *Australia* **63 E5** 30 15S 150 35 E
Nandi = Nadi, *Fiji* **59 C7** 17 42S 177 20 E
Nandigram, *India* **43 H12** 22 1N 87 58 E
Nandurbar, *India* **40 J9** 21 20N 74 15 E
Nandyal, *India* **40 M11** 15 30N 78 30 E
Nanga-Eboko, *Cameroon* **52 D2** 4 41N 12 22 E
Nanga Parbat, *Pakistan* **43 B6** 35 10N 74 35 E
Nangade, *Mozam.* **55 E4** 11 5S 39 36 E
Nangapinoh, *Indonesia* **36 E4** 0 20S 111 44 E
Nangarhār □, *Afghan.* **40 B7** 34 20N 70 0 E
Nangatayap, *Indonesia* **36 E4** 1 32S 110 34 E
Nangeya Mts., *Uganda* **54 B3** 3 30N 33 30 E
Nangong, *China* **34 F8** 37 23N 115 22 E
Nanhuang, *China* **35 F11** 36 58N 121 48 E
Nanjeko, *Zambia* **55 F1** 15 31S 23 30 E
Nanjing, *China* **33 C6** 32 2N 118 47 E
Nanjirinji, *Tanzania* **55 D4** 9 41S 39 5 E
Nankana Sahib, *Pakistan* **42 D5** 31 27N 73 38 E
Nanking = Nanjing, *China* **33 C6** 32 2N 118 47 E
Nankoku, *Japan* **31 H6** 33 39N 133 44 E
Nanning, *China* **32 D5** 22 48N 108 20 E
Nannup, *Australia* **61 F2** 33 59S 115 48 E
Nanpara, *India* **43 F9** 27 52N 81 33 E
Nanpi, *China* **34 E9** 38 2N 116 45 E
Nanping, *China* **33 D6** 26 38N 118 10 E
Nanripe, *Mozam.* **55 E4** 13 52S 38 52 E
Nansei-Shotō = Ryūkyū-rettō, *Japan* **31 M3** 26 0N 126 0 E
Nansen Sd., *Canada* **4 A3** 81 0N 91 0W
Nanshan I., *S. China Sea* **36 B5** 10 45N 115 49 E
Nansio, *Tanzania* **54 C3** 2 3S 33 4 E
Nantes, *France* **18 C3** 47 12N 1 33W
Nanticoke, *U.S.A.* **79 E8** 41 12N 76 0W
Nanton, *Canada* **72 C6** 50 21N 113 46W
Nantong, *China* **33 C7** 32 1N 120 52 E
Nantucket I., *U.S.A.* **76 E10** 41 16N 70 5W
Nantwich, *U.K.* **10 D5** 53 4N 2 31W
Nanty Glo, *U.S.A.* **78 F6** 40 28N 78 50W
Nanuque, *Brazil* **93 G10** 17 50S 40 21W
Nanusa, Kepulauan, *Indonesia* **37 D7** 4 45N 127 1 E
Nanutarra Roadhouse, *Australia* **60 D2** 22 32S 115 30 E
Nanyang, *China* **34 H7** 33 11N 112 30 E
Nanyuki, *Kenya* **54 B4** 0 2N 37 4 E
Nao, C. de la, *Spain* **19 C6** 38 44N 0 14 E
Naococane, L., *Canada* **71 B5** 52 50N 70 45W
Napa, *U.S.A.* **84 G4** 38 18N 122 17W
Napa →, *U.S.A.* **84 G4** 38 10N 122 19W
Napanee, *Canada* **78 B8** 44 15N 77 0W
Napanoch, *U.S.A.* **79 E10** 41 44N 74 22W
Nape, *Laos* **38 C5** 18 18N 105 6 E
Nape Pass = Keo Neua, Deo, *Vietnam* **38 C5** 18 23N 105 10 E
Napier, *N.Z.* **59 H6** 39 30S 176 56 E
Napier Broome B., *Australia* **60 B4** 14 2S 126 37 E
Napier Pen., *Australia* **62 A2** 12 4S 135 43 E
Napierville, *Canada* **79 A11** 45 11N 73 25W
Naples = Nápoli, *Italy* **20 D6** 40 50N 14 15 E
Naples, *U.S.A.* **77 M5** 26 8N 81 48W
Napo →, *Peru* **92 D4** 3 20S 72 40W
Napoleon, *N. Dak., U.S.A.* **80 B5** 46 30N 99 46W
Napoleon, *Ohio, U.S.A.* **76 E3** 41 23N 84 8W
Nápoli, *Italy* **20 D6** 40 50N 14 15 E
Napopo, *Dem. Rep. of the Congo* **54 B2** 4 15N 28 0 E
Naqb, Ra's an, *Jordan* **47 F4** 30 0N 35 29 E
Naqqāsh, *Iran* **45 C6** 35 40N 49 6 E
Nara, *Japan* **31 G7** 34 40N 135 49 E
Nara, *Mali* **50 E4** 15 10N 7 20W
Nara □, *Japan* **31 G8** 34 30N 136 0 E
Nara Canal, *Pakistan* **42 G3** 24 30N 69 20 E
Nara Visa, *U.S.A.* **81 H3** 35 37N 103 6W
Naracoorte, *Australia* **63 F3** 36 58S 140 45 E
Naradhan, *Australia* **63 E4** 33 34S 146 17 E
Naraini, *India* **43 G9** 25 11N 80 29 E
Narasapur, *India* **41 L12** 16 26N 81 40 E
Narathiwat, *Thailand* **39 J3** 6 30N 101 48 E
Narayanganj, *Bangla.* **41 H17** 23 40N 90 33 E
Narayanpet, *India* **40 L10** 16 45N 77 30 E
Narbonne, *France* **18 E5** 43 11N 3 0 E
Nardīn, *Iran* **45 B7** 37 3N 55 59 E
Nardò, *Italy* **21 D8** 40 11N 18 2 E
Narembeen, *Australia* **61 F2** 32 7S 118 24 E
Narendranagar, *India* **42 D8** 30 10N 78 18 E
Nares Str., *Arctic* **66 A13** 80 0N 70 0W
Naretha, *Australia* **61 F3** 31 0S 124 45 E
Narew →, *Poland* **17 B11** 52 26N 20 41 E
Nari →, *Pakistan* **42 F2** 28 0N 67 40 E
Narin, *Afghan.* **40 A6** 36 5N 69 0 E
Narindra, Helodranon' i, *Madag.* **57 A8** 14 55S 47 30 E
Narita, *Japan* **31 G10** 35 47N 140 19 E
Narmada →, *India* **42 J5** 21 38N 72 36 E
Narmland, *Sweden* **9 F15** 60 0N 13 30 E
Narnaul, *India* **42 E7** 28 5N 76 11 E
Narodnaya, *Russia* **24 A10** 65 5N 59 58 E
Narok, *Kenya* **54 C4** 1 55S 35 52 E
Narooma, *Australia* **63 F5** 36 14S 150 4 E
Narowal, *Pakistan* **42 C6** 32 6N 74 52 E
Narrabri, *Australia* **63 E4** 30 19S 149 46 E
Narran →, *Australia* **63 D4** 28 37S 148 12 E
Narrandera, *Australia* **63 E4** 34 42S 146 31 E
Narrogin, *Australia* **61 F2** 32 58S 117 14 E
Narromine, *Australia* **63 E4** 32 12S 148 12 E
Narrow Hills Prov. Park, *Canada* **73 C8** 54 0N 104 37W
Narsimhapur, *India* **43 H8** 22 54N 79 14 E
Narsinghgarh, *India* **42 H7** 23 45N 76 40 E
Naruto, *Japan* **31 G7** 34 11N 134 37 E
Narva, *Estonia* **24 C4** 59 23N 28 12 E
Narva →, *Russia* **9 G22** 59 27N 28 2 E
Narva Bay, *Estonia* **9 G19** 59 35N 27 35 E
Narvik, *Norway* **8 B17** 68 28N 17 26 E
Narwana, *India* **42 E7** 29 39N 76 6 E
Naryan-Mar, *Russia* **24 A9** 67 42N 53 12 E
Narym, *Russia* **26 D9** 59 0N 81 30 E
Naryn, *Kyrgyzstan* **26 E8** 41 26N 75 58 E
Nasa, *Norway* **8 C16** 66 29N 15 23 E
Naseby, *N.Z.* **59 L3** 45 1S 170 10 E
Naselle, *U.S.A.* **84 D3** 46 22N 123 49W
Naser, Buheirat en, *Egypt* **51 D12** 23 0N 32 30 E
Nashua, *Mont., U.S.A.* **82 B10** 48 8N 106 22W
Nashua, *N.H., U.S.A.* **79 D13** 42 45N 71 28W
Nashville, *Ark., U.S.A.* **81 J8** 33 57N 93 51W
Nashville, *Ga., U.S.A.* **77 K4** 31 12N 83 15W
Nashville, *Tenn., U.S.A.* **77 G2** 36 10N 86 47W
Nasik, *India* **40 K8** 19 58N 73 50 E
Nasirabad, *India* **42 F6** 26 15N 74 45 E
Nasirabad, *Pakistan* **42 E3** 28 23N 68 24 E
Naskaupi →, *Canada* **71 B7** 53 47N 60 51W
Naşrābād, *Iran* **45 C6** 34 8N 51 26 E
Naşriān-e Pā'īn, *Iran* **44 C5** 32 52N 46 52 E
Nass →, *Canada* **72 C3** 55 0N 129 40W
Nassau, *Bahamas* **88 A4** 25 5N 77 20W
Nassau, *U.S.A.* **79 D11** 42 31N 73 37W
Nassau, B., *Chile* **96 H3** 55 20S 68 0W
Nasser, L. = Naser, Buheirat en, *Egypt* **51 D12** 23 0N 32 30 E
Nasser City = Kôm Ombo, *Egypt* **51 D12** 24 25N 32 52 E
Nässjö, *Sweden* **9 H16** 57 39N 14 42 E
Nastapoka →, *Canada* **70 A4** 56 55N 76 33W
Nastapoka, Is., *Canada* **70 A4** 56 55N 76 50W
Nata, *Botswana* **56 C4** 20 12S 26 12 E
Nata →, *Botswana* **56 C4** 20 14S 26 10 E
Natal, *Brazil* **93 E11** 5 47S 35 13W
Natal, *Indonesia* **36 D1** 0 35N 99 7 E
Natal, *S. Africa* **53 K6** 28 30S 30 30 E
Naţanz, *Iran* **45 C6** 33 30N 51 55 E
Natashquan, *Canada* **71 B7** 50 14N 61 46W
Natashquan →, *Canada* **71 B7** 50 7N 61 50W
Natchez, *U.S.A.* **81 K9** 31 34N 91 24W
Natchitoches, *U.S.A.* **81 K8** 31 46N 93 5W
Nathalia, *Australia* **63 F4** 36 1S 145 13 E
Nathdwara, *India* **42 G5** 24 55N 73 50 E
Nati, Pta., *Spain* **22 A10** 40 3N 3 50 E
Natimuk, *Australia* **63 F3** 36 42S 142 0 E
Nation →, *Canada* **72 B4** 55 30N 123 32W
National City, *U.S.A.* **85 N9** 32 41N 117 6W
Natitingou, *Benin* **50 F6** 10 20N 1 26 E
Natividad, I., *Mexico* **86 B1** 27 50N 115 10W
Natkyizin, *Burma* **38 E1** 14 57N 97 59 E
Natron, L., *Tanzania* **54 C4** 2 20S 36 0 E
Natrona Heights, *U.S.A.* **78 F5** 40 37N 79 44W
Natukanaoka Pan, *Namibia* **56 B2** 18 40S 15 45 E
Natuna Besar, Kepulauan, *Indonesia* **39 L7** 4 0N 108 15 E
Natuna Is. = Natuna Besar, Kepulauan, *Indonesia* **39 L7** 4 0N 108 15 E
Natuna Selatan, Kepulauan, *Indonesia* **39 L7** 2 45N 109 0 E
Natural Bridge, *U.S.A.* **79 B9** 44 5N 75 30W
Naturaliste, C., *Australia* **62 G4** 40 50S 148 15 E
Nau Qala, *Afghan.* **42 B3** 34 5N 68 5 E
Naugatuck, *U.S.A.* **79 E11** 41 30N 73 3W
Naujaat = Repulse Bay, *Canada* **69 B11** 66 30N 86 30W
Naumburg, *Germany* **16 C6** 51 9N 11 47 E
Nā'ūr at Tunayb, *Jordan* **47 D4** 31 48N 35 57 E
Nauru ■, *Pac. Oc.* **64 H8** 1 0S 166 0 E
Naushahra = Nowshera, *Pakistan* **40 C8** 34 0N 72 0 E
Naushahro, *Pakistan* **42 F3** 26 50N 68 7 E
Naushon I., *U.S.A.* **79 E14** 41 29N 70 45W
Nauta, *Peru* **92 D4** 4 31S 73 35W
Nautanwa, *India* **41 F13** 27 20N 83 25 E
Nautla, *Mexico* **87 C5** 20 20N 96 50W
Nava, *Mexico* **86 B4** 28 25N 100 46W
Navadwip, *India* **43 H13** 23 34N 88 20 E
Navahrudak, *Belarus* **17 B13** 53 40N 25 50 E
Navajo Reservoir, *U.S.A.* **83 H10** 36 48N 107 36W
Navalmoral de la Mata, *Spain* **19 C3** 39 52N 5 33W
Navan = An Uaimh, *Ireland* **13 C5** 53 39N 6 41W
Navarino, I., *Chile* **96 H3** 55 0S 67 40W
Navarra □, *Spain* **19 A5** 42 40N 1 40W
Navarre, *U.S.A.* **78 F3** 40 43N 81 31W
Navarro →, *U.S.A.* **84 F3** 39 11N 123 45W
Navasota, *U.S.A.* **81 K6** 30 23N 96 5W
Navassa I., *W. Indies* **89 C5** 18 30N 75 0W
Naver →, *U.K.* **12 C4** 58 32N 4 14W
Navibandar, *India* **42 J3** 21 26N 69 48 E
Navidad, *Chile* **94 C1** 33 57S 71 50W
Navirai, *Brazil* **95 A5** 23 8S 54 13W
Navlakhi, *India* **42 H4** 22 58N 70 28 E
Năvodari, *Romania* **17 F15** 44 19N 28 36 E
Navoi = Nawoiy, *Uzbekistan* **26 E7** 40 9N 65 22 E
Navojoa, *Mexico* **86 B3** 27 0N 109 30W
Navolato, *Mexico* **86 C3** 24 47N 107 42W
Návpaktos, *Greece* **21 E9** 38 24N 21 50 E
Návplion, *Greece* **21 F10** 37 33N 22 50 E
Navsari, *India* **40 J8** 20 57N 72 59 E
Nawa Kot, *Pakistan* **42 E4** 28 21N 71 24 E
Nawab Khan, *Pakistan* **42 D3** 30 17N 69 12 E
Nawabganj, *Ut. P., India* **43 F9** 26 56N 81 14 E
Nawabganj, *Ut. P., India* **43 E8** 28 32N 79 40 E
Nawabshah, *Pakistan* **42 F3** 26 15N 68 25 E
Nawada, *India* **43 G11** 24 50N 85 33 E
Nawakot, *Nepal* **43 F11** 27 55N 85 10 E
Nawalgarh, *India* **42 F6** 27 50N 75 15 E
Nawanshahr, *India* **43 C6** 32 33N 74 48 E
Nawar, Dasht-i-, *Afghan.* **42 C3** 33 52N 68 0 E
Nawoiy, *Uzbekistan* **26 E7** 40 9N 65 22 E
Naxçıvan, *Azerbaijan* **25 G8** 39 12N 45 15 E
Naxçıvan □, *Azerbaijan* **25 G8** 39 25N 45 26 E
Náxos, *Greece* **21 F11** 37 8N 25 25 E
Nay, Mui, *Vietnam* **36 B3** 12 55N 109 23 E
Nāy Band, *Būshehr, Iran* **45 E7** 27 20N 52 40 E
Nāy Band, *Khorāsān, Iran* **45 C8** 32 20N 57 34 E
Nayakhan, *Russia* **27 C16** 61 56N 159 0 E
Nayarit □, *Mexico* **86 C4** 22 0N 105 0W
Nayoro, *Japan* **30 B11** 44 21N 142 28 E
Nayyāl, W. →, *Si. Arabia* **44 D3** 28 35N 39 4 E
Nazaré, *Brazil* **93 F11** 13 2S 39 0W
Nazareth = Naẕerat, *Israel* **47 C4** 32 42N 35 17 E
Nazareth, *U.S.A.* **79 F9** 40 44N 75 19W
Nazas, *Mexico* **86 B4** 25 10N 104 6W
Nazas →, *Mexico* **86 B4** 25 35N 103 25W
Nazca, *Peru* **92 F4** 14 50S 74 57W
Naze, The, *U.K.* **11 F9** 51 53N 1 18 E
Naẕerat, *Israel* **47 C4** 32 42N 35 17 E
Nāzīk, *Iran* **44 B5** 39 1N 45 4 E
Nazilli, *Turkey* **21 F13** 37 55N 28 15 E
Nazko, *Canada* **72 C4** 53 1N 123 37W
Nazko →, *Canada* **72 C4** 53 7N 123 34W
Nazret, *Ethiopia* **46 F2** 8 32N 39 22 E
Nazwa, *Oman* **46 C6** 22 56N 57 32 E
Nchanga, *Zambia* **55 E2** 12 30S 27 49 E
Ncheu, *Malawi* **55 E3** 14 50S 34 47 E
Ndala, *Tanzania* **54 C3** 4 45S 33 15 E
Ndalatando, *Angola* **52 F2** 9 12S 14 48 E
Ndareda, *Tanzania* **54 C4** 4 12S 35 30 E
Ndélé, *C.A.R.* **52 C4** 8 25N 20 36 E
Ndjamena, *Chad* **51 F8** 12 10N 14 59 E
Ndola, *Zambia* **55 E2** 13 0S 28 34 E
Ndoto Mts., *Kenya* **54 B4** 2 0N 37 0 E
Nduguti, *Tanzania* **54 C3** 4 18S 34 41 E
Neagh, Lough, *U.K.* **13 B5** 54 37N 6 25W
Neah Bay, *U.S.A.* **84 B2** 48 22N 124 37W
Neale, L., *Australia* **60 D5** 24 15S 130 0 E
Neápolis, *Greece* **23 D7** 35 15N 25 37 E
Near Is., *U.S.A.* **68 C1** 52 30N 174 0 E
Neath, *U.K.* **11 F4** 51 39N 3 48W
Neath Port Talbot □, *U.K.* **11 F4** 51 42N 3 45W
Nebine Cr. →, *Australia* **63 D4** 29 27S 146 56 E
Nebitdag, *Turkmenistan* **25 G9** 39 30N 54 22 E
Nebo, *Australia* **62 C4** 21 42S 148 42 E
Nebraska □, *U.S.A.* **80 E5** 41 30N 99 30W
Nebraska City, *U.S.A.* **80 E7** 40 41N 95 52W
Nébrodi, Monti, *Italy* **20 F6** 37 54N 14 35 E
Necedah, *U.S.A.* **80 C9** 44 2N 90 4W
Nechako →, *Canada* **72 C4** 53 30N 122 44W
Neches →, *U.S.A.* **81 L8** 29 58N 93 51W
Neckar →, *Germany* **16 D5** 49 27N 8 29 E
Necochea, *Argentina* **94 D4** 38 30S 58 50W
Needles, *Canada* **72 D5** 49 53N 118 7W
Needles, *U.S.A.* **85 L12** 34 51N 114 37W
Needles, The, *U.K.* **11 G6** 50 39N 1 35W
Ñeembucú □, *Paraguay* **94 B4** 27 0S 58 0W
Neemuch = Nimach, *India* **42 G6** 24 30N 74 56 E
Neenah, *U.S.A.* **76 C1** 44 11N 88 28W
Neepawa, *Canada* **73 C9** 50 15N 99 30W
Neftçala, *Azerbaijan* **25 G8** 39 19N 49 12 E
Neftekumsk, *Russia* **25 F7** 44 46N 44 50 E
Nefyn, *U.K.* **10 E3** 52 56N 4 31W
Negapatam = Nagappattinam, *India* **40 P11** 10 46N 79 51 E
Negaunee, *U.S.A.* **76 B2** 46 30N 87 36W
Negele, *Ethiopia* **46 F2** 5 20N 39 36 E
Negev Desert = Hanegev, *Israel* **47 E4** 30 50N 35 0 E
Negombo, *Sri Lanka* **40 R11** 7 12N 79 50 E
Negotin, *Serbia, Yug.* **21 B10** 44 16N 22 37 E
Negra, Pta., *Peru* **92 E2** 6 6S 81 10W
Negrais, C. = Maudin Sun, *Burma* **41 M19** 16 0N 94 30 E
Negril, *Jamaica* **88 C4** 18 22N 78 20W
Negro →, *Argentina* **96 E4** 41 2S 62 47W
Negro →, *Brazil* **92 D7** 3 0S 60 0W
Negro →, *Uruguay* **95 C4** 33 24S 58 22W
Negros, *Phil.* **37 C6** 9 30N 122 40 E
Neguac, *Canada* **71 C6** 47 15N 65 5W
Nehalem →, *U.S.A.* **84 E3** 45 40N 123 56W
Nehāvand, *Iran* **45 C6** 35 56N 49 31 E
Nehbandān, *Iran* **45 D9** 31 35N 60 5 E
Nei Monggol Zizhiqu □, *China* **34 D7** 42 0N 112 0 E
Neijiang, *China* **32 D5** 29 35N 104 55 E
Neillsville, *U.S.A.* **80 C9** 44 34N 90 36W
Neilton, *U.S.A.* **82 C2** 47 25N 123 53W
Neiqiu, *China* **34 F8** 37 15N 114 30 E
Neiva, *Colombia* **92 C3** 2 56N 75 18W
Neixiang, *China* **34 H6** 33 10N 111 52 E
Nejanilini L., *Canada* **73 B9** 59 33N 97 48W
Nejd = Najd, *Si. Arabia* **46 B3** 26 30N 42 0 E
Nekā, *Iran* **45 B7** 36 39N 53 19 E
Nekemte, *Ethiopia* **46 F2** 9 4N 36 30 E
Neksø, *Denmark* **9 J16** 55 4N 15 8 E
Nelia, *Australia* **62 C3** 20 39S 142 12 E
Neligh, *U.S.A.* **80 D5** 42 8N 98 2W
Nelkan, *Russia* **27 D14** 57 40N 136 4 E
Nellore, *India* **40 M11** 14 27N 79 59 E
Nelson, *Canada* **72 D5** 49 30N 117 20W
Nelson, *N.Z.* **59 J4** 41 18S 173 16 E
Nelson, *U.K.* **10 D5** 53 50N 2 13W
Nelson, *Ariz., U.S.A.* **83 J7** 35 31N 113 19W
Nelson, *Nev., U.S.A.* **85 K12** 35 42N 114 50W
Nelson →, *Canada* **73 C9** 54 33N 98 2W
Nelson, C., *Australia* **63 F3** 38 26S 141 32 E
Nelson, Estrecho, *Chile* **96 G2** 51 30S 75 0W
Nelson Forks, *Canada* **72 B4** 59 30N 124 0W
Nelson House, *Canada* **73 B9** 55 47N 98 51W
Nelson L., *Canada* **73 B8** 55 48N 100 7W
Nelspoort, *S. Africa* **56 E3** 32 7S 23 0 E
Nelspruit, *S. Africa* **57 D5** 25 29S 30 59 E
Néma, *Mauritania* **50 E4** 16 40N 7 15W
Neman, *Russia* **9 J20** 55 2N 22 2 E
Neman →, *Lithuania* **9 J19** 55 25N 21 10 E
Nemeiben L., *Canada* **73 B7** 55 20N 105 20W
Némiscau, *Canada* **70 B4** 51 18N 76 54W
Némiscau, L., *Canada* **70 B4** 51 25N 76 40W
Nemunas = Neman →, *Lithuania* **9 J19** 55 25N 21 10 E
Nemuro, *Japan* **30 C12** 43 20N 145 35 E
Nemuro-Kaikyō, *Japan* **30 C12** 43 30N 145 30 E
Nen Jiang →, *China* **35 B13** 45 28N 124 30 E
Nenagh, *Ireland* **13 D3** 52 52N 8 11W
Nenasi, *Malaysia* **39 L4** 3 9N 103 23 E
Nene →, *U.K.* **11 E8** 52 49N 0 11 E
Nenjiang, *China* **33 B7** 49 10N 125 10 E
Neno, *Malawi* **55 F3** 15 25S 34 40 E
Neodesha, *U.S.A.* **81 G7** 37 25N 95 41W
Neosho, *U.S.A.* **81 G7** 36 52N 94 22W
Neosho →, *U.S.A.* **81 H7** 36 48N 95 18W
Nepal ■, *Asia* **43 F11** 28 0N 84 30 E
Nepalganj, *Nepal* **43 E9** 28 5N 81 40 E
Nepalganj Road, *India* **43 E9** 28 1N 81 41 E
Nephi, *U.S.A.* **82 G8** 39 43N 111 50W
Nephin, *Ireland* **13 B2** 54 1N 9 22W
Neptune, *U.S.A.* **79 F10** 40 13N 74 2W
Nerang, *Australia* **63 D5** 27 58S 153 20 E
Nerchinsk, *Russia* **27 D12** 52 0N 116 39 E
Neret, L., *Canada* **71 B5** 54 45N 70 44W
Neretva →, *Croatia* **21 C7** 43 1N 17 27 E
Neringa, *Lithuania* **9 J19** 55 20N 21 5 E
Neryungri, *Russia* **27 D13** 57 38N 124 28 E
Nescopeck, *U.S.A.* **79 E8** 41 3N 76 12W
Ness, L., *U.K.* **12 D4** 57 15N 4 32W
Ness City, *U.S.A.* **80 F5** 38 27N 99 54W
Nesterov, *Poland* **17 C12** 50 4N 23 58 E
Nesvizh = Nyasvizh, *Belarus* **17 B14** 53 14N 26 38 E
Netanya, *Israel* **47 C3** 32 20N 34 51 E
Netarhat, *India* **43 H11** 23 29N 84 16 E
Nete →, *Belgium* **15 C4** 51 7N 4 14 E
Netherdale, *Australia* **62 C4** 21 10S 148 33 E
Netherlands ■, *Europe* **15 C5** 52 0N 5 30 E
Netherlands Antilles ■, *W. Indies* **92 A5** 12 15N 69 0W
Netrang, *India* **42 J5** 21 39N 73 21 E
Nettilling L., *Canada* **69 B12** 66 30N 71 0W
Netzahualcoyotl, Presa, *Mexico* **87 D6** 17 10N 93 30W
Neubrandenburg, *Germany* **16 B7** 53 33N 13 15 E
Neuchâtel, *Switz.* **18 C7** 47 0N 6 55 E
Neuchâtel, Lac de, *Switz.* **18 C7** 46 53N 6 50 E
Neufchâteau, *Belgium* **15 E5** 49 50N 5 25 E
Neumünster, *Germany* **16 A5** 54 4N 9 58 E
Neunkirchen, *Germany* **16 D4** 49 20N 7 9 E
Neuquén, *Argentina* **96 D3** 38 55S 68 0W

Norderstedt

Neuquén □, Argentina **94 D2** 38 0S 69 50W
Neuruppin, Germany **16 B7** 52 55N 12 48 E
Neuse →, U.S.A. **77 H7** 35 6N 76 29W
Neusiedler See, Austria **17 E9** 47 50N 16 47 E
Neustrelitz, Germany **16 B7** 53 21N 13 4 E
Neva →, Russia **24 C5** 59 50N 30 30 E
Nevada, Iowa, U.S.A. **80 D8** 42 1N 93 27W
Nevada, Mo., U.S.A. **81 G7** 37 51N 94 22W
Nevada □, U.S.A. **82 G5** 39 0N 117 0W
Nevada City, U.S.A. **84 F6** 39 16N 121 1W
Nevado, Cerro, Argentina **94 D2** 35 30S 68 32W
Nevel, Russia **24 C4** 56 0N 29 55 E
Nevers, France **18 C5** 47 0N 3 9 E
Nevertire, Australia **63 E4** 31 50S 147 44 E
Neville, Canada **73 D7** 49 58N 107 39W
Nevinnomyssk, Russia **25 F7** 44 40N 42 0 E
Nevis, St. Kitts & Nevis **89 C7** 17 0N 62 30W
Nevşehir, Turkey **44 B2** 38 33N 34 40 E
Nevyansk, Russia **24 C11** 57 30N 60 13 E
New →, U.S.A. **76 F5** 38 10N 81 12W
New Aiyansh, Canada **72 B3** 55 12N 129 4W
New Albany, Ind., U.S.A. **76 F3** 38 18N 85 49W
New Albany, Miss., U.S.A. **81 H10** 34 29N 89 0W
New Albany, Pa., U.S.A. **79 E8** 41 36N 76 27W
New Amsterdam, Guyana **92 B7** 6 15N 57 36W
New Angledool, Australia **63 D4** 29 5S 147 55 E
New Baltimore, U.S.A. **78 D2** 42 41N 82 44W
New Bedford, U.S.A. **79 E14** 41 38N 70 56W
New Berlin, N.Y., U.S.A. **79 D9** 42 37N 75 20W
New Berlin, Pa., U.S.A. **78 F8** 40 50N 76 57W
New Bern, U.S.A. **77 H7** 35 7N 77 3W
New Bethlehem, U.S.A. **78 F5** 41 0N 79 20W
New Bloomfield, U.S.A. **78 F7** 40 25N 77 11W
New Boston, U.S.A. **81 J7** 33 28N 94 25W
New Braunfels, U.S.A. **81 L5** 29 42N 98 8W
New Brighton, N.Z. **59 K4** 43 29S 172 43 E
New Brighton, U.S.A. **78 F4** 40 42N 80 19W
New Britain, Papua N. G. **64 H7** 5 50S 150 20 E
New Britain, U.S.A. **79 E12** 41 40N 72 47W
New Brunswick, U.S.A. **79 F10** 40 30N 74 27W
New Brunswick □, Canada **71 C6** 46 50N 66 30W
New Caledonia ■, Pac. Oc. **64 K8** 21 0S 165 0 E
New Castile = Castilla-La Mancha □, Spain **19 C4** 39 30N 3 30W
New Castle, Ind., U.S.A. **76 F3** 39 55N 85 22W
New Castle, Pa., U.S.A. **78 F4** 41 0N 80 21W
New City, U.S.A. **79 E11** 41 9N 73 59W
New Concord, U.S.A. **78 G3** 39 59N 81 54W
New Cumberland, U.S.A. **78 F4** 40 30N 80 36W
New Cuyama, U.S.A. **85 L7** 34 57N 119 38W
New Delhi, India **42 E7** 28 37N 77 13 E
New Denver, Canada **72 D5** 50 0N 117 25W
New Don Pedro Reservoir, U.S.A. **84 H6** 37 43N 120 24W
New England, U.S.A. **80 B3** 46 32N 102 52W
New England Ra., Australia **63 E5** 30 20S 151 45 E
New Forest, U.K. **11 G6** 50 53N 1 34W
New Galloway, U.K. **12 F4** 55 5N 4 9W
New Glasgow, Canada **71 C7** 45 35N 62 36W
New Guinea, Oceania **28 K17** 4 0S 136 0 E
New Hamburg, Canada **78 C4** 43 23N 80 42W
New Hampshire □, U.S.A. **79 C13** 44 0N 71 30W
New Hampton, U.S.A. **80 D8** 43 3N 92 19W
New Hanover, S. Africa **57 D5** 29 22S 30 31 E
New Hartford, U.S.A. **79 C9** 43 4N 75 18W
New Haven, Conn., U.S.A. **79 E12** 41 18N 72 55W
New Haven, Mich., U.S.A. **78 D2** 42 44N 82 48W
New Hazelton, Canada **72 B3** 55 20N 127 30W
New Hebrides = Vanuatu ■, Pac. Oc. **64 J8** 15 0S 168 0 E
New Holland, U.S.A. **79 F8** 40 6N 76 5W
New Iberia, U.S.A. **81 K9** 30 1N 91 49W
New Ireland, Papua N. G. **64 H7** 3 20S 151 50 E
New Jersey □, U.S.A. **76 E8** 40 0N 74 30W
New Kensington, U.S.A. **78 F5** 40 34N 79 46W
New Lexington, U.S.A. **76 F4** 39 43N 82 13W
New Liskeard, Canada **70 C4** 47 31N 79 41W
New London, Conn., U.S.A. **79 E12** 41 22N 72 6W
New London, Ohio, U.S.A. **78 E2** 41 5N 82 24W
New London, Wis., U.S.A. **80 C10** 44 23N 88 45W
New Madrid, U.S.A. **81 G10** 36 36N 89 32W
New Martinsville, U.S.A. **76 F5** 39 39N 80 52W
New Meadows, U.S.A. **82 D5** 44 58N 116 18W
New Melones L., U.S.A. **84 H6** 37 57N 120 31W
New Mexico □, U.S.A. **83 J10** 34 30N 106 0W
New Milford, Conn., U.S.A. **79 E11** 41 35N 73 25W
New Milford, Pa., U.S.A. **79 E9** 41 52N 75 44W
New Norcia, Australia **61 F2** 30 57S 116 13 E
New Norfolk, Australia **62 G4** 42 46S 147 2 E
New Orleans, U.S.A. **81 L9** 29 58N 90 4W
New Philadelphia, U.S.A. **78 F3** 40 30N 81 27W
New Plymouth, N.Z. **59 H5** 39 4S 174 5 E
New Plymouth, U.S.A. **82 E5** 43 58N 116 49W
New Port Richey, U.S.A. **77 L4** 28 16N 82 43W
New Providence, Bahamas **88 A4** 25 25N 78 35W
New Quay, U.K. **11 E3** 52 13N 4 21W
New Radnor, U.K. **11 E4** 52 15N 3 9W
New Richmond, Canada **71 C6** 48 15N 65 45W
New Richmond, U.S.A. **80 C8** 45 7N 92 32W
New Roads, U.S.A. **81 K9** 30 42N 91 26W
New Rochelle, U.S.A. **79 F11** 40 55N 73 47W
New Rockford, U.S.A. **80 B5** 47 41N 99 8W
New Romney, U.K. **11 G8** 50 59N 0 57 E
New Ross, Ireland **13 D5** 52 23N 6 57W
New Salem, U.S.A. **80 B4** 46 51N 101 25W
New Scone, U.K. **12 E5** 56 25N 3 24W
New Siberian I. = Novaya Sibir, Ostrov, Russia **27 B16** 75 10N 150 0 E
New Siberian Is. = Novosibirskiye Ostrova, Russia **27 B15** 75 0N 142 0 E
New Smyrna Beach, U.S.A. **77 L5** 29 1N 80 56W
New South Wales □, Australia **63 E4** 33 0S 146 0 E
New Town, U.S.A. **80 B3** 47 59N 102 30W
New Tredegar, U.K. **11 F4** 51 44N 3 16W
New Ulm, U.S.A. **80 C7** 44 19N 94 28W
New Waterford, Canada **71 C7** 46 13N 60 4W
New Westminster, Canada **84 A4** 49 13N 122 55W
New York, U.S.A. **79 F11** 40 45N 74 0W
New York □, U.S.A. **79 D9** 43 0N 75 0W
New York Mts., U.S.A. **83 J6** 35 0N 115 20W
New Zealand ■, Oceania **59 J6** 40 0S 176 0 E
Newaj →, India **42 G7** 24 24N 76 49 E
Newala, Tanzania **55 E4** 10 58S 39 18 E
Newark, Del., U.S.A. **76 F8** 39 41N 75 46W
Newark, N.J., U.S.A. **79 F10** 40 44N 74 10W
Newark, N.Y., U.S.A. **78 C7** 43 3N 77 6W
Newark, Ohio, U.S.A. **78 F2** 40 3N 82 24W
Newark-on-Trent, U.K. **10 D7** 53 5N 0 48W
Newark Valley, U.S.A. **79 D8** 42 14N 76 11W
Newberg, U.S.A. **82 D2** 45 18N 122 58W
Newberry, Mich., U.S.A. **76 B3** 46 21N 85 30W
Newberry, S.C., U.S.A. **77 H5** 34 17N 81 37W
Newberry Springs, U.S.A. **85 L10** 34 50N 116 41W
Newboro L., Canada **79 B8** 44 38N 76 20W
Newbridge = Droichead Nua, Ireland **13 C5** 53 11N 6 48W
Newburgh, Canada **78 B8** 44 19N 76 52W
Newburgh, U.S.A. **79 E10** 41 30N 74 1W
Newbury, U.K. **11 F6** 51 24N 1 20W
Newbury, N.H., U.S.A. **79 B12** 43 19N 72 3W
Newbury, Vt., U.S.A. **79 B12** 44 5N 72 4W
Newburyport, U.S.A. **77 D10** 42 49N 70 53W
Newcastle, Australia **63 E5** 33 0S 151 46 E
Newcastle, N.B., Canada **71 C6** 47 1N 65 38W
Newcastle, Ont., Canada **70 D4** 43 55N 78 35W
Newcastle, S. Africa **57 D4** 27 45S 29 58 E
Newcastle, U.K. **13 B6** 54 13N 5 54W
Newcastle, Calif., U.S.A. **84 G5** 38 53N 121 8W
Newcastle, Wyo., U.S.A. **80 D2** 43 50N 104 11W
Newcastle Emlyn, U.K. **11 E3** 52 2N 4 28W
Newcastle Ra., Australia **60 C5** 15 45S 130 15 E
Newcastle-under-Lyme, U.K. **10 D5** 53 1N 2 14W
Newcastle-upon-Tyne, U.K. **10 C6** 54 58N 1 36W
Newcastle Waters, Australia **62 B1** 17 30S 133 28 E
Newcastle West, Ireland **13 D2** 52 27N 9 3W
Newcomb, U.S.A. **79 C10** 43 58N 74 10W
Newcomerstown, U.S.A. **78 F3** 40 16N 81 36W
Newdegate, Australia **61 F2** 33 6S 119 0 E
Newell, Australia **62 B4** 16 20S 145 16 E
Newell, U.S.A. **80 C3** 44 43N 103 25W
Newfane, U.S.A. **78 C6** 43 17N 78 43W
Newfield, U.S.A. **79 D8** 42 18N 76 33W
Newfound L., U.S.A. **79 C13** 43 40N 71 47W
Newfoundland, Canada **66 E14** 49 0N 55 0W
Newfoundland, U.S.A. **79 E9** 41 18N 75 19W
Newfoundland □, Canada **71 B8** 53 0N 58 0W
Newhall, U.S.A. **85 L8** 34 23N 118 32W
Newhaven, U.K. **11 G8** 50 47N 0 3 E
Newkirk, U.S.A. **81 G6** 36 53N 97 3W
Newlyn, U.K. **11 G2** 50 6N 5 34W
Newman, Australia **60 D2** 23 18S 119 45 E
Newman, U.S.A. **84 H5** 37 19N 121 1W
Newmarket, Canada **78 B5** 44 3N 79 28W
Newmarket, Ireland **13 D2** 52 13N 9 0W
Newmarket, U.K. **11 E8** 52 15N 0 25 E
Newmarket, U.S.A. **79 C14** 43 4N 70 56W
Newnan, U.S.A. **77 J3** 33 23N 84 48W
Newport, Ireland **13 C2** 53 53N 9 33W
Newport, I. of W., U.K. **11 G6** 50 42N 1 17W
Newport, Newp., U.K. **11 F5** 51 35N 3 0W
Newport, Ark., U.S.A. **81 H9** 35 37N 91 16W
Newport, Ky., U.S.A. **76 F3** 39 5N 84 30W
Newport, N.H., U.S.A. **79 C12** 43 22N 72 10W
Newport, N.Y., U.S.A. **79 C9** 43 11N 75 1W
Newport, Oreg., U.S.A. **82 D1** 44 39N 124 3W
Newport, Pa., U.S.A. **78 F7** 40 29N 77 8W
Newport, R.I., U.S.A. **79 E13** 41 29N 71 19W
Newport, Tenn., U.S.A. **77 H4** 35 58N 83 11W
Newport, Vt., U.S.A. **79 B12** 44 56N 72 13W
Newport, Wash., U.S.A. **82 B5** 48 11N 117 3W
Newport □, U.K. **11 F4** 51 33N 3 1W
Newport Beach, U.S.A. **85 M9** 33 37N 117 56W
Newport News, U.S.A. **76 G7** 36 59N 76 25W
Newport Pagnell, U.K. **11 E7** 52 5N 0 43W
Newquay, U.K. **11 G2** 50 25N 5 6W
Newry, U.K. **13 B5** 54 11N 6 21W
Newton, Ill., U.S.A. **80 F10** 38 59N 88 10W
Newton, Iowa, U.S.A. **80 E8** 41 42N 93 3W
Newton, Kans., U.S.A. **81 F6** 38 3N 97 21W
Newton, Mass., U.S.A. **79 D13** 42 21N 71 12W
Newton, Miss., U.S.A. **81 J10** 32 19N 89 10W
Newton, N.C., U.S.A. **77 H5** 35 40N 81 13W
Newton, N.J., U.S.A. **79 E10** 41 3N 74 45W
Newton, Tex., U.S.A. **81 K8** 30 51N 93 46W
Newton Abbot, U.K. **11 G4** 50 32N 3 37W
Newton Aycliffe, U.K. **10 C6** 54 37N 1 34W
Newton Falls, U.S.A. **78 E4** 41 11N 80 59W
Newton Stewart, U.K. **12 G4** 54 57N 4 30W
Newtonmore, U.K. **12 D4** 57 4N 4 8W
Newtown, U.K. **11 E4** 52 31N 3 19W
Newtownabbey, U.K. **13 B6** 54 40N 5 56W
Newtownards, U.K. **13 B6** 54 36N 5 42W
Newtownbarry = Bunclody, Ireland **13 D5** 52 39N 6 40W
Newtownstewart, U.K. **13 B4** 54 43N 7 23W
Newville, U.S.A. **78 F7** 40 10N 77 24W
Neya, Russia **24 C7** 58 21N 43 49 E
Neyrīz, Iran **45 D7** 29 15N 54 19 E
Neyshābūr, Iran **45 B8** 36 10N 58 50 E
Nezhin = Nizhyn, Ukraine **25 D5** 51 5N 31 55 E
Nezperce, U.S.A. **82 C5** 46 14N 116 14W
Ngabang, Indonesia **36 D3** 0 23N 109 55 E
Ngabordamlu, Tanjung, Indonesia **37 F8** 6 56S 134 11 E
N'Gage, Angola **52 F3** 7 46S 15 16 E
Ngami Depression, Botswana **56 C3** 20 30S 22 46 E
Ngamo, Zimbabwe **55 F2** 19 3S 27 32 E
Nganglong Kangri, China **41 C12** 33 0N 81 0 E
Ngao, Thailand **38 C2** 18 46N 99 59 E
Ngaoundéré, Cameroon **52 C2** 7 15N 13 35 E
Ngapara, N.Z. **59 L3** 44 57S 170 46 E
Ngara, Tanzania **54 C3** 2 29S 30 40 E
Ngawi, Indonesia **37 G14** 7 24S 111 26 E
Nghia Lo, Vietnam **38 B5** 21 33N 104 28 E
Ngoma, Malawi **55 E3** 13 8S 33 45 E
Ngomahura, Zimbabwe **55 G3** 20 26S 30 43 E
Ngomba, Tanzania **55 D3** 8 20S 32 53 E
Ngoring Hu, China **32 C4** 34 55N 97 5 E
Ngorongoro, Tanzania **54 C4** 3 11S 35 32 E
Ngozi, Burundi **54 C2** 2 54S 29 50 E
Ngudu, Tanzania **54 C3** 2 58S 33 25 E
Nguigmi, Niger **51 F8** 14 20N 13 20 E
Nguiu, Australia **60 B5** 11 46S 130 38 E
Ngukurr, Australia **62 A1** 14 44S 134 44 E
Ngunga, Tanzania **54 C3** 3 37S 33 37 E
Nguru, Nigeria **51 F8** 12 56N 10 29 E
Nguru Mts., Tanzania **54 D4** 6 0S 37 30 E
Ngusi, Malawi **55 E3** 14 0S 34 50 E
Nguyen Binh, Vietnam **38 A5** 22 39N 105 56 E
Nha Trang, Vietnam **39 F7** 12 16N 109 10 E
Nhacoongo, Mozam. **57 C6** 24 18S 35 14 E
Nhamaabué, Mozam. **55 F4** 17 25S 35 5 E
Nhamundá →, Brazil **93 D7** 2 12S 56 41W
Nhangulaze, L., Mozam. **57 C5** 24 0S 34 30 E
Nhill, Australia **63 F3** 36 18S 141 40 E
Nho Quan, Vietnam **38 B5** 20 18N 105 45 E
Nhulunbuy, Australia **62 A2** 12 10S 137 20 E
Nia-nia, Dem. Rep. of the Congo **54 B2** 1 30N 27 40 E
Niagara Falls, Canada **78 C5** 43 7N 79 5W
Niagara Falls, U.S.A. **78 C6** 43 5N 79 4W
Niagara-on-the-Lake, Canada **78 C5** 43 15N 79 4W
Niah, Malaysia **36 D4** 3 58N 113 46 E
Niamey, Niger **50 F6** 13 27N 2 6 E
Niangara, Dem. Rep. of the Congo **54 B2** 3 42N 27 50 E
Niantic, U.S.A. **79 E12** 41 20N 72 11W
Nias, Indonesia **36 D1** 1 0N 97 30 E
Niassa □, Mozam. **55 E4** 13 30S 36 0 E
Nibāk, Si. Arabia **45 E7** 24 25N 50 50 E
Nicaragua ■, Cent. Amer. **88 D2** 11 40N 85 30W
Nicaragua, L. de, Nic. **88 D2** 12 0N 85 30W
Nicastro, Italy **20 E7** 38 59N 16 19 E
Nice, France **18 E7** 43 42N 7 14 E
Niceville, U.S.A. **77 K2** 30 31N 86 30W
Nichicun, L., Canada **71 B5** 53 5N 71 0W
Nichinan, Japan **31 J5** 31 38N 131 23 E
Nicholás, Canal, W. Indies **88 B3** 23 30N 80 5W
Nicholasville, U.S.A. **76 G3** 37 53N 84 34W
Nichols, U.S.A. **79 D8** 42 1N 76 22W
Nicholson, Australia **60 C4** 18 2S 128 54 E
Nicholson, U.S.A. **79 E9** 41 37N 75 47W
Nicholson →, Australia **62 B2** 17 31S 139 36 E
Nicholson L., Canada **73 A8** 62 40N 102 40W
Nicholson Ra., Australia **61 E2** 27 15S 116 45 E
Nicholville, U.S.A. **79 B10** 44 41N 74 39W
Nicobar Is., Ind. Oc. **29 J13** 8 0N 93 30 E
Nicola, Canada **72 C4** 50 12N 120 40W
Nicolls Town, Bahamas **88 A4** 25 8N 78 0W
Nicosia, Cyprus **23 D12** 35 10N 33 25 E
Nicoya, Costa Rica **88 D2** 10 9N 85 27W
Nicoya, G. de, Costa Rica **88 E3** 10 0N 85 0W
Nicoya, Pen. de, Costa Rica **88 E2** 9 45N 85 40W
Nidd →, U.K. **10 D6** 53 59N 1 23W
Niedersachsen □, Germany **16 B5** 52 50N 9 0 E
Niekerkshoop, S. Africa **56 D3** 29 19S 22 51 E
Niemba, Dem. Rep. of the Congo **54 D2** 5 58S 28 24 E
Niemen = Neman →, Lithuania **9 J19** 55 25N 21 10 E
Nienburg, Germany **16 B5** 52 39N 9 13 E
Nieu Bethesda, S. Africa **56 E3** 31 51S 24 34 E
Nieuw Amsterdam, Surinam **93 B7** 5 53N 55 5W
Nieuw Nickerie, Surinam **93 B7** 6 0N 56 59W
Nieuwoudtville, S. Africa **56 E2** 31 23S 19 7 E
Nieuwpoort, Belgium **15 C2** 51 8N 2 45 E
Nieves, Pico de las, Canary Is. **22 G4** 27 57N 15 35W
Niğde, Turkey **25 G5** 37 58N 34 40 E
Nigel, S. Africa **57 D4** 26 27S 28 25 E
Niger ■, W. Afr. **50 E7** 17 30N 10 0 E
Niger →, W. Afr. **50 G7** 5 33N 6 33 E
Nigeria ■, W. Afr. **50 G7** 8 30N 8 0 E
Nighasin, India **43 E9** 28 14N 80 52 E
Nightcaps, N.Z. **59 L2** 45 57S 168 2 E
Nii-Jima, Japan **31 G9** 34 20N 139 15 E
Niigata, Japan **30 F9** 37 58N 139 0 E
Niigata □, Japan **31 F9** 37 15N 138 45 E
Niihama, Japan **31 H6** 33 55N 133 16 E
Niihau, U.S.A. **74 H14** 21 54N 160 9W
Niimi, Japan **31 G6** 34 59N 133 28 E
Niitsu, Japan **30 F9** 37 48N 139 7 E
Nijil, Jordan **47 E4** 30 32N 35 33 E
Nijkerk, Neths. **15 B5** 52 13N 5 30 E
Nijmegen, Neths. **15 C5** 51 50N 5 52 E
Nijverdal, Neths. **15 B6** 52 22N 6 28 E
Nīk Pey, Iran **45 B6** 36 50N 48 10 E
Nikiniki, Indonesia **37 F6** 9 49S 124 30 E
Nikkō, Japan **31 F9** 36 45N 139 35 E
Nikolayev = Mykolayiv, Ukraine **25 E5** 46 58N 32 0 E
Nikolayevsk, Russia **25 E8** 50 0N 45 35 E
Nikolayevsk-na-Amur, Russia **27 D15** 53 8N 140 44 E
Nikolskoye, Russia **27 D17** 55 12N 166 0 E
Nikopol, Ukraine **25 E5** 47 35N 34 25 E
Nīkshahr, Iran **45 E9** 26 15N 60 10 E
Nikšić, Montenegro, Yug. **21 C8** 42 50N 18 57 E
Nîl, Nahr en →, Africa **51 B12** 30 10N 31 6 E
Nîl el Abyad →, Sudan **51 E12** 15 38N 32 31 E
Nîl el Azraq →, Sudan **51 E12** 15 38N 32 31 E
Nila, Indonesia **37 F7** 6 44S 129 31 E
Niland, U.S.A. **85 M11** 33 14N 115 31W
Nile = Nîl, Nahr en →, Africa **51 B12** 30 10N 31 6 E
Niles, Mich., U.S.A. **76 E2** 41 50N 86 15W
Niles, Ohio, U.S.A. **78 E4** 41 11N 80 46W
Nim Ka Thana, India **42 F6** 27 44N 75 48 E
Nimach, India **42 G6** 24 30N 74 56 E
Nimbahera, India **42 G6** 24 37N 74 45 E
Nîmes, France **18 E6** 43 50N 4 23 E
Nimfaíon, Ákra = Pínnes, Ákra, Greece **21 D11** 40 5N 24 20 E
Nimmitabel, Australia **63 F4** 36 29S 149 15 E
Ninawá, Iraq **44 B4** 36 25N 43 10 E
Nindigully, Australia **63 D4** 28 21S 148 50 E
Nineveh = Ninawá, Iraq **44 B4** 36 25N 43 10 E
Ning Xian, China **34 G4** 35 30N 107 58 E
Ning'an, China **35 B15** 44 22N 129 20 E
Ningbo, China **33 D7** 29 51N 121 28 E
Ningcheng, China **35 D10** 41 32N 119 53 E
Ningjin, China **34 F8** 37 35N 114 57 E
Ningjing Shan, China **32 D4** 30 0N 98 20 E
Ningling, China **34 G8** 34 25N 115 22 E
Ningpo = Ningbo, China **33 D7** 29 51N 121 28 E
Ningqiang, China **34 H4** 32 47N 106 15 E
Ningshan, China **34 H5** 33 21N 108 21 E
Ningsia Hui A.R. = Ningxia Huizu Zizhiqu □, China **34 F4** 38 0N 106 0 E
Ningwu, China **34 E7** 39 0N 112 18 E
Ningxia Huizu Zizhiqu □, China **34 F4** 38 0N 106 0 E
Ningyang, China **34 G9** 35 47N 116 45 E
Ninh Binh, Vietnam **38 B5** 20 15N 105 55 E
Ninh Giang, Vietnam **38 B6** 20 44N 106 24 E
Ninh Hoa, Vietnam **38 F7** 12 30N 109 7 E
Ninh Ma, Vietnam **38 F7** 12 48N 109 21 E
Ninove, Belgium **15 D4** 50 51N 4 2 E
Nioaque, Brazil **95 A4** 21 5S 55 50W
Niobrara, U.S.A. **80 D6** 42 45N 98 2W
Niobrara →, U.S.A. **80 D6** 42 46N 98 3W
Nioro du Sahel, Mali **50 E4** 15 15N 9 30W
Niort, France **18 C3** 46 19N 0 29W
Nipawin, Canada **73 C8** 53 20N 104 0W
Nipigon, Canada **70 C2** 49 0N 88 17W
Nipigon, L., Canada **70 C2** 49 50N 88 30W
Nipishish L., Canada **71 B7** 54 12N 60 45W
Nipissing, L., Canada **70 C4** 46 20N 80 0W
Nipomo, U.S.A. **85 K6** 35 3N 120 29W
Nipton, U.S.A. **85 K11** 35 28N 115 16W
Niquelândia, Brazil **93 F9** 14 33S 48 23W
Nīr, Iran **44 B5** 38 2N 47 59 E
Nirasaki, Japan **31 G9** 35 42N 138 27 E
Nirmal, India **40 K11** 19 3N 78 20 E
Nirmali, India **43 F12** 26 20N 86 35 E
Niš, Serbia, Yug. **21 C9** 43 19N 21 58 E
Nişāb, Si. Arabia **44 D5** 29 11N 44 43 E
Nişāb, Yemen **46 E4** 14 25N 46 29 E
Nishinomiya, Japan **31 G7** 34 45N 135 20 E
Nishino'omote, Japan **31 J5** 30 43N 130 59 E
Nishiwaki, Japan **31 G7** 34 59N 134 58 E
Niskibi →, Canada **70 A2** 56 29N 88 9W
Nisqually →, U.S.A. **84 C4** 47 6N 122 42W
Nissáki, Greece **23 A3** 39 43N 19 52 E
Nissum Bredning, Denmark **9 H13** 56 40N 8 20 E
Nistru = Dnister →, Europe **17 E16** 46 18N 30 17 E
Nisutlin →, Canada **72 A2** 60 14N 132 34W
Nitchequon, Canada **71 B5** 53 10N 70 58W
Niterói, Brazil **95 A7** 22 52S 43 0W
Nith →, Canada **78 C4** 43 12N 80 23W
Nith →, U.K. **12 F5** 55 14N 3 33W
Nitra, Slovak Rep. **17 D10** 48 19N 18 4 E
Nitra →, Slovak Rep. **17 E10** 47 46N 18 10 E
Niuafo'ou, Tonga **59 B11** 15 30S 175 58W
Niue, Cook Is. **65 J11** 19 2S 169 54W
Niut, Indonesia **36 D4** 0 55N 110 6 E
Niuzhuang, China **35 D12** 40 58N 122 28 E
Nivala, Finland **8 E21** 63 56N 24 57 E
Nivelles, Belgium **15 D4** 50 35N 4 20 E
Nivernais, France **18 C5** 47 15N 3 30 E
Niwas, India **43 H9** 23 3N 80 26 E
Nixon, U.S.A. **81 L6** 29 16N 97 46W
Nizamabad, India **40 K11** 18 45N 78 7 E
Nizamghat, India **41 E19** 28 20N 95 45 E
Nizhne Kolymsk, Russia **27 C17** 68 34N 160 55 E
Nizhnekamsk, Russia **24 C9** 55 38N 51 49 E
Nizhneudinsk, Russia **27 D10** 54 54N 99 3 E
Nizhnevartovsk, Russia **26 C8** 60 56N 76 38 E
Nizhniy Novgorod, Russia **24 C7** 56 20N 44 0 E
Nizhniy Tagil, Russia **24 C10** 57 55N 59 57 E
Nizhyn, Ukraine **25 D5** 51 5N 31 55 E
Nizip, Turkey **44 B3** 37 5N 37 50 E
Nízké Tatry, Slovak Rep. **17 D10** 48 55N 19 30 E
Njakwa, Malawi **55 E3** 11 1S 33 56 E
Njanji, Zambia **55 E3** 14 25S 31 46 E
Njinjo, Tanzania **55 D4** 8 48S 38 54 E
Njombe, Tanzania **55 D3** 9 20S 34 50 E
Njombe →, Tanzania **54 D4** 6 56S 35 6 E
Nkana, Zambia **55 E2** 12 50S 28 8 E
Nkandla, S. Africa **57 D5** 28 37S 31 5 E
Nkayi, Zimbabwe **55 F2** 19 41S 29 20 E
Nkhotakota, Malawi **55 E3** 12 56S 34 15 E
Nkongsamba, Cameroon **52 D1** 4 55N 9 55 E
Nkurenkuru, Namibia **56 B2** 17 42S 18 32 E
Nmai →, Burma **41 G20** 25 30N 97 25 E
Noakhali = Maijdi, Bangla. **41 H17** 22 48N 91 10 E
Nobel, Canada **78 A4** 45 25N 80 6W
Nobeoka, Japan **31 H5** 32 36N 131 41 E
Noblesville, U.S.A. **76 E3** 40 3N 86 1W
Nocera Inferiore, Italy **20 D6** 40 44N 14 38 E
Nocona, U.S.A. **81 J6** 33 47N 97 44W
Noda, Japan **31 G9** 35 56N 139 52 E
Nogales, Mexico **86 A2** 31 20N 110 56W
Nogales, U.S.A. **83 L8** 31 20N 110 56W
Nōgata, Japan **31 H5** 33 48N 130 44 E
Noggerup, Australia **61 F2** 33 32S 116 5 E
Noginsk, Russia **27 C10** 64 30N 90 50 E
Nogoa →, Australia **62 C4** 23 40S 147 55 E
Nogoyá, Argentina **94 C4** 32 24S 59 48W
Nohar, India **42 E6** 29 11N 74 49 E
Nohta, India **43 H8** 23 40N 79 34 E
Noires, Mts., France **18 B2** 48 11N 3 40W
Noirmoutier, Î. de, France **18 C2** 46 58N 2 10W
Nojane, Botswana **56 C3** 23 15S 20 14 E
Nojima-Zaki, Japan **31 G9** 34 54N 139 53 E
Nok Kundi, Pakistan **40 E3** 28 50N 62 45 E
Nokaneng, Botswana **56 B3** 19 40S 22 17 E
Nokia, Finland **9 F20** 61 30N 23 30 E
Nokomis, Canada **73 C8** 51 35N 105 0W
Nokomis L., Canada **73 B8** 57 0N 103 0W
Nola, C.A.R. **52 D3** 3 35N 16 4 E
Noma Omuramba →, Namibia **56 B3** 18 52S 20 53 E
Nombre de Dios, Panama **88 E4** 9 34N 79 28W
Nome, U.S.A. **68 B3** 64 30N 165 25W
Nomo-Zaki, Japan **31 H4** 32 35N 129 44 E
Nonacho L., Canada **73 A7** 61 42N 109 40W
Nonda, Australia **62 C3** 20 40S 142 28 E
Nong Chang, Thailand **38 E2** 15 23N 99 51 E
Nong Het, Laos **38 C4** 19 29N 103 59 E
Nong Khai, Thailand **38 D4** 17 50N 102 46 E
Nong'an, China **35 B13** 44 25N 125 5 E
Nongoma, S. Africa **57 D5** 27 58S 31 35 E
Nonoava, Mexico **86 B3** 27 28N 106 44W
Nonoava →, Mexico **86 B3** 27 29N 106 45W
Nonthaburi, Thailand **38 F3** 13 51N 100 34 E
Noonamah, Australia **60 B5** 12 40S 131 4 E
Noord Brabant □, Neths. **15 C5** 51 40N 5 0 E
Noord Holland □, Neths. **15 B4** 52 30N 4 45 E
Noordbeveland, Neths. **15 C3** 51 35N 3 50 E
Noordoostpolder, Neths. **15 B5** 52 45N 5 45 E
Noordwijk, Neths. **15 B4** 52 14N 4 26 E
Nootka I., Canada **72 D3** 49 32N 126 42W
Nopiming Prov. Park, Canada **73 C9** 50 30N 95 37W
Noralee, Canada **72 C3** 53 59N 126 26W
Noranda = Rouyn-Noranda, Canada **70 C4** 48 20N 79 0W
Norco, U.S.A. **85 M9** 33 56N 117 33W
Nord-Kivu □, Dem. Rep. of the Congo **54 C2** 1 0S 29 0 E
Nord-Ostsee-Kanal, Germany **16 A5** 54 12N 9 32 E
Nordaustlandet, Svalbard **4 B9** 79 14N 23 0 E
Nordegg, Canada **72 C5** 52 29N 116 5W
Norderney, Germany **16 B4** 53 42N 7 9 E
Norderstedt, Germany **16 B5** 53 42N 10 1 E

O

Organos, Pta. de los

Organos, Pta. de los, *Canary Is.* **22 F2** 28 12N 17 17W
Orgaz, *Spain* **19 C4** 39 39N 3 53W
Orgeyev = Orhei, *Moldova* **17 E15** 47 24N 28 50 E
Orhaneli, *Turkey* **21 E13** 39 54N 28 59 E
Orhangazi, *Turkey* **21 D13** 40 29N 29 18 E
Orhei, *Moldova* **17 E15** 47 24N 28 50 E
Orhon Gol →, *Mongolia* **32 A5** 50 21N 106 0 E
Oriental, Cordillera, *Colombia* **92 B4** 6 0N 73 0W
Oriental, Grand Erg, *Algeria* **50 B7** 30 0N 6 30 E
Orientale □, *Dem. Rep. of the Congo* **54 B2** 2 20N 26 0 E
Oriente, *Argentina* **94 D3** 38 44S 60 37W
Orihuela, *Spain* **19 C5** 38 7N 0 55W
Orillia, *Canada* **78 B5** 44 40N 79 24W
Orinoco →, *Venezuela* **92 B6** 9 15N 61 30W
Orion, *Canada* **73 D6** 49 27N 110 49W
Oriskany, *U.S.A.* **79 C9** 43 10N 75 20W
Orissa □, *India* **41 K14** 20 0N 84 0 E
Orissaare, *Estonia* **9 G20** 58 34N 23 5 E
Oristano, *Italy* **20 E3** 39 54N 8 36 E
Oristano, G. di, *Italy* **20 E3** 39 50N 8 29 E
Orizaba, *Mexico* **87 D5** 18 51N 97 6W
Orkanger, *Norway* **8 E13** 63 18N 9 52 E
Orkla →, *Norway* **8 E13** 63 18N 9 51 E
Orkney, *S. Africa* **56 D4** 26 58S 26 40 E
Orkney □, *U.K.* **12 B5** 59 2N 3 13W
Orkney Is., *U.K.* **12 B6** 59 0N 3 0W
Orland, *U.S.A.* **84 F4** 39 45N 122 12W
Orlando, *U.S.A.* **77 L5** 28 33N 81 23W
Orléanais, *France* **18 C5** 48 0N 2 0 E
Orléans, *France* **18 C4** 47 54N 1 52 E
Orleans, *U.S.A.* **79 B12** 44 49N 72 12W
Orléans, I. d', *Canada* **71 C5** 46 54N 70 58W
Ormara, *Pakistan* **40 G4** 25 16N 64 33 E
Ormoc, *Phil.* **37 B6** 11 0N 124 37 E
Ormond, *N.Z.* **59 H6** 38 33S 177 56 E
Ormond Beach, *U.S.A.* **77 L5** 29 17N 81 3W
Ormskirk, *U.K.* **10 D5** 53 35N 2 54W
Ormstown, *Canada* **79 A11** 45 8N 74 0W
Örnsköldsvik, *Sweden* **8 E18** 63 17N 18 40 E
Oro, *N. Korea* **35 D14** 40 1N 127 27 E
Oro →, *Mexico* **86 B3** 25 35N 105 2W
Oro Grande, *U.S.A.* **85 L9** 34 36N 117 20W
Oro Valley, *U.S.A.* **83 K8** 32 26N 110 58W
Orocué, *Colombia* **92 C4** 4 48N 71 20W
Orofino, *U.S.A.* **82 C5** 46 29N 116 15W
Orol Dengizi = Aral Sea, *Asia* **26 E7** 44 30N 60 0 E
Oromocto, *Canada* **71 C6** 45 54N 66 29W
Orono, *Canada* **78 C6** 43 59N 78 37W
Orono, *U.S.A.* **77 C11** 44 53N 68 40W
Oronsay, *U.K.* **12 E2** 56 1N 6 15W
Oroqen Zizhiqi, *China* **33 A7** 50 34N 123 43 E
Oroquieta, *Phil.* **37 C6** 8 32N 123 44 E
Orosháza, *Hungary* **17 E11** 46 32N 20 42 E
Orotukan, *Russia* **27 C16** 62 16N 151 42 E
Oroville, *Calif., U.S.A.* **84 F5** 39 31N 121 33W
Oroville, *Wash., U.S.A.* **82 B4** 48 56N 119 26W
Oroville, L., *U.S.A.* **84 F5** 39 33N 121 29W
Orroroo, *Australia* **63 E2** 32 43S 138 38 E
Orrville, *U.S.A.* **78 F3** 40 50N 81 46W
Orsha, *Belarus* **24 D5** 54 30N 30 25 E
Orsk, *Russia* **26 D6** 51 12N 58 34 E
Orşova, *Romania* **17 F12** 44 41N 22 25 E
Ortaca, *Turkey* **21 F13** 36 49N 28 45 E
Ortegal, C., *Spain* **19 A2** 43 43N 7 52W
Orthez, *France* **18 E3** 43 29N 0 48W
Ortigueira, *Spain* **19 A2** 43 40N 7 50W
Orting, *U.S.A.* **84 C4** 47 6N 122 12W
Ortles, *Italy* **18 C9** 46 31N 10 33 E
Ortón →, *Bolivia* **92 F5** 10 50S 67 0W
Ortonville, *U.S.A.* **80 C6** 45 19N 96 27W
Orūmīyeh, *Iran* **44 B5** 37 40N 45 0 E
Orūmīyeh, Daryācheh-ye, *Iran* **44 B5** 37 50N 45 30 E
Oruro, *Bolivia* **92 G5** 18 0S 67 9W
Orust, *Sweden* **9 G14** 58 10N 11 40 E
Oruzgān □, *Afghan.* **40 C5** 33 30N 66 0 E
Orvieto, *Italy* **20 C5** 42 43N 12 7 E
Orwell, *N.Y., U.S.A.* **79 C9** 43 35N 75 50W
Orwell, *Ohio, U.S.A.* **78 E4** 41 32N 80 52W
Orwell →, *U.K.* **11 F9** 51 59N 1 18 E
Orwigsburg, *U.S.A.* **79 F8** 40 38N 76 6W
Oryakhovo, *Bulgaria* **21 C10** 43 40N 23 57 E
Osa, *Russia* **24 C10** 57 17N 55 26 E
Osa, Pen. de, *Costa Rica* **88 E3** 8 0N 84 0W
Osage, *U.S.A.* **80 D8** 43 17N 92 49W
Osage →, *U.S.A.* **80 F9** 38 35N 91 57W
Osage City, *U.S.A.* **80 F7** 38 38N 95 50W
Ōsaka, *Japan* **31 G7** 34 40N 135 30 E
Osan, *S. Korea* **35 F14** 37 11N 127 4 E
Osawatomie, *U.S.A.* **80 F7** 38 31N 94 57W
Osborne, *U.S.A.* **80 F5** 39 26N 98 42W
Osceola, *Ark., U.S.A.* **81 H10** 35 42N 89 58W
Osceola, *Iowa, U.S.A.* **80 E8** 41 2N 93 46W
Oscoda, *U.S.A.* **78 B1** 44 26N 83 20W
Ösel = Saaremaa, *Estonia* **9 G20** 58 30N 22 30 E
Osgoode, *Canada* **79 A9** 45 8N 75 36W
Osh, *Kyrgyzstan* **26 E8** 40 37N 72 49 E
Oshakati, *Namibia* **53 H3** 17 45S 15 40 E
Oshawa, *Canada* **78 C6** 43 50N 78 50W
Oshigambo, *Namibia* **56 B2** 17 45S 16 5 E
Oshkosh, *Nebr., U.S.A.* **80 E3** 41 24N 102 21W
Oshkosh, *Wis., U.S.A.* **80 C10** 44 1N 88 33W
Oshmyany = Ashmyany, *Belarus* **9 J21** 54 26N 25 52 E
Oshnovīyeh, *Iran* **44 B5** 37 2N 45 6 E
Oshogbo, *Nigeria* **50 G6** 7 48N 4 37 E
Oshtorīnān, *Iran* **45 C6** 34 1N 48 38 E
Oshwe, *Dem. Rep. of the Congo* **52 E3** 3 25S 19 28 E
Osijek, *Croatia* **21 B8** 45 34N 18 41 E
Osipenko = Berdyansk, *Ukraine* **25 E6** 46 45N 36 50 E
Osipovichi = Asipovichy, *Belarus* **17 B15** 53 19N 28 33 E
Osiyan, *India* **42 F5** 26 43N 72 55 E
Osizweni, *S. Africa* **57 D5** 27 49S 30 7 E
Oskaloosa, *U.S.A.* **80 E8** 41 18N 92 39W
Oskarshamn, *Sweden* **9 H17** 57 15N 16 27 E
Oskélanéo, *Canada* **70 C4** 48 5N 75 15W
Öskemen, *Kazakstan* **26 E9** 50 0N 82 36 E
Oslo, *Norway* **9 G14** 59 55N 10 45 E
Oslofjorden, *Norway* **9 G14** 59 20N 10 35 E
Osmanabad, *India* **40 K10** 18 5N 76 10 E
Osmaniye, *Turkey* **25 G6** 37 5N 36 10 E
Osnabrück, *Germany* **16 B5** 52 17N 8 3 E
Osorio, *Brazil* **95 B5** 29 53S 50 17W
Osorno, *Chile* **96 E2** 40 25S 73 0W
Osoyoos, *Canada* **72 D5** 49 0N 119 30W
Osøyro, *Norway* **9 F11** 60 9N 5 30 E
Ospika →, *Canada* **72 B4** 56 20N 124 0W
Osprey Reef, *Australia* **62 A4** 13 52S 146 36 E
Oss, *Neths.* **15 C5** 51 46N 5 32 E
Ossa, Mt., *Australia* **62 G4** 41 52S 146 3 E
Óssa, Óros, *Greece* **21 E10** 39 47N 22 42 E
Ossabaw I., *U.S.A.* **77 K5** 31 50N 81 5W
Ossining, *U.S.A.* **79 E11** 41 10N 73 55W
Ossipee, *U.S.A.* **79 C13** 43 41N 71 7W
Ossokmanuan L., *Canada* **71 B7** 53 25N 65 0W
Ossora, *Russia* **27 D17** 59 20N 163 13 E
Ostend = Oostende, *Belgium* **15 C2** 51 15N 2 54 E
Oster, *Ukraine* **17 C16** 50 57N 30 53 E
Osterburg, *U.S.A.* **78 F6** 40 16N 78 31W
Österdalälven, *Sweden* **9 F16** 61 30N 13 45 E
Østerdalen, *Norway* **9 F14** 61 40N 10 50 E
Östersund, *Sweden* **8 E16** 63 10N 14 38 E
Ostfriesische Inseln, *Germany* **16 B4** 53 42N 7 0 E
Ostrava, *Czech Rep.* **17 D10** 49 51N 18 18 E
Ostróda, *Poland* **17 B10** 53 42N 19 58 E
Ostroh, *Ukraine* **17 C14** 50 20N 26 30 E
Ostrołęka, *Poland* **17 B11** 53 4N 21 32 E
Ostrów Mazowiecka, *Poland* **17 B11** 52 50N 21 51 E
Ostrów Wielkopolski, *Poland* **17 C9** 51 36N 17 44 E
Ostrowiec-Świętokrzyski, *Poland* **17 C11** 50 55N 21 22 E
Ostuni, *Italy* **21 D7** 40 44N 17 35 E
Ōsumi-Kaikyō, *Japan* **31 J5** 30 55N 131 0 E
Ōsumi-Shotō, *Japan* **31 J5** 30 30N 130 0 E
Osuna, *Spain* **19 D3** 37 14N 5 8W
Oswegatchie →, *U.S.A.* **79 B9** 44 42N 75 30W
Oswego, *U.S.A.* **79 C8** 43 27N 76 31W
Oswego →, *U.S.A.* **79 C8** 43 27N 76 30W
Oswestry, *U.K.* **10 E4** 52 52N 3 3W
Oświęcim, *Poland* **17 C10** 50 2N 19 11 E
Otago □, *N.Z.* **59 L2** 45 15S 170 0 E
Otago Harbour, *N.Z.* **59 L3** 45 47S 170 42 E
Ōtake, *Japan* **31 G6** 34 12N 132 13 E
Otaki, *N.Z.* **59 J5** 40 45S 175 10 E
Otaru, *Japan* **30 C10** 43 10N 141 0 E
Otaru-Wan = Ishikari-Wan, *Japan* **30 C10** 43 25N 141 1 E
Otavalo, *Ecuador* **92 C3** 0 13N 78 20W
Otavi, *Namibia* **56 B2** 19 40S 17 24 E
Otchinjau, *Angola* **56 B1** 16 30S 13 56 E
Otelnuk L., *Canada* **71 A6** 56 9N 68 12W
Othello, *U.S.A.* **82 C4** 46 50N 119 10W
Otjiwarongo, *Namibia* **56 C2** 20 30S 16 33 E
Otoineppu, *Japan* **30 B11** 44 44N 142 16 E
Otorohanga, *N.Z.* **59 H5** 38 12S 175 14 E
Otoskwin →, *Canada* **70 B2** 52 13N 88 6W
Otra →, *Norway* **9 G13** 58 9N 8 1 E
Otranto, *Italy* **21 D8** 40 9N 18 28 E
Otranto, C. d', *Italy* **21 D8** 40 7N 18 30 E
Otranto, Str. of, *Italy* **21 D8** 40 15N 18 40 E
Otse, *S. Africa* **56 D4** 25 2S 25 45 E
Ōtsu, *Japan* **31 G7** 35 0N 135 50 E
Ōtsuki, *Japan* **31 G9** 35 36N 138 57 E
Ottawa = Outaouais →, *Canada* **70 C5** 45 27N 74 8W
Ottawa, *Canada* **79 A9** 45 27N 75 42W
Ottawa, *Ill., U.S.A.* **80 E10** 41 21N 88 51W
Ottawa, *Kans., U.S.A.* **80 F7** 38 37N 95 16W
Ottawa Is., *Canada* **69 C11** 59 35N 80 10W
Otter Cr. →, *U.S.A.* **79 B11** 44 13N 73 17W
Otter L., *Canada* **73 B8** 55 35N 104 39W
Otterville, *Canada* **78 D4** 42 55N 80 36W
Ottery St. Mary, *U.K.* **11 G4** 50 44N 3 17W
Otto Beit Bridge, *Zimbabwe* **55 F2** 15 59S 28 56 E
Ottosdal, *S. Africa* **56 D4** 26 46S 25 59 E
Ottumwa, *U.S.A.* **80 E8** 41 1N 92 25W
Oturkpo, *Nigeria* **50 G7** 7 16N 8 8 E
Otway, B., *Chile* **96 G2** 53 30S 74 0W
Otway, C., *Australia* **63 F3** 38 52S 143 30 E
Otwock, *Poland* **17 B11** 52 5N 21 20 E
Ou →, *Laos* **38 B4** 20 4N 102 13 E
Ou Neua, *Laos* **38 A3** 22 18N 101 48 E
Ou-Sammyaku, *Japan* **30 E10** 39 20N 140 35 E
Ouachita →, *U.S.A.* **81 K9** 31 38N 91 49W
Ouachita, L., *U.S.A.* **81 H8** 34 34N 93 12W
Ouachita Mts., *U.S.A.* **81 H7** 34 40N 94 25W
Ouagadougou, *Burkina Faso* **50 F5** 12 25N 1 30W
Ouahran = Oran, *Algeria* **50 A5** 35 45N 0 39W
Ouallene, *Algeria* **50 D6** 24 41N 1 11 E
Ouargla, *Algeria* **50 B7** 31 59N 5 16 E
Ouarzazate, *Morocco* **50 B4** 30 55N 6 50W
Oubangi →, *Dem. Rep. of the Congo* **52 E3** 0 30S 17 50 E
Ouddorp, *Neths.* **15 C3** 51 50N 3 57 E
Oude Rijn →, *Neths.* **15 B4** 52 12N 4 24 E
Oudenaarde, *Belgium* **15 D3** 50 50N 3 37 E
Oudtshoorn, *S. Africa* **56 E3** 33 35S 22 14 E
Ouessant, Î. d', *France* **18 B1** 48 28N 5 6W
Ouesso, *Congo* **52 D3** 1 37N 16 5 E
Ouest, Pte. de l', *Canada* **71 C7** 49 52N 64 40W
Ouezzane, *Morocco* **50 B4** 34 51N 5 35W
Oughterard, *Ireland* **13 C2** 53 26N 9 18W
Oujda, *Morocco* **50 B5** 34 41N 1 55W
Oulainen, *Finland* **8 D21** 64 17N 24 47 E
Oulu, *Finland* **8 D21** 65 1N 25 29 E
Oulujärvi, *Finland* **8 D22** 64 25N 27 15 E
Oulujoki →, *Finland* **8 D21** 65 1N 25 30 E
Oum Chalouba, *Chad* **51 E10** 15 48N 20 46 E
Oum Hadjer, *Chad* **51 F9** 13 18N 19 41 E
Ounasjoki →, *Finland* **8 C21** 66 31N 25 40 E
Ounguati, *Namibia* **56 C2** 22 0S 15 46 E
Ounianga Sérir, *Chad* **51 E10** 18 54N 20 51 E
Our →, *Lux.* **15 E6** 49 55N 6 5 E
Ouray, *U.S.A.* **83 G10** 38 1N 107 40W
Ourense, *Spain* **19 A2** 42 19N 7 55W
Ouricuri, *Brazil* **93 E10** 7 53S 40 5W
Ourinhos, *Brazil* **95 A6** 23 0S 49 54W
Ouro Fino, *Brazil* **95 A6** 22 16S 46 25W
Ouro Prêto, *Brazil* **95 A7** 20 20S 43 30W
Ourthe →, *Belgium* **15 D5** 50 29N 5 35 E
Ouse →, *E. Susx., U.K.* **11 G8** 50 47N 0 4 E
Ouse →, *N. Yorks., U.K.* **10 D7** 53 44N 0 55W
Outaouais →, *Canada* **70 C5** 45 27N 74 8W
Outardes →, *Canada* **71 C6** 49 24N 69 30W
Outer Hebrides, *U.K.* **12 D1** 57 30N 7 40W
Outjo, *Namibia* **56 C2** 20 5S 16 7 E
Outlook, *Canada* **73 C7** 51 30N 107 0W
Outokumpu, *Finland* **8 E23** 62 43N 29 1 E
Ouyen, *Australia* **63 F3** 35 1S 142 22 E
Ovalau, *Fiji* **59 C8** 17 40S 178 48 E
Ovalle, *Chile* **94 C1** 30 33S 71 18W
Ovamboland, *Namibia* **56 B2** 18 30S 16 0 E
Overflakkee, *Neths.* **15 C4** 51 44N 4 10 E
Overijssel □, *Neths.* **15 B6** 52 25N 6 35 E
Overland Park, *U.S.A.* **80 F7** 38 55N 94 50W
Overton, *U.S.A.* **85 J12** 36 33N 114 27W
Övertorneå, *Sweden* **8 C20** 66 23N 23 38 E
Ovid, *U.S.A.* **79 D8** 42 41N 76 49W
Oviedo, *Spain* **19 A3** 43 25N 5 50W
Oviši, *Latvia* **9 H19** 57 33N 21 44 E
Ovoot, *Mongolia* **34 B7** 45 21N 113 45 E
Övör Hangay □, *Mongolia* **34 B2** 45 0N 102 30 E
Øvre Årdal, *Norway* **9 F12** 61 19N 7 48 E
Ovruch, *Ukraine* **17 C15** 51 25N 28 45 E
Owaka, *N.Z.* **59 M2** 46 27S 169 40 E
Owambo = Ovamboland, *Namibia* **56 B2** 18 30S 16 0 E
Owasco L., *U.S.A.* **79 D8** 42 50N 76 31W
Owase, *Japan* **31 G8** 34 7N 136 12 E
Owatonna, *U.S.A.* **80 C8** 44 5N 93 14W
Owbeh, *Afghan.* **40 B3** 34 28N 63 10 E
Owego, *U.S.A.* **79 D8** 42 6N 76 16W
Owen Falls Dam, *Uganda* **54 B3** 0 30N 33 5 E
Owen Sound, *Canada* **78 B4** 44 35N 80 55W
Owens →, *U.S.A.* **84 J9** 36 32N 117 59W
Owens L., *U.S.A.* **85 J9** 36 26N 117 57W
Owensboro, *U.S.A.* **76 G2** 37 46N 87 7W
Owl →, *Canada* **73 B10** 57 51N 92 44W
Owo, *Nigeria* **50 G7** 7 10N 5 39 E
Owosso, *U.S.A.* **76 D3** 43 0N 84 10W
Owyhee, *U.S.A.* **82 F5** 41 57N 116 6W
Owyhee →, *U.S.A.* **82 E5** 43 49N 117 2W
Owyhee, L., *U.S.A.* **82 E5** 43 38N 117 14W
Ox Mts. = Slieve Gamph, *Ireland* **13 B3** 54 6N 9 0W
Öxarfjörður, *Iceland* **8 C5** 66 15N 16 45W
Oxbow, *Canada* **73 D8** 49 14N 102 10W
Oxelösund, *Sweden* **9 G17** 58 43N 17 5 E
Oxford, *N.Z.* **59 K4** 43 18S 172 11 E
Oxford, *U.K.* **11 F6** 51 46N 1 15W
Oxford, *Mass., U.S.A.* **79 D13** 42 7N 71 52W
Oxford, *Miss., U.S.A.* **81 H10** 34 22N 89 31W
Oxford, *N.C., U.S.A.* **77 G6** 36 19N 78 35W
Oxford, *N.Y., U.S.A.* **79 D9** 42 27N 75 36W
Oxford, *Ohio, U.S.A.* **76 F3** 39 31N 84 45W
Oxford L., *Canada* **73 C9** 54 51N 95 37W
Oxfordshire □, *U.K.* **11 F6** 51 48N 1 16W
Oxnard, *U.S.A.* **85 L7** 34 12N 119 11W
Oxus = Amudarya →, *Uzbekistan* **26 E6** 43 58N 59 34 E
Oya, *Malaysia* **36 D4** 2 55N 111 55 E
Oyama, *Japan* **31 F9** 36 18N 139 48 E
Oyem, *Gabon* **52 D2** 1 34N 11 31 E
Oyen, *Canada* **73 C6** 51 22N 110 28W
Oykel →, *U.K.* **12 D4** 57 56N 4 26W
Oymyakon, *Russia* **27 C15** 63 25N 142 44 E
Oyo, *Nigeria* **50 G6** 7 46N 3 56 E
Oyster Bay, *U.S.A.* **79 F11** 40 52N 73 32W
Ōyübari, *Japan* **30 C11** 43 1N 142 5 E
Ozamiz, *Phil.* **37 C6** 8 15N 123 50 E
Ozark, *Ala., U.S.A.* **77 K3** 31 28N 85 39W
Ozark, *Ark., U.S.A.* **81 H8** 35 29N 93 50W
Ozark, *Mo., U.S.A.* **81 G8** 37 1N 93 12W
Ozark Plateau, *U.S.A.* **81 G9** 37 20N 91 40W
Ozarks, L. of the, *U.S.A.* **80 F8** 38 12N 92 38W
Ózd, *Hungary* **17 D11** 48 14N 20 15 E
Ozette L., *U.S.A.* **84 B2** 48 6N 124 38W
Ozona, *U.S.A.* **81 K4** 30 43N 101 12W
Ozuluama, *Mexico* **87 C5** 21 40N 97 50W

P

Pa-an, *Burma* **41 L20** 16 51N 97 40 E
Pa Mong Dam, *Thailand* **38 D4** 18 0N 102 22 E
Pa Sak →, *Thailand* **36 B2** 15 30N 101 0 E
Paamiut, *Greenland* **4 C5** 62 0N 49 43W
Paarl, *S. Africa* **56 E2** 33 45S 18 56 E
Pab Hills, *Pakistan* **42 F2** 26 30N 66 45 E
Pabbay, *U.K.* **12 D1** 57 46N 7 14W
Pabianice, *Poland* **17 C10** 51 40N 19 20 E
Pabna, *Bangla.* **41 G16** 24 1N 89 18 E
Pabo, *Uganda* **54 B3** 3 1N 32 10 E
Pacaja →, *Brazil* **93 D8** 1 56S 50 50W
Pacaraima, Sa., *S. Amer.* **92 C6** 4 0N 62 30W
Pacasmayo, *Peru* **92 E3** 7 20S 79 35W
Pachhar, *India* **42 G7** 24 40N 77 42 E
Pachitea →, *Peru* **92 E4** 8 46S 74 33W
Pachmarhi, *India* **43 H8** 22 28N 78 26 E
Pachpadra, *India* **40 G8** 25 58N 72 10 E
Pachuca, *Mexico* **87 C5** 20 10N 98 40W
Pacific, *Canada* **72 C3** 54 48N 128 28W
Pacific-Antarctic Ridge, *Pac. Oc.* **65 M16** 43 0S 115 0W
Pacific Grove, *U.S.A.* **84 J5** 36 38N 121 56W
Pacific Ocean, *Pac. Oc.* **65 G14** 10 0N 140 0W
Pacific Rim Nat. Park, *Canada* **84 B2** 48 40N 124 45W
Pacifica, *U.S.A.* **84 H4** 37 36N 122 30W
Pacitan, *Indonesia* **37 H14** 8 12S 111 7 E
Packwood, *U.S.A.* **84 D5** 46 36N 121 40W
Padaido, Kepulauan, *Indonesia* **37 E9** 1 15S 136 30 E
Padang, *Indonesia* **36 E2** 1 0S 100 20 E
Padang Endau, *Malaysia* **39 L4** 2 40N 103 38 E
Padangpanjang, *Indonesia* **36 E2** 0 40S 100 20 E
Padangsidempuan, *Indonesia* **36 D1** 1 30N 99 15 E
Paddle Prairie, *Canada* **72 B5** 57 57N 117 29W
Paddockwood, *Canada* **73 C7** 53 30N 105 30W
Paderborn, *Germany* **16 C5** 51 42N 8 45 E
Padma, *India* **43 G11** 24 12N 85 22 E
Pádova, *Italy* **20 B4** 45 25N 11 53 E
Padra, *India* **42 H5** 22 15N 73 7 E
Padrauna, *India* **43 F10** 26 54N 83 59 E
Padre I., *U.S.A.* **81 M6** 27 10N 97 25W
Padstow, *U.K.* **11 G3** 50 33N 4 58W
Padua = Pádova, *Italy* **20 B4** 45 25N 11 53 E
Paducah, *Ky., U.S.A.* **76 G1** 37 5N 88 37W
Paducah, *Tex., U.S.A.* **81 H4** 34 1N 100 18W
Paengnyŏng-do, *S. Korea* **35 F13** 37 57N 124 40 E
Paeroa, *N.Z.* **59 G5** 37 23S 175 41 E
Pafúri, *Mozam.* **57 C5** 22 28S 31 17 E
Pag, *Croatia* **16 F8** 44 25N 15 3 E
Pagadian, *Phil.* **37 C6** 7 55N 123 30 E
Pagai Selatan, Pulau, *Indonesia* **36 E2** 3 0S 100 15 E
Pagai Utara, Pulau, *Indonesia* **36 E2** 2 35S 100 0 E
Pagalu = Annobón, *Atl. Oc.* **49 G4** 1 25S 5 36 E
Pagara, *India* **43 G9** 24 22N 80 1 E
Pagastikós Kólpos, *Greece* **21 E10** 39 15N 23 0 E
Pagatan, *Indonesia* **36 E5** 3 33S 115 59 E
Page, *U.S.A.* **83 H8** 36 57N 111 27W
Pago Pago, *Amer. Samoa* **59 B13** 14 16S 170 43W
Pagosa Springs, *U.S.A.* **83 H10** 37 16N 107 1W
Pagwa River, *Canada* **70 B2** 50 2N 85 14W
Pahala, *U.S.A.* **74 J17** 19 12N 155 29W
Pahang →, *Malaysia* **39 L4** 3 30N 103 9 E
Pahiatua, *N.Z.* **59 J5** 40 27S 175 50 E
Pahokee, *U.S.A.* **77 M5** 26 50N 80 40W
Pahrump, *U.S.A.* **85 J11** 36 12N 115 59W
Pahute Mesa, *U.S.A.* **84 H10** 37 20N 116 45W
Pai, *Thailand* **38 C2** 19 19N 98 27 E
Paicines, *U.S.A.* **84 J5** 36 44N 121 17W
Paide, *Estonia* **9 G21** 58 57N 25 31 E
Paignton, *U.K.* **11 G4** 50 26N 3 35W
Päijänne, *Finland* **9 F21** 61 30N 25 30 E
Pailani, *India* **43 G9** 25 45N 80 26 E
Pailin, *Cambodia* **38 F4** 12 46N 102 36 E
Painan, *Indonesia* **36 E2** 1 21S 100 34 E
Painesville, *U.S.A.* **78 E3** 41 43N 81 15W
Paint Hills = Wemindji, *Canada* **70 B4** 53 0N 78 49W
Paint L., *Canada* **73 B9** 55 28N 97 57W
Painted Desert, *U.S.A.* **83 J8** 36 0N 111 0W
Paintsville, *U.S.A.* **76 G4** 37 49N 82 48W
País Vasco □, *Spain* **19 A4** 42 50N 2 45W
Paisley, *Canada* **78 B3** 44 18N 81 16W
Paisley, *U.K.* **12 F4** 55 50N 4 25W
Paisley, *U.S.A.* **82 E3** 42 42N 120 32W
Paita, *Peru* **92 E2** 5 11S 81 9W
Pajares, Puerto de, *Spain* **19 A3** 42 58N 5 46W
Pak Lay, *Laos* **38 C3** 18 15N 101 27 E
Pak Phanang, *Thailand* **39 H3** 8 21N 100 12 E
Pak Sane, *Laos* **38 C4** 18 22N 103 39 E
Pak Song, *Laos* **38 E6** 15 11N 106 14 E
Pak Suong, *Laos* **38 C4** 19 58N 102 15 E
Pakaur, *India* **43 G12** 24 38N 87 51 E
Pakenham, *Canada* **79 A8** 45 18N 76 18W
Pákhnes, *Greece* **23 D6** 35 16N 24 4 E
Pakhuis, *S. Africa* **56 E2** 32 9S 19 5 E
Pakistan ■, *Asia* **42 E4** 30 0N 70 0 E
Pakkading, *Laos* **38 C4** 18 19N 103 59 E
Pakokku, *Burma* **41 J19** 21 20N 95 0 E
Pakowki L., *Canada* **73 D6** 49 20N 111 0W
Pakpattan, *Pakistan* **42 D5** 30 25N 73 27 E
Paktīā □, *Afghan.* **40 C6** 33 0N 69 15 E
Pakwach, *Uganda* **54 B3** 2 28N 31 27 E
Pakxe, *Laos* **38 E5** 15 5N 105 52 E
Pal Lahara, *India* **43 J11** 21 27N 85 11 E
Pala, *Chad* **51 G9** 9 25N 15 5 E
Pala, *Dem. Rep. of the Congo* **54 D2** 6 45S 29 30 E
Pala, *U.S.A.* **85 M9** 33 22N 117 5W
Palabek, *Uganda* **54 B3** 3 22N 32 33 E
Palacios, *U.S.A.* **81 L6** 28 42N 96 13W
Palagruža, *Croatia* **20 C7** 42 24N 16 15 E
Palaiókastron, *Greece* **23 D8** 35 12N 26 15 E
Palaiokhóra, *Greece* **23 D5** 35 16N 23 39 E
Palam, *India* **40 K10** 19 0N 77 0 E
Palampur, *India* **42 C7** 32 10N 76 30 E
Palana, *Australia* **62 F4** 39 45S 147 55 E
Palana, *Russia* **27 D16** 59 10N 159 59 E
Palanan, *Phil.* **37 A6** 17 8N 122 29 E
Palanan Pt., *Phil.* **37 A6** 17 17N 122 30 E
Palandri, *Pakistan* **43 C5** 33 42N 73 40 E
Palanga, *Lithuania* **9 J19** 55 58N 21 3 E
Palangkaraya, *Indonesia* **36 E4** 2 16S 113 56 E
Palani Hills, *India* **40 P10** 10 14N 77 33 E
Palanpur, *India* **42 G5** 24 10N 72 25 E
Palapye, *Botswana* **56 C4** 22 30S 27 7 E
Palas, *Pakistan* **43 B5** 35 4N 73 14 E
Palashi, *India* **43 H13** 23 47N 88 15 E
Palasponga, *India* **43 J11** 21 47N 85 34 E
Palatka, *Russia* **27 C16** 60 6N 150 54 E
Palatka, *U.S.A.* **77 L5** 29 39N 81 38W
Palau ■, *Pac. Oc.* **28 J17** 7 30N 134 30 E
Palauk, *Burma* **38 F2** 13 10N 98 40 E
Palawan, *Phil.* **36 C5** 9 30N 118 30 E
Palayankottai, *India* **40 Q10** 8 45N 77 45 E
Paldiski, *Estonia* **9 G21** 59 23N 24 9 E
Paleleh, *Indonesia* **37 D6** 1 10N 121 50 E
Palembang, *Indonesia* **36 E2** 3 0S 104 50 E
Palencia, *Spain* **19 A3** 42 1N 4 34W
Palenque, *Mexico* **87 D6** 17 31N 91 58W
Paleokastrítsa, *Greece* **23 A3** 39 40N 19 41 E
Paleometokho, *Cyprus* **23 D12** 35 7N 33 11 E
Palermo, *Italy* **20 E5** 38 7N 13 22 E
Palermo, *U.S.A.* **82 G3** 39 26N 121 33W
Palestina, *Chile* **96 A3** 23 50S 69 47W
Palestine, *Asia* **47 D4** 32 0N 35 0 E
Palestine, *U.S.A.* **81 K7** 31 46N 95 38W
Paletwa, *Burma* **41 J18** 21 10N 92 50 E
Palghat, *India* **40 P10** 10 46N 76 42 E
Palgrave, Mt., *Australia* **60 D2** 23 22S 115 58 E
Pali, *India* **42 G5** 25 50N 73 20 E
Palikir, *Micronesia* **64 G7** 6 55N 158 9 E
Palioúrion, Ákra, *Greece* **21 E10** 39 57N 23 45 E
Palisades Reservoir, *U.S.A.* **82 E8** 43 20N 111 12W
Paliseul, *Belgium* **15 E5** 49 54N 5 8 E
Palitana, *India* **42 J4** 21 32N 71 49 E
Palizada, *Mexico* **87 D6** 18 18N 92 8W
Palk Bay, *Asia* **40 Q11** 9 30N 79 15 E
Palk Strait, *Asia* **40 Q11** 10 0N 79 45 E
Palkānah, *Iraq* **44 C5** 35 49N 44 26 E
Palkot, *India* **43 H11** 22 53N 84 39 E
Palla Road = Dinokwe, *Botswana* **56 C4** 23 29S 26 37 E
Pallanza = Verbánia, *Italy* **18 D8** 45 56N 8 33 E
Pallarenda, *Australia* **62 B4** 19 12S 146 46 E
Pallinup →, *Australia* **61 F2** 34 27S 118 50 E
Pallisa, *Uganda* **54 B3** 1 12N 33 43 E
Pallu, *India* **42 E6** 28 59N 74 14 E
Palm Bay, *U.S.A.* **77 L5** 28 2N 80 35W
Palm Beach, *U.S.A.* **77 M6** 26 43N 80 2W
Palm Coast, *U.S.A.* **77 L5** 29 35N 81 12W
Palm Desert, *U.S.A.* **85 M10** 33 43N 116 22W
Palm Is., *Australia* **62 B4** 18 40S 146 35 E
Palm Springs, *U.S.A.* **85 M10** 33 50N 116 33W
Palma, *Mozam.* **55 E5** 10 46S 40 29 E
Palma, B. de, *Spain* **22 B9** 39 30N 2 39 E

Peera Peera Poolanna L.

Palma de Mallorca, Spain 22 B9 39 35N 2 39 E
Palma Soriano, Cuba 88 B4 20 15N 76 0W
Palmares, Brazil 93 E11 8 41S 35 28W
Palmas, Brazil 95 B5 26 29S 52 0W
Palmas, C., Liberia 50 H4 4 27N 7 46W
Pálmas, G. di, Italy 20 E3 39 0N 8 30 E
Palmdale, U.S.A. 85 L8 34 35N 118 7W
Palmeira das Missões, Brazil 95 B5 27 55S 53 17W
Palmeira dos Índios, Brazil 93 E11 9 25S 36 37W
Palmer, U.S.A. 68 B5 61 36N 149 7W
Palmer →, Australia 62 B3 16 0S 142 26 E
Palmer Arch., Antarctica 5 C17 64 15S 65 0W
Palmer Lake, U.S.A. 80 F2 39 7N 104 55W
Palmer Land, Antarctica 5 D18 73 0S 63 0W
Palmerston, Canada 78 C4 43 50N 80 51W
Palmerston, N.Z. 59 L3 45 29S 170 43 E
Palmerston North, N.Z. 59 J5 40 21S 175 39 E
Palmerton, U.S.A. 79 F9 40 48N 75 37W
Palmetto, U.S.A. 77 M4 27 31N 82 34W
Palmi, Italy 20 E6 38 21N 15 51 E
Palmira, Argentina 94 C2 32 59S 68 34W
Palmira, Colombia 92 C3 3 32N 76 16W
Palmyra = Tudmur, Syria 44 C3 34 36N 38 15 E
Palmyra, Mo., U.S.A. 80 F9 39 48N 91 32W
Palmyra, N.J., U.S.A. 79 F9 40 1N 75 1W
Palmyra, N.Y., U.S.A. 78 C7 43 5N 77 18W
Palmyra, Pa., U.S.A. 79 F8 40 18N 76 36W
Palmyra Is., Pac. Oc. 65 G11 5 52N 162 5W
Palo Alto, U.S.A. 84 H4 37 27N 122 10W
Palo Verde, U.S.A. 85 M12 33 26N 114 44W
Palopo, Indonesia 37 E6 3 0S 120 16 E
Palos, C. de, Spain 19 D5 37 38N 0 40W
Palos Verdes, U.S.A. 85 M8 33 48N 118 23W
Palos Verdes, Pt., U.S.A. 85 M8 33 43N 118 26W
Palu, Indonesia 37 E5 1 0S 119 52 E
Palu, Turkey 25 G7 38 45N 40 0 E
Palwal, India 42 E7 28 8N 77 19 E
Pamanukan, Indonesia 37 G12 6 16S 107 49 E
Pamiers, France 18 E4 43 7N 1 39 E
Pamir, Tajikistan 26 F8 37 40N 73 0 E
Pamlico →, U.S.A. 77 H7 35 20N 76 28W
Pamlico Sd., U.S.A. 77 H8 35 20N 76 0W
Pampa, U.S.A. 81 H4 35 32N 100 58W
Pampa de las Salinas, Argentina 94 C2 32 1S 66 58W
Pampanua, Indonesia 37 E6 4 16S 120 8 E
Pampas, Argentina 94 D3 35 0S 63 0W
Pampas, Peru 92 F4 12 20S 74 50W
Pamplona, Colombia 92 B4 7 23N 72 39W
Pamplona, Spain 19 A5 42 48N 1 38W
Pampoenpoort, S. Africa 56 E3 31 3S 22 40 E
Pana, U.S.A. 80 F10 39 23N 89 5W
Panaca, U.S.A. 83 H6 37 47N 114 23W
Panaitan, Indonesia 37 G11 6 36S 105 12 E
Panaji, India 40 M8 15 25N 73 50 E
Panamá, Panama 88 E4 9 0N 79 25W
Panama ■, Cent. Amer. 88 E4 8 48N 79 55W
Panamá, G. de, Panama 88 E4 8 4N 79 20W
Panama Canal, Panama 88 E4 9 10N 79 37W
Panama City, U.S.A. 77 K3 30 10N 85 40W
Panamint Range, U.S.A. 85 J9 36 20N 117 20W
Panamint Springs, U.S.A. 85 J9 36 20N 117 28W
Panão, Peru 92 E3 9 55S 75 55W
Panare, Thailand 39 J3 6 51N 101 30 E
Panay, Phil. 37 B6 11 10N 122 30 E
Panay, G., Phil. 37 B6 11 0N 122 30 E
Pančevo, Serbia, Yug. 21 B9 44 52N 20 41 E
Panda, Mozam. 57 C5 24 2S 34 45 E
Pandan, Phil. 37 B6 11 45N 122 10 E
Pandegelang, Indonesia 37 G12 6 25S 106 5 E
Pandhana, India 42 J7 21 42N 76 13 E
Pandharpur, India 40 L9 17 41N 75 20 E
Pando, Uruguay 95 C4 34 44S 56 0W
Pando, L. = Hope, L., Australia 63 D2 28 24S 139 18 E
Pandokrátor, Greece 23 A3 39 45N 19 50 E
Pandora, Costa Rica 88 E3 9 43N 83 3W
Panevežys, Lithuania 9 J21 55 42N 24 25 E
Panfilov, Kazakstan 26 E8 44 10N 80 0 E
Pang-Long, Burma 41 H21 23 11N 98 45 E
Pang-Yang, Burma 41 H21 22 7N 98 48 E
Panga, Dem. Rep. of the Congo 54 B2 1 52N 26 18 E
Pangalanes, Canal des = Ampangalana, Lakandranon', Madag. 57 C8 22 48S 47 50 E
Pangani, Tanzania 54 D4 5 25S 38 58 E
Pangani →, Tanzania 54 D4 5 26S 38 58 E
Pangfou = Bengbu, China 35 H9 32 58N 117 20 E
Pangil, Dem. Rep. of the Congo 54 C2 3 10S 26 35 E
Pangkah, Tanjung, Indonesia 37 G15 6 51S 112 33 E
Pangkajene, Indonesia 37 E5 4 46S 119 34 E
Pangkalanbrandan, Indonesia 36 D1 4 1N 98 20 E
Pangkalanbuun, Indonesia 36 E4 2 41S 111 37 E
Pangkalpinang, Indonesia 36 E3 2 0S 106 0 E
Pangnirtung, Canada 69 B13 66 8N 65 54W
Pangong Tso, India 42 B8 34 40N 78 40 E
Panguitch, U.S.A. 83 H7 37 50N 112 26W
Pangutaran Group, Phil. 37 C6 6 18N 120 34 E
Panhandle, U.S.A. 81 H4 35 21N 101 23W
Pani Mines, India 42 H5 22 29N 73 50 E
Pania-Mutombo, Dem. Rep. of the Congo 54 D1 5 11S 23 51 E
Panikota I., India 42 J4 20 46N 71 21 E
Panipat, India 42 E7 29 25N 77 2 E
Panjal Range = Pir Panjal Range, India 42 C7 32 30N 76 50 E
Panjang, Hon, Vietnam 39 H4 9 20N 103 28 E
Panjgur, Pakistan 40 F4 27 0N 64 5 E
Panjim = Panaji, India 40 M8 15 25N 73 50 E
Panjin, China 35 D12 41 3N 122 2 E
Panjinad Barrage, Pakistan 40 E7 29 22N 71 15 E
Panjnad →, Pakistan 42 E4 28 57N 70 30 E
Panjwai, Afghan. 42 D1 31 26N 65 27 E
Panmunjŏm, N. Korea 35 F14 37 59N 126 38 E
Panna, India 43 G9 24 40N 80 15 E
Panna Hills, India 43 G9 24 40N 81 15 E
Pannawonica, Australia 60 D2 21 39S 116 19 E
Pannirtuuq = Pangnirtung, Canada 69 B13 66 8N 65 54W
Pano Akil, Pakistan 42 F3 27 51N 69 7 E
Pano Lefkara, Cyprus 23 E12 34 53N 33 20 E
Pano Panayia, Cyprus 23 E11 34 55N 32 38 E
Panorama, Brazil 95 A5 21 21S 51 51W
Pánormon, Greece 23 D6 35 25N 24 41 E
Pansemal, India 42 J6 21 39N 74 42 E
Panshan = Panjin, China 35 D12 41 3N 122 2 E
Panshi, China 35 C14 42 58N 126 5 E
Pantanal, Brazil 92 H7 17 30S 57 40W
Pantar, Indonesia 37 F6 8 28S 124 10 E
Pante Macassar, E. Timor 37 F6 9 30S 123 58 E
Pante Makasar = Pante Macassar, E. Timor 37 F6 9 30S 123 58 E
Pantelleria, Italy 20 F4 36 50N 11 57 E
Pánuco, Mexico 87 C5 22 0N 98 15W
Paola, Malta 23 D2 35 52N 14 30 E
Paola, U.S.A. 80 F7 38 35N 94 53W
Paonia, U.S.A. 83 G10 38 52N 107 36W
Paoting = Baoding, China 34 E8 38 50N 115 28 E
Paot'ou = Baotou, China 34 D6 40 32N 110 2 E
Paoua, C.A.R. 52 C3 7 9N 16 20 E
Pápa, Hungary 17 E9 47 22N 17 30 E
Papa Stour, U.K. 12 A7 60 20N 1 42W
Papa Westray, U.K. 12 B6 59 20N 2 55W
Papagayo →, Mexico 87 D5 16 36N 99 43W
Papagayo, G. de, Costa Rica 88 D2 10 30N 85 50W
Papakura, N.Z. 59 G5 37 4S 174 59 E
Papantla, Mexico 87 C5 20 30N 97 30W
Papar, Malaysia 36 C5 5 45N 116 0 E
Papeete, Tahiti 65 J13 17 32S 149 34W
Paphos, Cyprus 23 E11 34 46N 32 25 E
Papien Chiang = Da →, Vietnam 38 B5 21 15N 105 20 E
Papigochic →, Mexico 86 B3 29 9N 109 40W
Paposo, Chile 94 B1 25 0S 70 30W
Papoutsa, Cyprus 23 E12 34 54N 33 4 E
Papua New Guinea ■, Oceania 64 H6 8 0S 145 0 E
Papudo, Chile 94 C1 32 29S 71 27W
Papun, Burma 41 K20 18 2N 97 30 E
Papunya, Australia 60 D5 23 15S 131 54 E
Pará = Belém, Brazil 93 D9 1 20S 48 30W
Pará □, Brazil 93 D8 3 20S 52 0W
Paraburdoo, Australia 60 D2 23 14S 117 32 E
Paracatu, Brazil 93 G9 17 10S 46 50W
Paracel Is., S. China Sea 36 A4 15 50N 112 0 E
Parachilna, Australia 63 E2 31 10S 138 21 E
Parachinar, Pakistan 42 C4 33 55N 70 5 E
Paradhísi, Greece 23 C10 36 18N 28 7 E
Paradip, India 41 J15 20 15N 86 35 E
Paradise, Calif., U.S.A. 84 F5 39 46N 121 37W
Paradise, Nev., U.S.A. 85 J11 36 9N 115 10W
Paradise →, Canada 71 B8 53 27N 57 19W
Paradise Hill, Canada 73 C7 53 32N 109 28W
Paradise River, Canada 71 B8 53 27N 57 17W
Paradise Valley, U.S.A. 82 F5 41 30N 117 32W
Parado, Indonesia 37 F5 8 42S 118 30 E
Paragould, U.S.A. 81 G9 36 3N 90 29W
Paragua →, Venezuela 92 B6 6 55N 62 55W
Paraguaçu →, Brazil 93 F11 12 45S 38 54W
Paraguaçu Paulista, Brazil 95 A5 22 22S 50 35W
Paraguaná, Pen. de, Venezuela 92 A5 12 0N 70 0W
Paraguarí, Paraguay 94 B4 25 36S 57 0W
Paraguarí □, Paraguay 94 B4 26 0S 57 10W
Paraguay ■, S. Amer. 94 A4 23 0S 57 0W
Paraguay →, Paraguay 94 B4 27 18S 58 38W
Paraíba = João Pessoa, Brazil 93 E12 7 10S 34 52W
Paraíba □, Brazil 93 E11 7 0S 36 0W
Paraíba do Sul →, Brazil 95 A7 21 37S 41 3W
Parainen, Finland 9 F20 60 18N 22 18 E
Paraiso, Mexico 87 D6 18 24N 93 14W
Parak, Iran 45 E7 27 38N 52 25 E
Parakou, Benin 50 G6 9 25N 2 40 E
Paralimni, Cyprus 23 D12 35 2N 33 58 E
Paramaribo, Surinam 93 B7 5 50N 55 10W
Paramushir, Ostrov, Russia 27 D16 50 24N 156 0 E
Paran →, Israel 47 E4 30 20N 35 10 E
Paraná, Argentina 94 C3 31 45S 60 30W
Paraná, Brazil 93 F9 12 30S 47 48W
Paraná □, Brazil 95 A5 24 30S 51 0W
Paraná →, Argentina 94 C4 33 43S 59 15W
Paranaguá, Brazil 95 B6 25 30S 48 30W
Paranaíba, Brazil 93 G8 19 40S 51 11W
Paranaíba →, Brazil 93 H8 20 6S 51 4W
Paranapanema →, Brazil 95 A5 22 40S 53 9W
Paranapiacaba, Serra do, Brazil 95 A6 24 31S 48 35W
Paranavaí, Brazil 95 A5 23 4S 52 56W
Parang, Maguindanao, Phil. 37 C6 7 23N 124 16 E
Parang, Sulu, Phil. 37 C6 5 55N 120 54 E
Parângul Mare, Vf., Romania 17 F12 45 20N 23 37 E
Paraparaumu, N.Z. 59 J5 40 57S 175 3 E
Parbati →, Mad. P., India 42 G7 25 50N 76 30 E
Parbati →, Raj., India 42 F7 26 54N 77 53 E
Parbhani, India 40 K10 19 8N 76 52 E
Parchim, Germany 16 B6 53 26N 11 52 E
Pardes Hanna-Karkur, Israel 47 C3 32 28N 34 57 E
Pardo →, Bahia, Brazil 93 G11 15 40S 39 0W
Pardo →, Mato Grosso, Brazil 95 A5 21 46S 52 9W
Pardubice, Czech Rep. 16 C8 50 3N 15 45 E
Pare, Indonesia 37 G15 7 43S 112 12 E
Pare Mts., Tanzania 54 C4 4 0S 37 45 E
Parecis, Serra dos, Brazil 92 F7 13 0S 60 0W
Paren, Russia 27 C17 62 30N 163 15 E
Parent, Canada 70 C5 47 55N 74 35W
Parent, L., Canada 70 C4 48 31N 77 1W
Parepare, Indonesia 37 E5 4 0S 119 40 E
Párga, Greece 21 E9 39 15N 20 29 E
Pargo, Pta. do, Madeira 22 D2 32 49N 17 17W
Pariaguán, Venezuela 92 B6 8 51N 64 34W
Paricutín, Cerro, Mexico 86 D4 19 28N 102 15W
Parigi, Indonesia 37 E6 0 50S 120 5 E
Parika, Guyana 92 B7 6 50N 58 20W
Parima, Serra, Brazil 92 C6 2 30N 64 0W
Parinari, Peru 92 D4 4 35S 74 25W
Pariñas, Pta., S. Amer. 90 D2 4 30S 82 0W
Parintins, Brazil 93 D7 2 40S 56 50W
Pariparit Kyun, Burma 41 M18 14 55N 93 45 E
Paris, Canada 78 C4 43 12N 80 25W
Paris, France 18 B5 48 50N 2 20 E
Paris, Idaho, U.S.A. 82 E8 42 14N 111 24W
Paris, Ky., U.S.A. 76 F3 38 13N 84 15W
Paris, Tenn., U.S.A. 77 G1 36 18N 88 19W
Paris, Tex., U.S.A. 81 J7 33 40N 95 33W
Parish, U.S.A. 79 C8 43 25N 76 8W
Parishville, U.S.A. 79 B10 44 38N 74 49W
Park, U.S.A. 84 B4 48 45N 122 18W
Park City, U.S.A. 81 G6 37 48N 97 20W
Park Falls, U.S.A. 80 C9 45 56N 90 27W
Park Head, Canada 78 B3 44 36N 81 9W
Park Hills, U.S.A. 81 G9 37 53N 90 28W
Park Range, U.S.A. 82 G10 40 0N 106 30W
Park Rapids, U.S.A. 80 B7 46 55N 95 4W
Park River, U.S.A. 80 A6 48 24N 97 45W
Park Rynie, S. Africa 57 E5 30 25S 30 45 E
Parkā Bandar, Iran 45 E8 25 55N 59 35 E
Parkano, Finland 9 E20 62 1N 23 0 E
Parker, Ariz., U.S.A. 85 L12 34 9N 114 17W
Parker, Pa., U.S.A. 78 E5 41 5N 79 41W
Parker Dam, U.S.A. 85 L12 34 18N 114 8W
Parkersburg, U.S.A. 76 F5 39 16N 81 34W
Parkes, Australia 63 E4 33 9S 148 11 E
Parkfield, U.S.A. 84 K6 35 54N 120 26W
Parkhill, Canada 78 C3 43 15N 81 38W
Parkland, U.S.A. 84 C4 47 9N 122 26W
Parkston, U.S.A. 80 D6 43 24N 97 59W
Parksville, Canada 72 D4 49 20N 124 21W
Parla, Spain 19 B4 40 14N 3 46W
Parma, Italy 18 D9 44 48N 10 20 E
Parma, Idaho, U.S.A. 82 E5 43 47N 116 57W
Parma, Ohio, U.S.A. 78 E3 41 23N 81 43W
Parnaguá, Brazil 93 F10 10 10S 44 38W
Parnaíba, Brazil 93 D10 2 54S 41 47W
Parnaíba →, Brazil 93 D10 3 0S 41 50W
Parnassós, Greece 21 E10 38 35N 22 30 E
Pärnu, Estonia 9 G21 58 28N 24 33 E
Paroo →, Australia 63 E3 31 28S 143 32 E
Páros, Greece 21 F11 37 5N 25 12 E
Parowan, U.S.A. 83 H7 37 51N 112 50W
Parral, Chile 94 D1 36 10S 71 52W
Parras, Mexico 86 B4 25 30N 102 20W
Parrett →, U.K. 11 F4 51 12N 3 1W
Parris I., U.S.A. 77 J5 32 20N 80 41W
Parrsboro, Canada 71 C7 45 30N 64 25W
Parry I., Canada 78 A4 45 18N 80 10W
Parry Is., Canada 4 B2 77 0N 110 0W
Parry Sound, Canada 78 A5 45 20N 80 0W
Parsnip →, Canada 72 B4 55 10N 123 2W
Parsons, U.S.A. 81 G7 37 20N 95 16W
Parsons Ra., Australia 62 A2 13 30S 135 15 E
Partinico, Italy 20 E5 38 3N 13 7 E
Partridge I., Canada 70 A2 55 59N 87 37W
Paru →, Brazil 93 D8 1 33S 52 38W
Parvān □, Afghan. 40 B6 35 0N 69 0 E
Parvatipuram, India 41 K13 18 50N 83 25 E
Parvatsar, India 42 F6 26 52N 74 49 E
Parys, S. Africa 56 D4 26 52S 27 29 E
Pas, Pta. des, Spain 22 C7 38 46N 1 26 E
Pasadena, Canada 71 C8 49 1N 57 36W
Pasadena, Calif., U.S.A. 85 L8 34 9N 118 9W
Pasadena, Tex., U.S.A. 81 L7 29 43N 95 13W
Pasaje →, Argentina 94 B3 25 39S 63 56W
Pascagoula, U.S.A. 81 K10 30 21N 88 33W
Pascagoula →, U.S.A. 81 K10 30 23N 88 37W
Paşcani, Romania 17 E14 47 14N 26 45 E
Pasco, U.S.A. 82 C4 46 14N 119 6W
Pasco, Cerro de, Peru 92 F3 10 45S 76 10W
Pasco I., Australia 60 D2 20 57S 115 20 E
Pascoag, U.S.A. 79 E13 41 57N 71 42W
Pascua, I. de, Chile 65 K17 27 7S 109 23W
Pasfield L., Canada 73 B7 58 24N 105 20W
Pashmakli = Smolyan, Bulgaria 21 D11 41 36N 24 38 E
Pasir Mas, Malaysia 39 J4 6 2N 102 8 E
Pasir Putih, Malaysia 39 K4 5 50N 102 24 E
Pasirian, Indonesia 37 H15 8 13S 113 8 E
Pasirkuning, Indonesia 36 E2 0 30S 104 33 E
Paskūh, Iran 45 E9 27 34N 61 39 E
Pasley, C., Australia 61 F3 33 52S 123 35 E
Pašman, Croatia 16 G8 43 58N 15 20 E
Pasni, Pakistan 40 G3 25 15N 63 27 E
Paso Cantinela, Mexico 85 N11 32 33N 115 47W
Paso de Indios, Argentina 96 E3 43 55S 69 0W
Paso de los Libres, Argentina 94 B4 29 44S 57 10W
Paso de los Toros, Uruguay 94 C4 32 45S 56 30W
Paso Robles, U.S.A. 83 J3 35 38N 120 41W
Paspébiac, Canada 71 C6 48 3N 65 17W
Pasrur, Pakistan 42 C6 32 16N 74 43 E
Passage West, Ireland 13 E3 51 52N 8 21W
Passaic, U.S.A. 79 F10 40 51N 74 7W
Passau, Germany 16 D7 48 34N 13 28 E
Passero, C., Italy 20 F6 36 41N 15 10 E
Passo Fundo, Brazil 95 B5 28 10S 52 20W
Passos, Brazil 93 H9 20 45S 46 37W
Pastavy, Belarus 9 J22 55 4N 26 50 E
Pastaza →, Peru 92 D3 4 50S 76 52W
Pasto, Colombia 92 C3 1 13N 77 17W
Pasuruan, Indonesia 37 G15 7 40S 112 44 E
Patagonia, Argentina 96 F3 45 0S 69 0W
Patagonia, U.S.A. 83 L8 31 33N 110 45W
Patambar, Iran 45 D9 29 45N 60 17 E
Patan = Lalitapur, Nepal 43 F11 27 40N 85 20 E
Patan, Gujarat, India 40 H8 23 54N 72 14 E
Patan, Maharashtra, India 42 H5 23 54N 72 14 E
Patani, Indonesia 37 D7 0 20N 128 50 E
Pataudi, India 42 E7 28 18N 76 48 E
Patchewollock, Australia 63 F3 35 22S 142 12 E
Patchogue, U.S.A. 79 F11 40 46N 73 1W
Patea, N.Z. 59 H5 39 45S 174 30 E
Patensie, S. Africa 56 E3 33 46S 24 49 E
Paternò, Italy 20 F6 37 34N 14 54 E
Pateros, U.S.A. 82 B4 48 3N 119 54W
Paterson, U.S.A. 79 F10 40 55N 74 11W
Paterson Ra., Australia 60 D3 21 45S 122 10 E
Pathankot, India 42 C6 32 18N 75 45 E
Pathein = Bassein, Burma 41 L19 16 45N 94 30 E
Pathfinder Reservoir, U.S.A. 82 E10 42 28N 106 51W
Pathiu, Thailand 39 G2 10 42N 99 19 E
Pathum Thani, Thailand 38 E3 14 1N 100 32 E
Pati, Indonesia 37 G14 6 45S 111 1 E
Patía →, Colombia 92 C3 2 13N 78 40W
Patiala, Punjab, India 42 D7 30 23N 76 26 E
Patiala, Ut. P., India 43 F8 27 43N 79 1 E
Patkai Bum, India 41 F19 27 0N 95 30 E
Pátmos, Greece 21 F12 37 21N 26 36 E
Patna, India 43 G11 25 35N 85 12 E
Pato Branco, Brazil 95 B5 26 13S 52 40W
Patonga, Uganda 54 B3 2 45N 33 15 E
Patos, Brazil 93 E11 6 55S 37 16W
Patos, L. dos, Brazil 95 C5 31 20S 51 0W
Patos, Rio de los →, Argentina 94 C2 31 18S 69 25W
Patos de Minas, Brazil 93 G9 18 35S 46 32W
Patquía, Argentina 94 C2 30 2S 66 55W
Pátrai, Greece 21 E9 38 14N 21 47 E
Pátraikós Kólpos, Greece 21 E9 38 17N 21 30 E
Patras = Pátrai, Greece 21 E9 38 14N 21 47 E
Patrocínio, Brazil 93 G9 18 57S 47 0W
Patta, Kenya 54 C5 2 10S 41 0 E
Pattani, Thailand 39 J3 6 48N 101 15 E
Pattaya, Thailand 36 B2 12 52N 100 55 E
Patten, U.S.A. 77 C11 46 0N 68 38W
Patterson, Calif., U.S.A. 84 H5 37 28N 121 8W
Patterson, La., U.S.A. 81 L9 29 42N 91 18W
Patterson, Mt., U.S.A. 84 G7 38 29N 119 20W
Patti, Punjab, India 42 D6 31 17N 74 54 E
Patti, Ut. P., India 43 G10 25 55N 82 12 E
Pattoki, Pakistan 42 D5 31 5N 73 52 E
Patton, U.S.A. 78 F6 40 38N 78 39W
Patuakhali, Bangla. 41 H17 22 20N 90 25 E
Patuanak, Canada 73 B7 55 55N 107 43W
Patuca →, Honduras 88 C3 15 50N 84 18W
Patuca, Punta, Honduras 88 C3 15 49N 84 14W
Pátzcuaro, Mexico 86 D4 19 30N 101 40W
Pau, France 18 E3 43 19N 0 25W
Pauk, Burma 41 J19 21 27N 94 30 E
Paul I., Canada 71 A7 56 30N 61 20W
Paul Smiths, U.S.A. 79 B10 44 26N 74 15W
Paulatuk, Canada 68 B7 69 25N 124 0W
Paulis = Isiro, Dem. Rep. of the Congo 54 B2 2 53N 27 40 E
Paulistana, Brazil 93 E10 8 9S 41 9W
Paulo Afonso, Brazil 93 E11 9 21S 38 15W
Paulpietersburg, S. Africa 57 D5 27 23S 30 50 E
Pauls Valley, U.S.A. 81 H6 34 44N 97 13W
Pauma Valley, U.S.A. 85 M10 33 16N 116 58W
Pauri, India 43 D8 30 9N 78 47 E
Pāveh, Iran 44 C5 35 3N 46 22 E
Pavia, Italy 18 D8 45 7N 9 8 E
Pavilion, U.S.A. 78 D6 42 52N 78 1W
Pāvilosta, Latvia 9 H19 56 53N 21 14 E
Pavlodar, Kazakstan 26 D8 52 33N 77 0 E
Pavlograd = Pavlohrad, Ukraine 25 E6 48 30N 35 52 E
Pavlohrad, Ukraine 25 E6 48 30N 35 52 E
Pavlovo, Russia 24 C7 55 58N 43 5 E
Pavlovsk, Russia 25 D7 50 26N 40 5 E
Pavlovskaya, Russia 25 E6 46 17N 39 47 E
Pawayan, India 43 E9 28 4N 80 6 E
Pawhuska, U.S.A. 81 G6 36 40N 96 20W
Pawling, U.S.A. 79 E11 41 34N 73 36W
Pawnee, U.S.A. 81 G6 36 20N 96 48W
Pawnee City, U.S.A. 80 E6 40 7N 96 9W
Pawtucket, U.S.A. 79 E13 41 53N 71 23W
Paximádhia, Greece 23 E6 35 0N 24 35 E
Paxoí, Greece 21 E9 39 14N 20 12 E
Paxton, Ill., U.S.A. 76 E1 40 27N 88 6W
Paxton, Nebr., U.S.A. 80 E4 41 7N 101 21W
Payakumbuh, Indonesia 36 E2 0 20S 100 35 E
Payette, U.S.A. 82 D5 44 5N 116 56W
Payne Bay = Kangirsuk, Canada 69 B13 60 0N 70 0W
Payne L., Canada 69 C12 59 30N 74 30W
Paynes Find, Australia 61 E2 29 15S 117 42 E
Paynesville, U.S.A. 80 C7 45 23N 94 43W
Paysandú, Uruguay 94 C4 32 19S 58 8W
Payson, U.S.A. 83 J8 34 14N 111 20W
Paz →, Guatemala 88 D1 13 44N 90 10W
Paz, B. de la, Mexico 86 C2 24 15N 110 25W
Pāzanān, Iran 45 D6 30 35N 49 59 E
Pazardzhik, Bulgaria 21 C11 42 12N 24 20 E
Pe Ell, U.S.A. 84 D3 46 34N 123 18W
Peabody, U.S.A. 79 D14 42 31N 70 56W
Peace →, Canada 72 B6 59 0N 111 25W
Peace Point, Canada 72 B6 59 7N 112 27W
Peace River, Canada 72 B5 56 15N 117 18W
Peach Springs, U.S.A. 83 J7 35 32N 113 25W
Peachland, Canada 72 D5 49 47N 119 45W
Peachtree City, U.S.A. 77 J3 33 25N 84 35W
Peak, The = Kinder Scout, U.K. 10 D6 53 24N 1 52W
Peak District, U.K. 10 D6 53 10N 1 50W
Peak Hill, N.S.W., Australia 63 E4 32 47S 148 11 E
Peak Hill, W. Austral., Australia 61 E2 25 35S 118 43 E
Peak Ra., Australia 62 C4 22 50S 148 20 E
Peake Cr. →, Australia 63 D2 28 2S 136 7 E
Peale, Mt., U.S.A. 83 G9 38 26N 109 14W
Pearblossom, U.S.A. 85 L9 34 30N 117 55W
Pearl →, U.S.A. 81 K10 30 11N 89 32W
Pearl City, U.S.A. 74 H16 21 24N 157 59W
Pearl Harbor, U.S.A. 74 H16 21 21N 157 57W
Pearl River, U.S.A. 79 E10 41 4N 74 2W
Pearsall, U.S.A. 81 L5 28 54N 99 6W
Peary Land, Greenland 4 A6 82 40N 33 0W
Pease →, U.S.A. 81 H5 34 12N 99 2W
Peawanuck, Canada 69 C11 55 15N 85 12W
Pebane, Mozam. 55 F4 17 10S 38 8 E
Pebas, Peru 92 D4 3 10S 71 46W
Pebble Beach, U.S.A. 84 J5 36 34N 121 57W
Peć, Kosovo, Yug. 21 C9 42 40N 20 17 E
Pechenga, Russia 24 A5 69 29N 31 4 E
Pechenizhyn, Ukraine 17 D13 48 30N 24 48 E
Pechiguera, Pta., Canary Is. 22 F6 28 51N 13 53W
Pechora, Russia 24 A10 65 10N 57 11 E
Pechora →, Russia 24 A9 68 13N 54 15 E
Pechorskaya Guba, Russia 24 A9 68 40N 54 0 E
Pečory, Russia 9 H22 57 48N 27 40 E
Pecos, U.S.A. 81 K3 31 26N 103 30W
Pecos →, U.S.A. 81 L3 29 42N 101 22W
Pécs, Hungary 17 E10 46 5N 18 15 E
Pedder, L., Australia 62 G4 42 55S 146 10 E
Peddie, S. Africa 57 E4 33 14S 27 7 E
Pedernales, Dom. Rep. 89 C5 18 2N 71 44W
Pedieos →, Cyprus 23 D12 35 10N 33 54 E
Pedirka, Australia 63 D2 26 40S 135 14 E
Pedra Azul, Brazil 93 G10 16 2S 41 17W
Pedreiras, Brazil 93 D10 4 32S 44 40W
Pedro Afonso, Brazil 93 E9 9 0S 48 10W
Pedro Cays, Jamaica 88 C4 17 5N 77 48W
Pedro de Valdivia, Chile 94 A2 22 55S 69 38W
Pedro Juan Caballero, Paraguay 95 A4 22 30S 55 40W
Pee Dee →, U.S.A. 77 J6 33 22N 79 16W
Peebinga, Australia 63 E3 34 52S 140 57 E
Peebles, U.K. 12 F5 55 40N 3 11W
Peekskill, U.S.A. 79 E11 41 17N 73 55W
Peel, U.K. 10 C3 54 13N 4 40W
Peel →, Australia 63 E5 30 50S 150 29 E
Peel →, Canada 68 B6 67 0N 135 0W
Peel Sound, Canada 68 A10 73 0N 96 0W
Peera Peera Poolanna L., Australia 63 D2 26 30S 138 0 E

Port Washington

Pinglu, *China* **34 E7** 39 31N 112 30 E
Pingluo, *China* **34 E4** 38 52N 106 30 E
Pingquan, *China* **35 D10** 41 1N 118 37 E
Pingrup, *Australia* **61 F2** 33 32S 118 29 E
P'ingtung, *Taiwan* **33 D7** 22 38N 120 30 E
Pingwu, *China* **34 H3** 32 25N 104 30 E
Pingxiang, *China* **32 D5** 22 6N 106 46 E
Pingyao, *China* **34 F7** 37 12N 112 10 E
Pingyi, *China* **35 G9** 35 30N 117 35 E
Pingyin, *China* **34 F9** 36 20N 116 25 E
Pingyuan, *China* **34 F9** 37 10N 116 22 E
Pinhal, *Brazil* **95 A6** 22 10S 46 46W
Pinheiro, *Brazil* **93 D9** 2 31S 45 5W
Pinheiro Machado, *Brazil* **95 C5** 31 34S 53 23W
Pinhel, *Portugal* **19 B2** 40 50N 7 1W
Pini, *Indonesia* **36 D1** 0 10N 98 40 E
Piniós →, *Greece* **21 E10** 39 55N 22 41 E
Pinjarra, *Australia* **61 F2** 32 37S 115 52 E
Pink Mountain, *Canada* **72 B4** 57 3N 122 52W
Pinnacles, *U.S.A.* **84 J5** 36 33N 121 19W
Pinnaroo, *Australia* **63 F3** 35 17S 140 53 E
Pínnes, Ákra, *Greece* **21 D11** 40 5N 24 20 E
Pinon Hills, *U.S.A.* **85 L9** 34 26N 117 39W
Pinos, *Mexico* **86 C4** 22 20N 101 40W
Pinos, Mt., *U.S.A.* **85 L7** 34 49N 119 8W
Pinos Pt., *U.S.A.* **83 H3** 36 38N 121 57W
Pinotepa Nacional, *Mexico* **87 D5** 16 19N 98 3W
Pinrang, *Indonesia* **37 E5** 3 46S 119 41 E
Pins, Pte. aux, *Canada* **78 D3** 42 15N 81 51W
Pinsk, *Belarus* **17 B14** 52 10N 26 1 E
Pintados, *Chile* **92 H5** 20 35S 69 40W
Pinyug, *Russia* **24 B8** 60 5N 48 0 E
Pioche, *U.S.A.* **83 H6** 37 56N 114 27W
Piombino, *Italy* **20 C4** 42 55N 10 32 E
Pioner, Ostrov, *Russia* **27 B10** 79 50N 92 0 E
Piorini, L., *Brazil* **92 D6** 3 15S 62 35W
Piotrków Trybunalski, *Poland* **17 C10** 51 23N 19 43 E
Pīp, *Iran* **45 E9** 26 45N 60 10 E
Pipar, *India* **42 F5** 26 25N 73 31 E
Pipar Road, *India* **42 F5** 26 27N 73 27 E
Piparia, *Mad. P., India* **42 H8** 22 45N 78 23 E
Piparia, *Mad. P., India* **42 J7** 21 49N 77 37 E
Pipestone, *U.S.A.* **80 D6** 44 0N 96 19W
Pipestone →, *Canada* **70 B2** 52 53N 89 23W
Pipestone Cr. →, *Canada* **73 D8** 49 38N 100 15W
Piplan, *Pakistan* **42 C4** 32 17N 71 21 E
Piploda, *India* **42 H6** 23 37N 74 56 E
Pipmuacan, Rés., *Canada* **71 C5** 49 45N 70 30W
Pippingarra, *Australia* **60 D2** 20 27S 118 42 E
Piqua, *U.S.A.* **76 E3** 40 9N 84 15W
Piquiri →, *Brazil* **95 A5** 24 3S 54 14W
Pir Panjal Range, *India* **42 C7** 32 30N 76 50 E
Pīr Sohrāb, *Iran* **45 E9** 25 44N 60 54 E
Piracicaba, *Brazil* **95 A6** 22 45S 47 40W
Piracuruca, *Brazil* **93 D10** 3 50S 41 50W
Piræus = Piraiévs, *Greece* **21 F10** 37 57N 23 42 E
Piraiévs, *Greece* **21 F10** 37 57N 23 42 E
Pirajuí, *Brazil* **95 A6** 21 59S 49 29W
Piram I., *India* **42 J5** 21 36N 72 21 E
Pirané, *Argentina* **94 B4** 25 42S 59 6W
Pirapora, *Brazil* **93 G10** 17 20S 44 56W
Pirawa, *India* **42 G7** 24 10N 76 2 E
Pírgos, *Greece* **21 F9** 37 40N 21 27 E
Piribebuy, *Paraguay* **94 B4** 25 26S 57 2W
Pirimapun, *Indonesia* **37 F9** 6 20S 138 24 E
Pirin Planina, *Bulgaria* **21 D10** 41 40N 23 30 E
Pírineos = Pyrénées, *Europe* **18 E4** 42 45N 0 18 E
Piripiri, *Brazil* **93 D10** 4 15S 41 46W
Pirmasens, *Germany* **16 D4** 49 12N 7 36 E
Pirot, *Serbia, Yug.* **21 C10** 43 9N 22 33 E
Piru, *Indonesia* **37 E7** 3 4S 128 12 E
Piru, *U.S.A.* **85 L8** 34 25N 118 48W
Pisa, *Italy* **20 C4** 43 43N 10 23 E
Pisagua, *Chile* **92 G4** 19 40S 70 15W
Pisco, *Peru* **92 F3** 13 50S 76 12W
Písek, *Czech Rep.* **16 D8** 49 19N 14 10 E
Pishan, *China* **32 C2** 37 30N 78 33 E
Pīshīn, *Iran* **45 E9** 26 6N 61 47 E
Pishin, *Pakistan* **42 D2** 30 35N 67 0 E
Pishin Lora →, *Pakistan* **42 E1** 29 9N 64 5 E
Pising, *Indonesia* **37 F6** 5 8S 121 53 E
Pismo Beach, *U.S.A.* **85 K6** 35 9N 120 38W
Pissis, Cerro, *Argentina* **94 B2** 27 45S 68 48W
Pissouri, *Cyprus* **23 E11** 34 40N 32 42 E
Pistóia, *Italy* **20 C4** 43 55N 10 54 E
Pistol B., *Canada* **73 A10** 62 25N 92 37W
Pisuerga →, *Spain* **19 B3** 41 33N 4 52W
Pit →, *U.S.A.* **82 F2** 40 47N 122 6W
Pitarpunga, L., *Australia* **63 E3** 34 24S 143 30 E
Pitcairn I., *Pac. Oc.* **65 K14** 25 5S 130 5W
Pite älv →, *Sweden* **8 D19** 65 20N 21 25 E
Piteå, *Sweden* **8 D19** 65 20N 21 25 E
Piteşti, *Romania* **17 F13** 44 52N 24 54 E
Pithapuram, *India* **41 L13** 17 10N 82 15 E
Pithara, *Australia* **61 F2** 30 20S 116 35 E
Pithoragarh, *India* **43 E9** 29 35N 80 13 E
Pithoro, *Pakistan* **42 G3** 25 31N 69 23 E
Pitlochry, *U.K.* **12 E5** 56 42N 3 44W
Pitsilia, *Cyprus* **23 E12** 34 55N 33 0 E
Pitt I., *Canada* **72 C3** 53 30N 129 50W
Pittsburg, *Calif., U.S.A.* **84 G5** 38 2N 121 53W
Pittsburg, *Kans., U.S.A.* **81 G7** 37 25N 94 42W
Pittsburg, *Tex., U.S.A.* **81 J7** 33 0N 94 59W
Pittsburgh, *U.S.A.* **78 F5** 40 26N 80 1W
Pittsfield, *Ill., U.S.A.* **80 F9** 39 36N 90 49W
Pittsfield, *Maine, U.S.A.* **77 C11** 44 47N 69 23W
Pittsfield, *Mass., U.S.A.* **79 D11** 42 27N 73 15W
Pittsfield, *N.H., U.S.A.* **79 C13** 43 18N 71 20W
Pittston, *U.S.A.* **79 E9** 41 19N 75 47W
Pittsworth, *Australia* **63 D5** 27 41S 151 37 E
Pituri →, *Australia* **62 C2** 22 35S 138 30 E
Piura, *Peru* **92 E2** 5 15S 80 38W
Pixley, *U.S.A.* **84 K7** 35 58N 119 18W
Pizhou, *China* **34 G9** 34 44N 116 55 E
Placentia, *Canada* **71 C9** 47 20N 54 0W
Placentia B., *Canada* **71 C9** 47 0N 54 40W
Placerville, *U.S.A.* **84 G6** 38 44N 120 48W
Placetas, *Cuba* **88 B4** 22 15N 79 44W
Plainfield, *N.J., U.S.A.* **79 F10** 40 37N 74 25W
Plainfield, *Ohio, U.S.A.* **78 F3** 40 13N 81 43W
Plainfield, *Vt., U.S.A.* **79 B12** 44 17N 72 26W
Plains, *Mont., U.S.A.* **82 C6** 47 28N 114 53W
Plains, *Tex., U.S.A.* **81 J3** 33 11N 102 50W
Plainview, *Nebr., U.S.A.* **80 D6** 42 21N 97 47W
Plainview, *Tex., U.S.A.* **81 H4** 34 11N 101 43W
Plainwell, *U.S.A.* **76 D3** 42 27N 85 38W
Plaistow, *U.S.A.* **79 D13** 42 50N 71 6W
Pláka, Ákra, *Greece* **23 D8** 35 11N 26 19 E
Plana Cays, *Bahamas* **89 B5** 22 38N 73 30W
Planada, *U.S.A.* **84 H6** 37 16N 120 19W
Plano, *U.S.A.* **81 J6** 33 1N 96 42W
Plant City, *U.S.A.* **77 M4** 28 1N 82 7W
Plaquemine, *U.S.A.* **81 K9** 30 17N 91 14W
Plasencia, *Spain* **19 B2** 40 3N 6 8W
Plaster City, *U.S.A.* **85 N11** 32 47N 115 51W
Plaster Rock, *Canada* **71 C6** 46 53N 67 22W
Plastun, *Russia* **30 B8** 44 45N 136 19 E
Plata, Río de la, *S. Amer.* **94 C4** 34 45S 57 30W
Plátani →, *Italy* **20 F5** 37 23N 13 16 E
Plátanos, *Greece* **23 D5** 35 28N 23 33 E
Platte, *U.S.A.* **80 D5** 43 23N 98 51W
Platte →, *Mo., U.S.A.* **80 F7** 39 16N 94 50W
Platte →, *Nebr., U.S.A.* **80 E7** 41 4N 95 53W
Platteville, *U.S.A.* **80 D9** 42 44N 90 29W
Plattsburgh, *U.S.A.* **79 B11** 44 42N 73 28W
Plattsmouth, *U.S.A.* **80 E7** 41 1N 95 53W
Plauen, *Germany* **16 C7** 50 30N 12 8 E
Plavinas, *Latvia* **9 H21** 56 35N 25 46 E
Playa Blanca, *Canary Is.* **22 F6** 28 55N 13 37W
Playa Blanca Sur, *Canary Is.* **22 F6** 28 51N 13 50W
Playa de las Americas,
Canary Is. **22 F3** 28 5N 16 43W
Playa de Mogán, *Canary Is.* **22 G4** 27 48N 15 47W
Playa del Inglés, *Canary Is.* **22 G4** 27 45N 15 33W
Playa Esmerelda, *Canary Is.* **22 F5** 28 8N 14 16W
Playgreen L., *Canada* **73 C9** 54 0N 98 15W
Pleasant Bay, *Canada* **71 C7** 46 51N 60 48W
Pleasant Hill, *U.S.A.* **84 H4** 37 57N 122 4W
Pleasant Mount, *U.S.A.* **79 E9** 41 44N 75 26W
Pleasanton, *Calif., U.S.A.* **84 H5** 37 39N 121 52W
Pleasanton, *Tex., U.S.A.* **81 L5** 28 58N 98 29W
Pleasantville, *N.J., U.S.A.* **76 F8** 39 24N 74 32W
Pleasantville, *Pa., U.S.A.* **78 E5** 41 35N 79 34W
Plei Ku, *Vietnam* **38 F7** 13 57N 108 0 E
Plenty →, *Australia* **62 C2** 23 25S 136 31 E
Plenty, B. of, *N.Z.* **59 G6** 37 45S 177 0 E
Plentywood, *U.S.A.* **80 A2** 48 47N 104 34W
Plesetsk, *Russia* **24 B7** 62 43N 40 20 E
Plessisville, *Canada* **71 C5** 46 14N 71 47W
Plétipi, L., *Canada* **71 B5** 51 44N 70 6W
Pleven, *Bulgaria* **21 C11** 43 26N 24 37 E
Plevlja, *Montenegro, Yug.* **21 C8** 43 21N 19 21 E
Plevna, *Canada* **78 B8** 44 58N 76 59W
Płock, *Poland* **17 B10** 52 32N 19 40 E
Plöckenstein, *Germany* **16 D7** 48 46N 13 51 E
Ploieşti, *Romania* **17 F14** 44 57N 26 5 E
Plonge, Lac la, *Canada* **73 B7** 55 8N 107 20W
Plovdiv, *Bulgaria* **21 C11** 42 8N 24 44 E
Plum, *U.S.A.* **78 F5** 40 29N 79 47W
Plum I., *U.S.A.* **79 E12** 41 11N 72 12W
Plumas, *U.S.A.* **84 F7** 39 45N 120 4W
Plummer, *U.S.A.* **82 C5** 47 20N 116 53W
Plumtree, *Zimbabwe* **55 G2** 20 27S 27 55 E
Plungė, *Lithuania* **9 J19** 55 53N 21 59 E
Plymouth, *U.K.* **11 G3** 50 22N 4 10W
Plymouth, *Calif., U.S.A.* **84 G6** 38 29N 120 51W
Plymouth, *Ind., U.S.A.* **76 E2** 41 21N 86 19W
Plymouth, *Mass., U.S.A.* **79 E14** 41 57N 70 40W
Plymouth, *N.C., U.S.A.* **77 H7** 35 52N 76 43W
Plymouth, *N.H., U.S.A.* **79 C13** 43 46N 71 41W
Plymouth, *Pa., U.S.A.* **79 E9** 41 14N 75 57W
Plymouth, *Wis., U.S.A.* **76 D2** 43 45N 87 59W
Plynlimon = Pumlumon Fawr,
U.K. **11 E4** 52 28N 3 46W
Plzeň, *Czech Rep.* **16 D7** 49 45N 13 22 E
Po →, *Italy* **20 B5** 44 57N 12 4 E
Po Hai = Bo Hai, *China* **35 E10** 39 0N 119 0 E
Pobeda, *Russia* **27 C15** 65 12N 146 12 E
Pobedy, Pik, *Kyrgyzstan* **26 E8** 42 0N 79 58 E
Pocahontas, *Ark., U.S.A.* **81 G9** 36 16N 90 58W
Pocahontas, *Iowa, U.S.A.* **80 D7** 42 44N 94 40W
Pocatello, *U.S.A.* **82 E7** 42 52N 112 27W
Pochutla, *Mexico* **87 D5** 15 50N 96 31W
Pocito Casas, *Mexico* **86 B2** 28 32N 111 6W
Pocomoke City, *U.S.A.* **76 F8** 38 5N 75 34W
Poços de Caldas, *Brazil* **95 A6** 21 50S 46 33W
Podgorica, *Montenegro, Yug.* **21 C8** 42 30N 19 19 E
Podilska Vysochyna, *Ukraine* **17 D14** 49 0N 28 0 E
Podolsk, *Russia* **24 C6** 55 25N 37 30 E
Podporozhye, *Russia* **24 B5** 60 55N 34 2 E
Pofadder, *S. Africa* **56 D2** 29 10S 19 22 E
Pogranitšnyi, *Russia* **30 B5** 44 25N 131 24 E
Poh, *Indonesia* **37 E6** 0 46S 122 51 E
P'ohang, *S. Korea* **35 F15** 36 1N 129 23 E
Pohjanmaa, *Finland* **8 E20** 62 58N 22 50 E
Pohnpei, *Micronesia* **64 G7** 6 55N 158 10 E
Pohri, *India* **42 G6** 25 32N 77 22 E
Poinsett, C., *Antarctica* **5 C8** 65 42S 113 18 E
Point Arena, *U.S.A.* **84 G3** 38 55N 123 41W
Point Baker, *U.S.A.* **72 B2** 56 21N 133 37W
Point Edward, *Canada* **70 D3** 43 0N 82 30W
Point Hope, *U.S.A.* **68 B3** 68 21N 166 47W
Point L., *Canada* **68 B8** 65 15N 113 4W
Point Pedro, *Sri Lanka* **40 Q12** 9 50N 80 15 E
Point Pleasant, *N.J., U.S.A.* **79 F10** 40 5N 74 4W
Point Pleasant, *W. Va., U.S.A.* **76 F4** 38 51N 82 8W
Pointe-à-Pitre, *Guadeloupe* **89 C7** 16 10N 61 32W
Pointe-Claire, *Canada* **79 A11** 45 26N 73 50W
Pointe-Gatineau, *Canada* **79 A9** 45 28N 75 42W
Pointe-Noire, *Congo* **52 E2** 4 48S 11 53 E
Poisonbush Ra., *Australia* **60 D3** 22 30S 121 30 E
Poissonnier Pt., *Australia* **60 C2** 19 57S 119 10 E
Poitiers, *France* **18 C4** 46 35N 0 20 E
Poitou, *France* **18 C3** 46 40N 0 10W
Pojoaque, *U.S.A.* **83 J11** 35 54N 106 1W
Pokaran, *India* **40 F7** 27 0N 71 50 E
Pokataroo, *Australia* **63 D4** 29 30S 148 36 E
Pokhara, *Nepal* **43 E10** 28 14N 83 58 E
Poko, *Dem. Rep. of the Congo* **54 B2** 3 7N 26 52 E
Pokrovsk = Engels, *Russia* **25 D8** 51 28N 46 6 E
Pokrovsk, *Russia* **27 C13** 61 29N 129 0 E
Pola = Pula, *Croatia* **16 F7** 44 54N 13 57 E
Polacca, *U.S.A.* **83 J8** 35 50N 110 23W
Polan, *Iran* **45 E9** 25 30N 61 10 E
Poland ■, *Europe* **17 C10** 52 0N 20 0 E
Polar Bear Prov. Park, *Canada* **70 A2** 55 0N 83 45W
Polatsk, *Belarus* **24 C4** 55 30N 28 50 E
Polcura, *Chile* **94 D1** 37 17S 71 43W
Polessk, *Russia* **9 J19** 54 50N 21 8 E
Polesye = Pripet Marshes,
Europe **17 B15** 52 10N 28 10 E
Polevskoy, *Russia* **24 C11** 56 26N 60 11 E
Pŏlgyo-ri, *S. Korea* **35 G14** 34 51N 127 21 E
Police, *Poland* **16 B8** 53 33N 14 33 E
Polillo Is., *Phil.* **37 B6** 14 56N 122 0 E
Polis, *Cyprus* **23 D11** 35 2N 32 26 E
Políyiros, *Greece* **21 D10** 40 23N 23 25 E
Polk, *U.S.A.* **78 E5** 41 22N 79 56W
Pollachi, *India* **40 P10** 10 35N 77 0 E
Pollença, *Spain* **22 B10** 39 54N 3 1 E
Pollença, B. de, *Spain* **22 B10** 39 53N 3 8 E
Polnovat, *Russia* **26 C7** 63 50N 65 54 E
Polonne, *Ukraine* **17 C14** 50 6N 27 30 E
Polonnoye = Polonne,
Ukraine **17 C14** 50 6N 27 30 E
Polson, *U.S.A.* **82 C6** 47 41N 114 9W
Poltava, *Ukraine* **25 E5** 49 35N 34 35 E
Põltsamaa, *Estonia* **9 G21** 58 41N 25 58 E
Polunochnoye, *Russia* **26 C7** 60 52N 60 25 E
Põlva, *Estonia* **9 G22** 58 3N 27 3 E
Polyarny, *Russia* **24 A5** 69 8N 33 20 E
Polynesia, *Pac. Oc.* **65 J11** 10 0S 162 0W
Polynésie française = French
Polynesia ■, *Pac. Oc.* **65 K13** 20 0S 145 0W
Pomaro, *Mexico* **86 D4** 18 20N 103 18W
Pombal, *Portugal* **19 C1** 39 55N 8 40W
Pómbia, *Greece* **23 E6** 35 0N 24 51 E
Pomene, *Mozam.* **57 C6** 22 53S 35 33 E
Pomeroy, *Ohio, U.S.A.* **76 F4** 39 2N 82 2W
Pomeroy, *Wash., U.S.A.* **82 C5** 46 28N 117 36W
Pomézia, *Italy* **20 D5** 41 40N 12 30 E
Pomona, *Australia* **63 D5** 26 22S 152 52 E
Pomona, *U.S.A.* **85 L9** 34 4N 117 45W
Pomorskie, Pojezierze, *Poland* **17 B9** 53 40N 16 37 E
Pomos, *Cyprus* **23 D11** 35 9N 32 33 E
Pomos, C., *Cyprus* **23 D11** 35 10N 32 33 E
Pompano Beach, *U.S.A.* **77 M5** 26 14N 80 8W
Pompeys Pillar, *U.S.A.* **82 D10** 45 59N 107 57W
Pompton Lakes, *U.S.A.* **79 F10** 41 0N 74 17W
Ponape = Pohnpei,
Micronesia **64 G7** 6 55N 158 10 E
Ponask L., *Canada* **70 B1** 54 0N 92 41W
Ponca, *U.S.A.* **80 D6** 42 34N 96 43W
Ponca City, *U.S.A.* **81 G6** 36 42N 97 5W
Ponce, *Puerto Rico* **89 C6** 18 1N 66 37W
Ponchatoula, *U.S.A.* **81 K9** 30 26N 90 26W
Poncheville, L., *Canada* **70 B4** 50 10N 76 55W
Pond, *U.S.A.* **85 K7** 35 43N 119 20W
Pond Inlet, *Canada* **69 A12** 72 40N 77 0W
Pondicherry, *India* **40 P11** 11 59N 79 50 E
Ponds, I. of, *Canada* **71 B8** 53 27N 55 52W
Ponferrada, *Spain* **19 A2** 42 32N 6 35W
Ponnani, *India* **40 P9** 10 45N 75 59 E
Ponoka, *Canada* **72 C6** 52 42N 113 40W
Ponorogo, *Indonesia* **37 G14** 7 52S 111 27 E
Ponoy, *Russia* **24 A7** 67 0N 41 13 E
Ponoy →, *Russia* **24 A7** 66 59N 41 17 E
Ponta do Sol, *Madeira* **22 D2** 32 42N 17 7W
Ponta Grossa, *Brazil* **95 B5** 25 7S 50 10W
Ponta Pora, *Brazil* **95 A4** 22 20S 55 35W
Pontarlier, *France* **18 C7** 46 54N 6 20 E
Pontchartrain L., *U.S.A.* **81 K10** 30 5N 90 5W
Ponte do Pungué, *Mozam.* **55 F3** 19 30S 34 33 E
Ponte Nova, *Brazil* **95 A7** 20 25S 42 54W
Ponteix, *Canada* **73 D7** 49 46N 107 29W
Pontevedra, *Spain* **19 A1** 42 26N 8 40W
Pontiac, *Ill., U.S.A.* **80 E10** 40 53N 88 38W
Pontiac, *Mich., U.S.A.* **76 D4** 42 38N 83 18W
Pontian Kecil, *Malaysia* **39 M4** 1 29N 103 23 E
Pontianak, *Indonesia* **36 E3** 0 3S 109 15 E
Pontine Is. = Ponziane, Ísole,
Italy **20 D5** 40 55N 12 57 E
Pontine Mts. = Kuzey Anadolu
Dağları, *Turkey* **25 F6** 41 30N 35 0 E
Pontivy, *France* **18 B2** 48 5N 2 58W
Pontoise, *France* **18 B5** 49 3N 2 5 E
Ponton →, *Canada* **72 B5** 58 27N 116 11W
Pontypool, *Canada* **78 B6** 44 6N 78 38W
Pontypool, *U.K.* **11 F4** 51 42N 3 2W
Ponziane, Ísole, *Italy* **20 D5** 40 55N 12 57 E
Poochera, *Australia* **63 E1** 32 43S 134 51 E
Poole, *U.K.* **11 G6** 50 43N 1 59W
Poole □, *U.K.* **11 G6** 50 43N 1 59W
Poona = Pune, *India* **40 K8** 18 29N 73 57 E
Pooncarie, *Australia* **63 E3** 33 22S 142 31 E
Poopelloe L., *Australia* **63 E3** 31 40S 144 0 E
Poopó, L. de, *Bolivia* **92 G5** 18 30S 67 35W
Popayán, *Colombia* **92 C3** 2 27N 76 36W
Poperinge, *Belgium* **15 D2** 50 51N 2 42 E
Popilta L., *Australia* **63 E3** 33 10S 141 42 E
Popio L., *Australia* **63 E3** 33 10S 141 52 E
Poplar, *U.S.A.* **80 A2** 48 7N 105 12W
Poplar →, *Canada* **73 C9** 53 0N 97 19W
Poplar Bluff, *U.S.A.* **81 G9** 36 46N 90 24W
Poplarville, *U.S.A.* **81 K10** 30 51N 89 32W
Popocatépetl, Volcán, *Mexico* **87 D5** 19 2N 98 38W
Popokabaka, *Dem. Rep. of*
the Congo **52 F3** 5 41S 16 40 E
Poprad, *Slovak Rep.* **17 D11** 49 3N 20 18 E
Porali →, *Pakistan* **42 G2** 25 58N 66 26 E
Porbandar, *India* **42 J3** 21 44N 69 43 E
Porcher I., *Canada* **72 C2** 53 50N 130 30W
Porcupine →, *Canada* **73 B8** 59 11N 104 46W
Porcupine →, *U.S.A.* **68 B5** 66 34N 145 19W
Pordenone, *Italy* **20 B5** 45 57N 12 39 E
Pori, *Finland* **9 F19** 61 29N 21 48 E
Porlamar, *Venezuela* **92 A6** 10 57N 63 51W
Poronaysk, *Russia* **27 E15** 49 13N 143 0 E
Poroshiri-Dake, *Japan* **30 C11** 42 41N 142 52 E
Poroto Mts., *Tanzania* **55 D3** 9 0S 33 30 E
Porpoise B., *Antarctica* **5 C9** 66 0S 127 0 E
Porreres, *Spain* **22 B10** 39 31N 3 2 E
Porsangen, *Norway* **8 A21** 70 40N 25 40 E
Porsgrunn, *Norway* **9 G13** 59 10N 9 40 E
Port Alberni, *Canada* **72 D4** 49 14N 124 50W
Port Alfred, *S. Africa* **56 E4** 33 36S 26 55 E
Port Alice, *Canada* **72 C3** 50 20N 127 25W
Port Allegany, *U.S.A.* **78 E6** 41 48N 78 17W
Port Allen, *U.S.A.* **81 K9** 30 27N 91 12W
Port Alma, *Australia* **62 C5** 23 38S 150 53 E
Port Angeles, *U.S.A.* **84 B3** 48 7N 123 27W
Port Antonio, *Jamaica* **88 C4** 18 10N 76 30W
Port Aransas, *U.S.A.* **81 M6** 27 50N 97 4W
Port Arthur = Lüshun, *China* **35 E11** 38 45N 121 15 E
Port Arthur, *Australia* **62 G4** 43 7S 147 50 E
Port Arthur, *U.S.A.* **81 L8** 29 54N 93 56W
Port au Choix, *Canada* **71 B8** 50 43N 57 22W
Port au Port B., *Canada* **71 C8** 48 40N 58 50W
Port-au-Prince, *Haiti* **89 C5** 18 40N 72 20W
Port Augusta, *Australia* **63 E2** 32 30S 137 50 E
Port Austin, *U.S.A.* **78 B2** 44 3N 83 1W
Port Bell, *Uganda* **54 B3** 0 18N 32 35 E
Port Bergé Vaovao, *Madag.* **57 B8** 15 33S 47 40 E
Port Blandford, *Canada* **71 C9** 48 20N 54 10W
Port Bradshaw, *Australia* **62 A2** 12 30S 137 20 E
Port Broughton, *Australia* **63 E2** 33 37S 137 56 E
Port Burwell, *Canada* **78 D4** 42 40N 80 48W
Port Canning, *India* **43 H13** 22 23N 88 40 E
Port-Cartier, *Canada* **71 B6** 50 2N 66 50W
Port Chalmers, *N.Z.* **59 L3** 45 49S 170 30 E
Port Charlotte, *U.S.A.* **77 M4** 26 59N 82 6W
Port Chester, *U.S.A.* **79 F11** 41 0N 73 40W
Port Clements, *Canada* **72 C2** 53 40N 132 10W
Port Clinton, *U.S.A.* **76 E4** 41 31N 82 56W
Port Colborne, *Canada* **78 D5** 42 50N 79 10W
Port Coquitlam, *Canada* **72 D4** 49 15N 122 45W
Port Credit, *Canada* **78 C5** 43 33N 79 35W
Port Curtis, *Australia* **62 C5** 23 57S 151 20 E
Port d'Alcúdia, *Spain* **22 B10** 39 50N 3 7 E
Port Dalhousie, *Canada* **78 C5** 43 13N 79 16W
Port d'Andratx, *Spain* **22 B9** 39 32N 2 23 E
Port Darwin, *Australia* **60 B5** 12 24S 130 45 E
Port Darwin, *Falk. Is.* **96 G5** 51 50S 59 0W
Port Davey, *Australia* **62 G4** 43 16S 145 55 E
Port-de-Paix, *Haiti* **89 C5** 19 50N 72 50W
Port de Pollença, *Spain* **22 B10** 39 54N 3 4 E
Port de Sóller, *Spain* **22 B9** 39 48N 2 42 E
Port Dickson, *Malaysia* **39 L3** 2 30N 101 49 E
Port Douglas, *Australia* **62 B4** 16 30S 145 30 E
Port Dover, *Canada* **78 D4** 42 47N 80 12W
Port Edward, *Canada* **72 C2** 54 12N 130 10W
Port Elgin, *Canada* **78 B3** 44 25N 81 25W
Port Elizabeth, *S. Africa* **56 E4** 33 58S 25 40 E
Port Ellen, *U.K.* **12 F2** 55 38N 6 11W
Port Erin, *U.K.* **10 C3** 54 5N 4 45W
Port Essington, *Australia* **60 B5** 11 15S 132 10 E
Port Etienne = Nouâdhibou,
Mauritania **50 D2** 20 54N 17 0W
Port Ewen, *U.S.A.* **79 E11** 41 54N 73 59W
Port Fairy, *Australia* **63 F3** 38 22S 142 12 E
Port Gamble, *U.S.A.* **84 C4** 47 51N 122 35W
Port-Gentil, *Gabon* **52 E1** 0 40S 8 50 E
Port Germein, *Australia* **63 E2** 33 1S 138 1 E
Port Gibson, *U.S.A.* **81 K9** 31 58N 90 59W
Port Glasgow, *U.K.* **12 F4** 55 56N 4 41W
Port Harcourt, *Nigeria* **50 H7** 4 40N 7 10 E
Port Hardy, *Canada* **72 C3** 50 41N 127 30W
Port Harrison = Inukjuak,
Canada **69 C12** 58 25N 78 15W
Port Hawkesbury, *Canada* **71 C7** 45 36N 61 22W
Port Hedland, *Australia* **60 D2** 20 25S 118 35 E
Port Henry, *U.S.A.* **79 B11** 44 3N 73 28W
Port Hood, *Canada* **71 C7** 46 0N 61 32W
Port Hope, *Canada* **78 C6** 43 56N 78 20W
Port Hope, *U.S.A.* **78 C2** 43 57N 82 43W
Port Hope Simpson, *Canada* **71 B8** 52 33N 56 18W
Port Hueneme, *U.S.A.* **85 L7** 34 7N 119 12W
Port Huron, *U.S.A.* **78 D2** 42 58N 82 26W
Port Jefferson, *U.S.A.* **79 F11** 40 57N 73 3W
Port Jervis, *U.S.A.* **79 E10** 41 22N 74 41W
Port Kelang = Pelabuhan
Kelang, *Malaysia* **39 L3** 3 0N 101 23 E
Port Kenny, *Australia* **63 E1** 33 10S 134 41 E
Port Lairge = Waterford,
Ireland **13 D4** 52 15N 7 8W
Port Laoise, *Ireland* **13 C4** 53 2N 7 18W
Port Lavaca, *U.S.A.* **81 L6** 28 37N 96 38W
Port Leyden, *U.S.A.* **79 C9** 43 35N 75 21W
Port Lincoln, *Australia* **63 E2** 34 42S 135 52 E
Port Loko, *S. Leone* **50 G3** 8 48N 12 46W
Port Louis, *Mauritius* **49 H9** 20 10S 57 30 E
Port MacDonnell, *Australia* **63 F3** 38 5S 140 48 E
Port McNeill, *Canada* **72 C3** 50 35N 127 6W
Port Macquarie, *Australia* **63 E5** 31 25S 152 25 E
Port Maria, *Jamaica* **88 C4** 18 25N 76 55W
Port Matilda, *U.S.A.* **78 F6** 40 48N 78 3W
Port Mellon, *Canada* **72 D4** 49 32N 123 31W
Port-Menier, *Canada* **71 C7** 49 51N 64 15W
Port Moody, *Canada* **84 A4** 49 17N 122 51W
Port Morant, *Jamaica* **88 C4** 17 54N 76 19W
Port Moresby, *Papua N. G.* **64 H6** 9 24S 147 8 E
Port Musgrave, *Australia* **62 A3** 11 55S 141 50 E
Port Neches, *U.S.A.* **81 L8** 30 0N 93 59W
Port Nolloth, *S. Africa* **56 D2** 29 17S 16 52 E
Port Nouveau-Québec =
Kangiqsualujjuaq, *Canada* **69 C13** 58 30N 65 59W
Port of Spain, *Trin. & Tob.* **89 D7** 10 40N 61 31W
Port Orange, *U.S.A.* **77 L5** 29 9N 80 59W
Port Orchard, *U.S.A.* **84 C4** 47 32N 122 38W
Port Orford, *U.S.A.* **82 E1** 42 45N 124 30W
Port Pegasus, *N.Z.* **59 M1** 47 12S 167 41 E
Port Perry, *Canada* **78 B6** 44 6N 78 56W
Port Phillip B., *Australia* **63 F3** 38 10S 144 50 E
Port Pirie, *Australia* **63 E2** 33 10S 138 1 E
Port Radium = Echo Bay,
Canada **68 B8** 66 5N 117 55W
Port Renfrew, *Canada* **72 D4** 48 30N 124 20W
Port Roper, *Australia* **62 A2** 14 45S 135 25 E
Port Rowan, *Canada* **78 D4** 42 40N 80 30W
Port Safaga = Bûr Safâga,
Egypt **44 E2** 26 43N 33 57 E
Port Said = Bûr Sa'îd, *Egypt* **51 B12** 31 16N 32 18 E
Port St. Joe, *U.S.A.* **77 L3** 29 49N 85 18W
Port St. Johns = Umzimvubu,
S. Africa **57 E4** 31 38S 29 33 E
Port St. Lucie, *U.S.A.* **77 M5** 27 20N 80 20W
Port Sanilac, *U.S.A.* **78 C2** 43 26N 82 33W
Port Severn, *Canada* **78 B5** 44 48N 79 43W
Port Shepstone, *S. Africa* **57 E5** 30 44S 30 28 E
Port Simpson, *Canada* **72 C2** 54 30N 130 20W
Port Stanley = Stanley,
Falk. Is. **96 G5** 51 40S 59 51W
Port Stanley, *Canada* **78 D3** 42 40N 81 10W
Port Sudan = Bûr Sûdân,
Sudan **51 E13** 19 32N 37 9 E
Port Sulphur, *U.S.A.* **81 L10** 29 29N 89 42W
Port Talbot, *U.K.* **11 F4** 51 35N 3 47W
Port Townsend, *U.S.A.* **84 B4** 48 7N 122 45W
Port-Vendres, *France* **18 E5** 42 32N 3 8 E
Port Vila, *Vanuatu* **64 J8** 17 45S 168 18 E
Port Vladimir, *Russia* **24 A5** 69 25N 33 6 E
Port Wakefield, *Australia* **63 E2** 34 12S 138 10 E
Port Washington, *U.S.A.* **76 D2** 43 23N 87 53W

Port Weld

Port Weld = Kuala Sepetang, Malaysia 39 K3 4 49N 100 28 E
Porta Orientalis, Romania 17 F12 45 6N 22 18 E
Portadown, U.K. 13 B5 54 25N 6 27W
Portaferry, U.K. 13 B6 54 23N 5 33W
Portage, Pa., U.S.A. 78 F6 40 23N 78 41W
Portage, Wis., U.S.A. 80 D10 43 33N 89 28W
Portage La Prairie, Canada 73 D9 49 58N 98 18W
Portageville, U.S.A. 81 G10 36 26N 89 42W
Portalegre, Portugal 19 C2 39 19N 7 25W
Portales, U.S.A. 81 H3 34 11N 103 20W
Portarlington, Ireland 13 C4 53 9N 7 14W
Portbou, Spain 19 A7 42 25N 3 9 E
Porter L., N.W.T., Canada 73 A7 61 41N 108 5W
Porter L., Sask., Canada 73 B7 56 20N 107 20W
Porterville, S. Africa 56 E2 33 0S 19 0 E
Porterville, U.S.A. 84 J8 36 4N 119 1W
Porthcawl, U.K. 11 F4 51 29N 3 42W
Porthill, U.S.A. 82 B5 48 59N 116 30W
Porthmadog, U.K. 10 E3 52 55N 4 8W
Portile de Fier, Europe 17 F12 44 44N 22 30 E
Portimão, Portugal 19 D1 37 8N 8 32W
Portishead, U.K. 11 F5 51 29N 2 46W
Portknockie, U.K. 12 D6 57 42N 2 51W
Portland, N.S.W., Australia 63 E5 33 20S 150 0 E
Portland, Vic., Australia 63 F3 38 20S 141 35 E
Portland, Canada 79 B8 44 42N 76 12W
Portland, Conn., U.S.A. 79 E12 41 34N 72 38W
Portland, Maine, U.S.A. 69 D12 43 39N 70 16W
Portland, Mich., U.S.A. 76 D3 42 52N 84 54W
Portland, Oreg., U.S.A. 84 E4 45 32N 122 37W
Portland, Pa., U.S.A. 79 F9 40 55N 75 6W
Portland, Tex., U.S.A. 81 M6 27 53N 97 20W
Portland, I. of, U.K. 11 G5 50 33N 2 26W
Portland B., Australia 63 F3 38 15S 141 45 E
Portland Bill, U.K. 11 G5 50 31N 2 28W
Portland Canal, U.S.A. 72 B2 55 56N 130 0W
Portmadoc = Porthmadog, U.K. 10 E3 52 55N 4 8W
Porto, Portugal 19 B1 41 8N 8 40W
Pôrto Alegre, Brazil 95 C5 30 5S 51 10W
Porto Amboim = Gunza, Angola 52 G2 10 50S 13 50 E
Porto Cristo, Spain 22 B10 39 33N 3 20 E
Pôrto de Móz, Brazil 93 D8 1 41S 52 13W
Porto Empédocle, Italy 20 F5 37 17N 13 32 E
Pôrto Esperança, Brazil 92 G7 19 37S 57 29W
Pôrto Franco, Brazil 93 E9 6 20S 47 24W
Pôrto Mendes, Brazil 95 A5 24 30S 54 15W
Porto Moniz, Madeira 22 D2 32 52N 17 11W
Pôrto Murtinho, Brazil 92 H7 21 45S 57 55W
Pôrto Nacional, Brazil 93 F9 10 40S 48 30W
Porto-Novo, Benin 50 G6 6 23N 2 42 E
Porto Petro, Spain 22 B10 39 22N 3 13 E
Porto Santo, I. de, Madeira 50 B2 33 45N 16 25W
Pôrto São José, Brazil 95 A5 22 43S 53 10W
Pôrto Seguro, Brazil 93 G11 16 26S 39 5W
Porto Tórres, Italy 20 D3 40 50N 8 24 E
Pôrto União, Brazil 95 B5 26 10S 51 10W
Pôrto Válter, Brazil 92 E4 8 15S 72 40W
Porto-Vecchio, France 18 F8 41 35N 9 16 E
Pôrto Velho, Brazil 92 E6 8 46S 63 54W
Portobelo, Panama 88 E4 9 35N 79 42W
Portoferràio, Italy 20 C4 42 48N 10 20 E
Portola, U.S.A. 84 F6 39 49N 120 28W
Portoscuso, Italy 20 E3 39 12N 8 24 E
Portoviejo, Ecuador 92 D2 1 7S 80 28W
Portpatrick, U.K. 12 G3 54 51N 5 7W
Portree, U.K. 12 D2 57 25N 6 12W
Portrush, U.K. 13 A5 55 12N 6 40W
Portsmouth, Domin. 89 C7 15 34N 61 27W
Portsmouth, U.K. 11 G6 50 48N 1 6W
Portsmouth, N.H., U.S.A. 77 D10 43 5N 70 45W
Portsmouth, Ohio, U.S.A. 76 F4 38 44N 82 57W
Portsmouth, R.I., U.S.A. 79 E13 41 36N 71 15W
Portsmouth, Va., U.S.A. 76 G7 36 50N 76 18W
Portsmouth □, U.K. 11 G6 50 48N 1 6W
Portsoy, U.K. 12 D6 57 41N 2 41W
Portstewart, U.K. 13 A5 55 11N 6 43W
Porttipahtan tekojärvi, Finland 8 B22 68 5N 26 40 E
Portugal ■, Europe 19 C1 40 0N 8 0W
Portumna, Ireland 13 C3 53 6N 8 14W
Portville, U.S.A. 78 D6 42 3N 78 20W
Porvenir, Chile 96 G2 53 10S 70 16W
Porvoo, Finland 9 F21 60 24N 25 40 E
Posadas, Argentina 95 B4 27 30S 55 50W
Poshan = Boshan, China 35 F9 36 28N 117 49 E
Posht-e-Badam, Iran 45 C7 33 2N 55 23 E
Poso, Indonesia 37 E6 1 20S 120 55 E
Posong, S. Korea 35 G14 34 46N 127 5 E
Posse, Brazil 93 F9 14 4S 46 18W
Possession I., Antarctica 5 D11 72 4S 172 0 E
Possum Kingdom L., U.S.A. 81 J5 32 52N 98 26W
Post, U.S.A. 81 J4 33 12N 101 23W
Post Falls, U.S.A. 82 C5 47 43N 116 57W
Postavy = Pastavy, Belarus 9 J22 55 4N 26 50 E
Poste-de-la-Baleine = Kuujjuarapik, Canada 70 A4 55 20N 77 35W
Postmasburg, S. Africa 56 D3 28 18S 23 5 E
Postojna, Slovenia 16 F8 45 46N 14 12 E
Poston, U.S.A. 85 M12 34 0N 114 24W
Postville, Canada 71 B8 54 54N 59 47W
Potchefstroom, S. Africa 56 D4 26 41S 27 7 E
Poteau, U.S.A. 81 H7 35 3N 94 37W
Poteet, U.S.A. 81 L5 29 2N 98 35W
Potenza, Italy 20 D6 40 38N 15 48 E
Poteriteri, L., N.Z. 59 M1 46 5S 167 10 E
Potgietersrus, S. Africa 57 C4 24 10S 28 55 E
Poti, Georgia 25 F7 42 10N 41 38 E
Potiskum, Nigeria 51 F8 11 39N 11 2 E
Potomac →, U.S.A. 76 G7 38 0N 76 23W
Potosí, Bolivia 92 G5 19 38S 65 50W
Potosi Mt., U.S.A. 85 K11 35 57N 115 29W
Pototan, Phil. 37 B6 10 54N 122 38 E
Potrerillos, Chile 94 B2 26 30S 69 30W
Potsdam, Germany 16 B7 52 25N 13 4 E
Potsdam, U.S.A. 79 B10 44 40N 74 59W
Pottersville, U.S.A. 79 C11 43 43N 73 50W
Pottstown, U.S.A. 79 F9 40 15N 75 39W
Pottsville, U.S.A. 79 F8 40 41N 76 12W
Pottuvil, Sri Lanka 40 R12 6 55N 81 50 E
Pouce Coupé, Canada 72 B4 55 40N 120 10W
Poughkeepsie, U.S.A. 79 E11 41 42N 73 56W
Poulaphouca Res., Ireland 13 C5 53 8N 6 30W
Poulsbo, U.S.A. 84 C4 47 44N 122 39W
Poultney, U.S.A. 79 C11 43 31N 73 14W
Poulton-le-Fylde, U.K. 10 D5 53 51N 2 58W
Pouso Alegre, Brazil 95 A6 22 14S 45 57W
Pouthisat, Cambodia 38 F4 12 34N 103 50 E
Považská Bystrica, Slovak Rep. 17 D10 49 8N 18 27 E
Povenets, Russia 24 B5 62 50N 34 50 E
Poverty B., N.Z. 59 H7 38 43S 178 2 E
Póvoa de Varzim, Portugal 19 B1 41 25N 8 46W
Povungnituk = Puvirnituq, Canada 69 B12 60 2N 77 10W
Powassan, Canada 70 C4 46 5N 79 25W
Poway, U.S.A. 85 N9 32 58N 117 2W
Powder →, U.S.A. 80 B2 46 45N 105 26W
Powder River, U.S.A. 82 E10 43 2N 106 59W
Powell, U.S.A. 82 D9 44 45N 108 46W
Powell, L., U.S.A. 83 H8 36 57N 111 29W
Powell River, Canada 72 D4 49 50N 124 35W
Powers, U.S.A. 76 C2 45 41N 87 32W
Powys □, U.K. 11 E4 52 20N 3 20W
Poyang Hu, China 33 D6 29 5N 116 20 E
Poyarkovo, Russia 27 E13 49 36N 128 41 E
Poza Rica, Mexico 87 C5 20 33N 97 27W
Požarevac, Serbia, Yug. 21 B9 44 35N 21 18 E
Poznań, Poland 17 B9 52 25N 16 55 E
Pozo, U.S.A. 85 K6 35 20N 120 24W
Pozo Almonte, Chile 92 H5 20 10S 69 50W
Pozo Colorado, Paraguay 94 A4 23 30S 58 45W
Pozoblanco, Spain 19 C3 38 23N 4 51W
Pozzuoli, Italy 20 D6 40 49N 14 7 E
Prachin Buri, Thailand 38 E3 14 0N 101 25 E
Prachuap Khiri Khan, Thailand 39 G2 11 49N 99 48 E
Prado, Brazil 93 G11 17 20S 39 13W
Prague = Praha, Czech Rep. 16 C8 50 5N 14 22 E
Praha, Czech Rep. 16 C8 50 5N 14 22 E
Praia, C. Verde Is. 49 E1 15 2N 23 34W
Prainha, Amazonas, Brazil 92 E6 7 10S 60 30W
Prainha, Pará, Brazil 93 D8 1 45S 53 30W
Prairie, Australia 62 C3 20 50S 144 35 E
Prairie City, U.S.A. 82 D4 44 28N 118 43W
Prairie Dog Town Fork →, U.S.A. 81 H5 34 30N 99 23W
Prairie du Chien, U.S.A. 80 D9 43 3N 91 9W
Prairies, L. of the, Canada 73 C8 51 16N 101 32W
Pran Buri, Thailand 38 F2 12 23N 99 55 E
Prapat, Indonesia 36 D1 2 41N 98 58 E
Prasonísi, Ákra, Greece 23 D9 35 42N 27 46 E
Prata, Brazil 93 G9 19 25S 48 54W
Pratabpur, India 43 H10 23 28N 83 15 E
Pratapgarh, Raj., India 42 G6 24 2N 74 40 E
Pratapgarh, Ut. P., India 43 G9 25 56N 81 59 E
Prato, Italy 20 C4 43 53N 11 6 E
Pratt, U.S.A. 81 G5 37 39N 98 44W
Prattville, U.S.A. 77 J2 32 28N 86 29W
Pravia, Spain 19 A2 43 30N 6 12W
Praya, Indonesia 36 F5 8 39S 116 17 E
Precordillera, Argentina 94 C2 30 0S 69 1W
Preeceville, Canada 73 C8 51 57N 102 40W
Preiļi, Latvia 9 H22 56 18N 26 43 E
Premont, U.S.A. 81 M5 27 22N 98 7W
Prentice, U.S.A. 80 C9 45 33N 90 17W
Preobrazheniye, Russia 30 C6 42 54N 133 54 E
Preparis North Channel, Ind. Oc. 41 M18 15 12N 93 40 E
Preparis South Channel, Ind. Oc. 41 M18 14 36N 93 40 E
Přerov, Czech Rep. 17 D9 49 28N 17 27 E
Prescott, Canada 79 B9 44 45N 75 30W
Prescott, Ariz., U.S.A. 83 J7 34 33N 112 28W
Prescott, Ark., U.S.A. 81 J8 33 48N 93 23W
Prescott Valley, U.S.A. 83 J7 34 40N 112 18W
Preservation Inlet, N.Z. 59 M1 46 8S 166 35 E
Presho, U.S.A. 80 D4 43 54N 100 3W
Presidencia de la Plaza, Argentina 94 B4 27 0S 59 50W
Presidencia Roque Saenz Peña, Argentina 94 B3 26 45S 60 30W
Presidente Epitácio, Brazil 93 H8 21 56S 52 6W
Presidente Hayes □, Paraguay 94 A4 24 0S 59 0W
Presidente Prudente, Brazil 95 A5 22 5S 51 25W
Presidio, Mexico 86 B4 29 29N 104 23W
Presidio, U.S.A. 81 L2 29 34N 104 22W
Prešov, Slovak Rep. 17 D11 49 0N 21 15 E
Prespa, L. = Prespansko Jezero, Macedonia 21 D9 40 55N 21 0 E
Prespansko Jezero, Macedonia 21 D9 40 55N 21 0 E
Presque I., U.S.A. 78 D4 42 9N 80 6W
Presque Isle, U.S.A. 77 B12 46 41N 68 1W
Prestatyn, U.K. 10 D4 53 20N 3 24W
Presteigne, U.K. 11 E5 52 17N 3 0W
Preston, Canada 78 C4 43 23N 80 21W
Preston, U.K. 10 D5 53 46N 2 42W
Preston, Idaho, U.S.A. 82 E8 42 6N 111 53W
Preston, Minn., U.S.A. 80 D8 43 40N 92 5W
Preston, C., Australia 60 D2 20 51S 116 12 E
Prestonburg, U.S.A. 76 G4 37 39N 82 46W
Prestwick, U.K. 12 F4 55 29N 4 37W
Pretoria, S. Africa 57 D4 25 44S 28 12 E
Préveza, Greece 21 E9 38 57N 20 45 E
Prey Veng, Cambodia 39 G5 11 35N 105 29 E
Pribilof Is., U.S.A. 68 C2 57 0N 170 0W
Příbram, Czech Rep. 16 D8 49 41N 14 2 E
Price, U.S.A. 82 G8 39 36N 110 49W
Price I., Canada 72 C3 52 23N 128 41W
Prichard, U.S.A. 77 K1 30 44N 88 5W
Priekule, Latvia 9 H19 56 26N 21 35 E
Prienai, Lithuania 9 J20 54 38N 23 57 E
Prieska, S. Africa 56 D3 29 40S 22 42 E
Priest L., U.S.A. 82 B5 48 35N 116 52W
Priest River, U.S.A. 82 B5 48 10N 116 54W
Priest Valley, U.S.A. 84 J6 36 10N 120 39W
Prievidza, Slovak Rep. 17 D10 48 46N 18 36 E
Prikaspiyskaya Nizmennost = Caspian Depression, Eurasia 25 E8 47 0N 48 0 E
Prilep, Macedonia 21 D9 41 21N 21 32 E
Priluki = Pryluky, Ukraine 25 D5 50 30N 32 24 E
Prime Seal I., Australia 62 G4 40 3S 147 43 E
Primrose L., Canada 73 C7 54 55N 109 45W
Prince Albert, Canada 73 C7 53 15N 105 50W
Prince Albert, S. Africa 56 E3 33 12S 22 2 E
Prince Albert Mts., Antarctica 5 D11 76 0S 161 30 E
Prince Albert Nat. Park, Canada 73 C7 54 0N 106 25W
Prince Albert Pen., Canada 68 A8 72 30N 116 0W
Prince Albert Sd., Canada 68 A8 70 25N 115 0W
Prince Alfred, C., Canada 4 B1 74 20N 124 40W
Prince Charles I., Canada 69 B12 67 47N 76 12W
Prince Charles Mts., Antarctica 5 D6 72 0S 67 0 E
Prince Edward I. □, Canada 71 C7 46 20N 63 20W
Prince Edward Is., Ind. Oc. 3 G11 46 35S 38 0 E
Prince Edward Pt., Canada 78 C8 43 56N 76 52W
Prince George, Canada 72 C4 53 55N 122 50W
Prince of Wales, C., U.S.A. 66 C3 65 36N 168 5W
Prince of Wales I., Australia 62 A3 10 40S 142 10 E
Prince of Wales I., Canada 68 A10 73 0N 99 0W
Prince of Wales I., U.S.A. 68 C6 55 47N 132 50W
Prince Patrick I., Canada 4 B2 77 0N 120 0W
Prince Regent Inlet, Canada 4 B3 73 0N 90 0W
Prince Rupert, Canada 72 C2 54 20N 130 20W
Princess Charlotte B., Australia 62 A3 14 25S 144 0 E
Princess May Ranges, Australia 60 C4 15 30S 125 30 E
Princess Royal I., Canada 72 C3 53 0N 128 40W
Princeton, Canada 72 D4 49 27N 120 30W
Princeton, Calif., U.S.A. 84 F4 39 24N 122 1W
Princeton, Ill., U.S.A. 80 E10 41 23N 89 28W
Princeton, Ind., U.S.A. 76 F2 38 21N 87 34W
Princeton, Ky., U.S.A. 76 G2 37 7N 87 53W
Princeton, Mo., U.S.A. 80 E8 40 24N 93 35W
Princeton, N.J., U.S.A. 79 F10 40 21N 74 39W
Princeton, W. Va., U.S.A. 76 G5 37 22N 81 6W
Principe, I. de, Atl. Oc. 48 F4 1 37N 7 27 E
Principe da Beira, Brazil 92 F6 12 20S 64 30W
Prineville, U.S.A. 82 D3 44 18N 120 51W
Prins Harald Kyst, Antarctica 5 D4 70 0S 35 1 E
Prinsesse Astrid Kyst, Antarctica 5 D3 70 45S 12 30 E
Prinsesse Ragnhild Kyst, Antarctica 5 D4 70 15S 27 30 E
Prinzapolca, Nic. 88 D3 13 20N 83 35W
Priozersk, Russia 24 B5 61 2N 30 7 E
Pripet = Prypyat →, Europe 17 C16 51 20N 30 15 E
Pripet Marshes, Europe 17 B15 52 10N 28 10 E
Pripyat Marshes = Pripet Marshes, Europe 17 B15 52 10N 28 10 E
Pripyats = Prypyat →, Europe 17 C16 51 20N 30 15 E
Priština, Kosovo, Yug. 21 C9 42 40N 21 13 E
Privas, France 18 D6 44 45N 4 37 E
Privolzhskaya Vozvyshennost, Russia 25 D8 51 0N 46 0 E
Prizren, Kosovo, Yug. 21 C9 42 13N 20 45 E
Probolinggo, Indonesia 37 G15 7 46S 113 13 E
Proctor, U.S.A. 79 C11 43 40N 73 2W
Proddatur, India 40 M11 14 45N 78 30 E
Prodhromos, Cyprus 23 E11 34 57N 32 50 E
Profitis Ilías, Greece 23 C9 36 17N 27 56 E
Profondeville, Belgium 15 D4 50 23N 4 52 E
Progreso, Coahuila, Mexico 86 B4 27 28N 101 4W
Progreso, Yucatán, Mexico 87 C7 21 20N 89 40W
Prokopyevsk, Russia 26 D9 54 0N 86 45 E
Prokuplje, Serbia, Yug. 21 C9 43 16N 21 36 E
Prome, Burma 41 K19 18 49N 95 13 E
Prophet →, Canada 72 B4 58 48N 122 40W
Prophet River, Canada 72 B4 58 6N 122 43W
Propriá, Brazil 93 F11 10 13S 36 51W
Proserpine, Australia 62 C4 20 21S 148 36 E
Prosna →, Poland 17 B9 52 6N 17 44 E
Prospect, U.S.A. 79 C9 43 18N 75 9W
Prosser, U.S.A. 82 C4 46 12N 119 46W
Prostějov, Czech Rep. 17 D9 49 30N 17 9 E
Proston, Australia 63 D5 26 8S 151 32 E
Provence, France 18 E6 43 40N 5 46 E
Providence, Ky., U.S.A. 76 G2 37 24N 87 46W
Providence, R.I., U.S.A. 79 E13 41 49N 71 24W
Providence Bay, Canada 70 C3 45 41N 82 15W
Providence Mts., U.S.A. 85 K11 35 10N 115 15W
Providencia, I. de, Colombia 88 D3 13 25N 81 26W
Provideniya, Russia 27 C19 64 23N 173 18W
Provins, France 18 B5 48 33N 3 15 E
Provo, U.S.A. 82 F8 40 14N 111 39W
Provost, Canada 73 C6 52 25N 110 20W
Prudhoe Bay, U.S.A. 68 A5 70 18N 148 22W
Prudhoe I., Australia 62 C4 21 19S 149 41 E
Prud'homme, Canada 73 C7 52 20N 105 54W
Pruszków, Poland 17 B11 52 9N 20 49 E
Prut →, Romania 17 F15 45 28N 28 10 E
Pruzhany, Belarus 17 B13 52 33N 24 28 E
Prydz B., Antarctica 5 C6 69 0S 74 0 E
Pryluky, Ukraine 25 D5 50 30N 32 24 E
Pryor, U.S.A. 81 G7 36 19N 95 19W
Prypyat →, Europe 17 C16 51 20N 30 15 E
Przemyśl, Poland 17 D12 49 50N 22 45 E
Przhevalsk = Karakol, Kyrgyzstan 26 E8 42 30N 78 20 E
Psará, Greece 21 E11 38 37N 25 38 E
Psira, Greece 23 D7 35 12N 25 52 E
Pskov, Russia 24 C4 57 50N 28 25 E
Ptich = Ptsich →, Belarus 17 B15 52 9N 28 52 E
Ptolemaís, Greece 21 D9 40 30N 21 43 E
Ptsich →, Belarus 17 B15 52 9N 28 52 E
Pu Xian, China 34 F6 36 24N 111 6 E
Pua, Thailand 38 C3 19 11N 100 55 E
Puán, Argentina 94 D3 37 30S 62 45W
Puan, S. Korea 35 G14 35 44N 126 44 E
Pucallpa, Peru 92 E4 8 25S 74 30W
Pudasjärvi, Finland 8 D22 65 23N 26 53 E
Pudozh, Russia 24 B6 61 48N 36 32 E
Puduchcheri = Pondicherry, India 40 P11 11 59N 79 50 E
Pudukkottai, India 40 P11 10 28N 78 47 E
Puebla, Mexico 87 D5 19 3N 98 12W
Puebla □, Mexico 87 D5 18 30N 98 0W
Pueblo, U.S.A. 80 F2 38 16N 104 37W
Pueblo Hundido, Chile 94 B1 26 20S 70 5W
Puelches, Argentina 94 D2 38 5S 65 51W
Puelén, Argentina 94 D2 37 32S 67 38W
Puente Alto, Chile 94 C1 33 32S 70 35W
Puente-Genil, Spain 19 D3 37 22N 4 47W
Puerco →, U.S.A. 83 J10 34 22N 107 50W
Puerto, Canary Is. 22 F2 28 5N 17 20W
Puerto Aisén, Chile 96 F2 45 27S 73 0W
Puerto Ángel, Mexico 87 D5 15 40N 96 29W
Puerto Arista, Mexico 87 D6 15 56N 93 48W
Puerto Armuelles, Panama 88 E3 8 20N 82 51W
Puerto Ayacucho, Venezuela 92 B5 5 40N 67 35W
Puerto Barrios, Guatemala 88 C2 15 40N 88 32W
Puerto Bermejo, Argentina 94 B4 26 55S 58 34W
Puerto Bermúdez, Peru 92 F4 10 20S 74 58W
Puerto Bolívar, Ecuador 92 D3 3 19S 79 55W
Puerto Cabello, Venezuela 92 A5 10 28N 68 1W
Puerto Cabezas, Nic. 88 D3 14 0N 83 30W
Puerto Cabo Gracias á Dios, Nic. 88 D3 15 0N 83 10W
Puerto Carreño, Colombia 92 B5 6 12N 67 22W
Puerto Castilla, Honduras 88 C2 16 0N 86 0W
Puerto Chicama, Peru 92 E3 7 45S 79 20W
Puerto Coig, Argentina 96 G3 50 54S 69 15W
Puerto Cortés, Costa Rica 88 E3 8 55N 84 0W
Puerto Cortés, Honduras 88 C2 15 51N 88 0W
Puerto Cumarebo, Venezuela 92 A5 11 29N 69 30W
Puerto de Alcudia = Port d'Alcúdia, Spain 22 B10 39 50N 3 7 E
Puerto de Cabrera, Spain 22 B9 39 8N 2 56 E
Puerto de Gran Tarajal, Canary Is. 22 F5 28 13N 14 1W
Puerto de la Cruz, Canary Is. 22 F3 28 24N 16 32W
Puerto de Pozo Negro, Canary Is. 22 F6 28 19N 13 55W
Puerto de Sóller = Port de Sóller, Spain 22 B9 39 48N 2 42 E
Puerto del Carmen, Canary Is. 22 F6 28 55N 13 38W
Puerto del Rosario, Canary Is. 22 F6 28 30N 13 52W
Puerto Deseado, Argentina 96 F3 47 55S 66 0W
Puerto Escondido, Mexico 87 D5 15 50N 97 3W
Puerto Heath, Bolivia 92 F5 12 34S 68 39W
Puerto Inírida, Colombia 92 C5 3 53N 67 52W
Puerto Juárez, Mexico 87 C7 21 11N 86 49W
Puerto La Cruz, Venezuela 92 A6 10 13N 64 38W
Puerto Leguízamo, Colombia 92 D4 0 12S 74 46W
Puerto Limón, Colombia 92 C4 3 23N 73 30W
Puerto Lobos, Argentina 96 E3 42 0S 65 3W
Puerto Madryn, Argentina 96 E3 42 48S 65 4W
Puerto Maldonado, Peru 92 F5 12 30S 69 10W
Puerto Manotí, Cuba 88 B4 21 22N 76 50W
Puerto Montt, Chile 96 E2 41 28S 73 0W
Puerto Morazán, Nic. 88 D2 12 51N 87 11W
Puerto Morelos, Mexico 87 C7 20 49N 86 52W
Puerto Natales, Chile 96 G2 51 45S 72 15W
Puerto Padre, Cuba 88 B4 21 13N 76 35W
Puerto Páez, Venezuela 92 B5 6 13N 67 28W
Puerto Peñasco, Mexico 86 A2 31 20N 113 33W
Puerto Pinasco, Paraguay 94 A4 22 36S 57 50W
Puerto Plata, Dom. Rep. 89 C5 19 48N 70 45W
Puerto Pollensa = Port de Pollença, Spain 22 B10 39 54N 3 4 E
Puerto Princesa, Phil. 37 C5 9 46N 118 45 E
Puerto Quepos, Costa Rica 88 E3 9 29N 84 6W
Puerto Rico, Canary Is. 22 G4 27 47N 15 42W
Puerto Rico ■, W. Indies 89 C6 18 15N 66 45W
Puerto Rico Trench, Atl. Oc. 89 C6 19 50N 66 0W
Puerto San Julián, Argentina 96 F3 49 18S 67 43W
Puerto Sastre, Paraguay 94 A4 22 2S 57 55W
Puerto Suárez, Bolivia 92 G7 18 58S 57 52W
Puerto Vallarta, Mexico 86 C3 20 36N 105 15W
Puerto Wilches, Colombia 92 B4 7 21N 73 54W
Puertollano, Spain 19 C3 38 43N 4 7W
Pueyrredón, L., Argentina 96 F2 47 20S 72 0W
Puffin I., Ireland 13 E1 51 50N 10 24W
Pugachev, Russia 24 D8 52 0N 48 49 E
Pugal, India 42 E5 28 30N 72 48 E
Puge, Tanzania 54 C3 4 45S 33 11 E
Puget Sound, U.S.A. 82 C2 47 50N 122 30W
Pugŏdong, N. Korea 35 C16 42 5N 130 0 E
Pugu, Tanzania 54 D4 6 55S 39 4 E
Pūgūnzi, Iran 45 E8 25 49N 59 10 E
Puig Major, Spain 22 B9 39 48N 2 47 E
Puigcerdà, Spain 19 A6 42 24N 1 50 E
Puigpunyent, Spain 22 B9 39 38N 2 32 E
Pujon-chŏsuji, N. Korea 35 D14 40 35N 127 35 E
Pukaki, L., N.Z. 59 L3 44 4S 170 1 E
Pukapuka, Cook Is. 65 J11 10 53S 165 49W
Pukaskwa Nat. Park, Canada 70 C2 48 20N 86 0W
Pukatawagan, Canada 73 B8 55 45N 101 20W
Pukchin, N. Korea 35 D13 40 12N 125 45 E
Pukch'ŏng, N. Korea 35 D15 40 14N 128 10 E
Pukekohe, N.Z. 59 G5 37 12S 174 55 E
Pukhrayan, India 43 F8 26 14N 79 51 E
Pula, Croatia 16 F7 44 54N 13 57 E
Pulacayo, Bolivia 92 H5 20 25S 66 41W
Pulandian, China 35 E11 39 25N 121 58 E
Pularumpi, Australia 60 B5 11 24S 130 26 E
Pulaski, N.Y., U.S.A. 79 C8 43 34N 76 8W
Pulaski, Tenn., U.S.A. 77 H2 35 12N 87 2W
Pulaski, Va., U.S.A. 76 G5 37 3N 80 47W
Pulau →, Indonesia 37 F9 5 50S 138 15 E
Puławy, Poland 17 C11 51 23N 21 59 E
Pulga, U.S.A. 84 F5 39 48N 121 29W
Pulicat L., India 40 N12 13 40N 80 15 E
Pullman, U.S.A. 82 C5 46 44N 117 10W
Pulog, Mt., Phil. 37 A6 16 40N 120 50 E
Pułtusk, Poland 17 B11 52 43N 21 6 E
Pumlumon Fawr, U.K. 11 E4 52 28N 3 46W
Puná, I., Ecuador 92 D2 2 55S 80 5W
Punakha, Bhutan 41 F16 27 42N 89 52 E
Punasar, India 42 F5 27 6N 73 6 E
Punata, Bolivia 92 G5 17 32S 65 50W
Punch, India 43 C6 33 48N 74 4 E
Punch →, Pakistan 42 C5 33 12N 73 40 E
Punda Maria, S. Africa 57 C5 22 40S 31 5 E
Pune, India 40 K8 18 29N 73 57 E
P'ungsan, N. Korea 35 D15 40 50N 128 9 E
Pungue, Ponte de, Mozam. 55 F3 19 0S 34 0 E
Punjab □, India 42 D7 31 0N 76 0 E
Punjab □, Pakistan 42 E6 32 0N 72 30 E
Puno, Peru 92 G4 15 55S 70 3W
Punpun →, India 43 G11 25 31N 85 18 E
Punta Alta, Argentina 96 D4 38 53S 62 4W
Punta Arenas, Chile 96 G2 53 10S 71 0W
Punta de Díaz, Chile 94 B1 28 0S 70 45W
Punta del Hidalgo, Canary Is. 22 F3 28 33N 16 19W
Punta Gorda, Belize 87 D7 16 10N 88 45W
Punta Gorda, U.S.A. 77 M5 26 56N 82 3W
Punta Prieta, Mexico 86 B2 28 58N 114 17W
Punta Prima, Spain 22 B11 39 48N 4 16 E
Puntarenas, Costa Rica 88 E3 10 0N 84 50W
Punto Fijo, Venezuela 92 A4 11 50N 70 13W
Punxsatawney, U.S.A. 78 F6 40 57N 78 59W
Puquio, Peru 92 F4 14 45S 74 10W
Pur →, Russia 26 C8 67 31N 77 55 E
Purace, Vol., Colombia 92 C3 2 21N 76 23W
Puralia = Puruliya, India 43 H12 23 17N 86 24 E
Puranpur, India 43 E9 28 31N 80 9 E
Purbeck, Isle of, U.K. 11 G6 50 39N 1 59W

Randalstown

Purcell, *U.S.A.* **81 H6** 35 1N 97 22W
Purcell Mts., *Canada* **72 D5** 49 55N 116 15W
Puri, *India* **41 K14** 19 50N 85 58 E
Purmerend, *Neths.* **15 B4** 52 32N 4 58 E
Purnia, *India* **43 G12** 25 45N 87 31 E
Pursat = Pouthisat, *Cambodia* **38 F4** 12 34N 103 50 E
Purukcahu, *Indonesia* **36 E4** 0 35S 114 35 E
Puruliya, *India* **43 H12** 23 17N 86 24 E
Purus →, *Brazil* **92 D6** 3 42S 61 28W
Purvis, *U.S.A.* **81 K10** 31 9N 89 25W
Purwa, *India* **43 F9** 26 28N 80 47 E
Purwakarta, *Indonesia* **37 G12** 6 35S 107 29 E
Purwodadi, *Indonesia* **37 G14** 7 7S 110 55 E
Purwokerto, *Indonesia* **37 G13** 7 25S 109 14 E
Puryŏng, *N. Korea* **35 C15** 42 5N 129 43 E
Pusa, *India* **43 G11** 25 59N 85 41 E
Pusan, *S. Korea* **35 G15** 35 5N 129 0 E
Pushkino, *Russia* **25 D8** 51 16N 47 0 E
Putahow L., *Canada* **73 B8** 59 54N 100 40W
Putao, *Burma* **41 F20** 27 28N 97 30 E
Putaruru, *N.Z.* **59 H5** 38 2S 175 50 E
Putignano, *Italy* **20 D7** 40 51N 17 7 E
Puting, Tanjung, *Indonesia* **36 E4** 3 31S 111 46 E
Putnam, *U.S.A.* **79 E13** 41 55N 71 55W
Putorana, Gory, *Russia* **27 C10** 69 0N 95 0 E
Puttalam, *Sri Lanka* **40 Q11** 8 1N 79 55 E
Puttgarden, *Germany* **16 A6** 54 30N 11 10 E
Putumayo →, *S. Amer.* **92 D5** 3 7S 67 58W
Putussibau, *Indonesia* **36 D4** 0 50N 112 56 E
Puvirnituq, *Canada* **69 B12** 60 2N 77 10W
Puy-de-Dôme, *France* **18 D5** 45 46N 2 57 E
Puyallup, *U.S.A.* **84 C4** 47 12N 122 18W
Puyang, *China* **34 G8** 35 40N 115 1 E
Pūzeh Rīg, *Iran* **45 E8** 27 20N 58 40 E
Pwani □, *Tanzania* **54 D4** 7 0S 39 0 E
Pweto, *Dem. Rep. of the Congo* **55 D2** 8 25S 28 51 E
Pwllheli, *U.K.* **10 E3** 52 53N 4 25W
Pya-ozero, *Russia* **24 A5** 66 5N 30 58 E
Pyapon, *Burma* **41 L19** 16 20N 95 40 E
Pyasina →, *Russia* **27 B9** 73 30N 87 0 E
Pyatigorsk, *Russia* **25 F7** 44 2N 43 6 E
Pyè = Prome, *Burma* **41 K19** 18 49N 95 13 E
Pyetrikaw, *Belarus* **17 B15** 52 11N 28 29 E
Pyhäjoki, *Finland* **8 D21** 64 28N 24 14 E
Pyinmana, *Burma* **41 K20** 19 45N 96 12 E
Pyla, C., *Cyprus* **23 E12** 34 56N 33 51 E
Pymatuning Reservoir, *U.S.A.* **78 E4** 41 30N 80 28W
Pyŏktong, *N. Korea* **35 D13** 40 50N 125 50 E
Pyŏnggang, *N. Korea* **35 E14** 38 24N 127 17 E
P'yŏngt'aek, *S. Korea* **35 F14** 37 1N 127 4 E
P'yŏngyang, *N. Korea* **35 E13** 39 0N 125 30 E
Pyote, *U.S.A.* **81 K3** 31 32N 103 8W
Pyramid L., *U.S.A.* **82 G4** 40 1N 119 35W
Pyramid Pk., *U.S.A.* **85 J10** 36 25N 116 37W
Pyrénées, *Europe* **18 E4** 42 45N 0 18 E
Pyu, *Burma* **41 K20** 18 30N 96 28 E

Q

Qaanaaq, *Greenland* **4 B4** 77 40N 69 0W
Qachasnek, *S. Africa* **57 E4** 30 6S 28 42 E
Qa'el Jafr, *Jordan* **47 E5** 30 20N 36 25 E
Qa'emābād, *Iran* **45 D9** 31 44N 60 2 E
Qā'emshahr, *Iran* **45 B7** 36 30N 52 53 E
Qagan Nur, *China* **34 C8** 43 30N 114 55 E
Qahar Youyi Zhongqi, *China* **34 D7** 41 12N 112 40 E
Qahremānshahr = Bākhtarān, *Iran* **44 C5** 34 23N 47 0 E
Qaidam Pendi, *China* **32 C4** 37 0N 95 0 E
Qajarīyeh, *Iran* **45 D6** 31 1N 48 22 E
Qala, Ras il, *Malta* **23 C1** 36 2N 14 20 E
Qala-i-Jadid = Spīn Būldak, *Afghan.* **42 D2** 31 1N 66 25 E
Qala Point = Qala, Ras il, *Malta* **23 C1** 36 2N 14 20 E
Qala Viala, *Pakistan* **42 D2** 30 49N 67 17 E
Qala Yangi, *Afghan.* **42 B2** 34 20N 66 30 E
Qal'at al Akhḑar, *Si. Arabia* **44 E3** 28 0N 37 10 E
Qal'at Dīzah, *Iraq* **44 B5** 36 11N 45 7 E
Qal'at Şāliḩ, *Iraq* **44 D5** 31 31N 47 16 E
Qal'at Sukkar, *Iraq* **44 D5** 31 51N 46 5 E
Qamani'tuaq = Baker Lake, *Canada* **68 B10** 64 20N 96 3W
Qamdo, *China* **32 C4** 31 15N 97 6 E
Qamruddin Karez, *Pakistan* **42 D3** 31 45N 68 20 E
Qandahār, *Afghan.* **40 D4** 31 32N 65 43 E
Qandahār □, *Afghan.* **40 D4** 31 0N 65 0 E
Qapān, *Iran* **45 B7** 37 40N 55 47 E
Qapshaghay, *Kazakstan* **26 E8** 43 51N 77 14 E
Qaqortoq, *Greenland* **69 B6** 60 43N 46 0W
Qara Qash →, *China* **43 B8** 35 0N 78 30 E
Qarabutaq, *Kazakstan* **26 E7** 49 59N 60 14 E
Qaraghandy, *Kazakstan* **26 E8** 49 50N 73 10 E
Qārah, *Si. Arabia* **44 D4** 29 55N 40 3 E
Qarataū, *Kazakstan* **26 E8** 43 10N 70 28 E
Qarataū, *Kazakstan* **26 E7** 43 30N 69 30 E
Qardho = Gardo, *Somali Rep.* **46 F4** 9 30N 49 6 E
Qareh →, *Iran* **44 B5** 39 25N 47 22 E
Qareh Tekān, *Iran* **45 B6** 36 38N 49 29 E
Qarqan He →, *China* **32 C3** 39 30N 88 30 E
Qarqaraly, *Kazakstan* **26 E8** 49 26N 75 30 E
Qarshi, *Uzbekistan* **26 F7** 38 53N 65 48 E
Qartabā, *Lebanon* **47 A4** 34 4N 35 50 E
Qaryat al Gharab, *Iraq* **44 D5** 31 27N 44 48 E
Qaryat al 'Ulyā, *Si. Arabia* **44 E5** 27 33N 47 42 E
Qasr 'Amra, *Jordan* **44 D3** 31 48N 36 35 E
Qaşr-e Qand, *Iran* **45 E9** 26 15N 60 45 E
Qasr Farâfra, *Egypt* **51 C11** 27 0N 28 1 E
Qatanā, *Syria* **47 B5** 33 26N 36 4 E
Qatar ■, *Asia* **46 B5** 25 30N 51 15 E
Qatlīsh, *Iran* **45 B8** 37 50N 57 19 E
Qattâra, Munkhafed el, *Egypt* **51 C11** 29 30N 27 30 E
Qattâra Depression = Qattâra, Munkhafed el, *Egypt* **51 C11** 29 30N 27 30 E
Qawām al Ḩamzah, *Iraq* **44 D5** 31 43N 44 58 E
Qāyen, *Iran* **45 C8** 33 40N 59 10 E
Qazaqstan = Kazakstan ■, *Asia* **26 E7** 50 0N 70 0 E
Qazimämmäd, *Azerbaijan* **45 A6** 40 3N 49 0 E
Qazvin, *Iran* **45 B6** 36 15N 50 0 E
Qena, *Egypt* **51 C12** 26 10N 32 43 E
Qeqertarsuaq, *Greenland* **4 C5** 69 15N 53 38W
Qeqertarsuaq, *Greenland* **69 B5** 69 45N 53 30W
Qeshlāq, *Iran* **44 C5** 34 55N 46 28 E
Qeshm, *Iran* **45 E8** 26 55N 56 10 E
Qeys, *Iran* **45 E7** 26 32N 53 58 E
Qezel Owzen →, *Iran* **45 B6** 36 45N 49 22 E
Qezi'ot, *Israel* **47 E3** 30 52N 34 26 E
Qi Xian, *China* **34 G8** 34 40N 114 48 E
Qian Gorlos, *China* **35 B13** 45 5N 124 42 E
Qian Xian, *China* **34 G5** 34 31N 108 15 E
Qianyang, *China* **34 G4** 34 40N 107 8 E
Qikiqtarjuaq, *Canada* **69 B13** 67 33N 63 0W
Qila Safed, *Pakistan* **40 E2** 29 0N 61 30 E
Qila Saifullāh, *Pakistan* **42 D3** 30 45N 68 17 E
Qilian Shan, *China* **32 C4** 38 30N 96 0 E
Qin He →, *China* **34 G7** 35 1N 113 22 E
Qin Ling = Qinling Shandi, *China* **34 H5** 33 50N 108 10 E
Qin'an, *China* **34 G3** 34 48N 105 40 E
Qing Xian, *China* **34 E9** 38 35N 116 45 E
Qingcheng, *China* **35 F9** 37 15N 117 40 E
Qingdao, *China* **35 F11** 36 5N 120 20 E
Qingfeng, *China* **34 G8** 35 52N 115 8 E
Qinghai □, *China* **32 C4** 36 0N 98 0 E
Qinghai Hu, *China* **32 C5** 36 40N 100 10 E
Qinghecheng, *China* **35 D13** 41 28N 124 15 E
Qinghemen, *China* **35 D11** 41 48N 121 25 E
Qingjian, *China* **34 F6** 37 8N 110 8 E
Qingjiang = Huaiyin, *China* **35 H10** 33 30N 119 2 E
Qingshui, *China* **34 G4** 34 48N 106 8 E
Qingshuihe, *China* **34 E6** 39 55N 111 35 E
Qingtongxia Shuiku, *China* **34 F3** 37 50N 105 58 E
Qingxu, *China* **34 F7** 37 34N 112 22 E
Qingyang, *China* **34 F4** 36 2N 107 55 E
Qingyuan, *China* **35 C13** 42 10N 124 55 E
Qingyun, *China* **35 F9** 37 45N 117 20 E
Qinhuangdao, *China* **35 E10** 39 56N 119 30 E
Qinling Shandi, *China* **34 H5** 33 50N 108 10 E
Qinshui, *China* **34 G7** 35 40N 112 8 E
Qinyang = Jiyuan, *China* **34 G7** 35 7N 112 57 E
Qinyuan, *China* **34 F7** 36 29N 112 20 E
Qinzhou, *China* **32 D5** 21 58N 108 38 E
Qionghai, *China* **38 C8** 19 15N 110 26 E
Qiongzhou Haixia, *China* **38 B8** 20 10N 110 15 E
Qiqihar, *China* **27 E13** 47 26N 124 0 E
Qiraîya, W. →, *Egypt* **47 E3** 30 27N 34 0 E
Qiryat Ata, *Israel* **47 C4** 32 47N 35 6 E
Qiryat Gat, *Israel* **47 D3** 31 32N 34 46 E
Qiryat Mal'akhi, *Israel* **47 D3** 31 44N 34 44 E
Qiryat Shemona, *Israel* **47 B4** 33 13N 35 35 E
Qiryat Yam, *Israel* **47 C4** 32 51N 35 4 E
Qishan, *China* **34 G4** 34 25N 107 38 E
Qitai, *China* **32 B3** 44 2N 89 35 E
Qixia, *China* **35 F11** 37 17N 120 52 E
Qızılağac Körfäzi, *Azerbaijan* **45 B6** 39 9N 49 0 E
Qojūr, *Iran* **44 B5** 36 12N 47 55 E
Qom, *Iran* **45 C6** 34 40N 51 0 E
Qomolangma Feng = Everest, Mt., *Nepal* **43 E12** 28 5N 86 58 E
Qomsheh, *Iran* **45 D6** 32 0N 51 55 E
Qoraqalpoghistan □, *Uzbekistan* **26 E6** 43 0N 58 0 E
Qostanay, *Kazakstan* **26 D7** 53 10N 63 35 E
Quabbin Reservoir, *U.S.A.* **79 D12** 42 20N 72 20W
Quairading, *Australia* **61 F2** 32 0S 117 21 E
Quakertown, *U.S.A.* **79 F9** 40 26N 75 21W
Qualicum Beach, *Canada* **72 D4** 49 22N 124 26W
Quambatook, *Australia* **63 F3** 35 49S 143 34 E
Quambone, *Australia* **63 E4** 30 57S 147 53 E
Quamby, *Australia* **62 C3** 20 22S 140 17 E
Quan Long = Ca Mau, *Vietnam* **39 H5** 9 7N 105 8 E
Quanah, *U.S.A.* **81 H5** 34 18N 99 44W
Quang Ngai, *Vietnam* **38 E7** 15 13N 108 58 E
Quang Tri, *Vietnam* **38 D6** 16 45N 107 13 E
Quang Yen, *Vietnam* **38 B6** 20 56N 106 52 E
Quantock Hills, *U.K.* **11 F4** 51 8N 3 10W
Quanzhou, *China* **33 D6** 24 55N 118 34 E
Qu'Appelle, *Canada* **73 C8** 50 33N 103 53W
Quaqtaq, *Canada* **69 B13** 60 55N 69 40W
Quaraí, *Brazil* **94 C4** 30 15S 56 20W
Quartu Sant'Élena, *Italy* **20 E3** 39 15N 9 10 E
Quartzsite, *U.S.A.* **85 M12** 33 40N 114 13W
Quatsino Sd., *Canada* **72 C3** 50 25N 127 58W
Quba, *Azerbaijan* **25 F8** 41 21N 48 32 E
Qūchān, *Iran* **45 B8** 37 10N 58 27 E
Queanbeyan, *Australia* **63 F4** 35 17S 149 14 E
Québec, *Canada* **71 C5** 46 52N 71 13W
Québec □, *Canada* **71 C6** 48 0N 74 0W
Queen Alexandra Ra., *Antarctica* **5 E11** 85 0S 170 0 E
Queen Charlotte City, *Canada* **72 C2** 53 15N 132 2W
Queen Charlotte Is., *Canada* **72 C2** 53 20N 132 10W
Queen Charlotte Sd., *Canada* **72 C3** 51 0N 128 0W
Queen Charlotte Strait, *Canada* **72 C3** 50 45N 127 10W
Queen Elizabeth Is., *Canada* **66 B10** 76 0N 95 0W
Queen Mary Land, *Antarctica* **5 D7** 70 0S 95 0 E
Queen Maud G., *Canada* **68 B9** 68 15N 102 30W
Queen Maud Land, *Antarctica* **5 D3** 72 30S 12 0 E
Queen Maud Mts., *Antarctica* **5 E13** 86 0S 160 0W
Queens Chan., *Australia* **60 C4** 15 0S 129 30 E
Queenscliff, *Australia* **63 F3** 38 16S 144 39 E
Queensland □, *Australia* **62 C3** 22 0S 142 0 E
Queenstown, *Australia* **62 G4** 42 4S 145 35 E
Queenstown, *N.Z.* **59 L2** 45 1S 168 40 E
Queenstown, *S. Africa* **56 E4** 31 52S 26 52 E
Queets, *U.S.A.* **84 C2** 47 32N 124 20W
Queguay Grande →, *Uruguay* **94 C4** 32 9S 58 9W
Queimadas, *Brazil* **93 F11** 11 0S 39 38W
Quelimane, *Mozam.* **55 F4** 17 53S 36 58 E
Quellón, *Chile* **96 E2** 43 7S 73 37W
Quelpart = Cheju do, *S. Korea* **35 H14** 33 29N 126 34 E
Quemado, *N. Mex., U.S.A.* **83 J9** 34 20N 108 30W
Quemado, *Tex., U.S.A.* **81 L4** 28 58N 100 35W
Quemú-Quemú, *Argentina* **94 D3** 36 3S 63 36W
Quequén, *Argentina* **94 D4** 38 30S 58 30W
Querétaro, *Mexico* **86 C4** 20 36N 100 23W
Querétaro □, *Mexico* **86 C5** 20 30N 100 0W
Queshan, *China* **34 H8** 32 55N 114 2 E
Quesnel, *Canada* **72 C4** 53 0N 122 30W
Quesnel →, *Canada* **72 C4** 52 58N 122 29W
Quesnel L., *Canada* **72 C4** 52 30N 121 20W
Questa, *U.S.A.* **83 H11** 36 42N 105 36W
Quetico Prov. Park, *Canada* **70 C1** 48 30N 91 45W
Quetta, *Pakistan* **42 D2** 30 15N 66 55 E
Quezaltenango, *Guatemala* **88 D1** 14 50N 91 30W
Quezon City, *Phil.* **37 B6** 14 38N 121 0 E
Qufār, *Si. Arabia* **44 E4** 27 26N 41 37 E
Qui Nhon, *Vietnam* **38 F7** 13 40N 109 13 E
Quibaxe, *Angola* **52 F2** 8 24S 14 27 E
Quibdo, *Colombia* **92 B3** 5 42N 76 40W
Quiberon, *France* **18 C2** 47 29N 3 9W
Quiet L., *Canada* **72 A2** 61 5N 133 5W
Quiindy, *Paraguay* **94 B4** 25 58S 57 14W
Quila, *Mexico* **86 C3** 24 23N 107 13W
Quilán, C., *Chile* **96 E2** 43 15S 74 30W
Quilcene, *U.S.A.* **84 C4** 47 49N 122 53W
Quilimarí, *Chile* **94 C1** 32 5S 71 30W
Quilino, *Argentina* **94 C3** 30 14S 64 29W
Quill Lakes, *Canada* **73 C8** 51 55N 104 13W
Quillabamba, *Peru* **92 F4** 12 50S 72 50W
Quillagua, *Chile* **94 A2** 21 40S 69 40W
Quillaicillo, *Chile* **94 C1** 31 17S 71 40W
Quillota, *Chile* **94 C1** 32 54S 71 16W
Quilmes, *Argentina* **94 C4** 34 43S 58 15W
Quilon, *India* **40 Q10** 8 50N 76 38 E
Quilpie, *Australia* **63 D3** 26 35S 144 11 E
Quilpué, *Chile* **94 C1** 33 5S 71 33W
Quilua, *Mozam.* **55 F4** 16 17S 39 54 E
Quimilí, *Argentina* **94 B3** 27 40S 62 30W
Quimper, *France* **18 B1** 48 0N 4 9W
Quimperlé, *France* **18 C2** 47 53N 3 33W
Quinault →, *U.S.A.* **84 C2** 47 21N 124 18W
Quincy, *Calif., U.S.A.* **84 F6** 39 56N 120 57W
Quincy, *Fla., U.S.A.* **77 K3** 30 35N 84 34W
Quincy, *Ill., U.S.A.* **80 F9** 39 56N 91 23W
Quincy, *Mass., U.S.A.* **79 D14** 42 15N 71 0W
Quincy, *Wash., U.S.A.* **82 C4** 47 22N 119 56W
Quines, *Argentina* **94 C2** 32 13S 65 48W
Quinga, *Mozam.* **55 F5** 15 49S 40 15 E
Quinns Rocks, *Australia* **61 F2** 31 40S 115 42 E
Quintana Roo □, *Mexico* **87 D7** 19 0N 88 0W
Quintanar de la Orden, *Spain* **19 C4** 39 36N 3 5W
Quintero, *Chile* **94 C1** 32 45S 71 30W
Quirihue, *Chile* **94 D1** 36 15S 72 35W
Quirindi, *Australia* **63 E5** 31 28S 150 40 E
Quirinópolis, *Brazil* **93 G8** 18 32S 50 30W
Quissanga, *Mozam.* **55 E5** 12 24S 40 28 E
Quissico, *Mozam.* **57 C5** 24 42S 34 44 E
Quitilipi, *Argentina* **94 B3** 26 50S 60 13W
Quitman, *U.S.A.* **77 K4** 30 47N 83 34W
Quito, *Ecuador* **92 D3** 0 15S 78 35W
Quixadá, *Brazil* **93 D11** 4 55S 39 0W
Quixaxe, *Mozam.* **55 F5** 15 17S 40 4 E
Qulan, *Kazakstan* **26 E8** 42 55N 72 43 E
Qul'ân, Jazâ'ir, *Egypt* **44 E2** 24 22N 35 31 E
Qumbu, *S. Africa* **57 E4** 31 10S 28 48 E
Quneitra, *Syria* **47 B4** 33 7N 35 48 E
Qŭnghirot, *Uzbekistan* **26 E6** 43 6N 58 54 E
Quoin I., *Australia* **60 B4** 14 54S 129 32 E
Quoin Pt., *S. Africa* **56 E2** 34 46S 19 37 E
Quorn, *Australia* **63 E2** 32 25S 138 5 E
Qŭqon, *Uzbekistan* **26 E8** 40 30N 70 57 E
Qurnat as Sawdā', *Lebanon* **47 A5** 34 18N 36 6 E
Quşaybā', *Si. Arabia* **44 E4** 26 53N 43 35 E
Qusaybah, *Iraq* **44 C4** 34 24N 40 59 E
Quseir, *Egypt* **44 E2** 26 7N 34 16 E
Qūshchī, *Iran* **44 B5** 37 59N 45 3 E
Quthing, *Lesotho* **57 E4** 30 25S 27 36 E
Qūţīābād, *Iran* **45 C6** 35 47N 48 30 E
Quwo, *China* **34 G6** 35 38N 111 25 E
Quyang, *China* **34 E8** 38 35N 114 40 E
Quynh Nhai, *Vietnam* **38 B4** 21 49N 103 33 E
Quyon, *Canada* **79 A8** 45 31N 76 14W
Quzhou, *China* **33 D6** 28 57N 118 54 E
Quzi, *China* **34 F4** 36 20N 107 20 E
Qyzylorda, *Kazakstan* **26 E7** 44 48N 65 28 E

R

Ra, Ko, *Thailand* **39 H2** 9 13N 98 16 E
Raahe, *Finland* **8 D21** 64 40N 24 28 E
Raalte, *Neths.* **15 B6** 52 23N 6 16 E
Raasay, *U.K.* **12 D2** 57 25N 6 4W
Raasay, Sd. of, *U.K.* **12 D2** 57 30N 6 8W
Raba, *Indonesia* **37 F5** 8 36S 118 55 E
Rába →, *Hungary* **17 E9** 47 38N 17 38 E
Rabai, *Kenya* **54 C4** 3 50S 39 31 E
Rabat = Victoria, *Malta* **23 C1** 36 3N 14 14 E
Rabat, *Malta* **23 D1** 35 53N 14 24 E
Rabat, *Morocco* **50 B4** 34 2N 6 48W
Rabaul, *Papua N. G.* **64 H7** 4 24S 152 18 E
Rābigh, *Si. Arabia* **46 C2** 22 50N 39 5 E
Râbniţa, *Moldova* **17 E15** 47 45N 29 0 E
Rābor, *Iran* **45 D8** 29 17N 56 55 E
Race, C., *Canada* **71 C9** 46 40N 53 5W
Rach Gia, *Vietnam* **39 G5** 10 5N 105 5 E
Rachid, *Mauritania* **50 E3** 18 45N 11 35W
Racibórz, *Poland* **17 C10** 50 7N 18 18 E
Racine, *U.S.A.* **76 D2** 42 41N 87 51W
Rackerby, *U.S.A.* **84 F5** 39 26N 121 22W
Radama, Nosy, *Madag.* **57 A8** 14 0S 47 47 E
Radama, Saikanosy, *Madag.* **57 A8** 14 16S 47 53 E
Rădăuţi, *Romania* **17 E13** 47 50N 25 59 E
Radcliff, *U.S.A.* **76 G3** 37 51N 85 57W
Radekhiv, *Ukraine* **17 C13** 50 25N 24 32 E
Radekhov = Radekhiv, *Ukraine* **17 C13** 50 25N 24 32 E
Radford, *U.S.A.* **76 G5** 37 8N 80 34W
Radhanpur, *India* **42 H4** 23 50N 71 38 E
Radhwa, Jabal, *Si. Arabia* **44 E3** 24 34N 38 18 E
Radisson, *Qué., Canada* **70 B4** 53 47N 77 37W
Radisson, *Sask., Canada* **73 C7** 52 30N 107 20W
Radium Hot Springs, *Canada* **72 C5** 50 35N 116 2W
Radnor Forest, *U.K.* **11 E4** 52 17N 3 10W
Radom, *Poland* **17 C11** 51 23N 21 12 E
Radomsko, *Poland* **17 C10** 51 5N 19 28 E
Radomyshl, *Ukraine* **17 C15** 50 30N 29 12 E
Radstock, C., *Australia* **63 E1** 33 12S 134 20 E
Radviliškis, *Lithuania* **9 J20** 55 49N 23 33 E
Radville, *Canada* **73 D8** 49 30N 104 15W
Rae, *Canada* **72 A5** 62 50N 116 3W
Rae Bareli, *India* **43 F9** 26 18N 81 20 E
Rae Isthmus, *Canada* **69 B11** 66 40N 87 30W
Raeren, *Belgium* **15 D6** 50 41N 6 7 E
Raeside, L., *Australia* **61 E3** 29 20S 122 0 E
Raetihi, *N.Z.* **59 H5** 39 25S 175 17 E
Rafaela, *Argentina* **94 C3** 31 10S 61 30W
Rafah, *Gaza Strip* **47 D3** 31 18N 34 14 E
Rafai, *C.A.R.* **54 B1** 4 59N 23 58 E
Rafḩā, *Si. Arabia* **44 D4** 29 35N 43 35 E
Rafsanjān, *Iran* **45 D8** 30 30N 56 5 E
Raft Pt., *Australia* **60 C3** 16 4S 124 26 E
Râgâ, *Sudan* **51 G11** 8 28N 25 41 E
Ragachow, *Belarus* **17 B16** 53 8N 30 5 E
Ragama, *Sri Lanka* **40 R11** 7 0N 79 50 E
Ragged, Mt., *Australia* **61 F3** 33 27S 123 25 E
Raghunathpalli, *India* **43 H11** 22 14N 84 48 E
Raghunathpur, *India* **43 H12** 23 33N 86 40 E
Raglan, *N.Z.* **59 G5** 37 55S 174 55 E
Ragusa, *Italy* **20 F6** 36 55N 14 44 E
Raha, *Indonesia* **37 E6** 4 55S 123 0 E
Rahaeng = Tak, *Thailand* **38 D2** 16 52N 99 8 E
Rahatgarh, *India* **43 H8** 23 47N 78 22 E
Rahimyar Khan, *Pakistan* **42 E4** 28 30N 70 25 E
Rāhjerd, *Iran* **45 C6** 34 22N 50 22 E
Rahon, *India* **42 D7** 31 3N 76 7 E
Raichur, *India* **40 L10** 16 10N 77 20 E
Raiganj, *India* **43 G13** 25 37N 88 10 E
Raigarh, *India* **41 J13** 21 56N 83 25 E
Raijua, *Indonesia* **37 F6** 10 37S 121 36 E
Raikot, *India* **42 D6** 30 41N 75 42 E
Railton, *Australia* **62 G4** 41 25S 146 28 E
Rainbow Lake, *Canada* **72 B5** 58 30N 119 23W
Rainier, *U.S.A.* **84 D4** 46 53N 122 41W
Rainier, Mt., *U.S.A.* **84 D5** 46 52N 121 46W
Rainy L., *Canada* **73 D10** 48 42N 93 10W
Rainy River, *Canada* **73 D10** 48 43N 94 29W
Raippaluoto, *Finland* **8 E19** 63 13N 21 14 E
Raipur, *India* **41 J12** 21 17N 81 45 E
Raisen, *India* **42 H8** 23 20N 77 48 E
Raisio, *Finland* **9 F20** 60 28N 22 11 E
Raj Nandgaon, *India* **41 J12** 21 5N 81 5 E
Raj Nilgiri, *India* **43 J12** 21 28N 86 46 E
Raja, Ujung, *Indonesia* **36 D1** 3 40N 96 25 E
Raja Ampat, Kepulauan, *Indonesia* **37 E7** 0 30S 130 0 E
Rajahmundry, *India* **41 L12** 17 1N 81 48 E
Rajang →, *Malaysia* **36 D4** 2 30N 112 0 E
Rajanpur, *Pakistan* **42 E4** 29 6N 70 19 E
Rajapalaiyam, *India* **40 Q10** 9 25N 77 35 E
Rajasthan □, *India* **42 F5** 26 45N 73 30 E
Rajasthan Canal, *India* **42 F5** 28 0N 72 0 E
Rajauri, *India* **43 C6** 33 25N 74 21 E
Rajgarh, *Mad. P., India* **42 G7** 24 2N 76 45 E
Rajgarh, *Raj., India* **42 F7** 27 14N 76 38 E
Rajgarh, *Raj., India* **42 E6** 28 40N 75 25 E
Rajgir, *India* **43 G11** 25 2N 85 25 E
Rajkot, *India* **42 H4** 22 15N 70 56 E
Rajmahal Hills, *India* **43 G12** 24 30N 87 30 E
Rajpipla, *India* **40 J8** 21 50N 73 30 E
Rajpur, *India* **42 H6** 22 18N 74 21 E
Rajpura, *India* **42 D7** 30 25N 76 32 E
Rajshahi, *Bangla.* **41 G16** 24 22N 88 39 E
Rajshahi □, *Bangla.* **43 G13** 25 0N 89 0 E
Rajula, *India* **42 J4** 21 3N 71 26 E
Rakaia, *N.Z.* **59 K4** 43 45S 172 1 E
Rakaia →, *N.Z.* **59 K4** 43 36S 172 15 E
Rakan, Ra's, *Qatar* **45 E6** 26 10N 51 20 E
Rakaposhi, *Pakistan* **43 A6** 36 10N 74 25 E
Rakata, Pulau, *Indonesia* **36 F3** 6 10S 105 20 E
Rakhiv, *Ukraine* **17 D13** 48 3N 24 12 E
Rakhni, *Pakistan* **42 D3** 30 4N 69 56 E
Rakhni →, *Pakistan* **42 E3** 29 31N 69 36 E
Rakitnoye, *Russia* **30 B7** 45 36N 134 17 E
Rakops, *Botswana* **56 C3** 21 1S 24 28 E
Rakvere, *Estonia* **9 G22** 59 20N 26 25 E
Raleigh, *U.S.A.* **77 H6** 35 47N 78 39W
Ralls, *U.S.A.* **81 J4** 33 41N 101 24W
Ralston, *U.S.A.* **78 E8** 41 30N 76 57W
Ram →, *Canada* **72 A4** 62 1N 123 41W
Rām Allāh, *West Bank* **47 D4** 31 55N 35 10 E
Rama, *Nic.* **88 D3** 12 9N 84 15W
Ramakona, *India* **43 J8** 21 43N 78 50 E
Raman, *Thailand* **39 J3** 6 29N 101 18 E
Ramanathapuram, *India* **40 Q11** 9 25N 78 55 E
Ramanetaka, B. de, *Madag.* **57 A8** 14 13S 47 52 E
Ramanujganj, *India* **43 H10** 23 48N 83 42 E
Ramat Gan, *Israel* **47 C3** 32 4N 34 48 E
Ramatlhabama, *S. Africa* **56 D4** 25 37S 25 33 E
Ramban, *India* **43 C6** 33 14N 75 12 E
Rambipuji, *Indonesia* **37 H15** 8 12S 113 37 E
Rame Hd., *Australia* **63 F4** 37 47S 149 30 E
Ramechhap, *Nepal* **43 F12** 27 25N 86 10 E
Ramganga →, *India* **43 F8** 27 5N 79 58 E
Ramgarh, *Jharkhand, India* **43 H11** 23 40N 85 35 E
Ramgarh, *Raj., India* **42 F6** 27 16N 75 14 E
Ramgarh, *Raj., India* **42 F4** 27 30N 70 36 E
Rāmhormoz, *Iran* **45 D6** 31 15N 49 35 E
Ramiān, *Iran* **45 B7** 37 3N 55 16 E
Ramingining, *Australia* **62 A2** 12 19S 135 3 E
Ramla, *Israel* **47 D3** 31 55N 34 52 E
Ramnad = Ramanathapuram, *India* **40 Q11** 9 25N 78 55 E
Ramnagar, *Jammu & Kashmir, India* **43 C6** 32 47N 75 18 E
Ramnagar, *Uttaranchal, India* **43 E8** 29 24N 79 7 E
Râmnicu Sărat, *Romania* **17 F14** 45 26N 27 3 E
Râmnicu Vâlcea, *Romania* **17 F13** 45 9N 24 21 E
Ramona, *U.S.A.* **85 M10** 33 2N 116 52W
Ramore, *Canada* **70 C3** 48 30N 80 25W
Ramotswa, *Botswana* **56 C4** 24 50S 25 52 E
Rampur, *H.P., India* **42 D7** 31 26N 77 43 E
Rampur, *Mad. P., India* **42 H5** 23 25N 73 53 E
Rampur, *Ut. P., India* **43 E8** 28 50N 79 5 E
Rampur Hat, *India* **43 G12** 24 10N 87 50 E
Rampura, *India* **42 G6** 24 30N 75 27 E
Ramrama Tola, *India* **43 J8** 21 52N 79 55 E
Ramree I., *Burma* **41 K19** 19 0N 93 40 E
Rāmsar, *Iran* **45 B6** 36 53N 50 41 E
Ramsey, *U.K.* **10 C3** 54 20N 4 22W
Ramsey, *U.S.A.* **79 E10** 41 4N 74 9W
Ramsey L., *Canada* **70 C3** 47 13N 82 15W
Ramsgate, *U.K.* **11 F9** 51 20N 1 25 E
Ramtek, *India* **40 J11** 21 20N 79 15 E
Rana Pratap Sagar Dam, *India* **42 G6** 24 58N 75 38 E
Ranaghat, *India* **43 H13** 23 15N 88 35 E
Ranahu, *Pakistan* **42 G3** 25 55N 69 45 E
Ranau, *Malaysia* **36 C5** 6 2N 116 40 E
Rancagua, *Chile* **94 C1** 34 10S 70 50W
Rancheria →, *Canada* **72 A3** 60 13N 129 7W
Ranchester, *U.S.A.* **82 D10** 44 54N 107 10W
Ranchi, *India* **43 H11** 23 19N 85 27 E
Rancho Cucamonga, *U.S.A.* **85 L9** 34 10N 117 30W
Randalstown, *U.K.* **13 B5** 54 45N 6 19W

Randers

Randers, *Denmark* 9 **H14** 56 29N 10 1 E
Randfontein, *S. Africa* 57 **D4** 26 8S 27 45 E
Randle, *U.S.A.* 84 **D5** 46 32N 121 57W
Randolph, *Mass., U.S.A.* 79 **D13** 42 10N 71 2W
Randolph, *N.Y., U.S.A.* 78 **D6** 42 10N 78 59W
Randolph, *Utah, U.S.A.* 82 **F8** 41 40N 111 11W
Randolph, *Vt., U.S.A.* 79 **C12** 43 55N 72 40W
Randsburg, *U.S.A.* 85 **K9** 35 22N 117 39W
Råne älv →, *Sweden* 8 **D20** 65 50N 22 20 E
Rangae, *Thailand* 39 **J3** 6 19N 101 44 E
Rangaunu B., *N.Z.* 59 **F4** 34 51S 173 15 E
Rangeley, *U.S.A.* 79 **B14** 44 58N 70 39W
Rangeley L., *U.S.A.* 79 **B14** 44 55N 70 43W
Rangely, *U.S.A.* 82 **F9** 40 5N 108 48W
Ranger, *U.S.A.* 81 **J5** 32 28N 98 41W
Rangia, *India* 41 **F17** 26 28N 91 38 E
Rangiora, *N.Z.* 59 **K4** 43 19S 172 36 E
Rangitaiki →, *N.Z.* 59 **G6** 37 54S 176 49 E
Rangitata →, *N.Z.* 59 **K3** 43 45S 171 15 E
Rangkasbitung, *Indonesia* 37 **G12** 6 21S 106 15 E
Rangon →, *Burma* 41 **L20** 16 28N 96 40 E
Rangoon, *Burma* 41 **L20** 16 45N 96 20 E
Rangpur, *Bangla.* 41 **G16** 25 42N 89 22 E
Rangsit, *Thailand* 38 **F3** 13 59N 100 37 E
Ranibennur, *India* 40 **M9** 14 35N 75 30 E
Raniganj, *Ut. P., India* 43 **F9** 27 3N 82 13 E
Raniganj, *W. Bengal, India* 41 **H15** 23 40N 87 5 E
Ranikhet, *India* 43 **E8** 29 39N 79 25 E
Raniwara, *India* 40 **G8** 24 50N 72 10 E
Rāniyah, *Iraq* 44 **B5** 36 15N 44 53 E
Ranka, *India* 43 **H10** 23 59N 83 47 E
Ranken →, *Australia* 62 **C2** 20 31S 137 36 E
Rankin, *U.S.A.* 81 **K4** 31 13N 101 56W
Rankin Inlet, *Canada* 68 **B10** 62 30N 93 0W
Rankins Springs, *Australia* 63 **E4** 33 49S 146 14 E
Rannoch, L., *U.K.* 12 **E4** 56 41N 4 20W
Rannoch Moor, *U.K.* 12 **E4** 56 38N 4 48W
Ranobe, Helodranon' i, *Madag.* 57 **C7** 23 3S 43 33 E
Ranohira, *Madag.* 57 **C8** 22 29S 45 24 E
Ranomafana, *Toamasina, Madag.* 57 **B8** 18 57S 48 50 E
Ranomafana, *Toliara, Madag.* 57 **C8** 24 34S 47 0 E
Ranomena, *Madag.* 57 **C8** 23 25S 47 17 E
Ranong, *Thailand* 39 **H2** 9 56N 98 40 E
Ranotsara Nord, *Madag.* 57 **C8** 22 48S 46 36 E
Rānsa, *Iran* 45 **C6** 33 39N 48 18 E
Ransiki, *Indonesia* 37 **E8** 1 30S 134 10 E
Rantabe, *Madag.* 57 **B8** 15 42S 49 39 E
Rantauprapat, *Indonesia* 36 **D1** 2 15N 99 50 E
Rantemario, *Indonesia* 37 **E5** 3 15S 119 57 E
Rantoul, *U.S.A.* 76 **E1** 40 19N 88 9W
Raoyang, *China* 34 **E8** 38 15N 115 45 E
Rapa, *Pac. Oc.* 65 **K13** 27 35S 144 20W
Rapa Nui = Pascua, I. de, *Chile* 65 **K17** 27 7S 109 23W
Rapallo, *Italy* 18 **D8** 44 21N 9 14 E
Rapar, *India* 42 **H4** 23 34N 70 38 E
Rāpch, *Iran* 45 **E8** 25 40N 59 15 E
Raper, C., *Canada* 69 **B13** 69 44N 67 6W
Rapid City, *U.S.A.* 80 **D3** 44 5N 103 14W
Rapid River, *U.S.A.* 76 **C2** 45 55N 86 58W
Rapla, *Estonia* 9 **G21** 59 1N 24 52 E
Rapti →, *India* 43 **F10** 26 18N 83 41 E
Raquette →, *U.S.A.* 79 **B10** 45 0N 74 42W
Raquette Lake, *U.S.A.* 79 **C10** 43 49N 74 40W
Rarotonga, *Cook Is.* 65 **K12** 21 30S 160 0W
Ra's al 'Ayn, *Syria* 44 **B4** 36 45N 40 12 E
Ra's al Khaymah, *U.A.E.* 46 **B6** 25 50N 55 59 E
Rasca, Pta. de la, *Canary Is.* 22 **G3** 27 59N 16 41W
Raseiniai, *Lithuania* 9 **J20** 55 25N 23 5 E
Rashmi, *India* 42 **G6** 25 4N 74 22 E
Rasht, *Iran* 45 **B6** 37 20N 49 40 E
Rasi Salai, *Thailand* 38 **E5** 15 20N 104 9 E
Rason L., *Australia* 61 **E3** 28 45S 124 25 E
Rasra, *India* 43 **G10** 25 50N 83 50 E
Rasul, *Pakistan* 42 **C5** 32 42N 73 34 E
Rat Buri, *Thailand* 38 **F2** 13 30N 99 54 E
Rat Islands, *U.S.A.* 68 **C1** 52 0N 178 0 E
Rat L., *Canada* 73 **B9** 56 10N 99 40W
Ratangarh, *India* 42 **E6** 28 5N 74 35 E
Raṭāwī, *Iraq* 44 **D5** 30 38N 47 13 E
Rath, *India* 43 **G8** 25 36N 79 37 E
Rath Luirc, *Ireland* 13 **D3** 52 21N 8 40W
Rathdrum, *Ireland* 13 **D5** 52 56N 6 14W
Rathenow, *Germany* 16 **B7** 52 37N 12 19 E
Rathkeale, *Ireland* 13 **D3** 52 32N 8 56W
Rathlin I., *U.K.* 13 **A5** 55 18N 6 14W
Rathmelton, *Ireland* 13 **A4** 55 2N 7 38W
Ratibor = Racibórz, *Poland* 17 **C10** 50 7N 18 18 E
Ratlam, *India* 42 **H6** 23 20N 75 0 E
Ratnagiri, *India* 40 **L8** 16 57N 73 18 E
Ratodero, *Pakistan* 42 **F3** 27 48N 68 18 E
Raton, *U.S.A.* 81 **G2** 36 54N 104 24W
Rattaphum, *Thailand* 39 **J3** 7 8N 100 16 E
Rattray Hd., *U.K.* 12 **D7** 57 38N 1 50W
Ratz, Mt., *Canada* 72 **B2** 57 23N 132 12W
Raub, *Malaysia* 39 **L3** 3 47N 101 52 E
Rauch, *Argentina* 94 **D4** 36 45S 59 5W
Raudales de Malpaso, *Mexico* 87 **D6** 17 30N 23 30W
Raufarhöfn, *Iceland* 8 **C6** 66 27N 15 57W
Raufoss, *Norway* 9 **F14** 60 44N 10 37 E
Raukumara Ra., *N.Z.* 59 **H6** 38 5S 177 55 E
Rauma, *Finland* 9 **F19** 61 10N 21 30 E
Raurkela, *India* 43 **H11** 22 14N 84 50 E
Rausu-Dake, *Japan* 30 **B12** 44 4N 145 7 E
Rava-Ruska, *Poland* 17 **C12** 50 15N 23 42 E
Rava Russkaya = Rava-Ruska, *Poland* 17 **C12** 50 15N 23 42 E
Ravalli, *U.S.A.* 82 **C6** 47 17N 114 11W
Ravānsar, *Iran* 44 **C5** 34 43N 46 40 E
Rāvar, *Iran* 45 **D8** 31 20N 56 51 E
Ravena, *U.S.A.* 79 **D11** 42 28N 73 49W
Ravenna, *Italy* 20 **B5** 44 25N 12 12 E
Ravenna, *Nebr., U.S.A.* 80 **E5** 41 1N 98 55W
Ravenna, *Ohio, U.S.A.* 78 **E3** 41 9N 81 15W
Ravensburg, *Germany* 16 **E5** 47 46N 9 36 E
Ravenshoe, *Australia* 62 **B4** 17 37S 145 29 E
Ravensthorpe, *Australia* 61 **F3** 33 35S 120 2 E
Ravenswood, *Australia* 62 **C4** 20 6S 146 54 E
Ravenswood, *U.S.A.* 76 **F5** 38 57N 81 46W
Ravi →, *Pakistan* 42 **D4** 30 35N 71 49 E
Rawalpindi, *Pakistan* 42 **C5** 33 38N 73 8 E
Rawāndūz, *Iraq* 44 **B5** 36 40N 44 30 E
Rawang, *Malaysia* 39 **L3** 3 20N 101 35 E
Rawene, *N.Z.* 59 **F4** 35 25S 173 32 E
Rawlinna, *Australia* 61 **F4** 30 58S 125 28 E
Rawlins, *U.S.A.* 82 **F10** 41 47N 107 14W
Rawlinson Ra., *Australia* 61 **D4** 24 40S 128 30 E
Rawson, *Argentina* 96 **E3** 43 15S 65 5W
Raxaul, *India* 43 **F11** 26 59N 84 51 E
Ray, *U.S.A.* 80 **A3** 48 21N 103 10W
Ray, C., *Canada* 71 **C8** 47 33N 59 15W
Rayadurg, *India* 40 **M10** 14 40N 76 50 E
Rayagada, *India* 41 **K13** 19 15N 83 20 E
Raychikhinsk, *Russia* 27 **E13** 49 46N 129 25 E
Rāyen, *Iran* 45 **D8** 29 34N 57 26 E
Rayleigh, *U.K.* 11 **F8** 51 36N 0 37 E
Raymond, *Canada* 72 **D6** 49 30N 112 35W
Raymond, *Calif., U.S.A.* 84 **H7** 37 13N 119 54W
Raymond, *N.H., U.S.A.* 79 **C13** 43 2N 71 11W
Raymond, *Wash., U.S.A.* 84 **D3** 46 41N 123 44W
Raymondville, *U.S.A.* 81 **M6** 26 29N 97 47W
Raymore, *Canada* 73 **C8** 51 25N 104 31W
Rayón, *Mexico* 86 **B2** 29 43N 110 35W
Rayong, *Thailand* 38 **F3** 12 40N 101 20 E
Rayville, *U.S.A.* 81 **J9** 32 29N 91 46W
Raz, Pte. du, *France* 18 **C1** 48 2N 4 47W
Razan, *Iran* 45 **C6** 35 23N 49 2 E
Razdel'naya = Rozdilna, *Ukraine* 17 **E16** 46 50N 30 2 E
Razdolnoye, *Russia* 30 **C5** 43 30N 131 52 E
Razeh, *Iran* 45 **C6** 32 47N 48 9 E
Razgrad, *Bulgaria* 21 **C12** 43 33N 26 34 E
Razim, Lacul, *Romania* 17 **F15** 44 50N 29 0 E
Razmak, *Pakistan* 42 **C3** 32 45N 69 50 E
Ré, Î. de, *France* 18 **C3** 46 12N 1 30W
Reading, *U.K.* 11 **F7** 51 27N 0 58W
Reading, *U.S.A.* 79 **F9** 40 20N 75 56W
Reading □, *U.K.* 11 **F7** 51 27N 0 58W
Realicó, *Argentina* 94 **D3** 35 0S 64 15W
Ream, *Cambodia* 39 **G4** 10 34N 103 39 E
Reata, *Mexico* 86 **B4** 26 8N 101 5W
Reay Forest, *U.K.* 12 **C4** 58 22N 4 55W
Rebi, *Indonesia* 37 **F8** 6 23S 134 7 E
Rebiana, *Libya* 51 **D10** 24 12N 22 10 E
Rebun-Tō, *Japan* 30 **B10** 45 23N 141 2 E
Recherche, Arch. of the, *Australia* 61 **F3** 34 15S 122 50 E
Rechna Doab, *Pakistan* 42 **D5** 31 35N 73 30 E
Rechytsa, *Belarus* 17 **B16** 52 21N 30 24 E
Recife, *Brazil* 93 **E12** 8 0S 35 0W
Recklinghausen, *Germany* 15 **C7** 51 37N 7 12 E
Reconquista, *Argentina* 94 **B4** 29 10S 59 45W
Recreo, *Argentina* 94 **B2** 29 25S 65 10W
Red →, *La., U.S.A.* 81 **K9** 31 1N 91 45W
Red →, *N. Dak., U.S.A.* 68 **C10** 49 0N 97 15W
Red Bank, *U.S.A.* 79 **F10** 40 21N 74 5W
Red Bay, *Canada* 71 **B8** 51 44N 56 25W
Red Bluff, *U.S.A.* 82 **F2** 40 11N 122 15W
Red Bluff L., *U.S.A.* 81 **K3** 31 54N 103 55W
Red Cliffs, *Australia* 63 **E3** 34 19S 142 11 E
Red Cloud, *U.S.A.* 80 **E5** 40 5N 98 32W
Red Creek, *U.S.A.* 79 **C8** 43 14N 76 45W
Red Deer, *Canada* 72 **C6** 52 20N 113 50W
Red Deer →, *Alta., Canada* 73 **C7** 50 58N 110 0W
Red Deer →, *Man., Canada* 73 **C8** 52 53N 101 1W
Red Deer L., *Canada* 73 **C8** 52 55N 101 20W
Red Hook, *U.S.A.* 79 **E11** 41 55N 73 53W
Red Indian L., *Canada* 71 **C8** 48 35N 57 0W
Red L., *Canada* 73 **C10** 51 3N 93 49W
Red Lake, *Canada* 73 **C10** 51 3N 93 49W
Red Lake Falls, *U.S.A.* 80 **B6** 47 53N 96 16W
Red Lake Road, *Canada* 73 **C10** 49 59N 93 25W
Red Lodge, *U.S.A.* 82 **D9** 45 11N 109 15W
Red Mountain, *U.S.A.* 85 **K9** 35 37N 117 38W
Red Oak, *U.S.A.* 80 **E7** 41 1N 95 14W
Red Rock, *Canada* 70 **C2** 48 55N 88 15W
Red Rock, L., *U.S.A.* 80 **E8** 41 22N 92 59W
Red Rocks Pt., *Australia* 61 **F4** 32 13S 127 32 E
Red Sea, *Asia* 46 **C2** 25 0N 36 0 E
Red Slate Mt., *U.S.A.* 84 **H8** 37 31N 118 52W
Red Sucker L., *Canada* 70 **B1** 54 9N 93 40W
Red Tower Pass = Turnu Roşu, P., *Romania* 17 **F13** 45 33N 24 17 E
Red Wing, *U.S.A.* 80 **C8** 44 34N 92 31W
Redang, *Malaysia* 36 **C2** 5 49N 103 2 E
Redange, *Lux.* 15 **E5** 49 46N 5 52 E
Redcar, *U.K.* 10 **C6** 54 37N 1 4W
Redcar & Cleveland □, *U.K.* 10 **C7** 54 29N 1 0W
Redcliff, *Canada* 73 **C6** 50 10N 110 50W
Redcliffe, *Australia* 63 **D5** 27 12S 153 0 E
Redcliffe, Mt., *Australia* 61 **E3** 28 30S 121 30 E
Reddersburg, *S. Africa* 56 **D4** 29 41S 26 10 E
Redding, *U.S.A.* 82 **F2** 40 35N 122 24W
Redditch, *U.K.* 11 **E6** 52 18N 1 55W
Redfield, *U.S.A.* 80 **C5** 44 53N 98 31W
Redford, *U.S.A.* 79 **B11** 44 38N 73 48W
Redlands, *U.S.A.* 85 **M9** 34 4N 117 11W
Redmond, *Oreg., U.S.A.* 82 **D3** 44 17N 121 11W
Redmond, *Wash., U.S.A.* 84 **C4** 47 41N 122 7W
Redon, *France* 18 **C2** 47 40N 2 6W
Redonda, *Antigua* 89 **C7** 16 58N 62 19W
Redondela, *Spain* 19 **A1** 42 15N 8 38W
Redondo Beach, *U.S.A.* 85 **M8** 33 50N 118 23W
Redruth, *U.K.* 11 **G2** 50 14N 5 14W
Redvers, *Canada* 73 **D8** 49 35N 101 40W
Redwater, *Canada* 72 **C6** 53 55N 113 6W
Redwood, *U.S.A.* 79 **B9** 44 18N 75 48W
Redwood City, *U.S.A.* 84 **H4** 37 30N 122 15W
Redwood Falls, *U.S.A.* 80 **C7** 44 32N 95 7W
Redwood Nat. Park, *U.S.A.* 82 **F1** 41 40N 124 5W
Ree, L., *Ireland* 13 **C3** 53 35N 8 0W
Reed, L., *Canada* 73 **C8** 54 38N 100 30W
Reed City, *U.S.A.* 76 **D3** 43 53N 85 31W
Reedley, *U.S.A.* 84 **J7** 36 36N 119 27W
Reedsburg, *U.S.A.* 80 **D9** 43 32N 90 0W
Reedsport, *U.S.A.* 82 **E1** 43 42N 124 6W
Reedsville, *U.S.A.* 78 **F7** 40 39N 77 35W
Reefton, *N.Z.* 59 **K3** 42 6S 171 51 E
Reese →, *U.S.A.* 82 **F5** 40 48N 117 4W
Refugio, *U.S.A.* 81 **L6** 28 18N 97 17W
Regensburg, *Germany* 16 **D7** 49 1N 12 6 E
Reggâne = Zaouiet Reggâne, *Algeria* 50 **C6** 26 32N 0 3 E
Réggio di Calábria, *Italy* 20 **E6** 38 6N 15 39 E
Réggio nell'Emília, *Italy* 20 **B4** 44 43N 10 36 E
Reghin, *Romania* 17 **E13** 46 46N 24 42 E
Regina, *Canada* 73 **C8** 50 27N 104 35W
Regina Beach, *Canada* 73 **C8** 50 47N 105 0W
Registro, *Brazil* 95 **A6** 24 29S 47 49W
Rehar →, *India* 43 **H10** 23 55N 82 40 E
Rehli, *India* 43 **H8** 23 38N 79 5 E
Rehoboth, *Namibia* 56 **C2** 23 15S 17 4 E
Rehovot, *Israel* 47 **D3** 31 54N 34 48 E
Reichenbach, *Germany* 16 **C7** 50 37N 12 17 E
Reid, *Australia* 61 **F4** 30 49S 128 26 E
Reidsville, *U.S.A.* 77 **G6** 36 21N 79 40W
Reigate, *U.K.* 11 **F7** 51 14N 0 12W
Reims, *France* 18 **B6** 49 15N 4 1 E
Reina Adelaida, Arch., *Chile* 96 **G2** 52 20S 74 0W
Reindeer →, *Canada* 73 **B8** 55 36N 103 11W
Reindeer I., *Canada* 73 **C9** 52 30N 98 0W
Reindeer L., *Canada* 73 **B8** 57 15N 102 15W
Reinga, C., *N.Z.* 59 **F4** 34 25S 172 43 E
Reinosa, *Spain* 19 **A3** 43 2N 4 15W
Reitz, *S. Africa* 57 **D4** 27 48S 28 29 E
Reivilo, *S. Africa* 56 **D3** 27 36S 24 8 E
Reliance, *Canada* 73 **A7** 63 0N 109 20W
Remarkable, Mt., *Australia* 63 **E2** 32 48S 138 10 E
Rembang, *Indonesia* 37 **G14** 6 42S 111 21 E
Remedios, *Panama* 88 **E3** 8 15N 81 50W
Remeshk, *Iran* 45 **E8** 26 55N 58 50 E
Remich, *Lux.* 15 **E6** 49 32N 6 22 E
Remscheid, *Germany* 15 **C7** 51 11N 7 12 E
Ren Xian, *China* 34 **F8** 37 8N 114 40 E
Rendsburg, *Germany* 16 **A5** 54 17N 9 39 E
Renfrew, *Canada* 79 **A8** 45 30N 76 40W
Renfrewshire □, *U.K.* 12 **F4** 55 49N 4 38W
Rengat, *Indonesia* 36 **E2** 0 30S 102 45 E
Rengo, *Chile* 94 **C1** 34 24S 70 50W
Reni, *Ukraine* 17 **F15** 45 28N 28 15 E
Renmark, *Australia* 63 **E3** 34 11S 140 43 E
Rennell Sd., *Canada* 72 **C2** 53 23N 132 35W
Renner Springs, *Australia* 62 **B1** 18 20S 133 47 E
Rennes, *France* 18 **B3** 48 7N 1 41W
Rennie L., *Canada* 73 **A7** 61 32N 105 35W
Reno, *U.S.A.* 84 **F7** 39 31N 119 48W
Reno →, *Italy* 20 **B5** 44 38N 12 16 E
Renovo, *U.S.A.* 78 **E7** 41 20N 77 45W
Renqiu, *China* 34 **E9** 38 43N 116 5 E
Rensselaer, *Ind., U.S.A.* 76 **E2** 40 57N 87 9W
Rensselaer, *N.Y., U.S.A.* 79 **D11** 42 38N 73 45W
Rentería, *Spain* 19 **A5** 43 19N 1 54W
Renton, *U.S.A.* 84 **C4** 47 29N 122 12W
Reotipur, *India* 43 **G10** 25 33N 83 45 E
Republic, *Mo., U.S.A.* 81 **G8** 37 7N 93 29W
Republic, *Wash., U.S.A.* 82 **B4** 48 39N 118 44W
Republican →, *U.S.A.* 80 **F6** 39 4N 96 48W
Repulse Bay, *Canada* 69 **B11** 66 30N 86 30W
Requena, *Peru* 92 **E4** 5 5S 73 52W
Requena, *Spain* 19 **C5** 39 30N 1 4W
Reşadiye = Datça, *Turkey* 21 **F12** 36 46N 27 40 E
Reserve, *U.S.A.* 83 **K9** 33 43N 108 45W
Resht = Rasht, *Iran* 45 **B6** 37 20N 49 40 E
Resistencia, *Argentina* 94 **B4** 27 30S 59 0W
Reşiţa, *Romania* 17 **F11** 45 18N 21 53 E
Resolution I., *Canada* 69 **B13** 61 30N 65 0W
Resolution I., *N.Z.* 59 **L1** 45 40S 166 40 E
Ressano Garcia, *Mozam.* 57 **D5** 25 25S 32 0 E
Reston, *Canada* 73 **D8** 49 33N 101 6W
Retalhuleu, *Guatemala* 88 **D1** 14 33N 91 46W
Retenue, L. de, *Dem. Rep. of the Congo* 55 **E2** 11 0S 27 0 E
Retford, *U.K.* 10 **D7** 53 19N 0 56W
Réthímnon, *Greece* 23 **D6** 35 18N 24 30 E
Réthímnon □, *Greece* 23 **D6** 35 23N 24 28 E
Reti, *Pakistan* 42 **E3** 28 5N 69 48 E
Réunion ■, *Ind. Oc.* 49 **J9** 21 0S 56 0 E
Reus, *Spain* 19 **B6** 41 10N 1 5 E
Reutlingen, *Germany* 16 **D5** 48 29N 9 12 E
Reval = Tallinn, *Estonia* 9 **G21** 59 22N 24 48 E
Revda, *Russia* 24 **C10** 56 48N 59 57 E
Revelganj, *India* 43 **G11** 25 50N 84 40 E
Revelstoke, *Canada* 72 **C5** 51 0N 118 10W
Reventazón, *Peru* 92 **E2** 6 10S 80 58W
Revillagigedo, Is. de, *Pac. Oc.* 86 **D2** 18 40N 112 0W
Revuè →, *Mozam.* 55 **F3** 19 50S 34 0 E
Rewa, *India* 43 **G9** 24 33N 81 25 E
Rewari, *India* 42 **E7** 28 15N 76 40 E
Rexburg, *U.S.A.* 82 **E8** 43 49N 111 47W
Rey, *Iran* 45 **C6** 35 35N 51 25 E
Rey, I. del, *Panama* 88 **E4** 8 20N 78 30W
Rey Malabo, *Eq. Guin.* 52 **D1** 3 45N 8 50 E
Reyðarfjörður, *Iceland* 8 **D6** 65 2N 14 13W
Reyes, Pt., *U.S.A.* 84 **H3** 38 0N 123 0W
Reykjahlið, *Iceland* 8 **D5** 65 40N 16 55W
Reykjanes, *Iceland* 8 **E2** 63 48N 22 40W
Reykjavík, *Iceland* 8 **D3** 64 10N 21 57W
Reynolds Ra., *Australia* 60 **D5** 22 30S 133 0 E
Reynoldsville, *U.S.A.* 78 **E6** 41 5N 78 58W
Reynosa, *Mexico* 87 **B5** 26 5N 98 18W
Rēzekne, *Latvia* 9 **H22** 56 30N 27 17 E
Rezvān, *Iran* 45 **E8** 27 34N 56 6 E
Rhayader, *U.K.* 11 **E4** 52 18N 3 29W
Rhein →, *Europe* 15 **C6** 51 52N 6 2 E
Rhein-Main-Donau-Kanal, *Germany* 16 **D6** 49 1N 11 27 E
Rheine, *Germany* 16 **B4** 52 17N 7 26 E
Rheinland-Pfalz □, *Germany* 16 **C4** 50 0N 7 0 E
Rhin = Rhein →, *Europe* 15 **C6** 51 52N 6 2 E
Rhine = Rhein →, *Europe* 15 **C6** 51 52N 6 2 E
Rhinebeck, *U.S.A.* 79 **E11** 41 56N 73 55W
Rhineland-Palatinate = Rheinland-Pfalz □, *Germany* 16 **C4** 50 0N 7 0 E
Rhinelander, *U.S.A.* 80 **C10** 45 38N 89 25W
Rhinns Pt., *U.K.* 12 **F2** 55 40N 6 29W
Rhino Camp, *Uganda* 54 **B3** 3 0N 31 22 E
Rhir, Cap, *Morocco* 50 **B4** 30 38N 9 54W
Rhode Island □, *U.S.A.* 79 **E13** 41 40N 71 30W
Rhodes = Ródhos, *Greece* 23 **C10** 36 15N 28 10 E
Rhodesia = Zimbabwe ■, *Africa* 55 **F3** 19 0S 30 0 E
Rhodope Mts. = Rhodopi Planina, *Bulgaria* 21 **D11** 41 40N 24 20 E
Rhodopi Planina, *Bulgaria* 21 **D11** 41 40N 24 20 E
Rhön, *Germany* 16 **C5** 50 24N 9 58 E
Rhondda, *U.K.* 11 **F4** 51 39N 3 31W
Rhondda Cynon Taff □, *U.K.* 11 **F4** 51 42N 3 27W
Rhône →, *France* 18 **E6** 43 28N 4 42 E
Rhum, *U.K.* 12 **E2** 57 0N 6 20W
Rhyl, *U.K.* 10 **D4** 53 20N 3 29W
Riachão, *Brazil* 93 **E9** 7 20S 46 37W
Riasi, *India* 43 **C6** 33 10N 74 50 E
Riau □, *Indonesia* 36 **D2** 0 0 102 35 E
Riau, Kepulauan, *Indonesia* 36 **D2** 0 30N 104 20 E
Riau Arch. = Riau, Kepulauan, *Indonesia* 36 **D2** 0 30N 104 20 E
Ribadeo, *Spain* 19 **A2** 43 35N 7 5W
Ribas do Rio Pardo, *Brazil* 93 **H8** 20 27S 53 46W
Ribauè, *Mozam.* 55 **E4** 14 57S 38 17 E
Ribble →, *U.K.* 10 **D5** 53 52N 2 25W
Ribe, *Denmark* 9 **J13** 55 19N 8 44 E
Ribeira Brava, *Madeira* 22 **D2** 32 41N 17 4W
Ribeirão Prêto, *Brazil* 95 **A6** 21 10S 47 50W
Riberalta, *Bolivia* 92 **F5** 11 0S 66 0W
Riccarton, *N.Z.* 59 **K4** 43 32S 172 37 E
Rice, *U.S.A.* 85 **L12** 34 5N 114 51W
Rice L., *Canada* 78 **B6** 44 12N 78 10W
Rice Lake, *U.S.A.* 80 **C9** 45 30N 91 44W
Rich, C., *Canada* 78 **B4** 44 43N 80 38W
Richards Bay, *S. Africa* 57 **D5** 28 48S 32 6 E
Richardson →, *Canada* 73 **B6** 58 25N 111 14W
Richardson Lakes, *U.S.A.* 76 **C10** 44 46N 70 58W
Richardson Springs, *U.S.A.* 84 **F5** 39 51N 121 46W
Riche, C., *Australia* 61 **F2** 34 36S 118 47 E
Richey, *U.S.A.* 80 **B2** 47 39N 105 4W
Richfield, *U.S.A.* 83 **G8** 38 46N 112 5W
Richfield Springs, *U.S.A.* 79 **D10** 42 51N 74 59W
Richford, *U.S.A.* 79 **B12** 45 0N 72 40W
Richibucto, *Canada* 71 **C7** 46 42N 64 54W
Richland, *Ga., U.S.A.* 77 **J3** 32 5N 84 40W
Richland, *Wash., U.S.A.* 82 **C4** 46 17N 119 18W
Richland Center, *U.S.A.* 80 **D9** 43 21N 90 23W
Richlands, *U.S.A.* 76 **G5** 37 6N 81 48W
Richmond, *Australia* 62 **C3** 20 43S 143 8 E
Richmond, *N.Z.* 59 **J4** 41 20S 173 12 E
Richmond, *U.K.* 10 **C6** 54 25N 1 43W
Richmond, *Calif., U.S.A.* 84 **H4** 37 56N 122 21W
Richmond, *Ind., U.S.A.* 76 **F3** 39 50N 84 53W
Richmond, *Ky., U.S.A.* 76 **G3** 37 45N 84 18W
Richmond, *Mich., U.S.A.* 78 **D2** 42 49N 82 45W
Richmond, *Mo., U.S.A.* 80 **F8** 39 17N 93 58W
Richmond, *Tex., U.S.A.* 81 **L7** 29 35N 95 46W
Richmond, *Utah, U.S.A.* 82 **F8** 41 56N 111 48W
Richmond, *Va., U.S.A.* 76 **G7** 37 33N 77 27W
Richmond, *Vt., U.S.A.* 79 **B12** 44 24N 72 59W
Richmond Hill, *Canada* 78 **C5** 43 52N 79 27W
Richmond Ra., *Australia* 63 **D5** 29 0S 152 45 E
Richwood, *U.S.A.* 76 **F5** 38 14N 80 32W
Ridder = Leninogorsk, *Kazakstan* 26 **D9** 50 20N 83 30 E
Riddlesburg, *U.S.A.* 78 **F6** 40 9N 78 15W
Ridgecrest, *U.S.A.* 85 **K9** 35 38N 117 40W
Ridgefield, *Conn., U.S.A.* 79 **E11** 41 17N 73 30W
Ridgefield, *Wash., U.S.A.* 84 **E4** 45 49N 122 45W
Ridgeland, *U.S.A.* 77 **J5** 32 29N 80 59W
Ridgetown, *Canada* 78 **D3** 42 26N 81 52W
Ridgewood, *U.S.A.* 79 **F10** 40 59N 74 7W
Ridgway, *U.S.A.* 78 **E6** 41 25N 78 44W
Riding Mountain Nat. Park, *Canada* 73 **C9** 50 50N 100 0W
Ridley, Mt., *Australia* 61 **F3** 33 12S 122 7 E
Riebeek-Oos, *S. Africa* 56 **E4** 33 10S 26 10 E
Ried, *Austria* 16 **D7** 48 14N 13 30 E
Riesa, *Germany* 16 **C7** 51 17N 13 17 E
Riet →, *S. Africa* 56 **D3** 29 0S 23 54 E
Rietbron, *S. Africa* 56 **E3** 32 54S 23 10 E
Rietfontein, *Namibia* 56 **C3** 21 58S 20 58 E
Rieti, *Italy* 20 **C5** 42 24N 12 51 E
Rif, Er = Er Rif, *Morocco* 50 **A5** 35 1N 4 1W
Riffe L., *U.S.A.* 84 **D4** 46 32N 122 26W
Rifle, *U.S.A.* 82 **G10** 39 32N 107 47W
Rift Valley □, *Kenya* 54 **B4** 0 20N 36 0 E
Rīga, *Latvia* 9 **H21** 56 53N 24 8 E
Riga, G. of, *Latvia* 9 **H20** 57 40N 23 45 E
Rīgān, *Iran* 45 **D8** 28 37N 58 58 E
Rīgas Jūras Līcis = Riga, G. of, *Latvia* 9 **H20** 57 40N 23 45 E
Rigaud, *Canada* 79 **A10** 45 29N 74 18W
Rigby, *U.S.A.* 82 **E8** 43 40N 111 55W
Rīgestān, *Afghan.* 40 **D4** 30 15N 65 0 E
Riggins, *U.S.A.* 82 **D5** 45 25N 116 19W
Rigolet, *Canada* 71 **B8** 54 10N 58 23W
Rihand Dam, *India* 43 **G10** 24 9N 83 2 E
Riihimäki, *Finland* 9 **F21** 60 45N 24 48 E
Riiser-Larsen-halvøya, *Antarctica* 5 **C4** 68 0S 35 0 E
Rijeka, *Croatia* 16 **F8** 45 20N 14 21 E
Rijssen, *Neths.* 15 **B6** 52 19N 6 31 E
Rikuzentakada, *Japan* 30 **E10** 39 0N 141 40 E
Riley, *U.S.A.* 82 **E4** 43 32N 119 28W
Rimah, Wadi ar →, *Si. Arabia* 44 **E4** 26 5N 41 30 E
Rimbey, *Canada* 72 **C6** 52 35N 114 15W
Rimersburg, *U.S.A.* 78 **E5** 41 3N 79 30W
Rimini, *Italy* 20 **B5** 44 3N 12 33 E
Rimouski, *Canada* 71 **C6** 48 27N 68 30W
Rimrock, *U.S.A.* 84 **D5** 46 38N 121 10W
Rinca, *Indonesia* 37 **F5** 8 45S 119 35 E
Rincón de Romos, *Mexico* 86 **C4** 22 14N 102 18W
Rinconada, *Argentina* 94 **A2** 22 26S 66 10W
Rind →, *India* 43 **G9** 25 53N 80 33 E
Ringas, *India* 42 **F6** 27 21N 75 34 E
Ringkøbing, *Denmark* 9 **H13** 56 5N 8 15 E
Ringvassøy, *Norway* 8 **B18** 69 56N 19 15 E
Ringwood, *U.S.A.* 79 **E10** 41 7N 74 15W
Rinjani, *Indonesia* 36 **F5** 8 24S 116 28 E
Rio Branco, *Brazil* 92 **E5** 9 58S 67 49W
Río Branco, *Uruguay* 95 **C5** 32 40S 53 40W
Río Bravo del Norte →, *Mexico* 87 **B5** 25 57N 97 9W
Rio Brilhante, *Brazil* 95 **A5** 21 48S 54 33W
Rio Claro, *Brazil* 95 **A6** 22 19S 47 35W
Rio Claro, *Trin. & Tob.* 89 **D7** 10 20N 61 25W
Río Colorado, *Argentina* 96 **D4** 39 0S 64 0W
Río Cuarto, *Argentina* 94 **C3** 33 10S 64 25W
Rio das Pedras, *Mozam.* 57 **C6** 23 8S 35 28 E
Rio de Janeiro, *Brazil* 95 **A7** 23 0S 43 12W
Rio de Janeiro □, *Brazil* 95 **A7** 22 50S 43 0W
Rio do Sul, *Brazil* 95 **B6** 27 13S 49 37W
Río Gallegos, *Argentina* 96 **G3** 51 35S 69 15W
Rio Grande = Grande, Rio →, *U.S.A.* 81 **N6** 25 58N 97 9W
Río Grande, *Argentina* 96 **G3** 53 50S 67 45W
Rio Grande, *Brazil* 95 **C5** 32 0S 52 20W
Río Grande, *Mexico* 86 **C4** 23 50N 103 2W
Río Grande, *Nic.* 88 **D3** 12 54N 83 33W
Rio Grande City, *U.S.A.* 81 **M5** 26 23N 98 49W
Río Grande de Santiago →, *Mexico* 86 **C3** 21 36N 105 26W
Rio Grande do Norte □, *Brazil* 93 **E11** 5 40S 36 0W
Rio Grande do Sul □, *Brazil* 95 **C5** 30 0S 53 0W

Russell

Rio Hato, *Panama* 88 E3 8 22N 80 10W
Rio Lagartos, *Mexico* 87 C7 21 36N 88 10W
Rio Largo, *Brazil* 93 E11 9 28S 35 50W
Rio Mulatos, *Bolivia* 92 G5 19 40S 66 50W
Rio Muni □, *Eq. Guin.* 52 D2 1 30N 10 0 E
Rio Negro, *Brazil* 95 B6 26 0S 49 55W
Rio Pardo, *Brazil* 95 C5 30 0S 52 30W
Rio Rancho, *U.S.A.* 83 J10 35 14N 106 38W
Rio Segundo, *Argentina* 94 C3 31 40S 63 59W
Rio Tercero, *Argentina* 94 C3 32 15S 64 8W
Rio Verde, *Brazil* 93 G8 17 50S 51 0W
Rio Verde, *Mexico* 87 C5 21 56N 99 59W
Rio Vista, *U.S.A.* 84 G5 38 10N 121 42W
Riobamba, *Ecuador* 92 D3 1 50S 78 45W
Riohacha, *Colombia* 92 A4 11 33N 72 55W
Riosucio, *Colombia* 92 B3 7 27N 77 7W
Riou L., *Canada* 73 B7 59 7N 106 25W
Ripley, *Canada* 78 B3 44 4N 81 35W
Ripley, *Calif., U.S.A.* 85 M12 33 32N 114 39W
Ripley, *N.Y., U.S.A.* 78 D5 42 16N 79 43W
Ripley, *Tenn., U.S.A.* 81 H10 35 45N 89 32W
Ripley, *W. Va., U.S.A.* 76 F5 38 49N 81 43W
Ripon, *U.K.* 10 C6 54 9N 1 31W
Ripon, *Calif., U.S.A.* 84 H5 37 44N 121 7W
Ripon, *Wis., U.S.A.* 76 D1 43 51N 88 50W
Rishā', W. ar →, *Si. Arabia* 44 E5 25 33N 44 5 E
Rishiri-Tō, *Japan* 30 B10 45 11N 141 15 E
Rishon le Ẓiyyon, *Israel* 47 D3 31 58N 34 48 E
Rison, *U.S.A.* 81 J8 33 58N 92 11W
Risør, *Norway* 9 G13 58 43N 9 13 E
Rita Blanca Cr. →, *U.S.A.* 81 H3 35 40N 102 29W
Ritter, Mt., *U.S.A.* 84 H7 37 41N 119 12W
Rittman, *U.S.A.* 78 F3 40 58N 81 47W
Ritzville, *U.S.A.* 82 C4 47 8N 118 23W
Riva del Garda, *Italy* 20 B4 45 53N 10 50 E
Rivadavia, *Buenos Aires, Argentina* 94 D3 35 29S 62 59W
Rivadavia, *Mendoza, Argentina* 94 C2 33 13S 68 30W
Rivadavia, *Salta, Argentina* 94 A3 24 5S 62 54W
Rivadavia, *Chile* 94 B1 29 57S 70 35W
Rivas, *Nic.* 88 D2 11 30N 85 50W
River Cess, *Liberia* 50 G4 5 30N 9 32W
River Jordan, *Canada* 84 B2 48 26N 124 3W
Rivera, *Argentina* 94 D3 37 12S 63 14W
Rivera, *Uruguay* 95 C4 31 0S 55 50W
Riverbank, *U.S.A.* 84 H6 37 44N 120 56W
Riverdale, *U.S.A.* 84 J7 36 26N 119 52W
Riverhead, *U.S.A.* 79 F12 40 55N 72 40W
Riverhurst, *Canada* 73 C7 50 55N 106 50W
Rivers, *Canada* 73 C8 50 2N 100 14W
Rivers Inlet, *Canada* 72 C3 51 42N 127 15W
Riversdale, *S. Africa* 56 E3 34 7S 21 15 E
Riverside, *U.S.A.* 85 M9 33 59N 117 22W
Riverton, *Australia* 63 E2 34 10S 138 46 E
Riverton, *Canada* 73 C9 51 1N 97 0W
Riverton, *N.Z.* 59 M2 46 21S 168 0 E
Riverton, *U.S.A.* 82 E9 43 2N 108 23W
Riverton Heights, *U.S.A.* 84 C4 47 28N 122 17W
Riviera, *U.S.A.* 85 K12 35 4N 114 35W
Riviera di Levante, *Italy* 18 D8 44 15N 9 30 E
Riviera di Ponente, *Italy* 18 D8 44 10N 8 20 E
Rivière-au-Renard, *Canada* 71 C7 48 59N 64 23W
Rivière-du-Loup, *Canada* 71 C6 47 50N 69 30W
Rivière-Pentecôte, *Canada* 71 C6 49 57N 67 1W
Rivière-Pilote, *Martinique* 89 D7 14 26N 60 53W
Rivière St. Paul, *Canada* 71 B8 51 28N 57 45W
Rivne, *Ukraine* 17 C14 50 40N 26 10 E
Rívoli, *Italy* 18 D7 45 3N 7 31 E
Rivoli B., *Australia* 63 F3 37 32S 140 3 E
Riyadh = Ar Riyāḑ, *Si. Arabia* 46 C4 24 41N 46 42 E
Rize, *Turkey* 25 F7 41 0N 40 30 E
Rizhao, *China* 35 G10 35 25N 119 30 E
Rizokarpaso, *Cyprus* 23 D13 35 36N 34 23 E
Rizzuto, C., *Italy* 20 E7 38 53N 17 5 E
Rjukan, *Norway* 9 G13 59 54N 8 33 E
Road Town, *Br. Virgin Is.* 89 C7 18 27N 64 37W
Roan Plateau, *U.S.A.* 82 G9 39 20N 109 20W
Roanne, *France* 18 C6 46 3N 4 4 E
Roanoke, *Ala., U.S.A.* 77 J3 33 9N 85 22W
Roanoke, *Va., U.S.A.* 76 G6 37 16N 79 56W
Roanoke →, *U.S.A.* 77 H7 35 57N 76 42W
Roanoke I., *U.S.A.* 77 H8 35 55N 75 40W
Roanoke Rapids, *U.S.A.* 77 G7 36 28N 77 40W
Roatán, *Honduras* 88 C2 16 18N 86 35W
Robāt Sang, *Iran* 45 C8 35 35N 59 10 E
Robbins I., *Australia* 62 G4 40 42S 145 0 E
Robe →, *Australia* 60 D2 21 42S 116 15 E
Robert Lee, *U.S.A.* 81 K4 31 54N 100 29W
Robertsdale, *U.S.A.* 78 F6 40 11N 78 6W
Robertsganj, *India* 43 G10 24 44N 83 4 E
Robertson, *S. Africa* 56 E2 33 46S 19 50 E
Robertson I., *Antarctica* 5 C18 65 15S 59 30W
Robertson Ra., *Australia* 60 D3 23 15S 121 0 E
Robertstown, *Australia* 63 E2 33 58S 139 5 E
Roberval, *Canada* 71 C5 48 32N 72 15W
Robeson Chan., *Greenland* 4 A4 82 0N 61 30W
Robesonia, *U.S.A.* 79 F8 40 21N 76 8W
Robinson, *U.S.A.* 76 F2 39 0N 87 44W
Robinson →, *Australia* 62 B2 16 3S 137 16 E
Robinson Ra., *Australia* 61 E2 25 40S 119 0 E
Robinvale, *Australia* 63 E3 34 40S 142 45 E
Roblin, *Canada* 73 C8 51 14N 101 21W
Roboré, *Bolivia* 92 G7 18 10S 59 45W
Robson, *Canada* 72 D5 49 20N 117 41W
Robson, Mt., *Canada* 72 C5 53 10N 119 10W
Robstown, *U.S.A.* 81 M6 27 47N 97 40W
Roca, C. da, *Portugal* 19 C1 38 40N 9 31W
Roca Partida, I., *Mexico* 86 D2 19 1N 112 2W
Rocas, I., *Brazil* 93 D12 4 0S 34 1W
Rocha, *Uruguay* 95 C5 34 30S 54 25W
Rochdale, *U.K.* 10 D5 53 38N 2 9W
Rochefort, *Belgium* 15 D5 50 9N 5 12 E
Rochefort, *France* 18 D3 45 56N 0 57W
Rochelle, *U.S.A.* 80 E10 41 56N 89 4W
Rocher River, *Canada* 72 A6 61 23N 112 44W
Rochester, *U.K.* 11 F8 51 23N 0 31 E
Rochester, *Ind., U.S.A.* 76 E2 41 4N 86 13W
Rochester, *Minn., U.S.A.* 80 C8 44 1N 92 28W
Rochester, *N.H., U.S.A.* 79 C14 43 18N 70 59W
Rochester, *N.Y., U.S.A.* 78 C7 43 10N 77 37W
Rock →, *Canada* 72 A3 60 7N 127 7W
Rock Creek, *U.S.A.* 78 E4 41 40N 80 52W
Rock Falls, *U.S.A.* 80 E10 41 47N 89 41W
Rock Hill, *U.S.A.* 77 H5 34 56N 81 1W
Rock Island, *U.S.A.* 80 E9 41 30N 90 34W
Rock Rapids, *U.S.A.* 80 D6 43 26N 96 10W
Rock Sound, *Bahamas* 88 B4 24 54N 76 12W
Rock Springs, *Mont., U.S.A.* 82 C10 46 49N 106 15W
Rock Springs, *Wyo., U.S.A.* 82 F9 41 35N 109 14W
Rock Valley, *U.S.A.* 80 D6 43 12N 96 18W
Rockall, *Atl. Oc.* 6 D3 57 37N 13 42W
Rockdale, *Tex., U.S.A.* 81 K6 30 39N 97 0W
Rockdale, *Wash., U.S.A.* 84 C5 47 22N 121 28W
Rockefeller Plateau, *Antarctica* 5 E14 80 0S 140 0W
Rockford, *U.S.A.* 80 D10 42 16N 89 6W
Rockglen, *Canada* 73 D7 49 11N 105 57W
Rockhampton, *Australia* 62 C5 23 22S 150 32 E
Rockingham, *Australia* 61 F2 32 15S 115 38 E
Rockingham, *U.S.A.* 77 H6 34 57N 79 46W
Rockingham B., *Australia* 62 B4 18 5S 146 10 E
Rocklake, *U.S.A.* 80 A5 48 47N 99 15W
Rockland, *Canada* 79 A9 45 33N 75 17W
Rockland, *Idaho, U.S.A.* 82 E7 42 34N 112 53W
Rockland, *Maine, U.S.A.* 77 C11 44 6N 69 7W
Rockland, *Mich., U.S.A.* 80 B10 46 44N 89 11W
Rocklin, *U.S.A.* 84 G5 38 48N 121 14W
Rockmart, *U.S.A.* 77 H3 34 0N 85 3W
Rockport, *Mass., U.S.A.* 79 D14 42 39N 70 37W
Rockport, *Mo., U.S.A.* 80 E7 40 25N 95 31W
Rockport, *Tex., U.S.A.* 81 L6 28 2N 97 3W
Rocksprings, *U.S.A.* 81 K4 30 1N 100 13W
Rockville, *Conn., U.S.A.* 79 E12 41 52N 72 28W
Rockville, *Md., U.S.A.* 76 F7 39 5N 77 9W
Rockwall, *U.S.A.* 81 J6 32 56N 96 28W
Rockwell City, *U.S.A.* 80 D7 42 24N 94 38W
Rockwood, *Canada* 78 C4 43 37N 80 8W
Rockwood, *Maine, U.S.A.* 77 C11 45 41N 69 45W
Rockwood, *Tenn., U.S.A.* 77 H3 35 52N 84 41W
Rocky Ford, *U.S.A.* 80 F3 38 3N 103 43W
Rocky Gully, *Australia* 61 F2 34 30S 116 57 E
Rocky Harbour, *Canada* 71 C8 49 36N 57 55W
Rocky Island L., *Canada* 70 C3 46 55N 83 0W
Rocky Lane, *Canada* 72 B5 58 31N 116 22W
Rocky Mount, *U.S.A.* 77 H7 35 57N 77 48W
Rocky Mountain House, *Canada* 72 C6 52 22N 114 55W
Rocky Mountain Nat. Park, *U.S.A.* 82 F11 40 25N 105 45W
Rocky Mts., *N. Amer.* 82 G10 49 0N 115 0W
Rocky Point, *Namibia* 56 B2 19 3S 12 30 E
Rod, *Pakistan* 40 E3 28 10N 63 5 E
Rødbyhavn, *Denmark* 9 J14 54 39N 11 22 E
Roddickton, *Canada* 71 B8 50 51N 56 8W
Rodez, *France* 18 D5 44 21N 2 33 E
Rodhopoú, *Greece* 23 D5 35 34N 23 45 E
Ródhos, *Greece* 23 C10 36 15N 28 10 E
Rodney, *Canada* 78 D3 42 34N 81 41W
Rodney, C., *N.Z.* 59 G5 36 17S 174 50 E
Rodriguez, *Ind. Oc.* 3 E13 19 45S 63 20 E
Roe →, *U.K.* 13 A5 55 6N 6 59W
Roebling, *U.S.A.* 79 F10 40 7N 74 47W
Roebourne, *Australia* 60 D2 20 44S 117 9 E
Roebuck B., *Australia* 60 C3 18 5S 122 20 E
Roermond, *Neths.* 15 C6 51 12N 6 0 E
Roes Welcome Sd., *Canada* 69 B11 65 0N 87 0W
Roeselare, *Belgium* 15 D3 50 57N 3 7 E
Rogachev = Ragachow, *Belarus* 17 B16 53 8N 30 5 E
Rogagua, L., *Bolivia* 92 F5 13 43S 66 50W
Rogatyn, *Ukraine* 17 D13 49 24N 24 36 E
Rogdhia, *Greece* 23 D7 35 22N 25 1 E
Rogers, *U.S.A.* 81 G7 36 20N 94 7W
Rogers City, *U.S.A.* 76 C4 45 25N 83 49W
Rogersville, *Canada* 71 C6 46 44N 65 26W
Roggan →, *Canada* 70 B4 54 24N 79 25W
Roggan L., *Canada* 70 B4 54 8N 77 50W
Roggeveldberge, *S. Africa* 56 E3 32 10S 20 10 E
Rogoaguado, L., *Bolivia* 92 F5 13 0S 65 30W
Rogue →, *U.S.A.* 82 E1 42 26N 124 26W
Róhda, *Greece* 23 A3 39 48N 19 46 E
Rohnert Park, *U.S.A.* 84 G4 38 16N 122 40W
Rohri, *Pakistan* 42 F3 27 45N 68 51 E
Rohri Canal, *Pakistan* 42 F3 26 15N 68 27 E
Rohtak, *India* 42 E7 28 55N 76 43 E
Roi Et, *Thailand* 38 D4 16 4N 103 40 E
Roja, *Latvia* 9 H20 57 29N 22 43 E
Rojas, *Argentina* 94 C3 34 10S 60 45W
Rojo, C., *Mexico* 87 C5 21 33N 97 20W
Rokan →, *Indonesia* 36 D2 2 0N 100 50 E
Rokiškis, *Lithuania* 9 J21 55 55N 25 35 E
Rolândia, *Brazil* 95 A5 23 18S 51 23W
Rolla, *U.S.A.* 81 G9 37 57N 91 46W
Rolleston, *Australia* 62 C4 24 28S 148 35 E
Rollingstone, *Australia* 62 B4 19 2S 146 24 E
Roma, *Australia* 63 D4 26 32S 148 49 E
Roma, *Italy* 20 D5 41 54N 12 29 E
Roma, *Sweden* 9 H18 57 32N 18 26 E
Roma, *U.S.A.* 81 M5 26 25N 99 1W
Romain C., *U.S.A.* 77 J6 33 0N 79 22W
Romaine, *Canada* 71 B7 50 13N 60 40W
Romaine →, *Canada* 71 B7 50 18N 63 47W
Roman, *Romania* 17 E14 46 57N 26 55 E
Romang, *Indonesia* 37 F7 7 30S 127 20 E
Români, *Egypt* 47 E1 30 59N 32 38 E
Romania ■, *Europe* 17 F12 46 0N 25 0 E
Romano, Cayo, *Cuba* 88 B4 22 0N 77 30W
Romanovka = Basarabeasca, *Moldova* 17 E15 46 21N 28 58 E
Romans-sur-Isère, *France* 18 D6 45 3N 5 3 E
Romblon, *Phil.* 37 B6 12 33N 122 17 E
Rome = Roma, *Italy* 20 D5 41 54N 12 29 E
Rome, *Ga., U.S.A.* 77 H3 34 15N 85 10W
Rome, *N.Y., U.S.A.* 79 C9 43 13N 75 27W
Rome, *Pa., U.S.A.* 79 E8 41 51N 76 21W
Romney, *U.S.A.* 76 F6 39 21N 78 45W
Romney Marsh, *U.K.* 11 F8 51 2N 0 54 E
Rømø, *Denmark* 9 J13 55 10N 8 30 E
Romorantin-Lanthenay, *France* 18 C4 47 21N 1 45 E
Romsdalen, *Norway* 9 E12 62 25N 7 52 E
Romsey, *U.K.* 11 G6 51 0N 1 29W
Ron, *Vietnam* 38 D6 17 53N 106 27 E
Rona, *U.K.* 12 D3 57 34N 5 59W
Ronan, *U.S.A.* 82 C6 47 32N 114 6W
Roncador, Cayos, *Colombia* 88 D3 13 32N 80 4W
Roncador, Serra do, *Brazil* 93 F8 12 30S 52 30W
Ronda, *Spain* 19 D3 36 46N 5 12W
Rondane, *Norway* 9 F13 61 57N 9 50 E
Rondônia □, *Brazil* 92 F6 11 0S 63 0W
Rondonópolis, *Brazil* 93 G8 16 28S 54 38W
Rong, Koh, *Cambodia* 39 G4 10 45N 103 15 E
Ronge, L. la, *Canada* 73 B7 55 6N 105 17W
Rønne, *Denmark* 9 J16 55 6N 14 43 E
Ronne Ice Shelf, *Antarctica* 5 D18 78 0S 60 0W
Ronsard, C., *Australia* 61 D1 24 46S 113 10 E
Ronse, *Belgium* 15 D3 50 45N 3 35 E
Roodepoort, *S. Africa* 57 D4 26 11S 27 54 E
Roof Butte, *U.S.A.* 83 H9 36 28N 109 5W
Rooiboklaagte →, *Namibia* 56 C3 20 50S 21 0 E
Roorkee, *India* 42 E7 29 52N 77 59 E
Roosendaal, *Neths.* 15 C4 51 32N 4 29 E
Roosevelt, *U.S.A.* 82 F8 40 18N 109 59W
Roosevelt →, *Brazil* 92 E6 7 35S 60 20W
Roosevelt, Mt., *Canada* 72 B3 58 26N 125 20W
Roosevelt I., *Antarctica* 5 D12 79 30S 162 0W
Roper →, *Australia* 62 A2 14 43S 135 27 E
Roper Bar, *Australia* 62 A1 14 44S 134 44 E
Roque Pérez, *Argentina* 94 D4 35 25S 59 24W
Roquetas de Mar, *Spain* 19 D4 36 46N 2 36W
Roraima □, *Brazil* 92 C6 2 0N 61 30W
Roraima, Mt., *Venezuela* 92 B6 5 10N 60 40W
Røros, *Norway* 9 E14 62 35N 11 23 E
Rosa, *Zambia* 55 D3 9 33S 31 15 E
Rosa, L., *Bahamas* 89 B5 21 0N 73 30W
Rosa, Monte, *Europe* 18 D7 45 57N 7 53 E
Rosalia, *U.S.A.* 82 C5 47 14N 117 22W
Rosamond, *U.S.A.* 85 L8 34 52N 118 10W
Rosario, *Argentina* 94 C3 33 0S 60 40W
Rosário, *Brazil* 93 D10 3 0S 44 15W
Rosario, *Baja Calif., Mexico* 86 B1 30 0N 115 50W
Rosario, *Sinaloa, Mexico* 86 C3 23 0N 105 52W
Rosario, *Paraguay* 94 A4 24 30S 57 35W
Rosario de la Frontera, *Argentina* 94 B3 25 50S 65 0W
Rosario de Lerma, *Argentina* 94 A2 24 59S 65 35W
Rosario del Tala, *Argentina* 94 C4 32 20S 59 10W
Rosário do Sul, *Brazil* 95 C5 30 15S 54 55W
Rosarito, *Mexico* 85 N9 32 18N 117 4W
Roscoe, *U.S.A.* 79 E10 41 56N 74 55W
Roscommon, *Ireland* 13 C3 53 38N 8 11W
Roscommon □, *Ireland* 13 C3 53 49N 8 23W
Roscrea, *Ireland* 13 D4 52 57N 7 49W
Rose →, *Australia* 62 A2 14 16S 135 45 E
Rose Blanche, *Canada* 71 C8 47 38N 58 45W
Rose Pt., *Canada* 72 C2 54 11N 131 39W
Rose Valley, *Canada* 73 C8 52 19N 103 49W
Roseau, *Domin.* 89 C7 15 20N 61 24W
Roseau, *U.S.A.* 80 A7 48 51N 95 46W
Rosebery, *Australia* 62 G4 41 46S 145 33 E
Rosebud, *S. Dak., U.S.A.* 80 D4 43 14N 100 51W
Rosebud, *Tex., U.S.A.* 81 K6 31 4N 96 59W
Roseburg, *U.S.A.* 82 E2 43 13N 123 20W
Rosedale, *U.S.A.* 81 J9 33 51N 91 2W
Roseland, *U.S.A.* 84 G4 38 25N 122 43W
Rosemary, *Canada* 72 C6 50 46N 112 5W
Rosenberg, *U.S.A.* 81 L7 29 34N 95 49W
Rosenheim, *Germany* 16 E7 47 51N 12 7 E
Roses, G. de, *Spain* 19 A7 42 10N 3 15 E
Rosetown, *Canada* 73 C7 51 35N 107 59W
Roseville, *Calif., U.S.A.* 84 G5 38 45N 121 17W
Roseville, *Mich., U.S.A.* 78 D2 42 30N 82 56W
Rosewood, *Australia* 63 D5 27 38S 152 36 E
Roshkhvār, *Iran* 45 C8 34 58N 59 37 E
Rosignano Maríttimo, *Italy* 20 C4 43 24N 10 28 E
Rosignol, *Guyana* 92 B7 6 15N 57 30W
Roşiori de Vede, *Romania* 17 F13 44 9N 25 0 E
Roskilde, *Denmark* 9 J15 55 38N 12 3 E
Roslavl, *Russia* 24 D5 53 57N 32 55 E
Rosmead, *S. Africa* 56 E4 31 29S 25 8 E
Ross, *Australia* 62 G4 42 2S 147 30 E
Ross, *N.Z.* 59 K3 42 53S 170 49 E
Ross I., *Antarctica* 5 D11 77 30S 168 0 E
Ross Ice Shelf, *Antarctica* 5 E12 80 0S 180 0 E
Ross L., *U.S.A.* 82 B3 48 44N 121 4W
Ross-on-Wye, *U.K.* 11 F5 51 54N 2 34W
Ross River, *Australia* 62 C1 23 44S 134 30 E
Ross River, *Canada* 72 A2 62 30N 131 30W
Ross Sea, *Antarctica* 5 D11 74 0S 178 0 E
Rossall Pt., *U.K.* 10 D4 53 55N 3 3W
Rossan Pt., *Ireland* 13 B3 54 42N 8 47W
Rossano, *Italy* 20 E7 39 36N 16 39 E
Rossburn, *Canada* 73 C8 50 40N 100 49W
Rosseau, *Canada* 78 A5 45 16N 79 39W
Rosseau L., *Canada* 78 A5 45 10N 79 35W
Rosses, The, *Ireland* 13 A3 55 2N 8 20W
Rossignol, L., *Canada* 70 B5 52 43N 73 40W
Rossignol Res., *Canada* 71 D6 44 12N 65 10W
Rossland, *Canada* 72 D5 49 6N 117 50W
Rosslare, *Ireland* 13 D5 52 17N 6 24W
Rosso, *Mauritania* 50 E2 16 40N 15 45W
Rossosh, *Russia* 25 D6 50 15N 39 28 E
Røssvatnet, *Norway* 8 D16 65 45N 14 5 E
Røst, *Norway* 8 C15 67 32N 12 0 E
Rosthern, *Canada* 73 C7 52 40N 106 20W
Rostock, *Germany* 16 A7 54 5N 12 8 E
Rostov, *Don, Russia* 25 E6 47 15N 39 45 E
Rostov, *Yaroslavl, Russia* 24 C6 57 14N 39 25 E
Roswell, *Ga., U.S.A.* 77 H3 34 2N 84 22W
Roswell, *N. Mex., U.S.A.* 81 J2 33 24N 104 32W
Rotan, *U.S.A.* 81 J4 32 51N 100 28W
Rother →, *U.K.* 11 G8 50 59N 0 45 E
Rotherham, *U.K.* 10 D6 53 26N 1 20W
Rothes, *U.K.* 12 D5 57 32N 3 13W
Rothesay, *Canada* 71 C6 45 23N 66 0W
Rothesay, *U.K.* 12 F3 55 50N 5 3W
Roti, *Indonesia* 37 F6 10 50S 123 0 E
Roto, *Australia* 63 E4 33 0S 145 30 E
Rotondo, Mte., *France* 18 E8 42 14N 9 8 E
Rotoroa, L., *N.Z.* 59 J4 41 55S 172 39 E
Rotorua, *N.Z.* 59 H6 38 9S 176 16 E
Rotorua, L., *N.Z.* 59 H6 38 5S 176 18 E
Rotterdam, *Neths.* 15 C4 51 55N 4 30 E
Rotterdam, *U.S.A.* 79 D10 42 48N 74 1W
Rottnest I., *Australia* 61 F2 32 0S 115 27 E
Rottumeroog, *Neths.* 15 A6 53 33N 6 34 E
Rottweil, *Germany* 16 D5 48 9N 8 37 E
Rotuma, *Fiji* 64 J9 12 25S 177 5 E
Roubaix, *France* 18 A5 50 40N 3 10 E
Rouen, *France* 18 B4 49 27N 1 4 E
Rouleau, *Canada* 73 C8 50 10N 104 56W
Round Mountain, *U.S.A.* 82 G5 38 43N 117 4W
Round Mt., *Australia* 63 E5 30 26S 152 16 E
Round Rock, *U.S.A.* 81 K6 30 31N 97 41W
Roundup, *U.S.A.* 82 C9 46 27N 108 33W
Rousay, *U.K.* 12 B5 59 10N 3 2W
Rouses Point, *U.S.A.* 79 B11 44 59N 73 22W
Rouseville, *U.S.A.* 78 E5 41 28N 79 42W
Roussillon, *France* 18 E5 42 30N 2 35 E
Rouxville, *S. Africa* 56 E4 30 25S 26 50 E
Rouyn-Noranda, *Canada* 70 C4 48 20N 79 0W
Rovaniemi, *Finland* 8 C21 66 29N 25 41 E
Rovereto, *Italy* 20 B4 45 53N 11 3 E
Rovigo, *Italy* 20 B4 45 4N 11 47 E
Rovinj, *Croatia* 16 F7 45 5N 13 40 E
Rovno = Rivne, *Ukraine* 17 C14 50 40N 26 10 E
Rovuma = Ruvuma →, *Tanzania* 55 E5 10 29S 40 28 E
Row'ān, *Iran* 45 C6 35 8N 48 51 E
Rowena, *Australia* 63 D4 29 48S 148 55 E
Rowley Shoals, *Australia* 60 C2 17 30S 119 0 E
Roxas, *Phil.* 37 B6 11 36N 122 49 E
Roxboro, *U.S.A.* 77 G6 36 24N 78 59W
Roxburgh, *N.Z.* 59 L2 45 33S 169 19 E
Roxbury, *U.S.A.* 78 F7 40 6N 77 39W
Roy, *Mont., U.S.A.* 82 C9 47 20N 108 58W
Roy, *N. Mex., U.S.A.* 81 H2 35 57N 104 12W
Roy, *Utah, U.S.A.* 82 F7 41 10N 112 2W
Royal Canal, *Ireland* 13 C4 53 30N 7 13W
Royal Leamington Spa, *U.K.* 11 E6 52 18N 1 31W
Royal Tunbridge Wells, *U.K.* 11 F8 51 7N 0 16 E
Royale, Isle, *U.S.A.* 80 B10 48 0N 88 54W
Royan, *France* 18 D3 45 37N 1 2W
Royston, *U.K.* 11 E7 52 3N 0 0W
Rozdilna, *Ukraine* 17 E16 46 50N 30 2 E
Rozhyshche, *Ukraine* 17 C13 50 54N 25 15 E
Rtishchevo, *Russia* 24 C7 52 18N 43 46 E
Ruacaná, *Namibia* 56 B1 17 27S 14 21 E
Ruahine Ra., *N.Z.* 59 H6 39 55S 176 2 E
Ruapehu, *N.Z.* 59 H5 39 17S 175 35 E
Ruapuke I., *N.Z.* 59 M2 46 46S 168 31 E
Ruâq, W. →, *Egypt* 47 F2 30 0N 33 49 E
Rub' al Khālī, *Si. Arabia* 46 D4 19 0N 48 0 E
Rubeho Mts., *Tanzania* 54 D4 6 50S 36 25 E
Rubh a' Mhail, *U.K.* 12 F2 55 56N 6 8W
Rubha Hunish, *U.K.* 12 D2 57 42N 6 20W
Rubha Robhanais = Lewis, Butt of, *U.K.* 12 C2 58 31N 6 16W
Rubicon →, *U.S.A.* 84 G5 38 53N 121 4W
Rubio, *Venezuela* 92 B4 7 43N 72 22W
Rubtsovsk, *Russia* 26 D9 51 30N 81 10 E
Ruby L., *U.S.A.* 82 F6 40 10N 115 28W
Ruby Mts., *U.S.A.* 82 F6 40 30N 115 20W
Rubyvale, *Australia* 62 C4 23 25S 147 42 E
Rūd Sar, *Iran* 45 B6 37 8N 50 18 E
Rudall, *Australia* 63 E2 33 43S 136 17 E
Rudall →, *Australia* 60 D3 22 34S 122 13 E
Rudewa, *Tanzania* 55 E3 10 7S 34 40 E
Rudnyy, *Kazakstan* 26 D7 52 57N 63 7 E
Rudolfa, Ostrov, *Russia* 26 A6 81 45N 58 30 E
Rudyard, *U.S.A.* 76 B3 46 14N 84 36W
Rufiji →, *Tanzania* 54 D4 7 50S 39 15 E
Rufino, *Argentina* 94 C3 34 20S 62 50W
Rufunsa, *Zambia* 55 F2 15 4S 29 34 E
Rugby, *U.K.* 11 E6 52 23N 1 16W
Rugby, *U.S.A.* 80 A5 48 22N 100 0W
Rügen, *Germany* 16 A7 54 22N 13 24 E
Ruhengeri, *Rwanda* 54 C2 1 30S 29 36 E
Ruhnu, *Estonia* 9 H20 57 48N 23 15 E
Ruhr →, *Germany* 16 C4 51 27N 6 43 E
Ruhuhu →, *Tanzania* 55 E3 10 31S 34 34 E
Ruidoso, *U.S.A.* 83 K11 33 20N 105 41W
Ruivo, Pico, *Madeira* 22 D3 32 45N 16 56W
Rujm Tal'at al Jamā'ah, *Jordan* 47 E4 30 24N 35 30 E
Ruk, *Pakistan* 42 F3 27 50N 68 42 E
Rukhla, *Pakistan* 42 C4 32 27N 71 57 E
Ruki →, *Dem. Rep. of the Congo* 52 E3 0 5N 18 17 E
Rukwa □, *Tanzania* 54 D3 7 0S 31 30 E
Rukwa, L., *Tanzania* 54 D3 8 0S 32 20 E
Rulhieres, C., *Australia* 60 B4 13 56S 127 22 E
Rum = Rhum, *U.K.* 12 E2 57 0N 6 20W
Rum Cay, *Bahamas* 89 B5 23 40N 74 58W
Rum Jungle, *Australia* 60 B5 13 0S 130 59 E
Rumāḩ, *Si. Arabia* 44 E5 25 29N 47 10 E
Rumania = Romania ■, *Europe* 17 F12 46 0N 25 0 E
Rumaylah, *Iraq* 44 D5 30 47N 47 37 E
Rumbêk, *Sudan* 51 G11 6 54N 29 37 E
Rumford, *U.S.A.* 77 C10 44 33N 70 33W
Rumia, *Poland* 17 A10 54 37N 18 25 E
Rumoi, *Japan* 30 C10 43 56N 141 39 E
Rumonge, *Burundi* 54 C2 3 59S 29 26 E
Rumson, *U.S.A.* 79 F11 40 23N 74 0W
Rumuruti, *Kenya* 54 B4 0 17N 36 32 E
Runan, *China* 34 H8 33 0N 114 30 E
Runanga, *N.Z.* 59 K3 42 25S 171 15 E
Runaway, C., *N.Z.* 59 G6 37 32S 177 59 E
Runcorn, *U.K.* 10 D5 53 21N 2 44W
Rundu, *Namibia* 56 B2 17 52S 19 43 E
Rungwa, *Tanzania* 54 D3 6 55S 33 32 E
Rungwa →, *Tanzania* 54 D3 7 36S 31 50 E
Rungwe, *Tanzania* 55 D3 9 11S 33 32 E
Rungwe, Mt., *Tanzania* 52 F6 9 8S 33 40 E
Runton Ra., *Australia* 60 D3 23 31S 123 6 E
Ruoqiang, *China* 32 C3 38 55N 88 10 E
Rupa, *India* 41 F18 27 15N 92 21 E
Rupar, *India* 42 D7 31 2N 76 38 E
Rupat, *Indonesia* 36 D2 1 45N 101 40 E
Rupen →, *India* 42 H4 23 28N 71 31 E
Rupert, *U.S.A.* 82 E7 42 37N 113 41W
Rupert →, *Canada* 70 B4 51 29N 78 45W
Rupert B., *Canada* 70 B4 51 35N 79 0W
Rupert House = Waskaganish, *Canada* 70 B4 51 30N 78 40W
Rupsa, *India* 43 J12 21 37N 87 1 E
Rurrenabaque, *Bolivia* 92 F5 14 30S 67 32W
Rusambo, *Zimbabwe* 55 F3 16 30S 32 4 E
Rusape, *Zimbabwe* 55 F3 18 35S 32 8 E
Ruschuk = Ruse, *Bulgaria* 21 C12 43 48N 25 59 E
Ruse, *Bulgaria* 21 C12 43 48N 25 59 E
Rush, *Ireland* 13 C5 53 31N 6 6W
Rushan, *China* 35 F11 36 56N 121 30 E
Rushden, *U.K.* 11 E7 52 18N 0 35W
Rushmore, Mt., *U.S.A.* 80 D3 43 53N 103 28W
Rushville, *Ill., U.S.A.* 80 E9 40 7N 90 34W
Rushville, *Ind., U.S.A.* 76 F3 39 37N 85 27W
Rushville, *Nebr., U.S.A.* 80 D3 42 43N 102 28W
Russas, *Brazil* 93 D11 4 55S 37 50W
Russell, *Canada* 73 C8 50 50N 101 20W
Russell, *Kans., U.S.A.* 80 F5 38 54N 98 52W

S

Söderhamn

Sierra Blanca, U.S.A. 83 L11 31 11N 105 22W
Sierra Blanca Peak, U.S.A. 83 K11 33 23N 105 49W
Sierra City, U.S.A. 84 F6 39 34N 120 38W
Sierra Colorada, Argentina 96 E3 40 35S 67 50W
Sierra Gorda, Chile 94 A2 22 50S 69 15W
Sierra Leone ■, W. Afr. 50 G3 9 0N 12 0W
Sierra Madre, Mexico 87 D6 16 0N 93 0W
Sierra Mojada, Mexico 86 B4 27 19N 103 42W
Sierra Nevada, Spain 19 D4 37 3N 3 15W
Sierra Nevada, U.S.A. 84 H8 39 0N 120 30W
Sierra Vista, U.S.A. 83 L8 31 33N 110 18W
Sierraville, U.S.A. 84 F6 39 36N 120 22W
Sífnos, Greece 21 F11 37 0N 24 45 E
Sifton, Canada 73 C8 51 21N 100 8W
Sifton Pass, Canada 72 B3 57 52N 126 15W
Sighetu-Marmaţiei, Romania 17 E12 47 57N 23 52 E
Sighişoara, Romania 17 E13 46 12N 24 50 E
Sigli, Indonesia 36 C1 5 25N 96 0 E
Siglufjörður, Iceland 8 C4 66 12N 18 55W
Signal, U.S.A. 85 L13 34 30N 113 38W
Signal Pk., U.S.A. 85 M12 33 20N 114 2W
Sigsig, Ecuador 92 D3 3 0S 78 50W
Sigüenza, Spain 19 B4 41 3N 2 40W
Siguiri, Guinea 50 F4 11 31N 9 10W
Sigulda, Latvia 9 H21 57 10N 24 55 E
Sihanoukville = Kampong Saom, Cambodia 39 G4 10 38N 103 30 E
Sihora, India 43 H9 23 29N 80 6 E
Siikajoki →, Finland 8 D21 64 50N 24 43 E
Siilinjärvi, Finland 8 E22 63 4N 27 39 E
Sijarira Ra. = Chizarira, Zimbabwe 55 F2 17 36S 27 45 E
Sika, India 42 H3 22 26N 69 47 E
Sikao, Thailand 39 J2 7 34N 99 21 E
Sikar, India 42 F6 27 33N 75 10 E
Sikasso, Mali 50 F4 11 18N 5 35W
Sikeston, U.S.A. 81 G10 36 53N 89 35W
Sikhote Alin, Khrebet, Russia 27 E14 45 0N 136 0 E
Sikhote Alin Ra. = Sikhote Alin, Khrebet, Russia 27 E14 45 0N 136 0 E
Síkinos, Greece 21 F11 36 40N 25 8 E
Sikkani Chief →, Canada 72 B4 57 47N 122 15W
Sikkim □, India 41 F16 27 50N 88 30 E
Sikotu-Ko, Japan 30 C10 42 45N 141 25 E
Sil →, Spain 19 A2 42 27N 7 43W
Silacayoapan, Mexico 87 D5 17 30N 98 9W
Silawad, India 42 J6 21 54N 74 54 E
Silchar, India 41 G18 24 49N 92 48 E
Siler City, U.S.A. 77 H6 35 44N 79 28W
Silesia = Śląsk, Poland 16 C9 51 0N 16 30 E
Silgarhi Doti, Nepal 43 E9 29 15N 81 0 E
Silghat, India 41 F18 26 35N 93 0 E
Silifke, Turkey 25 G5 36 22N 33 58 E
Siliguri = Shiliguri, India 41 F16 26 45N 88 25 E
Siling Co, China 32 C3 31 50N 89 20 E
Silistra, Bulgaria 21 B12 44 6N 27 19 E
Silivri, Turkey 21 D13 41 4N 28 14 E
Siljan, Sweden 9 F16 60 55N 14 45 E
Silkeborg, Denmark 9 H13 56 10N 9 32 E
Silkwood, Australia 62 B4 17 45S 146 2 E
Sillajhuay, Cordillera, Chile 92 G5 19 46S 68 40W
Sillamäe, Estonia 9 G22 59 24N 27 45 E
Silloth, U.K. 10 C4 54 52N 3 23W
Siloam Springs, U.S.A. 81 G7 36 11N 94 32W
Silsbee, U.S.A. 81 K7 30 21N 94 11W
Šilutė, Lithuania 9 J19 55 21N 21 33 E
Silva Porto = Kuito, Angola 53 G3 12 22S 16 55 E
Silvani, India 43 H8 23 18N 78 25 E
Silver City, U.S.A. 83 K9 32 46N 108 17W
Silver Cr. →, U.S.A. 82 E4 43 16N 119 13W
Silver Creek, U.S.A. 78 D5 42 33N 79 10W
Silver L., U.S.A. 84 G6 38 39N 120 6W
Silver Lake, Calif., U.S.A. 85 K10 35 21N 116 7W
Silver Lake, Oreg., U.S.A. 82 E3 43 8N 121 3W
Silverton, Colo., U.S.A. 83 H10 37 49N 107 40W
Silverton, Tex., U.S.A. 81 H4 34 28N 101 19W
Silvies →, U.S.A. 82 E4 43 34N 119 2W
Simaltala, India 43 G12 24 43N 86 33 E
Simanggang = Bandar Sri Aman, Malaysia 36 D4 1 15N 111 32 E
Simard, L., Canada 70 C4 47 40N 78 40W
Simav, Turkey 21 E13 39 4N 28 58 E
Simba, Tanzania 54 C4 2 10S 37 36 E
Simbirsk, Russia 24 D8 54 20N 48 25 E
Simbo, Tanzania 54 C2 4 51S 29 41 E
Simcoe, Canada 78 D4 42 50N 80 20W
Simcoe, L., Canada 78 B5 44 25N 79 20W
Simdega, India 43 H11 22 37N 84 31 E
Simeria, Romania 17 F12 45 51N 23 1 E
Simeulue, Indonesia 36 D1 2 45N 95 45 E
Simferopol, Ukraine 25 F5 44 55N 34 3 E
Sími, Greece 21 F12 36 35N 27 50 E
Simi Valley, U.S.A. 85 L8 34 16N 118 47W
Simikot, Nepal 43 E9 30 0N 81 50 E
Simla, India 42 D7 31 2N 77 9 E
Simmie, Canada 73 D7 49 56N 108 6W
Simmler, U.S.A. 85 K7 35 21N 119 59W
Simojoki →, Finland 8 D21 65 35N 25 1 E
Simojovel, Mexico 87 D6 17 12N 92 38W
Simonette →, Canada 72 B5 55 9N 118 15W
Simonstown, S. Africa 56 E2 34 14S 18 26 E
Simplonpass, Switz. 18 C8 46 15N 8 3 E
Simpson Desert, Australia 62 D2 25 0S 137 0 E
Simpson Pen., Canada 69 B11 68 34N 88 45W
Simpungdong, N. Korea 35 D15 40 56N 129 29 E
Simrishamn, Sweden 9 J16 55 33N 14 22 E
Simsbury, U.S.A. 79 E12 41 53N 72 48W
Simushir, Ostrov, Russia 27 E16 46 50N 152 30 E
Sin Cowe I., S. China Sea 36 C4 9 53N 114 19 E
Sinabang, Indonesia 36 D1 2 30N 96 24 E
Sinadogo, Somali Rep. 46 F4 5 50N 47 0 E
Sinai = Es Sînâ', Egypt 47 F3 29 0N 34 0 E
Sinai, Mt. = Mûsa, Gebel, Egypt 44 D2 28 33N 33 59 E
Sinai Peninsula, Egypt 47 F3 29 30N 34 0 E
Sinaloa □, Mexico 86 C3 25 0N 107 30W
Sinaloa de Leyva, Mexico 86 B3 25 50N 108 20W
Sinarádhes, Greece 23 A3 39 34N 19 51 E
Sincelejo, Colombia 92 B3 9 18N 75 24W
Sinch'ang, N. Korea 35 D15 40 7N 128 28 E
Sinchang-ni, N. Korea 35 E14 39 24N 126 8 E
Sinclair, U.S.A. 82 F10 41 47N 107 7W
Sinclair Mills, Canada 72 C4 54 5N 121 40W
Sinclair's B., U.K. 12 C5 58 31N 3 5W
Sinclairville, U.S.A. 78 D5 42 16N 79 16W
Sincorá, Serra do, Brazil 93 F10 13 30S 41 0W
Sind, Pakistan 42 G3 26 0N 68 30 E
Sind □, Pakistan 42 G3 26 0N 69 0 E
Sind →, Jammu & Kashmir, India 43 B6 34 18N 74 45 E
Sind →, Mad. P., India 43 F8 26 26N 79 13 E
Sind Sagar Doab, Pakistan 42 D4 32 0N 71 30 E
Sindangan, Phil. 37 C6 8 10N 123 5 E
Sindangbarang, Indonesia 37 G12 7 27S 107 1 E
Sinde, Zambia 55 F2 17 28S 25 51 E
Sindh = Sind □, Pakistan 42 G3 26 0N 69 0 E
Sindri, India 43 H12 23 45N 86 42 E
Sines, Portugal 19 D1 37 56N 8 51W
Sines, C. de, Portugal 19 D1 37 58N 8 53W
Sineu, Spain 22 B10 39 38N 3 1 E
Sing Buri, Thailand 38 E3 14 53N 100 25 E
Singa, Sudan 51 F12 13 10N 33 57 E
Singapore ■, Asia 39 M4 1 17N 103 51 E
Singapore, Straits of, Asia 39 M5 1 15N 104 0 E
Singaraja, Indonesia 36 F5 8 7S 115 6 E
Singida, Tanzania 54 C3 4 49S 34 48 E
Singida □, Tanzania 54 D3 6 0S 34 30 E
Singitikós Kólpos, Greece 21 D11 40 6N 24 0 E
Singkaling Hkamti, Burma 41 G19 26 0N 95 39 E
Singkang, Indonesia 37 E6 4 8S 120 1 E
Singkawang, Indonesia 36 D3 1 0N 108 57 E
Singkep, Indonesia 36 E2 0 30S 104 25 E
Singleton, Australia 63 E5 32 33S 151 0 E
Singleton, Mt., N. Terr., Australia 60 D5 22 0S 130 46 E
Singleton, Mt., W. Austral., Australia 61 E2 29 27S 117 15 E
Singoli, India 42 G6 25 0N 75 22 E
Singora = Songkhla, Thailand 39 J3 7 13N 100 37 E
Singosan, N. Korea 35 E14 38 52N 127 25 E
Sinhung, N. Korea 35 D14 40 11N 127 34 E
Sînî □, Egypt 47 F3 30 0N 34 0 E
Sinjai, Indonesia 37 F6 5 7S 120 20 E
Sinjār, Iraq 44 B4 36 19N 41 52 E
Sinkat, Sudan 51 E13 18 55N 36 49 E
Sinkiang Uighur = Xinjiang Uygur Zizhiqu □, China 32 C3 42 0N 86 0 E
Sinmak, N. Korea 35 E14 38 25N 126 14 E
Sinnamary, Fr. Guiana 93 B8 5 25N 53 0W
Sinni →, Italy 20 D7 40 8N 16 41 E
Sinop, Turkey 25 F6 42 1N 35 11 E
Sinor, India 42 J5 21 55N 73 20 E
Sinp'o, N. Korea 35 E15 40 0N 128 13 E
Sinsk, Russia 27 C13 61 8N 126 48 E
Sintang, Indonesia 36 D4 0 5N 111 35 E
Sinton, U.S.A. 81 L6 28 2N 97 31W
Sintra, Portugal 19 C1 38 47N 9 25W
Sinŭiju, N. Korea 35 D13 40 5N 124 24 E
Siocon, Phil. 37 C6 7 40N 122 10 E
Siófok, Hungary 17 E10 46 54N 18 3 E
Sion, Switz. 18 C7 46 14N 7 20 E
Sion Mills, U.K. 13 B4 54 48N 7 29W
Sioux City, U.S.A. 80 D6 42 30N 96 24W
Sioux Falls, U.S.A. 80 D6 43 33N 96 44W
Sioux Lookout, Canada 70 B1 50 10N 91 50W
Sioux Narrows, Canada 73 D10 49 25N 94 10W
Siping, China 35 C13 43 8N 124 21 E
Sipiwesk L., Canada 73 B9 55 5N 97 35W
Sipra →, India 42 H6 23 55N 75 28 E
Sipura, Indonesia 36 E1 2 18S 99 40 E
Siquia →, Nic. 88 D3 12 10N 84 20W
Siquijor, Phil. 37 C6 9 12N 123 35 E
Siquirres, Costa Rica 88 D3 10 6N 83 30W
Şīr Banī Yās, U.A.E. 45 E7 24 19N 52 37 E
Sir Edward Pellew Group, Australia 62 B2 15 40S 137 10 E
Sir Graham Moore Is., Australia 60 B4 13 53S 126 34 E
Sir James MacBrien, Mt., Canada 68 B7 62 8N 127 40W
Sira →, Norway 9 G12 58 23N 6 34 E
Siracusa, Italy 20 F6 37 4N 15 17 E
Sirajganj, Bangla. 43 G13 24 25N 89 47 E
Sirathu, India 43 G9 25 39N 81 19 E
Sīrdān, Iran 45 B6 36 39N 49 12 E
Sirdaryo = Syrdarya →, Kazakstan 26 E7 46 3N 61 0 E
Siren, U.S.A. 80 C8 45 47N 92 24W
Sirer, Spain 22 C7 38 56N 1 22 E
Siret →, Romania 17 F14 45 24N 28 1 E
Sirghāyā, Syria 47 B5 33 51N 36 8 E
Sirmaur, India 43 G9 24 51N 81 23 E
Sirohi, India 42 G5 24 52N 72 53 E
Sironj, India 42 G7 24 5N 77 39 E
Síros, Greece 21 F11 37 28N 24 57 E
Sirretta Pk., U.S.A. 85 K8 35 56N 118 19W
Sirrī, Iran 45 E7 25 55N 54 32 E
Sirsa, India 42 E6 29 33N 75 4 E
Sirsa →, India 43 F8 26 51N 79 4 E
Sisak, Croatia 16 F9 45 30N 16 21 E
Sisaket, Thailand 38 E5 15 8N 104 23 E
Sishen, S. Africa 56 D3 27 47S 22 59 E
Sishui, Henan, China 34 G7 34 48N 113 15 E
Sishui, Shandong, China 35 G9 35 42N 117 18 E
Sisipuk L., Canada 73 B8 55 45N 101 50W
Sisophon, Cambodia 38 F4 13 38N 102 59 E
Sisseton, U.S.A. 80 C6 45 40N 97 3W
Sīstān, Asia 45 D9 30 50N 61 0 E
Sīstān, Daryācheh-ye, Iran 45 D9 31 0N 61 0 E
Sīstān va Balūchestān □, Iran 45 E9 27 0N 62 0 E
Sisters, U.S.A. 82 D3 44 18N 121 33W
Siswa Bazar, India 43 F10 27 9N 83 46 E
Sitamarhi, India 43 F11 26 37N 85 30 E
Sitampiky, Madag. 57 B8 16 41S 46 6 E
Sitapur, India 43 F9 27 38N 80 45 E
Siteki, Swaziland 57 D5 26 32S 31 58 E
Sitges, Spain 19 B6 41 17N 1 47 E
Sitia, Greece 23 D8 35 13N 26 6 E
Sitka, U.S.A. 72 B1 57 3N 135 20W
Sitoti, Botswana 56 C3 23 15S 23 40 E
Sittang Myit →, Burma 41 L20 17 20N 96 45 E
Sittard, Neths. 15 C5 51 0N 5 52 E
Sittingbourne, U.K. 11 F8 51 21N 0 45 E
Sittoung = Sittang Myit →, Burma 41 L20 17 20N 96 45 E
Sittwe, Burma 41 J18 20 18N 92 45 E
Situbondo, Indonesia 37 G16 7 42S 114 0 E
Siuna, Nic. 88 D3 13 37N 84 45W
Siuri, India 43 H12 23 50N 87 34 E
Sīvand, Iran 45 D7 30 5N 52 55 E
Sivas, Turkey 25 G6 39 43N 36 58 E
Siverek, Turkey 44 B3 37 50N 39 19 E
Sivomaskinskiy, Russia 24 A11 66 40N 62 35 E
Sivrihisar, Turkey 25 G5 39 30N 31 35 E
Sîwa, Egypt 51 C11 29 11N 25 31 E
Sîwa, El Wâhât es, Egypt 48 D6 29 10N 25 30 E
Siwa Oasis = Sîwa, El Wâhât es, Egypt 48 D6 29 10N 25 30 E
Siwalik Range, Nepal 43 F10 28 0N 83 0 E
Siwan, India 43 F11 26 13N 84 21 E
Siwana, India 42 G5 25 38N 72 25 E
Sixmilebridge, Ireland 13 D3 52 44N 8 46W
Sixth Cataract, Sudan 51 E12 16 20N 32 42 E
Siziwang Qi, China 34 D6 41 25N 111 40 E
Sjælland, Denmark 9 J14 55 30N 11 30 E
Sjumen = Shumen, Bulgaria 21 C12 43 18N 26 55 E
Skadarsko Jezero, Montenegro, Yug. 21 C8 42 10N 19 20 E
Skaftafell, Iceland 8 D5 64 1N 17 0W
Skagafjörður, Iceland 8 D4 65 54N 19 35W
Skagastølstindane, Norway 9 F12 61 28N 7 52 E
Skagaströnd, Iceland 8 D3 65 50N 20 19W
Skagen, Denmark 9 H14 57 43N 10 35 E
Skagerrak, Denmark 9 H13 57 30N 9 0 E
Skagit →, U.S.A. 84 B4 48 23N 122 22W
Skagway, U.S.A. 68 C6 59 28N 135 19W
Skala-Podilska, Ukraine 17 D14 48 50N 26 15 E
Skala Podolskaya = Skala-Podilska, Ukraine 17 D14 48 50N 26 15 E
Skalat, Ukraine 17 D13 49 23N 25 55 E
Skåne, Sweden 9 J15 55 59N 13 30 E
Skaneateles, U.S.A. 79 D8 42 57N 76 26W
Skaneateles L., U.S.A. 79 D8 42 51N 76 22W
Skara, Sweden 9 G15 58 25N 13 30 E
Skardu, Pakistan 43 B6 35 20N 75 44 E
Skarżysko-Kamienna, Poland 17 C11 51 7N 20 52 E
Skeena →, Canada 72 C2 54 9N 130 5W
Skeena Mts., Canada 72 B3 56 40N 128 30W
Skegness, U.K. 10 D8 53 9N 0 20 E
Skeldon, Guyana 92 B7 5 55N 57 20W
Skellefte älv →, Sweden 8 D19 64 45N 21 10 E
Skellefteå, Sweden 8 D19 64 45N 20 50 E
Skelleftehamn, Sweden 8 D19 64 40N 21 9 E
Skerries, The, U.K. 10 D3 53 25N 4 36W
Ski, Norway 9 G14 59 43N 10 52 E
Skíathos, Greece 21 E10 39 12N 23 30 E
Skibbereen, Ireland 13 E2 51 33N 9 16W
Skiddaw, U.K. 10 C4 54 39N 3 9W
Skidegate, Canada 72 C2 53 15N 132 1W
Skien, Norway 9 G13 59 12N 9 35 E
Skierniewice, Poland 17 C11 51 58N 20 10 E
Skikda, Algeria 50 A7 36 50N 6 58 E
Skilloura, Cyprus 23 D12 35 14N 33 10 E
Skipton, U.K. 10 D5 53 58N 2 3W
Skirmish Pt., Australia 62 A1 11 59S 134 17 E
Skíros, Greece 21 E11 38 55N 24 34 E
Skive, Denmark 9 H13 56 33N 9 2 E
Skjálfandafljót →, Iceland 8 D5 65 59N 17 25W
Skjálfandi, Iceland 8 C5 66 5N 17 30W
Skoghall, Sweden 9 G15 59 20N 13 30 E
Skole, Ukraine 17 D12 49 3N 23 30 E
Skópelos, Greece 21 E10 39 9N 23 47 E
Skopí, Greece 23 D8 35 11N 26 2 E
Skopje, Macedonia 21 C9 42 1N 21 26 E
Skövde, Sweden 9 G15 58 24N 13 50 E
Skovorodino, Russia 27 D13 54 0N 124 0 E
Skowhegan, U.S.A. 77 C11 44 46N 69 43W
Skull, Ireland 13 E2 51 32N 9 34W
Skunk →, U.S.A. 80 E9 40 42N 91 7W
Skuodas, Lithuania 9 H19 56 16N 21 33 E
Skvyra, Ukraine 17 D15 49 44N 29 40 E
Skye, U.K. 12 D2 57 15N 6 10W
Skykomish, U.S.A. 82 C3 47 42N 121 22W
Skyros = Skíros, Greece 21 E11 38 55N 24 34 E
Slættaratindur, Færoe Is. 8 E9 62 18N 7 1W
Slagelse, Denmark 9 J14 55 23N 11 19 E
Slamet, Indonesia 37 G13 7 16S 109 8 E
Slaney →, Ireland 13 D5 52 26N 6 33W
Slangberge, S. Africa 56 E3 31 32S 20 48 E
Śląsk, Poland 16 C9 51 0N 16 30 E
Slate Is., Canada 70 C2 48 40N 87 0W
Slatina, Romania 17 F13 44 28N 24 22 E
Slatington, U.S.A. 79 F9 40 45N 75 37W
Slaton, U.S.A. 81 J4 33 26N 101 39W
Slave →, Canada 72 A6 61 18N 113 39W
Slave Coast, W. Afr. 50 G6 6 0N 2 30 E
Slave Lake, Canada 72 B6 55 17N 114 43W
Slave Pt., Canada 72 A5 61 11N 115 56W
Slavgorod, Russia 26 D8 53 1N 78 37 E
Slavonski Brod, Croatia 21 B8 45 11N 18 1 E
Slavuta, Ukraine 17 C14 50 15N 27 2 E
Slavyanka, Russia 30 C5 42 53N 131 21 E
Slavyansk = Slovyansk, Ukraine 25 E6 48 55N 37 36 E
Slawharad, Belarus 17 B16 53 27N 31 0 E
Sleaford, U.K. 10 D7 53 0N 0 24W
Sleaford B., Australia 63 E2 34 55S 135 45 E
Sleat, Sd. of, U.K. 12 D3 57 5N 5 47W
Sleeper Is., Canada 69 C11 58 30N 81 0W
Sleepy Eye, U.S.A. 80 C7 44 18N 94 43W
Slemon L., Canada 72 A5 63 13N 116 4W
Slide Mt., U.S.A. 79 E10 42 0N 74 25W
Slidell, U.S.A. 81 K10 30 17N 89 47W
Sliema, Malta 23 D2 35 55N 14 30 E
Slieve Aughty, Ireland 13 C3 53 4N 8 30W
Slieve Bloom, Ireland 13 C4 53 4N 7 40W
Slieve Donard, U.K. 13 B6 54 11N 5 55W
Slieve Gamph, Ireland 13 B3 54 6N 9 0W
Slieve Gullion, U.K. 13 B5 54 7N 6 26W
Slieve Mish, Ireland 13 D2 52 12N 9 50W
Slievenamon, Ireland 13 D4 52 25N 7 34W
Sligeach = Sligo, Ireland 13 B3 54 16N 8 28W
Sligo, Ireland 13 B3 54 16N 8 28W
Sligo, U.S.A. 78 E5 41 6N 79 29W
Sligo □, Ireland 13 B3 54 8N 8 42W
Sligo B., Ireland 13 B3 54 18N 8 40W
Slippery Rock, U.S.A. 78 E4 41 4N 80 3W
Slite, Sweden 9 H18 57 42N 18 48 E
Sliven, Bulgaria 21 C12 42 42N 26 19 E
Sloan, U.S.A. 85 K11 35 57N 115 13W
Sloansville, U.S.A. 79 D10 42 45N 74 22W
Slobodskoy, Russia 24 C9 58 40N 50 6 E
Slobozia, Romania 17 F14 44 34N 27 23 E
Slocan, Canada 72 D5 49 48N 117 28W
Slonim, Belarus 17 B13 53 4N 25 19 E
Slough, U.K. 11 F7 51 30N 0 36W
Slough □, U.K. 11 F7 51 30N 0 36W
Sloughhouse, U.S.A. 84 G5 38 26N 121 12W
Slovak Rep. ■, Europe 17 D10 48 30N 20 0 E
Slovakia = Slovak Rep. ■, Europe 17 D10 48 30N 20 0 E
Slovakian Ore Mts. = Slovenské Rudohorie, Slovak Rep. 17 D10 48 45N 20 0 E
Slovenia ■, Europe 16 F8 45 58N 14 30 E
Slovenija = Slovenia ■, Europe 16 F8 45 58N 14 30 E
Slovenské Rudohorie, Slovak Rep. 17 D10 48 45N 20 0 E
Slovyansk, Ukraine 25 E6 48 55N 37 36 E
Sluch →, Ukraine 17 C14 51 37N 26 38 E
Sluis, Neths. 15 C3 51 18N 3 23 E
Słupsk, Poland 17 A9 54 30N 17 3 E
Slurry, S. Africa 56 D4 25 49S 25 42 E
Slutsk, Belarus 17 B14 53 2N 27 31 E
Slyne Hd., Ireland 13 C1 53 25N 10 10W
Slyudyanka, Russia 27 D11 51 40N 103 40 E
Småland, Sweden 9 H16 57 15N 15 25 E
Smalltree L., Canada 73 A8 61 0N 105 0W
Smallwood Res., Canada 71 B7 54 0N 64 0W
Smarhon, Belarus 17 A14 54 20N 26 24 E
Smartt Syndicate Dam, S. Africa 56 E3 30 45S 23 10 E
Smartville, U.S.A. 84 F5 39 13N 121 18W
Smeaton, Canada 73 C8 53 30N 104 49W
Smederevo, Serbia, Yug. 21 B9 44 40N 20 57 E
Smerwick Harbour, Ireland 13 D1 52 12N 10 23W
Smethport, U.S.A. 78 E6 41 49N 78 27W
Smidovich, Russia 27 E14 48 36N 133 49 E
Smith, Canada 72 B6 55 10N 114 0W
Smith Center, U.S.A. 80 F5 39 47N 98 47W
Smith Sund, Greenland 4 B4 78 30N 74 0W
Smithburne →, Australia 62 B3 17 3S 140 57 E
Smithers, Canada 72 C3 54 45N 127 10W
Smithfield, S. Africa 57 E4 30 9S 26 30 E
Smithfield, N.C., U.S.A. 77 H6 35 31N 78 21W
Smithfield, Utah, U.S.A. 82 F8 41 50N 111 50W
Smiths Falls, Canada 79 B9 44 55N 76 0W
Smithton, Australia 62 G4 40 53S 145 6 E
Smithville, Canada 78 C5 43 6N 79 33W
Smithville, U.S.A. 81 K6 30 1N 97 10W
Smoky →, Canada 72 B5 56 10N 117 21W
Smoky Bay, Australia 63 E1 32 22S 134 13 E
Smoky Hill →, U.S.A. 80 F6 39 4N 96 48W
Smoky Hills, U.S.A. 80 F5 39 15N 99 30W
Smoky Lake, Canada 72 C6 54 10N 112 30W
Smøla, Norway 8 E13 63 23N 8 3 E
Smolensk, Russia 24 D5 54 45N 32 5 E
Smolikas, Óros, Greece 21 D9 40 9N 20 58 E
Smolyan, Bulgaria 21 D11 41 36N 24 38 E
Smooth Rock Falls, Canada 70 C3 49 17N 81 37W
Smoothstone L., Canada 73 C7 54 40N 106 50W
Smorgon = Smarhon, Belarus 17 A14 54 20N 26 24 E
Smyrna = İzmir, Turkey 21 E12 38 25N 27 8 E
Smyrna, U.S.A. 76 F8 39 18N 75 36W
Snæfell, Iceland 8 D6 64 48N 15 34W
Snaefell, U.K. 10 C3 54 16N 4 27W
Snæfellsjökull, Iceland 8 D2 64 49N 23 46W
Snake →, U.S.A. 82 C4 46 12N 119 2W
Snake I., Australia 63 F4 38 47S 146 33 E
Snake Range, U.S.A. 82 G6 39 0N 114 20W
Snake River Plain, U.S.A. 82 E7 42 50N 114 0W
Snåsavatnet, Norway 8 D14 64 12N 12 0 E
Sneek, Neths. 15 A5 53 2N 5 40 E
Sneeuberge, S. Africa 56 E3 31 46S 24 20 E
Snelling, U.S.A. 84 H6 37 31N 120 26W
Sněžka, Europe 16 C8 50 41N 15 50 E
Snizort, L., U.K. 12 D2 57 33N 6 28W
Snøhetta, Norway 9 E13 62 19N 9 16 E
Snohomish, U.S.A. 84 C4 47 55N 122 6W
Snoul, Cambodia 39 F6 12 4N 106 26 E
Snow Hill, U.S.A. 76 F8 38 11N 75 24W
Snow Lake, Canada 73 C8 54 52N 100 3W
Snow Mt., Calif., U.S.A. 84 F4 39 23N 122 45W
Snow Mt., Maine, U.S.A. 79 A14 45 18N 70 48W
Snow Shoe, U.S.A. 78 E7 41 2N 77 57W
Snowbird L., Canada 73 A8 60 45N 103 0W
Snowdon, U.K. 10 D3 53 4N 4 5W
Snowdrift →, Canada 73 A6 62 24N 110 44W
Snowflake, U.S.A. 83 J8 34 30N 110 5W
Snowshoe Pk., U.S.A. 82 B6 48 13N 115 41W
Snowtown, Australia 63 E2 33 46S 138 14 E
Snowville, U.S.A. 82 F7 41 58N 112 43W
Snowy →, Australia 63 F4 37 46S 148 30 E
Snowy Mt., U.S.A. 79 C10 43 42N 74 23W
Snowy Mts., Australia 63 F4 36 30S 148 20 E
Snug Corner, Bahamas 89 B5 22 33N 73 52W
Snyatyn, Ukraine 17 D13 48 27N 25 38 E
Snyder, Okla., U.S.A. 81 H5 34 40N 98 57W
Snyder, Tex., U.S.A. 81 J4 32 44N 100 55W
Soahanina, Madag. 57 B7 18 42S 44 13 E
Soalala, Madag. 57 B8 16 6S 45 20 E
Soaloka, Madag. 57 B8 18 32S 45 15 E
Soamanonga, Madag. 57 C7 23 52S 44 47 E
Soan →, Pakistan 42 C4 33 1N 71 44 E
Soanierana-Ivongo, Madag. 57 B8 16 55S 49 35 E
Soanindraniny, Madag. 57 B8 19 54S 47 14 E
Soavina, Madag. 57 C8 20 23S 46 56 E
Soavinandriana, Madag. 57 B8 19 9S 46 45 E
Sobat, Nahr →, Sudan 51 G12 9 22N 31 33 E
Sobhapur, India 42 H8 22 47N 78 17 E
Sobradinho, Reprêsa de, Brazil 93 E10 9 30S 42 0 E
Sobral, Brazil 93 D10 3 50S 40 20W
Soc Giang, Vietnam 38 A6 22 54N 106 1 E
Soc Trang, Vietnam 39 H5 9 37N 105 50 E
Socastee, U.S.A. 77 J6 33 41N 79 1W
Soch'e = Shache, China 32 C2 38 20N 77 10 E
Sochi, Russia 25 F6 43 35N 39 40 E
Société, Is. de la, Pac. Oc. 65 J12 17 0S 151 0W
Society Is. = Société, Is. de la, Pac. Oc. 65 J12 17 0S 151 0W
Socompa, Portezuelo de, Chile 94 A2 24 27S 68 18W
Socorro, N. Mex., U.S.A. 83 J10 34 4N 106 54W
Socorro, Tex., U.S.A. 83 L10 31 39N 106 18W
Socorro, I., Mexico 86 D2 18 45N 110 58W
Socotra, Yemen 46 E5 12 30N 54 0 E
Soda L., U.S.A. 83 J5 35 10N 116 4W
Soda Plains, India 43 B8 35 30N 79 0 E
Soda Springs, U.S.A. 82 E8 42 39N 111 36W
Sodankylä, Finland 8 C22 67 29N 26 40 E
Soddy-Daisy, U.S.A. 77 H3 35 17N 85 10W
Söderhamn, Sweden 9 F17 61 18N 17 10 E

Söderköping

Söderköping, *Sweden* **9 G17** 58 31N 16 20 E
Södermanland, *Sweden* **9 G17** 58 56N 16 55 E
Södertälje, *Sweden* **9 G17** 59 12N 17 39 E
Sodiri, *Sudan* **51 F11** 14 27N 29 0 E
Sodus, *U.S.A.* **78 C7** 43 14N 77 4W
Soekmekaar, *S. Africa* **57 C4** 23 30S 29 55 E
Soest, *Neths.* **15 B5** 52 9N 5 19 E
Sofala □, *Mozam.* **57 B5** 19 30S 34 30 E
Sofia = Sofiya, *Bulgaria* **21 C10** 42 45N 23 20 E
Sofia →, *Madag.* **57 B8** 15 27S 47 23 E
Sofiya, *Bulgaria* **21 C10** 42 45N 23 20 E
Sōfu-Gan, *Japan* **31 K10** 29 49N 140 21 E
Sogamoso, *Colombia* **92 B4** 5 43N 72 56W
Sogār, *Iran* **45 E8** 25 53N 58 6 E
Sogndalsfjøra, *Norway* **9 F12** 61 14N 7 5 E
Søgne, *Norway* **9 G12** 58 5N 7 48 E
Sognefjorden, *Norway* **9 F11** 61 10N 5 50 E
Sŏgwipo, *S. Korea* **35 H14** 33 13N 126 34 E
Soh, *Iran* **45 C6** 33 26N 51 27 E
Sohâg, *Egypt* **51 C12** 26 33N 31 43 E
Sohagpur, *India* **42 H8** 22 42N 78 12 E
Sŏhori, *N. Korea* **35 D15** 40 7N 128 23 E
Soignies, *Belgium* **15 D4** 50 35N 4 5 E
Soissons, *France* **18 B5** 49 25N 3 19 E
Sōja, *Japan* **31 G6** 34 40N 133 45 E
Sojat, *India* **42 G5** 25 55N 73 45 E
Sokal, *Ukraine* **17 C13** 50 31N 24 15 E
Söke, *Turkey* **21 F12** 37 48N 27 28 E
Sokelo, *Dem. Rep. of the Congo* **55 D1** 9 55S 24 36 E
Sokhumi, *Georgia* **25 F7** 43 0N 41 0 E
Sokodé, *Togo* **50 G6** 9 0N 1 11 E
Sokol, *Russia* **24 C7** 59 30N 40 5 E
Sokółka, *Poland* **17 B12** 53 25N 23 30 E
Sokołów Podlaski, *Poland* **17 B12** 52 25N 22 15 E
Sokoto, *Nigeria* **50 F7** 13 2N 5 16 E
Sol Iletsk, *Russia* **24 D10** 51 10N 55 0 E
Solai, *Kenya* **54 B4** 0 2N 36 12 E
Solan, *India* **42 D7** 30 55N 77 7 E
Solano, *Phil.* **37 A6** 16 31N 121 15 E
Solapur, *India* **40 L9** 17 43N 75 56 E
Soldotna, *U.S.A.* **68 B4** 60 29N 151 3W
Soléa, *Cyprus* **23 D12** 35 5N 33 4 E
Soledad, *Colombia* **92 A4** 10 55N 74 46W
Soledad, *U.S.A.* **84 J5** 36 26N 121 20W
Soledad, *Venezuela* **92 B6** 8 10N 63 34W
Solent, The, *U.K.* **11 G6** 50 45N 1 25W
Solfonn, *Norway* **9 F12** 60 2N 6 57 E
Solhan, *Turkey* **44 B4** 38 57N 41 3 E
Soligalich, *Russia* **24 C7** 59 5N 42 10 E
Soligorsk = Salihorsk, *Belarus* **17 B14** 52 51N 27 27 E
Solihull, *U.K.* **11 E6** 52 26N 1 47W
Solikamsk, *Russia* **24 C10** 59 38N 56 50 E
Solila, *Madag.* **57 C8** 21 25S 46 37 E
Solimões = Amazonas →, *S. Amer.* **93 D9** 0 5S 50 0W
Solingen, *Germany* **16 C4** 51 10N 7 5 E
Sollefteå, *Sweden* **8 E17** 63 12N 17 20 E
Sóller, *Spain* **22 B9** 39 46N 2 43 E
Solo →, *Indonesia* **37 G15** 6 47S 112 22 E
Sologne, *France* **18 C4** 47 40N 1 45 E
Solok, *Indonesia* **36 E2** 0 45S 100 40 E
Sololá, *Guatemala* **88 D1** 14 49N 91 10W
Solomon, N. Fork →, *U.S.A.* **80 F5** 39 29N 98 26W
Solomon, S. Fork →, *U.S.A.* **80 F5** 39 25N 99 12W
Solomon Is. ■, *Pac. Oc.* **64 H7** 6 0S 155 0 E
Solon, *China* **33 B7** 46 32N 121 10 E
Solon Springs, *U.S.A.* **80 B9** 46 22N 91 49W
Solor, *Indonesia* **37 F6** 8 27S 123 0 E
Solothurn, *Switz.* **18 C7** 47 13N 7 32 E
Šolta, *Croatia* **20 C7** 43 24N 16 15 E
Solṭānābād, *Khorāsān, Iran* **45 C8** 34 13N 59 58 E
Solṭānābād, *Khorāsān, Iran* **45 B8** 36 29N 58 5 E
Solunska Glava, *Macedonia* **21 D9** 41 44N 21 31 E
Solvang, *U.S.A.* **85 L6** 34 36N 120 8W
Solvay, *U.S.A.* **79 C8** 43 3N 76 13W
Sölvesborg, *Sweden* **9 H16** 56 5N 14 35 E
Solvychegodsk, *Russia* **24 B8** 61 21N 46 56 E
Solway Firth, *U.K.* **10 C4** 54 49N 3 35W
Solwezi, *Zambia* **55 E2** 12 11S 26 21 E
Sōma, *Japan* **30 F10** 37 40N 140 50 E
Soma, *Turkey* **21 E12** 39 10N 27 35 E
Somabhula, *Zimbabwe* **57 B4** 19 42S 29 40 E
Somali Pen., *Africa* **48 F8** 7 0N 46 0 E
Somali Rep. ■, *Africa* **46 F4** 7 0N 47 0 E
Somalia = Somali Rep. ■, *Africa* **46 F4** 7 0N 47 0 E
Sombor, *Serbia, Yug.* **21 B8** 45 46N 19 9 E
Sombra, *Canada* **78 D2** 42 43N 82 29W
Sombrerete, *Mexico* **86 C4** 23 40N 103 40W
Sombrero, *Anguilla* **89 C7** 18 37N 63 30W
Somdari, *India* **42 G5** 25 47N 72 38 E
Somers, *U.S.A.* **82 B6** 48 5N 114 13W
Somerset, *Ky., U.S.A.* **76 G3** 37 5N 84 36W
Somerset, *Mass., U.S.A.* **79 E13** 41 47N 71 8W
Somerset, *Pa., U.S.A.* **78 F5** 40 1N 79 5W
Somerset □, *U.K.* **11 F5** 51 9N 3 0W
Somerset East, *S. Africa* **56 E4** 32 42S 25 35 E
Somerset I., *Canada* **68 A10** 73 30N 93 0W
Somerset West, *S. Africa* **56 E2** 34 8S 18 50 E
Somersworth, *U.S.A.* **79 C14** 43 16N 70 52W
Somerton, *U.S.A.* **83 K6** 32 36N 114 43W
Somerville, *U.S.A.* **79 F10** 40 35N 74 38W
Someş →, *Romania* **17 D12** 47 49N 22 43 E
Somme →, *France* **18 A4** 50 11N 1 38 E
Somnath, *India* **42 J4** 20 53N 70 22 E
Somosierra, Puerto de, *Spain* **19 B4** 41 4N 3 35W
Somoto, *Nic.* **88 D2** 13 28N 86 37W
Somport, Puerto de, *Spain* **18 E3** 42 48N 0 31W
Son →, *India* **43 G11** 25 42N 84 52 E
Son Ha, *Vietnam* **38 E7** 15 3N 108 34 E
Son Hoa, *Vietnam* **38 F7** 13 2N 108 58 E
Son La, *Vietnam* **38 B4** 21 20N 103 50 E
Son Serra, *Spain* **22 B10** 39 43N 3 13 E
Son Tay, *Vietnam* **38 B5** 21 8N 105 30 E
Soná, *Panama* **88 E3** 8 0N 81 20W
Sonamarg, *India* **43 B6** 34 18N 75 21 E
Sonamukhi, *India* **43 H12** 23 18N 87 27 E
Sonar →, *India* **43 G8** 24 24N 79 56 E
Sŏnch'ŏn, *N. Korea* **35 E13** 39 48N 124 55 E
Sondags →, *S. Africa* **56 E4** 33 44S 25 51 E
Sondar, *India* **43 C6** 33 28N 75 56 E
Sønderborg, *Denmark* **9 J13** 54 55N 9 49 E
Sóndrio, *Italy* **18 C8** 46 10N 9 52 E
Sone, *Mozam.* **55 F3** 17 23S 34 55 E
Sonepur, *India* **41 J13** 20 55N 83 50 E
Song, *Thailand* **38 C3** 18 28N 100 11 E
Song Cau, *Vietnam* **38 F7** 13 27N 109 18 E
Song Xian, *China* **34 G7** 34 12N 112 8 E
Songch'ŏn, *N. Korea* **35 E14** 39 12N 126 15 E
Songea, *Tanzania* **55 E4** 10 40S 35 40 E
Songhua Hu, *China* **35 C14** 43 35N 126 50 E
Songhua Jiang →, *China* **33 B8** 47 45N 132 30 E
Songjin, *N. Korea* **35 D15** 40 40N 129 10 E
Songjŏng-ni, *S. Korea* **35 G14** 35 8N 126 47 E
Songkhla, *Thailand* **39 J3** 7 13N 100 37 E
Songnim, *N. Korea* **35 E13** 38 45N 125 39 E
Songo, *Mozam.* **53 H6** 15 34S 32 38 E
Songo, *Sudan* **51 G10** 9 47N 24 21 E
Songpan, *China* **32 C5** 32 40N 103 30 E
Songwe, *Dem. Rep. of the Congo* **54 C2** 3 20S 26 16 E
Songwe →, *Africa* **55 D3** 9 44S 33 58 E
Sonhat, *India* **43 H10** 23 29N 82 31 E
Sonid Youqi, *China* **34 C7** 42 45N 112 48 E
Sonipat, *India* **42 E7** 29 0N 77 5 E
Sonkach, *India* **42 H7** 22 59N 76 21 E
Sonmiani, *Pakistan* **42 G2** 25 25N 66 40 E
Sonmiani B., *Pakistan* **42 G2** 25 15N 66 30 E
Sono →, *Brazil* **93 E9** 9 58S 48 11W
Sonoma, *U.S.A.* **84 G4** 38 18N 122 28W
Sonora, *Calif., U.S.A.* **84 H6** 37 59N 120 23W
Sonora, *Tex., U.S.A.* **81 K4** 30 34N 100 39W
Sonora □, *Mexico* **86 B2** 29 0N 111 0W
Sonora →, *Mexico* **86 B2** 28 50N 111 33W
Sonoran Desert, *U.S.A.* **85 L12** 33 40N 114 15W
Sonoyta, *Mexico* **86 A2** 31 51N 112 50W
Sŏnsan, *S. Korea* **35 F15** 36 14N 128 17 E
Sonsonate, *El Salv.* **88 D2** 13 43N 89 44W
Soochow = Suzhou, *China* **33 C7** 31 19N 120 38 E
Sooke, *Canada* **84 B3** 48 13N 123 43W
Sop Hao, *Laos* **38 B5** 20 33N 104 27 E
Sop Prap, *Thailand* **38 D2** 17 53N 99 20 E
Sopi, *Indonesia* **37 D7** 2 34N 128 28 E
Sopot, *Poland* **17 A10** 54 27N 18 31 E
Sopron, *Hungary* **17 E9** 47 45N 16 32 E
Sopur, *India* **43 B6** 34 18N 74 27 E
Sør-Rondane, *Antarctica* **5 D4** 72 0S 25 0 E
Sorah, *Pakistan* **42 F3** 27 13N 68 56 E
Soraon, *India* **43 G9** 25 37N 81 51 E
Sorel, *Canada* **70 C5** 46 0N 73 10W
Sórgono, *Italy* **20 D3** 40 1N 9 6 E
Soria, *Spain* **19 B4** 41 43N 2 32W
Soriano, *Uruguay* **94 C4** 33 24S 58 19W
Sorkh, Kuh-e, *Iran* **45 C8** 35 40N 58 30 E
Soroca, *Moldova* **17 D15** 48 8N 28 12 E
Sorocaba, *Brazil* **95 A6** 23 31S 47 27W
Sorochinsk, *Russia* **24 D9** 52 26N 53 10 E
Soroki = Soroca, *Moldova* **17 D15** 48 8N 28 12 E
Sorong, *Indonesia* **37 E8** 0 55S 131 15 E
Soroni, *Greece* **23 C10** 36 21N 28 1 E
Soroti, *Uganda* **54 B3** 1 43N 33 35 E
Sørøya, *Norway* **8 A20** 70 40N 22 30 E
Sørøysundet, *Norway* **8 A20** 70 25N 23 0 E
Sorrell, *Australia* **62 G4** 42 47S 147 34 E
Sorsele, *Sweden* **8 D17** 65 31N 17 30 E
Sorsogon, *Phil.* **37 B6** 13 0N 124 0 E
Sortavala, *Russia* **24 B5** 61 42N 30 41 E
Sortland, *Norway* **8 B16** 68 42N 15 25 E
Sŏsan, *S. Korea* **35 F14** 36 47N 126 27 E
Soscumica, L., *Canada* **70 B4** 50 15N 77 27W
Sosnogorsk, *Russia* **24 B9** 63 37N 53 51 E
Sosnowiec, *Poland* **17 C10** 50 20N 19 10 E
Sossus Vlei, *Namibia* **56 C2** 24 40S 15 23 E
Sŏsura, *N. Korea* **35 C16** 42 16N 130 36 E
Sot →, *India* **43 F8** 27 27N 79 37 E
Sotkamo, *Finland* **8 D23** 64 8N 28 23 E
Soto la Marina →, *Mexico* **87 C5** 23 40N 97 40W
Sotuta, *Mexico* **87 C7** 20 29N 89 43W
Souanké, *Congo* **52 D2** 2 10N 14 3 E
Souderton, *U.S.A.* **79 F9** 40 19N 75 19W
Soúdha, *Greece* **23 D6** 35 29N 24 4 E
Soúdhas, Kólpos, *Greece* **23 D6** 35 25N 24 10 E
Soufrière, *St. Lucia* **89 D7** 13 51N 61 3W
Soukhouma, *Laos* **38 E5** 14 38N 105 48 E
Sŏul, *S. Korea* **35 F14** 37 31N 126 58 E
Sound, The, *U.K.* **11 G3** 50 20N 4 10W
Sources, Mt. aux, *Lesotho* **57 D4** 28 45S 28 50 E
Soure, *Brazil* **93 D9** 0 35S 48 30W
Souris, *Man., Canada* **73 D8** 49 40N 100 20W
Souris, *P.E.I., Canada* **71 C7** 46 21N 62 15W
Souris →, *Canada* **80 A5** 49 40N 99 34W
Sousa, *Brazil* **93 E11** 6 45S 38 10W
Sousse, *Tunisia* **51 A8** 35 50N 10 38 E
Sout →, *S. Africa* **56 E2** 31 35S 18 24 E
South Africa ■, *Africa* **56 E3** 32 0S 23 0 E
South America **90 E5** 10 0S 60 0W
South Atlantic Ocean **90 H7** 20 0S 10 0W
South Aulatsivik I., *Canada* **71 A7** 56 45N 61 30W
South Australia □, *Australia* **63 E2** 32 0S 139 0 E
South Ayrshire □, *U.K.* **12 F4** 55 18N 4 41W
South Baldy, *U.S.A.* **83 J10** 33 59N 107 11W
South Bass I., *U.S.A.* **78 E2** 41 38N 82 53W
South Bend, *Ind., U.S.A.* **76 E2** 41 41N 86 15W
South Bend, *Wash., U.S.A.* **84 D3** 46 40N 123 48W
South Boston, *U.S.A.* **77 G6** 36 42N 78 54W
South Branch, *Canada* **71 C8** 47 55N 59 2W
South Brook, *Canada* **71 C8** 49 26N 56 5W
South Carolina □, *U.S.A.* **77 J5** 34 0N 81 0W
South Charleston, *U.S.A.* **76 F5** 38 22N 81 44W
South China Sea, *Asia* **36 C4** 10 0N 113 0 E
South Dakota □, *U.S.A.* **80 C5** 44 15N 100 0W
South Deerfield, *U.S.A.* **79 D12** 42 29N 72 37W
South Downs, *U.K.* **11 G7** 50 52N 0 25W
South East C., *Australia* **62 G4** 43 40S 146 50 E
South East Is., *Australia* **61 F3** 34 17S 123 30 E
South Esk →, *U.K.* **12 E6** 56 43N 2 31W
South Foreland, *U.K.* **11 F9** 51 8N 1 24 E
South Fork American →, *U.S.A.* **84 G5** 38 45N 121 5W
South Fork Feather →, *U.S.A.* **84 F5** 39 17N 121 36W
South Fork Grand →, *U.S.A.* **80 C3** 45 43N 102 17W
South Fork Republican →, *U.S.A.* **80 E4** 40 3N 101 31W
South Georgia, *Antarctica* **96 G9** 54 30S 37 0W
South Gloucestershire □, *U.K.* **11 F5** 51 32N 2 28W
South Hadley, *U.S.A.* **79 D12** 42 16N 72 35W
South Haven, *U.S.A.* **76 D2** 42 24N 86 16W
South Henik, L., *Canada* **73 A9** 61 30N 97 30W
South Honshu Ridge, *Pac. Oc.* **64 E6** 23 0N 143 0 E
South Horr, *Kenya* **54 B4** 2 12N 36 56 E
South I., *Kenya* **54 B4** 2 35N 36 35 E
South I., *N.Z.* **59 L3** 44 0S 170 0 E
South Indian Lake, *Canada* **73 B9** 56 47N 98 56W
South Invercargill, *N.Z.* **59 M2** 46 26S 168 23 E
South Knife →, *Canada* **73 B10** 58 55N 94 37W
South Koel →, *India* **43 H11** 22 32N 85 14 E
South Korea ■, *Asia* **35 G15** 36 0N 128 0 E
South Lake Tahoe, *U.S.A.* **84 G6** 38 57N 119 59W
South Lanarkshire □, *U.K.* **12 F5** 55 37N 3 53W
South Loup →, *U.S.A.* **80 E5** 41 4N 98 39W
South Magnetic Pole, *Antarctica* **5 C9** 64 8S 138 8 E
South Milwaukee, *U.S.A.* **76 D2** 42 55N 87 52W
South Molton, *U.K.* **11 F4** 51 1N 3 51W
South Moose L., *Canada* **73 C8** 53 46N 100 8W
South Nahanni →, *Canada* **72 A4** 61 3N 123 21W
South Nation →, *Canada* **79 A9** 45 34N 75 6W
South Natuna Is. = Natuna Selatan, Kepulauan, *Indonesia* **39 L7** 2 45N 109 0 E
South Negril Pt., *Jamaica* **88 C4** 18 14N 78 30W
South Orkney Is., *Antarctica* **5 C18** 63 0S 45 0W
South Ossetia □, *Georgia* **25 F7** 42 21N 44 2 E
South Pagai, I. = Pagai Selatan, Pulau, *Indonesia* **36 E2** 3 0S 100 15 E
South Paris, *U.S.A.* **79 B14** 44 14N 70 31W
South Pittsburg, *U.S.A.* **77 H3** 35 1N 85 42W
South Platte →, *U.S.A.* **80 E4** 41 7N 100 42W
South Pole, *Antarctica* **5 E** 90 0S 0 0W
South Porcupine, *Canada* **70 C3** 48 30N 81 12W
South Portland, *U.S.A.* **77 D10** 43 38N 70 15W
South Pt., *U.S.A.* **78 B1** 44 52N 83 19W
South River, *Canada* **70 C4** 45 52N 79 23W
South River, *U.S.A.* **79 F10** 40 27N 74 23W
South Ronaldsay, *U.K.* **12 C6** 58 48N 2 58W
South Sandwich Is., *Antarctica* **5 B1** 57 0S 27 0W
South Saskatchewan →, *Canada* **73 C7** 53 15N 105 5W
South Seal →, *Canada* **73 B9** 58 48N 98 8W
South Shetland Is., *Antarctica* **5 C18** 62 0S 59 0W
South Shields, *U.K.* **10 C6** 55 0N 1 25W
South Sioux City, *U.S.A.* **80 D6** 42 28N 96 24W
South Taranaki Bight, *N.Z.* **59 H5** 39 40S 174 5 E
South Thompson →, *Canada* **72 C4** 50 40N 120 20W
South Twin I., *Canada* **70 B4** 53 7N 79 52W
South Tyne →, *U.K.* **10 C5** 54 59N 2 8W
South Uist, *U.K.* **12 D1** 57 20N 7 15W
South West Africa = Namibia ■, *Africa* **56 C2** 22 0S 18 9 E
South West C., *Australia* **62 G4** 43 34S 146 3 E
South Williamsport, *U.S.A.* **78 E8** 41 13N 77 0W
South Yorkshire □, *U.K.* **10 D6** 53 27N 1 36W
Southampton, *Canada* **78 B3** 44 30N 81 25W
Southampton, *U.K.* **11 G6** 50 54N 1 23W
Southampton, *U.S.A.* **79 F12** 40 53N 72 23W
Southampton □, *U.K.* **11 G6** 50 54N 1 23W
Southampton I., *Canada* **69 B11** 64 30N 84 0W
Southaven, *U.S.A.* **81 H9** 34 59N 90 2W
Southbank, *Canada* **72 C3** 54 2N 125 46W
Southbridge, *N.Z.* **59 K4** 43 48S 172 16 E
Southbridge, *U.S.A.* **79 D12** 42 5N 72 2W
Southend, *Canada* **73 B8** 56 19N 103 22W
Southend-on-Sea, *U.K.* **11 F8** 51 32N 0 44 E
Southend-on-Sea □, *U.K.* **11 F8** 51 32N 0 44 E
Southern □, *Malawi* **55 F4** 15 0S 35 0 E
Southern □, *Zambia* **55 F2** 16 20S 26 20 E
Southern Alps, *N.Z.* **59 K3** 43 41S 170 11 E
Southern Cross, *Australia* **61 F2** 31 12S 119 15 E
Southern Indian L., *Canada* **73 B9** 57 10N 98 30W
Southern Ocean, *Antarctica* **5 C6** 62 0S 60 0 E
Southern Pines, *U.S.A.* **77 H6** 35 11N 79 24W
Southern Uplands, *U.K.* **12 F5** 55 28N 3 52W
Southington, *U.S.A.* **79 E12** 41 36N 72 53W
Southland □, *N.Z.* **59 L1** 45 30S 168 0 E
Southold, *U.S.A.* **79 E12** 41 4N 72 26W
Southport, *Australia* **63 D5** 27 58S 153 25 E
Southport, *U.K.* **10 D4** 53 39N 3 0W
Southport, *Fla., U.S.A.* **77 K3** 30 17N 85 38W
Southport, *N.Y., U.S.A.* **78 D8** 42 3N 76 49W
Southwest C., *N.Z.* **59 M1** 47 17S 167 28 E
Southwold, *U.K.* **11 E9** 52 20N 1 41 E
Soutpansberg, *S. Africa* **57 C4** 23 0S 29 30 E
Sovetsk, *Kaliningd., Russia* **9 J19** 55 6N 21 50 E
Sovetsk, *Kirov, Russia* **24 C8** 57 38N 48 53 E
Sovetskaya Gavan = Vanino, *Russia* **27 E15** 48 50N 140 5 E
Soweto, *S. Africa* **57 D4** 26 14S 27 54 E
Sōya-Kaikyō = La Perouse Str., *Asia* **30 B11** 45 40N 142 0 E
Sōya-Misaki, *Japan* **30 B10** 45 30N 141 55 E
Sozh →, *Belarus* **17 B16** 51 57N 30 48 E
Spa, *Belgium* **15 D5** 50 29N 5 53 E
Spain ■, *Europe* **19 B4** 39 0N 4 0W
Spalding, *Australia* **63 E2** 33 30S 138 37 E
Spalding, *U.K.* **10 E7** 52 48N 0 9W
Spangler, *U.S.A.* **78 F6** 40 39N 78 48W
Spanish, *Canada* **70 C3** 46 12N 82 20W
Spanish Fork, *U.S.A.* **82 F8** 40 7N 111 39W
Spanish Town, *Jamaica* **88 C4** 18 0N 76 57W
Sparks, *U.S.A.* **84 F7** 39 32N 119 45W
Sparta = Spárti, *Greece* **21 F10** 37 5N 22 25 E
Sparta, *Mich., U.S.A.* **76 D3** 43 10N 85 42W
Sparta, *N.J., U.S.A.* **79 E10** 41 2N 74 38W
Sparta, *Wis., U.S.A.* **80 D9** 43 56N 90 49W
Spartanburg, *U.S.A.* **77 H5** 34 56N 81 57W
Spartansburg, *U.S.A.* **78 E5** 41 49N 79 41W
Spárti, *Greece* **21 F10** 37 5N 22 25 E
Spartivento, C., *Calabria, Italy* **20 F7** 37 55N 16 4 E
Spartivento, C., *Sard., Italy* **20 E3** 38 53N 8 50 E
Sparwood, *Canada* **72 D6** 49 44N 114 53W
Spassk Dalniy, *Russia* **27 E14** 44 40N 132 48 E
Spátha, Ákra, *Greece* **23 D5** 35 42N 23 43 E
Spatsizi →, *Canada* **72 B3** 57 42N 128 7W
Spatsizi Plateau Wilderness Park, *Canada* **72 B3** 57 40N 128 0W
Spean →, *U.K.* **12 E4** 56 55N 4 59W
Spearfish, *U.S.A.* **80 C3** 44 30N 103 52W
Spearman, *U.S.A.* **81 G4** 36 12N 101 12W
Speculator, *U.S.A.* **79 C10** 43 30N 74 25W
Speightstown, *Barbados* **89 D8** 13 15N 59 39W
Speke Gulf, *Tanzania* **54 C3** 2 20S 32 50 E
Spencer, *Idaho, U.S.A.* **82 D7** 44 22N 112 11W
Spencer, *Iowa, U.S.A.* **80 D7** 43 9N 95 9W
Spencer, *N.Y., U.S.A.* **79 D8** 42 13N 76 30W
Spencer, *Nebr., U.S.A.* **80 D5** 42 53N 98 42W
Spencer, C., *Australia* **63 F2** 35 20S 136 53 E
Spencer B., *Namibia* **56 D1** 25 30S 14 47 E
Spencer G., *Australia* **63 E2** 34 0S 137 20 E
Spencerville, *Canada* **79 B9** 44 51N 75 33W
Spences Bridge, *Canada* **72 C4** 50 25N 121 20W
Spennymoor, *U.K.* **10 C6** 54 42N 1 36W
Spenser Mts., *N.Z.* **59 K4** 42 15S 172 45 E
Sperrin Mts., *U.K.* **13 B5** 54 50N 7 0W
Spey →, *U.K.* **12 D5** 57 40N 3 6W
Speyer, *Germany* **16 D5** 49 29N 8 25 E
Spezand, *Pakistan* **42 E2** 29 59N 67 0 E
Spíli, *Greece* **23 D6** 35 13N 24 31 E
Spin Būldak, *Afghan.* **42 D2** 31 1N 66 25 E
Spinalónga, *Greece* **23 D7** 35 18N 25 44 E
Spirit Lake, *U.S.A.* **84 D4** 46 15N 122 9W
Spirit River, *Canada* **72 B5** 55 45N 118 50W
Spiritwood, *Canada* **73 C7** 53 24N 107 33W
Spithead, *U.K.* **11 G6** 50 45N 1 10W
Spitzbergen = Svalbard, *Arctic* **4 B8** 78 0N 17 0 E
Spjelkavik, *Norway* **9 E12** 62 28N 6 22 E
Split, *Croatia* **20 C7** 43 31N 16 26 E
Split L., *Canada* **73 B9** 56 8N 96 15W
Split Lake, *Canada* **73 B9** 56 8N 96 15W
Spofford, *U.S.A.* **81 L4** 29 10N 100 25W
Spokane, *U.S.A.* **82 C5** 47 40N 117 24W
Spoleto, *Italy* **20 C5** 42 44N 12 44 E
Spooner, *U.S.A.* **80 C9** 45 50N 91 53W
Sporyy Navolok, Mys, *Russia* **26 B7** 75 50N 68 40 E
Sprague, *U.S.A.* **82 C5** 47 18N 117 59W
Spratly I., *S. China Sea* **36 C4** 8 38N 111 55 E
Spratly Is., *S. China Sea* **36 C4** 8 20N 112 0 E
Spray, *U.S.A.* **82 D4** 44 50N 119 48W
Spree →, *Germany* **16 B7** 52 32N 13 13 E
Sprengisandur, *Iceland* **8 D5** 64 52N 18 7W
Spring City, *U.S.A.* **79 F9** 40 11N 75 33W
Spring Creek, *U.S.A.* **82 F6** 40 45N 115 38W
Spring Garden, *U.S.A.* **84 F6** 39 52N 120 47W
Spring Hill, *U.S.A.* **77 L4** 28 27N 82 41W
Spring Mts., *U.S.A.* **83 H6** 36 0N 115 45W
Spring Valley, *U.S.A.* **85 N10** 32 45N 117 5W
Springbok, *S. Africa* **56 D2** 29 42S 17 54 E
Springboro, *U.S.A.* **78 E4** 41 48N 80 22W
Springdale, *Canada* **71 C8** 49 30N 56 6W
Springdale, *U.S.A.* **81 G7** 36 11N 94 8W
Springer, *U.S.A.* **81 G2** 36 22N 104 36W
Springerville, *U.S.A.* **83 J9** 34 8N 109 17W
Springfield, *Canada* **78 D4** 42 50N 80 56W
Springfield, *N.Z.* **59 K3** 43 19S 171 56 E
Springfield, *Colo., U.S.A.* **81 G3** 37 24N 102 37W
Springfield, *Ill., U.S.A.* **80 F10** 39 48N 89 39W
Springfield, *Mass., U.S.A.* **79 D12** 42 6N 72 35W
Springfield, *Mo., U.S.A.* **81 G8** 37 13N 93 17W
Springfield, *Ohio, U.S.A.* **76 F4** 39 55N 83 49W
Springfield, *Oreg., U.S.A.* **82 D2** 44 3N 123 1W
Springfield, *Tenn., U.S.A.* **77 G2** 36 31N 86 53W
Springfield, *Vt., U.S.A.* **79 C12** 43 18N 72 29W
Springfontein, *S. Africa* **56 E4** 30 15S 25 40 E
Springhill, *Canada* **71 C7** 45 40N 64 4W
Springhill, *U.S.A.* **81 J8** 33 0N 93 28W
Springhouse, *Canada* **72 C4** 51 56N 122 7W
Springs, *S. Africa* **57 D4** 26 13S 28 25 E
Springsure, *Australia* **62 C4** 24 8S 148 6 E
Springvale, *U.S.A.* **79 C14** 43 28N 70 48W
Springville, *Calif., U.S.A.* **84 J8** 36 8N 118 49W
Springville, *N.Y., U.S.A.* **78 D6** 42 31N 78 40W
Springville, *Utah, U.S.A.* **82 F8** 40 10N 111 37W
Springwater, *U.S.A.* **78 D7** 42 38N 77 35W
Spruce-Creek, *U.S.A.* **78 F6** 40 36N 78 9W
Spruce Mt., *U.S.A.* **79 B12** 44 12N 72 19W
Spur, *U.S.A.* **81 J4** 33 28N 100 52W
Spurn Hd., *U.K.* **10 D8** 53 35N 0 8 E
Spuzzum, *Canada* **72 D4** 49 37N 121 23W
Squam L., *U.S.A.* **79 C13** 43 45N 71 32W
Squamish, *Canada* **72 D4** 49 45N 123 10W
Square Islands, *Canada* **71 B8** 52 47N 55 47W
Squires, Mt., *Australia* **61 E4** 26 14S 127 28 E
Srbija = Serbia □, *Yugoslavia* **21 C9** 43 30N 21 0 E
Sre Ambel, *Cambodia* **39 G4** 11 8N 103 46 E
Sre Khtum, *Cambodia* **39 F6** 12 10N 106 52 E
Sre Umbell = Sre Ambel, *Cambodia* **39 G4** 11 8N 103 46 E
Srebrenica, *Bos.-H.* **21 B8** 44 6N 19 18 E
Sredinny Ra. = Sredinnyy Khrebet, *Russia* **27 D16** 57 0N 160 0 E
Sredinnyy Khrebet, *Russia* **27 D16** 57 0N 160 0 E
Srednekolymsk, *Russia* **27 C16** 67 27N 153 40 E
Śrem, *Poland* **17 B9** 52 6N 17 2 E
Sremska Mitrovica, *Serbia, Yug.* **21 B8** 44 59N 19 38 E
Srepok →, *Cambodia* **38 F6** 13 33N 106 16 E
Sretensk, *Russia* **27 D12** 52 10N 117 40 E
Sri Lanka ■, *Asia* **40 R12** 7 30N 80 50 E
Srikakulam, *India* **41 K13** 18 14N 83 58 E
Srinagar, *India* **43 B6** 34 5N 74 50 E
Staaten →, *Australia* **62 B3** 16 24S 141 17 E
Stade, *Germany* **16 B5** 53 35N 9 29 E
Stadskanaal, *Neths.* **15 A6** 53 4N 6 55 E
Staffa, *U.K.* **12 E2** 56 27N 6 21W
Stafford, *U.K.* **10 E5** 52 49N 2 7W
Stafford, *U.S.A.* **81 G5** 37 58N 98 36W
Stafford Springs, *U.S.A.* **79 E12** 41 57N 72 18W
Staffordshire □, *U.K.* **10 E5** 52 53N 2 10W
Staines, *U.K.* **11 F7** 51 26N 0 29W
Stakhanov, *Ukraine* **25 E6** 48 35N 38 40 E
Stalingrad = Volgograd, *Russia* **25 E7** 48 40N 44 25 E
Staliniri = Tskhinvali, *Georgia* **25 F7** 42 14N 44 1 E
Stalino = Donetsk, *Ukraine* **25 E6** 48 0N 37 45 E
Stalinogorsk = Novomoskovsk, *Russia* **24 D6** 54 5N 38 15 E
Stalis, *Greece* **23 D7** 35 17N 25 25 E
Stalowa Wola, *Poland* **17 C12** 50 34N 22 3 E
Stalybridge, *U.K.* **10 D5** 53 28N 2 3W
Stamford, *Australia* **62 C3** 21 15S 143 46 E
Stamford, *U.K.* **11 E7** 52 39N 0 29W
Stamford, *Conn., U.S.A.* **79 E11** 41 3N 73 32W
Stamford, *N.Y., U.S.A.* **79 D10** 42 25N 74 38W
Stamford, *Tex., U.S.A.* **81 J5** 32 57N 99 48W
Stampriet, *Namibia* **56 C2** 24 20S 18 28 E
Stamps, *U.S.A.* **81 J8** 33 22N 93 30W
Standerton, *S. Africa* **57 D4** 26 55S 29 7 E
Standish, *U.S.A.* **76 D4** 43 59N 83 57W
Stanford, *S. Africa* **56 E2** 34 26S 19 29 E
Stanford, *U.S.A.* **82 C8** 47 9N 110 13W
Stanger, *S. Africa* **57 D5** 29 27S 31 14 E
Stanislaus →, *U.S.A.* **84 H5** 37 40N 121 14W

Suphan Buri

Stanislav = Ivano-Frankivsk, *Ukraine* **17 D13** 48 40N 24 40 E
Stanke Dimitrov, *Bulgaria* **21 C10** 42 17N 23 9 E
Stanley, *Australia* **62 G4** 40 46S 145 19 E
Stanley, *Canada* **73 B8** 55 24N 104 22W
Stanley, *Falk. Is.* **96 G5** 51 40S 59 51W
Stanley, *U.K.* **10 C6** 54 53N 1 41W
Stanley, *Idaho, U.S.A.* **82 D6** 44 13N 114 56W
Stanley, *N. Dak., U.S.A.* **80 A3** 48 19N 102 23W
Stanley, *N.Y., U.S.A.* **78 D7** 42 48N 77 6W
Stanovoy Khrebet, *Russia* **27 D13** 55 0N 130 0 E
Stanovoy Ra. = Stanovoy Khrebet, *Russia* **27 D13** 55 0N 130 0 E
Stansmore Ra., *Australia* **60 D4** 21 23S 128 33 E
Stanthorpe, *Australia* **63 D5** 28 36S 151 59 E
Stanton, *U.S.A.* **81 J4** 32 8N 101 48W
Stanwood, *U.S.A.* **84 B4** 48 15N 122 23W
Staples, *U.S.A.* **80 B7** 46 21N 94 48W
Star City, *Canada* **73 C8** 52 50N 104 20W
Star Lake, *U.S.A.* **79 B9** 44 10N 75 2W
Stara Planina, *Bulgaria* **21 C10** 43 15N 23 0 E
Stara Zagora, *Bulgaria* **21 C11** 42 26N 25 39 E
Starachowice, *Poland* **17 C11** 51 3N 21 2 E
Staraya Russa, *Russia* **24 C5** 57 58N 31 23 E
Starbuck I., *Kiribati* **65 H12** 5 37S 155 55W
Stargard Szczeciński, *Poland* **16 B8** 53 20N 15 0 E
Staritsa, *Russia* **24 C5** 56 33N 34 55 E
Starke, *U.S.A.* **77 L4** 29 57N 82 7W
Starogard Gdański, *Poland* **17 B10** 53 59N 18 30 E
Starokonstantinov = Starokonstyantyniv, *Ukraine* **17 D14** 49 48N 27 10 E
Starokonstyantyniv, *Ukraine* **17 D14** 49 48N 27 10 E
Start Pt., *U.K.* **11 G4** 50 13N 3 39W
Staryy Chartoriysk, *Ukraine* **17 C13** 51 15N 25 54 E
Staryy Oskol, *Russia* **25 D6** 51 19N 37 55 E
State College, *U.S.A.* **78 F7** 40 48N 77 52W
Stateline, *U.S.A.* **84 G7** 38 57N 119 56W
Staten, I. = Estados, I. de Los, *Argentina* **96 G4** 54 40S 64 30W
Staten I., *U.S.A.* **79 F10** 40 35N 74 9W
Statesboro, *U.S.A.* **77 J5** 32 27N 81 47W
Statesville, *U.S.A.* **77 H5** 35 47N 80 53W
Stauffer, *U.S.A.* **85 L7** 34 45N 119 3W
Staunton, *Ill., U.S.A.* **80 F10** 39 1N 89 47W
Staunton, *Va., U.S.A.* **76 F6** 38 9N 79 4W
Stavanger, *Norway* **9 G11** 58 57N 5 40 E
Staveley, *N.Z.* **59 K3** 43 40S 171 32 E
Stavelot, *Belgium* **15 D5** 50 23N 5 55 E
Stavern, *Norway* **9 G14** 59 0N 10 1 E
Stavoren, *Neths.* **15 B5** 52 53N 5 22 E
Stavropol, *Russia* **25 E7** 45 5N 42 0 E
Stavros, *Cyprus* **23 D11** 35 1N 32 38 E
Stavrós, *Greece* **23 D6** 35 12N 24 45 E
Stavrós, Ákra, *Greece* **23 D6** 35 26N 24 58 E
Stawell, *Australia* **63 F3** 37 5S 142 47 E
Stawell →, *Australia* **62 C3** 20 20S 142 55 E
Stayner, *Canada* **78 B4** 44 25N 80 5W
Stayton, *U.S.A.* **82 D2** 44 48N 122 48W
Steamboat Springs, *U.S.A.* **82 F10** 40 29N 106 50W
Steele, *U.S.A.* **80 B5** 46 51N 99 55W
Steelton, *U.S.A.* **78 F8** 40 14N 76 50W
Steen River, *Canada* **72 B5** 59 40N 117 12W
Steenkool = Bintuni, *Indonesia* **37 E8** 2 7S 133 32 E
Steens Mt., *U.S.A.* **82 E4** 42 35N 118 40W
Steenwijk, *Neths.* **15 B6** 52 47N 6 7 E
Steep Pt., *Australia* **61 E1** 26 8S 113 8 E
Steep Rock, *Canada* **73 C9** 51 30N 98 48W
Stefanie L. = Chew Bahir, *Ethiopia* **46 G2** 4 40N 36 50 E
Stefansson Bay, *Antarctica* **5 C5** 67 20S 59 8 E
Steiermark □, *Austria* **16 E8** 47 26N 15 0 E
Steilacoom, *U.S.A.* **84 C4** 47 10N 122 36W
Steilrandberge, *Namibia* **56 B1** 17 45S 13 20 E
Steinbach, *Canada* **73 D9** 49 32N 96 40W
Steinhausen, *Namibia* **56 C2** 21 49S 18 20 E
Steinkjer, *Norway* **8 D14** 64 1N 11 31 E
Steinkopf, *S. Africa* **56 D2** 29 18S 17 43 E
Stellarton, *Canada* **71 C7** 45 32N 62 30W
Stellenbosch, *S. Africa* **56 E2** 33 58S 18 50 E
Stendal, *Germany* **16 B6** 52 36N 11 53 E
Steornabhaigh = Stornoway, *U.K.* **12 C2** 58 13N 6 23W
Stepanakert = Xankändi, *Azerbaijan* **25 G8** 39 52N 46 49 E
Stephens Creek, *Australia* **63 E3** 31 50S 141 30 E
Stephens I., *Canada* **72 C2** 54 10N 130 45W
Stephens L., *Canada* **73 B9** 56 32N 95 0W
Stephenville, *Canada* **71 C8** 48 31N 58 35W
Stephenville, *U.S.A.* **81 J5** 32 13N 98 12W
Stepnoi = Elista, *Russia* **25 E7** 46 16N 44 14 E
Steppe, *Asia* **28 D9** 50 0N 50 0 E
Sterkstroom, *S. Africa* **56 E4** 31 32S 26 32 E
Sterling, *Colo., U.S.A.* **80 E3** 40 37N 103 13W
Sterling, *Ill., U.S.A.* **80 E10** 41 48N 89 42W
Sterling, *Kans., U.S.A.* **80 F5** 38 13N 98 12W
Sterling City, *U.S.A.* **81 K4** 31 51N 101 0W
Sterling Heights, *U.S.A.* **76 D4** 42 35N 83 0W
Sterling Run, *U.S.A.* **78 E6** 41 25N 78 12W
Sterlitamak, *Russia* **24 D10** 53 40N 56 0 E
Stérnes, *Greece* **23 D6** 35 30N 24 9 E
Stettin = Szczecin, *Poland* **16 B8** 53 27N 14 27 E
Stettiner Haff, *Germany* **16 B8** 53 47N 14 15 E
Stettler, *Canada* **72 C6** 52 19N 112 40W
Steubenville, *U.S.A.* **78 F4** 40 22N 80 37W
Stevenage, *U.K.* **11 F7** 51 55N 0 13W
Stevens Point, *U.S.A.* **80 C10** 44 31N 89 34W
Stevenson, *U.S.A.* **84 E5** 45 42N 121 53W
Stevenson L., *Canada* **73 C9** 53 55N 96 0W
Stevensville, *U.S.A.* **82 C6** 46 30N 114 5W
Stewart, *Canada* **72 B3** 55 56N 129 57W
Stewart, *U.S.A.* **84 F7** 39 5N 119 46W
Stewart →, *Canada* **68 B6** 63 19N 139 26W
Stewart, C., *Australia* **62 A1** 11 57S 134 56 E
Stewart, I., *Chile* **96 G2** 54 50S 71 15W
Stewart I., *N.Z.* **59 M1** 46 58S 167 54 E
Stewarts Point, *U.S.A.* **84 G3** 38 39N 123 24W
Stewartville, *U.S.A.* **80 D8** 43 51N 92 29W
Stewiacke, *Canada* **71 C7** 45 9N 63 22W
Steynsburg, *S. Africa* **56 E4** 31 15S 25 49 E
Steyr, *Austria* **16 D8** 48 3N 14 25 E
Steytlerville, *S. Africa* **56 E3** 33 17S 24 19 E
Stigler, *U.S.A.* **81 H7** 35 15N 95 8W
Stikine →, *Canada* **72 B2** 56 40N 132 30W
Stilfontein, *S. Africa* **56 D4** 26 51S 26 50 E
Stillwater, *N.Z.* **59 K3** 42 27S 171 20 E
Stillwater, *Minn., U.S.A.* **80 C8** 45 3N 92 49W
Stillwater, *N.Y., U.S.A.* **79 D11** 42 55N 73 41W
Stillwater, *Okla., U.S.A.* **81 G6** 36 7N 97 4W
Stillwater Range, *U.S.A.* **82 G4** 39 50N 118 5W
Stillwater Reservoir, *U.S.A.* **79 C9** 43 54N 75 3W
Stilwell, *U.S.A.* **81 H7** 35 49N 94 38W
Štip, *Macedonia* **21 D10** 41 42N 22 10 E
Stirling, *Canada* **78 B7** 44 18N 77 33W
Stirling, *U.K.* **12 E5** 56 8N 3 57W
Stirling □, *U.K.* **12 E4** 56 12N 4 18W
Stirling Ra., *Australia* **61 F2** 34 23S 118 0 E
Stittsville, *Canada* **79 A9** 45 15N 75 55W
Stjernøya, *Norway* **8 A20** 70 20N 22 40 E
Stjørdalshalsen, *Norway* **8 E14** 63 29N 10 51 E
Stockerau, *Austria* **16 D9** 48 24N 16 12 E
Stockholm, *Sweden* **9 G18** 59 20N 18 3 E
Stockport, *U.K.* **10 D5** 53 25N 2 9W
Stocksbridge, *U.K.* **10 D6** 53 29N 1 35W
Stockton, *Calif., U.S.A.* **84 H5** 37 58N 121 17W
Stockton, *Kans., U.S.A.* **80 F5** 39 26N 99 16W
Stockton, *Mo., U.S.A.* **81 G8** 37 42N 93 48W
Stockton-on-Tees, *U.K.* **10 C6** 54 35N 1 19W
Stockton-on-Tees □, *U.K.* **10 C6** 54 35N 1 19W
Stockton Plateau, *U.S.A.* **81 K3** 30 30N 102 30W
Stoeng Treng, *Cambodia* **38 F5** 13 31N 105 58 E
Stoer, Pt. of, *U.K.* **12 C3** 58 16N 5 23W
Stoke-on-Trent, *U.K.* **10 D5** 53 1N 2 11W
Stoke-on-Trent □, *U.K.* **10 D5** 53 1N 2 11W
Stokes Pt., *Australia* **62 G3** 40 10S 143 56 E
Stokes Ra., *Australia* **60 C5** 15 50S 130 50 E
Stokksnes, *Iceland* **8 D6** 64 14N 14 58W
Stokmarknes, *Norway* **8 B16** 68 34N 14 54 E
Stolac, *Bos.-H.* **21 C7** 43 5N 17 59 E
Stolbovoy, Ostrov, *Russia* **27 B14** 74 44N 135 14 E
Stolbtsy = Stowbtsy, *Belarus* **17 B14** 53 30N 26 43 E
Stolin, *Belarus* **17 C14** 51 53N 26 50 E
Stomion, *Greece* **23 D5** 35 21N 23 32 E
Stone, *U.K.* **10 E5** 52 55N 2 9W
Stoneboro, *U.S.A.* **78 E4** 41 20N 80 7W
Stonehaven, *U.K.* **12 E6** 56 59N 2 12W
Stonehenge, *Australia* **62 C3** 24 22S 143 17 E
Stonehenge, *U.K.* **11 F6** 51 9N 1 45W
Stonewall, *Canada* **73 C9** 50 10N 97 19W
Stony L., *Man., Canada* **73 B9** 58 51N 98 40W
Stony L., *Ont., Canada* **78 B6** 44 30N 78 5W
Stony Point, *U.S.A.* **79 E11** 41 14N 73 59W
Stony Pt., *U.S.A.* **79 C8** 43 50N 76 18W
Stony Rapids, *Canada* **73 B7** 59 16N 105 50W
Stony Tunguska = Tunguska, Podkamennaya →, *Russia* **27 C10** 61 50N 90 13 E
Stonyford, *U.S.A.* **84 F4** 39 23N 122 33W
Stora Lulevatten, *Sweden* **8 C18** 67 10N 19 30 E
Storavan, *Sweden* **8 D18** 65 45N 18 10 E
Stord, *Norway* **9 G11** 59 52N 5 23 E
Store Bælt, *Denmark* **9 J14** 55 20N 11 0 E
Storm B., *Australia* **62 G4** 43 10S 147 30 E
Storm Lake, *U.S.A.* **80 D7** 42 39N 95 13W
Stormberge, *S. Africa* **56 E4** 31 16S 26 17 E
Stormsrivier, *S. Africa* **56 E3** 33 59S 23 52 E
Stornoway, *U.K.* **12 C2** 58 13N 6 23W
Storozhinets = Storozhynets, *Ukraine* **17 D13** 48 14N 25 45 E
Storozhynets, *Ukraine* **17 D13** 48 14N 25 45 E
Storrs, *U.S.A.* **79 E12** 41 49N 72 15W
Storsjön, *Sweden* **8 E16** 63 9N 14 30 E
Storuman, *Sweden* **8 D17** 65 5N 17 10 E
Storuman, sjö, *Sweden* **8 D17** 65 13N 16 50 E
Stouffville, *Canada* **78 C5** 43 58N 79 15W
Stoughton, *Canada* **73 D8** 49 40N 103 0W
Stour →, *Dorset, U.K.* **11 G6** 50 43N 1 47W
Stour →, *Kent, U.K.* **11 F9** 51 18N 1 22 E
Stour →, *Suffolk, U.K.* **11 F9** 51 57N 1 4 E
Stourbridge, *U.K.* **11 E5** 52 28N 2 8W
Stout L., *Canada* **73 C10** 52 0N 94 40W
Stove Pipe Wells Village, *U.S.A.* **85 J9** 36 35N 117 11W
Stow, *U.S.A.* **78 E3** 41 10N 81 27W
Stowbtsy, *Belarus* **17 B14** 53 30N 26 43 E
Stowmarket, *U.K.* **11 E9** 52 12N 1 0 E
Strabane, *U.K.* **13 B4** 54 50N 7 27W
Strahan, *Australia* **62 G4** 42 9S 145 20 E
Stralsund, *Germany* **16 A7** 54 18N 13 4 E
Strand, *S. Africa* **56 E2** 34 9S 18 48 E
Stranda, *Møre og Romsdal, Norway* **9 E12** 62 19N 6 58 E
Stranda, *Nord-Trøndelag, Norway* **8 E14** 63 33N 10 14 E
Strangford L., *U.K.* **13 B6** 54 30N 5 37W
Stranraer, *U.K.* **12 G3** 54 54N 5 1W
Strasbourg, *Canada* **73 C8** 51 4N 104 55W
Strasbourg, *France* **18 B7** 48 35N 7 42 E
Stratford, *Canada* **78 C4** 43 23N 81 0W
Stratford, *N.Z.* **59 H5** 39 20S 174 19 E
Stratford, *Calif., U.S.A.* **84 J7** 36 11N 119 49W
Stratford, *Conn., U.S.A.* **79 E11** 41 12N 73 8W
Stratford, *Tex., U.S.A.* **81 G3** 36 20N 102 4W
Stratford-upon-Avon, *U.K.* **11 E6** 52 12N 1 42W
Strath Spey, *U.K.* **12 D5** 57 9N 3 49W
Strathalbyn, *Australia* **63 F2** 35 13S 138 53 E
Strathaven, *U.K.* **12 F4** 55 40N 4 5W
Strathcona Prov. Park, *Canada* **72 D3** 49 38N 125 40W
Strathmore, *Canada* **72 C6** 51 5N 113 18W
Strathmore, *U.K.* **12 E5** 56 37N 3 7W
Strathmore, *U.S.A.* **84 J7** 36 9N 119 4W
Strathnaver, *Canada* **72 C4** 53 20N 122 33W
Strathpeffer, *U.K.* **12 D4** 57 35N 4 32W
Strathroy, *Canada* **78 D3** 42 58N 81 38W
Strathy Pt., *U.K.* **12 C4** 58 36N 4 1W
Strattanville, *U.S.A.* **78 E5** 41 12N 79 19W
Stratton, *U.S.A.* **79 A14** 45 8N 70 26W
Stratton Mt., *U.S.A.* **79 C12** 43 4N 72 55W
Straubing, *Germany* **16 D7** 48 52N 12 34 E
Straumnes, *Iceland* **8 C2** 66 26N 23 8W
Strawberry →, *U.S.A.* **82 F8** 40 10N 110 24W
Streaky B., *Australia* **63 E1** 32 48S 134 13 E
Streaky Bay, *Australia* **63 E1** 32 51S 134 18 E
Streator, *U.S.A.* **80 E10** 41 8N 88 50W
Streetsboro, *U.S.A.* **78 E3** 41 14N 81 21W
Streetsville, *Canada* **78 C5** 43 35N 79 42W
Strelka, *Russia* **27 D10** 58 5N 93 3 E
Streng →, *Cambodia* **38 F4** 13 12N 103 37 E
Streymoy, *Færoe Is.* **8 E9** 62 8N 7 5W
Strezhevoy, *Russia* **26 C8** 60 42N 77 34 E
Strimón →, *Greece* **21 D10** 40 46N 23 51 E
Strimonikós Kólpos, *Greece* **21 D11** 40 33N 24 0 E
Stroma, *U.K.* **12 C5** 58 41N 3 7W
Strómboli, *Italy* **20 E6** 38 47N 15 13 E
Stromeferry, *U.K.* **12 D3** 57 21N 5 33W
Stromness, *U.K.* **12 C5** 58 58N 3 17W
Stromsburg, *U.S.A.* **80 E6** 41 7N 97 36W
Strömstad, *Sweden* **9 G14** 58 56N 11 10 E
Strömsund, *Sweden* **8 E16** 63 51N 15 33 E
Strongsville, *U.S.A.* **78 E3** 41 19N 81 50W
Stronsay, *U.K.* **12 B6** 59 7N 2 35W
Stroud, *U.K.* **11 F5** 51 45N 2 13W
Stroud Road, *Australia* **63 E5** 32 18S 151 57 E
Stroudsburg, *U.S.A.* **79 F9** 40 59N 75 12W
Stroumbi, *Cyprus* **23 E11** 34 53N 32 29 E
Struer, *Denmark* **9 H13** 56 30N 8 35 E
Strumica, *Macedonia* **21 D10** 41 28N 22 41 E
Struthers, *Canada* **70 C2** 48 41N 85 51W
Struthers, *U.S.A.* **78 E4** 41 4N 80 39W
Stryker, *U.S.A.* **82 B6** 48 41N 114 46W
Stryy, *Ukraine* **17 D12** 49 16N 23 48 E
Strzelecki Cr. →, *Australia* **63 D2** 29 37S 139 59 E
Stuart, *Fla., U.S.A.* **77 M5** 27 12N 80 15W
Stuart, *Nebr., U.S.A.* **80 D5** 42 36N 99 8W
Stuart →, *Canada* **72 C4** 54 0N 123 35W
Stuart Bluff Ra., *Australia* **60 D5** 22 50S 131 52 E
Stuart L., *Canada* **72 C4** 54 30N 124 30W
Stuart Ra., *Australia* **63 D1** 29 10S 134 56 E
Stull L., *Canada* **70 B1** 54 24N 92 34W
Stung Treng = Stoeng Treng, *Cambodia* **38 F5** 13 31N 105 58 E
Stupart →, *Canada* **70 A1** 56 0N 93 25W
Sturgeon B., *Canada* **73 C9** 52 0N 97 50W
Sturgeon Bay, *U.S.A.* **76 C2** 44 50N 87 23W
Sturgeon Falls, *Canada* **70 C4** 46 25N 79 57W
Sturgeon L., *Alta., Canada* **72 B5** 55 6N 117 32W
Sturgeon L., *Ont., Canada* **70 C1** 50 0N 90 45W
Sturgeon L., *Ont., Canada* **78 B6** 44 28N 78 43W
Sturgis, *Canada* **73 C8** 51 56N 102 36W
Sturgis, *Mich., U.S.A.* **76 E3** 41 48N 85 25W
Sturgis, *S. Dak., U.S.A.* **80 C3** 44 25N 103 31W
Sturt Cr. →, *Australia* **60 C4** 19 8S 127 50 E
Stutterheim, *S. Africa* **56 E4** 32 33S 27 28 E
Stuttgart, *Germany* **16 D5** 48 48N 9 11 E
Stuttgart, *U.S.A.* **81 H9** 34 30N 91 33W
Stuyvesant, *U.S.A.* **79 D11** 42 23N 73 45W
Stykkishólmur, *Iceland* **8 D2** 65 2N 22 40W
Styria = Steiermark □, *Austria* **16 E8** 47 26N 15 0 E
Su Xian = Suzhou, *China* **34 H9** 33 41N 116 59 E
Suakin, *Sudan* **51 E13** 19 8N 37 20 E
Suan, *N. Korea* **35 E14** 38 42N 126 22 E
Suaqui, *Mexico* **86 B3** 29 12N 109 41W
Suar, *India* **43 E8** 29 2N 79 3 E
Subang, *Indonesia* **37 G12** 6 34S 107 45 E
Subansiri →, *India* **41 F18** 26 48N 93 50 E
Subarnarekha →, *India* **43 H12** 22 34N 87 24 E
Subayhah, *Si. Arabia* **44 D3** 30 2N 38 50 E
Subi, *Indonesia* **39 L7** 2 58N 108 50 E
Subotica, *Serbia, Yug.* **21 A8** 46 6N 19 39 E
Suceava, *Romania* **17 E14** 47 38N 26 16 E
Suchan, *Russia* **30 C6** 43 8N 133 9 E
Suchitoto, *El Salv.* **88 D2** 13 56N 89 0W
Suchou = Suzhou, *China* **33 C7** 31 19N 120 38 E
Süchow = Xuzhou, *China* **35 G9** 34 18N 117 10 E
Suck →, *Ireland* **13 C3** 53 17N 8 3W
Sucre, *Bolivia* **92 G5** 19 0S 65 15W
Sucuriú →, *Brazil* **93 H8** 20 47S 51 38W
Sud, Pte. du, *Canada* **71 C7** 49 3N 62 14W
Sud-Kivu □, *Dem. Rep. of the Congo* **54 C2** 3 0S 28 30 E
Sud-Ouest, Pte. du, *Canada* **71 C7** 49 23N 63 36W
Sudan, *U.S.A.* **81 H3** 34 4N 102 32W
Sudan ■, *Africa* **51 E11** 15 0N 30 0 E
Sudbury, *Canada* **70 C3** 46 30N 81 0W
Sudbury, *U.K.* **11 E8** 52 2N 0 45 E
Sûdd, *Sudan* **51 G12** 8 20N 30 0 E
Sudeten Mts. = Sudety, *Europe* **17 C9** 50 20N 16 45 E
Sudety, *Europe* **17 C9** 50 20N 16 45 E
Suðuroy, *Færoe Is.* **8 F9** 61 32N 6 50W
Sudi, *Tanzania* **55 E4** 10 11S 39 57 E
Sudirman, Pegunungan, *Indonesia* **37 E9** 4 30S 137 0 E
Sueca, *Spain* **19 C5** 39 12N 0 21W
Suemez I., *U.S.A.* **72 B2** 55 15N 133 20W
Suez = El Suweis, *Egypt* **51 C12** 29 58N 32 31 E
Suez, G. of = Suweis, Khalîg el, *Egypt* **51 C12** 28 40N 33 0 E
Suez Canal = Suweis, Qanâ es, *Egypt* **51 B12** 31 0N 32 20 E
Suffield, *Canada* **72 C6** 50 12N 111 10W
Suffolk, *U.S.A.* **76 G7** 36 44N 76 35W
Suffolk □, *U.K.* **11 E9** 52 16N 1 0 E
Sugargrove, *U.S.A.* **78 E5** 41 59N 79 21W
Sugarive →, *India* **43 F12** 26 16N 86 24 E
Sugluk = Salluit, *Canada* **69 B12** 62 14N 75 38W
Şuḩār, *Oman* **46 C6** 24 20N 56 40 E
Sühbaatar □, *Mongolia* **34 B8** 45 30N 114 0 E
Suhl, *Germany* **16 C6** 50 36N 10 42 E
Sui, *Pakistan* **42 E3** 28 37N 69 19 E
Sui Xian, *China* **34 G8** 34 25N 115 2 E
Suide, *China* **34 F6** 37 30N 110 12 E
Suifenhe, *China* **35 B16** 44 25N 131 10 E
Suihua, *China* **33 B7** 46 32N 126 55 E
Suining, *China* **35 H9** 33 56N 117 58 E
Suiping, *China* **34 H7** 33 10N 113 59 E
Suir →, *Ireland* **13 D4** 52 16N 7 9W
Suisun City, *U.S.A.* **84 G4** 38 15N 122 2W
Suiyang, *China* **35 B16** 44 30N 130 56 E
Suizhong, *China* **35 D11** 40 21N 120 20 E
Sujangarh, *India* **42 F6** 27 42N 74 31 E
Sukabumi, *Indonesia* **37 G12** 6 56S 106 50 E
Sukadana, *Indonesia* **36 E3** 1 10S 110 0 E
Sukagawa, *Japan* **31 F10** 37 17N 140 23 E
Sukaraja, *Indonesia* **36 E4** 2 28S 110 25 E
Sukarnapura = Jayapura, *Indonesia* **37 E10** 2 28S 140 38 E
Sukch'ŏn, *N. Korea* **35 E13** 39 22N 125 35 E
Sukhona →, *Russia* **24 C6** 61 15N 46 39 E
Sukhothai, *Thailand* **38 D2** 17 1N 99 49 E
Sukhumi = Sokhumi, *Georgia* **25 F7** 43 0N 41 0 E
Sukkur, *Pakistan* **42 F3** 27 42N 68 54 E
Sukkur Barrage, *Pakistan* **42 F3** 27 40N 68 50 E
Sukri →, *India* **42 G4** 25 4N 71 43 E
Sukumo, *Japan* **31 H6** 32 56N 132 44 E
Sukunka →, *Canada* **72 B4** 55 45N 121 15W
Sula, Kepulauan, *Indonesia* **37 E7** 1 45S 125 0 E
Sulaco →, *Honduras* **88 C2** 15 2N 87 44W
Sulaiman Range, *Pakistan* **42 D3** 30 30N 69 50 E
Sūlār, *Iran* **45 D6** 31 53N 51 54 E
Sulawesi Sea = Celebes Sea, *Indonesia* **37 D6** 3 0N 123 0 E
Sulawesi Selatan □, *Indonesia* **37 E6** 2 30S 120 0 E
Sulawesi Utara □, *Indonesia* **37 D6** 1 0N 122 30 E
Sulima, *S. Leone* **50 G3** 6 58N 11 32W
Sulina, *Romania* **17 F15** 45 10N 29 40 E
Sulitjelma, *Norway* **8 C17** 67 9N 16 3 E
Sullana, *Peru* **92 D2** 4 52S 80 39W
Sullivan, *Ill., U.S.A.* **80 F10** 39 36N 88 37W
Sullivan, *Ind., U.S.A.* **76 F2** 39 6N 87 24W
Sullivan, *Mo., U.S.A.* **80 F9** 38 13N 91 10W
Sullivan Bay, *Canada* **72 C3** 50 55N 126 50W
Sullivan I. = Lanbi Kyun, *Burma* **39 G2** 10 50N 98 20 E
Sulphur, *La., U.S.A.* **81 K8** 30 14N 93 23W
Sulphur, *Okla., U.S.A.* **81 H6** 34 31N 96 58W
Sulphur Pt., *Canada* **72 A6** 60 56N 114 48W
Sulphur Springs, *U.S.A.* **81 J7** 33 8N 95 36W
Sultan, *Canada* **70 C3** 47 36N 82 47W
Sultan, *U.S.A.* **84 C5** 47 52N 121 49W
Sultanpur, *Mad. P., India* **42 H8** 23 9N 77 56 E
Sultanpur, *Punjab, India* **42 D6** 31 13N 75 11 E
Sultanpur, *Ut. P., India* **43 F10** 26 18N 82 4 E
Sulu Arch., *Phil.* **37 C6** 6 0N 121 0 E
Sulu Sea, *E. Indies* **37 C6** 8 0N 120 0 E
Suluq, *Libya* **51 B10** 31 44N 20 14 E
Sulzberger Ice Shelf, *Antarctica* **5 D10** 78 0S 150 0 E
Sumalata, *Indonesia* **37 D6** 1 0N 122 31 E
Sumampa, *Argentina* **94 B3** 29 25S 63 29W
Sumatera □, *Indonesia* **36 D2** 0 40N 100 20 E
Sumatera Barat □, *Indonesia* **36 E2** 1 0S 101 0 E
Sumatera Utara □, *Indonesia* **36 D1** 2 30N 98 0 E
Sumatra = Sumatera □, *Indonesia* **36 D2** 0 40N 100 20 E
Sumba, *Indonesia* **37 F5** 9 45S 119 35 E
Sumba, Selat, *Indonesia* **37 F5** 9 0S 118 40 E
Sumbawa, *Indonesia* **36 F5** 8 26S 117 30 E
Sumbawa Besar, *Indonesia* **36 F5** 8 30S 117 26 E
Sumbawanga □, *Tanzania* **52 F6** 8 0S 31 30 E
Sumbe, *Angola* **52 G2** 11 10S 13 48 E
Sumburgh Hd., *U.K.* **12 B7** 59 52N 1 17W
Sumdeo, *India* **43 D8** 31 26N 78 44 E
Sumdo, *China* **43 B8** 35 6N 78 41 E
Sumedang, *Indonesia* **37 G12** 6 52S 107 55 E
Šumen = Shumen, *Bulgaria* **21 C12** 43 18N 26 55 E
Sumenep, *Indonesia* **37 G15** 7 1S 113 52 E
Sumgait = Sumqayıt, *Azerbaijan* **25 F8** 40 34N 49 38 E
Summer L., *U.S.A.* **82 E3** 42 50N 120 45W
Summerland, *Canada* **72 D5** 49 32N 119 41W
Summerside, *Canada* **71 C7** 46 24N 63 47W
Summersville, *U.S.A.* **76 F5** 38 17N 80 51W
Summerville, *Ga., U.S.A.* **77 H3** 34 29N 85 21W
Summerville, *S.C., U.S.A.* **77 J5** 33 1N 80 11W
Summit Lake, *Canada* **72 C4** 54 20N 122 40W
Summit Peak, *U.S.A.* **83 H10** 37 21N 106 42W
Sumner, *Iowa, U.S.A.* **80 D8** 42 51N 92 6W
Sumner, *Wash., U.S.A.* **84 C4** 47 12N 122 14W
Sumoto, *Japan* **31 G7** 34 21N 134 54 E
Šumperk, *Czech Rep.* **17 D9** 49 59N 16 59 E
Sumqayıt, *Azerbaijan* **25 F8** 40 34N 49 38 E
Sumter, *U.S.A.* **77 J5** 33 55N 80 21W
Sumy, *Ukraine* **25 D5** 50 57N 34 50 E
Sun City, *S. Africa* **56 D4** 25 17S 27 3 E
Sun City, *Ariz., U.S.A.* **83 K7** 33 36N 112 17W
Sun City, *Calif., U.S.A.* **85 M9** 33 42N 117 11W
Sun City Center, *U.S.A.* **77 M4** 27 43N 82 18W
Sun Lakes, *U.S.A.* **83 K8** 33 10N 111 52W
Sun Valley, *U.S.A.* **82 E6** 43 42N 114 21W
Sunagawa, *Japan* **30 C10** 43 29N 141 55 E
Sunan, *N. Korea* **35 E13** 39 15N 125 40 E
Sunart, L., *U.K.* **12 E3** 56 42N 5 43W
Sunburst, *U.S.A.* **82 B8** 48 53N 111 55W
Sunbury, *Australia* **63 F3** 37 35S 144 44 E
Sunbury, *U.S.A.* **79 F8** 40 52N 76 48W
Sunchales, *Argentina* **94 C3** 30 58S 61 35W
Suncho Corral, *Argentina* **94 B3** 27 55S 63 27W
Sunch'ŏn, *S. Korea* **35 G14** 34 52N 127 31 E
Suncook, *U.S.A.* **79 C13** 43 8N 71 27W
Sunda, Selat, *Indonesia* **36 F3** 6 20S 105 30 E
Sunda Is., *Indonesia* **28 K14** 5 0S 105 0 E
Sunda Str. = Sunda, Selat, *Indonesia* **36 F3** 6 20S 105 30 E
Sundance, *Canada* **73 B10** 56 32N 94 4W
Sundance, *U.S.A.* **80 C2** 44 24N 104 23W
Sundar Nagar, *India* **42 D7** 31 32N 76 53 E
Sundarbans, *Asia* **41 J16** 22 0N 89 0 E
Sundargarh, *India* **41 H14** 22 4N 84 5 E
Sundays = Sondags →, *S. Africa* **56 E4** 33 44S 25 51 E
Sunderland, *Canada* **78 B5** 44 16N 79 4W
Sunderland, *U.K.* **10 C6** 54 55N 1 23W
Sundre, *Canada* **72 C6** 51 49N 114 38W
Sundsvall, *Sweden* **9 E17** 62 23N 17 17 E
Sung Hei, *Vietnam* **39 G6** 10 20N 106 2 E
Sungai Kolok, *Thailand* **39 J3** 6 2N 101 58 E
Sungai Lembing, *Malaysia* **39 L4** 3 55N 103 3 E
Sungai Petani, *Malaysia* **39 K3** 5 37N 100 30 E
Sungaigerong, *Indonesia* **36 E2** 2 59S 104 52 E
Sungailiat, *Indonesia* **36 E3** 1 51S 106 8 E
Sungaipenuh, *Indonesia* **36 E2** 2 1S 101 20 E
Sungari = Songhua Jiang →, *China* **33 B8** 47 45N 132 30 E
Sunghua Chiang = Songhua Jiang →, *China* **33 B8** 47 45N 132 30 E
Sunland Park, *U.S.A.* **83 L10** 31 50N 106 40W
Sunndalsøra, *Norway* **9 E13** 62 40N 8 33 E
Sunnyside, *U.S.A.* **82 C3** 46 20N 120 0W
Sunnyvale, *U.S.A.* **84 H4** 37 23N 122 2W
Suntar, *Russia* **27 C12** 62 15N 117 30 E
Suomenselkä, *Finland* **8 E21** 62 52N 24 0 E
Suomussalmi, *Finland* **8 D23** 64 54N 29 10 E
Suoyarvi, *Russia* **24 B5** 62 3N 32 20 E
Supai, *U.S.A.* **83 H7** 36 15N 112 41W
Supaul, *India* **43 F12** 26 10N 86 40 E
Superior, *Ariz., U.S.A.* **83 K8** 33 18N 111 6W
Superior, *Mont., U.S.A.* **82 C6** 47 12N 114 53W
Superior, *Nebr., U.S.A.* **80 E5** 40 1N 98 4W
Superior, *Wis., U.S.A.* **80 B8** 46 44N 92 6W
Superior, L., *N. Amer.* **70 C2** 47 0N 87 0W
Suphan Buri, *Thailand* **38 E3** 14 14N 100 10 E

T

Tethul

Tethul →, Canada 72 A6 60 35N 112 12W
Tetiyev, Ukraine 17 D15 49 22N 29 38 E
Teton →, U.S.A. 82 C8 47 56N 110 31W
Tétouan, Morocco 50 A4 35 35N 5 21W
Tetovo, Macedonia 21 C9 42 1N 20 59 E
Teuco →, Argentina 94 B3 25 35S 60 11W
Teulon, Canada 73 C9 50 23N 97 16W
Teun, Indonesia 37 F7 6 59S 129 8 E
Teutoburger Wald, Germany 16 B5 52 5N 8 22 E
Tevere →, Italy 20 D5 41 44N 12 14 E
Teverya, Israel 47 C4 32 47N 35 32 E
Teviot →, U.K. 12 F6 55 29N 2 38W
Tewantin, Australia 63 D5 26 27S 153 3 E
Tewkesbury, U.K. 11 F5 51 59N 2 9W
Texada I., Canada 72 D4 49 40N 124 25W
Texarkana, Ark., U.S.A. 81 J8 33 26N 94 2W
Texarkana, Tex., U.S.A. 81 J7 33 26N 94 3W
Texas, Australia 63 D5 28 49S 151 9 E
Texas □, U.S.A. 81 K5 31 40N 98 30W
Texas City, U.S.A. 81 L7 29 24N 94 54W
Texel, Neths. 15 A4 53 5N 4 50 E
Texline, U.S.A. 81 G3 36 23N 103 2W
Texoma, L., U.S.A. 81 J6 33 50N 96 34W
Tezin, Afghan. 42 B3 34 24N 69 30 E
Teziutlán, Mexico 87 D5 19 50N 97 22W
Tezpur, India 41 F18 26 40N 92 45 E
Tezzeron L., Canada 72 C4 54 43N 124 30W
Tha-anne →, Canada 73 A10 60 31N 94 37W
Tha Deua, Laos 38 D4 17 57N 102 53 E
Tha Deua, Laos 38 C3 19 26N 101 50 E
Tha Pla, Thailand 38 D3 17 48N 100 32 E
Tha Rua, Thailand 38 E3 14 34N 100 44 E
Tha Sala, Thailand 39 H2 8 40N 99 56 E
Tha Song Yang, Thailand 38 D1 17 34N 97 55 E
Thaba Putsoa, Lesotho 57 D4 29 45S 28 0 E
Thabana Ntlenyana, Lesotho 57 D4 29 30S 29 16 E
Thabazimbi, S. Africa 57 C4 24 40S 27 21 E
Thādiq, Si. Arabia 44 E5 25 18N 45 52 E
Thai Binh, Vietnam 38 B6 20 35N 106 1 E
Thai Muang, Thailand 39 H2 8 24N 98 16 E
Thai Nguyen, Vietnam 38 B5 21 35N 105 55 E
Thailand ■, Asia 38 E4 16 0N 102 0 E
Thailand, G. of, Asia 39 G3 11 30N 101 0 E
Thakhek, Laos 38 D5 17 25N 104 45 E
Thal, Pakistan 42 C4 33 28N 70 33 E
Thal Desert, Pakistan 42 D4 31 10N 71 30 E
Thala La = Hkakabo Razi, Burma 41 E20 28 25N 97 23 E
Thalabarivat, Cambodia 38 F5 13 33N 105 57 E
Thallon, Australia 63 D4 28 39S 148 49 E
Thames, N.Z. 59 G5 37 7S 175 34 E
Thames →, Canada 78 D2 42 20N 82 25W
Thames →, U.K. 11 F8 51 29N 0 34 E
Thames →, U.S.A. 79 E12 41 18N 72 5W
Thames Estuary, U.K. 11 F8 51 29N 0 52 E
Thamesford, Canada 78 C4 43 4N 81 0W
Thamesville, Canada 78 D3 42 33N 81 59W
Than, India 42 H4 22 34N 71 11 E
Than Uyen, Vietnam 38 B4 22 0N 103 54 E
Thana Gazi, India 42 F7 27 25N 76 19 E
Thandla, India 42 H6 23 0N 74 34 E
Thane, India 40 K8 19 12N 72 59 E
Thanesar, India 42 D7 30 1N 76 52 E
Thanet, I. of, U.K. 11 F9 51 21N 1 20 E
Thangool, Australia 62 C5 24 38S 150 42 E
Thanh Hoa, Vietnam 38 C5 19 48N 105 46 E
Thanh Hung, Vietnam 39 H5 9 55N 105 43 E
Thanh Pho Ho Chi Minh, Vietnam 39 G6 10 58N 106 40 E
Thanh Thuy, Vietnam 38 A5 22 55N 104 51 E
Thanjavur, India 40 P11 10 48N 79 12 E
Thano Bula Khan, Pakistan 42 G2 25 22N 67 50 E
Thaolinta L., Canada 73 A9 61 30N 96 25W
Thap Sakae, Thailand 39 G2 11 30N 99 37 E
Thap Than, Thailand 38 E2 15 27N 99 54 E
Thar Desert, India 42 F5 28 0N 72 0 E
Tharad, India 42 G4 24 30N 71 44 E
Thargomindah, Australia 63 D3 27 58S 143 46 E
Tharrawaddy, Burma 41 L19 17 38N 95 48 E
Tharthār, Mileh, Iraq 44 C4 34 0N 43 15 E
Tharthār, W. ath →, Iraq 44 C4 33 59N 43 12 E
Thásos, Greece 21 D11 40 40N 24 40 E
That Khe, Vietnam 38 A6 22 16N 106 28 E
Thatcher, Ariz., U.S.A. 83 K9 32 51N 109 46W
Thatcher, Colo., U.S.A. 81 G2 37 33N 104 7W
Thaton, Burma 41 L20 16 55N 97 22 E
Thaungdut, Burma 41 G19 24 30N 94 40 E
Thayer, U.S.A. 81 G9 36 31N 91 33W
Thayetmyo, Burma 41 K19 19 20N 95 10 E
Thazi, Burma 41 J20 21 0N 96 5 E
The Alberga →, Australia 63 D2 27 6S 135 33 E
The Bight, Bahamas 89 B4 24 19N 75 24W
The Dalles, U.S.A. 82 D3 45 36N 121 10W
The English Company's Is., Australia 62 A2 11 50S 136 32 E
The Frome →, Australia 63 D2 29 8S 137 54 E
The Great Divide = Great Dividing Ra., Australia 62 C4 23 0S 146 0 E
The Hague = 's-Gravenhage, Neths. 15 B4 52 7N 4 17 E
The Hamilton →, Australia 63 D2 26 40S 135 19 E
The Macumba →, Australia 63 D2 27 52S 137 12 E
The Neales →, Australia 63 D2 28 8S 136 47 E
The Officer →, Australia 61 E5 27 46S 132 30 E
The Pas, Canada 73 C8 53 45N 101 15W
The Range, Zimbabwe 55 F3 19 2S 31 2 E
The Rock, Australia 63 F4 35 15S 147 2 E
The Salt L., Australia 63 E3 30 6S 142 8 E
The Sandheads, India 43 J13 21 10N 88 20 E
The Stevenson →, Australia 63 D2 27 6S 135 33 E
The Warburton →, Australia 63 D2 28 4S 137 28 E
The Woodlands, U.S.A. 81 K7 30 9N 95 27W
Thebes = Thívai, Greece 21 E10 38 19N 23 19 E
Thebes, Egypt 51 C12 25 40N 32 35 E
Thedford, Canada 78 C3 43 9N 81 51W
Thedford, U.S.A. 80 E4 41 59N 100 35W
Theebine, Australia 63 D5 25 57S 152 34 E
Thekulthili L., Canada 73 A7 61 3N 110 0W
Thelon →, Canada 73 A8 62 35N 104 3W
Theodore, Australia 62 C5 24 55S 150 3 E
Theodore, Canada 73 C8 51 26N 102 55W
Theodore, U.S.A. 77 K1 30 33N 88 10W
Theodore Roosevelt Nat. Memorial Park, U.S.A. 80 B3 47 0N 103 25W
Theodore Roosevelt Res., U.S.A. 83 K8 33 46N 111 0W
Thepha, Thailand 39 J3 6 52N 100 58 E
Theresa, U.S.A. 79 B9 44 13N 75 48W
Thermaïkós Kólpos, Greece 21 D10 40 15N 22 45 E
Thermopolis, U.S.A. 82 E9 43 39N 108 13W
Thermopylae P., Greece 21 E10 38 48N 22 35 E
Thessalon, Canada 70 C3 46 20N 83 30W
Thessaloníki, Greece 21 D10 40 38N 22 58 E
Thessaloniki, Gulf of = Thermaïkós Kólpos, Greece 21 D10 40 15N 22 45 E
Thetford, U.K. 11 E8 52 25N 0 45 E
Thetford Mines, Canada 71 C5 46 8N 71 18W
Theun →, Laos 38 C5 18 19N 104 0 E
Theunissen, S. Africa 56 D4 28 26S 26 43 E
Thevenard, Australia 63 E1 32 9S 133 38 E
Thibodaux, U.S.A. 81 L9 29 48N 90 49W
Thicket Portage, Canada 73 B9 55 19N 97 42W
Thief River Falls, U.S.A. 80 A6 48 7N 96 10W
Thiel Mts., Antarctica 5 E16 85 15S 91 0W
Thiers, France 18 D5 45 52N 3 33 E
Thiès, Senegal 50 F2 14 50N 16 51W
Thika, Kenya 54 C4 1 1S 37 5 E
Thikombia, Fiji 59 B9 15 44S 179 55W
Thimphu, Bhutan 41 F16 27 31N 89 45 E
Þingvallavatn, Iceland 8 D3 64 11N 21 9W
Thionville, France 18 B7 49 20N 6 10 E
Thíra, Greece 21 F11 36 23N 25 27 E
Third Cataract, Sudan 51 E12 19 42N 30 20 E
Thirsk, U.K. 10 C6 54 14N 1 19W
Thiruvananthapuram = Trivandrum, India 40 Q10 8 41N 77 0 E
Thisted, Denmark 9 H13 56 58N 8 40 E
Thistle I., Australia 63 F2 35 0S 136 8 E
Thívai, Greece 21 E10 38 19N 23 19 E
Þjórsá →, Iceland 8 E3 63 47N 20 48W
Thlewiaza →, Man., Canada 73 B8 59 43N 100 5W
Thlewiaza →, N.W.T., Canada 73 A10 60 29N 94 40W
Thmar Puok, Cambodia 38 F4 13 57N 103 4 E
Tho Vinh, Vietnam 38 C5 19 16N 105 42 E
Thoa →, Canada 73 A7 60 31N 109 47W
Thoen, Thailand 38 D2 17 43N 99 12 E
Thoeng, Thailand 38 C3 19 41N 100 12 E
Thohoyandou, S. Africa 53 J6 22 58S 30 29 E
Tholdi, Pakistan 43 B7 35 5N 76 6 E
Thomas, U.S.A. 81 H5 35 45N 98 45W
Thomas, L., Australia 63 D2 26 4S 137 58 E
Thomaston, U.S.A. 77 J3 32 53N 84 20W
Thomasville, Ala., U.S.A. 77 K2 31 55N 87 44W
Thomasville, Ga., U.S.A. 77 K4 30 50N 83 59W
Thomasville, N.C., U.S.A. 77 H5 35 53N 80 5W
Thompson, Canada 73 B9 55 45N 97 52W
Thompson, U.S.A. 79 E9 41 52N 75 31W
Thompson →, Canada 72 C4 50 15N 121 24W
Thompson →, U.S.A. 80 F8 39 46N 93 37W
Thompson Falls, U.S.A. 82 C6 47 36N 115 21W
Thompson Pk., U.S.A. 82 F2 41 0N 123 0W
Thompson Springs, U.S.A. 83 G9 38 58N 109 43W
Thompsontown, U.S.A. 78 F7 40 33N 77 14W
Thomson, U.S.A. 77 J4 33 28N 82 30W
Thomson →, Australia 62 C3 25 11S 142 53 E
Thomson's Falls = Nyahururu, Kenya 54 B4 0 2N 36 27 E
Þórisvatn, Iceland 8 D4 64 20N 18 55W
Thornaby on Tees, U.K. 10 C6 54 33N 1 18W
Thornbury, Canada 78 B4 44 34N 80 26W
Thorne, U.K. 10 D7 53 37N 0 57W
Thornhill, Canada 72 C3 54 31N 128 32W
Thorold, Canada 78 C5 43 7N 79 12W
Þórshöfn, Iceland 8 C6 66 12N 15 20W
Thouin, C., Australia 60 D2 20 20S 118 10 E
Thousand Oaks, U.S.A. 85 L8 34 10N 118 50W
Thrace, Turkey 21 D12 41 0N 27 0 E
Three Forks, U.S.A. 82 D8 45 54N 111 33W
Three Hills, Canada 72 C6 51 43N 113 15W
Three Hummock I., Australia 62 G3 40 25S 144 55 E
Three Points, C., Ghana 50 H5 4 42N 2 6W
Three Rivers, Calif., U.S.A. 84 J8 36 26N 118 54W
Three Rivers, Tex., U.S.A. 81 L5 28 28N 98 11W
Three Sisters, U.S.A. 82 D3 44 4N 121 51W
Three Springs, Australia 61 E2 29 32S 115 45 E
Throssell, L., Australia 61 E3 27 33S 124 10 E
Throssell Ra., Australia 60 D3 22 3S 121 43 E
Thuan Hoa, Vietnam 39 H5 8 58N 105 30 E
Thubun Lakes, Canada 73 A6 61 30N 112 0W
Thuin, Belgium 15 D4 50 20N 4 17 E
Thule = Qaanaaq, Greenland 4 B4 77 40N 69 0W
Thun, Switz. 18 C7 46 45N 7 38 E
Thunder B., U.S.A. 78 B1 45 0N 83 20W
Thunder Bay, Canada 70 C2 48 20N 89 15W
Thung Song, Thailand 39 H2 8 10N 99 40 E
Thunkar, Bhutan 41 F17 27 55N 91 0 E
Thuong Tra, Vietnam 38 D6 16 2N 107 42 E
Thüringer Wald, Germany 16 C6 50 35N 11 0 E
Thurles, Ireland 13 D4 52 41N 7 49W
Thurrock □, U.K. 11 F8 51 31N 0 23 E
Thursday I., Australia 62 A3 10 30S 142 3 E
Thurso, Canada 70 C4 45 36N 75 15W
Thurso, U.K. 12 C5 58 36N 3 32W
Thurso →, U.K. 12 C5 58 36N 3 32W
Thurston I., Antarctica 5 D16 72 0S 100 0W
Thutade L., Canada 72 B3 57 0N 126 55W
Thyolo, Malawi 55 F4 16 7S 35 5 E
Thysville = Mbanza Ngungu, Dem. Rep. of the Congo 52 F2 5 12S 14 53 E
Ti Tree, Australia 62 C1 22 5S 133 22 E
Tian Shan, Asia 32 B3 40 30N 76 0 E
Tianjin, China 35 E9 39 8N 117 10 E
Tianshui, China 34 G3 34 32N 105 40 E
Tianzhen, China 34 D8 40 24N 114 5 E
Tianzhuangtai, China 35 D12 40 43N 122 5 E
Tiaret, Algeria 50 A6 35 20N 1 21 E
Tibagi, Brazil 95 A5 24 30S 50 24W
Tibagi →, Brazil 95 A5 22 47S 51 1W
Tiber = Tevere →, Italy 20 D5 41 44N 12 14 E
Tiberias = Teverya, Israel 47 C4 32 47N 35 32 E
Tiberias, L. = Yam Kinneret, Israel 47 C4 32 45N 35 35 E
Tibesti, Chad 51 D9 21 0N 17 30 E
Tibet = Xizang Zizhiqu □, China 32 C3 32 0N 88 0 E
Tibet, Plateau of, Asia 28 F12 32 0N 86 0 E
Tibnī, Syria 44 C3 35 36N 39 50 E
Tibooburra, Australia 63 D3 29 26S 142 1 E
Tiburón, I., Mexico 86 B2 29 0N 112 30W
Ticino →, Italy 18 D8 45 9N 9 14 E
Ticonderoga, U.S.A. 79 C11 43 51N 73 26W
Ticul, Mexico 87 C7 20 20N 89 31W
Tidaholm, Sweden 9 G15 58 12N 13 58 E
Tiddim, Burma 41 H18 23 28N 93 45 E
Tidioute, U.S.A. 78 E5 41 41N 79 24W
Tidjikja, Mauritania 50 E3 18 29N 11 35W
Tidore, Indonesia 37 D7 0 40N 127 25 E
Tiel, Neths. 15 C5 51 53N 5 26 E
Tieling, China 35 C12 42 20N 123 55 E
Tielt, Belgium 15 C3 51 0N 3 20 E
Tien Shan = Tian Shan, Asia 32 B3 40 30N 76 0 E
Tien-tsin = Tianjin, China 35 E9 39 8N 117 10 E
Tien Yen, Vietnam 38 B6 21 20N 107 24 E
T'ienching = Tianjin, China 35 E9 39 8N 117 10 E
Tienen, Belgium 15 D4 50 48N 4 57 E
Tientsin = Tianjin, China 35 E9 39 8N 117 10 E
Tieri, Australia 62 C4 23 2S 148 21 E
Tierra Amarilla, Chile 94 B1 27 28S 70 18W
Tierra Amarilla, U.S.A. 83 H10 36 42N 106 33W
Tierra Colorada, Mexico 87 D5 17 10N 99 35W
Tierra de Campos, Spain 19 A3 42 10N 4 50W
Tierra del Fuego, I. Gr. de, Argentina 96 G3 54 0S 69 0W
Tiétar →, Spain 19 C3 39 50N 6 1W
Tieté →, Brazil 95 A5 20 40S 51 35W
Tiffin, U.S.A. 76 E4 41 7N 83 11W
Tiflis = Tbilisi, Georgia 25 F7 41 43N 44 50 E
Tifton, U.S.A. 77 K4 31 27N 83 31W
Tifu, Indonesia 37 E7 3 39S 126 24 E
Tighina, Moldova 17 E15 46 50N 29 30 E
Tigil, Russia 27 D16 57 49N 158 40 E
Tignish, Canada 71 C7 46 58N 64 2W
Tigre →, Peru 92 D4 4 30S 74 10W
Tigre →, Venezuela 92 B6 9 20N 62 30W
Tigris = Dijlah, Nahr →, Asia 44 D5 31 0N 47 25 E
Tigyaing, Burma 41 H20 23 45N 96 10 E
Tijara, India 42 F7 27 56N 76 31 E
Tijuana, Mexico 85 N9 32 30N 117 10W
Tikal, Guatemala 88 C2 17 13N 89 24W
Tikamgarh, India 43 G8 24 44N 78 50 E
Tikhoretsk, Russia 25 E7 45 56N 40 5 E
Tikhvin, Russia 24 C5 59 35N 33 30 E
Tikrīt, Iraq 44 C4 34 35N 43 37 E
Tiksi, Russia 27 B13 71 40N 128 45 E
Tilamuta, Indonesia 37 D6 0 32N 122 23 E
Tilburg, Neths. 15 C5 51 31N 5 6 E
Tilbury, Canada 78 D2 42 17N 82 23W
Tilbury, U.K. 11 F8 51 27N 0 22 E
Tilcara, Argentina 94 A2 23 36S 65 23W
Tilden, U.S.A. 80 D6 42 3N 97 50W
Tilhar, India 43 F8 28 0N 79 45 E
Tilichiki, Russia 27 C17 60 27N 166 5 E
Tílissos, Greece 23 D7 35 20N 25 1 E
Till →, U.K. 10 B5 55 41N 2 13W
Tillamook, U.S.A. 82 D2 45 27N 123 51W
Tillsonburg, Canada 78 D4 42 53N 80 44W
Tillyeria, Cyprus 23 D11 35 6N 32 40 E
Tílos, Greece 21 F12 36 27N 27 27 E
Tilpa, Australia 63 E3 30 57S 144 24 E
Tilsit = Sovetsk, Russia 9 J19 55 6N 21 50 E
Tilt →, U.K. 12 E5 56 46N 3 51W
Tilton, U.S.A. 79 C13 43 27N 71 36W
Tiltonsville, U.S.A. 78 F4 40 10N 80 41W
Timagami, L., Canada 70 C3 47 0N 80 10W
Timanskiy Kryazh, Russia 24 A9 65 58N 50 5 E
Timaru, N.Z. 59 L3 44 23S 171 14 E
Timau, Kenya 54 B4 0 4N 37 15 E
Timbákion, Greece 23 D6 35 4N 24 45 E
Timber Creek, Australia 60 C5 15 40S 130 29 E
Timber Lake, U.S.A. 80 C4 45 26N 101 5W
Timber Mt., U.S.A. 84 H10 37 6N 116 28W
Timbuktu = Tombouctou, Mali 50 E5 16 50N 3 0W
Timi, Cyprus 23 E11 34 44N 32 31 E
Timimoun, Algeria 50 C6 29 14N 0 16 E
Timirist, Râs, Mauritania 50 E2 19 21N 16 30W
Timişoara, Romania 17 F11 45 43N 21 15 E
Timmins, Canada 70 C3 48 28N 81 25W
Timok →, Serbia, Yug. 21 B10 44 10N 22 40 E
Timor, Indonesia 37 F7 9 0S 125 0 E
Timor Sea, Ind. Oc. 60 B4 12 0S 127 0 E
Timor Timur = East Timor ■, Asia 37 F7 8 50S 126 0 E
Tin Can Bay, Australia 63 D5 25 56S 153 0 E
Tin Mt., U.S.A. 84 J9 36 50N 117 10W
Tina →, S. Africa 57 E4 31 18S 29 13 E
Tinaca Pt., Phil. 37 C7 5 30N 125 25 E
Tinajo, Canary Is. 22 E6 29 4N 13 42W
Tindal, Australia 60 B5 14 31S 132 22 E
Tindouf, Algeria 50 C4 27 42N 8 10W
Tinggi, Pulau, Malaysia 39 L5 2 18N 104 7 E
Tingo Maria, Peru 92 E3 9 10S 75 54W
Tingrela, Ivory C. 50 F4 10 27N 6 25W
Tinh Bien, Vietnam 39 G5 10 36N 104 57 E
Tinnevelly = Tirunelveli, India 40 Q10 8 45N 77 45 E
Tinogasta, Argentina 94 B2 28 5S 67 32W
Tínos, Greece 21 F11 37 33N 25 8 E
Tinpahar, India 43 G12 24 59N 87 44 E
Tintina, Argentina 94 B3 27 2S 62 45W
Tintinara, Australia 63 F3 35 48S 140 2 E
Tioga, N. Dak., U.S.A. 80 A3 48 23N 102 56W
Tioga, Pa., U.S.A. 78 E7 41 55N 77 8W
Tioman, Pulau, Malaysia 39 L5 2 50N 104 10 E
Tionesta, U.S.A. 78 E5 41 30N 79 28W
Tipongpani, India 41 F19 27 20N 95 55 E
Tipperary, Ireland 13 D3 52 28N 8 10W
Tipperary □, Ireland 13 D4 52 37N 7 55W
Tipton, Calif., U.S.A. 84 J7 36 4N 119 19W
Tipton, Iowa, U.S.A. 80 E9 41 46N 91 8W
Tipton Mt., U.S.A. 85 K12 35 32N 114 12W
Tiptonville, U.S.A. 81 G10 36 23N 89 29W
Tīrān, Iran 45 C6 32 45N 51 8 E
Tiranë, Albania 21 D8 41 18N 19 49 E
Tiraspol, Moldova 17 E15 46 55N 29 35 E
Tire, Turkey 21 E12 38 5N 27 45 E
Tirebolu, Turkey 25 F6 40 58N 38 45 E
Tiree, U.K. 12 E2 56 31N 6 55W
Tiree, Passage of, U.K. 12 E2 56 30N 6 30W
Tîrgovişte = Târgovişte, Romania 17 F13 44 55N 25 27 E
Tîrgu-Jiu = Târgu-Jiu, Romania 17 F12 45 5N 23 19 E
Tîrgu Mureş = Târgu Mureş, Romania 17 E13 46 31N 24 38 E
Tirich Mir, Pakistan 40 A7 36 15N 71 55 E
Tírnavos, Greece 21 E10 39 45N 22 18 E
Tirodi, India 40 J11 21 40N 79 44 E
Tirol □, Austria 16 E6 47 3N 10 43 E
Tirso →, Italy 20 E3 39 53N 8 32 E
Tiruchchirappalli, India 40 P11 10 45N 78 45 E
Tirunelveli, India 40 Q10 8 45N 77 45 E
Tirupati, India 40 N11 13 39N 79 25 E
Tiruppur, India 40 P10 11 5N 77 22 E
Tiruvannamalai, India 40 N11 12 15N 79 5 E
Tisa, India 42 C7 32 50N 76 9 E
Tisa →, Serbia, Yug. 21 B9 45 15N 20 17 E
Tisdale, Canada 73 C8 52 50N 104 0W
Tishomingo, U.S.A. 81 H6 34 14N 96 41W
Tisza = Tisa →, Serbia, Yug. 21 B9 45 15N 20 17 E
Tit-Ary, Russia 27 B13 71 55N 127 2 E
Tithwal, Pakistan 43 B5 34 21N 73 50 E
Titicaca, L., S. Amer. 92 G5 15 30S 69 30W
Titograd = Podgorica, Montenegro, Yug. 21 C8 42 30N 19 19 E
Titule, Dem. Rep. of the Congo 54 B2 3 15N 25 31 E
Titusville, Fla., U.S.A. 77 L5 28 37N 80 49W
Titusville, Pa., U.S.A. 78 E5 41 38N 79 41W
Tivaouane, Senegal 50 F2 14 56N 16 45W
Tiverton, U.K. 11 G4 50 54N 3 29W
Tívoli, Italy 20 D5 41 58N 12 45 E
Tizi-Ouzou, Algeria 50 A6 36 42N 4 3 E
Tizimín, Mexico 87 C7 21 0N 88 1W
Tjeggelvas, Sweden 8 C17 66 37N 17 45 E
Tjirebon = Cirebon, Indonesia 36 F3 6 45S 108 32 E
Tjörn, Sweden 9 G14 58 0N 11 35 E
Tlacotalpan, Mexico 87 D5 18 37N 95 40W
Tlahualilo, Mexico 86 B4 26 20N 103 30W
Tlaquepaque, Mexico 86 C4 20 39N 103 19W
Tlaxcala, Mexico 87 D5 19 20N 98 14W
Tlaxcala □, Mexico 87 D5 19 30N 98 20W
Tlaxiaco, Mexico 87 D5 17 18N 97 40W
Tlemcen, Algeria 50 B5 34 52N 1 21W
To Bong, Vietnam 38 F7 12 45N 109 16 E
Toad →, Canada 72 B4 59 25N 124 57W
Toad River, Canada 72 B3 58 51N 125 14W
Toamasina, Madag. 57 B8 18 10S 49 25 E
Toamasina □, Madag. 57 B8 18 0S 49 0 E
Toay, Argentina 94 D3 36 43S 64 38W
Toba, Japan 31 G8 34 30N 136 51 E
Toba, Danau, Indonesia 36 D1 2 30N 97 30 E
Toba Kakar, Pakistan 42 D3 31 30N 69 0 E
Toba Tek Singh, Pakistan 42 D5 30 55N 72 25 E
Tobago, Trin. & Tob. 89 D7 11 10N 60 30W
Tobelo, Indonesia 37 D7 1 45N 127 56 E
Tobermory, Canada 78 A3 45 12N 81 40W
Tobermory, U.K. 12 E2 56 38N 6 5W
Tobi, Pac. Oc. 37 D8 2 40N 131 10 E
Tobin, U.S.A. 84 F5 39 55N 121 19W
Tobin, L., Australia 60 D4 21 45S 125 49 E
Tobin L., Canada 73 C8 53 35N 103 30W
Toboali, Indonesia 36 E3 3 0S 106 25 E
Tobol →, Russia 26 D7 58 10N 68 12 E
Toboli, Indonesia 37 E6 0 38S 120 5 E
Tobolsk, Russia 26 D7 58 15N 68 10 E
Tobruk = Tubruq, Libya 51 B10 32 7N 23 55 E
Tobyhanna, U.S.A. 79 E9 41 11N 75 25W
Tobyl = Tobol →, Russia 26 D7 58 10N 68 12 E
Tocantinópolis, Brazil 93 E9 6 20S 47 25W
Tocantins □, Brazil 93 F9 10 0S 48 0W
Tocantins →, Brazil 93 D9 1 45S 49 10W
Toccoa, U.S.A. 77 H4 34 35N 83 19W
Tochi →, Pakistan 42 C4 32 49N 70 41 E
Tochigi, Japan 31 F9 36 25N 139 45 E
Tochigi □, Japan 31 F9 36 45N 139 45 E
Toconao, Chile 94 A2 23 11S 68 1W
Tocopilla, Chile 94 A1 22 5S 70 10W
Tocumwal, Australia 63 F4 35 51S 145 31 E
Tocuyo →, Venezuela 92 A5 11 3N 68 23W
Todd →, Australia 62 C2 24 52S 135 48 E
Todeli, Indonesia 37 E6 1 40S 124 29 E
Todenyang, Kenya 54 B4 4 35N 35 56 E
Todgarh, India 42 G5 25 42N 73 58 E
Todos os Santos, B. de, Brazil 93 F11 12 48S 38 38W
Todos Santos, Mexico 86 C2 23 27N 110 13W
Toe Hd., U.K. 12 D1 57 50N 7 8W
Tofield, Canada 72 C6 53 25N 112 40W
Tofino, Canada 72 D3 49 11N 125 55W
Tofua, Tonga 59 D11 19 45S 175 5W
Tōgane, Japan 31 G10 35 33N 140 22 E
Togian, Kepulauan, Indonesia 37 E6 0 20S 121 50 E
Togliatti, Russia 24 D8 53 32N 49 24 E
Togo ■, W. Afr. 50 G6 8 30N 1 35 E
Togtoh, China 34 D6 40 15N 111 10 E
Tōhoku □, Japan 30 E10 39 50N 141 45 E
Töhöm, Mongolia 34 B5 44 27N 108 2 E
Toinya, Sudan 51 G11 6 17N 29 46 E
Toiyabe Range, U.S.A. 82 G5 39 30N 117 0W
Tojikiston = Tajikistan ■, Asia 26 F8 38 30N 70 0 E
Tojo, Indonesia 37 E6 1 20S 121 15 E
Tōjō, Japan 31 G6 34 53N 133 16 E
Tok, U.S.A. 68 B5 63 20N 142 59W
Tok-do, Japan 31 F5 37 15N 131 52 E
Tokachi-Dake, Japan 30 C11 43 17N 142 5 E
Tokachi-Gawa →, Japan 30 C11 42 44N 143 42 E
Tokala, Indonesia 37 E6 1 30S 121 40 E
Tōkamachi, Japan 31 F9 37 8N 138 43 E
Tokanui, N.Z. 59 M2 46 34S 168 56 E
Tokara-Rettō, Japan 31 K4 29 37N 129 43 E
Tokarahi, N.Z. 59 L3 44 56S 170 39 E
Tokashiki-Shima, Japan 31 L3 26 11N 127 21 E
Tokat □, Turkey 25 F6 40 15N 36 30 E
Tŏkch'ŏn, N. Korea 35 E14 39 45N 126 18 E
Tokeland, U.S.A. 84 D3 46 42N 123 59W
Tokelau Is., Pac. Oc. 64 H10 9 0S 171 45W
Tokmak, Kyrgyzstan 26 E8 42 49N 75 15 E
Toko Ra., Australia 62 C2 23 5S 138 20 E
Tokoro-Gawa →, Japan 30 B12 44 7N 144 5 E
Tokuno-Shima, Japan 31 L4 27 56N 128 55 E
Tokushima, Japan 31 G7 34 4N 134 34 E
Tokushima □, Japan 31 H7 33 55N 134 0 E
Tokuyama, Japan 31 G5 34 3N 131 50 E
Tōkyō, Japan 31 G9 35 45N 139 45 E
Tolaga Bay, N.Z. 59 H7 38 21S 178 20 E
Tolbukhin = Dobrich, Bulgaria 21 C12 43 37N 27 49 E
Toledo, Brazil 95 A5 24 44S 53 45W
Toledo, Spain 19 C3 39 50N 4 2W
Toledo, Ohio, U.S.A. 76 E4 41 39N 83 33W
Toledo, Oreg., U.S.A. 82 D2 44 37N 123 56W
Toledo, Wash., U.S.A. 82 C2 46 26N 122 51W
Toledo, Montes de, Spain 19 C3 39 33N 4 20W
Toledo Bend Reservoir, U.S.A. 81 K8 31 11N 93 34W
Tolga, Australia 62 B4 17 15S 145 29 E

Tubruq

Toliara, Madag. 57 C7 23 21S 43 40 E
Toliara □, Madag. 57 C8 21 0S 45 0 E
Tolima, Colombia 92 C3 4 40N 75 19W
Tolitoli, Indonesia 37 D6 1 5N 120 50 E
Tollhouse, U.S.A. 84 H7 37 1N 119 24W
Tolo, Teluk, Indonesia 37 E6 2 20S 122 10 E
Toluca, Mexico 87 D5 19 20N 99 40W
Tom Burke, S. Africa 57 C4 23 5S 28 0 E
Tom Price, Australia 60 D2 22 40S 117 48 E
Tomah, U.S.A. 80 D9 43 59N 90 30W
Tomahawk, U.S.A. 80 C10 45 28N 89 44W
Tomakomai, Japan 30 C10 42 38N 141 36 E
Tomales, U.S.A. 84 G4 38 15N 122 53W
Tomales B., U.S.A. 84 G3 38 15N 123 58W
Tomar, Portugal 19 C1 39 36N 8 25W
Tomaszów Mazowiecki, Poland 17 C10 51 30N 20 2 E
Tomatlán, Mexico 86 D3 19 56N 105 15W
Tombador, Serra do, Brazil 92 F7 12 0S 58 0W
Tombigbee →, U.S.A. 77 K2 31 8N 87 57W
Tombouctou, Mali 50 E5 16 50N 3 0W
Tombstone, U.S.A. 83 L8 31 43N 110 4W
Tombua, Angola 56 B1 15 55S 11 55 E
Tomé, Chile 94 D1 36 36S 72 57W
Tomelloso, Spain 19 C4 39 10N 3 2W
Tomini, Indonesia 37 D6 0 30N 120 30 E
Tomini, Teluk, Indonesia 37 E6 0 10S 121 0 E
Tomintoul, U.K. 12 D5 57 15N 3 23W
Tomkinson Ranges, Australia 61 E4 26 11S 129 5 E
Tommot, Russia 27 D13 59 4N 126 20 E
Tomnop Ta Suos, Cambodia 39 G5 11 20N 104 15 E
Tomo →, Colombia 92 B5 5 20N 67 48W
Toms Place, U.S.A. 84 H8 37 34N 118 41W
Toms River, U.S.A. 79 G10 39 58N 74 12W
Tomsk, Russia 26 D9 56 30N 85 5 E
Tonalá, Mexico 87 D6 16 8N 93 41W
Tonantins, Brazil 92 D5 2 45S 67 45W
Tonasket, U.S.A. 82 B4 48 42N 119 26W
Tonawanda, U.S.A. 78 D6 43 1N 78 53W
Tonbridge, U.K. 11 F8 51 11N 0 17 E
Tondano, Indonesia 37 D6 1 35N 124 54 E
Tondoro, Namibia 56 B2 17 45S 18 50 E
Tone →, Australia 61 F2 34 25S 116 25 E
Tone-Gawa →, Japan 31 F9 35 44N 140 51 E
Tonekābon, Iran 45 B6 36 45N 51 12 E
Tong Xian, China 34 E9 39 55N 116 35 E
Tonga ■, Pac. Oc. 59 D11 19 50S 174 30W
Tonga Trench, Pac. Oc. 64 J10 18 0S 173 0W
Tongaat, S. Africa 57 D5 29 33S 31 9 E
Tongareva, Cook Is. 65 H12 9 0S 158 0W
Tongatapu Group, Tonga 59 E12 21 0S 175 0W
Tongchŏn-ni, N. Korea 35 E14 39 50N 127 25 E
Tongchuan, China 34 G5 35 6N 109 3 E
Tongeren, Belgium 15 D5 50 47N 5 28 E
Tongguan, China 34 G6 34 40N 110 25 E
Tonghua, China 35 D13 41 42N 125 58 E
Tongjosŏn Man, N. Korea 35 E15 39 30N 128 0 E
Tongking, G. of = Tonkin, G. of, Asia 32 E5 20 0N 108 0 E
Tongliao, China 35 C12 43 38N 122 18 E
Tongling, China 33 C6 30 55N 117 48 E
Tongnae, S. Korea 35 G15 35 12N 129 5 E
Tongobory, Madag. 57 C7 23 32S 44 20 E
Tongoy, Chile 94 C1 30 16S 71 31W
Tongres = Tongeren, Belgium 15 D5 50 47N 5 28 E
Tongsa Dzong, Bhutan 41 F17 27 31N 90 31 E
Tongue, U.K. 12 C4 58 29N 4 25W
Tongue →, U.S.A. 80 B2 46 25N 105 52W
Tongwei, China 34 G3 35 0N 105 5 E
Tongxin, China 34 F3 36 59N 105 58 E
Tongyang, N. Korea 35 E14 39 9N 126 53 E
Tongyu, China 35 B12 44 45N 123 4 E
Tonj, Sudan 51 G11 7 20N 28 44 E
Tonk, India 42 F6 26 6N 75 54 E
Tonkawa, U.S.A. 81 G6 36 41N 97 18W
Tonkin = Bac Phan, Vietnam 38 B5 22 0N 105 0 E
Tonkin, G. of, Asia 32 E5 20 0N 108 0 E
Tonle Sap, Cambodia 38 F4 13 0N 104 0 E
Tono, Japan 30 E10 39 19N 141 32 E
Tonopah, U.S.A. 83 G5 38 4N 117 14W
Tonosí, Panama 88 E3 7 20N 80 20W
Tons →, Haryana, India 42 D7 30 30N 77 39 E
Tons →, Ut. P., India 43 F10 26 1N 83 33 E
Tønsberg, Norway 9 G14 59 19N 10 25 E
Toobanna, Australia 62 B4 18 42S 146 9 E
Toodyay, Australia 61 F2 31 34S 116 28 E
Tooele, U.S.A. 82 F7 40 32N 112 18W
Toompine, Australia 63 D3 27 15S 144 19 E
Toora, Australia 63 F4 38 39S 146 23 E
Toora-Khem, Russia 27 D10 52 28N 96 17 E
Toowoomba, Australia 63 D5 27 32S 151 56 E
Top-ozero, Russia 24 A5 65 35N 32 0 E
Top Springs, Australia 60 C5 16 37S 131 51 E
Topaz, U.S.A. 84 G7 38 41N 119 30W
Topeka, U.S.A. 80 F7 39 3N 95 40W
Topley, Canada 72 C3 54 49N 126 18W
Topocalma, Pta., Chile 94 C1 34 10S 72 2W
Topock, U.S.A. 85 L12 34 46N 114 29W
Topol'čany, Slovak Rep. 17 D10 48 35N 18 12 E
Topolobampo, Mexico 86 B3 25 40N 109 4W
Toppenish, U.S.A. 82 C3 46 23N 120 19W
Toraka Vestale, Madag. 57 B7 16 20S 43 58 E
Torata, Peru 92 G4 17 23S 70 1W
Torbalı, Turkey 21 E12 38 10N 27 21 E
Torbat-e Heydārīyeh, Iran 45 C8 35 15N 59 12 E
Torbat-e Jām, Iran 45 C9 35 16N 60 35 E
Torbay, Canada 71 C9 47 40N 52 42W
Torbay □, U.K. 11 G4 50 26N 3 31W
Tordesillas, Spain 19 B3 41 30N 5 0W
Torfaen □, U.K. 11 F4 51 43N 3 3W
Torgau, Germany 16 C7 51 34N 13 0 E
Torhout, Belgium 15 C3 51 5N 3 7 E
Tori-Shima, Japan 31 J10 30 29N 140 19 E
Torin, Mexico 86 B2 27 33N 110 15W
Torino, Italy 18 D7 45 3N 7 40 E
Torit, Sudan 51 H12 4 27N 32 31 E
Torkamān, Iran 44 B5 37 35N 47 23 E
Tormes →, Spain 19 B2 41 18N 6 29W
Tornado Mt., Canada 72 D6 49 55N 114 40W
Torne älv →, Sweden 8 D21 65 50N 24 12 E
Torneå = Tornio, Finland 8 D21 65 50N 24 12 E
Torneträsk, Sweden 8 B18 68 24N 19 15 E
Tornio, Finland 8 D21 65 50N 24 12 E
Tornionjoki →, Finland 8 D21 65 50N 24 12 E
Tornquist, Argentina 94 D3 38 8S 62 15W
Toro, Spain 22 B11 39 59N 4 8 E
Toro, Cerro del, Chile 94 B2 29 10S 69 50W
Toro Pk., U.S.A. 85 M10 33 34N 116 24W
Toroníios Kólpos, Greece 21 D10 40 5N 23 30 E
Toronto, Canada 78 C5 43 39N 79 20W
Toronto, U.S.A. 78 F4 40 28N 80 36W
Toropets, Russia 24 C5 56 30N 31 40 E
Tororo, Uganda 54 B3 0 45N 34 12 E
Toros Dağları, Turkey 25 G5 37 0N 32 30 E
Torpa, India 43 H11 22 57N 85 6 E
Torquay, U.K. 11 G4 50 27N 3 32W
Torrance, U.S.A. 85 M8 33 50N 118 19W
Torre de Moncorvo, Portugal 19 B2 41 12N 7 8W
Torre del Greco, Italy 20 D6 40 47N 14 22 E
Torrejón de Ardoz, Spain 19 B4 40 27N 3 29W
Torrelavega, Spain 19 A3 43 20N 4 5W
Torremolinos, Spain 19 D3 36 38N 4 30W
Torrens, L., Australia 63 E2 31 0S 137 50 E
Torrens Cr. →, Australia 62 C4 22 23S 145 9 E
Torrens Creek, Australia 62 C4 20 48S 145 3 E
Torrent, Spain 19 C5 39 27N 0 28W
Torreón, Mexico 86 B4 25 33N 103 26W
Torres, Brazil 95 B5 29 21S 49 44W
Torres, Mexico 86 B2 28 46N 110 47W
Torres Strait, Australia 64 H6 9 50S 142 20 E
Torres Vedras, Portugal 19 C1 39 5N 9 15W
Torrevieja, Spain 19 D5 37 59N 0 42W
Torrey, U.S.A. 83 G8 38 18N 111 25W
Torridge →, U.K. 11 G3 51 0N 4 13W
Torridon, L., U.K. 12 D3 57 35N 5 50W
Torrington, Conn., U.S.A. 79 E11 41 48N 73 7W
Torrington, Wyo., U.S.A. 80 D2 42 4N 104 11W
Tórshavn, Færoe Is. 8 E9 62 5N 6 56W
Tortola, Br. Virgin Is. 89 C7 18 19N 64 45W
Tortosa, Spain 19 B6 40 49N 0 31 E
Tortosa, C., Spain 19 B6 40 41N 0 52 E
Tortue, I. de la, Haiti 89 B5 20 5N 72 57W
Torūd, Iran 45 C7 35 25N 55 5 E
Toruń, Poland 17 B10 53 2N 18 39 E
Tory I., Ireland 13 A3 55 16N 8 14W
Tosa, Japan 31 H6 33 24N 133 23 E
Tosa-Shimizu, Japan 31 H6 32 52N 132 58 E
Tosa-Wan, Japan 31 H6 33 15N 133 30 E
Toscana □, Italy 20 C4 43 25N 11 0 E
Toshkent, Uzbekistan 26 E7 41 20N 69 10 E
Tostado, Argentina 94 B3 29 15S 61 50W
Tostón, Pta. de, Canary Is. 22 F5 28 42N 14 2W
Tosu, Japan 31 H5 33 22N 130 31 E
Toteng, Botswana 56 C3 20 22S 22 58 E
Totma, Russia 24 C7 60 0N 42 40 E
Totnes, U.K. 11 G4 50 26N 3 42W
Totness, Surinam 93 B7 5 53N 56 19W
Totonicapán, Guatemala 88 D1 14 58N 91 12W
Totten Glacier, Antarctica 5 C8 66 45S 116 10 E
Tottenham, Australia 63 E4 32 14S 147 21 E
Tottenham, Canada 78 B5 44 1N 79 49W
Tottori, Japan 31 G7 35 30N 134 15 E
Tottori □, Japan 31 G7 35 30N 134 12 E
Toubkal, Djebel, Morocco 50 B4 31 0N 8 0W
Tougan, Burkina Faso 50 F5 13 11N 2 58W
Touggourt, Algeria 50 B7 33 6N 6 4 E
Toul, France 18 B6 48 40N 5 53 E
Toulon, France 18 E6 43 10N 5 55 E
Toulouse, France 18 E4 43 37N 1 27 E
Toummo, Niger 51 D8 22 45N 14 8 E
Toungoo, Burma 41 K20 19 0N 96 30 E
Touraine, France 18 C4 47 20N 0 30 E
Tourane = Da Nang, Vietnam 38 D7 16 4N 108 13 E
Tourcoing, France 18 A5 50 42N 3 10 E
Touriñán, C., Spain 19 A1 43 3N 9 18W
Tournai, Belgium 15 D3 50 35N 3 25 E
Tournon-sur-Rhône, France 18 D6 45 4N 4 50 E
Tours, France 18 C4 47 22N 0 40 E
Toussora, Mt., C.A.R. 52 C4 9 7N 23 14 E
Touws →, S. Africa 56 E3 33 45S 21 11 E
Touwsrivier, S. Africa 56 E3 33 20S 20 2 E
Towada, Japan 30 D10 40 37N 141 13 E
Towada-Ko, Japan 30 D10 40 28N 140 55 E
Towanda, U.S.A. 79 E8 41 46N 76 27W
Towang, India 41 F17 27 37N 91 50 E
Tower, U.S.A. 80 B8 47 48N 92 17W
Towerhill Cr. →, Australia 62 C3 22 28S 144 35 E
Towner, U.S.A. 80 A4 48 21N 100 25W
Townsend, U.S.A. 82 C8 46 19N 111 31W
Townshend I., Australia 62 C5 22 10S 150 31 E
Townsville, Australia 62 B4 19 15S 146 45 E
Towson, U.S.A. 76 F7 39 24N 76 36W
Towuti, Danau, Indonesia 37 E6 2 45S 121 32 E
Toya-Ko, Japan 30 C10 42 35N 140 51 E
Toyama, Japan 31 F8 36 40N 137 15 E
Toyama □, Japan 31 F8 36 45N 137 30 E
Toyama-Wan, Japan 31 F8 37 0N 137 30 E
Toyohashi, Japan 31 G8 34 45N 137 25 E
Toyokawa, Japan 31 G8 34 48N 137 27 E
Toyonaka, Japan 31 G7 34 50N 135 28 E
Toyooka, Japan 31 G7 35 35N 134 48 E
Toyota, Japan 31 G8 35 3N 137 7 E
Tozeur, Tunisia 50 B7 33 56N 8 8 E
Trá Li = Tralee, Ireland 13 D2 52 16N 9 42W
Tra On, Vietnam 39 H5 9 58N 105 55 E
Trabzon, Turkey 25 F6 41 0N 39 45 E
Tracadie, Canada 71 C7 47 30N 64 55W
Tracy, Calif., U.S.A. 84 H5 37 44N 121 26W
Tracy, Minn., U.S.A. 80 C7 44 14N 95 37W
Trafalgar, C., Spain 19 D2 36 10N 6 2W
Trail, Canada 72 D5 49 5N 117 40W
Trainor L., Canada 72 A4 60 24N 120 17W
Trákhonas, Cyprus 23 D12 35 12N 33 21 E
Tralee, Ireland 13 D2 52 16N 9 42W
Tralee B., Ireland 13 D2 52 17N 9 55W
Tramore, Ireland 13 D4 52 10N 7 10W
Tramore B., Ireland 13 D4 52 9N 7 10W
Tran Ninh, Cao Nguyen, Laos 38 C4 19 30N 103 10 E
Tranås, Sweden 9 G16 58 3N 14 59 E
Trancas, Argentina 94 B2 26 11S 65 20W
Trang, Thailand 39 J2 7 33N 99 38 E
Trangahy, Madag. 57 B7 19 7S 44 31 E
Trangan, Indonesia 37 F8 6 40S 134 20 E
Trangie, Australia 63 E4 32 4S 148 0 E
Trani, Italy 20 D7 41 17N 16 25 E
Tranoroa, Madag. 57 C8 24 42S 45 4 E
Tranqueras, Uruguay 95 C4 31 13S 55 45W
Transantarctic Mts., Antarctica 5 E12 85 0S 170 0W
Transilvania, Romania 17 E12 46 30N 24 0 E
Transilvanian Alps = Carpaţii Meridionali, Romania 17 F13 45 30N 25 0 E
Transvaal, S. Africa 53 K5 25 0S 29 0 E
Transylvania = Transilvania, Romania 17 E12 46 30N 24 0 E
Trápani, Italy 20 E5 38 1N 12 29 E
Trapper Pk., U.S.A. 82 D6 45 54N 114 18W
Traralgon, Australia 63 F4 38 12S 146 34 E
Trasimeno, L., Italy 20 C5 43 8N 12 6 E
Trat, Thailand 39 F4 12 14N 102 33 E
Tratani →, Pakistan 42 E3 29 19N 68 20 E
Traun, Austria 16 D8 48 14N 14 15 E
Traveller's L., Australia 63 E3 33 20S 142 0 E
Travemünde, Germany 16 B6 53 57N 10 52 E
Travers, Mt., N.Z. 59 K4 42 1S 172 45 E
Traverse City, U.S.A. 76 C3 44 46N 85 38W
Travis, L., U.S.A. 81 K5 30 24N 97 55W
Travnik, Bos.-H. 21 B7 44 17N 17 39 E
Trébbia →, Italy 18 D8 45 4N 9 41 E
Třebíč, Czech Rep. 16 D8 49 14N 15 55 E
Trebinje, Bos.-H. 21 C8 42 44N 18 22 E
Trebonne, Australia 62 B4 18 37S 146 5 E
Tregaron, U.K. 11 E4 52 14N 3 56W
Tregrosse Is., Australia 62 B5 17 41S 150 43 E
Treherne, Canada 73 D9 49 38N 98 42W
Treinta y Tres, Uruguay 95 C5 33 16S 54 17W
Trelawney, Zimbabwe 57 B5 17 30S 30 30 E
Trelew, Argentina 96 E3 43 10S 65 20W
Trelleborg, Sweden 9 J15 55 20N 13 10 E
Tremadog Bay, U.K. 10 E3 52 51N 4 18W
Tremonton, U.S.A. 82 F7 41 43N 112 10W
Tremp, Spain 19 A6 42 10N 0 52 E
Trenche →, Canada 70 C5 47 46N 72 53W
Trenčín, Slovak Rep. 17 D10 48 52N 18 4 E
Trenggalek, Indonesia 37 H14 8 3S 111 43 E
Trenque Lauquen, Argentina 94 D3 36 5S 62 45W
Trent →, Canada 78 B7 44 6N 77 34W
Trent →, U.K. 10 D7 53 41N 0 42W
Trento, Italy 20 A4 46 4N 11 8 E
Trenton, Canada 78 B7 44 10N 77 34W
Trenton, Mo., U.S.A. 80 E8 40 5N 93 37W
Trenton, N.J., U.S.A. 79 F10 40 14N 74 46W
Trenton, Nebr., U.S.A. 80 E4 40 11N 101 1W
Trepassey, Canada 71 C9 46 43N 53 25W
Tres Arroyos, Argentina 94 D3 38 26S 60 20W
Três Corações, Brazil 95 A6 21 44S 45 15W
Três Lagoas, Brazil 93 H8 20 50S 51 43W
Tres Lomas, Argentina 94 D3 36 27S 62 51W
Tres Marías, Islas, Mexico 86 C3 21 25N 106 28W
Tres Montes, C., Chile 96 F1 46 50S 75 30W
Tres Pinos, U.S.A. 84 J5 36 48N 121 19W
Três Pontas, Brazil 95 A6 21 23S 45 29W
Tres Puentes, Chile 94 B1 27 50S 70 15W
Tres Puntas, C., Argentina 96 F3 47 0S 66 0W
Três Rios, Brazil 95 A7 22 6S 43 15W
Tres Valles, Mexico 87 D5 18 15N 96 8W
Tresco, U.K. 11 H1 49 57N 6 20W
Treviso, Italy 20 B5 45 40N 12 15 E
Triabunna, Australia 62 G4 42 30S 147 55 E
Triánda, Greece 23 C10 36 25N 28 10 E
Triangle, Zimbabwe 57 C5 21 2S 31 28 E
Tribal Areas □, Pakistan 42 C4 33 0N 70 0 E
Tribulation, C., Australia 62 B4 16 5S 145 29 E
Tribune, U.S.A. 80 F4 38 28N 101 45W
Trichinopoly = Tiruchchirappalli, India 40 P11 10 45N 78 45 E
Trichur, India 40 P10 10 30N 76 18 E
Trida, Australia 63 E4 33 1S 145 1 E
Trier, Germany 16 D4 49 45N 6 38 E
Trieste, Italy 20 B5 45 40N 13 46 E
Triglav, Slovenia 16 E7 46 21N 13 50 E
Tríkkala, Greece 21 E9 39 34N 21 47 E
Trikomo, Cyprus 23 D12 35 17N 33 52 E
Trikora, Puncak, Indonesia 37 E9 4 15S 138 45 E
Trim, Ireland 13 C5 53 33N 6 48W
Trincomalee, Sri Lanka 40 Q12 8 38N 81 15 E
Trindade, Brazil 93 G9 16 40S 49 30W
Trindade, I., Atl. Oc. 2 F8 20 20S 29 50W
Trinidad, Bolivia 92 F6 14 46S 64 50W
Trinidad, Cuba 88 B4 21 48N 80 0W
Trinidad, Trin. & Tob. 89 D7 10 30N 61 15W
Trinidad, Uruguay 94 C4 33 30S 56 50W
Trinidad, U.S.A. 81 G2 37 10N 104 31W
Trinidad →, Mexico 87 D5 17 49N 95 9W
Trinidad & Tobago ■, W. Indies 89 D7 10 30N 61 20W
Trinity, Canada 71 C9 48 59N 53 55W
Trinity, U.S.A. 81 K7 30 57N 95 22W
Trinity →, Calif., U.S.A. 82 F2 41 11N 123 42W
Trinity →, Tex., U.S.A. 81 L7 29 45N 94 43W
Trinity B., Canada 71 C9 48 20N 53 10W
Trinity Is., U.S.A. 68 C4 56 33N 154 25W
Trinity Range, U.S.A. 82 F4 40 15N 118 45W
Trinkitat, Sudan 51 E13 18 45N 37 51 E
Trinway, U.S.A. 78 F2 40 9N 82 1W
Tripoli = Tarābulus, Lebanon 47 A4 34 31N 35 50 E
Tripoli = Tarābulus, Libya 51 B8 32 49N 13 7 E
Trípolis, Greece 21 F10 37 31N 22 25 E
Tripolitania, N. Afr. 51 B8 31 0N 13 0 E
Tripura □, India 41 H18 24 0N 92 0 E
Tripylos, Cyprus 23 E11 34 59N 32 41 E
Tristan da Cunha, Atl. Oc. 49 K2 37 6S 12 20W
Trisul, India 43 D8 30 19N 79 47 E
Trivandrum, India 40 Q10 8 41N 77 0 E
Trnava, Slovak Rep. 17 D9 48 23N 17 35 E
Trochu, Canada 72 C6 51 50N 113 13W
Trodely I., Canada 70 B4 52 15N 79 26W
Troglav, Croatia 20 C7 43 56N 16 36 E
Troilus, L., Canada 70 B5 50 50N 74 35W
Trois-Pistoles, Canada 71 C6 48 5N 69 10W
Trois-Rivières, Canada 70 C5 46 25N 72 34W
Troitsk, Russia 26 D7 54 10N 61 35 E
Troitsko Pechorsk, Russia 24 B10 62 40N 56 10 E
Trölladyngja, Iceland 8 D5 64 54N 17 16W
Trollhättan, Sweden 9 G15 58 17N 12 20 E
Trollheimen, Norway 8 E13 62 46N 9 1 E
Trombetas →, Brazil 93 D7 1 55S 55 35W
Tromsø, Norway 8 B18 69 40N 18 56 E
Trona, U.S.A. 85 K9 35 46N 117 23W
Tronador, Mte., Argentina 96 E2 41 10S 71 50W
Trøndelag, Norway 8 D14 64 17N 11 50 E
Trondheim, Norway 8 E14 63 36N 10 25 E
Trondheimsfjorden, Norway 8 E14 63 35N 10 30 E
Troodos, Cyprus 23 E11 34 55N 32 52 E
Troon, U.K. 12 F4 55 33N 4 39W
Tropic, U.S.A. 83 H7 37 37N 112 5W
Trostan, U.K. 13 A5 55 3N 6 10W
Trout →, Canada 72 A5 61 19N 119 51W
Trout L., N.W.T., Canada 72 A4 60 40N 121 14W
Trout L., Ont., Canada 73 C10 51 20N 93 15W
Trout Lake, Canada 72 B6 56 30N 114 32W
Trout Lake, U.S.A. 84 E5 46 0N 121 32W
Trout River, Canada 71 C8 49 29N 58 8W
Trout Run, U.S.A. 78 E7 41 23N 77 3W
Trouville-sur-Mer, France 18 B4 49 21N 0 5 E
Trowbridge, U.K. 11 F5 51 18N 2 12W
Troy, Turkey 21 E12 39 57N 26 12 E
Troy, Ala., U.S.A. 77 K3 31 48N 85 58W
Troy, Kans., U.S.A. 80 F7 39 47N 95 5W
Troy, Mo., U.S.A. 80 F9 38 59N 90 59W
Troy, Mont., U.S.A. 82 B6 48 28N 115 53W
Troy, N.Y., U.S.A. 79 D11 42 44N 73 41W
Troy, Ohio, U.S.A. 76 E3 40 2N 84 12W
Troy, Pa., U.S.A. 79 E8 41 47N 76 47W
Troyes, France 18 B6 48 19N 4 3 E
Truchas Peak, U.S.A. 81 H2 35 58N 105 39W
Trucial States = United Arab Emirates ■, Asia 46 C5 23 50N 54 0 E
Truckee, U.S.A. 84 F6 39 20N 120 11W
Trudovoye, Russia 30 C6 43 17N 132 5 E
Trujillo, Honduras 88 C2 16 0N 86 0W
Trujillo, Peru 92 E3 8 6S 79 0W
Trujillo, Spain 19 C3 39 28N 5 55W
Trujillo, U.S.A. 81 H2 35 32N 104 42W
Trujillo, Venezuela 92 B4 9 22N 70 38W
Truk, Micronesia 64 G7 7 25N 151 46 E
Trumann, U.S.A. 81 H9 35 41N 90 31W
Trumansburg, U.S.A. 79 D8 42 33N 76 40W
Trumbull, Mt., U.S.A. 83 H7 36 25N 113 8W
Trundle, Australia 63 E4 32 53S 147 35 E
Trung-Phan = Annam, Vietnam 38 E7 16 0N 108 0 E
Truro, Canada 71 C7 45 21N 63 14W
Truro, U.K. 11 G2 50 16N 5 4W
Truskavets, Ukraine 17 D12 49 17N 23 30 E
Trutch, Canada 72 B4 57 44N 122 57W
Truth or Consequences, U.S.A. 83 K10 33 8N 107 15W
Trutnov, Czech Rep. 16 C8 50 37N 15 54 E
Truxton, U.S.A. 79 D8 42 45N 76 2W
Tryonville, U.S.A. 78 E5 41 42N 79 48W
Tsandi, Namibia 56 B1 17 42S 14 50 E
Tsaratanana, Madag. 57 B8 16 47S 47 39 E
Tsaratanana, Mt. de, Madag. 57 A8 14 0S 49 0 E
Tsarevo = Michurin, Bulgaria 21 C12 42 9N 27 51 E
Tsau, Botswana 56 C3 20 8S 22 22 E
Tselinograd = Astana, Kazakstan 26 D8 51 10N 71 30 E
Tses, Namibia 56 D2 25 58S 18 8 E
Tsetserleg, Mongolia 32 B5 47 36N 101 32 E
Tshabong, Botswana 56 D3 26 2S 22 29 E
Tshane, Botswana 56 C3 24 5S 21 54 E
Tshela, Dem. Rep. of the Congo 52 E2 4 57S 13 4 E
Tshesebe, Botswana 57 C4 21 51S 27 32 E
Tshibeke, Dem. Rep. of the Congo 54 C2 2 40S 28 35 E
Tshibinda, Dem. Rep. of the Congo 54 C2 2 23S 28 43 E
Tshikapa, Dem. Rep. of the Congo 52 F4 6 28S 20 48 E
Tshilenge, Dem. Rep. of the Congo 54 D1 6 17S 23 48 E
Tshinsenda, Dem. Rep. of the Congo 55 E2 12 20S 28 0 E
Tshofa, Dem. Rep. of the Congo 54 D2 5 13S 25 16 E
Tshwane, Botswana 56 C3 22 24S 22 1 E
Tsigara, Botswana 56 C4 20 22S 25 54 E
Tsihombe, Madag. 57 D8 25 10S 45 41 E
Tsiigehtchic, Canada 68 B6 67 15N 134 0W
Tsimlyansk Res. = Tsimlyanskoye Vdkhr., Russia 25 E7 48 0N 43 0 E
Tsimlyanskoye Vdkhr., Russia 25 E7 48 0N 43 0 E
Tsinan = Jinan, China 34 F9 36 38N 117 1 E
Tsineng, S. Africa 56 D3 27 5S 23 5 E
Tsinghai = Qinghai □, China 32 C4 36 0N 98 0 E
Tsingtao = Qingdao, China 35 F11 36 5N 120 20 E
Tsinjoarivo, Madag. 57 B8 19 37S 47 40 E
Tsinjomitondraka, Madag. 57 B8 15 40S 47 8 E
Tsiroanomandidy, Madag. 57 B8 18 46S 46 2 E
Tsitondroina, Madag. 57 C8 21 19S 46 0 E
Tsivory, Madag. 57 C8 24 4S 46 5 E
Tskhinvali, Georgia 25 F7 42 14N 44 1 E
Tsna →, Russia 24 D7 54 55N 41 58 E
Tso Moriri, L., India 43 C8 32 50N 78 20 E
Tsobis, Namibia 56 B2 19 27S 17 30 E
Tsodilo Hill, Botswana 56 B3 18 49S 21 43 E
Tsogttsetsiy = Baruunsuu, Mongolia 34 C3 43 43N 105 35 E
Tsolo, S. Africa 57 E4 31 18S 28 37 E
Tsomo, S. Africa 57 E4 32 0S 27 42 E
Tsu, Japan 31 G8 34 45N 136 25 E
Tsu L., Canada 72 A6 60 40N 111 52W
Tsuchiura, Japan 31 F10 36 5N 140 15 E
Tsugaru-Kaikyō, Japan 30 D10 41 35N 141 0 E
Tsumeb, Namibia 56 B2 19 9S 17 44 E
Tsumis, Namibia 56 C2 23 39S 17 29 E
Tsuruga, Japan 31 G8 35 45N 136 2 E
Tsurugi-San, Japan 31 H7 33 51N 134 6 E
Tsuruoka, Japan 30 E9 38 44N 139 50 E
Tsushima, Gifu, Japan 31 G8 35 10N 136 43 E
Tsushima, Nagasaki, Japan 31 G4 34 20N 129 20 E
Tsuyama, Japan 31 G7 35 3N 134 0 E
Tsyelyakhany, Belarus 17 B13 52 30N 25 46 E
Tual, Indonesia 37 F8 5 38S 132 44 E
Tuam, Ireland 13 C3 53 31N 8 51W
Tuamotu Arch. = Tuamotu Is., Pac. Oc. 65 J13 17 0S 144 0W
Tuamotu Is., Pac. Oc. 65 J13 17 0S 144 0W
Tuamotu Ridge, Pac. Oc. 65 K14 20 0S 138 0W
Tuao, Phil. 37 A6 17 55N 121 22 E
Tuapse, Russia 25 F6 44 5N 39 10 E
Tuatapere, N.Z. 59 M1 46 8S 167 41 E
Tuba City, U.S.A. 83 H8 36 8N 111 14W
Tuban, Indonesia 37 G15 6 54S 112 3 E
Tubani, Botswana 56 C3 24 46S 24 18 E
Tubarão, Brazil 95 B6 28 30S 49 0W
Tūbās, West Bank 47 C4 32 20N 35 22 E
Tubas →, Namibia 56 C2 22 54S 14 35 E
Tübingen, Germany 16 D5 48 31N 9 4 E
Tubruq, Libya 51 B10 32 7N 23 55 E

Tubuai Is.

U

World: Regions in the News

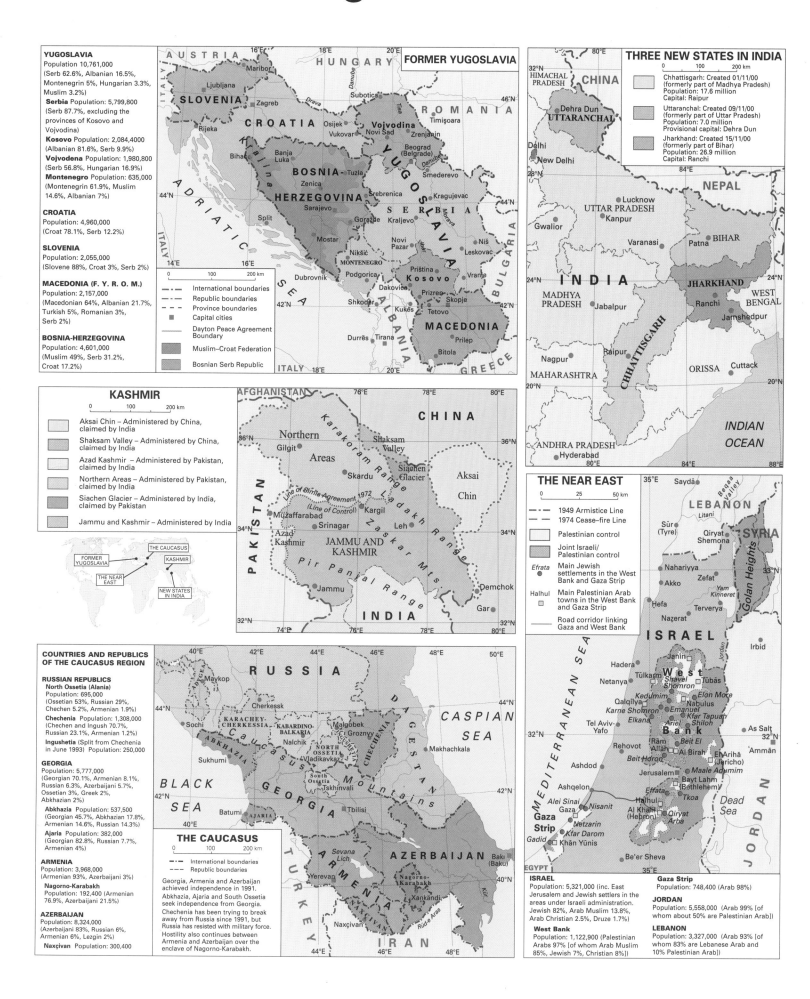

YUGOSLAVIA
Population 10,761,000
(Serb 62.6%, Albanian 16.5%,
Montenegrin 5%, Hungarian 3.3%,
Muslim 3.2%)
Serbia Population: 5,799,800
(Serb 87.7%, excluding the
provinces of Kosovo and
Vojvodina)
Kosovo Population: 2,084,4000
(Albanian 81.6%, Serb 9.9%)
Vojvodena Population: 1,980,800
(Serb 56.8%, Hungarian 16.9%)
Montenegro Population: 635,000
(Montenegrin 61.9%, Muslim
14.6%, Albanian 7%)

CROATIA
Population: 4,960,000
(Croat 78.1%, Serb 12.2%)

SLOVENIA
Population: 2,055,000
(Slovene 88%, Croat 3%, Serb 2%)

MACEDONIA (F. Y. R. O. M.)
Population: 2,157,000
(Macedonian 64%, Albanian 21.7%,
Turkish 5%, Romanian 3%,
Serb 2%)

BOSNIA-HERZEGOVINA
Population: 4,601,000
(Muslim 49%, Serb 31.2%,
Croat 17.2%)

FORMER YUGOSLAVIA

- – · – International boundaries
- – · – Republic boundaries
- – – Province boundaries
- ■ Capital cities
- ——— Dayton Peace Agreement Boundary
- Muslim–Croat Federation
- Bosnian Serb Republic

THREE NEW STATES IN INDIA
0   100   200 km

- Chhattisgarh: Created 01/11/00 (formerly part of Madhya Pradesh) Population: 17.6 million Capital: Raipur
- Uttaranchal: Created 09/11/00 (formerly part of Uttar Pradesh) Population: 7.0 million Provisional capital: Dehra Dun
- Jharkhand: Created 15/11/00 (formerly part of Bihar) Population: 26.9 million Capital: Ranchi

KASHMIR
0   100   200 km

- Aksai Chin – Administered by China, claimed by India
- Shaksam Valley – Administered by China, claimed by India
- Azad Kashmir – Administered by Pakistan, claimed by India
- Northern Areas – Administered by Pakistan, claimed by India
- Siachen Glacier – Administered by India, claimed by Pakistan
- Jammu and Kashmir – Administered by India

THE NEAR EAST
0   25   50 km

- – · – 1949 Armistice Line
- – – 1974 Cease–fire Line
- Palestinian control
- Joint Israeli/ Palestinian control
- *Efrata* Main Jewish settlements in the West Bank and Gaza Strip
- *Halhul* □ Main Palestinian Arab towns in the West Bank and Gaza Strip
- ——— Road corridor linking Gaza and West Bank

COUNTRIES AND REPUBLICS OF THE CAUCASUS REGION

RUSSIAN REPUBLICS
North Ossetia (Alania)
Population: 695,000
(Ossetian 53%, Russian 29%,
Chechen 5.2%, Armenian 1.9%)
Chechenia Population: 1,308,000
(Chechen and Ingush 70.7%,
Russian 23.1%, Armenian 1.2%)
Ingushetia (Split from Chechenia
in June 1993) Population: 250,000

GEORGIA
Population: 5,777,000
(Georgian 70.1%, Armenian 8.1%,
Russian 6.3%, Azerbaijani 5.7%,
Ossetian 3%, Greek 2%,
Abkhazian 2%)
Abkhazia Population: 537,500
(Georgian 45.7%, Abkhazian 17.8%,
Armenian 14.6%, Russian 14.3%)
Ajaria Population: 382,000
(Georgian 82.8%, Russian 7.7%,
Armenian 4%)

ARMENIA
Population: 3,968,000
(Armenian 93%, Azerbaijani 3%)
Nagorno-Karabakh
Population: 192,400 (Armenian
76.9%, Azerbaijani 21.5%)

AZERBAIJAN
Population: 8,324,000
(Azerbaijani 83%, Russian 6%,
Armenian 6%, Lezgin 2%)
Naxçivan Population: 300,400

THE CAUCASUS
0   100   200 km

- – · – International boundaries
- – · – Republic boundaries

Georgia, Armenia and Azerbaijan
achieved independence in 1991.
Abkhazia, Ajaria and South Ossetia
seek independence from Georgia.
Chechenia has been trying to break
away from Russia since 1991, but
Russia has resisted with military force.
Hostility also continues between
Armenia and Azerbaijan over the
enclave of Nagorno-Karabakh.

ISRAEL
Population: 5,321,000 (inc. East
Jerusalem and Jewish settlers in the
areas under Israeli administration.
Jewish 82%, Arab Muslim 13.8%,
Arab Christian 2.5%, Druze 1.7%)

West Bank
Population: 1,122,900 (Palestinian
Arabs 97% [of whom Arab Muslim
85%, Jewish 7%, Christian 8%])

Gaza Strip
Population: 748,400 (Arab 98%)

JORDAN
Population: 5,558,000 (Arab 99% [of
whom about 50% are Palestinian Arab])

LEBANON
Population: 3,327,000 (Arab 93% [of
whom 83% are Lebanese Arab and
10% Palestinian Arab])

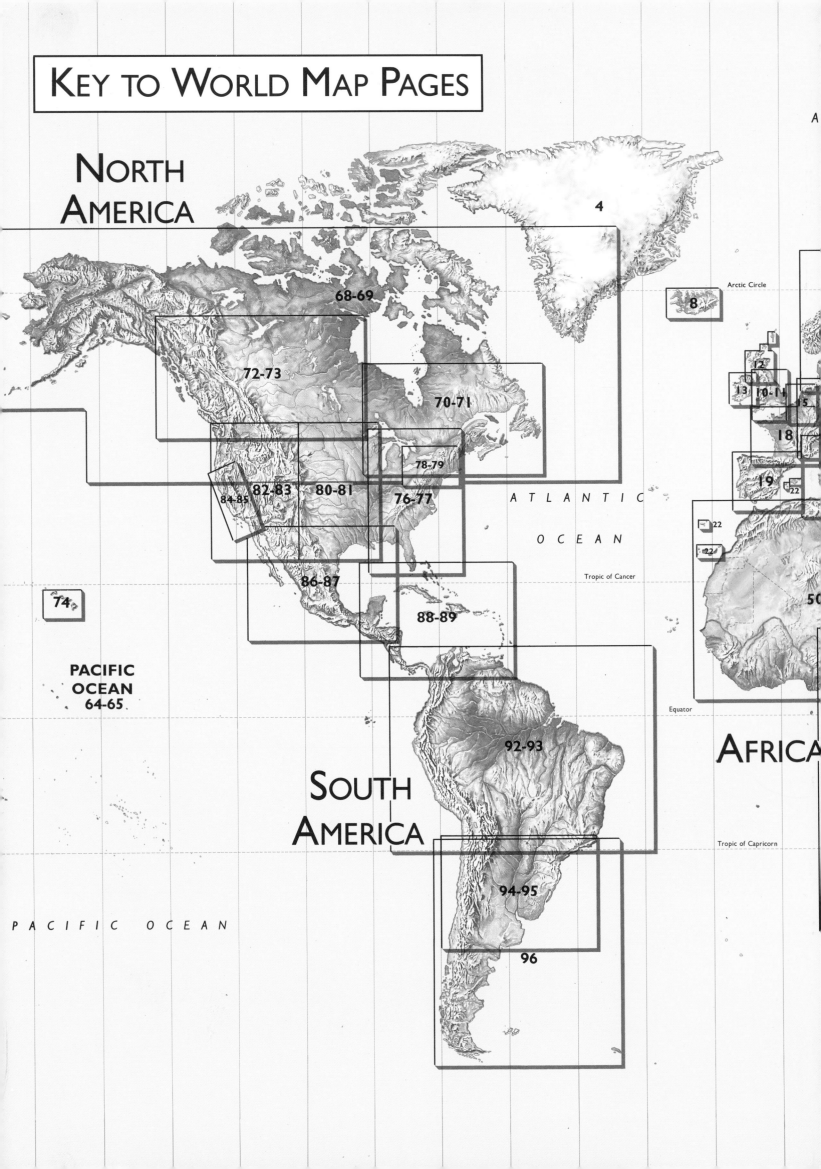

KEY TO WORLD MAP PAGES

NORTH AMERICA

SOUTH AMERICA

AFRICA

PACIFIC OCEAN

PACIFIC OCEAN 64-65

ATLANTIC OCEAN

Arctic Circle

Tropic of Cancer

Equator

Tropic of Capricorn

4

8

12

13

10-11

15

18

19

22

22

22

22

50

68-69

72-73

70-71

78-79

76-77

82-83

80-81

84-85

86-87

88-89

92-93

94-95

96

74